Stovall

ANTITRUST LAW, POLICY, AND PROCEDURE: CASES, MATERIALS, PROBLEMS
SEVENTH EDITION

ANTITRUST LAW, POLICY, AND PROCEDURE

Cases, Materials, Problems

Seventh Edition

E. Thomas Sullivan
President of The University of Vermont and
Dean Emeritus, University of Minnesota Law School

Herbert Hovenkamp
Ben and Dorothy Willie Professor
University of Iowa College of Law

Howard A. Shelanski
Professor of Law , Georgetown University Law Center
former Director, Bureau of Economics, Federal Trade Commission

Christopher R. Leslie
Professor of Law
School of Law, University of California Irvine

ISBN: 978-1-6304-3015-3
Looseleaf ISBN: 978-1-6304-3016-0
eBook ISBN: 978-1-6304-3017-7

Library of Congress Cataloging-in-Publication Data

Sullivan, E. Thomas, author.

Antitrust law, policy, and procedure : cases, materials, problems / E. Thomas Sullivan, President of the University of Vermont and Dean Emeritus, University of Minnesota Law School; Herbert Hovenkamp, Ben and Dorothy Willie Professor University of Iowa College of Law; Howard A. Shelanski, Professor of Law and Director, Berkeley Center for Law & Technology University of California Berkeley School of Law; Christopher R. Leslie, Professor of Law School of Law, University of California Irvine. — [Revised Sixth Edition].

pages cm

Includes index.

ISBN 978-1-63043-015-3

1. Antitrust law — United States — Cases. I. Hovenkamp, Herbert, 1948-author. II. Shelanski, Howard A., author. III. Leslie, Christopher R., author. IV. Title.

KF1649.S88 2014

343.7307'21 — dc23

2014003878

NOTE TO USERS

To ensure that you are using the latest materials available in this area, please be sure to periodically check the LexisNexis Law School web site for downloadable updates and supplements at www.lexisnexis.com/lawschool.

Editorial Offices

121 Chanlon Rd., New Providence, NJ 07974 (908) 464-6800

201 Mission St., San Francisco, CA 94105-1831 (415) 908-3200

www.lexisnexis.com

MATTHEW◆BENDER

Preface to the Seventh Edition

This Seventh Edition of *Antitrust Law, Policy, and Procedure* comes out as this casebook has entered its thirtieth year of continuous publication. This year we welcome a fourth author, Professor Christopher R. Leslie of the University of California, Irvine, a prolific and nationally known antitrust scholar with particular experience in the law of collusion and intellectual property rights.

The Seventh Edition is completely updated through 2013. As previously, we have attempted to select and edit cases so as to give balanced coverage of antitrust's various ideologies as well as its economics. All chapters have been completely revised.

Out of concern for publication costs and as a concession to classroom realities, we have moved the Chapter on secondary-line enforcement of the Robinson-Patman Act to SSRN's digital site. Few antitrust teachers continue to cover the materials in that chapter in a basic antitrust course, although it continues to be taught in some advanced or specialty classes or seminars. It can be found at http://papers.ssrn.com/sol3/papers.cfm?abstract_id=2319067. We will continue to keep that chapter up to date, and anyone who wishes may use it at no charge, including the printing of multiple copies for classroom use. We ask only that you preserve attribution of authorship.

E. Thomas Sullivan,
Burlington, Vermont
Herbert Hovenkamp,
Iowa City, Iowa
Howard A. Shelanski,
Washington, D.C.
Christopher R. Leslie,
Irvine, California
October, 2013

Preface to the Sixth Edition

This Sixth Edition is a substantial revision from the previous edition, with updating of all case law materials, including the recent decisions of the Roberts Supreme Court, and numerous lower court decisions. In particular we have expanded sections on pricing behavior, intellectual property, merger policy, regulatory policy, and added a great deal of comparative material focusing mainly on the competition law of the European Union.

Beginning with this edition we welcome Professor Howard A. Shelanski as a co-author. Professor Shelanski has been teaching and writing in antitrust and related fields for many years. He has particular expertise in the areas of regulated industries, telecommunications law, and mergers. His knowledge of antitrust policy in high technology industries is particularly welcome.

E. Thomas Sullivan,
Minneapolis, Minnesota
Herbert Hovenkamp,
Iowa City, Iowa
Howard A. Shelanski,
Washington, D.C.
June, 2009

Preface to the Fifth Edition

The structure and approach of the Fifth Edition of Antitrust Law, Policy and Procedure remain the same as we used in previous editions. The text has been updated fully with all the Supreme Court decisions and the most important appellate decisions issued since the Fourth Edition was published. In addition, we have updated and expanded notes on economics, international issues, and expert testimony, and we have greatly enlarged the treatment of intellectual property issues. We also include several new problems.

E. Thomas Sullivan,
Minneapolis, Minnesota
Herbert Hovenkamp,
Iowa City, Iowa
August, 2003

Preface to the Fourth Edition

This Fourth Edition of Antitrust Law, Policy and Procedure continues the basic approach of preceding editions. The central focus is on judicial decisions, supplemented by analytic, historical, and economic notes and questions. Principal decisions and note cases have been updated in all areas, as well as references to secondary sources, and we have added new problems. The edition also adjusts the coverage to include somewhat less in relatively quiet areas, such as vertical and conglomerate mergers, and more in areas of greater activity, such as technology and intellectual property. A few older decisions have been pruned, but we have tried not to change the book's general pitch any more than necessary to reflect new developments.

E. Thomas Sullivan,
Minneapolis, Minnesota
Herbert Hovenkamp,
Iowa City, Iowa
March, 1999

Preface to the Third Edition

This edition continues the same approach followed in earlier editions of heavy focus on the case law, together with simple economic analysis and notes representing a variety of ideological viewpoints. In the matter of antitrust ideology, the Supreme Court is as divided and undirected as it has ever been — witness the chasm between the 1992 Kodak decision and the 1993 Spectrum Sports and Brooke decisions.

The increase in the volume of Supreme Court opinions over the last five years has necessitated some pruning and editing of earlier opinions, but we have tried to leave all important concurrences and dissents as intact as possible. This edition also adds several new problems, expanded bibliographies, and all Supreme Court decisions through the October, 1992 term.

We thank Professor Richard D. Friedman of the University of Michigan Law School for numerous invaluable comments. We are also grateful to our research assistants Craig Marquiz, Hrayr A. Sayadian, and Ellen Szarleta for a variety of significant contributions.

E. Thomas Sullivan,
Tucson, Arizona
Herbert Hovenkamp,
Iowa City, Iowa
September, 1993

Preface to the Second Edition

We continue to believe that the best approach toward antitrust in the law school curriculum is through the cases. For that reason, this casebook emphasizes judicial opinions and contains relatively more of each one, including dissents, than other books in the field.

We also believe that antitrust should be taught with the "best" legal precedents available, and that sometimes a recent circuit court opinion is better than an outdated Supreme Court opinion. For this reason, some antitrust decisions that were important in the 1960s and earlier have been given very brief treatment or omitted as principal cases in this edition.

Finally, we believe that a casebook designed for a student's first or second antitrust course should not overwhelm the student with one particular ideology. Antitrust ideologies have come and gone, and they will continue to do so. The notes in this book are designed to take seriously the competing ideologies of left, right, and center, to confront their defects, and to present their strengths. Professors who are strongly committed to a particular ideology should find plenty of material to criticize or, alternatively, to illustrate their views.

This edition encompasses antitrust developments through the summer of 1988 and includes all Supreme Court decisions of the October, 1987 Term.

As a new feature in this edition, we offer a series of problems for class discussion or individual assignment. The problems are analyzed in detail in a Teacher's Problem Manual to be published as a companion to this volume.

E. Thomas Sullivan,
St. Louis, Missouri
Herbert Hovenkamp,
Iowa City, Iowa
January, 1989

Preface to the First Edition

We believe this book on federal antitrust law is a unique and valuable contribution to its genre. Although it covers the same general law as its peers, its perspective is different in several ways that make it particularly useful for teachers hoping to offer a sophisticated but litigation-oriented antitrust course.

First, this book is shorter than most others in the field. Many antitrust books have grown fat with overruled Supreme Court opinions, with opinions whose historical value far exceeds their usefulness as credible statements of current law, and long footnotes of string citations that do little for students facing their first experience in antitrust analysis and problem solving.

To be sure, brevity imposes certain costs. This book contains no separate sections on antitrust and the patent system, and no detailed discussion of the extraterritorial applications of antitrust law. It has only brief sections on antitrust in the regulated and so-called "exempt" industries. Although all these things are useful and can be profitably taught, it is our experience that few instructors emphasize them in the basic three-unit or four-unit antitrust class.

At the same time, this book offers a broader coverage than most on procedural issues, particularly on the law of private enforcement. Because more than ninety percent of all federal antitrust cases are now brought by private plaintiffs, the law of private enforcement has developed a rich and complex "substance" all its own. That law is more appropriate to a basic antitrust course than is the extensive discussion of patents or extraterritorial application.

Likewise this book focuses more than most on the process of antitrust litigation — on evidentiary standards, burden of proof requirements, and standards for judgment. These emphases seem appropriate because concepts such as "market power," "agreement," or "intent" are not merely abstractions of the substantive law: They are facts that must be established in court.

An additional, important difference between this book and many others in the field is ideological. This book attempts to strike a balanced, diversified approach in presenting a wide spectrum of ideas regarding the goals and economic underpinnings of antitrust law. The authors of this book disagree with each other about many questions that are central to antitrust policy making today, such as whether increased allocative efficiency should be the exclusive or only one of many antitrust enforcement goals. As a result this book both entertains and takes seriously alternative viewpoints and permits the students (or the teacher) a larger perspective for individual choice.

Ideological narrowness is nowhere more evident than in the editing of opinions. Antitrust casebooks have become notorious for "ideological editing" that either supports the view of the editor or else makes the court's position appear far less rational than it really was. Antitrust opinions are particularly conducive to such editing because they are so long — in many cases a fifty-page opinion must be reduced to five or six.

Neither of the authors has permitted an editorial atrocity that reflects too favorably on the ideology of the other. Although nonideological editing does not exist, nothing succeeds like competition in bringing differences of ideology into the light of day. The

Preface to the First Edition

result in most instances is that the edited opinions contained here are longer than those in other antitrust casebooks. Furthermore, this book prints excerpts from many more concurring and dissenting opinions, particularly when the secondary opinion foreshadowed a position later taken by the Supreme Court.

The book also employs the positive use of economic theories as an analytical device. As to the level of economic sophistication and difficulty, this book must be classified as "medium." Today no one can ask whether an antitrust casebook should develop price theory and industrial organization; the only question is how much. This book is addressed to students, however, who are assumed to have no prior experience in economics. Its approach centers on the fundamentals.

It offers an introductory chapter and then builds in succeeding chapters on the models created. Unlike casebooks in which economic analysis can be found only in an opening chapter or appendix, the economic analysis in this book is integrated into the notes and discussions following each case selection. Economics in antitrust is valuable only to the extent that it enhances our ability to analyze disputes and make useful policy judgments. For that, a few comments about price theory hidden in an appendix are simply inadequate. Famous and influential opinions such as Alcoa, du Pont, and Brown Shoe have an imposing if dubious economics content, but most students will not discern that content unless they are given at least minimal guidance. We attempt to do that.

In sum, this offering attempts to integrate into the traditional antitrust casebook an appreciation for the rich historical, socio-political, and economic development of the antitrust laws and policies. How the law has evolved and the implications for future development are central to this book's format. In addition to the doctrinal development, this book attempts to focus the attention of students on the evidentiary and procedural context within which the "substantive" material may be utilized. We hope these objectives will be successful.

E. Thomas Sullivan,
Columbia, Missouri
Herbert Hovenkamp,
San Francisco, California
February, 1984

Table of Contents

Table of Contents

Table of Contents

Table of Contents

Table of Contents

Table of Contents

Table of Contents

Table of Contents

Table of Contents

Table of Contents

Table of Contents

Table of Contents

Table of Contents

Chapter 1

INTRODUCTION TO THE COMPETITION MODEL

I OVERVIEW: THE POLICIES AND GOALS OF ANTITRUST REGULATION

Throughout history, antitrust law has been concerned with governmental control of business concentration and economic power. Since 1890, the antitrust laws have had varying interpretations in order to promote certain policies and goals perceived to underlie the original statutes. Antitrust analysis, like much of antitrust conduct, however, is cyclical in nature. As the decisional law indicates, at various times Congress and the courts have defined and refined the values sought to be advanced by enforcement of the antitrust laws. Current antitrust analysis suggests that courts interpret the law in order to promote the maximization of consumer welfare. Such an approach, however, deemphasizes certain prior precedents and displaces other analytical approaches toward antitrust. To put antitrust in perspective and to understand the analysis today, one must consider the interdisciplinary nature of the subject and the historical debates and enforcement trends that encircle the law's development.

Probably the single most important factor affecting antitrust analysis has been the introduction and application of economics into antitrust law. But the positive use or misuse of economics in antitrust decision making is of recent origin. As the judicial debate began concerning how "competition" as the goal of antitrust should be defined, economic models were introduced into the definitional analysis. If the challenged conduct was foreseen as unreasonably anticompetitive, then it was to be condemned under the antitrust laws. Economics was offered as an analytical measure to inform the content and rationale of the antitrust laws. But because economists differ markedly on the assumptions that underlie their economic modeling, no solid consensus emerged as to which models better inform and facilitate antitrust analysis and policy. This is so largely because economics is based, among other things, upon many assumptions concerning behavior. Some of the assumptions draw on social and political values as well as experience. Moreover, it is difficult to quantify or isolate with precision an economic model that measures all the relevant antitrust concerns. Consequently, many antitrust observers believe that there is a gap between economic theory and actual market conduct. With these limitations noted, the identified policies and goals of antitrust regulation will be explored.

Historically, two central themes have been recognized at one time or another as the underpinnings for antitrust policy. One supported the noneconomic approach that enforcement was to be carried out so as to control the economic concentration of industrial power. "Competition" was defined as the promotion of equality among businesses through the dispersion of economic power. Free access to markets was an objective. Economic power was the evil sought to be condemned. Freedom of individual choice, distributive justice, and pluralism were core values. The small entrepreneur was favored and protected against the encroaching economic leverage of the larger concentrated entity, even if the result was increased costs to the consumer.

The other theme viewed antitrust as a body of law designed to promote the goal of enhancing economic efficiency, without regard to the sociopolitical imbalance that such a goal might create between the large concentrated business and small struggling competitor. Under this approach, the antitrust laws were intended to protect competition rather than competitors. "The whole task of antitrust can be summed up as the effort to improve allocative efficiency without impairing productive efficiency so greatly as to produce either no gain or a net loss in consumer welfare." R. BORK, THE ANTITRUST PARADOX 91 (1978). Efficiency is frequently viewed in terms of whether the challenged conduct creates a restraint or limitation on output. Absent a finding of output limitation, the conduct is deemed efficient and beyond the condemnation of the antitrust laws. In practice, these goals often diverged, creating analytical and policy tensions, though few at first accepted the apparent inconsistencies. *Compare* Fox, *The Modernization of Antitrust: A New Equilibrium*, 66 CORNELL L. REV. 1140 (1981), *with* Posner, *The Chicago School of Antitrust Analysis*, 127 U. PA. L. REV. 925 (1979). *See* Hovenkamp, *Antitrust Policy After Chicago*, 84 MICH. L. REV. 213 (1985); Bruce H. Kobayashi, Timothy J. Muris, *Chicago, Post-Chicago, and Beyond: Time to Let Go of the 20th Century*, 78 ANTITRUST L.J. 147 (2012).

Central to the debate underlying the values inherent in antitrust policy is the issue of how "competition" ought to be defined. In one of the Supreme Court's first opinions on the subject, the Court suggested that one goal of the law was to protect small business units from reduced prices brought about by larger concerns. In *United States v. Trans-Missouri Freight Ass'n*, 166 U.S. 290, 322–323 (1897), Justice Peckham reasoned:

> Manufacturing or trading companies may also affect prices by joining together in forming a trust or other combination, and by making agreements in restraint of trade and commerce, which, when carried out, affect the interests of the public. . . . It is true the results of trusts, or combinations of that nature, may be different in different kinds of corporations, and yet they all have an essential similarity, and have been induced by motives of individual or corporate aggrandizement as against the public interest. In business or trading combinations they may even temporarily, or perhaps permanently, reduce the price of the article traded in or manufactured, by reducing the expense inseparable from the running of many different companies for the same purpose. Trade or commerce under those circumstances may nevertheless be badly and unfortunately restrained by driving out of business the small dealers and worthy men whose lives have been spent therein, and who might be unable to readjust themselves to their altered surroundings. Mere reduction in the price of the commodity dealt in might be dearly paid for by the ruin of such a class and

the absorption of control over one commodity by an all-powerful combination of capital.

This theme found expression, though not consistently, in many other Supreme Court opinions, particularly during the Warren Court era. An example can be found in *Northern Pac. Ry. v. United States*, 356 U.S. 1, 4 (1958), where the Court observed that:

> The Sherman Act was designed to be a comprehensive charter of economic liberty aimed at preserving free and unfettered competition as the rule of trade. It rests on the premise that the unrestrained interaction of competitive forces will yield the best allocation of our economic resources, the lowest prices, the highest quality and the greatest material progress, while at the same time providing an environment conducive to the preservation of our democratic, political and social institutions.

Citations to this Supreme Court statement have been made frequently in support of the argument that the antitrust laws have as their foundational goal the noneconomic objectives of preserving democratic institutions and industrial organization in the form of small units, and the encouragement of equal competitive opportunity. *See, e.g., United States v. Von's Grocery Co.*, 384 U.S. 270, 274–75 (1966); *Brown Shoe Co. v. United States*, 370 U.S. 294, 344 (1962); *United States v. Aluminum Co. of Am.*, 148 F.2d 416, 427 (2d Cir. 1945). *See also* 21 Cong. Rec. 2457, 2459–2460 (1890).

During the Warren Court era, antitrust law and remedies were used by the Court as corrective instruments to equalize the economic landscape. Many of the Court's decisions appeared to condemn conduct that "reduced costs" or improved product quality as it made competition more difficult for less-equipped rivals, even if the conduct ultimately benefitted consumers. For the favored class of small businesses, antitrust cases under the Warren Court were relatively likely to proceed to a successful jury trial. Generally, the Warren Court disfavored the concentration of power that could result from product innovation and favored a more decentralized economy. H. HOVENKAMP, THE ANTITRUST ENTERPRISE 1 (2005).

The most forceful articulation of this antitrust policy can be found in the Warren Court's *Brown Shoe* decision. Although the context was Section 7 of the Clayton Act, Chief Justice Warren stated in *Brown Shoe* that the Court had struck the balance in favor of competition "equity" rather than efficiency:

> "[W]e cannot fail to recognize Congress' desire to promote competition through the protection of viable, small, locally owned businesses. Congress appreciated that occasional higher costs and prices might result from the maintenance of fragmented industries and markets. It resolved these competing considerations in favor of decentralization."

370 U.S. 294, 344 (1961). Certain lower court opinions embraced the same values for antitrust. *See United States v. Aluminum Co. of Am.*, 148 F.2d 416 (2d Cir. 1945) ("Throughout the history of [antitrust] statutes it has been constantly assumed that one of their purposes was to perpetuate and preserve, for its own sake and in spite of possible costs, an organization of industry in small units which can effectively compete with each other.").

Evidence that the Supreme Court has accepted gradually the economic objectives of efficiency and increased consumer welfare as the underlying policies of antitrust has emerged from recent decisions. This is particularly true since 1974. For example, relying on earlier pronouncements by Justice Brandeis in *Chicago Board of Trade v. United States*, 246 U.S. 231 (1918), the Court in 1978 held that the trial court's responsibility is limited to determining the "competitive effect" of the challenged restraint. *National Soc'y of Prof. Eng'rs v. United States*, 435 U.S. 679, 691–95 (1978). Such an economic approach explores only "the facts peculiar to the business, the history of the restraint, and the reasons why it was imposed."

Thus, the analytical framework requires an economic inquiry that weighs the competitive harms and the economic benefits. The factual and economic issues in the final analysis are reduced to whether the challenged conduct promotes or suppresses competition. The weighing of economic and noneconomic goals was rejected, Justice Stevens concluded for the Court, because the underlying assumption of the Sherman Act implicitly dictates that "competition will produce not only lower prices, but also better goods and services." And, "the statutory policy precludes inquiry into the question whether competition is good or bad." Social benefits are not to be weighed against competition factors. The Court reasoned that a weighing of the public interest against the anticompetitive restraint would be beyond the judicial prerogative and "would be tantamount to a repeal of the statute."

Other decisions seem to conclude that the antitrust laws should be read as advancing only a consumer welfare prescription. Implicit in the Court's reasoning has been a call for performance efficiency criteria as the standard upon which competition ought to be judged. *See, e.g., Reiter v. Sonotone Corp.*, 442 U.S. 330 (1979); *Broadcast Music, Inc. v. Columbia Broadcasting Sys.*, 441 U.S. 1 (1979); *Continental T.V., Inc. v. GTE Sylvania, Inc.*, 433 U.S. 36 (1977); *Brunswick Corp. v. Pueblo Bowl-O-Mat, Inc.*, 429 U.S. 477 (1977). This theme continues with the Rehnquist Court. *Business Elec. Corp. v. Sharp Elec. Corp.*, 485 U.S. 717 (1988), reprinted in Chapter 5, *infra*; and *Brooke Group Ltd. v. Brown & Williamson Tobacco Corp.*, 509 U.S. 209 (1993), reprinted in Chapter 6.

As the study of antitrust reveals, the Supreme Court's interpretation of the policies and goals of the antitrust laws has neither been static nor consistent. The debate continues among the Court's members and, as the following suggests, also among the antitrust academic community.

Although economic factors always have been at the forefront of antitrust law, Professor Robert Pitofsky argues that the modern courts are mistaken to ignore the intended impact of antitrust legislation on non-economic concerns. Robert Pitofsky, *The Political Content of Antitrust*, 127 U. Pa. L. Rev. 1051, 1075 (1979).

> [T]he trend toward use of an exclusively economic approach to antitrust analysis excludes important political considerations that have in the past been seen as relevant by Congress and the courts.

Id.

The drafters of the Sherman Act and subsequent antitrust statutes were concerned with promoting democracy and individual freedom, as well as avoiding the need for governmental rescue of those abused by the inevitable rise of monopolistic giants. Moreover, Pitofsky notes that early judicial interpretations recognized the legislative intent to address the political implications of anticompetitive behavior.

> Such considerations as the fear that excessive concentration of economic power will foster antidemocratic political pressures, the desire to reduce the range of private discretion by a few in order to enhance individual freedom, and the fear that increased governmental intrusion will become necessary if the economy is dominated by the few, can and should be feasibly incorporated into the antitrust equation. Although economic concerns would remain paramount, to ignore these non-economic factors would be to ignore the bases of antitrust legislation and the political consensus by which antitrust has been supported.

Id.

Given antitrust's irreconcilable premises that strive to preserve competition in some instances by suppressing it in others, Judge Robert Bork contends that the law has denigrated into an "unknown policy" that threatens our society in part because this body of law is largely made by judges, not Congress. ROBERT BORK, THE ANTITRUST PARADOX: A POLICY AT WAR WITH ITSELF 6–11 (Basic Books 1992). He argues for a fundamental reform of antitrust law aimed at the maximization of consumer welfare in order to align antitrust theories with the goals and policies of our modern economic system. The direction taken by the courts presents the prospect of antitrust becoming "an internal tariff against domestic competition and free trade," which is harmful to the general public and "ultimately incompatible with the preservation of a liberal capitalist social order," he asserts. Instead, Bork encourages the courts to return to a consumer-oriented law that "understand[s] and give[s] proper weight to the crucial concept of business efficiency" no matter if the business is a competitor or a monopolist.

> A consumer-oriented law must employ economic theory to judge which market structures and practices are harmful and which beneficial. Modern antitrust has performed this task very poorly. Its version of economics is a mélange of valid insights and obviously incorrect — sometimes fantastic — assumptions about the motivations and effects of business behavior. There are many problems here, but perhaps the core of the difficulty is that the courts, and particularly the Supreme Court, have failed to understand and give proper weight to the crucial concept of business efficiency. Since productive efficiency is one of the two opposing forces that determine the degree of consumer well-being (the other being resource misallocation due to monopoly power), this failure has skewed legal doctrine disastrously. Business efficiency necessarily benefits consumers by lowering the costs of goods and services or by increasing the value of the product or service offered; this is true whether the business unit is a competitor or a monopolist. When efficiency is not counted, or when it is seen as a positive evil, it appears that no business structure or behavior has any potential for social good, and there is consequently no reason to uphold its legality if any remote danger can be imagined. The results could not have been worse, and

would probably have been better, if the Court had made the opposite mistake and refused to recognize any harm in cartels and monopolies. Yet neither mistake need have been made. The hopeful development in the current Supreme Court's approach to antitrust . . . is a single case weighing in favor of a business practice its capacity to create efficiency. That approach seems obvious, but against the background of the jurisprudence of the last two decades it appears revolutionary. Applied generally, it could save antitrust as useful and respectable policy. It is too soon to tell whether the Court will follow up its new beginning.

Id.

While disagreement about antitrust's ultimate goals may continue, general recognition of the doctrine's disruptive potential has led to a "far humbler enterprise" of antitrust jurisprudence than existed in the 1960s. H. HOVENKAMP, THE ANTITRUST ENTERPRISE 7 (2005). Because antitrust functions, in part, as a form of regulation, and an imperfect one at that, courts have become more restrained in intervening with antitrust solutions. Even practices that economists might agree have anticompetitive potential are more often left alone because the judiciary is unable to create administerable solutions. Frankly, antitrust intervention is more generally today viewed as "the exception rather than the rule." *Id.*

R.H. Lande,
Wealth Transfers as the Original and Primary Concern of Antitrust: The Efficiency Interpretation Challenged
32 HASTINGS L.J. 67, 67–106 (1982)*

Considerable dispute over the goals of the antitrust laws has surfaced in scholarly commentary on the subject. While it is unanimously agreed that Congress enacted these laws to encourage competition, disagreement continues over Congress' ultimate goals. . . .

The prevailing view is that Congress intended the antitrust laws only to increase economic efficiency. Others, however, contend that Congress was largely motivated by a number of social, moral, and political concerns. . . . Congress passed the antitrust laws to further economic objectives, but primarily objectives of a distributive rather than of an efficiency nature. In other words, Congress was concerned principally with preventing "unfair" transfers of wealth from consumers to firms with market power. . . . Congress intended to subordinate all other concerns to the basic purpose of preventing firms with market power from directly harming consumers. . . .

[T]he antitrust laws were passed primarily to further what may be called a distributive goal, the goal of preventing unfair acquisitions of consumers' wealth by firms with market power. It should be stressed, however, that Congress did not pass the antitrust laws to secure the "fair" overall distribution of wealth in our economy or even to help the poor. Congress merely wanted to prevent one transfer of wealth that it considered inequitable, and to promote the distribution of wealth that competitive markets would bring. In other words, Congress implicitly declared that "consumers' surplus"[1] was the rightful entitlement of consumers; consumers were given the right to purchase competitively priced goods. Firms with market power were condemned because they acquired this property right without compensation to consumers. . . . [T]he antitrust laws embody a strong preference for consumers over firms with market power.[2]

. . . .

Economic Effects of Monopoly Power: A Brief Overview

Modern economists have, of course, made many important advances in the theory of monopoly. The most important development may be the modern analysis of the implications of monopoly self-interest, long recognized as including higher prices and restricted output. These effects can be divided into three categories. The first, allocative inefficiency, describes the misallocation of resources, which diminishes the total wealth of society. A second effect is a transfer of wealth from consumers to monopolists. The third involves the effect of monopolies, and antimonopoly statutes, on firms' productive efficiency. . . .

Allocative Inefficiency

Monopoly pricing reduces the total amount of wealth in society. Because a monopolist produces less than would be produced under competitive conditions, some resources that would otherwise have been used to make the monopoly product will instead be used for other purposes, ones that consumers value demonstrably less. This misallocation of resources results in diminished satisfaction of society's wants, and thus, in terms of what society values, a reduction of society's total wealth. This effect is termed "allocative inefficiency." Elimination of monopoly pricing would, *ceteris paribus*, increase society's total wealth and, therefore, increase consumer satisfaction.

---

[1] Consumers' surplus is the difference between the maximum amount that a consumer would pay and the price that he or she actually pays. Suppose that widgets are priced at $2.00, the competitive price. Marginal consumers of widgets would be willing to pay only this amount. Some consumers, however, would particularly desire widgets and willingly pay more — as much as $3.00. These consumers receive $1.00 in consumers' surplus when they purchase competitively priced widgets. If a monopolist gained control of the widget market and raised the price of widgets to $3.00, marginal consumers would no longer purchase widgets, and nonmarginal consumers would lose their surplus. The widget monopoly would acquire $1.00 of monopoly profits at the expense of widget consumers. For a more detailed definition, see E. Mansfield, *Microeconomics: Theory and Applications* 15 (4th ed. 1982); G. Stigler, *The Theory of Price* 78–81 (1966).

[2] Thus, although Congress was strongly interested in increasing the size of the economic "pie" when it passed the antitrust laws, it was even more interested in ensuring its "fair" ownership. It should also be observed that all purchasers were to be protected, whether they were resellers, farmers or ultimate consumers.

Transfer of "Consumers' Surplus" from Consumers to Monopolists

The most visible and obvious result of monopoly pricing is a transfer of wealth from purchasers to the monopolist; consumers become poorer while the monopolist becomes richer. The relative size of the transferred wealth and the allocative inefficiency will vary considerably from case to case depending upon a number of factors. Under market conditions most likely to be encountered, however, the transferred wealth usually will be between two and forty times as great as the accompanying allocative inefficiency. Thus, the redistributive effects of market power generally exceed the allocative inefficiency effects by a substantial amount.

The two principal effects of monopolistic pricing, the transfer of wealth from consumers to monopolists and the decrease in allocative efficiency, are different in one fundamental manner: the latter represents a decrease in society's absolute wealth, while the former merely redistributes that wealth. As Professor Williamson has observed, "[t]his [redistributive] transformation of benefits from one form (consumers' surplus) to another (profit) is treated as a wash under the conventional welfare economics model."[3]

Nevertheless, this transfer of wealth raises a very controversial question: is the transfer of wealth a "good," "bad," or neutral result of monopoly pricing? The value-laden answer in large part is determined by whether anyone is thought to be entitled to the economic benefit of the "consumer's surplus." Under monopoly pricing, some consumers' surplus is acquired by the monopolist. Depending on one's perspective, one can be entirely indifferent to the result, or one can conclude either that the monopoly is "unfairly taking" property from consumers, or that the monopoly is only reaping its just reward.

The redistributive effects of monopoly power are clearly good or bad only with respect to the assumptions and welfare criteria that are used to evaluate them. Condemnation of the direct consumer impact of monopoly power is therefore normally and properly termed "subjective" or a "value judgment," because it is based upon a preference for consumers over monopolists. . . .

Congress decided that consumers were entitled to the benefits of a competitive economic system. Consumers were deemed entitled to the "consumer's surplus" because Congress regarded the competitive scenario as the normal one. Monopoly pricing represented a change from the norm which Congress condemned as an "unfair" taking of consumers' property.

. . . .

In summary, considerable controversy exists over the proper treatment of monopolistic transfers of wealth. . . . Congress believed consumers were entitled to products priced at competitive levels and to the opportunity to buy the quantity of products a competitive market would offer. . . . When Congress passed the antitrust laws it condemned the use of market power to interfere with these property rights or entitlements out of an explicit antimonopolistic, proconsumer bias.

---

[3] Williamson, *Economies as an Antitrust Defense Revisited*, 125 U. Pa. L. Rev. 699, 711 (1977).

. . . .

Congressional Goals

The antitrust laws are among the least precise statutes enacted by Congress. The central terms, including "competition," "unfair methods of competition," "conspiracy in restraint of trade," and "monopolize," are inherently vague and not self-defining.

It is not possible to ascertain with certainty the original goals of the antitrust laws. Not only are there conflicting statements of legislative purpose, but it is often difficult to decide whether certain statements represent isolated, unimportant views or infrequently mentioned but nevertheless significant motivating factors. . . .

The Sherman Act

[T]he legislative history of the Sherman Act reveals a total lack of concern for allocative inefficiency. Trusts and monopolies were condemned principally because they "unfairly" extracted wealth from consumers. Productive efficiency also was an aim of the Act. Congress wanted the economy to function efficiently primarily to provide consumers the benefits of free competition. . . . [I]n balancing the competing considerations, Congress condemned firms with monopoly power despite their acknowledged efficiencies, and with the knowledge that this condemnation might not maximize society's economic efficiency. Indeed, the evidence suggests that Congress was unwilling to subordinate its distributive-based distaste for trusts and monopolists to the goal of corporate efficiency when the efficiency gains would be retained by the monopolists. . . . Congress passed the Sherman Act because it believed that trusts and monopolies possess excessive social and political power, and reduce entrepreneurial liberty and opportunity.

. . . .

Protecting Consumers from Unfair Transfers of Wealth

In the legislative debates over the Sherman Act, Congress clearly condemned the use of market power to raise prices and restrict output. This condemnation, however, did not arise from concern with allocative efficiency. The debates strongly suggest that Congress condemned trusts and monopolies because they had enough market power to raise prices and "unfairly" extract wealth from consumers, turning it into monopoly profits.

In the legislative debates, Congress discussed at length price increases by trusts and the resulting higher consumer prices. For example, Senator Sherman, defending the bill's constitutionality, asked that Congress protect the public from trusts that "restrain commerce, turn it from its natural course, increase the price of articles, and therefore diminish the amount of commerce." From this and other similar evidence Judge Bork correctly concluded, "[t]he touchstone of illegality is raising prices to consumers. There were no exceptions."

The debates strongly suggest that higher prices to consumers were condemned because they unfairly extracted wealth from consumers and turned it into monopoly profit. For example, during the debates Senator Sherman termed monopolistic overcharges "extortion which makes the people poor," and "extorted wealth." Congressman Coke referred to the overcharges as "robbery." Representative Heard declared that the trusts, "without rendering the slightest equivalent," have "stolen untold millions from the people." Congressman Wilson complained that the beef trust "robs the farmer on the one hand and the consumer on the other." Representative Fithian declared that the trusts were "impoverishing" the people through "robbery." Senator Hoar declared that monopolistic pricing was "a transaction the direct purpose of which is to extort from the community . . . wealth which ought to be generally diffused over the whole community." Senator George complained that "[t]hey aggregate to themselves great enormous wealth by extortion which makes the people poor."

Congress condemned monopolistic overcharges in strong moral terms, rather than because of their efficiency effects. Purchasers, whether resellers or ultimate consumers, were entitled to purchase competitively priced products. Members of Congress also condemned the unequal distribution of wealth resulting from monopolistic overcharges. The legislators decided that competitive prices were "fair" whereas monopoly prices were not; therefore, consumers were entitled to own that quantity of wealth known today as "consumer surplus." The unfair prices, in effect, robbed consumers of that wealth. As a result, Congress was willing to risk some immediate efficiency losses in order to benefit consumers ultimately. Congress was willing to pass the Sherman Act in large part in an attempt to prevent such "unfair" transfers of wealth from consumers to monopolies.

Other Goals

Curbing the Social and Political Power of Trusts and Monopolies

. . . .

The legislative history demonstrates that Congress condemned monopolies in part because they increased the cost of goods to consumers. Logic would seem to indicate that pressure from consumers burdened by higher prices contributed to the passage of the Sherman Act. This cannot be the complete explanation, however, because just prior to the passage of the Act, price levels in the United States were stable or slowly decreasing. In 1890, American consumers paid less for goods than at almost any time since the end of the Civil War.

The legislative history reveals that a major factor leading to the passage of the Sherman Act was a congressional desire to curb the power of trusts. While Congress was concerned about the uses of this power to raise prices and restrict output, it also desired, as an end in itself, the prevention of accumulation of power by large corporations and the men who controlled them. Alarm over corporate aggrandizement of economic, social, and political power pervaded the debate. The legislators feared not only the economic consequences of monopoly power, but potential social disruptions as well. Moreover, this apprehension has been recognized repeatedly by courts interpreting the legislative history of the Act.

A review of the social history of the period illuminates the reasons underlying Congress' alarm. The post-Civil War period saw a rural agricultural nation transformed into an increasingly urban and industrial society. Work patterns changed. By the end of the Civil War individual yeoman farmers had all but vanished. In their places stood entrepreneurs and commercial farmers who shipped their goods to markets and then used the resulting cash to purchase goods from small businesses. Thus, traditional independence gradually changed into interdependence.

With the rise of trusts, interdependence became impotence. Decision making was transferred from traditional power centers to the great industrialists. Self-reliant farmers, business owners, and local leaders became dependant on the discretionary power of a few very rich men. Local control of society ended as numerous small power centers were swept away by the new class, one perceived as greedy and evil. This transfer of power generated hostility towards the trusts and resulted in political pressure on Congress to pass antitrust legislation.

Protecting Small Businesses

Congress also expressed concern for preserving business opportunities for small firms. The opportunity to compete has been viewed as particularly important for small entrepreneurs, perhaps because of their vulnerability to predatory activities. . . .

Judicial statements of congressional intention to assist small businesses have been frequent. Courts have even occasionally viewed congressional interest in protecting small businesses as overriding its consumer-oriented goals.

Despite clear judicial recognition, close examination reveals relatively little support in the legislative history, beyond the few references above, for the "small producer" rationale. Although there are a few statements suggesting that the protection of the opportunity of small business to compete was one motivating factor for the legislators, these statements do not imply that protection of small businesses was meant to override other goals. Congress probably did not intend to go further than establishment of an economic system providing free opportunities for entry and enough producers to ensure vigorous competition, a system in which no company became large enough to dominate.

Additionally, the congressional intent to assist small businesses can be interpreted as promoting distributive, rather than efficiency, considerations. Passage of the Sherman Act may have been intended, in part, to transfer wealth to small businesses. The legislative history does not indicate, however, that Congress intended to help small businesses as a means of improving the overall efficiency of the economy. The debate suggests only a possible intent to assist small businesses as an end in itself, not as a means of increasing total economic output.

Sympathetic to the plight of small businesses harmed by trusts, Congress expressed a desire to create an environment in which small businesses could effectively compete. It can fairly be said that one of Congress' goals was to assist small businesses; although consumers' interests were meant to be paramount, and conflicts between the welfare of consumers and small businesses were generally to be resolved in favor of consumers, Congress' desire to help small businesses certainly extended to those circumstances in which small businesses would be helped but consumers would not significantly suffer. . . . [T]his expression of sympathy did not amount to a congressional directive to assist small businesses in ways conflicting with the essential purpose of the Act, the protection of consumers.

Summary

Congress passed the Sherman Act to further a number of goals. Its main concern was with firms acquiring or possessing enough market power to raise prices artificially and to restrict output. Congress' primary aim was to enable consumers to purchase products at competitive prices. Artificially high prices were condemned not for causing allocative inefficiency but for "unfairly" transforming consumers' wealth into monopoly profits. All purchasers, whether consumers or businesses, were given the right to purchase competitively priced goods. All sellers were given the right to face rivals selling at competitive prices.

Concurrently, Congress was interested in encouraging efficient behavior in firms. Congress wanted a competitive economy to encourage the greater efficiencies resulting from competition. Efficiency gains were particularly desired when benefits passed through directly to consumers. A concern with productive efficiency could not, however, explain why Congress passed the Sherman Act. Congress condemned the relatively efficient trusts and monopolies for redistributive reasons. With the unlikely possibility of an exception for the "efficient monopolist," monopolizing conduct was not permitted merely because it produced efficiency gains for the monopolist.

The Act also involved efforts to decentralize economic, social, and political decision making to ensure that narrow private interests would be unable to override the public good flowing from free competition. The corporate power that the free market inadequately curbed was the target of the Act. Thus, the Act was also aimed at curbing the social and political power of large corporations and at encouraging opportunities for small entrepreneurs to compete, both thought to flow from the desired economic order as expressed in the Act.

The Sherman Act, the first antitrust law, set the tone for future antitrust legislation. Subsequent antitrust laws represented either extensions of the same ideas to different economic arenas, or attempts to better implement the same fundamental principles.

NOTE: ANTITRUST GOALS —
CONSUMER WELFARE v. GENERAL WELFARE

One widely debated issue is whether United States antitrust policy should adopt a "consumer welfare" principle rather than a more economic "total welfare" principle for determining illegality. "Total welfare" refers to the aggregate value that an economy produces, without regard for the way that gains or losses are distributed. For example, if a product costs $5 to make and is sold for $8, the $3 surplus goes to the seller. On the other side, if a customer would have been willing to pay $10 for a product but is able to purchase it for $8, then this $2 surplus is value added to the consumer. A perfectly competitive market maximizes total welfare, at least when we are not concerned about innovation. A perfectly competitive market also gives most of the surplus to consumers, however, because firms compete to the point that price equals marginal cost.

Formally, "consumer welfare" looks only at the surplus that goes to consumers, ignoring what goes to sellers. Suppose, for example, that a joint venture among the firms that dominate a market simultaneously (1) facilitates a collusive output reduction that raises consumer prices, but (2) reduces the firms' variable costs by permitting them to share production or distribution processes. In some cases the cost reduction might be so great that even the cartel price is lower than the pre-venture price. In that case this joint venture should be approved under general welfare grounds because it increases total wealth. It would also be approved under the consumer welfare principle because consumers actually benefit.

But suppose that the joint venture produces significant gains in production costs of, say, $100; however, it also facilitates a price fix that raises the overall price level by $80. In that case the joint venture would be efficient under total welfare criteria because the productive efficiency gains exceed the losses that result from collusion. The consumer welfare criterion would condemn it, however, because consumers are worse off.

The debate has both historical, or positive, as well as normative aspects. The historical debate concerns mainly whether the original intent of the framers of the Sherman Act or one of antitrust law's subsequent amendments was a general welfare test for legality, a consumer welfare test, or perhaps some alternative test. The normative debate is concerned with whether general welfare or consumer welfare should be the antitrust goal.

Concerns for administrability often favor the consumer welfare test. It does not require "balancing" to net out producer gains and consumer losses. If consumers are harmed (either by reduced output or product quality, or by higher prices resulting from the exercise of market power), then this fact trumps any amount of offsetting gains to producers, and presumably to others. Theoretically, even a minor injury to consumers outweighs significant efficiency gains. In this sense the consumer welfare test is easier to administer on a case-by-case basis than general welfare tests. Under a simple rule of reason test employing the consumer welfare principle one would have to consider whether the challenged practice creates a sufficient inference of higher prices resulting from lessened competition. If so it is presumptively unlawful. At that time the defendants will have an opportunity to show that the output model ignores efficiencies that the challenged practice produces, and that these efficiencies are so significant that the resulting price level is no higher than it had been before the venture was formed.

By contrast, a general welfare test requires a measure of net gains or losses. Some cases would not be difficult. For example, naked price fixing, unaccompanied by any integration of research, production, or output, produces no measurable efficiency gains and leads directly to higher prices. Total welfare "balancing" is easy because there is nothing to place on one side of the scale. On the other side, many purely vertical practices, including vertical territorial restraints, tying or exclusive dealing, may not result in higher consumer prices at all and have efficiency benefits that serve to explain them. In these cases the other side of the scale is empty and balancing is again easy. In the middle, however, are joint ventures with some integrative function, mergers, many unilateral practices, and at least a few vertical practices, including some instances of resale price maintenance, exclusive dealing, and tying. What these practices have in common is that under the right circumstances they can serve as an opportunity for exercising market power, but they can also produce considerable efficiencies. In these cases the market power requirement, which applies in some fashion to all of them, serves to distinguish cases where there is no consumer harm because a market wide output reduction is impossible. If market power is present, then the case is much more difficult.

The courts have rarely engaged this debate explicitly. It is worth noting, however, that any time the courts find that a limitation on competition has caused higher consumer prices or a significant threat of them they condemn the practice, without considering offsetting producer benefits. This suggests that they at least implicitly apply a consumer welfare test. *See* Herbert Hovenkamp, *Implementing Antitrust's Welfare Goals*, 81 FORDHAM L. REV. 2471 (2013). In the 2013 *Actavis* decision all eight Justices (Justice Alito did not participate) appeared to agree that consumer welfare should be the goal of the antitrust laws. Justice Breyer's opinion for the Court focused exclusively on consumer harm, saying nothing about producer gains. Chief Justice Roberts dissented (joined by Justices Scalia and Thomas), but he also concluded that "[t]he point of antitrust law is to encourage competitive markets to promote consumer welfare." By contrast, "[t]he point of patent law is to grant limited monopolies as a way of encouraging innovation." *FTC v. Actavis, Inc.*, 133 S. Ct. 2223, 2238 (2013).

II COMMON LAW LEGACIES

[A] English Foundations

Many of the framers of the Sherman Act believed they were merely enacting and federalizing the common law of trade restraints. 21 Cong. Rec. 2456, 3146, 3151–3152 (1890). But as the rich literature of today indicates, the common law had numerous branches, English and American, which included statutory as well as judge-made doctrines. H. THORELLI, THE FEDERAL ANTITRUST POLICY 10 (1954). Because of the diversity of the sources and versions of the common law up to the 1890s, no single integrated common law existed. No single standard governed the concept of restraint of competition. H. HOVENKAMP, ENTERPRISE AND AMERICAN LAW, 1836–1937, ch. 21 (1991); Dewey, *The Common-Law Background of Antitrust Policy*, 41 VA. L. REV. 759, 761 (1955). Of course, the framers of the Sherman Act believed that there was a single "general" common law. Consider *Swift v. Tyson*, 41 U.S. (16 Pet.) 1 (1842), which was not overruled until *Erie R.R. v. Tompkins*, 304 U.S. 64 (1938), decided almost 50 years after the Sherman Act was enacted. Certain developments in the common law are helpful for a general understanding of the status of the law on restraints of trade at the time of the passage of the first federal statute in 1890. *See generally* James May, *Antitrust Practice and*

Procedure in the Formative Era: The Constitutional and Conceptual Reach of State Antitrust Law, 1880–1918, 135 U. Pa. L. Rev. 495 (1987); Daniel A. Crane & Herbert Hovenkamp, *Classicism, Neoclassicism, and the Sherman Act*, in The Making of Competition Policy 71 (2013).

It seems clear that the common law developed and changed direction during the eighteenth and nineteenth centuries depending upon the economic policies being espoused at a particular time. That common-law development regarding monopolies has been described as follows:

W. Letwin, Law and Economic Policy in America: The Evolution of The Sherman Antitrust Act
18–32 (1995)*

Monopoly at Common Law

The Sherman Act was founded on the common law, the body of judicial decisions that the United States inherited from England. The common law, it has been widely believed, always favored freedom of trade. When English and American judges during the eighteenth and nineteenth centuries decided cases against monopolists, engrossers, or restrainers of trade, they thought they were continuing a tradition that reached back into "time of which no man hath memory." The congressmen who drafted and passed the Sherman Antitrust Law thought they were merely declaring the illegality of offenses that the common law had always prohibited. Those judges and legislators, like other lawyers, must have known, or at least would not have doubted, that the common-law rules on these subjects had changed in the course of time, for it is taken as axiomatic that the common law "grows." But it is not always recognized that the common law can change its direction, and without much warning begin to prohibit practices it had formerly endorsed, or to protect arrangements it had earlier condemned. Lawyers do not so readily see that the common law at any given time reflects the economic theories and policies then favored by the community, and may change as radically as those theories and policies. As a result they have too easily accepted the mistaken view that the attitude of the common law toward freedom of trade was essentially the same throughout its history.

The common law did not always defend freedom of trade and abhor monopoly. For a long time it did quite the opposite: it supported an economic order in which the individual's getting and spending were closely controlled by kings, parliaments, and mayors, statutes, and customs, and his opportunities limited by the exclusive powers of guilds, chartered companies, and patentees. The common law first began to oppose this system of regulation and privilege at the end of the sixteenth century; it did not do so wholeheartedly until the eighteenth century; and by the middle of the nineteenth century, it had again lost its enthusiasm for the task. It would have been surprising if the pattern of development had been different. Changes in the common law are changes in the attitudes of judges and lawyers; it would have been remarkable if they had persistently opposed monopoly when the rest of the

---

community did not know the word and considered the phenomenon natural or desirable. It would have been strange if lawyers had upheld *laissez faire* policies centuries before any statesman or economist had advocated or stated them, and had continued following them long after they had been abandoned or denied by the rest of the community. In fact, English laws governing monopoly and English policies for the economic organization of society changed together, except for minor differences in timing. The English law of monopoly traditionally includes four branches: the law on monopoly proper, whether by patent, charter, or custom; on forestalling, engrossing, and regrating; on contracts in restraint of trade; and on combinations in restraint of trade. These branches, distinct in form and based on more or less independent bodies of precedent, nevertheless show the same development from an active support of monopolies in the earliest period, through active opposition during an interlude of less than two centuries, to leniency and indifference which characterized them in 1890.

. . . .

The idea that the common law opposed monopolies from the earliest time onward was invented largely by Sir Edward Coke, who argued that monopoly was forbidden by the Civil Law, and implicitly by Magna Carta as well as by certain statutes of Edward III's reign. The earliest common-law precedent he could mention was a case that arose during the fourteenth century, and the modern lawyers and historians who follow his authority continue to cite that case as evidence of the ancient antagonism of common law to monopolies. Yet the case gives at least equally good evidence to the contrary.

. . . .

The great movement against the granting of monopolies by letter-patent began only at the end of the sixteenth century, although it was [so] strongly supported that within less than a hundred years the principle had been established that Parliament alone could grant a monopoly, and that generally even it could not, as the King had regularly done, sell a patent or award it on a whim or as a friendly gesture. By the end of the seventeenth century the royal letter-patent had been converted into a more or less modern version of the patent, justifiable only by a solid contribution to economic development. The process was not, however, moved by coherent opposition to monopoly; it was brought about mainly by disturbances within the monopolistic system administered largely by the guilds, and by objections not to the broad economic effect of monopolies but to the political power which the crown exercised in granting them.

The first recorded case on monopolies was *Davenant v. Hurdis*, or *The Merchant Tailors'* case decided in 1599, which shows not only the extent of monopolistic control that the guilds exercised, but also the ends that such controls were supposed to serve, and the collisions that were taking place between several guilds as each tried to maintain intact its power over a trade. The case arose under a by-law passed by the London tailors' guild in 1571. . . . [The ordinance required guild members who had clothes finished by others to have at least half the finishing done by a guild member. Plaintiff, a member of the tailors' guild, brought an action of trespass. Sir Edward Coke argued for Davenant that the by-law was unreasonable and illegal because it created a monopoly, although no clear basis in common law could be cited for the proposition. Judgment was unanimous that such a by-law that brought "all trade on traffic into the hands of one company, or one person, and to exclude all others, is illegal."]

. . . .

The decision represented an innovation in the law as much as in economic policy. There is no reported common-law case on monopoly prior to *Davenant v. Hurdis*; Coke later mentioned in Parliament some unreported cases, but their precise content is unknown. . . . A number of prior cases are known, but these were heard in the Star Chamber, Privy Council, and other prerogative courts, which generally defended such monopolies as proper exercises of the King's power. The law was still so divided on the validity of monopolies as late as 1624 that Parliament felt it necessary to include in the Statute of Monopolies a provision that "all monopolies . . . and the force and validity of them and of every of them, ought to be and shall be forever hereafter examined, heard, tried and determined by and according to the common laws of this Realm and not otherwise."

The next step, and perhaps the greatest single one, in creating the modern common law on monopolies was *Darcy v. Allen*, or *The Case of Monopolies*, decided in 1603. Where *Davenant v. Hurdis* established that a corporate by-law was invalid if it created a monopoly, *Darcy v. Allen* went further, laying down the principle that even a royal grant [by Queen Elizabeth] by patent would be invalid if it did so. . . . In short, Darcy's patent was held void on the argument that it violated the right of others to carry on their trade.

. . . .

There is no doubt that the series of cases at the turn of the seventeenth century radically changed the attitude of the common law toward monopolies.

. . . .

The first important law contributing to that result was the Statute of Monopolies of 1624, which, however, has a deceptive ring. For though it was certainly directed against monopolies, it was based not on a preference for competition, but on constitutional objections to the power which the Crown presumed in granting monopolies and to the arbitrary reasons for which it had granted them. Parliament did not at this period oppose monopolies in themselves. As Bacon told the House of Commons in 1601, its attitude was inconsistent and suspect: "If her Majesty make a patent or a monopoly unto any of her servants, that we must go and cry out against: but if she grant it to a number of burgesses or a corporation, that must stand, and that forsooth is no monopoly."

This inconsistency the House of Commons carried over into the Statute of Monopolies. The first section declared void "all monopolies and all commissions, grants, licenses, charters, and letter patents heretofore made or granted, or hereafter to be made or granted to any person or persons, bodies politic or corporate whatsoever, of or for the sole buying, selling, making, working, or using of anything, or of any other monopolies." The ninth section nevertheless provides that the Act shall not apply to any cities or towns, or any of their privileges, "or unto any corporations, companies, or fellowships of any trade, occupation, or mystery, or to any companies or societies of merchants within this Realm, erected for the maintenance, enlargement, or ordering of any trade of merchandise. . . ." And this inconsistency, which symbolized Parliament's willingness to have monopolies, provided Parliament alone granted them, was not merely a matter of words in statute. It justified the final irony in the case of *Darcy v. Allen*: only a few years after Darcy's monopoly of playing cards was judged void at common law, the same monopoly was given, under authority of the Statute of Monopolies, to the Company of Card Makers.

The Statute of Monopolies soon put an end to the arbitrary granting of private monopolies, but it was not intended to abolish customary monopoly privileges of corporations. Cities and boroughs, guilds, and chartered trading companies continued to exercise their monopoly powers to exclude strangers from various trades. The common law continued to protect them, though with lessening fervor as the influence of economic liberalism grew, and some of these monopolistic controls were finally abolished only by legislation in the nineteenth century.

[1] Contracts in Restraint of Trade

At common law, a contract in restraint of trade included agreements restricting a party from engaging in a particular trade or occupation or restricting the time, place, or manner in which that trade or occupation could be engaged. The earliest reported case was decided in 1414. In the *Case of John Dyer*, Y.B. 2 Hen. V, 5f. 5 (1414), the defendant was restricted from engaging in the trade of dyeing in a certain location for a prescribed period of time. The court condemned the restriction.

The most famous case of a common-law restraint was *Mitchel v. Reynolds*, 24 Eng. Rep. 347 (K.B. 1711). The plaintiff had entered a contract to lease a bakehouse for a period of years on the condition that the lessor, also a baker, would refrain from engaging in the bakery business for the term of the lease. Contrary to the decision in the *Dyer* case, the court held that a contract not to compete in a particular trade or occupation was valid and enforceable, as long as certain conditions were met. The first requirement was that the covenant not to compete was supported by valid consideration. Second, the covenant had to be voluntary. Third, a determination was to be made whether the contract was reasonable in limitations of time and place. Finally, the restraint could only be lawful if it were ancillary, that is secondary to an otherwise lawful main purpose. *See generally* W. Letwin, *supra*, at 42–44. *Mitchel v. Reynolds* thus established the "ancillary restraint" doctrine at common law: a contract not to compete which is ancillary to an otherwise lawful main purpose, such as the sale of a business or employment contract, is lawful when specifically limited in scope, time, and geographic area. To the extent that the court in *Mitchel v. Reynolds* required an inquiry into the purpose behind the restraint and the effects of the restraint, it established a "reasonableness" test, which later came to be known as the "rule of reason" standard.

During the nineteenth century, the English courts also considered whether the lawful purpose of the restraint could be obtained through less restrictive means. In *Horner v. Graves*, Chief Justice Tindal cautioned that the issue is:

whether the restraint is such only as to afford a fair protection to the interests of the party in favour of whom it is given, and not so large as to interfere with the interests of the public. Whatever restraint is larger than the necessary protection of the party, can be of no benefit to either, it can only be oppressive; and if oppressive, it is, in the eye of the law, unreasonable.

7 Bing. 735, 743, 131 Eng. Rep. 284, 287 (1831).

Not until some time later, however, did English courts consider whether the interest of the public was to be considered as well in determining the "reasonableness" of the restraint. The House of Lords settled the issue in 1894.

The public have an interest in every person's carrying on his trade freely: so has the individual. All interference with individual liberty of action in trading, and all restraints of trade of themselves, if there is nothing more, are contrary to public policy, and therefore void. That is the general rule. But there are exceptions: restraints of trade and interference with individual liberty of action may be justified by the special circumstances of a particular case. It is a sufficient justification, and indeed it is the only justification, if the restriction is reasonable — reasonable, that is, in reference to the interests of the parties concerned and reasonable in reference to the interests of the public, so framed and so guarded as to afford adequate protection to the party in whose favour it is imposed, while at the same time it is in no way injurious to the public.

Nordenfelt v. Maxim Nordenfelt Guns & Ammunition Co., [1894] App. Cas. 535, 565.

Letwin makes the point that by 1894:

English law on contracts in restraint of trade was not in any important respect an instrument for the maintenance of a competitive economic order. If ever, then only for a very short period after *Mitchel v. Reynolds* did the courts give the public policy of promoting competition an important part in deciding cases on contracts in restraint of trade. . . . [It seemed] that competition was no longer public policy, or at least that freedom of contract had become a more important end than freedom of trade.

W. Letwin, *supra*, at 45–46.

[2] Combinations in Restraint of Trade

The labor union movement in England during the nineteenth century had an effect on the development of the law on combinations in restraint of trade.

The common law, influenced by a feeling that employers should not be denied rights granted to workers, matched the new legal power of the latter with a solicitous concern for employers' combinations; in the end it came to put a higher value on the freedom of entrepreneurs to use any means short of violence to outstrip competitors than on the right of the public to enjoy the advantages of competition.

[A]fter the beginning of the nineteenth century, the common law came to regard an agreement between competitors to combine as analogous to a contract in restraint of trade, and judged such agreements by whether they left the parties reasonably free to act as they desired. All along less attention was paid to whether the agreement seriously interfered with competition.

W. Letwin, *supra*, at 46, 48–49. For the American developments, see Hovenkamp, *Labor Conspiracies in American Law, 1880–1930*, 66 TEX. L. REV. 919 (1988).

After a series of cases beginning in 1815 and continuing through the nineteenth century, it became rather clear that combinations or agreements in restraint of trade would be unenforceable as against public policy, but they were not deemed illegal in the sense that affirmative relief was available unless it became a conspiracy that sought unlawful means or ends. In the early 1800s, conspiracy was still considered a tort rather than a crime. H. Thorelli, *supra*, at 29. *But see* Dewey, *supra*, at 766–771. The doctrine of conspiracy in restraint of trade began to develop first as a means to control the organization of labor unions. Statutes in England were also adopted to make union combinations criminal offenses. W. Letwin, *supra*, at 46–48. By the middle of the nineteenth century, the courts were beginning to apply the law of combination in restraint of trade against manufacturers and merchants as well as labor unions, and refused to enforce agreements between competitors that set wages of employees. *Hilton v. Eckersly*, 6 El. & Bl. 47 (1855). The law also condemned production reductions, and price-fixing agreements among competitors as unenforceable combinations. *Mogul Steamship Co. v. McGregor, Gow & Co.*, 23 Q.B.D. 598 (1889), *aff'd*, A.C. 25 (1892).

But in England, the challenges to restraints of trade during the 1800s were in the context of private party litigation; public litigation at this time was out of the question.

By 1890, what little there had ever been of English common law against monopolies had become quite weak. The common law against monopoly proper had been superseded by the Statute of Monopolies. The common law against forestalling had been abolished by the statute of 1844. The common law against combinations of workmen and of masters had been overruled by the Trade Union Acts. The common law against contracts and combinations in restraint of trade alone remained in force, but it was governed by principles that condoned more than they prohibited. If monopolies were to be restrained, the common law would have to change its direction again, or legislation would have to remedy its weakness.

W. Letwin, *supra*, at 51. And as Letwin noted, English common law at the time of the adoption of the Sherman Act hardly could be considered coherent, integrated, or consistent in light of the interaction of the *laissez faire* movement with the law's development. For a good comparative study of British and American competition policy since the late nineteenth century, see T. FREYER, REGULATING BIG BUSINESS: ANTITRUST IN GREAT BRITAIN AND AMERICA, 1880–1990 (1992).

[B] American Common Law Tradition

The common law in the United States during the nineteenth century developed independently though similarly to the English common law on restraint of trade. That which did develop prior to 1890 was accomplished largely through state judge-made decisions. There was no significant integrated federal common law on restraint of trade. H. Thorelli, *supra*, at 36, 51–52. The exceptions to this were the English common-law restrictions of forestalling, engrossing, and regrating. Except in a few states, these crimes were never recognized as they were in England up to the end of the eighteenth century. On the other hand, the doctrine of restraint of trade did have a significant history in the American common law with regard to monopolies, combinations, and conspiracies.

The American common law against monopolies was particularly strong. To be sure, evidence exists that restrictions on monopoly were enforced even more rigorously in the American colonies than in England. The reasons for this vary, but critical to this development were the grants of monopoly to the English trading companies that were given charters in the colonies. Such monopolies ran counter to the individualistic character of liberty as espoused in the American colonies. Unless the monopoly was, by reason of a patent, for the purpose of invention, it was contrary to the American common law. Although there are few reported cases concerning monopoly prior to 1890, the antimonopoly sentiment was expressed for the most part in state constitutions and statutes. On the relationship between politics and the law of monopolies in nineteenth century America, see M. HORWITZ, THE TRANSFORMATION OF AMERICAN LAW, 1780–1860, 109–139 (1977); H. HOVENKAMP, ENTERPRISE, *supra*, chs. 2, 10, & 11. *See also* Jones, *Historical Development of the Law of Business Competition*, 36 YALE L.J. 207 (1926); MILLER, THE CASE OF MONOPOLIES — SOME OF ITS RESULTS AND SUGGESTIONS 1, 15–24 (1907); May, *Antitrust Practice and Procedure in the Formative Era: The Constitutional and Conceptual Reach of State Antitrust Law, 1880–1918*, 135 U. PA. L. REV. 495 (1987).

The common law regarding contracts and combinations in restraint of trade was the most developed in the United States prior to adoption of the Sherman Act. Contracts "in restraint of trade" originally included only covenants or restraints not to compete in a trade or occupation, whether restricted generally or within a stated place and time. The American common law was influenced significantly by the seminal English decision of *Mitchel v. Reynolds*, 24 Eng. Rep. 347 (K.B. 1711), discussed *supra*, which established the "ancillary restraint" doctrine. This doctrine distinguished between general (non-ancillary) restraints, which were purposefully designed to eliminate competition, and a partial (ancillary) restraint, which was secondary to the otherwise lawful main purpose of the contract. The former was held void, while the ancillary restraint was considered lawful if reasonably limited as to time, place, and scope.

In 1874, the United States Supreme Court recognized this common-law precedent by noting that it was a "well settled rule of law that an agreement in general restraint of trade is illegal and void; but an agreement which operates merely in partial restraint of trade is good, providing it be not unreasonable." *Oregon Steam Nav. Co. v. Winsor*, 87 U.S. (20 Wall.) 64, 66–67 (1874). The celebrated decision by Judge Taft in *United States v. Addyston Pipe & Steel Co.*, 85

F. 271 (6th Cir. 1898) 175 U.S. 211 (1899), is cited as the definitive authority for the acceptance of the ancillary restraint doctrine in the United States, although his analytical recapitulation of the common-law tradition regarding general (non-ancillary) restraints has been questioned. *See, e.g., United States v. Trenton Potteries Co.*, 273 U.S. 392 (1927); *Standard Oil Co. v. United States*, 221 U.S. 1 (1911).

In *Addyston Pipe & Steel*, Judge Taft surveyed the common law as it evolved from *Mitchel v. Reynolds* and suggested that partial or ancillary restraints were lawful if they were reasonably necessary to serve legitimate ends of the business arrangement, such as an employment contract or a contract to sell a business or trade. But this balancing approach, which turned on the "reasonableness" of the restraint was, according to Judge Taft's reading of the common law, applicable only in determining the legality of a restraint classified as "ancillary." If the restraint were determined to be of a "general" nature, then it was illegal as contrary to public policy, and the reviewing court would not be permitted to engage in "rule of reason" analysis to determine whether the challenged restraint was reasonable. 85 F. at 282–284. *But see Wickens v. Evans*, 3 Y. & J. 318, 148 Eng. Rep. 1202 (Ex. 1829); *Jones v. North*, 19 Eq. 426 (1875); *Collins v. Locks*, 4 App. Cas. 674 (P.C. 1879). *See generally* Arthur, *Farewell to the Sea of Doubt: Jettisoning the Constitutional Sherman Act*, 74 CAL. L. REV. 266 (1986). Thus, according to Judge Taft, restraints on trade were automatically (per se) illegal unless they were merely ancillary to one's business and reasonable. Others did not share Judge Taft's reading of the common law.

Chief Justice White, in the 1911 *Standard Oil* case, 221 U.S. 1, concluded that the rule of reason analysis should be applied regardless of whether the restraint was general or ancillary; under this standard, only "unreasonable" restraints were to be declared illegal. And in 1927, Justice (later Chief Justice) Stone, in *Trenton Potteries, supra*, stated further that restraints are illegal only if they affect price or prevent competition. 273 U.S. at 397. *See also* Dewey, *supra*, at 772–773. For a critique of Judge Taft's use of common-law sources, see H. Hovenkamp, *Enterprise, supra*, 285–287.

By the late 1800s, "restraint of trade" came to be used more generally than the law of covenants not to compete in a trade or occupation. It covered a broader array of restraints on trade, including monopolistic practices and combinations. At first in England and later in the United States, the term became part of the doctrines of conspiracy or combinations to restrain or monopolize trade. H. Thorelli, *supra*, at 53, 155. Only in the last half of the 1800s, however, were corporate trusts and pooling arrangements (e.g., agreements by competitors to "pool" and divide "all or part of the production, markets, sales, profits or patents") in the United States challenged, mainly on the theory that the corporations involved had acted beyond the power created in their charters. H. Hovenkamp, *Enterprise, supra*, chs. 6, 20. The rise of the corporate association, pooling arrangement, or trust, whereby competing businesses attempted to control prices and preserve profits by mutual agreement, came about largely as a result of the industrial development and expansion following the Civil War. The trust or pooling arrangement was an attempt to undermine the increased competition brought about by the post-war industrialization.

The state common-law precedents and statutes were not necessarily uniform and no strong federal common law of restraint of trade existed. Enforcement against restraints was weak, particularly since the trusts were multistate, and a state's jurisdictional reach was limited at this time to property and persons located within its territorial boundaries. The perceived jurisdictional limitation on state power, together with the commerce clause limitations on the federal government, necessitated new federal legislation. *See generally* Hovenkamp, *State Antitrust in the Federal Scheme*, 57 IND. L.J. 375 (1983).

[C]   Development of Legislation

The sociopolitical and economic background of the period between 1865 and 1890 set the stage for the adoption of the Sherman Act in 1890. Public antagonism towards corporate trusts and pooling arrangements, which permitted competitors to form combinations, to set prices, and divide markets, grew during this period. *See* W. Letwin, *supra*, at 54–70, 77–85. The growth of the trusts (e.g., tight combinations between competitors) occurred generally between the time of the Civil War and 1890. *See generally* H. Thorelli, *supra*, at 72–106. At first, the trusts were regional in nature. Only later did they become national in scope and control. In the 1880s and 1890s, the public focused on the large, national trusts, which were often the villains in popular literature. The Standard Oil Trust (1882), the American Cotton Trust (1884), the National Linseed Oil Trust (1885), the Sugar Trust (1887), the Whiskey Trust (1887), and the National Lead Trust (1887–1889) were all challenged legally, either on the theory that they acted *ultra vires* by entering into trust arrangements or that their trust practices were unreasonable restraints of trading tending to create a monopoly.

The period from 1865 to 1890 also witnessed the dramatic growth of the railroads. As the railroads became larger, unscrupulous, anticompetitive practices developed. People believed that charges for local traffic where monopolies existed were artificially inflated to subsidize rates for more competitive routes. This cross subsidization was thought to lead to monopoly pricing in many regions and ultimately developed into pooling agreements for the purpose of fixing rail rates. The economic probability of this, however, has been questioned. *See* Hovenkamp, *Regulatory Conflict in the Gilded Age: Federalism and the Railroad Problem*, 97 YALE L.J. 1017 (1988).

Granges and farmers felt the burden of these practices. In the mid-1870s, state Granger laws were enacted in an attempt to regulate the railroads. But the legality of these state statutes was quickly challenged on the ground such statutes were (1) not within the regulating authority of the state, (2) an unconstitutional interference with interstate commerce, and (3) a violation of the due process clause and obligation of contract clause. In a series of cases from 1876 to 1890, the Supreme Court changed course in several decisions and ultimately held that a state could not regulate rail rates and schedules even within its own territory when interstate commerce was involved. In addition, because of territorial jurisdictional limits on state common law against monopolies (or monopolistic practice) and combinations, the common law was considered ineffective as a device to control increased use of trusts and monopolies. Moreover, most suits against trust and monopolies in the last half of the 1800s were brought by private parties; only a small number of suits were initiated by public officials on behalf of their constituents, although by 1890, many states had constitutional and statutory provisions prohibiting monopolies. H. Thorelli, *supra*, at 155. Thus, it became clear that federal regulation was necessary. In 1887, Congress passed the Interstate Commerce Act to regulate the railroads; it was Congress' first attempt to enact a comprehensive economic regulatory measure. The Sherman Act in 1890 was the second.

A reading of the history, origins, and objectives of the Sherman Act indicates that there were differing views leading up to the legislation, as there had been with regard to the common-law development against restraint of trade.

The legislation was originally introduced in the Senate in 1888 by Senator John Sherman of Ohio. He argued initially that Congress could regulate trusts only through its taxing power, but later shifted his argument to include the power of Congress to regulate commerce through the commerce clause. W. Letwin, *supra*, at 87–90. During the two years that the legislation was debated in Congress, Senator Sherman opined that the legislation was intended "to destroy combinations, not all combinations, but all those which the common law had always condemned as unlawful." After floor debate, the bill was referred to the Senate Judiciary Committee, where it was redrafted. A lengthy conference committee between the Senate and House followed, with the Senate Judiciary Committee version finally prevailing. It was signed into law on July 2, 1890. No doubt, public hostility toward trusts, monopolies, and concentrations of power, however diffuse, played a role as did the "norm of free competition" in the enactment of the first federal antitrust law. *See* H. Thorelli, *supra*, at 162–163; W. Letwin, *supra*, at 53–85; A. Neale & D. Goyder, The Antitrust Laws of the U.S.A. 16–21 (3d ed. 1980).

Although the underlying economic theories of the Sherman Act were not seriously debated by its framers, many students of antitrust law have read the legislative history as promoting a particular economic ideology, such as consumer welfare. Bork, *Legislative Intent and the Policy of the Sherman Act*, 9 J.L. & Econ. 7 (1966). According to them, the purpose of the antitrust laws is to promote a market that improves (1) available productive forces and materials in accordance with consumer demands (allocative efficiency), and (2) effective use of resources by firms responding to consumer demands (productive efficiency). Other commentators have presented more broadly based interpretations of the legislative history.

According to Thorelli, there was a general consensus of the inherit value of "full and free" competition by the members of Congress who articulated the Sherman Act. In achieving this end, the goal of the government was to remove obstacles to the free flow of commerce, and not itself become an additional obstacle. Thorelli maintains that goal of Congress was ultimately to benefit the consumer, by allowing for a "continuous increase in production and commodity quality at a progressively lowered price." Yet, in "safeguarding the rights of the 'common man' in business 'equal' to those of evolving more 'ruthless' and impersonal forms enterprise the Sherman Act [also] embodies what is to be characterized as an eminently 'social' purpose." Indeed, Sherman himself held that the contemplated legislation represented a means of achieving "freedom from corruption and maintaining freedom of independent thinking in political life." While the goals behind the Sherman Act were thus nuanced, the driving force behind the Act stemmed from a common disdain of anticompetitive forces. Congress's "projection of the philosophy of competition on the plane of policy" hinged on the existence of a "direct and reversible relationship between competition on the one hand and monopoly on the other." It was not until antitrust policy had been confronted with "stark realities" that it became apparent that legislating against monopolies and other restraints on trades was not "necessarily . . . the same as enforc[ing], or maintain[ing], free competition."

[D]   Early Interpretations

Not until 1895 did the Supreme Court decide its first case under the Act. That holding bespoke of the enforcement difficulties that lay ahead in challenging trusts and monopolies. In *United States v. E.C. Knight Co.*, 156 U.S. 1 (1895), the Supreme Court, narrowly interpreting the Act's jurisdictional reach, held that the government failed to demonstrate that the sugar trust's monopoly of refining was a *direct* restraint on interstate commerce on the theory that the Sherman Act did not reach restraints affecting merely the manufacture of commodities. Under this reading, manufacturing did not come within the regulatory framework of the Sherman Act. Such a narrow holding as to what constitutes "commerce" threatened to derail the effective enforcement of the statute.

Two years later, the Court considered *United States v. Trans-Missouri Freight Ass'n*, 166 U.S. 290 (1897). A cartel was created by 18 railroads that provided rail service west of the Mississippi River for the purpose of setting freight schedules and rates for all railroads. The Department of Justice charged that the cartel was a restraint of trade in violation of Section 1 of the Sherman Act. The defense urged that such a commercial arrangement was not unlawful at common law since the fixed rates were reasonable and, therefore, the cartel was not unlawful under the Sherman Act. Justice Peckham, writing for the Court, declined to consider whether the challenged practice violated the common law. Instead, the Court interpreted Section 1 literally as condemning "every" restraint without exception as unlawful.

UNITED STATES v. TRANS-MISSOURI FREIGHT ASS'N
166 U.S. 290 (1897)

[After deciding that the Sherman Act covers railroad common carriers, the Court turned to the question of whether the railroad cartel violated any provision of the Sherman Act.]

JUSTICE PECKHAM delivered the opinion of the Court.

. . . .

The next question to be discussed . . . is the true construction of the statute. . . . Is it confined to a contract or combination which is only in unreasonable restraint of trade or commerce, or does it include what the language of the act plainly and in terms covers, all contracts of that nature?

We are asked to regard the title of this act as indicative of its purpose to include only those contracts which were unlawful at common law, but which require the sanction of a Federal statute in order to be dealt with in a Federal court. It is said that when terms which are known to the common law are used in a Federal statute those terms are to be given the same meaning that they received at common law, and that when the language of the title is "to protect trade and commerce against unlawful restraints and monopolies," it means those restraints and monopolies which the common law regarded as unlawful, and which were to be prohibited by the Federal statute. We are of opinion that the language used in the title refers to and includes and was intended to include those restraints and monopolies which are made unlawful in the body of the statute. It is to the statute itself that resort must be had to learn the meaning thereof, though a resort to the title here creates no doubt about the meaning of and does not alter the plain language contained in its text.

It is now with much amplification of argument urged that the statute, in declaring illegal every combination in the form of trust or otherwise, or conspiracy in restraint of trade or commerce, does not mean what the language used therein plainly imports, but that it only means to declare illegal any such contract which is in *unreasonable* restraint of trade, while leaving all others unaffected by the provisions of the act; that the common-law meaning of the term "contract in restraint of trade" includes only such contracts as are in *unreasonable* restraint of trade, and when that term is used in the Federal statute it is not intended to include all contracts in restraint of trade, but only those which are in unreasonable restraint thereof.

The term is not of such limited signification. Contracts in restraint of trade have been known and spoken of for hundreds of years both in England and in this country, and the term includes all kinds of those contracts which in fact restrain or may restrain trade. Some of such contracts have been held void and unenforceable in the courts by reason of their restraint being unreasonable, while others have been held valid because they were not of that nature. A contract may be in restraint of trade and still be valid at common law. Although valid, it is nevertheless a contract in restraint of trade, and would be so described either at common law or elsewhere. By the simple use of the term "contract in restraint of trade," all contracts of that nature, whether valid or otherwise, would be included, and not alone that kind of contract which was invalid and unenforceable as being in unreasonable restraint of trade. When, therefore, the body of an act pronounces as illegal every contract or combination in restraint of trade or commerce among the several States, etc., the plain and ordinary meaning of such language is not limited to that kind of contract alone which is in unreasonable restraint of trade, but all contracts are included in such language, and no exception or limitation can be added without placing in the act that which has been omitted by Congress. . . .

A contract which is the mere accompaniment of the sale of property, and thus entered into for the purpose of enhancing the price at which the vendor sells it, which in effect is collateral to such sale, and where the main purpose of the whole contract is accomplished by such sale, might not be included, within the letter or spirit of the statute in question. But we cannot see how the statute can be limited, as it has been by the courts below, without reading into its text an exception which alters the natural meaning of the language used, and that, too, upon a most material point, and where no sufficient reason is shown for believing that such alteration would make the statute more in accord with the intent of the law-making body that enacted it.

The great stress of the argument for the defendants on this branch of the case has been to show, if possible, some reason in the attendant circumstances, or some fact existing in the nature of railroad property and business upon which to found the claim, that although by the language of the statute agreements or combinations in restraint of trade or commerce are included, the statute really means to declare illegal only those contracts, etc., which are in unreasonable restraint of trade. . . .

The plaintiffs are, however, under no obligation in order to maintain this action to show that by the common law all agreements among competing railroad companies to keep up rates to such as are reasonable were void as in restraint of trade or commerce. There are many cases which look in that direction if they do not precisely decide that point. . . . But assuming that agreements of this nature are not void at common law and that the various cases cited by the learned courts below show it, the answer to the statement of their validity now is to be found in the terms of the statute under consideration. . . .

The claim that the company has the right to charge reasonable rates, and that, therefore, it has the right to enter into a combination with competing roads to maintain such rates, cannot be admitted. The conclusion does not follow from an admission of the premise. What one company may do in the way of charging reasonable rates is radically different from entering into an agreement with other and competing roads to keep up the rates to that point. If there be any competition the extent of the charge for the service will be seriously affected by that fact. Competition will itself bring charges down to what may be reasonable, while in the case of an agreement to keep prices up, competition is allowed no play; it is shut out, and the rate is practically fixed by the companies themselves by virtue of the agreement, so long as they abide by it. . . .

In the view we have taken of the question, the intent alleged by the Government is not necessary to be proved. The question is one of law in regard to the meaning and effect of the agreement itself, namely: Does the agreement restrain trade or commerce in any way so as to be a violation of the act? We have no doubt that it does. The agreement on its face recites that it is entered into "for the purpose of mutual protection by establishing and maintaining reasonable rates, rules and regulations on all freight traffic, both through and local." To that end the association is formed and a body created which is to adopt rates, which, when agreed to, are to be the governing rates for all the companies, and a violation of which subjects the defaulting company to the payment of a penalty, and although the parties have a right to withdraw from the agreement on giving thirty days' notice of a desire so to do, yet while in force and assuming it to be lived up to, there can be no doubt that its direct, immediate and necessary effect is to put a restraint upon trade or commerce as described in the act.

For these reasons the suit of the Government can be maintained without proof of the allegation that the agreement was entered into for the purpose of restraining trade or commerce or for maintaining rates above what was reasonable. The necessary effect of the agreement is to restrain trade or commerce, no matter what the intent was on the part of those who signed it. . . .

[In dissent, JUSTICE WHITE urged that the Sherman Act only condemned unreasonable restraints.]

NOTES AND QUESTIONS

1. The following year, the Court reconsidered its reasoning and concluded that its interpretation of Section 1 was overinclusive. In *United States v. Joint Traffic Ass'n*, 171 U.S. 505 (1898), Justice Peckham, for the Court, observed:

> We are not aware that it has ever been claimed that a lease or purchase by a farmer, manufacturer, or merchant of an additional farm, manufactory, or shop, or the withdrawal from business of any farmer, merchant, or manufacturer, restrained commerce or trade within any legal definition of that term; and the sale of a goodwill of a business with an accompanying agreement not to engage in a similar business was instanced in the *Trans-Missouri* case as a contract not within the meaning of the act; and it was said that such a contract was collateral to the main contract of sale, and was entered into for the purpose of enhancing the price at which the vendor sells his business. . . . [T]he statute applies only to those contracts whose direct and immediate effect is a restraint upon interstate commerce, and that to treat the act as condemning all agreements under which, as a result, the cost of conducting an interstate commercial business may be increased, would enlarge the application of the act far beyond the fair meaning of the language used. . . . An agreement entered into for the purpose of promoting the legitimate business of an individual or corporation, with no purpose to thereby affect or restrain interstate commerce, and which does not directly restrain such commerce, is not, as we think, covered by the act, although the agreement indirectly and remotely affects that commerce. . . . To suppose, as is assumed by counsel, that the effect of the decision in the *Trans-Missouri* case is to render illegal most business contracts or combinations, however indispensable and necessary they may be, because, as they assert, they all restrain trade in some remote and indirect degree, is to make a most violent assumption, and one not called for or justified by the decision mentioned, or by any other decision of this court.

2. Does Justice Peckham's opinion indicate that an arrangement that had only an incidental effect on competition would be lawful under the Sherman Act? Would it matter whether the purpose of the agreement was to lessen competition? Could the restraint be saved if its terms were reasonable in light of market conditions? What remains of *Trans-Missouri* after *Joint Traffic*? Does the Sherman Act extend beyond conduct condemned under the common law?

Implicit in Justice Peckham's opinion is a standard of competition under which subsequent cases have been judged. The decision suggests that concerted market practices, like price fixing, that affect competition directly are illegal and no inquiry as to the reasonableness of the price will be considered. *Joint Traffic* did indicate, however, that there may be market arrangements that do not directly or significantly affect competition and for which the Court should evaluate the reasonableness of the practice. The Court also alluded to the common-law "ancillary restraint" doctrine and in dicta suggested that such incidental restraints are not condemned under Section 1.

Consider also Justice Peckham's statement in *Trans-Missouri* that business agreements

> . . . may even temporarily, or perhaps permanently, reduce the price of the article traded in or manufactured, by reducing the expense inseparable from the running of many different companies for the same purpose. Trade or commerce under those circumstances may nevertheless be badly and unfortunately restrained by driving out of business the small dealers and worthy men whose lives have been spent therein, and who might be unable to readjust themselves to their altered surroundings. Mere reduction in the price of the commodity dealt in might be dearly paid for by the ruin of such a class.

166 U.S. at 323.

Does Justice Peckham's "small dealers and worthy men" phrase indicate that the Sherman Act is designed to protect small competitors and producers? If so, would this interpretation be compatible with the goal of protecting consumers? *See* R. Bork, The Antitrust Paradox 25 (1978).

The analysis introduced in *Joint Traffic* had been considered the same year by Judge Taft, later Chief Justice, in the famous case that established the American rule governing ancillary restraints and the standard employed in analyzing price-fixing cases.

UNITED STATES v. ADDYSTON PIPE & STEEL CO.
85 F. 271 (6th Cir. 1898), *aff'd*, 175 U.S. 211 (1899)

[Defendants were six corporations manufacturing cast iron pipe. They were charged with engaging in a cartel to divide competitive territories and to fix the price within the territories. Markets were divided in many of the southern and western states. Collusive bid practices were part of the scheme. The evidence tended to show that the cartel set the price of the iron pipe low enough to foreclose competition from east coast manufacturers, but high enough to deter competition among the defendants and that prices would have been lower had the local manufacturers competed. The questions presented were: (1) "was the association of the defendants a contract, combination, or conspiracy in restraint of trade . . . (2) was the trade thus restrained trade between the states?"]

Circuit Judge Taft delivered the opinion of the Court.

The contention on behalf of defendants is that the association would have been valid at common law, and that the federal anti-trust law was not intended to reach any agreements that were not void and unenforceable at common law. It might be a sufficient answer to this contention to point to the decision of the Supreme Court of the United States in *United States v. Trans-Missouri Freight Ass'n*, 166 U.S. 290, in which it was held that contracts in restraint of interstate transportation were within the statute, whether the restraints would be regarded as reasonable at common law or not. It is suggested, however, that the case related to a quasi public employment necessarily under public control, and affecting public interests, and that a less stringent rule of construction applies to contracts restricting parties in sales of merchandise, which is purely a private business, having in it no element of a public or quasi public character. Whether or not there is substance in such a distinction, — a question we do not decide, — it is certain that, if the contract of association which bound the defendants was void and unenforceable at the common law because of restraint of trade, it is within the inhibition of the statute if the trade it restrained was interstate. Contracts that were in unreasonable restraint of trade at common law were not unlawful in the sense of being criminal, or giving rise to a civil action for damages in favor of one prejudicially affected thereby, but were simply void, and were not enforced by the courts. . . . The effect of the act of 1890 is to render such contracts unlawful in an affirmative or positive sense, and punishable as a misdemeanor, and to create a right of civil action for damages in favor of those injured thereby, and a civil remedy by injunction in favor of both private persons and the public against the execution of such contracts and the maintenance of such trade restraints.

The argument for defendants is that their contract of association was not, and could not be, a monopoly, because their aggregate tonnage capacity did not exceed 30 per cent of the total tonnage capacity of the country; that the restraints upon the members of the association, if restraints they could be called, did not embrace all the states, and were not unlimited in space; that such partial restraints were justified and upheld at common law if reasonable, and only proportioned to the necessary protection of the parties; that in this case the partial restraints were reasonable, because without them each member would be subjected to ruinous competition by the other, and did not exceed in degree of stringency or scope what was necessary to protect the parties in securing prices for their product that were fair and reasonable to themselves and the public; that competition was not stifled by the association because the prices fixed by it had to be fixed with reference to the very active competition of pipe companies which were not members of the association, and which had more than double the defendants' capacity; that in this way the association only modified and restrained the evils of ruinous competition, while the public had all the benefit from competition which public policy demanded.

. . . .

The inhibition against restraints of trade at common law seems at first to have had no exception. . . . After a time it became apparent to the people and the courts that it was in the interest of trade that certain covenants in restraint of trade should be enforced. . . . [A]fter a man had built up a business with an extensive good will, he should be able to sell his business and good will to the best advantage, and he could not do so unless he could bind himself by an enforceable contract not to engage in the same business in such a way as to prevent injury to that which he was about to sell. It was equally for the good of the public and trade, when partners dissolved, and one took the business, or they divided the business, that each partner might bind himself not to do anything in trade thereafter which would derogate from his grant of the interest conveyed to his former partner. [T]his effect was only an incident to the main purpose of a union of their capital, enterprise, and energy to carry on a successful business, and one useful to the community. . . .

[C]ovenants in partial restraint of trade are generally upheld as valid when they are agreements (1) by the seller of property or business not to compete with the buyer in such a way as to derogate from the value of the property or business sold; (2) by a retiring partner not to compete with the firm; (3) by a partner pending the partnership not to do anything to interfere, by competition or otherwise, with the business of the firm; (4) by the buyer of property not to use the same in competition with the business retained by the seller; and (5) by an assistant, servant, or agent not to compete with his master or employer after the expiration of his time of service. Before such agreements are upheld, however, the court must find that the restraints attempted thereby are reasonably necessary (1, 2, and 3) to the enjoyment by the buyer of the property, good will, or interest in the partnership bought; or (4) to the legitimate ends of the existing partnership; or (5) to the prevention of possible injury to the business of the seller from use by the buyer of the thing sold; or (6) to protection from the danger of loss to the employer's business caused by the unjust use on the part of the employee of the confidential knowledge acquired in such business. . . .

It would be stating it too strongly to say that these five classes of covenants in restraint of trade include all of those upheld as valid at the common law; but it would certainly seem to follow from the tests laid down for determining the validity of such an agreement that no conventional restraint of trade can be enforced unless the covenant embodying it is merely ancillary to the main purpose of a lawful contract, and necessary to protect the covenantee in the enjoyment of the legitimate fruits of the contract, or to protect him from the dangers of an unjust use of those fruits by the other party. . . .

[T]he rule implies that the contract must be one in which there is a main purpose, to which the covenant in restraint of trade is merely ancillary. The covenant is inserted only to protect one of the parties from the injury which, in the execution of the contract or enjoyment of its fruits, he may suffer from the unrestrained competition of the other. The main purpose of the contract suggests the measure of protection needed, and furnishes a sufficiently uniform standard by which the validity of such restraints may be judicially determined. In such a case, if the restraint exceeds the necessity presented by the main purpose of the contract, it is void for two reasons: First, because it oppresses the covenantor, without any corresponding benefit to the covenantee; and, second, because it tends to a monopoly. But where the sole object of both parties in making the contract as expressed therein is merely to restrain competition, and enhance or maintain prices, it would seem that there was nothing to justify or excuse the restraint, that it would necessarily have a tendency to monopoly, and therefore would be void. In such a case there is no measure of what is necessary to the protection of either party, except the vague and varying opinion of judges as to how much, on principles of political economy, men ought to be allowed to restrain competition. There is in such contracts no main lawful purpose, to subserve which partial restraint is permitted, and by which its reasonableness is measured, but the sole object is to restrain trade in order to avoid the competition which it has always been the policy of the common law to foster.

Much has been said in regard to the relaxing of the original strictness of the common law in declaring contracts in restraint of trade void as conditions of civilization and public policy have changed, and the argument drawn therefrom is that the law now recognizes that competition may be so ruinous as to injure the public, and, therefore, that contracts made with a view to check such ruinous competition and regulate prices, though in restraint of trade, and having no other purpose, will be upheld. We think this conclusion is unwarranted by the authorities when all of them are considered. It is true that certain rules for determining whether a covenant in restraint of trade ancillary to the main purpose of a contract was reasonably adapted and limited to the necessary protection of a party in the carrying out of such purpose have been somewhat modified by modern authorities. . . . But these cases all involved contracts in which the covenant in restraint of trade was ancillary to the main and lawful purpose of the contract, and was necessary to the protection of the covenantee in the carrying out of that main purpose. They do not manifest any general disposition on the part of the courts to be more liberal in supporting contracts having for their sole object the restraint of trade than did the courts of an earlier time. It is true that there are some cases in which the courts, mistaking, as we conceive, the proper limits of the relaxation of the rules for determining the unreasonableness of restraints of trade, have set sail on a sea of doubt, and have assumed the power to say, in respect to contracts which have no other purpose and no other consideration on either side than the mutual restraint of the parties, how much restraint of competition is in the public interest, and how much is not.

The manifest danger in the administration of justice according to so shifting, vague, and indeterminate a standard would seem to be a strong reason against adopting it. . . .

Upon this review of the law and the authorities, we can have no doubt that the association of the defendants, however reasonable the prices they fixed, however great the competition they had to encounter, and however great the necessity for curbing themselves by joint agreement from committing financial suicide by ill-advised competition, was void at common law, because in restraint of trade, and tending to a monopoly. But the facts of the case do not require us to go so far as this, for they show that the attempted justification of this association on the grounds stated is without foundation.

. . . .

It has been earnestly pressed upon us that the prices at which the cast-iron pipe was sold in pay territory were reasonable. . . . We do not think the issue an important one, because, as already stated, we do not think that at common law there is any question of reasonableness open to the courts with reference to such a contract. Its tendency was certainly to give defendants the power to charge unreasonable prices, had they chosen to do so. But, if it were important, we should unhesitatingly find that the prices charged in the instances which were in evidence were unreasonable. . . .

Reversed.

[The case was affirmed the next year by the Supreme Court in an opinion by

Justice Peckham.]

NOTES AND QUESTIONS

1. On what ground did the Court find the challenged agreement to be illegal? Did the Court rely on the analysis of *Trans-Missouri* in finding a Sherman Act violation? What relevance did Judge Taft's discussion of ancillary restraints have on the cartel price-fixing agreement? Under what circumstances does the "ancillary restraint" doctrine protect a covenant not to compete?

Judge Taft's opinion on the ancillary restraint doctrine set the standard for the distinction between lawful and unlawful restraints. Moreover, he opined that if prices were set by means other than competition in the market, they were illegal regardless of their reasonableness. Thus a two-prong approach to antitrust jurisprudence emerged from Judge Taft's opinion. For Taft, the "reasonableness" test (later called the "rule of reason") was applied at common law only to ancillary restraints, but not to such direct restraints as price fixing, which he characterized as "naked restraints." According to Taft, this same standard was to be incorporated into the Sherman Act, as well. This approach was challenged by Chief Justice White, however, in *Standard Oil* (1911). He had dissented in *Trans-Missouri*. The opinion charts the so-called "rule of reason" approach to antitrust.

2. In *Standard Oil Co. v. United States*, 221 U.S. 1 (1911), a combination of 37 oil companies was managed through a holding company. The companies were brought together and joined through a series of devices and mergers. The combination was charged with predatory conduct and anti-competitive abuses, including price cutting and discriminatory pricing. Defendants were charged with violating Sections 1 and 2 of the Sherman Act. The Court found for the government and ordered dissolution of the combinations.

Chief Justice White delivered the opinion of the Court, holding that the standard of reason which had been applied at the common law and in this country in dealing with subjects of the character embraced by the statute was intended to be the measure used for the purpose of determining whether in a given case a particular act had or had not brought about the wrong against which the statute provided.

> [C]onsidering the contracts or agreements, their necessary effect and the character of the parties by whom they were made, they were clearly restraints of trade within the purview of the statute, they could not be taken out of that category by indulging in general reasoning as to the expediency or non-expediency of having made the contracts or the wisdom or want of wisdom of the statute which prohibited their being made. [T]he nature and character of the contracts, creating as they did a conclusive presumption which brought them within the statute, such result was not to be disregarded by the substitution of a judicial appreciation of what the law ought to be for the plain judicial duty of enforcing the law as it was made.

For a good historical discussion of the development of antitrust case law from the turn of the century through *Standard Oil*, see IX A. Bickel & B. Schmidt, *Holmes Devise History of the Supreme Court*, 86–199 (1984).

3. In *United States v. American Tobacco Co.*, 221 U.S. 106, 179 (1911), decided 14 days after *Standard Oil*, Chief Justice White observed further:

> Applying the rule of reason to the construction of the statute, it was held in the *Standard Oil Case*, that as the words 'restraint of trade' at common law . . . only embraced acts or contracts or agreements or combinations which operated to the prejudice of the public interests by unduly restricting competition or unduly obstructing the due course of trade or which, either because of their inherent nature or effect or because of the evident purpose of the acts, etc., injuriously restrained trade.

4. After *Standard Oil*, is the term "restraint of trade" restricted to its common-law meaning? How did Chief Justice White's Sherman Act analysis differ from Judge Taft's? Under Chief Justice White's approach, could direct and purposeful restraints ever be considered valid under Section 1? *See, e.g., Chicago Board of Trade v. United States*, 246 U.S. 231 (1918); *Appalachian Coals, Inc. v. United States*, 288 U.S. 344 (1933); *National Soc'y of Prof. Eng'rs v. United States*, 435 U.S. 679 (1978); *Broadcast Music, Inc. v. CBS*, 441 U.S. 1 (1979). What probative value would evidence of the "purpose" or "effect" of the combination have in determining the reasonableness of the restraint? Do we know from Chief Justice White's "standard of reason" whether harmful effects can be inferred from the purpose of the arrangement? Does the "reasonableness" standard permit defense counsel to argue that the challenged practice will promote the public interest better than market forces?

Chief Justice White's reasoning suggests that Judge Taft's line-drawing regarding the limits of judicial discretion in Section 1 cases was too narrow. Taft would have limited the judicial inquiry into reasonableness of the restraint only as to restraints classified as incidental or ancillary. If the restraint was not ancillary, it was automatically illegal. In *Addyston Pipe*, Taft made it clear that those defending deliberate restraints of trade as being within the public interest were setting "sail on a sea of doubt." White, however, would apply the rule of reason analysis to direct, as well as ancillary, restraints in determining whether they were reasonable. Only "unreasonable" or "undue" restraints of trade were illegal under the later view. The standard seemed to be whether there has been a significant interference with or impact on *competition*, although competition was never defined.

White's observation in *American Tobacco* sets forth the critical inquiry for determining this standard: an illegal restraint is one that includes a contract, agreement, or combination, which either by its inherent nature or anticompetitive purpose or effect unduly restricts competition. Consider *Standard Oil's* admonition that rate fixing between competitors is by its "nature, character and necessary effect" anticompetitive and hence subject to a "conclusive presumption" of invalidity. Thus, if the restraint is not by its nature or character inherently anticompetitive, then the purpose or effect of the contract, combination, or agreement must be considered. In sum, Chief Justice White focused the analysis on whether the nature, purpose, or effect of the restraint was unreasonably anticompetitive. Evidence or reasonable inferences therefrom could support a finding of unreasonableness. The rule of reason standard was thus created as a model of analysis and construction for decision making.

5. *Clayton Act and FTC Act.* Applying his newly articulated rule of reason, Chief Justice White found that the defendants in *Standard Oil* did in fact engage in unreasonable restraints of trade and ordered dissolution of Standard Oil. But the rule of reason approach announced by White caused critics to fear that the broader analysis set forth by White might weaken the statute, given its vagueness. Bills were introduced in Congress to amend the Sherman Act so that reasonable as well as unreasonable restraints of trade would come within its ambit. Because no consensus emerged on the proposed amendments, it was not until after the presidential elections of 1912 that new antitrust laws became a reality.

In 1914, President Wilson proposed that the Sherman Act not be amended, but that supplementary legislation be enacted which would be more explicit in condemning specific conduct. He advocated also the establishment of an independent trade commission, which was to be an expert body that would investigate trade practices and be involved in the remedial stage of antitrust suits. W. Letwin, *supra*, at 270–273.

As a result of Wilson's proposals, the Clayton Act and the Federal Trade Commission Act were adopted in 1914. These statutes were designed to reach trade practices in their "incipiency," before they reached monopoly status. The Clayton Act specifically targeted interlocking directors (Section 8), exclusive dealing and tying arrangements (Section 3), price discriminations (Section 2), and acquisitions or mergers (Section 7). The operative language qualifying the conduct was whether the effects of the challenged practice "may be to substantially lessen competition or tend to create a monopoly in any line of commerce."

The open-endedness of these standards defied specificity and clarity. The Conference Committee Report amplified why Congress was unable to be more precise regarding the prohibitive conducts:

> It is now generally recognized that the only effective means of establishing and maintaining monopoly, where there is no control of a natural resource as of transportation, is the use of unfair competition. The most certain way to stop monopoly at the threshold is to prevent unfair competition.
>
>   . . . .
>
> It is impossible to frame definitions which embrace all unfair practices. There is no limit to human inventiveness in this field. . . . If Congress were to adopt the method of definition, it would undertake an endless task.

63d Cong., 2d Sess., H.R. Rep. No. 1142, 18–29 (1914).

But subsequent interpretations have included within its scope practices found unlawful under the Sherman and Clayton Act, incipient conduct bordering on Sherman and Clayton Act violations, and there is indication that it might also include merely "unfair" conduct.

The Federal Trade Commission, also established in 1914, was designed to operate separately from the Antitrust Division of the Department of Justice. Originally its authority was limited to issuing cease and desist orders. No private right of action or criminal jurisdiction was provided. Its principal substantive provision declared illegal unfair methods of competition and unfair or deceptive acts or practices in or affecting commerce. Section 5 of the Act originally proscribed only "unfair methods of competition." The Wheeler-Lee Act of 1938 amended the statute to prohibit "unfair" or deceptive acts or practices." In general, the Commission and the Department of Justice have concurrent jurisdiction over enforcement of the Clayton Act, while the Department of Justice has primary responsibility over enforcement of the Sherman Act. The Department has no jurisdiction over the FTC Act.

Chapter 2

FRAMEWORK FOR ANALYSIS

I THE ECONOMIC PROBLEM

[A] Introduction

The economic theory of antitrust law is based on two parts of microeconomics called price theory and industrial organization. Together, these are concerned with the behavior and structure of firms under various competitive conditions.

Every society must make decisions regarding what products are to be produced, in what quantities, and to whom the products are to be distributed. Societies over the ages and those of contemporary times have found but three types of systems that separately or in combinations enable us to solve economic problems. These systems are economies run by tradition, economies run by command of the sovereign, and economies run by the market.

Although economies based on tradition or command may pre-date market economies, market economies today dominate the world. In the United States, notwithstanding a large government, most resources are still allocated through some type of market exchange.

Several important factors distinguish a market economy from any other form of economic organization. In a market economy, no central authority decides what to produce, how much of each product to produce, and what prices to charge. How then are these decisions made? They are made by individuals, both producers and consumers, seeking not the good of the community but only their own self-interest. Central to the economist's model of predicting behavior is the underlying assumption that each person in society strives to maximize his or her own personal wealth and by doing so, maximizes the wealth of the entire community. For instance, the microeconomic model predicts that consumers will make purchase decisions in order to maximize their own desires, given their income and the price. On the other side, producers will strive to satisfy consumer demands by producing products at output levels that maximize producer profits. The force that channels the avarice of individuals, whether consumers or producers, into socially productive ends is competition. Without competition, the "free enterprise" system falls apart: resources are used in a socially inefficient manner.

[B]   Law of Demand

The law of demand refers to a phenomenon each of us observes every day: more of a given product is purchased if its price is lowered, providing nothing else changes. Graphically, this corresponds to a downward sloping demand curve as pictured in Figure 1. At price P_1, only Q_1 units of the commodity are demanded while at the lower price, P_2, Q_2 units are demanded. As the price decreases from P_1 to P_2 the quantity demanded increases from Q_1 to Q_2. The demand curve in this figure is a straight line, implying that demand changes and price changes occur at exactly the same rate. In the real world, this is probably never the case. The linear demand curve oversimplifies the real-world dynamics but often makes market behavior easier to understand.

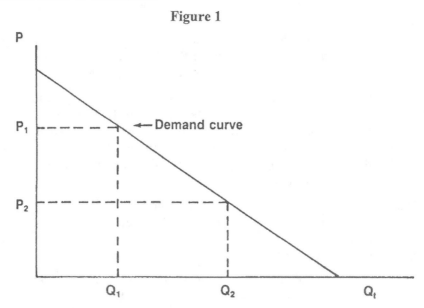

Figure 1

Of special importance are the determinants of the shape and slope (steepness) of the demand curve. Consider the two diagrams in Figure 2.

Panel (a) depicts a situation where the product in question is indispensable in some invariable amount. Therefore, a predetermined quantity of Q_1 will be demanded no matter what price is charged. We sometimes say that such a product has no substitutes. For example, only polio vaccine will prevent the disease of polio; no other will do. A product of this kind is said to be perfectly price-*inelastic*. Demand is called inelastic because even though the price is increased, the quantity demanded remains unchanged. But such products are extremely rare, and very likely not even polio vaccine qualifies. Some people will choose not to be vaccinated if the price goes too high. Thus, even this demand curve will probably have a slightly horizontal slope. In fact, few, if any, scarce resources have a perfectly vertical demand curve.

Panel (b) depicts the polar extreme. This product is so similar to others that a slight increase in its price will result in an immediate shift to the other products by consumers and leave zero demand for this product. For example, if farmer *A* attempts to market his wheat at prices higher than prevailing, then consumers will shift to farmer *B*'s wheat, a perfect substitute. From the farmer's point of view, the demand for wheat is said to be perfectly elastic.

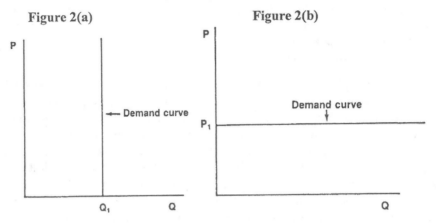

Consider the difference between a demand curve faced by an entire industry versus the demand curve faced by each of several firms within the industry. Figure 3 depicts the demand curve for the entire market for some product. Suppose that from the consumer's viewpoint all firms in the industry produce identical products. Then, any one firm in the industry will face a demand structure as pictured in Figure 2(b), above. A single firm acting alone cannot charge a price higher than P_1 without losing all sales and will not charge a price lower than P_1 because all output can be sold at price P_1. If a large number of firms produce identical products, each firm faces a perfectly elastic demand curve. This concept is crucial to understanding the respective performances of competitive and monopoly market structures.

Figure 3

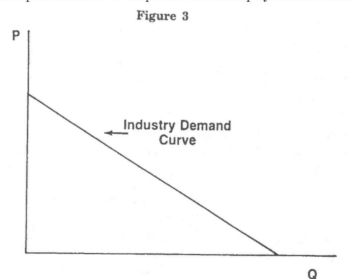

A final word on elasticities. The elasticity of demand facing a particular individual firm is a function not only of the price it attempts to charge but also of the ability of other firms to offer products that consumers view as substitutes. If firm *A* attempts to raise the price of product *X*, two things will happen: first, customers will try to switch away from *X*; second, competing producers will attempt to manufacture something that resembles *X*, or if they are already manufacturing a close substitute, to increase their production. The measurement of this latter phenomenon is called the market "elasticity of supply."

Elasticity of supply can be a function of many things: the closeness with which consumers view one product as a substitute for another one, excess capacity in the hands of competing producers, and the ease with which competing firms can enter firm *A*'s market. At the limit, elasticity of supply will be infinite and if firm *A* attempts to raise the price of product *X* by even a small amount, *A* will lose all its sales. Perhaps, for example, customers view product *Y* as a good substitute for *X*, and the firms manufacturing *Y* have unused capacity in their factories. These firms will respond to *A*'s price increase by producing more of *Y*. Likewise, if entry into manufacture of *X* is very easy, new firms will enter the market when the price of *X* rises. In an extreme case, *A* might have 100% of the market for *X* at the current price, but be absolutely unable to raise the price of *X* without losing all sales. Although economists commonly refer to this phenomenon as "elasticity of supply," courts have given it a number of names — such as "production substitutability" or "exchangeability."

In evaluating elasticity of supply, a court must consider not only the likelihood that new firms will enter the market, but also the amount of time that new entry will require. If entry into a market is relatively easy, but construction of a plant and creation of a distribution network takes five years, an existing monopolist in that market will be able to earn five years' worth of monopoly profits.

[C] The Theory of Costs

In order for production to occur, there must be some expenditure of land, raw materials, labor, and capital. Each of these factors of production requires compensation to bring it into the production process. An increase in output generally requires an increase in the amount of inputs that are needed. The result is increased costs.

Consider the situation where a plant already exists and we want to describe how costs vary as a result of differing plant utilization rates. Cost relationships may, of course, be quite different for a particular industry under study. We will describe this situation as short run because at least one element of the costs of production — the plant itself — will not vary with varying rates of production.

The costs associated with provision of the plant itself do not depend on the level of plant production. For example, the interest on the plant mortgage must be paid whether the plant operates or not. As a result, such costs are called "fixed costs." Figure 4 presents the graph of total fixed costs to the plant output level. By contrast, other costs change with the rate of output — the higher the output, the higher these costs become. Raw materials, utilities, and most kinds of labor are included in this category of "variable costs."

Figure 4

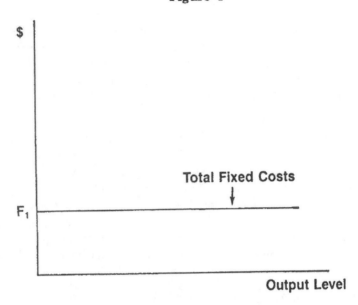

Figure 5, panel (a) presents the relationship of "total variable costs" to the plant output level. The graph is drawn to reflect phenomena observed in many production processes. At low levels of output (say below A), variable costs rise rather rapidly but at a decreasing rate. In the middle range of utilization,

Figure 5

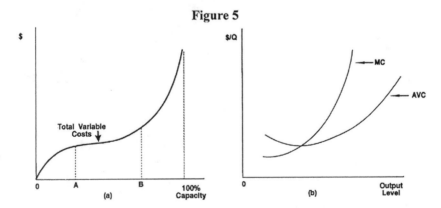

between points A and B, variable costs rise more slowly with increased output. At high levels of utilization, above point B, variable costs rise at an increasing rate. The shape of the total variable cost curve indicates that a plant operates most efficiently in certain ranges of output. If the plant is operated outside of these ranges, a substantial penalty is incurred in terms of higher per unit costs. Notice that panel (b) of Figure 5 presents the graph of variable costs per unit of output against the output level. These average variable costs are obtained by dividing total variable costs by the output level. In many industries, a plant's costs are fairly constant over a wide output range. In that case the average variable cost (AVC) curve will have a flatter bottom than the curve in Figure 5(b).

Because all costs are characterized as either a fixed cost or a variable cost, total fixed costs plus total variable costs equal total cost. Combining Figures 4 and 5, we obtain a total short run cost function illustrated in Figure 6, panel (a). Consider that its shape is identical to that of the total variable cost function, with the only difference being the addition of F_1 (fixed cost) at every output level.

Panel (b) of Figure 6 presents the average total cost curve and the marginal cost curve. Average total costs are calculated by dividing total cost at any given output level by the quantity produced. Marginal cost, on the other hand, refers to the cost associated with producing an additional unit of output or the value of resources that must be sacrificed to get an additional unit of output. Notice the relationship of the marginal to the average costs in Figure 6. When marginal cost is below average cost, the latter falls. When marginal cost is above average cost, the average value rises. Most students are quite aware of marginal-average relationships. If a student's grade average is 80 and the student receives a 70 in Torts (the marginal exam), then the average must fall. If he or she receives a 90 in Antitrust, it will rise.

Over the long run, nearly all costs must be counted as variable. For example, even the plant itself must eventually be replaced. Previously we assumed that a plant of a given size already existed and the rate of utilization was the only variable of interest. But how was the size of the plant determined initially? This question is answered by considering the relationship of costs to variation in plant size.

Figure 6

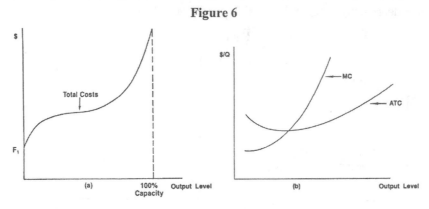

The plant cost structure shown in Figure 6(b) represents the minimum costs possible for a plant of that size. But suppose the plant size is doubled and the two cost structures are pictured as in Figure 7, where ATC_1 is the average total cost curve for the plant in Figure 6 and ATC_2 is the curve for a plant twice as big. The larger plant has the capability of producing the product at lower per unit costs if enough is produced. The production of this product in the range from A to B is said to be subject to economies of scale — that is, within that range the larger the plant, the lower the price.

Figure 7

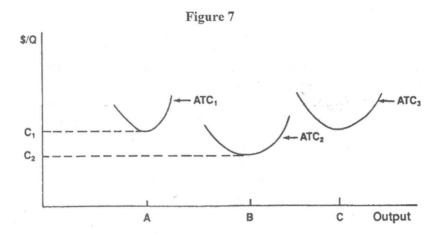

Suppose ATC_3 is the average total cost curve for a plant three times the size of the original plant. The minimum per unit costs associated with plant 3 are higher than those associated with plant 2. Consequently, in the range B to C, the production of the product is said to be subject to diseconomies of scale because costs per unit rise with increased plant size in that range. By considering a variety of plant sizes and the cost curves associated with each, it is possible to derive a new curve that relates the minimum achievable cost for each plant to the output level. This curve is called the long run average cost curve and is illustrated in Figure 8.

Figure 8

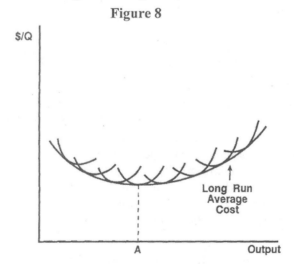

In the region to the left of point A, production is subject to economies of scale, and in the region to the right of point A, to diseconomies of scale. The plant associated with point A is said to be the optimally scaled plant since it is the one in which per unit costs are at an irreducible minimum.

The shape of the long run average cost curve of a given industry is of extreme importance to antitrust policy. For example, suppose that Figure 9 represents the cost and demand structure of a particular industry.

If a firm of size q_1 tries to compete in this industry, a larger firm could undercut the smaller firm's price because the larger scale of production would give the larger firm lower costs. In fact, in Figure 9, the long run average cost curve declines all the way to its intersection with the demand curve. In this case, the firm of most efficient size will be one capable of taking care of the entire market. If two or more firms competed in such a market, one of two things would inevitably happen: one of the firms would eventually obtain a

Figure 9

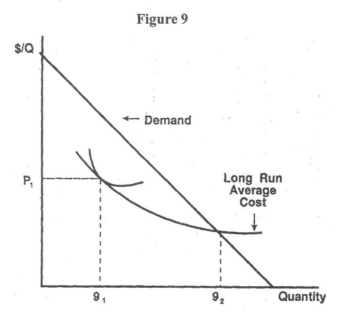

larger market share and a cost advantage over the other firm and drive it out of business. Otherwise, if the two firms continued to operate in the market, total market output would be lower than optimal and price would be higher than optimal. Such a market is called a natural monopoly. Examples of natural monopoly may include electric and gas distribution systems, many delivery routes (such as newspaper routes), and perhaps railroads and bridges. What characterizes many (although not all) such markets is either price regulation by the state or else outright public ownership. See discussion of natural monopoly and regulation in Chapter 9, *infra*.

Compare the natural monopoly market with the situation depicted in Figure 10. At price P_1, the market could support about five optimally sized plants (of size A).

Figure 10

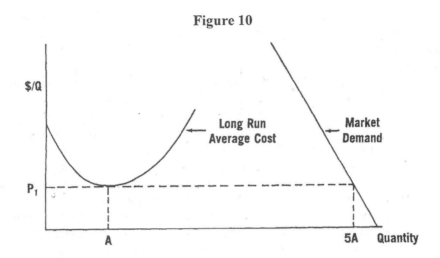

The cost characteristics of a particular industry, which are determined primarily by technological considerations and transaction costs, are a major factor in determining the maximum number of firms the industry will support. Industries with small scale requirements relative to market demand, such as agriculture, will be able to support a large number of firms, while industries with large scale requirements, such as automobile production, may have only a few firms. The technology of an industry is therefore of major importance in determining the level of industrial concentration and the parameters of competition, as those terms are defined under Sections 1 and 2 of the Sherman Act.

For more on industry cost characteristics, scale economies, and their effect on industrial structure, see F. M. SCHERER & D. ROSS, INDUSTRIAL MARKET STRUCTURE AND ECONOMIC PERFORMANCE (3d ed. 1990); W. K. VISCUSI, J. E. HARRINGTON, JR., & J. M. VERNON, ECONOMICS OF REGULATION AND ANTITRUST, ch. 3 (4th ed. 2005).

II   THE MARKET IN MOVEMENT

[A]   Perfect Competition

Given these basic ideas about demand and costs, we can understand how the perfectly competitive market adjusts to achieve a socially optimal mix of products. The driving force in a market system is the behavior of the competitive firm.

Within the competitive model, the perfectly competitive firm has the following characteristics:

1. It is only one among many firms producing identical products;

2. No individual firm is large enough to affect the market price by its individual actions; and

3. There are no significant inhibitions on entry into and exit from the industry.

Given these environmental assumptions, how does the profit maximizing firm determine the quantity to be produced? Referring to Figure 11, suppose the market price which the firm takes as quoted is P_1. Since there are a large number of firms producing identical products, the demand curve for any individual firm is perfectly elastic and is represented by the dashed line P_1 A. If this firm decided to produce q_0 units of output, it would not be making as much profit as it could. This can be seen by noting that at output level q0, the cost to produce an additional unit of output is C_0 while it can be sold for P_1. Therefore, by producing the additional unit, profit is increased by the quantity P_1-C_0. Now consider output level q_2. By producing this much, the firm has incurred a marginal loss of C_2 on the last unit of output but can sell it for only P_1. Therefore, by not producing this last unit, the firm avoids a loss of C_2-P_1 on this unit and profits rise. Without belaboring the point, it can be shown that the profit maximizing output level for this firm is q_1, the point that price equals marginal cost. Thus, the competitive firm attempts to maximize profits by setting output levels at the place where the firm's marginal costs equal the obtainable price. This market condition is the point of equilibrium.

Figure 11

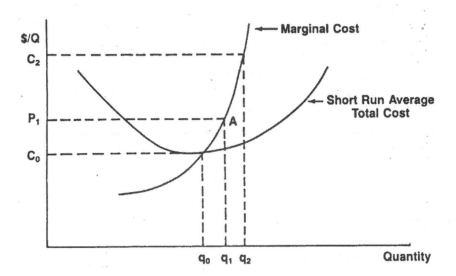

If each of the firms in the competitive industry follows this decision rule, then we can obtain a market supply curve by adding up the quantities produced by each firm at any given price. For example, if there were 100 identical firms in the industry and a price P_1 prevailed as in Figure 11, then the market supply of this product at price P_1 would be 100 q_1. If price rose to C_2, then market supply would rise to 100 q_2. The industry supply curve is traced out in Figure 12.

Figure 12

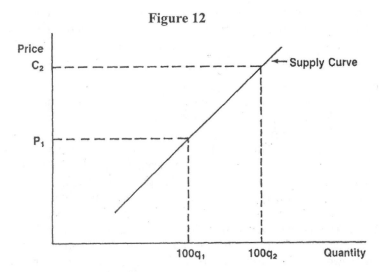

We are now ready to explain the adjustment process of a competitive market. As discussed above, consumers express their desires for goods and services in the marketplace by their willingness and ability to pay for items. This information is summarized in the schedule of quantities demanded at various price levels levels — the demand curve. The marketwide demand curve is calculated in the same manner as the industry supply curve: at each price, determine how many total units all consumers will demand and plot that point on the graph. Do this for every price, connect the dots, and you have drawn a demand curve. Producers express their willingness to provide products at various prices by adjusting output in order to maximize their profits. This information is expressed in the supply curve. By combining these two curves, an equilibrium price and quantity can be ascertained.

Figure 13 contains two diagrams. Panel (a) is a reproduction of Figure 11, which presents the cost curves for a representative firm in the industry. Panel

Figure 13

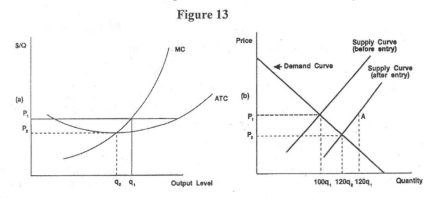

(b) is a reproduction of Figure 12 with the addition of a market demand curve. Referring to panel (b), it is seen that price P_1 is the price that initially "clears the market." That is, any price below P_1 would result in a shortage of the product and consumers bidding the price back up to P_1. Any price above P_1 would result in a surplus and producers would compete against each other to sell the excess products, thereby lowering the price to P_1. P_1 is the equilibrium price. But will P_1 prevail indefinitely in these circumstances?

The answer to this question highlights the integral role entry plays in a market system. At price P_1, notice what is happening to the representative firm in panel (a). First, price is significantly above average total cost. Since the latter quantity already includes a normal profit level, this firm is making profits in excess of what is necessary to attract and maintain investment in this industry. Enterprising individuals outside this industry see the high profit potential herein and decide to enter. Now, instead of 100 firms, the industry might have 120.* But with 120 firms, market supply rises to 120 q_1 with price at P_1 and results in a surplus as shown at point A of panel (b). The 120 producers now engage in price competition to sell the excess supply. This competition results in price being driven down to P_2 and the market clears again. Is this new equilibrium stable? Within the confines of the model, the answer is yes because at price P_2, the representative firm no longer makes extraordinary profits. Thus the inducement for further entry is gone and price will stay at P_2 so long as the demand and cost structures remain steady. In the real world, however, no market remains in equilibrium for long. Markets are subject to almost daily shocks — new technology and new uses for products, seasonal changes, wars, famines, and the weather can upset the market's balance and force it to seek a new equilibrium.

If demand conditions change, resulting in a shift to the left of the market demand curve, price would fall. This in turn would result in economic losses to the firm and ultimately cause some firms to exit the market or reduce their output. In turn, the reduction in total market output shifts the supply curve leftward and moves price up. Exit ceases when price reaches P_2.

P_2 is the stable equilibrium price because it is the only price where there are no economic profits or losses. Note further that price P_2 causes the firm to operate at the minimum of the average total cost curve. This has positive performance implications that will be discussed more fully below.

To summarize the market mechanism, briefly consider the following outline:

1. Consumers choose goods that satisfy their personal preferences.

2. Consumers reveal these preferences by making purchases in the market-place.

3. Producers choose a quantity of output that maximizes their profits at a given price.

4. If profits are above necessary levels in a given industry, other producers are attracted into the industry.

5. The excess supply at the high price forces producers to compete for sales; the result is that price is reduced so as to eliminate above normal profits.

---

* Alternatively, some or all of the existing firms might increase their internal production and sell more output. Or, there would be a combination of such expansion and new market entry.

6. The resulting equilibrium point is where marginal costs equal price.

7. The outcome is that products are supplied at prices which reflect minimum costs.

[B] Monopoly

Consider next a monopoly. By definition, there is only one firm producing the product in question and, for purposes of analysis, assume that there is no possibility of competitive entry. Even the monopolist is unable to charge an infinite price for its product because if price rises too high, some consumers will decide to forego the product altogether. However, the monopolist may be able to charge more than the competitive price without losing so many sales that the price increase is unprofitable. Assume that the monopolist desires to maximize profits and that it must charge all customers the same price. Since the monopolist is the only firm in the industry, the market demand curve is also the firm demand curve. The monopolist must choose how much to produce and also what price to charge. Figure 14 illustrates this point.

First, some explanation of the curve labeled "marginal revenue" is in order. Marginal revenue is the amount a seller receives by selling an additional unit, as opposed to marginal costs, which is the additional cost that the producer incurs in making one additional unit. Because the monopolist is unable to charge higher prices to those people willing to pay them and at the same time lower prices to others, each reduction in price loses some revenue that could have been earned from people willing to pay the higher price. Thus, for a one dollar reduction in selling price, the change in revenue is the difference between the new price times the new quantity and the old quantity times the old price.

What quantity of output will the monopolist choose so as to maximize profits? Consider the output level Q_m in Figure 14. If one more unit of output is produced at this point, it would have to be sold at a loss because marginal cost exceeds marginal revenue just to the right of point Q_m. If one less unit were produced, the monopolist would be missing an opportunity to increase profit because just to the left of point Q_m, marginal revenue exceeds marginal cost. Therefore, the point Q_m must be the profit maximizing output; the point where marginal revenue equals marginal cost.

Figure 14

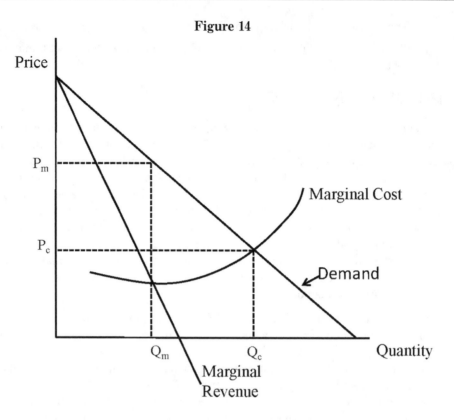

The monopoly price-output decision can be summarized as follows:

1. Consumers choose goods that satisfy their personal preferences.

2. These preferences are revealed by actual purchases of products.

3. The monopolist faces a downward sloping demand curve, which indicates that it can charge more by reducing output.

4. The monopolist maximizes its profits by choosing an output level that equates marginal cost to marginal revenue.

5. Profits can remain at supracompetitive levels because competitive entry is foreclosed.

6. The outcome is that products are supplied at prices higher than costs, and higher than prices in competitive markets, and market output is lower than it would be in a competitive market.

These same effects occur when competitors form a cartel and set the price or output by agreement.

[C] Relative Performances of Competition and Monopoly

What is wrong with monopoly? Why are "competitive" markets generally preferred to monopoly? The answers to these questions involve both economic and noneconomic considerations and values. The latter will be discussed first.

Monopoly industrial structure results in a concentration of power unknown to most competitive markets. The structure of a competitive market decentralizes and disperses power because competitive markets contain many firms each acting in its own self-interest. On the other hand, a monopoly capitalist social structure places a great deal of reliance on the decisions of a single firm and its managers. If these individuals make errors in judgment, the consequences reverberate throughout the economy.

A second political consideration associated with concentrated power is political influence. Certain monopolists may be able to exert extreme pressure on public officials to vote for measures that enhance their monopoly position. If this is true and practical, the monopolist can ensure its continued existence.

An important issue that lies somewhere between politics and economics is income redistribution. The monopolist who makes extraordinary profits redistributes income from consumers to corporate shareholders, officers, and perhaps to employees. Although the economist is generally unwilling to say that this redistribution of wealth results in a welfare loss to society, this is probably the most prominent reason that the public and perhaps Congress have condemned monopoly power.

From the economist's viewpoint, the greatest evil of monopoly is wasted resources. The waste can come in three forms: (a) failure to produce the "right" quantity of goods at minimum price; (b) the wasted resources the monopolist spends creating or preserving its monopoly position; and (c) the competitors' waste of resources.

A competitive market is said to be allocatively efficient because in equilibrium the market price equals the marginal cost of production. This means that in an economy where consumers dictate the mix of goods to be produced, by comparing their preferences for additional units of each good to the costs of additional units, it is imperative that accurate information regarding costs be communicated to the public. In most circumstances, the only piece of information that is available about the costs of production is the product price. Therefore, product price must reflect the cost of additional production. In short, price must equal marginal cost. If price is held above marginal cost then the consumer is receiving inaccurate signals and will make suboptimal choices. There will be less of the product produced than is socially desirable and more of some less desirable product will be produced. Figure 15 illustrates the point. For purposes of this comparison, assume that the firm has the same costs per unit of output, no matter how much it produces. This assumption will be discussed at length below.

The monopoly output in this case is Q_m and the price charged is P_m. Society is being told that the cost to produce an additional unit of output is P_m when in fact it is P_c. The competitive solution results in price stabilizing at the minimum of the average total cost curve. At this price, a quantity of Q_c is produced. Thus the monopolist restricts output relative to the competitive market and charges a higher price This reduction in output has two effects. First, for those buyers who are paying a higher price, wealth is transferred from consumers to the monopolist. This is represented in Figure 15 by the shaded rectangle labeled "Wealth Transfer." Second, some consumers are no longer able to purchase the product even though they value the product more than the cost of making it. This creates a form of inefficiency known as Deadweight Loss, illustrated in Figure 15 as the shaded area to the right of Q_m. Resources are wasted in the sense that they are diverted to less socially desirable ends.

Figure 15

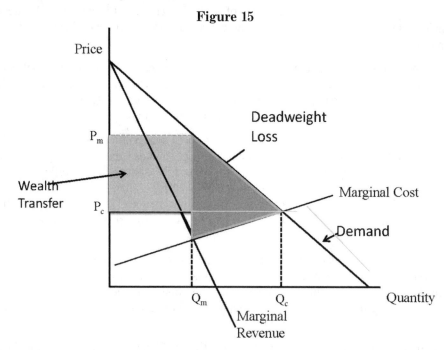

The other form of wasted resources is a result not of monopoly pricing, but of monopoly conduct. In the model, it was assumed that entry by potential competitors into the market controlled by the monopolist is impossible. As a general rule, that is not the case in real markets. In fact, the monopolist's high profits will be more attractive to people with capital to invest than the available profits in competitive markets. All things being equal, the investor would like to put his or her money where profits are the highest. The monopolist, by contrast, would prefer that the investor look somewhere else.

If a monopoly is worth $1,000,000 per year in monopoly profits to a particular firm, that firm will be willing to spend any amount up to $1,000,000 to exclude potential rivals from the market. In short, at the outer limit, the shaded box in Figure 14 does not represent monopoly profits at all, but money spent by the monopolist in order to exclude potential rivals. Some of this money might be spent in socially useful ways, such as cost-justified research and investment. Much of it may be spent in harmful ways, however: predatory pricing, false advertising, espionage or sabotage, or perhaps bribery or lobbying. It is possible that the social waste caused by these entry deterring practices is far larger than the social waste caused by monopoly pricing itself.

A third important social cost of monopoly that is often overlooked, because the economic model we have described does not account for it, is the social cost that results from the injuries that monopolistic exclusionary practices impose on others

— most frequently, the monopolist's competitors. To take an extreme example, suppose that a firm creates a monopoly by engaging in industrial sabotage: it dynamites its competitors' plants. The social cost of this monopoly will consist of three quite distinct elements: (1) the welfare loss caused by inefficient consumer substitutions; (2) the resources consumed by the monopolist in the (socially inefficient) activity of destroying its competitors' plants; and, importantly, (3) the social resources used to build the competitors' plants, which now have been destroyed. This third element in the social cost of monopoly could easily dwarf elements (1) and (2). The resources that a potential entrant invests to overcome artificial barriers to entry can represent a form of social waste. Yet, accounting for it may justify much broader use of competitor lawsuits in antitrust cases than some antitrust scholars believe appropriate. For more on the relationship between the social cost of monopoly and optimal rules of enforcement, see the note on damages in Chapter 3, *infra*.

[D]   The Competitive Continuum

Although competition and monopoly are often discussed as if they represent the two possible alternative states of an economy, perfectly competitive markets and true monopolies are rare. Instead, perfect competition and absolute monopoly are archetypes; they represent poles on a spectrum of competitiveness. Most markets fall somewhere in between and markets are analyzed with respect to where they fall on this continuum. For example, in general, a market with 100 firms is more competitive than a market with 30 firms. A market that is relatively concentrated — and thus closer to the monopoly side of the continuum — is sometimes described as an oligopoly, meaning that there are few sellers in the market.

Antitrust labels do not necessarily map precisely to the economic definitions of various market structures. For example, antitrust courts may refer to a market as "competitive" even though it does not meet the economics textbook definition of a perfectly competitive market. Similarly, a firm with a very high market share may be described as a monopolist for antitrust purposes even though there are competing firms in the market. As discussed in Chapter 6, much antitrust law involves the issue of when a firm with less than 100% market share should be considered a monopolist. Finally, it bears noting that antitrust enforcement is not likely to replace monopolies with perfect competition; rather, antitrust law is designed to make monopolized (or heavily concentrated) markets more competitive by reducing artificial barriers to competition.

III   JUDICIAL EMPHASIS ON ECONOMIC REASONING

[A]   Introduction

Before proceeding with the case analysis that comprises the remainder of this book, it is important to consider briefly the emphasis that the federal courts, primarily the Supreme Court, have placed on economic thinking in antitrust jurisprudence. As one might expect, the courts have changed their emphasis dramatically over the history of antitrust litigation. The early years of antitrust law can be characterized as years of socio-political concern. The emphasis of antitrust analysis was on fairness and equality in business dealings. The populist political tenor of the times condemned large enterprises because they threatened the fabric of a free society — the small business. The idea is ably presented by Judge Hand's oft-quoted passage from *United States v. Aluminum Co. of Am.*, 148 F.2d 416, 428–429 (2d Cir. 1945).

> We have been speaking only of the economic reasons which forbid monopoly; but, as we have already implied, there are others, based upon the belief that great industrial consolidations are inherently undesirable, regardless of their economic results. In the debates in Congress Senator Sherman himself . . . showed that among the purposes of Congress in 1890 was a desire to put an end to great aggregations of capital because of the helplessness of the individual before them. . . . Throughout the history of these statutes it has been constantly assumed that one of their purposes was to perpetuate and preserve, for its own sake and in spite of possible cost, an organization of industry in small units which can effectively compete with each other.

[B] Structuralist Analysis

Historically, federal antitrust policy has been dominated by an industrial organization theory called "structuralism." The premise of the structuralist approach is that the structure of the industry (basically the number and size distribution of the firms in the industry) *determines* the conduct and behavior of firms. The conduct in turn determines the economic performance of the industry in terms of prices, product quality, and output levels. For example, the majority opinion in *United States v. Container Corp. of Am.*, 393 U.S. 333 (1969), places great emphasis on the competitive consequences of markets dominated by a few sellers in the context of price information exchanges:

> Price information exchanged in some markets may have no effect on a truly competitive price. But the corrugated containers industry is domi-nated by relatively few sellers. . . . The inferences are irresistible that the exchange of price information has had an anticompetitive effect in the industry, chilling the vigor of price competition.

393 U.S. at 337. There was no finding of a formal agreement to fix prices. The Court reasoned, nevertheless, that the oligopolistic structure of the industry made price fixing likely. Thus any conduct that had the effect of facilitating the fixing of prices within a highly concentrated industry structure was said to be repugnant to public policy.

Structuralism in antitrust has been severely qualified by our knowledge that markets can vary greatly in their details but that the fact finding abilities of an antitrust tribunal, such as a court, are severely limited. For example, general principles of economic theory tell us that when a substantial portion of the market is shared by a few firms, these firms will recognize their interdependence and act accordingly. But how many firms are a few? Are all actions by oligopolists pernicious? Does every firm in a concentrated market actually act as the model predicts? The most famous economic expression of structuralism is the "Structure-Conduct-Performance Paradigm," which holds that highly concentrated market structures necessarily lead to anticompetitive conduct, which in turn leads to poor economic performance. The merits of the Structure-Conduct-Performance Paradigm are discussed more fully in Chapter 6 on monopolization and Chapter 7 on merger policy, *infra. See also* H. HOVENKAMP, FEDERAL ANTITRUST POLICY § 1.7 (4th ed. 2011).

Most significantly, the implications of forced changes in industry structure are usually unclear. If firms are subject to significant economies of scale, judicial intervention breaking up large firms may make the firms *behave* more competitively, by pricing closer to marginal costs. But their marginal costs could be significantly higher, given their smaller size. *See generally* E. Thomas Sullivan, *The Jurisprudence of Antitrust Divestiture: The Path Less Traveled*, 86 MINN. L. REV. 565 (2002).

[C]   Efficiency Analysis

At odds with the structuralist theory is the efficiency or Chicago school theory of industrial organization. The framework of this economic analysis is price theory as described in the first sections of this chapter. The underlying assumption is that the interaction of supply and demand will determine a set of prices that maximize society's economic welfare. The profit-maximizing firm will seek cost-reducing production techniques in order to enhance its own market position and in so doing, inadvertently improve economic welfare by charging lower prices. Monopoly power is limited, even for the firm with a high market share, by a vanguard of potential entrants ready, willing, and able to enter the industry if profit levels are attractive. Thus, under this view of the market, an economy dominated by a few large firms could indeed be socially optimal because (a) the large firms achieve production efficiency through economies of scale, and (b) the problems of allocative efficiency are eliminated by potential entry, because each firm knows that it will face additional competition if it charges too high a price. This view thus rejects the Structure-Conduct-Performance Paradigm, arguing instead that performance causes concentration, rather than vice-versa. Firms become big because they are innovative and do better than their competitors. As a result, high concentration in a market may be as much a sign of vigorous, innovative behavior as of anticompetitiveness. *See* JAMES W. MEEHAN, JR. & ROBERT J. LARNER, *The Structural School, Its Critics, and Its Progeny: An Assessment, in* ECONOMICS AND ANTITRUST POLICY 182 (Robert J. Larner & James W. Meehan, Jr., eds., New York: Quorum, 1989).

Recall the previous discussion of monopoly output and pricing decisions. In the absence of potential entry, the monopolist will set prices above marginal cost and thereby produce less of the product than socially desirable. This condition was referred to as allocative inefficiency. If it is assumed, however, that potential entry is easy, and can be accomplished in a short time, then the allocative efficiency problem is no longer pressing because entrants limit the monopolist's pricing prerogatives. This is to say that the potential entry causes the monopolist's demand curve to become more elastic and closer to that of a competitive firm. The implications of easy entry, as well as problems of measurement, are discussed in both Chapter 7, on mergers, and Chapter 9, on deregulation and its antitrust implications, *infra*.

The policy prescription of those who endorse the efficiency theory is as follows: If the conduct under scrutiny leads to lower potential costs and thus to lower prices to consumers, then the conduct should not be found unlawful. This analysis has received considerable but not unanimous acceptance in the courts. See especially the cases discussed in Chapter 6, *infra*. For example, in *Telex Corp. v. IBM Corp.*, 510 F.2d 894 (10th Cir.) 423 U.S. 802 (1975), the court of appeals reversed a finding of the district court that IBM had engaged in predatory behavior by lowering prices on its peripheral equipment. The court adopted the efficiency theory, stating: "The record shows, during the period under consideration, that the parties and others in the market produced more advanced products better suited to the needs of customers at lower prices." 510 F.2d at 926. Under the efficiency methodology, better products at lower prices is the *sine qua non* of legality.

The differences between the structuralist and efficiency schools of thought are more profound than is apparent from reading the material above. The efficiency school has a deeply held belief that competition will work even though only a few firms dominate the industry. Structuralists are much more suspicious, believing that a monopolist can do nothing other than act as a monopolist. Likewise, a group of oligopolists can do nothing other than act like a shared monopoly.

The debate continues both in the literature and the process of federal judicial appointments. As a consequence, analytical inconsistencies emerge in the case law and must ultimately be rationalized. For example, the Supreme Court decision in *Eastman Kodak Co. v. Image Technical Servs., Inc.*, 504 U.S. 451 (1992), reprinted in Chapter 5, reflects a deep-seated suspicion about dominant firms in product differentiated markets — largely the consequence of a structuralist approach. By contrast, the Supreme Court's decision only a year later in *Brooke Group Ltd. v. Brown & Williamson Tobacco Corp.*, 509 U.S. 209 (1993), reprinted in Chapter 6, reflects the Chicago School view that even highly concentrated markets are likely to reflect substantial amounts of competition.

[D] Strategic Behavior

A third approach that attempts to assimilate aspects of the other two is called the strategic behavior approach. It recognizes that structuralists probably err in placing too little emphasis on technological efficiencies and that the efficiency school ignores the dangers of increased market concentration, strategic creation of barriers to entry, and strategic raising of rivals' costs. This approach attempts to balance the conflicting aspects of a given business practice in order to assess the net competitive effect of any challenged conduct. The Federal Trade Commission case, *In re E.I. du Pont*, 96 F.T.C. 650 (1980), is a good example of this approach. The Commission concluded that it was essential to the analysis that it "weigh the relative competitive virtues and evils of dominant firm behavior even in the monopoly context." Note that this approach allows not only the efficiency defenses but also evidence of exclusionary effects of strategic planning. Perhaps most importantly, the approach attempts to incorporate the insights of game theory, which are just beginning to make their way into antitrust analysis.

Insofar as policy is concerned, the strategic approach to antitrust adjudication places a great deal of faith in the ability of courts to weigh competing economic models and make enlightened decisions that effectively determine the future structure of the United States economy. Increased emphasis is placed on expert economic testimony in trying to ascertain the viability of potential competition, the scale required for efficient production, the concentration of industry, the most likely responses of profit-maximizing firms, and other matters relevant to a full economic inquiry into strategic possibilities. Increasingly, courts focus on the economics of opportunistic behavior, the costs of consumer switching, and information costs. Whether these are fruitful avenues of inquiry remains to be seen, but for the time being at least they cannot be ignored. *See* Rudolph J.R. Peritz, *Toward a Dynamic Antitrust Analysis of Strategic Market Behavior*, 47 N.Y.L. SCH. L. REV. 101 (2003).

Chapter 3

SPECIAL PROBLEMS OF ANTITRUST ENFORCEMENT

I ENFORCEMENT

[A] Tripartite Approach

The antitrust and trade regulation laws are enforced by the U.S. Department of Justice, the Federal Trade Commission (FTC), and private individuals or entities. In addition, state attorneys general have authority under Section 4C of the Clayton Act to bring federal antitrust suits as parens patriae on behalf of natural persons residing within the state. Most states also have enacted statutes patterned after the federal antitrust and trade regulation laws.

The responsibility for enforcement of antitrust by the two federal agencies has been divided. The Antitrust Division of the Department of Justice is charged with enforcing the Sherman, Clayton, and Robinson-Patman Acts, through either civil or criminal prosecution. The FTC is the sole enforcer of the Federal Trade Commission Act with the exception of Section 12, and has concurrent jurisdiction with the Antitrust Division over Sections 2, 3, 7, and 8 of the Clayton Act. Since both agencies have jurisdiction over the Clayton Act, they have adopted informal clearance procedures, which are to be invoked before an investigation begins. *See* Trade Reg. Rep. (CCH) ¶ 9565.05.

[1] Department of Justice

The Antitrust Division of the Department of Justice, together with the offices of the United States Attorneys, is delegated the authority to enforce the antitrust laws. The enforcement can be through either civil or criminal means. Sections 1, 2, and 3 of the Sherman Act, Section 3 of the Robinson-Patman Act, and Section 14 of the Clayton Act all contain criminal penalties. Only the Department of Justice can seek criminal sanctions under any of these statutes. A violation of Section 12 of the FTC Act may also be a criminal violation; therefore, it is enforced by the Department. In addition, the Department may bring civil suits under Sections 1, 2, and 3 of the Sherman Act. Sections 2, 3, 7, and 8 of the Clayton Act, as amended by the Robinson-Patman Act, provide only for civil suits with enforcement either by the Antitrust Division or the FTC.

[a]   Civil Action

In investigating a civil charge, the Antitrust Division may discover and examine records of a business under investigation by issuing a civil investigative demand (CID) before a formal complaint has been filed. These means of compulsory process were first permitted in 1962 under the Antitrust Civil Process Act. 15 U.S.C. §§ 1311–1314. The original Act required that there be reason to believe that a "company" was in control or possession of documents relevant to the investigation . Section 3 of the Act required that before a CID could be enforced, the company to which it was directed must have been "under investigation" and the material sought to be discovered must have been relevant to the ongoing investigation. An individual's records were not subject to scrutiny under the original revision of the Act. Under the Hart-Scott-Rodino Antitrust Improvements Act of 1976, however, the Department may use a CID to discover information from individuals and third parties.

The enforcement of a CID is analogous to that of a subpoena duces tecum issued by a grand jury. Moreover, its scope is similar to that permitted under the Federal Rules of Civil Procedure. The information obtained through the CID cannot be turned over to the FTC, but it can be used by the Department in any related civil or criminal proceeding, including use before a grand jury. A CID enforcement suit must be brought in the federal district court where the target company is found or transacts business, or if it transacts business in more than one district, where its principal place of business is located.

After a civil suit has been filed, the Department can use the Federal Rules of Civil Procedure to acquire discoverable material. The civil action can be initiated for either injunctive relief under Section 4 of the Sherman Act and Section 15 of the Clayton Act, or damages under Section 4A of the Clayton Act if the U.S. government itself was injured by the violation. If the Department files a civil suit to recover damages, it is entitled to claim the same as that allowable to private parties when injured by reason of a price-fixing scheme.

Under Section 4B of the Clayton Act, the statute of limitations for a civil antitrust action for damages is four years from the time the claim for relief "accrues." Because suits for injunctive relief are equitable in nature, no statute of limitations governs the commencement of the suit. The equitable argument of laches does apply to an action for injunctive or other equitable relief brought by private parties but not generally to equitable suits brought by the government.

[b]   Criminal Prosecutions

A criminal proceeding generally is commenced by the Antitrust Division through use of a grand jury to investigate allegations of antitrust violations. The grand jury has authority to investigate alleged violations of Sections 1 and 2 of the Sherman Act and Section 3 of the Robinson-Patman Act. If conviction for a Sherman Act violation is obtained after grand jury indictment, it is considered a felony, and fines up to $1 million for an individual and up to $100 million dollars for a corporation may be imposed, as well as prison terms for individuals up to 10 years. 15 U.S.C. §§ 1 and 2. Violation of the criminal provision of Section 3 of the

Robinson-Patman Act can yield a fine up to $5,000 and a prison term up to one year. 15 U.S.C. § 21e. This provision has seldom been enforced. Indeed, the Department of Justice has not enforced any part of the Robinson-Patman Act in two decades.

In May 2010, Congress approved legislation to extend the Antitrust Criminal Penalties Enforcement and Reform Act (ACPERA). Originally passed in 2004, the law limits the civil liability available against cartel participants who have been accepted into the Department of Justice's leniency program to actual, rather than treble damages. This new legislation will extend the de-trebling provision to 2020.

The U.S. Sentencing Commission has had an increasingly important role to play in establishing antitrust sentencing guidelines. The new guidelines apply to market allocations, bid rigging, and cartel price-fixing schemes. Although the sentencing guidelines are complicated to apply and contain quantitative calculations, they do provide qualitative benchmarks. For example, in a price-fixing case, the sentencing judge will consider, among other issues, two factors: (1) the amount of the increase of the artificially inflated price and (2) the injury to the consumer who did not buy the product at the inflated, higher price. *See generally* 56 Fed. Reg. 22, 762 (1991).

Recently, the Eighth Circuit has permitted an upward departure under the Sentencing Guidelines, for an individual found guilty of price fixing. *See United States v. VandeBrake*, 679 F.3d 1030 (8th Cir. 2012). Upholding the district court's discretion for an "upward" adjustment in sentencing when there is such a disparity between antitrust and the fraud sentencing guidelines, the Eighth Circuit found the district court's departure from the sentencing guidelines for an antitrust offense was reasonable, given the district's court's policy disagreement with the guidelines to treat fraud more harshly than antitrust crimes and the defendant's lack of remorse. The circuit court affirmed the district court's use of the fraud sentencing guidelines rather than the sentencing guidelines for the antitrust offense in the price fixing case.

The federal sentencing guidelines, which guide federal judges in sentencing convicted violators of federal criminal statutes, distinguish between price fixing and bid rigging. Before the sentencing guidelines were enacted, "bid rigging" did not constitute a distinct offense but was "merely a descriptive term for a subset of price fixing cases." Many cases used the terms "bid rigging," "bid rotation," and "noncompetitive bidding" interchangeably. In *United States v. Heffernan*, 43 F.3d 1144, 1146 (7th Cir. 1994), the Seventh Circuit held that because the purchasers were private firms, not public entities, and because sealed bidding was not used in the conduct at issue, it was indistinguishable from price fixing and thus not entitled to the enhanced sentence contemplated by the sentencing guidelines for bid rigging. Bid rigging is given a higher sentence than price fixing because bid rigging disproportionately affects government agencies due to the frequent use of sealed bids, particularly when the bidding is on a fixed quantity of products.

Do you see why bid rigging is more dangerous than the general run of price fixes? When firms rig a bid and the winning bid is opened, all the cartel members know immediately whether one of their members "cheated" by supplying a lower bid than previously agreed. As a result, cartels in bidding markets where the winning bid is publicly announced are particularly susceptible to collusion. Since the government often purchases in this manner, it is a particularly vulnerable victim. In the more general run of price fixes, particularly where prices are discretely negotiated between buyer and seller, a firm could cheat on the cartel for a long period without getting caught. This makes cartels in such markets less stable.

United States v. Nippon Paper Indus. Co., 109 F.3d 1 (1st Cir. 1997), *cert. denied*, 522 U.S. 1044 (1998), held that price fixing that had occurred entirely in Japan could be the subject of a U.S. criminal indictment. Nippon and unnamed co-conspirators were accused of fixing the price of facsimile paper sold in North America, including the United States. The relevant meetings culminating in the challenged agreement all occurred in Japan. The alleged agreement was apparently facilitated with resale price maintenance agreements under which firms purchasing the paper in Japan promised to resell it at specified minimum prices in North America. Nippon then allegedly monitored resale prices within the United States in order to ensure that the maintained price was the one actually charged.

In concluding that the criminal jurisdiction of the federal antitrust laws could reach conduct abroad just as the civil jurisdiction could, the court stated that "one datum sticks out like a sore thumb" — namely, "in both criminal and civil cases, the claim that Section One applies extraterritorially is based on the same language in the same section of the same statute" and "common sense suggests that courts should interpret the same language in the same section of the same statute uniformly, regardless of whether the impetus for interpretation is criminal or civil."

The court rejected the defendant's argument that the lack of any precedent made the assertion of criminal liability improper — that is, the case law failed to give the foreign actor fair notice that its wholly extraterritorial act might subject it to criminal antitrust prosecution. But as the court noted, while there is little in the way of *antitrust* precedent for applying a U.S. criminal statute to extraterritorial conduct, there was ample precedent from other statutes. For example, the manufacturing and sale of addictive drugs abroad targeting U.S. markets has frequently been condemned under criminal statutes notwithstanding that the defendants performed no acts within the United States.

Perhaps the most important rationale for expansive reach and even criminal punishment in such cases is that the sovereign representing purchasers has a significantly greater interest at stake than the sovereign representing sellers. As a general matter, a cartel in one country fixing the price of its goods elsewhere transfers wealth away from the territory containing the buyers and toward the territory containing the sellers. As a result, sovereigns, including the United States itself, have typically been less concerned with condemning restraints on export trade where all the buyers are foreign, than with restraints on imports. *See generally* Joel I. Klein, *The War Against International Cartels: Lessons from the Battlefront* (Oct. 14, 1999), *available at* http://www.usdoj.gov/atr/public/speeches/3747.htm.

Venue Rule 18 of the Federal Rules of Criminal Procedure provides that suit is to be brought in the district where the offense is committed. Service of the summons or warrant may be nationwide. Removal of the suit under Rule 21 from the district where the offense was committed is possible if the district presents "so great a prejudice against the defendant" that a fair trial is not possible.

The statute of limitations governing a criminal antitrust violation requires that suit must be commenced within five years from the date of the offense. 18 U.S.C. § 3282. Whatever act triggers the substantive violation will also start the statute of limitations running. For a conspiracy which is continuing in nature, the statute commences to run from the last act in furtherance of the conspiracy. For a description and critique from a game theory perspective of the Department's amnesty policy, *see* C. Leslie, *Antitrust Amnesty, Game Theory, and Cartel Stability*, 31 J. CORP. L. 453 (2006).

The Department frequently has announced that criminal prosecution will be directed only at per se violations, such as price fixing, where the legality of the challenged conduct is unquestioned, and to cases where the defendant has willfully violated the law. This standard of prosecution has become problematic in recent years, however, as the per se classification has undergone reevaluation and reformulation. The Department has announced the following special circumstances "in which criminal sanctions might not be used even in *per se* cases: (1) confusion of law; (2) truly novel issues of law or fact; (3) confusion caused by past prosecutorial decisions; or (4) clear evidence that defendants did not appreciate the consequences of their actions." Remarks by John H. Shenefeld, "Antitrust Division Enforcement Policy," to the Federal Bar Association, Cleveland (Apr. 18, 1979). *See generally United States v. Taubman*, 297 F.3d 161 (2d Cir. 2002).

The Department recently has outlined seven steps it deemed "useful practices for the detection and prosecution of cartels." The seven steps are:

> (1) focus prosecutors on "hard core" collusive activity; (2) treat cartels as serious crimes; (3) provide an amnesty program and "amnesty plus"; (4) vigorously prosecute obstruction of justice; (5) charge cartels in conjunction with other offenses; (6) provide transparency and predictability; and (7) publicize these enforcement efforts.

Presentation by Thomas O. Barnett, *Seven Steps to Better Cartel Enforcement*, to the 11th Annual Competition Law & Policy Workshop, European Union Institute (June 2, 2006), *available at* http://www.usdoj.gov/atr/public/speeches/216453.pdf.

[2]   Federal Trade Commission

The FTC, together with the Antitrust Division, has authority to enforce the Clayton Act's civil provisions. It also has primary authority over the FTC Act, Section 5 of which prohibits unfair methods of competition and unfair or deceptive acts or practices. The agency mission is divided between antitrust enforcement (Bureau of Competition) and consumer protection (Bureau of Consumer Protection). It carries out its enforcement role through case-by-case adjudication or industry-wide rulemaking. Traditionally the FTC, composed of five Commissioners appointed by the President, functions through its power to issue cease and desist orders, which are enforced through civil penalties and court injunctions. The Commission's authority is exercised through administrative proceedings. Under Section 13(a), the Commission can also initiate civil actions in federal district courts to obtain injunctive relief for the maintenance of the status quo pending the outcome of an administrative hearing.

The FTC has broad power to conduct investigations under Section 6 of the FTC Act. *See* 16 C.F.R. § 2.1 *et seq.* (1988). Pursuant to its investigative powers, the Commission can issue subpoenas under Section 9 for allegations of unfair methods of competition during the precomplaint investigation stage. Moreover, since 1980, its precomplaint investigation of competition issues under Section 5(a) of the Act is governed by procedures akin to the Department of Justice's CID process. For example, a CID is the only "form of compulsory process issued in investigations with respect to unfair or deceptive acts." 16 C.F.R. § 2.7; 15 U.S.C. § 576-1 (1988 Supp.). It also can require the attendance and testimony of a witness at a precomplaint investigative hearing conducted by a Commission staff member authorized to administer oaths. Failure to comply with an FTC subpoena can lead to fines up to $5,000, or up to one year's imprisonment, or both.

Acting through its Commissioners, the FTC commences administrative adjudicative proceedings by issuing a complaint, setting forth a factual statement of the acts or practices alleged to be in violation of the law together with the legal authority for the action. 16 C.F.R. § 3.11 (1988). After completion of discovery, and if summary judgment has not been granted, an adjudicative hearing is held before an administrative law judge appointed by the Commission. The Commission is represented by staff counsel, called complaint counsel. After the hearing, the administrative law judge is required to file an "initial decision" within 90 days. On filing the initial decision, the jurisdiction of the administrative law judge is terminated. Under Section 5(b) of the Act, an appeal of the initial decision comes before the five Commissioners. A respondent, but not complaint counsel, may appeal a decision by the Commission to the U.S. Court of Appeals. The standard of review is whether the findings and conclusions are supported by substantial evidence in the record.

If the Commission's final cease and desist order is upheld or not appealed, the FTC has authority to seek enforcement and civil penalties in federal district court for "knowing violations." The penalties for each violation may be up to $10,000 , with a provision that a continuing failure to comply is considered to be a separate violation for each day of noncompliance.

As of 1975, the FTC also has authority to represent itself, either by commencing or defending an action in court, rather than having the Department of Justice as its counsel. Cases in which such authority exists include: (1) injunctions in false advertising cases; (2) judicial review of a rule promulgated by the FTC; (3) judicial review of a cease and desist order; (4) subpoena enforcement; (5) consumer redress cases (Section 19); and (6) cases involving collection of civil penalties.

The Commission, in addition to its adjudicative power, has adopted formal rulemaking procedures for the promulgation of industry-wide trade regulation rules. The authority to make rules and regulations is under Section 6(g) of the FTC Act. *See* 16 C.F.R. §§ 1.7 and 1.22 (1988). Notice of proposed rules is given in the Federal Register and interested parties are permitted participation in the rulemaking through submission of written and/or oral argument. 16 C.F.R. § 1.11. The Commission, in connection with its rulemaking, may conduct investigations, studies, conferences, and hearings. 16 C.F.R. §§ 1.13 and 1.26.

Rulemaking, other than of rules of practice and procedure, generally has been reserved for consumer protection issues rather than antitrust competition issues. But nothing in the rulemaking authority explicitly limits the FTC's power in this regard. *See National Petr. Refs. Ass'n v. FTC*, 482 F.2d 672 (D.C. Cir. 1973), *cert. denied*, 415 U.S. 951 (1974); 120 CONG. REC. 41407 (1974) (remarks of Rep. Broyhill, Conference Manager of the Magnuson-Moss Warranty FTC Improvement Act); 15 U.S.C. § 57a(a)(2) (1976).

[3] Private Suits

Section 4 of the Clayton Act provides that any person, whether an individual, business entity, or government, who has been injured in its "business or property" by reason of an antitrust violation may sue to recover treble damages, costs of the suit, and attorney's fees. 15 U.S.C. § 15. *See generally* Lande, *Are Antitrust "Treble" Damages Really Single Damages?* 54 OHIO ST. L.J. 115 (1993) (arguing that, as a result of numerous limitations, antitrust treble damages are really only "single" damages — only equal to or even less than the actual damages caused by antitrust violations). *See generally* D. FLOYD & E. THOMAS SULLIVAN, PRIVATE ANTITRUST ACTIONS § 6 (1996).

Once a violation, causation, and injury have been found, the award of attorney's fees, costs, and treble damages is mandatory. The trial judge or jury has no discretion to modify it. Indeed, the jury is not even informed of the trebling procedure. The trial judge automatically multiplies the damage award by three. *Pollock & Riley, Inc. v. Pearl Brewing Co.*, 498 F.2d 1240 (5th Cir. 1974), *cert. denied sub nom. Gulf Oil Corp. v. Wood*, 420 U.S. 992 (1975). This provision was designed to create deterrence from violations, monetary incentives to sue for violations, and compensation to victims. Since 1914 and the adoption of Section 16 of the Clayton Act, injunctive relief is also available for threatened loss or damage. 15 U.S.C. § 26 (1988 Supp.). Section 16 also gives attorney's fees to a prevailing plaintiff. *See Blue Cross and Blue Shield of Wis. v. Marshfield Clinic*, 152 F.3d 588 (7th Cir. 1998) (plaintiff who could not prove damages had an "inadequate remedy at law" and could thus still obtain an injunction).

One study demonstrates dramatically the influence of private antitrust actions in the development of the law. The 1985 Georgetown Study of Private Antitrust Litigation found that the filing of private cases outnumbered government cases twenty-to-one from the mid 1960s until the late 1970s. Until 1965, the ratio was six-to-one. In the 1980s, the ratio was ten-to-one. *See* Salop & White, *Economic Analysis of Private Antitrust Litigation*, 74 GEO. L.J. 1001 (1986). *See also* D. Rosenberg & J. Sullivan, *Coordinating Private Class Action and Public Agency Enforcement of Antitrust Law*, 2 J. COMPETITION L. & ECON. 159 (2006) (proposing an auction-like system to coordinate the enforcement efforts between public and private enforcers).

In order to maintain a private antitrust action, a plaintiff must demonstrate a causal connection among the following: (1) injury suffered, (2) to business or property, by (3) the violation of an antitrust law. *Brunswick Corp. v. Pueblo Bowl-O-Mat, Inc.*, 429 U.S. 477 (1977). The "antitrust" laws included within the meaning of Section 4 of the Clayton Act are: (1) Sections 1, 2, and 3 of the Sherman Act; (2) Section 2(a)–(f) of the Clayton Act (price discrimination); (3) Section 3 of the Clayton Act (exclusive dealing and tying arrangements); (4) Section 7 of the Clayton Act (merger); and (5) Section 8 of the Clayton Act (interlocking directorates). The FTC Act and Section 3 of the Robinson-Patman Act, amending the Clayton Act, are not considered "antitrust" laws; therefore, a private right of action for treble damages or injunctive relief does not exist under Section 4 of the Clayton Act for conduct within these statutes.

The pleading requirements for a private suit vary depending on which statute the conduct allegedly violated. Consider these recent pronouncements from the Supreme Court regarding the burden of pleading and proving an antitrust violation under Section 4.

> Section 4 . . . is in essence a remedial provision. . . . [T]reble damages . . . play an important role in penalizing wrongdoers and deterring wrongdoing . . . .
>
> [T]o recover damages . . . [plaintiff] must prove more than injury causally linked to an illegal [course of conduct]. Plaintiffs must prove *antitrust* injury, which is to say injury of the type the antitrust laws were intended to prevent and that flows from that which makes defendants' acts unlawful. The injury should reflect the anticompetitive effect either of the violation or of anticompetitive acts made possible by the violation. It should, in short, be "the type of loss that the claimed violations . . . would be likely to cause."

Brunswick Corp. v. Pueblo Bowl-O-Mat, Inc., 429 U.S. 477, 485–489 (1977).

> [In interpreting section 4 of the Clayton Act] we look (1) to the physical and economic nexus between the alleged violation and the harm to the plaintiff, and, (2) more particularly, to the relationship of the injury alleged with those forms of injury about which Congress was likely to have been concerned in making defendant's conduct unlawful and in providing a private remedy under § 4.

Blue Shield of Va. v. McCready, 457 U.S. 465, 477–478 (1982). The individual issues presented by these requirements are addressed next.

[a]   Jurisdiction, Venue, and Service

Sections 4 and 16 of the Clayton Act are jurisdiction-creating statutes. They require no minimum "amount in controversy." The jurisdiction is exclusive within the federal district courts, but it has been held that a prior state decision may operate as a bar to a subsequent federal antitrust claim, and that the subsequent federal antitrust court should consider the preclusive effect of the prior state judgment with regard to preclusion law of the state court. *Marrese v. American Academy of Orthopaedic Surgeons*, 470 U.S. 373 (1985). *See* discussion in this chapter, Section [I][E], *infra*.

Section 4 of the Clayton Act permits venue to be located where the defendant, including an individual, partnership, or unincorporated association, "resides, or is found, or has an agent." Section 12 of the Clayton Act provides that when the defendant is a corporation, venue is also appropriate "not only in the judicial district [where the corporate defendant] is an inhabitant, but also in any district wherein [defendant] may be found or transacts business." This special antitrust venue provision is supplemented by a general venue statute permitting venue in the district where the "defendant resides, if all defendants reside in the same state . . . or [where] a substantial part of the events or omissions giving rise to the claim occurred, or [where] a substantial part of property that is the subject of the action is situated, or [where] the defendant may be found [if there is no other district where the action may be brought]," or in the district where the corporate defendant is "subject to personal jurisdiction." 28 U.S.C. § 1391(b), (c).

These venue provisions have been construed liberally so as to interpret the requirements of identifying the district where the suit should be brought in a "practical, everyday business or commercial" context. The decisional law suggests that in interpreting the statutes, the "transacting business" test is broader than the "doing business" or "claim-arising" tests. As these statutes indicate, the law of venue is directed to an inquiry concerning the physical presence of the defendant so that the litigation can be located in a fair forum. *See* Hovenkamp, *Personal Jurisdiction and Venue in Private Antitrust Actions in the Federal Courts: A Policy Analysis*, 67 Iowa L. Rev. 485 (1982). When the Department of Justice sues for damages for its own injury, it is subject to these same venue provisions. 15 U.S.C. § 15a.

Daniel v. American Board of Emergency Medicine, 428 F.3d 408 (2d Cir. 2005), provides an example of activity within a judicial district that amounts to "transacting business" necessary for establishing venue in that district under Section 12 of the Clayton Act. The court wrote:

> [T]hese contacts must be considered in light of the nature of [American Board of Emergency Medicine's] business, which is certifying doctors who meet its training and testing standards in the field of emergency medicine. ABEM, which operates out of its headquarters in Michigan, neither develops its standards nor administers its certification examinations in the Western District of New York. It does not own or lease any real estate in the district. It does not maintain an office, telephone, bank account, or mailing address there. It employs no agent to carry on its operations or promote its activities in the Western District of New York. It does not advertise or solicit applicants for its certification examination in the district. Indeed, inquiries or contacts are initiated by potential applicants *to* ABEM, not the reverse. To the extent the district court found that 99% of ABEM's revenues derive from examination application fees, *see Daniel v. American Bd. of Emergency Med.*, 988 F. Supp. at 261, it made no finding as to how much of that fee revenue derived from applicants in the Western District of New York. Indeed, the only evidence on that point appears to be an affidavit of ABEM's executive director (in support of ABEM's motion to dismiss plaintiffs' Second Amended Complaint), which states that the revenue ABEM receives from examination applications in the Western District of New York is *de minimis* "in relation to ABEM's total revenues." Munger Aff. ¶ 7 (July 20, 1994).

With this understanding of ABEM's business, it is impossible to conclude that an unspecified number of communications by ABEM into the district in response to inquiries about tests to be administered outside the district, even when coupled with an unspecified but apparently minimal amount of revenue from test fees transmitted from applicants residing in the district, evidences the sort of "practical, everyday business or commercial concept of doing business or carrying on business of any substantial character" that the Supreme Court has equated to "transact[ing] business" for purposes of Section 12 venue (citing *United States v. Scophony Corp.*, 333 U.S. 795, 807 (1948).

Id. at 430.

The question of venue becomes problematic in a multiple defendant antitrust case. Generally, venue requirements must be met separately for each defendant. *See* Hovenkamp, *supra*, at 518. While substantively the co-conspiracy doctrine creates an agency relationship, this vicarious litigation strategy has not found acceptance in the interpretation of Section 4 of the Clayton Act or the supplementary provisions of the general revenue statute. The Supreme Court in *Bankers Life & Cas. Co. v. Holland*, 346 U.S. 379, 384 (1953), held that in government antitrust suits, venue is proper "where the conspiracy was formed or in part carried on or where an overt act was committed in furtherance thereof," but that in private suits under Section 4 for treble damages, Congress "placed definite limits on venue." *See also Piedmont Label Co. v. Sun Garden Packing Co.*, 598 F.2d 491, 495 (9th Cir. 1979); *Contra Giusti v. Pyrotechnic Indus.*, 156 F.2d 351 (9th Cir. 1946).

Venue may be changed, for the convenience of parties and witnesses and in the interest of justice, to any other district where the action "might have been brought" originally. 28 U.S.C. § 1404(a). This general venue transfer provision requires that before transfer is appropriate under Section 1404(a) three prerequisites are required: (1) that the venue is proper in the transferor forum court; (2) that the venue is proper in the transferee court; and (3) that the personal jurisdiction can be obtained over defendant in the transferee court. *Hoffman v. Blaski*, 363 U.S. 335 (1960). *See also Piper Aircraft Co. v. Reyno*, 454 U.S. 235 (1981). In addition, Section 1406(a) permits transfer to a district where the action could have been brought when in fact it was brought in a district where venue was improper. In order to invoke Section 1406(a), the transferor court must have the appropriate subject matter jurisdiction, but apparently it need not have personal jurisdiction over the defendant. *See Goldlawr, Inc. v. Heiman*, 369 U.S. 463 (1962).

The Second Circuit has held that in antitrust cases Section 1404(a) does not apply where the more convenient forum is outside the United States. *Capital Currency Exchange v. National Westminster Bank PLC*, 155 F.3d 603 (2d Cir. 1998), *cert. denied*, 526 U.S. 1067 (1999). In such cases, the common-law doctrine of forum non-conveniens governs, regardless of the Clayton Act's "special venue" provision.

Finally, 28 U.S.C. § 1407 permits the transfer of the case for pretrial discovery purposes to a single district when there are numerous related cases in several districts that involve common questions of fact. The transfer is accomplished by a petition to transfer, which is filed with the Judicial Panel on Multidistrict Litigation. The purpose underlying the multidistrict transfer provision is to achieve economies by avoiding duplication of effort in resolving common questions. Moreover, transfer is designed for the convenience of the parties and witnesses and should facilitate the promotion of the efficient conduct of the multidistrict actions. After the pretrial matters have been decided, the transferee court must remand the case back to the original transferor court. *See Lexecon Inc. v. Milberg Weiss Bershad Hynes & Lerach*, 523 U.S. 26 (1998).

Section 12 of the Clayton Act provides for service of process wherever the corporate defendant is an inhabitant or may be found. 15 U.S.C. § 22. This language has been interpreted to mean that service outside the forum district is proper "only when the action is brought in the district where the defendant resides, is found, or transacts business." Hovenkamp, *supra*, at 509. The extraterritorial service under Section 12 applies only to corporations, not to individuals, partnerships, or unincorporated associations. If there is an attempt to serve process outside the limits of Section 12, such as when the defendant is not a corporation, plaintiff must rely on the forum state's long arm statute. Otherwise, service is restricted to the judicial district where the suit is filed or, under Rule 4(f) of the Federal Rules of Civil Procedure, service may be made anywhere within the state where the forum court sits.

In *Go-Video v. Akai Elec. Co.*, 885 F.2d 1406 (9th Cir. 1989), the Ninth Circuit approved the use of worldwide service of process against an alien defendant even though venue was established under the Alien Venue Statute, which permits an alien to be sued in any district. Consider, for example, whether under that combination a foreign defendant doing business only in Iowa could be sued in Arizona.

Although the Ninth Circuit has adopted a national contacts test for personal jurisdiction under Section 12 of the Clayton Act, the District of Columbia Circuit has decided to adopt a local contacts test. *GTE New Media Servs. Inc. v. BellSouth Corp.*, 199 F.3d 1343 (D.C. Cir. 2000); *see also In re Vitamins Antitrust Litigation*, 94 F. Supp. 2d 26 (D.D.C. 2000). The District of Columbia Circuit flatly rejected the Ninth Circuit's interpretation of Section 12, choosing instead to align itself with the position taken by the Second Circuit. *See Goldlawr Inc. v. Heiman*, 288 F.2d 579, 581 (2d Cir. 1961), *rev'd on other grounds*, 369 U.S. 463 (1962).

The Ninth and the District of Columbia Circuits rely on differing interpretations of Section 12, which provides as follows:

> Any suit, action, or proceeding under the antitrust laws against a corporation may be brought not only in the judicial district whereof it is an inhabitant, but also in any district wherein it may be found or transacts business; and all process in such cases may be served in the district of which it is an inhabitant, or wherever it may be found.

Most recently, in *KM Enterp., Inc. v. Global Traffic Tech., Inc.*, 725 F.3d 718 (7th Cir. 2013), the Seventh Circuit chose the narrower reading, holding that ordinary rules of statutory interpretation required the court to give meaning to the phrase "in such cases." Further,

> the fact that Congress passed Section 12 with the intent to expand venue in antitrust cases does not indicate that Congress wanted *nationwide* venue. Congress said no such thing in Section 12. To the contrary, it created

specific limits on venue — limits that for many corporations would result in a set of permissible districts much smaller than the entire United States.

The difference between the circuits is whether the venue clause of the statute must be satisfied before nationwide, and subsequently worldwide, service of process is allowed: the District of Columbia Circuit believes that venue must be found before the extraterritorial service privilege is given; the Ninth Circuit does not. The Eleventh Circuit in *Prewitt* found the Clayton Act's worldwide service of process to be independent of its venue provisions.

In an important procedural decision, the Ninth Circuit has held that federal personal jurisdiction over a corporate antitrust defendant under Section 12 of the Clayton Act is independent of whether there is proper venue. Judge Fletcher (a long-time civil procedure teacher), writing for the court, reasoned that personal jurisdiction is satisfied when the corporation has minimum contacts with the United States as whole. Further, the court notes that the issue of personal jurisdiction should be resolved first, followed by whether the exercise of personal jurisdiction then raises issues of venue. Personal jurisdiction and venue are not to be read as "an integrated whole" but rather are two separate inquiries under Section 12. *Action Embroidery Corp. v. Atlantic Embroidery, Inc.*, 368 F.3d 1174 (9th Cir. 2004).

In a 2005 decision, *Daniel v. American Board of Emergency Med.*, 428 F.3d 408 (2d Cir. 2005), the Second Circuit confirmed its position expressed in *Goldlawr* that the venue clause of Section 12 must be satisfied before that section's worldwide service of process is allowed. In particular, this interpretation was supported by the fact that the "service of process" clause was separated from the "venue" clause by a semicolon, and by the use of the words "such cases" in the "service of process clause" to mandate that "all process *in such cases* may be served in the district of which it is an inhabitant, or wherever it may be found." (Italics added.) *Id.* at 422. Thus, if the general venue statute, 28 U.S.C. § 1391, is the basis for venue, Section 12's broad service of process cannot be employed. *Id.* at 427.

[b]   Statute of Limitations

Section 4B of the Clayton Act requires that a private treble damages suit be brought within four years after the claim for relief accrues. Under certain circumstances, the statute of limitations may be suspended, thus extending the time within which an action can be brought. Although suits seeking private treble damages fall under the four-year statute of limitations, courts uniformly have held that a suit brought for injunctive relief pursuant to Section 16 of the Clayton Act is not subject to the provisions of Section 4B.

As discussed *infra*, in order to allege a claim for relief, plaintiff must plead injury to business or property by reason of a violation of an antitrust law. Once damage or injury has been sustained, the statute of limitations commences to run. The question of when injury is sustained depends on the nature of the antitrust violation alleged. The Court in *Zenith Radio Corp. v. Hazeltine Research, Inc.*, 401 U.S. 321, 338–339 (1971), where the alleged damage occurred more than four years before suit was filed, held that:

> [A] cause of action accrues and the statute begins to run when a defendant commits an act that injures a plaintiff's business. . . . In the context of a continuing conspiracy to violate the antitrust laws, . . . this has usually been understood to mean that each time a plaintiff is injured by an act of the defendants a cause of action accrues to him to recover the damages caused by that act and that, as to those damages, the statute of limitation runs from the commission of the act. . . . [E]ach separate cause of action that so accrues entitles a plaintiff to recover not only those damages which he has suffered at the date of accrual, but also those which he will suffer in the future from the particular invasion.

The Court concluded that if damages are too speculative, no claim for relief has yet accrued, and the statute of limitations will not commence until the damages have been suffered.

The Sixth and Eighth Circuits have focused on the distinction between the defendant's initial "overt" action, which causes the plaintiff's injury, and the subsequent "effects" that the initial action may have. *See Concord Boat Corp. v. Brunswick Corp.*, 207 F.3d 1039 (8th Cir. 2000); *Grand Rapids Plastics Inc. v. Lakian*, 188 F.3d 401 (6th Cir. 1999). In general, the limitations period begins to run at "the point the act first causes injury." *Klehr v. A.O. Smith Corp.*, 521 U.S. 179, 190–191 (1997) (citing *Zenith Radio Corp.*, 401 U.S. at 339–340). In a continuing violation, however, there is an initial act that causes injury followed by a number of other acts that also cause injury. This type of violation typically occurs in the context of Sherman Act or RICO claims where multiple defendants are alleged to be part of an ongoing conspiracy. *Concord Boat Corp.*, 207 F.3d at 1051. In such a situation, the statute of limitations runs from the last "overt" act.

In determining what an overt act actually is, the Sixth Circuit has held that acts which simply reflect or implement a prior refusal to deal or acts that are merely unabated inertial consequences (of a single act) do not restart the statute of limitations. *DXS Inc. v. Siemans Med. Sys. Inc.*, 100 F.3d 462, 467–468 (6th Cir. 1996). In *Concord Boat, supra*, the court held that the four-year statute of limitations began to run on a merger when the transaction occurred, rejecting the plaintiff's claim that each subsequent sale that the firm made constituted a "continuing violation," just as each sale made by a cartel; rather, subsequent sales were merely the "inertial consequences" of the merger. If the plaintiff's theory were correct, would the statute of limitations ever run on a merger? If not, would that be wise antitrust policy? *See Midwestern Machinery v. Northwest Airlines, Inc.*, 2003-1 Trade Cas. 73,950, 2003 U.S. Dist. LEXIS 1827 (D. Minn. Feb. 5, 2003), *aff'd*, 392 F.3d 265 (8th Cir. 2004), where the district court ruled in a Section 7 merger challenge that the injury flows from the initial acquisition of stocks and assets and not from each ticket purchase. *But see Xechem, Inc. v. Bristol-Meyers Squibb Co.*, 372 F.3d 899, 902 (7th Cir. 2004) ("[T]hat it may be too late to complain in 2003 about what Bristol-Meyers did in 1997 does not imply that it is too late to complain about what it did in 2000 or 2002; improperly prolonging a monopoly is as much an offense against the Sherman Act as is wrongfully acquiring market power in the first place."). The Third Circuit has rejected the Sixth Circuit's interpretation of what constitutes an overt act for statute of limitations purposes. Relying on the *Grand Rapids Plastics*, defendants in *West Penn Allegheny Health System, Inc. v. UPMC*,

627 F.3d 85, 106 (3d Cir. 2010), argued that injurious acts occurring within the limitations period do not trigger the statute of limitations if they are merely "reaffirmations" of acts done, or decisions made outside of the limitations period. The Third Circuit, siding with the Fifth Circuit, rejected defendant's interpretation as inconsistent with *Hanover Shoe*. *Id.* at 106–107; *see also Bell v. Dow Chem. Co.*, 847 F.2d 1179, 1186–1187 (5th Cir. 1988). Thus plaintiff West Penn was allowed to proceed with its claim, even though the acts that occurred within the limitations period were the result of decisions and acts done outside of the limitations period. *West Penn Allegheny Health System*, 627 F.3d at 106.

Continuing conspiracies generally toll the statute of limitations. *See generally In re Issuer Plaintiff Initial Public Offering Antitrust Litigation*, 2004-1 Trade Cas. (CCH) 74,348, 2004 U.S. Dist. LEXIS 3892 (S.D.N.Y. Mar. 9, 2004) (finding that because of the nature of price-fixing conspiracies, the statute of limitations can be tolled by showing that the plaintiff had no knowledge of the underlying facts or could not have reasonably found them out); *Exhaust Unlimited, Inc. v. Cintas Corp.*, 326 F. Supp. 2d 928 (S.D. Ill. 2004) (allowing a cause of action to accrue each time the defendant allegedly imposed environmental charges in auto repair shops); *United States v. Therm-All, Inc.*, 373 F.3d 625 (5th Cir. 2003), *cert. denied*, 543 U.S. 1004 (2004) (tolling statute where price-setting scheme involved repeated setting of prices); *Varner v. Peterson Farms*, 371 F.3d 1011, 1020 (8th Cir. 2004) (refusing to toll statute where original contract claimed to contain tying provision had not been modified); *Southwire Co. v. J.P. Morgan Chase & Co.*, 307 F. Supp. 2d 1046, 1062 (W.D. Wis. 2004) (ruling that statute of limitations began to run when reports announcing investigation by Commodities Future Trading Commission were released, not three years later when a different party filed a lawsuit).

The statute of limitations can be tolled or suspended under certain circumstances. Fraudulent concealment of the claim for relief can suspend the running of the statute of limitations. When the fraud is discovered, or should have been discovered, the statute will begin to run. Likewise, evidence of duress may be grounds for tolling the statute of limitations, although the degree of duress required to toll the statute may be so substantial as to render the application of this exception very narrow. At least one court has held that the duress must result from a threat to do an unlawful act. *Philco Corp. v. Radio Corp. of Am.*, 186 F. Supp. 155 (E.D. Pa. 1960). *See* D. Floyd & E. Thomas Sullivan, Private Antitrust Actions § 5.4.1 (1998).

Recently, the Sixth Circuit looked at the plaintiff's role in a fraudulent concealment case. The Court held that a plaintiff who delays his or her suit must show a justifiable basis for the delay in order to overcome the per se hurdle of the limitations period. *Alba v. Marietta Mem'l Hosp.*, 202 F.3d 267 (6th Cir. 2000). To justify the concealment exception, the plaintiff must prove three things: (1) concealment of the material basis by the defendants; (2) failure to discover operative facts during the four-year period; and (3) plaintiff's due diligence to pursue operable and material information.

Some antitrust violations, such as naked price-fixing conspiracies, are "concealed" from victims by their very nature — i.e., the defendants knew that what they were doing was illegal and so hid it from the public. This has inspired some courts to develop the notion of a "self-concealing" conspiracy. If a plaintiff can prove such a conspiracy, the statute of limitations will not be tolled. *See Bethlehem Steel Corp. v. Fischbach & Moore*, 641 F. Supp. 271, 274 (E.D. Pa. 1986).

In addition to equitable justifications for tolling the statute of limitations, Section 5(i) of the Clayton Act provides that if a "civil or criminal proceeding is instituted by the United States" for violations of antitrust laws, a subsequent private action "based in whole or in part on any matter complained of" in the government suit is not barred until one year after the completion of the government suit. *See, e.g., Leh v. General Petr. Corp.*, 382 U.S. 54 (1965). While the statute is unclear whether the reference to the United States includes the FTC, the Supreme Court has held that actions by the FTC, at least when enforcing the Clayton Act, toll the statute for the one-year period. *Minnesota Mining & Mfg. Co. v. New Jersey Wood Fin. Co.*, 381 U.S. 311, 320–321 (1965). Whether FTC actions brought under statutes other than the Clayton Act (e.g., Section 5 of FTC Act) come within Section 5(i)'s tolling provision is unclear. *Compare Rader v. Balfour*, 440 F.2d 469, 473 (7th Cir.), *cert. denied*, 404 U.S. 983 (1971) (Section 5 of FTC Act included), *with Laitram Corp. v. Deepsouth Packing Co.*, 279 F. Supp. 883, 891 (E.D. La. 1968) (Section 5 of FTC Act not included because not an antitrust law). *See also Greyhound Corp. v. Mt. Hood Stages, Inc.*, 437 U.S. 322 (1978). It is clear, however, from the language of Section 5(i) that its tolling provision does not apply to government damage actions under Section 4A of the Clayton Act unless the government also seeks injunctive relief. *See, e.g., Chipanno v. Champion Int'l Corp.*, 702 F.2d 827 (9th Cir. 1983); 15 U.S.C. § 15a. The Seventh Circuit has held that the statute of limitations was not tolled during a patent-interference proceeding before the Patent Office because a patent validity claim is not within the Patent Office's primary jurisdiction. *Brunswick Corp. v. Riegel Textile Corp.*, 752 F.2d 261 (7th Cir. 1984), *cert. denied*, 472 U.S. 1018 (1985). This suggests that the one-year extension under Section 5(i) may have a narrower application than earlier thought.

The "identity of the issues" requirement under Section 5(i) is determined, regardless of the outcome of the first suit, by comparing the government and private complaints. *Leh v. General Petr. Corp.*, 382 U.S. 54 (1965). It does not matter whether the party defendants in the private suit are identical with defendants in the government suit in order for the statute of limitations to be suspended during the pendency of the government suit. *Zenith Radio Corp. v. Hazeltine Research, Inc.*, 401 U.S. 321 (1971).

Finally, it has been held that the one-year period begins to run when a final judgment as to all defendants in the government action has been resolved on appeal or when the time for filing the appeal has expired. *Russ Togs, Inc. v. Grinnell Corp.*, 426 F.2d 850 (2d Cir. 1970); *New Jersey v. Morton Salt Co.*, 387 F.2d 94 (3d Cir. 1967), *cert. denied*, 391 U.S. 967 (1968). *See Morton's Market Inc. v. Gustafson's Dairy Inc.*, 198 F.3d 823 (11th Cir. 1999) (providing a good illustration of a large portion of the principles addressed in this section, including the commencement of the statute of limitations, equitable tolling, and tolling due to a government proceeding).

[c]   Interstate Commerce Requirement

Congress' authority to regulate commercial transactions under the antitrust laws derives from its constitutional power to regulate interstate and foreign trade or commerce. Since the jurisdictional base of the antitrust laws rests on the Commerce Clause of the Constitution, a plaintiff must initially plead a statement invoking Commerce Clause jurisdiction for an alleged antitrust violation.

It is often said that, in passing the Sherman Act, Congress exerted its full power to regulate commerce. Initially the Supreme Court took the view, however, that the Commerce Clause permitted the national government to regulate only those activities "in the flow" of commerce. In *United States v. E.C. Knight Co.*, 156 U.S. 1, 12 (1895), the Court held that "[c]ommerce succeeds to manufacture, [but] is not a part of it." Under the *E.C. Knight* theory, the Sherman Act would not even reach a manufacturer who manufactured goods in several states and shipped them to other states if the restraint was in the goods, not in the commerce. Consistent with that rule, the Court had no problem finding jurisdiction two years later in *United States v. Trans-Missouri Freight Ass'n*, 166 U.S. 290 (1897), where the alleged price fixing involved interstate rail transportation.

E.C. Knight was overruled by *Mandeville Island Farms, Inc. v. American Crystal Sugar Co.*, 334 U.S. 219 (1948), where the Supreme Court held that the Sherman Act reaches restraints of trade which are either "in" interstate commerce, or which have a substantial "effect" on interstate commerce. As Justice Jackson once put it, "[i]f it is interstate commerce that feels the pinch, it does not matter how local the operation which applies the squeeze." *United States v. Women's Sportswear Mfrs. Ass'n*, 336 U.S. 460 (1949). Under this rule, the Sherman Act has been held to reach activities that are quite local in nature, if a substantial effect on interstate commerce is perceived. For example, in *McLain v. Real Estate Bd. of New Orleans*, 444 U.S. 232 (1980), the Supreme Court held that the Sherman Act would reach price fixing among real estate brokers in a single city, because many of the purchasers and sellers of those homes were either moving from or going to a different state, and because out-of-state lending institutions participated in the financing.

If the challenged restraint affects an "appreciable" amount of interstate commerce, defined qualitatively, the quantitative volume of commerce is not ordinarily measured. This is particularly true for per se violations where it has been held that the amount of commerce affected is immaterial. *United States v. Columbia Steel Co.*, 334 U.S. 495 (1948). This commerce requirement can initially be satisfied at the pleading stage through the filing of affidavits. *McLain, supra*.

Traditionally the key to Commerce Clause jurisdiction has been whether there is a causal connection between the restraint and a demonstrated consequence on interstate commerce. In this regard, consider the following case.

SUMMIT HEALTH, LTD. v. PINHAS
500 U.S. 322 (1991)

JUSTICE STEVENS delivered the opinion of the Court.

The question presented is whether the interstate commerce requirement of antitrust jurisdiction is satisfied by allegations that petitioners conspired to exclude respondent, a duly licensed and practicing physician and surgeon, from the market for ophthalmological services in Los Angeles because he refused to follow an unnecessarily costly surgical procedure. In 1987, respondent Dr. Simon J. Pinhas filed a complaint in District Court alleging that petitioners Summit Health, Ltd. (Summit), Midway Hospital Medical Center (Midway), its medical staff, and others, had entered into a conspiracy to drive him out of business "so that other ophthalmologists and eye physicians [including four of the petitioners] will have a greater share of the eye care and ophthalmic surgery in Los Angeles." Among his allegations was a claim that the conspiracy violated § 1 of the Sherman Act. The District Court granted defendants' (now petitioners') motion to dismiss the First Amended Complaint (complaint) without leave to amend, but the United States Court of Appeals for the Ninth Circuit reinstated the antitrust claim. 894 F.2d 1024 (1989).

. . . .

I

Because this case comes before us from the granting of a motion to dismiss on the pleadings, we must assume the truth of the material facts as alleged in the complaint. Respondent, a diplomat of the American Board of Ophthalmology, has earned a national and international reputation as a specialist in corneal eye problems. Since October 1981, he has been a member of the staff of Midway in Los Angeles, and because of his special skills, has performed more eye surgical procedures, including cornea transplants and cataract removals, than any other surgeon at the hospital. Prior to 1986, most eye surgeries in Los Angeles were performed by a primary surgeon with the assistance of a second surgeon. This practice significantly increased the cost of eye surgery. In February of that year, the administrators of the Medicare program announced that they would no longer reimburse physicians for the services of assistants, and most hospitals in southern California abolished the assistant surgeon requirement. Respondent, and certain other ophthalmologists, asked Midway to abandon the requirement, but the medical staff refused to do so. Respondent explained that because Medicare reimbursement was no longer available, the requirement would cost him about $60,000 per year in payments to competing surgeons for assistance that he did not need. Although respondent expressed a desire to maintain the preponderance of his practice at Midway, he nevertheless advised the hospital that he would leave if the assistant surgeon requirement were not eliminated.

Petitioners responded to respondent's request to forgo an assistant in two ways. First, Midway and its corporate parent offered the respondent a "sham" contract that provided for payments of $36,000 per year (later increased by oral offer to

$60,000) for services that he would not be asked to perform. Second, when respondent refused to sign or return the "sham" contract, petitioners initiated peer-review proceedings against him and summarily suspended, and subsequently terminated, his medical staff privileges. The proceedings were conducted in an unfair manner by biased decision makers, and ultimately resulted in an order upholding one of the seven charges against respondent, and imposing severe restrictions on his practice. When this action was commenced, petitioners were preparing to distribute an adverse report about respondent that would "preclude him from continued competition in the market place, not only at defendant Midway Hospital [but also] . . . in California, if not the United States." The defendants allegedly planned to disseminate the report "to all hospitals which Dr. Pinhas is a member, and to all hospitals to which he may apply so as to secure similar actions by those hospitals, thus effectuating a boycott of Dr. Pinhas." The complaint alleges that petitioner Summit owns and operates 19 hospitals, including Midway, and 49 other health care facilities in California, six other States, and Saudi Arabia. Summit, Midway, and each of the four ophthalmic surgeons named as individual defendants, as well as respondent, are all allegedly engaged in interstate commerce. The provision of ophthalmological services affects interstate commerce because both physicians and hospitals serve nonresident patients and receive reimbursement through Medicare payments. Reports concerning peer-review proceedings are routinely distributed across state lines and affect doctors' employment opportunities throughout the Nation.

. . . .

II

Petitioner Summit, the parent of Midway as well as several other general hospitals, is unquestionably engaged in interstate commerce. Moreover, although Midway's primary activity is the provision of health care services in a local market, it also engages in interstate commerce. A conspiracy to prevent Midway from expanding would be covered by the Sherman Act, even though any actual impact on interstate commerce would be "indirect" and "fortuitous." *Hospital Bldg. Co. v. Rex Hospital Trustees*, 425 U.S. 738, 744 (1976). No specific purpose to restrain interstate commerce is required. As a "matter of practical economics," the effect of such a conspiracy on the hospital's "purchases of out-of-state medicines and supplies as well as its revenues from out-of-state insurance companies," would establish the necessary interstate nexus.

This case does not involve the full range of activities conducted at a general hospital. Rather, this case involves the provision of ophthalmological services. It seems clear, however, that these services are regularly performed for out-of-state patients and generate revenues from out-of-state sources; their importance as part of the entire operation of the hospital is evident from the allegations of the complaint. A conspiracy to eliminate the entire ophthalmological department of the hospital, like a conspiracy to destroy the hospital itself, would unquestionably affect interstate commerce.

Petitioners contend, however, that a boycott of a single surgeon has no such obvious effect because the complaint does not deny the existence of an adequate supply of other surgeons to perform all of the services that respondent's current and future patients may ever require. Petitioners argue that respondent's complaint is insufficient because there is no factual nexus between the restraint on this one surgeon's practice and interstate commerce.

There are two flaws in petitioners' argument. First, because the essence of any violation of § 1 is the illegal agreement itself — rather than the overt acts performed in furtherance of it — proper analysis focuses, not upon actual consequences, but rather upon the potential harm that would ensue if the conspiracy were successful. As we explained in *McLain v. Real Estate Bd. of New Orleans, Inc.*, 444 U.S. 232 (1980): "If establishing jurisdiction required a showing that the unlawful conduct itself had an effect on interstate commerce, jurisdiction would be defeated by a demonstration that the alleged restraint failed to have its intended anticompetitive effect. A violation may still be found in such circumstances because in a civil action under the Sherman Act, liability may be established by proof of either an unlawful purpose or an anticompetitive effect." Thus, respondent need not allege, or prove, an actual effect on interstate commerce to support federal jurisdiction. Second, if the conspiracy alleged in the complaint is successful, "as a matter of practical economics" there will be a reduction in the provision of ophthalmological services in the Los Angeles market. In cases involving horizontal agreements to fix prices or allocate territories within a single State, we have based jurisdiction on a general conclusion that the defendants' agreement "almost surely" had a market-wide impact and therefore an effect on interstate commerce, *Burke v. Ford*, 389 U.S. 320, 322 (1967) (per curiam), or that the agreement "necessarily affect[ed]" the volume of residential sales and therefore the demand for financing and title insurance provided by out-of-state concerns. *McLain*, 444 U.S., at 246. In the latter, we explained: "To establish the jurisdictional element of a Sherman Act violation it would be sufficient for petitioners to demonstrate a substantial effect on interstate commerce generated by respondents' brokerage activity. Petitioners need not make the more particularized showing of an effect on interstate commerce caused by the alleged conspiracy to fix commission rates, or by those other aspects of respondents' activity that are alleged to be unlawful." Although plaintiffs in *McLain* were consumers of the conspirators' real estate brokerage services, and plaintiff in this case is a competing surgeon whose complaint identifies only himself as the victim of the alleged boycott, the same analysis applies. The case involves an alleged restraint on the practice of ophthalmological services. . . . The restraint was accomplished by an alleged misuse of a congressionally regulated peer-review process,[1] which respondent characterizes as the gateway that controls access to the market for his services. The gateway was closed to respondent, both at Midway and at other hospitals, because petitioners insisted upon adhering to an unnecessarily costly procedure.

The competitive significance of respondent's exclusion from the market must be measured, not just by a particularized evaluation of his own practice, but rather, by

---

[1] [FN 12] *See* Health Care Quality Improvement Act of 1986, 100 Stat. 3784, 42 U.S.C. § 11101 *et seq.* The statute provides for immunity from antitrust, and other, actions if the peer-review process proceeds in accordance with § 11112. Respondent alleges that the process did not conform with the requirements set forth in § 11112, such as adequate notice, representation by an attorney, access to a transcript of the proceedings, and the right to cross-examine witnesses. . . .

a general evaluation of the impact of the restraint on other participants and potential participants in the market from which he has been excluded. We have no doubt concerning the power of Congress to regulate a peer-review process controlling access to the market for ophthalmological surgery in Los Angeles. Thus respondent's claim that members of the peer-review committee conspired with others to abuse that process and thereby deny respondent access to the market for ophthalmological services provided by general hospitals in Los Angeles has a sufficient nexus with interstate commerce to support federal jurisdiction. The judgment of the Court of Appeals is affirmed.

It is so ordered.

JUSTICE SCALIA, with whom JUSTICE O'CONNOR, JUSTICE KENNEDY, and JUSTICE SOUTER join, dissenting.

[T]he question before us is not whether Congress could reach the activity before us here if it wanted to, but whether it has done so via the Sherman Act. That enactment does not prohibit all conspiracies using instrumentalities of commerce that Congress could regulate. Nor does it prohibit all conspiracies that have sufficient constitutional "nexus" to interstate commerce to be regulated. It prohibits only those conspiracies that are "in restraint of trade or commerce among the several States." This language commands a judicial inquiry into the nature and potential effect of each particular restraint. "The jurisdictional inquiry under general prohibitions . . . like § 1 of the Sherman Act, turning as it does on the circumstances presented in each case and requiring a particularized judicial determination, differs significantly from that required when Congress itself has defined the specific persons and activities that affect commerce and therefore require federal regulation." *Gulf Oil Corp. v. Copp Paving Co.*, 419 U.S. 186, 197, n.12 (1974).

Until 1980, the nature of this jurisdictional inquiry with respect to alleged restraints not targeted at the very flow of interstate commerce was clear: the question was whether the restraint at issue, if successful, would have a substantial effect on interstate commercial activity. . . . Unfortunately, in 1980, the Court seemed to abandon this approach. *McLain v. Real Estate Bd. of New Orleans, Inc.*, 444 U.S. 232 (1980), appeared to shift the inquiry away from the effects of the restraint itself, asking instead whether the "[defendants'] activities which allegedly have been infected by a price-fixing conspiracy . . . have a not insubstantial effect on the interstate commerce involved."

. . . .

With respect to a restraint like the one at issue here, for example, how does one decide which "activities of the defendants" are "infected"? Are they all the activities of the hospital? Only the activities of the eye surgery department? The entire practice of eye surgeons who use the hospital? Or, as the Ninth Circuit apparently found in this case, the peer review process itself? Today the Court could have cleared up the confusion created by *McLain*, refocused the inquiry along the lines marked out by our previous cases (and still adhered to by most circuits), and reversed the judgment below. Instead, it compounds the confusion by rejecting the two competing interpretations of *McLain* and adding yet a third candidate to the field, one that no court or commentator has ever suggested, let alone endorsed. To determine Sherman Act jurisdiction it looks neither to the effect on commerce of the restraint, nor to the effect on commerce of the defendants' infected activity, but rather, it seems, to the effect on commerce of the activity from which the plaintiff has been excluded. As I understand the Court's opinion, the test of Sherman Act jurisdiction is whether the entire line of commerce from which Dr. Pinhas has been excluded affects interstate commerce. Since excluding him from eye surgery at Midway Hospital effectively excluded him from the entire Los Angeles market for eye surgery (because no other Los Angeles hospital would accord him practice privileges after Midway rejected him), the jurisdictional question is simply whether that market affects interstate commerce, which of course it does. This analysis tells us nothing about the substantiality of the impact on interstate commerce generated by the particular conduct at issue here. Determining the "market" for a product or service, meaning the scope of other products or services against which it must compete, is of course necessary for many purposes of antitrust analysis. But today's opinion does not identify a relevant "market" in that sense. It declares Los Angeles to be the pertinent "market" only because that is the entire scope of Dr. Pinhas's exclusion from practice. If the scope of his exclusion had been national, it would have declared the entire United States to be the "market," though it is quite unlikely that all eye surgeons in the United States are in competition.

. . . .

NOTES AND QUESTIONS

1. Does the majority opinion require the restraining effect to be on the plaintiff's professional activities, or is the broader market of ophthalmological services by all doctors the affected commerce connection? Suppose a restraint covers an entire, properly defined relevant market but the market itself is located within a single state. Does *Summit* permit jurisdiction? For example, suppose the only three gasoline stations in a rural community fix their prices, and the court found the community to be a relevant geographic market. Would it matter where the stations purchased the gasoline? Where the gasoline was refined or the crude oil produced? Would it matter whether all or nearly all of the stations' customers were from within the state? How would you balance all of these factors? Note that four of the Justices in dissent urged a narrower reach for Sherman Act jurisdiction.

2. If a defendant wishes to challenge the "commerce" requirement after *Summit*, should he or she use a motion to dismiss under Fed. Rule 12(b)(1) (subject matter jurisdiction) or under Fed. Rule 12(b)(6) (failure to state a claim for relief)? *See* Calkins, *The 1990–91 Supreme Court Term and Antitrust*, 60 ANTITRUST L.J. 603, 631–634 (1991).

Following *Summit*, the Seventh Circuit reinstated a § 1 complaint, noting that the Commerce Clause requirements are met if the plaintiff alleges that the defendants' conduct restrained interstate commerce. *Hammes v. AAMCO Transmissions, Inc.*, 33 F.3d 774 (7th Cir. 1994). Judge Posner noted that it is "enough for the plaintiff to have alleged, without further particulars, that the defendants' conduct in excluding it from [the market] restrained (impeded, impaired, diminished — there is no magic word) interstate commerce." He offered that "[t]hough some cases state otherwise, the complaint would not have had to add that the restraint was substantial. No such limitations are stated in the Act." Although he admits that there is "a deep tension in commerce cases," he opts for "simplification" in holding that "[i]t is quite enough, probably more than enough, if the complaint alleges that the plaintiff was engaged in interstate commerce and was injured by the alleged antitrust violation." *Id.* at 779–782. Hence, no factual connection between commerce and the restraint needs to be alleged, at least in the Seventh Circuit. There is still some ambiguity about whether antitrust Commerce Clause jurisdiction is measured by the defendants' activities in or affecting interstate commerce or by the alleged restraint's effect on interstate commerce.

In *Hamilton Chapter of Alpha Delta Phi, Inc. v. Hamilton College*, 128 F.3d 59 (2d Cir. 1997), the Second Circuit reversed the dismissal of plaintiff's Sherman Act claim. At issue was the defendant college's requirement that all its students live in college-owned housing facilities and buy meal plans sponsored by the college. The parties disagreed on whether the plan had a commercial purpose, with the defendant claiming that it had the noncommercial purpose of making the college experience more pleasant for female students. The court admitted that, "[i]n the context of higher education, certain activities have been held to be so central to the educational mission, and so far removed from the 'business competition' regulated by the Sherman Act, that they are not 'trade or commerce.' " *Id.* at 64. The court also disagreed with the plaintiff's claim that *any* activity undertaken by a college or university to enhance its reputation is commercial and thus subject to antitrust scrutiny. *Id.* at 65. Nonetheless, the court found that the plaintiff had offered sufficient facts suggesting a nexus between the allegedly illegal behavior and interstate commerce, including the fact that the college solicited applicants from all over the globe and that plaintiff and other providers of off-campus housing stood to lose around $1 million per year if the new policy was upheld. Thus, the defendant's conduct had "a substantial effect on interstate commerce." *Id.* at 66.

3. The Federal Trade Commission and Department of Justice have clarified that Internet commerce gives rise to jurisdiction under the antitrust laws, but the fact that commerce will be structured or designed to take place on the Internet will not change which agency will review a proposed merger or joint venture. Under the merger clearance process, discussed *infra* in Chapter 7, the agencies will examine the nature of the commerce at issue — i.e., the industry of the proposed merger or joint venture — in order to determine which agency will bear primary responsibility for review.

[d]   Transnational Application of United States Antitrust Laws

The Sherman Act applies to restraints of trade with foreign nations, including the import or export of goods to or from the United States. The application of United States antitrust laws to transnational business goes back to at least 1906, when the Department of Justice started to bring suits against conduct that allegedly had substantial adverse "effects" on the United States economy. Even foreign firms acting outside of the United States are subject to U.S. subject matter jurisdiction if they act with the intent to affect United States commerce and cause a direct effect. *See* E. Fox & D. Crane, Global Issues in Antitrust and Competition Law, 454 (2010). In incorporating the "effects" doctrine within the interpretation of the jurisdictional reach of the Sherman Act, courts have held that the following conduct comes within the Sherman Act: (1) activities of foreign firms in the United States with an effect in this country; (2) activities of foreign firms outside the United States that have an effect on the United States economy; and (3) activities of United States firms outside the United States that have effects on the United States economy. Conversely, the antitrust laws generally have not been applied to overseas conduct by United States firms or foreign firms, the result of which does not affect United States markets, consumers, or export opportunities. The original Clayton Act and the Robinson-Patman Act have a jurisdictional reach narrower than the Sherman Act. These statutes apply only to persons or entities "in" interstate commerce. In 1980, Congress amended Section 7 of the Clayton Act to permit jurisdiction over mergers that meet only the "effects" test on commerce similar to that governing the Sherman Act.

Since 1976, the courts also have started to apply the doctrine of "comity" when the United States antitrust laws are applied extraterritorially. *See Mannington Mills, Inc. v. Congoleum Corp.*, 595 F.2d 1287 (3d Cir. 1979); *Timberlane Lumber Co. v. Bank of Am. (Timberlane I)*, 549 F.2d 597 (9th Cir. 1976); *Timberlane II*, 574 F. Supp. 1453 (N.D. Cal. 1983). This approach is essentially a balancing of interests test that seeks to evaluate the propriety of applying United States law as a matter of good relations with foreign countries. *See Laker Airways v. Sabena, Belgian World Airlines*, 731 F.2d 909, 937 (D.C. Cir. 1984) ("when possible, the decisions of foreign tribunals should be given effect in domestic courts, since recognition fosters international cooperation and encourages reciprocity, thereby promoting predictability and stability"); Restatement of Foreign Relations Law (Revised) §§ 402, 403, 415 (Tentative Draft No. 6 1985). *See also* Justice Department and Federal Trade Commission, *Antitrust Enforcement Guidelines for International Operations* (1995), available at http://www.justice.gov/atr/public/guidelines/internat. htm.

The issue of antitrust jurisdiction over extraterritorial conduct has turned on whether the comity analysis is part of the jurisdictional inquiry. *Compare Timberlane III*, 749 F.2d 1378 (9th Cir. 1984) (incorporating comity into jurisdictional analysis), *with Laker Airways* (comity not a part of jurisdiction). *See also* Note, *The Laker Antitrust Legislation: The Jurisdictional "Rule of Reason" Applied to Transnational Injunctive Relief*, 71 Cornell L. Rev. 645 (1986).

The Supreme Court considered the scope of international comity in *Hartford Fire Ins. Co. v. California*, 509 U.S. 764 (1993). Nineteen states and various private plaintiffs alleged that the defendants, both domestic and foreign insurance carriers, conspired to restrict the terms of coverage for commercial general liability (CGL) insurance within the United States. In their complaint, the plaintiffs alleged that the purpose behind the conspiracy was to force certain primary insurers (those insurers who sell insurance directly to consumers) to change the terms of their standard CGL insurance policies to conform with the policies the defendant insurers wanted to sell.

The foreign defendants argued that the principle of international comity precluded extraterritorial application of the Sherman Act to the alleged conduct. The Supreme Court affirmed the extraterritorial application of the Sherman Act to this anticompetitive conduct abroad, noting that it adversely affected commerce within the United States. The Court, commenting that "the Sherman Act applies to foreign conduct that was meant to produce and did in fact produce some substantial effect in the United States," held that the alleged conduct was within the purview of the Sherman Act and, therefore, was subject to federal jurisdiction. In reaching its decision, the Court relied on the Restatement (Third) Foreign Relations Law of the United States that provides "the fact that conduct is lawful in the state in which it took place will not, of itself, bar application of the United States antitrust laws." This standard applies even if the foreign state has a strong policy to permit or encourage such conduct. In this particular case, however, the only policy that the foreign state (Great Britain) cited was one of permitting its insurers to regulate themselves. The specific acts complained of were neither mandated nor prevented by British law.

In addition to considerations of comity, the extraterritorial reach of the United States antitrust laws has been limited by the substantive defenses of the "act of state" and "foreign sovereign immunity" doctrines. The "act of state" doctrine holds that a United States court cannot review or question the validity of a "sovereign" act by a foreign government or instrumentality of a foreign government when the act is consummated within the boundaries of the foreign country.

In *W.S. Kirkpatrick & Co. v. Environmental Tectonics Corp.*, 493 U.S. 400 (1990), the Supreme Court held that the act of state doctrine does not apply to a cause of action that does not rest upon the asserted invalidity of an official act of a foreign sovereign. The action was filed against a successful bidder on a foreign government contract by an unsuccessful bidder, on the theory that the successful bidder had violated federal racketeering and other statutes by paying bribes to foreign government officials in the Republic of Nigeria. The parties agreed "that Nigerian law prohibits both the payment and receipt of bribes in connection with the award of a government contract." In this case, the allegation was that Kirkpatrick paid a "commission" equal to 20% of the contract price as a bribe to officials of the Nigerian Government.

Defendants asked that the action be dismissed under Rule 12(b)(6) on the ground that the act of state doctrine barred the suit. The legal advisor to the United States Department of State filed a letter with the district court stating that the United States court's "judicial inquiry into the purpose behind the act of a foreign sovereign would not produce the 'unique embarrassment, and the particular interference with the conduct of foreign affairs, that may result from the judicial determination that a foreign sovereign's acts are invalid.'"

The Supreme Court determined that the factual predicate for application of the act of state doctrine did not exist in this case. "Neither the claim nor any asserted defense requires a determination that Nigeria's contract with Kirkpatrick was, or was not, effective." The Court observed that in each prior instance where it held the act of state doctrine applicable, the claim for relief or the defense required the Court to declare invalid the official act of a foreign sovereign performed within its own territory. But here the Court did not accept the invitation to apply the doctrine.

"Act of state issues only arise when a court *must decide* — that is, when the outcome of the case turns upon — the effect of official action by a foreign sovereign. When that question is not in the case, neither is the act of state doctrine." The Court held that the legality of the Nigerian contract — a prerequisite for the application of the act of state doctrine — "is simply not a question to be decided." Rather, the Court seemed persuaded by the State Department's logic that the act of state doctrine is neither applicable nor dispositive when the inquiry "involves only the 'motivation' for, rather than the 'validity' of, a foreign sovereign act." Because the claim for relief did not ask the Court to invalidate the contract entered into by the Nigerian Government — the official act of the sovereign performed within its own territory — the mere challenge to the motivation of the contract was insufficient to trigger the act of state doctrine. The Court did not suggest, given the factual record, that the award of the contract by the foreign government in this case qualified for the commercial activity exception to the act of state doctrine.

The *Kirkpatrick* decision opened the way for the Justice Department and the FTC to challenge conduct by private companies in foreign countries as long as the challenge does not seek directly to invalidate an official act of the sovereign. To be sure, the Justice Department has announced it will investigate conduct by foreign-owned companies if there is an anticompetitive effect on United States consumers in domestic or export markets. The fact that the conspiracy or conduct took place overseas will not prevent the United States from exercising jurisdiction, the Department has declared. *Kirkpatrick* seems to reduce a litigation barrier for these kinds of government enforcement actions. An example might be that, if the Japanese auto makers entered a conspiracy to restrict the markets for American cars or parts in Japan, the Justice Department could sue the American subsidiaries of the Japanese companies under the "effects doctrine." *See generally United States v. Aluminum Co. of Am.*, 148 F.2d 416 (2d Cir. 1945).

Related to, but distinct from, act of state is the doctrine of foreign sovereign immunity, which gives foreign governments and their instrumentalities a limited immunity from suit. The immunity applies when the sovereign is acting in a "sovereign" capacity, but not when it is merely pursuing "proprietary" or "commercial" interests. *Alfred Dunhill of London v. Republic of Cuba*, 425 U.S. 682 (1976). The Foreign Sovereign Immunities Act of 1976, 28 U.S.C. § 1330 and §§ 1602–1611 (1976), regulates personal jurisdiction and many elements of subject matter jurisdiction in all actions against foreign sovereigns and their agents, including actions brought under the federal antitrust laws. *See International Ass'n of Machinists v. Organization of Petr. Exporting Countries*, 649 F.2d 1354 (9th Cir. 1981), *cert. denied*, 454 U.S. 1163 (1982); Hovenkamp, *Sovereign Immunities Act Jurisdiction and Antitrust Policy*, 14 U.C. Davis L. Rev. 839 (1982); Hovenkamp, *Can a Foreign Sovereign Be an Antitrust Defendant?* 32 Syracuse L. Rev. 879 (1981).

Foreign Trade Antitrust Improvements Act

The Foreign Trade Antitrust Improvements Act of 1982 restricts the reach of the Sherman Act to protect United States companies in their foreign commerce. The Act prohibits the application of the Sherman Act to export or nonimport foreign commerce unless the alleged practice has a "direct, substantial and reasonably foreseeable effect" on domestic or export trade commerce and "such effect gives rise to a claim under the Sherman Act." FTAIA does not apply to import commerce, which is still governed by the basic effects test. *See* E. Fox & D. Crane, Global Issues in Antitrust and Competition Law, 455 (2010). This is the approach essentially taken under the revised Antitrust Enforcement Guidelines for International Operations, *supra*.

Traditionally, FTAIA has been view as a jurisdictional bar on antitrust claims. In 2011, the Third Circuit, in overturning its own precedent, held in *Animal Science Products Inc. v. China Minmetals Corp.*, 654 F.3d 462 (3d Cir. 2011) that FTAIA added only statutory elements for defining the "merits" of an antitrust claim alleging foreign conduct but did not restrict the federal subject matter jurisdiction of the federal courts. Plaintiffs, who were United States purchasers of magnesite, charged that Chinese producers and exporters conspired to fix the price of magnesite when sold in the United States. Subsequent to the Third Circuit's decision, the Seventh Circuit changed its position and agreed. *See Minn-Chem Inc v. Agrium Juc.*, 683 F.3d 845 (7th Cir. 2012). The practical consequence of this shifting view is that the defense challenge to a FTAIA claim is a motion to dismiss under Rule 12(b)(6), not Rule 12(b)(1) of the Federal Rules of Civil Procedure. Under Rule 12(b)(6) the judge must accept factual allegations in a complaint. By contrast, the court can make its own jurisdictional fact finding when assessing a 12(b)(1) motion. Further, because jurisdiction cannot be waived the judge can decide the jurisdictional issue at any time, even on its own motion. See generally *Carrier Corp. v. OntoKumpu Oyj*, 673 F.3d 430 (6th Cir. 2012), for a recent holding on the pleading standard (*Twombly*) necessary to plead the requisite "foreign conduct" to affect United States markets; and *see* Edward D. Cavanagh, *The FTAIA and Claims by Foreign Plaintiffs Under State Law*, 26 Antitrust 43 (Fall 2011).

The First Circuit, in 1997, added an important new development in extraterritorial enforcement in the criminal context. The court held that the Sherman Act applies to anticompetitive conduct that takes place *entirely* in another country, as long as it was intended to have, and does have, potential effects on the United States economy. "Common sense" dictates that the Sherman Act be read the same way in both civil and criminal actions, the court reasoned. *See United States v. Nippon Paper*, 109 F.3d 1 (1st Cir. 1997) (to dismiss on the basis of lack of subject matter jurisdiction would create a safe harbor for future cartels or price-fixers, who could simply erect territorial barriers outside the United States, while forgetting the United States economy). *Compare Metro Indus., Inc. v. Sammi Corp.*, 82 F.3d 839, 843 (9th Cir. 1996), *with Filetech S.A.R.L. v. France Telecom*, 978 F. Supp. 464, 476 (S.D.N.Y. 1997), *vacated on other grounds, Filetech v. France Telecom S.A.*, 157 F.3d 922 (2d. Cir. 1998).

The Supreme Court clarified this area in 2004 with its opinion in *F. Hoffmann-LaRoche Ltd. v. Empagran, S.A.*, 542 U.S. 155 (2004). The issue was whether foreign plaintiffs, who purchased vitamins outside the United States from foreign sellers, could sue under the Sherman Act in the United States to recover treble damages for price overcharges caused by a worldwide cartel.

First, the Court ruled that the price fixing alleged in the complaint did fall within the FTAIA's exclusion clause that "conduct involving trade or commerce with foreign nations" is not covered by the Sherman Act. Second, given this holding, the Court, then, had to decide whether this conduct came within the "exception" to the exclusion: whether the conduct had a "direct, substantial, and reasonably foreseeable effect" on domestic commerce, and that "such effect gives rise to a [Sherman Act] claim." The Court held that this exception, which would have swept the allegation back within the Sherman Act coverage, did not apply "where the plaintiff's claim rests solely on the independent foreign harm." In short, while a purchaser in the United States could bring a Sherman Act claim under FTAIA because of a domestic injury, a purchaser in a foreign country could not bring an action based on foreign harm.

The Court began by noting that the canons of statutory construction call for ambiguous statutes to be construed so as to avoid unreasonable interference with sovereign authority, a construction consistent with customary international laws. Here, the Court concluded it was unreasonable to apply American law to conduct in a foreign country that causes an "independent" foreign harm that alone gives rise to the claim by the plaintiff. The antitrust harm to the foreign plaintiffs was higher foreign prices charged by their own foreign seller, not higher prices charged in the United States. Purchasers in the United States could have brought antitrust claims in the United States for anticompetitive conduct here, but this was not the claim of the foreign plaintiffs. The Court reasoned, "the exception [effect on domestic commerce] applies if the conduct's domestic effect gives rise to 'a claim' not to 'the plaintiff's claim' or 'the claim at issue.'"

The statute permits suits if the conduct has harmful domestic effects and those effects give rise to "a" claim. The plaintiffs argued that this language could refer to *anyone*'s claim, not their own claim. Under that reading, which the Court rejected, the foreign plaintiff could bring an action against a foreign seller if it could point to some other person who purchased in the United States from that seller or a fellow cartel member, and that other person had a claim under the Sherman Act. The Court found this reading of the statute plausible, but rejected it as inconsistent with general principles of international comity, because it would interfere with the power of a nation to determine the consequences for competition law violations within its own sovereign territory.

The Court ended by noting that "[w]e have assumed that the anticompetitive conduct here independently caused foreign injury; that is, the conduct's domestic effects did not help to bring about the foreign injury." It remanded to the lower courts to determine whether this independence was actually the case. Thus the Court held open the possibility that a foreign plaintiff could maintain an action if it could show that its injury was closely linked to the injuries suffered within the United States. *See In re Dynamic Random Access Memory (DRAM) Antitrust Litig.*, 546 F.3d 981 (9th Cir. 2008) (holding that the domestic effects of an alleged price-fixing conspiracy did not proximately cause a British manufacturer's foreign injury). The Court did not specify what kind of violation might cause such an injury. Can you think of one?

For a discussion on the scope of discovery within the United States, see *Intel Corp. v. Advanced Micro Devices, Inc.*, 542 U.S. 241 (2004) (the Supreme Court, speaking through Justice Ginsburg, held that the statute authorized, but did not require, discovery).

NOTE: INTERNATIONAL ANTITRUST GUIDELINES

More than 25% of domestic output from the United States is directly related in some way to international trade. In 1995, the Federal Trade Commission and the Department of Justice issued joint guidelines designed to complement Congress' enactment of the International Antitrust Enforcement Assistance Act of 1994.

The Act allows the United States to enter into mutual legal assistance treaties with foreign governments and foreign agencies, to share antitrust evidence, and to assist each other in determining whether a person has violated or is about to violate any foreign antitrust law. Reciprocal assistance between foreign countries and enforcement officials from the United States is sanctioned. The intent of the Act, in substantial part, is to internationalize antitrust enforcement, and to promote free competition in global markets.

Specifically, the Guidelines (1) recognize the broader antitrust jurisdiction involving imports, recognized by the Supreme Court in *Hartford Fire Ins. Co. v. California*, 509 U.S. 764 (1993); (2) protect exports of the United States from anticompetitive foreign restraints; and (3) establish practices and policies for the Department to obtain evidence in foreign countries.

Hartford stated that "the Sherman Act applies to foreign conduct that was meant to produce and did in fact produce some substantial effect in the United States." 509 U.S. at 795. The Guidelines state that imports coming into the United States "by definition affect the U.S. market directly, and will, therefore, almost invariably satisfy the intent part of the *Hartford* test." Whether *Hartford*'s "substantial effects" test is met, however, will depend on a fact-specific analysis in each case. Generally, the present enforcement standard is that United States jurisdiction exists when the challenged conduct has "a direct, substantial, and reasonably foreseeable effect" on domestic, import, or export commerce of the United States. Interestingly, the Guidelines opine that if the substantial effects test is not met, jurisdiction might still be found if the United States acts: (1) as a commercial purchaser; or (2) in a financial role to finance the purchase for consumption or use in a foreign country.

The Guidelines take the position that a merger between two foreign firms with no United States subsidiaries is reachable under the antitrust laws if one or both firms have substantial United States sales. If such a merger is anticompetitive, the Guidelines reason, substantial effects in the United States are foreseeable, given the United States sales. To be sure, the Guidelines acknowledge that relief may be difficult to obtain.

The International Guidelines also claim jurisdiction over a foreign cartel that makes no sales into the United States directly, but that sells to an intermediary with the knowledge that the latter intends to resell into the United States. *Guidelines, id.* at § 3.13. Suppose a cartel in the country of Erehwon is completely legal under Erehwon law; should that cartel's members be forbidden from selling to a firm located in, say, France, simply because they know that the French firm intends to resell the product in the United States?

American antitrust courts generally hesitate to condemn a defendant for conduct compelled by a foreign sovereign with appropriate jurisdiction. United States courts may not order foreign firms to abstain from taking an action that is required by their home government. *See* E. Fox & D. Crane, Global Issues in Antitrust and Competition Law, 454 (2010). But permission or approval is not compulsion; the foreign law must *mandate* an act that is inconsistent with American law. *Hartford, supra*, 509 U.S. at 797–799. The sovereign compulsion defense is thus considerably narrower than the "state action" doctrine in domestic antitrust law. That doctrine grants immunity not only to conduct that is compelled by a domestic sovereign such as a state or municipality, but also to private conduct that is merely "authorized," provided that the conduct is also supervised by a public agency or official. *See, e.g., American Banana Co. v. United Fruit Co.*, 213 U.S. 347 (1909); *Interamerican Ref. Corp. v. Texaco Maracaibo, Inc.*, 307 F. Supp. 1291 (D. Del. 1970).

Traditionally, the foreign sovereign compulsion doctrine applied only to actions performed within the territory of the foreign sovereign, but that limitation seems unduly narrow when numerous sovereigns including the United States assert jurisdiction over business and activities outside their territory. The Guidelines insist that the key is not strict territoriality but the legitimate power of the foreign sovereign to force its law upon the firm in question. Still, the Guidelines disallow any foreign compulsion for conduct within the United States itself: No foreign sovereign has the power to force a firm or person claimed to be under its jurisdiction to commit a United States antitrust violation within United States territory. *Guidelines*, § 3.332.

The 1990s saw increased interest in the application of antitrust principles in the global marketplace. Following the fall of the Berlin Wall, numerous countries developed market systems and accompanying antitrust laws. With lower trading barriers, improved technologies, and a more integrated global economy, antitrust concerns became increasingly international and necessitated cooperation by sovereigns. *See* E. Fox & D. Crane, Global Issues in Antitrust and Competition Law, 505 (2010). In 1991 and 1998, the United States entered into a bilateral agreement with the Commission of the European Communities (the EC) that provides for notification and consultation on antitrust issues where there are important mutual interests. Similar agreements had been entered earlier with Germany, Australia, and Canada. But the agreement with the EC contemplates coordinated investigations, as well as requests ("positive comity") within the home country to invoke its own domestic antitrust laws against domestic defendants who engage in anticompetitive conduct. The United States signed a number of additional antitrust cooperation agreements in 1999, including agreements with Japan, Israel, and Brazil, in order to advance cooperation with these countries in enforcing antitrust and competition laws. *See* Antitrust & Trade Reg. Daily (BNA) (Oct. 27, 1999). Some commentators argue for an even more expansive international antitrust code. *See* Diane P. Wood, *Antitrust at the Global Level*, 72 U. Chi. L. Rev. 309 (2005).

PROBLEM 3.1

Suppose (a) that Mercedes and BMW are both German automobile manufactures; (b) neither produces anything in the United States; but (c) both sell a significant volume of automobiles to the United States. Mercedes now proposes to acquire BMW and the United States decides to challenge the merger. How should the Germans respond to an attempt by an American agency applying American law to restructure German industry? Should it matter that if Mercedes/BMW was able to obtain a monopoly of a market for luxury cars, that Germans as sellers would be the principal beneficiaries of the merger, while people in the United States as buyers would be the principal victims? *Compare Oerlikon-buhrle Holding AG*, 5 Trade Reg. Rep. ¶ 23697 (F.T.C. 1994) (consent decree requiring collateral divestitures and then approving Swiss scientific equipment manufacturer's acquisition of German competitor).

PROBLEM 3.2

Ten Japanese companies were members of a fish import association. Within the import association, the members exchanged market information about demand, supply, and prices paid for imported fish. During an 18-month period, all of the Alaska tanner crab that was purchased within Japan was purchased at the same price, regardless of demand or supply. The 10 Japanese import (buying) companies that regularly exchanged the commercial data controlled 80% of the crab import (buying) market. The Alaska tanner crab exporters believe that the Japanese fish import association was used to fix and coordinate at depressed levels the price paid for the processed crab imported into Japan. If you were the district court judge faced with a motion to dismiss a suit under the Sherman Act brought by the Alaska exporters against the 10 Japanese importers in federal district court in Alaska, how would you rule on the jurisdictional issue presented?

[e]   The Direct Purchaser Requirement and the Problem of Passing On

The "direct purchaser" and "antitrust injury" rules, which are discussed in this section and the next, are analytically distinct doctrines but often are confused or merged together with the "standing" requirement, which is discussed in the following section. Each of the three doctrines limits the domain of those who can recover for an antitrust violation.

ILLINOIS BRICK CO. v. ILLINOIS
431 U.S. 720 (1977)

JUSTICE WHITE delivered the opinion of the Court.

In *Hanover Shoe* this Court rejected as a matter of law the defense that indirect rather than direct purchasers were the parties injured by the antitrust violation. The Court held that except in certain limited circumstances,[2] a direct purchaser

---

[2] [FN 2] The Court cited, as an example of when a pass-on defense might be permitted, the situation

suing for treble damages under § 4 of the Clayton Act is injured within the meaning of § 4 by the full amount of the overcharge paid by it and that the antitrust defendant is not permitted to introduce evidence that indirect purchasers were in fact injured by the illegal overcharge. The first reason for the Court's rejection of this offer of proof was an unwillingness to complicate treble-damages actions with attempts to trace the effects of the overcharge on the purchaser's prices, sales, costs, and profits, and of showing that these variables would have behaved differently without the overcharge.[3]

A second reason for barring the pass-on defense was the Court's concern that unless direct purchasers were allowed to sue for the portion of the overcharge arguably passed on to indirect purchasers, antitrust violators "would retain the fruits of their illegality" because indirect purchasers "would have only a tiny stake in the lawsuit" and hence little incentive to sue.

In this case we once again confront the question whether the overcharged direct purchaser should be deemed for purposes of § 4 to have suffered the full injury from the overcharge; but the issue is presented in the context of a suit in which the plaintiff, an indirect purchaser, seeks to show its injury by establishing pass-on by the direct purchaser and in which the antitrust defendants rely on *Hanover Shoe*'s rejection of the pass-on theory. Having decided that in general a pass-on theory may not be used defensively by an antitrust violator against a direct purchaser plaintiff, we must now decide whether that theory may be used offensively by an indirect purchaser plaintiff against an alleged violator.

---

where "an overcharged buyer has a pre-existing 'cost-plus' contract, thus making it easy to prove that he has not been damaged. . . ."

 [3] [FN 3] The Court explained the economic uncertainties and complexities involved in proving pass-on as follows:

> A wide range of factors influence a company's pricing policies. Normally the impact of a single change in the relevant conditions cannot be measured after the fact; indeed a businessman may be unable to state whether, had one fact been different (a single supply less expensive, general economic conditions more buoyant, or the labor market tighter, for example), he would have chosen a different price. Equally difficult to determine, in the real economic world rather than an economist's hypothetical model, is what effect a change in a company's price will have on its total sales. Finally, costs per unit for a different volume of total sales are hard to estimate. Even if it could be shown that the buyer raised his price in response to, and in the amount of, the overcharge and that his margin of profit and total sales had not thereafter declined, there would remain the nearly insuperable difficulty of demonstrating that the particular plaintiff could not or would not have raised his prices absent the overcharge or maintained the higher price had the overcharge been discontinued. Since establishing the applicability of the passing-on defense would require a convincing showing of each of these virtually unascertainable figures, the task would normally prove insurmountable. On the other hand, it is not unlikely that if the existence of the defense is generally confirmed, antitrust defendants will frequently seek to establish its applicability. Treble-damage actions would often require additional long and complicated proceedings involving massive evidence and complicated theories.

392 U.S. at 492–493, 88 S. Ct. at 2231. (Footnote omitted.)

I

Petitioners manufacture and distribute concrete block in the Greater Chicago area. They sell the block primarily to masonry contractors, who submit bids to general contractors for the masonry portions of construction projects. The general contractors in turn submit bids for these projects to customers such as the respondents in this case, the State of Illinois and 700 local governmental entities in the Greater Chicago area, including counties, municipalities, housing authorities, and school districts. Respondents are thus indirect purchasers of concrete block, which passes through two separate levels in the chain of distribution before reaching respondents. The block is purchased directly from petitioners by masonry contractors and used by them to build masonry structures; those structures are incorporated into entire buildings by general contractors and sold to respondents.

Respondent State of Illinois, on behalf of itself and respondent local governmental entities, brought this antitrust treble-damages action under § 4 of the Clayton Act, alleging that petitioners had engaged in a combination and conspiracy to fix the prices of concrete block in violation of § 1 of the Sherman Act. The complaint alleged that the amounts paid by respondents for concrete block were more than $3 million higher by reason of this price-fixing conspiracy. The only way in which the antitrust violation alleged could have injured respondents is if all or part of the overcharge was passed on by the masonry and general contractors to respondents, rather than being absorbed at the first two levels of distribution.

Petitioner manufacturers moved for partial summary judgment against all plaintiffs that were indirect purchasers of concrete block from petitioners, contending that as a matter of law only direct purchasers could sue for the alleged overcharge. . . .

We granted certiorari, to resolve a conflict among the Courts of Appeals on the question whether the offensive use of pass-on authorized by the decision below is consistent with *Hanover Shoe*'s restrictions on the defensive use of pass-on. We hold that it is not, and we reverse. We reach this result in two steps. First, we conclude that whatever rule is to be adopted regarding pass-on in antitrust damages actions, it must apply equally to plaintiffs and defendants. Because *Hanover Shoe* would bar petitioners from using respondents' pass-on theory as a defense to a treble-damages suit by the direct purchasers (the masonry contractors), we are faced with the choice of overruling (or narrowly limiting) *Hanover Shoe* or of applying it to bar respondents' attempt to use this pass-on theory offensively. Second, we decline to abandon the construction given § 4 in *Hanover Shoe* — that the overcharged direct purchaser, and not others in the chain of manufacture or distribution, is the party "injured in his business or property" within the meaning of the section — in the absence of a convincing demonstration that the Court was wrong in *Hanover Shoe* to think that the effectiveness of the antitrust treble-damages action would be substantially reduced by adopting a rule that any party in the chain may sue to recover the fraction of the overcharge allegedly absorbed by it.

II

. . . .

First, allowing offensive but not defensive use of pass-on would create a serious risk of multiple liability for defendants. Even though an indirect purchaser had already recovered for all or part of an overcharge passed on to it, the direct purchaser would still recover automatically the full amount of the overcharge that the indirect purchaser had shown to be passed on; similarly, following an automatic recovery of the full overcharge by the direct purchaser, the indirect purchaser could sue to recover the same amount. The risk of duplicative recoveries created by unequal application of the *Hanover Shoe* rule is much more substantial than in the more usual situation where the defendant is sued in two different lawsuits by plaintiffs asserting conflicting claims to the same fund. A one-sided application of *Hanover Shoe* substantially increases the possibility of inconsistent adjudications — and therefore of unwarranted multiple liability for the defendant — by *presuming* that one plaintiff (the direct purchaser) is entitled to full recovery while preventing the defendant from using that presumption against the other plaintiff; overlapping recoveries are certain to result from the two lawsuits unless the indirect purchaser is unable to establish any pass-on whatsoever. . . .

Second, the reasoning of *Hanover Shoe* cannot justify unequal treatment of plaintiffs and defendants with respect to the permissibility of pass-on arguments. The principal basis for the decision in *Hanover Shoe* was the Court's perception of the uncertainties and difficulties in analyzing price and output decisions "in the real economic world rather than an economist's hypothetical model," and of the costs to the judicial system and the efficient enforcement of the antitrust laws of attempting to reconstruct those decisions in the courtroom. This perception that the attempt to trace the complex economic adjustments to a change in the cost of a particular factor of production would greatly complicate and reduce the effectiveness of already protracted treble-damages proceedings applies with no less force to the assertion of pass-on theories by plaintiffs than it does to the assertion by defendants. However "long and complicated" the proceedings would be when defendants sought to prove pass-on, *ibid.*, they would be equally so when the same evidence was introduced by plaintiffs. Indeed, the evidentiary complexities and uncertainties involved in the defensive use of pass-on against a direct purchaser are multiplied in the offensive use of pass-on by a plaintiff several steps removed from the defendant in the chain of distribution. The demonstration of how much of the overcharge was passed on by the first purchaser must be repeated at each point at which the price-fixed goods changed hands before they reached the plaintiff.

It is argued, however, that *Hanover Shoe* rests on a policy of ensuring that a treble-damages plaintiff is available to deprive antitrust violators of "the fruits of their illegality." . . .[4]

---

[4] [FN 14] . . . Congress made clear, however, that this legislation [Hart-Scott-Rodino Act] did not alter the definition of which overcharged persons were injured within the meaning of § 4. It simply created a new procedural device — *parens patriae* actions by States on behalf of their citizens — to enforce existing rights of recovery under § 4. The House Report quoted above stated that the *parens patriae* provision "creates no new substantive liability"; the relevant language of the newly enacted § 4C(a) of the Clayton Act tracks that of existing § 4, showing that it was intended only as "an alternative

We thus decline to construe § 4 to permit offensive use of a pass-on theory against an alleged violator that could not use the same theory as a defense in an action by direct purchasers. In this case, respondents seek to demonstrate that masonry contractors, who incorporated petitioners' block into walls and other masonry structures, passed on the alleged overcharge on the block to general contractors, who incorporated the masonry structures into entire buildings, and that the general contractors in turn passed on the overcharge to respondents in the bids submitted for those buildings. We think it clear that under a fair reading of *Hanover Shoe* petitioners would be barred from asserting this theory in a suit by the masonry contractors.

In *Hanover Shoe* this Court did not endorse the broad exception that had been recognized in that case by the courts below — permitting the pass-on defense against middlemen who did not alter the goods they purchased before reselling them. The masonry contractors here could not be included under this exception in any event, because they transform the concrete block purchased from defendants into the masonry portions of buildings. But this Court in *Hanover Shoe* indicated the narrow scope it intended for any exception to its rule barring pass-on defenses by citing, as the only example of a situation where the defense might be permitted, a pre-existing cost-plus contract. In such a situation, the purchaser is insulated from any decrease in its sales as a result of attempting to pass on the overcharge, because its customer is committed to buying a fixed quantity regardless of price. The effect of the overcharge is essentially determined in advance, without reference to the interaction of supply and demand that complicates the determination in the general case. The competitive bidding process by which the concrete block involved in this case was incorporated into masonry structures and then into entire buildings can hardly be said to circumvent complex market interactions as would a cost-plus contract.[5]

We are left, then, with two alternatives: either we must overrule *Hanover Shoe* (or at least narrowly confine it to its facts), or we must preclude respondents from seeking to recover on their pass-on theory. We choose the latter course.

---

means . . . for the vindication of existing substantive claims." H.R. Rep. No. 94-499, *supra*, at 9, 1976 U.S. Code Cong. & Admin. News, p. 2578. "The establishment of an alternative remedy does not increase any defendant's liability." *Ibid*. Representative Rodino himself acknowledged in the remarks cited above that this legislation did not create a right of recovery for consumers where one did not already exist.

We thus cannot agree with the dissenters that the legislative history of the 1976 Antitrust Improvements Act is dispositive as to the interpretation of § 4 of the Clayton Act, enacted in 1914, or the predecessor section of the Sherman Act, enacted in 1890. *Post*, at 2080–2081. . . .

While we do not lightly disagree with the reading of *Hanover Shoe* urged by these legislators [who regard *Hanover Shoe* as applying only to defendants], we think the construction of § 4 adopted in that decision cannot be applied for the exclusive benefit of plaintiffs. Should Congress disagree with this result, it may, of course, amend the section to change it. But it has not done so in the recent *parens patriae* legislation.

[5] [FN 16] Another situation in which market forces have been superseded and the pass-on defense might be permitted is where the direct purchaser is owned or controlled by its customer. . . .

III

In considering whether to cut back or abandon the *Hanover Shoe* rule, we must bear in mind that considerations of *stare decisis* weigh heavily in the area of statutory construction, where Congress is free to change this Court's interpretation of its legislation. . . . This presumption of adherence to our prior decisions construing legislative enactments would support our reaffirmance of the *Hanover Shoe* construction of § 4, joined by eight Justices without dissent only a few years ago, even if the Court were persuaded that the use of pass-on theories by plaintiffs and defendants in treble-damages actions is more consistent with the policies underlying the treble-damages action than is the *Hanover Shoe* rule. But we are not so persuaded.

Permitting the use of pass-on theories under § 4 essentially would transform treble-damages actions into massive efforts to apportion the recovery among all potential plaintiffs that could have absorbed part of the overcharge — from direct purchasers to middlemen to ultimate consumers. However appealing this attempt to allocate the overcharge might seem in theory, it would add whole new dimensions of complexity to treble-damages suits and seriously undermine their effectiveness.

As we have indicated, potential plaintiffs at each level in the distribution chain are in a position to assert conflicting claims to a common fund — the amount of the alleged overcharge — by contending that the entire overcharge was absorbed at that particular level in the chain.[6]

A treble-damages action brought by one of these potential plaintiffs (or one class of potential plaintiffs) to recover the overcharge implicates all three of the interests that have traditionally been thought to support compulsory joinder of absent and potentially adverse claimants; the interest of the defendant in avoiding multiple liability for the fund; the interest of the absent potential plaintiffs in protecting their right to recover for the portion of the fund allocable to them; and the social interest in the efficient administration of justice and the avoidance of multiple litigation. . . .

It is unlikely, of course, that all potential plaintiffs could or would be joined. Some may not wish to assert claims to the overcharge; others may be unmanageable as a class; and still others may be beyond the personal jurisdiction of the court. We can assume that ordinarily the action would still proceed, the absent parties not being deemed "indispensable" under Fed. Rule Civ. Proc. 19(b). But allowing indirect purchasers to recover using pass-on theories, even under the optimistic assumption that joinder of potential plaintiffs will deal satisfactorily with problems of multiple litigation and liability, would transform treble-damages actions into massive multiparty litigations involving many levels of distribution and including large classes of ultimate consumers remote from the defendant. In treble-damages actions by ultimate consumers, the overcharge would have to be apportioned among

---

[6] [FN 18] In this Part, we assume that use of pass-on will be permitted symmetrically, if at all. This assumption, of course, reduces the substantial risk of multiple liability for defendants that is posed by allowing indirect purchasers to recover for the overcharge passed on to them while at the same time allowing direct purchasers automatically to collect the entire overcharge. *See supra*, at 2067–2068. But the possibility of inconsistent judgments obtained by conflicting claimants remains nonetheless. Even this residual possibility justifies bringing potential and actual claimants together in one action if possible.

the relevant wholesalers, retailers, and other middlemen, whose representatives presumably should be joined. And in suits by direct purchasers or middlemen, the interests of ultimate consumers are similarly implicated.

There is thus a strong possibility that indirect purchasers remote from the defendant would be parties to virtually every treble-damages action (apart from those brought against defendants at the retail level). The Court's concern in *Hanover Shoe* to avoid weighing down treble-damages actions with the "massive evidence and complicated theories," involved in attempting to establish a pass-on defense against a direct purchaser applies *a fortiori* to the attempt to trace the effect of the overcharge through each step in the distribution chain from the direct purchaser to the ultimate consumer. We are no more inclined than we were in *Hanover Shoe* to ignore the burdens that such an attempt would impose on the effective enforcement of the antitrust laws.

. . . .

More important, as the *Hanover Shoe* Court observed, "in the real economic world rather than an economist's hypothetical model," the latter's drastic simplifications generally must be abandoned. Overcharged direct purchasers often sell in imperfectly competitive markets. They often compete with other sellers that have not been subject to the overcharge; and their pricing policies often cannot be explained solely by the convenient assumption of profit maximization. As we concluded in *Hanover Shoe*, attention to "sound laws of economics" can only heighten the awareness of the difficulties and uncertainties involved in determining how the relevant market variables would have behaved had there been no overcharge.

. . . .

We reject these attempts to carve out exceptions to the *Hanover Shoe* rule for particular types of markets. An exception allowing evidence of pass-on by middlemen that resell the goods they purchase of course would be of no avail to respondents, because the contractors that allegedly passed on the overcharge on the block incorporated it into buildings. An exception for the contractors here on the ground that they purport to charge a fixed percentage above their costs would substantially erode the *Hanover Shoe* rule without justification. Firms in many sectors of the economy rely to an extent on cost-based rules of thumb in setting prices. See F. Scherer, Industrial Market Structure and Economic Performance 173–179 (1970). These rules are not adhered to rigidly, however; the extent of the markup (or the allocation of costs) is varied to reflect demand conditions. The intricacies of tracing the effect of an overcharge on the purchaser's prices, costs, sales, and profits thus are not spared the litigants.

More generally, the process of classifying various market situations according to the amount of pass-on likely to be involved and its susceptibility of proof in a judicial forum would entail the very problems that the *Hanover Shoe* rule was meant to avoid. The litigation over where the line should be drawn in a particular class of cases would inject the same "massive evidence and complicated theories" into treble-damages proceedings, albeit at a somewhat higher level of generality. As we have noted, . . . *Hanover Shoe* itself implicitly discouraged the creation of exceptions to its rule barring pass-on defenses, and we adhere to the narrow scope of exemption indicated by our decision there.

The concern in *Hanover Shoe* for the complexity that would be introduced into treble-damages suits if pass-on theories were permitted was closely related to the Court's concern for the reduction in the effectiveness of those suits if brought by indirect purchasers with a smaller stake in the outcome than that of direct purchasers suing for the full amount of the overcharge. The apportionment of the recovery throughout the distribution chain would increase the overall costs of recovery by injecting extremely complex issues into the case; at the same time such an apportionment would reduce the benefits to each plaintiff by dividing the potential recovery among a much larger group. Added to the uncertainty of how much of an overcharge could be established at trial would be the uncertainty of how that overcharge would be apportioned among the various plaintiffs. This additional uncertainty would further reduce the incentive to sue. The combination of increasing the costs and diffusing the benefits of bringing a treble-damages action could seriously impair this important weapon of antitrust enforcement.

We think the longstanding policy of encouraging vigorous private enforcement of the antitrust laws, supports our adherence to the *Hanover Shoe* rule, under which direct purchasers are not only spared the burden of litigating the intricacies of pass-on but also are permitted to recover the full amount of the overcharge. We recognize that direct purchasers sometimes may refrain from bringing a treble-damages suit for fear of disrupting relations with their suppliers. But on balance, and until there are clear directions from Congress to the contrary, we conclude that the legislative purpose in creating a group of " 'private attorneys general' " to enforce the antitrust laws under § 4, is better served by holding direct purchasers to be injured to the full extent of the overcharge paid by them than by attempting to apportion the overcharge among all that may have absorbed a part of it.

It is true that, in elevating direct purchasers to a preferred position as private attorneys general, the *Hanover Shoe* rule denies recovery to those indirect purchasers who may have been actually injured by antitrust violations. Of course, as Mr. JUSTICE BRENNAN points out in dissent, "from the deterrence standpoint, it is irrelevant to whom damages are paid, so long as some one redresses the violation." But § 4 has another purpose in addition to deterring violators and depriving them of "the fruits of their illegality," it is also designed to compensate victims of antitrust violations for their injuries. *Hanover Shoe* does further the goal of compensation to the extent that the direct purchaser absorbs at least some and often most of the overcharge. In view of the considerations supporting the *Hanover Shoe* rule, we are unwilling to carry the compensation principle to its logical extreme by attempting to allocate damages among all "those within the defendant's chain of distribution," especially because we question the extent to which such an attempt would make individual victims whole for actual injuries suffered rather than simply depleting the overall recovery in litigation over pass-on issues. Many of the indirect purchasers barred from asserting pass-on claims under the *Hanover Shoe* rule have such a small stake in the lawsuit that even if they were to recover as part of a class, only a small fraction would be likely to come forward to collect their damages. And given the difficulty of ascertaining the amount absorbed by any particular indirect purchaser, there is little basis for believing that the amount of the recovery would reflect the actual injury suffered.

Reversed.

[JUSTICES BRENNAN, MARSHALL, and BLACKMUN dissented.]

NOTES AND QUESTIONS

1.   The Court made clear that a plaintiff did not state a claim for *damages* under Section 4 of the Clayton Act unless it alleged it was a "direct purchaser" from an antitrust violator. The issue was not "standing" as such. In light of this rule, which procedural option, a Rule 12(b)(6) motion to dismiss, a Rule 12(c) motion for judgment on the pleadings, or a Rule 56 summary judgment motion, would be preferred in challenging a claim by an indirect purchaser?

2.   Consider the Court's stated reasons for rejecting claims of indirect purchasers through the "pass-on" theory: (1) litigation complexity and uncertainty due to tracing problems; and (2) exposure to multiple liability or duplicative recovery. Would these same concerns be present should a plaintiff other than a direct purchaser seek *injunctive* relief rather than monetary damages? The courts generally have answered in the negative and permitted injunction suits. *E.g.*, *Mid-West Paper Prods. Co. v. Continental Group*, 596 F.2d 573, 590 (3d Cir. 1979).

The Court's approach represents a balancing of interests: in its view, antitrust policies are better served by permitting the direct purchaser to recover the full amount of the overcharge paid by the direct purchaser than apportionment of damages by all parties in the distribution process. Do you agree with the Court that the deterrent effect of the antitrust laws will increase by permitting only the direct purchaser to recover? Consider whether deterrence is enhanced by the risk of increased magnitude of the loss compared to increased detection of the violation by a larger class of potential plaintiffs.

3.   The *Illinois Brick* opinion discussed the Court's earlier decision in *Hanover Shoe, Inc. v. United Shoe Mach. Corp.*, 392 U.S. 481 (1968), where the Court held that an antitrust defendant could not defeat a private damages action by arguing that the plaintiff had suffered no financial injury, because the entire overcharge was "passed on" to consumers. Read together, *Hanover Shoe* and *Illinois Brick* prohibit both "defensive" and "offensive" use of passing on. Exceptions to this prohibition were noted by the Court. Presumably the exceptions apply to both offensive and defensive uses of passing on. Under the articulated exceptions, indirect purchasers may state a claim for relief and demonstrate that overcharges were passed on when (1) a preexisting (from before the cartel was formed) cost-plus contract existed between the first purchaser from the price fixer and the indirect purchaser (plaintiff) and (2) the first purchaser is "controlled or owned" by either the price fixer or the indirect purchaser. Under either exception, problems of tracing and duplicative recovery were considered manageable.

The rationale for the first exception is that the existing cost-plus contract, which automatically passes on the overcharge, determines in advance the effect of the overcharge because the indirect purchaser (the customer of the first purchaser) "is committed to buying a fixed quantity regardless of price." Without the additional contractual requirement of fixed quantities, however, this exception may not be applicable, for a purchaser under a fixed-cost contract would reduce the amount of its purchases in response to a cartel's price increase. In that instance the decrease in volume would create passing-on problems similar to those in *Illinois Brick*. *See generally* Hovenkamp, *The Indirect-Purchaser Rule and Cost-Plus Sales*, 103 HARV. L. REV. 1717 (1990). *Compare Mid-West Paper Prods. Co. v. Continental Group, Inc.*, 596 F.2d 573 (3d Cir. 1979), *with In re Beef Indus. Antitrust Litig.*, 600 F.2d 1148 (5th Cir. 1979).

The second exception (ownership *or* control) was not defined by the Court in *Illinois Brick*, although the latter term would seem easier to establish than ownership. The factual inquiry is directed toward answering whether the application of the exception will create multiple liability for the defendants and whether in reality one transaction has occurred.

Subsequent lower courts have also created an additional exception to the direct purchaser rule where a vertical agreement (resale price maintenance) is alleged between the price fixer and the middleman direct purchaser. In this instance, the plaintiff consumer becomes the direct purchaser from a co-conspirator; price tracing thus is not problematic. *See, e.g., Arizona v. Shamrock Foods Co.*, 729 F.2d 1208 (9th Cir. 1984); *Jewish Hosp. Ass'n v. Stewart Mech. Enters.*, 628 F.2d 971, 975 (6th Cir. 1980). Some courts have indicated, however, that the vertical price-fixing conspiracy will not be applicable unless the alleged co-conspirator middleman is a party to the suit. This requirement would foreclose the possibility of multiple liability. *See, e.g., In re Beef Indus. Antitrust Litig.*, 600 F.2d 1148, 1161–1163 (5th Cir. 1979). *But see Lowell v. American Cyanamid Co.*, 177 F.3d 1228 (11th Cir. 1999) (adopting the vertical conspiracy exception to *Illinois Brick without* requiring the joinder of intermediary parties).

4. Consider whether an indirect supplier can sue buyers for agreeing to set prices artificially low. *Illinois Brick* has been applied to deny recovery to an indirect seller for undercharges caused by the indirect buyer's illegal activities. In *Zinser v. Continental Grain Co.*, 660 F.2d 754 (10th Cir. 1981), defendant grain exporters allegedly conspired to suppress information regarding impending wheat sales to the Soviet Union. The result was a depressed market in which plaintiffs sold wheat to middlemen at reduced prices who, in turn, sold wheat to defendants. In rejecting plaintiffs' "inverted" chain of distribution theory, the Tenth Circuit said "in an antitrust treble damage case involving price-fixing the plaintiff must have dealt directly with the alleged violator." *Id.* at 760. *See also In re Beef Indus. Antitrust Litig.*, 600 F.2d 1148 (5th Cir. 1979) (where the court held that cattle feeders failed to establish that retail grocers engaged in a conspiracy to set wholesale beef prices; the cattle feeders did not sell directly to retailers but to beef packers).

5. In sum, four exceptions have been articulated to the *Illinois Brick* direct purchaser limitation: (1) preexisting, fixed quantity, cost-plus contract; (2) ownership or control over the first purchaser; (3) a vertical price-fixing conspiracy; and (4) injunctive relief.

6. The majority of the exceptions to *Illinois Brick*'s direct purchaser rule listed in Note 5 were discussed in the Third Circuit's opinion in *Howard Hess Dental*

Labs., Inc. v. Dentsply Int'l, Inc., 424 F.3d 363 (3d Cir. 2005). The opinion resolved two tag-along class action suits against Dentsply International, Inc., a producer of artificial teeth used by the dental labs to make dentures, which was found guilty of monopolization in *United States v. Dentsply Int'l, Inc.*, 399 F.3d 181 (3d Cir. 2005).

The defendant, Dentsply, included an "all or nothing" provision in its distribution contracts, which required the dealers exclusively to distribute Dentsply's teeth or distribute no Dentsply's teeth at all. *Id.* at 185. Even though a dealer could terminate the arrangement at any time, the realities of the market characterized by Dentsply's predominant position and the efficacy of its exclusionary conduct created strong incentives for the dealers to remain loyal to Dentsply. *Id.* at 193–194. As the key channel of distribution, the dealer's network became a "gateway" to the artificial teeth market. There were no comparable alternative channels of distribution. Moreover, Dentsply's "long-entrenched Dentsply dealer network with its ties to the laboratories [made] it impracticable for a manufacturer to rely on direct distribution to the laboratories in any significant amount." *Id.* at 193. Finally, dental laboratories preferred working with the dealers because they could purchase from the dealers all the necessary components for dentures. The dealer's role was so remarkable that the court considered foreclosure of Dentsply's competitors from the dealer distribution network to rise to the level of anticompetitive harm necessary to establish the offense of monopolization. *Id.* at 191.

The plaintiffs faced a significant obstacle to their recovery of compensation for harm caused by Dentsply's violations given the *Illinois Brick*'s direct purchaser requirement.

The court began by expressly stating that before the applicability of the co-conspirator exception to *Illinois Brick* — an exception not articulated in the *Illinois Brick* opinion itself, but readily adopted by some courts of appeals with respect to vertical restraints — will be considered, the alleged down-stream co-conspirators must be joined as co-defendants. *Howard Hess Dental Labs.*, 424 F.3d at 371. The court reasoned that the requirement of joinder would eliminate any possibility of a direct purchaser suit by the alleged down-stream co-conspirators against the up-stream manufacturer and, as a result, prevent duplicative recovery and complexities in apportioning harm among the direct and indirect purchasers.

Plaintiffs failed to clear the joinder requirement to qualify for standing under the co-conspirator exception to the *Illinois Brick* rule because they did not join any of the intermediary dealers who they claimed were Dentsply's co-conspirators. With respect to a comparison case, plaintiffs had named 26 of Dentsply's then 28 authorized dealers. Regarding these purchasers, the court proceeded to consider whether recognition of a co-conspirator exception would not undermine the goals of antitrust enforcement that triggered the *Illinois Brick* rule.

At the outset, the court considered the plaintiffs' claim that they have standing to recover overcharge damages from purchases they made from Dentsply's dealers, the members of its retail price-fixing conspiracy. The court accepted this claim as valid, observing that *Illinois Brick* does not limit suits "by consumers against a manufacturer who illegally contracted with its dealers to set the latter's resale price" because the consumer is the only party who paid the overcharge. *Id.* at 377. The dealers' claim for damages in the context of a price-fixing conspiracy would be for lost profits from lost sales caused by the constraint on their resale price. *Id.* The overcharge losses suffered by the *Jersey Dental* plaintiffs and the lost profits losses suffered by the dealers are not duplicative because both are caused by resale price maintenance. *Id.* (citing 2 PHILLIP E. AREEDA, HERBERT HOVENKAMP & ROGER D. BLAIR, ANTITRUST LAW ¶ 346h, at 369–370 (2d ed. 2000)). Furthermore, there are no evidentiary complexities typical to apportionment of overcharged damages mentioned in the *Illinois Brick* court as injurious to effective antitrust enforcement. *Id.* at 377–378. Finally, there is no dilution of enforcement as the scope of the dealers' lost profit recovery is not affected by the overcharge recovery of the *Jersey Dental* plaintiffs. *Id.* at 378.

Next the court considered whether there was a co-conspirator exception to non-retail-price-maintenance (non-RPM) conspiracies like an exclusive dealing conspiracy. The court held "that such an exception would only exist in circumstances where the middlemen [(dealers)] would be barred from bringing a claim against their former co-conspirator — the manufacturer — because their involvement in the conspiracy was 'truly complete' (*i.e.*, if the middlemen would be barred from suing by the 'complete involvement defense' of the manufacturer)." *Id.* at 378–379. In the court's opinion, it is somewhat economically implausible for direct purchasers to join a non-RPM conspiracy and "effectively agree to be overcharged (as input costs increase, profits decrease)." *Id.* at 379 n.12. It nonetheless had to take as true the plaintiffs' allegations because the case came to the court on a motion to dismiss. *Id..* The court did find a way in which Dentsply could compensate the dealers for joining its exclusive dealing conspiracy. Because a price-fixing conspiracy could be profitable to the dealers, Dentsply's participation in the retail price-fixing conspiracy could be a desirable consideration in exchange to the dealers' agreement not to deal with Dentsply's competitors and be overcharged. *Id.*

The court explained that the decision to adopt a limited co-conspirator exception was required to avoid the issues the *Illinois Brick* court sought to eliminate by adopting the direct purchaser requirement. A limited co-conspirator exception would eliminate the risk of duplicative recovery because its application is conditioned on barring the middlemen from recovery. *Id.* at 380. The second concern — evidentiary complexities of apportionment damages — militates against both the limited and the unlimited co-conspirator exception. This is so because non-RPM conspiracies distort the wholesale market allowing manufacturers to charge their dealers supra-competitive prices which the latter passes on to the final consumers. *Id.* Because the primary damages in the non-RPM context are overcharge damages, the concern with their apportionment exists whether the middlemen are barred from recovery or not. *Id.* If the middlemen are barred from recovery, the portion of the overcharge recoverable by them will need to be ascertained because the indirect purchasers are entitled pursuant to Section 4 of the Clayton Act to recovery only for the damage sustained by them by reasoning of passing on. *Id.* at 380 n.14. The third policy concern — the risk of dilution of antitrust enforcement — favors the limited co-conspirator exception because the incentive to sue will not decrease for the direct purchasers if they are not completely involved and the indirect purchasers are denied standing, and will exist for the indirect purchasers who will be granted standing to sue to the exclusion of the direct purchasers. *Id.* at 381. Despite *Illinois Brick*'s concern over evidentiary complexities of apportioning overcharge damages that remains valid with respect to a limited co-conspirator exception, the court held that it would be less desirable to have no co-conspirator exception applicable to non-RPM conspiracies at all. Complex apportionment problems cannot outweigh the need to have a private enforcing party outside the conspiracy between the initial seller and the completely involved direct purchasers. *Id.* One issue — whether, in light of the *Illinois Brick*'s policy considerations, there existed a "truly complete" involvement defense — had to be resolved by the court before allowing a special co-conspirator exception to *Illinois Brick* in non-RPM conspiracies. The court discussed the matters relevant to the complete involvement defense, but concluded that it did not need to decide on the permissibility of that defense under *Illinois Brick*, because the conditions for the defense were not met based on the facts of the case before the court. *Id.* at 381–383.

Plaintiffs also unsuccessfully attempted to argue that they fell within the control exception to the *Illinois Brick*'s direct purchaser requirement. The court rejected the argument, noting that the control exception applied when the initial seller owned the direct purchaser to ensure that indirect purchasers would have standing when they are the first non-controlled purchasers. *Id.* at 371. It further observed that even where the exception has been extended by other courts beyond a parent-subsidiary relationship, the courts require "relationships involving such functional economic or other unity between the direct purchaser and either the defendant or the indirect purchaser that there effectively has been only one sale." *Id.* at 372 (quoting *Jewish Hosp. Ass'n of Louisville, Ky. v. Stewart Mech. Enters.*, 628 F.2d 971, 975 (6th Cir. 1980)). The court listed the following modes of control that might qualify for the exception: "interlocking directorates, minority stock ownership, loan agreements that subject the wholesalers to the manufacturers' operating control, [or] trust agreements." *Id.* at 372 (alterations in original) (quoting *In re Brand Name Prescription Drugs Antitrust Litig.*, 123 F.3d 599, 605 (7th Cir. 1997)). In the case before the court, Dentsply's control over its dealers, if any, would not, according to the court, prevent the dealers from suing Dentsply. *Id.* at 372. Moreover, allowing the plaintiffs to sue on this theory, while the possibility of dealers' suing Dentsply existed, would cause duplicative recovery and inconsistent judgments, bring about the evidentiary complexities of allocating compensation for harm, and dilute the dealers' incentive to sue. *Id.*

Further, the court dealt with the argument by plaintiffs that they had standing because they sought lost profits damages caused by their lost opportunities to purchase and resell Dentsply's competitors' products. The court noted that when monopolization, a price-fixing conspiracy, or exclusionary conduct cause prices to increase, the members of a distribution chain suffer two types of injury: (1) overcharges paid for goods purchased; and (2) lost profits that members of the distribution chain incur when they are unable to buy and resell a greater volume of goods. *Id.* at 373 (citing Jeffrey L. Harrison, *The Lost Profits Measure of Damages in Price Enhancement Cases*, 64 MINN. L. REV. 751, 753, 770–772 (1980)). The court further observed that the overcharge paid minus overcharge passed on was also a form of lost profits. But it noted that the plaintiffs, realizing that this type of damages was precluded by the indirect purchaser rule of *Illinois Brick*, did not claim these lost profits but only those lost profits caused by the lost opportunity to buy and resell the goods of Dentsply's competitors. *Id.* at 374. Acknowledging that recovery of lost profits by indirect purchasers was not explicitly precluded by the *Illinois Brick* decision, the court nonetheless held that the plaintiffs did not have statutory standing to recover lost profits caused by their lost opportunities to purchase and resell Dentsply's competitors' products. *Id.* at 376. The court gave several reasons for this decision by pointing out the features of lost profits damages that make them inferior to overcharge damages, and by showing that the three rationales of *Illinois Brick* would make recovery of lost profits by indirect purchasers undesirable. For the first proposition — that lost profits are inferior antitrust damages to overcharge damages — the court cites Judge Easterbrook who wrote that:

> [t]he lure of damages for lost profits induces firms to make arguments that will injure rather than protect consumers. Profits get lost primarily from hard competition or from elimination of monopoly. . . . The more competitive the market, the more profits are "lost." . . . [Because] it is hard to tell competition from exclusion, . . . we must be wary of remedies that give the victims of hard competition a strong incentive to sue.

Id. at 375 (alterations in original) (quoting Frank H. Easterbrook, *Treble What?*, 55 ANTITRUST L.J. 95, 96–97, 100–101 (1986)). As to the failure of lost profit damages to accord with the goals of antitrust enforcement protected by the direct purchaser rule, the court showed that lost profits damages brought up the same evidentiary complexities of apportionment of damages among the members of the distribution chain, the avoidance of which was one of the rationales for the direct purchaser rule in *Illinois Brick*. *Id.* at 375–376 (citing Harrison, *supra* at 764–765).

7. To what extent does the *Illinois Brick* rule amount to a windfall for direct purchasers? At one extreme — where the direct purchaser is able to "pass on" the full overcharge and suffers no reduction in output — the direct purchaser suffers no injury but is given an action for three times the amount of the overcharge. At the other extreme, the direct purchaser must bear the full overcharge itself.

Neither of these extremes is likely to occur in the real world. Even a monopolist as direct purchaser would not be able to pass on the entire monopoly overcharge: although the monopolist's profit-maximizing price generally rises as its costs rise, it does not rise enough to offset the higher costs. The monopolist will make the highest profit if it can buy in a competitive market. It is possible to calculate the percentage of overcharge that a given direct purchaser will pass on to its customers. However, the formula requires knowledge of the elasticities of supply and demand, and these figures are very difficult if not impossible to measure, particularly in litigation.

8. Consider also whether the direct purchaser who passes on the complete overcharge has a claim for relief for lost customers (or potential customers) by reason of the increased price.

9. In *California v. ARC America Corp.*, 490 U.S. 93 (1989), the Supreme Court held that state antitrust laws permitting indirect purchasers to sue to recover illegal overcharges were not preempted by the federal statute. Sixteen states had enacted such laws in response to the Court's decision in *Illinois Brick. See also Free v. Abbott Laboratories Inc.*, 176 F.3d 298 (5th Cir. 1999)529 U.S. 333 (2000) (permit-

ting a state common-law interpretation to reach the same result); *Sea-Land Service Inc. v. Atlantic Pacific International*, 61 F. Supp. 2d 1092, 1097 (D. Haw. 1999) (providing an example of a state law indirect purchaser exemption). *See* William H. Page, *The Limits of State Indirect Purchaser Suits: Class Certification in the Shadow of* Illinois Brick, 67 ANTITRUST L.J. 1 (1999) (discussing why indirect purchaser suits have not been successful). Today, nearly half the states permit indirect purchaser antitrust suits and they have become almost routine in large multidistrict antitrust litigation. In its important decision in *AT&T Mobility, LLC v. AU Optronics Corp.*, 707 F.3d 1106 (9th Cir. 2013), the Ninth Circuit held that neither the Commerce Clause nor Due Process precluded the plaintiff indirect purchasers from relying on California's antitrust law, the Cartwright Act, to reach purchases that occurred outside the state, in both the United States and Asia, provided there was sufficient injury within the state. In this case price fixing in LCD electronic displays had occurred worldwide, and price-fixed units were shipped to producers and consumers located in California.

Under *ARC America*, downstream antitrust victims retain a remedy in those states that have enacted such statutes even though the damage recovery is not available in federal court. Consider whether these two approaches are complementary or inconsistent. How serious is the threat under *ARC America* to antitrust defendants of multiple liability from both indirect purchasers (in state court) and direct purchasers (in federal court)? Will this dual enforcement approach unfairly favor plaintiffs in settlement negotiations? Does it create over-deterrence from a public policy perspective? Or, does the Court's decision in both cases strike an appropriate balance for federalism?

10. Suppose that the direct purchaser is a price-regulated utility, forced to pay a cartel price for natural gas. Should *Illinois Brick* bar a damage action by the utility's customers? Suppose it could be shown that price-regulated utilities operate under rules that *always* permit them to pass their costs plus a "fair rate of return" on to their customers. Furthermore, customer use is very insensitive to price (that is, price elasticity of demand is low); as a result, the utility loses very little volume. Should *Illinois Brick* apply anyway? The Court answered yes in *Kansas and Missouri v. Utilicorp United, Inc.*, 497 U.S. 199 (1990). *See* 2 P. AREEDA & H. HOVENKAMP, ANTITRUST LAW ¶ 371 (4th ed. 2014).

Utilities, unlike firms in competitive markets, generally do not price at marginal cost. Rather, the regulatory agency grants them a rate predicated on direct costs (such as the price of natural gas), operating expenses, plus a "fair rate of return" on invested capital. This pricing formula suggests that some departures from *Illinois Brick* are in order. First, the utility, unlike the competitive firm, will probably be permitted to pass through its gas costs precisely. Second, in the short run, the utility may receive the same "fair rate of return" on its plant even if the plant is not operating at capacity. Thus, the utility suffers *neither* lost profits *nor* an overcharge when it is subjected to short-term price fixing. The overcharge is passed on directly; the rate of return is based on previous investment in plant and equipment, not on volume of sales. Over the long run, however, the reduced demand caused by a monopoly overcharge will make the construction of additional plants less likely. In that case, the utility will be denied a fair rate of return on these additional plants.

In addition, many studies suggest that the demand for electricity and natural gas is quite inelastic in the short run. As a result, the reduction in volume that follows a cartel's price increase may not be all that large. In that case, the utility's lost profits are not significant.

However, as the Supreme Court noted in *Utilicorp*, different regulatory agencies use different formulas for computing allowable rate increases, and some might permit increases even though "costs" have not gone up. But the formula itself is public information, much easier to parse out than is the pricing decision of the competitive firm. For example, the regulatory agency might decide (1) to raise the rate of return on invested capital from 7% to 7.3%; (2) to give a specified increase reflecting increased labor costs; and (3) to permit the utility to pass on a particular price increase in the cost of gas. But each of these three elements in the increase would usually be stated in the agency's decision, or in the regulated firm's application. Should that not make pass-on far easier to compute in the case of the regulated public utility?

Suppose a group of utility customers, who are indirect purchasers of natural gas, believe that the gas suppliers are fixing prices. They petition their utility to sue, but the utility refuses, saying (a) the suit will be expensive, and (b) suing is not in the best interest of the utility's shareholders, for any damage award would have to be reimbursed to the customers. What alternatives do the customers now have?

Suppose further that it could be shown that a public utility company was always permitted by the regulatory agency to pass on gas price increases to consumers dollar for dollar. In that case the utility would not be injured by an "overcharge" at all, for the entire overcharge is passed on. Rather, its injury comes from any loss in volume that results when its customers respond to the price increase by consuming less gas. Should not the utility's recovery be based on lost profits rather than a monopoly overcharge? *See* Hovenkamp, *The Indirect-Purchaser Rule and Cost-Plus Sales*, 103 Harv. L. Rev. 1717 (1990).

11. The Fourth Circuit affirmed the dismissal of the claims of 26 plaintiffs found to be indirect purchasers under *Illinois Brick*. The plaintiffs sought damages for overcharges on Microsoft software, including end user license agreements (EULA), purchased from retailers. While at first blush the plaintiffs fit squarely within *Illinois Brick*'s prohibition on indirect purchasers, they argued that the doctrine was not applicable in their case for a variety of reasons that the court ultimately rejected.

First, the plaintiffs argued that because the license agreement was between them and Microsoft directly, they were in fact direct purchasers. The court noted, however, that this argument fails to account for the role of the retailers in the licensing scheme. The plaintiffs could have acquired the license directly from Microsoft, as other litigants had done, but instead chose to purchase the licenses from retailers. *Kloth v. Microsoft Corp.*, 444 F.3d 312, 320–321 (4th Cir. 2006). Second, because the EULA provided for a refund directly from Microsoft in the event the plaintiffs did not ultimately use the software, the plaintiffs argued that the appropriate relationship for analyzing antitrust injury was between them and Microsoft. The plaintiffs did not *purchase* the software and EULAs from Microsoft, however, so Microsoft could not have controlled the retail price paid by plaintiffs, the court noted. *Id.* at 321.

Third, the court dismissed the plaintiff's estoppel claim because Microsoft had not adopted "mutually inconsistent positions" in previous litigation. The court distinguished the sell of title to OEMs — something Microsoft had previously denied doing — from the sell of the ability to charge for licenses — something never denied by Microsoft. *Id.* Fourth, the court construed the market forces exception narrowly to exclude its application to plaintiffs. Because the plaintiffs failed to plead "functional unity" with the direct purchaser (retailers and OEMs) and failed to assert "sufficient ownership interest in or control over" the same, it could not "overlook the Supreme Court's admonition against enlarging market-based exceptions that would undermine the indirect-purchaser rule." *Id.* at 321–322 (citing *Kansas v. UtiliCorp United, Inc.*, 497 U.S. 199, 216–217 (1990)).

PROBLEM 3.3

Zedco manufactures plywood bird houses and sells them to independent regional distributors, one of which is Quarty. Quarty in turn sells the bird houses to retail stores. On January 1, Retailer A entered into a contract with Quarty to supply it with 1,000 plywood bird houses yearly at Quarty's cost plus 10%. Later that year, Retailer A purchased an additional 400 bird houses from Quarty at the same price. At the same time, Retailer B contracted with Quarty to supply as many bird houses as Retailer B could sell at Quarty's cost plus 10%. Retailer B ended up purchasing 500 bird houses from Quarty. Quarty purchased all the bird houses from Zedco in March or later.

The following year Zedco and two other plywood bird house manufacturers were indicted for price fixing. The court found that the cartel came into existence on January 15, and that the competitive manufacturer's price for the bird houses should have been $8.00, but the cartel price was in fact $10.00.

Claiming offensive collateral estoppel (see the discussion *infra*), Quarty, Retailer A, and Retailer B all sought damages with respect to the above sales. Quarty claimed damages for the cartel overcharge on sales of 1,900 bird houses. Retailer A claimed damages for the cartel overcharge on sales of 1,400 bird houses. Retailer B claimed damages for the cartel overcharge on sales of 500 bird houses. To what extent will the court recognize each plaintiff's claim? How much will each receive?

[f]   "Business or Property" Requirement

In order for a plaintiff to bring a private treble damages suit under Section 4 of the Clayton Act, plaintiff's complaint must allege injuries to its "business or property." Frequently the issue has been whether this requires that the plaintiff have an injury to a "commercial interest." *Hawaii v. Standard Oil Co. of Cal.*, 405 U.S. 251, 264 (1972) (denying standing to states for injury to general economy). In 1979, the Supreme Court decided whether a consumer had standing to sue for damages by reason of injury to business or property caused by a price-fixing agreement. The Court distinguished between "business" and "property" injuries, and held that personal injuries alone would not suffice under Section 4.

REITER v. SONOTONE CORP.
442 U.S. 330 (1979)

CHIEF JUSTICE BURGER delivered the opinion of the Court.

Petitioner brought a class action on behalf of herself and all persons in the United States who purchased hearing aids manufactured by five corporations, respondents here. Her complaint alleges that respondents have committed a variety of antitrust violations, including vertical and horizontal price fixing.[7]

Because of these violations, the complaint alleges, petitioner and the class of persons she seeks to represent have been forced to pay illegally fixed higher prices for the hearing aids and related services they purchased from respondents' retail dealers. . . .

Respondents moved for dismissal of the complaint or summary judgment in the District Court. Among other things, respondents argued that Reiter, as a retail purchaser of hearing aids for personal use, lacked standing to sue for treble damages under § 4 of the Clayton Act because she had not been injured in her "business or property" within the meaning of the Act.

. . . .

[T]he word "property" has a naturally broad and inclusive meaning. In its dictionary definitions and in common usage "property" comprehends anything of material value owned or possessed. Money, of course, is a form of property. . . .

Respondents protest that, if the reference to "property" in § 4 means "money," the term "business" then becomes superfluous, for every injury in one's business necessarily involves a pecuniary injury. They argue that if Congress wished to permit one who lost only money to bring suit under § 4, it would not have used the restrictive phrase "business or property"; rather, it would have employed more generic language akin to that of § 16, for example, which provides for injunctive relief against any "threatened loss or damage." 15 U.S.C. § 26. Congress plainly intended to exclude *some* category of injury in choosing the phrase "business or property" for § 4. Only a "commercial interest" gloss, they argue, both gives the phrase the restrictive significance intended for it and at the same time gives independent significance to the word "business" and the word "property." The argument of respondents is straightforward: the phrase "business or property" means "business activity or property related to one's business."

That strained construction would have us ignore the disjunctive "or" and rob the term "property" of its independent and ordinary significance; moreover, it would convert the noun "business" into an adjective. In construing a statute we are obliged to give effect, if possible, to every word Congress used. Canons of construction ordinarily suggest that terms connected by a disjunctive be given separate

---

[7] [FN 1] She claims respondents restricted the territories, customers, and brands of hearing aids offered by their retail dealers, used the customer lists of their retail dealers for their own purposes, prohibited unauthorized retailers from dealing in or repairing their hearing aids, and conspired among themselves and with their retail dealers to fix the retail prices of the hearing aids.

meanings, unless the context dictates otherwise; here it does not. Congress' use of the word "or" makes plain that "business" was not intended to modify "property," nor was "property" intended to modify "business."

When a commercial enterprise suffers a loss of money it suffers an injury in both its "business" and its "property." But neither term is rendered redundant by recognizing that a consumer not engaged in a "business" enterprise, but rather acquiring goods or services for personal use, is injured in "property" when the price of those goods or services is artificially inflated by reason of the anticompetitive conduct complained of. The phrase "business or property" also retains restrictive significance. It would, for example, exclude personal injuries suffered. Congress must have intended to exclude some class of injuries by the phrase "business or property." But it taxes the ordinary meaning of common terms to argue, as respondents do, that a consumer's monetary injury arising directly out of a retail purchase is not comprehended by the natural and usual meaning of the phrase "business or property." We simply give the word "property" the independent significance to which it is entitled in this context. A consumer whose money has been diminished by reason of an antitrust violation has been injured "in his . . . property" within the meaning of § 4.

. . . .

Nor does her status as a "consumer" change the nature of the injury she suffered or the intrinsic meaning of "property" in § 4. That consumers of retail goods and services have standing to sue under § 4 is implicit in our decision in *Goldfarb v. Virginia State Bar*, 421 U.S. 773 (1975). There we held that a bar association was subject to a treble-damages suit brought under § 4 by persons who sought legal services in connection with the purchase of a residence. Furthermore, we have often referred to "consumers" as parties entitled to seek damages under § 4 without intimating that consumers of goods and services purchased for personal rather than commercial use were in any way foreclosed by the statutory language from asserting an injury in their "property." [Citing cases.]

Hawaii v. Standard Oil Co., is not to the contrary. There we held that injury to a state's total economy, for which the state sought redress in its *parens patriae* capacity, was not cognizable under § 4. It is true we noted that the words "business or property" refer to "commercial interests or enterprises," and reasoned that Hawaii could not recover on its claim for damage done to its "general economy" because such injury did not harm Hawaii's "commercial interests."

However, the language of an opinion is not always to be parsed as though we were dealing with language of a statute. Use of the phrase "commercial interests or enterprises," read in context, in no sense suggests that only injuries to a business entity are within the ambit of § 4. . . . The phrase "commercial interests" was used there as a generic reference to the interests of the State of Hawaii as a party to a commercial transaction. . . .

Nothing in the legislative history of § 4 conflicts with our holding today. . . .

Respondents also argue that allowing class actions to be brought by retail consumers like the petitioner here will add a significant burden to the already crowded dockets of the federal courts. That may well be true but cannot be a controlling consideration here. We must take the statute as we find it. Congress created the treble-damages remedy of § 4 precisely for the purpose of encouraging *private* challenges to antitrust violations. These private suits provide a significant supplement to the limited resources available to the Department of Justice for enforcing the antitrust laws and deterring violations. Indeed, nearly 20 times as many private antitrust actions are currently pending in the federal courts as actions filed by the Department of Justice. . . . To be sure, these private suits impose a heavy litigation burden on the federal courts; it is the clear responsibility of Congress to provide the judicial resources necessary to execute its mandates.

Finally, respondents argue that the cost of defending consumer class actions will have a potentially ruinous effect on small businesses in particular and will ultimately be paid by consumers in any event. These are not unimportant considerations, but they are policy considerations more properly addressed to Congress than to this Court. However accurate respondents' arguments may prove to be — and they are not without substance — they cannot govern our reading of the plain language in § 4.

District courts must be especially alert to identify frivolous claims brought to extort nuisance settlements; they have broad power and discretion vested in them by Fed. Rule Civ. Proc. 23 with respect to matters involving the certification and management of potentially cumbersome or frivolous class actions. . . . Recognition of the plain meaning of the statutory language "business or property" need not result in administrative chaos, class-action harassment, or "windfall" settlements if the district courts exercise sound discretion and use the tools available.

. . . .

Reversed.

NOTES AND QUESTIONS

1. Section 4 of the Clayton Act states that a private treble damages action may be maintained by "any person . . . injured in . . . business or property." It does not, however, define the class of individuals or entities that comes within the statutory language of "any person." That is partially done by Section 1 of the Clayton Act, which speaks in terms of foreign and domestic corporations and associations. 15 U.S.C. § 12 (1988 Supp.). Others have been included in the definition through decisional and statutory developments.

A state alleging a proprietary or commercial injury is a "person" for purposes of Section 4. A state also has authority to sue as parens patriae on behalf of its citizens who have been injured. Likewise, a city is a "person" within the statute. *Chattanooga Foundry & Pipe Works v. Atlanta*, 203 U.S. 390 (1906). The Court has even permitted foreign governments to sue for treble damages. *Pfizer, Inc. v. Government of India*, 434 U.S. 308 (1978). But the *Pfizer* rule permitting treble damages to foreign governments was modified in 1982 when Congress amended Section 4 of the Clayton Act limiting the right of foreign governments to recover only *actual* damages. Foreign Sovereign Antitrust Recoveries Act, Pub. L. No. 97-393. An amendment to Section 4A of the Clayton Act permits the United States Government to recover treble damages, the same as that allowable to private parties, when it is injured by an antitrust violation.

See also United States Postal Serv. v. Flamingo Indus. (USA) Ltd., 540 U.S. 736, 745–747 (2004) (holding that United States Postal Service is not a separate person with the antitrust laws).

2. While the Supreme Court has been liberal in interpreting the definition of "any person," the term is not without limitations. Indeed, the Court's definitional approach generally has included only consumers and competitors within the statutory term.

[g]   Antitrust Injury

Prior to the Supreme Court decision in *Klor's, Inc. v. Broadway-Hale Stores*, 359 U.S. 207 (1959), an antitrust plaintiff was required to plead and prove injury to the general public as well as specific injury to herself. In *Klor's*, the Supreme Court concluded that Congress had "determined its own criteria of public harm" and therefore it was unnecessary for the plaintiff to plead such harm, thus implying that public injury is inherent in antitrust violations. But *Klor's* and the subsequent case *Radiant Burners, Inc. v. Peoples Gas Light & Coke Co.*, 364 U.S. 656 (1961), dealt only with per se violations of Sections 1 and 2 of the Sherman Act. Other courts in rule of reason cases under the Sherman Act have suggested that where the offense is not per se unlawful, evidence that competition has been affected is the equivalent of a showing of public injury. The private plaintiff must also still prove injury to himself.

Another judicially created exception to treble damage liability is the "antitrust injury" requirement. It focuses on the "by reason of" language of Section 4.

BRUNSWICK CORP. v. PUEBLO BOWL-O-MAT, INC.
429 U.S. 477 (1977)

JUSTICE MARSHALL delivered the opinion of the Court.

I

Petitioner is one of the two largest manufacturers of bowling equipment in the United States. Respondents are three of the 10 bowling centers owned by Treadway Companies, Inc. Since 1965, petitioner has acquired and operated a large number of bowling centers, including six in the markets in which respondents operate. Respondents instituted this action contending that these acquisitions violated various provisions of the antitrust laws.

In the late 1950's, the bowling industry expanded rapidly, and petitioner's sales of lanes, automatic pinsetters, and ancillary equipment rose accordingly. . . .

In the early 1960's, the bowling industry went into a sharp decline. Petitioner's sales quickly dropped to preboom levels. . . .

To meet this difficulty, petitioner began acquiring and operating defaulting bowling centers when their equipment could not be resold and a positive cash flow could be expected from operating the centers. During the seven years preceding the trial in this case, petitioner acquired 222 centers, 54 of which it either disposed of or closed. These acquisitions made petitioner by far the largest operator of bowling centers, with over five times as many centers as its next largest competitor. . . .

At issue here are acquisitions by petitioner in the three markets in which respondents are located: Pueblo, Colo., Poughkeepsie, N. Y., and Paramus, N. J. In 1965, petitioner acquired one defaulting center in Pueblo, one in Poughkeepsie, and two in the Paramus area. In 1969, petitioner acquired a third defaulting center in the Paramus market, and in 1970 petitioner acquired a fourth. Petitioner closed its Poughkeepsie center in 1969 after three years of unsuccessful operation; the Paramus center acquired in 1970 also proved unsuccessful, and in March 1973 petitioner gave notice that it would cease operating the center when its lease expired. The other four centers were operational at the time of trial.

. . . .

II

The issue for decision is a narrow one. Petitioner does not presently contest the Court of Appeals' conclusion that a properly instructed jury could have found the acquisitions unlawful. Nor does petitioner challenge the Court of Appeals' determination that the evidence would support a finding that had petitioner not acquired these centers, they would have gone out of business and respondents' income would have increased. Petitioner questions only whether antitrust damages are available where the sole injury alleged is that competitors were continued in business, thereby denying respondents an anticipated increase in market shares.

To answer that question it is necessary to examine the antimerger and treble-damages provisions of the Clayton Act. Section 7 of the Act proscribes mergers whose effect *"may be* substantially to lessen competition, or *to tend to* create a monopoly."* (Emphasis added.) It is, as we have observed many times, a prophylactic measure, intended "primarily to arrest apprehended consequences of intercorporate relationships before those relationships could work their evil. . . ." [Citing cases.]

Section 4, in contrast, is in essence a remedial provision. It provides treble damages to "[a]ny person who shall be injured in his business or property by reason of anything forbidden in the antitrust laws. . . ." Of course, treble damages also play an important role in penalizing wrongdoers and deterring wrongdoing, as we also have frequently observed. . . . It nevertheless is true that the treble-damages provision, which makes awards available only to injured parties, and measures the awards by a multiple of the injury actually proved, is designed primarily as a remedy.

Intermeshing a statutory prohibition against acts that have a potential to cause certain harms with a damages action intended to remedy those harms is not without difficulty. Plainly, to recover damages respondents must prove more than that petitioner violated § 7, since such proof establishes only that injury may result. Respondents contend that the only additional element they need demonstrate is that they are in a worse position than they would have been had petitioner not committed those acts. The Court of Appeals agreed, holding compensable any loss "causally linked" to "the mere presence of the violator in the market." Because this holding divorces antitrust recovery from the purposes of the antitrust laws without a clear statutory command to do so, we cannot agree with it.

Every merger of two existing entities into one, whether lawful or unlawful, has the potential for producing economic readjustments that adversely affect some persons. But Congress has not condemned mergers on that account; it has condemned them only when they may produce anticompetitive effects. Yet under the Court of Appeals' holding, once a merger is found to violate § 7, all dislocations caused by the merger are actionable, regardless of whether those dislocations have anything to do with the reason the merger was condemned. This holding would make § 4 recovery entirely fortuitous, and would authorize damages for losses which are of no concern to the antitrust laws.

Both of these consequences are well illustrated by the facts of this case. If the acquisitions here were unlawful, it is because they brought a "deep pocket" parent into a market of "pygmies." Yet respondents' injury — the loss of income that would have accrued had the acquired centers gone bankrupt — bears no relationship to the size of either the acquiring company or its competitors. Respondents would have suffered the identical "loss" — but no compensable injury — had the acquired centers instead obtained refinancing or been purchased by "shallow pocket" parents as the Court of Appeals itself acknowledged. Thus, respondents' injury was not of "the type that the statute was intended to forestall," *Wyandotte Co. v. United States*, 389 U.S. 191.

But the antitrust laws are not merely indifferent to the injury claimed here. At base, respondents complain that by acquiring the failing centers petitioner preserved competition, thereby depriving respondents of the benefits of increased concentration. The damages respondents obtained are designed to provide them with the profits they would have realized had competition been reduced. The antitrust laws, however, were enacted for "the protection of *competition* not *competitors*," *Brown Shoe Co. v. United States*. It is inimical to the purposes of these laws to award damages for the type of injury claimed here.

Of course, Congress is free, if it desires, to mandate damages awards for all dislocations caused by unlawful mergers despite the peculiar consequences of so doing. But because of these consequences, "we should insist upon a clear expression of a congressional purpose," before attributing such an intent to Congress. We can find no such expression in either the language or the legislative history of § 4. To the contrary, it is far from clear that the loss of windfall profits that would have accrued had the acquired centers failed even constitutes "injury" within the meaning of § 4. And it is quite clear that if respondents were injured, it was not "by reason of anything forbidden in the antitrust laws": while respondents' loss occurred "by reason of" the unlawful acquisitions, it did not occur "by reason of" that which made the acquisitions unlawful.

We therefore hold that for the plaintiffs to recover treble damages on account of § 7 violations, they must prove more than injury causally linked to an illegal presence in the market. Plaintiffs must prove *antitrust* injury, which is to say injury of the type the antitrust laws were intended to prevent and that flows from that which makes defendants' acts unlawful. The injury should reflect the anticompetitive effect either of the violation or of anticompetitive acts made possible by the violation. It should, in short, be "the type of loss that the claimed violations . . . would be likely to cause." *Zenith Radio Corp. v. Hazeltine Research*, 395 U.S., at 125.

III

We come, then, to the question of appropriate disposition of this case. At the very least, petitioner is entitled to a new trial, not only because of the instructional errors noted by the Court of Appeals that are not at issue here but also because the District Court's instruction as to the basis for damages was inconsistent with our holding as outlined above. Our review of the record, however, persuades us that a new trial on the damages claim is unwarranted. Respondents based their case solely on their novel damages theory which we have rejected. While they produced some conclusory testimony suggesting that in operating the acquired centers petitioner had abused its deep pocket by engaging in anticompetitive conduct, they made no attempt to prove that they had lost any income as a result of such predation. Rather, their entire proof of damages was based on their claim to profits that would have been earned had the acquired centers closed. Since respondents did not prove any cognizable damages and have not offered any justification for allowing respondents, after two trials and over 10 years of litigation, yet a third opportunity to do so, it follows that, petitioner is entitled, in accord with its motion made pursuant to Rule 50(b), to judgment on the damages claim notwithstanding the verdict. . . .

Respondents' complaint also prayed for equitable relief, and the Court of Appeals held that if respondents established a § 7 violation, they might be entitled to an injunction against "those practices by which a deep pocket market entrant harms competition." Because petitioner has not contested this holding, respondents remain free, on remand, to seek such a decree.

NOTES AND QUESTIONS

1. Following its *Brunswick* decision, the Court in *J. Truett Payne Co. v. Chrysler Motors Corp.*, 451 U.S. 557 (1981), held that the "antitrust injury" limitation had application beyond Section 7, including price discrimination violations alleged under Section 2 of the Clayton Act, as amended by the Robinson-Patman Act. The Court in *Payne* reaffirmed that in order to meet the "antitrust injury" requirement, plaintiff must plead and demonstrate an actual diminution of competition.

2. In light of *Brunswick*, consider the accuracy of this rule: In order for plaintiff to recover for "antitrust injury" within the meaning of Section 4, it must plead, and ultimately establish, that the injury flowed from an antitrust violation which produced a decrease in competition. Is it accurate to state that the focus of *Brunswick*'s inquiry is on the "nature" of plaintiff's injury? Evaluate whether the "antitrust injury" test is discernibly different from the "standing" requirement. Is the latter limitation concerned only with the directness or remoteness of the injury from the antitrust violation? *See generally* Page, *Antitrust Damages and Economic Efficiency: An Approach to Antitrust Injury*, 47 U. Chi. L. Rev. 467 (1980).

3. In *Brunswick*, the plaintiff alleged that its competitor would have gone out of business but for the fact that it was acquired by the defendant. Why couldn't the defendant successfully assert the "failing company" defense, which permits mergers under certain circumstances when one of the parties is in danger of business failure? For an argument that the merger at issue in *Brunswick* was really legal because the defendant could have successfully raised the "failing company" defense, see Areeda, *Antitrust Violations Without Damage Recoveries*, 89 Harv. L. Rev. 1127 (1976). For more on the "failing company" defense, see Chapter 7, *infra*.

4. *Brunswick* left open the question whether the "antitrust injury" standard was a requirement in injunctive suits under Section 16 of the Clayton Act, where the statute speaks in terms of "threatened conduct that will cause loss or damages." The next case answers this issue.

CARGILL, INC. v. MONFORT OF COLORADO, INC.
479 U.S. 104 (1986)

Justice Brennan delivered the opinion of the Court.

Under § 16 of the Clayton Act private parties "threatened [with] loss or damage by a violation of the antitrust laws" may seek injunctive relief. This case presents two questions: whether a plaintiff seeking relief under § 16 must prove a threat of antitrust injury, and, if so, whether loss or damage due to increased competition constitutes such injury.

I

Respondent Monfort of Colorado, Inc. (Monfort), the plaintiff below, owns and operates three integrated beef-packing plants, that is, plants for both the slaughter of cattle and the fabrication of beef. Monfort operates in both the market for fed cattle (the input market) and the market for fabricated beef (the output market). These markets are highly competitive, and the profit margins of the major beef packers are low. The current markets are a product of two decades of intense competition, during which time packers with modern integrated plants have gradually displaced packers with separate slaughter and fabrication plants.

Monfort is the country's fifth-largest beef packer. Petitioner Excel Corporation (Excel), one of the two defendants below, is the second-largest packer. Excel operates five integrated plants and one fabrication plant. It is a wholly owned subsidiary of Cargill, Inc., the other defendant below, a large privately owned corporation with more than 150 subsidiaries in at least 35 countries.

On June 17, 1983, Excel signed an agreement to acquire the third-largest packer in the market, Spencer Beef, a division of the Land O'Lakes agricultural cooperative. Spencer Beef owned two integrated plants and one slaughtering plant. After the acquisition, Excel would still be the second-largest packer, but would command a market share almost equal to that of the largest packer, IBP, Inc. (IBP).[8]

Monfort brought an action under § 16 of the Clayton Act, 15 U.S.C. § 26, to enjoin the prospective merger. Its complaint alleged that the acquisition would "violat[e] Section 7 of the Clayton Act because the effect of the proposed acquisition may be substantially to lessen competition or tend to create a monopoly in several different ways. . . ." Monfort described the injury that it allegedly would suffer in this way: "(f) *Impairment of plaintiff's ability to compete.* The proposed acquisition will result in a concentration of economic power in the relevant markets which threatens Monfort's supply of fed cattle and its ability to compete in the boxed beef market."

II

This case requires us to decide, at the outset, a question we have not previously addressed: whether a private plaintiff seeking an injunction under § 16 of the Clayton Act must show a threat of antitrust injury. To decide the question, we must look first to the source of the antitrust injury requirement, which lies in a related provision of the Clayton Act, § 4, 15 U.S.C. § 15.

Like § 16, § 4 provides a vehicle for private enforcement of the antitrust laws. Under § 4, "any person who shall be injured in his business or property by reason of anything forbidden in the antitrust laws may sue therefor in any district court of the United States . . . , and shall recover threefold the damages by him sustained, and the cost of suit, including a reasonable attorney's fee." 15 U.S.C. § 15. In *Brunswick Corp. v. Pueblo Bowl-O-Mat, Inc.* we held that plaintiffs seeking treble damages under § 4 must show more than simply an "injury causally linked" to a particular merger; instead, "plaintiffs must prove *antitrust* injury, which is to say injury of the type the antitrust laws were intended to prevent and that flows from that which makes the defendants' acts unlawful." 429 U.S., at 489 (emphasis in original). . . .

Section 16 of the Clayton Act provides in part that "[a]ny person, firm, corporation, or association shall be entitled to sue for and have injunctive relief . . . against threatened loss or damage by a violation of the antitrust laws. . . ." 15 U.S.C. § 26. It is plain that § 16 and § 4 do differ in various ways. For example, § 4 requires a plaintiff to show actual injury, but § 16 requires a showing only of "threatened" loss or damage; similarly, § 4 requires a showing of injury to "business or property," while § 16 contains no such limitation.[9]

---

8 [FN 2] The District Court relied on the testimony of one of Monfort's witnesses in determining market share. 591 F. Supp. at 706–707. According to this testimony, Monfort's share of the cattle slaughter market was 5.5%, Excel's share was 13.3%, and IBP's was 24.4%. Monfort's share of the production market was 5.7%, Excel's share was 14.1%, and IBP's share was 27.3%. After the merger, Excel's share of each market would increase to 20.4%. *Id.* at 64, 69; 761 F.2d 570, 577 (10 Cir. 1985).

9 [FN 6] Standing analysis under § 16 will not always be identical to standing analysis under § 4. For example, the difference in the remedy each section provides means that certain considerations relevant to a determination of standing under § 4 are not relevant under § 16. The treble-damage remedy, if afforded to "every person tangentially affected by an antitrust violation," or for "all injuries that might conceivably be traced to an antitrust violation," would "open the door to duplicative recoveries," and to multiple lawsuits. In order to protect against multiple lawsuits and duplicative recoveries, courts should examine other factors in addition to antitrust injury, such as the potential for duplicative recovery, the

Although these differences do affect the nature of the injury cognizable under each section, the lower courts, including the courts below, have found that under both § 16 and § 4 the plaintiff must still allege an injury of the type the antitrust laws were designed to prevent. We agree.

The wording concerning the relationship of the injury to the violation of the antitrust laws in each section is comparable. Section 4 requires proof of injury "by reason of anything forbidden in the antitrust laws"; § 16 requires proof of "threatened loss or damage by a violation of the antitrust laws." It would be anomalous, we think, to read the Clayton Act to authorize a private plaintiff to secure an injunction against a threatened injury for which he would not be entitled to compensation if the injury actually occurred.

There is no indication that Congress intended such a result. Indeed, the legislative history of § 16 is consistent with the view that § 16 affords private plaintiffs injunction relief only for those injuries cognizable under § 4. According to the House Report,

> "Under section 7 of the act of July 2, 1890 [revised and incorporated into Clayton Act as § 4], a person injured in his business and property by corporations or combinations acting in violation of the Sherman antitrust law, may recover loss and damage for such wrongful act. There is, however, no provision in the existing law authorizing a person, firm, corporation, or association to enjoin threatened loss or damage to his business or property by the commission of *such unlawful acts, and the purpose of this section is to remedy such defect in the law.*" H.R. Rep. No. 627, pt. 1, 63d Cong., 2d Sess. 21 (1914) (emphasis added).

Sections 4 and 16 are thus best understood as providing complementary remedies for a single set of injuries. Accordingly, we conclude that in order to seek injunctive relief under § 16, a private plaintiff must allege threatened loss or damage "of the type the antitrust laws were designed to prevent and that flows from that which makes defendants' acts unlawful." *Brunswick*, 429 U.S., at 489. We therefore turn to the question of whether the proposed merger in this case threatened respondent with antitrust injury.

III

Initially, we confront the problem of determining what Monfort alleged the source of its injury to be. Monfort's complaint is of little assistance in this regard, since the injury alleged therein — "an impairment of plaintiff's ability to compete" — is alleged to result from "a concentration of economic power." The pretrial order largely restates these general allegations. At trial, however, Monfort did present

---

complexity of apportioning damages, and the existence of other parties that have been more directly harmed, to determine whether a party is a proper plaintiff under § 4. Conversely, under § 16, the only remedy available is equitable in nature, and, as we recognized in *Hawaii v. Standard Oil Co.*, "the fact is that one injunction is as effective as 100, and, concomitantly, that 100 injunctions are no more effective than one." 405 U.S., at 261. Thus, because standing under § 16 raises no threat of multiple lawsuits or duplicative recoveries, some of the factors other than antitrust injury that are appropriate to a determination of standing under § 4 are not relevant under § 16.

testimony and other evidence that helped define the threatened loss. Monfort alleged that after the merger, Excel would attempt to increase its market share at the expense of smaller rivals, such as Monfort. To that end, Monfort claimed, Excel would bid up the price it would pay for cattle, and reduce the price at which it sold boxed beef. Although such a strategy, which Monfort labeled a "cost-price squeeze," would reduce Excel's profits, Excel's parent corporation had the financial reserves to enable Excel to pursue such a strategy. Eventually, according to Monfort, smaller competitors lacking significant reserves and unable to match Excel's prices would be driven from the market; at this point Excel would raise the price of its boxed beef to supracompetitive levels, and would more than recoup the profits it lost during the initial phase.

From this scenario two theories of injury to Monfort emerge: (1) a threat of a loss of profits stemming from the possibility that Excel, after the merger, would lower its prices to a level at or only slightly above its costs; (2) a threat of being driven out of business by the possibility that Excel, after the merger, would lower its prices to a level below its costs.[10]

We discuss each theory in turn.

A

Monfort's first claim is that after the merger, Excel would lower its prices to some level at or slightly above its costs in order to compete with other packers for market share. Excel would be in a position to do this because of the multiplant efficiencies its acquisition of Spencer would provide. To remain competitive, Monfort would have to lower its prices; as a result, Monfort would suffer a loss in profitability, but would not be driven out of business.[11]

The question is whether Monfort's loss of profits in such circumstances constitutes antitrust injury.

To resolve the question, we look again to *Brunswick v. Pueblo Bowl-O-Mat, supra.* In *Brunswick*, we evaluated the antitrust significance of several competitors' loss of profits resulting from the entry of a large firm into its market. We concluded: "[T]he antitrust laws are not merely indifferent to the injury claimed here. At base, respondents complain that by acquiring the failing centers petitioner preserved competition, thereby depriving respondents of the benefits of increased concentration. The damages respondents obtained are designed to provide them with the profits they would have realized had competition been reduced. The antitrust laws, however, were enacted for 'the protection of *competition*, not *competitors*.' *Brown Shoe Co. v. United States*, 370 U.S., at 320. It is inimical to the purposes of these laws to award damages for the type of injury claimed here." "429 U.S., at 488."

---

[10] [FN 9] In its brief, Monfort also argues that it would be injured by "the trend toward oligopoly pricing" that could conceivably follow the merger. Brief for Respondent 18–20. There is no indication in the record that this claim was raised below, however, and so we do not address it here.

[11] [FN 10] In this case, Monfort has conceded that its viability would not be threatened by Excel's decision to lower prices: "Because Monfort's operations were as efficient as those of Excel, only below-cost pricing could remove Monfort as an obstacle." ("Monfort proved it was just as efficient as Excel"); ("Monfort would only be harmed by sustained predatory pricing").

The loss of profits to the competitors in *Brunswick* was not of concern under the antitrust laws, since it resulted only from continued competition. Respondent argues that the losses in *Brunswick* can be distinguished from the losses alleged here, since the latter will result from an increase, rather than from a mere continuation, of competition. The range of actions unlawful under § 7 of the Clayton Act is broad enough, respondent claims, to support a finding of antitrust injury whenever a competitor is faced with a threat of losses from increased competition.[12]

We find respondent's proposed construction of § 7 too broad, for reasons that *Brunswick* illustrates. *Brunswick* holds that the antitrust laws do not require the courts to protect small businesses from the loss of profits due to continued competition, but only against the loss of profits from practices forbidden by the antitrust laws. The kind of competition that Monfort alleges here, competition for increased market share, is not activity forbidden by the antitrust laws. It is simply, as petitioners claim, vigorous competition. To hold that the antitrust laws protect competitors from the loss of profits due to such price competition would, in effect, render illegal any decision by a firm to cut prices in order to increase market share. The antitrust laws require no such perverse result, for "[i]t is in the interest of competition to permit dominant firms to engage in vigorous competition, including price competition." *Arthur S. Langenderfer, Inc. v. S.E. Johnson Co.*, 729 F.2d 1050, 1057 (6th Cir.), *cert. denied*, 469 U.S. 1036 (1984). The logic of Brunswick compels the conclusion that the threat of loss of profits due to possible price competition following a merger does not constitute a threat of antitrust injury.

B

The second theory of injury argued here is that after the merger Excel would attempt to drive Monfort out of business by engaging in sustained predatory pricing. Predatory pricing may be defined as pricing below an appropriate measure of cost for the purpose of eliminating competitors in the short run and reducing competition in the long run. It is a practice that harms both competitors *and* competition. In contrast to price cutting aimed simply at increasing market share, predatory pricing has as its aim the elimination of competition. Predatory pricing is thus a practice "inimical to the purposes of [the antitrust] laws," *Brunswick*, 429 U.S., at 488, and one capable of inflicting antitrust injury.[13]

---

[12] [FN 11] Respondent finds support in the legislative history of the Hart-Scott Antitrust Improvements Act of 1976 for the view that Congress intends the courts to apply § 7 so as to protect the viability of small competitors. The Senate Report, for example, cites with approval this Court's statement in *United States v. Von's Grocery Co.*, 384 U.S. 270, 275 (1966) that "the basic purpose of the 1950 Celler-Kefauver Act [amending § 7 of the Clayton Act] was to prevent economic concentration in the American economy by keeping a large number of small competitors in business." S. Rep. No. 94-803, 63 (1976). Even if respondent is correct that Congress intended the courts to apply § 7 so as to keep small competitors in business at the expense of efficiency, a proposition about which there is considerable disagreement, such congressional intent is of no use to Monfort, which has conceded that it will suffer only a loss of profits, and not be driven from the market, should Excel engage in a cost-price squeeze.

[13] [FN 13] See also *Brunswick*, 429 U.S., at 489, n.14 ("The short-term effect of certain anticompetitive behavior — predatory below-cost pricing, for example — may be to stimulate price competition. But competitors may be able to prove antitrust injury before they actually are driven from the market and competition is thereby lessened.").

The Court of Appeals held that Monfort had alleged "what we consider to be a form of predatory pricing. . . ." 761 F.2d, at 575. The Court also found that Monfort "could only be harmed by sustained predatory pricing," and that "it is impossible to tell in advance of the acquisition" whether Excel would in fact engage in such a course of conduct; because it could not rule out the possibility that Excel would engage in predatory pricing, it found that Monfort was threatened with antitrust injury.

Although the Court of Appeals did not explicitly define what it meant by predatory pricing, two interpretations are plausible. First, the court can be understood to mean that Monfort's allegation of losses from the above-cost "cost-price squeeze" was equivalent to an allegation of injury from predatory conduct. If this is the proper interpretation, then the court's judgment is clearly erroneous because (a) Monfort made no allegation that Excel would act with predatory intent after the merger, and (b) price competition is not predatory activity, for the reason discussed in Part III-A, *supra*.

Second, the Court of Appeals can be understood to mean that Monfort had shown a credible threat of injury from below-cost pricing. To the extent the judgment rests on this ground, however, it must also be reversed, because Monfort did not allege injury from below-cost pricing before the District Court. The District Court twice noted that Monfort had made no assertion that Excel would engage in predatory pricing. See 591 F. Supp., at 691 ("Plaintiff does not contend that predatory practices would be engaged in by Excel or IBP."); *Id.*, at 710 ("Monfort does not allege that IBP and Excel will in fact engage in predatory activities as part of the cost-price squeeze").[14]

. . . We conclude that Monfort neither raised nor proved any claim of predatory pricing before the District Court.[15]

IV

In its *amicus* brief, the United States argues that the "danger of allowing a competitor to challenge an acquisition on the basis of necessarily speculative claims of post-acquisition predatory pricing far outweighs the danger that any anticompetitive merger will go unchallenged." On this basis, the United States invites the Court to adopt in effect a *per se* rule "denying competitors standing to challenge acquisitions on the basis of predatory pricing theories."

We decline the invitation. As the foregoing discussion makes plain, predatory pricing is an anticompetitive practice forbidden by the antitrust laws. While firms

---

[14] [FN 14] The Court of Appeals may have relied on the District Court's speculation that the merger raised "a distinct possibility . . . of predatory pricing." 591 F. Supp., at 710. This statement directly followed the District Court's second observation that Monfort did not raise such a claim, however, and thus was clearly dicta.

[15] [FN 15] Even had Monfort actually advanced a claim of predatory pricing, we doubt whether the facts as found by the District Court would have supported it. Although Excel may have had the financial resources to absorb losses over an extended period, other factors, such as Excel's share of market capacity and the barriers to entry after competitors have been driven from the market, must also be considered.

may engage in the practice only infrequently, there is ample evidence suggesting that the practice does occur.[16]

It would be novel indeed for a court to deny standing to a party seeking an injunction against threatened injury merely because such injuries rarely occur.[17]

In any case, nothing in the language or legislative history of the Clayton Act suggests that Congress intended this Court to ignore injuries caused by such anticompetitive practices as predatory pricing.

V

We hold that a plaintiff seeking injunctive relief under § 16 of the Clayton Act must show a threat of antitrust injury, and that a showing of loss or damage due merely to increased competition does not constitute such injury. The record below does not support a finding of antitrust injury, but only of threatened loss from increased competition. Because respondent has therefore failed to make the showing § 16 requires, we need not reach the question of whether the proposed merger violates § 7. The judgment of the Court of Appeals is reversed and the case is remanded for further proceedings consistent with this opinion.

NOTES AND QUESTIONS

1. Does *Cargill* also answer the issue of whether a target company suffers an antitrust injury by reason of a tender offer takeover? Is a target able to allege any diminution in competition? Consider the following problem: Company *A* seeks to "take over" Company *B* by means of a tender offer for *B*'s outstanding stock. *B* objects to the takeover. Its directors sue *A*, claiming that the proposed takeover would be an illegal merger. If the merger is illegal, however, it is because the post-merger firm, *AB*, will have more market power than the two firms did before the merger. *B* will therefore be the beneficiary, not the victim, of any illegal merger. Has *B* suffered antitrust injury? *See Anago, Inc. v. Tecnol Medical Products, Inc.*, 976 F.2d 248 (5th Cir. 1992). The court found that tender offer targets lack antitrust injury. *See* Easterbrook & Fischel, *Antitrust Suits by Targets of Tender Offers*, 80 Mich. L. Rev. 1155 (1982).

---

[16] [FN 16] See Koller, *The Myth of Predatory Pricing: An Empirical Study*, 4 Antitrust Law & Econ. Rev. 105 (1971); Miller, *Comments on Baumol and Ordover*, 28 J. Law & Econ. 267 (1985).

[17] [FN 17] Claims of threatened injury from predatory pricing must, of course, be evaluated with care. As we discussed in *Matsushita Electric Industrial Co. v. Zenith Radio Corp.*, the likelihood that predatory pricing will benefit the predator is "inherently uncertain: the short run loss [from pricing below cost] is definite, but the long-run gain depends on successfully neutralizing the competition. . . . [and] on maintaining monopoly power for long enough both to recoup the predator's losses and to harvest some additional gain." 475 U.S. 574, 588. Although the commentators disagree as to whether it is ever rational for a firm to engage in such conduct, it is plain that the obstacles to the successful execution of a strategy of predation are manifold, and that the disincentives to engage in such a strategy are accordingly numerous. As we stated in *Matsushita*, "predatory pricing schemes are rarely tried, and even more rarely successful." Moreover, the mechanism by which a firm engages in predatory pricing — lowering prices — is the same mechanism by which a firm stimulates competition; because "cutting prices in order to increase business often is the very essence of competition . . . mistaken inferences . . . are especially costly, because they chill the very conduct the antitrust laws are designed to protect."

2.   For further discussion of the "antitrust injury" in the context of Section 7 of the Clayton Act (mergers), *see* Chapter 7, *infra.*

3.   It seems clear after a review of the antitrust injury and direct purchaser limitations on Section 4 that the Supreme Court is concerned with litigation problems that implicate speculative injury claims, complex damage tracing problems, duplicative recoveries, and questionable causal connection theories.

4.   Foreign plaintiffs may have to prove that their antitrust injury derives from the result of competitive harm to the United States market in order to prevent their claim from being dismissed for lack of subject matter jurisdiction. In *Den Norske Stats Oljeselskap As v. HeereMac Vof*, 241 F.3d 420 (5th Cir. 2001), the Fifth Circuit dismissed the Norwegian state oil company's claim against foreign and domestic heavy-barge lift service providers who previously had been prosecuted by the Department of Justice for bid rigging and price fixing in the Gulf of Mexico, the North Sea, and South China Sea. The court stated that the plaintiffs failed to satisfy the requirements of the 1982 Foreign Trade Antitrust Improvements Act (FTAIA), 15 U.S.C. § 6a. Under the FTAIA, antitrust laws do not apply to foreign conduct, other than importing, unless the conduct has a "direct, substantial, and reasonably foreseeable effect" on United States commerce (§ 15 U.S.C. § 6a(1)) and "such effect gives rise to a claim" under the Sherman Act (§ 15 U.S.C. § 6a(2)). The Fifth Circuit interpreted the language "a claim" to mean the domestic effects had to be the basis for the plaintiff's claim. In this case, the oil company's injury could only be traced to the services in the North Sea.

The Second Circuit, in contrast, held that the effects of the defendant's conduct, and not the situs of the plaintiff's injury, should be the key to assessing whether the FTAIA prevents a Sherman Act claim from going forward. In *Kruman v. Christie's International PLC*, 284 F.3d 384 (2d Cir. 2002), plaintiffs sued the two largest auction houses in the world, alleging that they had paid inflated commissions to the defendants. The plaintiffs had purchased or sold goods at auctions held outside the United States. The court declined to interpret the words "a claim" to mean "the plaintiff's claim"; therefore, the alleged effect only had to violate the substantive provisions of the Sherman Act in order for subject matter jurisdiction to exist.

5.   After *Brunswick* and *Cargill* announced a new "antitrust injury" test to Sections 4 and 16 of the Clayton Act, the Court elaborated further in *Atlantic Richfield Co. v. USA Petroleum Co.*, 495 U.S. 328 (1990), when it held that a firm does not incur "an 'injury' within the meaning of the antitrust laws when it loses sales to a competitor charging nonpredatory prices pursuant to a vertical, maximum price-fixing scheme."

The Court reasoned:

> We reject respondent's argument. Although a vertical, maximum price-fixing agreement is unlawful under § 1 of the Sherman Act, it does not cause a competitor antitrust injury unless it results in predatory pricing. Antitrust injury does not arise for purposes of § 4 of the Clayton Act, until a private party is adversely affected by an anticompetitive aspect of the defendant's conduct . . . ; in the context of pricing practices, only predatory pricing has the requisite anticompetitive effect. . . . Low prices benefit

consumers regardless of how those prices are set, and so long as they are above predatory levels, they do not threaten competition. Hence, they cannot give rise to antitrust injury. We have adhered to this principle regardless of the type of antitrust claim involved. . . .

When prices are not predatory, any losses flowing from them cannot be said to stem from an anticompetitive aspect of the defendant's conduct. 'It is in the interest of competition to permit dominant firms to engage in vigorous competition, including price competition.' . . .

We also reject respondent's suggestion that no antitrust injury need be shown where a per se violation is involved. The per se rule is a method of determining whether § 1 of the Sherman Act has been violated, but it does not indicate whether a private plaintiff has suffered antitrust injury and thus whether he may recover damages under § 4 of the Clayton Act. Per se and rule-of-reason analysis are but two methods of determining whether a restraint is 'unreasonable,' i.e., whether its anticompetitive effects outweigh its procompetitive effects. The per se rule is a presumption of unreasonableness based on 'business certainty and litigation efficiency.' *Arizona v. Maricopa County Medical Society*, 457 U.S. at 332. It represents a 'long-standing judgment that the prohibited practices "by their nature have" a substantial potential for impact on competition.' *FTC v. Superior Court Trial Lawyers Assn.*, 493 U.S. 411, 432 (1990) (quoting *Jefferson Parish Hospital Dist. No. 2 v. Hyde*, 466 U.S. 2, 16 (1984)). 'Once experience with a particular kind of restraint enables the Court to predict with confidence that the rule of reason will condemn it, it has applied a conclusive presumption that the restraint is unreasonable.' *Maricopa County Medical Society, supra*, at 344.

The purpose of the antitrust injury requirement is different. It ensures that the harm claimed by the plaintiff corresponds to the rationale for finding a violation of the antitrust laws in the first place, and it prevents losses that stem from competition from supporting suits by private plaintiffs for either damages or equitable relief. Actions per se unlawful under the antitrust laws may nonetheless have some procompetitive effects, and private parties might suffer losses therefrom. Conduct in violation of the antitrust laws may have three effects, often interwoven: in some respects the conduct may reduce competition, in other respects it may increase competition, and in still other respects effects may be neutral as to competition. The antitrust injury requirement ensures that a plaintiff can recover only if the loss stems from a competition-*reducing* aspect or effect of the defendant's behavior. The need for this showing is at least as great under the per se rule as under the rule of reason. Indeed, in so far as the per se rule permits the prohibition of efficient practices in the name of simplicity, the need for the antitrust injury requirement is underscored. '[P]rocompetitive or efficiency-enhancing aspects of practices that nominally violate the antitrust laws may cause serious harm to individuals, but this kind of harm is the essence of competition and should play no role in the definition of antitrust damages.' Page, *The Scope of Liability for Antitrust Violations*, 37 STAN. L. REV. 1445, 1460 (1985). Thus, 'proof of a per se violation and of antitrust injury are distinct matters that must be shown independently.' P. Areeda & H. Hovenkamp, *Antitrust Law* ¶ 334.2c, at 330 (1989 Supp.).

6. On remand, 972 F.2d 1070 (9th Cir. 1992), the Ninth Circuit held that the Supreme Court's conclusion that the independent gasoline marketers lacked standing to challenge the alleged vertical maximum resale price maintenance scheme applied only in the absence of predatory pricing. But the plaintiffs might still have standing to prove that the maintained prices were predatory. Is this consistent with the Supreme Court's decision?

7. The Third Circuit has indicated that a plaintiff may be able to maintain a federal antitrust action based on allegations of lost profits and lost market shares stemming from an alleged vertical pricing agreement, without any allegations of predatory pricing. *West Penn Allegheny Health System*, 627 F.3d 85 (3d Cir. 2010). This ruling appears to create a conflict between the First, Third, and Ninth Circuit Courts of Appeals. *Monahan's Marine, Inc. v. Boston Whaler, Inc.*, 866 F.2d 525 (1st Cir. 1989); *Pool Water Products v. Olin Corp.*, 258 F.3d 1024 (9th Cir. 2001). The Third Circuit found that the plaintiff West Penn, the second largest hospital system in Pittsburgh, had "sustained an antitrust injury in the form of artificially depressed reimbursement rates." 627 F.3d at 103. Defendants UPMC and Highmark were the dominant hospital system and insurer in the city, respectively. *Id.* at 91. Pursuant to an agreement with UPMC, Highmark allegedly maintained West Penn's reimbursement rates at artificially depressed levels. *Id.* at 94. The court found that the "amount of the underpayments — *i.e.*, the difference between the reimbursements [plaintiff] would have received in a competitive market and those it actually received — constitute[d] an antitrust injury." *Id.* at 103. The court rejected defendants' argument that this injury was not part of the antitrust conduct because "low reimbursement rates translate into low premiums for subscribers, and that it would therefore be contrary to a key purpose of the antitrust laws — promoting consumer welfare — to allow West Penn to recover the amount of the underpayments." *Id.* Instead, the court determined that:

> First, even if it were true that paying West Penn depressed rates enabled Highmark to offer lower premiums, it is far from clear that this would have benefited consumers, because the premium reductions would have been achieved only by taking action that tends to diminish the quality and availability of hospital services. . . . Second, the complaint alleges that Highmark did *not* pass the savings on to consumers. It alleges, instead, that Highmark pocketed the savings, while repeatedly ratcheting up the insurance premiums.

Id. at 104. The court's analysis of the antitrust injury rested on the fact that defendants were exercising monopsony power. *Id.* at 105.

8. Does the majority opinion in *Atlantic Richfield* suggest that competitors lack antitrust injury in all pricing cases under Section 1, or only vertical, maximum price-fixing cases? What outcome if the Court's logic in *Atlantic Richfield* is applied to a vertical, minimum price-fixing agreement? Even where plaintiff competitors are unable to allege an antitrust injury because a defendant's price fixing has resulted in inflated prices that benefit not only the defendant but also the

defendant's competitors, they may still be able to allege that other anticompetitive behaviors constitute a sufficient antitrust injury. *See Morning Star Packing v. SK Foods*, 754 F. Supp. 2d 1230, 1232 (E.D. Cal. 2010) (Antitrust injury existed where plaintiffs alleged bribery and bid rigging, because "this type of conduct, unlike price fixing, can injure both customers and competitors. For example, bid rigging not only causes customers to pay more than they would have otherwise paid in a competitive market, but it can also result in a competitor being outbid on a contract they would have otherwise been awarded.").

9.   Is it clear after the decision that, even in per se cases under Section 1 of the Sherman Act, all plaintiffs must first demonstrate "antitrust injury"? Will antitrust injury be inferred in some cases? How about direct purchaser lawsuits against cartels? *See Rebel Oil Co. v. Atlantic Richfield Co.*, 51 F.3d 1421 (9th Cir.), *cert. denied*, 516 U.S. 987 (1995):

> Rebel argues that market power is not a prerequisite to antitrust injury if the claim is premised on Sherman Act § 1 . . . because vertical price fixing is per se illegal. . . . Rebel confuses proof of liability with proof of antitrust injury. . . . The "mere presence" of a per se violation under the Sherman Act § 1 "does not by itself bestow on any plaintiff a private right of action for damages." A plaintiff must prove that his injury flows from the anti-competitive aspect of the defendant's conduct. For example, in *USA Petroleum*, the plaintiff did not suffer antitrust injury from defendant's conspiracy to fix low prices. Although per se illegal, maximum price fixing cannot cause antitrust injury because low prices are the "very essence of competition." (Citing *Atlantic Richfield*, quoting *Matsushita*.)

10.   *Caribe BMW, Inc. v. Bayerische Motoren Werke Aktiengesellschaft*, 19 F.3d 745 (1st Cir. 1994), considered whether a dealer's lost profits resulting from a maximum resale price-fixing agreement constitutes antitrust injury. The court distinguished *Atlantic Richfield*, noting that the plaintiffs in that case were not dealers but *competitors* of the dealers. The court held that the district court erred in dismissing the antitrust claims because Caribe was the very firm that the alleged price maintenance agreement forced to keep its prices below the level that some customers — those seeking greater service, for example — presumably were willing to pay.

11.   In *State Oil v. Khan*, 522 U.S. 3 (1997), the court overruled *Albrecht* (discussed in the *Atlantic Richfield* decision) and held that vertical maximum price fixing is not per se unlawful. See Chapter 5, *infra. See also Pace Electronics, Inc. v. Canon Computer Systems, Inc.*, 213 F.3d 118 (3d Cir. 2000) (terminated dealer in vertical minimum price-fixing agreement suffers antitrust injury).

PROBLEM 3.4

Arlen, Inc. and Spectro, Inc., are the country's only two manufacturers of cardiac transponders, high-tech electronic devices for monitoring heart activity. Both the devices and the process by which they are manufactured are covered by several patents. Arlen is a large manufacturer, well established in the cardiac transponder business. Spectro is a small upstart that is not yet as well established and has a much smaller output, but it has patented some new transponder designs that have the potential to make its transponders superior to those of Arlen.

In 1987, Arlen made Spectro an offer it could not refuse: $10,000,000 for its plant and exclusive licenses on its patents, plus 10% of gross sales on all the transponders which were made in the acquired plant or which employed the acquired patents. Spectro sold both its plant and its patents to Arlen and went out of business.

A year later Arlen closed down the Spectro plant, announced to Spectro that it would continue to manufacture cardiac transponders under the old technology, and claimed that it thus owed Spectro no money under the "10% of gross sales" part of the sale agreement.

Spectro sued Arlen, alleging monopolization of the cardiac transponder market and that the Spectro-Arlen acquisition was an illegal merger. Does Spectro have standing? Does the Supreme Court's *Brunswick* decision apply? Would it make a difference if Spectro had owned two plants and Arlen had purchased only one of them? *See McDonald v. Johnson & Johnson*, 722 F.2d 1370 (8th Cir. 1983), *cert. denied*, 469 U.S. 870 (1984).

PROBLEM 3.5

The National Collegiate Athletic Association (NCAA) restricts member-school institutions in the amount of compensation student athletes may be paid while on an athletic scholarship. The NCAA rules provide sanctions against member schools, including suspension and expulsion, for violations of the compensation rule.

The Oxford Institute of Intelligence is a major football power and a member of the All-Academic Conference. In order to recruit football players, it made side payments in excess of the NCAA compensation rules. Each of its 30 football players received $200 per month more than the NCAA rules permit.

Upon investigation of the violations, the NCAA suspended Oxford Institute from NCAA-sponsored competitions for the 1990 season. Other penalties were imposed as well. A group of Oxford Institute alumni, students, football players, and cheerleaders challenged the NCAA suspensions, contending that the NCAA violated Section 1 of the Sherman Act by promulgating and enforcing rules restricting benefits that may be awarded to student athletes.

1. Consider whether each category of plaintiff (loyal students, alumni, football players, and cheerleaders) has:

(a) been injured in its "business or property";

(b) standing to bring suit; and

(c) alleged an "antitrust injury."

2. Would Oxford Institute meet these Section 4 requirements were it to bring an antitrust action against the NCAA? *See McCormack v. NCAA*, 845 F.2d 1338 (5th Cir. 1988).

PROBLEM 3.6

Plaintiff is a disabled person needing frequent medical care. Plaintiff's community contains two clinics, Clinic A and Clinic B. After obtaining services at Clinic A for several years, plaintiff has a bad experience there and files a malpractice action against one of Clinic A's physicians. Plaintiff then transfers his medical needs to Clinic B. Thereafter Clinic A and Clinic B merge. The management of the post-merger firm, Clinic AB, then informs plaintiff that he can no longer use the services of the clinic. Plaintiff sues, alleging that the merger of Clinic A and B has ended competition in the delivery of healthcare services in the community, that Clinic AB is restricting output after a merger giving it monopoly, and that plaintiff is therefore a victim of antitrust injury. What outcome? *See Nelson v. Monroe Regional Med. Center*, 925 F.2d 1555 (7th Cir. 1991). Query: When a monopolist reduces its output, does it arbitrarily divide its customer base into two classes and refuse to serve one class, or does it simply increase its price? Suppose Clinic AB can show that plaintiff was willing to pay the price that the clinic was charging following the merger. In that case, is plaintiff a victim of antitrust injury?

PROBLEM 3.7

Fuelco is the only company at a marina selling fuel to cruise ships. The owners of the ships believe that Fuelco is charging monopoly prices. They attempt to get another company, Gasco, to open a facility at the marina, but Gasco will not do so unless the ship owners agree to purchase half of the gasoline from Gasco. After speaking with one another, the ship owners agree that each will purchase one-half of its fuel needs from Gasco, and Gasco enters the market. Fuelco now sues, alleging that it has been the victim of an unlawful conspiracy. What outcome? *See Belcher Oil Co. v. Florida Fuels*, 749 F. Supp. 1104 (S.D. Fla. 1990).

PROBLEM 3.8

Yellow Pages Cost Consultants (YPCC) provides consulting advice to advertisers in yellow page directories. GTE, the publisher of a yellow page directory, decides to end its long-standing practice of allowing consultants like YPCC to order, place, and process advertisements on behalf of client advertisers. As soon as GTE refuses to deal with YPCC and other advertising consultants, YPCC sues GTE, claiming an illegal attempt to monopolize and a refusal to deal under Sections 1 and 2 of the Sherman Act. How should the court rule on YPCC's antitrust injury and standing?

[h]   Standing to Sue

Standing is a judicially created concept, which has the effect of limiting the class of persons who can sue for injuries. The analysis of the federal courts focuses on the "directness" of the injury to the plaintiff, or stated differently, the remoteness of the plaintiff's injury from the antitrust violation.

BLUE SHIELD OF VIRGINIA v. McCREADY
457 U.S. 465 (1982)

JUSTICE BRENNAN delivered the opinion of the Court.

The antitrust complaint at issue in this case alleges that a group health plan's practice of refusing to reimburse subscribers for psychotherapy performed by psychologists, while providing reimbursement for comparable treatment by psychiatrists, was in furtherance of an unlawful conspiracy to restrain competition in the psychotherapy market. The question presented is whether a subscriber who employed the services of a psychologist has standing to maintain an action under § 4 of the Clayton Act based upon the plan's failure to provide reimbursement for the costs of that treatment.

I

From September 1975 until January 1978, respondent Carol McCready was an employee of Prince William County, Virginia. As part of her compensation, the county provided her with coverage under a prepaid group health plan purchased from petitioner Blue Shield of Virginia (Blue Shield). The plan specifically provided reimbursement for a portion of the cost incurred by subscribers with respect to outpatient treatment for mental and nervous disorders, including psychotherapy. Pursuant to this provision, Blue Shield reimbursed subscribers for psychotherapy provided by *psychiatrists*. But Blue Shield did not provide reimbursement for the services of *psychologists* unless the treatment was supervised by and billed through a physician. While a subscriber to the plan, McCready was treated by a clinical psychologist. She submitted claims to Blue Shield for the costs of that treatment, but those claims were routinely denied because they had not been billed through a physician.

In 1978, McCready brought this class action . . . on behalf of all Blue Shield subscribers who had incurred costs for psychological services since 1973 but who had not been reimbursed. The complaint alleged that Blue Shield and petitioner Neuropsychiatric Society of Virginia, Inc., had engaged in an unlawful conspiracy in violation of § 1 of the Sherman Act, "to exclude and boycott clinical psychologists from receiving compensation under" the Blue Shield plans. McCready further alleged that Blue Shield's failure to reimburse had been in furtherance of the alleged conspiracy, and had caused injury to her business or property for which she was entitled to treble damages and attorney's fees under § 4 of the Clayton Act. . . .

B

Analytically distinct from the restrictions on the § 4 remedy recognized in *Hawaii* and *Illinois Brick*, there is the conceptually more difficult question "of which persons have sustained injuries *too remote* [from an antitrust violation] to give them standing to sue for damages under § 4." An antitrust violation may be expected to cause ripples of harm to flow through the Nation's economy; but "despite the broad wording of § 4 there is a point beyond which the wrongdoer should not be held liable." It is reasonable to assume that Congress did not intend to allow every person tangentially affected by an antitrust violation to maintain an action to recover threefold damages for the injury to his business or property. . . . In applying that elusive concept to this statutory action, we look (1) to the physical and economic nexus between the alleged violation and the harm to the plaintiff, and, (2) more particularly, to the relationship of the injury alleged with those forms of injury about which Congress was likely to have been concerned in making defendant's conduct unlawful and in providing a private remedy under § 4.

(1)

It is petitioners' position that McCready's injury is too "fortuitous," "incidental," and "remote" from the alleged violation to provide the basis for a § 4 action. At the outset, petitioners argue that because the alleged conspiracy was directed by its protagonists at psychologists, and not at subscribers to group health plans, only psychologists might maintain suit. This argument may be quickly disposed of.

We do not think that because the goal of the conspirators was to halt encroachment by psychologists into a market that physicians and psychiatrists sought to preserve for themselves, McCready's injury is rendered "remote." The availability of the § 4 remedy to some person who claims its benefit is not a question of the specific intent of the conspirators. Here the remedy cannot reasonably be restricted to those competitors whom the conspirators hoped to eliminate from the market. McCready claims that she has been the victim of a concerted refusal to pay on the part of Blue Shield, motivated by a desire to deprive psychologists of the patronage of Blue Shield subscribers. Denying reimbursement to subscribers for the cost of treatment was the very means by which it is alleged that Blue Shield sought to achieve its illegal ends. The harm to McCready and her class was clearly foreseeable; indeed, it was a necessary step in effecting the ends of the illegal conspiracy. Where the injury alleged is so integral an aspect of the conspiracy alleged, there can be no question but that the loss was precisely " 'the type of loss that the claimed violations . . . would be likely to cause.' " *Brunswick Corp. v. Pueblo Bowl-O-Mat, Inc.*, 429 U.S., at 489. . . .

Petitioners next argue that even if the § 4 remedy might be available to persons other than the competitors of the conspirators, it is not available to McCready because she was not an economic actor in the market that had been restrained. In petitioners' view, the proximate range of the violation is limited to the sector of the economy in which a violation of the type alleged would have its most direct anticompetitive effects. Here, petitioner contends that that market, for purposes of the alleged conspiracy, is the market in group health care plans. Thus, in petitioners' view, standing to redress the violation alleged in this case is limited to participants in that market — that is, to entities, such as McCready's employer, who were purchasers of group health plans, but not to McCready as a beneficiary of the Blue Shield plan.[18]

---

[18] [FN 16] Petitioners borrow selectively from *Brunswick Corp. v. Pueblo Bowl-O-Mat, Inc.*, 429 U.S. 477 (1979), in arguing that McCready's § 4 claim is "unrelated to any reduction in competition caused by the alleged boycott," because the injury she alleges "is the result of the terms of her insurance contract,

Petitioners misconstrue McCready's complaint. McCready does not allege a restraint in the market for group health plans. Her claim of injury is premised on a concerted refusal to reimburse under a plan that was, in fact, purchased and retained by her employer for her benefit, and that as a matter of contract construction and state law permitted reimbursement for the services of psychologists without any significant variation in the structure of the contractual relationship between her employer and Blue Shield. See n. 2, *supra*. As a consumer of psychotherapy services entitled to financial benefits under the Blue Shield plan, we think it clear that McCready was "within that area of the economy . . . endangered by [that] breakdown of competitive conditions" resulting from Blue Shield's selective refusal to reimburse. *Multidistrict Vehicle Air Pollution M.D.L. No. 31*, 481 F.2d 122, 129 (9th Cir. 1973).

(2)

We turn finally to the manner in which the injury alleged reflects Congress' core concerns in prohibiting the antitrust defendants' course of conduct. Petitioners phrase their argument on this point in a manner that concedes McCready's participation in the market for psychotherapy services and rests instead on the notion that McCready's injury does not reflect the "anti-competitive" effect of the alleged boycott. They stress that McCready did not visit a psychiatrist whose fees were artificially inflated as a result of the competitive advantage he gained by Blue Shield's refusal to reimburse for the services of psychologists; she did not pay additional sums for the services of a physician to supervise and bill for the psychotherapy provided by her psychologist; and that there is no "claim that her psychologist's bills are higher than they would have been had the conspiracy not existed." . . .

[W]hile an increase in price resulting from a dampening of competitive market forces is assuredly one type of injury for which § 4 potentially offers redress that is not the only form of injury remediable under § 4. We think it plain that McCready's injury was of a type that Congress sought to redress in providing a private remedy for violations of the antitrust laws.

McCready charges Blue Shield with a purposefully *anticompetitive scheme*. She seeks to recover as damages the sums lost to her as the consequence of Blue Shield's attempt to pursue that scheme.[19]

She alleges that Blue Shield sought to induce its subscribers into selecting psychiatrists over psychologists for the psychotherapeutic services they required, and that the heart of its scheme was the offer of a Hobson's choice to its subscribers.

---

and not the result of a reduction in competition." Extracting additional language from Brunswick, they argue that "McCready would have suffered the identical 'loss' — but no compensable 'injury' — as long as her employer, which acted independently in an unrestrained market, continued to purchase a group insurance contract that did not cover the services of clinical psychologists." *Id.*, at 16–17.

[19] [FN 19] . . . Most obviously, McCready's claim is quite unlike the claim asserted by the plaintiff in Brunswick for she does not seek to label increased competition as a harm to her. Nevertheless, we agree with petitioners that the relationship between the claimed injury and that which is unlawful in the defendant's conduct, as analyzed in Brunswick, is one factor to be considered in determining the redressability of a particular form of injury under § 4.

Those subscribers were compelled to choose between visiting a psychologist and forfeiting reimbursement, or receiving reimbursement by forgoing treatment by the practitioner of their choice. In the latter case, the antitrust injury would have been borne in the first instance by the competitors of the conspirators, and inevitably — though indirectly — by the customers of the competitors in the form of suppressed competition in the psychotherapy market; in the former case, as it happened, the injury was borne directly by the customers of the competitors. McCready did not yield to Blue Shield's coercive pressure, and bore Blue Shield's sanction in the form of an increase in the net cost of her psychologist's services. Although McCready was not a competitor of the conspirators, the injury she suffered was inextricably intertwined with the injury the conspirators sought to inflict on psychologists and the psychotherapy market. In light of the conspiracy here alleged we think that McCready's injury "flows from that which makes defendants' acts unlawful" within the meaning of *Brunswick*, and falls squarely within the area of congressional concern.

IV

Section 4 of the Clayton Act provides a remedy to "any person" injured "by reason of" anything prohibited in the antitrust laws. We are asked in this case to infer a limitation on the rule of recovery suggested by the plain language of § 4. But having reviewed our precedents and, more importantly, the policies of the antitrust laws, we are unable to identify any persuasive rationale upon which McCready might be denied redress under § 4 for the injury she claims. The judgment of the Court of Appeals is Affirmed.

[JUSTICES REHNQUIST, O'CONNOR, STEVENS, and CHIEF JUSTICE BURGER dissented.]

ASSOCIATED GENERAL CONTRACTORS v. CALIFORNIA STATE COUNCIL OF CARPENTERS
459 U.S. 519 (1983)

JUSTICE STEVENS delivered the opinion of the Court.

. . . .

This case arises out of a dispute between parties to a multiemployer collective bargaining agreement. The plaintiff unions allege that, in violation of the antitrust laws, the multiemployer association and its members coerced certain third parties, as well as some of the association's members, to enter into business relationships with nonunion firms. This coercion, according to the complaint, adversely affected the trade of certain unionized firms and thereby restrained the business activities of the unions. The question presented is whether the complaint sufficiently alleges that the unions have been "injured in [their] business or property by reason of anything forbidden in the antitrust laws" and may therefore recover treble damages under § 4 of the Clayton Act. 15 U.S.C. § 15. . . .

I

The two named plaintiffs (the "Union") — the California State Council of Carpenters and the Carpenters 46 Northern Counties Conference Board — are affiliated with the United Brotherhood of Carpenters and Joiners of America, AFL-CIO. The plaintiffs represent more than 50,000 individuals employed by the defendants in the carpentry, drywall, piledriving, and related industries throughout the state of California. The Union's complaint is filed as a class action on behalf of numerous affiliated local unions and district councils. The defendants are Associated General Contractors of California, Inc. ("Associated"), a membership corporation composed of various building and construction contractors, approximately 250 members of Associated who are identified by name in an exhibit attached to the complaint, and 1,000 unidentified co-conspirators.

The Union and Associated, and their respective predecessors, have been parties to collective bargaining agreements governing the terms and conditions of employment in construction-related industries in California for over 25 years. The wages and other benefits paid pursuant to these agreements amount to more than $750,000,000 per year. In addition, approximately 3,000 contractors who are not members of Associated have entered into separate "memorandum agreements" with the Union, which bind them to the terms of the master collective bargaining agreements between the Union and Associated. The amended complaint does not state the number of nonsignatory employers or the number of nonunion employees who are active in the relevant market.

. . . Paragraph 23 [of the amended complaint] alleges generally that the defendants conspired to abrogate and weaken the collective bargaining relationship between the Union and the signatory employers. . . . The most specific allegations relate to the labor relations between the parties. The complaint's description of actions affecting nonparties is both brief and vague. It is alleged that defendants:

". . . .

(3) Advocated, encouraged, induced, and aided nonmembers of defendant Associated General Contractors of California, Inc. to refuse to enter into collective bargaining relationships with plaintiffs and each of them;

(4) Advocated, encouraged, induced, *coerced*, aided and encouraged owners of land and other letters of construction contracts to hire contractors and subcontractors who are not signatories to collective bargaining agreements with plaintiffs and each of them;

(5) Advocated, induced, *coerced*, encouraged, and aided members of Associated General Contractors of California, Inc., non-members of Associated General Contractors of California, Inc., and 'memorandum contractors' to enter into subcontracting agreements with subcontractors who are not signatories to any collective bargaining agreements with plaintiffs and each of them; (emphasis added)."

. . . .

II

. . . .

We first note that the Union's most specific claims of injury involve matters that are not subject to review under the antitrust laws. The amended complaint alleges that the defendants have breached their collective bargaining agreements in various ways, and that they have manipulated their corporate names and corporate status in order to divert business to nonunion divisions or firms that they actually control. Such deceptive diversion of business to the nonunion portion of a so-called "double-breasted" operation might constitute a breach of contract, an unfair labor practice, or perhaps even a common-law fraud or deceit, but in the context of the bargaining relationship between the parties to this litigation, such activities are plainly not subject to review under the federal antitrust laws. Similarly, the charge that the defendants "advocated, encouraged, induced, and aided nonmembers . . . to refuse to enter into collective bargaining relationships" with the Union (23(3)) does not describe an antitrust violation.

The Union's antitrust claims arise from alleged restraints caused by defendants in the market for construction contracting and subcontracting. The complaint alleges that defendants "coerced" two classes of persons: (1) landowners and others who let construction contracts, i.e. the defendants' customers and potential customers; and (2) general contractors, i.e. defendants' competitors and defendants themselves. Coercion against the members of both classes was designed to induce them to give some of their business — but not necessarily all of it — to nonunion firms. Although the pleading does not allege that the coercive conduct increased the aggregate share of nonunion firms in the market, it does allege that defendants' activities weakened and restrained the trade "of certain contractors." . . . Thus, particular victims of coercion may have diverted particular contracts to nonunion firms and thereby caused certain unionized subcontractors to lose some business. . . .

III

. . . A literal reading of the statute is broad enough to encompass every harm that can be attributed directly or indirectly to the consequences of an antitrust violation. Some of our prior cases have paraphrased the statute in an equally expansive way. But before we hold that the statute is as broad as its words suggest, we must consider whether Congress intended such an open-ended meaning. . . .

As this Court has observed, the lower federal courts have been "virtually unanimous in concluding that Congress did not intend the antitrust laws to provide a remedy in damages for all injuries that might conceivably be traced to an antitrust violation." . . .

It is plain, therefore, that the question whether the Union may recover for the injury it allegedly suffered by reason of the defendants' coercion against certain third parties cannot be answered simply by reference to the broad language of § 4. Instead, as was required in common-law damages litigation in 1890, the question requires us to evaluate the plaintiff's harm, the alleged wrongdoing by the defendants, and the relationship between them.[20]

IV

. . . .

The factors that favor judicial recognition of the Union's antitrust claim are easily stated. The complaint does allege a causal connection between an antitrust violation and harm to the Union and further alleges that the defendants intended to cause that harm. As we have indicated, however, the mere fact that the claim is literally encompassed by the Clayton Act does not end the inquiry. We are also satisfied that an allegation of improper motive, although it may support a plaintiff's damages claim under § 4, is not a panacea that will enable any complaint to withstand a motion to dismiss. Indeed, in *McCready*, we specifically held: "The availability of the § 4 remedy to some person who claims its benefit is not a question of the specific intent of the conspirators."

A number of other factors may be controlling. In this case it is appropriate to focus on the nature of the plaintiff's alleged injury. As the legislative history shows, the Sherman Act was enacted to assure customers the benefits of price competition, and our prior cases have emphasized the central interest in protecting the economic freedom of participants in the relevant market. Last Term in *Blue Shield of Virginia v. McCready*, we identified the relevance of this central policy to a determination of the plaintiff's right to maintain an action under § 4. McCready alleged that she was a consumer of psychotherapeutic services and that she had been injured by the defendants' conspiracy to restrain competition in the market for such services. The Court stressed the fact that "McCready's injury was of a type that Congress sought to redress in providing a private remedy for violations of the antitrust laws." . . . After noting that her injury "was inextricably intertwined with the injury the conspirators sought to inflict on psychologists and the psychotherapy market," . . . the Court concluded that such an injury "falls squarely within the area of congressional concern."

In this case, however, the Union was neither a consumer nor a competitor in the market in which trade was restrained.[21]

It is not clear whether the Union's interests would be served or disserved by enhanced competition in the market. As a general matter, a union's primary goal is to enhance the earnings and improve the working conditions of its membership; that goal is not necessarily served, and indeed may actually be harmed, by uninhibited competition among employers striving to reduce costs in order to obtain a competitive advantage over their rivals. At common law — as well as in the early

---

[20] [FN 31] The label "antitrust standing" has traditionally been applied to some of the elements of this inquiry. As commentators have observed, the focus of the doctrine of "antitrust standing" is somewhat different from that of standing as a constitutional doctrine. Harm to the antitrust plaintiff is sufficient to satisfy the constitutional standing requirement of injury in fact, but the court must make a further determination whether the plaintiff is a proper party to bring a private antitrust action.

[21] [FN 40] Moreover, it has not even alleged any marketwide restraint of trade. The allegedly unlawful conduct involves predatory behavior directed at "certain" parties, rather than a claim that output has been curtailed or prices enhanced throughout an entire competitive market.

days of administration of the federal antitrust laws — the collective activities of labor unions were regarded as a form of conspiracy in restraint of trade. Federal policy has since developed not only a broad labor exemption from the antitrust laws, but also a separate body of labor law specifically designed to protect and encourage the organizational and representational activities of labor unions. Set against this background, a union, in its capacity as bargaining representative, will frequently not be part of the class the Sherman Act was designed to protect, especially in disputes with employers with whom it bargains. In each case its alleged injury must be analyzed to determine whether it is of the type that the antitrust statute was intended to forestall. . . . In this case, particularly in light of the longstanding collective bargaining relationship between the parties, the Union's labor-market interests seem to predominate, and the *Brunswick* test is not satisfied.

An additional factor is the directness or indirectness of the asserted injury. In this case, the chain of causation between the Union's injury and the alleged restraint in the market for construction subcontracts contains several somewhat vaguely defined links. According to the complaint, defendants applied coercion against certain landowners and other contracting parties in order to cause them to divert business from certain union contractors to nonunion contractors. As a result, the Union's complaint alleges, the Union suffered unspecified injuries in its "business activities." It is obvious that any such injuries were only an indirect result of whatever harm may have been suffered by "certain" construction contractors and subcontractors.

If either these firms, or the immediate victims of coercion by defendants, have been injured by an antitrust violation, their injuries would be direct and, as we held in *McCready, supra,* they would have a right to maintain their own treble damages actions against the defendants. An action on their behalf would encounter none of the conceptual difficulties that encumber the Union's claim. The existence of an identifiable class of persons whose self-interest would normally motivate them to vindicate the public interest in antitrust enforcement diminishes the justification for allowing a more remote party such as the Union to perform the office of a private attorney general. Denying the Union a remedy on the basis of its allegations in this case is not likely to leave a significant antitrust violation undetected or unremedied.

Partly because it is indirect, and partly because the alleged effects on the Union may have been produced by independent factors, the Union's damages claim is also highly speculative. There is, for example, no allegation that any collective bargaining agreement was terminated as a result of the coercion, no allegation that the aggregate share of the contracting market controlled by union firms has diminished, no allegation that the number of employed union members has declined, and no allegation that the Union's revenues in the form of dues or initiation fees have decreased. Moreover, although coercion against certain firms is alleged, there is no assertion that any such firm was prevented from doing business with any union firms or that any firm or group of firms was subjected to a complete boycott. Other than the alleged injuries flowing from breaches of the collective bargaining agreements — injuries that would be remediable under other laws — nothing but speculation informs the Union's claim of injury by reason of the alleged unlawful coercion. Yet, as we have recently reiterated, it is appropriate for § 4 purposes "to consider whether a claim rests at bottom on some abstract conception or speculative measure of harm."

The indirectness of the alleged injury also implicates the strong interest, identified in our prior cases, in keeping the scope of complex antitrust trials within judicially manageable limits. These cases have stressed the importance of avoiding either the risk of duplicate recoveries on the one hand, or the danger of complex apportionment of damages on the other. . . .

The same concerns should guide us in determining whether the Union is a proper plaintiff under § 4 of the Clayton Act. . . . In this case, if the Union's complaint asserts a claim for damages under § 4, the District Court would face problems of identifying damages and apportioning them among directly victimized contractors and subcontractors and indirectly affected employees and union entities. It would be necessary to determine to what extent the coerced firms diverted business away from union subcontractors, and then to what extent those subcontractors absorbed the damage to their businesses or passed it on to employees by reducing the workforce or cutting hours or wages. In turn it would be necessary to ascertain the extent to which the affected employees absorbed their losses and continued to pay union dues.

We conclude, therefore, that the Union's allegations of consequential harm resulting from a violation of the antitrust laws, although buttressed by an allegation of intent to harm the Union, are insufficient as a matter of law. Other relevant factors — the nature of the Union's injury, the tenuous and speculative character of the relationship between the alleged antitrust violation and the Union's alleged injury, the potential for duplicative recovery or complex apportionment of damages, and the existence of more direct victims of the alleged conspiracy — weigh heavily against judicial enforcement of the Union's antitrust claim. Accordingly, we hold that, based on the allegations of this complaint, the District Court was correct in concluding that the Union is not a person injured by reason of a violation of the antitrust laws within the meaning of § 4 of the Clayton Act.

The judgment of the Court of Appeals is Reversed.

[Only JUSTICE MARSHALL dissented.]

NOTES AND QUESTIONS

1. On the issue of standing, should courts distinguish between actions alleging violations of Section 1 of the Sherman Act and those alleging violations of Section 7 of the Clayton Act? What are the important differences?

Does Justice Stevens' opinion in *Associated General Contractors* further limit the scope of standing beyond the two-pronged "remoteness" inquiry articulated in *McCready*: (1) the physical and economic nexus between the antitrust violation and injury; and (2) the relationship of the injury and the intended scope of the statutes' coverage? Is the answer that *Associated General Contractors* limits Section 4 standing to consumers or competitors?

2. Does an employee who was discharged or disciplined because he refused to join in an antitrust violation have standing to sue his employer under Section 4? The courts of appeal are divided. While the Supreme Court has not explicitly decided this issue, *Associated General Contractors* may have signaled implicitly its resolution of this question. Subsequently, the Court denied review of the Seventh Circuit's opinion in *Bichan v. Chemetron Corp.*, 460 U.S. 1016, 681 F.2d 514 (7th Cir. 1982) (where the Seventh Circuit held that a discharged executive who refused to comply with his employer's illegal anticompetitive activities did not suffer "antitrust injury" and lacked standing under Section 4). On the same day the Court vacated the judgment of the Ninth Circuit in *Ostrofe v. H.S. Crocker Co.*, 670 F.2d 1378 (9th Cir. 1982) (where the Ninth Circuit had held that discharged employee had standing).

On remand after the Supreme Court decision in *Associated General*, the Ninth Circuit held that the discharged employee in *Ostrofe v. H.S. Crocker Co.* had standing to bring a treble damage claim against the employer under Section 4. Because the discharged employee was the victim of an intentional boycott, which resulted in the elimination of competition in a specific market, the court reasoned that the discharge was an "integral and inextricable" means of achieving the illegal scheme. 740 F.2d 739 (9th Cir. 1984). Other circuits have been less generous in granting standing.

3. In *McCready*, the Supreme Court treated the exclusion in Blue Shield's insurance policy as a concerted refusal to deal aimed at psychologists. For that reason, the standing of insured McCready, who was not the intended "target" of the conspiracy, gave the Court some pause. But why didn't the Court simply treat this as a price-fixing case? Hadn't the defendants agreed to reduce output — the amount of coverage to be provided by the policy — and wasn't Ms. McCready (or her employer) a direct purchaser of the policy? Direct purchasers of a cartelized product have virtually undisputed standing under the antitrust laws.

The answer is probably that the codefendants — Blue Shield and the Neuropsychiatric Society of Virginia — were not competitors. Suppose, however, that the Neuropsychiatric Society's motive in entering the agreement was to weaken the competitive position of psychologists; Blue Shield, on the other hand, was not particularly interested in competition between psychologists and psychiatrists but rather wanted to reduce the amount of coverage under its insurance policy. Is it clear that the case should be treated as a concerted refusal, and not as price fixing?

4. In *McCready*, the Court reiterated two types of limitations on treble damages: the denial of standing to prevent duplicative recovery and denial of standing because injuries are too remote from an antitrust violation. The distinction between these two Section 4 inquiries is evident when you compare *McCready* with *Illinois Brick, supra*.

[B] Parens Patriae

In *Hawaii v. Standard Oil Co. of Cal.*, 405 U.S. 251 (1972), the Supreme Court denied states the right to sue in their sovereign capacity as "parens patriae" for treble damages for injuries to their general economy under Section 4 of the Clayton Act. The Court concluded that the states could sue for injunctive relief as parens patriae, but that they did not have a cause of action in that capacity for treble damages. *See also Georgia v. Pennsylvania R.R.*, 324 U.S. 439 (1945).

In 1976, Congress passed the Hart-Scott-Rodino Antitrust Improvement Act, Pub. L. No. 94-435 (Sept. 30, 1976), which permits states, through their attorneys general, to sue in their parens patriae capacity for treble damages for "any violation of the Sherman Act." With this addition, parens patriae is an alternative to class action in situations where there are many individual victims, each of whom has sustained only modest monetary injury.

The monetary relief under parens patriae is threefold actual damages, excluding any damages that duplicate "amounts which have been awarded for the same injury." This provision is designed to prevent multiple liability. In addition, any state citizen who wishes to exclude her claim from the suit may opt out under Section 4C(b)(2), as is the case under a Rule 23(b)(3) class action.

Further limitations permit states to sue only on behalf of injured consumers, not businesses. Section 4G(3) specifically excludes partnerships and proprietor-ships from the "natural persons" definition.

In the first interpretation of the Hart-Scott-Rodino Amendments to come before the Court, the Supreme Court held in *Illinois Brick* that the parens patriae amendments did not create a new claim for relief. Therefore, if the consumer lacked an actionable claim under Section 4 because it was not a "direct purchaser," then the state attorney general also failed to state a claim when suing on behalf of the indirect consumer. In drawing the distinction between standing to sue and an actionable claim, the Court concluded that:

> Congress made clear, however, that this legislation did not alter the definition of which overcharged persons were injured within the meaning of § 4. It simply created a new procedural device — *parens patriae* actions by States on behalf of their citizens — to enforce existing rights of recovery under § 4. The House Report quoted above states that the *parens patriae* provision "creates no new substantive liability"; the relevant language of the newly enacted § 4C (a) of the Clayton Act tracks that of existing § 4, showing that it was intended only as "an alternative means . . . for the vindication of existing substantive claims." H. R. Rep. No. 94-499, *supra*, at 9. "The establishment of an alternative remedy does not increase any defendant's liability." *Ibid.* Representative Rodino himself acknowledged in the remarks cited above that this legislation did not create a right of recovery for consumers where one did not already exist.

431 U.S. 720, 734 n.14 (1977).

In the *Microsoft* litigation, discussed in Chapters 5 and 6, Microsoft sought to dismiss the equitable relief claims of a group of nine states that had become part of the consolidated litigation in 1998 but decided not to settle with Microsoft in 2001, as nine other states and the Department of Justice had. Microsoft argued that dismissal was warranted because the states could not define a "state-specific" antitrust injury. Judge Kollar-Kotelly invited the Department of Justice to deliver an amicus curiae brief on the issue. The brief stated that Microsoft's motion to dismiss was not mandated by either existing precedent or previous practice.

Although the agency stated that only the United States had the right to seek injunctive relief in a sovereign, law enforcement capacity, the states did have the "quasi-sovereign" right to seek monetary and injunctive relief in order to protect the economic well-being of their citizens. The states thus occupied the position of private parties when they sought relief under Section 16 of the Clayton Act. *See Memorandum Amicus Curiae of the United States Regarding Microsoft Corporation's Motion for Dismissal of the Non-Settling States' Demand for Equitable Relief, available at* www.usdoj.gov/atr/cases/f10900/10980.htm. Eventually, the district court denied Microsoft's motion to dismiss.

[C]   Advisory Opinions and Clearances Procedure

Upon request, both the Department of Justice and the FTC will review business conduct and give their opinions as to the legality of specific practices. The opinions are given in the form of statements regarding present enforcement intentions. The Federal Trade Commission will issue an "advisory opinion," while the Department of Justice will review the conduct through a "business review letter." Technically, the Department has no authority to give an advisory opinion. The submission of hypothetical questions will not result in a review by either agency.

Neither agency is legally bound by the issued opinion because both lack general authority to immunize antitrust conduct. Generally, the agencies reserve the option to commence enforcement proceedings at any time. If either agency decides to proceed against the firm that relied upon the advisory opinion or clearance, generally the firm, in the agency's discretion, will be given the opportunity to discontinue its practice before a proceeding will be instituted. *See* 16 C.F.R. § 1.3 (2007); 28 C.F.R. § 50.6 (2007). However, "[a]s to a stated present intention not to bring an action . . . the Division has never exercised its right to bring a criminal action where there has been full and true disclosure at the time of presenting the request." 28 C.F.R. § 50.6(9) (2007).

Both agencies' procedures require the submission of accurate and full information before the advisory opinion or business review letter will issue and before there can be reliance on the government's enforcement intentions. Supplemental data may also be required.

Until 1979, the FTC's advisory opinion program was limited to issuance of opinions on a firm's "proposed" course of action. The rules were amended in 1979 to include opinions concerning a firm's ongoing practices. The Department's business review clearance procedure is limited to reviewing "proposed business conduct." 28 C.F.R. § 50.6 (2007). The Commission rules state that the Commission "will not proceed against the requesting party with respect to any action taken in good faith reliance upon the Commission's advice . . . where all the relevant facts were fully, completely, and accurately presented . . . and where such action was promptly discontinued upon notification of rescission." 16 C.F.R. § 1.3 (2007). The Department's procedures are not as specific. 28 C.F.R. § 50.6(8) (2007). The FTC advisory opinions are published on a regular basis. 16 C.F.R. § 1.4 (2007).

It should be noted that the approval or clearance of a firm's conduct by one agency does not preclude enforcement action by the other. Nor does it prohibit suit by a private party challenging the conduct. Courts, likewise, are not bound by agencies' procedure or rulings, though weight may be given to the agencies' interpretations.

From time to time, both agencies issue specific enforcement guidelines, such as the recent merger guidelines discussed in Chapter 7. In addition, the FTC issues industry guidelines (sometimes referred to as trade practice rules) to regulate the practice of certain industries; noncompliance may result in the Commission bringing "corrective action." 16 C.F.R. § 1.5 (2007).

[D] Settlement

As would be expected, a large percentage (70–88%) of antitrust cases are settled. *See* S. Salop & L. White, *Private Antitrust Litigation: An Introduction and Framework, in* PRIVATE ANTITRUST LITIGATION 10–11 (L. White ed., 1988). Both the Antitrust Division and the FTC have established procedures for settlement of cases. The Antitrust Division's procedure permits entry of a consent decree following a settlement, while the FTC has authority to enter into a consent order. *See, e.g.,* 16 C.F.R. § 2.31 (1993). These procedures often represent an efficient means for management of limited litigation resources and the termination of the lawsuit.

Questions have been raised whether interested third parties can intervene under Rule 24 of the Federal Rules of Civil Procedure when a government suit is in the process of settlement. Unless the intervenor can demonstrate inadequate representation, bad faith, or malfeasance by government counsel, courts generally have not been inclined to permit intervention during the consent process. *Sam Fox Pub'g Co. v. United States*, 366 U.S. 683 (1961). The exception came in 1967 when the Supreme Court in *Cascade Nat. Gas Corp. v. El Paso Natural Gas Co.*, 386 U.S. 129 (1967), permitted intervention at the settlement stage after the case had been litigated and won by the government. In *Cascade Gas*, the Department settled for less than all the relief claimed and the Court apparently concluded that by settling for less than that demonstrated by the record, the Department "knuckled under to El Paso and [fell] far short of representing" the interest of the intervenor. Subsequent cases have narrowly interpreted *Cascade Gas* and have generally followed the rule established in *Sam Fox*, with the result that intervention is denied to third parties.

The issue of intervention has been less problematic since 1974. In that year, Congress amended the Clayton Act to require the Department to give public notice of proposed settlements 60 days prior to the entry of the consent decree. Antitrust Procedure and Penalties Act of 1974, 15 U.S.C. § 16(b)–(h) (1988) (the Tunney Act). *See also* 28 C.F.R. § 50.13 (1992). During the 60-day public comment period, interested persons are invited to submit comments. The Department is required also to file a "competitive impact statement" with the court. 15 U.S.C. § 16(b) (1988).

The 1974 amendments permit the reviewing court to enter the consent decree as a judgment only if the court finds that the decree is in the "public interest." This determination may require a hearing and testimony. In considering whether a consent judgment should enter, based on a finding of public interest,

> the court may consider — 1) the competitive impact of such judgment, including termination of alleged violations, provisions for enforcement and modification, duration of relief sought, anticipated effects of alternative remedies actually considered, and any other considerations bearing upon the adequacy of such judgment; 2) the impact of such entry of such judgment upon the public generally and individuals alleging specific injury from the violations set forth in the complaint, including consideration of the public benefit, if any, to be derived from a determination of the issues at trial.

Section 5(e) of Clayton Act, 15 U.S.C. § 16(e).

In most instances, the court's determination that a proposed consent decree is in the public interest is routine, and the court's judgment reaches that conclusion in a single sentence. Occasionally, however, where the case is complex and many interests are likely to be affected by the proposed consent decree, the public interest analysis is complex and extensive. For example, in examining the consent decree under which American Telephone and Telegraph Co. divested itself of many of its subsidiaries, the district court concluded that "Congress wanted the courts to act as an independent check on the terms of decrees negotiated by the Department of Justice." *United States v. AT&T*, 552 F. Supp. 131, 149 (D.D.C. 1982), *aff'd sub nom. Maryland v. United States*, 460 U.S. 1001 (1983). For that reason, the court concluded, it must analyze the effects on competition of each element in the proposed consent decree. The court noted, however, that it would approve a proposed decree "even if it falls short of the remedy the court would impose on its own, so long as it falls within the range of acceptability or is 'within the reaches of the public interest.' " *Id.* at 51. Having said that, the court went on to identify 10 modifications that must be made in the decree before it would win judicial approval.

More recently, District Court Judge Stanley Sporkin rejected the government-*Microsoft* consent decree in 1995 as not in the public interest. But the United States Court of Appeals for the District of Columbia reversed the decision as straying too far outside the boundaries of review set forth in the Tunney Act. In reversing, the court said:

> At the heart of this case, then, is the proper scope of the district court's inquiry into the "public interest." Is the district judge entitled to seize hold of the matter — the investigation into the putative defendant's business practices — and decide for himself the appropriate combined response of the executive and judicial branches to those practices? With respect to the specific allegations in the government's complaint, may the court interpose its own views of the appropriate remedy over those the government seeks as a part of its overall settlement? To be sure, Congress, in passing the Tunney Act, intended to prevent "judicial rubber stamping" of the Justice Department's proposed consent decree. . . . The Court was to "make an independent determination as to whether or not entry of a proposed consent decree [was] in the public interest."

. . . .

Although the language of section 16(e) is not precise, we think the government is correct in contending that section 16(e)(1)'s reference to the alleged violations suggests that Congress did not mean for a district judge to construct his own hypothetical case and then evaluate the decree against that case. Moreover, in section 16(e)(2), the court is authorized to consider "the public benefit . . . of the determination of the issues at trial." Putting aside the perplexing question of how the district judge could insure a trial if the government did not wish one, "the issues" referred to must be those formulated in the complaint. Congress surely did not contemplate that the district judge would, by reformulating the issues, effectively redraft the complaint himself. We therefore dismiss the claim that the last line in section 16(e)(1), the catchall clause allowing the district court to entertain "any other considerations bearing upon the adequacy of such judgment," authorizes the wide-ranging inquiry the district court wished to conduct in this case. That language recognizes, inter alia, that a consent decree might well do unexpected harm to persons other than those "alleging specific injury from the violations set forth in the complaint." 15 U.S.C. § 16(e)(2). And the district court might ponder those sort of concerns in determining whether to enter the judgment.

To be sure, the Act also authorizes the district judge to "take testimony of Government officials . . . as the court may deem appropriate." 15 U.S.C. § 16(f)(1) (1988). We do not read this language, however, to authorize the district judge to seek the kind of information concerning the government's investigation and settlement negotiations that he wished to obtain here. Even when a court is explicitly authorized to review government action under the Administrative Procedure Act, "there must be a strong showing of bad faith or improper behavior" before the court may "inquir[e] into the mental processes of administrative decisionmakers." Citizens to Preserve Overton Park, Inc. v. Volpe, 401 U.S. 402, 420 (1971). Here, the district court is not empowered to review the actions or behavior of the Department of Justice; the court is only authorized to review the decree itself. It is unnecessary to consider whether the district court might have broader authority to inquire into the Department's deliberations, even though not authorized to "review" the Department's action, if there were a credible showing of bad faith. . . . There is no such claim here.

The district court was troubled that if its review were limited to the market and practices within that market against which the complaint was directed, the government could, by narrow drafting, artificially limit the court's review under the Tunney Act. . . . We think, with all due respect, that the district court put the cart before the horse. The court's authority to review the decree depends entirely on the government's exercising its prosecutorial discretion by bringing a case in the first place.

United States v. Microsoft, 56 F.3d 1448, 1458–1460 (D.C. Cir. 1995).

The Court of Appeals also reversed the district court's finding of an inadequate remedy and an inadequate compliance mechanism in the consent decree. The Court of Appeals held that short of making a "mockery of judicial power," a decree should be respected as an aspect of prosecutorial discretion.

> [W]hen the government is challenged for not bringing as extensive an action as it might, a district judge must be careful not to exceed his or her constitutional role. A decree, even entered as a pretrial settlement, is a judicial act, and therefore the district judge is not obliged to accept one that, on its face and even after government explanation, appears to make a mockery of judicial power. Short of that eventuality, the Tunney Act cannot be interpreted as an authorization for a district judge to assume the role of Attorney General.

56 F.3d 1448, 1462.

Either party to the consent decree may seek modification of the consent decree once entered. The party seeking a change must make a "clear showing of grievous wrong evoked by new and unforeseen conditions." *United States v. Swift & Co.*, 286 U.S. 106, 119 (1932). Whether the burden is less on the government when seeking a modification is unclear. *Chrysler Corp. v. United States*, 316 U.S. 556 (1942); *Ford Motor Co. v. United States*, 335 U.S. 303 (1948). Generally, third parties not bound by the consent decree cannot seek to enforce the decree or seek damages under it even though they are beneficiaries of the decree.

[E] Preclusion Effects of a Prior Judgment on Subsequent Private Suits

Under certain circumstances, a final consent judgment or decree entered in a suit brought by the government can be used as prima facie evidence of a violation in a subsequent suit. Section 5(a) of the Clayton Act states:

> (a) A final judgment or decree . . . rendered in any civil or criminal proceeding brought by or on behalf of the United States under the antitrust laws to the effect that a defendant has violated said laws shall be prima facie evidence against such defendant in any action or proceeding brought by any other party against such defendant under said laws as to all matters respecting which said judgment or decree would be an estoppel as between the parties thereto: *Provided*, that this section shall not apply to consent judgments or decrees entered before any testimony has been taken. Nothing contained in this section shall be construed to impose any limitation on the application of collateral estoppel, except that, in any action or proceeding brought under the antitrust laws, collateral estoppel effect shall not be given to any finding made by the Federal Trade Commission under the antitrust laws or under section 5 of the Federal Trade Commission Act which could give rise to a claim for relief under the antitrust laws.

15 U.S.C. § 16(a) (1988). The statute was designed to ease a private plaintiff's burden of proof and to encourage the use of consent judgments or decrees in the disposition of government suits. In light of this provision, precise language in a judgment is necessary so that it can be accurately determined what issues were adjudged in the prior government suit. The problem of ambiguity is frequently present when the jury returns a general verdict.

Section 5(a) specifically states that the prima facie rule does *not* apply if the consent judgment or decree was entered before testimony was taken. This is designed to encourage settlement. In this regard, the entry of a consent decree prior to testimony has the same subsequent effect as a nolo contendere plea in a prior criminal case. *See* Fed. R. Crim. P. 11(b); *Burbank v. General Elec. Co.*, 329 F.2d 825, 834–836 (9th Cir. 1964). In neither situation is the earlier determination prima facie evidence in the subsequent private suit.

The case law has addressed several issues regarding the application of Section 5(a). First, does a consent order or agreement entered by the FTC come within Section 5(a)? The difficulty is presented because Section 5(a) speaks in terms of a proceeding "brought by . . . the United States under the antitrust laws." Frequently courts have held that the FTC Act (§ 5) is not an "antitrust law." *See, e.g.*, *Wendkos v. ABC Consol. Corp.*, 379 F. Supp. 15, 20 (E.D. Pa. 1974). But what if the FTC is proceeding to enforce the Clayton Act? *Purex Corp. v. Procter & Gamble Co.*, 453 F.2d 288 (9th Cir. 1971), *cert. denied*, 405 U.S. 1065 (1972) (holding that an order regarding Section 7 of the Clayton Act came within Section 5(a)).

Second, although Section 5(a) is rather clear that a consent judgment shall not be prima facie evidence in a second suit if entered before testimony, this provision has not been uniformly applied to consent decrees entered after testimony has commenced. *See* 2 P. Areeda & H. Hovenkamp, Antitrust Law ¶ 337 (4th ed. 2014).

As originally written, Section 5(a)'s prima facie rule, from an evidence standpoint, meant that once plaintiff in the second suit introduced the prior consent judgment, the first judgment was not considered conclusive but rather could be rebutted by the record evidence. This presumption, usable in the second suit, is available, however, "only on the basis of a judgment 'to the effect that a defendant has violated [the antitrust] laws.' " *United States v. AT&T*, 552 F. Supp. 131, 211 (D.D.C. 1982). Thus, the consent judgment must include a finding or admission that defendant violated the antitrust laws before the prima facie rule is applicable.

Today the value of Section 5(a) has been considerably mitigated by the doctrine of nonmutual, or offensive, collateral estoppel. In *Parklane Hosiery Co. v. Shore*, 439 U.S. 322 (1979), the Supreme Court held that a plaintiff, not a party to the first suit, could offensively use collateral estoppel to bar the defendant from relitigating issues in the second suit that were decided against the defendant in the first suit. In 1980, Congress amended Section 5(a) to clarify the use of the collateral estoppel doctrine in subsequently related antitrust suits. The section now provides that the "prima facie" language of Section 5(a) is not a limitation on the application of collateral estoppel. *See also Aluminum Co. of Am. v. United States*, 302 U.S. 230 (1937); *Cromwell v. County of Sac*, 94 U.S. 351 (1877); *United States v. AT&T*, 524 F. Supp. 1336, 1353 n.70 (D.D.C. 1981). Does the 1980 Amendment imply that collateral estoppel effect can be given to a consent judgment or decree entered before testimony begins? The answer is probably no because *Parklane* requires both "final" and "actual" litigation of an issue before offensive collateral estoppel will apply.

On the subject of the preclusion effects of a prior judgment, consider whether a prior action based on a state antitrust claim, which results in a judgment in favor of the defendant, can be refiled under the federal antitrust statute. Should the doctrine of res judicata be invoked? Does it matter to the outcome that jurisdiction over federal antitrust claims is exclusively within the federal courts?

In *Marrese v. American Academy of Orthopedic Surgeons*, 470 U.S. 373 (1985), the Supreme Court held that it was error to fail to consider the state law's interpretation of the preclusive effect of the state judgment before foreclosing suit in federal court. On remand, the district court held that the federal antitrust claim is not precluded by the prior Illinois judgment. The court reasoned that the Sherman Act claim was exclusively within the jurisdiction of the federal court, that it could not have been decided by the state court, that Illinois had adopted the Restatement (Second) of Judgments and "would seemingly accept the rule of inapplicability of *res judicata* to exclusively federal suits."

Consider whether a class member who opts out of a class action may invoke a favorable decision to the class by claiming issue preclusion under *Parklane Hosiery* in a subsequent suit against the common defendant. *See Premier Elec. Constr. Co. v. National Elec. Contrs. Ass'n*, 814 F.2d 358 (7th Cir. 1987) (holding that class member who opts out of class may not benefit from favorable decision to class by invoking offensive collateral estoppel). Judge Easterbrook, writing for the Seventh Circuit in *Premier Electrical*, held that the issue of whether class members should be entitled to benefit from a favorable judgment, despite not being bound by an unfavorable judgment, was considered when Rule 23 was amended in 1966. "Under the revised rule, a class member must cast his lot at the beginning of the suit and all parties are bound, for good or ill, by the results. Someone who opted out could take his chances separately, but the separate suit would proceed as if the class action had never been filed." *Id.*

Judge Easterbrook opined that:

> An approach that asks how to hold down the costs of litigation given the existence of multiple suits is an ex post perspective on judicial economy. It is the wrong perspective when inquiring about the consequences of a legal rule. A decision to make preclusion available to those who opt out of a class influences *whether* there will be multiple suits. The more class members who opt out may benefit from preclusion, the more class members will opt out. Preclusion thus may increase the number of suits, undermining the economy the district court hoped to achieve. The effect of the legal rule may be the opposite of the effect of applying preclusion to a given case. To determine whether a rule is beneficial, a court must examine how that rule influences future behavior. The influence of a rule of preclusion cannot be known for sure, but we are not confident that there would be net benefits.

An example of an issue preclusion may be found in the Ninth Circuit's decision in *Reyn's Pasta Bella, LLC v. Visa USA, Inc.*, 442 F.3d 741 (9th Cir. 2006). In this case, the plaintiffs alleged that the defendants, including Visa USA, Mastercard International, and several banks, conspired to fix prices on credit and debit card transactions. The court explained that each credit or debit card purchase is:

> a chain of transactions among the merchant, who sells the goods to the acquiring bank, who sells the goods to the issuing bank, who sells the goods

to the consumer. At each step, the buyer must purchase the goods at a price lower than its selling price — or make no profit.

Thus, a fixed high interchange rate claimed by the plaintiffs would lower the amount realized by the retailer on a sale of a good purchased with a debit or credit card. *Id.* at 744.

The defendants argued that because the plaintiffs were members of a class in an earlier action in which the plaintiffs sought antitrust recovery for the harm caused by high interchange rates obtained by the defendants in the present case by tying their debit cards to their credit cards, they were precluded from bringing the present claim. *Id.* at 745. The earlier case was ultimately settled, and Visa, Mastercard, and the bank defendants were released from "all antitrust liability arising out of conduct, prior to January 1, 2004, that is related to the claims asserted in the [previous case]." *Id.*

In approving the settlement in the earlier case, the court in that case "expressly determined that plaintiffs' price fixing claims were released." *Id.* Thus, the Ninth Circuit had to consider whether the plaintiffs' claims were barred by issue preclusion. It held that the three requirements of issue preclusion — whether "(1) the issue necessarily decided at the previous proceeding is identical to the one which is sought to be relitigated; (2) the first proceeding ended with a final judgment on the merits; and (3) the party against whom collateral estoppel is asserted was a party or in privity with a party at the first proceeding" — had been met. *Id.* at 746. The release of defendants from liability on the claims presented by the plaintiffs in the present case was necessary to the earlier judgment because the issues underlying the claims related to the "scope, and . . . substantive and procedural fairness" of the settlement agreement and had to be resolved by the court before it could approve the settlement, together with any objections made by the plaintiffs in that class action, including the question of release. *Id.* The approval of the settlement agreement constituted a final judgment. *Id.* Finally, the plaintiffs were parties to the proceeding in which the settlement agreement was approved. *Id.* at 747. The court noted that the argument raised by the plaintiffs that a judgment-rendering court may not determine the preclusive effect of its judgment was inapplicable in this case, as the court was responding to the plaintiffs' objections in the earlier case. *Id.*

Even if issue preclusion did not apply, a federal court would be entitled to "release not only those claims alleged in the complaint, but also a claim 'based on the identical factual predicate as that underlying the claims in the settled class action.'" *Id.* at 748 (citing *Class Plaintiffs v. City of Seattle*, 955 F.2d 1268, 1287–1289 (9th Cir. 1992)) (quoting *TBK Partners, Ltd. v. Western Union Corp.*, 675 F.2d 456, 460 (2d Cir. 1982)). Both the claim in this case and the claims in the earlier case were based on the same factual predicate — injury caused by an increase in interchange rates, which was occasioned by the defendants' anticompetitive behavior. *Id.* at 748–749. That the plaintiffs in both cases focused on different anticompetitive activity causing the described injury was, in the court's opinion, irrelevant to the determination whether the claims in this case arose from an identical factual predicate as the claims in the earlier case.

Recently, some nonantitrust cases have considered the expansion of the finality of judgments through the doctrine of res judicata by entertaining a theory of "virtual representation" when there is no client privity between the parties. This novel theory has not found wide acceptance. *See generally In re Estate of Lange*, 383 A.2d 1130 (N.J. 1978). The courts largely have concluded that absent privity in the traditional sense or control over the earlier litigation, or an express or implied legal relationship under which the party is accountable to the nonparty, or acquiescence, a nonparty may not be bound by the results of an action on the theory that its interests were adequately represented in that action. *See Becherer v. Merrill Lynch, Pierce, Fenner and Smith Inc.*, 193 F.3d 415 (6th Cir. 1999) (en banc); *Tice v. American Airlines Inc.*, 162 F.3d 966 (7th Cir. 1998), *cert. denied*, 527 U.S. 1036 (1999). *But see Boston Scientific Corp. v. Schneider (Europe) AG*, 983 F. Supp. 245 (D. Mass. 1997), *appeal dismissed*, 152 F.3d 947 (Fed. Cir. 1998). In the *Becherer* case, for example, a divided en banc Sixth Circuit concluded that plaintiffs who had opted out of a settlement class in federal securities litigation, leading to the collapse of the settlement, were not precluded by a later nonclass judgment adverse to the remaining plaintiffs; therefore, they were not properly enjoined from a subsequent proceeding with a Florida state court.

On the constitutional principles governing the binding of nonparties, see *Martin v. Wilks*, 490 U.S. 755 (1989); *Hansberry v. Lee*, 311 U.S. 32 (1940).

In the *Microsoft* litigation, the Fourth Circuit ruled that the doctrine of collateral estoppel could not be used offensively by private plaintiffs to block Microsoft from relitigating in subsequent private suits the 350 factual findings made earlier in the government's suit against Microsoft. The court held that unless those factual findings were "critical and necessary" to the prior government judgment against Microsoft, collateral estoppel could not apply. Subsequent litigation could not be foreclosed if the earlier facts were merely "supportive of" the prior judgment, the court reasoned. The "necessary and essential" standard is central to the preclusive doctrine of collateral estoppel, the court observed, in order to give the defendant the full opportunity to have litigated those issues in the earlier litigation. *In re Microsoft Corp. Antitrust Litigation*, 355 F.3d 322 (4th Cir. 2004).

[F]   Antitrust Counterclaims

When a claim and a counterclaim raise common issues of law and fact, involve largely the same evidence, are logically related, and would implicate the principle of res judicata if pursued separately, the counterclaim is deemed "compulsory." Fed. R. Civ. P. 13(a). Defendants are barred from bringing compulsory counterclaims in subsequent actions if they fail to bring them in the original suit, unless they are protected under a recognized exception to the rule.

One such exception involves antitrust counterclaims in patent infringement litigation. In *Mercoid Corp. v. Mid-Continent Investment Co.*, 320 U.S. 661, 671 (1944), the Supreme Court stated that although the antitrust claim in question could have been asserted as a counterclaim in the original patent infringement proceeding, res judicata did not bar the original defendant from bringing it in a subsequent action. Thus, the Court held that the antitrust counterclaim in a patent infringement action was "permissive" under Rule 13(b) of the Federal Rules of Civil Procedure.

The Fifth Circuit revisited the issue in *Tank Insulation International, Inc. v. Insultherm, Inc.*, 104 F.3d 83 (5th Cir. 1997), where the court held that the *Mercoid* exception to Rule 13(a) still applies to antitrust claims that otherwise would fall within the category of compulsory counterclaims. The court could not distinguish *Mercoid* on its facts, following the Ninth Circuit's decision to apply the exception in *Hydranautics v. Filmtec Corp.*, 70 F.3d 533, 536–537 (9th Cir. 1995). In so doing, the court refused to limit *Mercoid* to cases involving identical facts, as suggested by commentators and other courts.

[G] Expert Testimony After *Daubert*

In *Daubert v. Merrell Dow Pharmaceuticals, Inc.*, 509 U.S. 579 (1993), the Supreme Court held that district courts must evaluate expert testimony for reliability as well as relevance. The five factors listed by the Court in *Daubert* have become part of the Federal Rules of Evidence:

(1) whether the expert's technique or theory can be or has been tested — that is, whether the expert's theory can be challenged in some objective sense, or whether it is instead simply a subjective, conclusory approach that cannot reasonably be assessed for reliability;

(2) whether the technique or theory has been subject to peer review and publication;

(3) the known or potential rate of error for the technique or theory when applied;

(4) the existence and maintenance of standards and controls; and

(5) whether the technique or theory has been generally accepted in the scientific community.

Fed. R. Evid. 702 advisory committee's note.

After *Daubert* was decided, it was unclear to what extent its holding applied to antitrust law. The plaintiffs in *Daubert* alleged that Bendectin caused birth defects in children whose mothers took the drug while pregnant. The nature of this evidence was scientific, which the Court distinguished from the "technical" or "other specialized knowledge" also mentioned in Federal Rule of Evidence 702. The Supreme Court seemed to imply that *Daubert* did not apply to anything other than "hard science."

This uncertainty was resolved in 1999, when the Supreme Court decided *Kumho Tire Co. v. Carmichael*, 526 U.S. 137 (1999). The Court held that the gatekeeping role of the district court applied to all expert testimony, scientific or otherwise. The following case provides an example of the way courts have applied *Daubert* to antitrust law after *Kuhmo Tire*. For further discussion of this case, see Chapter 6.

CONCORD BOAT CORP. v. BRUNSWICK CORP.
207 F.3d 1039 (8th Cir.), *cert. denied*, 531 U.S. 979 (2000)

DIANA E. MURPHY, CIRCUIT JUDGE.

. . . During the course of the ten week trial, both parties called numerous witnesses and presented over 800 exhibits, including voluminous economic data, charts and graphs made in the course of business and for trial purposes, internal business memoranda, consultants' reports, deposition testimony, and much more. . . . Expert witnesses presented differing interpretations of stern drive engine market events and of Brunswick's conduct in that market.

The boat builders' primary evidence to establish Brunswick's antitrust liability was presented by their sole expert, Dr. Hall, a professor of economics at Stanford University. He testified that Brunswick had monopoly power in the stern drive market that enabled it to use its market share discount programs to impose a "tax" on boat builders and dealers who chose to purchase engines from other manufacturers. He defined the "tax" as the discount these purchasers gave up by not buying from Brunswick. He stated that Brunswick's program effectively required its competitors to charge substantially lower prices in order to convince customers to purchase from them and forgo the discount. Dr. Hall further testified that the discount programs, combined with the market power Brunswick acquired by purchasing Bayliner and Sea Ray, enabled Brunswick to capture 78% of the stern drive engine market. According to Dr. Hall, other manufacturers could not enter into stern drive engine manufacturing as a result of Brunswick's having such a high percentage of the market. He concluded that the discount programs were anticompetitive.

In support of the boat builders' damage claim, Dr. Hall relied on the Cournot model of economic theory that posits that a firm "maximizes its profits by assuming the observed output of other firms as a given, and then equating its own marginal cost and marginal revenue on that assumption." . . . Dr. Hall postulated that in a stern drive engine market that was competitive, Brunswick and some other firm would each maintain a 50% market share. Under this theory, any market share over 50% would be evidence of anticompetitive conduct on Brunswick's part. Since Brunswick at various points in time had garnered a market share as large as 78%, Dr. Hall concluded that it had engaged in anticompetitive conduct and that the boat builders had been overcharged at the moment Brunswick's market share surpassed the 50% threshold. . . .

A

Brunswick argues that Dr. Hall's expert opinion should have been excluded because it was contrary to undisputed record evidence and because it did not separate lawful from unlawful conduct. The district court recognized that

> the task Dr. Hall faced in analyzing this case was an enormous one. Notwithstanding the complex nature of the conduct at issue, Dr. Hall was required to construct a hypothetical market, a "but for" market, free of the

restraints and conduct alleged to be anticompetitive. The difficulty of such a task has long been recognized by courts in antitrust cases. . . .

Concord Boat Corp. v. Brunswick Corp., 21 F. Supp. 2d 923, 927 (E.D.Ark.1998). Despite the inherent difficulty of the task, counsel for the boat builders assured the district court before trial that Dr. Hall's model would reflect the reality of the market and would segregate any lawful acts and unrelated market events that might have contributed to Brunswick's market share from any anticompetitive conduct in order to enable the jury to assign damages only for illegal actions taken by Brunswick.

Counsel's assurances did not eliminate the need for a thorough analysis of the expert's economic model and his proffered opinion. Under Daubert the district court is to make a "preliminary assessment of whether the reasoning or methodology underlying the testimony is scientifically valid and of whether that reasoning or methodology properly can be applied to the facts in issue." Daubert, 509 U.S. at 592–93. Among the factors to consider is whether the " 'expert testimony proffered in the case is sufficiently tied to the facts of the case that it will aid the jury in resolving a factual dispute.' " Id. at 591. The Court referred to this requirement as "fit," meaning that the expert testimony must not only be based on reliable science but must also "fit" the particular facts of the case. See id.

In recent years the Supreme Court has put renewed emphasis on the importance of the "fit" of an expert's opinion to the data or facts in the case:

> [C]onclusions and methodology are not entirely distinct from one another. . . . [N]othing in either Daubert or the Federal Rules of Evidence requires a district court to admit opinion evidence that is connected to existing data only by the ipse dixit of the expert. A court may conclude that there is simply too great an analytic gap between the data and the opinion proffered.

General Elec. Co. v. Joiner, 522 U.S. 136, 146 (1997). A court must focus on the "reasonableness of using such an approach, along with [the expert's] particular method of analyzing the data thereby obtained, to draw a conclusion regarding the particular matter to which the expert testimony was directly relevant." Kumho Tire Co. v. Carmichael, 526 U.S. 137, 154, 119 S. Ct. 1167, 143 L. Ed. 2d 238 (1999) (emphasis in original).

The district court commented that because Brunswick had not challenged the Cournot model as a scientific theory, its "criticisms are reduced to complaints about how Dr. Hall applied the Cournot model to the facts of this case." Concord Boat Corp., 21 F. Supp. 2d at 934. If a party believes that an expert opinion has not considered all of the relevant facts, an objection to its admission is appropriate. See Kumho Tire Co., 526 U.S. at 154, 119 S. Ct. 1167; Joiner, 522 U.S. at 146, 118 S. Ct. 512. Even a theory that might meet certain Daubert factors, such as peer review and publication, testing, known or potential error rate, and general acceptance, should not be admitted if it does not apply to the specific facts of the case. See Kumho Tire Co., 526 U.S. at 154, 119 S. Ct. 1167; Joiner, 522 U.S. at 146, 118 S. Ct. 512.

Not all relevant circumstances were incorporated into the expert's method of analysis related to antitrust liability. Dr. Hall's opinion that Brunswick's discount programs imposed a tax on boat builders who chose to purchase engines from other manufacturers is not supported by the evidence that some boat builders chose to purchase 100% of their engines from Brunswick when they only needed to purchase 80% to qualify for the maximum discount. If Brunswick's market share had enabled it to charge supracompetitive high prices for its engines, presumably none of the boat builders would have chosen to purchase more than the minimum percentage required to receive the discount. There was other evidence that the boat builders were not unable to forgo Brunswick's discounts. For example, the boat builders wielded sufficient power over Brunswick to force it to scuttle its 1994 "Industry Growth Program," which would have raised the market share requirement to 95%, and their reaction led to a reduction in market share levels for the 1995 to 1997 model year program.

Dr. Hall used the Cournot model to construct a hypothetical market which was not grounded in the economic reality of the stern drive engine market, for it ignored inconvenient evidence. The basis for his model was a theoretical situation in which some other manufacturer's engine would be viewed as equal in quality to Brunswick's. In this hypothetical market, Dr. Hall assessed an overcharge on each engine sold at any point where Brunswick possessed over the 50% market share he deemed permissible. The overcharge was described as the difference between the actual price paid by the boat builders and the price that would theoretically have existed in a more competitive market. This approach was not affected by the actual price at which Brunswick's engines were sold since the overcharge percentage was applied any time its market share surpassed 50%. As Dr. Hall testified but his opinion did not reflect, Brunswick had achieved a 75% share in the mid 1980s, before it started the market share discounts and before it acquired Bayliner and Sea Ray.

The model also failed to account for market events that both sides agreed were not related to any anticompetitive conduct, such as the recall of OMC's Cobra engine and the problems associated with the Volvo/OMC merger. Dr. Hall admitted on cross examination that such facts could have been incorporated into his model but that he had not done so:

> I did not numerically attribute — in other words, it wasn't some specific adjustment that you'll see in my computer spread sheet saying, "Here's what I did because of OMC." And that's because of the framework that I was working in. Remember, I was stepping back and saying, "What's a reasonable benchmark for what a freer market would have been?". . . . Within that framework, there isn't a slot . . . [to get] down into the year by year details.
>
> . . . What I want to do is stand back and say what averaged over the years, with, of course, ups and downs.

Dr. Hall testified about OMC's recall of its Cobra engine and admitted that the "decline in OMC's market share and the corresponding increase during this time period of Brunswick's market share is very much related to the switch-over in engines previously supplied by OMC. . . ." The OMC/Volvo joint venture alone increased Brunswick's market share by as much as 10%. (Brunswick "picked up over 10 unearned market share points this past year due to the chaos created by the

Volvo/OMC joint venture announcement"). There was also evidence that the boat builders did not hesitate to switch to OMC and Volvo when they offered superior discounts.

Dr. Hall's expert opinion should not have been admitted because it did not incorporate all aspects of the economic reality of the stern drive engine market and because it did not separate lawful from unlawful conduct. Because of the deficiencies in the foundation of the opinion, the expert's resulting conclusions were "mere speculation." Virgin Atlantic Airways Ltd. v. British Airways PLC, 69 F. Supp. 2d 571, 580 (S.D.N.Y.1999) (summary judgment appropriate on Section 1 and 2 claims because "an expert's opinion is not a substitute for a plaintiff's obligation to provide evidence of facts that support the applicability of the expert's opinion to the case"). Expert testimony that is speculative is not competent proof and contributes "nothing to a 'legally sufficient evidentiary basis.' " Weisgram v. Marley Co., 528 U.S. 440, 120 S. Ct. 1011, 1015, 1020, 145 L. Ed. 2d 958 (2000) (citing Brooke Group Ltd. v. Brown & Williamson Tobacco Corp., 509 U.S. 209, 242 (1993)). "Expert testimony is useful as a guide to interpreting market facts, but it is not a substitute for them." Brooke Group Ltd., 509 U.S. at 242. . . .

An expert opinion cannot sustain a jury's verdict when it "is not supported by sufficient facts to validate it in the eyes of the law, or when indisputable record facts contradict or otherwise render the opinion unreasonable. . . ." Brooke Group Ltd., 509 U.S. at 242, 113 S. Ct. 2578. . . . An error in admission of evidence is reversible if the ruling affected a substantial right of a party. See Fed. R. Ev. 103(a). . . . Hall's expert opinion was the basis of the boat builders' damage case, and the jury clearly relied on his opinion in reaching its verdict because the damages it awarded to the individual boat builders were identical to the detailed figures Dr. Hall had calculated. It cannot be said that the verdict would have been the same without the expert testimony, and its admission affected Brunswick's substantial rights. Brunswick's motion for judgment should have therefore been granted.

NOTES AND QUESTIONS

1. A *Daubert* analysis performs two functions: It assesses both the reliability and the relevance of the proposed testimony. Courts talk about "fit" when discussing relevance — whether the methodology applies to the facts of a particular case. Does the Eighth Circuit maintain a clear distinction between reliability and relevance in its opinion?

2. A *Daubert* hearing should determine the admissibility of evidence but not its sufficiency. The judge acts as a gatekeeper, filtering unreliable or irrelevant information out before the jury hears it. Sufficiency is a matter for the trier of fact, unless the evidence is so insufficient that a directed verdict is proper. Does the Eighth Circuit address sufficiency in *Concord*?

3. What purpose does the new standard for expert testimony fulfill? Do *Daubert* hearings really help weed out "junk economics," or do they instead encourage a district court judge to make sufficiency determinations at too early a stage in litigation? While the impact of the new standard on the quality of expert testimony actually heard in trials is uncertain, the litigation costs added by *Daubert*

hearings are apparent. Some hearings turn into mini-trials, lasting two to six days and including opening and closing statements. See Andrew I. Gavil, *Defining Reliable Forensic Economics in the Post-Daubert/Kumho Tire Era: Case Studies from Antitrust*, 57 Wash. & Lee L. Rev. 831, 876–878 (2000) for an evaluation of courts' treatment of expert testimony after *Daubert* and *Kumho Tire.*

4. As the recent cases have suggested, parties have begun to argue for the application of *Daubert* in three distinctive pretrial settings: at summary judgment, at preliminary injunctions, and in class action certifications. *Compare Daubert v. Merrell Dow Pharmaceuticals, Inc.*, 509 U.S. 579, 583 (1993) (example of summary judgment), *with Scotts Co. v. United Indus. Corp.*, 315 F.3d 264 (4th Cir. 2002) (preliminary injunction application), *and In re St. Jude Med. Inc. Silzone Heart Valves Prods. Liab. Litig.*, MDL 01-1396, 2003 WL 1589527, at 11 17.14 (D. Minn. 2003) (class certification). Query whether *Daubert* was ever intended to cover the admissibility of expert testimony before trial or summary judgment where there are incomplete factual records and where the proceedings are not designed to resolve the merits. *See generally Wal-Mart Stores, Inc. v. Visa U.S.A. Inc.*, 280 F.3d 124 (2d Cir. 2001), *cert. denied*, 536 U.S. 917 (2002) (less exacting and less rigorous *Daubert* application at class certification stage); *In re Vitamins Antitrust Litigation*, 320 F. Supp. 2d 1 (D.D.C. 2004) (denying summary judgment motion on conspiracy claim when conspiracy seemed plausible); *R.J. Reynolds Tobacco Co. v. Premium Tobacco Stores, Inc.*, 2004-2 Trade Cas. (CCH) 74,491, 2004 U.S. Dist. LEXIS 13443 (N.D. Ill. July 16, 2004) (refusing to allow an expert's assessment of damages because other factors accounting for the plaintiff's performance were not considered); *U.S. Info. Sys., Inc. v. Int'l Bhd. of Elec. Workers Local Union No. 3, AFL-CIO*, 313 F. Supp. 2d 213 (S.D.N.Y. 2004) (excluding expert's testimony because it was based on an unreliable data sample); *Craftsmen Limousine, Inc. v. Ford Motor Co.*, 360 F.3d 865, 881–882 (8th Cir. 2004) (refusing to admit expert testimony that did not account for the entry of two direct competitors to plaintiff).

For a model-based discussion of expertise in judicial decision making, including an examination of the legitimacy of economic authority in the judicial system, see John E. Lopatka & William H. Page, *Economic Authority and the Limits of Expertise in Antitrust Cases*, 90 CORNELL L. REV. 617 (2005).

5. In all events, the purpose of expert testimony is to aid the fact finder. As a result, experts testify about questions of fact, not about questions of law. *See Cardizem Antitrust Litigation*, 105 F. Supp. 2d 682, 694 (E.D. Mich. 2000), which excluded the testimony of a forensic economist that certain activity should be analyzed under the rule of reason. The court held that an expert may not give testimony on questions of law, and the question whether a practice is governed by the per se rule or the rule of reason is one of law.

See also Weisgram v. Marley Co., 528 U.S. 440, 457 (2000) (if the trial judge erroneously admits expert testimony, without which the plaintiff cannot prove its case, the appellate court may order judgment for the defendant, rather than a new trial). *See generally* James Langenfeld & Christopher Alexander, *Daubert and Other Gate Keeping Challenges of Antitrust Experts*, 25 ANTITRUST 21 (2011).

II   ADDITIONAL ANTITRUST DEFENSES

[A]   First Amendment Protections

[1]   *Noerr-Pennington* Doctrine

The Supreme Court, in a series of decisions beginning in 1961, has recognized a First Amendment freedom of expression defense, regardless of anticompetitive intent, when competitors combine to influence governmental action. The defense is known as the *Noerr-Pennington* doctrine, named after the Court's two leading cases which developed the doctrine. The doctrine has received substantial attention and is used frequently as an antitrust defense. *See A.D. Bedell Wholesale Co., Inc. v. Phillip Morris, Inc.*, 263 F.3d 239 (3d Cir. 2001), *cert. denied*, 534 U.S. 1081 (2002) (settlement agreements that restrict competition as a basis for immunity); *Massachusetts School of Law v. ABA*, 107 F.3d 1026 (3d Cir. 1997) (lobbying of state supreme courts). For a narrow reading of the immunity, *see Prime Time 24 Joint Venture v. NBC*, 219 F.3d 92 (2d Cir. 2000). *But see Baltimore Scrap Corp. v. David J. Joseph Co.*, 237 F.3d 394 (4th Cir. 2001). It is discussed further in Chapter 9, *infra*.

[2]   Economic/Political Boycotts

In some cases, economic boycotts (concerted refusals to deal) which are motivated by political purposes have been immunized from antitrust scrutiny on the basis of the First Amendment right to petition government even when the boycott results in a commercial injury. See Chapter 4, Section I[E][5], *infra*, where the leading cases are discussed. *NAACP v. Claiborne Hdwe. Co.*, 458 U.S. 886 (1982); *Missouri v. National Org. for Women*, 620 F.2d 1301 (8th Cir. 1980). *But cf. Allied Tube & Conduit Corp. v. Indian Head, Inc.*, 486 U.S. 492 (1988); *FTC v. Superior Ct. Trial Lawyers Ass'n*, 493 U.S. 411 (1990), discussed in Chapter 9.

[3]   Overbroad Remedial Orders

A large part of the antitrust enforcement effort results in the issuance of judicial or FTC orders designed to regulate business behavior. The First Amendment is a relevant restraint on overbroad orders that invade constitutionally protected economic activity.

That the activity sought to be regulated is purely economic or commercial in nature does not mean that it is constitutionally insignificant or unprotected. Since 1975, the Supreme Court has signaled that overbroad governmental regulations could be challenged even if the activities sought to be regulated are commercial or economic in nature. *Virginia State Bd. of Pharmacy v. Virginia Citizens Consumer Council, Inc.*, 425 U.S. 748 (1976) (striking down state statute which declared it unprofessional conduct for a pharmacist to advertise prescription drug prices); *Bigelow v. Virginia*, 421 U.S. 809 (1975) (abortion advertising held constitutionally protected). Even in the absence of political content, First Amendment defenses are available to protect commercial speech because of its importance to the free market exchange of ideas in the allocation of resources. The Court has recognized that business speech has a marketplace focus and concern for both purchaser-oriented and seller-motivated profit interests. 425 U.S. 748, 761; *Bates v. State Bar*, 433 U.S. 350, 374–375 (1977) (where the Court held that a state could not prohibit price advertising for routine legal services).

When economically motivated communications are given First Amendment protection, tensions develop between the proper government regulation of that business and the values which underlie the First Amendment. It does seem evident, however, that the commercial speech component of the First Amendment is inapplicable if the speech sought to be protected is part of an illegal activity. *Pittsburgh Press Co. v. Pittsburgh Comm'n on Human Rels.*, 413 U.S. 376, 389 (1973) (Where the Court held that an ordinance prohibiting gender-designated captions in advertising did not violate the First Amendment. The advertisement could have facilitated the illegal activity of employment discrimination.).

In light of this developing defense, it is important for antitrust counsel to consider (1) whether and under what circumstances a remedial order can restrict economic conduct which arguably comes within the commercial speech doctrine, (2) whether any principles delimit the "illegal conduct" exception to the commercial speech defense, and (3) whether traditional standards of overbreadth analysis and vagueness are applicable.

Consider the Supreme Court's broad statement in *FTC v. National Lead Co.*, 352 U.S. 419, 429 (1957), that the government is not confined to blocking "the narrow lane the transgressor has traveled; it must be allowed effectively to close all roads to the prohibited goal." There the Court approved an FTC order prohibiting the quoting of prices calculated on a territorial zone price system. How can the parameters of such an order be defined? In Chapter 4, parallel conduct among competitors and the competitive consequences of such conduct are discussed. There it is noted that one enforcement theory is based on the price theory of interdependence: sellers in an oligopoly recognize that their own price and production decisions are dictated, given the industry structure, in large part by what the reactions of other sellers will be to price moves. Anticipating those reactions, competitors adopt parallel pricing. *See* Turner, *The Definition of Agreement Under the Sherman Act: Conscious Parallelism and Refusal to Deal*, 75 HARV. L. REV. 655 (1962). Would a remedial order, which prohibits public price announcements by competitors in an oligopolistic market, violate the First Amendment by reducing the amount of useful information in the marketplace?

On several occasions, the Supreme Court has implied that if the commercial speech is used to further or facilitate an illegal scheme, the speech (or conduct) is not protected. *See, e.g.*, *Bigelow v. Virginia*, 421 U.S. 809, 828 (1975). Thus, if the public price announcement was a facilitating device in an antitrust price-fixing scheme, the speech arguably would not be protected. Accordingly, an order could be drawn to fence in this otherwise protected conduct. The central inquiry is probably the remoteness of the challenged conduct to the demonstrated illegality. In short, the protection afforded to economic speech may depend on the illegality of the interest served by the speech and the closeness of the connection between the speech and the illegal conduct. *See* Sullivan, *First Amendment Defenses in Antitrust Litigation*, 46 MO. L. REV. 517 (1981).

The most definitive statement on constitutional protection from overbroad regulatory orders came in *Central Hudson Gas & Elec. Corp. v. Public Serv. Comm'n*, 447 U.S. 557 (1980). The New York Public Service Commission issued an order prohibiting the promotional advertising of the use of electricity. The state interest underlying the ban centered on energy conservation. After the energy shortage ended, the promotional ban continued, but the regulations permitted informational advertising designed to encourage time shifts in energy consumption. Central Hudson, a public utility, challenged the promotional ban, arguing that it violated the commercial speech doctrine. The New York Court of Appeals upheld the ban on the theory that there was "little value to advertising in 'the noncompetitive market in which electric corporations operate.' " *Id.* at 561. The Supreme Court reversed, holding that the ban violated Central Hudson's commercial speech rights.

The Court established a four-tiered analysis for scrutinizing regulations and orders that restrict commercial speech. The first question is whether the speech is protected, that is, whether it is commercial speech that is accurate and unrelated to illegal conduct. If it is inaccurate or related to illegal conduct, it is not entitled to constitutional protection. If it is not deceptive and does not encourage illegal activity, the speech is then protected and the second inquiry is whether the regulating authority has a substantial interest to be served by the regulation. Next, the restriction on the speech must advance directly the stated governmental interest. Finally, the restriction cannot be more extensive than necessary to serve that interest. *Id.* at 566.

The requirement that an order be no broader than necessary to achieve a governmental interest is one of the most litigated requirements in trade regulation. It mandates that the order can "extend only as far as the interest it serves." *Id.* at 565. If a less restrictive order will suffice to protect that interest, the order must be tailored to protect only the substantial governmental interest promoted. In other words, to support an order, the government must demonstrate that alternative means which would burden or impair the defendant less are unavailable.

In *Florida Bar v. Went For It, Inc.*, 515 U.S. 618 (1995), the Supreme Court reversed a Court of Appeals decision finding a violation of the *Central Hudson* test. The Eleventh Circuit had found that Florida Bar rules that prohibited lawyers from using direct mail to solicit injured clients until 30 days after the injury violated the First Amendment. But Justice O'Connor, applying the *Central Hudson* test, accepted the protection of potential clients' privacy and the preservation of the "integrity of the legal profession" as substantial Bar interests and found the rule "reasonably well-tailored to its stated objective of eliminating targeted mailings whose type and timing are a source of distress to Floridians, distress that has caused many of them to lose respect for the legal profession." 515 U.S. at 633.

In sum, the Supreme Court's opinions teach that economic conduct which is an essential, substantial, or facilitating part of an antitrust violation can be proscribed through a remedial order without violating the commercial speech protection. But care must be taken so that a conduct-oriented order does not sweep so broadly as to deter other conduct that may be competitive.

[B] *In Pari Delicto* and the Unclean Hands Doctrine

In pari delicto is a common-law defense raised when the plaintiff is a party to the alleged illegality. The term means "of equal fault." From its early application in *Eastman Kodak Co. v. Blackmore*, 277 F. 694 (2d Cir. 1921), the Supreme Court narrowly has restricted the use of the doctrine as an airtight defense to an antitrust charge. The following case discusses antitrust violations as a defense.

PERMA LIFE MUFFLERS, INC. v. INTERNATIONAL PARTS CORP.
392 U.S. 134 (1968)

JUSTICE BLACK delivered the opinion of the Court.

The principal question presented is whether the plaintiffs in this private antitrust action were barred from recovery by a doctrine known by the Latin phrase *in pari delicto*, which literally means "of equal fault." The plaintiffs, petitioners here, were all dealers who had operated "Midas Muffler Shops" under sales agreements granted by respondent Midas, Inc. Their complaint charged that Midas had entered into a conspiracy with the other named defendants — its parent corporation International Parts Corp., two other subsidiaries, and six individual defendants who were officers or agents of the corporations — to restrain and substantially lessen competition in violation of § 1 of the Sherman Act and § 3 of the Clayton Act. . . . In 1955 the owners of International initiated a detailed plan for promoting the sale of mufflers by extensively advertising the "Midas" trade name and establishing a nationwide chain of dealers who would specialize in selling exhaust system equipment. Each prospective dealer was offered a sales agreement prepared by Midas, Inc., a wholly owned subsidiary of International. The agreement obligated the dealer to purchase all his mufflers from Midas, to honor the Midas guarantee on mufflers sold by any dealer, and to sell the mufflers at resale prices fixed by Midas and at locations specified in the agreement. The dealers were also obligated to purchase all their exhaust system parts from Midas, to carry the complete line of Midas products, and in general to refrain from dealing with any of Midas' competitors. In return Midas promised to underwrite the cost of the muffler guarantee and gave the dealer permission to use the registered trademark "Midas" and the service mark "Midas Muffler Shops." The dealer was also granted the exclusive right to sell "Midas" products within his defined territory. He was not required to pay a franchise fee or to purchase or lease substantial capital equipment from Midas, and the agreement was cancelable by either party on 30 days' notice.

Petitioners' complaint challenged as illegal restraints of trade numerous provisions of the agreements, such as the terms barring them from purchasing from other sources of supply, preventing them from selling outside the designated territory, tying the sale of mufflers to the sale of other products in the Midas line, and requiring them to sell at fixed retail prices. Petitioners alleged that they had often requested Midas to eliminate these restrictions but that Midas had refused and had threatened to terminate their agreements if they failed to comply. Finally they alleged that one of the plaintiffs had his agreement canceled by Midas for purchasing exhaust parts from a Midas competitor, and that the other plaintiff dealers had themselves canceled their agreements. All the plaintiffs claimed treble damages for the monetary loss they had suffered from having to abide by the restrictive provisions.

The Court of Appeals . . . held the suit barred because petitioners were *in pari delicto*. The court noted that each of the petitioners had enthusiastically sought to acquire a Midas franchise with full knowledge of these provisions and had "solemnly subscribed" to the agreement containing the restrictive terms. Petitioners had all made enormous profits as Midas dealers, had eagerly sought to acquire additional franchises, and had voluntarily entered into additional franchise agreements, all while fully aware of the restrictions they now challenge. . . .

We find ourselves in complete disagreement with the Court of Appeals. There is nothing in the language of the antitrust acts which indicates that Congress wanted to make the common-law *in pari delicto* doctrine a defense to treble-damage actions, and the facts of this case suggest no basis for applying such a doctrine even if it did exist. Although *in pari delicto* literally means "of equal fault," the doctrine has been applied, correctly or incorrectly, in a wide variety of situations in which a plaintiff seeking damages or equitable relief is himself involved in some of the same sort of wrongdoing. We have often indicated the inappropriateness of invoking broad common-law barriers to relief where a private suit serves important public purposes. It was for this reason that we held in *Kiefer-Stewart Co. v. Joseph E. Seagram & Sons*, 340 U.S. 211 (1951), that a plaintiff in an antitrust suit could not be barred from recovery by proof that he had engaged in an unrelated conspiracy to commit some other antitrust violation. Similarly, in *Simpson v. Union Oil Co.*, 377 U.S. 13 (1964), we held that a dealer whose consignment agreement was canceled for failure to adhere to a fixed resale price could bring suit under the antitrust laws even though by signing the agreement he had to that extent become a participant in the illegal, competition-destroying scheme. Both *Simpson* and *Kiefer-Stewart* were premised on a recognition that the purposes of the antitrust laws are best served by insuring that the private action will be an ever-present threat to deter anyone contemplating business behavior in violation of the antitrust laws. The plaintiff who reaps the reward of treble damages may be no less morally reprehensible than the defendant, but the law encourages his suit to further the overriding public policy in favor of competition. A more fastidious regard for the relative moral worth of the parties would only result in seriously undermining the usefulness of the private action as a bulwark of antitrust enforcement. And permitting the plaintiff to recover a windfall gain does not encourage continued violations by those in his position since they remain fully subject to civil and criminal penalties for their own illegal conduct.

. . . Although petitioners may be subject to some criticism for having taken any part in respondents' allegedly illegal scheme and for eagerly seeking more franchises and more profits, their participation was not voluntary in any meaningful sense. They sought the franchises enthusiastically but they did not actively seek each and every clause of the agreement. Rather, many of the clauses were quite clearly detrimental to their interests, and they alleged that they had continually objected to them. Petitioners apparently accepted many of these restraints solely because their acquiescence was necessary to obtain an otherwise attractive business opportunity. . . . Moreover, even if petitioners actually favored and supported some of the other restrictions, they cannot be blamed for seeking to minimize the disadvantages of the agreement once they had been forced to accept its more onerous terms as a condition of doing business. The possible beneficial byproducts of a restriction from a plaintiff's point of view can of course be taken into consideration in computing damages, but once it is shown that the plaintiff did not aggressively support and further the monopolistic scheme as a necessary part and parcel of it, his understandable attempts to make the best of a bad situation should not be a ground for completely denying him the right to recover which the antitrust acts give him. We therefore hold that the doctrine of *in pari delicto*, with its complex scope, contents, and effects, is not to be recognized as a defense to an antitrust action.

Respondents, however, seek to support the judgment below on a considerably narrower ground. They picture petitioners as actively supporting the entire restrictive program as such, participating in its formulation and encouraging its continuation. We need not decide, however, whether such truly complete involvement and participation in a monopolistic scheme could ever be a basis, wholly apart from the idea of *in pari delicto*, for barring a plaintiff's cause of action, for in the present case the factual picture respondents attempt to paint is utterly refuted by the record. . . .

Reversed.

NOTES AND QUESTIONS

1. Justices White and Fortas suggested in their concurring opinions that if a plaintiff's participation in the antitrust violation is equal to or greater than the defendant's, the plaintiff may have difficulty proving causation of the injury, with the result that recovery would be denied.

2. In *Perma Life*, the Court was confronted with the determination of how best to maintain an effective deterrent policy for antitrust enforcement. Noting the "inappropriateness of invoking broad common-law barriers," the Supreme Court weighed the relative degrees of fault among alleged antitrust violators and held that the law's deterrent policies would be better served (maximized) if courts do not recognize the common rule of *in pari delicto* as a defense, even though the plaintiff had knowingly participated in the illegal scheme and could stand to recover a windfall. *See also Bangor Punta Opers., Inc. v. Bangor & A.R.R.*, 417 U.S. 703, 719 (1974) (Marshall, J., dissenting).

3. In evaluating the application of the defense to the facts, the Court apparently concluded that the antitrust violators were not of equal fault. Note the Court's conclusion that because of Perma Life's relative lack of bargaining power and unequal economic leverage, its participation in the illegal scheme "was not voluntary in any meaningful sense." Because the Court found that the wrongdoers were not of equal fault, perhaps the Court's language implied that the *in pari delicto* defense is available if the plaintiff's degree of fault was relatively equal with that of defendants. Consider Justice Black's statement that "[w]e need not decide, however, whether such truly complete involvement and participation in a monopo-

listic scheme could ever be a basis, wholly apart from the idea of *in pari delicto*, for barring a plaintiff's cause of action, for in the present case the factual picture respondents attempt to paint is utterly refuted by the record." 392 U.S. at 141. The four concurring opinions supported the continuing availability of the defense where the violators are of equal fault. The lower courts are in apparent agreement. *See, e.g., Bernstein v. Universal Pictures, Inc.*, 517 F.2d 976 (2d Cir. 1975); *THI-Hawaii, Inc. v. First Commerce Fin. Corp.*, 627 F.2d 991 (9th Cir. 1980).

4. Consider the separate question whether the jury should be instructed to consider the plaintiff's own antitrust conduct when determining the defendant's liability. *See* 2 P. AREEDA & H. HOVENKAMP, ANTITRUST LAWS ¶ 390 (4th ed. 2014). In *Eichler v. Berner*, 472 U.S. 299, 310–311 (1985), the Supreme Court observed that: "a private action for damages . . . may be barred on the grounds of the plaintiff's own culpability only where: (1) as a direct result of his own actions, the plaintiff bears at least substantially equal responsibility for the violations he seeks to redress, and (2) preclusion of suit would not significantly interfere with the effective enforcement of the . . . laws."

Is the *Eichler* test an easier standard for the defense to meet than that announced in *Perma Life*? At what time in the pretrial or trial stage is the defense assertable? Consider the two-part test. Is the first a jury question and the second a legal issue only the judge can determine? Could a summary judgment motion raise the defense? Consider how the Court has characterized its test in *Eichler*:

> The first prong of this test captures the essential elements of the classic *in pari delicto* doctrine. The second prong, which embodies the doctrine's traditional requirement that public policy implications be carefully considered before the defense is allowed, ensures that the broad judge-made law does not undermine the congressional policy favoring private suits as an important mode of enforcing federal . . . statutes.

Pinter v. Dahl, 486 U.S. 622, 633 (1988).

For a case where the Seventh Circuit affirmed a jury's special verdict finding that plaintiff "bore substantially equal responsibility" for a territorial restriction and rendered damages in the amount of "zero" dollars, see *General Leaseways, Inc. v. National Truck Leasing Ass'n*, 830 F.2d 716 (7th Cir. 1987). Subsequently, the Seventh Circuit, in a case between lawyers and former law partners, applied the equal responsibility defense announced in *Perma Life* and denied treble damages. In *Blackburn v. Sweeney*, 53 F.3d 825 (7th Cir. 1995), former partners in a law firm sued other former partners, alleging that the "withdrawal from partnership agreement" which they each entered was a horizontal market division agreement unlawful under the Sherman Act. Although agreeing that the agreement was unlawful, the court held that the former partners could not recover damages because the parties had relatively equal bargaining power and freely entered the restrictive agreement. The court also concluded that the plaintiff had not suffered antitrust injury because, as one of the two colluding competitors, he did not suffer from the effects of the collusion on competition.

However, the court declared the agreement illegal, and thus unenforceable. The result thus suggests this outcome: when *A* and *B* enter into a per se unlawful cartel or territorial division conspiracy, neither *A* nor *B* can later claim that the agreement is unlawful and obtain damages or an injunction (plus attorneys fees) against the other; however, neither can the agreement be enforced, and one party could presumably bring a Declaratory Judgment action to that effect. The ordinary rules of antitrust standing, injury, and probably *pari delicto* do not apply to the Declaratory Judgment Act — where, in any event, relief would ordinarily be limited to a declaration that the provision at issue is unlawful and unenforceable.

See subsection E, Chapter 3, *supra*. Note that in the state of New York, such a "no compete" restriction in a partnership agreement would be unethical, *Cohen v. Lord, Day & Lord*, 550 N.E.2d 410 (N.Y. 1989), but not in the state of California, *Howard v. Babcock*, 863 P.2d 150 (Cal. 1993). *See* Robert W. Hillman, *The Law Firm As Jurassic Park: Comments on Howard v. Babcock*, 27 U.C. Davis L. Rev. 533 (1994).

5. Generally, the equitable doctrine of unclean hands has been interpreted to have broader application than the *in pari delicto* defense. It has found expression when the plaintiff may have violated some other antitrust provision or related statute in a separate illegality. Its application, however, has been upheld rather infrequently. *See Kiefer-Stewart Co. v. Joseph E. Seagram & Sons*, 340 U.S. 211 (1951); Handler & Sacks, *The Continued Vitality of In Pari Delicto as an Antitrust Defense*, 70 Geo. L.J. 1123 (1982). *See also* ABA Section of Antitrust Law, Antitrust Law Developments 910 (5th ed. 2002).

The doctrine was applied in *Stokely-Van Camp, Inc. v. Coca-Cola Co.*, 646 F. Supp. 2d 510 (S.D.N.Y. 2009). Both the plaintiff and defendant had claimed that their energy drinks contained calcium and magnesium. *Id.* at 533. The court held that plaintiff SVC could not recover injunctive relief from defendant Coca-Cola banning them from making these claims where SVC had engaged in behavior that was "virtually identical" if not worse than the behavior of the plaintiffs. *Id.*

6. Chrysler Corp. challenged the 1983–1984 joint venture between General Motors and Toyota to build subcompact cars. The defendants argued that the joint venture was legal, and also that Chrysler had unclean hands because it had anticompetitive motives in bringing the antitrust action against its two competitors. After deciding that Chrysler had standing to challenge the joint venture and noting that the "lower courts have almost uniformly declined to permit the unclean hands defense in antitrust suits where injunctive relief is sought," the district court ruled that defendants could not raise unclean hands as an affirmative defense to block Chrysler's suit. Citing the "overriding public interest in preventing anticompetitive injury," the district court struck the unclean hands defense. *Chrysler Corp. v. General Motors Corp.*, 596 F. Supp. 416 (D.D.C. 1984).

III REMEDIES

United States v. Keyspan, 763 F. Supp. 2d 633 (S.D.N.Y. 2011), addressed for the first time the question of whether the Department of Justice can seek disgorgement as a remedy for a Sherman Act violation. The Government submitted to the court that it had never previously sought disgorgement as a remedy for a Sherman Act violation. *Id.* at 636. Finding no "decisions concerning a district court's power to order disgorgement to remedy a Sherman Act violation," the court turned to a Second Circuit opinion addressing the availability of disgorgement to remedy violations of the securities laws. *Id.* In *Sec & Exchange Comm'n v. Cavanagh*, 445 F.3d 105, 118 (2d Cir. 2006), the Second Circuit held that whether a district court could order disgorgement "requires an inquiry into whether the remedies available at chancery in 1789 included disgorgement." Ultimately, the Second Circuit concluded that because chancery courts had possessed the power to order disgorgement, contemporary district courts retain that power. *Id.* at 120. The *Keyspan* court accepted this analysis and also determined that traditional equity and antitrust principles did not preclude use of disgorgement as a remedy. *Keyspan*, 763 F. Supp. 2d 633. Disgorgement is an appropriate tool for the district court to use, because under antitrust law, district courts "are invested with large discretion to model their judgments to fit the exigencies of the particular case." *Id.* at 640–641 (quoting *Int'l Boxing Club of N.Y., Inc. v. United States*, 358 U.S. 242, 253 (1959)). Additionally, the court found disgorgement to be a "particularly appropriate" remedy where, as here, "the anticompetitive conduct in question has ceased." Because the Swap at issue had expired, there were no assets to be divested. Thus, absent disgorgement, the Government would be without any recourse to remedy Keyspan's anticompetitive conduct. "A rejection of disgorgement could incentivize other generators to manipulate the electricity markets using derivative instruments that expire in the short term, with the understanding that they will be permitted to retain their earnings because restitution for customers is unavailable." The *Keyspan* court declined to adopt the rationale given by circuit courts for limiting disgorgement as a remedy for RICO violations, finding that violations under the Sherman Act were distinguishable because "[a]ntitrust law is both forward- *and* backward-looking." (emphasis in original).

[A] Damages

Section 4 of the Clayton Act, 15 U.S.C. § 15, provides that "[a]ny person who shall be injured in his business or property by reason of anything forbidden in the antitrust laws may sue therefor . . . and shall recover threefold the damages by him sustained." Both the legislative history and judicial interpretations suggest that this statute has two central, but not always consistent, purposes. One is to deter potential antitrust violators; the other is to encourage private litigants to bring suit.

An antitrust plaintiff seeking damages must first show the "fact" of antitrust injury. This includes (1) the existence of an antitrust violation; (2) causation, or cause-in-fact, that is, the plaintiff cannot recover unless it can show that the violation was responsible for the injury; and (3) that the injury is of the type the antitrust laws were intended to prevent, that is, the plaintiff must make out the "antitrust injury" requirements of *Brunswick Corp. v. Pueblo Bowl-O-Mat, Inc.*, 429 U.S. 477 (1977), reprinted *supra*. After fact of injury has been established, the plaintiff must prove the amount of its injury. Most courts hold that the fact of injury has to be established with some rigor, but that proof standards respecting the amount of damages are far more relaxed. *See Bigelow v. RKO Radio Pictures*, 327 U.S. 251, 265 (1946). Plaintiffs who can establish the fact of injury, but who cannot establish the amount with sufficient precision, may be awarded nominal damages. *E.g., Rosebrough Monument Co. v. Memorial Park Cem. Ass'n*, 736 F.2d 441 (8th Cir. 1984).

Today courts recognize two types of damage measurement. If the plaintiffs are purchasers of a monopolized or cartelized product, their damages will generally be the "overcharge" — or the amount by which the illegal activity enhanced the price. The Supreme Court approved damage measurement based on "the difference between the price paid and the market or fair price" in *Chattanooga Foundry & Pipe Works v. Atlanta*, 203 U.S. 390, 396 (1906). If the plaintiffs are competitors or terminated dealers, damages are generally based on lost profits. *See Eastman Kodak Co. v. Southern Photo Materials Co.*, 273 U.S. 359, 379 (1927). Of course, under Section 4 of the Clayton Act, all damages are trebled. As a general rule, the jury is not instructed in advance that its damage award will be multiplied by three.

Today damages are most commonly proved by the "before-and-after" method and the "yardstick" method. Under the "before-and-after" method, a plaintiff tries to show what was happening in the market both before and after the violation occurred and argues that its damages should be based on these numbers. For example, if a purchaser from a cartel can show that widgets cost $1.00 before a cartel came into existence and $1.00 after it fell apart, but $1.25 during the cartel period, one can presume that the cartel raised prices by 25 cents. As you might suspect, a good deal of adjustment, guesswork, and even some speculation goes into such estimates. Under the "yardstick" method, the plaintiff looks at some other firm or some other market presumed to be similar to the market in which the antitrust violation occurred, except for the violation. Damages are then based on the difference between prices or profits in the "yardstick" market and the market at issue. For example, if the price of widgets was $1.35 in Boston during the operation of a local cartel, but only $1.00 in Chicago at the same time, where the market was presumably competitive, then the difference may approximate the amount of the cartel overcharge. These prices will have to be adjusted to account for differences in costs, taxes, etc. For more on the mechanics of damage measurement under these two methods, see H. HOVENKAMP, FEDERAL ANTITRUST POLICY, ch. 17 (4th ed. 2011).

Damage measurement becomes more difficult, and correspondingly more speculative, when the plaintiff was actually forced to exit the market as a result of a violation. The prevailing rules permit the plaintiff to show damages as a function of the business' value as a "going concern" — or its market value in a hypothetical market in which the antitrust violation had not occurred. Even more problematic is the plight of the "precluded entrant" — the plaintiff who was prohibited from ever entering a market as a result of an antitrust violation. Should such a plaintiff be entitled to show the "going concern" value of a business that never went anywhere? Or to show lost profits from a business that never made any sales? Courts generally permit such showings in principle, but few precluded plaintiffs have made substantial damage recoveries. Courts require that the plaintiff show both an "intention" to enter a market, and sufficient "preparedness" to do so to make the award of damages reasonable. *See Neumann v. Reinforced Earth Co.*, 786 F.2d 424 (9th Cir. 1986), which held that the plaintiff had not been sufficiently "prepared" to enter the market when all his applications for financing had been rejected. The sad irony of the precluded entrant cases is that people who have not yet entered a market may be uniquely vulnerable to certain kinds of antitrust violations. As a general rule, the less unrecoverable investment a firm has made in a market, the more easily it can be driven out. For example, predatory pricing strategies designed to deter firms thinking about entering a market might be much more successful than predatory pricing against established rivals. O. Williamson, *Predatory Pricing: A Strategic and Welfare Analysis*, 87 YALE L.J. 284 (1977).

If injured competitors are part of a certified class of litigants, they eventually will receive a distribution of damages. Under the *cy pres* doctrine a judge may equitably distribute any unclaimed funds, but may be required to distribute them according to the original purpose of the antitrust litigation. *See In re Airline Ticket Comm'n Antitrust Litig. I*, 268 F.3d 619 (8th Cir. 2001) (directing redistribution of funds slated through discretion to go to local law schools and charitable organizations to activities closer to the purpose of the cause of action); *In re Airline Ticket Comm'n Antitrust Litig. II*, 307 F.3d 679, 683 (8th Cir. 2002) (ordering the distribution of unclaimed funds to "the next best recipients" or those "agencies [who] would relate directly to the antitrust injury alleged in this lawsuit and settled by the parties"); *Diamond Chem. Co., Inc. v. Akzo Nobel Chems. B.V.*, 2007 U.S. Dist. LEXIS 49406 (D.D.C. July 10, 2007) (authorizing the distribution of remaining settlement funds to a local law school for the creation of a center for competition).

In sum, injured competitors may be awarded damages for: (1) recovery for increased costs; (2) recovery for lost profits of a continuing business; (3) recovery for lost profits of a terminated business; and (4) recovery for reduction in business value. *See* D. FLOYD & E. THOMAS SULLIVAN, PRIVATE ANTITRUST ACTIONS, § 9 (1996).

[1]   Optimal Antitrust Damages

The language of Section 4 of the Clayton Act permitting a private plaintiff to recover three times the damages "by him sustained" suggests rather strongly that compensation of victims, rather than deterrence of violators, is the principal goal of private damage actions under the antitrust laws.

Nevertheless, the Supreme Court has suggested that deterrence is an important goal of private antitrust enforcement. *Illinois Brick Co. v. Illinois*, 431 U.S. 720, 746 (1977); *Brunswick Corp. v. Pueblo Bowl-O-Mat, Inc.*, 429 U.S. 477, 485–486 (1977). Recent scholarship, which relies on an influential article by economist Gary Becker, *Crime and Punishment: An Economic Approach*, 76 J. POL. ECON. 169 (1968), argues that deterrence should be the *only* goal of private damage actions. This Optimal Deterrence Model begins with the premise that many of the things the antitrust laws condemn are efficient, largely because courts are unable to distinguish precisely between efficient and inefficient practices. An optimal damages rule should deter inefficient conduct, while permitting efficient conduct.

There is little correlation between the size of this optimal fine and the losses experienced by potential plaintiffs, particularly when the plaintiff is a competitor of the defendant rather than a seller or purchaser. Thus the model often yields results inconsistent with Section 4's mandate that the victim of an antitrust violation recover an award based on losses "by him sustained."

Within the neoclassical model, you may recall (*see* Chapter 2, *supra*), monopoly produces both a wealth transfer, caused by consumers forced to pay monopoly prices, and a "deadweight" loss, caused by those consumers who choose not to purchase the product at the higher price, but rather make inefficient substitutions to something else. In evaluating the social consequences of monopoly, the neoclassical economist views the wealth transfer as relatively unimportant. He or she is concerned principally with the overall size of the pie, not with how big the individual pieces are. However, the deadweight loss is a matter of great concern, for it represents lost social value. This has led some people to suppose that if the goal of private antitrust enforcement is efficiency, the optimal sanction must be a function of the deadweight loss. *E.g.*, Schwartz, *An Overview of the Economics of Antitrust Enforcement*, 68 GEO. L.J. 1075, 1081–1085 (1980).

But often a fine equal to the deadweight loss is too small to deter inefficient conduct. For example, in a market with a perfectly linear demand curve price fixing that produces $1,000 in excess profits to the violators will generate consumer overcharges of $1,000 and a deadweight loss of $500. A fine equal to the deadweight loss would be too small. The fine would have to be marginally greater than $1,000 in order to make the price fixing unprofitable.

The Optimal Deterrence Model identifies optimal damages as the *sum* of the wealth transfer and the deadweight loss. Requiring the violator to pay damages that include the deadweight loss will induce him to refrain from violating the antitrust laws only if his conduct is socially harmful. For example, an efficiency-producing merger or joint venture, or even some exclusionary practices by monopolists, may simultaneously increase firms' market power and reduce their production or distribution costs. In such cases, the size of the deadweight loss becomes theoretically relevant. Suppose that conduct which permits the defendant to charge monopoly prices produces a wealth transfer of $1,000 and a deadweight loss of $400. However, it also reduces the defendant's production costs. The conduct is efficient on balance if the production cost savings are greater than $400, but inefficient if the savings are less than $400. Under the Optimal Deterrence Model, the perfect penalty would be the *sum* of the monopoly overcharge and the deadweight loss, or $1,400. If the production cost savings are greater than $400, it will be worth more than $1,400 and the defendant will engage in it, the threat of a penalty notwithstanding. If the production cost savings are less than $400, and the activity inefficient, then it will be worth less to the defendant than the anticipated fine, and the defendant will not engage in the conduct. Thus the optimal fine will deter inefficient conduct but permit efficient conduct. *See* W. BREIT & K. ELZINGA, ANTITRUST PENALTY REFORM: AN ECONOMIC ANALYSIS (1986); Easterbrook, *Detrebling Antitrust Damages*, 28 J.L. & ECON. 445 (1985); Landes, *Optimal Sanctions for Antitrust Violations*, 50 U. CHI. L. REV. 652 (1983). For a critique, see H. HOVENKAMP, FEDERAL ANTITRUST POLICY, ch. 17 (4th ed. 2011).

One conceptual problem with the Optimal Deterrence Model is that it fails to account for the full social cost of monopoly in dynamic markets — i.e., markets where firms behave strategically. The incipient monopolist may consume many of its own resources or those of others in order to create or maintain its monopoly position. As a result, the social cost of *de facto* monopoly consists of three things:

(1) the deadweight loss triangle, which measures inefficient consumer substitutions away from the monopolized goods;

(2) that part of the wealth "transfer," as the neoclassical model identifies it, that the *de facto* monopolist or monopolist-to-be spends in socially harmful ways in order to retain or obtain monopoly power (see Chapter 2, *infra* on the social cost of monopoly); and importantly,

(3) the socially harmful losses that the monopolist or incipient monopolist imposes on competitors or others in the same effort.

The Optimal Deterrence Model expressly takes cost element (1) into account by including the deadweight loss triangle as part of the basis for damages. It also takes cost element (2) into account because the cost to the monopolist of its exclusionary practices reduces the anticipated profitability of monopoly. But the Model completely ignores the social cost of any injury that the monopolist's exclusionary practices may impose on others. For example, if Chrysler should bomb all the plants owned by General Motors, Ford, and its other competitors and murder their executives, it might attain a monopoly. But the social cost of that monopoly caused by inefficient consumer substitutions would be trivial in comparison to the social cost of the means by which Chrysler created it. Chrysler presumably will not spend more on arsonists and assassins than the value of the expected monopoly. But the social cost of the losses it imposes on its competitors could be far larger. The largest social cost of many forms of monopolizing conduct is the inefficient losses imposed on competitors or other nonconsumers.

By failing to consider this element of social cost, the "Optimal" Deterrence Model frequently yields suboptimal damages. For example, suppose a monopolist uses a combination of predatory pricing, exclusive contracts, and patent fraud to lengthen the duration of its monopoly. The activity permits the firm to earn $1,000 in additional monopoly profits, costs the firm $100, and produces a deadweight loss of $400. As a result of scale economies, the activity also generates cost savings. The Optimal Deterrence Model would assess a penalty of $1,400. In this case, the monopolist would pursue the activity only if the cost savings exceeded $500.

But suppose that the monopolistic activity additionally imposes $700 in inefficient losses on competitors whose plants must be dismantled, research discarded, opportunities lost, and contracts broken. In that case the Optimal Deterrence Model might end up approving socially costly activity simply because injuries to other firms, rather than injuries that accrue to consumers, are not calculated into the social cost of monopoly. An optimal model for antitrust damages would try to predicate damages on the sum of the monopoly overcharge plus the *entire* social cost of monopoly, and the deadweight loss alone reflects only part — sometimes a very small part — of the social cost of monopoly.

One important difference between that part of the social cost of monopoly that falls upon competitors and the social cost described by the traditional deadweight loss triangle is that society may have to pay the first cost whether or not the scheme succeeds. That is, some attempts to create monopolies fail, but they are costly to competitors and to society, nonetheless. It has been argued that such failed attempts should not be actionable, for they are self-deterring and the incipient monopolist bears the full social cost of its failures. Landes, *Optimal Sanctions, supra*, at 668–672.

The resources spent by the incipient monopolist in the monopolistic scheme are costs borne by itself, and if the scheme fails there will be no monopoly overcharge or deadweight loss. Once again, however, this perspective ignores the social cost that might be borne by competitors, whether or not the scheme fails. For example, suppose that a putative predator calculates that predatory pricing (discussed in Chapter 6) will cost $300 and generate monopoly returns of $2,000. It will also produce a deadweight loss of $800. Under the Optimal Deterrence Model, the penalty is $2,800 if the scheme succeeds, but zero if the scheme fails, for there will be neither a monopoly overcharge nor a deadweight loss. But suppose that the predation forces inefficient plant closings, bankruptcies, loss of contracts and jobs, and other social injuries that equal $2,000. Many of these inefficiencies may result whether or not the predation scheme succeeds.

This critique of the Optimal Deterrence Model suggests much more room for competitor lawsuits than its advocates would allow. For example, many failed attempts to monopolize impose socially harmful losses on competitors even though they never yield a monopoly overcharge and deadweight loss. But to deny that the inefficient losses imposed by failed attempts are social costs of "monopoly" is quite wrong. They are social costs of the *prospect* of monopoly, which tempts some people, and which the antitrust laws are designed to discourage. Competitors — who must be driven out of a market before a monopoly can be created — may be in a unique position to detect the *first* social costs of monopoly to be incurred, the money inefficiently spent, and the injuries inefficiently imposed by the monopolist or incipient monopolist in establishing its position. The social cost of waiting until the monopolist spends more of its own resources, inflicts more injuries on competitors, and begins charging monopoly prices could be enormous. Further, the chances of prosecution are less if we rely on consumers, for they are less likely to detect monopoly than are the immediate victims of exclusionary practices. *See* Hovenkamp, *Antitrust Policy and the Social Cost of Monopoly*, 78 Iowa L. Rev. 371 (1993).

[2] The Optimal Deterrence Model and Treble Damages

Section 4 of the Clayton Act also provides that the successful antitrust plaintiff is entitled to *three times* its losses. The requirement that antitrust damages be trebled is very old, going back at least as far as the English Statute of Monopolies, passed in 1623.

The Optimal Deterrence Model presents an economic argument for a damages multiplier — although the correct multiplier may not be three. Damages are trebled because there is a less than 100% likelihood that the violation will be detected and prosecuted, and the damages paid. Treble damages are appropriate on the assumption of a 0.33 probability that the fine will ever be paid. In short, an antitrust regime in which damages are based on three times the anticipated monopoly profits from a violation will deter such conduct if we can assume that such violators will have to pay the fine one time for every three such violations. As a general rule, the sanction should equal the sum of the monopoly overcharge plus the deadweight loss, multiplied by the reciprocal of the probability that the violation will be detected and prosecuted and the penalty paid.

But this economic rationale for treble damages meets substantial problems of both computation and strategy. First, coming up with the relevant data is well-nigh impossible. How many undetected cartels are there? Finding out would be difficult without detecting them.

More importantly, there is no single probability of detection for antitrust violations generally. At one extreme is naked bid rigging in which the conspirators know they are doing something criminal and take elaborate precautions to conceal it. Here the probability of detection is clearly less than 100%, or there would be no such conspiracies. At the other extreme are actions like airline or automobile company mergers which are announced to the Department of Justice before they occur and are described in public newspapers such as the *Wall Street Journal*. Here the probability of detection is so close to 100% that no firm could hope to escape antitrust liability by avoiding it. Rather, the firm must rely on its ability to convince an agency or court that its merger is legal. In between are explicit agreements that incorporate resale price maintenance and exclusive dealing or tying arrangements, and that are known to the parties to the agreement but perhaps not to the public generally. In many such cases the eventual plaintiff is a party to the agreement, so the probability of "detection" is very high, although the likelihood of successful prosecution is much lower. Likewise, ambiguous is monopolization where certain acts, such as an express refusal to deal or controlling an essential facility, are quite public, while other acts, such as patent fraud or predatory pricing, are concealed.

Perhaps the damage multiplier should consider the average of all of these. If we could identify the probability of detection of price fixing, resale price maintenance (RPM), exclusive dealing, monopolization and attempt, mergers, etc., weigh the numbers to account for the relative occurrence of each, and then average them, we might discover that, on the whole, one of every three antitrust violations is detected. As a result, treble damages is the optimal sanction.

But the immediate effect of our rule would be that firms bent on violating the antitrust laws would behave strategically. There would be relatively more of those violations where the probability of detection was less than one-third, and relatively fewer of those violations where the probability of detection was greater. Over time, the average probability of detection would decrease and our treble damage rule would prove underdeterrent.

Even if we segregated those antitrust offenses for which the probability of detection was relatively small and developed multiple damages rules for them, the problem would be the same. For example, suppose we decided that the probability that a cartel will be detected is one-third, and assigned a treble damage rule to naked price fixing. Were we omniscient, we would soon discover that, although the *average* probability that a cartel might be detected is one-third, not all cartels are alike. The probability that a cartel will be detected varies with the number of competitors, the extent of otherwise lawful communication among them, the presence or absence of nonparticipating competitors, the amount of detail with which price and output agreements have to be drawn, the nature of sales in the market, etc. Assuming an average probability of 0.33 that cartels will be detected, for some particular cartels that probability is far greater than 0.33 and for others it is far less. A treble damages rule will discourage cartels in the former category, where the rule will be overdeterrent, and encourage those in the latter category, where it is underdeterrent. Within a few years, the average probability of detection will no longer be one-third, and the number will have to be adjusted.

In short, there is no equilibrium in which a damage multiplier will work. As soon as one is established it will become underdeterrent, as firms choose those antitrust violations that are, on balance, more profitable. *See* Hovenkamp, *Antitrust Damages Reform*, 33 ANTITRUST BULL. 233 (1988).

[B] Award of Attorney's Fees

In addition to treble damages, costs and interest, a successful plaintiff, whether an individual, entity, or state attorney general, in an antitrust action is entitled to receive a "reasonable attorney's fee." Under Section 4 of the Clayton Act, the court is without discretion to decide whether the plaintiff who recovers damages is entitled to an attorney fee; the award is mandatory. Under Section 16 of the Clayton Act (15 U.S.C. § 26), the same rule applies to suits requesting injunctive relief. But the court does have discretion on how the fee is computed. *See* FLOYD & SULLIVAN, PRIVATE ANTITRUST ACTIONS 1047–1115 (1996). This discretion extends to the inherent power of the district court to review the amount of attorney's fees awarded pursuant to a class action settlement even when those fees are paid directly by the defendant and are not awarded out of the monetary recovery of the class. *Zucker v. Occidental Petroleum Corp.*, 192 F.3d 1323 (9th Cir. 1999). The court ruled that it must reserve this inherent power in order to "assure that the amount and mode of payment of attorney's fees are fair and proper." *Id.* at 1327.

Under Section 4C(d)(2) of the Hart-Scott-Rodino amendments of 1976, the district court has discretion to award a successful *defendant* attorney's fees, but only if a parens patriae suit has been brought by a state attorney general in "bad faith, vexatiously, wantonly or for oppressive reasons."

After experimenting with a formula based on a percentage of the recovery, courts have adopted through the years several methods of calculating the attorney fee based on the statutory requirement that the fee be "reasonable." While the methods vary, the outcome seems clear that attorney fees under Section 4 are to be awarded and calculated without regard to a preexisting contingent fee agreement between the plaintiff and counsel. *Farmington Dowel Prods. Co. v. Forster Mfg. Co.*, 421 F.2d 61 (1st Cir. 1969).

The trend in calculating the award has been towards establishing objective benchmarks rather than an evaluation based purely on subjective factors. The prevailing criterion today is known as the "lodestar" approach. In *Lindy Bros. Bldrs. v. American Radiator & Std. San. Corp.*, 487 F.2d 161 (3d Cir. 1973) (*Lindy I*), the Third Circuit stated that the computation should include the multiplication of the numbers of hours utilized by the normal billing rate for antitrust litigation, including the attorney's reputation and status, together with adjustments made for more subjective factors such as the likelihood of success or risk involved and quality of the professional service rendered. *See also Lindy Bros. Bldrs. v.*

American Radiator & Std. San. Corp., 540 F.2d 102 (3d Cir. 1976) (*Lindy II*). *Accord Strong v. BellSouth Telecomms. Inc.*, 137 F.3d 844 (5th Cir. 1998); *In re Petroleum Products Antitrust Litigation*, 109 F.3d 602 (9th Cir. 1997); *In re NASDAQ Market-Makers Antitrust Litigation*, 187 F.R.D. 465 (S.D.N.Y. 1998). *See generally Pennsylvania v. Delaware Valley Citizens' Council for Clean Air*, 483 U.S. 711 (1987) (where a majority of the Court agreed that federal fee-shifting statutes permit an upward adjustment of the lodestar for the risk of nonrecovery); Arthur J. Lachman, Note, *Attorney's Fee Contingency Enhancements*, 63 WASH. L. REV. 469 (1988).

The major criticism of the lodestar approach is that it creates a disincentive to settle because the attorney fee is largely based on the number of hours worked. Recently, the courts have seemed more willing to scrutinize the attorney's work in order to curtail the abuse of working excessive hours and prolonging the case so as to increase the award. *See, e.g., Arbor Hill Concerned Citizens Neighborhood Ass'n v. County of Albany*, 484 F.3d 162 (2d Cir. 2007); *City of Detroit v. Grinnell Corp.*, 495 F.2d 448 (2d Cir. 1974); Hornstein, *Legal Therapeutics: The "Salvage" Factor in Counsel Fee Awards*, 69 HARV. L. REV. 658 (1956). Another criticism of the lodestar method is that there is an inevitable waste of judicial resources. *In re Union Carbide Corp. Consumer Prod. Bus. Sec. Litig.*, 724 F. Supp. 160, 167–168 (S.D.N.Y. 1989). Citing the Third Circuit, the court stated that the lodestar approach is a "cumbersome, enervating, and often surrealistic process of preparing and evaluating fee petitions." *The Report of the Third Circuit Task Force, Court Awarded Attorney Fees*, 108 F.R.D. 237, 258 (3d Cir. 1985).

Several courts have held that the fee award must reflect the amount of damages won by the plaintiff, as well as other relief obtained. *Rosebrough Monument Co. v. Memorial Park Cem. Ass'n*, 572 F. Supp. 92, 94–95 (E.D. Mo. 1983) (citing *Hensley v. Eckerhart*, 461 U.S. 424 (1983)) (an award of attorney's fees should be based on "degree of success obtained"). But the Supreme Court in *City of Riverside v. Rivera*, 477 U.S. 561 (1986), by a divided majority, ruled against a general "requirement of proportionality between damages recovered and fees awardable." Rowe, *The Supreme Court on Attorney Fee Awards, 1985 and 1986 Terms: Economics, Ethics, and Ex Ante Analysis*, 1 GEO. J. LEGAL ETHICS 621, 623 (1988).

Is an award of attorney's fees permitted when the action is settled? The issue has been addressed most frequently in the settlement of antitrust class action suits. The Clayton Act does not specifically provide for the award of attorney fees when actions are settled. *Decorative Stone Co. v. Building Trades Council*, 23 F.2d 426, 428 (2d Cir. 1928). But the inherent equitable powers of the antitrust court have given rise to an "equitable fund doctrine," which has been used to permit the payment of attorney fees for an action resulting in settlement. *Compare Lindy I*, 487 F.2d 161, 165 (3d Cir. 1973), *with City of Detroit v. Grinnell Corp.*, 495 F.2d 448, 459 (2d Cir. 1974). *See Funeral Consumers Alliance, Inc. v. Serv. Corp. Int'l*, 695 F.3d 330 (5th Cir. 2012) (finding plaintiffs' settlement with one defendant does not prevent them from recovering costs and attorneys' fees from the remaining defendants).

The first exception to the "American Rule" requiring parties to pay their own attorney fees, absent a statutory authorization, came in *Trustees v. Greenough*, 105

U.S. 527 (1882). The Supreme Court held that a "common fund" is established for the payment of attorney's fees when a suit is brought that results in an economic benefit or increase of a fund, the interest in which is shared by many. This "common fund" doctrine provides an incentive to sue and prevents, at the time, unjust enrichment so that persons who obtain benefits of a lawsuit without contributing to its costs are not unjustly enriched at the successful litigants' expense. *See, e.g., Boeing Co. v. Van Gemert*, 444 U.S. 472, 478–482 (1980) (attorney's fees may be "assessed against the unclaimed portion" of the class action "fund created by the judgment"); *Mills v. Electric Auto Lite Co.*, 396 U.S. 375, 389–397 (1970). *See also Goldberger v. Integrated Resources Inc.*, 209 F.3d 43, 48 (2d Cir. 2000) (discretion in common fund cases).

In *United States Football League v. National Football League*, 887 F.2d 408 (2d Cir. 1989), the Second Circuit held that an attorney fee award of over $5.5 million was appropriate, even though a professional football league won only $1 in actual damages on its monopolization claim against the NFL. The court reasoned that the fact of injury, not the amount of damages, triggers the mandatory grant of fees under the Clayton Act. Although minimal damages may be relevant in determining the amount of fees allowed, it does not affect the entitlement, the court observed, because the policy behind fee awards is to encourage the detection and cessation of anticompetitive behavior. The court also held that in this case it was not necessary to apply the "prevailing party" standard to determine the fee entitlement because Section 4 requires only that there be injury, and once the jury makes a finding of injury, an award of attorney's fees will follow. The court proceeded to uphold a lodestar computation by the trial court. *See also Blue Cross & Blue Shield United v. Marshfield Clinic*, 152 F.3d 588 (7th Cir. 1998); *In re Synthroid Mktg. Litig.*, 325 F.3d 974 (7th Cir. 2003) (upholding a fee award amounting to over $10 million, 22% of the $46 million class fund).

One decision has required plaintiffs' attorneys to submit sealed bids to handle an antitrust case on a contingent-fee basis. *In re Oracle Securities Litig.*, 131 F.R.D. 688 (N.D. Cal. 1990).

Section 4 of the Clayton Act also permits the award of costs to the prevailing party. Recoverable costs have been defined as reimbursements for court filing fees, court reporter fees, transcript costs, witnesses' expenses, document copy expenses, etc. *See* Fed. R. Civ. P. 54(d). Other expenses, however, such as expert witness fees, are not included within the recoverable costs section of the Clayton Act, except by specific authorization. *See also* 28 U.S.C. § 1920 (2000).

[C]   Injunctive Relief and Structural Remedies

The Supreme Court in *Winter v. Natural Resources Defense Council, Inc.*, 555 U.S. 7 (2008), held that plaintiffs seeking preliminary injunctive relief must demonstrate that irreparable injury is likely in the absence of an injunction. There is a split in authority among the circuit courts with regard to whether the *Winter* decision prohibits the use of more flexible preliminary injunction standards, such as the sliding scale approach and the Second Circuit's "serious questions" standard. *Citigroup Global Markets Inc. v. VCG Special Opportunities Master Fund Ltd.*, 598 F.3d 30 (2d Cir. 2010). The *Winter* Court recited that the traditional standard for issuance of a preliminary injunction requires a party seeking the relief to demonstrate that (1) likely success on the merits, (2) likely to suffer irreparable harm in the absence of preliminary relief, (3) that the balance of equities tips in the requesting party's favor, and (4) that an injunction is in the public interest. *Winter*, 129 S. Ct. at 374 (citing *Munaf v. Green*, 553 U.S. 674, 690 (2008)). In *Winter*, however, even if the irreparable injury had been likely, any such injury was outweighed by the public interest and the Navy's interest in effectively training sailors.

With regard to likelihood of success, the circuit courts, post-*Winter*, now fall into roughly two categories. The first group interprets the traditional standard for granting a preliminary injunction to require a showing that the movant is likely to succeed on the merits. This group includes the First, Third, Fourth, Fifth, Eleventh, and Federal Circuits. *Bl(a)ck Tea Society v. City of Boston*, 378 F.3d 8 (1st Cir. 2004); *In re Arthur Treacher's Franchisee Litig.*, 689 F.2d 1137 (3d Cir. 1982); *Real Truth About Obama, Inc. v. Federal Election Comm'n*, 575 F.3d 342 (4th Cir. 2009), *vacated as moot*, 559 U.S. 1089 (2010); *Concerned Women for Am., Inc. v. Lafayette Cnty.*, 883 F.2d 32 (5th Cir. 1989); *Snook v. Trust Co. of Ga. Bank of Savannah, N.A.*, 909 F.2d 480 (11th Cir. 1990); *Am. Signature, Inc. v. United States.*, 598 F.3d 816 (Fed. Cir. 2010).

The second group uses a more lenient standard, serious question or sliding scale test regarding the likelihood of success on the merits. This group includes the Second, Sixth, Seventh, Eighth, Ninth, Tenth, and D.C. Circuits. *Citigroup*, 598 F.3d 30; *Mich. Bell Tel. Co. v. Engler*, 257 F.3d 587 (6th Cir. 2001); *Duct-O-Wire Co. v. U.S. Crane, Inc.*, 31 F.3d 506 (7th Cir. 1994); *Gen. Mills, Inc. v. Kellogg Co.*, 824 F.2d 622 (8th Cir. 1987); *Alliance for the Wild Rockies v. Cottrell*, 632 F.3d 1127 (9th Cir. 2011); *Okla. Tax Comm'n v. Int'l Registration Plan, Inc.*, 455 F.3d 1107 (10th Cir. 2006); *Davenport v. Int'l Bhd. of Teamsters*, 166 F.3d 356 (D.C. Cir. 1999).

The Second and Seventh Circuits have determined expressly that the serious question standard is in line with the Supreme Court's *Winter* ruling. *Citigroup*, 598 F.3d at 37–38 (2d Cir. 2010); *Hoosier Energy Rural Elec. Co-Op., Inc. v. John Hancock Life Ins. Co.*, 582 F.3d 721, 725 (7th Cir. 2009). Other circuits, however, that used a more flexible standard for granting preliminary injunctions prior to *Winter* have read the Court's language in *Winter* as a clear mandate to reverse course. The Fourth Circuit declared that is prior use of the serious question test stood in "fatal tension with [*Winter*]." *Real Truth About Obama*, 575 F.3d at 345–347 (4th Cir. 2009). The Ninth Circuit also indicated that it would abandon its flexible standard post-*Winter*. *Alliance for Wild Rockies v. Cottrell*, 613 F.3d 960 (9th Cir. 2010). However, two months after issuing that opinion, the Ninth Circuit amended the opinion to hold that *Winter* did not preclude use of the serious question standard. *Alliance for Wild Rockies v. Cottrell*, 622 F.3d 1045 (9th Cir. 2010), *withdrawn and superseded on denial of rehearing en banc by Alliance for Wild Rockies*, 632 F.3d 1127 (9th Cir. 2011).

Section 16 of the Clayton Act permits private suits for injunctive relief. Similarly, Section 4 of the Sherman Act and Section 15 of the Clayton Act grant jurisdiction to the district court to entertain actions brought by the government "in equity to prevent and restrain violations of these Acts." Injunctions sought by either private or government enforcement action generally focus on restraining anticompetitive conduct or behavior. Under certain circumstances, injunctive relief may also be brought to alter the structure of the corporation or industry under review.

Conduct-oriented injunctions are most generally in the form of "cease and desist" orders. Defendants are restrained from engaging in future violations of the statutes, or in addition, may be required to refrain from conduct not specifically forbidden by the statute. They have no effect on prior conduct, although the law may have been violated and anticompetitive profits obtained, unless the injunction is complementary to a damage award. If the injunction is violated, a "show cause" order may issue to determine whether defendant should be held in contempt of court, in addition to other sanctions.

In recent years, antitrust litigants have been bringing an increased number of appeals regarding the standards for the issuance of preliminary injunctions. The Seventh Circuit has been particularly active in articulating the prerequisites in antitrust cases:

(1) The plaintiff has no adequate remedy at law and will suffer irreparable harm if the preliminary injunction is not granted.

(2) The award of damages to the plaintiff would be inadequate.

(3) The court must consider any irreparable harm that the defendant might suffer from the injunction.

(4) The plaintiff must show some likelihood of success on the merits.

(5) The court must determine how likely the success of the plaintiff is because "[t]he more likely the plaintiff is to win, the less heavily need the balance of harms weigh in his favor."

(6) The public interest must be considered.

Roland Mach. Co. v. Dresser Indus., 749 F.2d 380 (7th Cir. 1984); *General Leaseways, Inc. v. National Leasing Ass'n*, 744 F.2d 588 (7th Cir. 1984). Appellate review is based on an "abuse of discretion."

Subsequent to *Roland*, Judge Posner of the Seventh Circuit attempted to express the standard for preliminary injunction in terms of a mathematical formula. The district court judge has discretion to grant a preliminary injunction if

$P * H_p > (1-P) * H_d$, where:

P = probability that the denial would be an error; ((1-P), in that case, refers to the possibility that granting of the injunction would be an error);

H_p = harm to the plaintiff;

H_d = harm to the defendant.

In other words, "only if harm to the plaintiff if the injunction is denied, multiplied by the probability that the denial would be an error, exceeds the harm to the defendant if the injunction is granted, multiplied by the probability that granting the injunction would be an error," should the injunction issue. *American Hosp.*

Supply Corp. v. Hospital Prods. Ltd., 780 F.2d 589 (7th Cir. 1986) (supplier terminated a distributor, who sued for breach of contract). The formula is designed to minimize the costs associated with a mistaken issuance of an injunction. Do you think this quantitative expression is merely a distillation of the six prerequisites set out above? If so, as the dissent in *American Hospital* opines, "why bother?" Specifically, does the formula include the equitable factors of irreparable injury, the balance of equities, the likelihood of success, and the public interest? Does it suggest a more rigid standard for issuance of a preliminary injunction? *See also Lawson Prods., Inc. v. Avnet, Inc.*, 782 F.2d 1429 (7th Cir. 1986). Remember that the standard of review on appeal is generally whether the district court abused its discretion in either granting or denying the injunction. This is in contrast to the Second Circuit's new standard which mandates that the court of appeal should engage in a *de novo* review of the factual findings. *Norlin Corp. v. Rooney, Pace, Inc.*, 744 F.2d 255 (2d Cir. 1984). Leubsdorf, *The Standard for Preliminary Injunctions*, 91 HARV. L. REV. 525 (1978).

Subsequent courts have framed Judge Posner's formulation more directly, in plain English, calling it the "sliding scale" approach. *Sofinet v. Immigration and Natural Service*, 188 F.3d 703 (7th Cir. 1999). *See Abbott Laboratories v. Mead Johnson & Co.*, 971 F.2d 6 (7th Cir. 1992); *Diginet Inc. v. Western Union ATS Inc.*, 958 F.2d 1388 (7th Cir. 1992). Under this approach, "the more likely it is that the plaintiff will succeed on the merits, the less the balance of irreparable harms need weigh towards its side; the less likely it is the plaintiff will succeed, the more the balance need weigh toward its side." *Sofinet*, 188 F.3d at 707. Once these two factors have been considered, the court is free to look at the other prerequisites of *Roland Mach.*

In contrast to conduct-directed injunctions, equitable relief may be fashioned so as to alter the structure of defendant's corporation, either through dissolution, divestiture, or divorcement. Litigation has addressed the question whether Section 16 of the Clayton Act limits a private plaintiff's options, in seeking equitable relief, to conduct-oriented injunctions, or whether structural remedies are available as well.

CALIFORNIA v. AMERICAN STORES CO.
495 U.S. 271 (1990)

STEVENS, J., delivered the opinion for a unanimous Court.

By merging with a major competitor, American Stores Co. (American) more than doubled the number of supermarkets that it owns in California. The State sued claiming that the merger violates the federal antitrust laws and will harm consumers in 62 California cities. The complaint prayed for a preliminary injunction requiring American to operate the acquired stores separately until the case is decided, and then to divest itself of all of the acquired assets located in California. . . . We conclude that [divesture] is [possible].

I

. . . .

On its face, the simple grant of authority in § 16 to "have injunctive relief" would seem to encompass divestiture just as plainly as the comparable language in § 15. Certainly § 16's reference to "injunctive relief . . . against threatened loss or damage" differs from § 15's grant of jurisdiction to "prevent and restrain violations," but it obviously does not follow that one grant encompasses remedies excluded from the other.[22]

Indeed, we think it could plausibly be argued that § 16's terms are the more expansive. In any event, . . . § 16 "states no restrictions or exceptions to the forms of injunctive relief a private plaintiff may seek, or that a court may order. . . . Rather, the statutory language indicates Congress' intention that traditional principles of equity govern the grant of injunctive relief." We agree that the plain text of § 16 authorizes divestiture decrees to remedy § 7 violations.

American rests its contrary argument upon two phrases in § 16 that arguably narrow its scope. The entitlement "to sue for and have injunctive relief" affords relief "against threatened loss or damage by a violation of the antitrust laws." Moreover, the right to such relief exists "when and under the same conditions and principles as injunctive relief against threatened conduct that will cause loss or damage is granted by courts of equity." . . . In this case, however, the requirement of "threatened loss or damage" is unquestionably satisfied. The allegations of the complaint, the findings of the District Court and the opinion of the Court of Appeals all assume that even if the merger is a completed violation of law, the threatened harm to California consumers exists. If divestiture is an appropriate means of preventing that harm, the statutory reference to "threatened loss or damage" surely does not negate the Court's power to grant such relief.

The second phrase, which refers to "threatened conduct that will cause loss or damage," is not drafted as a limitation on the power to grant relief, but rather is a part of the general reference to the standards that should be applied in fashioning injunctive relief. It is surely not the equivalent of a directive stating that unlawful conduct may be prohibited but structural relief may not be mandated. Indeed, as the Ninth Circuit's analysis of the issue demonstrates, the distinction between conduct and structure — or between prohibitory and mandatory relief — is illusory in a case of this kind. Thus, in the *IT&T* case, the Court recognized that an injunction prohibiting a parent company from voting the stock of the subsidiary should not be treated differently from a mandatory order of divestiture. And in this case the court treated the "Hold Separate Agreement" as a form of "indirect divestiture." In both cases the injunctive relief would unquestionably prohibit "conduct" by the defendants. American's textual arguments — which rely on a distinction between mandatory and prohibited relief — do not explain why such remedies would not be appropriate.

---

[22] [FN 7] That the two provisions do differ is not surprising at all, since § 15 was largely copied from § 4 of the Sherman Act while § 16, which had to incorporate standing limits appropriate to private actions — see *Cargill, Inc. v. Monfort of Colorado, Inc.*, 479 U.S. 104 (1986) — had no counterpart in the Sherman Act.

If we assume that the merger violated the antitrust laws, and if we agree with the District Court's finding that the conduct of the merged enterprise threatens economic harm to California consumers, the literal text of § 16 is plainly sufficient to authorize injunctive relief, including an order of divestiture, that will prohibit that conduct from causing that harm. This interpretation is consistent with our precedents, which have upheld injunctions issued pursuant to § 16 regardless of whether they were mandatory or prohibitory in character. *See Zenith Radio Corp. v. Hazeltine Research, Inc.*, 395 U.S. 100, 129–33 (1969) (reinstating injunction that required defendants to withdraw from patent pools); *see also Silver v. New York Stock Exchange*, 373 U.S. 341, 345, 365 (1963) (reinstating judgment for defendants in suit to compel installation of wire services). We have recognized when construing § 16 that it was enacted "not merely to provide private relief, but . . . to serve as well the high purpose of enforcing the antitrust laws." *Zenith Radio Corp. v. Hazeltine Research, Inc.*, 395 U.S., at 130–31. . . .

Finally, by construing § 16 to encompass divestiture decrees we are better able than American to harmonize the section with its statutory context. The Act's other provisions manifest a clear intent to encourage vigorous private litigation against anticompetitive mergers. Section 7 itself creates a relatively expansive definition of antitrust liability: to show that a merger is unlawful, a plaintiff need only prove that its effect *"may* be substantially to lessen competition." *See Brown Shoe Co. v. United States*, 370 U.S. 294, 323 (1962). In addition, § 5 of the Act provided that during the pendency of a government action, the statute of limitations for private actions would be tolled. The section also permitted plaintiffs to use the final judgment in a government antitrust suit as a prima facie evidence of liability in a later civil suit. Private enforcement of the Act was in no sense an afterthought; it was an integral part of the congressional plan for protecting competition. *See Minnesota Mining & Mfg. Co. v. New Jersey Wood Finishing Co.*, 381 U.S. 311, 318 (1965). Congress also made express its view that divestiture was the most suitable remedy in a suit for relief from a § 7 violation: in § 11 of the Act, Congress directed the Federal Trade Commission to issue [an] order requiring that a violator of § 7 "cease and desist from the violation," and, specifically, that the violator "divest itself of the stock held" in violation of the Act. Section 16, construed to authorize a private divestiture remedy when appropriate in light of equitable principles, fits well in a statutory scheme that favors private enforcement, subjects mergers to searching scrutiny, and regards divestiture as the remedy best suited to redress the ills of anticompetitive merger.

. . . .

IV

Our conclusion that a district court has the power to order divestiture in appropriate cases brought under § 16 of the Clayton Act does not, of course, mean that such power should be exercised in every situation in which the Government would be entitled to such relief under § 15. In a Government case the proof of a violation of law may itself establish sufficient public injury to warrant relief. . . . A private litigant, however, must have standing — in the words of § 16, he must prove "threatened loss or damage" to his own interests in order to obtain relief. *See*

Cargill, Inc. v. Monfort of Colorado, Inc., 479 U.S. 104 (1986). Moreover, equitable defenses such as laches, or perhaps "unclean hands," may protect consummated transactions from belated attacks by private parties when it would not be too late for the Government to vindicate the public interest.

Such questions, however, are not presented in this case. We are merely confronted with the naked question whether the District Court had the power to divest American of any part of its ownership interests in the acquired Lucky Stores either by forbidding the exercise of the owner's normal right to integrate the operations of the two previously separate companies, or by requiring it to sell certain assets located in California. We hold that such a remedy is a form of "injunctive relief" within the meaning of § 16 of the Clayton Act. Accordingly, the judgment of the Court of Appeals is reversed and the case is remanded for further proceedings consistent with this opinion. It is so ordered.

NOTES AND QUESTIONS

1.   Should it matter whether the private plaintiff seeking divestiture is a state suing as parens patriae, as in the *American Stores* decision, rather than a private competitor? What would a private competitor have to show in order to obtain divestiture of an admittedly illegal merger? When the state sues as parens patriae, whose interest is it protecting? Consumers'? Competitors'? Are state enforcement agencies ever "captured" by special interest groups? If so, should this be relevant in an antitrust case? Suppose it was widely known that the state attorney general's office was heavily lobbied to challenge a merger by a group of competitors who would be injured by the post-merger firm's increased efficiency. Would the state have standing? Could it obtain divestiture?

2.   Under Section 16 of the Clayton Act, indirect purchasers are private parties who may sue for injunctive relief. *See Campos v. Ticketmaster Corp.*, 140 F.3d 1166, 1172 (8th Cir. 1998). However, no federal court has ordered a divesture when the plaintiff was a private party who was neither a customer nor competitor of merging parties. *See Antoine Garabet, M.D., Inc. v. Autonomous Tech. Corp.*, 116 F. Supp. 2d 1159, 1173 n.13 (C.D. Cal. 2000); *Glendora v. Gannett Co.*, 858 F. Supp. 369, 372 (S.D.N.Y. 1994). In *Ginsburg v. InBev NV/SA*, 623 F.3d 1229, 1230 (8th Cir. 2010), plaintiffs were beer consumers who had filed suit to enjoin the consummated acquisition of Anheuser-Busch Companies by InBev NV/SA on the grounds that the transaction violated Section 7 of the Clayton Act.

The Eighth Circuit found that because plaintiffs were private, indirect purchasers "rather than a federal antitrust enforcement agency, divesture's 'far-reaching effects put it at the least accessible end of a spectrum of injunctive relief.' " *Id.* at 1234 (quoting *Antoine Garabet*, 116 F. Supp. 2d at 1172). The court noted that plaintiffs delay in filing their lawsuit until the merger had been consummated constituted a lack of diligence that counseled against divestiture as a remedy. *Id.* at 1235 (citing *Midwestern Mach. Co. v. Northwest Airlines, Inc.*, 392 F.3d 265, 277 (8th Cir. 2004)). Finally, the court found that the balance of equities tipped sharply in favor of the merging companies. "While the price benefit beer drinkers would gain from divestiture is unclear, a court decree splitting up the combined entities would impose obvious hardship on the employees and distributors of former

[Anheuser-Busch] and might well damage competition and consumers by crippling the operations of the largest domestic producers of immensely popular products." *Id.* at 1235–1236. The possibility of harm to a group of indirect purchasers was too remote to warrant "the extreme remedy of divesture." *Id.* (quoting *Broadcom Corp. v. Qualcomm Inc.*, 501 F.3d 297, 322 (3d Cir. 2007)).

3. What importance should a court attach to the fact that one of the enforcement agencies (FTC or Department of Justice Antitrust Division) had already reviewed and approved a merger that is now being challenged by a private party? As a basic premise, the agency decision is not binding on any private litigant. Suppose the agency decides that, although a merger may have some short-run anticompetitive effects within the United States, in the long run it will improve America's competitive position in world markets. Should a private plaintiff be able to "restructure" an industry by obtaining a divestiture decree in a way that conflicts with basic American economic policy? Could this problem be solved by any means other than new legislation?

4. At one time, there was a question whether the FTC, in addition to the Justice Department, had the authority to seek divestiture. In *FTC v. Eastman Kodak Co.*, 274 U.S. 619 (1927), the Supreme Court held that the FTC lacked authority to order divestiture of some of Kodak's laboratories. Later the Court changed its mind, however, and today the power of the FTC to order divestiture in appropriate circumstances is clearly established. *See FTC v. Procter & Gamble Co.*, 386 U.S. 568 (1967), reprinted in Chapter 7, *infra*.

5. The use of structural relief, in conjunction with conduct-directed injunction, might be particularly appropriate in remedying monopolization violations under Section 2 of the Sherman Act or illegal mergers under Section 7 of the Clayton Act. Violators of Section 1 of the Sherman Act might also be candidates, though to a lesser extent. Structural remedies might include an order to divest assets, stock, or securities, or to "spin off" a firm so that it can become an independent competitor in the market. *See* Sullivan, *The Antitrust Division as a Regulatory Agency: An Enforcement Policy in Transition*, 64 WASH. U.L.Q. 997 (1986). Consider whether a "spin off" divestiture which results in a dissolution of the firm might not create diseconomies of scale. Is a court equipped to determine the minimum output level below which a firm cannot survive? *See White House Task Force [Report] on Antitrust Policy* 311–312 (1968).

6. For a comparison of structural and behavioral remedies available in antitrust, see E. Thomas Sullivan, *Antitrust Remedies in the U.S. and E.U.: Advancing a Standard of Proportionality*, 48 ANTITRUST BULL. 377 (2003); E. Thomas Sullivan, *The Jurisprudence of Antitrust Divestiture: The Path Less Traveled*, 86 MINN. L. REV. 565 (2002); Howard A. Shelanski & J. Gregory Sidak, *Antitrust Divestiture in Network Industries*, 68 U. CHI. L. REV. 1 (2001).

[D] Contribution and Claim Reduction

Under present law, a plaintiff has a right to sue and attempt to recover all its damages against a single defendant, although other, perhaps more culpable, defendants exist. This is so because each defendant is liable for all of the treble damages caused by the antitrust violation — i.e., liability is "joint and several." In the absence of a rule permitting contribution, a sued defendant may pay damages far in excess of its responsibility, while others escape liability. *See generally* Sullivan, *New Perspectives in Antitrust Litigation: Toward a Right of Comparative Contribution*, 1980 U. ILL. L F. 389. This is true even when some direct purchasers in *Illinois Brick*-styled litigation choose not to sue. In *Paper Systems, Inc. v. Nippon Industries Co.*, 281 F.3d 629 (7th Cir. 2002), the court held that *Illinois Brick* does not preclude application of joint and several liability to a single defendant, even if some of the direct purchasers did not join the class of plaintiffs in the class action. If the three plaintiffs in the suit, and members of the class, could prove a conspiracy among the five manufacturers, then any single defendant could be responsible for the overcharge of all five manufacturers. All that *Illinois Brick* meant was that the total amount of recoverable damages would be reduced by the damages that the non-suing direct purchasers could recover.

The Supreme Court spoke to the issue of contribution in antitrust, in *Texas Indus., Inc. v. Radcliff Materials, Inc.*, 451 U.S. 630 (1981), when it held that Congress did not intend to create contribution rights when it adopted the Sherman and Clayton Acts. Thus the federal courts were without power to fashion common-law rules sanctioning contribution in antitrust litigation. The Court, although not signaling its own view on how the competing interests involved should be weighed, did invite Congress to consider the policies and values at issue.

Since the *Texas Industries* decision, Congress has considered a number of contribution and claim reduction bills. None has passed both houses of the Congress, although substantial support for some variation of a pro-contribution/claim reduction rule does exist. *See* E. Cavanagh, *Contribution, Claim Reduction and Individual Treble Damage Responsibility: Which Path to Reform of Antitrust Remedies*, 40 VAND. L. REV. 1278 (1987); D. Polden & E. Sullivan, *Contribution and Claim Reduction in Antitrust Litigation: A Legislative Analysis*, 20 HARV. J. ON LEGIS. 397 (1983).

On a related issue, the Fourth Circuit, subsequent to *Texas Industries*, held in *Burlington Indus. v. Milliken & Co.*, 690 F.2d 380, 390–395 (4th Cir. 1982) that *Texas Industries'* logic should extend to claim reductions. In *Burlington Industries*, the plaintiff had settled with one defendant before suit. The district court found for plaintiff, but reduced its damage judgment by treble the settlement figure. The Fourth Circuit overturned the district court when it reaffirmed the prevailing rule that any amount received in settlement should be deducted from plaintiff's damages after trebling, not before. Reasoning that claim reduction was analogous to contribution, the court held that the district court lacked the authority to implement claim reduction.

Chapter 4

CARTELS AND OTHER JOINT CONDUCT BY COMPETITORS

I HORIZONTAL RESTRAINTS

[A] The Development of Analytical and Evidentiary Rules

[1] Introduction: The Problems of Horizontal Arrangements

Section 1 of the Sherman Act is directed toward conduct which unreasonably interferes with trade and is the product of an "agreement" among two or more independent actors. When the agreement is among competitors, the conduct is classified as horizontal. Horizontal arrangements include, inter alia, price fixing, market divisions or allocations, bid rigging, group boycotts, and other concerted activities that restrict output or exclude competition. In contrast to Section 2 of the Sherman Act, which is concerned with single firm activity, Section 1 requires concerted conduct by more than one entity. However not all agreements — not even all agreements of competitors — are illegal. The problem is to characterize the conduct and understand how it affects competition.

The protection of competition is the central policy of the Sherman Act. In a competitive market, individual firms attempt to maximize profits within the context of consumer desires and limited available resources. Each firm takes costs and prices as given and sets output at a level maximizing returns at the given prices. But if the firms can agree on price and output, they will behave much more like a monopolist. Industry output will be lower and prices higher. Such an agreement is called a cartel.

The success of a cartel may depend upon the structure of industry in which it operates. Cooperation among cartel members is essential. The larger the number of firms in the cartel, the more likely that cartelization will be impracticable. Christopher R. Leslie, *Trust, Distrust, and Antitrust*, 82 Tex. L. Rev. 515 (2004); George A. Hay & Daniel Kelley, *An Empirical Survey of Price Fixing Conspiracies*, 17 J.L. & Econ. 13, 14, 27 (1974). For a cartel to work effectively, there must be an agreement on output and price. Some cartels set limits on inputs as well as outputs. Herbert Hovenkamp & Christopher R. Leslie, *The Firm as Cartel Manager*, 64 Vand. L. Rev. 813 (2011). When firms can agree on overall production limits, they must still decide how to apportion the total quantity produced.

Moreover, if the sellers have different costs, they will have different profit maximizing prices. As a result, it may be difficult for them to agree about either the resale price or the output quota for each member. Any agreement that they reach will necessarily be a compromise, and some firms are likely to feel cheated. For this reason, many cartels are inherently unstable. RICHARD POSNER, ANTITRUST LAW 66–68 (2d ed. 2001); *Business Elec. Corp. v. Sharp Elec. Corp.*, 485 U.S. 717 (1988) ("Cartels are neither easy to form nor easy to maintain. Uncertainty over the terms of the cartel, particularly the prices to be charged in the future, obstructs both formation and adherence by making cheating easier.").

In addition to administrative difficulties and costs of the cartel, which may increase the overall cartel price of the product, the cartel faces enforcement problems. First, if the cartel sets the price of the product too high, it may encourage new firms to enter the market, which will increase market output and reduce prices. Second, the cartel may be subject to cheating by cartel members. Individual competitors may wish to drop prices and undercut competitors in order to capture a larger share of the market. Under these conditions, the cartel will not survive unless artificial entry barriers are erected against the new entrant or unless the discounter is detected and persuaded to comply. Otherwise the other cartel members will individually increase output and reduce price in order to meet the new competition. Interdependence of conduct which was a prerequisite under the cartel arrangement will disappear. *See* HERBERT HOVENKAMP, FEDERAL ANTITRUST POLICY § 4.1 (4th ed. 2011). Section 1 of the Sherman Act addresses these types of cartel practices and interdependent conduct.

[2]   Rules of Reason and Per Se Illegality

As discussed in Chapter 1, the rule of reason developed as a rule of construction under the Sherman Act from Judge Taft's decision in *United States v. Addyston Pipe*, 85 F. 271 (6th Cir. 1898), *aff'd*, 175 U.S. 211 (1899), and Chief Justice White's opinions in *Standard Oil Co. v. United States*, 221 U.S. 1 (1911), and *United States v. American Tobacco Co.*, 221 U.S. 106 (1911). Unlike the ancillary-direct restraint dichotomy adopted in *Addyston Pipe*, Chief Justice White applied the rule of reason analysis to all trade restraints, whether ancillary or direct. The result was that only *unreasonable* restraints of trade were deemed illegal. But how was a court to determine the "reasonableness" of the restraint?

Chief Justice White set out a three-prong test for weighing the reasonableness of the restraint. He was particularly concerned with the competitive effects that an agreement between competing firms would have in the market. He expressed the belief that any analysis of Section 1 of the Sherman Act had to examine the effects of the challenged conduct. He implicitly recognized, however, that certain conduct is, by its nature or character, unreasonable because it is inherently anticompetitive. In the earlier Supreme Court case of *United States v. Joint Traffic Ass'n*, 171 U.S. 505, 568 (1898), the Court noted that price-fixing arrangements that have a "direct and immediate effect" are illegal.

From Chief Justice White's early reasoning, several methods of analyzing challenged conduct emerge. Initially, the court must find that a contract, combination, or agreement existed. The court must further inquire whether, because of the inherent nature of the practice, trade is restrained. If the conduct (such as a cartel arrangement) is likely to have no beneficial effect and if it significantly impairs competition, it is classified as "per se" illegal. From an evidentiary standpoint, the inquiry is over once the Court has determined that the conduct is, by its nature, inherently anticompetitive. No further inquiry is needed to determine the reasonableness of the restraint or actual competitive effect. Neither purpose nor market power to accomplish the anticompetitive effect will be examined. The per se analysis thus is a conclusive presumption of illegality. In application, it is the functional equivalent of a rule of evidence. Once the restrictive conduct is found to come within a category defined as per se illegal, evidentiary matters that might be relevant in a rule of reason case become irrelevant.

Not all restrictive conduct is inherently anticompetitive, however. If the court has not classified previously the challenged practice as per se illegal, or if the court has not had substantial experience with the practice, it will decide anew whether the practice has an unlawful purpose *or* anticompetitive effect. The rule of reason analysis will be applied in this situation by a detailed factual inquiry that will scrutinize the purpose and the effect of the practice and reasonable inferences derived therefrom. Beginning in the 1980s, courts developed a third mode of antitrust analysis, referred to as abbreviated rule of reason or "quick look" analysis. Quick look analysis is less rigid than the per se rule but less thorough than a full-blown rule of reason analysis.

As the cases in this chapter indicate, distinctions between the per se rule of illegality, the quick look approach, and the rule of reason analysis are sometimes confusing. The judicial function is to examine the challenged conduct within a limited range of judicial discretion. That discretion is guided by the rules of construction and rules of evidence discussed herein. The line drawing is not always clear; subtle distinctions are made and significant overlap exists between the various analyses.

Over the years, judges have drawn distinctions and established classifications that decide questions of fact and policy. By definition and practice, the process of decision-making is flexible and multifaceted. This is not only its strength but its weakness as well. Clear judicial guidelines are not always forthcoming. Ultimately, however, the question is whether the courts' approach to antitrust analysis is faithful to the legislative policy and intent. But see J. Flynn, *The Role of Rules in Antitrust Analysis*, 2006 UTAH L. REV. 605 (2006), for an argument that the economic theory behind the per se rules had led to "[r]ule rigidity and concept calcification."

[3] Guidelines for Collaboration Among Competitors

Both the Federal Trade Commission and the Department of Justice issued on April 7, 2000, the Guidelines for Collaborations Among Competitors. The Guidelines set forth an enforcement framework for understanding the government's current thinking on horizontal agreements among competitors so that businesses can assess whether an antitrust enforcement action is likely. The Guidelines do not have the force of law and are not binding on courts. Nevertheless, the Guidelines provide guidance to businesses as to whether their conduct will likely result in a government prosecution. Furthermore, some courts may find the Guidelines to be persuasive authority when deciding cases.

The Guidelines address rule of reason analysis and per se approaches to antitrust. Consistent with case law, the Guidelines treat conduct that raises price or reduces output as per se illegal (price fixing, bid rigging, and market divisions), while a more detailed factual inquiry will be undertaken for other agreements that do not always or usually tend to affect price or output. Under the rule of reason approach, market factors are considered. First, the nature of the agreement is considered in the context of a market power analysis. When considering market power, whether an increase or an ability to facilitate its exercise, the Guidelines indicate that the market will be defined, market shares calculated, and concentration factors determined. Second, an examination will occur whether under the agreement there is an ability for the participants to compete independently of each other. Entry into the market also will be considered. Finally, if the analyses of these factors reveal no anticompetitive harm, there will be no need to consider any offsetting procompetitive benefits. If there is evidence of some antitrust harm, the government will weigh whether the likely procompetitive features of the agreement will outweigh the anticompetitive harms. In achieving the substantial efficiencies, the methods chosen to accomplish the benefits cannot be broader than necessary.

The Guidelines establish "safe zones" for certain collaborations between competitors when anticompetitive effects are unlikely. These safe zones include (1) collaborations among competitors when the market share of the participants is 20% or less of the relevant market; (2) innovation markets (joint research or development activities) when there are three or more independently controlled research ventures that are close substitutes for joint research and development activities. If the collaborations among competitors fall outside these safety zones, then, under the Guidelines, the government's analysis will proceed either under the rule of reason or per se analysis. *See Guidelines for Collaborations Among Competitors* at Appendix E.

[B] Price Fixing

[1] The Foundation Cases

CHICAGO BOARD OF TRADE v. UNITED STATES
246 U.S. 231 (1918)

[The Board of Trade, which operated a commodity grain exchange, enacted rules that governed the regulation of grain sales. The first rule governed "spot sales," or the sale of grain which was located in Chicago and ready for delivery. The second concerned "future sales," or contracts which required the purchase of grain for future delivery. The third rule regulated "to arrive sales," or sales of grain which had not yet arrived in Chicago, but were enroute and would be ready for delivery upon arrival. During the regular hours of the Board, traders would buy and sell "spot and future sales." After the close of the regular hours, "call" sessions were held for the purpose of permitting traders to make sales for the "to arrive" grain. In addition, members of the Board were individually permitted to buy and sell "to arrive" grain during the nonregular hours.

In 1906, the Board established a "call" rule which precluded members of the Board from buying or selling "to arrive" grain during a period after the "call" session and before the exchange opened the next day at a price other than the one established as the closing price at the end of each call session. The Department of Justice challenged the "call" rule and sought an injunction to prohibit its enforcement. The Government argued that the rule amounted to an agreement to fix the price of the "to arrive" grain in violation of Section 1 of the Sherman Act, though the "call" did not purport to set the price level. The defendant maintained that the rule had neither an unlawful purpose or effect; that, in fact, the purpose was to restrict the hours of trading for the convenience of the exchange members; to reduce the monopoly held by a certain, though small, group of grain traders who bought and sold during the nonregular hours; and to promote more competition during the regular hours. The lower court, on a motion from the Government, struck the defense allegations concerning the purpose of the rule. The rule was found to be a restraint of trade and the Board was enjoined from acting on it.]

JUSTICE BRANDEIS delivered the opinion of the Court.

. . . The Government proved the existence of the rule and described its application and the change in business practice involved. It made no attempt to show that the rule was designed to or that it had the effect of limiting the amount of grain shipped to Chicago; or of retarding or accelerating shipment; or of raising or depressing prices; or of discriminating against any part of the public; or that it resulted in hardship to anyone. The case was rested upon the bald proposition, that a rule or agreement by which men occupying positions of strength in any branch of trade, fixed prices at which they would buy or sell during an important part of the business day, is an illegal restraint of trade under the Anti-Trust Law. But the legality of an agreement or regulation cannot be determined by so simple a test, as whether it restrains competition. Every agreement concerning trade, every regulation of trade, restrains. To bind, to restrain, is of their very essence. The true test of legality is whether the restraint imposed is such as merely regulates and perhaps thereby promotes competition or whether it is such as may suppress or even destroy competition. To determine that question the court must ordinarily consider the facts peculiar to the business to which the restraint is applied; its condition before and after the restraint was imposed; the nature of the restraint and its effect, actual or probable. The history of the restraint, the evil believed to exist, the reason for adopting the particular remedy, the purpose or end sought to be attained, are all relevant facts. This is not because a good intention will save an otherwise objectionable regulation or the reverse; but because knowledge of intent may help the court to interpret facts and to predict consequences. The District Court erred, therefore, in striking from the answer allegations concerning the history and purpose of the Call rule and in later excluding evidence on that subject. But the evidence admitted makes it clear that the rule was a reasonable regulation of business consistent with the provisions of the Anti-Trust Law.

First: The nature of the rule: The restriction was upon the period of price-making. It required members to desist from further price-making after the close of the Call until 9:30 A. M. the next business day: but there was no restriction upon the sending out of bids after close of the Call. Thus it required members who desired to buy grain "to arrive" to make up their minds before the close of the Call how much they were willing to pay during the interval before the next session of the Board. The rule made it to their interest to attend the Call; and if they did not fill their wants by purchases there, to make the final bid high enough to enable them to purchase from country dealers.

Second: The scope of the rule: It is restricted in operation to grain "to arrive." It applies only to a small part of the grain shipped from day to day to Chicago, and to an even smaller part of the day's sales: members were left free to purchase grain already in Chicago from anyone at any price throughout the day. It applies only during a small part of the business day; members were left free to purchase during the sessions of the Board grain "to arrive," at any price, from members anywhere and from non-members anywhere except on the premises of the Board. It applied only to grain shipped to Chicago: members were left free to purchase at any price throughout the day from either members or non-members, grain "to arrive" at any other market. . . .

Third: The effects of the rule: As it applies to only a small part of the grain shipped to Chicago and to that only during a part of the business day and does not apply at all to grain shipped to other markets, the rule had no appreciable effect on general market prices; nor did it materially affect the total volume of grain coming to Chicago. But within the narrow limits of its operation the rule helped to improve market conditions thus:

(a) It created a public market for grain "to arrive." Before its adoption, bids were made privately. Men had to buy and sell without adequate knowledge of actual market conditions. This was disadvantageous to all concerned, but particularly so to country dealers and farmers.

(b) It brought into the regular market hours of the Board sessions more of the trading in grain "to arrive."

(c) It brought buyers and sellers into more direct relations; because on the Call they gathered together for a free and open interchange of bids and offers.

(d) It distributed the business in grain "to arrive" among a far larger number of Chicago receivers and commission merchants than had been the case there before.

(e) It increased the number of country dealers engaging in this branch of the business; supplied them more regularly with bids from Chicago; and also increased the number of bids received by them from competing markets.

(f) It eliminated risks necessarily incident to a private market, and thus enabled country dealers to do business on a smaller margin. In that way the rule made it possible for them to pay more to farmers without raising the price to consumers.

(g) It enabled country dealers to sell some grain to arrive which they would otherwise have been obliged either to ship to Chicago commission merchants or to sell for "future delivery."

(h) It enables those grain merchants of Chicago who sell to millers and exporters to trade on a smaller margin and, by paying more for grain or selling it for less, to make the Chicago market more attractive for both shippers and buyers of grain.

(i) Incidentally it facilitated trading "to arrive" by enabling those engaged in these transactions to fulfil their contracts by tendering grain arriving at Chicago on any railroad, whereas formerly shipments had to be made over the particular railroad designated by the buyer.'

. . . Every board of trade and nearly every trade organization imposes some restraint upon the conduct of business by its members. Those relating to the hours in which business may be done are common; and they make a special appeal where, as here, they tend to shorten the working day or, at least, limit the period of most exacting activity. The decree of the District Court is reversed with directions to dismiss the bill.

Reversed.

NOTES AND QUESTIONS

1. At the time the call rule was adopted, the members of the Board of Trade also had fixed commission rates for executing sales. Should not Justice Brandeis have analyzed this fact? The Board members probably adopted the call rule to prevent members from "cheating" on the commission rates. For example, suppose that a commodity closed at the end of a trading session at a price of $10 per unit, and that the commission on 10 units was $10. An agent who negotiated a sale of 10 units at $10 would charge the buyer $110 and pay the seller $100. The agent would keep the $10 commission. On the floor, the commissions were fixed by agreement and all transactions had to take place at the posted price. The combination of these two rules effectively eliminated all price competition between agents. Before the call rule was adopted, however, an agent could "cheat" in order to obtain a particular transaction: although he still had to charge the $10 commission, he could shave $5 off the price to the buyer, effectively collecting $105 from the buyer and paying $100 to the seller. The call rule made price competition among the agents impossible both during the trading session and after it was over.

2. While the restraint in *Chicago Board of Trade* was deemed reasonable because it protected a socially desirable class of grain traders, Professor Carstensen posits that an alternative justification exists: the restraint controlled the risks of opportunistic behavior and was ancillary to a joint venture. *See* Peter C. Carstensen, *The Content of the Hollow Core of Antitrust: The Chicago Board of Trade Case and the Meaning of the "Rule of Reason" in Restraint of Trade Analysis*, *in* RESEARCH IN LAW AND ECONOMICS 1–88 (1992).

3. Justice Brandeis' opinion in *Chicago Board of Trade* should be compared with the next case, *Trenton Potteries*, where the Court rejected a rule of reason analysis for price fixing. What factors did Justice Brandeis say should be evaluated in determining the legality of the restraint? Does the Court's language indicate that in a price-fixing case it will consider the reasonableness of the price? Were other alternatives available to the Board that would have countered the monopoly enjoyed by the traders who conducted business during the nonregular hours?

UNITED STATES v. TRENTON POTTERIES CO.
273 U.S. 392 (1927)

[Twenty-three corporations and twenty individuals were indicted and charged with fixing the price of pottery for bathrooms. Defendants, members of a pottery trade association, controlled 82% of the sanitary pottery fixtures in the United States. Defendants were convicted in the district court, but the court of appeals reversed on the ground that the jury had been erroneously instructed on the law. The trial court charged that if the jury found "the agreements or combination complained of, it might return a verdict of guilty without regard to the reasonableness of the price fixed, or the good intentions of the combining units, whether prices were actually lowered or raised . . . since [such] agreements . . . were unreasonable restraints." Defendant argued that the challenged conduct was lawful because the established prices were reasonable and noninjurious to the public. The Supreme Court reversed the court of appeals, the effect of which was to reinstate the convictions.]

JUSTICE STONE delivered the opinion of the Court.

. . . Reasonableness is not a concept of definite and unchanging content. Its meaning necessarily varies in the different fields of the law, because it is used as a convenient summary of the dominant considerations which control in the application of legal doctrines. Our view of what is a reasonable restraint of commerce is controlled by the recognized purpose of the Sherman Law itself. Whether this type of restraint is reasonable or not must be judged in part at least in the light of its effect on competition, for whatever difference of opinion there may be among economists as to the social and economic desirability of an unrestrained competitive system, it cannot be doubted that the Sherman Law and the judicial decisions interpreting it are based upon the assumption that the public interest is best protected from the evils of monopoly and price control by the maintenance of competition.

The aim and result of every price-fixing agreement, if effective, is the elimination of one form of competition. The power to fix prices, whether reasonably exercised or not, involves power to control the market and to fix arbitrary and unreasonable prices. The reasonable price fixed today may through economic and business changes become the unreasonable price of tomorrow. Once established, it may be maintained unchanged because of the absence of competition secured by the agreement for a price reasonable when fixed. Agreements which create such potential power may well be held to be in themselves unreasonable or unlawful restraints, without the necessity of minute inquiry whether a particular price is reasonable or unreasonable as fixed and without placing on the government in enforcing the Sherman Law the burden of ascertaining from day to day whether it has become unreasonable through the mere variation of economic conditions. Moreover, in the absence of express legislation requiring it, we should hesitate to adopt a construction making the difference between legal and illegal conduct in the field of business relations depend upon so uncertain a test as whether prices are reasonable — a determination which can be satisfactorily made only after a complete survey of our economic organization and a choice between rival philosophies. . . . Thus viewed, the Sherman law is not only a prohibition against the infliction of a particular type of public injury. It is a limitation of rights, . . . which may be pushed to evil consequences and therefore restrained.

That such was the view of this Court in deciding the *Standard Oil* and *Tobacco* cases, and that such is the effect of its decisions both before and after those cases, does not seem fairly open to question. Beginning with *Trans-Missouri* [and] *Joint Traffic Association,* where agreements for establishing reasonable and uniform freight rates by competing lines of railroad were held unlawful, it has since often been decided and always assumed that uniform price-fixing by those controlling in any substantial manner a trade or business in interstate commerce is prohibited by the Sherman Law, despite the reasonableness of the particular prices agreed upon. In *Addyston Pipe & Steel Co. v. United States,* 175 U.S. 211, 237, a case involving a scheme for fixing prices, this Court quoted with approval the following passage from the lower court's opinion: " . . . the affiants say that, in their opinion, the prices at which pipe has been sold by defendants have been reasonable. We do not think the issue an important one, because, as already stated, we do not think that at common law there is any question of reasonableness open to the courts with reference to such a contract."

. . . .

That the opinions in the *Standard Oil* and *Tobacco* cases were not intended to affect this view of the illegality of price-fixing agreements affirmatively appears from the opinion in the *Standard Oil* case where . . . the court said:

> "That as considering the contracts or agreements, their necessary effect and the character of the parties by whom they were made, they were clearly restraints of trade within the purview of the statute, they could not be taken out of that category by indulging in general reasoning as to the expediency or non-expediency of having made the contracts or the wisdom or want of wisdom of the statute which prohibited their being made. That is to say, the cases but decided that the nature and character of the contracts, creating as they did a conclusive presumption which brought them within the statute, such result was not to be disregarded by the substitution of a judicial appreciation of what the law ought to be for the plain judicial duty of enforcing the law as it was made."

. . . .

Respondents rely upon *Chicago Board of Trade* in which an agreement by members of the Chicago Board of Trade controlling prices during certain hours of the day in a special class of grain contracts and affecting only a small proportion of the commerce in question was upheld. The purpose and effect of the agreement there was to maintain for a part of each business day the price which had been that day determined by open competition on the floor of the Exchange. That decision, dealing as it did with a regulation of a board of trade, does not sanction a price agreement among competitors in an open market such as is presented here.

The charge of the trial court, viewed as a whole, fairly submitted to the jury the question whether a price-fixing agreement as described in the first count was entered into by the respondents. Whether the prices actually agreed upon were reasonable or unreasonable was immaterial in the circumstances charged in the indictment and necessarily found by the verdict.

. . . .

It follows that the judgment of the circuit court of appeals must be reversed and the judgment of the district court reinstated.

Reversed.

[JUSTICE BRANDEIS, the author of the *Chicago Board of Trade* decision, took no part in the consideration of the decision.]

NOTES AND QUESTIONS

1. Did Justice Stone distinguish *Chicago Board of Trade* adequately? Or did *Trenton Potteries* implicitly overrule *Chicago Board of Trade*? Recall that in *Chicago Board of Trade*, the concerted arrangement established the price at which grain could be sold during nonregular hours. What if the arrangement merely fixed the hours during which trading was permissible? Is that a restraint of competition? Consider whether the degree of the restraint is relevant in determining legality. *See Detroit Auto Dealers v. FTC*, 955 F.2d 457 (6th Cir. 1992) (condemning an agreement among automobile dealers to restrict showroom hours, after applying the rule of reason). How would you distinguish *Chicago Board*?

2. Was it relevant to the Court that defendants controlled over 80% of the national production of sanitary pottery? Does it matter under a price-fixing charge whether the defendant has the ability (i.e., market power) actually to affect the price? Can market power be inferred from the fact that the defendants entered into the agreement? Can one infer market power from market share?

3. The Court in *Trenton Potteries* implied that the range of judicial discretion is narrow in a price-fixing case. The limited inquiry is whether an agreement to fix the price can be established. From the agreement, illegal purpose can be inferred. And from the nature of the conduct (i.e., price fixing), the inherent anticompetitive effects are obvious. Thus, the Court suggested that price fixing is illegal per se. Evidence demonstrating the reasonableness of the price and the circumstances surrounding the practice are, from an evidentiary standpoint, irrelevant.

A more careful reading of *Trenton Potteries* reveals, however, that Justice Stone assumed that the challenged price fix was effective, that is, that defendants had the market power to affect price. Defendants' control of over 80% of the market would support this conclusion. Perhaps, then, the per se approach to price fixing is applicable only where the price-fixing arrangement is effective because of the defendant's market power. But what if defendants lacked market power to affect price? Would the establishment of the illegal agreement be sufficient for the submission of a prima facie case on a per se theory?

4. A part of the opinion not reprinted details a second agreement by the defendants to destroy all "seconds" — i.e., imperfect products — or else to sell them abroad. What was the purpose of that agreement? Suppose that the defendants agreed that each would reduce its output by 30%, but the agreement contained no provision concerning "seconds." If the price for seconds was higher than the cost of producing them, it would be profitable for a cartel member to continue producing at full capacity but designate 30% of its output as "seconds" and sell them at a price lower than the cartel price, but a profitable price nevertheless. The manufacturer could achieve this either by designating perfect products as "seconds," or else by grading its output using extraordinarily high standards. If every manufacturer did this, the output restriction agreement would be undermined. The only way the cartel could effectively detect such cheating would be to prohibit the selling of seconds in the cartelized market.

In *Standard Mfg. Co. v. United States*, 226 U.S. 20 (1912), the Supreme Court held that a licensing agreement by manufacturers of sanitary enameled iron ware, such as bath tubs, violated Section 1 of the Sherman Act when it restricted the production and distribution of "seconds." Such licensing restriction, the Court reasoned, amounted to an output limitation and was not necessary to protect the use of the patent of the lawful monopoly conferred by the grant of the patent. The Court concluded that the agreement on "seconds" was for "the purpose and accomplished a restraint on trade," in that it affected price. *Id.* at 48.

APPALACHIAN COALS, INC. v. UNITED STATES
288 U.S. 344 (1933)

[Given the economic conditions caused, at least in part, by the Great Depression, 137 producers of bituminous coal in the Appalachian area entered into an arrangement to establish an exclusive selling agent. The agent, Appalachian Coals, Inc. was to sell, at the highest prices, the entire bituminous production for all 137 producers. The stock of the company was owned by the producers in proportion to their production percentages. Price of the coal was set by the selling agent. The 137 producers accounted for 12% of the bituminous production east of the Mississippi, but 74% of the Appalachian territory, including Tennessee, Kentucky, Virginia, and West Virginia.]

[Prior to implementation of the plan, Department of Justice approval was sought. Upon reviewing the exclusive selling arrangement, the Department sought and obtained an injunction against the plan, which had not yet gone into effect, on the theory that the concerted arrangement actually established a cartel which would eliminate competition between the member producers.]

CHIEF JUSTICE HUGHES delivered the opinion of the Court.

. . . .

Defendants insist that the primary purpose of the formation of the selling agency was to increase the sale, and thus the production, of Appalachian coal through better methods of distribution, intensive advertising and research; to achieve economies in marketing, and to eliminate abnormal, deceptive and destructive trade practices. They disclaim any intent to restrain or monopolize interstate commerce; and in justification of their design they point to the statement of the District Court that "it is but due to defendants to say that the evidence in the case clearly shows that they have been acting fairly and openly, in an attempt to organize the coal industry and to relieve the deplorable conditions resulting from over-expansion, destructive competition, wasteful trade practices, and the inroads of competing industries." . . . Defendants contend that the evidence establishes that the selling agency will not have the power to dominate or fix the price of coal in any consuming market; that the price of coal will continue to be set in an open competitive market; and that their plan by increasing the sale of bituminous coal from Appalachian territory will promote, rather than restrain, interstate commerce.

There is no question as to the test to be applied in determining the legality of the defendants' conduct. The purpose of the Sherman Anti-Trust Act is to prevent undue restraints of interstate commerce, to maintain its appropriate freedom in the public interest, to afford protection from the subversive or coercive influences of monopolistic endeavor. As a charter of freedom, the Act has a generality and adaptability comparable to that found to be desirable in constitutional provisions. It does not go into detailed definitions which might either work injury to legitimate enterprise or through particularization defeat its purposes by providing loopholes for escape. The restrictions the Act imposes are not mechanical or artificial. Its general phrases, interpreted to attain its fundamental objects, set up the essential standard of reasonableness. They call for vigilance in the detection and frustration of all efforts unduly to restrain the free course of interstate commerce, but they do not seek to establish a mere delusive liberty either by making impossible the normal and fair expansion of that commerce or the adoption of reasonable measures to protect it from injurious and destructive practices and to promote competition upon a sound basis. . . .

In applying this test, a close and objective scrutiny of particular conditions and purposes is necessary in each case. Realities must dominate the judgment. The mere fact that the parties to an agreement eliminate competition between themselves is not enough to condemn it. "The legality of an agreement or regulation cannot be determined by so simple a test, as whether it restrains competition. Every agreement concerning trade, every regulation of trade, restrains." *Chicago Board of Trade v. United States, supra.* The familiar illustrations of partnerships, and enterprises fairly integrated in the interest of the promotion of commerce, at once occur. The question of the application of the statute is one of intent and effect, and is not to be determined by arbitrary assumptions. It is therefore necessary in this instance to consider the economic conditions peculiar to the coal industry, the practices which have obtained, the nature of defendant's plan of making sales, the reasons which led to its adoption, and the probable consequences of the carrying out of that plan in relation to market prices and other matters affecting the public interest in interstate commerce in bituminous coal.

. . . .

With respect to defendant's purposes, we find no warrant for determining that they were other than those they declared. Good intentions will not save a plan otherwise objectionable, but knowledge of actual intent is an aid in the interpretation of facts and prediction of consequences. *Chicago Board of Trade v. United States, supra.* The evidence leaves no doubt of the existence of the evils at which defendants' plan was aimed. The industry was in distress. It suffered from over-expansion and from a serious relative decline through the growing use of substitute fuels. It was afflicted by injurious practices within itself, — practices which demanded correction. If evil conditions could not be entirely cured, they at least might be alleviated. The unfortunate state of the industry would not justify any attempt unduly to restrain competition or to monopolize, but the existing situation prompted defendants to make, and the statute did not preclude them from making, an honest effort to remove abuses, to make competition fairer, and thus to promote the essential interests of commerce. The interests of producers and consumers are interlinked. When industry is grievously hurt, when producing concerns fail, when unemployment mounts and communities dependent upon profitable production are prostrated, the wells of commerce go dry. So far as actual purposes are concerned, the conclusion of the court below was amply supported that defendants were engaged in a fair and open endeavor to aid the industry in a measurable recovery from its plight. The inquiry, then, must be whether despite this objective the inherent nature of their plan was such as to create an undue restraint upon interstate commerce.

The question thus presented chiefly concerns the effect upon prices. The evidence as to the conditions of the production and distribution of bituminous coal, the available facilities for its transportation, the extent of developed mining capacity, and the vast potential undeveloped capacity, makes it impossible to conclude that defendants through the operation of their plan will be able to fix the price of coal in the consuming markets. The ultimate finding of the District Court is that the defendants "will not have monopoly control of any market, nor the power to fix monopoly prices"; and in its opinion the court stated that "the selling agency will not be able, we think, to fix the market price of coal." Defendants' coal will continue to be subject to active competition. In addition to the coal actually produced and seeking markets in competition with defendants' coal, enormous additional quantities will be within reach and can readily be turned into the channels of trade if an advance of price invites that course. While conditions are more favorable to the position of defendants' group in some markets than in others, we think that the proof clearly shows that, wherever their selling agency operates, it will find itself confronted by effective competition backed by virtually inexhaustible sources of supply, and will also be compelled to cope with the organized buying power of large consumers. The plan cannot be said either to contemplate or to involve the fixing of market prices.

The contention is, and the court below found, that while defendants could not fix market prices, the concerted action would "affect" them, that is, that it would have a tendency to stabilize market prices and to raise them to a higher level than would otherwise obtain. But the facts found do not establish, and the evidence fails to show, that any effect will be produced which in the circumstances of this industry will be detrimental to fair competition. A cooperative enterprise, otherwise free from objection, which carries with it no monopolistic menace, is not to be condemned as an undue restraint merely because it may effect a change in market conditions, where the change would be in mitigation of recognized evils [distressed, over-expanded market] and would not impair, but rather foster, fair competitive opportunities. Voluntary action to rescue and preserve these opportunities, and thus to aid in relieving a depressed industry and in reviving commerce by placing competition upon a sounder basis, may be more efficacious than an attempt to provide remedies through legal processes. The fact that the correction of abuses may tend to stabilize a business, or to produce fairer price levels, does not mean that the abuses should go uncorrected or that cooperative endeavor to correct them necessarily constitutes an unreasonable restraint of trade. The intelligent conduct of commerce through the acquisition of full information of all relevant facts may properly be sought by the cooperation of those engaged in trade, although stabilization of trade and more reasonable prices may be the result. Putting an end to injurious practices, and the consequent improvement of the competitive position of a group of producers, is not a less worthy aim and may be entirely consonant with the public interest, where the group must still meet effective competition in a fair market and neither seeks nor is able to effect a domination of prices.

. . . Defendants insist that on the evidence adduced as to their competitive position in the consuming markets, and in the absence of proof of actual operations showing an injurious effect upon competition, either through possession or abuse of power, no valid objection could have been interposed under the Sherman Act if the defendants had eliminated competition between themselves by a complete integration of their mining properties in a single ownership. We agree that there is no ground for holding defendants' plan illegal merely because they have not integrated their properties and have chosen to maintain their independent plants, seeking not to limit but rather to facilitate production. . . . The question in either case is whether there is an unreasonable restraint of trade or an attempt to monopolize. If there is, the combination cannot escape because it has chosen corporate form; and, if there is not, it is not to be condemned because of the absence of corporate integration. As we stated at the outset, the question under the Act is not simply whether the parties have restrained competition between themselves but as to the nature and effect of that restraint.

The fact that the suit is brought under the Sherman Act does not change the principles which govern the granting of equitable relief. There must be "a definite factual showing of illegality." We think that the Government has failed to show adequate grounds for an injunction in this case. We recognize, however, that the case has been tried in advance of the operation of defendants' plan, and that it has been necessary to test that plan with reference to purposes and anticipated consequences without the advantage of the demonstrations of experience. If in actual operation it should prove to be an undue restraint upon interstate commerce, if it should appear that the plan is used to the impairment of fair competitive opportunities, the decision upon the present record should not preclude the Government from seeking the remedy which would be suited to such a state of facts.

. . . .

Reversed and remanded.

NOTES AND QUESTIONS

1. Can the Court's decision be reconciled with the earlier per se approach of *Trenton Potteries*? From a historical perspective, what occurred between these two opinions? Might the Court have been influenced by these economic conditions? If permitted, would this plan have had the effect of reducing price competition among the cartel members? Would it not also have had the effect of reducing the supply of distress or spot coal, with the result that prices would have been raised or stabilized? Would this have had a direct price effect on consumers purchasing coal? From Justice Hughes' opinion, how is a price-fixing arrangement to be defined? How direct must the effect be on prices before it is considered a price-fixing agreement? Should any practice that may affect price be viewed as price fixing within the category of conduct deemed per se illegal?

2. Like *Chicago Board of Trade* before it, *Appalachian Coals* sanctioned a rule of reason analysis in determining the legality of a scheme that, on its face, had characteristics of a price-fixing agreement. The Court in *Appalachian Coals* stated that its reasoning was justified because of the realities of "deplorable economic conditions in the industry." Moreover, after accepting the defendants' argument that their intent was benign, the Court implied that they lacked market power to affect price, having only a 12% market share nationally. The implication was that in order to establish a price-fixing arrangement, something more than the agreement itself was necessary. But what of the fact that the sales agent controlled 74% of the market in the Appalachian area? Isn't that market power within a definable market?

3. Hadn't the Supreme Court established in the *Trans-Missouri* and *Joint Traffic* cases, 30 years before *Trenton Potteries*, that price-fixing agreements were unlawful without regard to the "reasonableness" of the price that was fixed? (*See* Chapter 1, *supra*.) Why did the Supreme Court bother to entertain the question again? Perhaps it was because in 1897, Associate Justice White dissented in *Trans-Missouri* (a 5-4 decision), arguing that all restraints on trade ought to be governed by a rule of reason. White's dissent appeared to leave open the possibility that in a price-fixing case, he would accept the defense that the prices fixed were reasonable. In 1911, White, then Chief Justice, wrote the majority opinion adopting the "rule of reason" in *Standard Oil Co. v. United States*, 221 U.S. 1 (1911). Many people, reading the two opinions together, believed that *Standard Oil* effectively overruled older cases like *Trans-Missouri*, and adopted a rule of reason for all alleged antitrust violations, including price-fixing agreements. Whether Chief Justice White intended this in the *Standard Oil* opinion is unclear; however, the *Trenton Potteries* case made it plain that the pre-*Standard Oil* law of price fixing survived. Incidentally, three justices in *Trenton Potteries* dissented without opinion — Van Devanter, Sutherland, and Butler — probably the three most conservative judges on the Court.

[2]   Supply or Output Restrictions

UNITED STATES v. SOCONY-VACUUM OIL CO.
310 U.S. 150 (1940)

[Respondent oil companies were convicted by a jury under an indictment charging violations of Section 1 of the Sherman Act. It was alleged that the coconspirators met and coordinated their purchases of gasoline in spot markets with the effect, if not intent, of raising prices at the retail level. The Court of Appeals for the Seventh Circuit reversed and remanded for a new trial after finding the jury instructions to inappropriately imply that such a combination was illegal *per se*. The Circuit Court believed the behavior to be lawful unless it constituted an unreasonable restraint of trade.]

JUSTICE DOUGLAS delivered the opinion of the Court.

. . . .

III. *The Alleged Conspiracy*

[During February, 1935, the coconspirators met] . . . and decided that certain major companies (including the corporate respondents) would purchase gasoline from these refiners. . . . Each of the major companies was to select one (or more) of the independent refiners having distress gasoline as its "dancing partner," and would assume responsibility for purchasing its distress supply. In this manner buying power would be coordinated, purchases would be effectively placed, and the results would be much superior to the previous haphazard purchasing. There were to be no formal contractual commitments to purchase this gasoline, either between the major companies or between the majors and the independents. Rather it was an informal gentlemen's agreement or understanding whereby each undertook to perform his share of the joint undertaking. Purchases were to be made at the "fair going market price."

. . . .

As a result of these buying programs it was hoped and intended that both the tank car and the retail markets would improve. The conclusion is irresistible that defendants' purpose was not merely to raise the spot market prices but, as the real and ultimate end, to raise the price of gasoline in their sales to jobbers and consumers in the Mid-Western area. Their agreement or plan embraced not only buying on the spot markets but also, at least by clear implication, an understanding to maintain such improvements in Mid-Western prices as would result from those purchases of distress gasoline. . . . In essence the raising and maintenance of the spot market prices were but the means adopted for raising and maintaining prices to jobbers and consumers.

. . . .

The defendant companies sold about 83% of all gasoline sold in the Mid-Western area during 1935. . . . During the greater part of the indictment period the defendant companies owned and operated many retail service stations through which they sold about 20% of their Mid-Western gasoline in 1935 and about 12% during the first seven months of 1936.

. . . .

V. *Application of the Sherman Act*

The court charged the jury that it was a violation of the Sherman Act for a group of individuals or corporations to act together to raise the prices to be charged for the commodity which they manufactured where they controlled a substantial part of the interstate trade and commerce in that commodity. The court stated that where the members of a combination had the power to raise prices and acted together for that purpose, the combination was illegal; and that it was immaterial how reasonable or unreasonable those prices were or to what extent they had been affected by the combination. It further charged that if such illegal combination existed, it did not matter that there may also have been other factors which contributed to the raising of the prices. . . . The court then charged that, unless the jury found beyond a reasonable doubt that the price rise and its continuance were "caused" by the combination and not caused by those other factors, verdicts of "not guilty" should be returned. . . .

The Circuit Court of Appeals held this charge to be reversible error, since it was based upon the theory that such a combination was illegal *per se*. In its view respondents' activities were not unlawful unless they constituted an unreasonable restraint of trade. . . .

In *United States v. Trenton Potteries Co.*, 273 U.S. 392, this Court sustained a conviction under the Sherman Act where the jury was charged that an agreement on the part of the members of a combination, controlling a substantial part of an industry, upon the prices which the members are to charge for their commodity is in itself an unreasonable restraint of trade without regard to the reasonableness of the prices or the good intentions of the combining units.

. . . .

But respondents claim that other decisions of this Court afford them adequate defenses to the indictment. Among those on which they place reliance are *Appalachian Coals, Inc. v. United States*, 288 U.S. 344; *Chicago Board of Trade v. United States*, 246 U.S. 231; and the *American Tobacco* and *Standard Oil* cases, *supra*.

But we do not think that line of cases is apposite. As clearly indicated in the *Trenton Potteries* case, the *American Tobacco* and *Standard Oil* cases have no application to combinations operating directly on prices or price structures.

And we are of the opinion that *Appalachian Coals, Inc. v. United States*, is not in point.

. . . This Court concluded that so far as actual purpose was concerned, the defendant producers were engaged in a "fair and open endeavor to aid the industry in a measurable recovery from its plight." And it observed that the plan did not either contemplate or involve "the fixing of market prices"; that defendants would not be able to fix the price of coal in the consuming markets; that their coal would continue to be subject to "active competition." . . .

Thus in reality the only essential thing in common between the instant case and the *Appalachian Coals* case is the presence in each of so-called demoralizing or injurious practices. The methods of dealing with them were quite divergent. In the instant case there were buying programs of distress gasoline which had as their direct purpose and aim the raising and maintenance of spot market prices and of prices to jobbers and consumers in the Mid-Western area, by the elimination of distress gasoline as a market factor. The increase in the spot market prices was to be accomplished by a well organized buying program on that market: regular ascertainment of the amounts of surplus gasoline; assignment of sellers among the buyers; regular purchases at prices which would place and keep a floor under the market. Unlike the plan in the instant case, the plan in the *Appalachian Coals* case was not designed to operate *vis-à-vis* the general consuming market and to fix the prices on that market. Furthermore, the effect, if any, of that plan on prices was not only wholly incidental but also highly conjectural. For the plan had not then been put into operation. Hence this Court expressly reserved jurisdiction in the District Court to take further proceedings if, *inter alia*, in "actual operation" the plan proved to be "an undue restraint upon interstate commerce." And as we have seen it would *per se* constitute such a restraint if price-fixing were involved.

. . . .

Nor can respondents find sanction in *Chicago Board of Trade* for the buying programs here under attack. That case involved a prohibition on the members of the Chicago Board of Trade from purchasing or offering to purchase between the closing of the session and its opening the next day grains (under a special class of contracts) at a price other than the closing bid. The rule was somewhat akin to rules of an exchange limiting the period of trading, for as stated by this Court the "restriction was upon the period of price-making." No attempt was made to show that the purpose or effect of the rule was to raise or depress prices. The rule affected only a small proportion of the commerce in question. And among its effects was the creation of a public market for grains under that special contract class, where prices were determined competitively and openly. Since it was not aimed at price manipulation or the control of the market prices and since it had "no appreciable effect on general market prices," the rule survived as a reasonable restraint of trade.

. . . .

Thus for over forty years this Court has consistently and without deviation adhered to the principle that price-fixing agreements are unlawful *per se* under the Sherman Act and that no showing of so-called competitive abuses or evils which those agreements were designed to eliminate or alleviate may be interposed as a defense. . . .

Therefore the sole remaining question on this phase of the case is the applicability of the rule of the *Trenton Potteries* case to these facts.

. . . .

In the first place, there was abundant evidence that the combination had the purpose to raise prices. And likewise, there was ample evidence that the buying programs at least contributed to the price rise and the stability of the spot markets, and to increases in the price of gasoline sold in the Mid-Western area during the indictment period. That other factors also may have contributed to that rise and stability of the markets is immaterial. For in any such market movement, forces other than the purchasing power of the buyers normally would contribute to the price rise and the market stability. So far as cause and effect are concerned it is sufficient in this type of case if the buying programs of the combination resulted in a price rise and market stability which but for them would not have happened. For this reason the charge to the jury that the buying programs must have "caused" the price rise and its continuance was more favorable to respondents than they could have required. Proof that there was a conspiracy, that its purpose was to raise prices, and that it caused or contributed to a price rise is proof of the actual consummation or execution of a conspiracy under § 1 of the Sherman Act.

Secondly, the fact that sales on the spot markets were still governed by some competition is of no consequence. For it is indisputable that competition was restricted through the removal by respondents of a part of the supply which but for the buying programs would have been a factor in determining the going prices on those markets. But the vice of the conspiracy was not merely the restriction of supply of gasoline by removal of a surplus. . . .

The elimination of so-called competitive evils is no legal justification for such buying programs. The elimination of such conditions was sought primarily for its effect on the price structures. Fairer competitive prices, it is claimed, resulted when distress gasoline was removed from the market. But such defense is typical of the protestations usually made in price-fixing cases. Ruinous competition, financial disaster, evils of price cutting and the like appear throughout our history as ostensible justifications for price-fixing. If the so-called competitive abuses were to be appraised here, the reasonableness of prices would necessarily become an issue in every price-fixing case. In that event the Sherman Act would soon be emasculated; its philosophy would be supplanted by one which is wholly alien to a system of free competition; it would not be the charter of freedom which its framers intended.

The reasonableness of prices has no constancy due to the dynamic quality of business facts underlying price structures. Those who fixed reasonable prices today would perpetuate unreasonable prices tomorrow, since those prices would not be subject to continuous administrative supervision and readjustment in light of changed conditions. Those who controlled the prices would control or effectively dominate the market. And those who were in that strategic position would have it in their power to destroy or drastically impair the competitive system. But the thrust of the rule is deeper and reaches more than monopoly power. Any combination which tampers with price structures is engaged in an unlawful activity. Even though the members of the price-fixing group were in no position to control the market, to the extent that they raised, lowered, or stabilized prices they would be directly interfering with the free play of market forces. The Act places all such schemes beyond the pale and protects that vital part of our economy against any degree of interference. Congress has not left with us the determination of whether or not particular price-fixing schemes are wise or unwise, healthy or destructive. It has not permitted the age-old cry of ruinous competition and competitive evils to be a defense to price-fixing conspiracies. It has no more allowed genuine or fancied competitive abuses as a legal justification for such schemes than it has the good intentions of the members of the combination. If such a shift is to be made, it must be done by the Congress. Certainly Congress has not left us with any such choice. . . . There was accordingly no error in the refusal to charge that in order to convict the jury must find that the resultant prices were raised and maintained at "high, arbitrary and noncompetitive levels." The charge in the indictment to that effect was surplusage.

Nor is it important that the prices paid by the combination were not fixed in the sense that they were uniform and inflexible. Price-fixing as used in the *Trenton Potteries* case has no such limited meaning. An agreement to pay or charge rigid, uniform prices would be an illegal agreement under the Sherman Act. But so would agreements to raise or lower prices whatever machinery for price-fixing was used. That price-fixing includes more than the mere establishment of uniform prices is clearly evident from the *Trenton Potteries* case itself. . . . Hence, prices are fixed within the meaning of the *Trenton Potteries* case if the range within which purchases or sales will be made is agreed upon, if the prices paid or charged are to be at a certain level or on ascending or descending scales, if they are to be uniform, or if by various formulae they are related to the market prices. They are fixed because they are agreed upon. And the fact that, as here, they are fixed at the fair going market price is immaterial. For purchases at or under the market are one species of price-fixing. In this case, the result was to place a floor under the market — a floor which served the function of increasing the stability and firmness of market prices. That was repeatedly characterized in this case as stabilization. But in terms of market operations stabilization is but one form of manipulation. And market manipulation in its various manifestations is implicitly an artificial stimulus applied to (or at times a brake on) market prices, a force which distorts those prices, a factor which prevents the determination of those prices by free competition alone. . . .

As we have indicated, the machinery employed by a combination for price-fixing is immaterial.

Under the Sherman Act a combination formed for the purpose and with the effect of raising, depressing, fixing, pegging, or stabilizing the price of a commodity in interstate or foreign commerce is illegal *per se*. Where the machinery for price-fixing is an agreement on the prices to be charged or paid for the commodity in the interstate or foreign channels of trade, the power to fix prices exists if the combination has control of a substantial part of the commerce in that commodity. Where the means for price-fixing are purchases or sales of the commodity in a market operation or, as here, purchases of a part of the supply of the commodity for the purpose of keeping it from having a depressive effect on the markets, such power may be found to exist though the combination does not control a substantial part of the commodity. In such a case that power may be established if as a result of market conditions, the resources available to the combinations, the timing and the strategic placement of orders and the like, effective means are at hand to accomplish the desired objective. But there may be effective influence over the market though the group in question does not control it. Price-fixing agreements may have utility to members of the group though the power possessed or exerted falls far short of domination and control. Monopoly power (*United States v. Patten*, 226 U.S. 525) is not the only power which the Act strikes down, as we have said. Proof that a combination was formed for the purpose of fixing prices and that it caused them to be fixed or contributed to that result is proof of the completion of a price-fixing conspiracy under § 1 of the Act.[1]

The indictment in this case charged that this combination had that purpose and effect. And there was abundant evidence to support it. Hence the existence of power on the part of members of the combination to fix prices was but a conclusion from the finding that the buying programs caused or contributed to the rise and stability of prices.

. . . .

Accordingly we conclude that the Circuit Court of Appeals erred in reversing the judgments on this ground. *A fortiori* the position taken by respondents in their

---

[1] [FN 59] Under this indictment proof that prices in the Mid-Western area were raised as a result of the activities of the combination was essential, since sales of gasoline by respondents at the increased prices in that area were necessary in order to establish jurisdiction in the Western District of Wisconsin. Hence we have necessarily treated the case as one where exertion of the power to fix prices (i.e., the actual fixing of prices) was an ingredient of the offense. But that does not mean that both a purpose and a power to fix prices are necessary for the establishment of a conspiracy under § 1 of the Sherman Act. That would be true if power or ability to commit an offense was necessary in order to convict a person of conspiring to commit it. But it is well established that a person "may be guilty of conspiring although incapable of committing the objective offense."

. . . And it is likewise well settled that conspiracies under the Sherman Act are not dependent on any overt act other than the act of conspiring. It is the "contract, combination . . . or conspiracy in restraint of trade or commerce" which § 1 of the Act strikes down, whether the concerted activity be wholly nascent or abortive on the one hand, or successful on the other. See *United States v. Trenton Potteries Co.*, 273 U.S. 392, 402. And the amount of interstate or foreign trade involved is not material since § 1 of the Act brands as illegal the character of the restraint not the amount of commerce affected. In view of these considerations a conspiracy to fix prices violates § 1 of the Act though no overt act is shown, though it is not established that the conspirators had the means available for accomplishment of their objective, and though the conspiracy embraced but a part of the interstate or foreign commerce in the commodity. Whatever may have been the status of price-fixing agreements at common law the Sherman Act has a broader application to them than the common law prohibitions or sanctions. See *United States v. Trans-Missouri Freight Assn.*, 166 U.S. 290, 328. Price-fixing agreements may or may not be aimed at complete elimination of price competition. The group making those agreements may or may not have power to control the market. But the fact that the group cannot control the market prices does not necessarily mean that the agreement as to prices has no utility to the members of the combination. The effectiveness of price-fixing agreements is dependent on many factors, such as competitive tactics, position in the industry, the formula underlying price policies. Whatever economic justification particular price-fixing agreements may be thought to have, the law does not permit an inquiry into their reasonableness. They are all banned because of their actual or potential threat to the central nervous system of the economy.

The existence or exertion of power to accomplish the desired objective . . . becomes important only in cases where the offense charged is the actual monopolizing of any part of trade or commerce in violation of § 2 of the Act. An intent and a power to produce the result which the law condemns are then necessary. . . . But the crime under § 1 is legally distinct from that under § 2 . . . though the two sections overlap in the sense that a monopoly under § 2 is a species of restraint of trade under § 1. . . . Only a confusion between the nature of the offenses under those two sections . . . would lead to the conclusion that power to fix prices was necessary for proof of a price-fixing conspiracy under § 1.

cross petition that they were entitled to directed verdicts of acquittal is untenable.

Reversed.

NOTES AND QUESTIONS

1. Does Justice Douglas' opinion leave any doubt that price fixing cartels are illegal per se? Are the distinctions drawn by Justice Douglas between *Appalachian Coals* and *Socony-Vacuum* persuasive? Would Justice Douglas' conclusion, that "any combination which tampers with price structure," regardless of whether the defendant was in a "position to control the market," is unlawful, apply to a cartel scheme which introduced efficiencies into the market, as in *Chicago Board of Trade* and *Appalachian Coals*?

2. Does footnote 59 of the *Socony-Vacuum* opinion suggest that the prosecution need not introduce evidence of market power to effectuate the agreement — that the agreement to tamper with a component of price is itself illegal? Can one infer from such an agreement that the parties have the requisite market power? *See, e.g., United States v. General Motors Corp.*, 384 U.S. 127 (1966); *United States v. McKesson & Robbins, Inc.*, 351 U.S. 305 (1956). Consider whether an agreement between two sellers which together hold a 3% market share should be challenged as illegal price fixing under the Sherman Act.

3. Justice Douglas' statement in *Socony-Vacuum* that "[a]ny combination which tampers with price structure . . . is unlawful" stands as a classic definition of a price-fixing agreement. Its clearly articulated per se rule established firmly that price fixing, as a classification of conduct, was per se illegal. It drew this conclusion from the earlier pronouncements in *Joint Traffic, Standard Oil* and *Trenton Potteries.* Although not an explicit price-fixing agreement, the scheme in *Socony-Vacuum* to affect the flow of output and surplus in the market is the most basic method of affecting price. And it does not matter whether that market is depressed or the price reasonable. Under the per se evidentiary analysis, the judicial inquiry is limited to whether the challenged conduct, once established, comes within the price-fixing category.

The policy justification for the per se approach was described by the Supreme Court in *Northern Pac. Ry. v. United States*, 356 U.S. 1, 5 (1958):

> [T]here are certain agreements or practices which because of their pernicious effect on competition and lack of any redeeming virtue are conclusively presumed to be unreasonable and therefore illegal without elaborate inquiry as to the precise harm they have caused or the business excuse for their use. This principle of *per se* unreasonableness not only makes the type of restraints which are proscribed by the Sherman Act more certain to the benefit of everyone concerned, but it also avoids the necessity for an incredibly complicated and prolonged economic investigation into the entire history of the industry involved, as well as related industries, in an effort to determine at large whether a particular restraint has been unreasonable — an inquiry so often wholly fruitless when undertaken.

The per se rule of illegality, therefore, furthers the goals of clarifying the law for business certainty and promoting judicial economy.

4. In *Ezzo's Invs. v. Royal Beauty Supply, Inc.*, 243 F.3d 980 (6th Cir. 2001), defendant would only sell Matrix beauty products to salons that derived more than 50% of their revenue from hair-care services and not from product sales. Plaintiff sued contending that defendant's policy was a per se violation of Section 1 of the Sherman Act because it restricted output and discouraged price competition. The plaintiff argued the "50% rule" restricted output by creating a limit on product sales. The Sixth Circuit affirmed defendant's motion for partial summary judgment because the plaintiff had failed to show that defendant had market power to restrain trade and that plaintiff's argument that the 50% sales rule was a volume restriction was incorrectly based on the assumption that the volume of products sold determined the percentage of sales derived from the products. Instead, the court noted that salons could sell any desired volume of products and still achieve the desired balance of product and service sales by adjusting the product prices.

5. In *Continental Airlines Inc. v. United Air Lines Inc.*, 126 F. Supp. 2d 962 (E.D. Va. 2001), Continental Airlines sued United Air Lines and AMC, the unincorporated association of carriers servicing Dulles Airport, when defendants agreed to restrict the size of all carry-on luggage for all airlines. This restriction was enforced by installing a "template" over x-ray machines which prevented luggage larger than the agreed upon size from passing through x-ray machines located at all security gates. Continental Airlines sued claiming that such size restriction prevented the airlines from competing based on the allowed size of carry-on luggage. The court found the restriction was a horizontal agreement to restrict output because the restriction standardized the size of carry-on luggage and prevented the airlines from competing on this service. Under rule of reason analysis, defendants were unable to offer procompetitive justifications for the restriction. Therefore, the restriction was found to be an unreasonable restraint of trade.

On appeal, however, the United States Court of Appeals for the Fourth Circuit overturned the order of summary judgment and injunction against Dulles Airport Management Council, and award of treble damages to Continental Airlines, and remanded for further consideration. *Continental Airlines, Inc. v. Dulles Airport Airline Mgmt. Council*, 277 F.3d 499 (4th Cir. 2002). Plausible material issues of disputed fact existed between the parties, including whether there were procompetitive justifications for the templates. A competing airline had offered evidence that such templates improved both on-board safety and passenger comfort, but Continental had rejected such claims as illusory, and the district court agreed. The court determined that the district court's analysis was "too quick": while it was correct in rejecting a *per se* analysis, the context of the suit required a more extended analysis. For example, the district court had not considered carefully how the unique architectural configuration of the airport required consideration of the template program's competitive effect. In reaching this conclusion, the Fourth Circuit relied on a Supreme Court decision from the beginning of the 20th century, which held that the architectural configuration of a railroad terminal required railway companies to combine and submit to regulatory control. Last, the district court also was instructed to consider the potential impact of the events of

September 11, 2001 in fashioning the remedy on remand; while the Federal Aviation Administration had for security reasons only thus far restricted the number of carry-ons per person, it was possible that it could also restrict the size.

6. As evident from *Socony-Vacuum*, antitrust law condemns practices that drive up prices by curtailing output. Judge Easterbrook wrote in *Sanderson v. Culligan Int'l Co.*, 415 F.3d 620 (7th Cir. 2005), that false statements about competitors' goods "do not curtail output in either the short or the long run." *Id.* at 623. According to Judge Easterbrook, such false statements merely make competition in the advertising market more rigorous. Advertising is a tool of persuasion used by producers to convince consumers to buy their products, and its rigorous use is competition, not a practice prohibited by the antitrust laws, he reasoned. Falsehood of advertising alone is not targeted by the Sherman Act, the court concluded. *Id.* at 624. Finally, persuading a trade association to withhold an attribute of recognition from the plaintiffs' products did not render the defendant's practices anticompetitive because the attribute of recognition was a marketing device not made part of any governmental quality requirement. *Id.* at 623–624.

[3] Data Dissemination and Information Exchanges

It may be helpful to examine several related price-affecting practices in understanding the analytic progression achieved by the Court. The first issue presented is the effect that price or data disclosures among competitors have in the market and the role the structure of the industry might play in determining the legality of certain industry cooperative practices.

As the previous cases and discussions reveal, antitrust analysis, at least in part, centers on factual and economic distinctions between certain kinds of behavior. The nature, character, purpose, or effect of the conduct will be determinative of the conduct's classification and legality. How the conduct is to be characterized or classified is not, however, always easy to determine. The decisional process often involves borderline questions of fact which may alter the characterization of the conduct and, accordingly, its legality. Because not all agreements between competitors are inherently anticompetitive, courts must sometimes examine the competitive effect of the arrangement rather than engage only in a summary per se analysis.

A case in point is the exchange of information by competitors, often by means of a trade association, where competitors come together to share mutual industry interests and objectives and to collect and share industry data. *See generally* G. LAMB & C. SHIELDS, TRADE ASSOCIATION LAW AND PRACTICE (1971). The data exchanged between competitors include such things as statistics about production, inventory, sales, shipments, price, or plant capacity. Competitors may also engage in standardization programs for the industry, which attempt to set terms and guidelines for products, contracts, credit, freight charges, etc. Among the questions presented by such arrangements is whether the cooperative commercial arrangement has the effect of limiting competition by facilitating price coordination. The competitive effects of an exchange will vary, according to the following cases, depending on what data are exchanged, how firms react to the information, and the structure of the industry where the exchange takes place. Section 1 of the Sherman Act is implicated because trade associations constitute a "combination" within the meaning of the statute. Moreover, the "agreement" to exchange commercial information may come within the "contract" language of the statute. The following cases explore the antitrust limits of exchange agreements among competitors. In each case, you should compare the challenged conduct, market power, and the purpose and effect of the cooperative programs.

In *American Column & Lumber Co. v. United States*, 257 U.S. 377 (1921), the Supreme Court struck down a trade association program which mandated compliance with several restrictive requirements, including immediate reporting of price changes and the filing of daily reports on sales, production, and purchases. The dangers of overproduction were stressed in speeches and memoranda. Restrictions on output and price maintenance were discussed. Monthly meetings were held and members were encouraged to set high prices. The association's membership accounted for 33% of the industry production, but there was some evidence of increases in prices. Said the Court:

> Genuine competitors do not make daily, weekly and monthly reports of the minutest details of their business to their rivals, as the defendants did; they do not contract, as was done here, to submit their books to the discretionary audit and their stocks to the discretionary inspection of their rivals for the purpose of successfully competing with them; and they do not submit the details of their business to the analysis of an expert, jointly employed, and obtain from him a "harmonized" estimate of the market as it is and as, in his specially and confidentially informed judgment, it promises to be. This is not the conduct of competitors but is so clearly that of men united in an agreement, express or implied, to act together and pursue a common purpose under a common guide that, if it did not stand confessed a combination to restrict production and increase prices in interstate commerce and as, therefore, a direct restraint upon that commerce, as we have seen that it is, that conclusion must inevitably have been inferred from the facts which were proved. To pronounce such abnormal conduct on the part of 365 natural competitors, controlling one-third of the trade of the country in an article of prime necessity, a "new form of competition" and not an old form of combination in restraint of trade, as it so plainly is, would be for this court to confess itself blinded by words and forms to realities which men in general very plainly see and understand and condemn, as an old evil in a new dress and with a new name.

> . . . .

> In the presence of this record it is futile to argue that the purpose of the "Plan" was simply to furnish those engaged in this industry, with widely scattered units, the equivalent of such information as is contained in the newspaper and government publications with respect to the market for commodities sold on boards of trade or stock exchanges. One distinguishing and sufficient difference is that the published reports go to both seller and buyer, but these reports go to the seller only; and another is that there is no skilled interpreter of the published reports, such as we have in this case,

to insistently recommend harmony of action likely to prove profitable in proportion as it is unitedly pursued.

Convinced, as we are, that the purpose and effect of the activities of the "Open Competition Plan," here under discussion, were to restrict competition and thereby restrain interstate commerce in the manufacture and sale of hardwood lumber by concerted action in curtailing production and in increasing prices, we agree with the District Court that it constituted a combination and conspiracy in restraint of interstate commerce within the meaning of the Anti-Trust Act of 1890 and the decree of that court must be affirmed.

Justice Brandeis dissented, pointing out that the hardwood industry was populated by small, isolated manufacturers who had very poor access to information about market conditions and who might be taken advantage of by large buyers. The market would run more efficiently, Brandeis argued, if everyone in the market had access to the same reliable information about price and output conditions.

Two years after *American Column & Lumber*, the Supreme Court in *United States v. American Linseed Oil Co.*, 262 U.S. 371 (1923), followed the standard used in the earlier case and held that an association of 12 corporations, which manufactured linseed products and which exchanged detailed current price and production data through regular meetings and a coercive enforcement plan, was an illegal combination because the plan resulted in higher prices.

As the next case indicates, however, the legality of a cooperative plan may depend on the content of the exchange and the enforcement mechanism.

MAPLE FLOORING MANUFACTURERS ASS'N v. UNITED STATES
268 U.S. 563 (1925)

JUSTICE STONE delivered the opinion of the Court.

The defendants are the Maple Flooring Manufacturers Association, an unincorporated "trade association"; twenty-two corporate defendants, members of the Association, engaged in the business of selling and shipping maple, beech and birch flooring in interstate commerce, all but two of them having their principal places of business in Michigan, Minnesota or Wisconsin (one defendant being located in Illinois and one in New York). . . . Estimates submitted in behalf of the Government indicate that in the year 1922 the defendants produced 70% of the total production of these types of flooring. . . .

. . . The defendants have engaged in many activities to which no exception is taken by the Government and which are admittedly beneficial to the industry and to consumers; such as co-operative advertising and the standardization and improvement of the product. The activities, however, of the present Association of which the Government complains may be summarized as follows:

(1) The computation and distribution among the members of the association of the average cost to association members of all dimensions

and grades of flooring.

(2) The compilation and distribution among members of a booklet showing freight rates on flooring from Cadillac, Michigan, to between five and six thousand points of shipment in the United States.

(3) The gathering of statistics which at frequent intervals are supplied by each member of the Association to the Secretary of the Association giving complete information as to the quantity and kind of flooring sold and prices received by the reporting members, and the amount of stock on hand, which information is summarized by the Secretary and transmitted to members without, however, revealing the identity of the members in connection with any specific information thus transmitted.

(4) Meetings at which the representatives of members congregate and discuss the industry and exchange views as to its problems.

Before considering these phases of the activities of the Association, it should be pointed out that it is neither alleged nor proved that there was any agreement among the members of the Association either affecting production, fixing prices or for price maintenance. Both by the articles of association and in actual practice, members have been left free to sell their product at any price they choose and to conduct their business as they please. Although the bill alleges that the activities of the defendants hereinbefore referred to resulted in the maintenance of practical uniformity of net delivered prices as between the several corporate defendants, the evidence fails to establish such uniformity and it was not seriously urged before this Court that any substantial uniformity in price had in fact resulted from the activities of the Association, although it was conceded by defendants that the dissemination of information as to cost of the product and as to production and prices would tend to bring about uniformity in prices through the operation of economic law. Nor was there any direct proof that the activities of the Association had affected prices adversely to consumers. On the contrary, the defendants offered a great volume of evidence tending to show that the trend of prices of the product of the defendants corresponded to the law of supply and demand and that it evidenced no abnormality when compared with the price of commodities generally. There is undisputed evidence that the prices of members were fair and reasonable and that they were usually lower than the prices of non-members and there is no claim that defendants were guilty of unfair or arbitrary trade practices.

. . . .

Computation and distribution, among the members, of information as to the average cost of their product.

. . . .

In order to determine the cost of a given type or grade of flooring, it was necessary to distribute the total cost of the aggregate of the different types and grades of finished flooring produced from a given amount of rough lumber among the several types and grades thus produced. This distribution was made by the officials of the Association and the estimated cost thus determined was tabulated and distributed among the members of the Association. There is no substantial claim made on the part of the Government that the preparation of these estimates of cost was not made with all practicable accuracy . . . except that the point is made by the Government that the distribution of cost among the several types and grades of finished flooring produced from a given amount of rough lumber was necessarily arbitrary and that it might be or become a cover for price fixing. . . . [N]either the Government nor the defendants seem to have found it necessary to prove upon what principle of cost accounting this distribution of cost was made and there are no data from which any inference can be drawn as to whether or not it conformed to accepted practices.

The compilation and distribution among members of information as to freight rates.

Through the agency of the Secretary of the Association a booklet was compiled and distributed to members of the Association showing freight rates from Cadillac, Michigan, to numerous points throughout the United States to which the finished flooring is shipped by members of the Association. It appears from the evidence to have been the usual practice in the maple flooring trade, to quote flooring at a delivered price and that purchasers of flooring usually will not buy on any other basis. . . . It also appears that the mills of most of the members of the Association are located in small towns in Michigan and Wisconsin and that the average freight rates from these principal producing points in Michigan and Wisconsin to the principal centers of consumption in the United States are approximately the same as the freight rate from Cadillac, Michigan, to the same centers of consumption.

The Government bases its criticism of the use of the freight-rate book upon the fact that antecedent associations, maintained by defendants, incorporated in the freight-rate book a delivered price which was made up by adding the calculated freight rate from Cadillac, Michigan, to a minimum price under the so-called "minimum price plan" of previous associations, whereby the price was fixed at cost plus ten per cent of profit. It is conceded that the present Association does not include a delivered price in the freight-rate book, but it is urged by the Government that the circulation of the tables of estimated cost of flooring, together with a freight-rate book, enables members of the Association to fix a delivered price . . . whereby the defendants have continued the so-called minimum price plan formerly maintained by predecessor associations. . . .

. . . [D]ata as to the average cost of flooring circulated among the members of the Association when combined with a calculated freight rate which is either exactly or approximately the freight rate from the point of shipment, plus an arbitrary percentage of profit, could be made the basis for fixing prices or for an agreement for price maintenance, which, if found to exist, would under the decisions of this Court, constitute a violation of the Sherman Act. But, as we have already said, the record is barren of evidence that the published list of costs and the freight-rate book have been so used by the present Association. Consequently, the question which this Court must decide is whether the use of this material by members of the Association will necessarily have that effect so as to produce that unreasonable restraint of interstate commerce which is condemned by the Sherman Act.

The gathering and distributing among members of trade statistics.

. . . [M]embers reported weekly to the Secretary of the Association on forms showing dates of sales made by the reporting member, the quantity, the thickness and face, the grade, the kind of wood, the delivery, the prices at which sold, the average freight rate to destination and the rate of commission paid, if any. Members also reported monthly the amount of flooring on hand of each dimension and grade and the amount of unfilled orders. Monthly reports were also required showing the amount of production for each period and the new orders booked for each variety of flooring. . . . All reports of sales and prices dealt exclusively with past and closed transactions. The statistics gathered by the defendant Association are given wide publicity.

Association meetings.

The Government, however, does not charge, nor is it contended, that there was any understanding or agreement, either express or implied, at the meetings or elsewhere, with respect to prices.

Upon this state of the record, the District Court . . . held that the plan or system operated by the defendants had a direct and necessary tendency to destroy competition. . . .

. . . .

It is not, we think, open to question that the dissemination of pertinent information concerning any trade or business tends to stabilize that trade or business and to produce uniformity of price and trade practice. Exchange of price quotations of market commodities tends to produce uniformity of prices in the markets of the world. Knowledge of the supplies of available merchandise tends to prevent over-production and to avoid the economic disturbances produced by business crises resulting from over-production. But the natural effect of the acquisition of wider and more scientific knowledge of business conditions, on the minds of the individuals engaged in commerce, and its consequent effect in stabilizing production and price, can hardly be deemed a restraint of commerce or if so it cannot, we think, be said to be an unreasonable restraint, or in any respect unlawful.

. . . .

We do not conceive that the members of trade associations become such conspirators merely because they gather and disseminate information, such as is here complained of, bearing on the business in which they are engaged and make use of it in the management and control of their individual businesses; nor do we think that the proper application of the principles of decision of *American Column & Lumber Co. v. United States* . . . leads to any such result. . . .

We decide only that trade associations or combinations of persons or corporations which openly and fairly gather and disseminate information as to the cost of their product, the volume of production, the actual price which the product has brought in past transactions, stocks of merchandise on hand, approximate cost of transportation from the principal point of shipment to the points of consumption, as did these defendants, and who, as they did, meet and discuss such information and statistics without however reaching or attempting to reach any agreement or any concerted action with respect to prices or production or restraining competition, do not thereby engage in unlawful restraint of commerce.

Reversed.

[JUSTICES TAFT, SANFORD, and MCREYNOLDS dissented.]

NOTES AND QUESTIONS

1. In *Cement Mfrs. Protective Ass'n v. United States*, 268 U.S. 588 (1925), handed down the same day, the Court found no Section 1 violation where the government had challenged the statistical and credit activities of the association, but no charge had been made that the association had restricted production or prices. The evidence showed that the price of cement changed frequently though uniformly. The Court also found that inferences of any agreement or uniformity of trade practices could not be drawn from the exchange of statistics on production, shipments, stocks, or credit terms. Moreover, the Court opined that the exchange of information was necessary to inhibit customer fraud and misrepresentation.

2. Did the relatively small number of members (22) in the Maple Flooring Manufacturer's Association make it more or less likely that the information exchange would have an impact on price?

3. Why did the defendants compile and distribute to themselves a book showing freight rates from Cadillac, Michigan? One possibility is that Cadillac, Michigan, was a point central to all of them, from which freight rates could easily be computed. Another possibility, however, is that they were engaged in base-point pricing.

4. The next data exchange case to reach the Court was *Sugar Inst. v. United States*, 297 U.S. 553 (1936), where the Court decided whether a "code of ethics" which required sugar refiners not to deviate from announced prices violated Section 1. Intense competition characterized the sugar industry at this time. Because sugar was a homogenous product, competition focused on price. The agreement prohibited secret price concessions and discriminatory rebates. Refiners were free to set price and announce price changes; once announced, however, the code prevented price changes and discrimination unless openly announced in advance.

The Court held that it was a violation of Section 1 for the trade association members to agree to refrain from changing an announced price through a secret price concession. In delivering the opinion for the Court, Chief Justice Hughes reasoned as follows:

> We have said that the Sherman Act, as a charter of freedom, has a generality and adaptability comparable to that found to be desirable in constitutional provisions. It does not go into detailed definitions. Thus in applying its broad prohibitions, each case demands a close scrutiny of its own facts. Questions of reasonableness are necessarily questions of relation and degree. In the instant case, a fact of outstanding importance is the relative position of defendants in the sugar industry. We have noted that the fifteen refiners, represented in the Institute, refine practically all the imported raw sugar processed in this country. They supply from 70 to 80

per cent of the sugar consumed. Their refineries are in the East, South, and West, and their agreements and concerted action have a direct effect upon the entire sugar trade. While their product competes with beet sugar and "offshore" sugar, the maintenance of fair competition between the defendants themselves in the sale of domestic refined sugar is manifestly of serious public concern. Another outstanding fact is that defendants' product is a thoroughly standardized commodity. In their competition, price, rather than brand, is generally the vital consideration. The question of unreasonable restraint of competition thus relates in the main to competition in prices, terms and conditions of sales. The fact that, because sugar is a standardized commodity, there is a strong tendency to uniformity of price, makes it the more important that such opportunities as may exist for fair competition should not be impaired.

Defendants point to the abuses which existed before they formed the Institute, and to their remedial efforts. But the controversy that emerges is not as to the abuses which admittedly existed, but whether defendants' agreement and requirements went too far and imposed unreasonable restraints. After a hearing of extraordinary length, in which no pertinent fact was permitted to escape consideration, the trial court subjected the evidence to a thorough and acute analysis which has left but slight room for debate over matters of fact. Our examination of the record discloses no reason for overruling the court's findings in any matter essential to our decision.

In determining the relief to be afforded, appropriate regard should be had to the special and historic practice of the sugar industry. The restraints, found to be unreasonable, were the offspring of the basic agreement. The vice in that agreement was not in the mere open announcement of prices and terms in accordance with the custom of the trade. That practice which had grown out of the special character of the industry did not restrain competition. The trial court did not hold that practice to be illegal and we see no reason for condemning it. The unreasonable restraints which defendants imposed lay not in advance announcements, but in the steps taken to secure adherence, without deviation, to prices and terms thus announced. It was that concerted undertaking which cut off opportunities for variation in the course of competition however fair and appropriate they might be."

On the question of the proper remedy, *Sugar Institute* struck down as too expansive the injunction issued by the district court. The order entered by the trial court forbade conduct:

> "Effectuating   any   system   for . . . reporting . . . among . . . competitors or to a common agency, information as to current or future prices, terms, conditions. . . . 4. Relaying by or through The Sugar Institute . . . information as to current or future prices, terms, conditions. . . . 5. Giving any prior notice of any change or contemplated change in prices, terms, conditions . . . or

relaying, reporting or announcing any such change in advance there thereof."

297 U.S. at 603. In reviewing this decree, the Court said:

> The trial court left defendants free to provide for immediate publicity as to prices and terms in all closed transactions. We think that a limitation to that sort of publicity fails to take proper account of the practice of the trade in selling on "moves" [a condition of the industry which permitted a customer a grace period in which to purchase at the old price]. That custom involves advance announcements, and it does not appear that arrangements merely to circulate or relay such announcements threaten competitive opportunities. On the other hand, such provision for publicity may be helpful in promoting fair competition. If the requirement that there must be adherence to prices and terms openly announced in advance is abrogated and the restraints which followed that requirement are removed, the just interests of competition will be safeguarded and the trade will still be left with whatever advantage may be incidental to its established practice.

Id. at 601–602.

Thus the Court approved the advance announcement of price information, although the *agreement* not to deviate from the announced prices, which had the effect of eliminating price concessions and reductions, was found unlawful. *See* E. Thomas Sullivan, *First Amendment Defenses in Antitrust Litigation*, 46 Mo. L. REV. 517, 554 (1981). The Court's analysis suggests that before an order can enjoin the exchange of price information, there must be an inquiry into how closely the disclosure is related to an agreement that might affect prices and the role the price announcement or exchange played in the trade practice. *Cf. Broadcast Music, Inc. v. CBS, Inc.*, 441 U.S. 1 (1979) (Court examined market purpose of a blanket licensing agreement to determine whether it was a per se illegal price fixing arrangement).

Did the Court in the preceding cases articulate why it applies a rule of reason approach in data dissemination cases rather than a per se analysis? Consider whether the 1940 *Socony-Vacuum* decision implicitly overruled *Maple Flooring*. In comparing *Maple Flooring* to *Socony-Vacuum*, can you define what constitutes price fixing? Does it matter whether there is an agreement concerning the use of the disclosed prices? What advice can you give a trade association client in establishing guidelines for a lawful statistical exchange program?

Sugar Institute, and to a lesser extent the earlier cases, suggested that the structure of the industry might play a role in determining the legality of a cooperative exchange program. The Court noted that "[q]uestions of reasonableness are necessarily questions of relation and degree. . . . [A] fact of outstanding importance is the relative position of defendants in the . . . industry." 297 U.S. at 600. This comment foreshadowed the market structure analysis and economic theory that achieved acceptance in the next case. While *Sugar Institute* considered how the communication was affected by market conditions and trade practices, the following case focused on how market structure may be determinative of the legality of the communication.

UNITED STATES v. CONTAINER CORP. OF AMERICA
393 U.S. 333 (1969)

Justice Douglas delivered the opinion of the Court.

This is a civil antitrust action charging a price-fixing agreement in violation of § 1, of the Sherman Act. . . . The District Court dismissed the complaint. . . .

The case as proved is unlike any of other price decisions we have rendered. There was here an exchange of price information but no agreement to adhere to a price schedule. . . . There was here an exchange of information concerning specific sales to identified customers, not a statistical report on the average cost to all members, without identifying the parties to specific transactions. . . . While there was present here . . . an exchange of prices to specific customers, there was absent the controlling circumstance, [found in *Cement*] that cement manufacturers, to protect themselves from delivering to contractors more cement than was needed for a specific job and thus receiving a lower price, exchanged price information as a means of protecting their legal rights from fraudulent inducements to deliver more cement than needed for a specific job.

Here all that was present was a request by each defendant of its competitor for information as to the most recent price changed or quoted, whenever it needed such information and whenever it was not available from another source. Each defendant on receiving that request usually furnished the data with the expectation that it would be furnished reciprocal information when it wanted it. That concerted action is of course sufficient to establish the combination or conspiracy, the initial ingredient of a violation of § 1 of the Sherman Act.

There was of course freedom to withdraw from the agreement. But the fact remains that when a defendant requested and received price information, it was affirming its willingness to furnish such information in return.

There was to be sure an infrequency and irregularity of price exchanges between the defendants; and often the data were available from the records of the defendants or from the customers themselves. Yet the essence of the agreement was to furnish price information whenever requested.

Moreover, although the most recent price charged or quoted was sometimes fragmentary, each defendant had the manuals with which it could compute the price charged by a competitor on a specific order to a specific customer.

Further, the price quoted was the current price which a customer would need to pay in order to obtain products from the defendant furnishing the data.

The defendants account for about 90% of the shipment of corrugated containers from plants in the Southeastern United States. While containers vary as to dimensions, weight, color, and so on, they are substantially identical, no matter who produces them, when made to particular specifications. The prices paid depend on price alternatives. Suppliers when seeking new or additional business or keeping old customers, do not exceed a competitor's price. It is common for purchasers to buy from two or more suppliers concurrently. A defendant supplying a customer with containers would usually quote the same price on additional orders, unless costs had changed. Yet where a competitor was charging a particular price, a defendant would normally quote the same price or even a lower price.

The exchange of price information seemed to have the effect of keeping prices within a fairly narrow ambit. Capacity has exceeded the demand from 1955 to 1963, the period covered by the complaint, and the trend of corrugated container prices has been downward. Yet despite this excess capacity and the downward trend of prices, the industry has expanded in the Southeast from 30 manufacturers with 49 plants to 51 manufacturers with 98 plants. An abundance of raw materials and machinery makes entry into the industry easy with an investment of $50,000 to $75,000.

The result of this reciprocal exchange of prices was to stabilize prices though at a downward level. Knowledge of a competitor's price usually meant matching that price. The continuation of some price competition is not fatal to the Government's case. The limitation or reduction of price competition brings the case within the ban, for as we held in *United States v. Socony-Vacuum Oil Co.*, interference with the setting of price by free market forces is unlawful *per se.* Price information exchanged in some markets may have no effect on a truly competitive price. But the corrugated container industry is dominated by relatively few sellers. The product is fungible and the competition for sales is price. The demand is inelastic, as buyers place orders only for immediate, short-run needs. The exchange of price data tends toward price uniformity. For a lower price does not mean a larger share of the available business but a sharing of the existing business at a lower return. Stabilizing prices as well as raising them is within the ban of § 1 of the Sherman Act. As we said in *United States v. Socony-Vacuum Oil Co.*, "in terms of market operations stabilization is but one form of manipulation." The inferences are irresistible that the exchange of price information has had an anticompetitive effect in the industry, chilling the vigor of price competition. . . .

Price is too critical, too sensitive a control to allow it to be used even in an informal manner to restrain competition.

Reversed.

JUSTICE FORTAS, concurring.

I join in the judgment and opinion of the Court. I do not understand the Court's opinion to hold that the exchange of specific information among sellers as to prices charged to individual customers, pursuant to mutual arrangement, is a *per se* violation of the Sherman Act.

Absent *per se* violation, proof is essential that the practice resulted in an unreasonable restraint of trade. There is no single test to determine when the record adequately shows an "unreasonable restraint of trade"; but a practice such as that here involved, which is adopted for the purpose of arriving at a determination of prices to be quoted to individual customers, inevitably suggests the probability that it so materially interfered with the operation of the price mechanism of the marketplace as to bring it within the condemnation of this Court's decisions.

Theoretical probability, however, is not enough unless we are to regard mere exchange of current price information as so akin to price-fixing by combination or conspiracy as to deserve the *per se* classification. I am not prepared to do this, nor is it necessary here. In this case, the probability that the exchange of specific price information led to an unlawful effect upon prices is adequately buttressed by evidence in the record. This evidence, although not overwhelming, is sufficient in the special circumstances of this case to show an actual effect on pricing and to compel us to hold that the court below erred in dismissing the Government's complaint.

On this record, taking into account the specially sensitive function of the price term in the antitrust equation, I cannot see that we would be justified in reaching any conclusion other than that defendants' tacit agreement to exchange information about current prices to specific customers did in fact substantially limit the amount of price competition in the industry. That being so, there is no need to consider the possibility of a *per se* violation.

JUSTICE MARSHALL, with whom JUSTICE HARLAN and JUSTICE STEWART join, dissenting.

I agree with the Court's holding that there existed an agreement among the defendants to exchange price information whenever requested. However, I cannot agree that that agreement should be condemned, either as illegal *per se*, or as having had the purpose or effect of restricting price competition in the corrugated container industry in the Southeastern United States.

. . . .

Per se rules always contain a degree of arbitrariness. They are justified on the assumption that the gains from imposition of the rule will far outweigh the losses and that significant administrative advantages will result. In other words, the potential competitive harm plus the administrative costs of determining in what particular situations the practice may be harmful must far outweigh the benefits that may result. If the potential benefits in the aggregate are outweighed to this degree, then they are simply not worth identifying in individual cases.

I do not believe that the agreement in the present case is so devoid of potential benefit or so inherently harmful that we are justified in condemning it without proof that it was entered into for the purpose of restraining price competition or that it actually had that effect. . . .

Complete market knowledge is certainly not an evil in perfectly competitive markets. This is not, however, such a market, and there is admittedly some danger that price information will be used for anticompetitive purposes, particularly the maintenance of prices at a high level. If the danger that price information will be so used is particularly high in a given situation, then perhaps exchange of information should be condemned.

I do not think the danger is sufficiently high in the present case. Defendants are only 18 of the 51 producers of corrugated containers in the Southeastern United States. Together, they do make up 90% of the market and the six largest defendants do control 60% of the market. But entry is easy; an investment of $50,000 to $75,000 is ordinarily all that is necessary. In fact, the number of sellers has increased from 30 to the present 51 in the eight-year period covered by the complaint. The size of the market has almost doubled because of increased demand for corrugated containers. Nevertheless, some excess capacity is present. The products produced by defendants are undifferentiated. Industry demand is inelastic, so that price changes will not, up to a certain point, affect the total amount purchased. The only effect of price changes will be to reallocate market shares among sellers.

. . . .

In a competitive situation, each seller will cut his price in order to increase his share of the market, and prices will ultimately stabilize at a competitive level — i.e., price will equal cost, including a reasonable return on capital. Obviously, it would be to a seller's benefit to avoid such price competition and maintain prices at a higher level, with a corresponding increase in profit. In a market with very few sellers, and detailed knowledge of each other's price, such action is possible. However, I do not think it can be concluded that this particular market is sufficiently oligopolistic, especially in light of the ease of entry, to justify the inference that price information will necessarily be used to stabilize prices. Nor do I think that the danger of such a result is sufficiently high to justify imposing a *per se* rule without actual proof.

In this market, we have a few sellers presently controlling a substantial share of the market. We have a large number competing for the remainder of the market, also quite substantial. And total demand is increasing. In such a case, I think it just as logical to assume that the sellers, especially the smaller and newer ones will desire to capture a larger market share by cutting prices as it is that they will acquiesce in oligopolistic behavior. The likelihood that prices will be cut and that those lower prices will have to be met acts as a deterrent to setting prices at an artificially high level in the first place. Given the uncertainty about the probable effect of an exchange of price information in this context, I would require that the Government prove that the exchange was entered into for the purpose of, or that it had the effect of, restraining price competition.

NOTES AND QUESTIONS

1. Did Justice Douglas' opinion hold that price exchanges are illegal per se? Did the Court find that the exchange of price information was inherently anticompetitive? Or did the Court find anticompetitive purpose or effect?

2. Did Justice Douglas find an "agreement" to exchange price information? If so, how did he reach this conclusion? Consider the fact that the exchanges were infrequent; does this bode against an inference of agreement? What if it were an exchange of past sale transactions? Is an agreement to exchange price information the equivalent of an agreement to fix prices? If there was no "agreement" to exchange the information, could the defendants have violated Section 1?

3. Under the economic analysis employed by Justice Douglas, how concentrated must the market be before a price exchange will be considered illegal? What relevance should excess capacity, the collective market power of the defendants, and ease of entry into the market have on determining the legality of a price exchange? Do falling prices and increased costs indicate evidence of market power? If these economic conditions were present in the market, is it likely that the prices exceeded a competitive level? Under what structural conditions would you expect that exchange of prices would lead to more, rather than less, competition?

The *Container* decision was the first explicit indication that the Supreme Court would expand its analysis to consider the relationship between market structure and the effect of price exchanges. Previously, the Court had concentrated its analysis on conduct or behavior of the defendant. *Container* also raised the question as to the proper standard of analysis for price-affecting conduct, such as exchanges of price information. Although ambiguous, *Container* suggested a per se rule: it is not necessary to establish evidence of either unlawful purpose or actual anticompetitive effect in order to find a violation in an oligopolistic market. As an evidentiary and substantive law concern, the standard employed is obviously important. But as Justices Fortas and Marshall pointed out in their separate opinions in *Container*, there was uncertainty as to the actual approach utilized in the majority opinion.

The issue was clarified six years later when the Court, in *United States v. Citizens & S. Nat'l Bank*, 422 U.S. 86, 113 (1975), stated unequivocally that the disclosure or exchange of price information is not a per se violation. Interestingly, the Court cited Justice Fortas' concurring opinion in *Container* for his statement of the law, rather than Justice Douglas' majority opinion. For the antitrust lawyer, the message seemed clear: actual proof "that the practice resulted in an unreasonable restraint of trade" (Fortas, J., concurring) was necessary in a price or data exchange case. 393 U.S. at 339.

In the next case, the standard was applied in a criminal case where the issue was whether an interseller price verification plan among competitors, for the purpose of defending a price discrimination charge under the Robinson-Patman Act, was exempt from the Sherman Act's coverage. In addition to clarifying its analytic approach, the Court articulated distinctions between civil and criminal violations.

UNITED STATES v. UNITED STATES GYPSUM CO.
438 U.S. 422 (1978)

CHIEF JUSTICE BURGER delivered the opinion of the Court.

This case presents the following questions: (a) whether intent is an element of a criminal antitrust offense; (b) whether an exchange of price information for purposes of compliance with the Robinson-Patman Act is exempt from Sherman Act scrutiny. . . .

I

Gypsum board, a laminated type of wall board composed of paper, vinyl or other specially treated coverings over a gypsum core, has in the last 30 years substantially replaced wet plaster as the primary component of interior walls and ceilings in residential and commercial construction. The product is essentially fungible; differences in price, credit terms and delivery services largely dictate the purchasers' choice between competing suppliers. Overall demand, however, is governed by the level of construction activity and is only marginally affected by price fluctuations.

The gypsum board industry is highly concentrated with the number of producers ranging from nine to 15 in the period 1960–1973. The eight largest companies accounted for some 94% of the national sales with the seven "single plant producers" accounting for the remaining 6%. Most of the major producers and a large number of the single plant producers are members of the Gypsum Association which since 1930 has served as a trade association of gypsum board manufacturers.

. . . .

B

The focus of the Government's price fixing case at trial was interseller price verification — that is, the practice allegedly followed by the gypsum board manufacturers of telephoning a competing producer to determine the price currently being offered on gypsum board to a specific customer. The Government contended that these price exchanges were part of an agreement among the defendants, had the effect of stabilizing prices, and policing agreed upon price increases, and were undertaken on a frequent basis until sometime in 1973. Defendants disputed both the scope and duration of the verification activities, and further maintained that those exchanges of price information which did occur were for the purposes of complying with the Robinson-Patman Act and preventing customer fraud. These purposes, in defendants' view, brought the disputed communications among competitors within a "controlling circumstance" exception to Sherman Act liability — at the extreme, precluding, as a matter of law, consideration of verification by the jury in determining defendants' guilt on the price fixing charge, and at the minimum, making the defendants' purposes in engaging in such communications a threshold factual question.

The instructions on the verification issue given by the trial judge provided that if the exchanges of price information were deemed by the jury to have been undertaken "in a good faith effort to comply with the Robinson-Patman Act," verification standing alone would not be sufficient to establish an illegal price fixing agreement. The paragraphs immediately following, however, provided that the purpose was essentially irrelevant if the jury found that the effect of verification was to raise, fix, maintain or stabilize prices. The instructions on verification closed with the observation:

"The law presumes that a person intends the necessary and natural consequences of his acts. Therefore, if the effect of the exchanges of pricing information was to raise, fix, maintain and stabilize prices, then the parties to them are presumed, as a matter of law, to have intended that result."

. . . .

D

The Court of Appeals for the Third Circuit reversed the convictions.

. . . .

II

. . . .

We agree with the Court of Appeals that an effect on prices, without more, will not support a criminal conviction under the Sherman Act, but we do not base that conclusion on the existence of any conflict between the requirements of the Robinson-Patman and the Sherman Acts. Rather, we hold that a defendant's state of mind or intent is an element of a criminal antitrust offense which must be established by evidence and inferences drawn therefrom and cannot be taken from the trier of fact through reliance on a legal presumption of wrongful intent from proof of an effect on prices. Cf. *Morissette v. United States*, 342 U.S. 246, 274–275. Since the challenged instruction, as we read it, had this prohibited effect, it is disapproved. We are unwilling to construe the Sherman Act as mandating a regime of strict liability criminal offenses.[2]

A

We start with the familiar proposition that "[t]he existence of a *mens rea* is the rule of, rather than the exception to, the principles of Anglo-American criminal jurisprudence." . . . Although Blackstone's requisite "vicious will" has been replaced by more sophisticated and less colorful characterizations of the mental state required to support criminality, see ALI Model Penal Code § 2.02 (Prop. Official Draft 1962), intent generally remains an indispensable element of a criminal offense. This is as true in a sophisticated criminal antitrust case as in one involving any other criminal offense. . . .

While strict liability offenses are not unknown to the criminal law and do not invariably offend constitutional requirements, . . . the limited circumstances in which Congress has created and this Court has recognized such offenses, . . . attest to their generally disfavored status. Certainly far more than the simple omission of the appropriate phrase from the statutory definition is necessary to justify dispensing with an intent requirement. In the context of the Sherman Act, this generally inhospitable attitude to non-*mens rea* offenses is reinforced by an array of considerations arguing against treating antitrust violations as strict liability crimes.

---

[2] [FN 13] Our analysis focuses solely on the elements of a criminal offense under the antitrust laws, and leaves unchanged the general rule that a civil violation can be established by proof of either an unlawful purpose or an anticompetitive effect. See *United States v. Container Corp.*, 393 U.S. 333 (1969); (Marshall, J., dissenting). Of course, consideration of intent may play an important role in divining the actual nature and effect of the alleged anticompetitive conduct. See *Chicago Board of Trade v. United States*, 246 U.S. 231, 238.

B

The Sherman Act, unlike most traditional criminal statutes, does not, in clear and categorical terms, precisely identify the conduct which it proscribes. Both civil remedies and criminal sanctions are authorized with regard to the same generalized definitions of the conduct proscribed — restraints of trade or commerce and illegal monopolization — without reference to or mention of intent or state of mind. Nor has judicial elaboration of the Act always yielded the clear and definitive rules of conduct, which the statute omits; instead open-ended and fact-specific standards like the "rule of reason" have been applied to broad classes of conduct falling within the purview of the Act's general provisions. . . . Simply put the Act has not been interpreted as if it were primarily a criminal statute; it has been construed to have a "generality and adaptability comparable to that found desirable in constitutional provisions." . . .

. . . .

. . . With certain exceptions for conduct regarded as *per se* illegal because of its unquestionably anticompetitive effects, . . . the behavior proscribed by the Act is often difficult to distinguish from the gray zone of socially acceptable and economically justifiable business conduct. Indeed, the type of conduct charged in the indictment in this case — the exchange of price information among competitors — is illustrative in this regard.[3] The imposition of criminal liability on a corporate official, or for that matter on a corporation directly, for engaging in such conduct which only after the fact is determined to violate the statute because of anticompetitive effects, without inquiring into the intent with which it was undertaken, holds out the distinct possibility of overdeterrence; salutary and procompetitive conduct lying close to the borderline of impermissible conduct might be shunned by businessmen who chose to be excessively cautious in the face of uncertainty regarding possible exposure to criminal punishment for even a good- faith error of judgment. . . . Further, the use of criminal sanctions in such circumstances would be difficult to square with the generally accepted functions of the criminal law. . . . The criminal sanctions would be used not to punish conscious and calculated wrongdoing at odds with statutory proscriptions, but instead simply to *regulate* business practices regardless of the intent with which they were undertaken. . . .

For these reasons, we conclude that the criminal offenses defined by the

---

[3] [FN 16] The exchange of price data and other information among competitors does not invariably have anticompetitive effects; indeed such practices can in certain circumstances increase economic efficiency and render markets more, rather than less, competitive. For this reason, we have held that such exchanges of information do not constitute a *per se* violation of the Sherman Act. *See, e.g., United States v. Citizens & S. Nat. Bank*, 422 U.S. 86, 113 (1975); *United States v. Container Corp.*, 393 U.S., at 338 (Fortas, J., concurring). A number of factors including most prominently the structure of the industry involved and the nature of the information exchanged are generally considered in divining the procompetitive or anticompetitive effects of this type of interseller communication. See *United States v. Container Corp. See generally* L. Sullivan, Law of Antitrust 265–74 (1977). Exchanges of current price information, of course, have the greatest potential for generating anticompetitive effects and although not *per se* unlawful have consistently been held to violate the Sherman Act. See *American Column & Lumber Co. v. United States*, 257 U.S. 377 (1921); *United States v. American Linseed Oil Co.*, 262 U.S. 371 (1923); *United States v. Container Corp.*

Sherman Act should be construed as including intent as an element.

C

. . . .

. . . Our question . . . is whether a criminal violation of the antitrust laws requires, in addition to proof of anticompetitive effects, a demonstration that the disputed conduct was undertaken with the "conscious object" of producing such effects or whether it is sufficient that the conduct is shown to have been undertaken with knowledge that the proscribed effects would most likely follow. . . . [W]e conclude that action undertaken with knowledge of its probable consequences and having the requisite anticompetitive effects can be a sufficient predicate for a finding of criminal liability under the antitrust laws.[4]

Nothing in our analysis of the Sherman Act persuades us that this general understanding of intent should not be applied to criminal antitrust violations such as charged here. The business behavior which is likely to give rise to criminal antitrust charges is conscious behavior normally undertaken only after a full consideration of the desired results and a weighing of the costs, benefits and risks. A requirement of proof not only of this knowledge of likely effects, but also of a conscious desire to bring them to fruition or to violate the law would seem, particularly in such a context, both unnecessarily cumulative and unduly burdensome. Where carefully planned and calculated conduct is being scrutinized in the context of a criminal prosecution, the perpetrator's knowledge of the anticipated consequences is a sufficient predicate for a finding of criminal intent.

D

When viewed in terms of this standard, the jury instructions on the price fixing charge cannot be sustained. "A conclusive presumption [of intent], which testimony could not overthrow would effectively eliminate intent as an ingredient of the offense." The challenged jury instruction, as we read it, had precisely this effect; the jury was told that the requisite intent followed, *as a matter of law*, from a finding that the exchange of price information had an impact on prices. Although an effect on prices may well support an inference that the defendant had knowledge of the probability of such a consequence at the time he acted, the jury must remain free to consider additional evidence before accepting or rejecting the inference. Therefore, although it would be correct to instruct the jury that it may infer intent from an effect on prices, ultimately the decision on the issue of intent must be left to the trier of fact alone. The instruction given invaded this fact finding function.[5]

---

[4] [FN 21] In so holding, we do not mean to suggest that conduct undertaken with the purpose of producing anticompetitive effects would not also support criminal liability, even if such effects did not come to pass. *Cf. United States v. Griffith*, 334 U.S. 100, 105 (1948). We hold only that this elevated standard of intent need not be established in cases where anticompetitive effects have been demonstrated; instead, proof that the defendant's conduct was undertaken with knowledge of its probable consequences will satisfy the Government's burden.

[5] [FN 22] Respondents contend that "prior to the trial of this case, no court had ever held that a mere exchange of information which had a stabilizing effect on prices violated the Sherman Act, regardless of

Affirmed.

NOTES AND QUESTIONS

1.   Reflect on the distinctions drawn in *Gypsum* between a civil and criminal violation for an exchange of price information. What evidentiary factors are relevant, under *Gypsum*, for determining the legality of the price exchange? In defining a price-fixing agreement, does it matter that there is no agreement concerning the use of the prices exchanged? Does *Gypsum* stand for the proposition that an agreement that may affect price, though not a direct price-fixing arrangement, should be analyzed under the rule of reason? Did the *Gypsum* Court disavow *Container's* pronouncement that a concentrated industry is predisposed towards cartelization?

2.   How would you write a jury instruction in a criminal case on the intent element of a Section 1 charge? Is the standard specific intent or general intent? Consider whether intent can be presumed if the indictment charges only a per se violation, thus negating the *Gypsum* requirement that the issue be submitted to the jury. Can the requisite criminal intent be inferred if the agreement is established? See generally *United States v. Continental Group, Inc.*, 603 F.2d 444 (3d Cir. 1978); *Phillips v. Crown Cent. Petr. Corp.*, 602 F.2d 616 (4th Cir. 1979); *United States v. Brighton Bldg. & Main. Co.*, 598 F.2d 1101 (7th Cir. 1979); *United States v. Gillen*, 599 F.2d 541 (3d Cir. 1979), for a discussion of whether there is a distinction between an agreement to exchange prices (*Gypsum*) and an agreement to fix prices, and whether the prosecution in a criminal case must prove intent with respect to any anticompetitive effect beyond the existence of a price fixing agreement. Do you agree that "conduct that clearly constitutes a per se offense carries with it its own

---

the purposes of the exchange." Retroactive application of "this judicially expanded definition of the crime" would, the argument continues, "contravene the principles of fair notice in the Due Process Clause." While we have rejected on other grounds the "effects only" test in the context of criminal proceedings, we do not agree with respondents that the prior case law dealing with the exchange of price information required proof of a purpose to restrain competition in order to make out a Sherman Act violation.

Certainly our decision in *United States v. Container Corp.*, 393 U.S. 333 (1969), is fairly read as indicating that proof of an anticompetitive effect is a sufficient predicate for liability. In that case, liability followed from proof that "the exchange of price information had an anti-competitive effect in the industry," *Id.*, at 337, and no suggestion was made that proof of a purpose to restrain trade or competition was also required. Thus, at least in the post-*Container* period, which comprises almost the entire period at issue here, respondent's claimed lack of notice cannot be credited.

Nor are the prior cases treating exchanges of information among competitors more favorable to respondent's position. See *American Column Co. v. United States*, 257 U.S. 377, 400 (1921) ("any concerted action . . . to cause, or which in fact does cause . . . restraint of competition is unlawful"); *United States v. American Linseed Oil Co.*, 262 U.S. 371, 389 (1923) ("necessary tendency . . . to suppress competition is unlawful"); *Maple Flooring Mfrs. Ass'n v. United States*, 268 U.S. 563, 585 (1925) (purpose to restrain trade or conduct which "had resulted or would necessarily result in tendency to less production or increased prices" sufficient for liability). While in *Cement Mfrs. [Protective] Ass'n v. United States*, 268 U.S. 588 (1925), an exception from Sherman Act liability was recognized for conduct intended to prevent fraud, we do not read that case as repudiating the rule set out in prior cases; instead *Cement* highlighted a narrow limitation on the application of the general rule that either purpose or effect will support liability.

intent"? If price information exchanges are analyzed under the rule of reason, can they ever be a criminal violation?

3. In a civil case after *Gypsum*, are unlawful purpose and anticompetitive consequences prerequisites of a Section 1 violation? Can unlawful purpose be inferred from evidence of an effect on price? In either civil or criminal cases, what factors should the prosecutor or plaintiff's counsel consider in attempting to establish anticompetitive effect?

After *Gypsum*, Professor Milton Handler wrote that he was unaware "of any case in which a court has found that a defendant was civilly liable under Section 1 because he had a bad intent where his actions did not rise to the level of an unreasonable restraint of trade." He opined that "many cases have looked at the defendant's intent in determining the legality of challenged conduct. But these cases, while mouthing the . . . 'purpose and effect' test, in reality apply the . . . approach of considering intent merely as a means of determining the actual effect of an alleged restraint of trade." Milton Handler, *Antitrust — 1978*, 78 COLUM. L. REV. 1363, 1401–1402 (1978). The same standard was expressed before *Gypsum* by the Fifth Circuit in *Northwest Power Prods. v. Omark Indus.*, 576 F.2d 83, 90 (5th Cir. 1978), where the court said that "[a]n evil intent alone is insufficient to establish a violation under the rule of reason, although proof of intent may help a court assess the market impact of the defendants' conduct." Do you agree that in a civil case, intent evidence should be used only in determining the actual effect of the challenged action? Is this contradicted by *Gypsum?*

4. How workable is a rule that a price information exchange is illegal where the exchange has an "effect" on price? Prices in most markets change daily, and there are literally thousands of variables that determine them. How does one go about deciding whether a particular exchange of information has an "impact" on the price that a party to the exchange actually charges? One answer, of course, is that the parties also agree to be bound by the price information they obtain from a competitor. If this is true, however, they can be charged with price fixing, not merely with the exchange of price information.

PROBLEM 4.1

A group of oil companies responsible for about 80% of industry output periodically conducts, on an individual basis, salary surveys for nonunion, managerial employees. The companies submit this information to a third-party consultant, who compiles a "benchmark" database on job titles, which includes duties and salaries associated with particular positions and "job families" at each of the companies. The database is updated every few months, and therefore represents a current account of the compensation being paid in the industry. Representatives from the human resources departments of these companies also occasionally convene to discuss current and future salary budgets. None of this information is made available to the public. Under what circumstances would this amount to an unlawful information exchange? What is the antitrust injury? *See Todd v. Exxon Corp.*, 275 F.3d 191 (2d Cir. 2001).

[4]   The Meaning and Scope of the Rule of Reason

The distinction between per se conduct and conduct analyzed under the rule of reason standard has not always been clear. The problem of selecting the correct analysis arguably seems dependent upon the directness of the "agreement" to an effect on price. As Supreme Court opinions indicate, however, confusion still exists on how that standard is measured and when the per se rules of analysis will be employed. One conclusion is that not all concerted action that affects price is "price fixing."

NATIONAL SOCIETY OF PROFESSIONAL ENGINEERS v. UNITED STATES
435 U.S. 679 (1978)

JUSTICE STEVENS delivered the opinion of the Court.

This is a civil antitrust case brought by the United States to nullify an association's canon of ethics prohibiting competitive bidding by its members. The question is whether the canon may be justified under the Sherman Act, . . . because it was adopted by members of a learned profession for the purpose of minimizing the risk that competition would produce inferior engineering work endangering the public safety. . . . Because we are satisfied that the asserted defense rests on a fundamental misunderstanding of the Rule of Reason frequently applied in antitrust litigation, we affirm.

I

Engineering is an important and learned profession. There are over 750,000 graduate engineers in the United States, of whom about 325,000 are registered as professional engineers. Registration requirements vary from State to State, but usually require the applicant to be a graduate engineer with at least four years of practical experience and to pass a written examination. About half of those who are registered engage in consulting engineering on a fee basis. . . . Engineering fees, amounting to well over $2 billion each year, constitute about 5% of total construction costs. In any given facility, approximately 50% to 80% of the cost of construction is the direct result of work performed by an engineer concerning the systems and equipment to be incorporated in the structure.

The National Society of Professional Engineers (Society) was organized in 1935 to deal with the nontechnical aspects of engineering practice, including the promotion of the professional, social, and economic interests of its members. Its present membership of 69,000 resides throughout the United States and in some foreign countries. Approximately 12,000 members are consulting engineers who offer their services to governmental, industrial, and private clients. . . .

The charges of a consulting engineer may be computed in different ways. He may charge the client a percentage of the cost of the project, may set his fee at his actual cost plus overhead plus a reasonable profit, may charge fixed rates per hour for different types of work, may perform an assignment for a specific sum, or he may combine one or more of these approaches. Suggested fee schedules for particular types of services in certain areas have been promulgated from time to time by various local societies. This case does not, however, involve any claim that the National Society has tried to fix specific fees, or even a specific method of calculating fees. It involves a charge that the members of the Society have unlawfully agreed to refuse to negotiate or even to discuss the question of fees until after a prospective client has selected the engineer for a particular project. . . .

. . . The Society's Code of Ethics thus "prohibits engineers from both soliciting and submitting such price information," and seeks to preserve the profession's "traditional" method of selecting professional engineers. Under the traditional method, the client initially selects an engineer on the basis of background and reputation, not price.

. . . .

In its answer the Society admitted the essential facts alleged by the Government and pleaded a series of affirmative defenses, only one of which remains in issue. In that defense, the Society averred that the standard set out in the Code of Ethics was reasonable because competition among professional engineers was contrary to the public interest. It was averred that it would be cheaper and easier for an engineer "to design and specify inefficient and unnecessarily expensive structures and methods of construction." Accordingly, competitive pressure to offer engineering services at the lowest possible price would adversely affect the quality of engineering. Moreover, the practice of awarding engineering contracts to the lowest bidder, regardless of quality, would be dangerous to the public health, safety, and welfare. For these reasons, the Society claimed that its Code of Ethics was not an "unreasonable restraint of interstate trade or commerce."

. . . .

II

In *Goldfarb v. Virginia State Bar*, 421 U.S. 773, the Court held that a bar association's rule prescribing minimum fees for legal services violated § 1 of the Sherman Act. In that opinion the Court noted that certain practices by members of a learned profession might survive scrutiny under the Rule of Reason even though they would be viewed as a violation of the Sherman Act in another context. . . .

. . . .

A. *The Rule of Reason*

One problem presented by the language of § 1 of the Sherman Act is that it cannot mean what it says. The statute says that "every" contract that restrains trade is unlawful. But, as Mr. Justice Brandeis perceptively noted, restraint is the very essence of every contract; read literally, § 1 would outlaw the entire body of private contract law. Yet it is that body of law that establishes the enforceability of commercial agreements and enables competitive markets — indeed, a competitive economy — to function effectively.

Congress, however, did not intend the text of the Sherman Act to delineate the full meaning of the statute or its application in concrete situations. The legislative history makes it perfectly clear that it expected the courts to give shape to the statute's broad mandate by drawing on common-law tradition. The Rule of Reason, with its origins in common-law precedents long antedating the Sherman Act, has served that purpose. It has been used to give the Act both flexibility and definition, and its central principle of antitrust analysis has remained constant. Contrary to its name, the Rule does not open the field of antitrust inquiry to any argument in favor of a challenged restraint that may fall within the realm of reason. Instead, it focuses directly on the challenged restraint's impact on competitive conditions.

This principle is apparent in even the earliest of cases applying the Rule of Reason, *Mitchel v. Reynolds, supra. Mitchel* involved the enforceability of a promise by the seller of a bakery that he would not compete with the purchaser of his business. The covenant was for a limited time and applied only to the area in which the bakery had operated. It was therefore upheld as reasonable, even though it deprived the public of the benefit of potential competition. The long-run benefit of enhancing the marketability of the business itself — and thereby providing incentives to develop such an enterprise — outweighed the temporary and limited loss of competition.

The Rule of Reason suggested by *Mitchel v. Reynolds* has been regarded as a standard for testing the enforceability of covenants in restraint of trade which are ancillary to a legitimate transaction, such as an employment contract or the sale of a going business. Judge (later Mr. Chief Justice) Taft so interpreted the Rule in his classic rejection of the argument that competitors may lawfully agree to sell their goods at the same price as long as the agreed-upon price is reasonable. *United States v. Addyston Pipe & Steel Co.*, 85 F. 271, 282–283 (6th Cir. 1898), aff'd, 175 U.S. 211. That case, and subsequent decisions by this Court, unequivocally foreclose an interpretation of the Rule as permitting an inquiry into the reasonableness of the prices set by private agreement.

The early cases also foreclose the argument that because of the special characteristics of a particular industry, monopolistic arrangements will better promote trade and commerce than competition. . . . That kind of argument is properly addressed to Congress and may justify an exemption from the statute for specific industries, but it is not permitted by the Rule of Reason. As the Court observed in *Standard Oil Co. v. United States*, 221 U.S., at 65, "restraints of trade within the purview of the statute . . . [can]not be taken out of that category by indulging in general reasoning as to the expediency or nonexpediency of having made the contracts or the wisdom or want of wisdom of the statute which prohibited their being made."

The test prescribed in *Standard Oil* is whether the challenged contracts or acts "were unreasonably restrictive of competitive conditions." Unreasonableness under that test could be based either (1) on the nature or character of the contracts, or (2) on surrounding circumstances giving rise to the inference or presumption that they were intended to restrain trade and enhance prices. Under either branch of the test, the inquiry is confined to a consideration of impact on competitive conditions.

In this respect the Rule of Reason has remained faithful to its origins. From Mr.

Justice Brandeis' opinion for the Court in *Chicago Board of Trade* to the Court opinion written by Justice Powell in *Continental T.V., Inc.*, the Court has adhered to the position that the inquiry mandated by the Rule of Reason is whether the challenged agreement is one that promotes competition or one that suppresses competition. "The true test of legality is whether the restraint imposed is such as merely regulates and perhaps thereby promotes competition or whether it is such as may suppress or even destroy competition."

There are, thus, two complementary categories of antitrust analysis. In the first category are agreements whose nature and necessary effect are so plainly anticompetitive that no elaborate study of the industry is needed to establish their illegality — they are "illegal *per se.*" In the second category are agreements whose competitive effect can only be evaluated by analyzing the facts peculiar to the business, the history of the restraint, and the reasons why it was imposed. In either event, the purpose of the analysis is to form a judgment about the competitive significance of the restraint; it is not to decide whether a policy favoring competition is in the public interest, or in the interest of the members of an industry. Subject to exceptions defined by statute, that policy decision has been made by the Congress.

B. *The Ban on Competitive Bidding*

Price is the "central nervous system of the economy," *United States v. Socony-Vacuum Oil Co.*, 310 U.S. 150, and an agreement that "interfere[s] with the setting of price by free market forces" is illegal on its face. *United States v. Container Corp.*, 393 U.S. 333, 337. In this case we are presented with an agreement among competitors to refuse to discuss prices with potential customers until after negotiations have resulted in the initial selection of an engineer. While this is not price fixing as such, no elaborate industry analysis is required to demonstrate the anticompetitive character of such an agreement. It operates as an absolute ban on competitive bidding, applying with equal force to both complicated and simple projects and to both inexperienced and sophisticated customers. As the District Court found, the ban "impedes the ordinary give and take of the market place," and substantially deprives the customer of "the ability to utilize and compare prices in selecting engineering services." On its face, this agreement restrains trade within the meaning of § 1 of the Sherman Act.

The Society's affirmative defense confirms rather than refutes the anticompetitive purpose and effect of its agreement. The Society argues that the restraint is justified because bidding on engineering services is inherently imprecise, would lead to deceptively low bids, and would thereby tempt individual engineers to do inferior work with consequent risk to public safety and health. The logic of this argument rests on the assumption that the agreement will tend to maintain the price level; if it had no such effect, it would not serve its intended purpose. The Society nonetheless invokes the Rule of Reason, arguing that its restraint on price competition ultimately inures to the public benefit by preventing the production of inferior work and by insuring ethical behavior. As the preceding discussion of the Rule of Reason reveals, this Court has never accepted such an argument.

It may be, as petitioner argues, that competition tends to force prices down and that an inexpensive item may be inferior to one that is more costly. There is some risk, therefore, that competition will cause some suppliers to market a defective product. Similarly, competitive bidding for engineering projects may be inherently imprecise and incapable of taking into account all the variables which will be involved in the actual performance of the project. Based on these considerations, a purchaser might conclude that his interest in quality — which may embrace the safety of the end product — outweighs the advantages of achieving cost savings by pitting one competitor against another. Or an individual vendor might independently refrain from price negotiation until he has satisfied himself that he fully understands the scope of his customers' needs. These decisions might be reasonable; indeed, petitioner has provided ample documentation for that thesis. But these are not reasons that satisfy the Rule; nor are such individual decisions subject to antitrust attack.

The Sherman Act does not require competitive bidding; it prohibits unreasonable restraints on competition. Petitioner's ban on competitive bidding prevents all customers from making price comparisons in the initial selection of an engineer, and imposes the Society's views of the costs and benefits of competition on the entire marketplace. It is this restraint that must be justified under the Rule of Reason, and petitioner's attempt to do so on the basis of the potential threat that competition poses to the public safety and the ethics of its profession is nothing less than a frontal assault on the basic policy of the Sherman Act.

The Sherman Act reflects a legislative judgment that ultimately competition will produce not only lower prices, but also better goods and services. "The heart of our national economic policy long has been faith in the value of competition." *Standard Oil Co. v. FTC*, 340 U.S. 231, 248. The assumption that competition is the best method of allocating resources in a free market recognizes that all elements of a bargain — quality, service, safety, and durability — and not just the immediate cost, are favorably affected by the free opportunity to select among alternative offers. Even assuming occasional exceptions to the presumed consequences of competition, the statutory policy precludes inquiry into the question whether competition is good or bad.

The fact that engineers are often involved in large-scale projects significantly affecting the public safety does not alter our analysis. Exceptions to the Sherman Act for potentially dangerous goods and services would be tantamount to a repeal of the statute. In our complex economy the number of items that may cause serious harm is almost endless — automobiles, drugs, foods, aircraft components, heavy equipment, and countless others, cause serious harm to individuals or to the public at large if defectively made. The judiciary cannot indirectly protect the public against this harm by conferring monopoly privileges on the manufacturers.

By the same token, the cautionary footnote in *Goldfarb*, 421 U.S., at 788–789, n. 17, cannot be read as fashioning a broad exemption under the Rule of Reason for learned professions. We adhere to the view expressed in *Goldfarb* that, by their nature, professional services may differ significantly from other business services, and, accordingly, the nature of the competition in such services may vary. Ethical norms may serve to regulate and promote this competition, and thus fall within the

Rule of Reason.[6] But the Society's argument in this case is a far cry from such a position. We are faced with a contention that a total ban on competitive bidding is necessary because otherwise engineers will be tempted to submit deceptively low bids. Certainly, the problem of professional deception is a proper subject of an ethical canon. But, once again, the equation of competition with deception, like the similar equation with safety hazards, is simply too broad; we may assume that competition is not entirely conducive to ethical behavior, but that is not a reason, cognizable under the Sherman Act, for doing away with competition.

. . . .

In sum, the Rule of Reason does not support a defense based on the assumption that competition itself is unreasonable. Such a view of the Rule would create the "sea of doubt" on which Judge Taft refused to embark in *Addyston*, 85 F., at 284, and which this Court has firmly avoided ever since.

III

The judgment entered by the District Court, as modified by the Court of Appeals, prohibits the Society from adopting any official opinion, policy statement, or guideline stating or implying that competitive bidding is unethical. Petitioner argues that this judgment abridges its First Amendment rights. We find no merit in this contention.

Affirmed.

NOTES AND QUESTIONS

1. In determining whether to apply the per se rule or rule of reason analysis to a professional organization, the Court referred to *Goldfarb v. Virginia State Bar*, 421 U.S. 773 (1975), which considered whether a minimum fee schedule for lawyers — enforced by the state bar association — violated Section 1 of the Sherman Act. In holding that sellers of professional services come within the Sherman Act, Chief Justice Burger found that the minimum fee schedule constituted "price fixing."

> A purely advisory fee schedule issued to provide guidelines, or an exchange of price information without a showing of an actual restraint on trade, would present us with a different question. . . . The record here, however, reveals a situation quite different from what would occur under a purely advisory fee schedule. Here a fixed, rigid price floor arose from respondents' activities: every lawyer who responded to petitioners' inquiries adhered to the fee schedule, and no lawyer asked for additional information

---

[6] [FN 22] Courts have, for instance, upheld marketing restraints related to the safety of a product, provided that they have no anticompetitive effect and that they are reasonably ancillary to the seller's main purpose of protecting the public from harm or itself from product liability. *See, e.g., Tripoli Co. v. Wella Corp.*, 425 F.2d 932 (3d Cir. 1970) (en banc); *cf. Continental T.V.*, 433 U.S., at 55 n. 23. [In *Tripoli* the Third Circuit held that the restraint on wholesale distributors' reselling products to nonprofessionals was not a per se violation because some of the products could cause dangerous adverse effects, and the motivation for the restriction was to protect the public from harm or to protect defendant manufacturer from potential product liability. 425 F.2d, at 932, 936–37.]

in order to set an individualized fee. The price information disseminated did not concern past standards, . . . but rather minimum fees to be charged in future transactions, and those minimum rates were increased over time. The fee schedule was enforced through the prospective professional discipline from the State Bar, and the desire of attorneys to comply with announced professional norms . . . ; the motivation to conform was reinforced by the assurance that other lawyers would not compete by underbidding. This is not merely a case of an agreement that may be inferred from an exchange of price information, *United States v. Container Corp.*, 393 U.S. 333, 337 (1969), for here a naked agreement was clearly shown, and the effect on prices is plain.

. . . .

It is no disparagement of the practice of law as a profession to acknowledge that it has this business aspect, . . . In the modern world it cannot be denied that the activities of lawyers plays an important part in commercial intercourse, and that anticompetitive activities by lawyers may exert a restraint on commerce.

At points, the Court's opinion suggested greater toleration of a restraint imposed by a professional organization. It even suggested that the Court would adopt, at least for professions, a broader decisional analysis which would balance and perhaps accommodate noneconomic interests and policies. E. THOMAS SULLIVAN & JEFFREY L. HARRISON, UNDERSTANDING ANTITRUST AND ITS ECONOMIC IMPLICATIONS, ch. 4 (5th ed. 2008); *see* Mark D. Bauer, *The Licensed Professional Exemption in Consumer Protection: At Odds with Antitrust History and Precedent*, 73 TENN. L. REV. 131 (2006).

Nevertheless, Chief Justice Burger also described the minimum fee schedule as a "naked agreement," language generally used to connote per se illegality. In any event, the "professional organization" exemption to the per se approach soon came under increased attack, and was eventually at least partially repudiated. *See, e.g., Virginia State Bd. of Pharmacy v. Virginia Citizens Consumer Council*, 425 U.S. 748 (1976); *Bates v. State Bar of Ariz.*, 433 U.S. 350 (1977). In both cases, the Court struck down state enforced disciplinary rules restricting advertising by professions on the ground that the restrictions violated commercial speech rights protected under the First Amendment. Because of the significant state involvement in the adoption and enforcement of the regulation, the Court held that the restrictions were immune from antitrust scrutiny, under the state action doctrine (*see* Chapter 9, *infra*).

2. The Court's analysis in *Professional Engineers* raised the question of whether the defenses would be limited to economic justifications. In light of the broad per se rule announced in *Socony-Vacuum*, the resolution of these issues seemed crucial because after *Socony-Vacuum*, the continued vitality of *Chicago Board of Trade* and *Appalachian Coals* was questionable. But after *Professional Engineers*, the rule of reason analysis was ascendant and *Socony-Vacuum* seemed less important. A partial answer was forthcoming the next year.

BROADCAST MUSIC, INC. v. COLUMBIA BROADCASTING SYSTEM
441 U.S. 1 (1979)

JUSTICE WHITE delivered the opinion of the Court.

This case involves an action under the antitrust and copyright laws brought by respondent Columbia Broadcasting System, Inc. (CBS), against petitioners, American Society of Composers, Authors and Publishers (ASCAP) and Broadcast Music, Inc. (BMI), and their members and affiliates. The basic question presented is whether the issuance by ASCAP and BMI to CBS of blanket licenses to copyrighted musical compositions at fees negotiated by them is price fixing *per se* unlawful under the antitrust laws.

I

CBS operates one of three national commercial television networks, supplying programs to approximately 200 affiliated stations and telecasting approximately 7,500 network programs per year. Many, but not all, of these programs make use of copyrighted music recorded on the soundtrack. CBS also owns television and radio stations in various cities. . . .

Since 1897, the copyright laws have vested in the owner of a copyrighted musical composition the exclusive right to perform the work publicly for profit, but the legal right is not self-enforcing. In 1914, Victor Herbert and a handful of other composers organized ASCAP because those who performed copyrighted music for profit were so numerous and widespread, and most performances so fleeting, that as a practical matter it was impossible for the many individual copyright owners to negotiate with and license the users and to detect unauthorized uses. "ASCAP was organized as a 'clearing-house' for copyright owners and users to solve these problems" associated with the licensing of music. As ASCAP operates today, its 22,000 members grant it nonexclusive rights to license nondramatic performances of their works, and ASCAP issues licenses and distributes royalties to copyright owners in accordance with a schedule reflecting the nature and amount of the use of their music and other factors.

BMI, a nonprofit corporation owned by members of the broadcasting industry, was organized in 1939, is affiliated with or represents some 10,000 publishing companies and 20,000 authors and composers, and operates in much the same manner as ASCAP. Almost every domestic copyrighted composition is in the repertory either of ASCAP, with a total of three million compositions, or of BMI, with one million.

Both organizations operate primarily through blanket licenses, which give the licensees the right to perform any and all of the compositions owned by the members or affiliates as often as the licensees desire for a stated term. Fees for blanket licenses are ordinarily a percentage of total revenues or a flat dollar amount, and do not directly depend on the amount or type of music used. Radio and television broadcasters are the largest users of music, and almost all of them hold blanket licenses from both ASCAP and BMI. Until this litigation, CBS held blanket licenses from both organizations for its television network on a continuous basis since the late 1940's and had never attempted to secure any other form of license from either ASCAP or any of its members.

The complaint filed by CBS charged various violations of the Sherman Act and the copyright laws. CBS argued that ASCAP and BMI are unlawful monopolies and that the blanket license is illegal price fixing, an unlawful tying arrangement, a concerted refusal to deal, and a misuse of copyrights. The District Court, though denying summary judgment to certain defendants, ruled that the practice did not fall within the *per se* rule. After an 8-week trial, limited to the issue of liability, the court dismissed the complaint, rejecting again the claim that the blanket license was price fixing and a *per se* violation of § 1 of the Sherman Act, and holding that since direct negotiation with individual copyright owners is available and feasible there is no undue restraint of trade, illegal tying, misuse of copyrights, or monopolization.

Though agreeing with the District Court's factfinding and not disturbing its legal conclusions on the other antitrust theories of liability, the Court of Appeals held that the blanket license issued to television networks was a form of price fixing illegal *per se* under the Sherman Act. This conclusion, without more, settled the issue of liability under the Sherman Act, established copyright misuse, and required reversal of the District Court's judgment, as well as a remand to consider the appropriate remedy.[7]

. . . Because we disagree with the Court of Appeals' conclusions with respect to the *per se* illegality of the blanket license, we reverse its judgment and remand the cause for appropriate proceedings.

II

In construing and applying the Sherman Act's ban against contracts, conspiracies, and combinations in restraint of trade, the Court has held that certain agreements or practices are so "plainly anticompetitive," . . . and so often "lack . . . any redeeming virtue," . . . that they are conclusively presumed illegal

---

[7] [FN 10] The Court of Appeals went on to suggest some guidelines as to remedy, indicating that despite its conclusion on liability the blanket license was not totally forbidden. The Court of Appeals said:

> Normally, after a finding of price-fixing, the remedy is an injunction against the price-fixing — in this case, the blanket license. We think, however, that if on remand a remedy can be fashioned which will ensure that the blanket license will not affect the price or negotiations for direct licenses, the blanket license need not be prohibited in all circumstances. The blanket license is not simply a "naked restraint" ineluctably doomed to extinction. There is not enough evidence in the present record to compel a finding that the blanket license does not serve a market need for those who wish full protection against infringement suits or who, for some other business reason, deem the blanket license desirable. The blanket license includes a practical covenant not to sue for infringement of any ASCAP copyright as well as an indemnification against suits by others.

> Our objection to the blanket license is that it reduces price competition among the members and provides a disinclination to compete. We think that these objections may be removed if ASCAP itself is required to provide some form of per use licensing which will ensure competition among the individual members with respect to those networks which wish to engage in per use licensing. *Id.*, at 140 (footnotes omitted).

without further examination under the rule of reason generally applied in Sherman Act cases. This *per se* rule is a valid and useful tool of antitrust policy and enforcement.[8] And agreements among competitors to fix prices on their individual goods or services are among those concerted activities that the Court has held to be within the per se category. But easy labels do not always supply ready answers.

A

To the Court of Appeals and CBS, the blanket license involves "price fixing" in the literal sense: the composers and publishing houses have joined together into an organization that sets its price for the blanket license it sells. But this is not a question simply of determining whether two or more potential competitors have literally "fixed" a "price." As generally used in the antitrust field, "price fixing" is a shorthand way of describing certain categories of business behavior to which the *per se* rule has been held applicable. The Court of Appeals' literal approach does not alone establish that this particular practice is one of those types or that it is "plainly anticompetitive" and very likely without "redeeming virtue." Literalness is overly simplistic and often overbroad. When two partners set the price of their goods or services they are literally "price fixing," but they are not *per se* in violation of the Sherman Act. See *United States v. Addyston Pipe & Steel Co.*, 85 F. 271, 280 (6th Cir. 1898), aff'd, 175 U.S. 211 (1899). Thus, it is necessary to characterize the challenged conduct as falling within or without that category of behavior to which we apply the label *"per se* price fixing." That will often, but not always, be a simple matter.

Consequently, as we recognized in *United States v. Topco Associates, Inc.*, 405 U.S. 596, 607–608 (1972), "[i]t is only after considerable experience with certain business relationships that courts classify them as *per se* violations. . . . " We have never examined a practice like this one before; indeed, the Court of Appeals recognized that "[i]n dealing with performing rights in the music industry we confront conditions both in copyright law and in antitrust law which are *sui generis.*" And though there has been rather intensive antitrust scrutiny of ASCAP and its blanket licenses, that experience hardly counsels that we should outlaw the blanket license as a *per se* restraint of trade.

B

. . . .

The 1950 decree [which resulted from a consent decree entered by ASCAP and the Department of Justice "that imposed tight restrictions on ASCAP's operations," including giving ASCAP "only nonexclusive rights to license" works], as amended from time to time, continues in effect, and the blanket license continues to be the

---

[8] [FN 11] "This principle of *per se* unreasonableness not only makes the type of restraints which are proscribed by the Sherman Act more certain to the benefit of everyone concerned, but it also avoids the necessity for an incredibly complicated and prolonged economic investigation into the entire history of the industry involved, as well as related industries, in an effort to determine at large whether a particular restraint has been unreasonable — an inquiry so often wholly fruitless when undertaken." *Northern Pac. Ry. Co. v. United States*, 356 U.S. 1, 5 (1958).

primary instrument through which ASCAP conducts its business under the decree. The courts have twice construed the decree not to require ASCAP to issue licenses for selected portions of its repertory. It also remains true that the decree guarantees the legal availability of direct licensing of performance rights by ASCAP members; and the District Court found, and in this respect the Court of Appeals agreed, that there are no practical impediments preventing direct dealing by the television networks if they so desire. Historically, they have not done so. Since 1946, CBS and other television networks have taken blanket licenses from ASCAP and BMI. It was not until this suit arose that the CBS network demanded any other kind of license.

Of course, a consent judgment, even one entered at the behest of the Antitrust Division, does not immunize the defendant from liability for actions, including those contemplated by the decree, that violate the rights of nonparties. But it cannot be ignored that the Federal Executive and Judiciary have carefully scrutinized ASCAP and the challenged conduct, have imposed restrictions on various of ASCAP's practices, and, by the terms of the decree, stand ready to provide further consideration, supervision, and perhaps invalidation of asserted anticompetitive practices. In these circumstances, we have a unique indicator that the challenged practice may have redeeming competitive virtues and that the search for those values is not almost sure to be in vain.

III

Finally, we note that Congress itself, in the new Copyright Act, has chosen to employ the blanket license and similar practices. Congress created a compulsory blanket license for secondary transmissions by cable television systems and provided that "[n]otwithstanding any provisions of the antitrust laws, . . . any claimants may agree among themselves as to the proportionate division of compulsory licensing fees among them, may lump their claims together and file them jointly or as a single claim, or may designate a common agent to receive payment on their behalf." 17 U.S.C. App. § 111(d)(5)(A). And the newly created compulsory license for the use of copyrighted compositions in jukeboxes is also a blanket license, which is payable to the performing-rights societies such as ASCAP unless an individual copyright holder can prove his entitlement to a share. § 116 (c) (4). Moreover, in requiring noncommercial broadcasters to pay for their use of copyrighted music, Congress again provided that "[n]otwithstanding any provision of the antitrust laws" copyright owners "may designate common agents to negotiate, agree to, pay, or receive payments." § 118 (b). Though these provisions are not directly controlling, they do reflect an opinion that the blanket license, and ASCAP, are economically beneficial in at least some circumstances.

. . . .

As a preliminary matter, we are mindful that the Court of Appeals' holding would appear to be quite difficult to contain. If, as the court held, there is a *per se* antitrust violation whenever ASCAP issues a blanket license to a television network for a single fee, why would it not also be automatically illegal for ASCAP to negotiate and issue blanket licenses to individual radio or television stations or to other users who perform copyrighted music for profit? Likewise, if the present network licenses issued through ASCAP on behalf of its members are *per se* violations, why would it not be equally illegal for the members to authorize ASCAP to issue licenses establishing various categories of uses that a network might have for copyrighted music and setting a standard fee for each described use?

Although the Court of Appeals apparently thought the blanket license could be saved in some or even many applications, it seems to us that the *per se* rule does not accommodate itself to such flexibility and that the observations of the Court of Appeals with respect to remedy tend to impeach the *per se* basis for the holding of liability.[9]

CBS would prefer that ASCAP be authorized, indeed directed, to make all its compositions available at standard per-use rates within negotiated categories of use. . . . But if this in itself or in conjunction with blanket licensing constitutes illegal price fixing by copyright owners, CBS urges that an injunction issue forbidding ASCAP to issue any blanket license or to negotiate any fee except on behalf of an individual member for the use of his own copyrighted work or works. Thus, we are called upon to determine that blanket licensing is unlawful across the board. We are quite sure, however, that the *per se* rule does not require any such holding.

B

. . . Although the copyright laws confer no rights on copyright owners to fix prices among themselves or otherwise to violate the antitrust laws, we would not expect that any market arrangements reasonably necessary to effectuate the rights that are granted would be deemed a *per se* violation of the Sherman Act. Otherwise, the commerce anticipated by the Copyright Act and protected against restraint by the Sherman Act would not exist at all or would exist only as a pale reminder of what Congress envisioned.

C

More generally, in characterizing this conduct under the *per se* rule, our inquiry must focus on whether the effect and, here because it tends to show effect, the purpose of the practice are to threaten the proper operation of our predominantly free-market economy — that is, whether the practice facially appears to be one that

---

[9] [FN 27] The Court of Appeals would apparently not outlaw the blanket license across the board but would permit it in various circumstances where it is deemed necessary or sufficiently desirable. It did not even enjoin blanket licensing with the television networks, the relief it realized would normally follow a finding of *per se* illegality of the license in that context. Instead, as requested by CBS, it remanded to the District Court to require ASCAP to offer in addition to blanket licensing some competitive form or per-use licensing. But per-use licensing by ASCAP, as recognized in the consent decrees, might be even more susceptible to the *per se* rule than blanket licensing.

The rationale for this unusual relief in a *per se* case was that "[t]he blanket license is not simply a 'naked restraint' ineluctably doomed to extinction." 562 F.2d, at 130. To the contrary, the Court of Appeals found that the blanket license might well "serve a market need" for some. *Ibid.* This, it seems to us, is not the *per se* approach, which does not yield so readily to circumstances, but in effect is a rather bobtailed application of the rule of reason, bobtailed in the sense that it is unaccompanied by the necessary analysis demonstrating why the particular licensing system is an undue competitive restraint.

would always or almost always tend to restrict competition and decrease output, and in what portion of the market, or instead one designed to "increase economic efficiency and render markets more, rather than less, competitive." . . .

The blanket license, as we see it, is not a "naked restrain[t] of trade with no purpose except stifling of competition," but rather accompanies the integration of sales, monitoring, and enforcement against unauthorized copyright use. As we have already indicated, ASCAP and the blanket license developed together out of the practical situation in the marketplace: thousands of users, thousands of copyright owners, and millions of compositions. Most users want unplanned, rapid, and indemnified access to any and all of the repertory of compositions, and the owners want a reliable method of collecting for the use of their copyrights. Individual sales transactions in this industry are quite expensive, as would be individual monitoring and enforcement, especially in light of the resources of single composers. Indeed, as both the Court of Appeals and CBS recognize, the costs are prohibitive for licenses with individual radio stations, nightclubs, and restaurants, and it was in that milieu that the blanket license arose.

A middleman with a blanket license was an obvious necessity if the thousands of individual negotiations, a virtual impossibility, were to be avoided. Also, individual fees for the use of individual compositions would presuppose an intricate schedule of fees and uses, as well as a difficult and expensive reporting problem for the user and policing task for the copyright owner. Historically, the market for public-performance rights organized itself largely around the single-fee blanket license, which gave unlimited access to the repertory and reliable protection against infringement. When ASCAP's major and user-created competitor, BMI, came on the scene, it also turned to the blanket license.

With the advent of radio and television networks, market conditions changed, and the necessity for and advantages of a blanket license for those users may be far less obvious than is the case when the potential users are individual television or radio stations, or the thousands of other individuals and organizations performing copyrighted compositions in public. But even for television network licenses, ASCAP reduces costs absolutely by creating a blanket license that is sold only a few, instead of thousands, of times, and that obviates the need for closely monitoring the networks to see that they do not use more than they pay for. ASCAP also provides the necessary resources for blanket sales and enforcement, resources unavailable to the vast majority of composers and publishing houses. Moreover, a bulk license of some type is a necessary consequence of the integration necessary to achieve these efficiencies, and a necessary consequence of an aggregate license is that its price must be established.

D

This substantial lowering of costs, which is of course potentially beneficial to both sellers and buyers, differentiates the blanket license from individual use licenses. The blanket license is composed of the individual compositions plus the aggregating service. Here, the whole is truly greater than the sum of its parts; it is, to some extent, a different product. The blanket license has certain unique characteristics: It allows the licensee immediate use of covered compositions, without the delay of prior individual negotiations, and great flexibility in the choice of musical material. Many consumers clearly prefer the characteristics and cost advantages of this marketable package, and even small performing-rights societies that have occasionally arisen to compete with ASCAP and BMI have offered blanket licenses. Thus, to the extent the blanket license is a different product, ASCAP is not really a joint sales agency offering the individual goods of many sellers, but is a separate seller offering its blanket license, of which the individual compositions are raw material. ASCAP, in short, made a market in which individual composers are inherently unable to compete fully effectively.

E

Finally, we have some doubt — enough to counsel against application of the *per se* rule — about the extent to which this practice threatens the "central nervous system of the economy," *United States v. Socony-Vacuum Oil Co.*, 310 U.S. 150, 226 n. 59 (1940), that is, competitive pricing as the free market's means of allocating resources. Not all arrangements among actual or potential competitors that have an impact on price are *per se* violations of the Sherman Act or even unreasonable restraints. Mergers among competitors eliminate competition, including price competition, but they are not *per se* illegal, and many of them withstand attack under any existing antitrust standard. Joint ventures and other cooperative arrangements are also not usually unlawful, at least not as price-fixing schemes, where the agreement on price is necessary to market the product at all.

Here, the blanket-license fee is not set by competition among individual copyright owners, and it is a fee for the use of any of the compositions covered by the license. But the blanket license cannot be wholly equated with a simple horizontal arrangement among competitors. ASCAP does set the price for its blanket license, but that license is quite different from anything any individual owner could issue. The individual composers and authors have neither agreed not to sell individually in any other market nor use the blanket license to mask price fixing in such other markets. Moreover, the substantial restraints placed on ASCAP and its members by the consent decree must not be ignored. The District Court found that there was no legal, practical, or conspiratorial impediment to CBS's obtaining individual licenses; CBS, in short, had a real choice.

With this background in mind, which plainly enough indicates that over the years, and in the face of available alternatives, the blanket license has provided an acceptable mechanism for at least a large part of the market for the performing rights to copyrighted musical compositions, we cannot agree that it should automatically be declared illegal in all of its many manifestations. Rather, when attacked, it should be subjected to a more discriminating examination under the rule of reason. It may not ultimately survive that attack, but that is not the issue before us today.

IV

. . . We reverse that judgment [of the Court of Appeals] and the copyright misuse judgment dependent upon it, and remand for further proceedings to consider any unresolved issues that CBS may have properly brought to the Court of Appeals.

[The dissenting opinion of Justice Stevens is omitted. On remand, the Second Circuit held that under the efficiency standard employed by the Court, the blanket licensing did not create an unreasonable restraint because the individual transaction costs were too high for individual licensing to work competitively. *CBS, Inc. v. ASCAP*, 620 F.2d 930 (1st Cir. 1980). The Second Circuit also found that because the blanket license did not prohibit the freedom of individual composers from direct licensing, price competition was not eliminated by the arrangement.]

NOTES AND QUESTIONS

1. Did *Professional Engineers* and *Broadcast Music* indicate a shift away from a broad reading of the "tamper with price structure" standard of *Socony-Vacuum*? Can these cases be reconciled with *Socony-Vacuum*? Did the Court in each apply a rule of reason analysis? How does Justice Stevens define the boundaries of the decisional analysis after *Professional Engineers*? Under this standard, why did the engineers' defense fail? Are there any conditions under which the Court might accept the "quality/safety" defense? Might the ancillary restraint doctrine have application under this defense? Do you accept Justice Stevens' Sherman Act assumption that "competition will produce not only lower prices, but also better goods and services?" Might noneconomic values be important as well?

2. Does *Professional Engineers* articulate how a trial judge is to measure the net competitive effect of a restraint? In measuring the competitive benefits versus the costs of the restraint, might the outcome differ depending whether the restraint is engaged in by a professional organization rather than a commercial venture?

3. After *Professional Engineers* and *Broadcast Music*, how should you define the scope of the per se rule's application? Is a competitive benefit/harm analysis permitted before the per se label is attached? How direct must the effect on price be before a per se classification will result?

4. What justification did the Court give in *Broadcast Music* for approving one kind of analysis for the market facilitating scheme in *Socony-Vacuum* and another in *Broadcast Music*? Consider whether the distinction can be based on economic efficiency and the reduction of transaction costs and whether output is limited.

5. CBS asked the lower court to force ASCAP to "make all its compositions available at standard per-use rates within negotiated categories of use." Would not this be just as illegal under the Sherman Act as the blanket licensing scheme? Artists would still be "agreeing" on a uniform fee within a particular category of music, and ASCAP would obtain the fee for them.

The lower court actually found rather few alternatives to blanket licensing that would avoid all price agreements. One would be to require each radio station or network to purchase individually each right to play a composition from the owner of the performance right. A radio station that played 100 different songs would engage in 100 separate transactions. In this case, transaction costs alone (that is, the costs of negotiating the individual contracts) would have been far greater than the total price that many stations were paying for the right to play a particular composition. An alternative would have been for the purchaser to go to each composer and obtain performance rights for everything that composer owned. The district court expressly found that many artists would have been willing to negotiate with CBS for such rights. CBS represented thousands of affiliated radio stations, and could negotiate for all of them together. How about the small, unaffiliated radio station that would also have to negotiate with each artist individually?

Professor Richard Friedman posits this solution: What if the blanket license agreement were eliminated in favor of allowing ASCAP and BMI to license each artist's product at a rate posted by the artists, thus obviating the need for users to negotiate with each artist. Would his solution avoid the anticompetitive effect of the blanket license? Would it increase the costs to the user? Should the absence of a less restrictive alternative incline the court to condemn the current arrangement?

6.   The marginal cost to a performance right holder of having his or her composition played is virtually zero. Furthermore, capacity in the industry is infinite. Once a song is composed, it can be played 1,000,000 times as easily as 10 times. In a competitive market, wouldn't you therefore expect the performance rights to compositions to be sold for almost nothing? That would certainly be true if the product were fungible. For example, if one hundred different people owned performance rights to "Born in the U.S.A.," and competed with each other in the sale of those rights, we would expect the price of the right to perform "Born in the U.S.A.," to be extremely small. In fact, however, listeners differentiate substantially between songs. If one person owns the performance rights to "Born in the U.S.A.," another to "Graceland," a third to "Sergeant Pepper's Lonely Hearts Club Band," etc., we would expect each to sell performance rights at substantially above marginal cost. The different owners of the performance rights to different compositions are monopolists, some of whom have substantial market power, which is the power to set a profit-maximizing price above marginal cost. But if they are all monopolists, then the rights that each of them offers is a distinct "product."

7.   One reading of the opinions in *Professional Engineers* and *Broadcast Music* is that the Burger Court was more inclined to avoid initially a rigid per se analysis so that it could explore the business justification for the conduct and determine whether it promotes market integration and economic efficiency without sacrificing output. Implicitly, *Socony* seemed to be on the decline. The next term of the Court, however, signaled the continued validity of the summary per se analysis, though a subsequent opinion indicates that the Court continues to vacillate on where the line should be drawn in defining price-fixing agreements.

. . . .

CATALANO, INC. v. TARGET SALES, INC.
446 U.S. 643 (1980)

Per Curiam.

Petitioners, a conditionally certified class of brewer retailers in the Fresno, Cal. area, brought suit against respondent wholesalers alleging that they had conspired to eliminate short term trade credit formerly granted on beer purchases in violation of § 1 of the Sherman Act. The District Court entered an interlocutory order, which among other things, denied petitioners' "motion to declare this a case of *per se* illegality," and then certified to the United States Court of Appeals for the Ninth Circuit, pursuant to 28 U.S.C. § 1292(b), the question whether the alleged agreement among competitors fixing credit terms, if proven, was unlawful on its face. The Court of Appeals granted permission to appeal, and, with one judge dissenting, agreed with the District Court that a horizontal agreement among competitors to fix credit terms does not necessarily contravene the antitrust laws. . . .

For purposes of decision we assume the following facts alleged in the amended complaint to be true. Petitioners allege that, beginning in early 1967, respondent wholesalers secretly agreed, in order to eliminate competition among themselves, that as of December 1967 they would sell to retailers only if payment were made in advance or upon delivery. Prior to the agreement, the wholesalers had extended credit without interest up to the 30 and 42 day limits permitted by state law. According to the Petition, prior to the agreement wholesalers had competed with each other with respect to trade credit, and the credit terms for individual retailers had varied substantially. After entering into the agreement, respondents uniformly refused to extend any credit at all.

The Court of Appeals decided that the credit fixing agreement should not be characterized as a form of price fixing. The court suggested that such an agreement might actually enhance competition in two ways: (1) "by removing a barrier perceived by some sellers to entry," and (2) "by the increased visibility of prices made possible by the agreement to eliminate credit."

In dissent, Judge Blumenfeld expressed the opinion that an agreement to eliminate credit was a form of price fixing. He reasoned that the extension of interest-free credit is an indirect price reduction and that the elimination of such credit is therefore a method of raising prices:

> "The purchase of goods creates an obligation to pay for them. Credit is one component of the overall price paid for a product. The cost to a retailer of purchasing goods consists of (1) the amount he has to pay to obtain the goods, and (2) the date on which he has to make that payment. If there is a differential between a purchase for cash and one on time, that difference is not interest but part of the price. Allowing a retailer interest-free short-term credit on beer purchases effectively reduces the price of beer, when compared to a requirement that the retailer pay the same amount immediately in cash; and conversely, the elimination of free credit is the equivalent of price increase."

It followed, in his view, that the agreement was just as plainly anticompetitive as a direct agreement to raise prices. Consequently, no further inquiry under the rule of reason, *see National Society of Professional Engineers v. United States*, 435 U.S. 679 (1978), was required in order to establish the agreement's unlawfulness.

Our cases . . . foreclose both of the possible justifications on which the majority relied.[10] In *Broadcast Music*, we said:

> In construing and applying the Sherman Act's ban against contracts, conspiracies, and combinations in restraint of trade, the Court has held that certain agreements or practices are so "plainly anticompetitive," . . . and so often "lack . . . any redeeming virtue," that they are conclusively presumed illegal without further examination under the rule of reason generally applied in Sherman Act cases.

A horizontal agreement to fix prices is the archetypal example of such a practice. It has long been settled that an agreement to fix prices is unlawful *per se*. It is no excuse that the prices fixed are themselves reasonable. . . .

Thus, we have held agreements to be unlawful *per se* that had substantially less direct impact on price than the agreement alleged in this case. For example, in *Sugar Institute v. United States*, 297 U.S. 533, 601–602 (1933), the Court held unlawful an agreement to adhere to previously announced prices and terms of sale, even though advance price announcements are perfectly lawful and even though the particular prices and terms were not themselves fixed by private agreement. Similarly, an agreement among competing firms of professional engineers to refuse to discuss prices with potential customers until after negotiations have resulted in the initial selection of an engineer was held unlawful without requiring further inquiry. *National Society of Professional Engineers v. United States.* Indeed, a horizontal agreement among competitors to use a specific method of quoting prices [multiple basing point pricing system] may be unlawful. *Cf. Federal Trade Commission v. Cement Institute.*

It is virtually self evident that extending interest-free credit for a period of time is equivalent to giving a discount equal to the value of the use of the purchase price for that period of time. Thus, credit terms must be characterized as an inseparable part of the price. An agreement to terminate the practice of giving credit is thus tantamount to an agreement to eliminate discounts, and thus falls squarely within the traditional *per se* rule against price fixing. While it may be that the elimination of a practice of giving variable discounts will ultimately lead in a competitive market to corresponding decreases in the invoice price, that is surely not necessarily to be anticipated. It is more realistic to view an agreement to eliminate credit sales as extinguishing one form of competition among the sellers. In any event, when a particular concerted activity entails an obvious risk of anticompetitive impact with no apparent potentially redeeming value, the fact that a practice may turn out to be harmless in a particular set of circumstances will not prevent its being declared unlawful *per se*.

The majority of the panel of the Court of Appeals suggested, however, that a horizontal agreement to eliminate credit sales may remove a barrier to other sellers who may wish to enter the market. But in any case in which competitors are able to increase the price level or to curtail production by agreement, it could be argued that the agreement has the effect of making the market more attractive to potential

---

[10] [FN 8] Respondents nowhere suggest a procompetitive justification for a horizontal agreement to fix credit. Their argument is confined to disputing that settled case law establishes that such an agreement is unlawful on its face.

new entrants. If that potential justifies horizontal agreements among competitors imposing one kind of voluntary restraint or another on their competitive freedom, it would seem to follow that the more successful an agreement is in raising the price level, the safer it is from antitrust attack. Nothing could be more inconsistent with our cases.

Nor can the informing function of the agreement, the increased price visibility, justify its restraint on the individual wholesaler's freedom to select his own prices and terms of sale. For, again, it is obvious that any industry wide agreement on prices will result in a more accurate understanding of the terms offered by all parties to the agreement. As the *Sugar Institute* case demonstrates, however, there is a plain distinction between the lawful right to publish prices and terms of sale, on the one hand, and an agreement among competitors limiting action with respect to the published prices, on the other.

Thus, under the reasoning of our cases, an agreement among competing wholesaler to refuse to sell unless the retailer makes payment in cash either in advance or upon delivery is "plainly anticompetitive." Since it is merely one form of price fixing, and since price-fixing agreements have been adjudged to lack any "redeeming virtue," it is conclusively presumed illegal without further examination under the rule of reason.

Accordingly, the judgment of the Court of Appeals is reversed, and the case is remanded for further proceedings consistent with this opinion.

NOTES AND QUESTIONS

1.   Why is refusing to extend credit equivalent to raising price?

2.   Does *Catalano* forbid competitors from sharing information about buyers' creditworthiness? In *Burtch v. Milberg Factors, Inc.*, 662 F.3d 212 (3d Cir. 2011), the Third Circuit considered a claim that "the mere exchange of future credit information is a per se price-fixing claim." The court rejected the claim, holding:

> Exchanging information regarding the creditworthiness of customers does not violate the Sherman Act. Cement Mftrs. Protective Ass'n v. United States, 268 U.S. 588, 599–600 (1925). The Supreme Court has stated that the mere exchange of credit information without "any understanding on the basis of which credit has to be extended to customers or that any co-operation resulted from the distribution of this information, or that there were any consequences from it other than such as would naturally ensue from the exercise of the individual judgment of manufacturers in determining, on the basis of available information, whether to extend credit" does not violate the Sherman Act. Catalano v. Target, 446 U.S. 643, 648 n.12 (1980) (quoting *Cement Mfrs.*, 268 U.S. at 588).
>
> . . . [C]redit information and price are distinct. [Plaintiff] relies on the statement in *Catalano* that "credit terms must be characterized as an inseparable part of price." 446 U.S. at 648. However, [Plaintiff] mischaracterizes *Catalano*. *Catalano* did not suggest that price information and credit information are equivalent for purposes of antitrust violations. It

held that an agreement to temporarily extend interest-free credit was "equivalent to giving a discount equal to the value of the use of the purchase price for that period of time." *Id.* at 648.

Thus, we do not conclude based on *Catalano* that sharing information regarding the creditworthiness of a [person] without an agreement should be treated the same as discussions concerning price. Exchanges regarding price typically serve no other purpose than to suppress competition and violate the Sherman Act; conversely, information concerning the creditworthiness of customers can protect competitors from insolvent customers.

Id. at 222–23.

ARIZONA v. MARICOPA COUNTY MEDICAL SOCIETY
457 U.S. 332 (1982)

Justice Stevens delivered the opinion of the Court.

The question presented is whether § 1 of the Sherman Act, 15 U.S.C. § 1, has been violated by an agreement among competing physicians setting, by majority vote, the maximum fees that they may claim in full payment for health services provided to policyholders of specified insurance plans. The United States Court of Appeals for the Ninth Circuit held that the question could not be answered without evaluating the actual purpose and effect of the agreement at a full trial. . . . Because the undisputed facts disclose a violation of the statute, we granted certiorari, and now reverse.

. . . .

II

The Maricopa Foundation for Medical Care is a non-profit Arizona corporation composed of licensed doctors of medicine, osteopathy, and podiatry engaged in private practice. Approximately 1,750 doctors, representing about 70% of the practitioners in Maricopa County, are members.

. . . The foundation performs three primary activities. It establishes the schedule of maximum fees that participating doctors agree to accept as payment in full for services performed for patients insured under plans approved by the foundation. It reviews the medical necessity and appropriateness of treatment provided by its members to such insured persons. It is authorized to draw checks on insurance company accounts to pay doctors for services performed for covered patients. In performing these functions, the foundation is considered an "insurance administrator" by the Director of the Arizona Department of Insurance. Its participating doctors, however, have no financial interest in the operation of the foundation. [A similar foundation, the Pima Foundation for Medical Care, had 400 member doctors.]

At the time this lawsuit was filed, each foundation made use of "relative values" and "conversion factors" in compiling its fee schedule.

The fee schedules limit the amount that the member doctors may recover for services performed for patients insured under plans approved by the foundations. To obtain this approval the insurers — including self-insured employers as well as insurance companies — agree to pay the doctors' charges up to the scheduled amounts, and in exchange the doctors agree to accept those amounts as payment in full for their services. The doctors are free to charge higher fees to uninsured patients and they also may charge any patient less than the scheduled maxima. A patient who is insured by a foundation-endorsed plan is guaranteed complete coverage for the full amount of his medical bills only if he is treated by a foundation member. He is free to go to a nonmember physician and is still covered for charges that do not exceed the maximum fee schedule, but he must pay any excess that the nonmember physician may charge.

The impact of the foundation fee schedules on medical fees and on insurance premiums is a matter of dispute. The State of Arizona contends that the periodic upward revisions of the maximum fee schedules have the effect of stabilizing and enhancing the level of actual charges by physicians, and that the increasing level of their fees in turn increases insurance premiums. The foundations, on the other hand, argue that the schedules impose a meaningful limit on physicians' charges, and that the advance agreement by the doctors to accept the maxima enables the insurance carriers to limit and to calculate more efficiently the risks they underwrite and therefore serves as an effective cost containment mechanism that has saved patients and insurers millions of dollars. . . .

III

The respondents recognize that our decisions establish that price fixing agreements are unlawful on their face. But they argue that the *per se* rule does not govern this case because the agreements at issue are horizontal and fix maximum prices, are among members of a profession, are in an industry with which the judiciary has little antitrust experience, and are alleged to have procompetitive justifications. . . .

A

. . . .

We have not wavered in our enforcement of the *per se* rule against price fixing. Indeed, in our most recent price fixing case we summarily reversed the decision of another Ninth Circuit panel that a horizontal agreement among competitors to fix credit terms does not necessarily contravene the antitrust laws. *Catalano, Inc. v. Target Sales, Inc.*

B

Our decisions foreclose the argument that the agreements at issue escape *per se* condemnation because they are horizontal and fix maximum prices. *Kiefer-Stewart* and *Albrecht* place horizontal agreements to fix maximum prices on the same legal — even if not economic — footing as agreements to fix minimum or uniform prices.

The *per se* rule "is grounded on faith in price competition as a market force [and not] on a policy of low selling prices at the price of eliminating competition." In this case the rule is violated by a price restraint that tends to provide the same economic rewards to all practitioners regardless of their skill, their experience, their training, or their willingness to employ innovative and difficult procedures in individual cases. Such a restraint also may discourage entry into the market and may deter experimentation and new developments by individual entrepreneurs. It may be a masquerade for an agreement to fix uniform prices, or it may in the future take on that character.

Nor does the fact that doctors — rather than nonprofessionals — are the parties to the price fixing agreements support the respondents' position. . . . The price fixing agreements in this case . . . are not premised on public service or ethical norms. The respondents do not argue, . . . that the quality of the professional service that their members provide is enhanced by the price restraint. The respondents' claim for relief from the *per se* rule is simply that the doctors' agreement not to charge certain insureds more than a fixed price facilitates the successful marketing of an attractive insurance plan. But the claim that the price restraint will make it easier for customers to pay does not distinguish the medical profession from any other provider of goods or services.

We are equally unpersuaded by the argument that we should not apply the *per se* rule in this case because the judiciary has little antitrust experience in the health care industry.[11] The argument quite obviously is inconsistent with *Socony-Vacuum*. In unequivocal terms, we stated that, "[w]hatever may be its peculiar problems and characteristics, the Sherman Act, so far as price-fixing agreements are concerned, establishes one uniform rule applicable to all industries alike." Finally, the argument that the *per se* rule must be rejustified for every industry that has not been subject to significant antitrust litigation ignores the rationale for *per se* rules, which in part is to avoid "the necessity for an incredibly complicated and prolonged economic investigation into the entire history of the industry involved, as well as related industries, in an effort to determine at large whether a particular restraint has been unreasonable — an inquiry so often wholly fruitless when undertaken."

The respondents' principal argument is that the *per se* rule is inapplicable because their agreements are alleged to have procompetitive justifications. The argument indicates a misunderstanding of the *per se* concept. The anticompetitive potential inherent in all price fixing agreements justifies their facial invalidation even if procompetitive justifications are offered for some. Those claims of enhanced competition are so unlikely to prove significant in any particular case that we adhere to the rule of law that is justified in its general application. Even when the respondents are given every benefit of the doubt, the limited record in this case is not inconsistent with the presumption that the respondents' agreements will not significantly enhance competition.

The respondents contend that their fee schedules are procompetitive because

---

[11] [FN 19] The argument should not be confused with the established position that a *new per se* rule is not justified until the judiciary obtains considerable rule of reason experience with the particular type of restraint challenged.

they make it possible to provide consumers of health care with a uniquely desirable form of insurance coverage that could not otherwise exist. The features of the foundation-endorsed insurance plans that they stress are a choice of doctors, complete insurance coverage, and lower premiums. The first two characteristics, however, are hardly unique to these plans. Since only about 70% of the doctors in the relevant market are members of either foundation, the guarantee of complete coverage only applies when an insured chooses a physician in that 70%. If he elects to go to a non-foundation doctor, he may be required to pay a portion of the doctor's fee. It is fair to presume, however, that at least 70% of the doctors in other markets charge no more than the "usual, customary, and reasonable" fee that typical insurers are willing to reimburse in full. Thus, in Maricopa and Pima Counties as well as in most parts of the country, if an insured asks his doctor if the insurance coverage is complete, presumably in about 70% of the cases the doctor will say yes and in about 30% of the cases he will say no.

It is true that a binding assurance of complete insurance coverage — as well as most of the respondents' potential for lower insurance premiums — can be obtained only if the insurer and the doctor agree in advance on the maximum fee that the doctor will accept as full payment for a particular service. Even if a fee schedule is therefore desirable, it is not necessary that the doctors do the price fixing. The record indicates that the Arizona Comprehensive Medical Dental Program for Foster Children is administered by the Maricopa foundation pursuant to a contract under which the maximum fee schedule is prescribed by a state agency rather than by the doctors. . . .

Having declined the respondents' invitation to cut back on the *per se* rule against price fixing, we are left with the respondents' argument that their fee schedules involve price fixing in only a literal sense. For this argument, the respondents rely upon *Broadcast Music, Inc. v. Columbia Broadcasting System, Inc.*, 441 U.S. 1 (1979).

In *Broadcast Music* we were confronted with an antitrust challenge to the marketing of the right to use copyrighted compositions derived from the entire membership of ASCAP. The so-called "blanket license" was entirely different from the product that any one composer was able to sell by himself.[12] Although there was little competition among individual composers for their separate compositions, the blanket license arrangement did not place any restraint on the right of any individual copyright owner to sell his own compositions separately to any buyer at any price. But a "necessary consequence" of the creation of the blanket license was that its price had to be established. We held that the delegation by the composers to ASCAP of the power to fix the price for the blanket license was not a species of the price fixing agreements categorically forbidden by the Sherman Act. The record disclosed price fixing only in a "literal sense."

This case is fundamentally different. Each of the foundations is composed of individual practitioners who compete with one another for patients. Neither the

---

[12] [FN 31] "Thus, to the extent the blanket license is a different product, ASCAP is not really a joint sales agency offering the individual goods of many sellers, but is a separate seller offering its blanket license, of which the individual compositions are raw material." 441 U.S. 1, 22 (1979).

foundations nor the doctors sell insurance, and they derive no profits from the sale of health insurance policies. The members of the foundations sell medical services. Their combination in the form of the foundation does not permit them to sell any different product. Their combination has merely permitted them to sell their services to certain customers at fixed prices and arguably to affect the prevailing market price of medical care.

The foundations are not analogous to partnerships or other joint arrangements in which persons who would otherwise be competitors pool their capital and share the risks of loss as well as the opportunities for profit. In such joint ventures the partnership is regarded as a single firm competing with other sellers in the market. The agreement under attack is an agreement among hundreds of competing doctors concerning the price at which each will offer his own services to a substantial number of consumers. It is true that some are surgeons, some anesthesiologists, and some psychiatrists, but the doctors do not sell a package of three kinds of services. If a clinic offered complete medical coverage for a flat fee, the cooperating doctors would have the type of partnership arrangement in which a price fixing agreement among the doctors would be perfectly proper. But the fee agreements disclosed by the record in this case are among independent competing entrepreneurs. They fit squarely into the horizontal price fixing mold.

The judgment of the Court of Appeals is *reversed*.

Justice Powell dissenting, with whom the Chief Justice and Justice Rehnquist join.

I do not think today's decision on an incomplete record is consistent with proper judicial resolution of an issue of this complexity, novelty, and importance to the public. I therefore dissent.

. . . .

II

This case comes to us on a plaintiff's motion for summary judgment after only limited discovery. Therefore, as noted above, the inferences to be drawn from the record must be viewed in the light most favorable to the respondents. This requires, as the Court acknowledges, that we consider the foundation arrangement as one that "impose[s] a meaningful limit on physicians' charges," that "enables the insurance carriers to limit and to calculate more efficiently the risks they underwrite," and that "therefore serves as an effective cost containment mechanism that has saved patients and insurers millions of dollars." The question is whether we should condemn this arrangement forthwith under the Sherman Act, a law designed to *benefit* consumers.

Several other aspects of the record are of key significance but are not stressed by the Court. First, the foundation arrangement forecloses *no* competition. Unlike the classic cartel agreement, the foundation plan does not instruct potential competitors: "Deal with consumers on the following terms and no others." Rather, physicians who participate in the foundation plan are free both to associate with other medical insurance plans — at any fee level, high or low — and directly to serve uninsured patients — at any fee level, high or low. Similarly, insurers that participate in the foundation plan also remain at liberty to do business outside the plan with any physician — foundation member or not — at any fee level. Nor are physicians locked into a plan for more than one year's membership. Thus freedom to compete as well as freedom to withdraw, is preserved. The Court cites no case in which a remotely comparable plan or agreement is condemned on a *per se* basis.

Second, on this record we must find that insurers represent consumer interests. Normally consumers search for high quality at low prices. But once a consumer is insured — i.e. has chosen a medical insurance plan — he is largely indifferent to the amount that his physician charges if the coverage is full, as under the foundation-sponsored plan.

The insurer, however, is *not* indifferent. To keep insurance premiums at a competitive level and to remain profitable, insurers — including those who have contracts with the foundations — step into the consumer's shoes with his incentive to contain medical costs. Indeed, insurers may be the only parties who have the effective power to restrain medical costs, given the difficulty that patients experience in comparing price and quality for a professional service such as medical care.

. . . .

III

It is settled law that once an arrangement has been labeled as "price fixing" it is to be condemned *per se*. But it is equally well settled that this characterization is not to be applied as a talisman to every arrangement that involves a literal fixing of prices. Many lawful contracts, mergers, and partnerships fix prices. But our cases require a more discerning approach. The inquiry in an antitrust case is not simply one of "determining whether two or more potential competitors have literally 'fixed' a 'price.' . . . [Rather], it is necessary to characterize the challenged conduct as falling within or without that category of behavior to which we apply the label '*per se* price fixing.' That will often, but not always, be a simple matter."

Before characterizing an arrangement as a *per se* price fixing agreement meriting condemnation, a court should determine whether it is a "naked restrain[t] of trade with no purpose except stifling of competition." Such a determination is necessary because "departure from the rule-of-reason standard must be based upon demonstrable economic effect rather than . . . upon formalistic line drawing." As part of this inquiry, a court must determine whether the procompetitive economies that the arrangement purportedly makes possible are substantial and realizable in the absence of such an agreement.

In sum, the fact that a foundation sponsored health insurance plan *literally* involves the setting of ceiling prices among competing physicians does not, of itself, justify condemning the plan as *per se* illegal. Only if it is clear from the record that the agreement among physicians is "so plainly anticompetitive that no elaborate study of [its effects] is needed to establish [its] illegality" may a court properly make a *per se* judgment. *National Society of Professional Engineers v. United States, supra*, 435 U.S., at 692. And, as our cases demonstrate, the *per se* label should not be assigned without carefully considering substantial benefits and procompetitive justifications. This is especially true when the agreement under attack is novel, as in this case.

IV

The Court acknowledges that the *per se* ban against price fixing is not to be invoked every time potential competitors *literally* fix prices. One also would have expected it to acknowledge that *per se* characterization is inappropriate if the challenged agreement or plan achieves for the public procompetitive benefits that otherwise are not attainable. The Court does not do this. And neither does it provide alternative criteria by which the *per se* characterization is to be determined. It is content simply to brand this type of plan as "price fixing" and describe the agreement in *Broadcast Music* — which also literally involved the fixing of prices — as "fundamentally different."

In fact, however, the two agreements are similar in important respects. Each involved competitors and resulted in cooperative pricing. Each arrangement also was prompted by the need for better service to the consumers. And each arrangement apparently makes possible a new product by reaping otherwise unattainable efficiencies. The Court's effort to distinguish *Broadcast Music* thus is unconvincing.

. . . .

V

I believe the Court's action today loses sight of the basic purposes of the Sherman Act. As we have noted, the antitrust laws are a "consumer welfare prescription." *Reiter v. Sonotone*, 442 U.S. 330, 343 (1979). In its rush to condemn a novel plan about which it knows very little, the Court suggests that this end is achieved only by invalidating activities that *may* have some potential for harm. But the little that the record does show about the effect of the plan suggests that it is a means of providing medical services that in fact benefits rather than injures persons who need them.

In a complex economy, complex economic arrangements are commonplace. It is unwise for the Court, in a case as novel and important as this one, to make a final judgment in the absence of a complete record and where mandatory inferences create critical issues of fact.

NOTES AND QUESTIONS

1. Do you agree with the *Catalano* Court's characterization that *Professional Engineers* and *Sugar Institute* utilized per se approaches? Does the Court's analysis in *Catalano* and *Maricopa County* seem consistent with *Professional Engineers* and *Broadcast Music*? Did the Court in *Catalano* even attempt to reconcile these two earlier opinions? Perhaps the reason for the lack of a clear statement justifying the distinctions between the cases is the fact that *Catalano* was decided by summary reversal on a petition for certiorari that did not allow the parties to file briefs on the merits or argue the case orally.

2. After *Maricopa County*, what, if anything, is left of *Goldfarb's and Professional Engineers'* special protection for professionals? Did the Court, at least implicitly, draw an analytical distinction between ethical and commercial objectives?

3. The Court in *Maricopa* suggested that the "maximum" price fixing at issue may have been nothing more than disguised "minimum" price fixing if all doctors actually charged the agreed-upon price. In that case, why would the insurance companies participate in the scheme? The insurers and the doctors stand in a vertical relationship. Does it strike you as plausible that automobile insurers would participate in a price-fixing agreement among auto body repair shops? Isn't an insurer generally best off when the costs of the risk that it is insuring are minimized?

The Court in *Maricopa* referred to its earlier opinion in *Kiefer-Stewart Co. v. Joseph E. Seagram & Sons*, 340 U.S. 211 (1951), in which the Court was presented with the issue whether it was a violation of Section 1 for two distillers to agree on the maximum resale prices that they would permit their distributors to charge. The jury had returned a verdict for plaintiff. The Court of Appeals for the Seventh Circuit reversed, holding as a matter of law "that an agreement among respondents to fix maximum resale prices did not violate the Sherman Act because such prices promoted rather than restrained competition." *Id.* at 212.

Justice Black, writing for the Court, said:

> The Court of Appeals erred in holding that an agreement among competitors to fix maximum resale prices of their products does not violate the Sherman Act. For such agreements, no less than those to fix minimum prices, cripple the freedom of traders and thereby restrain their ability to sell in accordance with their own judgment. We reaffirm what we said in *United States v. Socony-Vacuum Oil Co.*, 310 U.S. 150, 223: "Under the Sherman Act a combination formed for the purpose and with the effect of raising, depressing, fixing, pegging, or stabilizing the price of a commodity in interstate or foreign commerce is illegal *per se.*"

For what reasons would sellers agree to fix a maximum price with the effect of holding prices down? It has been suggested that under certain conditions, such a practice does serve the self-interest of the seller. First, higher prices which result in greater profit could encourage entry of more competition into the market; thus, the price fixed may be an entry-deterring price. Is this theory plausible? Second, the maximum price fix may be an indirect method of achieving a minimum price; the price will rise to the level of the fixed price and not go below it. Third, by fixing the level of the price, above which the price will not rise, demand for the product may be increased. Fourth, it may be a means to establish price leadership. Fifth, it may have the result of inhibiting product innovation, which might result in higher prices and greater competition. Lawrence Sullivan, Handbook of the Law of Antitrust 211 (1977); *but see* Frank Easterbrook, *Maximum Price Fixing*, 48 U. Chi. L. Rev. 886 (1981), arguing that in markets with poorly informed buyers, advance announcement of maximum prices may enable customers to locate the most competitive sellers.

4. Do *Catalano* and *Maricopa County* give the lower courts a clear standard for subsequent litigation? Has business certainty been advanced by the Court's decisions? Can any systematic criteria for reviewing horizontal price-affecting conduct be stated after these decisions? *See* Peter M. Gerhart, *The Supreme Court and Antitrust Analysis: The (Near) Triumph of the Chicago School*, 1982 SUP. CT. REV. 319.

Consider whether *Maricopa County* can be distinguished from *Broadcast Music* in that the price-fixing agreement in the former was not central to the attainment of the procompetitive objective, while in *Broadcast Music*, the license agreement was found indispensable to increasing integration and efficiency in the market. Was it necessary in *Maricopa County* that the physicians be a party to the agreement for it to be effective?

The Court made clear in *Maricopa County* that weighing the competitive benefits and harms, which was the centerpiece of the analysis in *Professional Engineers* and *Broadcast Music*, has no place once inferences are drawn that the challenged conduct amounts to a price-fixing agreement. At that point in the analysis, "[t]he anticompetitive potential inherent in all price-fixing agreements justifies their facial invalidation even if procompetitive justifications are offered." Is this approach consistent with other Supreme Court opinions, discussed herein, which indicate that the goals of antitrust laws are efficiency and consumer welfare? *See, e.g., Reiter v. Sonotone Corp.*, 442 U.S. 330 (1979); *Brunswick Corp. v. Pueblo Bowl-O-Mat, Inc.*, 429 U.S. 477 (1977); *Continental T.V., Inc. v. GTE Sylvania, Inc.*, 433 U.S. 36 (1977).

5. After *Maricopa County*, would it be illegal for a health insurer, such as Blue Shield, to pay physicians for treating patients only on the condition that each doctor not charge the patient-subscriber an additional charge not covered under the policy? The First Circuit has held that such a "ban on balance billing" practices does not violate either Section 1 or 2 of the Sherman Act. *Kartell v. Blue Shield of Mass., Inc.*, 749 F.2d 922 (1st Cir. 1984) (see discussion in Chapter 6, *infra*). Is Blue Shield in essence the buyer of medical services for others? Is the holding consistent with *Maricopa County*? Is the difference that this arrangement is vertical (between buyer and seller) rather than horizontal as in *Maricopa County*?

NATIONAL COLLEGIATE ATHLETIC ASS'N v. BOARD OF REGENTS
468 U.S. 85 (1984)

JUSTICE STEVENS delivered the opinion of the Court.

The University of Oklahoma and the University of Georgia contend that the National Collegiate Athletic Association has unreasonably restrained trade in the televising of college football games. After an extended trial, the District Court found that the NCAA had violated § 1 of the Sherman Act and granted injunctive relief. . . . The Court of Appeals agreed that the statute had been violated but modified the remedy in some respects. . . .

We granted certiorari, . . . and now affirm.

I

The NCAA

Since its inception in 1905, the NCAA has played an important role in the regulation of amateur collegiate sports. It has adopted and promulgated playing rules, standards of amateurism, standards for academic eligibility, regulations concerning recruitment of athletes, and rules governing the size of athletic squads and coaching staffs. . . . With the exception of football, the NCAA has not undertaken any regulation of the televising of athletic events.

The NCAA has approximately 850 voting members. The regular members are classified into separate divisions to reflect differences in size and scope of their athletic programs. Division I includes 276 colleges with major athletic programs; in this group only 187 play intercollegiate football. Divisions II and III include approximately 500 colleges with less extensive athletic programs. Division I has been subdivided into Divisions I-A and I-AA for football.

. . . .

The Current Plan

The plan adopted in 1981 for the 1982–1985 seasons is at issue in this case. This plan, like each of its predecessors, recites that it is intended to reduce, insofar as possible, the adverse effects of live television upon football game attendance.[13] It provides that "all forms of television of the football games of NCAA member institutions during the Plan control periods shall be in accordance with this Plan." . . .

In separate agreements with each of the carrying networks, ABC and the Columbia Broadcasting System (CBS), the NCAA granted each the right to telecast the 14 live "exposures" described in the plan, in accordance with the "ground rules" set forth therein. Each of the networks agreed to pay a specified "minimum aggregate compensation to the participating NCAA member institutions" during the 4-year period in an amount that totaled $131,750,000. In essence the agreement authorized each network to negotiate directly with member schools for the right to televise their games. The agreement itself does not describe the method of computing the compensation for each game, but the practice that has developed over the years and that the District Court found would be followed under the current agreement involved the setting of a recommended fee by a representative of the NCAA for different types of telecasts, with national telecasts being the most valuable, regional telecasts being less valuable, and Division II or Division III games commanding a still lower price. The aggregate of all these payments presumably equals the total minimum aggregate compensation set forth in the basic

---

[13] [FN 6] "The purposes of this Plan shall be to reduce, insofar as possible, the adverse effects of live television upon football game attendance and, in turn, upon the athletic and related educational programs dependent upon the proceeds therefrom; to spread football television participation among as many colleges as practicable; to reflect properly the image of universities as educational institutions; to promote college football through the use of television, to advance the overall interests of intercollegiate athletics, and to provide college football television to the public to the extent compatible with these other objectives." *Id.*, at 35 (parenthetical omitted).

agreement. Except for differences in payment between national and regional telecasts, and with respect to Division II and Division III games, the amount that any team receives does not change with the size of the viewing audience, the number of markets in which the game is telecast, or the particular characteristic of the game or the participating teams. Instead, the "ground rules" provide that the carrying networks make alternate selections of those games they wish to televise, and thereby obtain the exclusive right to submit a bid at an essentially fixed price to the institutions involved.[14]

The plan also contains "appearance requirements" and "appearance limitations" which pertain to each of the 2-year periods that the plan is in effect. The basic requirement imposed on each of the two networks is that it must schedule appearances for at least 82 different member institutions during each 2-year period. Under the appearance limitations no member institution is eligible to appear on television more than a total of six times and more than four times nationally, with the appearances to be divided equally between the two carrying net-works. . . . The number of exposures specified in the contracts also sets an absolute maximum on the number of games that can be broadcast.

Thus, although the current plan is more elaborate than any of its predecessors, it retains the essential features of each of them. It limits the total amount of televised intercollegiate football and the number of games that any one team may televise. No member is permitted to make any sale of television rights except in accordance with the basic plan.

II

There can be no doubt that the challenged practices of the NCAA constitute a "restraint of trade" in the sense that they limit members' freedom to negotiate and enter into their own television contracts. In that sense, however, every contract is a restraint of trade, and as we have repeatedly recognized, the Sherman Act was intended to prohibit only unreasonable restraints of trade.

It is also undeniable that these practices share characteristics of restraints we have previously held unreasonable. The NCAA is an association of schools which compete against each other to attract television revenues, not to mention fans and athletes. As the District Court found, the policies of the NCAA with respect to television rights are ultimately controlled by the vote of member institutions. By participating in an association which prevents member institutions from competing against each other on the basis of price or kind of television rights that can be

---

[14] [FN 11] The District Court explained how the agreement eliminates competition for broadcasting rights: "First, the networks have no intention to engage in bidding. Second, once the network holding first choice for any given date has made its choice and agreed to a rights fee for that game with the two teams involved, the other network is then in a monopsony position. The schools cannot threaten to sell the broadcast rights to any other network. They cannot sell to NBC without committing a violation of NCAA rules. They cannot sell to the network which had first choice over that particular date because, again, they would be in violation of NCAA rules, and the network would be in violation of its agreement with NCAA. Thus, NCAA creates a single eligible buyer for the product of all but the two schools selected by the network having first choice. Free market competition is thus destroyed under the new plan." 546 F. Supp. at 1292–1293.

offered to broadcasters, the NCAA member institutions have created a horizontal restraint — an agreement among competitors on the way in which they will compete with one another. A restraint of this type has often been held to be unreasonable as a matter of law. Because it places a ceiling on the number of games member institutions may televise, the horizontal agreement places an artificial limit on the quantity of televised football that is available to broadcasters and consumers. By restraining the quantity of television rights available for sale, the challenged practices create a limitation on output; our cases have held that such limitations are unreasonable restraints of trade. Moreover, the District Court found that the minimum aggregate price in fact operates to preclude any price negotiation between broadcasters and institutions, thereby constituting horizontal price fixing, perhaps the paradigm of an unreasonable restraint of trade.

Horizontal price-fixing and output limitation are ordinarily condemned as a matter of law under an "illegal per se" approach because the probability that these practices are anticompetitive is so high; a *per se* rule is applied when "the practice facially appears to be one that would always or almost always tend to restrain competition and decrease output." *Broadcast Music, Inc. v. CBS*, 441 U.S. 1, 19–20 (1979). In such circumstances a restraint is presumed unreasonable without inquiry into the particular market context in which it is found. Nevertheless, we have decided that it would be inappropriate to apply a *per se* rule to this case. This decision is not based on a lack of judicial experience with this type of arrangement,[15] on the fact that the NCAA is organized as a nonprivate entity, or on our respect for the NCAA's historic role in the preservation and encouragement of intercollegiate amateur athletics. Rather, what is critical is that this case involves an industry in which horizontal restraints on competition are essential if the product is to be available at all.

As Judge Bork has noted: "[S]ome activities can only be carried out jointly. Perhaps the leading example is league sports. When a league of professional lacrosse teams is formed, it would be pointless to declare their cooperation illegal on the ground that there are no other professional lacrosse teams." R. Bork, The Antitrust Paradox 278 (1978). What the NCAA and its member institutions market in this case is competition itself — contests between competing institutions. Of course, this would be completely ineffective if there were no rules on which the competitors agreed to create and define the competition to be marketed. A myriad of rules affecting such matters as the size of the field, the number of players on a team, and the extent to which physical violence is to be encouraged or proscribed, all must be agreed upon, and all restrain the manner in which institutions compete. Moreover, the NCAA seeks to market a particular brand of football — college football. The identification of this "product" with an academic tradition differentiates college football from and makes it more popular than professional sports to which it might otherwise be comparable, such as, for example, minor league baseball. In order to preserve the character and quality of the "product," athletes must not be paid, must be required to attend class, and the like. And the integrity

---

[15] [FN 21] While judicial inexperience with a particular arrangement counsels against extending the reach of *per se* rules . . . the likelihood that horizontal price and output restrictions are anti-competitive is generally sufficient to justify application of the per se rule without inquiry into the special characteristics of a particular industry. . . .

of the "product" cannot be preserved except by mutual agreement; if an institution adopted such restrictions unilaterally, its effectiveness as a competitor on the playing field might soon be destroyed. Thus, the NCAA plays a vital role in enabling college football to preserve its character, and as a result enables the product to be marketed which might otherwise be unavailable. In performing this role, its actions widen consumer choice — not only the choices available to sports fans but also those available to athletes — and hence can be viewed as procompetitive.

Broadcast Music squarely holds that a joint selling arrangement may be so efficient that it will increase sellers' aggregate output and thus be procompetitive. . . . Similarly, as we indicated in *Continental T.V., Inc. v. GTE Sylvania Inc.*, 433 U.S. 36, 51–57 (1977), a restraint in a limited aspect of a market may actually enhance market-wide competition. Respondents concede that the great majority of the NCAA's regulations enhance competition among member institutions. Thus, despite the fact that this case involves restraints on the ability of member institutions to compete in terms of price and output, a fair evaluation of their competitive character requires consideration of the NCAA's justifications for the restraints.

Our analysis of this case under the Rule of Reason, of course, does not change the ultimate focus of our inquiry. Both per se rules and the Rule of Reason are employed "to form a judgment about the competitive significance of the restraint." *National Society of Professional Engineers v. United States*, 435 U.S. 679, 692 (1978). . . .

Per se rules are invoked when surrounding circumstances make the likelihood of anticompetitive conduct so great as to render unjustified further examination of the challenged conduct. But whether the ultimate finding is the product of a presumption or actual market analysis, the essential inquiry remains the same — whether or not the challenged restraint enhances competition.[16]

Under the Sherman Act the criterion to be used in judging the validity of a restraint on trade is its impact on competition.

III

Because it restrains price and output, the NCAA's television plan has a significant potential for anticompetitive effects.[17] The findings of the District Court

---

[16] [FN 26] Indeed, there is often no bright line separating *per se* from Rule of Reason analysis. *Per se* rules may require considerable inquiry into market conditions before the evidence justifies a presumption of anticompetitive conduct. For example, while the Court has spoken of a "per se" rule against tying arrangements, it has also recognized that tying may have procompetitive justifications that make it inappropriate to condemn without considerable market analysis. *See Jefferson Parish Hosp. Dist. No. 2 v. Hyde*, 466 U.S. 2 (1984).

[17] [FN 28] In this connection, it is not without significance that Congress felt the need to grant professional sports an exemption from the antitrust laws for joint marketing of television rights. See 15 U.S.C. §§ 1291–1295. The legislative history of this exemption demonstrates Congress' recognition that agreements among league members to sell television rights in a cooperative fashion could run afoul of the Sherman Act, and in particular reflects its awareness of the decision in *United States v. National Football League*, 116 F. Supp. 319 (E.D. Pa. 1953), which held that an agreement between the teams of the National Football League that each team would not permit stations within 75 miles of the home city

indicate that this potential has been realized. The District Court found that if member institutions were free to sell television rights, many more games would be shown on television, and that the NCAA's output restriction has the effect of raising the price the networks pay for television rights. Moreover, the court found that by fixing a price for television rights to all games, the NCAA creates a price structure that is unresponsive to viewer demand and unrelated to the prices that would prevail in a competitive market. And, of course, since as a practical matter all member institutions need NCAA approval, members have no real choice but to adhere to the NCAA's television controls.

The anticompetitive consequences of this arrangement are apparent. Individual competitors lose their freedom to compete. Price is higher and output lower than they would otherwise be, and both are unresponsive to consumer preference. This latter point is perhaps the most significant, since "Congress designed the Sherman Act as a 'consumer welfare prescription.'" . . . A restraint that has the effect of reducing the importance of consumer preference in setting price and output is not consistent with this fundamental goal of antitrust law. Restrictions on price and output are the paradigmatic examples of restraints of trade that the Sherman Act was intended to prohibit. . . . At the same time, the television plan eliminates competitors from the market, since only those broadcasters able to bid on television rights covering the entire NCAA can compete. Thus, as the District Court found, many telecasts that would occur in a competitive market are foreclosed by the NCAA's plan.

Petitioner argues, however, that its television plan can have no significant anticompetitive effect since the record indicates that it has no market power — no ability to alter the interaction of supply and demand in the market. We must reject this argument for two reasons, one legal, one factual.

As a matter of law, the absence of proof of market power does not justify a naked restriction on price or output. To the contrary, when there is an agreement not to compete in terms of price or output, "no elaborate industry analysis is required to demonstrate the anticompetitive character of such an agreement." *Professional Engineers*, 435 U.S. at 692. Petitioner does not quarrel with the District Court's finding that price and output are not responsive to demand. Thus the plan is inconsistent with the Sherman Act's command that price and supply be responsive to consumer preference. We have never required proof of market power in such a case. This naked restraint on price and output requires some competitive justification even in the absence of a detailed market analysis.[18]

---

of another team to telecast its games on a day when that team was playing at home violated § 1 of the Sherman Act. . . .

[18] [FN 42] The Solicitor General correctly observes: "There was no need for the respondents to establish monopoly power in any precisely defined market for television programming in order to prove the restraint unreasonable. Both lower courts found not only that NCAA has power over the market for intercollegiate sports, but also that in the market for television programming — no matter how broadly or narrowly the market is defined — the NCAA television restrictions have reduced output, subverted viewer choice, and distorted pricing. Consequently, unless the controls have some countervailing procompetitive justification, they should be deemed unlawful regardless of whether petitioner has substantial market power over advertising dollars. While the 'reasonableness' of a particular alleged restraint often depends on the market power of the parties involved, because a judgment about market

As a factual matter, it is evident that petitioner does possess market power. The District Court employed the correct test for determining whether college football broadcasts constitute a separate market — whether there are other products that are reasonably substitutable for televised NCAA football games. Petitioner's argument that it cannot obtain supracompetitive prices from broadcasters since advertisers, and hence broadcasters, can switch from college football to other types of programming simply ignores the findings of the District Court. It found that intercollegiate football telecasts generate an audience uniquely attractive to advertisers and that competitors are unable to offer programming that can attract a similar audience. These findings amply support its conclusion that the NCAA possesses market power. Indeed, the District Court's subsidiary finding that advertisers will pay a premium price per viewer to reach audiences watching college football because of their demographic characteristics is vivid evidence of the uniqueness of this product. . . . Thus, respondents have demonstrated that there is a separate market for telecasts of college football which "rest[s] on generic qualities differentiating" viewers. . . . It inexorably follows that if college football broadcasts be defined as a separate market — and we are convinced they are — then the NCAA's complete control over those broadcasts provides a solid basis for the District Court's conclusion that the NCAA possesses market power with respect to those broadcasts. . . .

Thus, the NCAA television plan on its face constitutes a restraint upon the operation of a free market, and the findings of the District Court establish that it has operated to raise price and reduce output. Under the Rule of Reason, these hallmarks of anticompetitive behavior place upon petitioner a heavy burden of establishing an affirmative defense which competitively justifies this apparent deviation from the operations of a free market. . . . We turn now to the NCAA's proffered justifications.

IV

Relying on *Broadcast Music*, petitioner argues that its television plan constitutes a cooperative "joint venture" which assists in the marketing of broadcast rights and hence is procompetitive. While joint ventures have no immunity from the antitrust laws, as *Broadcast Music* indicates, a joint selling arrangement may "mak[e] possible a new product by reaping otherwise unattainable efficiencies." . . . The essential contribution made by the NCAA's arrangement is to define the number of games that may be televised, to establish the price for each exposure, and to define the basic terms of each contract between the network and a home team. The NCAA does not, however, act as a selling agent for any school or for any conference of schools. The selection of individual games, and the negotiation of particular agreements, is a matter left to the networks and the individual schools. Thus, the effect of the network plan is not to eliminate individual sales of broadcasts, since these still occur albeit subject to fixed prices and output limitations. Unlike

---

power is the means by which the effects of the conduct on the market place can be assessed, market power is only one test of 'reasonableness.' And where the anticompetitive effects of conduct can be ascertained through means short of extensive market analysis, and where no countervailing competitive virtues are evident, a lengthy analysis of market power is not necessary." . . .

Broadcast Music's blanket license covering broadcast rights to a large number of individual compositions, here the same rights are still sold on an individual basis, only in a non-competitive market.

The District Court did not find that the NCAA's television plan produced any procompetitive efficiencies which enhanced the competitiveness of college football television rights; to the contrary it concluded that NCAA football could be marketed just as effectively without the television plan. There is therefore no predicate in the findings for petitioner's efficiency justification. Indeed, petitioner's argument is refuted by the District Court's finding concerning price and output. If the NCAA's television plan produced procompetitive efficiencies, the plan would increase output and reduce the price of televised games. The District Court's contrary findings accordingly undermine petitioner's position. In light of these findings, it cannot be said that "the agreement on price is necessary to market the product at all." . . . In *Broadcast Music* the availability of a package product that no individual could offer enhanced the total volume of music that was sold. Unlike this case, there was no limit of any kind placed on the volume that might be sold in the entire market and each individual remained free to sell his own music without restraint. Here production has been limited, not enhanced. No individual school is free to televise its own games without restraint. The NCAA's efficiency justification is not supported by the record.

. . . .

V

Throughout the history of its regulation of intercollegiate football telecasts, the NCAA has indicated its concern with protecting live attendance. This concern, it should be noted, it not with protecting live attendance at games which *are* shown on television; that type of interest is not at issue in this case. Rather, the concern is that fan interest in a televised game may adversely affect ticket sales for games that will not appear on television.

. . . Under the current plan, games are shown on television during all hours that college football games are played. The plan simply does not protect live attendance by ensuring that games will not be shown on television at the same time as live events.

There is, however, a more fundamental reason for rejecting this defense. The NCAA's argument that its television plan is necessary to protect live attendance is not based on a desire to maintain the integrity of college football as a distinct and attractive product, but rather on a fear that the product will not prove sufficiently attractive to draw live attendance when faced with competition from televised games. At bottom the NCAA's position is that ticket sales for most college games are unable to compete in a free market. The television plan protects ticket sales by limiting output — just as any monopolist increases revenues by reducing output. By seeking to insulate live ticket sales from the full spectrum of competition because of its assumption that the product itself is insufficiently attractive to consumers, petitioner forwards a justification that is inconsistent with the basic policy of the Sherman Act. "[T]he Rule of Reason does not support a defense based on the assumption that competition itself is unreasonable." . . .

VI

Petitioner argues that the interest in maintaining a competitive balance among amateur athletic teams is legitimate and important and that it justifies the regulations challenged in this case. We agree with the first part of the argument but not the second.

Our decision not to apply a *per se* rule to this case rests in large part on our recognition that a certain degree of cooperation is necessary if the type of competition that petitioner and its member institutions seek to market is to be preserved. It is reasonable to assume that most of the regulatory controls of the NCAA are justifiable means of fostering competition among amateur athletic teams and therefore procompetitive because they enhance public interest in intercollegiate athletics. The specific restraints on football telecasts, that are challenged in this case do not, however, fit into the same mold as do rules defining the conditions of the contest, the eligibility of participants, or the manner in which members of a joint enterprise shall share the responsibilities and the benefits of the total venture.

. . . .

The television plan is not even arguably tailored to serve such an interest. It does not regulate the amount of money that any college may spend on its football program, nor the way in which the colleges may use the revenues that are generated by their football programs, whether derived from the sale of television rights, the sale of tickets, or the sale of concessions or program advertising. The plan simply imposes a restriction on one source of revenue that is more important to some colleges than to others. There is no evidence that this restriction produces any greater measure of equality throughout the NCAA than would a restriction on alumni donations, tuition rates, or any other revenue producing activity. At the same time, as the District Court found, the NCAA imposes a variety of other restrictions designed to preserve amateurism which are much better tailored to the goal of competitive balance than is the television plan, and which are "clearly sufficient" to preserve competitive balance to the extent it is within the NCAA's power to do so. And much more than speculation supported the District Court's findings on this score. No other NCAA sport employs a similar plan, and in particular the court found that in the most closely analogous sport, college basketball, competitive balance has been maintained without resort to a restrictive television plan.

Perhaps the most important reason for rejecting the argument that the interest in competitive balance is served by the television plan is the District Court's unambiguous and well supported finding that many more games would be televised in a free market than under the NCAA plan. The hypothesis that legitimates the maintenance of competitive balance as a procompetitive justification under the Rule of Reason is that equal competition will maximize consumer demand for the product. The finding that consumption will materially increase if the controls are removed is a compelling demonstration that they do not in fact serve any such legitimate purpose.

VII

The NCAA plays a critical role in the maintenance of a revered tradition of amateurism in college sports. There can be no question but that it needs ample latitude to play that role, or that the preservation of the student-athlete in higher education adds richness and diversity to intercollegiate athletics and is entirely consistent with the goals of the Sherman Act. But consistent with the Sherman Act, the role of the NCAA must be to *preserve* a tradition that might otherwise die; rules that restrict output are hardly consistent with this role. Today we hold only that the record supports the District Court's conclusion that by curtailing output and blunting the ability of member institutions to respond to consumer preference, the NCAA has restricted rather than enhanced the place of intercollegiate athletics in the Nation's life. Accordingly, the judgment of the Court of Appeals is

Affirmed.

NOTES AND QUESTIONS

1. After *NCAA*, what is the plaintiff's burden in proving a per se violation? If an agreement to fix price and output is not analyzed as per se unlawful, is any conduct hereafter? What remains of *Socony*'s per se test: "any combination which tampers with price structure"?

2. The Court in *NCAA* used the associational nature of defendant and the need for economic interdependence among competitors in this market as justification for applying a rule of reason approach. Did the Court give any guidance when cooperation among competitors and the resulting restraint will be deemed legal? Does the nature and purpose of the joint undertaking indicate the result? Or is it determined by whether the challenged practice produces countervailing procompetitive benefits? Is that the difference between the results in *Broadcast Music* and *NCAA*? Or is the difference the fact that in *Broadcast Music*, unlike *NCAA*, there was no output limitation? If the latter argument is determinative, why then is there no per se standard in *NCAA*?

3. *NCAA* focused on an output-restriction analysis more than previous cases. Does it necessarily follow that an agreement on price will lead to a decrease in output and in turn an increase in price? Consider whether a decrease in price competition might result in an increase in nonprice competition, such as increased product quality and service. Is it possible that nonprice competition could increase output, and hence be procompetitive? Does *NCAA* suggest that the link between the variables of price and nonprice competition is output, with output-expanding agreements deemed competitive? *See also* E. Thomas Sullivan, *On Nonprice Competition: An Economic and Marketing Analysis*, 45 U. PITT. L. REV. 771 (1984).

4. *NCAA* held that output-restricting agreements are anticompetitive. Was the Court's market power analysis essential to the finding that output was reduced? Does the Court imply that market power is a prerequisite for finding a Section 1 violation? Have any other Section 1 cases used this standard? Consider the Court's reasoning: If the market indicates that price and supply, by reason of the agreement, are not responsive to consumer preferences, a market power analysis is not required. Is an output restriction enough to condemn the practice regardless of market power?

5. Does the *NCAA* decision foreclose the NCAA or a conference from limiting the number of times a school might have its games shown on television, or enforcing a television blackout rule to avoid competition between gate attendance and television audiences? *See generally* Richard B. McKenzie & E. Thomas Sullivan, *Does the NCAA Exploit College Athletes? An Economics and Legal Reinterpretation*, 32 ANTITRUST BULL. 373 (1987).

6. Consider whether a television viewer would have standing to bring an action to challenge the NCAA plan or whether a consumer had suffered "antitrust injury." Does *NCAA* turn on a finding that viewers were adversely affected by the NCAA plan? Would an advertiser have standing?

7. In evaluating the Court's economic theory in *NCAA*, consider the 1984 college football television revenue compared to the year before the Court's decision: In 1983, a total of 89 TV games produced revenues of $69 million. And in 1984, 195 games produced only $45 million (including regional and local syndication). By 1986, 99 games on TV (excluding regional and local telecasts) produced $53 million.

8. On a request for a permanent injunction, consider whether a district court needs to define the relevant market under Section 1 when there is an output restriction shown and the defendant fails to offer a pro-consumer justification for the challenged output restriction. In *Chicago Prof. Sport, Ltd. Pt'ship v. National Basketball Ass'n*, 961 F.2d 667 (7th Cir. 1992), Judge Easterbrook, writing for the court, held that the issuance of a permanent injunction barring the NBA from enforcing a rule reducing the number of games from 25 to 20, broadcast over certain superstations, was proper because plaintiff demonstrated that an agreement to reduce the number of games shown was an output restriction without an offsetting efficiency justification. Because defendant failed to show some explanation connecting the restriction to consumers' benefits, there was no need to define the relevant market, as it was clear that the output restriction was enough to condemn the practice under a "quick look" analysis under the rule of reason.

9. The NCAA was condemned for capping the salaries for entry-level basketball coaches. In *Law v. National Collegiate Athletic Association*, 134 F.3d 1010 (10th Cir.), *cert. denied*, 525 U.S. 822 (1998), the Tenth Circuit applied a quick look rule of reason analysis to uphold the NCAA's Section 1 liability. The court decided that evidence suggested an anticompetitive effect because the NCAA used the rule to reduce part-time coaches' salaries from up to $60,000 to $16,000 per year. None of the justifications offered by the NCAA was found sufficient to overcome this presumption of anticompetitive effect.

10. While the NCAA has been condemned for regulating monetary decisions of the schools it regulates, the NCAA's ability to regulate the sports which it oversees was recently affirmed in *Warrior Sports, Inc. v. National Collegiate Athletic Association*, 623 F.3d 281 (6th Cir. 2010). The NCAA attempted to change a rule regarding the design of lacrosse stick heads allowed for use in NCAA games. If the rule were changed it would affect stick manufacturers because high schools and lower leagues would then adopt the new NCAA rule, requiring all lacrosse stick heads to be redesigned. There were three iterations to the rule. Many stick manufacturers, including Warrior, were consulted during each of the rule change processes. Warrior filed suit against the first rule change, which was dropped when the NCAA agreed to reconsider the proposed change. The second iteration of the rule included language that would have made a design patented by Warrior the only legal design. When the NCAA discovered that Warrior was the exclusive patent holder on that design the rule was changed to allow both Warrior's design as well as the design of other companies. The third rule was adopted and Warrior challenged it under the Sherman Act, claiming collusion between the NCAA and Warrior's competition. The court decided that Warrior's claim failed under a rule of reason analysis, because it did not identify any anticompetitive effects on the market for lacrosse sticks. The court emphasized that in performing rule of reason analysis there must be an adverse effect on the market, not just the individuals making the challenge. Since all lacrosse stick manufacturers were affected by the rule change in the same way, the court found that there was no anticompetitive effect to the rule change. In addition, the court noted that the rule as adopted would increase competition since the previous version of the rule would have given Warrior monopoly as the patent holder of the proposed design.

Similarly, in two decisions in 2010, the Third Circuit held that a sanctioning body's decisions regarding equipment and structure are not unreasonable, and hence not Sherman Act violations. In *Deustcher Tennis Bund v. ATP Tour, Inc.*, 610 F.3d 820 (3d Cir. 2010), the Third Circuit held that the Association of Tennis Professionals (ATP) did not violate the Sherman Act when it reorganized the structure of its tournaments, demoting the plaintiff's tournament from first tier to second tier status for lack of performance. The court held that a full-scale rule of reason analysis was appropriate, rather than a "quick-look" rule of reason or *per se* rule approach. The reason the "quick-look" approach was not appropriate was because under that approach the anticompetitive effects on markets and consumers are obvious. In this case, the definition of the market affected was hotly contested at trial. The court then decided that the plaintiff had failed to prove the existence of a relevant market and therefore a Sherman Act claim was precluded.

In *Race Tires America, Inc. v. Hoosier Racing Tire Corp.*, 614 F.3d 57 (3d Cir. 2010), the court held that a "single tire rule," which required the use of a single tire brand on vehicles in races at sanctioned dirt tracks, was reasonable even though the tire manufacturer was a race sponsor. A competitor that was not awarded the exclusive contract by the sanctioning body brought suit alleging conspiracy to restrain trade and coercion. In addition to finding no coercion, and good faith justifications on the part of the governing body, the court found that there was no injury to the market, which must be present for antitrust violation to take place. The court concluded:

> [T]he Sherman Act does not forbid sanctioning bodies and other sports-related organizations from freely (i.e., without any coercion or improper interference) adopting exclusive equipment requirements, so long as such organizations otherwise possess, in good faith, sufficient pro-competitive or business justifications for their actions. At the same time, we wish to make it clear that we are not granting any king of antitrust immunity. . . . For instance, we are not confronted with a situation in which the sanctioning

body offers absolutely no justification whatsoever for its actions or its justifications are offered in bad faith or are otherwise nonsensical. Instead, we will affirm the District Court's ruling because there are several good faith justifications for the sanctioning bodies' single tire rule.

11. In *Agnew v. NCAA*, 683 F.3d 328 (7th Cir. 2012), two college football players, whose athletic scholarships were not renewed following injuries that prevented them from playing football, challenged two NCAA regulations — a cap on the number of scholarships given per team and a prohibition of multi-year scholarships. The plaintiffs claimed that these rules had prevented them from receiving scholarships to cover the entire cost of their college education and violated Section 1 of the Sherman Act. The district court dismissed their amended complaint for failure to allege a relevant market on which the NCAA's bylaws could have an anticompetitive effect. On appeal, the plaintiffs urged the court to use quick-look analysis and asserted that they did not have to define a relevant market under the quick-look approach. The Seventh Circuit explained that while "[t]he quick-look doctrine permits plaintiffs to forgo any strict showing of market power, and thus a specific definition of the relevant market," there still must exist "a relevant market on which [defendants'] actions have an anticompetitive effect." *Id.* at 337. Although on appeal the plaintiffs claimed to have asserted a market for bachelor's degrees and a market for student-athlete labor, the Seventh Circuit found no such allegations in the plaintiffs' amended complaint and affirmed dismissal.

CALIFORNIA DENTAL ASS'N v. FEDERAL TRADE COMM'N
526 U.S. 756 (1999)

JUSTICE SOUTER delivered the opinion of the Court.

There are two issues in this case: whether the jurisdiction of the Federal Trade Commission extends to the California Dental Association (CDA), a nonprofit professional association, and whether a "quick look" sufficed to justify finding that certain advertising restrictions adopted by the CDA violated the antitrust laws. We hold that the Commission's jurisdiction under the Federal Trade Commission Act (FTC Act) extends to an association that, like the CDA, provides substantial economic benefit to its for-profit members, but that where, as here, any anticompetitive effects of given restraints are far from intuitively obvious, the rule of reason demands a more thorough enquiry into the consequences of those restraints than the Court of Appeals performed.

The CDA is a voluntary nonprofit association of local dental societies to which some 19,000 dentists belong, including about three-quarters of those practicing in the State. . . . The CDA is exempt from federal income tax under 26 U.S.C. § 501(c)(6), covering "[b]usiness leagues, chambers of commerce, real-estate boards, [and] boards of trade," although it has for-profit subsidiaries that give its members advantageous access to various sorts of insurance, including liability coverage, and to financing for their real estate, equipment, cars, and patients' bills. The CDA lobbies and litigates in its members' interests, and conducts marketing and public relations campaigns for their benefit. . . .

The dentists who belong to the CDA through these associations agree to abide by a Code of Ethics (Code) including the following § 10:

"Although any dentist may advertise, no dentist shall advertise or solicit patients in any form of communication in a manner that is false or misleading in any material respect. In order to properly serve the public, dentists should represent themselves in a manner that contributes to the esteem of the public. Dentists should not misrepresent their training and competence in any way that would be false or misleading in any material respect."

The CDA has issued a number of advisory opinions interpreting this section . . . and . . . has advised its dentists of disclosures they must make under state law when engaging in discount advertising.[19]

. . . .

The Commission brought a complaint against the CDA, alleging that it applied its guidelines so as to restrict truthful, nondeceptive advertising, and so violated § 5 of the FTC Act, 38 Stat. 717, 15 U.S.C. § 45.[20] The complaint alleged that the CDA had unreasonably restricted two types of advertising: price advertising, particularly discounted fees, and advertising relating to the quality of dental services. . . . An Administrative Law Judge ("ALJ") held the Commission to have jurisdiction over the CDA, which, the ALJ noted, had itself "stated that a selection of its programs and services has a potential value to members of between $22,739 and $65,127". . . . He found that although there had been no proof that the CDA exerted market power, no such proof was required to establish an antitrust violation under *In re Mass. Bd. of Registration in Optometry*, 110 F.T.C. 549 (1988), since the CDA had unreasonably prevented members and potential members from using truthful, nondeceptive advertising, all to the detriment of both dentists and consumers of dental services. He accordingly found a violation of § 5 of the FTC Act. . . .

The Commission adopted the factual findings of the ALJ except for his conclusion that the CDA lacked market power, with which the Commission disagreed. The Commission treated the CDA's restrictions on discount advertising as illegal *per se*. . . . In the alternative, the Commission held the price advertising (as well as the nonprice) restrictions to be violations of the Sherman and FTC Acts under an

---

[19] [FN 2] The disclosures include:

"1. The dollar amount of the nondiscounted fee for the service[.]

"2. Either the dollar amount of the discount fee or the percentage of the discount for the specific service[.]

"3. The length of time that the discount will be offered[.]

"4. Verifiable fees[.]

"5. [The identity of] [s]pecific groups who qualify for the discount or any other terms and conditions or restrictions for qualifying for the discount.". . . .

[20] [FN 3] The FTC Act's prohibition of unfair competition and deceptive acts or practices, 15 U.S.C. § 45(a)(1), overlaps the scope of § 1 of the Sherman Act, 15 U.S.C. § 1, aimed at prohibiting restraint of trade, FTC v. Indiana Federation of Dentists, 476 U.S. 447, 454–455 (1986), and the Commission relied upon Sherman Act law in adjudicating this case.

abbreviated rule-of-reason analysis. . . .

The Court of Appeals for the Ninth Circuit affirmed, sustaining the Commission's assertion of jurisdiction over the CDA and its ultimate conclusion on the merits. . . . The court thought it error for the Commission to have applied *per se* analysis to the price advertising restrictions, finding analysis under the rule of reason required for all the restrictions. But the Court of Appeals went on to explain that the Commission had properly

> applied an abbreviated, or 'quick look,' rule of reason analysis designed for restraints that are not *per se* unlawful but are sufficiently anticompetitive on their face that they do not require a full-blown rule of reason inquiry. . . . It allows the condemnation of a 'naked restraint' on price or output without an 'elaborate industry analysis. . . . .

The Court of Appeals thought truncated rule-of-reason analysis to be in order for several reasons. As for the restrictions on discount advertising, they "amounted in practice to a fairly 'naked' restraint on price competition itself." . . . The CDA's procompetitive justification, that the restrictions encouraged disclosure and prevented false and misleading advertising, carried little weight because "it is simply infeasible to disclose all of the information that is required" . . . and "the record provides no evidence that the rule has in fact led to increased disclosure and transparency of dental pricing." . . . As to non-price advertising restrictions, the court said that

> [t]hese restrictions are in effect a form of output limitation, as they restrict the supply of information about individual dentists' services. *See* Areeda & Hovenkamp, Antitrust Law ¶ 1505 at 693–694 (Supp. 1997). . . . The restrictions may also affect output more directly, as quality and comfort advertising may induce some customers to obtain nonemergency care when they might not otherwise do so. . . . Under these circumstances, we think that the restriction is a sufficiently naked restraint on output to justify quick look analysis. . . . .

The Court of Appeals went on to hold that the Commission's findings with respect to the CDA's agreement and intent to restrain trade, as well as on the effect of the restrictions and the existence of market power, were all supported by substantial evidence. . . .

We granted certiorari to resolve conflicts among the Circuits on the Commission's jurisdiction over a nonprofit professional association . . . and the occasions for abbreviated rule-of-reason analysis. . . . We now vacate the judgment of the Court of Appeals and remand.

II

The FTC Act gives the Commission authority over "persons, partnerships, or corporations," 15 U.S.C. § 45(a)(2), and defines "corporation" to include "any company . . . or association, incorporated or unincorporated, without shares of capital or capital stock or certificates of interest, except partnerships, which is organized to carry on business for its own profit or that of its members," § 44.

. . . .

We therefore conclude that the Commission had jurisdiction to pursue the claim here, and turn to the question whether the Court of Appeals devoted sufficient analysis to sustain the claim that the advertising restrictions promulgated by the CDA violated the FTC Act.

III

The Court of Appeals treated as distinct questions the sufficiency of the analysis of anticompetitive effects and the substantiality of the evidence supporting the Commission's conclusions. Because we decide that the Court of Appeals erred when it held as a matter of law that quick-look analysis was appropriate . . . we do not reach the question of the substantiality of the evidence supporting the Commission's conclusion. . . .

In *National Collegiate Athletic Assn. v. Board of Regents of Univ. of Okla.*, 468 U.S. 85 (1984), we held that a "naked restraint on price and output requires some competitive justification even in the absence of a detailed market analysis.". . . . Elsewhere, we held that "no elaborate industry analysis is required to demonstrate the anticompetitive character of" horizontal agreements among competitors to refuse to discuss prices, *National Soc. of Professional Engineers v. United States*, 435 U.S. 679, 692 (1978), or to withhold a particular desired service, *FTC v. Indiana Federation of Dentists*, 476 U.S. 447, 459 (1986) (quoting *National Soc. of Professional Engineers, supra*, at 692). In each of these cases, which have formed the basis for what has come to be called abbreviated or "quick-look" analysis under the rule of reason, an observer with even a rudimentary understanding of economics could conclude that the arrangements in question would have an anticompetitive effect on customers and markets. [Q]uick-look analysis carries the day when the great likelihood of anticompetitive effects can easily be ascertained. *See Law v. National Collegiate Athletic Assn.*, 134 F.3d 1010, 1020 (C.A.10 1998) (explaining that quick-look analysis applies "where a practice has obvious anticompetitive effects"); *Chicago Professional Sports Limited Partnership v. National Basketball Assn.*, 961 F.2d 667, 674–676 (C.A.7 1992) (finding quick-look analysis adequate after assessing and rejecting logic of proffered procompetitive justifications); *cf. United States v. Brown University*, 5 F.3d 658, 677–678 (C.A.3 1993) (finding full rule-of-reason analysis required where universities sought to provide financial aid to needy students and noting by way of contrast that the agreements in *National Soc. of Professional Engineers* and *Indiana Federation of Dentists* "embodied a strong economic self-interest of the parties to them").

The case before us, however, fails to present a situation in which the likelihood of anticompetitive effects is comparably obvious. Even on Justice Breyer's view that bars on truthful and verifiable price and quality advertising are *prima facie* anticompetitive . . . and place the burden of procompetitive justification on those who agree to adopt them, the very issue at the threshold of this case is whether professional price and quality advertising is sufficiently verifiable in theory and in fact to fall within such a general rule. Ultimately our disagreement with Justice Breyer turns on our different responses to this issue. Whereas he accepts, as the Ninth Circuit seems to have done, that the restrictions here were like restrictions on advertisement of price and quality generally . . . it seems to us that the CDA's advertising restrictions might plausibly be thought to have a net procompetitive effect, or possibly no effect at all on competition. The restrictions on both discount and nondiscount advertising are, at least on their face, designed to avoid false or deceptive advertising . . . in a market characterized by striking disparities between the information available to the professional and the patient. . . .

The explanation proffered by the Court of Appeals for the likely anticompetitive effect of the CDA's restrictions on discount advertising began with the unexceptionable statements that "price advertising is fundamental to price competition" . . . and that "[r]estrictions on the ability to advertise prices normally make it more difficult for consumers to find a lower price and for dentists to compete on the basis of price." . . . The court then acknowledged that, according to the CDA, the restrictions nonetheless furthered the "legitimate, indeed procompetitive, goal of preventing false and misleading price advertising." . . . The Court of Appeals might, at this juncture, have recognized that the restrictions at issue here are very far from a total ban on price or discount advertising, and might have considered the possibility that the particular restrictions on professional advertising could have different effects from those "normally" found in the commercial world, even to the point of promoting competition by reducing the occurrence of unverifiable and misleading across-the-board discount advertising.[21] Instead, the Court of Appeals confined itself to the brief assertion that the "CDA's disclosure requirements appear to prohibit across-the-board discounts because it is simply infeasible to disclose all of the information that is required" . . . followed by the observation that "the record provides no evidence that the rule has in fact led to increased disclosure and transparency of dental pricing." . . .

But these observations brush over the professional context and describe no anticompetitive effects. Assuming that the record in fact supports the conclusion that the CDA disclosure rules essentially bar advertisement of across-the-board discounts, it does not obviously follow that such a ban would have a net anticompetitive effect here. Whether advertisements that announced discounts for, say, first-time customers, would be less effective at conveying information relevant to competition if they listed the original and discounted prices for checkups, X-rays, and fillings, than they would be if they simply specified a percentage discount across the board, seems to us a question susceptible to empirical but not *a priori* analysis. . . . [T]he CDA's rule appears to reflect the prediction that any costs to competition associated with the elimination of across-the-board advertising will be outweighed by gains to consumer information (and hence competition) created by discount advertising that is exact, accurate, and more easily verifiable (at least by regulators). As a matter of economics this view may or may not be correct, but it is not implausible, and neither a court nor the Commission may initially dismiss it as presumptively wrong.[22]

---

[21] [FN 11] Justice Breyer claims that "the Court of Appeals did consider the relevant differences." . . . But the language he cites says nothing more than that per se analysis is inappropriate here and that "some caution" was appropriate where restrictions purported to restrict false advertising. . . . Caution was of course appropriate, but this statement by the Court of Appeals does not constitute a consideration of the possible differences between these and other advertising restrictions.

[22] [FN 12] Justice Breyer suggests that our analysis is "of limited relevance" . . . because "the basic

In theory, it is true, the Court of Appeals neither ruled out the plausibility of some procompetitive support for the CDA's requirements nor foreclosed the utility of an evidentiary discussion on the point. The court indirectly acknowledged the plausibility of procompetitive justifications for the CDA's position when it stated that "the record provides no evidence that the rule has in fact led to increased disclosure and transparency of dental pricing." . . . But because petitioner alone would have had the incentive to introduce such evidence, the statement sounds as though the Court of Appeals may have thought it was justified without further analysis to shift a burden to the CDA to adduce hard evidence of the procompetitive nature of its policy; the court's adversion to empirical evidence at the moment of this implicit burden-shifting underscores the leniency of its enquiry into evidence of the restrictions' anticompetitive effects.

The Court of Appeals was comparably tolerant in accepting the sufficiency of abbreviated rule-of-reason analysis as to the nonprice advertising restrictions. The court began with the argument that "[t]hese restrictions are in effect a form of output limitation, as they restrict the supply of information about individual dentists' services." . . . Although this sentence does indeed appear as cited, it is puzzling, given that the relevant output for antitrust purposes here is presumably not information or advertising, but dental services themselves. The question is not whether the universe of possible advertisements has been limited (as assuredly it has), but whether the limitation on advertisements obviously tends to limit the total delivery of dental services. The court came closest to addressing this latter question when it went on to assert that limiting advertisements regarding quality and safety "prevents dentists from fully describing the package of services they offer" . . . adding that "[t]he restrictions may also affect output more directly, as quality and comfort advertising may induce some customers to obtain nonemergency care when they might not otherwise do so." . . . This suggestion about output is also puzzling. If quality advertising actually induces some patients to obtain more care than they would in its absence, then restricting such advertising would reduce the demand for dental services, not the supply; and it is of course the producers' supply of a good in relation to demand that is normally relevant in determining whether a producer-imposed output limitation has the anticompetitive effect of artificially raising prices. . . .

Although the Court of Appeals acknowledged the CDA's view that "claims about quality are inherently unverifiable and therefore misleading" . . . it responded that this concern "does not justify banning all quality claims without regard to whether they are, in fact, false or misleading." . . . As a result, the court said, "the restriction is a sufficiently naked restraint on output to justify quick look analy-

---

question is whether this . . . theoretically redeeming virtue in fact offsets the restrictions' anticompetitive effects in this case". . . . He thinks that the Commission and the Court of Appeals "adequately answered that question" . . . but the absence of any empirical evidence on this point indicates that the question was not answered, merely avoided by implicit burden-shifting of the kind accepted by Justice Breyer. The point is that before a theoretical claim of anticompetitive effects can justify shifting to a defendant the burden to show empirical evidence of procompetitive effects, as quick-look analysis in effect requires, there must be some indication that the court making the decision has properly identified the theoretical basis for the anticompetitive effects and considered whether the effects actually are anticompetitive. Where, as here, the circumstances of the restriction are somewhat complex, assumption alone will not do.

sis." . . . The court assumed, in these words, that some dental quality claims may escape justifiable censure, because they are both verifiable and true. But its implicit assumption fails to explain why it gave no weight to the countervailing, and at least equally plausible, suggestion that restricting difficult-to-verify claims about quality or patient comfort would have a procompetitive effect by preventing misleading or false claims that distort the market. It is, indeed, entirely possible to understand the CDA's restrictions on unverifiable quality and comfort advertising as nothing more than a procompetitive ban on puffery . . . notwithstanding Justice Breyer's citation (to a Commission discussion that never faces the issue of the unverifiability of professional quality claims, raised in *Bates*) . . . .[23]

The point is not that the CDA's restrictions necessarily have the procompetitive effect claimed by the CDA; it is possible that banning quality claims might have no effect at all on competitiveness if, for example, many dentists made very much the same sort of claims. And it is also of course possible that the restrictions might in the final analysis be anticompetitive. The point, rather, is that the plausibility of competing claims about the effects of the professional advertising restrictions rules out the indulgently abbreviated review to which the Commission's order was treated. The obvious anticompetitive effect that triggers abbreviated analysis has not been shown.

In light of our focus on the adequacy of the Court of Appeals's analysis, Justice Breyer's thorough-going, *de novo* antitrust analysis contains much to impress on its own merits but little to demonstrate the sufficiency of the Court of Appeals's review. The obligation to give a more deliberate look than a quick one does not arise at the door of this Court and should not be satisfied here in the first instance. Had the Court of Appeals engaged in a painstaking discussion in a league with Justice Breyer's (compare his 14 pages with the Ninth Circuit's 8), and had it confronted the comparability of these restrictions to bars on clearly verifiable advertising, its reasoning might have sufficed to justify its conclusion. Certainly Justice Breyer's treatment of the antitrust issues here is no "quick look." Lingering is more like it, and indeed Justice Breyer, not surprisingly, stops short of endorsing the Court of Appeals's discussion as adequate to the task at hand.

Saying here that the Court of Appeals's conclusion at least required a more extended examination of the possible factual underpinnings than it received is not, of course, necessarily to call for the fullest market analysis. Although we have said that a challenge to a "naked restraint on price and output" need not be supported by "a detailed market analysis" in order to "requir[e] some competitive justification," *National Collegiate Athletic Assn.*, 468 U.S., at 110, it does not follow that every case attacking a less obviously anticompetitive restraint (like this one) is a candidate for plenary market examination. The truth is that our categories of analysis of anticompetitive effect are less fixed than terms like "*per se*," "quick look," and "rule of reason" tend to make them appear. We have recognized, for example, that "there is often no bright line separating *per se* from Rule of Reason analysis," since "considerable inquiry into market conditions" may be required before the

---

[23] [FN 14] The Commission said only that " 'mere puffing' deceives no one and has never been subject to regulation.' " . . . The question here, of course, is not whether puffery may be subject to governmental regulation, but whether a professional organization may ban it.

application of any so-called *"per se"* condemnation is justified. *Id.*, at 104, n.26. "[W]hether the ultimate finding is the product of a presumption or actual market analysis, the essential inquiry remains the same — whether or not the challenged restraint enhances competition." *Id.*, at 104. Indeed, the scholar who enriched antitrust law with the metaphor of "the twinkling of an eye" for the most condensed rule-of-reason analysis himself cautioned against the risk of misleading even in speaking of a 'spectrum' of adequate reasonableness analysis for passing upon antitrust claims: "There is always something of a sliding scale in appraising reasonableness, but the sliding scale formula deceptively suggests greater precision than we can hope for. . . . Nevertheless, the quality of proof required should vary with the circumstances." P. Areeda, Antitrust Law ¶ 1507, p. 402 (1986). . . . At the same time, Professor Areeda also emphasized the necessity, particularly great in the quasi-common law realm of antitrust, that courts explain the logic of their conclusions. "By exposing their reasoning, judges . . . are subjected to others' critical analyses, which in turn can lead to better understanding for the future." *Id.*, ¶ 1500, at 364. As the circumstances here demonstrate, there is generally no categorical line to be drawn between restraints that give rise to an intuitively obvious inference of anticompetitive effect and those that call for more detailed treatment. What is required, rather, is an enquiry meet for the case, looking to the circumstances, details, and logic of a restraint. The object is to see whether the experience of the market has been so clear, or necessarily will be, that a confident conclusion about the principal tendency of a restriction will follow from a quick (or at least quicker) look, in place of a more sedulous one. And of course what we see may vary over time, if rule-of-reason analyses in case after case reach identical conclusions. For now, at least, a less quick look was required for the initial assessment of the tendency of these professional advertising restrictions. Because the Court of Appeals did not scrutinize the assumption of relative anticompetitive tendencies, we vacate the judgment and remand the case for a fuller consideration of the issue.

It is so ordered.

JUSTICE BREYER, with whom JUSTICE STEVENS, JUSTICE KENNEDY, and JUSTICE GINS-BURG join, concurring in part and dissenting in part.

I agree with the Court that the Federal Trade Commission has jurisdiction over petitioner, and I join Parts I and II of its opinion. I also agree that in a "rule of reason" antitrust case "the quality of proof required should vary with the circumstances," that "[w]hat is required . . . is an enquiry meet for the case," and that the object is a "confident conclusion about the principal tendency of a restriction." But I do not agree that the Court has properly applied those unobjectionable principles here. In my view, a traditional application of the rule of reason to the facts as found by the Commission requires affirming the Commission — just as the Court of Appeals did below.

I

The Commission's conclusion is lawful if its "factual findings," insofar as they are supported by "substantial evidence," "make out a violation of Sherman Act § 1."

FTC v. Indiana Federation of Dentists, 476 U.S. 447, 454–455 (1986). To determine whether that is so, I would not simply ask whether the restraints at issue are anticompetitive overall. Rather, like the Court of Appeals (and the Commission), I would break that question down into four classical, subsidiary antitrust questions: (1) What is the specific restraint at issue? (2) What are its likely anticompetitive effects? (3) Are there offsetting procompetitive justifications? (4) Do the parties have sufficient market power to make a difference?

A

The most important question is the first: What are the specific restraints at issue?. . . . Those restraints do not include merely the agreement to which the California Dental Association's . . . ethical rule literally refers, namely, a promise to refrain from advertising that is " 'false or misleading in any material respect.' ". . . . Instead, the Commission found a set of restraints arising out of the way the Dental Association implemented this innocent-sounding ethical rule in practice , through advisory opinions, guidelines, enforcement policies, and review of membership applications. . . . As implemented, the ethical rule reached beyond its nominal target, to prevent truthful and nondeceptive advertising. In particular, the Commission determined that the rule, in practice:

(1) "precluded advertising that characterized a dentist's fees as being low, reasonable, or affordable." . . .

(2) "precluded advertising . . . of across the board discounts." . . .

(3) "prohibit[ed] all quality claims." . . .

Whether the Dental Association's basic rule as implemented actually restrained the truthful and nondeceptive advertising of low prices, across-the-board discounts, and quality service are questions of fact. The Administrative Law Judge ("ALJ") and the Commission may have found those questions difficult ones. But both the ALJ and the Commission ultimately found against the Dental Association in respect to these facts. And the question for us-whether those agency findings are supported by substantial evidence . . . is not difficult.

The Court of Appeals referred explicitly to some of the evidence that it found adequate to support the Commission's conclusions. It pointed out, for example, that the Dental Association's "advisory opinions and guidelines indicate that . . . descriptions of prices as 'reasonable' or 'low' do not comply" with the Association's rule; that in "numerous cases" the Association "advised members of objections to special offers, senior citizen discounts, and new patient discounts, apparently without regard to their truth"; and that one advisory opinion "expressly states that claims as to the quality of services are inherently likely to be false or misleading," all "without any particular consideration of whether" such statements were "true or false." . . .

The Commission itself had before it far more evidence. It referred to instances in which the Association, without regard for the truthfulness of the statements at issue, recommended denial of membership to dentists wishing to advertise, for example, "reasonable fees quoted in advance," "major savings," or "making teeth cleaning . . . inexpensive." . . . It referred to testimony that "across-the-board discount advertising in literal compliance with the requirements 'would probably take two pages in the telephone book' and '[n]obody is going to really advertise in that fashion.' " . . . And it pointed to many instances in which the Dental Association suppressed such advertising claims as "we guarantee all dental work for 1 year," "latest in cosmetic dentistry," and "gentle dentistry in a caring environment." . . .

I need not review the evidence further, for this Court has said that "substantial evidence" is a matter for the courts of appeals, and that it "will intervene only in what ought to be the rare instance when the standard appears to have been misapprehended or grossly misapplied." *Universal Camera Corp. v. NLRB*, 340 U.S. 474 (1951). I have said enough to make clear that this is not a case warranting our intervention. Consequently, we must decide only the basic legal question whether the three restraints described above unreasonably restrict competition.

B

Do each of the three restrictions mentioned have "the potential for genuine adverse effects on competition"? *Indiana Federation*, 476 U.S., at 460; 7 P. Areeda, Antitrust Law ¶ 1503a, pp. 372–377 (1986). . . . I should have thought that the anticompetitive tendencies of the three restrictions were obvious. An agreement not to advertise that a fee is reasonable, that service is inexpensive, or that a customer will receive a discount makes it more difficult for a dentist to inform customers that he charges a lower price. If the customer does not know about a lower price, he will find it more difficult to buy lower price service. That fact, in turn, makes it less likely that a dentist will obtain more customers by offering lower prices. And that likelihood means that dentists will prove less likely to offer lower prices. But why should I have to spell out the obvious? To restrain truthful advertising about lower prices is likely to restrict competition in respect to price — "the central nervous system of the economy." *United States v. Socony-Vacuum Oil Co.*, 310 U.S. 150, 226, n.59 (1940). . . . The Commission thought this fact sufficient to hold (in the alternative) that the price advertising restrictions were unlawful *per se*. . . . For present purposes, I need not decide whether the Commission was right in applying a *per se* rule. I need only assume a rule of reason applies, and note the serious anticompetitive tendencies of the price advertising restraints.

The restrictions on the advertising of service quality also have serious anticompetitive tendencies. This is not a case of "mere puffing," as the FTC recognized. . . . The days of my youth, when the billboards near Emeryville, California, home of AAA baseball's Oakland Oaks, displayed the name of "Painless" Parker, Dentist, are long gone — along with the Oakland Oaks. But some parents may still want to know that a particular dentist makes a point of "gentle care." Others may want to know about 1-year dental work guarantees. To restrict that kind of service quality advertisement is to restrict competition over the quality of service itself, for, unless consumers know, they may not purchase, and dentists may not compete to supply that which will make little difference to the demand for their services. That, at any rate, is the theory of the Sherman Act. And it is rather late in the day for anyone to deny the significant anticompetitive tendencies of an agreement that restricts competition in any legitimate respect . . . let alone one that inhibits customers from learning about the quality of a dentist's service.

Nor did the Commission rely solely on the unobjectionable proposition that a restriction on the ability of dentists to advertise on quality is likely to limit their incentive to compete on quality. Rather, the Commission pointed to record evidence affirmatively establishing that quality-based competition is important to dental consumers in California. . . .

The FTC found that the price advertising restrictions amounted to a "naked attempt to eliminate price competition." . . . It found that the service quality advertising restrictions "deprive consumers of information they value and of healthy competition for their patronage." It added that the "anticompetitive nature of these restrictions" was "plain." . . . The Court of Appeals agreed. I do not believe it possible to deny the anticompetitive tendencies I have mentioned.

C

We must also ask whether, despite their anticompetitive tendencies, these restrictions might be justified by other procompetitive tendencies or redeeming virtues. *See* 7 Areeda, ¶ 1504, at 377–383. This is a closer question — at least in theory. The Dental Association argues that the three relevant restrictions are inextricably tied to a legitimate Association effort to restrict false or misleading advertising. The Association, the argument goes, had to prevent dentists from engaging in the kind of truthful, nondeceptive advertising that it banned in order effectively to stop dentists from making unverifiable claims about price or service quality, which claims would mislead the consumer.

The problem with this or any similar argument is an empirical one. Notwithstanding its theoretical plausibility, the record does not bear out such a claim.

In the usual Sherman Act § 1 case, the defendant bears the burden of establishing a procompetitive justification. . . . And the Court of Appeals was correct when it concluded that no such justification had been established here.

D

I shall assume that the Commission must prove one additional circumstance, namely, that the Association's restraints would likely have made a real difference in the marketplace. *See* 7 Areeda, ¶ 1503, at 376–377. The Commission, disagreeing with the ALJ on this single point, found that the Association did possess enough market power to make a difference. In at least one region of California, the mid-Peninsula, its members accounted for more than 90% of the marketplace; on average they accounted for 75%. In addition, entry by new dentists into the marketplace is fairly difficult. Dental education is expensive . . . as is opening a new dentistry office. . . . And Dental Association members believe membership in the Association is important, valuable, and recognized as such by the public. . . .

These facts, in the Court of Appeals' view, were sufficient to show "enough market power to harm competition through [the Association's] standard setting in the area of advertising." . . . And that conclusion is correct. Restrictions on advertising price discounts in Palo Alto may make a difference because potential patients may not respond readily to discount advertising by the handful (10%) of dentists who are not members of the Association. And that fact, in turn, means that the remaining 90% will prove less likely to engage in price competition. Facts such as these have previously led this Court to find market power — unless the defendant has overcome the showing with strong contrary evidence. . . . I can find no reason for departing from that precedent here.

II

In the Court's view, the legal analysis conducted by the Court of Appeals was insufficient, and the Court remands the case for a more thorough application of the rule of reason. But in what way did the Court of Appeals fail? I find the Court's answers to this question unsatisfactory — when one divides the overall Sherman Act question into its traditional component parts and adheres to traditional judicial practice for allocating the burdens of persuasion in an antitrust case.

Did the Court of Appeals misconceive the anticompetitive tendencies of the restrictions? After all, the object of the rule of reason is to separate those restraints that "may suppress or even destroy competition" from those that "merely regulat[e] and perhaps thereby promot[e] competition." *Board of Trade of Chicago v. United States*, 246 U.S. 231, 238 (1918). The majority says that the Association's "advertising restrictions might plausibly be thought to have a net procompetitive effect, or possibly no effect at all on competition." . . . It adds that

> "advertising restrictions arguably protecting patients from misleading or irrelevant advertising call for more than cursory treatment as obviously comparable to classic horizontal agreements to limit output or price competition." . . .

> And it criticizes the Court of Appeals for failing to recognize that "the restrictions at issue here are very far from a total ban on price or discount advertising" and that "the particular restrictions on professional advertising could have different effects from those 'normally' found in the commercial world, even to the point of promoting competition . . . "

The problem with these statements is that the Court of Appeals did consider the relevant differences. It rejected the legal "treatment" customarily applied "to classic horizontal agreements to limit output or price competition" — i.e., the FTC's (alternative) *per se* approach. . . . It did so because the Association's "policies do not, on their face, ban truthful nondeceptive ads"; instead, they "have been enforced in a way that restricts truthful advertising." . . . It added that "[t]he value of restricting false advertising . . . counsels some caution in attacking rules that purport to do so but merely sweep too broadly." . . .

Did the Court of Appeals misunderstand the nature of an anticompetitive effect? The Court says:

> "If quality advertising actually induces some patients to obtain more care than they would in its absence, then restricting such advertising would reduce the demand for dental services, not the supply; and . . . the producers' supply . . . is normally relevant in determining whether

a . . . limitation has the anticompetitive effect of artificially raising prices. . . . "

But if the Court means this statement as an argument against the anticompetitive tendencies that flow from an agreement not to advertise service quality, I believe it is the majority, and not the Court of Appeals, that is mistaken. An agreement not to advertise, say, "gentle care" is anticompetitive because it imposes an artificial barrier against each dentist's independent decision to advertise gentle care. That barrier, in turn, tends to inhibit those dentists who want to supply gentle care from getting together with those customers who want to buy gentle care. *See* P. Areeda & H. Hovenkamp, Antitrust Law ¶ 1505, p. 404 (Supp. 1998). There is adequate reason to believe that tendency present in this case. . . .

Did the Court of Appeals inadequately consider possible procompetitive justifications? The Court seems to think so, for it says:

"[T]he [Association's] rule appears to reflect the prediction that any costs to competition associated with the elimination of across-the-board advertising will be outweighed by gains to consumer information (and hence competition) created by discount advertising that is exact, accurate, and more easily verifiable (at least by regulators)." . . .

That may or may not be an accurate assessment of the Association's motives in adopting its rule, but it is of limited relevance. *Cf. Chicago Board of Trade, supra,* at 238. The basic question is whether this, or some other, theoretically redeeming virtue in fact offsets the restrictions' anticompetitive effects in this case. Both court and Commission adequately answered that question.

The Commission found that the defendant did not make the necessary showing that a redeeming virtue existed in practice. . . . The Court of Appeals, asking whether the rules, as enforced, "augment[ed] competition and increase[d] market efficiency," found the Commission's conclusion supported by substantial evidence. . . . That is why the court said that "the record provides no evidence that the rule has in fact led to increased disclosure and transparency of dental pricing" — which is to say that the record provides no evidence that the effects, though anticompetitive, are nonetheless redeemed or justified. . . .

The majority correctly points out that "petitioner alone would have had the incentive to introduce such evidence" of procompetitive justification. . . . But despite this incentive, petitioner's brief in this Court offers nothing concrete to counter the Commission's conclusion that the record does not support the claim of justification. Petitioner's failure to produce such evidence itself "explain[s] why [the lower court] gave no weight to the . . . suggestion that restricting difficult-to-verify claims about quality or patient comfort would have a procompetitive effect by preventing misleading or false claims that distort the market." . . .

With respect to the restraint on advertising across-the-board discounts, the majority summarizes its concerns as follows: "Assuming that the record in fact supports the conclusion that the [Association's] disclosure rules essentially bar advertisement of [such] discounts, it does not obviously follow that such a ban would have a net anticompetitive effect here." . . . I accept, rather than assume, the premise: The FTC found that the disclosure rules did bar advertisement of across-the-board discounts, and that finding is supported by substantial evidence. . . . And I accept as literally true the conclusion that the Court says follows from that premise, namely, that "net anticompetitive effects" do not "obviously" follow from that premise. But obviousness is not the point. With respect to any of the three restraints found by the Commission, whether "net anticompetitive effects" follow is a matter of how the Commission, and, here, the Court of Appeals, have answered the questions I laid out at the beginning. . . . Has the Commission shown that the restriction has anticompetitive tendencies? It has. Has the Association nonetheless shown offsetting virtues? It has not. Has the Commission shown market power sufficient for it to believe that the restrictions will likely make a real world difference? It has.

The upshot, in my view, is that the Court of Appeals, applying ordinary antitrust principles, reached an unexceptional conclusion. It is the same legal conclusion that this Court itself reached in *Indiana Federation* — a much closer case than this one. There the Court found that an agreement by dentists not to submit dental X rays to insurers violated the rule of reason. The anticompetitive tendency of that agreement was to reduce competition among dentists in respect to their willingness to submit X rays to insurers . . . — a matter in respect to which consumers are relatively indifferent, as compared to advertising of price discounts and service quality, the matters at issue here. . . . The redeeming virtue in *Indiana Federation* was the alleged undesirability of having insurers consider a range of matters when deciding whether treatment was justified — a virtue no less plausible, and no less proved, than the virtue offered here. The "power" of the dentists to enforce their agreement was no greater than that at issue here (control of 75% to 90% of the relevant markets). . . . It is difficult to see how the two cases can be reconciled.

I would note that the form of analysis I have followed is not rigid; it admits of some variation according to the circumstances. The important point, however, is that its allocation of the burdens of persuasion reflects a gradual evolution within the courts over a period of many years. That evolution represents an effort carefully to blend the procompetitive objectives of the law of antitrust with administrative necessity. It represents a considerable advance, both from the days when the Commission had to present and/or refute every possible fact and theory, and from antitrust theories so abbreviated as to prevent proper analysis. The former prevented cases from ever reaching a conclusion . . . and the latter called forth the criticism that the "Government always wins," *United States v. Von's Grocery Co.*, 384 U.S. 270, 301 (1966) (Stewart, J., dissenting). I hope that this case does not represent an abandonment of that basic, and important, form of analysis.

For these reasons, I respectfully dissent from Part III of the Court's opinion.

NOTES AND QUESTIONS

1. How would you describe "a sliding scale" analysis discussed both in the majority and dissenting opinions? Is the "quick look" analysis now no longer permissible in antitrust?

The District of Columbia Court of Appeals discussed the "sliding scale" analysis in *Polygram Holding, Inc. v. FTC*, 416 F.3d 29 (D.C. Cir. 2005). The Court of

Appeals affirmed a finding of violation of Section 1 of the Sherman Act in an agreement between Polygram Holding and Warner Communications to suspend advertising and discounting of two earlier Three Tenor Albums, issued by these companies independently, to ensure the commercial success of their joint project to create an album for the third concert by the Three Tenors (José, Carreras, Plácido Domingo, and Luciano Pavarotti) at the July 1998 World Soccer Cup. Before this joint venture, Polygram distributed an earlier album of the Three Tenors Concert at the 1990 World Soccer Cup. Warner Communications distributed the 1994 concert. The companies publicly renounced their suspension agreement, but privately agreed to adhere to it. The most important of Polygram's four objections was that the Commission was required to show that the contested agreement actually harmed competition before it could require Polygram to provide a procompetitive justification for its conduct. *Id.* at 33.

The Court of Appeals indicated that the Supreme Court had moved away from a dichotomous approach toward detecting conduct violative of Section 1 of the Sherman Act. Instead of categorizing conduct as *per se* unlawful, or subject to a full-blown rule of reason analysis, the inquiry in each case is tailored to the nature of contested conduct. *Id.* at 34. In order to make the determination whether a restraint was unlawful, "a court must make 'an enquiry meet for the case, looking to the circumstances, details, and logic of [the] restraint.'" *Id.* at 35 (quoting *California Dental Assn. v. FTC*, 526 U.S. 756, 781 (1999)). "The object is to see whether the experience of the market has been so clear, or necessarily will be, that a confident conclusion about the principle tendency of a restriction will follow from a quick (or at least quicker) look, in place of a more sedulous one." *Id.*

The Court of Appeals approved the FTC's approach to review of restraints of trade under Section 1 of the Sherman Act. If, based on the economic knowledge and market experience, a restraint of trade is obviously likely to impair competition, "the restraint is presumed unlawful and, in order to avoid liability, the defendant must either identify some reason the restraint is unlikely to harm consumers or identify some competitive benefit that plausibly offsets the apparent or anticipated harm." *Id.* at 36 (citing *NCAA v. Board of Regents*, 468 U.S. 85, 110 (1984) (holding that "a naked restraint on price and output requires some competitive justification even in the absence of a detailed market analysis")). Despite using the term "inherently suspect" to describe restraints of trade likely harmful to consumers, the rebuttable presumption of market impairment is based on the resemblance of the contested conduct to conduct already determined to harm consumers. *Id.* at 37. A presumption of competition impairment or any similar generalization is possible in situations where rule of reason decisions have reached an identical conclusion with respect to the contested conduct. *Id.* (Citing *California Dental Assn. v. FTC*, 526 U.S. 756, 781 (1999).)

The court found that the agreement between Polygram and Warner in this case was a good candidate for the rebuttable presumption of competition impairment. A joint venture agreement restricting advertising and marketing of products outside the joint venture in the eyes of the court was very like a naked restraint of price traditionally treated as *per se* unlawful. *Id.* at 37. Thus, according to the Commission approach ratified by the court, Polygram had to proffer a procompetitive justification for the arrangement. The court rejected Polygram's assertion that the "restrictions on discounting and advertising enhanced the long-term profitability of all three concert albums and promoted the 'Three Tenors' brand." *Id.* Polygram argued that the restraints would take care of the potential free riding by each joint venturer on the venture's advertising and marketing of the third album to sell earlier Three Tenor albums. *Id.* The court held that profitability of a joint venture was not a sufficient justification, especially when the restraint pertained to products outside of the joint venture. Such a restraint was more like a *per se* illegal naked restraint on pricing. *Id.* at 38. Examples of acceptable justifications included measures "increasing output, creating operating efficiencies, making a new product available, enhancing service or quality, and widening consumer choice." *Id.* (Quoting *Law v. NCAA*, 134 F.3d 1010, 1023 (10th Cir. 1998).)

2.   On remand, the Ninth Circuit determined that the Federal Trade Commission's challenge to the advertising restrictions of the *California Dental Association* must be dismissed. *California Dental Ass'n v. FTC*, 224 F.3d 942 (9th Cir. 2000). On the continuum of rule-of-reason analysis from abbreviated to full-blown, the court's level of inquiry was closer to full-blown. The court held that the FTC failed to prove that the restrictions on advertising had a net anticompetitive effect. Although the court thought the advertising restrictions had anticompetitive effects, the procompetitive justifications of the restrictions outweighed the anticompetitive effects and therefore, no antitrust violation could be sustained.

3.   The Court holds in *California Dental* that the FTC has jurisdiction over this nonprofit association because "substantial benefits" are conferred on its for-profit members, such as "advantageous insurance and preferential financing arrangements" and because the association engages in lobbying, litigation, and public relations activities as marketing for the interest of its members. Because the association went beyond "professional education," the Court found FTC jurisdiction, when a substantial part of defendant's total activities "engender a pecuniary benefit to its members." On the applicability of antitrust law to non-profit entities, see Srikanth Srinivasan, *Note, College Financial Aid and Antitrust: Applying the Sherman Act to Collaborative Nonprofit Activity*, 46 STAN. L. REV. 919 (1994); Einer Richard Elhauge, *The Scope of Antitrust Process*, 104 HARV. L. REV. 667, 739–43 (1991); *Note, Antitrust and Nonprofit Entities*, 94 HARV. L. REV. 802 (1981).

4.   On the narrow range for the application of the quick look analysis, see Stephen Calkins, *California Dental Association: Not a Quick Look But Not the Full Monty*, 67 ANTITRUST L.J. 495 (2000); Timothy J. Muris, California Dental Assoc. v. FTC: *The Revenge of Footnote 17*, 8 SUP. CT. ECON. REV. 265 (2000).

5.   The majority in *California Dental* cited the *Brown University* case where the Third Circuit required a full rule-of-reason analysis before the Ivy League financial aid agreements could be considered illegal. Eight Ivy League colleges and MIT formed an "Ivy Overlap Group" agreement that effectively established the price at which each would offer needy students (each of who had applied to more than one Ivy League school) financial assistance. The district court found against the universities. In requiring a more extensive rule of reason consideration, the Third Circuit signaled the potential meritorious justification that such an agreement "promoted the social ideal of equality of educational access and opportunity." *United States v. Brown University*, 5 F.3d 658 (3d Cir. 1993). Are these noneco-

nomic goals expressed by the Third Circuit in tension with the analysis set forth by the Supreme Court in *Professional Engineers*? Recall Justice Stevens admonition in *Professional Engineers*: "[T]he purpose of the analysis is to form a judgment about the competitive significance of the restrain; it is not to decide whether a policy favoring competition is in the public interest, or in the interest of the members of the industry." at 692. The case was settled by the parties after the remand to the district court. According to the majority in *Professional Engineers*, to weigh the public interest would be beyond the Court's discretion. The judicial inquiry into the competitive significance was limited to an economic analysis of the challenged agreement's competitive impact. In short, the Sherman Act does not permit competitors to agree on one form of competition over another. *See also Reiter v. Sonotone Corp.*, 442 U.S. 330, 344–345 (1979).

6. After *NCAA* and *California Dental*, is the per se rule of illegality dead, or has its scope of application merely shrunk? Is it still accurate to say that per se standards apply in horizontal price fixing and market division cases, but that in most other areas of antitrust law, plaintiff's counsel would be well advised to prepare the case under the rule of reason, and thus to produce evidence of actual anticompetitive effects? *See Craftsmen Limousine, Inc. v. Ford Motor Co.*, 363 F.3d 761 (8th Cir. 2004) (where a $5.9 million group boycott award was reversed when the district court applied a per se test, but the Eighth Circuit held that the rule of reason should have been applied); *International Healthcare Management v. Hawaii Coalition for Health*, 332 F.3d 600 (9th Cir. 2003) (rejecting a per se approach when physician and consumers attempt to influence managed health care plans). Even so, does the evolution of § 1 cases suggest that defendants cannot advance the defenses that the price set is reasonable or that competition in a particular market is unsafe or ruinous?

TEXACO, INC. v. DAGHER
547 U.S. 1 (2006)

JUSTICE THOMAS delivered the opinion of the Court.

From 1998 until 2002, petitioners Texaco Inc. and Shell Oil Co. collaborated in a joint venture, Equilon Enterprises, to refine and sell gasoline in the western United States under the original Texaco and Shell Oil brand names. Respondents, a class of Texaco and Shell Oil service station owners, allege that petitioners engaged in unlawful price fixing when Equilon set a single price for both Texaco and Shell Oil brand gasoline. We granted certiorari to determine whether it is *per se* illegal under § 1 of the Sherman Act, 15 U.S.C. § 1, for a lawful, economically integrated joint venture to set the prices at which the joint venture sells its products. We conclude that it is not, and accordingly we reverse the contrary judgment of the Court of Appeals.

I

Historically, Texaco and Shell Oil have competed with one another in the national and international oil and gasoline markets. Their business activities include refining crude oil into gasoline, as well as marketing gasoline to downstream purchasers, such as the service stations represented in respondents' class action.

In 1998, Texaco and Shell Oil formed a joint venture, Equilon, to consolidate their operations in the western United States, thereby ending competition between the two companies in the domestic refining and marketing of gasoline. Under the joint venture agreement, Texaco and Shell Oil agreed to pool their resources and share the risks of and profits from Equilon's activities. Equilon's board of directors would comprise representatives of Texaco and Shell Oil, and Equilon gasoline would be sold to downstream purchasers under the original Texaco and Shell Oil brand names. The formation of Equilon was approved by consent decree, subject to certain divestments and other modifications, by the Federal Trade Commission, see *In re Shell Oil Co.*, 125 F.T.C. 769 (1998), as well as by the state attorneys general of California, Hawaii, Oregon, and Washington. Notably, the decrees imposed no restrictions on the pricing of Equilon gasoline.

After the joint venture began to operate, respondents brought suit in district court, alleging that, by unifying gasoline prices under the two brands, petitioners had violated the *per se* rule against price fixing that this Court has long recognized under § 1 of the Sherman Act. *See, e.g., Catalano, Inc. v. Target Sales, Inc.*, 446 U.S. 643, 647 (1980) *(per curiam)*. The District Court awarded summary judgment to Texaco and Shell Oil. It determined that the rule of reason, rather than a *per se* rule or the quick look doctrine, governs respondents' claim, and that, by eschewing rule of reason analysis, respondents had failed to raise a triable issue of fact. The Ninth Circuit reversed, characterizing petitioners' position as a request for an "exception to the *per se* prohibition on price fixing," and rejecting that request. *Dagher v. Saudi Refining, Inc.*, 369 F.3d 1108, 1116 (2004). We consolidated Texaco's and Shell Oil's separate petitions and granted certiorari to determine the extent to which the *per se* rule against price fixing applies to an important and increasingly popular form of business organization, the joint venture.

II

Section 1 of the Sherman Act prohibits "[e]very contract, combination in the form of trust or otherwise, or conspiracy, in restraint of trade or commerce among the several States." 15 U.S.C. § 1. This Court has not taken a literal approach to this language, however. *See, e.g., State Oil Co. v. Khan*, 522 U.S. 3, 10 (1997) ("[T]his Court has long recognized that Congress intended to outlaw only *unreasonable* restraints" (emphasis added)). Instead, this Court presumptively applies rule of reason analysis, under which antitrust plaintiffs must demonstrate that a particular contract or combination is in fact unreasonable and anticompetitive before it will be found unlawful. *Per se* liability is reserved for only those agreements that are "so plainly anticompetitive that no elaborate study of the industry is needed to establish their illegality." *National Soc. of Professional Engineers v. United States*, 435 U.S. 679, 692 (1978). Accordingly, "we have expressed reluctance to adopt *per se* rules . . . 'where the economic impact of certain practices is not immediately obvious.'" *State Oil, supra*, at 10 (quoting *FTC v. Indiana Federation of Dentists*, 476 U.S. 447, 458–459 (1986)).

Price-fixing agreements between two or more competitors, otherwise known as horizontal price-fixing agreements, fall into the category of arrangements that are *per se* unlawful. *See, e.g., Catalano, supra*, at 647. These cases do not present such an agreement, however, because Texaco and Shell Oil did not compete with one another in the relevant market — namely, the sale of gasoline to service stations in the western United States — but instead participated in that market jointly through their investments. . . . [24] In other words, the pricing policy challenged here amounts to little more than price setting by a single entity — albeit within the context of a joint venture — and not a pricing agreement between competing entities with respect to their competing products. Throughout Equilon's existence, Texaco and Shell Oil shared in the profits of Equilon's activities in their role as investors, not competitors. When "persons who would otherwise be competitors pool their capital and share the risks of loss as well as the opportunities for profit . . . such joint ventures [are] regarded as a single firm competing with other sellers in the market." *Arizona v. Maricopa County Medical Soc.*, 457 U.S. 332, 356 (1982). As such, though Equilon's pricing policy may be price fixing in a literal sense, it is not price fixing in the antitrust sense. See *Broadcast Music, Inc. v. Columbia Broadcasting System, Inc.*, 441 U.S. 1, 9 (1979) ("When two partners set the price of their goods or services they are literally 'price fixing,' but they are not *per se* in violation of the Sherman Act").

This conclusion is confirmed by respondents' apparent concession that there would be no *per se* liability had Equilon simply chosen to sell its gasoline under a single brand. We see no reason to treat Equilon differently just because it chose to sell gasoline under two distinct brands at a single price. As a single entity, a joint venture, like any other firm, must have the discretion to determine the prices of the products that it sells, including the discretion to sell a product under two different brands at a single, unified price. If Equilon's price unification policy is anticompetitive, then respondents should have challenged it pursuant to the rule of reason.[25] But it would be inconsistent with this Court's antitrust precedents to condemn the internal pricing decisions of a legitimate joint venture as *per se* unlawful.[26]

The court below reached the opposite conclusion by invoking the ancillary

---

[24] [FN 1] We presume for purposes of these cases that Equilon is a lawful joint venture. Its formation has been approved by federal and state regulators, and there is no contention here that it is a sham. As the court below noted: "There is a voluminous record documenting the economic justifications for creating the joint ventures. [T]he defendants concluded that numerous synergies and cost efficiencies would result" by creating Equilon as well as a parallel venture, Motiva Enterprises, in the eastern United States, and "that nationwide there would be up to $800 million in cost savings annually." 369 F.3d 1108, 1111 (C.A.9 2004). Had respondents challenged Equilon itself, they would have been required to show that its creation was anticompetitive under the rule of reason. See *Copperweld Corp. v. Independence Tube Corp.*, 467 U.S. 752, 768 (1984).

[25] [FN 2] Respondents have not put forth a rule of reason claim. 369 F.3d at 1113. Accordingly, we need not address petitioners' alternative argument that § 1 of the Sherman Act is inapplicable to joint ventures.

[26] [FN 3] Respondents alternatively contend that petitioners should be held liable under the quick look doctrine. To be sure, we have applied the quick look doctrine to business activities that are so plainly anticompetitive that courts need undertake only a cursory examination before imposing antitrust liability. See *California Dental Assn. v. FTC*, 526 U.S. 756, 770 (1999). But for the same reasons that *per se* liability is unwarranted here, we conclude that petitioners cannot be held liable under the quick look doctrine.

restraints doctrine. 369 F.3d, at 1118–1124. That doctrine governs the validity of restrictions imposed by a legitimate business collaboration, such as a business association or joint venture, on nonventure activities. *See, e.g., National Collegiate Athletic Assn. v. Board of Regents of Univ. of Okla.*, 468 U.S. 85, 113–115 (1984); *Citizen Publishing Co. v. United States*, 394 U.S. 131, 135–136 (1969). Under the doctrine, courts must determine whether the nonventure restriction is a naked restraint on trade, and thus invalid, or one that is ancillary to the legitimate and competitive purposes of the business association, and thus valid. We agree with petitioners that the ancillary restraints doctrine has no application here, where the business practice being challenged involves the core activity of the joint venture itself — namely, the pricing of the very goods produced and sold by Equilon. And even if we were to invoke the doctrine in these cases, Equilon's pricing policy is clearly ancillary to the sale of its own products. Judge Fernandez, dissenting from the ruling of the court below, put it well:

"In this case, nothing more radical is afoot than the fact that an entity, which now owns all of the production, transportation, research, storage, sales and distribution facilities for engaging in the gasoline business, also prices its own products. It decided to price them the same, as any other entity could. What could be more integral to the running of a business than setting a price for its goods and services?" 369 F.3d at 1127.

See also Broadcast Music, supra, at 23 ("Joint ventures and other cooperative arrangements are . . . not usually unlawful, at least not as price-fixing schemes, where the agreement on price is necessary to market the product at all").

*   *   *

Because the pricing decisions of a legitimate joint venture do not fall within the narrow category of activity that is *per se* unlawful under § 1 of the Sherman Act, respondents' antitrust claim cannot prevail. Accordingly, the judgment of the Court of Appeals is reversed.

NOTES AND QUESTIONS

1. The question presented in *Dagher* is whether a joint venture, lawful when created, may enter agreements that set the price of the product or whether such agreements on price are per se unlawful? Should it matter that the joint venture unified downstream production and manufacturing functions and that Equilon was a "legitimate," efficiency enhancing joint venture? Consider also the finding that Texaco and Shell ended competition between themselves in refining and retail sale of gasoline in the western United States after they entered the joint venture. If this is true, did the agreements on price eliminate competition? Is the Ninth Circuit's holding consistent with *BMI?*

2. When two firms lawfully merge, the resulting entity has the ability to lawfully set price. Is that what happened here, functionally, with the downstream operations? What arguments to the contrary can you make?

3. Regarding the ancillary restraint doctrine, does it matter that the constraints in the joint venture were to its own conduct inside the venture, not that of conduct outside the joint venture?

4.   Should it matter to the legality of the venture's pricing conduct how much the individual members contributed proportionally to the final product? If the individual member's input was small compared to the total output — the retail product — would the antitrust law permit the members to set the price of the finished product? Does such a proportionality examination tell us how much competition was eliminated relevant to the finished product? *See* HERBERT HOVENKAMP ¶ 2132 (3d ed. 2012).

PROBLEM 4.2

Bank credit cards, such as VISA and MasterCard, are issued by individual banks, and each bank ordinarily sets the terms of its own card: user annual fees, interest rates, and merchant fees. Suppose that all the banks that issue VISA cards agree with each other that (1) they will charge their individual card holders a $15.00 annual fee for card membership; (2) they will charge individual card holders an interest rate of 18% annually on unpaid charges; (3) they will charge merchants who accept the VISA card a fee of 1.5% of each transaction in which the card is used; (4) they will exchange with each other the names of people who are in substantial default on their VISA payments; and (5) they will not issue a VISA card to someone who has lost a VISA card issued by another bank because of nonpayment.

Which of these agreements would receive per se treatment? Which would be analyzed under the rule of reason? What would be the consequences of each bank's determining for itself what merchant transaction fee to charge? Suppose that a merchant were willing to accept VISA if the transaction fee were 1.5%, but not if it were higher. It would then have to call the issuing bank each time a potential customer presented a VISA card to see what its transaction fee was. Should this fact be sufficient to justify rule of reason treatment for agreement (3)? Should it matter that VISA transactions collectively account for 55% of all bank credit card transactions? That VISA transactions account for only.05% of all transactions, including cash and check transactions?

On agreement (3), see *National Bancard Corp. v. VISA U.S.A., Inc.*, 779 F.2d 592 (11th Cir. 1986); Baxter, *Bank Interchange of Transactional Paper: Legal and Economic Perspectives*, 26 J.L. & ECON. 541, 572–582 (1983).

PROBLEM 4.3

Each year the top 10 most elite and selective colleges get together through their financial aid officers to determine financial aid awards for those applicants who have been accepted by more than one of the schools in this elite group. Each year the schools agree to offer the same financial aid package to each applicant who had applied and was accepted.

Does the agreement violate Section 1? Would the answer change if at this yearly meeting the colleges also set, either explicitly or implicitly, the tuition at the respective schools? *See United States v. Brown Univ.*, 5 F.3d 658 (3d Cir. 1993).

Consider whether it violates Section 1 if certain colleges decide not to disclose to Barrons or any other publisher of college guidebooks the yearly admission data on each school, which could result in changes in the ranking of the individual schools. Does it matter to the antitrust conclusion if all the colleges that entered into these agreements are not-for-profit corporations? *Compare Hospital Corp. of Am. v. FTC*, in Chapter 7, *infra, and United States v. Carilion Health Sys.*, 707 F. Supp. 840 (W.D. Va.), *aff'd*, 892 F.2d 1042 (4th Cir. 1989).

PROBLEM 4.4

Troubled by escalating costs of recruiting law students for law firm positions, several law firms in San Francisco, Atlanta, Chicago, New York, and Los Angeles get together yearly to establish guidelines and rules that limit the amount of money law students can spend during recruiting trips to the participating law firms. Such guidelines include the requirements that students can only fly economy-class on airlines and that they take shuttle buses instead of taxis to and from the airports. Does the agreement that sets these guidelines and requirements violate Section 1? Who would have standing and antitrust injury to bring the antitrust suit? What if these same law firms arrange for all the airline tickets and hotel rooms for interviewing students through a travel agent shared by the firms?

PROBLEM 4.5

The City of Cosmos contains nine physicians practicing in the field of internal medicine (internists); they all have independent practices. A new machine called the Diagnition was invented, which scans the bodies of people with certain symptoms, and greatly aids internists in diagnosing what is wrong. Several of the Cosmos internists would like to own a Diagnition, but these machines are extremely expensive to purchase and to operate because they require a specialized technician, and a single internist would probably use it only three or four times a month. One day, six of the internists happen to meet at a local athletic club and decide to invest jointly in a Diagnition, share the cost of the technician's salary, and share the rent for an office where it can be located. In reaching their decision, the six physicians agree that they will (1) split the initial cost of the technician's salary on a per use basis; (2) allocate the operating costs and the technician's salary on a per use basis, with each internist initially paying $500 into a central pool each time a patient of that particular internist uses the Diagnition; (3) charge patients $700 for one use of the Diagnition; and (4) permit other internists in Cosmos to prescribe the Diagnition for their patients, but only if they pay $1000 per use. Discuss likely antitrust consequences of each of the four agreements; assume there is adequate federal jurisdiction under the commerce clause.

PROBLEM 4.6

Every year, graduating medical students anxiously await the "Match Day" rite of passage. On Match Day, a computer database matches students to teaching hospitals, where they will spend the next three to eight years completing a medical residency program. Traditionally, residency programs have been considered a continuation of a medical student's classroom education, and their length varies according to the type of specialty the student chooses. The match program is nationally coordinated by the Association of American Medical Colleges. Matches are based on ranked lists submitted by participating hospitals, and both students and hospitals agree in advance that they will accept the match. Residents cannot negotiate the terms of their employment, including salary and the number of hours they will work, which can exceed 100 hours a week. Hospitals maintain salaries at generally uniform levels, but compensation does vary according to the region of the country where the resident works.

Does the program violate Section 1? Does the conclusion change if the residents could not otherwise receive final professional accreditation without completing a residency? Is there an agreement among the hospitals to set salaries? For antitrust purposes, should it matter that the hospitals are teaching hospitals?

Congress passed and the President signed into law on April 10, 2004, legislation that exempts from antitrust coverage the medical school graduate residency matching program, which severely limits the number of hospitals at which new medical school graduates can seek residency. But the new exemptions do not include any agreement by two or more programs from fixing the amount of the stipends or other benefits that the medical residents might receive. The exemption applies to pending cases challenging the "match" program. *See* Section 207 of the Peason Equity Act of 2004. CCH Trade Reg. R. No. 835 (Apr. 2004), codified at 15 U.S.C. § 37(b).

The Act contains two additional and important provisions. First, evidence of participation in a matching program cannot be used "to support any claim or action alleging a violation of the antitrust laws," *Id.* § 37b(b)(2). Second, the Section 207 exemption is inapplicable when two or more graduate medical programs agree "to fix the amount of the stipend or other benefits received by students participating in such programs." *Id.* § 37b(b)(3).

[5]   Most-Favored-Nation (MFN) clauses

Some pricing practices raise antitrust concerns, though clear antitrust rules governing them do not yet exist. Most-favored-nation (MFN) clauses are a case in point. Although they come in different forms, in the most traditional MFN clause a seller agrees to give a lower price (sometimes retroactively) to a customer, if the seller, after the first purchase, sells to another customer at that lower price. Depending on the context, MFN clauses may be considered horizontal restraints or vertical restraints. Jonathan B. Baker, *Vertical Restraints with Horizontal Consequences: Competitive Effects of "Most-Favored-Customer" Clauses*, 64 ANTITRUST L.J. 517 (1996).

If such practices are industrywide, are they more likely to have anticompetitive or procompetitive effects? Do such practices inure to the benefit of the customer? Or do they make price cutting by the seller more expensive? *See* George A. Hay, *Oligopoly, Shared Monopoly, and Antitrust Law*, 67 CORNELL L. REV. 439 (1982). On the one hand, MFN clauses seem to protect consumers by guaranteeing them the lowest available price. On the other hand, MFN clauses are potentially anticompetitive because they may facilitate price coordination or stabilization among rivals. *See* Steven C. Salop & Fiona Scott Morton, *Developing an Administrable MFN Enforcement Policy*, 27 ANTITRUST 15 (2013). If an explicit price-fixing agreement exists, an agreement among the conspirators to all employ MFN clauses could theoretically reduce the risk of cheating on the cartel price because each cartel member would have less ability to target price cuts to its co-conspirators' customers without having to reduce its price to all of its customers. The MFN clause could effectively turn customers into cartel enforcers, as each customer has an incentive to see whether its supplier is charging a lower price to other customers and to report that price discrepancy. Furthermore, MFN clauses may discourage targeted price-cutting because if the seller charges a lower price to some customers, it must offer lower prices to all of its customers subject to MFN clauses.

Most courts to consider MFN provisions have accepted them as a mechanism to keep prices lower. *See Kartell v. Blue Shield of Massachusetts, Inc.*, 749 F.2d 922 (1st Cir. 1984); *Ocean State Physicians Health Plan v. Blue Cross and Blue Shield of Rhode Island*, 883 F.2d 1101 (1st Cir. 1989).

Some other courts, however, have questioned this logic. In *U.S. v. Delta Dental of Rhode Island*, 943 F. Supp. 172 (D.R.I. 1996), the district court denied a motion to dismiss a government challenge to the use of MFN clauses by a dental insurer — Delta Dental — in its contracts with participating dentists. The MFN clause at issue required dentists who accepted fees lower than Delta's to accept the lower fees from Delta as well. The court noted that some prior cases had seemed to validate MFN clauses. *Id.* at 176 (citing *Kartell* and *Ocean State*). But the court distinguished these cases by noting that the effect of the MFN clauses in Delta's contracts was to prevent dentists from participating in lower-cost insurance programs and thus to increase the price of dental services. The court noted that MFN "clauses may '(1) eliminate a dynamic mechanism by which prices are racheted down to the competitive level; (2) reduce [output of medical services]; and (3) prevent the market from rewarding more efficient distribution systems.' Celnicker, *A Competitive Analysis of Most Favored Nations Clauses in Contracts Between Health Care Providers and Insurers*, 69 N.C. L. Rev. 863, 884 (1991)." *Id.* at 182 (quoting *Willamette Dental Group, P.C. v. Oregon Dental Service Corporation*, 882 P.2d 637, 642–43 (Or. Ct. App. 1994)). Following the denial of its motion to dismiss, Delta settled with the government through a consent decree that precluded Delta from enforcing its MFN provisions. *U.S. v. Delta Dental of Rhode Island*, 1997 U.S. Dist. LEXIS 11239, 1997-2 Trade Cases P 71,860 (D.R.I. July 2, 1997).

Several factors may help determine whether the use of MFN provisions will likely have anticompetitive effects. First, are MFN provisions ubiquitous throughout the industry? If MFN clauses are sporadic, they are less likely to have anticompetitive marketwide effects. Second, are the MFN clauses the product of horizontal agreement? In *E.I. du Pont de Nemours & Co. v. F.T.C.*, 729 F.2d 128 (2d Cir. 1984), the Second Circuit declined to condemn the use of MFN provisions (along with other pricing provisions) under Section 5 of the FTC Act because each firm in the market had adopted the challenged practice "independently and unilaterally." *Id.* at 140. Third, does the firm imposing MFN agreements possess market power? For example, in *Delta Dental*, the DOJ alleged that Delta had MFN agreements with approximately 90% of practicing dentists in Rhode Island. W. Stephen Smith, *When Most-Favored Is Disfavored: A Counselor's Guide to MFNs*, 27 Antitrust 10, 11 (2013). Fourth, are there plausible efficiency justifications for the challenged MFN agreement? *See* Jonathan B. Baker & Judith A. Chevalier, *The*

Competitive Consequences of Most-Favored-Nation Provisions, 27 ANTITRUST 20, 20–22 (2013) (noting how MFN clauses can reduce transactions costs and delays in transacting). Finally, how businesses negotiate and implement their MFN provisions can be important. For example, the Second Circuit reversed the district court's grant of a motion to dismiss an antitrust challenge to an alleged conspiracy to fix the price of digital music, in part because of MFN clauses. *Starr v. Sony BMG Music Entertainment*, 592 F.3d 314 (2d Cir. 2010). The court found the defendants' use of MFN clauses particularly troubling as the "defendants attempted to hide their MFNs because they knew they would attract antitrust scrutiny." *Id.* at 324. In their secret communications, they noted that "there are legal/antitrust reasons why it would be bad idea to have MFN clauses in any, or certainly all, of these agreements." *Id.*

Although antitrust agencies generally challenge MFN clauses under the rule of reason, not the per se rule, MFN clauses can play an important part in an overall per se violation. In *U.S. v. Apple, Inc.*, ___ F. Supp. 2d ___, 2013 U.S. Dist. LEXIS 96424, 2013 WL 3454986 (S.D.N.Y. July 10, 2013), publishers of electronic books (ebooks) wanted to increase the price above the $9.99 per e-book that Amazon was charging. Apple wanted to enter the retail market for e-books but not at the $9.99 price point. Apple conspired with the publishers to construct an agency model that nominally gave the publishers the ability to set the resale price of ebooks — while giving Apple a 30% commission on e-book sales — but allowed Apple to set a price cap of $12.99 and $14.99 for bestsellers and electronic versions of higher-priced hardbacks. To prevent Apple from being undersold, in each of its contracts with a publisher, Apple included a most-favored-nation (MFN) clause, which gave Apple the ability to match the lowest retail price listed by any competing seller of e-books. This forced the publishers to impose the agency model on other e-book retailers, including Amazon, because if Amazon sold ebooks at a lower price than Apple then the MFN would force the publishers to charge the same low price through Apple. The arrangement succeeded in increasing the price of ebooks. After the DOJ Antitrust Division brought suit, the publishers all settled with the government. Apple went to trial and was found liable under the per se rule for knowingly participating in and facilitating a horizontal price-fixing conspiracy, including using MFN clauses to protect itself against retail price competition as part of the conspiracy. The court noted "entirely lawful contracts may include an MFN, price caps, or pricing tiers. Lawful distribution arrangements between suppliers and distributors certainly include agency arrangements. . . . That does not, however, make it lawful for a company to use those business practices to effect an unreasonable restraint of trade." *Id.* at *48.

[C]   Proof of Agreement

[1]   Introduction

Section 1 of the Sherman Act requires a "contract, combination or conspiracy" in restraint of trade before a violation can be found. Although the principal basis for a monopolization charge under Section 2 of the Sherman Act is single firm conduct, it is not covered by Section 1. Two or more parties must be engaged in the restraint. The "agreement" requirement raises problems in litigation because the requisite agreement is often difficult to establish. The cases and discussion that follow are concerned with how one proves "agreement."

The antitrust lawyer confronts this problem in both a procedural and evidentiary sense. There must be sufficient evidence of an "agreement" to survive a motion for judgment as a matter of law ("JMOL") and post-trial motions on the sufficiency of the evidence. A motion for JMOL will generally only be granted when "the court finds that a reasonable jury would not have a legally sufficient evidentiary basis to find for the party on that issue." Fed. R. Civ. P. 50(a). Under this rule, courts will construe the proof in a manner most favorable to the party against whom the motion is made.

Agreement in antitrust cases can be demonstrated through circumstantial evidence. Inferences can usually be drawn from conduct evidence about the existence of a common understanding, agreement, or conspiracy. Suffice it to say that the agreement requirement under Section 1 does not require proof of explicit collusion. The agreement can be tacit (silent, unspoken, implied) and still be illegal. Evidence showing that there has been a "meeting of the minds," concerted action, or mutual understanding is sufficient to support an inference of agreement. More than one antitrust lawyer has argued to a jury that "*but for* an agreement this type of joint conduct would not have occurred." Thus the inquiry is largely fact-oriented: from specific behavior indicating a common course of action, an agreement can be drawn inferentially.

Several courts have considered whether evidence of coercion precludes a finding of conspiracy — for example, when one or more co-conspirators act unwillingly, reluctantly, or under duress. The Seventh Circuit said that the combination or conspiracy element of Section 1 is not negated by coercion or reluctance. *MCM Partners, Inc. v. Andrews-Bartlett & Assoc.*, 62 F.3d 967 (7th Cir. 1995). Defendants urged the court to vary the remedy for anticompetitive conduct when coerced defendants are involved, but the court declined, though acknowledging that there was some support for this approach. Said the Seventh Circuit: "[S]o long as defendants knew that they were acquiescing in conduct that was in all likelihood unlawful, we have no difficulty concluding that they thereby joined a combination or conspiracy for which they can be held accountable under [Section] 1." *Id.* at 975.

The cases that follow discuss the standard of proof that is required to establish an "agreement" under Section 1. Concepts such as conscious parallelism, oligopoly pricing, and facilitating devices have emerged as theories under which the "agreement" requirement can be satisfied. These theories attempt to explain the nature of agreements in the context of market structure. The first issue is whether parallel conduct engaged in by competitors with knowledge of each other's actions constitutes an "agreement" in restraint of trade within Section 1.

[2]   Conscious Parallelism and the *Interstate Circuit* Doctrine

INTERSTATE CIRCUIT v. UNITED STATES
306 U.S. 208 (1939)

JUSTICE STONE delivered the opinion of the Court.

[The case is] now before us on findings of the District Court specifically stating that appellants did in fact agree with each other to enter into and carry out the contracts, which the court found to result in unreasonable and therefore unlawful restraints of interstate commerce.

Appellants comprise the two groups of defendants in the District Court. . . . The distributor appellants are engaged in the business of distributing in interstate commerce motion picture films, copyrights on which they own or control, for exhibition in theatres throughout the United States. They distribute about 75 per cent of all first-class feature films exhibited in the United States.

The exhibitor group of appellants consists of Interstate Circuit, Inc., and Texas Consolidated Theatres, Inc., and Hoblitzelle and O'Donnell, who are respectively president and general manager of both and in active charge of their business operations. The two corporations are affiliated with each other and with Paramount Pictures Distributing Co., Inc., one of the distributor appellants.

Interstate operates forty-three first-run and second-run motion picture theatres, located in six Texas cities. It has a complete monopoly of first-run theatres in these cities, except for one in Houston operated by one distributor's Texas agent. In most of these theatres the admission price for adults for the better seats at night is 40 cents or more. Interstate also operates several subsequent-run theatres in each of these cities, twenty-two in all, but in all but Galveston there are other subsequent-run theatres which compete with both its first- and subsequent-run theatres in those cities.

Texas Consolidated operates sixty-six theatres, some first- and some subsequent-run houses, in various cities and towns in the Rio Grande Valley and elsewhere in Texas and in New Mexico. In some of these cities there are no competing theatres, and in six leading cities there are no competing first-run theatres. It has no theatres in the six Texas cities in which Interstate operates. That Interstate and Texas Consolidated dominate the motion picture business in the cities where their theatres are located is indicated by the fact that at the time of the contracts in question Interstate and Consolidated each contributed more than 74 per cent of all the license fees paid by the motion picture theatres in their respective territories to the distributor appellants.

On July 11, 1934, following a previous communication on the subject to the eight branch managers of the distributor appellants, O'Donnell, the manager of Inter-state and Consolidated, sent to each of them a letter on the letterhead of Inter-state, each letter naming all of them as addressees, in which he asked compliance with two demands as a condition of Interstate's continued exhibition of the distributors' films in its "A" or first-run theatres at a night admission of 40 cents or more. One demand was that the distributors "agree that in selling their product to subsequent runs, that this "A" product will never be exhibited at any time or in any theatre at a smaller admission price than 25 cents for adults in the evening." The other was that "on 'A' pictures which are exhibited at a night admission of 40 cents or more — they shall never be exhibited in conjunction with another feature picture under the so-called policy of double features." The letter added that with respect to the "Rio Grande Valley situation," with which Consolidated alone was concerned, "We must insist that all pictures exhibited in our 'A' theatres at a maximum night admission price of 35 cents must also be restricted to subsequent runs in the Valley at 25 cents."

The admission price customarily charged for preferred seats at night in independently operated subsequent-run theatres in Texas at the time of these letters was less than 25 cents. In seventeen of the eighteen independent theatres of this kind whose operations were described by witnesses the admission price was less than 25 cents. In one only was it 25 cents. In most of them the admission was 15 cents or less. It was also the general practice in those theatres to provide double bills either on certain days of the week or with any feature picture which was weak in drawing power. The distributor appellants had generally provided in their license contracts for a minimum admission price of 10 or 15 cents, and three of them had included provisions restricting double billing. But none was at any time previously subject to contractual compulsion to continue the restrictions. The trial court found that the proposed restrictions constituted an important departure from prior practice.

The local representatives of the distributors, having no authority to enter into the proposed agreements, communicated the proposal to their home offices. Conferences followed between Hoblitzelle and O'Donnell, acting for Interstate and Consolidated, and the representatives of the various distributors. In these conferences each distributor was represented by its local branch manager and by one or more superior officials from outside the state of Texas. In the course of them each distributor agreed with Interstate for the 1934–35 season to impose both the demanded restrictions upon their subsequent-run licensees in the six Texas cities served by Interstate, except Austin and Galveston. While only two of the distributors incorporated the agreement to impose the restrictions in their license contracts with Interstate, the evidence establishes, and it is not denied, that all joined in the agreement, four of them after some delay in negotiating terms other than the restrictions and not now material. These agreements for the restrictions . . . were carried into effect by each of the distributors' imposing them on their subsequent-run licensees in the four Texas cities during the 1934–35 season. One agreement, that of Metro-Goldwyn-Mayer Distributing Corporation, was for three years. The others were renewed in the two following seasons and all were in force when the present suit was begun.

None of the distributors yielded to the demand that subsequent runs in towns in the Rio Grande Valley served by Consolidated should be restricted. One distributor, Paramount, which was affiliated with Consolidated, agreed to impose the restrictions in certain other Texas and New Mexico cities.

. . . .

The trial court drew the inference of agreement from the nature of the proposals made on behalf of Interstate and Consolidated; from the manner in which they were made; from the substantial unanimity of action taken upon them by the distributors; and from the fact that appellants did not call as witnesses any of the superior officials who negotiated the contracts with Interstate or any official who, in the normal course of business, would have had knowledge of the existence or non-existence of such an agreement among the distributors. This conclusion is challenged by appellants because not supported by subsidiary findings or by the evidence. We think this inference of the trial court was rightly drawn from the evidence. In the view we take of the legal effect of the cooperative action of the distributor appellants in carrying into effect the restrictions imposed upon subsequent-run theatres in the four Texas cities and of the legal effect of the separate agreements for the imposition of those restrictions entered into between Interstate and each of the distributors, it is unnecessary to discuss in great detail the evidence concerning this aspect of the case.

The O'Donnell letter named on its face as addressees the eight local representatives of the distributors, and so from the beginning each of the distributors knew that the proposals were under consideration by the others. Each was aware that all were in active competition and that without substantially unanimous action with respect to the restrictions for any given territory there was risk of a substantial loss of the business and good will of the subsequent-run and independent exhibitors, but that with it there was the prospect of increased profits. There was, therefore, strong motive for concerted action, full advantage of which was taken by Interstate and Consolidated in presenting their demands to all in a single document.

There was risk, too, that without agreement diversity of action would follow. Compliance with the proposals involved a radical departure from the previous business practices of the industry and a drastic increase in admission prices of most of the subsequent-run theatres. Acceptance of the proposals was discouraged by at least three of the distributors' local managers. Independent exhibitors met and organized a futile protest which they presented to the representatives of Interstate and Consolidated. . . .

. . . .

. . . Taken together, the circumstances of the case which we have mentioned, when uncontradicted and with no more explanation than the record affords, justify the inference that the distributors acted in concert and in common agreement in imposing the restrictions upon their licensees in the four Texas cities.

This inference was supported and strengthened when the distributors, with like unanimity, failed to tender the testimony, at their command, of any officer or agent of a distributor who knew, or was in a position to know, whether in fact an agreement had been reached among them for concerted action. When the proof supported, as we think it did, the inference of such concert, the burden rested on appellants of going forward with the evidence to explain away or contradict it. They undertook to carry that burden by calling upon local managers of the distributors to testify that they had acted independently of the other distributors, and that they did not have conferences with or reach agreements with the other distributors or their representatives. The failure under the circumstances to call as witnesses those officers who did have authority to act for the distributors and who were in a position to know whether they had acted in pursuance of agreement is itself persuasive that their testimony, if given, would have been unfavorable to appellants. The production of weak evidence when strong is available can lead only to the conclusion that the strong would have been adverse. [Cases cited.]

While the District Court's finding of an agreement of the distributors among themselves is supported by the evidence, we think that in the circumstances of this case such agreement for the imposition of the restrictions upon subsequent-run exhibitors was not a prerequisite to an unlawful conspiracy. It was enough that, knowing that concerted action was contemplated and invited, the distributors gave their adherence to the scheme and participated in it. Each distributor was advised that the others were asked to participate; each knew that cooperation was essential to successful operation of the plan. They knew that the plan, if carried out, would result in a restraint of commerce, which, we will presently point out, was unreasonable within the meaning of the Sherman Act, and knowing it, all participated in the plan. The evidence is persuasive that each distributor early became aware that the others had joined. With that knowledge they renewed the arrangement and carried it into effect for the two successive years.

It is elementary that an unlawful conspiracy may be and often is formed without simultaneous action or agreement on the part of the conspirators. Acceptance by competitors, without previous agreement, of an invitation to participate in a plan, the necessary consequence of which, if carried out, is restraint of interstate commerce, is sufficient to establish an unlawful conspiracy under the Sherman Act. . . .

. . . .

We think the conclusion is unavoidable that the conspiracy and each contract between Interstate and the distributors by which those consequences were effected are violations of the Sherman Act and that the District Court rightly enjoined enforcement and renewal of these agreements, as well as of the conspiracy among the distributors.

Affirmed.

[JUSTICES ROBERTS, MCREYNOLDS, AND BUTLER dissented, arguing that the Court should not have found a conspiracy under the stipulated facts and that these kinds of agreements were not contemplated by earlier courts as conspiracies under the Sherman Act. JUSTICE FRANKFURTER did not participate.]

NOTES AND QUESTIONS

1. *American Tobacco Co. v. United States*, 328 U.S. 781 (1946), held that firms which engaged in monopolization under Section 2 could be enjoined without any proof of an agreement to monopolize. The Court indicated:

No formal agreement is necessary to constitute an unlawful conspiracy. Often crimes are a matter of inference deduced from the acts of the person accused and done in pursuance of a criminal purpose. . . . The essential combination or conspiracy in violation of the Sherman Act may be found in a course of dealing or other circumstances as well as in an exchange of words. . . . Where the circumstances are such as to warrant a jury in finding that the conspirators had a unity of purpose or a common design and understanding or a meeting of minds in an unlawful arrangement, the conclusion that a conspiracy is established is justified.

Id. at 809–810.

In *United States v. Masonite Corp.*, 316 U.S. 265 (1942), the Court said "[i]t was enough that, knowing that concerted action was contemplated and invited, the distributors gave their adherence to the scheme and participated in it. . . . The fixing of prices by one member of a group pursuant to express delegation, acquiescence, or understanding is just as illegal as the fixing of prices by direct, joint action." Further, in *United States v. Paramount Pictures, Inc.*, 334 U.S. 131 (1948), the Court concluded that "it is not necessary to find an express agreement in order to find a conspiracy. It is enough that a concert of action is contemplated and that defendants conformed to the arrangement." *See also United States v. United States Gypsum Co.*, 333 U.S. 364, 394 (1948), where the Court said that "when a group of competitors enters into a series of separate but similar agreements with competitors or others, a strong inference arises that such agreements are the result of concerted action. That inference is strengthened when contemporaneous declarations indicate that supposedly separate actions are part of a common plan."

2. Did the Court in *Interstate Circuit* and its subsequent opinions hold that an agreement is not a prerequisite to a conspiracy charge under Section 1 where there is evidence of conscious parallelism? In other words, will mere evidence of parallel conduct by competitors with knowledge of each other's actions establish a prima facie case in support of an unlawful agreement?

3. Proof of withdrawal from a conspiracy is an effective affirmative defense to a Section 1 claim. To withdraw effectively, one must either report the conspiracy to the proper authorities or clearly communicate an intent to withdraw. *In re Brand Name Prescription Drugs Antitrust Litigation*, 123 F.3d 599, 616 (7th Cir. 1997); *In re TFT-LCD (Flat Panel) Antitrust Litigation*, 820 F. Supp. 2d 1055 (N.D. Cal. 2011). However, withdrawal does not protect the once-conspiring party from liability under other theories or causes of action, such as Section 2 of the Sherman Act. For example, the Seventh Circuit in *In re Brand Name Prescription Drugs Antitrust Litigation* held that the withdrawal of a particular drug manufacturer defendant from a price-fixing activity in the form of specialized discounts to preferred customers did not prevent subsequent liability under Section 2.

4. In *Toys "R" Us v. FTC*, 221 F.3d 928 (7th Cir. 2000), the Seventh Circuit upheld a remedial order by the FTC prohibiting Toys from boycotting warehouse clubs. The FTC found that Toys' "special warehouse club policy" was a boycott because it prevented warehouse clubs from being sold trendy toys by toy manufacturers. Although the evidence showed a series of vertical agreements between Toys and its manufacturers in which each manufacturer agreed to restrict sales to warehouse clubs if all the other manufacturers agreed, the FTC inferred a horizontal agreement under *Interstate Circuit v. U.S.*, 306 U.S. 208 (1939). The remedial order prevented Toys from entering into vertical agreements with its suppliers to limit the supply or refuse sales to discounters.

5. In *Spectators' Communication Network, Inc. v. Colonial Country Club*, 231 F.3d 1005 (5th Cir. 2000), the Fifth Circuit determined that the plaintiff had made an adequate showing of antitrust conspiracy even though one conspirator lacked a direct interest in precluding competition, but may have been enticed or coerced into knowingly curtailing competition by another conspirator who had an anticompetitive motive. In this case, although Anheuser-Busch would have nothing to gain if a competitor were eliminated, "the [Professional Golfers Association] made it worth Anheuser-Busch's while to cooperate" by offering Michelob the opportunity to replace Anheuser-Busch as the official beer of the PGA tournament.

THEATRE ENTERPRISES, INC. v. PARAMOUNT FILM DISTRIBUTING CORP.
346 U.S. 537 (1954)

JUSTICE CLARK delivered the opinion of the Court.

Petitioner brought this suit for treble damages and an injunction under §§ 4 and 16 of the Clayton Act, alleging that respondent motion picture producers and distributors had violated the antitrust laws by conspiring to restrict "first-run" pictures to downtown Baltimore theatres, thus confining its suburban theatre to subsequent runs and unreasonable "clearances." After hearing the evidence a jury returned a general verdict for respondents. The Court of Appeals for the Fourth Circuit affirmed the judgment based on the verdict. We granted certiorari.

Petitioner now urges, as it did in the Court of Appeals, that the trial judge should have directed a verdict in its favor and submitted to the jury only the question of the amount of damages. Alternatively, petitioner claims that the trial judge erred by inadequately instructing the jury as to the scope and effect of the decrees in *United States v. Paramount Pictures, Inc.*, the Government's prior equity suit against respondents. We think both contentions are untenable.

. . . Petitioner owns and operates the Crest Theatre, located in a neighborhood shopping district some six miles from the downtown shopping center in Baltimore, Maryland. The Crest, possessing the most modern improvements and appointments, opened on February 26, 1949. Before and after the opening, petitioner, through its president, repeatedly sought to obtain first-run features for the theatre. Petitioner approached each respondent separately, initially requesting exclusive first-runs, later asking for first-runs on a "day and date" basis. But respondents uniformly rebuffed petitioner's efforts and adhered to an established policy of restricting first-runs in Baltimore to the eight downtown theatres. Admittedly there is no direct evidence of illegal agreement between the respondents and no conspiracy is charged as to the independent exhibitors in Baltimore, who account for 63% of first-run exhibitions. The various respondents advanced much the same reasons for denying petitioner's offers. Among other reasons, they asserted that day-and-date first-runs are normally granted only to noncompeting theatres. Since the Crest is in "substantial competition" with the downtown theatres, a day-and-date arrangement would be economically unfeasible. And even if respondents wished to grant petitioner such a license, no downtown exhibitor would waive his clearance rights over the Crest and agree to a simultaneous showing. As a result, if petitioner were to receive first-runs, the license would have to be an exclusive one. However, an exclusive license would be economically unsound because the Crest is a suburban theatre, located in a small shopping center, and served by limited public transportation facilities; and, with a drawing area of less than one-tenth that of a downtown theatre, it cannot compare with those easily accessible theatres in the power to draw patrons. Hence the downtown theatres offer far greater opportunities for the widespread advertisement and exploitation of newly released features, which is thought necessary to maximize the over-all return from subsequent runs as well as first-runs. The respondents, in the light of these conditions, attacked the guaranteed offers of petitioner, one of which occurred during the trial, as not being made in good faith. Respondents Loew's and Warner refused petitioner an exclusive license because they owned the three downtown theatres receiving their first-run product.

The crucial question is whether respondents' conduct toward petitioner stemmed from independent decision or from an agreement, tacit or express. To be sure, business behavior is admissible circumstantial evidence from which the fact finder may infer agreement. *Interstate Circuit, Inc. v. United States*, 306 U.S. 208 (1939). . . . But this Court has never held that proof of parallel business behavior conclusively establishes agreement or, phrased differently, that such behavior itself constitutes a Sherman Act offense. Circumstantial evidence of consciously parallel behavior may have made heavy inroads into the traditional judicial attitude toward conspiracy; but "conscious parallelism" has not yet read conspiracy out of the Sherman Act entirely. Realizing this, petitioner attempts to bolster its argument for a directed verdict by urging that the conscious unanimity of action by respondents should be "measured against the background and findings in the *Paramount* case." In other words, since the same respondents had conspired in the *Paramount* case to impose a uniform system of runs and clearances without adequate explanation to sustain them as reasonable restraints of trade, use of the same device in the present case should be legally equated to conspiracy. But the *Paramount* decrees, even if admissible, were only prima facie evidence of a conspiracy covering the area and existing during the period there involved. Alone or in conjunction with the other proof of the petitioner, they would form no basis for a directed verdict. Here each of the respondents had denied the existence of any collaboration and in addition had introduced evidence of the local conditions surrounding the Crest operation which, they contended, precluded it from being a successful first-run house. They also attacked the good faith of the guaranteed offers of the petitioner for first-run pictures and attributed uniform action to individual business judgment motivated by the desire for maximum revenue. This evidence, together with other testimony of an explanatory nature, raised fact issues requiring the trial judge to submit the issue of conspiracy to the jury.

Affirmed.[27]

---

[27] [FN *] Justice Black dissented on other grounds. Justice Douglas took no part in the decision.

NOTES AND QUESTIONS

1. What probative evidence supports the inference of agreement in *Interstate Circuit*? Note that the Court inferred collusion from defendants' failure to present evidence. Who has the burden of proof on the issue of an "agreement"? What evidence might defendant introduce to rebut plaintiff's evidence, for example, of common price? When might that burden shift? Can the burden of proving noncollusion be placed on the defendant in a criminal case? *See Patterson v. New York*, 432 U.S. 197 (1977); *Mullaney v. Wilbur*, 421 U.S. 684 (1975); *Barnes v. United States*, 412 U.S. 837 (1973).

2. Do the different procedural issues addressed by the Court in *Interstate Circuit* and *Theatre Enterprises* account for the different results? Does the Court apply one standard when the issue is whether a motion for judgment as a matter of law should have been granted in defendant's favor, and another when the issue is whether there was sufficient evidence to sustain a jury finding of conspiracy?

[3]   Surviving a Motion to Dismiss

BELL ATLANTIC CORP. v. TWOMBLY
550 U.S. 544 (2007)

JUSTICE SOUTER delivered the opinion of the Court.

Liability under § 1 of the Sherman Act, 15 U.S.C. § 1, requires a "contract, combination . . . , or conspiracy, in restraint of trade or commerce." The question in this putative class action is whether a § 1 complaint can survive a motion to dismiss when it alleges that major telecommunications providers engaged in certain parallel conduct unfavorable to competition, absent some factual context suggesting agreement, as distinct from identical, independent action. We hold that such a complaint should be dismissed.

I

. . . .

Respondents William Twombly and Lawrence Marcus (hereinafter plaintiffs) represent a putative class consisting of all "subscribers of local telephone and/or high speed Internet services . . . from February 8, 1996 to present." . . .

The complaint alleges that the [defendants] conspired to restrain trade in two ways, each supposedly inflating charges for local telephone and high-speed Internet services. Plaintiffs say, first, that the [defendants] "engaged in parallel conduct" in their respective service areas to inhibit the growth of upstart [competitive local exchange carriers]. Their actions allegedly included making unfair agreements with the [competitive local exchange carriers] . . . , providing inferior connections to the networks, overcharging, and billing in ways designed to sabotage the [competitive local exchange carriers]' relations with their own customers. . . . .

Second, the complaint charges agreements by the [defendants] to refrain from competing against one another. These are to be inferred from the [defendants]' common failure "meaningfully [to] pursu[e]" "attractive business opportunit[ies]" in contiguous markets where they possessed "substantial competitive advantages." . . .

The complaint couches its ultimate allegations this way:

> "In the absence of any meaningful competition between the [(defendants)] in one another's markets, and in light of the parallel course of conduct that each engaged in to prevent competition from [competitive local exchange carriers] within their respective local telephone and/or high speed internet services markets and the other facts and market circumstances alleged above, Plaintiffs allege upon information and belief that [the (defendants)] have entered into a contract, combination or conspiracy to prevent competitive entry in their respective local telephone and/or high speed internet services markets and have agreed not to compete with one another and otherwise allocated customers and markets to one another.' '
> Id., ¶ 51, App. 27.[28]

The United States District Court for the Southern District of New York dismissed the complaint for failure to state a claim upon which relief can be granted. The District Court acknowledged that "plaintiffs may allege a conspiracy by citing instances of parallel business behavior that suggest an agreement," but emphasized that "while '[c]ircumstantial evidence of consciously parallel behavior may have made heavy inroads into the traditional judicial attitude toward conspiracy[, . . .] "conscious parallelism" has not yet read conspiracy out of the Sherman Act entirely.' " 313 F. Supp. 2d 174, 179 (2003) (quoting Theatre Enterprises, Inc. v. Paramount Film Distributing Corp., 346 U.S. 537, 541 (1954); alterations in original). Thus, the District Court understood that allegations of parallel business conduct, taken alone, do not state a claim under § 1; plaintiffs must allege additional facts that "ten[d] to exclude independent self-interested conduct as an explanation for defendants' parallel behavior." 313 F. Supp. 2d, at 179. . . .

The Court of Appeals for the Second Circuit reversed, holding that the District Court tested the complaint by the wrong standard. It held that "plus factors are not required to be pleaded to permit an antitrust claim based on parallel conduct to survive dismissal." 425 F.3d 99, 114 (2005) (emphasis in original). Although the Court of Appeals took the view that plaintiffs must plead facts that "include conspiracy among the realm of 'plausible' possibilities in order to survive a motion to dismiss," it then said that "to rule that allegations of parallel anticompetitive conduct fail to support a plausible conspiracy claim, a court would have to conclude

---

[28] [FN 2] In setting forth the grounds for § 1 relief, the complaint repeats these allegations in substantially similar language:

> "Beginning at least as early as February 6, 1996, and continuing to the present, the exact dates being unknown to Plaintiffs, Defendants and their co-conspirators engaged in a contract, combination or conspiracy to prevent competitive entry in their respective local telephone and/or high speed internet services markets by, among other things, agreeing not to compete with one another and to stifle attempts by others to compete with them and otherwise allocating customers and markets to one another in violation of Section 1 of the Sherman Act."
> Id., ¶ 64, App. 30–31.

that there is no set of facts that would permit a plaintiff to demonstrate that the particular parallelism asserted was the product of collusion rather than coincidence." *Ibid.*

We granted certiorari to address the proper standard for pleading an antitrust conspiracy through allegations of parallel conduct. . . .

II

A

Because § 1 of the Sherman Act "does not prohibit [all] unreasonable restraints of trade . . . but only restraints effected by a contract, combination, or conspiracy," *Copperweld Corp. v. Independence Tube Corp.*, 467 U.S. 752, 775 (1984), "[t]he crucial question" is whether the challenged anticompetitive conduct "stem[s] from independent decision or from an agreement, tacit or express," *Theatre Enterprises*, 346 U.S., at 540. While a showing of parallel "business behavior is admissible circumstantial evidence from which the fact finder may infer agreement," it falls short of "conclusively establish[ing] agreement or . . . itself constitut[ing] a Sherman Act offense." *Id.*, at 540–541. Even "conscious parallelism," a common reaction of "firms in a concentrated market [that] recogniz[e] their shared economic interests and their interdependence with respect to price and output decisions" is "not in itself unlawful." *Brooke Group Ltd. v. Brown & Williamson Tobacco Corp.*, 509 U.S. 209, 227 (1993); see 6 P. Areeda & H. Hovenkamp, Antitrust Law ¶ 1433a, p. 236 (2d ed. 2003) (hereinafter Areeda & Hovenkamp) ("The courts are nearly unanimous in saying that mere interdependent parallelism does not establish the contract, combination, or conspiracy required by Sherman Act § 1"). . . .

. . . .

Accordingly, we have previously hedged against false inferences from identical behavior at a number of points in the trial sequence. An antitrust conspiracy plaintiff with evidence showing nothing beyond parallel conduct is not entitled to a directed verdict, *see Theatre Enterprises*, *supra*; proof of a § 1 conspiracy must include evidence tending to exclude the possibility of independent action, *see Monsanto Co. v. Spray-Rite Service Corp.*, 465 U.S. 752 (1984); and at the summary judgment stage a § 1 plaintiff's offer of conspiracy evidence must tend to rule out the possibility that the defendants were acting independently, *see Matsushita Elec. Industrial Co. v. Zenith Radio Corp.*, 475 U.S. 574 (1986).

B

This case presents the antecedent question of what a plaintiff must plead in order to state a claim under § 1 of the Sherman Act. Federal Rule of Civil Procedure 8(a)(2) requires only "a short and plain statement of the claim showing that the pleader is entitled to relief," in order to "give the defendant fair notice of what the . . . claim is and the grounds upon which it rests," *Conley v. Gibson*, 355 U.S. 41, 47 (1957). While a complaint attacked by a Rule 12(b)(6) motion to dismiss does not need detailed factual allegations, ibid., a plaintiff's obligation to provide the "grounds" of his "entitle[ment] to relief" requires more than labels and conclusions, and a formulaic recitation of the elements of a cause of action will not do, *see Papasan v. Allain*, 478 U.S. 265, 286 (1986) (on a motion to dismiss, courts "are not bound to accept as true a legal conclusion couched as a factual allegation"). Factual allegations must be enough to raise a right to relief above the speculative level. ("[T]he pleading must contain something more . . . than . . . a statement of facts that merely creates a suspicion [of] a legally cognizable right of action"),[29] on the assumption that all the allegations in the complaint are true (even if doubtful in fact). . . .

In applying these general standards to a § 1 claim, we hold that stating such a claim requires a complaint with enough factual matter (taken as true) to suggest that an agreement was made. Asking for plausible grounds to infer an agreement does not impose a probability requirement at the pleading stage; it simply calls for enough fact to raise a reasonable expectation that discovery will reveal evidence of illegal agreement. And, of course, a well-pleaded complaint may proceed even if it strikes a savvy judge that actual proof of those facts is improbable, and "that a recovery is very remote and unlikely." In identifying facts that are suggestive enough to render a § 1 conspiracy plausible, we have the benefit of the prior rulings and considered views of leading commentators, already quoted, that lawful parallel conduct fails to bespeak unlawful agreement. It makes sense to say, therefore, that an allegation of parallel conduct and a bare assertion of conspiracy will not suffice. Without more, parallel conduct does not suggest conspiracy, and a conclusory allegation of agreement at some unidentified point does not supply facts adequate to show illegality. Hence, when allegations of parallel conduct are set out in order to make a § 1 claim, they must be placed in a context that raises a suggestion of a preceding agreement, not merely parallel conduct that could just as well be independent action.

The need at the pleading stage for allegations plausibly suggesting (not merely consistent with) agreement reflects the threshold requirement of Rule 8(a)(2) that the "plain statement" possess enough heft to "sho[w] that the pleader is entitled to relief." A statement of parallel conduct, even conduct consciously undertaken, needs some setting suggesting the agreement necessary to make out a § 1 claim; without that further circumstance pointing toward a meeting of the minds, an account of a defendant's commercial efforts stays in neutral territory. An allegation of parallel conduct is thus much like a naked assertion of conspiracy in a § 1 complaint: it gets the complaint close to stating a claim, but without some further factual enhance-

---

[29] [FN 3] The dissent greatly oversimplifies matters by suggesting that the Federal Rules somehow dispensed with the pleading of facts altogether. See post, at 1979 (opinion of STEVENS, J.) (pleading standard of Federal Rules "does not require, or even invite, the pleading of facts"). While, for most types of cases, the Federal Rules eliminated the cumbersome requirement that a claimant "set out in detail the facts upon which he bases his claim," Conley v. Gibson, 355 U.S. 41, 47, Rule 8(a)(2) still requires a "showing," rather than a blanket assertion, of entitlement to relief. Without some factual allegation in the complaint, it is hard to see how a claimant could satisfy the requirement of providing not only "fair notice" of the nature of the claim, but also "grounds" on which the claim rests. See 5 Wright & Miller § 1202, at 94, 95 (Rule 8(a) "contemplate[s] the statement of circumstances, occurrences, and events in support of the claim presented" and does not authorize a pleader's "bare averment that he wants relief and is entitled to it").

ment it stops short of the line between possibility and plausibility of "entitle[ment] to relief."

. . . .

Thus, it is one thing to be cautious before dismissing an antitrust complaint in advance of discovery, cf. *Poller v. Columbia Broadcasting System, Inc.*, 368 U.S. 464, 473 (1962), but quite another to forget that proceeding to antitrust discovery can be expensive. As we indicated over 20 years ago in *Associated Gen. Contractors of Cal., Inc. v. Carpenters*, 459 U.S. 519, 528, n. 17 (1983), "a district court must retain the power to insist upon some specificity in pleading before allowing a potentially massive factual controversy to proceed." . . .

It is no answer to say that a claim just shy of a plausible entitlement to relief can, if groundless, be weeded out early in the discovery process through "careful case management," post at 1975, given the common lament that the success of judicial supervision in checking discovery abuse has been on the modest side. . . . And it is self-evident that the problem of discovery abuse cannot be solved by "careful scrutiny of evidence at the summary judgment stage," much less "lucid instructions to juries," post, at 1975; the threat of discovery expense will push cost-conscious defendants to settle even anemic cases before reaching those proceedings. Probably, then, it is only by taking care to require allegations that reach the level suggesting conspiracy that we can hope to avoid the potentially enormous expense of discovery in cases with no " 'reasonably founded hope that the [discovery] process will reveal relevant evidence' " to support a § 1 claim.

. . . .

III

When we look for plausibility in this complaint, we agree with the District Court that plaintiffs' claim of conspiracy in restraint of trade comes up short. To begin with, the complaint leaves no doubt that plaintiffs rest their § 1 claim on descriptions of parallel conduct and not on any independent allegation of actual agreement among the [defendants]. . . . Although in form a few stray statements speak directly of agreement, on fair reading these are merely legal conclusions resting on the prior allegations. Thus, the complaint first takes account of the alleged "absence of any meaningful competition between [the (defendants)] in one another's markets," "the parallel course of conduct that each [defendant] engaged in to prevent competition from [competitive local exchange carriers]," "and the other facts and market circumstances alleged [earlier]"; "in light of" these, the complaint concludes "that [the [defendants]] have entered into a contract, combination or conspiracy to prevent competitive entry into their . . . markets and have agreed not to compete with one another." The nub of the complaint, then, is the [defendants]' parallel behavior, consisting of steps to keep the [competitive local exchange carriers] out and manifest disinterest in becoming [competitive local exchange carriers] themselves, and its sufficiency turns on the suggestions raised by this conduct when viewed in light of common economic experience.

We think that nothing contained in the complaint invests either the action or inaction alleged with a plausible suggestion of conspiracy. As to the [defendants]' supposed agreement to disobey the 1996 Act and thwart the [competitive local exchange carriers]' attempts to compete, we agree with the District Court that nothing in the complaint intimates that the resistance to the upstarts was anything more than the natural, unilateral reaction of each ILEC intent on keeping its regional dominance. The 1996 Act did more than just subject the [defendants] to competition; it obliged them to subsidize their competitors with their own equipment at wholesale rates. . . .

The complaint makes its closest pass at a predicate for conspiracy with the claim that collusion was necessary because success by even one CLEC in an ILEC's territory "would have revealed the degree to which competitive entry by [competitive local exchange carriers] would have been successful in the other territories." But, its logic aside, this general premise still fails to answer the point that there was just no need for joint encouragement to resist the 1996 Act; as the District Court said, "each ILEC has reason to want to avoid dealing with [competitive local exchange carriers]" and "each ILEC would attempt to keep [competitive local exchange carriers] out, regardless of the actions of the other [defendants]."

. . . .

Plaintiffs say that our analysis runs counter to *Swierkiewicz v. Sorema N. A.*, 534 U.S. 506, 508 (2002)[30], which held that "a complaint in an employment discrimination lawsuit [need] not contain specific facts establishing a prima facie case of discrimination under the framework set forth in *McDonnell Douglas Corp. v. Green*, 411 U.S. 792 (1973)." They argue that just as the prima facie case is a "flexible evidentiary standard" that "should not be transposed into a rigid pleading standard for discrimination cases," *Swierkiewicz, supra*, at 512, "transpos[ing] 'plus factor' summary judgment analysis woodenly into a rigid Rule 12(b)(6) pleading standard . . . would be unwise," Brief for Respondents 39. As the District Court correctly understood, however, "*Swierkiewicz* did not change the law of pleading, but simply re-emphasized . . . that the Second Circuit's use of a heightened pleading standard for Title VII cases was contrary to the Federal Rules' structure of liberal pleading requirements." 313 F. Supp. 2d, at 181 (citation and footnote omitted). Even though Swierkiewicz's pleadings "detailed the events leading to his termination, provided relevant dates, and included the ages and nationalities of at least some of the relevant persons involved with his termination," the Court of Appeals dismissed his complaint for failing to allege certain additional facts that Swierkiewicz would need at the trial stage to support his claim in the absence of direct evidence of discrimination. *Swierkiewicz*, 534 U.S., at 514. We reversed on the ground that the Court of Appeals had impermissibly applied what amounted to a heightened pleading requirement by insisting that Swierkiewicz allege "specific

---

[30] [FN 14] In reaching this conclusion, we do not apply any "heightened" pleading standard, nor do we seek to broaden the scope of Federal Rule of Civil Procedure 9, which can only be accomplished " 'by the process of amending the Federal Rules, and not by judicial interpretation.' " *Swierkiewicz v. Sorema N. A.*, 534 U.S. 506, 515 (2002) (quoting *Leatherman v. Tarrant County Narcotics Intelligence and Coordination Unit*, 507 U.S. 163, 168 (1993)). On certain subjects understood to raise a high risk of abusive litigation, a plaintiff must state factual allegations with greater particularity than Rule 8 requires. Fed. Rules Civ. Proc. 9(b)–(c). Here, our concern is not that the allegations in the complaint were insufficiently "particular[ized]", ibid.; rather, the complaint warranted dismissal because it failed *in toto* to render plaintiffs' entitlement to relief plausible.

facts" beyond those necessary to state his claim and the grounds showing entitlement to relief. *Id.*, at 508.

Here, in contrast, we do not require heightened fact pleading of specifics, but only enough facts to state a claim to relief that is plausible on its face. Because the plaintiffs here have not nudged their claims across the line from conceivable to plausible, their complaint must be dismissed.

* * *

The judgment of the Court of Appeals for the Second Circuit is reversed, and the cause is remanded for further proceedings consistent with this opinion.

It is so ordered.

JUSTICE STEVENS, with whom JUSTICE GINSBURG joins except as to Part IV, dissenting.

. . . .

[T]his is a case in which there is no dispute about the substantive law. If the defendants acted independently, their conduct was perfectly lawful. If, however, that conduct is the product of a horizontal agreement among potential competitors, it was unlawful. Plaintiffs have alleged such an agreement and, because the complaint was dismissed in advance of answer, the allegation has not even been denied. Why, then, does the case not proceed? Does a judicial opinion that the charge is not "plausible" provide a legally acceptable reason for dismissing the complaint? I think not.

Respondents' amended complaint describes a variety of circumstantial evidence and makes the straightforward allegation that petitioners

> "entered into a contract, combination or conspiracy to prevent competitive entry in their respective local telephone and/or high speed internet services markets and have agreed not to compete with one another and otherwise allocated customers and markets to one another." Amended Complaint in No. 02 CIV. 10220 (GEL) (SDNY) ¶ 51, App. 27 (hereinafter Complaint).

. . . .

In sum, respondents allege that petitioners entered into an agreement that has long been recognized as a classic per se violation of the Sherman Act.

Under rules of procedure that have been well settled since well before our decision in *Theatre Enterprises*, a judge ruling on a defendant's motion to dismiss a complaint, "must accept as true all of the factual allegations contained in the complaint."

. . . .

Two practical concerns presumably explain the Court's dramatic departure from settled procedural law. Private antitrust litigation can be enormously expensive, and there is a risk that jurors may mistakenly conclude that evidence of parallel conduct has proved that the parties acted pursuant to an agreement when they in fact merely made similar independent decisions. Those concerns merit careful case management, including strict control of discovery, careful scrutiny of evidence at the summary judgment stage, and lucid instructions to juries; they do not, however, justify the dismissal of an adequately pleaded complaint without even requiring the defendants to file answers denying a charge that they in fact engaged in collective decisionmaking. More importantly, they do not justify an interpretation of Federal Rule of Civil Procedure 12(b)(6) that seems to be driven by the majority's appraisal of the plausibility of the ultimate factual allegation rather than its legal sufficiency.

. . . .

II

. . . .

Today, however, in its explanation of a decision to dismiss a complaint that it regards as a fishing expedition, the Court scraps [the] "no set of facts" language [from *Conley v. Gibson*, 355 U.S. 41, 47 (1957)]. Concluding that the phrase has been "questioned, criticized, and explained away long enough," the Court dismisses it as careless composition.

If *Conley*'s "no set of facts" language is to be interred, let it not be without a eulogy. That exact language, which the majority says has "puzzl[ed] the profession for 50 years," *ibid.*, has been cited as authority in a dozen opinions of this Court and four separate writings. In not one of those 16 opinions was the language "questioned," "criticized," or "explained away." Indeed, today's opinion is the first by any Member of this Court to express any doubt as to the adequacy of the *Conley* formulation. Taking their cues from the federal courts, 26 States and the District of Columbia utilize as their standard for dismissal of a complaint the very language the majority repudiates: whether it appears "beyond doubt" that "no set of facts" in support of the claim would entitle the plaintiff to relief.

. . . .

Today's majority calls *Conley*'s " 'no set of facts' " language "an incomplete, negative gloss on an accepted pleading standard: once a claim has been stated adequately, it may be supported by showing any set of facts consistent with the allegations in the complaint." Ante, at 1969. This is not and cannot be what the *Conley* Court meant. First, as I have explained, and as the *Conley* Court well knew, the pleading standard the Federal Rules meant to codify does not require, or even invite, the pleading of facts. The "pleading standard" label the majority gives to what it reads into the *Conley* opinion — a statement of the permissible factual support for an adequately pleaded complaint — would not, therefore, have impressed the *Conley* Court itself. Rather, that Court would have understood the majority's remodeling of its language to express an evidentiary standard, which the *Conley* Court had neither need nor want to explicate. Second, it is pellucidly clear that the *Conley* Court was interested in what a complaint must contain, not what it may contain. In fact, the Court said without qualification that it was "appraising the sufficiency of the complaint." 355 U.S., at 45 (emphasis added). It was, to paraphrase today's majority, describing "the minimum standard of adequate pleading to govern a complaint's survival," *ante*, at 1969.

We can be triply sure as to *Conley*'s meaning by examining the three Court of Appeals cases the *Conley* Court cited as support for the "accepted rule" that "a complaint should not be dismissed for failure to state a claim unless it appears beyond doubt that the plaintiff can prove no set of facts in support of his claim which would entitle him to relief." 355 U.S., at 45–46.

. . . .

As in the discrimination context, we have developed an evidentiary framework for evaluating claims under § 1 of the Sherman Act when those claims rest on entirely circumstantial evidence of conspiracy. *See Matsushita Elec. Industrial Co. v. Zenith Radio Corp.*, 475 U.S. 574 (1986). Under *Matsushita*, a plaintiff's allegations of an illegal conspiracy may not, at the summary judgment stage, rest solely on the inferences that may be drawn from the parallel conduct of the defendants. In order to survive a Rule 56 motion, a § 1 plaintiff "must present evidence 'that tends to exclude the possibility' that the alleged conspirators acted independently.' " *Id.*, at 588 (quoting *Monsanto Co. v. Spray-Rite Service Corp.*, 465 U.S. 752, 764 (1984)). That is, the plaintiff "must show that the inference of conspiracy is reasonable in light of the competing inferences of independent action or collusive action." 475 U.S., at 588.

Everything today's majority says would therefore make perfect sense if it were ruling on a Rule 56 motion for summary judgment and the evidence included nothing more than the Court has described. But it should go without saying . . . that a heightened production burden at the summary judgment stage does not translate into a heightened pleading burden at the complaint stage. The majority rejects the complaint in this case because — in light of the fact that the parallel conduct alleged is consistent with ordinary market behavior — the claimed conspiracy is "conceivable" but not "plausible." I have my doubts about the majority's assessment of the plausibility of this alleged conspiracy. But even if the majority's speculation is correct, its "plausibility" standard is irreconcilable with Rule 8 and with our governing precedents. . . .

This case is a poor vehicle for the Court's new pleading rule, for we have observed that "in antitrust cases, where 'the proof is largely in the hands of the alleged conspirators,' . . . dismissals prior to giving the plaintiff ample opportunity for discovery should be granted very sparingly." *Hospital Building Co. v. Trustees of Rex Hospital*, 425 U.S. 738, 746 (1976) (quoting *Poller v. Columbia Broadcasting System, Inc.*, 368 U.S. 464, 473 (1962)); *see also Knuth v. Erie-Crawford Dairy Cooperative Assn.*, 395 F.2d 420, 423 (C.A.3 1968) ("The 'liberal' approach to the consideration of antitrust complaints is important because inherent in such an action is the fact that all the details and specific facts relied upon cannot properly be set forth as part of the pleadings"). Moreover, the fact that the Sherman Act authorizes the recovery of treble damages and attorney's fees for successful plaintiffs indicates that Congress intended to encourage, rather than discourage, private enforcement of the law. *See Radovich v. National Football League*, 352 U.S. 445, 454 (1957) ("Congress itself has placed the private antitrust litigant in a most favorable position. . . . In the face of such a policy this Court should not add requirements to burden the private litigant beyond what is specifically set forth by Congress in those laws"). It is therefore more, not less, important in antitrust cases to resist the urge to engage in armchair economics at the pleading stage.

. . . .

IV

Just a few weeks ago some of my colleagues explained that a strict interpretation of the literal text of statutory language is essential to avoid judicial decisions that are not faithful to the intent of Congress. *Zuni Public School Dist. No. 89 v. Department of Education*, 551 U.S. ___, ___ (2007) (SCALIA, J., dissenting). I happen to believe that there are cases in which other tools of construction are more reliable than text, but I agree of course that congressional intent should guide us in matters of statutory interpretation. *Id.*, at 1534 (STEVENS, J., concurring). This is a case in which the intentions of the drafters of three important sources of law — the Sherman Act, the Telecommunications Act of 1996, and the Federal Rules of Civil Procedure — all point unmistakably in the same direction, yet the Court marches resolutely the other way. Whether the Court's actions will benefit only defendants in antitrust treble-damages cases, or whether its test for the sufficiency of a complaint will inure to the benefit of all civil defendants, is a question that the future will answer. But that the Court has announced a significant new rule that does not even purport to respond to any congressional command is glaringly obvious.

. . . .

If the allegation of conspiracy happens to be true, today's decision obstructs the congressional policy favoring competition that undergirds both the Telecommunications Act of 1996 and the Sherman Act itself. More importantly, even if there is abundant evidence that the allegation is untrue, directing that the case be dismissed without even looking at any of that evidence marks a fundamental — and unjustified — change in the character of pretrial practice.

Accordingly, I respectfully dissent.

NOTES AND QUESTIONS

1. After *Twombly*, how much factual matter must be pleaded to survive a motion to dismiss under Rule 12(b)(6)? Is the threshold, now, one of "plausible grounds to infer an agreement," rather than one of "probability" that the parties entered into an agreement? Had the plaintiffs pleaded at least one "plus factor" beyond the parallel behavior, would the motion under the new standard applied in *Twombly* have been denied?

2. In announcing this new pleading standard, what risk did the cost of discovery play in the court's reasoning? Will the federal courts now be reluctant to permit initial discovery to go forward without a clear articulation by plaintiff's counsel of a factual predicate from which there could be reasonable expectations of an illegal agreement?

3. The Supreme Court in 2005 declined to limit *Twombly* to antitrust cases. Its opinion in *Ashcroft v. Iqbal*, 556 U.S. 662 (2009), a case brought by a Muslim Pakistani pretrial detainee against the former U.S. Attorney General alleging unconstitutional actions against him during his confinement, held that *Twombly*'s restricted pleading requirements apply to "all civil actions." *Id.* at 684.

IN RE TEXT MESSAGING ANTITRUST LITIGATION
630 F.3d 622 (7th Cir. 2010)

Posner, Circuit Judge.

A class action suit that has been consolidated for pretrial proceedings in the district court in Chicago charges the defendants with conspiring to fix prices of text messaging services in violation of federal antitrust law. The district court allowed the plaintiffs to file a second amended complaint despite the defendants' objection, based on *Bell Atlantic Corp. v. Twombly*, 550 U.S. 544 (2007), that the second complaint like the first failed to state a claim. . . .

The complaint in *Twombly* alleged that the regional telephone companies that were the successors to the Bell Operating Companies which AT & T had been forced to divest in settlement of the government's antitrust suit against it were engaged in "parallel behavior." Bluntly, they were not competing. But section 1 of the Sherman Act, under which the suit had been brought, does not require sellers to compete; it just forbids their agreeing or conspiring not to compete. So as the Court pointed out, a complaint that merely alleges parallel behavior alleges facts that are equally consistent with an inference that the defendants are conspiring and an inference that the conditions of their market have enabled them to avoid competing without having to agree not to compete. . . .

Our defendants contend that in this case too the complaint alleges merely that they are not competing. But we agree with the district judge that the complaint alleges a conspiracy with sufficient plausibility to satisfy the pleading standard of *Twombly*. . . .

The second amended complaint alleges a mixture of parallel behaviors, details of industry structure, and industry practices, that facilitate collusion. There is nothing incongruous about such a mixture. If parties agree to fix prices, one expects that as a result they will not compete in price — that's the purpose of price fixing. Parallel behavior of a sort anomalous in a competitive market is thus a symptom of price fixing, though standing alone it is not proof of it; and an industry structure that facilitates collusion constitutes supporting evidence of collusion. An accusation that the thousands of children who set up makeshift lemonade stands all over the country on hot summer days were fixing prices would be laughed out of court because the retail sale of lemonade from lemonade stands constitutes so dispersed and heterogeneous and uncommercial a market as to make a nationwide conspiracy of the sellers utterly implausible. But the complaint in this case alleges that the four defendants sell 90 percent of U.S. text messaging services, and it would not be difficult for such a small group to agree on prices and to be able to detect "cheating" (underselling the agreed price by a member of the group) without having to create elaborate mechanisms, such as an exclusive sales agency, that could not escape discovery by the antitrust authorities.

Of note is the allegation in the complaint that the defendants belonged to a trade association and exchanged price information directly at association meetings. This allegation identifies a practice, not illegal in itself, that facilitates price fixing that would be difficult for the authorities to detect. The complaint further alleges that the defendants, along with two other large sellers of text messaging services, constituted and met with each other in an elite "leadership council" within the association — and the leadership council's stated mission was to urge its members to substitute "co-opetition" for competition.

The complaint also alleges that in the face of steeply falling costs, the defendants increased their prices. This is anomalous behavior because falling costs increase a seller's profit margin at the existing price, motivating him, in the absence of agreement, to reduce his price slightly in order to take business from his competitors, and certainly not to increase his price. And there is more: there is an allegation that all at once the defendants changed their pricing structures, which were heterogeneous and complex, to a uniform pricing structure, and then simultaneously jacked up their prices by a third. The change in the industry's pricing structure was so rapid, the complaint suggests, that it could not have been accomplished without agreement on the details of the new structure, the timing of its adoption, and the specific uniform price increase that would ensue on its adoption.

A footnote in *Twombly* had described the type of evidence that enables parallel conduct to be interpreted as collusive: "Commentators have offered several examples of parallel conduct allegations that would state a [Sherman Act] § 1 claim under this standard . . . [namely,] 'parallel behavior that would probably not result from chance, coincidence, independent responses to common stimuli, or mere interdependence unaided by an advance understanding among the parties' . . .[;] 'conduct [that] indicates the sort of restricted freedom of action and sense of obligation that one generally associates with agreement.' The parties in this case agree that 'complex and historically unprecedented changes in pricing structure made at the very same time by multiple competitors, and made for no other discernible reason' would support a plausible inference of conspiracy." *Bell Atlantic Corp. v. Twombly, supra*, 550 U.S. at 557 n. 4 (citations omitted). That is the kind of "parallel plus" behavior alleged in this case.

What is missing, as the defendants point out, is the smoking gun in a price-fixing case: direct evidence, which would usually take the form of an admission by an employee of one of the conspirators, that officials of the defendants had met and agreed explicitly on the terms of a conspiracy to raise price. The second amended complaint does allege that the defendants "agreed to uniformly charge an unprecedented common per-unit price of ten cents for text messaging services," but does not allege direct evidence of such an agreement; the allegation is an inference from circumstantial evidence. Direct evidence of conspiracy is not a sine qua non, however. Circumstantial evidence can establish an antitrust conspiracy. We need not decide whether the circumstantial evidence that we have summarized is sufficient to compel an inference of conspiracy; the case is just at the complaint stage and the test for whether to dismiss a case at that stage turns on the complaint's "plausibility."

The Court said in *Iqbal* that the "plausibility standard is not akin to a 'probability requirement,' but it asks for more than a sheer possibility that a defendant has acted unlawfully." 129 S. Ct. at 1949. This is a little unclear because plausibility, probability, and possibility overlap. Probability runs the gamut from a zero likelihood to a certainty. What is impossible has a zero likelihood of occurring and what is plausible has a moderately high likelihood of occurring. The fact that the allegations undergirding a claim could be true is no longer enough to save a complaint from being dismissed; the complaint must establish a nonnegligible probability that the claim is valid; but the probability need not be as great as such terms as "preponderance of the evidence" connote.

The plaintiffs have conducted no discovery. Discovery may reveal the smoking gun or bring to light additional circumstantial evidence that further tilts the balance in favor of liability. All that we conclude at this early stage in the litigation is that the district judge was right to rule that the second amended complaint provides a sufficiently plausible case of price fixing to warrant allowing the plaintiffs to proceed to discovery.

NOTES AND QUESTIONS

1. Why did the complaint in *In re Text Messaging* survive a motion to dismiss when the complaint in *Twombly* did not?

2. The pre-*Twombly* earlier standard, overturned by *Twombly* and *Iqbal*, called for the pleading to show only the "sheer possibility that a defendant has acted unlawfully." *Iqbal*, 556 U.S. at 678. The new standard required a plaintiff to plead that the violation reaches the level of plausibility, a higher bar than merely possibility. The Court also notes that this does not require the pleading to reach the level of probability. Debate continues in the lower courts as to where precisely the lines between possible, plausible, and probably fall. Does Judge Posner's opinion in *In re Text Messaging* help determine where those lines are?

This debate is apparent when comparing the majority and minority opinions in *Tam Travel, Inc. v. Delta Airlines, Inc. (In re Travel Agent Comm'n Antitrust Litig.)*, 583 F.3d 896 (6th Cir. 2009). A divided Sixth Circuit panel applied the *Twombly* standard to dismiss conspiracy claims by a group of travel agents against several major airlines. Affirming the judgment of the district court, the Sixth Circuit majority held that "allegations of parallel conduct and bare assertions of conspiracy no longer supply an adequate foundation to support a plausible S 1 claim." The dissent argued that the majority had misapplied *Twombly* and required the plaintiff to show probability of success in their claims rather than simply plausibility as required by *Twombly*.

In *Starr v. Sony BMG Music Entm't*, 592 F.3d 314 (2d Cir. 2010), the Second Circuit addressed similar allegations of parallel conduct that were at issue in *Twombly*, coming to the opposite conclusion as the Supreme Court and holding that sufficient factual material was pleaded to state a claim plausible on its face. In a concurring opinion, Judge Jon O. Newman addressed a "perplexing" aspect of *Twombly*.

> The perplexing aspect of the Court's opinion is contained in the very first paragraph of the Court's substantive discussion. The Court there stated:
>
>> While a showing of parallel "business behavior is admissible circumstantial evidence *from which the fact finder may infer agreement*," it falls short of "conclusively establish[ing] agreement or . . . itself constitut[ing] a Sherman Act offense.
>
> Twombly, 550 U.S. at 553 (emphasis added) (citing Theatre Enterprises v. Paramount Film Distributing Corp., 346 U.S. 537, 540–41 (1954)) (alterations and ellipsis in original).
>
> . . . If, as the Court states in the first part of this sentence, a fact-finder is entitled to infer agreement from parallel conduct, one may wonder why a complaint alleging such conduct does not survive a motion to dismiss.
>
> In view of the Court's initial observation in *Twombly* that parallel conduct is sufficient to support a permissible inference of an agreement, the reason for the rejection of the complaint in *Twombly* must arise from something other than the plaintiff's reliance on parallel conduct. That reason is not difficult to find. It is the context in which the defendants' parallel conduct occurred.

592 F.3d at 328.

3. Allegations of guilty pleas or investigation of the same or similar anticompetitive behavior have been used by plaintiffs to try and meet the *Twombly* standard. In *In re Korean Air Lines Co. Antitrust Litig.*, 2008 U.S. Dist. LEXIS 111722 (C.D. Cal. June 25, 2008), defendant Korean Air Lines moved to dismiss the claim of conspiracy to fix prices on flights between the U.S. and Korea, in spite of the fact that Korean Air Lines had pleaded guilty and paid a fine following a U.S. Department of Justice investigation into substantially similar charges. The court held that the guilty plea was not sufficient to sustain allegations of a conspiracy broader than the specific limits of the plea.

In other cases, guilty pleas involving the same or seminal conduct as alleged in the claim have been held as sufficient, combined with other factual allegations, to reach *Twombly*'s plausibility threshold. *See In re Aid Cargo Shipping Services Antitrust Litigation*, 2009 U.S. Dist. LEXIS 97365 (E.D.N.Y. Aug. 21, 2009) ("[A]dmissions of price-fixing by [nine] defendants certainly is 'suggestive enough to render a § 1 conspiracy plausible.'") (quoting *Twombly*).

4. In attempting to clarify the *Twombly*/*Iqbal* intersection, the Second Circuit reversed a "improperty dismissal" complaint by noting that the proper inquiry by the district court is "whether there are sufficient factual allegations to make the complaint's claim plausible," rather than "whether there is a plausible alternative to the plaintiff's theory." *See Anderson News, LLC v. American Media Inc.* 680 F.3d 162 (2d Cir. 2012) (Kearse, J). See also *Carrier Corp. v. Outokumpu Oyj*, 673 F.3d 430 (6th Cir. 2012) on *Twombly*'s application to pleading "foreign conduct" affecting United States markets. *See generally* Gregory G. Wrobel, Michael J. Waters &

Joshua Dunn, *Judicial Application of the Twombly/Iqbal Plausibility Standard in Antitrust Cases*, 26 ANTITRUST 8 (2011).

PROBLEM 4.7

Major medical research has discovered that aspirin can prevent heart attacks. (In a study, more than 11,000 physicians over age 40 took one aspirin every other day, while another group of physicians took placebos. At the end of 57 months, the study showed that those taking aspirin had 47% fewer heart attacks.) Upon news of this discovery, the five major pharmaceutical companies that produce aspirin, with a total market share of 86% of the over-the-counter (OTC) pain-reliever market, each began advertising separately its aspirin product with a spectacular campaign of claims about the link of its product to heart attack avoidance.

After each company's ads had run for three weeks, representatives of the five majors met to discuss the impact of the ads and whether they should be withdrawn. There were statements at this meeting that the Food and Drug Administration was opposed to the ads because they may be misleading to the public, given the nature of the medical information. But most of the representatives at the meeting were not concerned with the FDA's warning; they were concerned that each ad was conveying essentially the same message but pitched to the particular brand of the product.

When the majors could not agree on the form of the future ads, they discussed withdrawing the ads. The week following the meeting, all ads regarding the aspirin-heart attack avoidance link were canceled.

Discuss what, if any, antitrust issues are presented by these facts, and how they would be decided by a court.

[4]   Surviving a Motion for Summary Judgment

MATSUSHITA ELECTRIC INDUSTRIAL CO. v. ZENITH RADIO CORP.
475 U.S. 574 (1986)

JUSTICE POWELL delivered the opinion of the Court.

This case requires that we again consider the standard district courts must apply when deciding whether to grant summary judgment in an antitrust conspiracy case.

I

. . . .

. . . What follows is a summary of this case's long history.

A

Petitioners, defendants below, are 21 corporations that manufacture or sell "consumer electronic products" (CEPs) — for the most part, television sets. Petitioners include both Japanese manufacturers of CEPs and American firms, controlled by Japanese parents, that sell the Japanese-manufactured products. Respondents, plaintiffs below, are Zenith Radio Corporation (Zenith) and National Union Electric Corporation (NUE). Zenith is an American firm that manufactures and sells television sets. NUE is the corporate successor to Emerson Radio Company, an American firm that manufactured and sold television sets until 1970, when it withdrew from the market after sustaining substantial losses. Zenith and NUE began this lawsuit in 1974, claiming that petitioners had illegally conspired to drive American firms from the American CEP market. According to respondents, the gist of this conspiracy was a " 'scheme to raise, fix and maintain artificially *high* prices for television receivers sold by [petitioners] in Japan and, at the same time, to fix and maintain *low* prices for television receivers exported to and sold in the United States.' " 723 F.2d at 251. These "low prices" were allegedly at levels that produced substantial losses for petitioners. 513 F. Supp., at 1125. The conspiracy allegedly began as early as 1953, and according to respondents was in full operation by sometime in the late 1960's. Respondents claimed that various portions of this scheme violated §§ 1 and 2 of the Sherman Act, § 2(a) of the Robinson-Patman Act, § 73 of the Wilson Tariff Act, and the Antidumping Act of 1916.

After several years of detailed discovery, petitioners filed motions for summary judgment on all claims against them. . . .

. . . [T]he court found that the admissible evidence did not raise a genuine issue of material fact as to the existence of the alleged conspiracy. At bottom, the court found, respondents' claims rested on the inferences that could be drawn from petitioners' parallel conduct in the Japanese and American markets, and from the effects of that conduct on petitioners' American competitors. 513 F. Supp., at 1125–1127. After reviewing the evidence both by category and *in toto*, the court found that any inference of conspiracy was unreasonable, because (i) some portions of the evidence suggested that petitioners conspired in ways that did not injure respondents, and (ii) the evidence that bore directly on the alleged price-cutting conspiracy did not rebut the more plausible inference that petitioners were cutting prices to compete in the American market and not to monopolize it. Summary judgment therefore was granted on respondents' claims under § 1 of the Sherman Act and the Wilson Tariff Act. Because the Sherman Act § 2 claims, which alleged that petitioners had combined to monopolize the American CEP market, were functionally indistinguishable from the § 1 claims, the court dismissed them also. Finally, the court found that the Robinson-Patman Act claims depended on the same supposed conspiracy as the Sherman Act claims. Since the court had found no genuine issue of fact as to the conspiracy, it entered judgment in petitioners' favor on those claims as well.

B

The Court of Appeals for the Third Circuit reversed. . . .

On the merits, and based on the newly enlarged record, the court found that the District Court's summary judgment decision was improper. The court acknowledged that "there are legal limitations upon the inferences which may be drawn from circumstantial evidence," 723 F.2d, at 304, but it found that "the legal problem . . . is different" when "there is direct evidence of concert of action." *Ibid.* Here, the court concluded, "there is both direct evidence of certain kinds of concert of action and circumstantial evidence having some tendency to suggest that other kinds of concert of action may have occurred." *Id.*, at 304–305. Thus, the court reasoned, cases concerning the limitations on inferring conspiracy from ambiguous evidence were not dispositive. *Id.*, at 305. [T]he court determined that a fact finder reasonably could draw the following conclusions:

> "1. The Japanese market for CEPs was characterized by oligopolistic behavior, with a small number of producers meeting regularly and exchanging information on price and other matters. *Id.*, at 307. This created the opportunity for a stable combination to raise both prices and profits in Japan. American firms could not attack such a combination because the Japanese government imposed significant barriers to entry. *Ibid.*

> 2. Petitioners had relatively higher fixed costs than their American counterparts, and therefore needed to operate at something approaching full capacity in order to make a profit. *Ibid.*

> 3. Petitioners' plant capacity exceeded the needs of the Japanese market. *Ibid.*

> 4. By formal agreements arranged in cooperation with Japan's Ministry of International Trade and Industry (MITI), petitioners fixed minimum prices for CEPs exported to the American market. *Id.*, at 310. The parties refer to these prices as the "check prices," and to the agreements that require them as the "check price agreements."

> 5. Petitioners agreed to distribute their products in the United States according to a "five-company rule": each Japanese producer was permitted to sell only to five American distributors. *Ibid.*

> 6. Petitioners undercut their own check prices by a variety of rebate schemes. *Id.*, at 311. Petitioners sought to conceal these rebate schemes both from the United States Customs Service and from MITI, the former to avoid various customs regulations as well as action under the antidumping laws, and the latter to cover up petitioners' violations of the check price agreements."

Based on inferences from the foregoing conclusions,[31] the Court of Appeals

---

[31] [FN 5] In addition to these inferences, the court noted that there was expert opinion evidence that petitioners' export sales "generally were at prices which produced losses, often as high as twenty-five percent on sales." 723 F.2d, at 311. The court did not identify any direct evidence of below-cost pricing; nor did it place particularly heavy reliance on this aspect of the expert evidence.

concluded that a reasonable fact finder could find a conspiracy to depress prices in the American market in order to drive out American competitors, which conspiracy was funded by excess profits obtained in the Japanese market. The court apparently did not consider whether it was as plausible to conclude that petitioners' price-cutting behavior was independent and not conspiratorial.

The court found it unnecessary to address petitioners' claim that they could not be held liable under the antitrust laws for conduct that was compelled by a foreign sovereign. The claim, in essence, was that because MITI required petitioners to enter into the check price agreements, liability could not be premised on those agreements. The court concluded that this case did not present any issue of sovereign compulsion, because the check price agreements were being used as "evidence of a low export price conspiracy" and not as an independent basis for finding antitrust liability. The court also believed it was unclear that the check prices in fact were mandated by the Japanese government, notwithstanding a statement to that effect by MITI itself. *Id.*, at 315.

We granted certiorari to determine (i) whether the Court of Appeals applied the proper standards in evaluating the District Court's decision to grant petitioners' motion for summary judgment, and (ii) whether petitioners could be held liable under the antitrust laws for a conspiracy in part compelled by a foreign sovereign. We reverse on the first issue, but do not reach the second.

II

We begin by emphasizing what respondents' claim is *not*. Respondents cannot recover antitrust damages based solely on an alleged cartelization of the Japanese market, because American antitrust laws do not regulate the competitive conditions of other nations' economies. *United States v. Aluminum Company of America*, 148 F.2d 416, 443 (2d Cir. 1945) (L. Hand, J.); 1 P. Areeda & D. Turner, *Antitrust Law* ¶ 236d (1978).[32] Nor can respondents recover damages for any conspiracy by petitioners to charge higher than competitive prices in the American market. Such conduct would indeed violate the Sherman Act, but it could not injure respondents: as petitioners' competitors, respondents stand to gain from any conspiracy to raise the market price in CEPs. Cf. *Brunswick Corp. v. Pueblo Bowl-O-Mat, Inc.*, 429

---

[32] [FN 6] The Sherman Act does reach conduct outside our borders, but only when the conduct has an effect on American commerce. *Continental Ore Co. v. Union Carbide & Carbon Corp.*, 370 U.S. 690, 704 (1962) ("A conspiracy to monopolize or restrain the domestic or foreign commerce of the United States is not outside the reach of the Sherman Act just because part of the conduct complained of occurs in foreign countries"). The effect on which respondents rely is the artificially depressed level of prices for CEPs in the United States.

Petitioners' alleged cartelization of the Japanese market could not have caused that effect over a period of some two decades. Once petitioners decided, as respondents allege, to reduce output and raise prices in the Japanese market, they had the option of either producing fewer goods or selling more goods in other markets. The most plausible conclusion is that petitioners chose the latter option because it would be more profitable than the former. That choice does not flow from the cartelization of the Japanese market. On the contrary, were the Japanese market perfectly competitive petitioners would still have to choose whether to sell goods overseas, and would still presumably make that choice based on their profit expectations. For this reason, respondents' theory of recovery depends on proof of the asserted price-cutting conspiracy in this country.

U.S. 477, 488–489 (1977). Finally, for the same reason, respondents cannot recover for a conspiracy to impose nonprice restraints that have the effect of either raising market price or limiting output. Such restrictions, though harmful to competition, actually benefit competitors by making supracompetitive pricing more attractive. Thus, neither petitioners' alleged supracompetitive pricing in Japan, nor the five-company rule that limited distribution in this country, nor the check prices insofar as they established minimum prices in this country, can by themselves give respondents a cognizable claim against petitioners for antitrust damages. The Court of Appeals therefore erred to the extent that it found evidence of these alleged conspiracies to be "direct evidence" of a conspiracy that injured respondents.

Respondents nevertheless argue that these supposed conspiracies, if not themselves grounds for recovery of antitrust damages, are circumstantial evidence of another conspiracy that *is* cognizable: a conspiracy to monopolize the American market by means of pricing below the market level.[33] The thrust of respondents' argument is that petitioners used their monopoly profits from the Japanese market to fund a concerted campaign to price predatorily and thereby drive respondents and other American manufacturers of CEPs out of business. Once successful, according to respondents, petitioners would cartelize the American CEP market, restricting output and raising prices above the level that fair competition would produce. The resulting monopoly profits, respondents contend, would more than compensate petitioners for the losses they incurred through years of pricing below market level.

The Court of Appeals found that respondents' allegation of a horizontal conspiracy to engage in predatory pricing,[34] if proved,[35] would be a *per se* violation of

---

[33] [FN 7] Respondents also argue that the check prices, the five-company rule, and the price-fixing in Japan are all part of one large conspiracy that includes monopolization of the American market through predatory pricing. The argument is mistaken. However one decides to describe the contours of the asserted conspiracy — whether there is one conspiracy or several — respondents must show that the conspiracy caused them an injury for which the antitrust laws provide relief. *Associated General Contractors v. California State Council of Carpenters*, 459 U.S. 519, 538–540 (1983); *Brunswick Corp. v. Pueblo Bowl-O-Mat, Inc.*, 429 U.S. 477, 488–489 (1977). That showing depends in turn on proof that petitioners conspired to price predatorily in the American market, since the other conduct involved in the alleged conspiracy cannot have caused such an injury.

[34] [FN 8] Throughout this opinion, we refer to the asserted conspiracy as one to price "predatorily." This term has been used chiefly in cases in which a single firm, having a dominant share of the relevan t market, cuts its prices in order to force competitors out of the market, or perhaps to deter potential entrants from coming in. *E.g.*, *Southern Pacific Communications Co. v. American Telephone & Telegraph Co.*, 238 U.S. App. D.C. 309, 331–336, 740 F.2d 980, 1002–1007 (1984), *cert. denied*, 470 U.S. 1005 (1985). In such cases, "predatory pricing" means pricing below some appropriate measure of cost. *E.g.*, *Barry Wright Corp. v. ITT Grinnell Corp.*, 724 F.2d 227, 232–235 (1st Cir. 1983); see *Utah Pie Co. v. Continental Baking Co.*, 386 U.S. 685, 698, 701, 702, n. 14 (1967).

There is a good deal of debate, both in the cases and in the law reviews, about what "cost" is relevant in such cases. We need not resolve this debate here, because unlike the cases cited above, this is a Sherman Act § 1 case. For purposes of this case, it is enough to note that respondents have not suffered an antitrust injury unless petitioners conspired to drive respondents out of the relevant markets by (i) pricing below the level necessary to sell their products, or (ii) pricing below some appropriate measure of cost. An agreement without these features would either leave respondents in the same position as would market forces or would actually benefit respondents by raising market prices. Respondents

§ 1 of the Sherman Act. 723 F.2d, at 306. Petitioners did not appeal from that conclusion. The issue in this case thus becomes whether respondents adduced sufficient evidence in support of their theory to survive summary judgment. We therefore examine the principles that govern the summary judgment determination.

III

To survive petitioners' motion for summary judgment, respondents must establish that there is a genuine issue of material fact as to whether petitioners entered into an illegal conspiracy that caused respondents to suffer a cognizable injury. Fed. Rule Civ. Proc. 56(e); *First National Bank of Arizona v. Cities Service Co.*, 391 U.S. 253, 288–289 (1968). This showing has two components. First, respondents must show more than a conspiracy in violation of the antitrust laws; they must show an injury to them resulting from the illegal conduct. Respondents charge petitioners with a whole host of conspiracies in restraint of trade. Except for the alleged conspiracy to monopolize the American market through predatory pricing, these alleged conspiracies could not have caused respondents to suffer an "antitrust injury," *Brunswick Corp. v. Pueblo Bowl-O-Mat*, 429 U.S., at 489, because they actually tended to benefit respondents. Therefore, unless, in context, evidence of these "other" conspiracies raises a genuine issue concerning the existence of a predatory pricing conspiracy, that evidence cannot defeat petitioners' summary judgment motion.

Second, the issue of fact must be "genuine." When the moving party has carried its burden under Rule 56(c), its opponent must do more than simply show that there is some metaphysical doubt as to the material facts. In the language of the Rule, the non-moving party must come forward with "specific facts showing that there is a *genuine issue for trial.*" Where the record taken as a whole could not lead a rational trier of fact to find for the non-moving party, there is no "genuine issue for trial."

It follows from these settled principles that if the factual context renders respondents' claim implausible — if the claim is one that simply makes no economic sense — respondents must come forward with more persuasive evidence to support their claim than would otherwise be necessary. . . .

Respondents correctly note that "[o]n summary judgment the inferences to be drawn from the underlying facts . . . must be viewed in the light most favorable to the party opposing the motion." But antitrust law limits the range of permissible inferences from ambiguous evidence in a § 1 case. Thus, in *Monsanto Co. v. Spray-Rite Service Corp.*, 465 U.S. 752 (1984), we held that conduct as consistent with permissible competition as with illegal conspiracy does not, standing alone,

---

therefore may not complain of conspiracies that, for example, set maximum prices above market levels, or that set minimum prices at *any* level.

[35] [FN 9] We do not consider whether recovery should ever be available on a theory such as respondents' when the pricing in question is above some measure of incremental cost. See generally Areeda & Turner, *Predatory Pricing and Related Practices Under Section 2 of the Sherman Act*, 88 Harv. L. Rev. 697, 709–718 (1975) (discussing cost-based test for use in § 2 cases). As a practical matter, it may be that only direct evidence of below-cost pricing is sufficient to overcome the strong inference that rational businesses would not enter into conspiracies such as this one. See Part IV-A, *infra*.

support an inference of antitrust conspiracy. To survive a motion for summary judgment or for a directed verdict, a plaintiff seeking damages for a violation of § 1 must present evidence "that tends to exclude the possibility" that the alleged conspirators acted independently. 465 U.S., at 764. Respondents in this case, in other words, must show that the inference of conspiracy is reasonable in light of the competing inferences of independent action or collusive action that could not have harmed respondents.

Petitioners argue that these principles apply fully to this case. According to petitioners, the alleged conspiracy is one that is economically irrational and practically infeasible. Consequently, petitioners contend, they had no motive to engage in the alleged predatory pricing conspiracy; indeed, they had a strong motive *not* to conspire in the manner respondents allege. Petitioners argue that, in light of the absence of any apparent motive and the ambiguous nature of the evidence of conspiracy, no trier of fact reasonably could find that the conspiracy with which petitioners are charged actually existed. This argument requires us to consider the nature of the alleged conspiracy and the practical obstacles to its implementation.

IV

A

A predatory pricing conspiracy is by nature speculative. Any agreement to price below the competitive level requires the conspirators to forego profits that free competition would offer them. The foregone profits may be considered an investment in the future. For the investment to be rational, the conspirators must have a reasonable expectation of recovering, in the form of later monopoly profits, more than the losses suffered. As then-Professor Bork, discussing predatory pricing by a single firm, explained:

> "Any realistic theory of predation recognizes that the predator as well as his victims will incur losses during the fighting, but such a theory supposes it may be a rational calculation for the predator to view the losses as an investment in future monopoly profits (where rivals are to be killed) or in future undisturbed profits (where rivals are to be disciplined). The future flow of profits, appropriately discounted, must then exceed the present size of the losses." R. Bork, *The Antitrust Paradox* 145 (1978).

See also McGee, *Predatory Pricing Revisited*, 23 J. Law & Econ. 289, 295–297 (1980). As this explanation shows, the success of such schemes is inherently uncertain: the short-run loss is definite, but the long-run gain depends on successfully neutralizing the competition. Moreover, it is not enough simply to achieve monopoly power, as monopoly pricing may breed quick entry by new competitors eager to share in the excess profits. The success of any predatory scheme depends on *maintaining* monopoly power for long enough both to recoup the predator's losses and to harvest some additional gain. Absent some assurance that the hoped-for monopoly will materialize, *and* that it can be sustained for a significant period of time, "[t]he predator must make a substantial investment with no assurance that it will pay off." Easterbrook, *Predatory Strategies and Counter-strategies*, 48 U. Chi. L. Rev. 263, 268 (1981). For this reason, there is a consensus among commentators that predatory pricing schemes are rarely tried, and even more rarely successful.

These observations apply even to predatory pricing by a *single firm* seeking monopoly power. In this case, respondents allege that a large number of firms have conspired over a period of many years to charge below-market prices in order to stifle competition. Such a conspiracy is incalculably more difficult to execute than an analogous plan undertaken by a single predator. The conspirators must allocate the losses to be sustained during the conspiracy's operation, and must also allocate any gains to be realized from its success. Precisely because success is speculative and depends on a willingness to endure losses for an indefinite period, each conspirator has a strong incentive to cheat, letting its partners suffer the losses necessary to destroy the competition while sharing in any gains if the conspiracy succeeds. The necessary allocation is therefore difficult to accomplish. Yet if conspirators cheat to any substantial extent, the conspiracy must fail, because its success depends on depressing the market price for *all* buyers of CEPs. If there are too few goods at the artificially low price to satisfy demand, the would-be victims of the conspiracy can continue to sell at the "real" market price, and the conspirators suffer losses to little purpose.

Finally, if predatory pricing conspiracies are generally unlikely to occur, they are especially so where, as here, the prospects of attaining monopoly power seem slight. In order to recoup their losses, petitioners must obtain enough market power to set higher than competitive prices, and then must sustain those prices long enough to earn in excess profits what they earlier gave up in below-cost prices. Two decades after their conspiracy is alleged to have commenced, petitioners appear to be far from achieving this goal: the two largest shares of the retail market in television sets are held by RCA and respondent Zenith, not by any of the petitioners. Moreover, those shares, which together approximate 40% of sales, did not decline appreciably during the 1970's. *Ibid.* Petitioners' collective share rose rapidly during this period, from one-fifth or less of the relevant markets to close to 50%.[36] Neither the District Court nor the Court of Appeals found, however, that petitioners' share presently allows them to charge monopoly prices; to the contrary, respondents contend that the conspiracy is ongoing — that petitioners are still artificially *depressing* the market price in order to drive Zenith out of the market. The data in the record strongly suggests that that goal is yet far distant.[37]

---

[36] [FN 14] During the same period, the number of American firms manufacturing television sets declined from 19 to 13. 5 App. to Brief for Appellant in No. 81-2331 (3d Cir.), p. 1961a. This decline continued a trend that began at least by 1960, when petitioners' sales in the United States market were negligible. *Ibid.* See Zenith Complaint ¶¶ 35, 37.

[37] [FN 15]Respondents offer no reason to suppose that entry into the relevant market is especially difficult, yet without barriers to entry it would presumably be impossible to maintain supracompetitive prices for an extended time. Judge Easterbrook, commenting on this case in a law review article, offers the following sensible assessment:

> The plaintiffs [in this case] maintain that for the last fifteen years or more at least ten Japanese manufacturers have sold TV sets at less than cost in order to drive United States firms out of business. Such conduct cannot possibly produce profits by harming competition,

The alleged conspiracy's failure to achieve its ends in the two decades of its asserted operation is strong evidence that the conspiracy does not in fact exist. Since the losses in such a conspiracy accrue before the gains, they must be "repaid" with interest. And because the alleged losses have accrued over the course of two decades, the conspirators could well require a correspondingly long time to recoup. Maintaining supracompetitive prices in turn depends on the continued cooperation of the conspirators, on the inability of other would-be competitors to enter the market, and (not incidentally) on the conspirators' ability to escape antitrust liability for their *minimum* price-fixing cartel.[38] Each of these factors weighs more heavily as the time needed to recoup losses grows. If the losses have been substantial — as would likely be necessary in order to drive out the competition[39] — petitioners would most likely have to sustain their cartel for years simply to break even.

Nor does the possibility that petitioners have obtained supracompetitive profits in the Japanese market change this calculation. Whether or not petitioners have the *means* to sustain substantial losses in this country over a long period of time, they have no *motive* to sustain such losses absent some strong likelihood that the alleged conspiracy in this country will eventually pay off. The courts below found no evidence of any such success, and — as indicated above — the facts actually are to the contrary: RCA and Zenith, not any of the petitioners, continue to hold the largest share of the American retail market in color television sets. More important, there is nothing to suggest any relationship between petitioners' profits in Japan and the amount petitioners could expect to gain from a conspiracy to monopolize the American market. In the absence of any such evidence, the possible existence of supracompetitive profits in Japan simply cannot overcome the economic obstacles to the ultimate success of this alleged predatory conspiracy.[40]

---

however. If the Japanese firms drive some United States firms out of business, they could not recoup. Fifteen years of losses could be made up only by very high prices for the indefinite future. (The losses are like investments, which must be recovered with compound interest.) If the defendants should try to raise prices to such a level, they would attract new competition. There are no barriers to entry into electronics, as the proliferation of computer and audio firms shows. The competition would come from resurgent United States firms, from other foreign firms (Korea and many other nations make TV sets), and from defendants themselves. In order to recoup, the Japanese firms would need to suppress competition among themselves. On plaintiffs' theory, the cartel would need to last at least thirty years, far longer than any in history, even when cartels were not illegal. None should be sanguine about the prospects of such a cartel, given each firm's incentive to shave price and expand its share of sales. The predation-recoupment story therefore does not make sense, and we are left with the more plausible inference that the Japanese firms did not sell below cost in the first place. They were just engaged in hard competition.

Easterbrook, *The Limits of Antitrust*, 63 Texas L. Rev. 1, 26–27 (1984) (footnotes omitted).

[38] [FN 16] The alleged predatory scheme makes sense only if petitioners can recoup their losses. In light of the large number of firms involved here, petitioners can achieve this only by engaging in some form of price-fixing after they have succeeded in driving competitors from the market. Such price-fixing would, of course, be an independent violation of § 1 of the Sherman Act. *United States v. Socony-Vacuum Oil Co.*, 310 U.S. 150 (1940).

[39] [FN 17] The predators' losses must actually increase as the conspiracy nears its objective: the greater the predators' market share, the more products the predators sell; but since every sale brings with it a loss, an increase in market share also means an increase in predatory losses.

[40] [FN 18] The same is true of any supposed excess production capacity that petitioners may have

V

. . . The Court of Appeals did not take account of the absence of a plausible motive to enter into the alleged predatory pricing conspiracy. It focused instead on whether there was "direct evidence of concert of action." 723 F.2d, at 304. The Court of Appeals erred in two respects: (i) the "direct evidence" on which the court relied had little, if any, relevance to the alleged predatory pricing conspiracy; and (ii) the court failed to consider the absence of a plausible motive to engage in predatory pricing.

The "direct evidence" on which the court relied was evidence of *other* combinations, not of a predatory pricing conspiracy. Evidence that petitioners conspired to raise prices in Japan provides little, if any, support for respondents' claims: a conspiracy to increase profits in one market does not tend to show a conspiracy to sustain losses in another. Evidence that petitioners agreed to fix *minimum* prices (through the "check price" agreements) for the American market actually works in petitioners' favor, because it suggests that petitioners were seeking to place a floor under prices rather than to lower them. The same is true of evidence that petitioners agreed to limit the number of distributors of their products in the American market — the so-called "Five Company Rule." That practice may have facilitated a horizonal territorial allocation, see *United States v. Topco Associates, Inc.*, 405 U.S. 596 (1972), but its natural effect would be to raise market prices rather than reduce them. Evidence that tends to support any of these collateral conspiracies thus says little, if anything, about the existence of a conspiracy to charge below-market prices in the American market over a period of two decades.

That being the case, the absence of any plausible motive to engage in the conduct charged is highly relevant to whether a "genuine issue for trial" exists within the meaning of Rule 56(e). Lack of motive bears on the range of permissible conclusions that might be drawn from ambiguous evidence: if petitioners had no rational economic motive to conspire, and if their conduct is consistent with other, equally plausible explanations, the conduct does not give rise to an inference of conspiracy. Here, the conduct in question consists largely of (i) pricing at levels that succeeded in taking business away from respondents, and (ii) arrangements that may have limited petitioners' ability to compete with each other (and thus kept prices from going even lower). This conduct suggests either that petitioners behaved competitively, or that petitioners conspired to *raise* prices. Neither possibility is consistent with an agreement among 21 companies to price below market levels. Moreover, the predatory pricing scheme that this conduct is said to prove is one that makes no practical sense: it calls for petitioners to destroy companies larger and better established than themselves, a goal that remains far distant more than two decades after the conspiracy's birth. Even had they succeeded in obtaining their monopoly, there is nothing in the record to suggest that they could recover the losses they would need to sustain along the way. In sum, in light of the absence of any rational motive to conspire, neither petitioners' pricing practices, nor their conduct in the

---

possessed. The existence of plant capacity that exceeds domestic demand does tend to establish the ability to sell products abroad. It does not, however, provide a motive for selling at prices lower than necessary to obtain sales; nor does it explain why petitioners would be willing to *lose* money in the United States market without some reasonable prospect of recouping their investment.

Japanese market, nor their agreements respecting prices and distribution in the American market, suffice to create a "genuine issue for trial." Fed. Rule Civ. Proc. 56(e).**41**

On remand, the Court of Appeals is free to consider whether there is other evidence that is sufficiently unambiguous to permit a trier of fact to find that petitioners conspired to price predatorily for two decades despite the absence of any apparent motive to do so. The evidence must "tend[] to exclude the possibility" that petitioners underpriced respondents to compete for business rather than to implement an economically senseless conspiracy. In the absence of such evidence, there is no "genuine issue for trial" under Rule 56(e), and petitioners are entitled to have summary judgment reinstated.

VI

Our decision makes it unnecessary to reach the sovereign compulsion issue. . . .

The decision of the Court of Appeals is reversed, and the case is remanded for further proceedings consistent with this opinion.

It is so ordered.

JUSTICE WHITE, with whom JUSTICE BRENNAN, JUSTICE BLACKMUN, and JUSTICE STEVENS join, dissenting.

It is indeed remarkable that the Court, in the face of the long and careful opinion of the Court of Appeals, reaches the result it does. The Court of Appeals faithfully followed the relevant precedents, and it kept firmly in mind the principle that proof of a conspiracy should not be fragmented. After surveying the massive record, including very significant evidence that the District Court erroneously had excluded, the Court of Appeals concluded that the evidence taken as a whole creates a genuine issue of fact whether petitioners engaged in a conspiracy in violation of §§ 1 and 2 of the Sherman Act, and § 2(a) of the Robinson-Patman Act. In my view, the Court of Appeals' opinion more than adequately supports this judgment.

The Court's opinion today, far from identifying reversible error, only muddies the waters. In the first place, the Court makes confusing and inconsistent statements about the appropriate standard for granting summary judgment. Second, the Court makes a number of assumptions that invade the factfinder's province. Third, the Court faults the Third Circuit for nonexistent errors and remands the case although it is plain that respondents' evidence raises genuine issues of material fact.

---

41 [FN 21] We do not imply that, if petitioners had a plausible reason to conspire, ambiguous conduct could suffice to create a triable issue of conspiracy. Our decision in *Monsanto Co. v. Spray-Rite Service Corp.*, 465 U.S. 752 (1984), establishes that conduct that is as consistent with permissible competition as with illegal conspiracy does not, without more, support even an inference of conspiracy. *Id.*, at 763–764.

I

. . . [T]he Court summarizes *Monsanto v. Spray-Rite Corp.* as holding that "courts should not permit factfinders to infer conspiracies when such inferences are implausible. . . . " Such language suggests that a judge hearing a defendant's motion for summary judgment in an antitrust case should go beyond the traditional summary judgment inquiry and decide for himself whether the weight of the evidence favors the plaintiff. *Cities Service* and *Monsanto* do not stand for any such proposition. Each of those cases simply held that a particular piece of evidence standing alone was insufficiently probative to justify sending a case to the jury. These holdings in no way undermine the doctrine that all evidence must be construed in the light most favorable to the party opposing summary judgment.

If the Court intends to give every judge hearing a motion for summary judgment in an antitrust case the job of determining if the evidence makes the inference of conspiracy more probable than not, it is overturning settled law. If the Court does not intend such a pronouncement, it should refrain from using unnecessarily broad and confusing language.

II

In defining what respondents must show in order to recover, the Court makes assumptions that invade the factfinder's province. The Court states with very little discussion that respondents can recover under § 1 of the Sherman Act only if they prove that "petitioners conspired to drive respondents out of the relevant markets by (i) pricing below the level necessary to sell their products, or (ii) pricing below some appropriate measure of cost." This statement is premised on the assumption that "[a]n agreement without these features would either leave respondents in the same position as would market forces or would actually benefit respondents by raising market prices." *Ibid.* In making this assumption, the Court ignores the contrary conclusions of respondents' expert DePodwin, whose report in very relevant part was erroneously excluded by the District Court.

The DePodwin Report, on which the Court of Appeals relied along with other material, indicates that respondents were harmed in two ways that are independent of whether petitioners priced their products below "the level necessary to sell their products or . . . some appropriate measure of cost." First, the Report explains that the price-raising scheme in Japan resulted in lower consumption of petitioners' goods in that country and the exporting of more of petitioners' goods to this country than would have occurred had prices in Japan been at the competitive level. Increasing exports to this country resulted in depressed prices here, which harmed respondents. Second, the DePodwin Report indicates that petitioners exchanged confidential proprietary information and entered into agreements such as the five-company rule with the goal of avoiding intragroup competition in the United States market. The Report explains that petitioners' restrictions on intragroup competition caused respondents to lose business that they would not have lost had petitioners competed with one another.[42]

---

[42] [FN 3] The DePodwin Report has this, among other things, to say in summarizing the harm to

The DePodwin Report alone creates a genuine factual issue regarding the harm to respondents caused by Japanese cartelization and by agreements restricting competition among petitioners in this country. No doubt the Court prefers its own economic theorizing to Dr. DePodwin's, but that is not a reason to deny the fact finder an opportunity to consider Dr. DePodwin's views on how petitioners' alleged collusion harmed respondents.

The Court, in discussing the unlikelihood of a predatory conspiracy, also consistently assumes that petitioners valued profit-maximization over growth. In light of the evidence that petitioners sold their goods in this country at substantial losses over a long period of time, I believe that this is an assumption that should be argued to the factfinder, not decided by the Court.

III

In reversing the Third Circuit's judgment, the Court identifies two alleged errors: "(i) [T]he direct evidence on which the [Court of Appeals] relied had little, if any, relevance to the alleged predatory pricing conspiracy, and (ii) the court failed to consider the absence of a plausible motive to engage in predatory pricing." The Court's position is without substance.

A

The first claim of error is that the Third Circuit treated evidence regarding price-fixing in Japan and the so-called five-company rule and check prices as " 'direct evidence' of a conspiracy that injured respondents." The passage from the Third Circuit's opinion in which the Court locates this alleged error makes what I consider to be a quite simple and correct observation, namely, that this case is distinguishable from traditional "conscious parallelism" cases, in that there is direct evidence of concert of action among petitioners. The Third Circuit did not, as the

---

respondents caused by the five-company rule, exchange of production data, price coordination, and other allegedly anti-competitive practices of petitioners:

> The impact of Japanese anti-competitive practices on United States manufacturers is evident when one considers the nature of competition. When a market is fully competitive, firms pit their resources against one another in an attempt to secure the business of individual customers. However, when firms collude, they violate a basic tenet of competitive behavior, i.e., that they act independently. United States firms were confronted with Japanese competitors who collusively were seeking to destroy their established customer relationships. Each Japanese company had targeted customers which it could service with reasonable assurance that its fellow Japanese cartel members would not become involved. But just as importantly, each Japanese firm would be assured that what was already a low price level for Japanese television receivers in the United States market would not be further depressed by the actions of its Japanese associates.

> The result was a phenomenal growth in exports, particularly to the United States. Concurrently, Japanese manufacturers, and the defendants in particular, made large investments in new plant and equipment and expanded production capacity. It is obvious, therefore, that the effect of the Japanese cartel's concerted actions was to generate a larger volume of investment in the Japanese television industry than would otherwise have been the case. This added capacity both enabled and encouraged the Japanese to penetrate the United States market more deeply than they would have had they competed lawfully." 5 App. to Brief for Appellant in No. 81-2331 (3d Cir.), pp. 1628a–1629a. . . .

Court implies, jump unthinkingly from this observation to the conclusion that evidence regarding the five-company rule could support a finding of antitrust injury to respondents. The Third Circuit twice specifically noted that horizontal agreements allocating customers, though illegal, do not ordinarily injure competitors of the agreeing parties. However, after reviewing evidence of cartel activity in Japan, collusive establishment of dumping prices in this country, and long-term, below-cost sales, the Third Circuit held that a factfinder could reasonably conclude that the five-company rule was not a simple price-raising device:

> "[A] factfinder might reasonably infer that the allocation of customers in the United States, combined with price-fixing in Japan, was intended to permit concentration of the effects of dumping upon American competitors while eliminating competition among the Japanese manufacturers in either market." *Id.*, at 311.

I see nothing erroneous in this reasoning.

B

The Court's second charge of error is that the Third Circuit was not sufficiently skeptical of respondents' allegation that petitioners engaged in predatory pricing conspiracy. But the Third Circuit is not required to engage in academic discussions about predation; it is required to decide whether respondents' evidence creates a genuine issue of material fact. The Third Circuit did its job, and remanding the case so that it can do the same job again is simply pointless.

The Third Circuit indicated that it considers respondents' evidence sufficient to create a genuine factual issue regarding long-term, below-cost sales by petitioners. The Court tries to whittle away at this conclusion by suggesting that the "expert opinion evidence of below-cost pricing has little probative value in comparison with the economic factors . . . that suggest that such conduct is irrational." But the question is not whether the Court finds respondents' experts persuasive, or prefers the District Court's analysis; it is whether, viewing the evidence in the light most favorable to respondents, a jury or other factfinder could reasonably conclude that petitioners engaged in long-term below-cost sales. I agree with the Third Circuit that the answer to this question is yes.

. . . .

IV

Because I believe that the Third Circuit was correct in holding that respondents have demonstrated the existence of genuine issues of material fact, I would affirm the judgment below and remand this case for trial.

NOTES AND QUESTIONS

1. As a matter of procedure, the Court holds that when a defendant files a motion for summary judgment, the burden shifts to the plaintiff to demonstrate that there exists a dispute as to a material fact, and that the burden is increased when the court in the first instance determines that plaintiff's underlying theory is implausible. This burden of persuasion, the Court opines, requires more evidence than is normally required under a summary judgment motion. This burden includes the requirement that plaintiff produce evidence, in rebuttal to the motion, showing that under a Section 1 theory, defendants acted in concert and not independently.

Consider whether the Court's approach in *Matsushita* now sanctions the use of summary judgment as a means of disposing of complex antitrust cases. Has the Court amended Rule 56, giving the trial judge broader discretion in granting summary judgment? Compare the Court's standard for motions to dismiss in *Twombly* for 12(b)(6) motions with the *Matsushita* standard for granting summary judgment under Rule 56. Does one standard help inform the other?

Do you agree with the Court that a plaintiff has the burden on a defendant's summary judgment motion to establish that there is a genuine issue of material fact as to the existence of a conspiracy and that injury flowed from the conspiratorial conduct? Or, is the majority opinion a reformulation of the traditional summary judgment standard?

2. Throughout its opinion, the *Matsushita* Court refers, as it does in its remand order to the Third Circuit, to the plaintiffs' obligation to produce "unambiguous" evidence of predatory pricing. Doesn't the fact that the evidence is or may be ambiguous suggest the presence of a genuine fact issue?

In *Corner Pocket of Sioux Falls, Inc. v. Video Lottery Technologies*, 123 F.3d 1107 (8th Cir. 1997), the court applied *Matsushita* to ambiguous evidence concerning an alleged conspiracy between the owners of stores featuring video lottery machines and a trade association of video lottery distributors. The plaintiffs, owners of lottery machines other than Video Lottery Technologies (VLT) machines, claimed that the Section 1 conspiracy was enforced by VLT, the most popular producer of the machines, in an attempt to assist distributors in allocating territories and fixing prices. The theory was that VLT had agreed to engage in the conspiracy as a favor to the trade association, the Music & Vending Association (MVA), and as repayment for the lobbying activities of MVA, which helped to legalize video gambling in South Dakota.

VLT argued that its policy was not to sell directly to retail establishments, but, instead, to distributors. This prevented VLT or bar/restaurant owners from being charged with maintaining the machines, making them better serviced through the distributors. This also made VLT machines more popular and profitable.

The Eighth Circuit found that, given the defendant's description of the marketplace, the district court acted properly in inferring lawful conduct on the part of VLT. Because the evidence was ambiguous, the court, following *Matsushita*, had to weigh the evidence presented by each side to determine whether the non-movant's evidence "tend[ed] to exclude the possibility that the alleged conspirators acted independently." *Id.* at 1112. The Eighth Circuit sided with VLT's assertions of unilateral action without conspiracy.

3. In discussing the summary judgment standard, the *Matsushita* Court reasoned that plaintiffs' underlying claim was implausible — that in this factual context, there was no conspiracy to predatorily price. "The alleged conspiracy's failure to achieve its ends in the two decades of its asserted operation is strong evidence that the conspiracy does not in fact exist." The Court chided the Third Circuit for "relying on 'direct evidence' that had little, if any, relevance to the alleged conspiracy and in failing to consider the lack of a plausible motive to engage in predatory pricing."

The "direct evidence" the Court referred to was evidence that defendants conspired to raise prices in Japan as a means of cross-subsidizing the losses in the United States market. Does the Court explain how it concluded that this evidence was not related to the domestic predatory pricing conspiracy? The Court states "a conspiracy to increase profits in one market does not tend to show a conspiracy to sustain losses in another." Is any reasoned explanation given for this conclusion? Is this the type of fact issue that juries traditionally decide? Is it plausible that a predator might use profits from one market to fund a scheme in another market that would produce losses? *See generally United States v. AT&T*, 524 F. Supp. 1336 (D.D.C. 1981), *later proceeding at* 552 F. Supp. 131 (D.D.C. 1982), *aff'd*, 460 U.S. 1001 (1983) (AT&T charged with cross-subsidization from one market to another).

On the issue of "motive," is it not possible that defendants miscalculated the length of time needed to complete successfully the predation and raise the price to recoup lost profits? Does the fact that the scheme continued to last into its twentieth year necessarily mean, through hindsight, that predatory pricing could not possibly have been intended? Again, does the Court's use of a motive and intent standard suggest the resolution of fact questions? Can motive and intent be determined through objective criteria? *See* Christopher R. Leslie, *Rationality Analysis in Antitrust*, 158 U. Pa. L. Rev. 261, 309–14 (2010) (discussing hindsight bias in *Matsushita*).

4. Does the Court's opinion hold that as a matter of law, the threat of predatory pricing is an implausible basis for relief? Does *Matsushita*, at least, make it very difficult for a plaintiff who asserts injury due to predatory pricing to ever survive a motion to dismiss or a motion for summary judgment?

In *Cargill*, reprinted *supra*, Chapter 3, the Supreme Court declined to reject predatory pricing as a cognizable claim for relief. Said the Court, "It would be novel indeed for a court to deny standing to a party seeking an injunction against threatened injury merely because such injuries rarely occur. In any case, nothing in the language or legislative history of the Clayton Act suggests that Congress intended this Court to ignore injuries caused by such anticompetitive practices as predatory pricing." Does this language suggest a substantive change from *Matsushita*, or merely the different burdens placed on litigants depending on the statute invoked (i.e., Section 4 or Section 16) or the procedure employed (i.e., motion to dismiss or motion for summary judgment)?

Even before *Matsushita*, only a few plaintiffs were successful in winning on predatory pricing theories, at least since the Areeda-Turner test for predatory pricing was adopted in 1975. See discussion in Chapter 6.

5. In attempting to harmonize the Supreme Court's *Matsushita* holding with the Constitution's right to a jury trial, the Ninth Circuit said:

We do not [interpret *Matsushita* to hold] that a district court may grant summary judgment to antitrust defendants whenever the court concludes that inferences of conspiracy and inferences of innocent conduct are equally plausible. Allowing the district court to make that decision would lead to a dramatic judicial encroachment on the province of the jury. To read *Matsushita* as requiring judges to ask whether the circumstantial evidence is more "consistent" with the defendants' theory than with the plaintiff's theory would imply that the jury should be permitted to chose an inference of conspiracy *only* if the judge has first decided that he would himself draw that inference. This approach would essentially convert the judge into a thirteenth juror, who must be persuaded before an antitrust violation may be found.

Petroleum Prods. Antitrust Litig., 906 F.2d 432, 438 (9th Cir. 1990).

6. Clearly, the *Matsushita* summary judgment standard was designed for plaintiffs who must prove an agreement on the basis of circumstantial evidence. What if there is explicit evidence of a written agreement? *See* discussion of *Palmer v. BRG of Georgia, Inc.*, 498 U.S. 46 (1990), *infra.*

7. *Expert Testimony. Matsushita* has strong implications for the use of expert witness affidavits in antitrust cases. Applying the criteria for the admissibility of expert testimony from *Daubert v. Merrell Dow Pharmaceutical*, 509 U.S. 579 (1993), discussed in Chapter 3, several antitrust decisions have held that the testimony of an economic expert did not create a fact issue precluding summary judgment. For example, in *City of Tuscaloosa v. Harcros Chemicals*, 877 F. Supp. 1504 (N.D. Ala. 1995), the plaintiffs' expert offered his opinion that the defendants were engaged in collusion by noting that (a) there were few defendants with similar cost structures and standardized products, thus making collusion easier; (b) the market was subject to frequent, predictable sales by means of sealed bids with announced winners, thus making bid rigging more plausible; and (c) price-cost margins suggested prices above the competitive level. In addition, there was some evidence that the defendant's employees were instructed not to deviate from published list prices and that one firm had used a price change as a "signal to get prices up." From such evidence, the expert opined that the market was subject to tacit collusion by "signalling." He testified that "[d]efendants were using explicit price signals through bids not intended to win contracts in order to reach an agreement to bid (and quote) higher prices, while always honoring one another's incumbencies." *Id.* at 1516.

On appeal, the Eleventh Circuit reversed, holding first that the economist had used methods that were acceptable within the discipline of economics, and thus admissible. Second, the court held that the testimony, once admitted, was sufficient to entitle the plaintiffs to go to trial. *Tuscaloosa*, 158 F.3d 548 (11th Cir. 1998). *See also Maiz v. Virani*, 253 F.3d 641 (11th Cir. 2001). See generally Chapter 3 Section G for a discussion of the *Daubert* requirements.

8. Some circuits have adopted a slightly stronger version of *Matsushita*, but most continue to profess that they are merely following the standard set out by the Supreme Court. For example, the Second Circuit, in *Apex Oil Co. v. Dimauro*, 822 F.2d 246, 253 (2d Cir. 1987), stated that the evidence necessary to properly infer a conscious commitment to an unlawful conspiracy must be *strong* direct or circum-stantial evidence. Similarly, the Fourth Circuit, in *Laurel Sand & Gravel, Inc. v. CSX Transp., Inc.*, 924 F.2d 539, 543 (4th Cir. 1991), claimed that the plaintiff, in order to succeed in a summary judgment motion, must bring evidence that does not just "tend to" exclude the possibility of independent conduct, but *actually excludes* such an inference. For further examples of stricter applications of *Matsushita*, see *Dimidowich v. Bell & Howell*, 803 F.2d 1473 (9th Cir. 1986) and *Flegel v. Christian Hosp., Northeast-Northwest*, 4 F.3d 682 (8th Cir. 1993).

On the other hand, the Third Circuit has adopted a more liberal version of the *Matsushita* standard. It has been more willing to deduce that evidence excludes all possibility of independent action than other circuits. *Id.* This suggests a propensity to side with plaintiffs in antitrust summary judgment issues. Many Third Circuit cases have contained vigorous dissents, however, often faulting the majority for confusing evidence showing an *opportunity* to conspire with evidence excluding the possibility that the defendant did anything other than conspire. The Third Circuit has accepted business necessity defenses to summary judgment motions, however. See *Houser v. Fox Theatres Management Corp.*, 845 F.2d 1225 (3d Cir. 1988). *See generally* O'Connor Murphy, *Survey of the Circuits: Standard of Review for Summary Judgment in Sherman Act § 1 Conspiracy Cases-Third Circuit*, 27 ANTITRUST LITIGATOR 2, 6 (1997).

The rest of the circuits strike a middle ground, with some adopting *Matsushita*'s exact wording and some varying the standard by applying step-by-step tests to summary judgment motions in antitrust cases. The First Circuit follows the language of *Matsushita* without variance, requiring the plaintiff to present "evidence reasonably tending to show a conscious commitment by [the alleged conspirators] to a common scheme designed to achieve an unlawful objective." *Moffat v. Lane Co.*, 595 F. Supp. 43 (D. Mass. 1984). The Fifth Circuit uses this language as well. *See, e.g., Johnson v. Hosp. Corp. of Am.*, 95 F.3d 383 (5th Cir. 1996). The Sixth, Seventh, Tenth, and Eleventh Circuits undertake an initial consideration of the plausibility of the plaintiff's evidence, then apply *Matsushita*'s "tending to exclude" language should any ambiguity exist. Sometimes, these circuits weigh business justifications into the initial balance. *See Riverview Invest-ments, Inc. v. Ottawa Community Improvement Corp.*, 899 F.2d 474 (6th Cir. 1990); *Gibson v. Greater Park City Co.*, 818 F.2d 722 (10th Cir. 1987). The Sixth and Seventh Circuits also employ "plus factors," or supplementary evidence, in deciding whether a violation has occurred.

9. In a six-five decision by the Eighth Circuit, the court makes clear that it is very difficult for a plaintiff, when confronted with a motion for summary judgment, to prove conspiracy from circumstantial evidence.

In *Blomkest Fertilizer, Inc. v. Potash Corp. of Saskatchewan, Inc.*, 203 F.3d 1028 (8th Cir. 2000), the Eighth Circuit ruled that parallel pricing followed by price verifications on completed sales falls short of *Monsanto*'s and *Matsushita*'s burden on the plaintiff to establish evidence that excludes the possibility of independent action. The court reasoned that this conduct is normal in a market characterized as an oligopoly "where conscious parallelism is the norm." 203 F.3d at 1036.

[T]he [plaintiff] may not proceed by first assuming a conspiracy and then setting out to prove it. If the [plaintiff] were to present independent evidence tending to exclude an inference that the producers acted independently, then, and only then, could it use these communications for whatever additional evidence of conspiracy they may provide. As the record stands. . . . These contacts [are] far too ambiguous to defeat summary judgment.

Id. at 1037.

Five judges on the court dissented from the majority's narrow reading of *Monsanto* and *Matsushita*. The dissent, written by Judge John R. Gibson, read the majority opinion as requiring direct evidence of the conspiracy in order for a plaintiff to overcome a summary judgment motion by a defendant. The dissent found that there was enough circumstantial evidence that prices resulted from collusion to withstand summary judgment. The different viewpoints were characterized by Judge Gibson:

The Court today concludes that voluntarily revealing secret price-cutting to one's competitors is not probative of conspiracy, for three reasons, each of which is unsound. First, the price verification communications involved completed sales, not future sales. The Court states: "Common sense dictates that a conspiracy to fix a price would involve one company communicating with another company before the price quotation to the customer." . . . This misconceives the purpose for which the price communications are being offered. The communications are not supposed to be direct evidence of a one-time mini-conspiracy to fix the price on one sale. Rather, they are circumstantial evidence of a type of behavior one would not expect in the absence of an agreement to cooperate. If no cartel was in place, each competitor would seek to benefit from high prices generally, while secretly shading prices when it would gain a customer without provoking retaliation. Confessing price-cutting when one needn't do so would only invite retaliation and guarantee that one's competitors could match the discounted price exactly next time. This is contrary to self-interest. On the other hand, if the producers were cooperating in a cartel, a necessary feature of their arrangement would be some way to determine who was discounting. Thus, confessing price-cutting to competitors makes no economic sense for independent actors, but makes perfect economic sense for cartel members.

The Court has rejected circumstantial evidence of an agreement because it is not direct evidence.

The Court's second reason for dismissing the price verification evidence is that "[t]here is no evidence to support the inference that the verifications had an impact on price increases." . . . The class points to the price verifications as circumstantial evidence of a broader conspiracy. Parallel price increases are the starting point for the class's case, so that if the conspiracy is proved, effect on prices has been proved at the first step. . . . The Court argues that prices eventually went down . . . but this glosses over the fact that they first rose dramatically, then remained above both the forecasted price based on market factors and the suspension agreement price until 1992 (with the exception of the two-month dip caused by the PCS "market correction program"). If, to prove collusion, a plaintiff has to prove that there was no cheating, thus no downward pressure on prices, cartels will be quite safe from the Sherman Act.

. . . .

To support its proposition that there is nothing suspicious about oligopolists exchanging non-public price information, the Court relies on *In re Baby Food Antitrust Litigation*, where the Third Circuit stated: "No evidence . . . shows that any executive of any defendant exchanged price or market information with any other executive." 166 F.3d at 135. The court held that price discussions among low level employees did not show a conspiracy. *Id.* at 137. This reasoning implies that if high-level executives had been involved, it would have constituted evidence of conspiracy (if, indeed, the plaintiffs had been able to prove parallel pricing, which they did not in *In re Baby Food, id.* at 128–32). In our case there is a wealth of evidence that high level executives, who were in a position to respond to what they learned, were directly involved in exchanging secret price information. Citing *In re Baby Food* in a case with this kind of evidence vitiates the distinction on which the Third Circuit relied.

. . . .

The Court's third reason for dismissing the price verifications is that the verifications were "sporadic." . . . The evidence indicates that the producers called each other when they had reason to think their competitors were cutting prices, and that they responded to each other's inquiries. The total number of such inquiries is difficult to set, but the defendants characterize it as "no more than several dozen" — surely more than a scintilla. *Cf. Container Corp.*, 393 U.S. at 335 (liability where "all that was present was a request by each defendant of its competitor [s] for information as to the most recent price charged or quoted, whenever it needed such information" . . .; "[t]here was to be sure an infrequency and irregularity of price exchanges").

This "sporadic" argument seems to be directed to the quantum of proof, rather than the quality of it. In other words, it is an argument that more proof should exist, rather than an argument that the existing proof is not probative. If the plaintiff adduces evidence of the kind that tends to prove the existence of a conspiracy, I do not believe that *Monsanto* and *Matsushita* give a justification for rejecting it. *Monsanto* and *Matsushita* lay out a test for the kind of proof necessary in antitrust cases, not the quantity of it. *Compare Monsanto*, 465 U.S. at 764; and *Matsushita*, 475 U.S. at 587–88 ("antitrust law limits the range of permissible inferences from ambiguous evidence"; if claim makes no economic sense, plaintiff's evidence must be "more persuasive" than would otherwise be necessary) *with Anderson v. Liberty Lobby, Inc.*, 477 U.S. 242, 254–55 (1986) (where substantive law imposes a heightened standard of proof, as in libel cases, a higher quantum of proof is required to survive summary judgment). . . . There is no heightened "clear and convincing" standard of proof in civil antitrust conspiracy cases, requiring a greater quantum of proof than the ordinary "preponderance of the evidence" standard. *See In re Brand Name Prescription Drugs Antitrust Litig.*, 186 F.3d 781, 787–88 (7th Cir. 1999), *cert. denied*, 120 S. Ct. 1220 (2000). The plaintiff's evidence must amount to more than a scintilla, but the plaintiff does not have to outweigh the defendant's evidence item by item. *See Rossi v. Standard Roofing, Inc.*, 156 F.3d 452, 466 (3d Cir. 1998).

. . . .

The Court states in this case that the fact that there were "several dozen communications" among competitors is not "significant." . . . I would hold that evidence of several dozen communications of the type that tends to prove conspiracy creates a genuine issue of material fact.

In addition to the price verification practices, evidence concerning PCS's "market correction program" in December 1989 also tends to exclude the hypothesis of independent action. . . .

. . . .

Again, the Court misconceives the import of this evidence, rejecting it as direct evidence of an attempt to reach an agreement, when the class offers it as circumstantial evidence of an agreement that already existed. The Court considers it crucial to establish who received the Canpotex memorandum . . . apparently reasoning that if the memorandum was meant to negotiate an agreement, only people who got the memorandum could respond to it. Instead, the class offers this memorandum as circumstantial evidence tending to show that Canpotex knew on Friday, January 8, of an existing agreement to raise prices. The prophecy by Canpotex that its members would issue new "price lists" with particular prices does indeed tend to show the price increase was coordinated, because otherwise it would have been impossible to know in advance what the individual producers would do.

In sum, the class has adduced evidence of a market structure ripe for collusion, a sudden change from price war to supra-competitive pricing, price-fixing overtures from one competitor to another, voluntary disclosure of secret price concessions, an explicitly discussed cheater punishment program, and advance knowledge of other producers' price moves. Taken together, this list of "plus factors" adds up to evidence that satisfies the *Monsanto* standard.

For other cases on this issue of requisite proof on summary judgment motions, see *DM Research, Inc. v. College of American Pathologists*, 170 F.3d 53 (1st Cir. 1999) (upholding summary judgment where plaintiff's conspiracy theory was highly implausible and supported by "nothing more than unlikely speculations"); *In re Baby Food Antitrust Litig.*, 166 F.3d 112 (3d Cir. 1999) (finding the need for "plus factors" to be present and the need to consider whether the information exchanges by low-level employees had an impact on pricing decisions); *In re Citric Acid Litig.*, 191 F.3d 1090 (9th Cir. 1999) (concluding that "sporadic price discussions" are inadequate to meet preponderance of evidence test on summary judgment motion);

Mitchael v. Intracorp, Inc., 179 F.3d 847 (10th Cir. 1999) (affirming summary judgment where plaintiff's circumstantial evidence of conspiracy at most showed defendants' common concern for cost containment, and failed to meet the *Matsushita* standard of presenting evidence "tending to exclude the possibility that the defendants acted independently out of a legitimate and reasonable" business concern); *In re Brand Name Prescription Drugs Antitrust Litig.*, 186 F.3d 781, 787–788 (7th Cir. 1999), *cert. denied*, 528 U.S. 1181 (2000) (granting summary judgment where plaintiff's conspiracy evidence is ambiguous, defendant's pricing decisions were a legitimate business activity and the plaintiffs were unable to produce any evidence tending "to exclude the possibility" that the defendant was pursuing legitimate business interests); *see also Super Sulky, Inc. v. United States Trotting Ass'n*, 174 F.3d 733 (6th Cir.), *cert. denied*, 528 U.S. 871 (1999) (upholding district court's decision to set aside jury verdict against defendant; plaintiff's conspiracy evidence was "based upon circumstantial evidence, coincidence, and speculation," without any evidence tending to exclude the possibility that the defendants acted independently in pursuing allegedly anticompetitive conduct). *But see City of Tuscaloosa v. Harcros Chemicals, Inc.*, 158 F.3d 548 (11th Cir. 1998), *cert. denied*, 528 U.S. 812 (1999) (denying summary judgment based on expert evidence of consciously parallel behavior and "plus factor" that the companies enjoyed an unlikely economic combination of high profits and high contract retention during the period of the alleged conspiracy). *But see S & S Forage & Equip. Co. v. Up North Plastics, Inc.*, 2002 U.S. Dist. LEXIS 5732 (D. Minn. Mar. 31, 2002) (granting summary judgment for plaintiff despite "high standard of proof" because both direct and circumstantial evidence could support a jury finding that defendants entered and executed agreements to fix prices and allocate customers).

In 2011, the First Circuit Court of Appeals decided that gas retailers in Martha's Vineyard did not engage in price fixing, despite maintaining prices that were considerably higher than on the Cape Cod mainland. *White v. R.M. Packer Co.*, 635 F.3d 571 (1st Cir. 2011). The plaintiffs complained that four of the nine gas retailers conspired to fix prices and to price-gouge in the wake of Hurricanes Katrina and Rita in 2005. The defendants prevailed on summary judgment at the district court level, which the court of appeals then affirmed. The court held that the plaintiffs could not establish that it was plausible that the retailers were engaged in more than a mere conscious parallelism. In order for the plaintiffs' to have survived summary judgment they would have to produce direct or circumstantial evidence showing not only conspiracy but also tending to exclude the possibility of independent action. The evidence must show parallel behavior resulting not from chance or independent responses to market factors. The evidence presented by the plaintiffs failed in the court's eyes to show more than a mere conscious parallelism among the retailers.

10. Different courts have interpreted *Matsushita* and the role of plus factors — and what constitutes a plus factor — in very divergent ways. Compare the following two case excerpts and consider which court does the better job of applying the holding and rationale of *Matsushita* to price-fixing defendants' motion for summary judgment.

IN RE HIGH FRUCTOSE CORN SYRUP ANTITRUST LITIGATION,

295 F.3d 651 (7th Cir. 2002)

POSNER, CIRCUIT JUDGE.

The plaintiffs appeal from the grant of summary judgment for the defendants in an antitrust class action charging price fixing in violation of section 1 of the Sherman Act, 15 U.S.C. § 1. The defendants are the principal manufacturers of high fructose corn syrup (HFCS) — Archer Daniels Midland (ADM), A.E. Staley, Cargill, American Maize-Products, and CPC International ***. The plaintiffs represent a certified class consisting of direct purchasers from the defendants.

HFCS is a sweetener manufactured from corn and used in soft drinks and other food products. There are two grades, HFCS 42 and HFCS 55, the numbers referring to the percentage of fructose. HFCS 55, which constitutes about 60 percent of total sales of HFCS, is bought mostly by producers of soft drinks, with Coca-Cola and Pepsi-Cola between them accounting for about half the purchases. But many purchasers, of both grades of HFCS, are small. Industry sales exceeded $1 billion a year during the relevant period.

The plaintiffs claim that in 1988 the defendants secretly agreed to raise the prices of HFCS, that the conspiracy was implemented the following year, and that it continued until mid-1995 when the FBI raided ADM in search of evidence of another price-fixing conspiracy. Billions of dollars in treble damages are sought ***. The suit was brought in 1995 and though an enormous amount of evidence was amassed in pretrial discovery, the district judge concluded that "no reasonable jury could find in [the plaintiffs'] favor on the record presented in this case without resorting to pure speculation or conjecture." The soundness of this conclusion is the basic issue presented by the appeal. ***

Because price fixing is a per se violation of the Sherman Act, an admission by the defendants that they agreed to fix their prices is all the proof a plaintiff needs. In the absence of such an admission, the plaintiff must present evidence from which the existence of such an agreement can be inferred — and remember that the plaintiffs in this case concede that it must be an explicit, manifested agreement rather than a purely tacit meeting of the minds. The evidence upon which a plaintiff will rely will usually be and in this case is of two types — economic evidence suggesting that the defendants were not in fact competing, and noneconomic evidence suggesting that they were not competing because they had agreed not to compete. The economic evidence will in turn generally be of two types, and is in this case: evidence that the structure of the market was such as to make secret price fixing feasible (almost any market can be cartelized if the law permits sellers to establish formal, overt mechanisms for colluding, such as exclusive sales agencies); and evidence that the market behaved in a noncompetitive manner. Neither form of economic evidence is strictly necessary, since price-fixing agreements are illegal even if the parties were completely unrealistic in supposing they could influence the market price. But economic evidence is important in a case such as this in which, although there is noneconomic evidence, that evidence is suggestive rather than conclusive.

In deciding whether there is enough evidence of price fixing to create a jury issue, a court asked to dismiss a price-fixing suit on summary judgment must be careful to avoid three traps that the defendants in this case have cleverly laid in their brief. The first is to weigh conflicting evidence (the job of the jury), and is illustrated by a dispute between the parties over testimony by an executive of A.E. Staley that Coca-Cola, a major customer, suggested that the prices of HFCS 42 and HFCS 55 be fixed in a ratio of 9 to 10. The fact that the defendants all adopted this ratio is part of the plaintiffs' evidence of conspiracy, and the inference of conspiracy would be weakened if the initiative for the adoption had come from a customer. The defendants treat the Staley testimony as uncontradicted because Coca-Cola's witness did not deny having suggested the 9:10 ratio but instead testified that he didn't recall having suggested it and was not aware of his company's ever having such a preference. The absence of a flat denial by Coca-Cola's witness of the Staley testimony would not as the defendants contend require a reasonable jury to accept that testimony, which is self-serving, uncorroborated, implausible (because the defendants achieved the ratio by raising the price of HFCS 42 rather than by lowering the price of HFCS 55, so Coca-Cola could not have benefited unless it just bought 55 and a competitor 42, which is not suggested), and inconsistent with the overall evidence of conspiracy, which as we shall see was abundant although not conclusive. A plaintiff cannot make his case just by asking the jury to disbelieve the defendant's witnesses, but there is much more here. The defendants' handling of the 90 percent issue illustrates how the statement of facts in the defendants' brief combines a recital of the facts favorable to the defendants with an interpretation favorable to them of the remaining evidence; and that is the character of a trial brief rather than of a brief defending a grant of summary judgment.

The second trap to be avoided in evaluating evidence of an antitrust conspiracy for purposes of ruling on the defendants' motion for summary judgment is to suppose that if no single item of evidence presented by the plaintiff points unequivocally to conspiracy, the evidence as a whole cannot defeat summary judgment. It is true that zero plus zero equals zero. But evidence can be susceptible of different interpretations, only one of which supports the party sponsoring it, without being wholly devoid of probative value for that party. Otherwise what need would there ever be for a trial? The question for the jury in a case such as this would simply be whether, when the evidence was considered as a whole, it was more likely that the defendants had conspired to fix prices than that they had not conspired to fix prices. E.g., *In re Brand Name Prescription Drugs Antitrust Litigation*, 186 F.3d 781, 787 (7th Cir. 1999).

The third trap is failing to distinguish between the existence of a conspiracy and its efficacy. The defendants point out that many of the actual sales of HFCS during the period of the alleged conspiracy were made at prices below the defendants' list prices, and they intimate, without quite saying outright, that therefore even a bald-faced agreement to fix list prices would not be illegal in this industry. (Their brief states, for example, that "list prices are irrelevant here because the vast majority of HFCS sales were *not* made at list price" (emphasis in original).) That is wrong. An agreement to fix list prices is, as the defendants' able counsel reluctantly conceded at the argument of the appeal, a per se violation of the

Sherman Act even if most or for that matter all transactions occur at lower prices. Anyway sellers would not bother to fix list prices if they thought there would be no effect on transaction prices. Many sellers are blessed with customers who are "sleepers," that is, customers who don't shop around for the best buy; and even for those who do bargain for a lower price, the list price is usually the starting point for the bargaining and the higher it is (within reason) the higher the ultimately bargained price is likely to be. ***

Let us turn to the evidence that the HFCS market is one in which secret price fixing might actually have an effect on price and thus be worth attempting. The fact that price fixing has to be kept secret in order to avoid immediate detection followed promptly by punishment tends to rule out price fixing in markets that have many sellers selling a product heterogeneous with regard to quality and specifications and having good substitutes in production or consumption; that are concentrated on the buying side, enabling the buyers to tempt sellers to shade any agreed-upon price in order to obtain a big bloc of business; and that have other characteristics, unnecessary to detail here, that make it irrational to run the legal and business risks of fixing prices.

The plaintiffs' economic expert opined in his report and the defendants pretty much concede that the structure of the HFCS market, far from being inimical to secret price fixing, is favorable to it. We need not go into great detail on the point as it is not seriously contested. There are few sellers of HFCS. The five original defendants *** accounted during the period of the alleged conspiracy for 90 percent of the sales of the product. Therefore elaborate communications, quick to be detected, would not have been necessary to enable pricing to be coordinated. And if one seller broke ranks, the others would quickly discover the fact, and so the seller would have gained little from cheating on his coconspirators; the threat of such discovery tends to shore up a cartel. In addition, the product, HFCS, is highly standardized. Remember that there are only two grades, 42 and 55; and both are uniform. So colluding sellers would not have to agree not only on price but also on quality, design, post-sale services, and the like. This is another reason why a successful conspiracy would not require such frequent communications as to make prompt detection likely. There also are no close substitutes for HFCS. Not that there aren't plenty of other sweeteners, such as sugar; but apparently they are not perceived as close substitutes by soft-drink manufacturers and other purchasers of HFCS. An attempt to raise price above cost would not be likely to come to grief by causing a hemorrhage of business to sellers in other markets.

And the defendants had a lot of excess capacity, a condition that makes price competition more than usually risky and collusion more than usually attractive. When a market's productive capacity exceeds the demand for the market's product, a very low price will cover the incremental cost of additional output because capacity will not have to be expanded in order to enable additional production. Competition will tend to drive price down to that level because any price above it will make some contribution to the seller's fixed costs (the costs that do not vary with output, such as the cost of building the seller's plant). But it will not be remunerative pricing, because it will not cover those costs in full. ***

The defendants continued to add to their capacity during the period of the alleged conspiracy. This behavior does not disprove the existence of the conspiracy, as the defendants argue. Maintenance of excess capacity discourages new entry, which supracompetitive prices would otherwise attract, and also shores up a cartel by increasing the risk that its collapse will lead to a devastating price war ending in the bankruptcy of some or all of the former cartelists.

The principal features of the HFCS market that might seem to bear against an inference that secret price fixing was feasible and attractive during the period of the alleged conspiracy [include] *** there are some very large buyers of HFCS, notably Coca-Cola and Pepsi-Cola, and, as theory predicts, they drove hard bargains and obtained large discounts from the list price of HFCS 55. But it does not follow that the defendants could not and did not fix the price of HFCS 55. There is a difference between a market in which all or virtually all the buyers are large and one in which there are some large and some small buyers. Suppose the buying side of the HFCS market were as concentrated as the selling side, meaning that five firms bought 90 percent of all the HFCS sold. They would be able to whipsaw the sellers into granting large discounts, and probably therefore any effort at fixing prices would quickly collapse. When instead there are some large and some small buyers, which is the situation here, this need not prevent price fixing; it may simply cause the price fixers to engage in price discrimination, giving large discounts to the big buyers and no (or small) discounts to the small ones.

Market-wide price discrimination is a symptom of price fixing when, as in this case, the product sold by the market is uniform. If the product is differentiated and as a result each seller has a little pocket of monopoly power, enabling it to charge some of its customers a price above cost without their switching to its competitors, no inference of collusion can be drawn from the fact that the sellers are all discriminating. Id. In this case, however, the product is uniform (a "commodity"), so that competition would be expected to prevent any one seller from raising his price to any of his customers above his cost. If sellers are competing in the sale of an identical product which costs each of them $1 to produce (including in cost the market return on equity capital, "profit" in a financial but not in an economic sense), so that the competitive price, which is the market price because the sellers are competing, is $1, no one of them can sell his product to some of his customers for $2, for they can buy from his competitors for $1-unless the sellers collude, and agree not to cut price to the disfavored buyers. This is a highly simplified example, obviously. It ignores and the parties do not discuss the possible erosion of price discrimination by arbitrage, that is, by the favored buyers' buying more than they need and reselling the excess to the disfavored, a process that may continue until all buyers obtain the seller's product at the same price. *Id.* But the example does illustrate an economic logic that favors the plaintiffs.

We turn now to the evidence of noncompetitive behavior, as distinct from evidence that the structure of the market was conducive to such behavior. Early in 1988, which is to say at the outset of the alleged conspiracy, ADM announced that it was raising its price for HFCS 42 to 90 percent of the price of HFCS 55, and the other defendants quickly followed suit. The defendants offer various explanations, of which the most plausible is that HFCS 42 is 90 percent as sweet as HFCS 55. Even if this is correct (there is evidence that the true percentage is only 71 percent), it does not counter an inference of price fixing. In a competitive market, price is based on cost rather than on value. Therefore the fact that buyers of HFCS are willing to pay more for HFCS 55 than for HFCS 42 because it is sweeter just shows that a monopolist or cartel could charge more for the higher grade whereas competition would bid price down to cost. (That was our $1-$2 example; the fact that some customers would pay $2 did not make that a competitive price.) Under competition, if the cost of the lower grade were, say, half the cost of the higher, so would the price be. There is no evidence that HFCS 42 costs 90 percent as much to produce as HFCS 55. Nor is there any evidence that industry-wide adoption of the 90 percent rule followed or anticipated a change in relative costs. In fact, the evidence suggests that it costs only 65 percent as much to manufacture HFCS 42, implying that under competition its price would be 65 percent — not 90 percent — of the price of HFCS 55.

A few months after the adoption of the 90 percent rule, the defendants switched from making contracts with their customers that specified the contract price for an entire year to contracts in which price was negotiated quarterly. They did this although virtually all their customers preferred the former system in order to minimize risk. In other words, the defendants shifted risk to their customers *** at the same time that, according to evidence discussed below, the defendants were raising their prices net of cost, rather than lowering them to compensate the customers for assuming additional risk. That is not competitive behavior.

There is evidence that defendants bought HFCS from one another even when the defendant doing the buying could have produced the amount bought at a lower cost than the purchase price. There is nothing suspicious about a firm's occasionally buying from a competitor to supply a customer whom the firm for one reason or another can't at the moment supply. The firm would rather buy from a competitor to supply its customer than tell the customer to buy from the competitor, lest the customer never return. But if the firm could supply its customer (remember there was a lot of excess capacity in the HFCS industry during the period of the alleged conspiracy) and at a lower cost than its competitor would charge, why would it buy from the competitor rather than expanding its own production? The possibility that springs immediately to mind is that this is a way of shoring up a sellers' cartel by protecting the market share of each seller. A seller who experiences a surge in demand, but meets the surge by buying what it needs from another seller rather than by expanding its own production, protects the other firm's market share and so preserves peace among the cartelists. It is pertinent to note that these inter-competitor transactions ended with the end of the alleged conspiracy.

In part because of those transactions the market shares of the defendants changed very little during the period of the alleged conspiracy, which is just what one would expect of a group of sellers who are all charging the same prices for a uniform product and trying to keep everyone happy by maintaining the relative sales positions of the group's members. This evidence probably does not deserve as much weight as the plaintiffs give it. They don't point us to any evidence of how market shares fluctuated before or after the period of the alleged conspiracy; and without such evidence there is no benchmark against which to assess the stability of the defendants' market shares during that period. But it is something, the evidence of stable market shares, for two reasons. First, had they gyrated wildly, this would be some evidence of active competition. The defendants argue that they did gyrate wildly, but their evidence involves comparing pre-conspiracy (1988) market shares with market shares during the period of the alleged conspiracy (the district court followed them in this mistake). If, consistent with that evidence, the gyrations moderated during the period of the alleged conspiracy, this would be evidence for the plaintiffs.

Second and much more important, the output of HFCS grew during this period and one might expect that growth to have brought about changes in market shares; for it would be unlikely that all the sellers had the same ability to exploit the new sales opportunities opened by the growing demand. This is why a growth in demand usually makes it more difficult for a cartel to hold together than if demand is steady. If demand is growing it is difficult for a seller to determine whether a decline in its market share is due to cheating by another member of the cartel or just to the superior ability of some other member or members of the cartel to attract new business without cutting price. The defendants emphasize that point but fail to acknowledge that the fact that market shares did not fluctuate significantly during the period of the alleged HFCS conspiracy may indicate that the sellers had agreed tacitly or otherwise to share the sales opportunities created by the growth in demand. This is conjecture, but conjecture has its place in building a case out of circumstantial evidence.

The plaintiffs' economic expert witness conducted a regression analysis that found, after correcting for other factors likely to influence prices of HFCS, that those prices were higher during the period of the alleged conspiracy than they were before or after. *** The defendants presented a competing regression analysis done by one of their economic experts ***. The plaintiffs rebutted with still another expert ***. Resolving this dispute requires a knowledge of statistical inference that judges do not possess. *** But in the present state of the record we must accept that the plaintiffs have presented some admissible evidence that higher prices during the period of the alleged conspiracy cannot be fully explained by causes consistent with active competition, such as changes in the price of corn. ***

To summarize the discussion to this point, there is evidence both that the HFCS market has a structure that is auspicious for price fixing and that during the period of the alleged conspiracy the defendants avoided or at least limited price competition. But as the defendants point out (when they are not arguing, inconsistently, that the industry was in fact fiercely competitive), all of this evidence is consistent with the hypothesis that they had a merely tacit agreement, which at least for purposes of this appeal the plaintiffs concede is not actionable under section 1 of the Sherman Act. The question then becomes whether there is enough evidence for a reasonable jury to find that there was an explicit agreement, not merely a tacit one. To repeat, there is evidence that the defendants were not competing; we might go so far as to say they had tacitly agreed not to compete, or at least to compete as little as possible; but the plaintiffs must prove that there was an actual, manifest agreement not to compete. Another and equivalent way to put this is that they must present evidence that would enable a reasonable jury to reject the hypothesis that the defendants foreswore price competition without actually agreeing to do so. See, e.g., *Matsushita Electric Industrial Co. v. Zenith Radio Corp.*, 475 U.S. 574, 588 (1986).

More evidence is required the less plausible the charge of collusive conduct. In *Matsushita*, for example, the charge was that the defendants had conspired to lower prices below cost in order to drive out competitors, and then to raise prices to monopoly levels. This was implausible for a variety of reasons, such as that it would mean that losses would be incurred in the near term in exchange for the speculative possibility of more than making them up in the uncertain and perhaps remote future — when, moreover, the competitors might come right back into the market as soon as (or shortly after) prices rose above cost, thus thwarting the conspirators' effort at recouping their losses with a commensurate profit. But the charge in this case involves no implausibility. The charge is of a garden-variety price-fixing conspiracy orchestrated by a firm, ADM, conceded to have fixed prices on related products (lysine and citric acid) during a period overlapping the period of the alleged conspiracy to fix the prices of HFCS. ***

Here *** is the plaintiffs' evidence, which the district judge should not have disregarded, that there was an explicit agreement to fix prices: One of Staley's HFCS plant managers was heard to say: "We have an understanding within the industry not to undercut each other's prices." *** A Staley document states that Staley will "support efforts to limit [HFCS] pricing to a quarterly basis." Presumably the reference is to efforts by its competitors. The president of ADM stated that "our competitors are our friends. Our customers are the enemy." This sentiment, which will win no friends for capitalism, was echoed by a director of Staley's parent company who said in a memo to Staley executives that "competitors['] happiness is at least as important as customers['] happiness." A director of Staley was reported to have said that "every business I'm in is an organization" (emphasis added) — which sounds innocuous enough, but he said it in reference to the conspiracy to fix the price of lysine ("lysine is an organization") and so in context it appears that "organization" meant price-fixing conspiracy. Michael Andreas, the vice chairman and executive vice president of ADM, said: "What are you gonna tell [Keough, the recently retired president of Coca-Cola], that we gotta [i.e., have a] deal with . . . our two biggest competitors to f**k ya over[?]" Andreas, a principal figure in the lysine and citric-acid price-fixing conspiracies, also referred to Cargill's president as a "friendly competitor" and mentioned an "understanding between the companies that . . . causes us not to . . . make irrational decisions." In a discussion with a Japanese businessman indicted along with Andreas for fixing the price of lysine, Andreas compared the relations between ADM and Cargill to those between Mitsubishi and Mitsui, two Japanese conglomerates widely believed to fix prices and allocate markets.

A handwritten Cargill document refers under the heading "competitors" to "entry of new entrants (barriers) and will they play by the rules (discipline)." A price-fixing conspiracy increases the attractiveness of entry into a market by creating a wedge between price and cost. And so conspirators will naturally worry whether, if there is entry, the new entrant will join rather than compete with the conspiracy and, if he refuses to join, whether the conspirators can punish him in some way. This is not the only possible interpretation of the document, but it is a plausible one.

Shortly after the FBI raided ADM's headquarters seeking evidence of the company's involvement in the lysine and citric-acid conspiracies, Terrence Wilson, the head of ADM's corn processing division — the division responsible for HFCS as well as for the other two products — said he didn't know "what other companies [the FBI] hit . . . I don't know . . . if they hit Staley or not." Since Staley did not manufacture lysine or citric acid, but did of course manufacture HFCS, Wilson may have been expressing a concern that the FBI would uncover evidence of an HFCS price-fixing conspiracy as well. It is further worth noting that the alleged HFCS conspiracy began shortly after Wilson became head of ADM's corn products division — which raises the question why, if as the defendants argue the 90 percent rule and the other parallel behavior that is the plaintiffs' evidence of a lack of price competition in the HFCS market were just the natural expression of the oligopolistic structure of the market, this behavior should have begun when Wilson, later to be imprisoned for price fixing, took charge of ADM's HFCS operations. There may be an answer (pure coincidence, perhaps, or a change in the structure of the HFCS industry that suddenly made tacit collusion more attractive) — a point with general application to our review of the evidence that favors the plaintiffs — but its adequacy presents a genuine issue of material fact and therefore cannot be determined on summary judgment. And in a civil case price fixing need be proved only by a preponderance of the evidence.

There is some more evidence of the kind we've just been discussing, that is, evidence of explicit agreement, and other economic evidence as well that bolsters the plaintiffs' case, evidence for example that ADM had significant ownership interests in two of the other defendants. But we can stop here because the evidence that we have summarized would have been enough to enable a reasonable jury to infer that the agreement to fix prices was express rather than tacit. The evidence is not conclusive by any means — there are alternative interpretations of every bit of it — but it is highly suggestive of the existence of an explicit though of course covert agreement to fix prices. ***

Reversed and Remanded.

WILLIAMSON OIL CO. v. PHILIP MORRIS USA
346 F.3d 1287 (11th Cir. 2003)

Marcus, Circuit Judge:

This is an antitrust action brought pursuant to section 1 of the Sherman Act, 15 U.S.C. § 1, and sections 4 and 16 of the Clayton Act, 15 U.S.C. §§ 15 and 26, by a class of several hundred cigarette wholesalers ("the class" or "the wholesalers") against Philip Morris, Inc. ("PM"), R.J. Reynolds Tobacco Co. ("RJR"), Brown & Williamson Tobacco Corp. ("B&W") and Lorillard Tobacco Co. ("Lorillard") (collectively "the manufacturers"). The class alleges that the manufacturers conspired between 1993 and 2000 to fix cigarette prices at unnaturally high levels, and that this collusion resulted in wholesale list price overcharges of nearly $12 billion. The district court ultimately entered summary judgment in favor of the manufacturers. It reasoned that the wholesalers had failed to demonstrate the existence of a "plus factor," as is necessary to create an inference of a price fixing conspiracy, and that even if the class had shown that a plus factor was present, the manufacturers were able to rebut fully the inference of collusion, as the economic realities of the 1990s cigarette market rendered the class's conspiracy theory untenable. Rather, the district court held that the manufacturers' pricing behavior evidenced nothing more than "conscious parallelism," a perfectly legal phenomenon commonly associated with oligopolistic industries. . . .

I

The modern American tobacco industry is a classic oligopoly. Between 1993 and 1999, appellees — the nation's four largest cigarette manufacturers — along with Liggett Group, Inc., manufactured more than 97% of the cigarettes sold in the United States. Moreover, the composition of the industry has been remarkably stable over time, a condition that has resulted largely from the fact that during the twentieth century the major tobacco players engaged in minimal price competition. *** [During the early 1990s, however, discount brands had cut into PM's market share profits. PM attempted increase profits by raising price but failed because no rivals followed suit.] ***

On April 2, 1993, PM decided to take what appellants refer to as "the single boldest commercial move in U.S. cigarette market history": it announced that it was cutting the retail price of Marlboro cigarettes — which were by far the single best selling brand in America, enjoying a 21% market share — by 40 cents per pack and foregoing price increases on other premium brands "for the foreseeable future." April 2, 1993 subsequently became widely known throughout the industry as "Marlboro Friday." *** [I]t set off a price war among appellees ***. [T]his vast decrease in cigarette prices was disastrous for PM, RJR, B&W and Lorillard alike in terms of profits, and appellees were forced to rethink their profitability strategies. ***

Appellants contend that it is only at this point that PM, RJR, B&W and Lorillard began conspiring to fix and steadily increase prices to make up for the tremendous financial losses they suffered as a consequence of this price war. *** By appellants' account, the manufacturers' conspiracy began in earnest when appellees began using trade press — i.e., tobacco industry financial analysts like Gary Black — to "signal" each other regarding their willingness to comply with PM's implicit demands so as to facilitate price increases. For example, the class points to a statement made by Martin Broughton, the CEO and Deputy Chairman of British American Tobacco ("BAT"), B&W's parent company, that "BAT may be one of those who started the price war in the U.S., but we have no wish to escalate it." ***

Appellants say that PM signaled its acceptance of its competitors' overtures by putting its distributors on "permanent allocation" — that is, limiting the quantities of product the distributors could order — on November 5, 1993. ***

Appellants suggest that RJR responded to PM's signal on November 8, 1993 with one last signal of its own. Specifically, the class argues that by announcing an increase of $2 per thousand cigarettes (4¢ per pack) in both the premium and discount categories, and thus maintaining the constricted discount/premium price gap, RJR indicated that it was acceding to PM's conditions for increasing prices. By November 22, 1993, PM, B&W and Lorillard had matched RJR's increase. The class argues that it was in the economic interests of RJR and B&W to attempt to widen the premium-discount price gap, and that their failure to do so is evidence of collusion.

This initial RJR-led price increase was followed by eleven more parallel increases between May 4, 1995 and January 14, 2000. ***

The class also labels as part of the conspiracy appellees' adoption of permanent allocation programs despite the fact that they each had excess manufacturing capacities. According to the class, restricting supply in the face of consumer demand for more product was directly contrary to the manufacturers' economic interests and thus indicative of illegal collusion.

Appellants also argue PM, RJR, B&W and Lorillard furthered their collusive enterprise by exchanging sales data through a common consultant, Management Science Associates ("MSA"), which allegedly enabled appellees to ensure that all were adhering to their allocation programs and to detect and punish what plaintiffs' expert Franklin M. Fisher termed "defections from an industry understanding on price." The MSA system tracks shipments from the manufacturers to wholesalers and from the wholesalers to retailers and provides reports to each appellee regarding the shipments of its competitors. Appellants allege that although in 1994 PM began collecting sales data on RJR, B&W and Lorillard through MSA,[43] and thereby incurred a great competitive advantage, in 1995 it inexplicably began sharing this system with its competitors. Moreover, the class posits, over time the MSA system has been modified to make the cigarette market more transparent, and all of these alterations have been implemented with the unanimous consent of PM, RJR, B&W and Lorillard. ***

*** [O]n February 8, 2002, PM, RJR, B&W and Lorillard moved for final summary judgment on all claims against them. *** [T]he district court granted this motion ***. *** The wholesalers then identify 11 "plus factors," and argue that each plus factor creates a presumption that PM, RJR, B&W and Lorillard conspired to fix cigarette prices. They say that this presumption enables them to survive appellees' summary judgment motion. ***

II

*** [W]e have fashioned a test under which price fixing plaintiffs must demonstrate the existence of "plus factors" that remove their evidence from the realm of equipoise and render that evidence more probative of conspiracy than of conscious parallelism.

Although our caselaw has identified some specific plus factors, for example, "a showing that the defendants' behavior would not be reasonable or explicable (i.e. not in their legitimate economic self-interest) if they were not conspiring to fix prices or otherwise restrain trade," Harcros, 158 F.3d at 572, any showing by appellants that "tend[s] to exclude the possibility of independent action" can qualify as a "plus factor." Id. at 571 n.35. In cases where the plaintiff establishes the existence of one or more "plus factors," these factors "only create a rebuttable presumption of a

---

[43] [FN 8] Specifically, PM required its wholesale distributors to provide it with information concerning their shipments of all brands of cigarettes.

conspiracy which the defendant may defeat with his own evidence . . . ." Todorov, 921 F.2d at 1456 n.30.

In short, there are three steps to the summary judgment analysis in the price fixing context. First, the court must determine whether the plaintiff has established a pattern of parallel behavior. Second, it must decide whether the plaintiff has demonstrated the existence of one or more plus factors that "tends to exclude the possibility that the alleged conspirators acted independently." Matsushita, 475 U.S. at 588 (internal punctuation and citation omitted). The existence of such a plus factor generates an inference of illegal price fixing. Third, if the first two steps are satisfied, the defendants may rebut the inference of collusion by presenting evidence establishing that no reasonable factfinder could conclude that they entered into a price fixing conspiracy. ***

B. The District Court's Application of the Antitrust Summary Judgment Standard in This Case

As a preliminary matter, no party contests the satisfaction of the first prong of our inquiry, viz., the existence of parallel pricing behavior. As evidenced by the repeated, synchronous pricing decisions that occurred within the tobacco industry between 1993 and 2000, appellees plainly priced their products in parallel. Similarly uncontroversial is appellants' lack of direct evidence of a price fixing conspiracy among PM, RJR, B&W and Lorillard. *** Accordingly, the key questions on appeal are (1) whether appellants have shown the existence of a plus factor so as to create an inference of conspiracy; and (2) if so, whether appellees are able to rebut that inference.

1. Appellants' Alleged Plus Factors

After articulating the summary judgment standard in an antitrust case, the district court delineated eleven distinct factors that appellants had denominated "plus factors." These are: "(1) signaling of intentions; (2) permanent allocations programs; (3) monitoring of sales; (4) actions taken contrary to economic self-interest, including (a) little analysis of whether to follow price increases, (b) B&W and RJR pulling away from the discount cigarette market, (c) the May 1995 price increase lead by RJR and followed by Philip Morris, (d) Philip Morris' agreement to base the initial [Management Science Associates] . . . payments on market capitalization rather than market share, and (e) 'excessive' price increases after the MSA; (5) nature of the market; (6) strong motivation; (7) reduction in the number of price tiers; (8) opportunities to conspire; (9) pricing decisions made at high levels; (10) the smoking and health conspiracy; and (11) foreign conspiracies." ***

a. Signaling

First, appellants identify several "signals" that allegedly were transmitted among PM, RJR, B&W and Lorillard as to their pricing intentions. The class claims that these signals were the means by which appellees' price fixing conspiracy was carried out, as the manufacturers formulated and cemented their plans to collusively fix cigarette prices by indirectly communicating with each other through media outlets and other public announcements. ***

None of the actions taken by PM, RJR or B&W that appellants label "signals" tend to exclude the possibility that the primary players in the tobacco industry were engaged in rational, lawful, parallel pricing behavior that is typical of an oligopoly. Nor, conversely, do they tend to establish that a price fixing conspiracy was afoot. Notably, this conclusion does not change when we consider these actions cumulatively. In other words, in this case the whole of the manufacturers' actions is no greater than the sum of its parts. Because none of appellees' largely ambiguous statements and actions come close to meeting the mark, it is unhelpful to the class to consider those actions in concert.

b. Actions Against the Manufacturers' Economic Interests

It is firmly established that actions that are contrary to an actor's economic interest constitute a plus factor that is sufficient to satisfy a price fixing plaintiff's burden in opposing a summary judgment motion.

However, we must exercise prudence in labeling a given action as being contrary to the actor's economic interests, lest we be too quick to second-guess well-intentioned business judgments of all kinds. Accordingly, appellants must show more than that a particular action did not ultimately work to a manufacturer's financial advantage. Instead, in the terms employed by *Matsushita*, the action must "tend[ ] to exclude the possibility of independent action." Thus, if a benign explanation for the action is equally or more plausible than a collusive explanation, the action cannot constitute a plus factor. Equipoise is not enough to take the case to the jury.

The district court identified 7 actions taken by PM, RJR, B&W and/or Lorillard that the class said were contrary to the actor's economic interest:

> (1) non-initiating Defendants always followed price increases; (2) after Marlboro Friday, B&W and RJR turned away from discount cigarettes; (3) RJR led, and Philip Morris followed, a price increase despite planning documents which reflected they would not take increases; (4) each Defendant exchanged information through [MSA]; (5) each Defendant had permanent allocation programs; (6) Philip Morris based settlement payments on market capitalization and not market share; and (7) Defendants agreed to pay "excessive" settlement price increases.

Simply put, we find each of the class's arguments to be unpersuasive. None of the actions on which appellants focus tends to exclude the possibility of independent behavior (or tends to establish a price fixing conspiracy), and accordingly they do not constitute plus factors. ***

[A]ppellees' only viable route back to profitability was to increase prices; that they did so in a parallel manner does not establish collusion. Because the decisions to follow price increases were in the economic interests of RJR and B&W, these actions are not plus factors.

Nor can the lack of analysis that preceded the decisions to match each such individual increase be construed as evidence of collusion. Once appellees perceived that raising prices was their wisest economic strategy, no extensive discussion or planning was needed to implement this strategy each time a competitor initiated a price increase. As the district court put it in discussing RJR: "Once RJR determined what its strategic response would be to Marlboro Friday, there was no need to re-complete that evaluation each time RJR needed to decide whether to respond to a price increase." ***

Appellants next raise two arguments related to the exchange by each appellee of wholesale-to-retail sales information through Management Science Associates ["MSA"]. Around 1993-94, PM developed with MSA a system for tracking wholesale to retail shipments of its products, which it believed would afford it a great competitive advantage. Subsequently, in 1995, PM permitted MSA to share this service with its competitors. In exchange for their acceptance of the service, RJR, B&W and Lorillard agreed to share their own sales information.

Appellants first argue that PM's decision to share this service cannot be seen as being in its economic interest, and instead must be viewed as a means of facilitating the monitoring of the conspiracy by all of the conspirators. PM responds that by sharing the MSA service it shifted the financial burden of gathering sales and market share data for its competitors to RJR, B&W and Lorillard, and that as a result it actually realized an annual savings of millions of dollars. Viewed in the light most favorable to appellants, both explanations are plausible, and thus, at the most, this action by PM stands in equipoise; that is, it is equally consistent with collusion as with lawful competition, and accordingly, under *Matsushita* ***, it cannot represent a plus factor. Second, appellants argue that the participation by all appellees in the MSA data sharing system was contrary to their respective interests.

Preliminarily (and quite significantly), we note that the evidence establishes that appellees exchanged only sales, not pricing, information through MSA. Simply put, it is far less indicative of a price fixing conspiracy to exchange information relating to sales as opposed to prices. Moreover, it plainly was economically beneficial for each individual appellee to keep tabs on the commercial activities of its competitors, so the receipt of information concerning their sales does not tend to exclude the possibility of independent action or to establish anticompetitive collusion. ***

Thus, although the sharing of information can be seen as suggesting conspiracy, as appellants allege, it also can be seen equally as a necessary means to the receipt of its competitors' information. *** [T]he delivery of wholesale-to-retail sales information to MSA does not tend to exclude the possibility of independent action (or tend to establish a price fixing conspiracy), and thus cannot constitute a plus factor. ***

c. Monitoring of Sales through MSA

Previously, we indicated that the district court correctly concluded that appellees' provision of sales and pricing information to MSA was not a plus factor. However, the class raises a separate argument related to this monitoring. In particular, it says that "MSA solicited and received each [appellee's] approval for the modification of its services and the introduction of new services and specifically conditioned them on [appellees'] unanimous approval," and that this concerted behavior tends to exclude the possibility of independent action.

*** To the extent that appellants argue that the very joint nature of this system gives rise to a reasonable inference of collusion, we already have discussed the practical and financial advantages that stem from the ability to monitor the sales of one's competitors and from the spreading of the responsibility for providing market share and pricing data to those competitors. ***

d. Smoking and Health Conspiracy

Appellants say that beginning in 1953, PM, RJR and B&W conspired to restrict competition on the basis of health. They assert that this agreement remained effective throughout the alleged conspiracy and that it evidences appellees' agreement to fix prices. ***

In essence, for a jury to infer from this evidence that appellees collusively fixed prices during the 1990s, it would have to engage in propensity reasoning, i.e., "they did it 40 years before so they probably did it again," albeit now with Lorillard on board and with the object of the conspiracy being prices as opposed to health. ***

The "smoking and health conspiracy" does not tend to exclude the possibility that appellees were engaged in lawful, competitive pricing behavior or to establish a price fixing conspiracy, and cannot constitute a plus factor.

e. Foreign Conspiracies

The class also suggests that appellees conspired to fix prices in 10 different foreign countries during and prior to the alleged American conspiracy around which this lawsuit centers. *** [The district court] summarized its disposition of the foreign conspiracy claim by saying that:

> [Appellants] [ ]assert that they have "extensive evidence of anticompetitive activity" by [appellees] in Hungary, France, Argentina, Venezuela, and Panama. [Appellants] fail, however, to address the court's previous ruling that "price-fixing agreements were not at all times unlawful under the laws" of these countries. Furthermore, [appellants] baldly contend that [appellees], or their affiliates, undertook anticompetitive price fixing agreements in Canada, Costa Rica, El Salvador, Guatemala, and Saudi Arabia (Gulf States). Nowhere do [appellants] describe the legal landscape in these countries that would make any such activities unlawful, nor do [they] do any more than cite to documents in describing the nature of these alleged anticompetitive activities. This is simply too thin a reed upon which to allege that [the manufacturers'] "foreign conspiracies" are a "plus factor" in the instant litigation.

Holiday Wholesale Grocery, 231 F. Supp. 2d at 1312.

On appeal, the class cites Professor Fisher's testimony for the proposition that regardless of the legality of the manufacturers' activities in these countries, the foreign agreements provided a mechanism to "establish and revise, and to monitor and enforce agreements to coordinate." Appellants say that a reasonable jury could infer the existence of such an American conspiracy from these allegedly anticompetitive activities abroad.

*** In the absence of some palpable tie between these overseas activities and appellees' pricing actions in the United States, the foreign undertakings of PM, RJR, B&W and Lorillard do not tend to exclude the possibility of independent action in the setting of domestic cigarette prices any more than does the health conspiracy that allegedly began during the 1950s. Nor does the evidence readily establish a prior crime, wrong or act where appellants ultimately have failed to establish that the foreign conduct was a crime or wrong under the laws of the foreign sovereigns. See generally Fed. R. Evid. 404(b). Accordingly, appellants' alleged evidence of foreign agreements to collude does not rise to the level of a plus factor.

f. History and Structure of the Tobacco Industry

First, appellants say that the structure of the tobacco industry is conducive to price fixing agreements because of a concentration of sellers, inelastic demand at competitive prices, high barriers to entry, a fungible product, principal firms selling at the same level in the chain of distribution, prices that can be changed quickly, cooperative practices and a record of antitrust violations. In support of the contention that this industry structure constitutes a plus factor, the class cites *In re High Fructose Corn Syrup Antitrust Litig.*, 295 F.3d 651, 655 (7th Cir.2002). The problem with this argument, however, is that the majority of the market characteristics on which the class focuses are simply indicia that the tobacco industry is an oligopoly, which is perfectly legal. Moreover, as Judge Posner recognized in *In re High Fructose Corn Syrup*, "almost any market can be cartelized if the law permits sellers to establish formal, overt mechanisms for colluding, such as exclusive sales agencies." 295 F.3d at 655.

As for the industry's history of antitrust violations, the district court noted that the class had failed to direct it to any precedent for holding such to be indicative of a present antitrust violation. Appellants have failed to do so on appeal as well. ***

i. Opportunities to Conspire and the Restriction of Decisionmaking Authority to High-Ranking Corporate Officers

The class posits that PM, RJR, B&W and Lorillard enjoyed numerous opportunities to conspire, and that this supports their collusion claim. We unambiguously held in Todorov, however, that "the mere opportunity to conspire among antitrust defendants does not, standing alone, permit the inference of conspiracy." Indeed, the opportunity to fix prices without any showing that appellees actually conspired does not tend to exclude the possibility that they did not avail themselves of such opportunity or, conversely, that they actually did conspire. Appellants may not rely on this proposition to support their allegations in this case. ***

Thus, after thorough review of this case, we are satisfied that none of the actions on which appellants' arguments are based rise to the level of plus factors. Nor do they constitute plus factors when considered in concert. Indeed, when all of appellees' actions are considered together, the class has established nothing more than that the tobacco industry is a classic oligopoly, replete with consciously parallel pricing behavior, and that its members act as such. ***

V

Because appellants cannot demonstrate the existence of a plus factor, they cannot establish an inference of conspiracy, as they must to carry the burden imposed on them at the summary judgment stage of a collusive price fixing case. Moreover, appellees would have rebutted any inference that they conspired to fix prices by demonstrating that the class's conspiracy theory is utterly implausible. *** Accordingly, we affirm in all respects the district court's final summary judgment in favor of the manufacturers.

Affirmed.

NOTES AND QUESTIONS

1. In the absence of direct evidence of price-fixing conspiracy, antitrust plaintiffs generally use of the process of showing conscious parallelism and the presence of plus factors. *See* William E. Kovacic, Robert C. Marshall, Leslie M. Marx & Halbert L. White, *Plus Factors and Agreement in Antitrust Law*, 110 MICH. L. REV. 393 (2011) (categorizing plus factors based on their probative value); RICHARD A. POSNER, ANTITRUST LAW 55–93 (2d ed. 2001) (identifying plus factors).

In the preceding two cases, the Seventh Circuit and the Eleventh Circuit seem to take different approaches to evaluating plus factors. Can the opinions be reconciled with each other? Which opinion is more faithful to *Matsushita*?

After *Williamson*, what would an antitrust plaintiff in the Eleventh Circuit need to do in order to make a circumstantial case that the defendants had an agreement to fix prices?

2. Does Judge Posner's opinion lower the bar for a plaintiff to avoid suffering a summary judgment? In reversing a summary judgment in favor of the defendant, the Seventh Circuit seems to be reading *Matsushita*, unlike other circuits, more narrowly. This opinion suggests that if the plaintiff can show that its theory makes economic sense and even if the plaintiff's evidence is contested by alternative explanations, it should be enough to send the case to the jury, thus making the evidentiary portion of the plaintiff's case easier than *Matsushita*'s formulation that the evidence must "tend to exclude the possibility" that defendants acted independently. *See* David L. Meyer, *The Seventh Circuit's High Fructose Corn Syrup Decision — Sweet for Plaintiffs, Sticky for Defendants*, 17 ANTITRUST 67 (2002).

3. One type of plus factor is the presence of facilitating practices. The Second Circuit has explained that "a horizontal price-fixing agreement may be inferred on the basis of conscious parallelism, when such interdependent conduct is accompanied by circumstantial evidence and plus factors such as defendants' use of facilitating practices." *Todd v. Exxon Corp.*, 275 F.3d 191, 198 (2d Cir. 2001) ("Information exchange is an example of a facilitating practice that can help support an inference of a price-fixing agreement."). Professor William Page has explained that "[t]he category of facilitating practices now includes systems for reporting transaction prices, most favored customer clauses, meeting competition clauses, delivered or basing point pricing, industry-wide resale price maintenance, and public price announcements." William H. Page, *A Neo-Chicago Approach to Concerted Action*, 78 ANTITRUST L.J. 173, 180 (2012). How do these practices facilitate price-fixing cartels? Do they make it easier for price-fixing firms to prevent or to detect cheating on a cartel agreement? For example, basing-point pricing is the practice of requiring consumers to pay transportation costs based on shipment for a particular location, regardless of actual delivery costs and where the goods are actually shipped from. Why would an agreement to use delivered pricing from a common base point stabilize a cartel? For an example of base-point pricing, see *FTC v. Cement Inst.*, 333 U.S. 683 (1948).

Professor Page's list of facilitating practices is neither exhaustive nor static. John E. Lopatka & William H. Page, *State Action and the Meaning of Agreement Under the Sherman Act: An Approach to Hybrid Restraints*, 20 YALE J. ON REG. 269, 309 (2003) ("the list of facilitating practices is not fixed; it expands as economic models and actual experience demonstrate that particular conduct can be conducive to collusion"). Can you think of other facilitating practices?

The unilateral adoption of facilitating practices may violate Section 5 of the FTC Act, which does not require proof of an agreement for liability. *See* Susan S. DeSanti & Ernest A. Nagata, *Competitor Communications: Facilitating Practices or Invitations to Collude?*, 63 ANTITRUST L.J. 93 (1994). But to be illegal, noncollusive facilitating practices must have an anticompetitive effect or purpose. In *E.I. du Pont de Nemours & Co. v. F.T.C.*, 729 F.2d 128 (2d Cir. 1984), the Second Circuit rejected an FTC complaint brought under Section 5 of the FTC Act that challenged Du Pont's unilateral decisions to: sell only on the basis of a delivered price that included the cost of transportation; use "most favored nation" clauses; require at least 30 days advance notice to customers of changes in price; and provide advance notice of price increases to the press. The Second Circuit opined:

> When a business practice is challenged by the Commission, even though, as here, it does not violate the antitrust or other laws and is not collusive, coercive, predatory or exclusionary in character, standards for determining whether it is "unfair" within the meaning of § 5 must be formulated to discriminate between normally acceptable business behavior and conduct that is unreasonable or unacceptable. Otherwise the door would be open to arbitrary or capricious administration of § 5; the FTC could, whenever it believed that an industry was not achieving its maximum competitive potential, ban certain practices in the hope that its action would increase competition. The mere existence of an oligopolistic market structure in which a small group of manufacturers engage in consciously parallel pricing of an identical product does not violate the antitrust laws. *Theatre Enterprises, Inc. v. Paramount Film Distributing Corp.*, 346 U.S. 537 (1954). It represents a condition, not a "method;" indeed it could be consistent with intense competition. Labelling one producer's price change in such a market as a "signal," parallel price changes as "lock-step," or prices as "supracompetitive," hardly converts its pricing into an "unfair" method of competition. To so hold would be to condemn any such price

increase or moves, however independent; yet the FTC has not suggested that § 5 authorizes it to ban all price increases in an oligopolistic market. On the contrary, it states that "Section 5 should not prohibit oligopolistic pricing *alone*, even supracompetitive parallel prices, in the absence of specific conduct which promotes such a result." (Emphasis in original). This fine distinction creates doubt as to the types of otherwise legitimate conduct that are lawful and those that are not. The doubt is increased by the Commission's concession that price uniformity is normal in a market with few sellers and homogeneous products . . . .

In our view, before business conduct in an oligopolistic industry may be labelled "unfair" within the meaning of § 5 a minimum standard demands that, absent a tacit agreement, at least some indicia of oppressiveness must exist such as (1) evidence of anticompetitive intent or purpose on the part of the producer charged, or (2) the absence of an independent legitimate business reason for its conduct. If, for instance, a seller's conduct, even absent identical behavior on the part of its competitors, is contrary to its independent self-interest, that circumstance would indicate that the business practice is "unfair" within the meaning of § 5. In short, in the absence of proof of a violation of the antitrust laws or evidence of collusive, coercive, predatory, or exclusionary conduct, business practices are not "unfair" in violation of § 5 unless those practices either have an anticompetitive purpose or cannot be supported by an independent legitimate reason. To suggest, as does the Commission in its opinion, that the defendant can escape violating § 5 only by showing that there are "countervailing procompetitive justifications" for the challenged business practices goes too far.

Id. at 138–40.

4. Antitrust plaintiffs do not need to rely on circumstantial evidence if they have direct evidence of a price-fixing agreement. Direct evidence can come in the form of recordings of cartel meetings or testimony from cartel participants. A former price fixer may testify against his former co-conspirators in exchange for immunity from criminal prosecution. In 1993, the DOJ Antitrust Division revised its Corporate Leniency Policy to make immunity relatively automatic for the first cartel participant to expose a cartel to the DOJ in exchange for leniency. Corporate Leniency Policy, available at http://www.justice.gov/atr/public/guidelines/0091.htm. The new policy has significantly increased the discovery and prosecution rates of price-fixing cartels. *See* Christopher R. Leslie, *Antitrust Amnesty, Game Theory and Cartel Stability*, 31 J. CORP. L. 453 (2006).

5. The *Williamson* opinion treats the increases in price as symptoms of oligopoly pricing. In a perfectly competitive market, any one competitor cannot have an effect on price or output. The number of buyers or sellers is too large. However, in a market with only a few sellers — an oligopoly — each seller may take into account the pricing and output decisions of the other competitors. This "interdependence" may lead sellers into foregoing price cuts for fear that if one seller were to drop the price, each would follow with a retaliatory price, the result of which would nullify a gain achieved by reason of the initial price decrease.

Knowing that this response will follow, the original seller will not reduce prices in order to increase sales or market share. This theory posits that in a highly concentrated industry, interdependent pricing and production decisions will be the norm. Consequently, price competition is avoided.

Antitrust scholars have long debated whether oligopoly pricing — absent actual agreement — should violate antitrust law. On the one hand, Donald Turner argued in the 1960s that it is rational for an oligopolist to price its product and determine its output by anticipating the reaction of its competitors in exactly the same way we would expect a seller to react in a competitive market. No agreement is necessarily involved, he argues, but rather merely a prudential judgment about probable reactions. Rational and lawful in one market but not another, he asks? Under his theory, if conscious parallelism is the only evidence before the court, then the "agreement" requirement has not been fulfilled and interdependent pricing should not be illegal. Anticipating a rival's market reaction is thus inherent in competition and the structure of the market. Therefore, injunctive relief would be inadequate because it would condemn rational market behavior. Donald Turner, *The Definition of Agreement Under the Sherman Act: Conscious Parallelism and Refusals to Deal*, 75 HARV. L. REV. 655 (1962).

Professor (now Judge) Posner challenged Turner's approach and argued that while noncompetitive pricing by oligopolists may be facilitated by market structure, it was not inevitably compelled. Posner, *Oligopoly and the Antitrust Laws: A Suggested Approach*, 21 STAN. L. REV. 1562 (1969). He urged that such conduct required voluntary and coordinated action among sellers, similar to that found in the traditional cartel. Because of the market structure, however, no explicit agreement was necessary to accomplish the objective. Thus, from a combination of voluntary price moves such as price signaling and acceptances, and market structure, the agreement requirement could be proven by an inference of tacit collusion. Posner would not, however, prove evidence of a "meeting of the minds" solely through traditional conduct evidence such as a price exchange or announcement. The burden of proof would also be carried by the introduction of economic evidence.

The debate started by Turner and Posner is still ongoing. *See* LOUIS KAPLOW, COMPETITION POLICY AND PRICE FIXING (2013) (arguing strenuously for rules permitting collusion to be inferred from economic behavior, without necessarily requiring explicit communication); William H. Page, *A Neo-Chicago Approach to Concerted Action*, 78 ANTITRUST L.J. 173, 184 (2012); J. Brock, *Antitrust Policy and the Oligopoly Problem*, 51 ANTITRUST BULL. 227 (2006) (critiquing the hyper-theoretical literature on oligopolies through an empirical perspective on the structure and behavior of highly concentrated industries in America); Thomas A. Piraino Jr., *Regulating Oligopoly Conduct Under the Antitrust Laws*, 89 MINN. L. REV. 9 (2004); Gregory J. Werden, *Economic Evidence on the Existence of Collusion: Reconciliation, Antitrust Law and Oligopoly Theory*, 71 ANTITRUST L.J. 719 (2004).

[5]   Intra-Enterprise Conspiracy

As the previous cases in this chapter have pointed out, Section 1 of the Sherman Act requires a contract, combination, or conspiracy between two or more legal persons. In defining the requirement of plurality, the question arises whether concerted conduct by persons within a single legal entity comes within the statutory proscription of an agreement in restraint of trade. Literally, of course, conduct entered between two or more persons would come within the definition. Since a corporation can act only through its officers and employees, however, it would be impossible for it to conduct its affairs if its every conduct comes within the agreement requirement. *See Report of the Attorney General's National Committee to Study the Antitrust Laws* 30–36 (1955). The decisional law has created exceptions to Section 1's application where there is concerted action on the corporations' behalf by officers of a single corporation. The rule is generally that a single corporation cannot conspire with itself under Section 1. Related questions are raised regarding conduct by subsidiary corporations and by unincorporated divisions on behalf of a parent corporation. Central to the inquiry is whether concerted action has been engaged in by separate economic entities. Still other questions raised under the plurality requirement concern the coverage of conduct by agents. The following cases set forth the standards that have been applied to these categories under the doctrine of intra-enterprise (intracorporate) conspiracy.

On the issue of affiliated corporate status where there is concerted action, the Supreme Court said in *United States v. Yellow Cab Co.*, 332 U.S. 218, 227 (1947), that the legality may depend on whether the actual creation of the affiliation was illegal. The Court said "a conspiracy among those who are affiliated or integrated under common ownership" may violate Section 1 as if it were a conspiracy between independent firms. In *Yellow Cab*, the Court was addressing a potential restraint, where a cab manufacturer acquired several cab operating companies that were joined as a single entity. The restraint concerned cab purchasing contracts which allegedly foreclosed competitors of the manufacturer from selling cabs to the operating companies. The Court found that, notwithstanding the resulting single business entity, an illegal "combination" may have been formed during the creation of the enterprise, and if so, Section 1 would be violated if a restraint were found. While the language of the Court was broader than the ultimate holding, subsequent opinions are in agreement. See 338 U.S. 338 (1949), where the Court eventually affirmed the district court's finding that the cab operating companies had been obtained lawfully.

COPPERWELD CORP. v. INDEPENDENCE TUBE CORP.
467 U.S. 752 (1984)

CHIEF JUSTICE BURGER delivered the opinion of the Court.

We granted certiorari to determine whether a parent corporation and its wholly owned subsidiary are legally capable of conspiring with each other under § 1 of the Sherman Act.

I

A

In May 1972, David Grohne formed respondent Independence Tube Corp. to compete in the steel tubing business against petitioner Regal Tube Co. Grohne previously was an executive with Regal when it was purchased from its parent corporation, Lear Siegler, Inc., by Copperweld Corp. After the acquisition, Grohne stayed as an executive with Lear Siegler. The sale agreement between Lear Siegler and Copperweld contained a provision barring Lear Siegler from competing against Regal for five years.

When respondent attempted to purchase supplies from Yoder Co., executives at Copperweld sent Yoder a letter expressing concern with protecting its rights under the non-compete agreement. After initially accepting respondent's offer to purchase the supplies, Yoder voided its acceptance two days after receiving Copperweld's letter. Consequently, respondent was unable to begin operations for nine additional months.

B

In 1976 respondent filed this action in the District Court against petitioners and Yoder. The jury found that Copperweld and Regal had conspired to violate § 1 of the Sherman Act . . . but that Yoder was not part of the conspiracy. . . .

. . . The jury then awarded $2,499,009 against petitioners on the antitrust claim, which was trebled to $7,497,027. . . .

C

The United States Court of Appeals for the Seventh Circuit affirmed. . . . It noted that the exoneration of Yoder from antitrust liability left a parent corporation and its wholly owned subsidiary as the only parties to the § 1 conspiracy. The court questioned the wisdom of subjecting an "intra-enterprise" conspiracy to antitrust liability, when the same conduct by a corporation and an unincorporated division would escape liability for lack of the requisite two legal persons. However, relying on its decision in *Photovest Corp. v. Fotomat Corp.*, 606 F.2d 704 (1979), *cert. denied*, 445 U.S. 917 (1980), the Court of Appeals held that liability was appropriate "when there is enough separation between the two entities to make treating them as two independent actors sensible." . . .

We granted certiorari to reexamine the intra-enterprise conspiracy doctrine . . . and we reverse.

II

Review of this case calls directly into question whether the coordinated acts of a parent and its wholly owned subsidiary can, in the legal sense contemplated by § 1 of the Sherman Act, constitute a combination or conspiracy. The so-called "intra-enterprise conspiracy" doctrine provides that § 1 liability is not foreclosed merely because a parent and its subsidiary are subject to common ownership. The doctrine derives from declarations in several of this Court's opinions.

In no case has the Court considered the merits of the intra-enterprise conspiracy doctrine in depth. Indeed, the concept arose from a far narrower rule. Although the Court has expressed approval of the doctrine on a number of occasions, a finding of intra-enterprise conspiracy was in all but perhaps one instance unnecessary to the result.

The problem began with *United States v. Yellow Cab Co.*, 332 U.S. 218 (1947). The controlling shareholder of the Checker Cab Manufacturing Corp., Morris Markin, also controlled numerous companies operating taxicabs in four cities. With few exceptions, the operating companies had once been independent and had come under Markin's control by acquisition or merger. The complaint alleged conspiracies under §§ 1 and 2 of the Sherman Act among Markin, Checker, and five corporations in the operating system. The Court stated that even restraints in a vertically integrated enterprise were not "necessarily" outside of the Sherman Act, observing that an unreasonable restraint

> may result as readily from a conspiracy among those who are affiliated or integrated under common ownership as from a conspiracy among those who are otherwise independent. Similarly, any affiliation or integration flowing from an illegal conspiracy cannot insulate the conspirators from the sanctions which Congress has imposed. The corporate interrelationships of the conspirators, in other words, are not determinative of the applicability of the Sherman Act. That statute is aimed at substance rather than form. . . .
>
> And so in this case, the common ownership and control of the various corporate appellees are impotent to liberate the alleged combination and conspiracy from the impact of the Act. The complaint charges that the restraint of interstate trade was not only effected by the combination of the appellees but was the primary object of the combination. The theory of the complaint . . . is that 'dominating power' over the cab operating companies 'was not obtained by normal expansion . . . but by deliberate, calculated purchase for control.' . . .

It is the underscored language that later breathed life into the intra-enterprise conspiracy doctrine. The passage as a whole, however, more accurately stands for a quite different proposition. It has long been clear that a pattern of acquisitions may itself create a combination illegal under § 1, especially when an original anticompetitive purpose is evident from the affiliated corporations' subsequent conduct. The *Yellow Cab* passage is most fairly read in light of this settled rule. In *Yellow Cab*, the affiliation of the defendants was irrelevant because the original acquisitions were *themselves* illegal.[44] An affiliation "flowing from an illegal conspiracy" would not avert sanctions. Common ownership and control are irrel-

---

[44] [FN 5] Contrary to the dissent's suggestion . . . our point is not that *Yellow Cab* found only the initial acquisition illegal; our point is that the illegality of the initial acquisition was a predicate for its holding that any post-acquisition conduct violated the Act.

evant because restraint of trade was "the primary object of the combination," which was created in a " 'deliberate, calculated' " manner. . . .

The ambiguity of the *Yellow Cab* holding yielded the one case giving support to the intra-enterprise conspiracy doctrine. In *Kiefer-Stewart Co. v. Joseph E. Seagram & Sons, Inc.*, 340 U.S. 211 (1951), the Court held that two wholly owned subsidiaries of a liquor distiller were guilty under § 1 of the Sherman Act for jointly refusing to supply a wholesaler who declined to abide by a maximum resale pricing scheme. The Court off-handedly dismissed the defendants' argument that "their status as 'mere instrumentalities of a single manufacturing-merchandizing unit' makes it impossible for them to have conspired in a manner forbidden by the Sherman Act." . . . With only a citation to *Yellow Cab* and no further analysis, the Court stated that the suggestion runs counter to our past decisions that common ownership and control does not liberate corporations from the impact of the antitrust laws and stated that this rule was "especially applicable" when defendants "hold themselves out as competitors." . . .

Unlike the *Yellow Cab* passage, this language does not pertain to corporations whose initial affiliation was itself unlawful. In straying beyond *Yellow Cab*, the *Kiefer-Stewart* Court failed to confront the anomalies an intra-enterprise doctrine entails. It is relevant nonetheless that, were the case decided today, the same result probably could be justified on the ground that the subsidiaries conspired with wholesalers other than the plaintiff.[45] An intra-enterprise conspiracy doctrine thus would no longer be necessary to a finding of liability on the facts of *Kiefer-Stewart*. . . .

In short, while this Court has previously seemed to acquiesce in the intra-enterprise conspiracy doctrine, it has never explored or analyzed in detail the justifications for such a rule; the doctrine has played only a relatively minor role in the Court's Sherman Act holdings.

III

We limit our inquiry to the narrow issue squarely presented: whether a parent and its wholly owned subsidiary are capable of conspiring in violation of § 1 of the Sherman Act. We do not consider under what circumstances, if any, a parent may be liable for conspiring with an affiliated corporation it does not completely own.

A

The Sherman Act contains a "basic distinction between concerted and independent action." . . . The conduct of a single firm is governed by § 2 alone and is unlawful only when it threatens actual monopolization. It is not enough that a single

---

[45] [FN 9] Although the plaintiff apparently never acquiesced in the resale price maintenance scheme, *Kiefer-Stewart Co. v. Joseph E. Seagram & Sons, Inc.*, 182 F.2d 228, 231 (7th Cir. 1950), *rev'd*, 340 U.S. 211 (1951), one of the subsidiaries did gain the compliance of other wholesalers after once terminating them for refusing to abide by the pricing scheme. . . . A theory of combination between the subsidiaries and the wholesalers could now support § 1 relief, whether or not it could have when *Kiefer-Stewart* was decided.

firm appears to "restrain trade" unreasonably, for even a vigorous competitor may leave that impression. . . .

Section 1 of the Sherman Act, in contrast, reaches unreasonable restraints of trade effected by a "contract, combination . . . or conspiracy" between *separate* entities. It does not reach conduct that is "wholly unilateral." . . . Concerted activity subject to § 1 is judged more sternly than unilateral activity under § 2. . . .

The reason Congress treated concerted behavior more strictly than unilateral behavior is readily appreciated. Concerted activity inherently is fraught with anticompetitive risk. It deprives the marketplace of the independent centers of decision making that competition assumes and demands. In any conspiracy, two or more entities that previously pursued their own interests separately are combining to act as one for their common benefit. This not only reduces the diverse directions in which economic power is aimed but suddenly increases the economic power moving in one particular direction. . . .

B

The distinction between unilateral and concerted conduct is necessary for a proper understanding of the terms "contract, combination . . . or conspiracy" in § 1. Nothing in the literal meaning of those terms excludes coordinated conduct among officers or employees of the *same* company. But it is perfectly plain that an internal "agreement" to implement a single, unitary firm's policies does not raise the antitrust dangers that § 1 was designed to police. The officers of a single firm are not separate economic actors pursuing separate economic interests, so agreements among them do not suddenly bring together economic power that was previously pursuing divergent goals. Coordination within a firm is as likely to result from an effort to compete as from an effort to stifle competition. In the marketplace, such coordination may be necessary if a business enterprise is to compete effectively. For these reasons, officers or employees of the same firm do not provide the plurality of actors imperative for a § 1 conspiracy.

There is also general agreement that § 1 is not violated by the internally coordinated conduct of a corporation and one of its unincorporated divisions. Although this Court has not previously addressed the question, there can be little doubt that the operations of a corporate enterprise organized into divisions must be judged as the conduct of a single actor. The existence of an unincorporated division reflects no more than a firm's decision to adopt an organizational division of labor. A division within a corporate structure pursues the common interests of the whole rather than interests separate from those of the corporation itself; a business enterprise establishes divisions to further its own interests in the most efficient manner. Because coordination between a corporation and its division does not represent a sudden joining of two independent sources of economic power previously pursuing separate interests, it is not an activity that warrants § 1 scrutiny.

Indeed, a rule that punished coordinated conduct simply because a corporation delegated certain responsibilities to autonomous units might well discourage corporations from creating divisions with their presumed benefits. This would serve no useful antitrust purpose but could well deprive consumers of the efficiencies that decentralized management may bring.

C

For similar reasons, the coordinated activity of a parent and its wholly owned subsidiary must be viewed as that of a single enterprise for purposes of § 1 of the Sherman Act. A parent and its wholly owned subsidiary have a complete unity of interest. Their objectives are common, not disparate; their general corporate actions are guided or determined not by two separate corporate consciousnesses, but one. They are not unlike a multiple team of horses drawing a vehicle under the control of a single driver. With or without a formal "agreement," the subsidiary acts for the benefit of the parent, its sole shareholder. If a parent and a wholly owned subsidiary do "agree" to a course of action, there is no sudden joining of economic resources that had previously served different interests, and there is no justification for § 1 scrutiny.

Indeed, the very notion of an "agreement" in Sherman Act terms between a parent and a wholly owned subsidiary lacks meaning. A § 1 agreement may be found when "the conspirators had a unity of purpose or a common design and understanding, or a meeting of minds in an unlawful arrangement." *American Tobacco Co. v. United States*, 328 U.S. 781, 810 (1946). But in reality a parent and a wholly owned subsidiary *always* have a "unity of purpose or a common design." They share a common purpose whether or not the parent keeps a tight rein over the subsidiary; the parent may assert full control at any moment if the subsidiary fails to act in the parent's best interests.

The intra-enterprise conspiracy doctrine looks to the form of an enterprise's structure and ignores the reality. Antitrust liability should not depend on whether a corporate sub-unit is organized as an unincorporated division or a wholly owned subsidiary. A corporation has complete power to maintain a wholly owned subsidiary in either form. The economic, legal, or other considerations that lead corporate management to choose one structure over the other are not relevant to whether the enterprise's conduct seriously threatens competition. Rather, a corporation may adopt the subsidiary form of organization for valid management and related purposes. Separate incorporation may improve management, avoid special tax problems arising from multistate operations, or serve other legitimate interests. Especially in view of the increasing complexity of corporate operations, a business enterprise should be free to structure itself in ways that serve efficiency of control, economy of operations, and other factors dictated by business judgment without increasing its exposure to antitrust liability. Because there is nothing inherently anticompetitive about a corporation's decision to create a subsidiary, the intra-enterprise conspiracy doctrine "impose[s] grave legal consequences upon organizational distinctions that are of *de minimis* meaning and effect." . . .

If antitrust liability turned on the garb in which a corporate subunit was clothed, parent corporations would be encouraged to convert subsidiaries into unincorporated divisions. Indeed, this is precisely what the Seagram company did after this Court's decision in *Kiefer-Stewart Co. v. Joseph E. Seagram & Sons, Inc.*, 340 U.S. 211 (1951). Such an incentive serves no valid antitrust goals but merely deprives consumers and producers of the benefits that the subsidiary form may yield.

The error of treating a corporate division differently from a wholly owned subsidiary is readily seen from the facts of this case. Regal was operated as an unincorporated division of Lear Siegler for four years before it became a wholly owned subsidiary of Copperweld. Nothing in this record indicates any meaningful difference between Regal's operations as a division and its later operations as a separate corporation. Certainly nothing suggests that Regal was a greater threat to competition as a subsidiary of Copperweld than as a division of Lear Siegler. Under either arrangement, Regal might have acted to bar a new competitor from entering the market. In one case it could have relied on economic power from other quarters of the Lear Siegler corporation; instead it drew on the strength of its separately incorporated parent, Copperweld. From the standpoint of the antitrust laws, there is no reason to treat one more harshly than the other. . . .

D

Any reading of the Sherman Act that remains true to the Act's distinction between unilateral and concerted conduct will necessarily disappoint those who find that distinction arbitrary. It cannot be denied that § 1's focus on concerted behavior leaves a "gap" in the Act's proscription against unreasonable restraints of trade. . . . An unreasonable restraint of trade may be effected not only by two independent firms acting in concert; a single firm may restrain trade to precisely the same extent if it alone possesses the combined market power of those same two firms. Because the Sherman Act does not prohibit unreasonable restraints of trade as such — but only restraints effected by a contract, combination, or conspiracy — it leaves untouched a single firm's anticompetitive conduct (short of threatened monopolization) that may be indistinguishable in economic effect from the conduct of two firms subject to § 1 liability.

We have already noted that Congress left this "gap" for eminently sound reasons. Subjecting a single firm's every action to judicial scrutiny for reasonableness would threaten to discourage the competitive enthusiasm that the antitrust laws seek to promote. . . . Moreover, whatever the wisdom of the distinction, the Act's plain language leaves no doubt that Congress made a purposeful choice to accord different treatment to unilateral and concerted conduct. Had Congress intended to outlaw unreasonable restraints of trade as such, § 1's requirement of a contract, combination, or conspiracy would be superfluous, as would the entirety of § 2. Indeed, this Court has recognized that § 1 is limited to concerted conduct at least since the days of *United States v. Colgate & Co.*, 250 U.S. 300 (1919). . . .

Although we recognize that any "gap" the Sherman Act leaves is the sensible result of a purposeful policy decision by Congress, we also note that the size of any such gap is open to serious question. Any anticompetitive activities of corporations and their wholly owned subsidiaries meriting antitrust remedies may be policed adequately without resort to an intra-enterprise conspiracy doctrine. A corporation's initial acquisition of control will always be subject to scrutiny under § 1 of the Sherman Act and § 7 of the Clayton Act. . . . Thereafter, the enterprise is fully subject to § 2 of the Sherman Act and § 5 of the Federal Trade Commission Act. . . . That these statutes are adequate to control dangerous anticompetitive conduct is suggested by the fact that not a single holding of antitrust liability by this Court would today be different in the absence of an intra-enterprise conspiracy doctrine. It is further suggested by the fact that the Federal Government, in its administration of the antitrust laws, no longer accepts the concept that a corporation and its wholly owned subsidiaries can "combine" or "conspire" under § 1. Elimination of the intra-enterprise conspiracy doctrine with respect to corporations and their wholly owned subsidiaries will therefore not cripple antitrust enforcement. It will simply eliminate treble damages from private state tort suits masquerading as antitrust actions.

IV

We hold that Copperweld and its wholly owned subsidiary Regal are incapable of conspiring with each other for purposes of § 1 of the Sherman Act. To the extent that prior decisions of this Court are to the contrary, they are disapproved and overruled. Accordingly, the judgment of the Court of Appeals is reversed.

NOTES AND QUESTIONS

1. The Court in *Copperweld* held that a corporation and its wholly owned subsidiary are a single enterprise and thus are incapable of conspiring under Section 1. In so doing, a rule of per se legality under Section 1 was created for the corporation and its wholly owned subsidiary. In light of the Court's rationale, is a corporation legally capable of conspiring with a firm it controls through a 60% ownership interest? *See Fishman v. Estate of Wirtz*, 807 F.2d 520 (7th Cir. 1986) (requiring a complete unity of interests). What in the Court's economic reasoning would support the same result announced in *Copperweld*? Consider whether the Court's functional "unity of interest" test is determinative. Or, is the severity of the restraint a factor in determining whether there is a single enterprise? The First and Third Circuits have suggested that *Copperweld* does not shield a parent corporation from the legal ability to enter a conspiracy with a less than wholly owned subsidiary. *Tunis Bros. v. Ford Motor Co.*, 763 F.2d 1482 (3d Cir. 1985) (defendant owned 100% of voting stock and 79% of equity stock); *Computer Identics Corp. v. Southern Pac. Co.*, 756 F.2d 200 (1st Cir. 1985) (defendant owned 80% of subsidiary). The *Computer Identics* court approved a jury instruction which avoids a direct numerical analysis in favor of a functional test: "If the defendants were so closely related that they were in fact one entity, there can be no conspiracy. . . . You are to decide whether the defendant corporations acted as a single entity sharing common management. . . . If they operated separately, then they are capable of conspiracy. If they acted as one common entity, then they could not enter into a conspiracy." *Id.* at 204–205. In practice, it may not be critical to focus on the relationship between the parent and partially owned subsidiary because the plurality requirement might be satisfied by the conduct of the other owner; partial ownership of the subsidiary means that the subsidiary has at least two owners. The Fourth Circuit has held in *Advanced Health-Care Servs. v. Radford Community Hosp.*, 910 F.2d 139 (4th Cir. 1990), that two subsidiaries wholly owned by the same parent corporation are not legally capable of conspiring with one another for purposes of the Sherman Act.

2. After *Copperweld*, is it likely that the Court will consider efficiency as a valid defense to the corporate structure? Consider the Court's language: "a business enterprise should be free to structure itself in ways that serve efficiency of control, economy of operations, and other factors dictated by business judgment without increasing its exposure to antitrust liability." Are there reasons for distinguishing between a parent and subsidiary and vertical integration if both are designed to achieve competitive efficiencies?

3. In 1986, the Supreme Court in *Fisher v. City of Berkeley*, 475 U.S. 260 (1986), held that a municipality could not conspire with itself or its officials within the meaning of Section 1 in adopting a rent control ordinance where there was no private influence alleged. The *Fisher* decision is reprinted *infra*, Chapter 9.

4. The Sixth Circuit held that *Copperweld* precludes a finding of conspiracy between a hospital and its medical staff but that the requisite agreement might be found among individual obstetricians who agreed to block medical care by midwives. *Nurse Midwifery Ass'n v. Hibbett*, 918 F.2d 605 (6th Cir. 1990). The difference, the court observed, is that the medical staff, when making staff-privilege decisions, only act as officers of the hospital who cannot compete with the hospital. But when the medical staff employee has a personal stake in the outcome, as when a competitor is denied staff privileges by a hospital board composed of physicians with independent practices, the board members may not be immune from antitrust suit under the intracorporate conspiracy doctrine. The court also suggested that concerns about competition emerged only when the doctors on the staff were in competition with those excluded:

> When the staff as a group makes decisions or recommendations for the hospital in areas that do not affect the market in which they compete as individuals, there is no reason not to treat them as agents of the hospital. However, when competing physicians are making privilege recommendations concerning another competitor, sufficient anticompetitive concerns are raised to warrant a conclusion that the members of the medical staff are not acting as agents of the hospital for purposes of applying the intracorporate conspiracy doctrine. . . .

Under the court's reasoning, an obstetrician on a hospital board who had an independent practice might be suable for voting to deny hospital staff privileges to a competing obstetrician; however, an anesthesiologist would not be suable because anesthesiologists do not compete directly with obstetricians as a general matter. Query: suppose that the obstetricians agreed to defer to the opinion of the anesthesiologists when an anesthesiologist's application for staff privileges was being considered, and vice-versa? The Supreme Court, over the objection of Justice White, refused to grant certiorari from the Sixth Circuit's decision in *Nurse Midwifery*. See also *Weiss v. York Hosp.*, 745 F.2d 786, 813–817 (3d Cir. 1984).

AMERICAN NEEDLE, INC. v. NATIONAL FOOTBALL LEAGUE
560 U.S. 183 (2010)

JUSTICE STEVENS delivered the opinion of the Court.

"Every contract, combination in the form of a trust or otherwise, or, conspiracy, in restraint of trade" is made illegal by § 1 of the Sherman Act. The question whether an arrangement is a contract, combination, or conspiracy is different from and antecedent to the question whether it unreasonably restrains trade. This case raises that antecedent question about the business of the 32 teams in the National Football League (NFL) and a corporate entity that they formed to manage their intellectual property. We conclude that the NFL's licensing activities constitute concerted action that is not categorically beyond the coverage of § 1. The legality of that concerted action must be judged under the Rule of Reason.

I

Originally organized in 1920, the NFL is an unincorporated association that now includes 32 separately owned professional football teams. Each team has its own name, colors, and logo, and owns related intellectual property. Like each of the other teams in the league, the New Orleans Saints and the Indianapolis Colts, for example, have their own distinctive names, colors, and marks that are well known to millions of sports fans.

Prior to 1963, the teams made their own arrangements for licensing their intellectual property and marketing trademarked items such as caps and jerseys. In 1963, the teams formed National Football League Properties (NFLP) to develop, license, and market their intellectual property. Most, but not all, of the substantial revenues generated by NFLP have either been given to charity or shared equally among the teams. However, the teams are able to and have at times sought to withdraw from this arrangement.

Between 1963 and 2000, NFLP granted nonexclusive licenses to a number of vendors, permitting them to manufacture and sell apparel bearing team insignias. Petitioner, American Needle, Inc., was one of those licensees. In December 2000, the teams voted to authorize NFLP to grant exclusive licenses, and NFLP granted Reebok International Ltd. an exclusive 10-year license to manufacture and sell trademarked headwear for all 32 teams. It thereafter declined to renew American Needle's nonexclusive license.

American Needle filed this action . . . , alleging that the agreements between the NFL, its teams, NFLP, and Reebok violated §§ 1 and 2 of the Sherman Act. In their answer to the complaint, the defendants averred that the teams, NFL, and NFLP were incapable of conspiring within the meaning of § 1 "because they are a single economic enterprise, at least with respect to the conduct challenged." . . .

II

As the case comes to us, we have only a narrow issue to decide: whether the NFL respondents are capable of engaging in a "contract, combination . . . , or conspiracy" as defined by § 1 of the Sherman Act, 15 U.S.C. § 1, or, as we have sometimes phrased it, whether the alleged activity by the NFL respondents "must be viewed as that of a single enterprise for purposes of § 1." *Copperweld Corp.* v. *Independence Tube Corp.*, 467 U.S. 752, 771 (1984). . . .

The meaning of the term "contract, combination . . . or conspiracy" is informed by the " 'basic distinction' " in the Sherman Act " 'between concerted and independent action' " that distinguishes § 1 of the Sherman Act from § 2. *Copperweld*, 467 U.S., at 767 (quoting *Monsanto Co.* v. *Spray-Rite Service Corp.*, 465 U.S. 752, 761 (1984)). Section 1 applies only to concerted action that restrains trade. Section 2, by contrast, covers both concerted and independent action, but only if that action "monopolize[s],"15 U.S.C. § 2, or "threatens actual monopolization," *Copperweld*, 467 U.S., at 767, a category that is narrower than restraint of trade. Monopoly power may be equally harmful whether it is the product of joint action or individual action. . . .

III

We have long held that concerted action under § 1 does not turn simply on whether the parties involved are legally distinct entities. Instead, we have eschewed such formalistic distinctions in favor of a functional consideration of how the parties involved in the alleged anticompetitive conduct actually operate. As a result, we have repeatedly found instances in which members of a legally single entity violated § 1 when the entity was controlled by a group of competitors and served, in essence, as a vehicle for ongoing concerted activity. In *United States* v. *Sealy, Inc.*, 388 U.S. 350 (1967), for example, a group of mattress manufacturers operated and controlled Sealy, Inc., a company that licensed the Sealy trademark to the manufacturers, and dictated that each operate within a specific geographic area. *Id.*, at 352–353. The Government alleged that the licensees and Sealy were conspiring in violation of § 1, and we agreed. *Id.*, at 352–354. We explained that "[w]e seek the central substance of the situation" and therefore "we are moved by the identity of the persons who act, rather than the label of their hats." *Id.*, at 353. We thus held that Sealy was not a "separate entity, but . . . an instrumentality of the individual manufacturers." *Id.*, at 356. In similar circumstances, we have found other formally distinct business organizations covered by § 1.

Conversely, there is not necessarily concerted action simply because more than one legally distinct entity is involved. Although, under a now-defunct doctrine known as the "intraenterprise conspiracy doctrine," we once treated cooperation between legally separate entities as necessarily covered by § 1, we now embark on a more functional analysis.

The roots of this functional analysis can be found in the very decision that established the intraenterprise conspiracy doctrine. In *United States* v. *Yellow Cab Co.*, 332 U.S. 218 (1947), we observed that "corporate interrelationships . . . are not determinative of the applicability of the Sherman Act" because the Act "is aimed at substance rather than form." *Id.*, at 227. We nonetheless held that cooperation between legally separate entities was necessarily covered by § 1 because an unreasonable restraint of trade "may result as readily from a conspiracy among those who are affiliated or integrated under common ownership as from a conspiracy among those who are otherwise independent." *Ibid.* . . .

We finally reexamined the intraenterprise conspiracy doctrine in *Copperweld Corp. v. Independence Tube Corp.*, 467 U.S. 752 (1984), and concluded that it was inconsistent with the " 'basic distinction between concerted and independent action.' " *Id.*, at 767. Considering it "perfectly plain that an internal agreement to implement a single, unitary firm's policies does not raise the antitrust dangers that § 1 was designed to police," *id.*, at 769, we held that a parent corporation and its wholly owned subsidiary "are incapable of conspiring with each other for purposes of § 1 of the Sherman Act," *id.*, at 777. We explained that although a parent corporation and its wholly owned subsidiary are "separate" for the purposes of incorporation or formal title, they are controlled by a single center of decision-making and they control a single aggregation of economic power. Joint conduct by two such entities does not "depriv[e] the marketplace of independent centers of decision-making," *id.*, at 769, and as a result, an agreement between them does not constitute a "contract, combination . . . or conspiracy" for the purposes of § 1.

IV

As *Copperweld* exemplifies, "substance, not form, should determine whether a[n] . . . entity is capable of conspiring under § 1." 467 U.S., at 773, n. 21. This inquiry is sometimes described as asking whether the alleged conspirators are a single entity. That is perhaps a misdescription, however, because the question is not whether the defendant is a legally single entity or has a single name; nor is the question whether the parties involved "seem" like one firm or multiple firms in any metaphysical sense. The key is whether the alleged "contract, combination . . . , or conspiracy" is concerted action — that is, whether it joins together separate decision makers. The relevant inquiry, therefore, is whether there is a "contract, combination . . . or conspiracy" amongst "separate economic actors pursuing separate economic interests," *id.*, at 769, such that the agreement "deprives the marketplace of independent centers of decision-making," *ibid.*, and therefore of "diversity of entrepreneurial interests," . . . .

Thus, while the president and a vice president of a firm could (and regularly do) act in combination, their joint action generally is not the sort of "combination" that § 1 is intended to cover. Such agreements might be described as "really unilateral behavior flowing from decisions of a single enterprise." *Copperweld*, 467 U.S., at 767. Nor, for this reason, does § 1 cover "internally coordinated conduct of a corporation and one of its unincorporated divisions," *id.*, at 770, because "[a] division within a corporate structure pursues the common interests of the whole," *ibid.*, and therefore "coordination between a corporation and its division does not represent a sudden joining of two independent sources of economic power previously pursuing separate interests," *id.*, at 770–771. Nor, for the same reasons, is "the coordinated activity of a parent and its wholly owned subsidiary" covered. See *id.*, at 771. They "have a complete unity of interest" and thus "[w]ith or without a formal 'agreement,' the subsidiary acts for the benefit of the parent, its sole shareholder."

Because the inquiry is one of competitive reality, it is not determinative that two parties to an alleged § 1 violation are legally distinct entities. Nor, however, is it determinative that two legally distinct entities have organized themselves under a single umbrella or into a structured joint venture. The question is whether the agreement joins together "independent centers of decision-making." *Id.*, at 769. If it does, the entities are capable of conspiring under § 1, and the court must decide whether the restraint of trade is an unreasonable and therefore illegal one.

V

The NFL teams do not possess either the unitary decision-making quality or the single aggregation of economic power characteristic of independent action. Each of the teams is a substantial, independently owned, and independently managed business. "[T]heir general corporate actions are guided or determined" by "separate corporate consciousnesses," and "[t]heir objectives are" not "common." *Copperweld*, 467 U.S., at 771; see also *North American Soccer League* v. *NFL*, 670 F.2d 1249, 1252 (CA2 1982) (discussing ways that "the financial performance of each team, while related to that of the others, does not . . . necessarily rise and fall with that of the others"). The teams compete with one another, not only on the playing field, but to attract fans, for gate receipts and for contracts with managerial and playing personnel. . . .

Directly relevant to this case, the teams compete in the market for intellectual property. To a firm making hats, the Saints and the Colts are two potentially competing suppliers of valuable trademarks. When each NFL team licenses its intellectual property, it is not pursuing the "common interests of the whole" league but is instead pursuing interests of each "corporation itself," *Copperweld*, 467 U.S., at 770; teams are acting as "separate economic actors pursuing separate economic interests," and each team therefore is a potential "independent cente[r] of decision-making," *id.*, at 769. Decisions by NFL teams to license their separately owned trademarks collectively and to only one vendor are decisions that "depriv[e] the marketplace of independent centers of decision-making," *ibid.*, and therefore of actual or potential competition. . . .

In defense, respondents argue that by forming NFLP, they have formed a single entity, akin to a merger, and market their NFL brands through a single outlet. But it is not dispositive that the teams have organized and own a legally separate entity that centralizes the management of their intellectual property. An ongoing § 1 violation cannot evade § 1 scrutiny simply by giving the ongoing violation a name and label. "Perhaps every agreement and combination in restraint of trade could be so labeled." *Timken Roller Bearing Co. v. United States*, 341 U.S. 593, 598 (1951).

The NFL respondents may be similar in some sense to a single enterprise that owns several pieces of intellectual property and licenses them jointly, but they are not similar in the relevant functional sense. Although NFL teams have common interests such as promoting the NFL brand, they are still separate, profit-maximizing entities, and their interests in licensing team trademarks are not necessarily aligned. See generally Hovenkamp, Exclusive Joint Ventures and

Antitrust Policy, 1995 Colum. Bus. L. Rev. 1, 52–61 (1995). . . .

Respondents argue that . . . , as the Court of Appeals held, they constitute a single entity because without their cooperation, there would be no NFL football. It is true that "the clubs that make up a professional sports league are not completely independent economic competitors, as they depend upon a degree of cooperation for economic survival." *Brown*, 518 U.S., at 248. But the Court of Appeals' reasoning is unpersuasive.

The justification for cooperation is not relevant to whether that cooperation is concerted or independent action. A "contract, combination . . . or conspiracy," § 1, that is necessary or useful to a joint venture is still a "contract, combination . . . or conspiracy" if it "deprives the marketplace of independent centers of decisionmaking," *Copperweld*, 467 U.S., at 769. See *NCAA*, 468 U.S., at 113 ("[J]oint ventures have no immunity from antitrust laws"). Any joint venture involves multiple sources of economic power cooperating to produce a product. And for many such ventures, the participation of others is necessary. But that does not mean that necessity of cooperation transforms concerted action into independent action; a nut and a bolt can only operate together, but an agreement between nut and bolt manufacturers is still subject to § 1 analysis. Nor does it mean that once a group of firms agree to produce a joint product, cooperation amongst those firms must be treated as independent conduct. The mere fact that the teams operate jointly in some sense does not mean that they are immune.

The question whether NFLP decisions can constitute concerted activity covered by § 1 is closer than whether decisions made directly by the 32 teams are covered by § 1. This is so both because NFLP is a separate corporation with its own management and because the record indicates that most of the revenues generated by NFLP are shared by the teams on an equal basis. Nevertheless we think it clear that for the same reasons the 32 teams' conduct is covered by § 1, NFLP's actions also are subject to § 1, at least with regards to its marketing of property owned by the separate teams. NFLP's licensing decisions are made by the 32 potential competitors, and each of them actually owns its share of the jointly managed assets. Cf. *Sealy*, 388 U.S., at 352–354. Apart from their agreement to cooperate in exploiting those assets, including their decisions as the NFLP, there would be nothing to prevent each of the teams from making its own market decisions relating to purchases of apparel and headwear, to the sale of such items, and to the granting of licenses to use its trademarks.

We generally treat agreements within a single firm as independent action on the presumption that the components of the firm will act to maximize the firm's profits. But in rare cases, that presumption does not hold. Agreements made within a firm can constitute concerted action covered by § 1 when the parties to the agreement act on interests separate from those of the firm itself,[46] and the intrafirm

---

[46] [FN 8] See Areeda & Hovenkamp ¶ 1471; Elhauge & Geradin 786–787, and n. 6; see also *Capital Imaging Assoc.* v. *Mohawk Valley Medical Assoc., Inc.*, 996 F.2d 537, 544 (CA2 1993); *Bolt v. Halifax Hospital Medical Center*, 891 F.2d 810, 819 (CA11 1990); *Oksanen v. Page Memorial Hospital*, 945 F.2d 696, 706 (CA4 1991); *Motive Parts Warehouse v. Facet Enterprises*, 774 F.2d 380, 387–388 (CA10 1985); *Victorian House, Inc. v. Fisher Camuto Corp.*, 769 F.2d 466, 469 (CA8 1985); *Weiss v. York Hospital*, 745 F.2d 786, 828 (CA3 1984).

agreements may simply be a formalistic shell for ongoing concerted action. See, *e.g.*, *Topco Associates, Inc.*, 405 U.S., at 609; *Sealy*, 388 U.S., at 352–354.

For that reason, decisions by the NFLP regarding the teams' separately owned intellectual property constitute concerted action. Thirty-two teams operating independently through the vehicle of the NFLP are not like the components of a single firm that act to maximize the firm's profits. The teams remain separately controlled, potential competitors with economic interests that are distinct from NFLP's financial well-being. See generally Hovenkamp, 1995 Colum. Bus. L. Rev., at 52–61. Unlike typical decisions by corporate shareholders, NFLP licensing decisions effectively require the assent of more than a mere majority of shareholders. And each team's decision reflects not only an interest in NFLP's profits but also an interest in the team's individual profits. See generally Shusido, 39 Hastings L.J., at 69–71. The 32 teams capture individual economic benefits separate and apart from NFLP profits as a result of the decisions they make for the NFLP. NFLP's decisions thus affect each team's profits from licensing its own intellectual property. "Although the business interests of" the teams "will *often* coincide with those of the" NFLP "as an entity in itself, that commonality of interest exists in every cartel." *Los Angeles Memorial Coliseum Comm'n v. NFL*, 726 F.2d 1381, 1389 (CA9 1984) (emphasis added). In making the relevant licensing decisions, NFLP is therefore "an instrumentality" of the teams. *Sealy*, 388 U.S., at 352–354; see also *Topco Associates, Inc.*, 405 U.S., at 609.

If the fact that potential competitors shared in profits or losses from a venture meant that the venture was immune from § 1, then any cartel "could evade the antitrust law simply by creating a 'joint venture' to serve as the exclusive seller of their competing products." *Major League Baseball Properties, Inc. v. Salvino, Inc.*, 542 F.3d 290, 335 (CA2 2008) (Sotomayor, J., concurring in judgment). "So long as no agreement," other than one made by the cartelists sitting on the board of the joint venture, "explicitly listed the prices to be charged, the companies could act as monopolies through the 'joint venture.' "*Ibid.* (Indeed, a joint venture with a single management structure is generally a better way to operate a cartel because it decreases the risks of a party to an illegal agreement defecting from that agreement). However, competitors "cannot simply get around" antitrust liability by acting "through a third-party intermediary or 'joint venture'." *Id.*, at 336.[47]

---

[47] [FN 9] For the purposes of resolving this case, there is no need to pass upon the Government's position that entities are incapable of conspiring under § 1 if they "have effectively merged the relevant aspect of their operations, thereby eliminating actual and potential competition . . . in that operational sphere" and "the challenged restraint [does] not significantly affect actual or potential competition . . . outside their merged operations." Brief for United States as *Amicus Curiae* 17. The Government urges that the choices "to offer only a blanket license" and "to have only a single headwear licensee" might not constitute concerted action under its test. *Id.*, at 32. However, because the teams still own their own trademarks and are free to market those trademarks as they see fit, even those two choices were agreements amongst potential competitors and would constitute concerted action under the Government's own standard. At any point, the teams could decide to license their own trademarks. It is significant, moreover, that the teams here control NFLP. The two choices that the Government might treat as independent action, although nominally made by NFLP, are for all functional purposes choices made by the 32 entities with potentially competing interests.

VI

Football teams that need to cooperate are not trapped by antitrust law. "[T]he special characteristics of this industry may provide a justification" for many kinds of agreements. *Brown*, 518 U.S., at 252 (STEVENS, J., dissenting). The fact that NFL teams share an interest in making the entire league successful and profitable, and that they must cooperate in the production and scheduling of games, provides a perfectly sensible justification for making a host of collective decisions. But the conduct at issue in this case is still concerted activity under the Sherman Act that is subject to § 1 analysis.

When "restraints on competition are essential if the product is to be available at all," *per se* rules of illegality are inapplicable, and instead the restraint must be judged according to the flexible Rule of Reason.[48] *NCAA*, 468 U.S., at 101; see *id.*, at 117 ("Our decision not to apply a *per se* rule to this case rests in large part on our recognition that a certain degree of cooperation is necessary if the type of competition that petitioner and its member institutions seek to market is to be preserved"); see also *Dagher*, 547 U.S., at 6. In such instances, the agreement is likely to survive the Rule of Reason. See *Broadcast Music, Inc. v. Columbia Broadcasting System, Inc.*, 441 U.S. 1, 23 (1979) ("Joint ventures and other cooperative arrangements are also not usually unlawful . . . where the agreement . . . is necessary to market the product at all"). And depending upon the concerted activity in question, the Rule of Reason may not require a detailed analysis; it "can sometimes be applied in the twinkling of an eye." *NCAA*, 468 U.S., at 109, n. 39.

Other features of the NFL may also save agreements amongst the teams. We have recognized, for example, "that the interest in maintaining a competitive balance" among "athletic teams is legitimate and important," *NCAA*, 468 U.S., at 117. While that same interest applies to the teams in the NFL, it does not justify treating them as a single entity for § 1 purposes when it comes to the marketing of the teams' individually owned intellectual property. It is, however, unquestionably an interest that may well justify a variety of collective decisions made by the teams. What role it properly plays in applying the Rule of Reason to the allegations in this case is a matter to be considered on remand.

---

[48] [FN 10] Justice Brandeis provided the classic formulation of the Rule of Reason in *Board of Trade of Chicago v. United States*, 246 U.S. 231, 238 (1918):

> "The true test of legality is whether the restraint imposed is such as merely regulates and perhaps thereby promotes competition or whether it is such as may suppress or even destroy competition. To determine that question the court must ordinarily consider the facts peculiar to the business to which the restraint is applied; its condition before and after the restraint is imposed; the nature of the restraint and its effect, actual or probable. The history of the restraint, the evil believed to exist, the reason for adopting the particular remedy, the purpose or end sought to be attained, are all relevant facts. This is not because a good intention will save an otherwise objectionable regulation or the reverse; but because knowledge of intent may help the court to interpret facts and to predict consequences." . . .

NOTES AND QUESTIONS

1. What standard of review does the Court use in evaluating the claims in this case? Does it apply a traditional Rule of Reason approach (*Chicago Board of Trade*) or some other analytical framework?

2. Does the Court distinguish between when the NFL is acting as a single entity rather than as 32 separate entities? Does the Court say that the teams ever really act as one entity? Is this analysis broader than NFL apparel licensing? Other than joint action, is there any other way to promote the NFL brand or trademark? *See generally* Michael A. McCann, American Needle v. NFL: *An Opportunity to Reshape Sports Law*, 119 YALE L.J. 726, 778–780 (2010). How does the Court apply the *Copperweld* doctrine in this case? Does the Court apply it strictly or does it modify the doctrine in some way?

3. As the Supreme Court's decision makes clear, a decision that is formally by a single entity can operate to facilitate collusion if the entity has contractual control over either its shareholders or other entities that it controls. *See* Herbert Hovenkamp & Christopher R. Leslie, *The Firm as Cartel Manager*, 64 VAND. L. REV. 813 (2011). Some analytic difficulties can emerge however, in distinguishing vertical from horizontal agreements. For example, if Ford sets the resale prices of cars sold by six Chicago Area Ford Dealers the resale price maintenance at issue would be addressed under the rule of reason. But suppose Ford simply orders the six dealers to fix prices among themselves?

4. If the teams are acting as economic competitors, how should a court rule if a high school football player challenged the NFL's requirement that in order to qualify for the NFL draft, a player must be at least three years out of high school? Similarly, how should a court rule on the NBA's recent policy of requiring athletes to spend at least one year out of high school before being eligible for the draft? Are these policies similar to the one struck down in *American Needle* since the teams should be competing for the best possible talent at any given time?

5. What effect does or should this decision have on other sports leagues such as the National Basketball Association, Major League Baseball, the National Hockey League, and Major League Soccer? Does this case open the gates to more antitrust claims against sports leagues? Are there any circumstances under which these leagues should be allowed exemptions or be considered for single entity status?

6. Interesting in *American Needle*, the unanimous Court ruled in favor of the plaintiff, which was a departure for the Court, having ruled before in eight straight antitrust cases in favor of the antitrust defendants.

7. The issue in *Robertson v. Sea Pines Real Estate Cos. Inc.*, 679 F.3d 278 (4th Cir. 2012) was whether members of two local multiple listing services in South Carolina qualified for immunity under the intracorporate immunity doctrine or "whether they were separate economic actors capable of conspiring" under Section 1 of the Sherman Act. The Fourth Circuit, speaking through Judge Wilkinson, held that "the defendants acted 'on interests separate from those of the firm itself" when they attempted to exclude innovative competitors, such conduct having conflicted with the economic interests of multiple listing services. The court concluded that the "plurality of actors" requirement under Section I had been met.

PROBLEM 4.8

Samaritan Hospital is a corporation operated by a Board of Directors composed entirely of physicians. Four of the seven members of the Board are currently pediatricians, each of whom has an extensive private practice. The Board members are not paid for being on the Board. Dr. Smith is the proprietor of the "Pediatric Health Clinic," an outpatient pediatric clinic offering cut-rate health care services. Over the past years, all four of the pediatricians on the Board have complained to Dr. Smith about his fees.

Dr. Smith would like to have staff privileges at Samaritan Hospital so he can better serve his patients who need hospital care. He applies, but the Board declines his application by a vote of 4-3, the four pediatricians voting against him. Smith sues, alleging that the hospital conspired with members of its Board of Directors to exclude Smith from the market. Should *Copperweld* preclude his suit? Suppose that at the same meeting, the Board voted 4-3 to raise the price of hospital rooms by $10.00 per day. The hospital is sued for engaging in price fixing with its Board. Should *Copperweld* preclude the second suit? *See Bahn v. NME Hosps.*, 669 F. Supp. 998 (E.D. Cal. 1987); *Smith v. Underwood Mem. Hosp.*, 1987-1 Trade Cas. ¶ 67,538 at 60,275 (D.N.J.).

PROBLEM 4.9

1. A group of rural electric corporations, which are separately incorporated and owned companies, comprises a part of a rural electric cooperative. The cooperative is organized on three functional levels. It is a three-tier organization made up of one corporation which owns nearly all of the cooperative's electric generating capacity and the power lines. The next level is six generation/transmission companies responsible for transporting and selling wholesale power. The third group consists of 43 local retail/distribution cooperatives, which are owned by 425,000 consumer-members. These retail cooperatives buy electric power wholesale and, in turn, sell it to their consumer-members in certain service areas.

The cooperative management flows from the top to the bottom, but ownership runs from the bottom up. For example, the 425,000 consumer-members own the 43 local retail distribution cooperatives. Members join the cooperative that sells them retail electricity, and each distribution cooperative is managed by a board of directors elected by its members. Each local cooperative owns part of one or more of the six wholesale companies that transmit and sell the power, and the wholesale company boards of directors are elected by the cooperative members. Moreover, the six wholesale generation transmission companies, in turn, are common owners of the company that owns the generating capacity and power lines.

Although each cooperative is autonomous, setting its own rates for the power it sells and managing its own profits and losses, the organization is "linked" by long-term requirements contracts. The owner of the power capacity and power lines supplies the wholesalers, which in turn sell to the retail cooperatives. They then sell to the cooperative members.

2. The City of Mount Pleasant, a non-member of the cooperative, entered a contract to buy a certain amount of energy from a cooperative. Thereafter, the city,

believing that it had been economically injured by reason of the cooperative's pricing schedule, sued numerous members of the cooperative, including the corporation that owned nearly all of the electric generating capacity and power lines and the companies responsible for the transmission and wholesale distribution of the power.

3. Counsel for the plaintiff city alleges that defendant members of the cooperative have: (1) participated in a "price-squeeze" conspiracy; (2) monopolized the relevant markets for wholesale electricity and for transporting electricity; and (3) charged the city a higher price for wholesale electricity than that charged retail cooperative members.

4. As counsel for defendants, what arguments would you make under *Copperweld*? Should your arguments be directed to the court as a question of law in a motion for a summary judgment, or is the *Copperweld* defense a question of fact which must be presented to a jury? *See City of Mt. Pleasant v. Associated Elec. Coop.*, 838 F.2d 268 (8th Cir. 1988).

PROBLEM 4.10

Jim and Tammy own 100% of the shares of Alpha Corporation which manufactures and distributes leather gloves. Jim, Tammy, and Francis own 100% of Beta Corporation which manufactures similar gloves. Together, Jim and Tammy's shares of Beta constitute 53% of the whole, and they have effective control. Alpha and Beta agree with each other to set the same price for gloves. Do the two firms have conspiratorial capacity under the Sherman Act? *See American Vision Centers v. Cohen*, 711 F. Supp. 721 (E.D.N.Y. 1989).

PROBLEM 4.11

Consider whether a patent holder can conspire with a sublicensee under the intra-enterprise conspiracy doctrine.

Larry Shea holds a patent on air conditioning ductwork. In order to market and exploit the patent, he incorporates ATS Products and conveys to ATS an exclusive license to use the patent. Later, Shea and ATS enter into a contract to give a nonexclusive license for use of the patent to Levi Co. to manufacture ductwork. Thereafter, ATS and Levi Co. agree that ATS would not give a similar license to Levi's chief competitor, Case Systems. Case sues ATS and Levi on a refusal to deal theory under Section 1 of the Sherman Act. Does the intra-enterprise conspiracy doctrine apply? What outcome?

[D] Market Allocation

[1] Joint Ventures and Cooperative Research Ventures

Before proceeding into the cases that evaluate the evidence and standards relevant to market allocation agreements, it may be helpful to discuss briefly other kinds of market-sharing arrangements. One such arrangement is the joint venture, which is an agreement between firms to carry on a business or activity of some nature in a cooperative fashion. See also Chapter 7, where joint ventures are discussed as mergers which may violate Section 7 of the Clayton Act. As one antitrust commentator has observed, "[t]he very definition of a joint venture is unclear. More than a simple contract yet less than a merger . . . the key element is continuity . . . [of the] association of two or more to carry on as co-owners an enterprise for one or a series of transactions." Joseph F. Brodley, *The Legal Status of Joint Ventures Under the Antitrust Laws: A Summary Assessment*, 21 ANTITRUST BULL. 453, 454 (1976).

When firms engage in joint activities, there is a potential for anticompetitive conduct that can violate Section 1 of the Sherman Act. Specifically, the anticompetitive risks involved are collusion, loss of competition, and market exclusion. Joseph F. Brodley, *Joint Ventures and Antitrust Policy*, 95 HARV. L. REV. 1521, 1530 (1982). With regard to cartel behavior, "the joint venture has been used as a means of restraining competition between the participants, typically by fixing prices and dividing markets, thus depriving the public of the benefits of competition." Though the joint venture may have a legitimate purpose, the Sherman Act is concerned with measuring the competitive consequences of the restraint that may result.

Chicago Board of Trade, Appalachian Coals, Broadcast Music, NCAA, and *Dagher* all involved joint ventures. In those cases, the legality of the arrangement and its consequence were examined under Section 1. See also *United States v. Penn-Olin Chem. Co.*, 378 U.S. 158 (1964), reprinted *infra*, where the Court began examining joint ventures under Section 7 of the Clayton Act. In all the cases, the Supreme Court was reluctant to apply a per se rule. Instead, it employed a balancing analysis, even where the defendants had significant market power, so that the benefits of the venture could be weighed against the resulting restraint. In each of the cases, the Court, using rule of reason analysis, balanced the economic efficiencies achieved by the joint venture against the social costs and potential harms.

In essence, the analysis centered on whether the joint venture (generally a joint sales agency) was formed to accomplish a competitively beneficial purpose; if so, the Court applied a rule of reason. *See also United States v. Morgan*, 118 F. Supp. 621 (S.D.N.Y. 1953). But see *Citizen Pub'g Co. v. United States*, 394 U.S. 131 (1969), where the Court held that horizontal joint ventures may be inherently unlawful. However, as the cases which follow in this subsection imply, the directness of the effect of the joint venture on price, and whether markets are actually divided, significantly alters the standards of analysis under Section 1.

Cooperation among businesses often involves research. Joint ventures may facilitate business research given the risks and costs involved. Furthermore, research activities often generate external benefits that can give rise to substantial "free rider" problems. Once a firm has put the results of expensive research to profitable use — for example, by marketing a product incorporating the new innovations — they become public information. If the innovations cannot easily be patented, or if a copyist can "invent around" the patents, the second and subsequent firms will be able to take advantage of the first firm's research at a far lower cost. These free rider problems can become a substantial disincentive to research and development — particularly where research costs are relatively high and the protection afforded by the patent laws is relatively low. The well constructed research joint venture can help solve this free rider problem by ensuring that all the firms in a position to profit from a particular innovation will also share in its costs. Joint research among competitors can maximize resources but it can also affect competition, giving rise to antitrust concerns. Pure research joint ventures are not problematic from an antitrust standpoint. They become so, however, when they are accompanied by restrictive agreements among the parties to the joint project or with outsiders.

In 1980, the Department of Justice issued guidelines for businesses engaged in or contemplating research joint ventures. The antitrust scrutiny of research joint ventures centers on the activities' effect on competition between existing competitors, whether the joint venture imposes specific restrictions on participants or outsiders that restrain trade, and whether other parties will have access to the benefits of the project. Antitrust Guide Concerning Research Joint Ventures, U.S. Dep't of Justice (Nov. 1980).

In 1984, Congress passed the National Cooperative Research Act of 1984. The purpose of the legislation was to encourage procompetitive joint research and development ventures and to decrease antitrust liability over such activity. The legislative history reveals that Congress believed that the perceived antitrust risk and the uncertainty of the law's application may have prevented procompetitive research and development.

Among other provisions, the statute detrebles antitrust damages to actual damages through a notification procedure, excludes per se liability, and allows the prevailing defendants to recover attorney's fees and costs attributable to frivolous claims or conduct. In order to come within the Act, defendants must give notification of the intended venture to the Department of Justice and FTC and identify the parties involved and the nature and goals of the undertaking. If the notification procedures are satisfied, an antitrust claimant under either federal or state law is limited to single (actual) damages. The Act does not cover (1) commercial data exchanges among competitors relating to costs, prices, marketing, or distribution unless reasonably required to carry out the venture, (2) marketing or distribution agreements which are restrictive, other than proprietary information (patents and trade secrets) that develop from the joint venture, and (3) unrelated conduct not reasonably required for the success of the venture.

In 1993, President Clinton signed the National Cooperative Production Amendments Act of 1993. As an extension of the 1984 Act, it applies to *production* joint ventures. It accomplishes several objectives: (1) it permits parties participating in joint research and development ventures to limit their antitrust damage exposure to actual, rather than treble, damages for qualifying ventures; (2) it requires a voluntary notification procedure in order for its provisions to apply; (3) it employs a rule of reason analysis to assess the alleged restraint; and (4) it provides special attorneys' fees in any antitrust case where the joint venture is challenged.

However, contrary to the 1984 Act, the new statute limits the actual damage recovery only in cases where the principal facilities for production are located in the United States or its territories, and then only to United States companies that control such ventures or companies from foreign countries whose law accords antitrust treatment "no less favorable to United States persons than to such country's domestic persons regarding participation in joint ventures for production." Further, except for the product manufactured by the joint venture, marketing and distribution agreements are excluded from the antitrust immunity.

In the last several years, a large volume of literature on joint ventures and innovation has developed. Much of the attention has been on collaborative high technology industries, with criticism that traditional antitrust interpretation inhibits the creation of cooperative, procompetitive ventures, and dynamic innovation. In substantial part, the new 1993 joint venture statute is in response to the contemporary literature. *See generally* T. JORDE & D. TEECE, ANTITRUST, INNOVATION AND COMPETITIVENESS (1992); Katten, *Antitrust Analysis of Technology Joint Ventures: Allocative Efficiency and the Rewards of Innovation*, 61 ANTITRUST L.J. 937 (1993); Jorde & Teece, *Rule of Reason Analysis of Horizontal Arrangements: Agreements Designed to Advance Innovation and Commercialize Technology*, 61 ANTITRUST L.J. 579 (1993); Jorde & Teece, *Acceptable Cooperation Among Competitors in the Face of Growing International Competition*, 58 ANTITRUST L.J. 2 (1989); P. STONEMAN, THE ECONOMIC ANALYSIS OF TECHNOLOGICAL CHANGE (1993); Ordover & Willig, *Antitrust for High Technology Industries: Assessing Research Joint Ventures and Mergers*, 28 J.L. & ECON. 311 (1985). William E. Kovacic, *Antitrust in High-Tech Industries: Improving the Federal Antitrust Joint Venture*, 19 GEO. MASON L. REV. 1097 (2012); Stephen F. Ross, *The Supreme Court's Renewed Focus on Inefficiently Structured Joint Ventures*, 14 U. PA. J. BUS. L. 261 (2011). Some joint ventures have been called "strategic alliances," especially in the airline industry. Michael J. AuBuchon, *Testing the Limits of Federal Tolerance: Strategic Alliances in the Airline Industry*, 26 TRANSP. L.J. 219 (1999).

The cases that follow establish the analytical process by which the courts have evaluated objectionable exclusionary agreements such as market divisions and concerted refusals to deal. Such agreements can arise from joint ventures in the form of restrictions on the venture members or outsiders regarding exclusion of access to markets. They can be created, in addition, through a more traditional cartel agreement that lacks any lawful purpose.

[2]   Horizontal Market Divisions

A market division agreement is one in which firms agree not to compete in a designated market. Agreements between competitors to divide markets (whether territories, customers, or products) can be as anticompetitive as price-fixing agreements. Indeed, such agreements can be the means by which competitors may avoid competing on price, enhance market power without an explicit price-fixing agreement, and thus facilitate creation of a monopoly in a given area. Generally, such agreements serve the direct purpose of controlling market entry by new competitors who are parties to the agreement or regulating the exit from the market of old competitors. In short, the purpose or effect of a market allocation agreement is often the reduction of competition. Analysis of such agreements may raise the same evidentiary question that alleged price-fixing agreements raise, such as how collusion can be established, and whether an express agreement is necessary.

In *Timken Roller Bearing Co. v. United States*, 341 U.S. 593 (1951), a corporation and its partially owned subsidiaries were parties to agreements that licensed a trademark, allocated territories for marketing purposes, and set prices within the territories. The United States firm owned 30% of the British firm and, with another firm, it owned all of a French firm (*see* discussion in *Sealy*, *infra*). In rejecting defendants' argument that the joint venture restrictions were ancillary and necessary to protect the trademark, the Court found that the challenged agreement was overbroad. The main purpose of the agreement, the Court held, was not trademark protection but rather market division. Moreover, the restraints affected interbrand competition as well as intrabrand competition. But the Court did not state with clarity whether a market division was *per se* illegal.

Sixteen years later, the Court made clear in *United States v. Sealy*, 388 U.S. 350 (1967), that if the market allocation is horizontal and a part of "an aggregation of trade restraints including unlawful price-fixing and policing," it is per se unlawful. In *Sealy*, the government challenged Sealy's policy of granting exclusive territories to its licensees who manufactured Sealy-brand mattresses. The government characterized the agreements as horizontal because the licensees controlled the Sealy Board of Directors. Sealy argued that each licensee was in a vertical relationship with Sealy and, thus, its policy should be evaluated under the more lenient Rule of Reason. The Court sided with the government. Treating the arrangements as horizontal and per se illegal, the Court noted, "they are unlawful under § 1 of the Sherman Act without the necessity for an inquiry in each particular case as to their business or economic justification, their impact in the marketplace, or their reasonableness."

UNITED STATES v. TOPCO ASSOCIATES
405 U.S. 596 (1972)

JUSTICE MARSHALL delivered the opinion of the Court.

The United States brought this action for injunctive relief against alleged violation by Topco Associates, Inc. (Topco), of § 1 of the Sherman Act. . . .

I

Topco is a cooperative association of approximately 25 small and medium-sized regional supermarket chains that operate stores in some 33 States. Each of the member chains operates independently; there is no pooling of earnings, profits, capital, management, or advertising resources. No grocery business is conducted under the Topco name. Its basic function is to serve as a purchasing agent for its members. In this capacity, it procures and distributes to the members more than 1,000 different food and related nonfood items, most of which are distributed under brand names owned by Topco. The association does not itself own any manufacturing, processing, or warehousing facilities, and the items that it procures for members are usually shipped directly from the packer or manufacturer to the members. Payment is made either to Topco or directly to the manufacturer at a cost that is virtually the same for the members as for Topco itself.

All of the stock in Topco is owned by the members, with the common stock, the only stock having voting rights, being equally distributed. The board of directors, which controls the operation of the association, is drawn from the members and is normally composed of high-ranking executive officers of member chains. It is the board that elects the association's officers and appoints committee members, and it is from the board that the principal executive officers of Topco must be drawn. . . .

Topco was founded in the 1940's by a group of small, local grocery chains, independently owned and operated, that desired to cooperate to obtain high quality merchandise under private labels in order to compete more effectively with larger national and regional chains.[49] With a line of canned, dairy, and other products, the association began. . . . By 1964, Topco's members had combined retail sales of more than $2 billion; by 1967, their sales totaled more than $2.3 billion, a figure exceeded by only three national grocery chains.

Members of the association vary in the degree of market share that they possess in their respective areas. The range is from 1.5% to 16%, with the average being approximately 6%. While it is difficult to compare these figures with the market shares of larger regional and national chains because of the absence in the record of accurate statistics for these chains, there is much evidence in the record that Topco members are frequently in as strong a competitive position in their respective areas as any other chain. The strength of this competitive position is due, in some measure, to the success of Topco-brand products. Although only 10% of the total goods sold by Topco members bear the association's brand names, the profit on these goods is substantial and their very existence has improved the competitive potential of Topco members with respect to other large and powerful chains.

. . . Topco has developed into a purchasing association . . . , which possess much economic muscle, individually as well as cooperatively.

II

. . . The United States charged that, beginning at least as early as 1960 and continuing up to the time that the complaint was filed, Topco had combined and

---

[49] [FN 3] The founding members of Topco were having difficulty competing with larger chains. This difficulty was attributable in some degree to the fact that the larger chains were capable of developing their own private-label programs. Private-labeled products differ from other brand-name products in that they are sold at a limited number of easily ascertainable stores. A&P, for example, was a pioneer in developing a series of products that were sold under an A&P label and that were only available in A&P stores. It is obvious that by using private-label products, a chain can achieve significant cost economies in purchasing, transportation, warehousing, promotion, and advertising. These economies may afford the chain opportunities for offering private-label products at lower prices than other brand-name products. This, in turn, provides many advantages of which some of the more important are: a store can offer national-brand products at the same price as other stores, while simultaneously offering a desirable, lower priced alternative; or, if the profit margin is sufficiently high on private-brand goods, national-brand products may be sold at reduced price. Other advantages include: enabling a chain to bargain more favorably with national-brand manufacturers by creating a broader supply base of manufacturers, thereby decreasing dependence on a few, large national-brand manufacturers; enabling a chain to create a "price-mix" whereby prices on special items can be lowered to attract customers while profits are maintained on other items; and creation of general goodwill by offering lower priced, higher quality goods.

conspired with its members to violate § 1 in two respects. First, the Government alleged that there existed:

> a continuing agreement, understanding and concert of action among the co-conspirator member firms acting through Topco, the substantial terms of which have been and are that each co-conspirator member firm will sell Topco-controlled brands only within the marketing territory allocated to it, and will refrain from selling Topco-controlled brands outside such marketing territory.

[Second,] [m]embership must first be approved by the board of directors, and thereafter by an affirmative vote of 75% of the association's members. If, however, the member whose operations are closest to those of the applicant, or any member whose operations are located within 100 miles of the applicant, votes against approval, an affirmative vote of 85% of the members is required for approval. Bylaws, Art. I, § 5. Because, as indicated by the record, members cooperate in accommodating each other's wishes, the procedure for approval provides, in essence, that members have a veto of sorts over actual or potential competition in the territorial areas in which they are concerned.

Following approval, each new member signs an agreement with Topco designating the territory in which that member may sell Topco-brand products. No member may sell these products outside the territory in which it is licensed. Most licenses are exclusive, and even those denominated "coextensive" or "non-exclusive" prove to be *de facto* exclusive. Exclusive territorial areas are often allocated to members who do no actual business in those areas on the theory that they may wish to expand at some indefinite future time and that expansion would likely be in the direction of the allocated territory. When combined with each member's veto power over new members, provisions for exclusivity work effectively to insulate members from competition in Topco-brand goods. Should a member violate its license agreement and sell in areas other than those in which it is licensed, its membership can be terminated. . . . Once a territory is classified as exclusive, either formally or *de facto*, it is extremely unlikely that the classification will ever be changed. . . .

Topco's answer to the complaint is illustrative of its posture in the District Court and before this Court. . . .

Topco essentially maintains that it needs territorial divisions to compete with larger chains; that the association could not exist if the territorial divisions were anything but exclusive; and that by restricting competition in the sale of Topco-brand goods, the association actually increases competition by enabling its members to compete successfully with larger regional and national chains.

. . . .

III

. . . .

It is only after considerable experience with certain business relationships that courts classify them as *per se* violations of the Sherman Act. One of the classic examples of a *per se* violation of § 1 is an agreement between competitors at the same level of the market structure to allocate territories in order to minimize competition. . . . This Court has reiterated time and time again that "[h]orizontal territorial limitations . . . are naked restraints of trade with no purpose except stifling of competition." [Citing cases.]

We think that it is clear that the restraint in this case is a horizontal one, and, therefore, a *per se* violation of § 1. The District Court failed to make any determination as to whether there were *per se* horizontal territorial restraints in this case and simply applied a rule of reason in reaching its conclusions that the restraints were not illegal. In so doing, the District Court erred.

. . . .

Whether or not we would decide this case the same way under the rule of reason used by the District Court is irrelevant to the issue before us. The fact is that courts are of limited utility in examining difficult economic problems.[50] Our inability to weigh, in any meaningful sense, destruction of competition in one sector of the economy against promotion of competition in another sector is one important reason we have formulated *per se* rules.

In applying these rigid rules, the Court has consistently rejected the notion that naked restraints of trade are to be tolerated because they are well intended or because they are allegedly developed to increase competition.

. . . .

The District Court determined that by limiting the freedom of its individual members to compete with each other, Topco was doing a greater good by fostering competition between members and other large supermarket chains. But, the fallacy in this is that Topco has no authority under the Sherman Act to determine the respective values of competition in various sectors of the economy. On the contrary, the Sherman Act gives to each Topco member and to each prospective member the right to ascertain for itself whether or not competition with other supermarket chains is more desirable than competition in the sale of Topco-brand products. Without territorial restrictions, Topco members may indeed "[cut] each other's throats." But, we have never found this possibility sufficient to warrant condoning horizontal restraints of trade.

. . . .

Just as the territorial restrictions on retailing Topco-brand products must fall, so must the territorial restrictions on wholesaling. The considerations are the same, and the Sherman Act requires identical results.

We also strike down Topco's other restrictions on the right of its members to wholesale goods. These restrictions amount to regulation of the customers to whom

---

[50] [FN 10] There has been much recent commentary on the wisdom of per se rules. . . . Without the *per se* rules, businessmen would be left with little to aid them in predicting in any particular case what courts will find to be legal and illegal under the Sherman Act. Should Congress ultimately determine that predictability is unimportant in this area of the law, it can, of course, make per se rules inapplicable in some or all cases, and leave courts free to ramble through the wilds of economic theory in order to maintain a flexible approach.

members of Topco may sell Topco-brand goods. Like territorial restrictions, limitations on customers are intended to limit intra-brand competition and to promote inter-brand competition. For the reasons previously discussed, the arena in which Topco members compete must be left to their unfettered choice absent a contrary congressional determination.

We reverse the judgment of the District Court and remand the case for entry of an appropriate decree.

CHIEF JUSTICE BURGER, dissenting.

This case does not involve restraints on interbrand competition or an allocation of markets by an association with monopoly or near-monopoly control of the sources of supply of one or more varieties of staple goods. Rather, we have here an agreement among several small grocery chains to join in a cooperative endeavor that, in my view, has an unquestionably lawful principal purpose; in pursuit of that purpose they have mutually agreed to certain minimal ancillary restraints that are fully reasonable in view of the principal purpose and that have never before today been held by this Court to be *per se* violations of the Sherman Act.

In joining in this cooperative endeavor, these small chains did not agree to the restraints here at issue in order to make it possible for them to exploit an already established line of products through noncompetitive pricing. There was no such thing as a Topco line of products until this cooperative was formed. The restraints to which the cooperative's members have agreed deal only with the marketing of the products in the Topco line, and the only function of those restraints is to permit each member chain to establish, within its own geographical area and through its own local advertising and marketing efforts, a local consumer awareness of the trademarked family of products as that member's "private label" line. The goal sought was the enhancement of the individual members' abilities to compete, albeit to a modest degree, with the large national chains which had been successfully marketing private-label lines for several years. The sole reason for a cooperative endeavor was to make economically feasible such things as quality control, large quantity purchases at bulk prices, the development of attractively printed labels, and the ability to offer a number of different lines of trademarked products. All these things, of course, are feasible for the large national chains operating individually, but they are beyond the reach of the small operators proceeding alone.

After a careful review of the economic considerations bearing upon this case, the District Court determined that "the relief which the government here seeks would not increase competition in Topco private label brands"; on the contrary, such relief "would substantially diminish competition in the supermarket field." . . .

I do not believe that our prior decisions justify the result reached by the majority. Nor do I believe that a new *per se* rule should be established in disposing of this case, for the judicial convenience and ready predictability that are made possible by *per se* rules are not such overriding considerations in antitrust law as to justify their promulgation without careful prior consideration of the relevant economic realities in the light of the basic policy and goals of the Sherman Act.

. . . .

II

With all respect, I believe that there are two basic fallacies in the Court's approach here. First, while I would not characterize our role under the Sherman Act as one of "rambl[ing] through the wilds," it is indeed one that requires our "examin[ation of] difficult economic problems." We can undoubtedly ease our task, but we should not abdicate that role by formulation of *per se* rules with no justification other than the enhancement of predictability and the reduction of judicial investigation. Second, from the general proposition that *per se* rules play a necessary role in antitrust law, it does not follow that the particular *per se* rule promulgated today is an appropriate one. Although it might well be desirable in a proper case for this Court to formulate a *per se* rule dealing with horizontal territorial limitations, it would not necessarily be appropriate for such a rule to amount to a blanket prohibition against all such limitations. More specifically, it is far from clear to me why such a rule should cover those division-of-market agreements that involve no price fixing and which are concerned only with trademarked products that are not in a monopoly or near-monopoly position with respect to competing brands. The instant case presents such an agreement; I would not decide it upon the basis of a *per se* rule.

The District Court specifically found that the horizontal restraints involved here tend positively to promote competition in the supermarket field and to produce lower costs for the consumer. The Court seems implicitly to accept this determination, but says that the Sherman Act does not give Topco the authority to determine for itself "whether or not competition with other supermarket chains is more desirable than competition in the sale of Topco-brand products." But the majority overlooks a further specific determination of the District Court, namely, that the invalidation of the restraints here at issue "would not increase competition in Topco private label brands." Indeed, the District Court seemed to believe that it would, on the contrary, lead to the likely demise of those brands in time. And the evidence before the District Court would appear to justify that conclusion.

. . . .

[After remand, the Supreme Court affirmed the district court's order permitting Topco to engage in areas of "primary responsibility," thereby permitting individual members to select designated warehouse locations, to identify locations of places of business for trademark licensees, and to terminate membership of businesses not adequately promoting Topco products, unless the practices resulted in territorial exclusivity. *United States v. Topco Assocs.*, 319 F. Supp. 1031 (N.D. Ill. 1970), *aff'd*, 414 U.S. 801 (1973).]

NOTES AND QUESTIONS

1.   What was the basis for the district court's refusal to apply a per se rule? Does the *per se* analysis adopted by the Supreme Court meet the previously announced test that such a standard be employed only when the conduct has a "pernicious effect on competition" and lacks "any redeeming virtue"? Does the Court in *Sealy* and *Topco* indicate that market division agreements will be considered illegal per se without regard to market power or countervailing procompetitive efficiency conse-

quences? Do the Court's holdings in *Sealy* and *Topco* imply that any agreement among competitors that alters competition is, by definition, a price-fixing agreement and subject to per se treatment? Do you agree with the Court in *Topco*, that these arrangements were horizontal between competitors? Was Justice Marshall characterizing the per se rule correctly when he said "whether or not we would decide this case the same way under the rule of reason . . . is irrelevant"?

In light of the rule of reason approach utilized in the *Broadcast Music* decision for a joint sales agency, do you consider *Topco* implicitly overruled? Given the language and analysis in *California Dental, infra,* is *Topco*'s approach still valid? Consider whether a market allocation agreement between competitors is more pernicious than a price-fixing agreement. Does the latter still permit room for competition on nonprice factors such as service and quality?

2. Is there any authority in *Topco* for treating joint ventures differently if the restrictions are imposed by smaller firms seeking to be more competitively efficient? Recall that the Court permitted the continuance of the independent grocers' joint purchasing agency.

3. After *Sealy* and *Topco*, what would you advise a client who is a manufacturer or trademark licensor, utilizing independent distributors, who wants to impose territorial restrictions on them? Does your analysis depend on whether the client competes with its own distributors? *Compare Williams & Co. v. Williams & Co.-East,* 542 F.2d 1053 (9th Cir. 1976), *cert. denied,* 433 U.S. 908 (1977), *with American Motor Inns, Inc. v. Holiday Inns, Inc.,* 521 F.2d 1230, 1253–1254 (3d Cir. 1975), *and Hobart Bros. v. Malcolm T. Gilliland, Inc.,* 471 F.2d 894 (5th Cir.), *cert. denied,* 412 U.S. 923 (1973). Are you persuaded by Chief Justice Burger's argument that the legal distinctions should turn on whether the restraint affects *interbrand* competition rather than *intrabrand* competition? What effect would there be on competition if such a standard were adopted? Can the effect on consumers be predicted? Should the legal analysis (and outcome) be dependent upon the conduct characterization employed (horizontal vs. vertical) or whether the defendants have market power to restrict output or affect price in the interbrand market? *See* Liebeler, *Book Review,* 66 CAL. L. REV. 1317, 1333–1341 (1978). *See* Mark A. Lemley & Christopher R. Leslie, *Categorical Analysis in Antitrust Jurisprudence,* 93 IOWA L. REV. 1207 (2008). See also Chapter 5, where the standard for analyzing intrabrand restraints is discussed in the context of *Continental T.V., Inc. v. GTE Sylvania, Inc.,* 433 U.S. 36 (1977).

4. How could the individual members of Topco reduce output or raise prices if each controlled, on average, only 6% of the retail grocery trade in its area?

5. Consider whether *Sealy* and *Topco* leave any room for a rule of reason analysis when the agreement between the "competitors" does not divide the entire market, but leaves the parties a residual zone in which to compete. On this question, the Supreme Court in 1984 denied certiorari in a case in which the lower appellate court held that the per se rule of illegality is applicable only when the entire geographic market is divided. *Atkin v. Union Processing Corp.,* 453 N.E.2d 522 (N.Y. 1983), *cert. denied,* 465 U.S. 1038 (1984). The three dissenting Justices from the certiorari denial believed that the New York Court of Appeals decision conflicted with *Topco,* and thus presented a substantial federal question.

POLK BROS. v. FOREST CITY ENTERPRISES
776 F.2d 185 (7th Cir. 1985)

JUDGE EASTERBROOK.

In 1972 Polk Bros., which owned some land in Burbank, Illinois, discussed with Forest City Enterprises the possibility of building a store large enough for both firms. Polk sells appliances and home furnishings; Forest City sells building materials, lumber, tools, and related products. Both have substantial chains of stores. They reached an agreement. Polk built a single building on a large parcel of land. The building is partitioned internally; Polk and Forest City have separate entrances; Polk's store contains 64,000 square feet, Forest City's 68,000 square feet. One parking lot serves both businesses. Forest City became Polk's lessee in 1973. The stores opened in 1975. In 1978 Forest City exercised its option to buy, and Polk took back a mortgage for some $1.4 million.

The attraction of the arrangement was the complementary nature of the firms' products. The two stores together could offer a full line of goods for furnishing and maintaining a home. Both Polk and Forest City were concerned, however, that competition might replace cooperation. They negotiated a covenant restricting the products each could sell. Forest City promised not to sell "major appliances and furniture," although it reserved the right to sell "built-in appliances in connection with Kitchen-Build-In business." Polk Bros. promised not to "stock or sell Toro and Lawnboy products including lawn mowers, building materials, lumber and related products, tools, paints and sundries, hardware, garden supplies, automotive supplies or plumbing supplies." The parties agreed on a long list of things that both could sell, including "Gas & Electric Heaters[,] Built-In-Ranges[,] . . . Snow Blowers[,] Lawn Mowers[,] . . . [and] Hardware/Garden Mdse." When Forest City became an owner in 1978 the parties agreed that the restrictions in the lease would become covenants running with the land for 50 years.

Forest City's management changed in 1982. The new managers were concerned about declining profits from its three stores near Chicago. Two stores sold some major appliances; the one at Burbank did not. Forest City found it uneconomical to advertise the large appliances when one of the three outlets could not sell them. Forest City asked to be relieved of its covenant at Burbank. Polk said no. In January 1983 Forest City informed Polk that it considered the covenant invalid; Polk responded with a suit in state court seeking an injunction. Forest City removed the action to the district court under 28 U.S.C. § 1441, where it could have been filed initially under the diversity jurisdiction.

. . . .

I

The district court held the covenant invalid under § 3(1)(c) of the antitrust law of Illinois, which declares unlawful contracts "allocating or dividing customers, territories, supplies, sales or markets, functional or geographical, for any commodity." That state's antitrust law, however, refers courts to federal antitrust law as a guide to questions of interpretation. In order to find out what Illinois law forbids, we inquire what federal antitrust law forbids. Cf. *Marrese v. American Academy of Orthopaedic Surgeons*, 726 F.2d 1150, 1155 (7th Cir. 1984) (en banc), *rev'd on other grounds*, 470 U.S. 373 (1985).

Like federal law, Illinois law recognizes a difference between contracts unlawful *per se* and those that must be assessed under a Rule of Reason. Although federal law treats almost all contracts allocating products and markets as unlawful *per se*, the *per se* rule is designed for "naked" restraints rather than agreements that facilitate productive activity. Any firm involves cooperation among people who could otherwise be competitors. Polk Bros. and Forest City each comprise many stores. The managers of each store could set prices independently, competing against each other, but antitrust law does not require this.

Cooperation is the basis of productivity. It is necessary for people to cooperate in some respects before they may compete in others, and cooperation facilitates efficient production. See *Monsanto Co. v. Spray-Rite Service Corp.*, 465 U.S. 752 (1984). Joint ventures, mergers, systems of distribution — all these and more require extensive cooperation, and all are assessed under a Rule of Reason that focuses on market power and the ability of the cooperators to raise price by restricting output. The war of all against all is not a good model for any economy. Antitrust law is designed to ensure an appropriate blend of cooperation and competition, not to require all economic actors to compete full tilt at every moment. When cooperation contributes to productivity through integration of efforts, the Rule of Reason is the norm. *National Collegiate Athletic Association v. Board of Regents of University of Oklahoma*, 468 U.S. 85 (1984) (*NCAA*).

A court must distinguish between "naked" restraints, those in which the restriction on competition is unaccompanied by new production or products, and "ancillary" restraints, those that are part of a larger endeavor whose success they promote. If two people meet one day and decide not to compete, the restraint is "naked"; it does nothing but suppress competition. If A hires B as a salesman and passes customer lists to B, then B's reciprocal covenant not to compete with A is "ancillary." At the time A and B strike their bargain, the enterprise (viewed as a whole) expands output and competition by putting B to work. The covenant not to compete means that A may trust B with broader responsibilities, the better to compete against third parties. Covenants of this type are evaluated under the Rule of Reason as ancillary restraints, and unless they bring a large market share under a single firm's control they are lawful. See *United States v. Addyston Pipe & Steel Co.*, 85 F. 271, 280–83 (6th Cir. 1898) (Taft, J.), *aff'd*, 172 U.S. 211 (1899).

The evaluation of ancillary restraints under the Rule of Reason does not imply that ancillary agreements are not real horizontal restraints. They are. A covenant not to compete following employment does not operate any differently from a horizontal market division among competitors — not at the time the covenant has its bite, anyway. The difference comes at the time people enter beneficial arrangements. A legal rule that enforces covenants not to compete, even after an employee has launched his own firm, makes it easier for people to cooperate productively in the first place. Knowing that he is not cutting his own throat by doing so, the employer will train the employee, giving him skills, knowledge, and trade secrets that make the firm more productive. Once that employment ends, there is nothing left but restraint — but the aftermath is the wrong focus.

A court must ask whether an agreement promoted enterprise and productivity at the time it was adopted. If it arguably did, then the court must apply the Rule of Reason to make a more discriminating assessment. "[I]t is sometimes difficult to distinguish robust competition from conduct with long-run anti-competitive effects" (*Copperweld Corp. v. Independence Tube Corp.*, 467 U.S. 752), and so a court must be very sure that a category of acts is anti-competitive before condemning that category *per se*. Both *BMI* and *NCAA* emphasize that condemnation *per se* is an unusual step, one that depends on confidence that a whole category of restraints is so likely to be anticompetitive that there is no point in searching for a potentially beneficial instance.

A restraint is ancillary when it may contribute to the success of a cooperative venture that promises greater productivity and output. If the restraint, viewed at the time it was adopted, may promote the success of this more extensive cooperation, then the court must scrutinize things carefully under the Rule of Reason. Only when a quick look reveals that "the practice facially appears to be one that would always or almost always tend to restrict competition and decrease output" should a court cut off further inquiry.

Polk Bros. and Forest City were deciding in 1972–73 whether to embark on a new venture — the building of a joint facility — that would expand output. The endeavor not only would increase the retail selling capacity in Burbank but also would provide a convenience to consumers. Polk Bros. does about 80% of its business in large appliances. If it could bring to the same location building supplies and the other items in which Forest City specializes, shopping would be more convenient for consumers. As the district court put it, the parties "hoped to attract more customers because of the proximity of two stores, selling different but complementary items for the home."

This was productive cooperation. The covenant allocating items between the retailers played an important role in inducing the two retailers to cooperate. The district court found that Polk "would not have entered into this arrangement, however, unless it had received assurances that [Forest City] would not compete with it in the sale of products that are the 'foundation of [Polk's] business.' . . . The agreement not to compete was an integral part of the lease and land sale."

It is easy to see why. Polk spent substantial sums in advertising to attract customers to its stores, where it displayed and demonstrated the appliances. It might be tempting for another retailer to take a free ride on these efforts. Once Polk had persuaded a customer to purchase a color TV, its next door neighbor might try to lure the customer away by quoting a lower price. It could afford to do this if, for example, it simply kept the TV sets in boxes and let Polk bear the costs of sales personnel and demonstrations. Polk would not continue doing the work while its neighbor took the sales. It would do less demonstrating and promotion, to the detriment of consumers who valued the information. The Supreme Court has recognized that the control of free riding is a legitimate objective of a system of distribution. See *Monsanto Co. v. Spray-Rite Serv. Corp.*, 465 U.S. 752; *Continental T.V., Inc. v. GTE Sylvania, Inc.*, 433 U.S. at 55–57.

The district court nonetheless concluded that the covenant is not ancillary because it was an essential part of the arrangement. It reasoned: "The agreement not to compete was an integral part of the lease and land sale. This was not a sale with an ancillary agreement designed to protect an original owner's established business interests. The lease and land sale would not have been made by Polk Bros. absent an agreement not to compete. . . . Because the covenant not to compete was not merely ancillary to a sale of land or business, it constitutes a horizontal restraint of trade and a *per se* violation of the Illinois Antitrust Act. . . ." There are two possible interpretations of this reasoning. One is that this covenant is not ancillary because it is so important. The other is that the agreement is not ancillary when it is part of the establishment of a new business, as opposed to the sale of an existing business. Neither is correct.

The reason for distinguishing between "ancillary" and "naked" restraints is to determine whether the agreement is part of a cooperative venture with prospects for increasing output. If it is, it should not be condemned *per se*. Only by exalting Webster's Third over the function of antitrust law could a court determine that a restraint is not "ancillary" because it was so important to the productive undertaking. The suggestion that the ancillary restraints doctrine does not apply to new ventures also slights the functions of the rule. The partners of a newly-formed law firm agree on fees and allocate subjects of specialty and clients among them; this "price fixing" and "market division" do not become unlawful just because the firm is new. The benefits of cooperation may be greatest when launching a new venture.

Polk Bros. and Forest City were cooperating to produce, not to curtail output; the cooperation increased the amount of retail space available and was at least potentially beneficial to consumers; the restrictive covenant made the cooperation possible. The Rule of Reason therefore applies. . . .

. . . .

Polk is entitled to the permanent injunction it seeks. Polk's relief may be conditioned, however, on its iron-clad undertaking to live up to its end of the bargain, and the district court should incorporate this into the injunction. Forest City also has an action for damages caused by Polk's sales, if it can establish any and if it has preserved the claim.

. . . .

Reversed.

NOTE

In *Palmer v. BRG of Georgia, Inc.*, 498 U.S. 46 (1990), the Supreme Court reaffirmed with both clarity and brevity that horizontal market division is unlawful per se. The per curiam opinion cited *Socony-Vacuum* and *Topco* for the rule that an allocation of markets or submarkets by competitors is unlawful whether or not the competitors had previously competed between themselves in the same market.

In *Palmer*, HBJ offered on a limited basis, in 1976, a bar review course in Georgia in competition with BRG. In 1980, they entered an agreement that gave BRG an exclusive license to use HBJ's written materials in Georgia, along with the trade name Bar/Bri. In return, the parties agreed that HBJ would not compete in Georgia and BRG would not compete outside Georgia. In this agreement, HBJ received $100 per student enrolled in Georgia by BRG and 40% of all revenues over $350. After the 1980 agreement became effective, the price of BRG's bar review course went from $150 to $400.

Said the Court: "The revenue-sharing formula in the 1980 agreement between BRG and HBJ, coupled with the price increase that took place immediately after the parties agreed to cease competing with each other in 1980, indicates that this agreement was 'formed for the purpose and with the effect of raising' the price of the bar review course." Does this language suggest that for a market division agreement to be per se unlawful, it must have a direct effect on price?

Relying on *Topco*, the Court answered in the negative. "Here, HBJ and BRG had previously competed in the Georgia market; under their allocation agreement, BRG received that market, while HBJ received the remainder of the United States. Each agreed not to compete in the other's territories. Such agreements are anticompetitive regardless of whether the parties split a market within which both do business or whether they merely reserve one market for one and another for the other. Thus, the 1980 agreement between HBJ and BRG was unlawful on its face."

Palmer makes clear that market allocations between competitors are per se unlawful even (1) in the absence of an agreement on price or evidence that one party has the right to be consulted about the other's prices, and (2) when the parties had not previously competed in the same market.

Interestingly, the district court had granted a summary judgment for the defendants under the authority of *Matsushita*, and the Court of Appeals had affirmed. Perhaps *Palmer* is the first signal from the Court to the lower courts that its expansive language in *Matsushita* in favor of granting a summary judgment is not applicable when the underlying theory of enforcement rests on a traditional per se theory. As Judge Clark observed in his dissent from the Court of Appeal decision, "it is . . . doubtful whether the standards announced in *Matsushita* and *Monsanto* apply in situations, such as the instant action, where the direct evidence of concerted action is manifest in explicit written agreements between dominant firms allocating and monopolizing the market and interfering with independent price setting," 874 F.2d 1417, 1431 (11th Cir. 1989) (Clark, J., dissenting). *See also In re Coordinated Pretrial Proceedings in Petroleum Prods. Antitrust Litig.*, 915 F.2d 542 (9th Cir. 1990).

Horizontal market division can affect professionals once in practice as well. Consider the traditional partnership agreement, which may contain a "no compete" clause within a certain territory if one leaves the partnership. Is a partnership agreement that limits the geographic area in which each partner or former partner can practice and advertise an enforceable contract or illegal under the Sherman Act? Does it matter if the agreement only restricts advertising and not areas of practice? Are such restrictions ancillary to the larger agreement to form or dissolve the partnership and thus legal?

Blackburn v. Sweeney, 53 F.3d 825 (7th Cir. 1995), applied the per se rule to an agreement not to advertise in one another's territories entered by two lawyers who had previously dissolved their relationship. The court found that the agreement "sufficiently approximate[d] an agreement to allocate markets so that the per se rule of illegality" applied. The court rejected the defense that the agreement was ancillary to the larger partnership dissolution agreement because the partnership had already been dissolved when the territorial agreement was entered.

Although the agreement was held per se illegal, treble damages and attorneys fees were denied because the parties were adjudged of equal fault or responsibility. See Chapter 3, *supra*, on the defenses of *in pari delicto* and unclean hands.

Query: How anticompetitive is an agreement between two lawyers (in this case, personal injury lawyers) dividing their territory when the market contains dozens or perhaps even hundreds of other lawyers in competition with them?

The Ninth Circuit has held that per se rule against horizontal market divisions does not apply in the international context. In *Metro Industries, Inc. v. Sammi Corp.*, 82 F.3d 839 (9th Cir. 1996), a domestic importer of Korean kitchenware alleged that the Korean system of export registration constituted an illegal market division. After determining that it had jurisdiction to rule on the claim, the court granted the defendant's motion for summary judgment. According to the court, even if the defendant's conduct was so inherently suspect that it would be subject to per se analysis had it occurred domestically, "application of the per se rule is not appropriate where the conduct in question occurred in another country. Determining whether the registration system was a violation of the antitrust laws would still require an examination of the impact of the system on commerce in the United States. . . ." The court proceeded to award summary judgment in favor of the defendant because the plaintiff did nothing more than suggest it could produce evidence of injury to itself and its customers.

[E]　Boycotts and Other Concerted Refusals to Deal

Up to this point in the study of cartel-like horizontal behavior, we have seen the Court adopt per se standards of analysis for conduct characterized as price fixing or market division. Exclusionary arrangements can also take the form of collective agreements designed to limit competition either by creating barriers to entry for new competition or facilitating market exit by existing competitors. Group boycotts or concerted refusals to deal are examples. The boycott, a refusal to deal with a particular firm, can be aimed at competitors on the same level of competition or at customers or suppliers on different levels of the market. The objective of the refusal to deal and the effect on competition influence the Court's analysis. The objective and effect will also determine how the boycott will be classified for purposes of analysis. As the following cases indicate, the legality of the boycott is determined by examining how essential the design of the agreement is to a lawful objective.

[1] Development of a Per Se Analysis: Collective Agreements Aimed at Competitors

EASTERN STATES RETAIL LUMBER DEALERS' ASS'N v. UNITED STATES
234 U.S. 600 (1914)

JUSTICE DAY delivered the opinion of the Court.

[Defendants were lumber trade associations composed largely of retail lumber dealers. The associations circulated among themselves the membership lists of wholesalers who also sold lumber retail directly to consumers. "The particular thing which this case concerns is the retailers' efforts . . . by the circulation of the reports in question, to keep the wholesalers from selling directly to the local trade."]

. . . When viewed in the light of the history of these associations and the conflict in which they were engaged to keep the retail trade to themselves and to prevent wholesalers from interfering with what they regarded as their rights in such trade there can be but one purpose in giving the information in this form to the members of the retail associations of the names of all wholesalers who by their attempt to invade the exclusive territory of the retailers, as they regard it, have been guilty of unfair competitive trade. These lists were quite commonly spoken of as blacklists, and when the attention of a retailer was brought to the name of a wholesaler who had acted in this wise it was with the evident purpose that he should know of such conduct and act accordingly. True it is that there is no agreement among the retailers to refrain from dealing with listed wholesalers, nor is there any penalty annexed for the failure so to do, but he is blind indeed who does not see the purpose in the predetermined and periodical circulation of this report to put the ban upon wholesale dealers whose names appear in the list of unfair dealers trying by methods obnoxious to the retail dealers to supply the trade which they regard as their own. . . .

[T]he circulation of such information among the hundreds of retailers as to the alleged delinquency of a wholesaler with one of their number had and was intended to have the natural effect of causing such retailers to withhold their patronage from the concern listed.

. . . .

Here are wholesale dealers in large number engaged in interstate trade upon whom it is proposed to impose as a condition of carrying on that trade that they shall not sell in such manner that a local retail dealer may regard such sale as an infringement of his exclusive right to trade, upon pain of being reported as an unfair dealer to a large number of other retail dealers associated with the offended dealer, the purpose being to keep the wholesaler from dealing not only with the particular dealer who reports him but with all others of the class who may be informed of his delinquency. . . . This record abounds in instances where the offending dealer was thus reported, the hoped for effect, unless he discontinued the offending practice, realized, and his trade directly and appreciably impaired.

But it is said that in order to show a combination or conspiracy within the Sherman Act some agreement must be shown under which the concerted action is taken. It is elementary, however, that conspiracies are seldom capable of proof by direct testimony and may be inferred from the things actually done, and when in this case by concerted action the names of wholesalers who were reported as having made sales to consumers were periodically reported to the other members of the associations, the conspiracy to accomplish that which was the natural consequence of such action may be readily inferred.

The circulation of these reports not only tends to directly restrain the freedom of commerce by preventing the listed dealers from entering into competition with retailers, as was held by the District Court, but it directly tends to prevent other retailers who have no personal grievance against him and with whom he might trade from so doing, they being deterred solely because of the influence of the report circulated among the members of the associations. . . .

A retail dealer has the unquestioned right to stop dealing with a wholesaler for reasons sufficient to himself, and may do so because he thinks such dealer is acting unfairly in trying to undermine his trade. "But," as was said . . . in *Grenada Lumber Co. v. Mississippi*, 217 U.S. 433, 440, "when the plaintiffs in error combine and agree that no one of them will trade with any producer or wholesaler who shall sell to a consumer within the trade range of any of them, quite another case is presented. An act harmless when done by one may become a public wrong when done by many acting in concert, for it then takes on the form of a conspiracy, and may be prohibited or punished, if the result be hurtful to the public or to the individual against whom the concerted action is directed."

When the retailer goes beyond his personal right, and, conspiring and combining with others of like purpose, seeks to obstruct the free course of interstate trade and commerce and to unduly suppress competition by placing obnoxious wholesale dealers under the coercive influence of a condemnatory report circulated among others, actual or possible customers of the offenders, he exceeds his lawful rights, and such action brings him and those acting with him within the condemnation of the act of Congress, and the District Court was right in so holding. It follows that its decree must be Affirmed.

NOTES AND QUESTIONS

1. Did the Court find an agreement to boycott or merely an agreement to exchange data? Does a distinction between the two matter with regard to the analysis utilized? Did the Court conclude that this boycott was per se illegal? Did it imply that competitive injury can be inferred without regard to market power?

2. Did the Court in *Eastern States* suggest that a unilateral refusal to deal is lawful? *See Lorain Journal Co. v. United States*, 342 U.S. 143 (1951). Consider the analysis adopted subsequently in *Interstate Circuit* and *Container*.

3. In *Fashion Originator's Guild of Am. ("FOGA") v. FTC*, 312 U.S. 457 (1941), the Court reached the same conclusion as in *Eastern States*. Defendant manufacturers of fashionable clothes for women in *Fashion Guild* attempted to prevent "style piracy" by agreeing to boycott retailers who purchased from the defendants' competitors that dealt in copied designs. As a result of the Guild's collective action, 12,000 retailers signed agreements to cooperate with the boycott in refusing to buy from the targeted discount manufacturers.

The Court affirmed the FTC's refusal to consider the "reasonableness" of the Guild's methods. Said the Court: "reasonableness of the methods pursued by the combination to accomplish its unlawful object is no more material than would be the reasonableness of the prices fixed by unlawful combination." The effect of this refusal to deal, the Court concluded, was to foreclose access to retail outlets and thus to reduce competition from lower-priced competitors.

KLOR'S, INC. v. BROADWAY-HALE STORES, INC.
359 U.S. 207 (1959)

JUSTICE BLACK delivered the opinion of the Court.

Klor's, Inc., operates a retail store on Mission Street, San Francisco, California; Broadway-Hale Stores, Inc., a chain of department stores, operates one of its stores next door. The two stores compete in the sale of radios, television sets, refrigerators and other household appliances. Claiming that Broadway-Hale and 10 national manufacturers and their distributors have conspired to restrain and monopolize commerce in violation of §§ 1 and 2 of the Sherman Act, Klor's brought this action for treble damages and injunction in the United States District Court.

In support of its claim Klor's made the following allegations: George Klor started an appliance store some years before 1952 and has operated it ever since either individually or as Klor's, Inc. Klor's is as well equipped as Broadway-Hale to handle all brands of appliances. Nevertheless, manufacturers and distributors of such well-known brands as General Electric, RCA, Admiral, Zenith, Emerson and others have conspired among themselves and with Broadway-Hale either not to sell to Klor's or to sell to it only at discriminatory prices and highly unfavorable terms. Broadway-Hale has used its "monopolistic" buying power to bring about this situation. The business of manufacturing, distributing and selling household appliances is in interstate commerce. The concerted refusal to deal with Klor's has seriously handicapped its ability to compete and has already caused it a great loss of profits, goodwill, reputation and prestige.

The defendants did not dispute these allegations, but sought summary judgment and dismissal of the complaint for failure to state a cause of action. They submitted unchallenged affidavits which showed that there were hundreds of other household appliance retailers, some within a few blocks of Klor's who sold many competing brands of appliances, including those the defendants refused to sell to Klor's. From the allegations of the complaint, and from the affidavits supporting the motion for summary judgment, the District Court concluded that the controversy was a "purely private quarrel" between Klor's and Broadway-Hale, which did not amount to a "public wrong proscribed by the [Sherman] Act." On this ground the complaint was dismissed and summary judgment was entered for the defendants. The Court of Appeals for the Ninth Circuit affirmed the summary judgment. It stated that "a violation of the Sherman Act requires conduct of defendants by which the public is or conceivably may be ultimately injured." It held that here the required public injury was missing since "there was no charge or proof that by any act of defendants the price, quantity, or quality offered the public was affected, nor that there was any intent or purpose to effect a change in, or an influence on, prices, quantity, or quality. . . ." The holding, if correct, means that unless the opportunities for customers to buy in a competitive market are reduced, a group of powerful businessmen may act in concert to deprive a single merchant like Klor, of the goods he needs to compete effectively. . . .

We think Klor's allegations clearly show one type of trade restraint and public harm the Sherman Act forbids, and that defendants' affidavits provide no defense to the charges. . . .

Group boycotts, or concerted refusals by traders to deal with other traders, have long been held to be in the forbidden category. They have not been saved by allegations that they were reasonable in the specific circumstances, nor by a failure to show that they "fixed or regulated prices, parcelled out or limited production, or brought about a deterioration in quality." . . .

Plainly the allegations of this complaint disclose such a boycott. This is not a case of a single trader refusing to deal with another, nor even of a manufacturer and a dealer agreeing to an exclusive distributorship. Alleged in this complaint is a wide combination consisting of manufacturers, distributors and a retailer. This combination takes from Klor's its freedom to buy appliances in an open competitive market and drives it out of business as a dealer in the defendants' products. It deprives the manufacturers and distributors of their freedom to sell to Klor's at the same prices and conditions made available to Broadway-Hale, and in some instances forbids them from selling to it on any terms whatsoever. It interferes with the natural flow of interstate commerce. It clearly has, by its "nature" and "character," a "monopolistic tendency." As such it is not to be tolerated merely because the victim is just one merchant whose business is so small that his destruction makes little difference to the economy.[51] Monopoly can as surely thrive by the elimination of such small businessmen, one at a time, as it can by driving them out in large groups. In recognition of this fact the Sherman Act has consistently been read to forbid all contracts and combinations "which 'tend to create a monopoly,' " whether "the tendency is a creeping one" or "one that proceeds at full gallop."

The judgment of the Court of Appeals is reversed and the cause is remanded to the District Court for trial.

---

[51] [FN 7] The court below relied heavily on *Apex Hosiery Co. v. Leader*, 310 U.S. 469, in reaching its conclusion. While some language in that case can be read as supporting the position that no restraint on trade is prohibited by § 1 of the Sherman Act unless it has or is intended to have an effect on market prices, such statements must be considered in the light of the fact that the defendant in that case was a labor union. The Court in *Apex* recognized that the Act is aimed primarily at combinations having commercial objectives and is applied only to a very limited extent to organizations, like labor unions, which normally have other objectives. Moreover, cases subsequent to *Apex* have made clear that an effect on prices is not essential to a Sherman Act violation. *See, e.g., Fashion Originators' Guild v. Federal Trade Comm'n*, 312 U.S. 457, 466.

NOTES AND QUESTIONS

1. Since the Court reversed the grant of summary judgment for the defendant, what would the plaintiff have to prove at trial to establish a prima facie case? Will actual competitive injury have to be demonstrated? If Klor's is not required to establish actual competitive injury, why wasn't summary judgment entered for plaintiff? What levels of competition were affected in both *FOGA* and *Klor's*? Does *Klor's* require a showing of market power before a Section 1 violation is found?

The complaint in *Klor's* alleged that Broadway-Hale Stores, Inc., used its "monopolistic" buying power to force General Electric, RCA, Admiral, Zenith, Emerson, and other large appliance manufacturers not to deal with Klor's. Because the Supreme Court merely reversed a grant of summary judgment for the defendant, it never dealt with the plausibility of such a scheme. Is it likely that a small retail chain had monopsony power vis-à-vis General Electric, RCA, and such companies? Much more likely, the companies were engaged in resale price maintenance (*see* discussion, *infra*) and Broadway-Hale was merely reporting Klor's violation of the resale price maintenance provision.

It is also possible that Klor's was injuring Broadway-Hale, which was right next door, by taking a "free ride" on Broadway-Hale's efforts to service its customers. Customers would go to a "full service" store like Broadway-Hale to see a complex item described and to receive helpful information about purchasing — then they would go next door to Klor's and purchase it at a discount price.

2. How did defendants' defense in *Klor's* differ from those posited in *FOGA* and *Eastern States*? Does the decisional analysis change accordingly?

3. The Court said that the challenged agreement in *Klor's* was something more than a vertical arrangement between customer (dealer) and supplier (manufacturer). Explain. Did the Court imply that the standard of analysis will vary according to the relationship between the parties involved? Should it matter whether the plaintiff is an excluded competitor or a consumer denied an opportunity to buy something at a lower price? What is the legal and economic rationale for such a distinction? If such an inference can be drawn from the opinion, is it unlawful per se to have an exclusive distributorship (such as an exclusive franchise) where a manufacturer agrees to sell only to a single retailer? What economic rationale supports such an arrangement? Will the boycott doctrine be applied to such a case?

When the members of a conspiracy share both vertical and horizontal relationships with their co-conspirators, it can complicate the antitrust analysis. However, when an antitrust conspiracy involves a horizontal component, a conspirator with a vertical relationship to its co-conspirators can be brought within the per se rule. A price-fixing example illustrates the point. When competing sellers of electronic books ("ebooks") wanted to raise the price of their products, Apple — a reseller of ebooks — offered to create an agency model of resale that allowed ebook publishers to raise considerably. When the government brought a per se claim against Apple, the company argued that the per se rule should not apply because Apple was in a vertical relationship with the publishers. *U.S. v. Apple, Inc.*, ___ F. Supp. 2d ___, 2013 U.S. Dist. LEXIS 96424, 2013 WL 3454986 (S.D.N.Y. July 10, 2013). The court rejected that argument, reasoning:

Per se price-fixing agreements may also include those where a vertical player participates in and facilitates a horizontal conspiracy. Where a vertical actor is alleged to have participated in an unlawful horizontal agreement, plaintiffs must demonstrate both that a horizontal conspiracy existed, and that the vertical player was a knowing participant in that agreement and facilitated the scheme.

Id. at 41 (citing *Toys "R" Us, Inc. v. FTC*, 221 F.3d 928, 934, 936 (7th Cir. 2000) and *Interstate Circuit v. United States*, 306 U.S. 208, 225–229 (1939)). The court found Apple liable per se for participating in and facilitating a horizontal price-fixing conspiracy.

NYNEX CORPORATION v. DISCON, INC.
525 U.S. 128 (1998)

Justice Breyer delivered the opinion of the Court.

In this case we ask whether the antitrust rule that group boycotts are illegal per se as set forth in *Klor's, Inc. v. Broadway-Hale Stores, Inc.*, 359 U.S. 207, 212 (1959), applies to a buyer's decision to buy from one seller rather than another, when that decision cannot be justified in terms of ordinary competitive objectives. We hold that the per se group boycott rule does not apply.

I

Before 1984 American Telephone and Telegraph Company (AT&T) supplied most of the Nation's telephone service and, through wholly owned subsidiaries such as Western Electric, it also supplied much of the Nation's telephone equipment. In 1984 an antitrust consent decree took AT&T out of the *local* telephone service business and left AT&T a *long-distance* telephone service provider, competing with such firms as MCI and Sprint. . . . The decree transformed AT&T's formerly owned local telephone companies into independent firms. At the same time, the decree insisted that those local firms help assure competitive long-distance service by guaranteeing long-distance companies physical access to their systems and to their local customers. See *United States v. American Telephone & Telegraph Co.*, 552 F. Supp. 131, 225, 227 (DC 1982), *aff'd sub nom. Maryland v. United States*, 460 U. S 1001 (1983). To guarantee that physical access, some local telephone firms had to install new call-switching equipment; and to install new call-switching equipment, they often had to remove old call-switching equipment. This case involves the business of removing that old switching equipment (and other obsolete telephone equipment) — a business called *"removal services."*

Discon, Inc., the respondent, sold removal services used by New York Telephone Company, a firm supplying local telephone service in much of New York State and parts of Connecticut. New York Telephone is a subsidiary of NYNEX Corporation. NYNEX also owns Materiel Enterprises Company, a purchasing entity that bought removal services for New York Telephone. Discon, in a lengthy detailed complaint, alleged that the NYNEX defendants (namely, NYNEX, New York Telephone, Materiel Enterprises, and several NYNEX related individuals) engaged in unfair, improper, and anticompetitive activities in order to hurt Discon and to benefit Discon's removal services competitor, AT&T Technologies, a lineal descendant of Western Electric. The Federal District Court dismissed Discon's complaint for failure to state a claim. The Court of Appeals for the Second Circuit affirmed that dismissal with an exception, and that exception is before us for consideration.

The Second Circuit focused on one of Discon's specific claims, a claim that Materiel Enterprises had switched its purchases from Discon to Discon's competitor, AT&T Technologies, as part of an attempt to defraud local telephone service customers by hoodwinking regulators. According to Discon, Materiel Enterprises would pay AT&T Technologies more than Discon would have charged for similar removal services. It did so because it could pass the higher prices on to New York Telephone, which in turn could pass those prices on to telephone consumers in the form of higher regulatory-agency-approved telephone service charges. At the end of the year, Materiel Enterprises would receive a special rebate from AT&T Technologies, which Materiel Enterprises would share with its parent, NYNEX. Discon added that it refused to participate in this fraudulent scheme, with the result that Materiel Enterprises would not buy from Discon, and Discon went out of business.

These allegations, the Second Circuit said, state a cause of action under § 1 of the Sherman Act, though under a "different legal theory" from the one articulated by Discon. 93 F.3d 1055, 1060 (1996). The Second Circuit conceded that ordinarily "the decision to discriminate in favor of one supplier over another will have a pro-competitive intent and effect." *Id.*, at 1061. But, it added, in this case, "no such pro-competitive rationale appears on the face of the complaint." *Ibid.* Rather, the complaint alleges Materiel Enterprises' decision to buy from AT&T Technologies, rather than from Discon, was intended to be, and was, "anti-competitive." *Ibid.* Hence, "Discon has alleged a cause of action under, at least, the rule of reason, and possibly under the per se rule applied to group boycotts in *Klor's*, if the restraint of trade " 'has no purpose except stifling competition.' "" *Ibid.* (quoting *Oreck Corp. v. Whirlpool Corp.*, 579 F.2d 126, 131 (CA2) (en banc) (in turn quoting *White Motor Co. v. United States*, 372 U.S. 253, 263 (1963)), *cert. denied*, 439 U.S. 946 (1978)). For somewhat similar reasons the Second Circuit believed the complaint stated a valid claim of conspiracy to monopolize under § 2 of the Sherman Act. See 93 F.3d at 1061–1062.

. . . .

II

As this Court has made clear, the Sherman Act's prohibition of "[e]very" agreement in "restraint of trade," . . . prohibits only agreements that *unreasonably* restrain trade. See *Business Electronics Corp. v. Sharp Electronics Corp.*, 485 U.S. 717, 723 (1988) (citing *National Collegiate Athletic Assn. v. Board of Regents of Univ. of Okla.*, 468 U.S. 85, 98 (1984)); *Standard Oil Co. of N. J. v. United States*, 221 U.S. 1, 59–62 (1911); 2 P. Areeda & H. Hovenkamp, Antitrust Law ¶ 320b, p. 49 (1995). Yet certain kinds of agreements will so often prove so harmful to competition and so rarely prove justified that the antitrust laws do not require proof that an agreement of that kind is, in fact, anticompetitive in the particular circumstances. See *State Oil Co. v. Khan*, 522 U.S. 3, 10 (1997); *Northwest Wholesale Stationers*,

Inc. v. Pacific Stationery & Printing Co., 472 U.S. 284, 289–290 (1985); 2 Areeda & Hovenkamp, *supra*, ¶ 320b, at 49–52. An agreement of such a kind is unlawful *per se*. *See, e.g., United States v. Socony-Vacuum Oil Co.*, 310 U.S. 150, 218 (1940) (finding horizontal price-fixing agreement *per se* illegal); *Dr. Miles Medical Co. v. John D. Park & Sons Co.*, 220 U.S. 373, 408 (1911) (finding vertical price-fixing agreement *per se* illegal); *Palmer v. BRG of Ga., Inc.*, 498 U.S. 46, 49–50 (1990) (*per curiam*) (finding horizontal market division *per se* illegal).

The Court has found the *per se* rule applicable in certain group boycott cases. Thus, in *Fashion Originators' Guild of America, Inc. v. FTC*, 312 U.S. 457 (1941), this Court considered a group boycott created by an agreement among a group of clothing designers, manufacturers, suppliers, and retailers. The defendant designers, manufacturers, and suppliers had promised not to sell their clothes to retailers who bought clothes from competing manufacturers and suppliers. The defendants wanted to present evidence that would show their agreement was justified because the boycotted competitors used "pira[ted]" fashion designs. *Id.*, at 467. But the Court wrote that "it was not error to refuse to hear the evidence offered" — evidence that the agreement was reasonable and necessary to "protect . . . against the devastating evils" of design pirating — for that evidence "is no more material than would be the reasonableness of the prices fixed" by a price-fixing agreement. *Id.*, at 467–468.

In *Klor's* the Court also applied the *per se* rule. The Court considered a boycott created when a retail store, Broadway-Hale, and 10 household appliance manufacturers and their distributors agreed that the distributors would not sell, or would sell only at discriminatory prices, household appliances to Broadway-Hale's small, nearby competitor, namely, Klor's. 359 U.S., at 208–209. The defendants had submitted undisputed evidence that their agreement hurt only one competitor (Klor's) and that so many other nearby appliance-selling competitors remained that competition in the marketplace continued to thrive. *Id.*, at 209–210. The Court held that this evidence was beside the point. The conspiracy was "not to be tolerated merely because the victim is just one merchant." *Id.*, at 213. The Court thereby inferred injury to the competitive process itself from the nature of the boycott agreement. And it forbade, as a matter of law, a defense based upon a claim that only one small firm, not competition itself, had suffered injury.

The case before us involves *Klor's*. The Second Circuit did not forbid the defendants to introduce evidence of "justification." To the contrary, it invited the defendants to do so, for it said that the "*per se* rule" would apply only if no "pro-competitive justification" were to be found. 93 F.3d at 1061; *cf.* 7 P. Areeda & H. Hovenkamp, Antitrust Law ¶ 1510, p. 416 (1986) ("Boycotts are said to be unlawful per se but justifications are routinely considered in defining the forbidden category"). Thus, the specific legal question before us is whether an antitrust court considering an agreement by a buyer to purchase goods or services from one supplier rather than another should (after examining the buyer's reasons or justifications) apply the *per se* rule if it finds no legitimate business reason for that purchasing decision. We conclude no boycott-related *per se* rule applies and that the plaintiff here must allege and prove harm, not just to a single competitor, but to the competitive process, i.e., to competition itself.

Our conclusion rests in large part upon precedent, for precedent limits the *per se* rule in the boycott context to cases involving horizontal agreements among direct competitors. The agreement in *Fashion Originators' Guild* involved what may be called a group boycott in the strongest sense: A group of competitors threatened to withhold business from third parties unless those third parties would help them injure their directly competing rivals. Although *Klor's* involved a threat made by a *single* powerful firm, it also involved a horizontal agreement among those threatened, namely, the appliance suppliers, to hurt a competitor of the retailer who made the threat. See 359 U.S. at 208–209; see also P. Areeda & L. Kaplow, Antitrust Analysis: Problems, Text, and Cases 333 (5th ed. 1997) (defining paradigmatic boycott as "collective action among a group of competitors that may inhibit the competitive vitality of rivals"); 11 H. Hovenkamp, Antitrust Law ¶ 1901e, pp. 189–190 (1998). This Court emphasized in *Klor's* that the agreement at issue was "not a case of a single trader refusing to deal with another, nor even of a manufacturer and a dealer agreeing to an exclusive distributorship. Alleged in this complaint is a wide combination consisting of manufacturers, distributors and a retailer." 359 U.S. at 212–213 (footnote omitted).

This Court subsequently pointed out specifically that *Klor's* was a case involving not simply a "vertical" agreement between supplier and customer, but a case that also involved a "horizontal" agreement among competitors. See *Business Electronics*, 485 U.S. at 734. And in doing so, the Court held that a "vertical restraint is not illegal *per se* unless it includes some agreement on price or price levels." *Id.*, at 735–736. This precedent makes the *per se* rule inapplicable, for the case before us concerns only a vertical agreement and a vertical restraint, a restraint that takes the form of depriving a supplier of a potential customer. *See* 11 Hovenkamp, *supra*, ¶ 1902d, at 198.

. . . .

To apply the *per se* rule here — where the buyer's decision, though not made for competitive reasons, composes part of a regulatory fraud — would transform cases involving business behavior that is improper for various reasons, say, cases involving nepotism or personal pique, into treble-damages antitrust cases. And that *per se* rule would discourage firms from changing suppliers — even where the competitive process itself does not suffer harm. Cf. *Poller v. Columbia Broadcasting System, Inc.*, 368 U.S. 464, 484 (1962) (Harlan, J., dissenting) (citing *Packard Motor Car Co. v. Webster Motor Car Co.*, 243 F.2d 418, 421 (CADC 1957)).

The freedom to switch suppliers lies close to the heart of the competitive process that the antitrust laws seek to encourage. Cf. *Standard Oil*, 221 U.S., at 62 (noting "the freedom of the individual right to contract when not unduly or improperly exercised [is] the most efficient means for the prevention of monopoly"). At the same time, other laws, for example, "unfair competition" laws, business tort laws, or regulatory laws, provide remedies for various "competitive practices thought to be offensive to proper standards of business morality." 3 P. Areeda & H. Hovenkamp, Antitrust Law ¶ 651d, p. 78 (1996). Thus, this Court has refused to apply *per se* reasoning in cases involving that kind of activity. See *Brooke Group Ltd. v. Brown & Williamson Tobacco Corp.*, 509 U.S. 209, 225 (1993) ("Even an act of pure malice by one business competitor against another does not, without more, state a claim under the federal antitrust laws."); 3 Areeda & Hovenkamp, *supra*, ¶ 651d, at 80 ("[I]n the presence of substantial market power, some kinds of tortious behavior could anticompetitively create or sustain a monopoly, [but] it is wrong categorically to condemn such practices . . . or categorically to excuse them").

Discon points to another special feature of its complaint, namely, its claim that Materiel Enterprises hoped to drive Discon from the market lest Discon reveal its behavior to New York Telephone or to the relevant regulatory agency. That hope, says Discon, amounts to a special anticompetitive motive.

We do not see how the presence of this special motive, however, could make a significant difference. That motive does not turn Materiel Enterprises' actions into a "boycott" within the meaning of this Court's precedents. . . .

Finally, we shall consider an argument that is related tangentially to Discon's *per se* claims. The complaint alleges that New York Telephone (through Materiel Enterprises) was the largest buyer of removal services in New York State . . . and that only AT&T Technologies competed for New York Telephone's business. . . . One might ask whether these accompanying allegations are sufficient to warrant application of a *Klor's*-type presumption of consequent harm to the competitive process itself.

We believe that these allegations do not do so, for, as we have said . . . antitrust law does not permit the application of the *per se* rule in the boycott context in the absence of a horizontal agreement. (Though in other contexts, say, vertical price fixing, conduct may fall within the scope of a *per se* rule not at issue here. *See, e.g., Dr. Miles Medical Co.*, 220 U.S., at 408.) The complaint itself explains why any such presumption would be particularly inappropriate here, for it suggests the presence of other potential or actual competitors, which fact, in the circumstances, could argue against the likelihood of anticompetitive harm. The complaint says, for example, that New York Telephone itself was a potential competitor in that New York Telephone considered removing its equipment by itself, and in fact did perform a few jobs itself. . . . The complaint also suggests that other nearby small local telephone companies needing removal services must have worked out some way to supply them . . . The complaint's description of the removal business suggests that entry was easy, perhaps to the point where other firms, employing workers who knew how to remove a switch and sell it for scrap, might have entered that business almost at will. . . . To that extent, the complaint suggests other actual or potential competitors might have provided roughly similar checks upon "equipment removal" prices and services with or without Discon. At the least, the complaint provides no sound basis for assuming the contrary. Its simple allegation of harm to Discon does not automatically show injury to competition.

III

The Court of Appeals also upheld the complaint's charge of a conspiracy to monopolize in violation of § 2 of the Sherman Act. It did so, however, on the understanding that the conspiracy in question consisted of the very same purchasing practices that we have previously discussed. Unless those agreements harmed the competitive process, they did not amount to a conspiracy to monopolize. We do not see, on the basis of the facts alleged, how Discon could succeed on this claim without prevailing on its § 1 claim. See 3 Areeda & Hovenkamp, *supra*, ¶ 651e, at 81–82. Given our conclusion that Discon has not alleged a § 1 *per se* violation, we think it prudent to vacate this portion of the Court of Appeals' decision and allow the court to reconsider its finding of a § 2 claim.

. . . .

V

For these reasons, the judgment of the Court of Appeals is vacated, and the case is remanded for further proceedings consistent with this opinion.

NOTES AND QUESTIONS

1. The Court likens its decision to *Business Electronics Corp. v. Sharp Electronics Corp.*, 485 U.S. 717, 723 (1988), which involved an intrabrand restraint. But don't the facts resemble an "interbrand" restraint? Isn't *NYNEX* just a garden variety exclusive dealing claim, but for the claim of fraudulent overcharging by a price regulated utility? What if *NYNEX* had simply contracted with a single firm to perform all its removal services? How would a court have analyzed exclusive dealing? What would the likely outcome have been?

2. After *NYNEX*, can you name the kinds of boycotts that would still be illegal per se under the Sherman Act? Suppose that two equipment removal companies had agreed with each other, as well as with *NYNEX*, to participate in the fraudulent scheme and to exclude Discon for refusing to participate. What would the outcome have been? Do you agree with Justice Breyer's characterization that this decision made virtually no new law, but was driven entirely by existing precedent?

3. The only apparent purpose of the kickback scheme challenged in *NYNEX* was to defraud consumers by inflating their telephone bills. Doesn't that make this a "naked" restraint? Does the case stand for the proposition that there is no such thing as "naked" vertical exclusion — at least not for purposes of employing the *per se* rule. Consider the practice briefly described in Chapter 6 in which Alcoa, an aluminum monopolist, entered into contracts with electric utilities under which they promised not to provide electricity to any competitor of Alcoa's. Presumably, those agreements were unlawful only because Alcoa had substantial market power, but they were also "naked" in the sense that they had no redeeming virtue. Would you agree with the proposition that if NYNEX had substantial market power in the purchase of telephone removal services, then the agreement at issue should be *per se* unlawful? Given that NYNEX is a regulated monopolist in the supply of local telephone services in New York, isn't monopoly power almost a foregone conclusion?

4. In *Diaz v. Farley*, 215 F.3d 1175 (10th Cir. 2000), an alleged boycott of three anesthesiologists was not a *per se* violation of Section 1 of the Sherman Act. Physicians at Cottonwood Ob/Gyn and Dr. Matthews agreed that Dr. Matthews either would personally perform anesthesiology services to Cottonwood Ob/Gyn's patients in the labor and delivery room or would choose another physician to provide the services when plaintiff doctors were scheduled for shifts in the labor and delivery room. There was evidence that physicians at Cottonwood were concerned with plaintiff doctors' skills. Plaintiffs alleged that defendants had engaged in a horizontal group boycott. The Tenth Circuit concluded that this case did not exemplify a group boycott situation because the plaintiffs did not define a relevant market, the plaintiffs' ability to compete was not restrained because they were able to practice anesthesiology in other departments at Cottonwood and were free to compete for increased access to ob/gyn patients, and because the agreements had the procompetitive effect of allowing doctors to choose a particular anesthesiologist.

[2] The Modern "Per Se Rule" Against Group Boycotts

NORTHWEST WHOLESALE STATIONERS, INC. v. PACIFIC STATIONERY & PRINTING CO.
472 U.S. 284 (1985)

JUSTICE BRENNAN delivered the opinion of the Court.

This case requires that we decide whether a *per se* violation of § 1 of the Sherman Act . . . occurs when a cooperative buying agency comprising various retailers expels a member without providing any procedural means for challenging the expulsion. The case also raises broader questions as to when per se antitrust analysis is appropriately applied to joint activity that is susceptible of being characterized as a concerted refusal to deal.

I

Because the District Court ruled on cross-motions for summary judgment after only limited discovery, this case comes to us on a sparse record. Certain background facts are undisputed. Petitioner Northwest Wholesale Stationers is a purchasing cooperative made up of approximately 100 office supply retailers in the Pacific Northwest States. The cooperative acts as the primary wholesaler for the retailers. Retailers that are not members of the cooperative can purchase wholesale supplies from Northwest at the same price as members. At the end of each year, however, Northwest distributes its profits to members in the form of a percentage rebate on purchases. Members therefore effectively purchase supplies at a price significantly lower than do nonmembers. Northwest also provides certain warehousing facilities. The cooperative arrangement thus permits the participating retailers to achieve economies of scale in purchasing and warehousing that would otherwise be unavailable to them. In fiscal 1978 Northwest had $5.8 million in sales. . . .

Respondent Pacific Stationery, Inc., sells office supplies at both the retail and wholesale levels. Its total sales in fiscal 1978 were approximately $7.6 million; the record does not indicate what percentage of revenue is attributable to retail and what percentage is attributable to wholesale. Pacific became a member of Northwest in 1958. In 1974 Northwest amended its bylaws to prohibit members from engaging in both retail and wholesale operations. . . . A grandfather clause preserved Pacific's membership rights. . . . In 1977 ownership of a controlling share of the stock of Pacific changed hands . . . and the new owners did not officially bring this change to the attention of the directors of Northwest. This failure to notify apparently violated another of Northwest's bylaws. . . .

In 1978 the membership of Northwest voted to expel Pacific. Most factual matters relevant to the expulsion are in dispute. No explanation for the expulsion was advanced at the time and Pacific was given neither notice, a hearing, nor any other opportunity to challenge the decision. Pacific argues that the expulsion resulted from Pacific's decision to maintain a wholesale operation. . . . Northwest contends that the expulsion resulted from Pacific's failure to notify the cooperative members of the change in stock ownership. . . . The minutes of the meeting of Northwest's directors do not definitively indicate the motive for the expulsion. . . . It is undisputed that Pacific received approximately $10,000 in rebates from Northwest in 1978, Pacific's last year of membership. Beyond a possible inference of loss from this fact, however, the record is devoid of allegations indicating the nature and extent of competitive injury the expulsion caused Pacific to suffer.

Pacific brought suit in 1980 in the United States District Court for the District of Oregon alleging a violation of § 1 of the Sherman Act. . . . Finding no anticompetitive effect on the basis of the record as presented, the court granted summary judgment for Northwest. . . .

The Court of Appeals for the Ninth Circuit reversed, holding "that the uncontroverted facts of this case support a finding of *per se* liability." . . .

II

The decision of the cooperative members to expel Pacific was certainly a restraint of trade in the sense that every commercial agreement restrains trade. . . . Whether this action violates § 1 of the Sherman Act depends on whether it is adjudged an *unreasonable* restraint. . . . Rule-of-reason analysis guides the inquiry, . . . unless the challenged action falls into the category of "agreements or practices which because of their pernicious effect on competition and lack of any redeeming virtue are conclusively presumed to be unreasonable and therefore illegal without elaborate inquiry as to the precise harm they have caused or the business excuse for their use." . . .

This *per se* approach permits categorical judgments with respect to certain business practices that have proved to be predominantly anticompetitive. Courts can thereby avoid the "significant costs" in "business certainty and litigation efficiency" that a full-fledged rule-of-reason inquiry entails. . . . The decision to apply the *per se* rule turns on "whether the practice facially appears to be one that would always or almost always tend to restrict competition and decrease output . . . or instead one designed to 'increase economic efficiency and render markets more, rather than less, competitive.' " . . .

This Court has long held that certain concerted refusals to deal or group boycotts are so likely to restrict competition without any offsetting efficiency gains that they should be condemned as *per se* violations of § 1 of the Sherman Act. . . . The question presented in this case is whether Northwest's decision to expel Pacific should fall within this category of activity that is conclusively presumed to be anticompetitive. . . .

A

The Court of Appeals drew from *Silver v. New York Stock Exchange* a broad rule that the conduct of a cooperative venture — including a concerted refusal to deal — undertaken pursuant to a legislative mandate for self-regulation is immune from *per se* scrutiny and subject to rule of reason analysis only if adequate procedural safeguards accompany self-regulation. We disagree and conclude that the approach of the Court in *Silver* has no proper application to the present controversy.

The Court in *Silver* framed the issue as follows:

> "[W]hether the New York Stock Exchange is to be held liable to a nonmember broker-dealer under the antitrust laws or regarded as impliedly immune therefrom when, pursuant to rules the Exchange has adopted under the Securities Exchange Act of 1934, it orders a number of its members to remove private direct telephone wire connections previously in operation between their offices and those of the nonmember, without giving the nonmember notice, assigning him any reason for the action, or affording him an opportunity to be heard." 373 U.S., at 343.

Because the New York Stock Exchange occupied such a dominant position in the securities trading markets that the boycott would devastate the nonmember, the Court concluded that the refusal to deal with the nonmember would amount to a *per se* violation of § 1 unless the Securities Exchange Act provided an immunity. . . . The question for the Court thus was whether effectuation of the policies of the Securities Exchange Act required partial repeal of the Sherman Act insofar as it proscribed this aspect of exchange self-regulation.

Finding exchange self-regulation — including the power to expel members and limit dealings with nonmembers — to be an essential policy of the Securities Exchange Act, the Court held that the Sherman Act should be construed as having been partially repealed to permit the type of exchange activity at issue. But the interpretive maxim disfavoring repeals by implication led the Court to narrow permissible self-policing to situations in which adequate procedural safeguards had been provided.

> " 'Congress . . . cannot be thought to have sanctioned and protected self-regulative activity when carried out in a fundamentally unfair manner. The point is not that the antitrust laws impose the requirement of notice and a hearing here, but rather that, in acting without according petitioners these safeguards in response to their request, the Exchange has plainly exceeded the scope of its authority under the Securities Exchange Act to engage in self-regulation.' . . ."

Thus it was the specific need to accommodate the important national policy of promoting effective exchange self-regulation, tempered by the principle that the Sherman Act should be narrowed only to the extent necessary to effectuate that policy, that dictated the result in *Silver.*

Section 4 of the Robinson-Patman Act is not comparable to the self-policing provisions of the Securities Exchange Act. That section is no more than a narrow immunity from the price discrimination prohibitions of the Robinson-Patman Act itself. The Conference Report makes clear that the exception was intended solely to "safeguard producer and consumer cooperatives against any charge of violation of the act *based on their distribution of earnings or surplus among their members on a patronage basis.*" H.R. Conf. Rep. No. 2951, 74th Cong., 2d Sess., 9 (1936) (emphasis added). This section has never been construed as granting cooperatives a blanket exception from the Robinson-Patman Act and cannot plausibly be construed as an exemption to or repeal of any portion of the Sherman Act. . . .

In light of this circumscribed congressional intent, there can be no argument that § 4 of the Robinson-Patman Act should be viewed as a broad mandate for industry self-regulation. No need exists, therefore, to narrow the Sherman Act in order to accommodate any competing congressional policy requiring discretionary self-policing. Indeed, Congress would appear to have taken some care to make clear that no constriction of the Sherman Act was intended. In any event, the absence of procedural safeguards can in no sense determine the antitrust analysis. If the challenged concerted activity of Northwest's members would amount to a *per se* violation of § 1 of the Sherman Act, no amount of procedural protection would save it. If the challenged action would not amount to a violation of § 1, no lack of procedural protections would convert it into a *per se* violation because the antitrust laws do not themselves impose on joint ventures a requirement of process.

B

This case therefore turns not on the lack of procedural protections but on whether the decision to expel Pacific is properly viewed as a group boycott or concerted refusal to deal mandating *per se* invalidation. "Group boycotts" are often listed among the classes of economic activity that merit *per se* invalidation under § 1. . . . Exactly what types of activity fall within the forbidden category is, however, far from certain. "[T]here is more confusion about the scope and operation of the *per se* rule against group boycotts than in reference to any other aspect of the *per se* doctrine." L. Sullivan, Law of Antitrust 229–230 (1977). Some care is therefore necessary in defining the category of concerted refusals to deal that mandate *per se* condemnation. . . .

Cases to which this Court has applied the *per se* approach have generally involved joint efforts by a firm or firms to disadvantage competitors by "either directly denying or persuading or coercing suppliers or customers to deny relationships the competitors need in the competitive struggle." . . . In these cases, the boycott often cut off access to a supply, facility, or market necessary to enable the boycotted firm to compete, . . . and frequently the boycotting firms possessed a dominant position in the relevant market. . . . In addition, the practices were generally not justified by plausible arguments that they were intended to enhance overall efficiency and make markets more competitive. Under such circumstances the likelihood of anticompetitive effects is clear and the possibility of countervailing procompetitive effects is remote.

Although a concerted refusal to deal need not necessarily possess all of these traits to merit *per se* treatment, not every cooperative activity involving a restraint or exclusion will share with the *per se* forbidden boycotts the likelihood of predominantly anticompetitive consequences. For example, we recognized last Term in *National Collegiate Athletic Assn. v. Board of Regents of University of Oklahoma* that *per se* treatment of the NCAA's restrictions on the marketing of televised college football was inappropriate — despite the obvious restraint on output — because the "case involves an industry in which horizontal restraints on competition are essential if the product is to be available at all." . . .

Wholesale purchasing cooperatives such as Northwest are not a form of concerted activity characteristically likely to result in predominantly anticompetitive effects. Rather, such cooperative arrangements would seem to be "designed to increase economic efficiency and render markets more, rather than less, competitive." . . . The arrangement permits the participating retailers to achieve economies of scale in both the purchase and warehousing of wholesale supplies, and also ensures ready access to a stock of goods that might otherwise be unavailable on short notice. The cost savings and order-filling guarantees enable smaller retailers to reduce prices and maintain their retail stock so as to compete more effectively with larger retailers.

Pacific, of course, does not object to the existence of the cooperative arrangement, but rather raises an antitrust challenge to Northwest's decision to bar Pacific from continued membership.[52] It is therefore the action of expulsion that must be evaluated to determine whether *per se* treatment is appropriate. The act of expulsion from a wholesale cooperative does not necessarily imply anticompetitive animus and thereby raise a probability of anticompetitive effect. . . . Wholesale purchasing cooperatives must establish and enforce reasonable rules in order to function effectively. Disclosure rules, such as the one on which Northwest relies, may well provide the cooperative with a needed means for monitoring the creditworthiness of its members. Nor would the expulsion characteristically be likely to result in predominantly anticompetitive effects, at least in the type of situation this case presents. Unless the cooperative possesses market power or exclusive access to an element essential to effective competition, the conclusion that expulsion is virtually always likely to have an anticompetitive effect is not warranted. . . . Absent such a showing with respect to a cooperative buying arrangement, courts should apply a rule-of-reason analysis. At no time has Pacific made a threshold showing that these structural characteristics are present in the case. . . .

. . . [I]n our judgment the District Court rejection of *per se* analysis in this case was correct. A plaintiff seeking application of the *per se* rule must present a threshold case that the challenged activity falls into a category likely to have

---

[52] [FN 6] Because Pacific has not been wholly excluded from access to Northwest's wholesale operations, there is perhaps some question whether the challenged activity is properly characterized a concerted refusal to deal. To be precise, Northwest's activity is a concerted refusal to deal with Pacific on substantially equal terms. Such activity might justify *per se* invalidation if it placed a competing firm at a severe competitive disadvantage. *See generally* Brodley, *Joint Ventures and Antitrust Policy*, 95 Harv. L. Rev. 1521, 1532 (1982) ("Even if the joint venture does deal with outside firms, it may place them at a severe competitive disadvantage by treating them less favorably than it treats the [participants in the joint venture.]").

predominantly anticompetitive effects. The mere allegation of a concerted refusal to deal does not suffice because not all concerted refusals to deal are predominantly anticompetitive. . . . Pacific did not allege any such facts. Because the Court of Appeals applied an erroneous *per se* analysis in this case, the court never evaluated the District Court's rule-of-reason analysis rejecting Pacific's claim. A remand is therefore appropriate for the limited purpose of permitting appellate review of that determination.

III

. . . In this case, the Court of Appeals failed to exercise the requisite care and applied *per se* analysis inappropriately. The judgment of the Court of Appeals is therefore reversed, and the case is remanded for further proceedings consistent with this opinion.

It is so ordered.

JUSTICE MARSHALL and JUSTICE POWELL took no part in the decision of this case.

NOTES AND QUESTIONS

1. In *Silver v. New York Stock Exch.*, 373 U.S. 341 (1963), the stock exchange denied access to facilities (wire service) to nonmember broker-dealers. In refusing to deal with Mr. Silver, the NYSE relied on what it thought was an implied, qualified immunity from antitrust coverage under the federal securities law. The Supreme Court found, however, that immunity from antitrust coverage under the federal securities laws is "implied only if necessary to make the Securities Exchange Act work and even then only to the minimum extent necessary."

The Court concluded by holding that the self-regulation by the NYSE was not justified here because it did not comport with basic due process; Mr. Silver was "not informed of the charges underlying the decision to invoke the Exchange rules and was not afforded an appropriate opportunity to explain or refute the charge against [him]." Before self-regulation and anticompetitive collective action will be approved under an implied exception to antitrust, procedures must be established that satisfy fundamental fairness. By failing to provide notice and opportunity for hearing, the NYSE had "plainly exceeded the scope of its authority under the SEC Act to engage in self-regulation and therefore [had] not even reached the threshold of justification under the statute for what would otherwise be an antitrust violation." In passing, the Court made clear that in an unregulated industry the challenged conduct at issue here — a refusal to deal with a competitor — would have been a per se violation.

2. Is it clear that *Northwest Stationers* has abandoned the per se rule for group boycott cases except where defendant possesses market power or where access to supply is cut off? How would you state the qualified per se application for a concerted refusal to deal after *Northwest Stationers*? Does one efficiency analysis (or defense) play any role in the qualified approach?

In *In re Tableware Antitrust Litigation*, 484 F. Supp. 2d 1059 (N.D. Cal. 2007), the plaintiffs alleged a group boycott coordinated by May Department Stores Co ("May") and Federated Department Stores, Inc ("Federated"). Bed, Bath & Beyond wanted to sell fine tableware and arranged to sell lines made by Lenox, Inc ("Lenox") and Waterford Wedgwood, USA ("Waterford"). Executives at May and Federated opposed these new relationships and communicated their displeasure to executives at Lenox and Waterford, who subsequently terminated their arrangements with Bed, Bath & Beyond. The plaintiffs — purchasers of fine tableware — alleged a series of agreements among the defendants — May, Federated, Lenox, and Waterford — including a horizontal agreement between May and Federated to orchestrate a per se illegal group boycott. The defendants made a summary judgment motion, asking that the per se rule against group boycotts not apply, thus requiring plaintiffs to prove liability under the rule of reason. The district court denied this motion, explaining:

> The Ninth Circuit reads *Northwest Wholesale* and its progeny as establishing three criteria for determining whether the per se standard applies to a group boycott:
>
> > (1) the boycott cuts off access to a supply, facility, or market necessary to enable the victim firm to compete;
>
> > (2) the boycotting firm possesses a dominant market position; and
>
> > (3) the practices are not justified by plausible arguments that they enhanced overall efficiency or competition.
>
> Adaptive Power Solutions, LLC v. Hughes Missile Systems Co., 141 F.3d 947, 950 (9th Cir. 1998). In the Ninth Circuit, these three criteria "are indicative of per se illegal conduct." *Adaptive Power Solutions*, 141 F.3d at 950.
>
> *** With respect to the first factor, the court notes that Waterford and Lennox were suppliers of tableware products necessary to enable Bed, Bath & Beyond to compete in the high-end tableware market. Further, defendants allegedly cut off this essential supply in order to obstruct Bed, Bath & Beyond's access to this market. The second factor (whether the boycotting firm possesses a "dominant" position in the market) is difficult to assess on the present record. In 2001, Federated and May were the third and fourth largest department store chains in the United States, respectively. Although this ranking among department stores does not imply market power, it may suggest that defendants held a "dominant" position. As the Seventh Circuit observed in *Toys "R" Us, Inc. v. FTC*, 221 F.3d 928 (7th Cir. 2000), the term "dominant" was "plainly chosen to stand for something different from antitrust's term of art 'monopoly.' " Id at 936. In view of this uncertainty, the court finds that this second factor weighs in neither party's favor.
>
> Most damaging to Federated's argument in favor of rule of reason review is the third factor — whether the boycott arguably enhances efficiency or competition. In accordance with this consideration, courts have noted that in the following factual settings, the effect of a refusal to deal is "more complex" than in the "classic boycott" scenario: industry self-

regulation, sports leagues, health care, noneconomic boycotts and access to joint venture facilities. The conduct alleged by plaintiffs falls within none of these exceptions. Nor does Federated proffer an independent pro-competitive justification for the alleged horizontal agreements to boycott Bed, Bath and Beyond. This silence is unsurprising, as the alleged horizontal agreement falls squarely within the ambit of per se treatment as dictated by *Northwest Wholesale*: "joint efforts by a firm or firms to disadvantage competitors by either directly denying or persuading or coercing suppliers or customers to deny relationships the competitors need in the competitive struggle." *Northwest Wholesale*, 472 U.S. at 294. Accordingly, the court concludes that the alleged horizontal agreement between Federated and May constitutes a classic boycott and thus warrants per se treatment.

Id. at 1070–1071.

3. On the issue of contract integration between legally separable companies, consider the interstate system of van line moving companies. Would it violate Section 1 of the Sherman Act if a national van line company such as Atlas agreed with its agents to adopt a policy of terminating ("boycotting") independent, local agents who pursued their own accounts or competed against the national van line, or who dealt with another national carrier as their local agent while using the Atlas name? Does the language in *BMI*, *NCAA*, and *Northwest Stationers* suggest that the Supreme Court implicitly has overruled *Sealy* and *Topco* as they apply to the horizontal restraints of this problem? *See Rothery Storage & Van Co. v. Atlas Van Lines*, 792 F.2d 210 (D.C. Cir. 1986) (where Judge Bork ruled that horizontal restraints such as boycotts that reduce free rider problems and promote efficiency are legal, absent market power, even when the shipping rates are established by the national van line). The Court in *Rothery* stated:

> If *Topco* and *Sealy*, rather than *Addyston Pipe*, state the law of horizontal restraints, the restraints imposed by Atlas would appear to be a per se violation of the Sherman Act. An examination of more recent Supreme Court decisions [*BMI*, *NCAA*, and *Northwest*], however, demonstrates that, to the extent that *Topco* and *Sealy* stand for the proposition that all horizontal restraints are illegal per se, they must be regarded as effectively overruled. *Id.* at 226, 229.

Petition for certiorari was denied without dissent.

FTC v. INDIANA FEDERATION OF DENTISTS
476 U.S. 447 (1986)

JUSTICE WHITE delivered the opinion of the Court.

This case concerns commercial relations among certain Indiana dentists, their patients, and the patients' dental health care insurers. The question presented is whether the Federal Trade Commission correctly concluded that a conspiracy among dentists to refuse to submit x rays to dental insurers for use in benefits determinations constituted an "unfair method of competition" in violation of § 5 of the Federal Trade Commission Act.

I

[In an attempt to contain costs, dental health insurers since the 1970's have undertaken an effort to limit the payment of benefits to the "least expensive yet adequate treatment." To this end, insurers frequently request that dental x-rays accompany insurance claim forms. These x-rays are then reviewed by the insurers to determine the value of the claim.]

. . . .

Such review of diagnostic and treatment decisions has been viewed by some dentists as a threat to their professional independence and economic well-being. In the early 1970's, the Indiana Dental Association, a professional organization comprising some 85% of practicing dentists in the State of Indiana, initiated an aggressive effort to hinder insurers' efforts to implement alternative benefits plans by enlisting member dentists to pledge not to submit x rays in conjunction with claim forms. The Association's efforts met considerable success: large numbers of dentists signed the pledge, and insurers operating in Indiana found it difficult to obtain compliance with their requests for x rays and accordingly had to choose either to employ more expensive means of making alternative benefits determinations (for example, visiting the office of the treating dentist or conducting an independent oral examination) or to abandon such efforts altogether.

By the mid-1970's, fears of possible antitrust liability had dampened the Association's enthusiasm for opposing the submission of x rays to insurers. In 1979, the Association and a number of its constituent societies consented to a Federal Trade Commission order requiring them to cease and desist from further efforts to prevent member dentists from submitting x rays. *In re Indiana Dental Assn.*, 93 F.T.C. 392 (1979). Not all Indiana dentists were content to leave the matter of submitting x rays to the individual dentist. In 1976, a group of such dentists formed the Indiana Federation of Dentists, respondent in this case, in order to continue to pursue the Association's policy of resisting insurers' requests for x rays. The Federation . . . immediately promulgated a "work rule" forbidding its members to submit x rays to dental insurers in conjunction with claim forms. Although the Federation's membership was small, numbering less than 100, its members were highly concentrated in and around three Indiana communities: Anderson, Lafayette, and Fort Wayne. The Federation succeeded in enlisting nearly 100% of the dental specialists in the Anderson area, and approximately 67% of the dentists in and around Lafayette. In the areas of its strength, the Federation was successful in continuing to enforce the Association's prior policy of refusal to submit x rays to dental insurers.

In 1978, the Federal Trade Commission issued a complaint against the Federation, alleging in substance that its efforts to prevent its members from complying with insurers' requests for x rays constituted an unfair method of competition in violation of § 5 of the Federal Trade Commission Act. . . .

The Commission found that the Federation had conspired both with the Indiana

Dental Association and with its own members to withhold cooperation with dental insurers' requests for x rays; that absent such a restraint, competition among dentists for patients would have tended to lead dentists to compete with respect to their policies in dealing with patients' insurers; and that in those areas where the Federation's membership was strong, the Federation's policy had had the actual effect of eliminating such competition among dentists and preventing insurers from obtaining access to x rays in the desired manner. These findings of anticompetitive effect, the Commission concluded, were sufficient to establish that the restraint was unreasonable even absent proof that the Federation's policy had resulted in higher costs to the insurers and patients than would have occurred had the x rays been provided. Further, the Commission rejected the Federation's argument that its policy of withholding x rays was reasonable because the provision of x rays might lead the insurers to make inaccurate determinations of the proper level of care and thus injure the health of the insured patients: the Commission found no evidence that use of x rays by insurance companies in evaluating claims would result in inadequate dental care. Finally, the Commission rejected the Federation's contention that its actions were exempt from antitrust scrutiny because the withholding of x rays was consistent with the law and policy of the State of Indiana against the use of x rays in benefit determination by insurance companies. The Commission concluded that no such policy existed, and that in any event the existence of such a policy would not have justified the dentists' private and unsupervised conspiracy in restraint of trade.

. . . .

II

The issue is whether the Commission erred in holding that the Federation's policy of refusal to submit x rays to dental insurers for use in benefits determinations constituted an "unfair method of competition," unlawful under § 5 of the Federal Trade Commission Act. The question involves review of both factual and legal determinations. As to the former, our review is governed by 15 U.S.C. § 45(c), which provides that "[t]he findings of the Commission as to the facts, if supported by evidence, shall be conclusive." The statute forbids a court to "make its own appraisal of the testimony, picking and choosing for itself among uncertain and conflicting inferences." Rather, as under the essentially identical "substantial evidence" standard for review of agency factfinding, the court must accept the Commission's findings of fact if they are supported by "such relevant evidence as a reasonable mind might accept as adequate to support a conclusion."

. . . The standard of "unfairness" under the FTC Act is, by necessity, an elusive one, encompassing not only practices that violate the Sherman Act and the other antitrust laws, but also practices that the Commission determines are against public policy for other reasons. In the case now before us, the sole basis of the FTC's finding of an unfair method of competition was the Commission's conclusion that the Federation's collective decision to withhold x rays from insurers was an unreasonable and conspiratorial restraint of trade in violation of § 1 of the Sherman Act. Accordingly, the legal question before us is whether the Commission's factual findings, if supported by evidence, make out a violation of Sherman Act § 1.

III

The relevant factual findings are that the members of the Federation conspired among themselves to withhold x rays requested by dental insurers for use in evaluating claims for benefits, and that this conspiracy had the effect of suppressing competition among dentists with respect to cooperation with the requests of the insurance companies. As to the first of these findings there can be no serious dispute; abundant evidence in the record reveals that one of the primary reasons — if not *the* primary reason — for the Federation's existence was the promulgation and enforcement of the so-called "work rule" against submission of x rays in conjunction with insurance claim forms.

. . . The Commission's finding that "[i]n the absence of . . . concerted behavior, individual dentists would have been subject to market forces of competition, creating incentives for them to . . . comply with the requests of patients' third-party insurers," finds support not only in common sense and economic theory, upon both of which the FTC may reasonably rely, but also in record documents, including newsletters circulated among Indiana dentists, revealing that Indiana dentists themselves perceived that unrestrained competition tended to lead their colleagues to comply with insurers' requests for x rays. Moreover, there was evidence that outside of Indiana, in States where dentists had not collectively refused to submit x rays, insurance companies found little difficulty in obtaining compliance by dentists with their requests. A "reasonable mind" could conclude on the basis of this evidence that competition for patients, who have obvious incentives for seeking dentists who will cooperate with their insurers, would tend to lead dentists in Indiana (and elsewhere) to cooperate with requests for information by their patients' insurers.

The Commission's finding that such competition was actually diminished where the Federation held sway also finds adequate support in the record. The Commission found that in the areas where Federation membership among dentists was most significant (that is, in the vicinity of Anderson and Lafayette) insurance companies were unable to obtain compliance with their requests for submission of x rays in conjunction with claim forms and were forced to resort to other, more costly, means of reviewing diagnoses for the purpose of benefit determination. . . . The Federation's collective activities resulted in the denial of the information the customers requested in the form that they requested it, and forced them to choose between acquiring that information in a more costly manner or foregoing it altogether. To this extent, at least, competition among dentists with respect to cooperation with the requests of insurers was restrained.

IV

The question remains whether these findings are legally sufficient to establish a violation of § 1 of the Sherman Act — that is, whether the Federation's collective refusal to cooperate with insurers' requests for x rays constitutes an "unreasonable" restraint of trade. Under our precedents, a restraint may be adjudged unreasonable either because it fits within a class of restraints that has been held to be "*per se*" unreasonable, or because it violates what has come to be known as the "Rule of Reason," under which the "test of legality is whether the restraint imposed is such as merely regulates and perhaps thereby promotes competition or whether it is such as may suppress or even destroy competition." *Chicago Board of Trade v. United States*, 246 U.S., at 238.

The policy of the Federation with respect to its members' dealings with third-party insurers resembles practices that have been labeled "group boycotts": the policy constitutes a concerted refusal to deal on particular terms with patients covered by group dental insurance. Although this Court has in the past stated that group boycotts are unlawful *per se*, see *United States v. General Motors Corp.*, 384 U.S. 127 (1966); *Klor's, Inc. v. Broadway-Hale Stores, Inc.*, 359 U.S. 207 (1959), we decline to resolve this case by forcing the Federation's policy into the "boycott" pigeonhole and invoking the *per se* rule. As we observed last Term in *Northwest Wholesale Stationers, Inc. v. Pacific Stationery and Printing Co.*, 472 U.S. 284 (1985), the category of restraints classed as group boycotts is not to be expanded indiscriminately, and the *per se* approach has generally been limited to cases in which firms with market power boycott suppliers or customers in order to discourage them from doing business with a competitor — a situation obviously not present here. Moreover, we have been slow to condemn rules adopted by professional associations as unreasonable *per se*, see *National Society of Professional Engineers v. United States*, 435 U.S. 679 (1978), and, in general, to extend *per se* analysis to restraints imposed in the context of business relationships where the economic impact of certain practices is not immediately obvious, see *Broadcast Music, Inc. v. CBS*, 441 U.S. 1 (1979). Thus, as did the FTC, we evaluate the restraint at issue in this case under the Rule of Reason rather than a rule of *per se* illegality.

Application of the Rule of Reason to these facts is not a matter of any great difficulty. The Federation's policy takes the form of a horizontal agreement among the participating dentists to withhold from their customers a particular service that they desire — the forwarding of x rays to insurance companies along with claim forms. "While this is not price fixing as such, no elaborate industry analysis is required to demonstrate the anticompetitive character of such an agreement." *Society of Professional Engineers, supra*, at 692. A refusal to compete with respect to the package of services offered to customers, no less than a refusal to compete with respect to the price term of an agreement, impairs the ability of the market to advance social welfare by ensuring the provision of desired goods and services to consumers at a price approximating the marginal cost of providing them. Absent some countervailing procompetitive virtue — such as, for example, the creation of efficiencies in the operation of a market or the provision of goods and services, see *Broadcast Music, Inc. v. CBS, supra; Chicago Board of Trade, supra;* cf. *NCAA v. Board of Regents of Univ. of Okla.*, 468 U.S. 85 (1984)— such an agreement limiting consumer choice by impeding the "ordinary give and take of the market place," *Society of Professional Engineers, supra*, at 692, cannot be sustained under the Rule of Reason. No credible argument has been advanced for the proposition that making it more costly for the insurers and patients who are the dentists' customers to obtain information needed for evaluating the dentists' diagnoses has any such procompetitive effect.

The Federation advances three principal arguments for the proposition that, notwithstanding its lack of competitive virtue, the Federation's policy of withholding x rays should not be deemed an unreasonable restraint of trade. First . . . the Federation suggests that in the absence of specific findings by the Commission concerning the definition of the market in which the Federation allegedly restrained trade and the power of the Federation's members in that market, the conclusion that the Federation unreasonably restrained trade is erroneous as a matter of law, regardless of whether the challenged practices might be impermissibly anticompetitive if engaged in by persons who together possessed power in a specifically defined market. This contention, however, runs counter to the Court's holding in *NCAA v. Board of Regents, supra,* that "[a]s a matter of law, the absence of proof of market power does not justify a naked restriction on price or output," and that such a restriction "requires some competitive justification even in the absence of a detailed market analysis." 468 U.S., at 109–110. Moreover, even if the restriction imposed by the Federation is not sufficiently "naked" to call this principle into play, the Commission's failure to engage in detailed market analysis is not fatal to its finding of a violation of the Rule of Reason. The Commission found that in two localities in the State of Indiana (the Anderson and Lafayette areas), Federation dentists constituted heavy majorities of the practicing dentists and that as a result of the efforts of the Federation, insurers in those areas were, over a period of years, actually unable to obtain compliance with their requests for submission of x rays. Since the purpose of the inquiries into market definition and market power is to determine whether an arrangement has the potential for genuine adverse effects on competition, "proof of actual detrimental effects, such as a reduction of output" can obviate the need for an inquiry into market power, which is but a "surrogate for detrimental effects." 7 P. Areeda, Antitrust Law ¶ 1511, p. 429 (1986). In this case, we conclude that the finding of actual, sustained adverse effects on competition in those areas where IFD dentists predominated, viewed in light of the reality that markets for dental services tend to be relatively localized, is legally sufficient to support a finding that the challenged restraint was unreasonable even in the absence of elaborate market analysis.[53]

Second, the Federation . . . argues that a holding that its policy of withholding x rays constituted an unreasonable restraint of trade is precluded by the Commission's failure to make any finding that the policy resulted in the provision of dental services that were more costly than those that the patients and their insurers would have chosen were they able to evaluate x rays in conjunction with claim forms. This argument, too, is unpersuasive. Although it is true that the goal of the insurers in seeking submission of x rays for use in their review of benefits claims was to minimize costs by choosing the least expensive adequate course of dental treatment, a showing that this goal was actually achieved through the means chosen is not an essential step in establishing that the dentists' attempt to thwart its achievement by collectively refusing to supply the requested information was an unreasonable restraint of trade. A concerted and effective effort to withhold (or make more costly) information desired by consumers for the purpose of determining whether a

---

[53] [FN 3] Because we find that the Commission's findings can be sustained on this basis, we do not address the Commission's contention that the Federation's activities can be condemned regardless of market power or actual effect merely because they constitute a continuation of the restraints formerly imposed by the Indiana Dental Association, which allegedly had market power throughout the State of Indiana.

particular purchase is cost-justified is likely enough to disrupt the proper functioning of the price-setting mechanism of the market that it may be condemned even absent proof that it resulted in higher prices or, as here, the purchase of higher-priced services, than would occur in its absence. *Society of Professional Engineers, supra.* Moreover, even if the desired information were in fact completely useless to the insurers and their patients in making an informed choice regarding the least costly adequate course of treatment — or, to put it another way, if the costs of evaluating the information were far greater than the cost savings resulting from its use — the Federation would still not be justified in deciding on behalf of its members' customers that they did not need the information: presumably, if that were the case, the discipline of the market would itself soon result in the insurers' abandoning their requests for x rays. The Federation is not entitled to pre-empt the working of the market by deciding for itself that its customers do not need that which they demand.

Third, the Federation complains that the Commission erred in failing to consider, as relevant to its Rule of Reason analysis, noncompetitive "quality of care" justifications for the prohibition on provision of x rays to insurers in conjunction with claim forms. . . . The gist of the claim is that x rays, standing alone, are not adequate bases for diagnosis of dental problems or for the formulation of an acceptable course of treatment. Accordingly, if insurance companies are permitted to determine whether they will pay a claim for dental treatment on the basis of x rays as opposed to a full examination of all the diagnostic aids available to the examining dentist, there is a danger that they will erroneously decline to pay for treatment that is in fact in the interest of the patient, and that the patient will as a result be deprived of fully adequate care.

The Federation's argument is flawed both legally and factually. The premise of the argument is that, far from having no effect on the cost of dental services chosen by patients and their insurers, the provision of x rays will have too great an impact: it will lead to the reduction of costs through the selection of inadequate treatment. Precisely such a justification for withholding information from customers was rejected as illegitimate in the *Society of Professional Engineers* case. The argument is, in essence, that an unrestrained market in which consumers are given access to the information they believe to be relevant to their choices will lead them to make unwise and even dangerous choices. Such an argument amounts to "nothing less than a frontal assault on the basic policy of the Sherman Act." *Society of Professional Engineers, supra,* at 695. Moreover, there is no particular reason to believe that the provision of information will be more harmful to consumers in the market for dental services than in other markets. Insurers deciding what level of care to pay for are not themselves the recipients of those services, but it is by no means clear that they lack incentives to consider the welfare of the patient as well as the minimization of costs. They are themselves in competition for the patronage of the patients — or, in most cases, the unions or businesses that contract on their behalf for group insurance coverage — and must satisfy their potential customers not only that they will provide coverage at a reasonable cost, but also that coverage will be adequate to meet their customers' dental needs. There is thus no more reason to expect dental insurance companies to sacrifice quality in return for cost savings than to believe this of consumers in, say, the market for engineering services. Accordingly, if noncompetitive quality-of-service justifications are inadmissible to justify the denial of information to consumers in the latter market, there is little reason to credit such justifications here.

In any event, the Commission did not, as the Federation suggests, refuse even to consider the quality of care justification for the withholding of x rays. Rather, the Commission held that the Federation had failed to introduce sufficient evidence to establish such a justification: "IFD has not pointed to any evidence — or even argued — that any consumers have in fact been harmed by alternative benefits determinations, or that actual determinations have been medically erroneous." 101 F.T.C., at 177. The evidence before the Administrative Law Judge on this issue appears to have consisted entirely of expert opinion testimony, with the Federation's experts arguing that x rays generally provide an insufficient basis, standing alone, for dental diagnosis, and the Commission's experts testifying that x rays may be useful in assessing diagnosis of and appropriate treatment for a variety of dental complaints. The Commission was amply justified in concluding on the basis of this conflicting evidence that even if concern for the quality of patient care could under some circumstances serve as a justification for a restraint of the sort imposed here, the evidence did not support a finding that the careful use of x rays as a basis for evaluating insurance claims is in fact destructive of proper standards of dental care.

In addition to arguing that its conspiracy did not effect an unreasonable restraint of trade, the Federation appears to renew its argument . . . that the conspiracy to withhold x rays is immunized from antitrust scrutiny by virtue of a supposed policy of the State of Indiana against the evaluation of dental x rays by lay employees of insurance companies. Allegedly, such use of x rays by insurance companies — even where no claim was actually denied without examination of an x ray by a licensed dentist — would constitute unauthorized practice of dentistry by the insurance company and its employees. The Commission found that this claim had no basis in any authoritative source of Indiana law and the Federation has not identified any adequate reason for rejecting the Commission's conclusion. Even if the Commission were incorrect in its reading of the law, however, the Federation's claim of immunity would fail. That a particular practice may be unlawful is not, in itself, a sufficient justification for collusion among competitors to prevent it. See *Fashion Originators' Guild of America, Inc. v. FTC*, 312 U.S. 457, 468 (1941). Anticompetitive collusion among private actors, even when its goal is consistent with state policy, acquires antitrust immunity only when it is actively supervised by the State. See *Southern Motor Carriers Rate Conference, Inc. v. United States*, 471 U.S. 48, 57 (1985). There is no suggestion of any such active supervision here; accordingly, whether or not the policy that Federation has taken upon itself to advance is consistent with the policy of the State of Indiana, the Federation's activities are subject to Sherman Act condemnation.

V

The factual findings of the Commission regarding the effect of the Federation's policy of withholding x rays are supported by substantial evidence, and those findings are sufficient as a matter of law to establish a violation of § 1 of the Sherman Act, and, hence, § 5 of the Federal Trade Commission Act. . . . The judgment of the Court of Appeals is accordingly

Reversed.

NOTES AND QUESTIONS

1. Did the Court explain why it did not apply a per se analysis to this boycott? Is it because the dentists were professionals or because they lacked market power, or both? Is a boycott per se unlawful only when the concerted action is horizontal, supported with market power, without business justification, and aimed at a competitor?

2. Consider whether the legal and economic arguments in *Indiana Federation* are the same as those in *Professional Engineers.* Was the purpose behind the insurance requirement of submitting X-rays to reduce the marginal costs of providing insurance in the dental services market? If so, does *Professional Engineers* permit this evidence to be weighed against noneconomic patient care objectives (*e.g.*, preventing the illegal practice of dentistry)? Does the Court make clear that only economic factors that promote competition are acceptable business justifications for trade restraints?

If the X-ray submission requirement reduced the costs of insurance, was the Federation's refusal to submit X-rays the equivalent of an overcharge to the patient-consumer? If so, does the Court require evidence of a price increase before finding a violation? Did the Court conclude that the boycott was illegal because it interfered with the normal market forces of cost containment, which resulted in increased costs to the consumer (patients and insurers)?

3. Do you think the burden of establishing a violation under Section 5 of the Federal Trade Act is less than under Section 1 of the Sherman Act?

4. In a 6-3 decision, the Supreme Court ruled in *FTC v. Superior Court Trial Lawyers Ass'n*, 493 U.S. 411 (1990) (reprinted in Chapter 9, *infra*), that private attorneys who represent indigent criminal defendants may not agree to withhold professional services in order to pressure the local government to increase professional fees under the Criminal Justice Act. Because of the effectiveness of the lawyers' boycott, the city raised the attorneys' fees to $35 an hour from the previous $20 an hour. But the Court found that the concerted refusal to take more indigent cases was a "classic restraint of trade." The means employed (the boycott) to obtain favorable legislation was commercial, not political, in nature, and was designed to increase the price that the lawyers would be paid for services. Unlike *Claiborne Hardware* (*infra* this chapter) where the boycott was designed to achieve "equality and freedom," the boycott in *Superior Court Trial Lawyers Ass'n* was character-ized as purely commercial, although there was a political impact. Moreover, the Court reasoned that such boycotts were not entitled to First Amendment protec-tion. Said the Court, "Every concerted refusal to do business with a potential customer or supplier has an expressive component." To recognize an exception to Section 1 "whenever an economic boycott has an expressive component, would create a gaping hole in the fabric of [the law]." Finally, the Court seemed to invoke a per se test of illegality for this commercial boycott. It rebuked the appellate court for implying that per se rules were designed only for "administrative convenience and efficiency." "The per se rules are, of course, the product of judicial interpretations of the Sherman Act, but the rules nevertheless have the same force and effect as any other statutory commands." Rather, the per se characterization is applied, the Court noted, when the conduct under challenge is inherently dangerous, regardless of whether actual harm results. Furthermore, market power is not necessarily a precondition to finding liability. "Conspirators need not achieve the dimensions of a monopoly, or even a degree of market power any greater than that already disclosed by this record [the boycott achieved a crisis in the administration of criminal justice in the District of Columbia and it achieved its economic goal of higher salaries], to warrant condemnation under the antitrust laws."

5. Consider these facts. Medical doctors in New Jersey, complaining of high malpractice insurance caused, they said, by high jury awards, staged a four-day work stoppage where they refused to see patients. In effect, all medical coverage in the state, except for emergency care, was terminated for four days. Does the doctors' boycott implicate the per se test of illegality announced in *Superior Court Trial Lawyer's Ass'n*? Did their actions violate the antitrust laws?

[4] Naked and Ancillary Concerted Refusals to Deal

ASSOCIATED PRESS v. UNITED STATES
326 U.S. 1 (1945)

JUSTICE BLACK delivered the opinion of the Court.

The publishers of more than 1,200 newspapers are members of the Associated Press (AP), a cooperative association incorporated under the Membership Corporation Law of the State of New York. Its business is the collection, assembly and distribution of news. The news it distributes is originally obtained by direct employees of the Association, employees of the member newspapers, and the employees of foreign independent news agencies with which AP has contractual relations, such as the Canadian Press. Distribution of the news is made through interstate channels of communication to the various newspaper members of the Association, who pay for it under an assessment plan which contemplates no profit to AP.

. . . .

The heart of the government's charge was that appellants had by concerted action set up a system of By-Laws which prohibited all AP members from selling news to non-members, and which granted each member powers to block its non-member competitors from membership. These By-Laws, to which all AP members had assented, were, in the context of the admitted facts, charged to be in violation of the Sherman Act. . . .

The District Court found that the By-Laws in and of themselves were contracts in restraint of commerce in that they contained provisions designed to stifle competition in the newspaper publishing field. The court also found that AP's restrictive By-Laws had hindered and impeded the growth of competing newspapers. This latter finding, as to the *past* effect of the restrictions, is challenged. We are inclined to think that it is supported by undisputed evidence, but we do not stop to labor the point. For the court below found, and we think correctly, that the By-Laws on their face, and without regard to their past effect, constitute restraints of trade. Combinations are no less unlawful because they have not as yet resulted in restraint. An agreement or combination to follow a course of conduct which will necessarily restrain or monopolize a part of trade or commerce may violate the Sherman Act, whether it be "wholly nascent or abortive on the one hand, or successful on the other." For these reasons the argument, repeated here in various forms, that AP had not yet achieved a complete monopoly is wholly irrelevant. Undisputed evidence did show, however, that its By-Laws had tied the hands of all of its numerous publishers, to the extent that they could not and did not sell any part of their news so that it could reach any of their non-member competitors. In this respect the court did find, and that finding cannot possibly be challenged, that AP's By-Laws had hindered and restrained the sale of interstate news to non-members who competed with members.

Inability to buy news from the largest news agency, or any one of its multitude of members, can have most serious effects on the publication of competitive newspapers, both those presently published and those which, but for these restrictions, might be published in the future. . . . The net effect is seriously to limit the opportunity of any new paper to enter these cities. Trade restraints of this character, aimed at the destruction of competition, tend to block the initiative which brings newcomers into a field of business and to frustrate the free enterprise system which it was the purpose of the Sherman Act to protect.

. . . .

It has been argued that the restrictive By-Laws should be treated as beyond the prohibitions of the Sherman Act, since the owner of the property can choose his associates and can, as to that which he has produced by his own enterprise and sagacity, efforts or ingenuity, decide for himself whether and to whom to sell or not to sell. While it is true in a very general sense that one can dispose of his property as he pleases, he cannot "go beyond the exercise of this right, and by contracts or combinations, express or implied, unduly hinder or obstruct the free and natural flow of commerce in the channels of interstate trade." The Sherman Act was specifically intended to prohibit independent businesses from becoming "associates" in a common plan which is bound to reduce their competitor's opportunity to buy or sell the things in which the groups compete. Victory of a member of such a combination over its business rivals achieved by such collective means cannot consistently with the Sherman Act or with practical, everyday knowledge be attributed to *individual* "enterprise and sagacity"; such hampering of business rivals can only be attributed to that which really makes it possible — the collective power of an unlawful combination. That the object of sale is the creation or product of a man's ingenuity does not alter this principle. *Fashion Originators' Guild v. Federal Trade Commission*, 312 U.S. 457. It is obviously fallacious to view the By-Laws here in issue as instituting a program to encourage and permit full freedom of sale and disposal of property by its owners. Rather, these publishers have, by concerted arrangements, pooled their power to acquire, to purchase, and to dispose of news reports through the channels of commerce. They have also pooled their economic and news control power and, in exerting that power, have entered into agreements which the District Court found to be "plainly designed in the interest of preventing competition."

It is further contended that, since there are other news agencies which sell news, it is not a violation of the Act for an overwhelming majority of American publishers to combine to decline to sell their news to the minority. But the fact that an agreement to restrain trade does not inhibit competition in all of the objects of that trade cannot save it from the condemnation of the Sherman Act. It is apparent that the exclusive right to publish news in a given field, furnished by AP and all of its members, gives many newspapers a competitive advantage over their rivals. Conversely, a newspaper without AP service is more than likely to be at a competitive disadvantage. . . . And the District Court's unchallenged finding was that "AP is a vast, intricately reticulated organization, the largest of its kind, gathering news from all over the world, the chief single source of news for the American press, universally agreed to be of great consequence."

. . . .

Here as in *Fashion Originators' Guild* . . . "the combination is in reality an extra-governmental agency, which prescribes rules for the regulation and restraint of interstate commerce, and provides extra-judicial tribunals for determination and punishment of violations, and thus 'trenches upon the power of the national legislature and violates the statute.'" By the restrictive By-Laws each of the publishers in the combination has, in effect, "surrendered himself completely to the control of the association," in respect to the disposition of news in interstate commerce. Therefore this contractual restraint of interstate trade, "designed in the interest of preventing competition," cannot be one of the "normal and usual agreements in aid of trade and commerce which may be found not to be within the [Sherman] Act. . . ." *Eastern States Lumber Dealers' Assn. v. United States.* It is further said that we reach our conclusion by application of the "public utility" concept to the newspaper business. This is not correct. We merely hold that arrangements or combinations designed to stifle competition cannot be immunized by adopting a membership device accomplishing that purpose.

Affirmed.

[JUSTICES DOUGLAS and FRANKFURTER concurred. CHIEF JUSTICE STONE and JUSTICES ROBERTS and MURPHY dissented. JUSTICE JACKSON did not participate.]

NOTES AND QUESTIONS

1. Were the by-laws held illegal per se? In determining this, consider whether the Court weighed the economies achieved by the integration against the anticompetitive harm. How did the Court measure the legality of the restraint? Was market power a factor? Was the concerted refusal to deal merely ancillary to an otherwise lawful purpose (attainment of economies of scale) and, if so, would such a defense be entertained? Consider whether the Court's analysis of the joint venture boycott issue is consistent with those cases discussed *supra* concerning price fixing or market division by joint ventures. Indeed, does the Court's analysis survive *Klor's* and *Silver's* per se prescription against boycotts aimed at competitors?

The Court in *Associated Press* ordered AP to make its membership available to nonmembers on a reasonable basis and, although admission could be restricted, it prohibited members from imposing discriminatory conditions that took into account possible competitive consequences of the new entrant into a member's geographical market. 326 U.S. at 21.

2. Isn't news simply a form of property? *See International News Serv. v. Associated Press*, 248 U.S. 215 (1918); Reich, *The New Property*, 73 YALE L.J. 733 (1964). Wasn't the holding in *Associated Press* simply a requirement that the members of Associated Press sell their property to others?

If three firms join in a research venture and develop a new invention, should they be required to share the invention with all other competitors? The "competitive advantage" that AP obtained over its rivals was merely an advantage that accrued from the fact that they produced better news than anyone else. Should anyone who develops a better device or scheme than someone else be required to sell it? Should it make a difference that two or more people developed it jointly?

In short, is *Associated Press* really a "boycott" case at all? The members of AP developed a product jointly and used it among themselves. No outsiders were excluded from having something that they had before AP was created. "Associated Press News" did not exist until Associated Press came into existence.

3. Consider the following refusal to deal within a credit card joint venture. Visa is a joint venture of some 5000 firms (mostly banks and other financial institutions) that issue VISA credit cards. Visa USA provides technology to process credit card transactions and coordinates individual credit card programs through rules and by-laws proposed by management and adopted by its Board of Directors. The Visa Board adopts an amendment that states that Visa "shall not accept for membership any applicant which is issuing, directly or indirectly, Discover cards or American Express cards, or any other cards deemed competitive by the Board of Directors; an applicant shall be deemed to be issuing such cards if its parent, subsidiary or affiliate issues such cards." Sears, which issues the Discover card, is denied membership in Visa USA pursuant to this regulation. What results if Sears sues?

See *SCFC ILC, Inc. v. Visa USA, Inc.*, 36 F.3d 958 (10th Cir. 1994), where the issue presented was whether the refusal to admit Sears (the Discover Card) to this joint venture violated Section 1 of the Sherman Act. The district court found in favor of Sears, after a jury verdict rejected Visa's legal and factual arguments. The Tenth Circuit reversed, rejecting per se treatment, and observing that the "[r]ule of reason analysis first asks whether the offending competitor, here Visa USA, possesses market power in the relevant market where the alleged anti-competitive activity occurs."

The parties had agreed that the relevant market was the "general purpose charge card market in the United States," of which there were six market participants, including Visa and Discover. The court found, however, that the relevant market was the "issuing" market, as opposed to the "systems" market. Although only six issuers participated at the "systems" level (Visa, MasterCard, American Express, Diners Club, Carte Blanche, and Discover), there were some 19,000 "participating members" offering cards. The court concluded that this atomistic market precluded a finding of power as a matter of law.

But query: when exclusion is undertaken by means of an explicit and enforced by-law, does the number of members matter to the exercise of market power? *Cf. American Society of Mechanical Engineers, Inc. v. Hydrolevel*, 456 U.S. 556 (1982) (association of 90,000 members held liable when members of one of its Committees conspired with each other to withhold approval of plaintiff's production innovation; no price fixing); *National Society of Professional Engineers v. United States*, 435 U.S. 679 (1978) (69,000 members; condemning canon against competitive bidding); *Associated Press v. United States*, 326 U.S. 1, 3 (1945) (condemning joint-venture rule excluding competitors as members; approximately 1200 members at time of litigation); *Indiana Federation of Dentists*, 476 U.S. 447 (1986) (condemning collective refusal to provide X-rays by federation of some 2500 dentists, 84 of whom participated in the agreement); *National Collegiate Athletic Ass'n (NCAA) v. Board of Regents of the Univ. of Oklahoma*, 468 U.S. 85, 89 (1984) (striking down output limitation agreement among collegiate athletic association with 850 members); *Arizona v. Maricopa County Medical Society*, 457 U.S. 332 (1982) (condemning maximum price-fixing agreement involving 1750 physicians).

The Tenth Circuit then considered the efficiency justification offered by Visa USA. The court found that the by-law that prohibited Sears from joining the network was ancillary to effectuate Visa's business and was no broader than necessary to achieve its business purpose. The court cited "free-rider" problems associated with Visa's competitors and concluded that the by-law was "reasonably necessary to ensure the effective operation of its credit card services." The court concluded:

> Bylaw 2.06 did not alter the character of the general purpose credit card market or change any present pattern of distribution. Nor did it bar Sears from access to this market. There was no evidence that Sears could only introduce a . . . card with Visa USA's help or that Visa USA's exclusion from its joint venture disabled Sears from developing its new card under the Discover mantle. More importantly, there was no evidence that the by-law harms consumers, the focus of the alleged violation.

36 F.3d at 971–972.

[Two of the authors of the Casebook jointly filed an amicus brief in this case.]

[5] Noncommercial Boycotts

In addressing the legality of boycotts, one needs to inquire to what extent a "noneconomic" political or social boycott is covered under Section 1 of the Sherman Act. First, it should be noted that the District of Columbia Circuit in *Smith v. Pro Football, Inc.*, 593 F.2d 1173, 1178 (D.C. Cir. 1978), distinguished a boycott of competitors at one level of competition by competitors on the same level (horizontal boycott) from other refusals to deal where the target is on a different level of competition (vertical boycott). The former was characterized as a classic per se illegal boycott. The latter was evaluated under a rule of reason.

Are consumers liable for treble damages under the antitrust laws for economic injury caused by a consumer boycott? Should the fact that the consumer might have an economic interest in the result affect the standard of analysis? Suppose the boycott is directed at a merchant that is forced, by reason of the boycott, to suffer substantial loss. Is there a distinction between this and a politically motivated boycott? Should legality turn on whether economic means (such as a boycott) are used to achieve a political result or whether political means are used to achieve an economic result? *See* Chapter 3, Section II[A]. *See also* Comment, *Protest Boycotts Under the Sherman Act*, 128 U. PA. L. REV. 1131 (1980); Note, *Concerted Refusals to Deal by Non-Business Groups: A Critique of* Missouri v. NOW, 49 GEO. WASH. L. REV. 143 (1980); Note, *Political Boycott Activity and the First Amendment*, 91 HARV. L. REV. 659 (1978).

Should the commercial or business interest of the participant in the boycott play a role in the decisional analysis? Recall the Supreme Court's earlier cautions in *Apex Hosiery* and *Klor's* that the Sherman Act is directed at commercial transactions or combinations having commercial objectives. 310 U.S. at 492–493; 359 U.S. at 213 n.7. The Ninth Circuit has ruled that lobbying activities with anticompetitive effects do not lose their First Amendment protection merely because the government entity is involved in a commercial enterprise. The Court distinguished the First Amendment protection from the state-action doctrine (*see* Chapter 3) where the commercial nature of the government's conduct becomes relevant. *In re Airport Car Rental Antitrust Litig.*, 693 F.2d 84 (9th Cir. 1982). Finally, if the protest boycott is not outside the scope of the Sherman Act, should its legality be tested by the per se rule or by an open-end Sherman Act balancing analysis that considers reasonableness in the context of purpose and effects? While few cases have addressed these issues, two decisions are worth noting.

In the following case, the Eighth Circuit considered whether a concerted convention boycott directed at several states that failed to ratify the Equal Rights Amendment (ERA) violated Section 1 of the Sherman Act. The defendant (NOW) was a nonprofit organization established for the purpose of furthering the legal rights of women. The convention boycott was designed to influence the Missouri Legislature, but the economic victims were Missouri motels, restaurants, and convention centers. The conduct challenged by Missouri was characterized by the court as "an economic boycott, politically motivated, to achieve a legislative goal." 620 F.2d at 1309.

MISSOURI v. NATIONAL ORGANIZATION FOR WOMEN
620 F.2d 1301 (8th Cir.), *cert. denied*, 449 U.S. 842 (1980)

JUDGE STEPHENSON.

[Finding the concerted boycott protected by the First Amendment, Judge Stephenson reasoned that the] ERA is not a "financial," "economic," or "commercial" piece of legislation. It is a social or political piece of legislation. While it is obviously perceived by the members of NOW as beneficial, the record indicates, and it seems apparent, that the orientation of both parties, NOW and Missouri, to the ERA is not one of profit motivation. The only financial, economic or commercial matter involved here is Missouri's concern about the financial repercussion of the boycott.

Keeping in mind that what we are discussing is the applicability of the Sherman Act to the facts, and the intent of the Congress to cover such situations, the difference in the content of the legislation — if anything — makes it more clear that NOW's efforts to influence the legislature's action on the ERA are beyond the scope and intent of the Sherman Act. A social piece of legislation and the efforts involved in influencing the legislature's actions on such legislation is further afield from the central focus of the Sherman Act than a commercial piece of legislation and the petitioning efforts associated therewith.

. . . .

Here, NOW's concerted activities and publicity campaign were initiated to show that in not ratifying the ERA, Missouri was denying rights to women, and in order to show displeasure with Missouri and to show support for the ERA, organizations were urged by NOW not to hold their conventions in Missouri. The ultimate goal was to have the ERA ratified and the hope was that by boycotting the state for as long as the ERA remained unratified in that state, it would result in a favorable legislative vote.

It is true that there were active solicitations by NOW followed by a boycott decision by the recipients of the solicitation. And yet, borrowing from the Supreme Court's language in *Noerr*, the finding by the district court in the instant case that NOW's campaign was intended to and did in fact injure Missouri in its relationship with its convention customers can mean no more than that Missouri sustained a *direct injury* as an incidental effect of NOW's campaign to influence governmental action.

"It is inevitable, whenever an attempt is made to influence legislation by a campaign of publicity, that an incidental effect of that campaign may be the infliction of some direct injury upon the interests of the party against whom the campaign is directed. . . . To hold that the knowing infliction of such injury renders the campaign itself illegal would thus be tantamount to outlawing all such campaigns."

NOW appears to have utilized its political power to bring about the ratification of the ERA by the State of Missouri. The tool it chose was a boycott, a device economic by nature. However, using a boycott in a non-competitive political arena for the purpose of influencing legislation is not proscribed by the Sherman Act.

. . . .

There resulted a restraint of trade in the *Noerr* case just as has occurred in this case. In *Noerr* it was accomplished by means of a publicity campaign with the ultimate goal of obtaining legislation that commercially or competitively affected the competitor-campaigners and competitor-target. In the instant case, it was accomplished by means of a publicity-boycott campaign with the ultimate goal of obtaining socially or politically-oriented legislation that had no effect upon the campaigners or target, at least in a commercial or business sense. These distinctions are not where our focus should be.

. . . .

[M]any of the cases do focus on the *Noerr* Court's reliance on the right of petition and the important constitutional questions that would be raised should the Court impute to Congress via the Sherman Act an intent to cover the *Noerr* activities. [Citing cases.]

Of those cases that emphasize the *Noerr* Court's reference to the constitutional concerns involved in *Noerr*, *California Motor Transport Co. v. Trucking Unlimited* was the one that dealt with it in the most expanded manner. In *Motor Transport*, Justice Douglas stated that the *Noerr* decision rested upon two grounds: (1) that there was no basis in the Sherman Act's legislative history by which to impute a purpose to regulate political activity and (2) that "[t]he right of petition is one of the freedoms protected by the Bill of Rights, and we cannot, of course, lightly impute to Congress an intent to invade these freedoms." *Id.*, 404 U.S. at 510. After stating this, the Court then extended the *Noerr* philosophy to the use of the channels and procedures of state and federal agencies and courts on the basis that not to do so would be destructive of the rights of association and of petition. *Id.*, 404 U.S. at 510. More importantly, in the course of invoking the sham exception to the *Noerr* case, the Court's focus is on the First Amendment rights. "First Amendment rights may not be used as the means or the pretext for achieving 'substantive evils' . . . which the legislature has the power to control." *Id.* at 515.

The parties do not even argue that there is a sham in this case; indeed, Missouri specifically argues that even those residents of Missouri who support the ERA must suffer as a result of this boycott. Thus the central point in *California Motor* and the other cases citing *Noerr* is the shift in focus from the *Noerr* holding that the railroads' activities are beyond the intent of Congress, insofar as the Sherman Act is concerned, to the *Noerr* statement that there are serious constitutional questions involved also.

The Court continued its mention of the constitutional issue presented in *Noerr* in *Lafayette v. Louisiana Power & Light Co., supra*, 435 U.S. at 399 and in *First National Bank v. Bellotti, supra*, 435 U.S. at 792 n.31.

In *Lafayette*, the Court stated that only two policies have been held to be "sufficiently weighty to override the presumption against implied exclusions from coverage of the antitrust laws" — one of which was the *Noerr* doctrine. (The other was the *Parker* state action exemption.) "[A] contrary construction [in *Noerr*] would impede the open communication between the polity and its lawmakers which is vital to the functioning of a representative democracy. . . . '[A]nd of at least equal significance,' is the threat to the constitutionally protected right of petition which a contrary construction would entail."

Thus, we feel that the Supreme Court's treatment of its *Noerr* doctrine requires recognition of the constitutional ramifications inherent in prohibiting, or considering as improper, activities such as NOW's boycott. . . . We hold that Missouri has no common law tort claim against NOW.

We hold today that the Sherman Act does not cover NOW's boycott activities on the basis of the legislative history of the Act and of the Supreme Court's consideration of the legislative history. We hold the same reasoning is applicable to Missouri's Antitrust Act. We hold that NOW's boycott activities are privileged on the basis of the First Amendment right to petition and the Supreme Court's recognition

of that important right when it collides with commercial effects of trade restraints.
. . .

NOTES AND QUESTIONS

1. In 1982, the Supreme Court decided whether a civil rights boycott by members of the National Association for the Advancement of Colored People (NAACP) against local merchants in Mississippi was protected under the First Amendment. *NAACP v. Claiborne Hardware Co.*, 458 U.S. 886 (1982). The purpose of the boycott was to secure compliance with a list of demands for social and racial justice. The state trial court found the NAACP members guilty of, inter alia, the tort of malicious interference with plaintiffs' business, a secondary boycott, and the state antitrust statute. The Mississippi Supreme Court held that the secondary boycott statute was inapplicable and the court "declined to rely on the restraint of trade statute, noting that the 'United States Supreme Court has seen fit to hold boycotts to achieve political ends are not a violation of the Sherman Act.' " The trial court's liability finding was upheld by the Mississippi Supreme Court, however, on a common law tort theory which outlawed boycotts. In reversing on First Amendment grounds, Justice Stevens, writing for the Court, concluded that:

> The boycott of white merchants at issue in this case took many forms. The boycott was launched at a meeting of a local branch of the NAACP attended by several hundred persons. Its acknowledged purpose was to secure compliance by both civic and business leaders with a lengthy list of demands for equality and racial justice. The boycott was supported by speeches and nonviolent picketing. Participants repeatedly encouraged others to join in its cause.

> Each of these elements of the boycott is a form of speech or conduct that is ordinarily entitled to protection under the First and Fourteenth Amendments. The black citizens named as defendants in this action banded together and collectively expressed their dissatisfaction with a social structure that had denied them rights to equal treatment and respect. As we so recently acknowledged, . . . "the practice of persons sharing common views banding together to achieve a common end is deeply embedded in the American political process." We recognized that "by collective effort individuals can make their views known, when, individually, their voices would be faint or lost. . . . There are, of course, some activities, legal if engaged in by one, yet illegal if performed in concert with others, but political expression is not one of them.

> . . . .

> Speech itself also was used to further the aims of the boycott. Nonparticipants repeatedly were urged to join the common cause, both through public address and through personal solicitation. These elements of the boycott involve speech in its most direct form. . . . Speech does not lose its protected character, however, simply because it may embarrass others or coerce them into action. . . .

In sum, the boycott clearly involved constitutionally protected activity.
. . .

The presence of protected activity, however, does not end the relevant constitutional inquiry. . . .

While States have broad power to regulate economic activity, we do not find a comparable right to prohibit peaceful political activity such as that found in the boycott in this case. This Court has recognized that expression on public issues "has always rested on the highest rung of the hierarchy of First Amendment values." "[S]peech concerning public affairs is more than self-expression; it is the essence of self-government." There is a "profound national commitment" to the principle that "debate on public issues should be uninhibited, robust, and wide-open."

. . . .

It is not disputed that a major purpose of the boycott in this case was to influence governmental action. [T]he petitioners certainly foresaw — and directly intended — that the merchants would sustain economic injury as a result of their campaign. [T]he purpose of petitioners' campaign was not to destroy legitimate competition. Petitioners sought to vindicate rights of equality and of freedom that lie at the heart of the Fourteenth Amendment itself. The right of the States to regulate economic activity could not justify a complete prohibition against a nonviolent, politically-motivated boycott designed to force governmental and economic change and to effectuate rights guaranteed by the Constitution itself.

. . . We hold that the nonviolent elements of petitioners' activities are entitled to the protection of the First Amendment.

458 U.S. at 907–915.

2. *The Sherman Act and Nonprofit Organizations.* Do the antitrust laws reach the activities of nonprofit organizations, such as church-sponsored hospitals? Does *NOW* speak to that proposition? To be sure, nonprofit institutions do not necessarily "maximize profits" in the sense of equating marginal cost and marginal revenue. But nonprofits may seek monopoly profits and cause competitive injury even when acting for purely charitable purposes. For example, the Sisters of Mercy may own a nonprofit hospital and a soup kitchen and conclude that, while all patrons of the soup kitchen are needy, not all patients at the hospital are. As a result, they may use monopoly profits from the hospital to subsidize the activities of the soup kitchen. If this completely charitable set of intentions is accompanied by power and exclusionary practices in the hospital, its patients have suffered competitive injury notwithstanding the Sisters' good motives. *See* W. Lynk, *Property Rights and the Presumptions of Merger Analysis*, 39 ANTITRUST BULL. 363, 377 (1994).

Two things seem fairly well settled. *First*, nonprofit organizations do not enjoy any general exemption from the Sherman or Clayton Acts. The antitrust laws presumptively apply to them. *Second*, although *NOW* and other cases declare an exemption for noncommercial activities, the exemption question responds to the nature of the *activity being challenged*, not to the nature of the organization engaging in it. Thus, if a nonprofit organization such as *NOW* engages in a purely economic boycott, the Sherman Act applies. By contrast, if Campbell's Soup Company gave free soup to a local charitable organization on the condition that they not charge more than 25 cents a bowl, the conduct would presumably be exempt.

Did the *NOW* and *NAACP* opinions express an unqualified immunity from the antitrust laws for noncommercial concerted refusals to deal? Even though these cases were decided under the First Amendment, at least in part, could such refusals to deal be found lawful under the prior boycott decisional law? If so, by what analysis, per se or rule of reason, would you reach your decision? Consider the analytical themes expressed throughout the prior decisions studied: (1) whether the boycott had a commercial objective; (2) whether the boycott was explicitly formed, or merely an incidental effect of some other agreement; (3) whether it had an otherwise lawful self-regulatory purpose; (4) whether it was a horizontal agreement entered between competitors; (5) whether its aim was horizontal, that is, in the direction of a competitor; (6) whether it was directed vertically to a supplier or customer; and (7) whether there were elements of coercion.

Determining whether the boycott is commercial in purpose or effect is sometimes problematic. Compare the language in *NOW* and *NAACP* with the results in *Allied Tube & Conduit Corp. v. Indian Head, Inc.*, 486 U.S. 492 (1988); *Superior Court Trial Lawyers Ass'n v. FTC*, 856 F.2d 226 (D.C. Cir. 1988). *See* Calkins, *Developments in Antitrust and the First Amendment: The Disaggregation of* Noerr, 57 ANTITRUST L.J. 327 (1988).

For an extended discussion of the *Noerr* doctrine, see Chapter 9, *infra*.

3. While boycotts can sometimes be delineated between economic and non-economic speech purposes, use of boycotts is generally a combination of the two, using the economic factors to make a non-economic point. As a result, there is opportunity for the First Amendment and the Sherman Act to directly conflict. The question, then, becomes whether speech protections should outweigh the antitrust concerns. *See* Hillary Greene, *Antitrust Censorship of Economic Protest*, 59 DUKE L.J. 1037, 1043 (2010). Professor Greene argues that in order to maintain the power of consumers to speak with their dollar, that boycotts must be subject to a more nuanced rule of reason approach then they currently are, focusing more attention on whether the boycott has a bona fide speech interest. *See Id.* at 1087–1088. What role should freedom of speech interest play in antitrust analysis? Which factor should get greater weight, speech interests, or antitrust concerns? Should boycotts get an exemption whenever there is a bona fide speech interest at stake regardless of the possibility for economic coercion?

[F]   Agreements Involving Intellectual Property

FEDERAL TRADE COMMISSION v. ACTAVIS, INC.
133 S. Ct. 2223 (2013)

JUSTICE BREYER delivered the opinion of the Court.

Company A sues Company B for patent infringement. The two companies settle under terms that require (1) Company B, the claimed infringer, not to produce the patented product until the patent's term expires, and (2) Company A, the patentee, to pay B many millions of dollars. Because the settlement requires the patentee to pay the alleged infringer, rather than the other way around, this kind of settlement agreement is often called a "reverse payment" settlement agreement. And the basic question here is whether such an agreement can sometimes unreasonably diminish competition in violation of the antitrust laws.

In this case, the Eleventh Circuit dismissed a Federal Trade Commission (FTC) complaint claiming that a particular reverse payment settlement agreement violated the antitrust laws. In doing so, the Circuit stated that a reverse payment settlement agreement generally is "immune from antitrust attack so long as its anticompetitive effects fall within the scope of the exclusionary potential of the patent." *FTC v. Watson Pharmaceuticals, Inc.*, 677 F.3d 1298, 1312 (2012). And since the alleged infringer's promise not to enter the patentee's market expired before the patent's term ended, the Circuit found the agreement legal and dismissed the FTC complaint. *Id.*, at 1315. In our view, however, reverse payment settlements such as the agreement alleged in the complaint before us can sometimes violate the antitrust laws. We consequently hold that the Eleventh Circuit should have allowed the FTC's lawsuit to proceed.

I

A

Apparently most if not all reverse payment settlement agreements arise in the context of pharmaceutical drug regulation, and specifically in the context of suits brought under statutory provisions allowing a generic drug manufacturer (seeking speedy marketing approval) to challenge the validity of a patent owned by an already-approved brand-name drug owner. See Brief for Petitioner 29; 12 P. Areeda & H. Hovenkamp, Antitrust Law ¶ 2046, p. 338 (3d ed. 2012) (hereinafter Areeda); Hovenkamp, Sensible Antitrust Rules for Pharmaceutical Competition, 39 U.S.F.L. .Rev. 11, 24 (2004). We consequently describe four key features of the relevant drug-regulatory framework established by the Drug Price Competition and Patent Term Restoration Act of 1984, 98 Stat. 1585, as amended. That Act is commonly known as the Hatch–Waxman Act.

First, a drug manufacturer, wishing to market a new prescription drug, must submit a New Drug Application to the federal Food and Drug Administration (FDA) and undergo a long, comprehensive, and costly testing process, after which, if successful, the manufacturer will receive marketing approval from the FDA. ***

Second, once the FDA has approved a brand-name drug for marketing, a manufacturer of a generic drug can obtain similar marketing approval through use of abbreviated procedures. The Hatch-Waxman Act permits a generic manufacturer to file an Abbreviated New Drug Application specifying that the generic has the "same active ingredients as," and is "biologically equivalent" to, the already-approved brand-name drug. In this way the generic manufacturer can obtain approval while avoiding the "costly and time-consuming studies" needed to obtain approval "for a pioneer drug." The Hatch-Waxman process, by allowing the generic to piggy-back on the pioneer's approval efforts, "speed[s] the introduction of low-cost generic drugs to market," thereby furthering drug competition.

Third, the Hatch-Waxman Act sets forth special procedures for identifying, and resolving, related patent disputes. It requires the pioneer brand-name manufacturer to list in its New Drug Application the "number and the expiration date" of any relevant patent. And it requires the generic manufacturer in its Abbreviated New Drug Application to "assure the FDA" that the generic "will not infringe" the brand-name's patents.

The generic *** can certify that any relevant patents have expired. It can request approval to market beginning when any still-in-force patents expire. Or, it can certify that any listed, relevant patent "is invalid or will not be infringed by the manufacture, use, or sale" of the drug described in the Abbreviated New Drug Application. Taking this last-mentioned route (called the "paragraph IV" route), automatically counts as patent infringement, and often "means provoking litigation." If the brand-name patentee brings an infringement suit within 45 days, the FDA then must withhold approving the generic, usually for a 30-month period, while the parties litigate patent validity (or infringement) in court. If the courts decide the matter within that period, the FDA follows that determination; if they do not, the FDA may go forward and give approval to market the generic product.

Fourth, Hatch-Waxman provides a special incentive for a generic to be the first to file an Abbreviated New Drug Application taking the paragraph IV route. That applicant will enjoy a period of 180 days of exclusivity (from the first commercial marketing of its drug). During that period of exclusivity no other generic can compete with the brand-name drug. If the first-to-file generic manufacturer can overcome any patent obstacle and bring the generic to market, this 180-day period of exclusivity can prove valuable, possibly "worth several hundred million dollars." Hemphill, Paying for Delay: Pharmaceutical Patent Settlement as a Regulatory Design Problem, 81 N.Y. U. L. Rev. 1553, 1579 (2006). *** The 180-day exclusivity period, however, can belong only to the first generic to file. Should that first-to-file generic forfeit the exclusivity right in one of the ways specified by statute, no other generic can obtain it.

B

1

In 1999, Solvay Pharmaceuticals, a respondent here, filed a New Drug Application for a brand-name drug called AndroGel. The FDA approved the application in 2000. In 2003, Solvay obtained a relevant patent and disclosed that fact to the FDA, as Hatch-Waxman requires.

Later the same year another respondent, Actavis, Inc. (then known as Watson Pharmaceuticals), filed an Abbreviated New Drug Application for a generic drug modeled after AndroGel. Subsequently, Paddock Laboratories, also a respondent, separately filed an Abbreviated New Drug Application for its own generic product. Both Actavis and Paddock certified under paragraph IV that Solvay's listed patent was invalid and their drugs did not infringe it. A fourth manufacturer, Par Pharmaceutical, likewise a respondent, did not file an application of its own but joined forces with Paddock, agreeing to share the patent litigation costs in return for a share of profits if Paddock obtained approval for its generic drug.

Solvay initiated paragraph IV patent litigation against Actavis and Paddock. Thirty months later the FDA approved Actavis' first-to-file generic product, but, in 2006, the patent-litigation parties all settled. Under the terms of the settlement Actavis agreed that it would not bring its generic to market until August 31, 2015, 65 months before Solvay's patent expired (unless someone else marketed a generic sooner). Actavis also agreed to promote AndroGel to urologists. The other generic manufacturers made roughly similar promises. And Solvay agreed to pay millions of dollars to each generic — $12 million in total to Paddock; $60 million in total to Par; and an estimated $19–$30 million annually, for nine years, to Actavis. The companies described these payments as compensation for other services the generics promised to perform, but the FTC contends the other services had little value. According to the FTC the true point of the payments was to compensate the generics for agreeing not to compete against AndroGel until 2015.

2

On January 29, 2009, the FTC filed this lawsuit against all the settling parties, namely, Solvay, Actavis, Paddock, and Par. The FTC's complaint (as since amended) alleged that respondents violated § 5 of the Federal Trade Commission Act, 15 U.S.C. § 45, by unlawfully agreeing "to share in Solvay's monopoly profits, abandon their patent challenges, and refrain from launching their low-cost generic products to compete with AndroGel for nine years." The District Court held that these allegations did not set forth an antitrust law violation. It accordingly dismissed the FTC's complaint. The FTC appealed.

The Court of Appeals for the Eleventh Circuit affirmed the District Court. It wrote that "absent sham litigation or fraud in obtaining the patent, a reverse payment settlement is immune from antitrust attack so long as its anticompetitive effects fall within the scope of the exclusionary potential of the patent." The court recognized that "antitrust laws typically prohibit agreements where one company pays a potential competitor not to enter the market." But, the court found that "reverse payment settlements of patent litigation presen[t] atypical cases because one of the parties owns a patent." Patent holders have a "lawful right to exclude others from the market," ibid. (internal quotation marks omitted); thus a patent "conveys the right to cripple competition." The court recognized that, if the parties to this sort of case do not settle, a court might declare the patent invalid. But, in light of the public policy favoring settlement of disputes (among other considerations) it held that the courts could not require the parties to continue to litigate in order to avoid antitrust liability.

The FTC sought certiorari. Because different courts have reached different conclusions about the application of the antitrust laws to Hatch-Waxman-related patent settlements, we granted the FTC's petition.

II

A

Solvay's patent, if valid and infringed, might have permitted it to charge drug prices sufficient to recoup the reverse settlement payments it agreed to make to its potential generic competitors. And we are willing to take this fact as evidence that the agreement's "anticompetitive effects fall within the scope of the exclusionary potential of the patent." But we do not agree that that fact, or characterization, can immunize the agreement from antitrust attack.

For one thing, to refer, as the Circuit referred, simply to what the holder of a valid patent could do does not by itself answer the antitrust question. The patent here may or may not be valid, and may or may not be infringed. "[A] *valid* patent excludes all except its owner from the use of the protected process or product," *United States v. Line Material Co.*, 333 U.S. 287, 308 (1948) (emphasis added). And that exclusion may permit the patent owner to charge a higher-than-competitive price for the patented product. But an invalidated patent carries with it no such right. And even a valid patent confers no right to exclude products or processes that do not actually infringe. The paragraph IV litigation in this case put the patent's validity at issue, as well as its actual preclusive scope. The parties' settlement ended that litigation. The FTC alleges that in substance, the plaintiff agreed to pay the defendants many millions of dollars to stay out of its market, even though the defendants did not have any claim that the plaintiff was liable to them for damages. That form of settlement is unusual. And, for reasons discussed in Part II-B, infra, there is reason for concern that settlements taking this form tend to have significant adverse effects on competition.

Given these factors, it would be incongruous to determine antitrust legality by measuring the settlement's anticompetitive effects solely against patent law policy, rather than by measuring them against procompetitive antitrust policies as well. And indeed, contrary to the Circuit's view that the only pertinent question is whether "the settlement agreement . . . fall[s] within" the legitimate "scope" of the patent's "exclusionary potential," this Court has indicated that patent and antitrust policies are both relevant in determining the "scope of the patent monopoly" — and consequently antitrust law immunity — that is conferred by a patent.

Thus, the Court in *Line Material* explained that "the improper use of [a patent] monopoly," is "invalid" under the antitrust laws and resolved the antitrust question in that case by seeking an accommodation "between the lawful restraint on trade of the patent monopoly and the illegal restraint prohibited broadly by the Sherman Act." To strike that balance, the Court asked questions such as whether "the patent statute specifically gives a right" to restrain competition in the manner challenged; and whether "competition is impeded to a greater degree" by the restraint at issue than other restraints previously approved as reasonable. *Id.*, at 311. In short, rather than measure the length or amount of a restriction solely against the length of the patent's term or its earning potential, as the Court of Appeals apparently did here, this Court answered the antitrust question by considering traditional antitrust factors such as likely anticompetitive effects, redeeming virtues, market power, and potentially offsetting legal considerations present in the circumstances, such as here those related to patents. See Part II-B, *infra*. ***

For another thing, this Court's precedents make clear that patent-related settlement agreements can sometimes violate the antitrust laws. In *United States v. Singer Mfg. Co.*, 374 U.S. 174 (1963), for example, two sewing machine companies possessed competing patent claims; a third company sought a patent under circumstances where doing so might lead to the disclosure of information that would invalidate the other two firms' patents. All three firms settled their patent-related disagreements while assigning the broadest claims to the firm best able to enforce the patent against yet other potential competitors. *Id.*, at 190–192. The Court did not examine whether, on the assumption that all three patents were valid, patent law would have allowed the patents' holders to do the same. Rather, emphasizing that the Sherman Act "imposes strict limitations on the concerted activities in which patent owners may lawfully engage," *id.*, at 197, it held that the agreements, although settling patent disputes, violated the antitrust laws. *Id.*, at 195, 197. And that, in important part, was because "the public interest in granting patent monopolies" exists only to the extent that "the public is given a novel and useful invention" in "consideration for its grant." *Id.*, at 199 (White, J., concurring). See also *United States v. New Wrinkle, Inc.*, 342 U.S. 371, 378 (1952) (applying antitrust scrutiny to patent settlement); *Standard Oil Co. (Indiana) v. United States*, 283 U.S. 163 (1931) (same).

Similarly, both within the settlement context and without, the Court has struck down overly restrictive patent licensing agreements — irrespective of whether those agreements produced supra-patent-permitted revenues. We concede that in *United States v. General Elec. Co.*, 272 U.S. 476, 489 (1926), the Court permitted a single patentee to grant to a single licensee a license containing a minimum resale price requirement. But in Line Material, supra, at 308, 310–311, the Court held that the antitrust laws forbid a group of patentees, each owning one or more patents, to cross-license each other, and, in doing so, to insist that each licensee maintain retail prices set collectively by the patent holders. The Court was willing to presume that the single-patentee practice approved in *General Electric* was a "reasonable restraint" that "accords with the patent monopoly granted by the patent law," 333 U.S., at 312, but declined to extend that conclusion to multiple-patentee agreements: "As the Sherman Act prohibits agreements to fix prices, any arrangement between patentees runs afoul of that prohibition and is outside the patent monopoly." *Ibid. In New Wrinkle*, 342 U.S., at 378, the Court held roughly the same, this time in respect to a similar arrangement in settlement of a litigation between two patentees, each of which contended that its own patent gave it the exclusive right to control production. That one or the other company (we may presume) was right about its patent did not lead the Court to confer antitrust immunity. Far from it, the agreement was found to violate the Sherman Act. *Id.*, at 380.

Finally in Standard Oil Co. (Indiana), the Court upheld cross-licensing agreements among patentees that settled actual and impending patent litigation, 283 U.S., at 168, which agreements set royalty rates to be charged third parties for a license to practice all the patents at issue (and which divided resulting revenues). But, in doing so, Justice Brandeis, writing for the Court, warned that such an arrangement would have violated the Sherman Act had the patent holders thereby "dominate[d]" the industry and "curtail[ed] the manufacture and supply of an unpatented product." *Id.*, at 174. These cases do not simply ask whether a hypothetically valid patent's holder would be able to charge, e.g., the high prices that the challenged patent-related term allowed. Rather, they seek to accommodate patent and antitrust policies, finding challenged terms and conditions unlawful unless patent law policy offsets the antitrust law policy strongly favoring competition.

*** Finally, the Hatch-Waxman Act itself does not embody a statutory policy that supports the Eleventh Circuit's view. Rather, the general procompetitive thrust of the statute, its specific provisions facilitating challenges to a patent's validity, see Part I-A, supra, and its later-added provisions requiring parties to a patent dispute triggered by a paragraph IV filing to report settlement terms to the FTC and the Antitrust Division of the Department of Justice, all suggest the contrary. Those interested in legislative history may also wish to examine the statements of individual Members of Congress condemning reverse payment settlements in advance of the 2003 amendments. See, e.g., 148 Cong. Rec. 14437 (2002) (remarks of Sen. Hatch) ("It was and is very clear that the [Hatch-Waxman Act] was not designed to allow deals between brand and generic companies to delay competition"); 146 Cong. Rec. 18774 (2000) (remarks of Rep. Waxman) (introducing bill to deter companies from "strik[ing] collusive agreements to trade multimillion dollar payoffs by the brand company for delays in the introduction of lower cost, generic alternatives").

B

The Eleventh Circuit's conclusion finds some degree of support in a general legal policy favoring the settlement of disputes. The Circuit's related underlying practical concern consists of its fear that antitrust scrutiny of a reverse payment agreement would require the parties to litigate the validity of the patent in order to demonstrate what would have happened to competition in the absence of the settlement. Any such litigation will prove time consuming, complex, and expensive. The antitrust game, the Circuit may believe, would not be worth that litigation candle.

We recognize the value of settlements and the patent litigation problem. But we nonetheless conclude that this patent-related factor should not determine the result here. Rather, five sets of considerations lead us to conclude that the FTC should have been given the opportunity to prove its antitrust claim.

First, the specific restraint at issue has the "potential for genuine adverse effects on competition." *Indiana Federation of Dentists*, 476 U.S., at 460–461 (citing 7 Areeda ¶ 1511, at 429 (1986)). The payment in effect amounts to a purchase by the patentee of the exclusive right to sell its product, a right it already claims but would lose if the patent litigation were to continue and the patent were held invalid or not infringed by the generic product. Suppose, for example, that the exclusive right to sell produces $50 million in supracompetitive profits per year for the patentee. And suppose further that the patent has 10 more years to run. Continued litigation, if it results in patent invalidation or a finding of noninfringement, could cost the patentee $500 million in lost revenues, a sum that then would flow in large part to consumers in the form of lower prices.

We concede that settlement on terms permitting the patent challenger to enter the market before the patent expires would also bring about competition, again to the consumer's benefit. But settlement on the terms said by the FTC to be at issue here — payment in return for staying out of the market — simply keeps prices at patentee-set levels, potentially producing the full patent-related $500 million monopoly return while dividing that return between the challenged patentee and the patent challenger. The patentee and the challenger gain; the consumer loses. Indeed, there are indications that patentees sometimes pay a generic challenger a sum even larger than what the generic would gain in profits if it won the paragraph IV litigation and entered the market. See Hemphill, 81 N.Y. U. L. Rev., at 1581. See also Brief for 118 Law, Economics, and Business Professors et al. as Amici Curiae 25 (estimating that this is true of the settlement challenged here). The rationale behind a payment of this size cannot in every case be supported by traditional settlement considerations. The payment may instead provide strong evidence that the patentee seeks to induce the generic challenger to abandon its claim with a share of its monopoly profits that would otherwise be lost in the competitive market.

But, one might ask, as a practical matter would the parties be able to enter into such an anticompetitive agreement? Would not a high reverse payment signal to other potential challengers that the patentee lacks confidence in its patent, thereby provoking additional challenges, perhaps too many for the patentee to "buy off?" Two special features of Hatch-Waxman mean that the answer to this question is "not necessarily so." First, under Hatch-Waxman only the first challenger gains the special advantage of 180 days of an exclusive right to sell a generic version of the brand-name product. See Part I-A, *supra*. And as noted, that right has proved valuable — indeed, it can be worth several hundred million dollars. Subsequent challengers cannot secure that exclusivity period, and thus stand to win significantly less than the first if they bring a successful paragraph IV challenge. That is, if subsequent litigation results in invalidation of the patent, or a ruling that the patent is not infringed, that litigation victory will free not just the challenger to compete, but all other potential competitors too (once they obtain FDA approval). The potential reward available to a subsequent challenger being significantly less, the patentee's payment to the initial challenger (in return for not pressing the patent challenge) will not necessarily provoke subsequent challenges. Second, a generic that files a paragraph IV after learning that the first filer has settled will (if sued by the brand-name) have to wait out a stay period of (roughly) 30 months before the FDA may approve its application, just as the first filer did. These features together mean that a reverse payment settlement with the first filer (or, as in this case, all of the initial filers) "removes from consideration the most motivated challenger, and the one closest to introducing competition." Hemphill, *supra*, at 1586. *** [S]cholars in the field tell us that "where only one party owns a patent, it is virtually unheard of outside of pharmaceuticals for that party to pay an accused infringer to settle the lawsuit." 1 H. Hovenkamp, M. Janis, M. Lemley, & C. Leslie, IP and Antitrust § 15.3, p. 15–45, n. 161 (2d ed. Supp. 2011). It may well be that Hatch-Waxman's unique regulatory framework, including the special advantage that the 180-day exclusivity period gives to first filers, does much to explain why in this context, but not others, the patentee's ordinary incentives to resist paying off challengers (*i.e.*, the fear of provoking myriad other challengers) appear to be more frequently overcome. See 12 Areeda ¶ 2046, at 341 (3d ed. 2010) (noting that these provisions, no doubt unintentionally, have created special incentives for collusion).

Second, these anticompetitive consequences will at least sometimes prove unjustified. As the FTC admits, offsetting or redeeming virtues are sometimes present. The reverse payment, for example, may amount to no more than a rough approximation of the litigation expenses saved through the settlement. That payment may reflect compensation for other services that the generic has promised to perform — such as distributing the patented item or helping to develop a market for that item. There may be other justifications. Where a reverse payment reflects traditional settlement considerations, such as avoided litigation costs or fair value for services, there is not the same concern that a patentee is using its monopoly profits to avoid the risk of patent invalidation or a finding of noninfringement. In such cases, the parties may have provided for a reverse payment without having sought or brought about the anticompetitive consequences we mentioned above. But that possibility does not justify dismissing the FTC's complaint. An antitrust defendant may show in the antitrust proceeding that legitimate justifications are present, thereby explaining the presence of the challenged term and showing the lawfulness of that term under the rule of reason. See, e.g., *Indiana Federation of Dentists, supra*, at 459; 7 Areeda ¶¶ 1504a–1504b, at 401–404 (3d ed. 2010).

Third, where a reverse payment threatens to work unjustified anticompetitive harm, the patentee likely possesses the power to bring that harm about in practice. See *id.*, ¶ 1503, at 392–393. At least, the "size of the payment from a branded drug manufacturer to a prospective generic is itself a strong indicator of power" — namely, the power to charge prices higher than the competitive level. 12 *id.*, ¶ 2046, at 351. An important patent itself helps to assure such power. Neither is a firm without that power likely to pay "large sums" to induce "others to stay out of its market." *Ibid.* In any event, the Commission has referred to studies showing that reverse payment agreements are associated with the presence of higher-than-competitive profits — a strong indication of market power.

Fourth, an antitrust action is likely to prove more feasible administratively than the Eleventh Circuit believed. The Circuit's holding does avoid the need to litigate the patent's validity (and also, any question of infringement). But to do so, it throws the baby out with the bath water, and there is no need to take that drastic step. That is because it is normally not necessary to litigate patent validity to answer the antitrust question (unless, perhaps, to determine whether the patent litigation is a sham, see 677 F.3d, at 1312). An unexplained large reverse payment itself would normally suggest that the patentee has serious doubts about the patent's survival. And that fact, in turn, suggests that the payment's objective is to maintain supracompetitive prices to be shared among the patentee and the challenger rather than face what might have been a competitive market — the very anticompetitive consequence that underlies the claim of antitrust unlawfulness. The owner of a particularly valuable patent might contend, of course, that even a small risk of invalidity justifies a large payment. But, be that as it may, the payment (if otherwise unexplained) likely seeks to prevent the risk of competition. And, as we have said, that consequence constitutes the relevant anticompetitive harm. In a word, the size of the unexplained reverse payment can provide a workable surrogate for a patent's weakness, all without forcing a court to conduct a detailed exploration of the validity of the patent itself. 12 Areeda ¶ 2046, at 350–352.

Fifth, the fact that a large, unjustified reverse payment risks antitrust liability does not prevent litigating parties from settling their lawsuit. They may, as in other industries, settle in other ways, for example, by allowing the generic manufacturer to enter the patentee's market prior to the patent's expiration, without the patentee paying the challenger to stay out prior to that point. Although the parties may have reasons to prefer settlements that include reverse payments, the relevant antitrust question is: What are those reasons? If the basic reason is a desire to maintain and to share patent-generated monopoly profits, then, in the absence of some other justification, the antitrust laws are likely to forbid the arrangement.

In sum, a reverse payment, where large and unjustified, can bring with it the risk of significant anticompetitive effects; one who makes such a payment may be unable to explain and to justify it; such a firm or individual may well possess market power derived from the patent; a court, by examining the size of the payment, may well be able to assess its likely anticompetitive effects along with its potential justifications without litigating the validity of the patent; and parties may well find ways to settle patent disputes without the use of reverse payments. In our view, these considerations, taken together, outweigh the single strong consideration — the desirability of settlements — that led the Eleventh Circuit to provide near-automatic antitrust immunity to reverse payment settlements.

III

The FTC urges us to hold that reverse payment settlement agreements are presumptively unlawful and that courts reviewing such agreements should proceed via a "quick look" approach, rather than applying a "rule of reason." See *California Dental*, 526 U.S., at 775, n. 12, ("Quick-look analysis in effect" shifts to "a defendant the burden to show empirical evidence of procompetitive effects"); 7 Areeda ¶ 1508, at 435–440 (3d ed. 2010). We decline to do so. In *California Dental*, we held (unanimously) that abandonment of the "rule of reason" in favor of presumptive rules (or a "quick-look" approach) is appropriate only where "an observer with even a rudimentary understanding of economics could conclude that the arrangements in question would have an anticompetitive effect on customers and markets." 526 U.S., at 770 (BREYER, J., concurring in part and dissenting in part). We do not believe that reverse payment settlements, in the context we here discuss, meet this criterion.

That is because the likelihood of a reverse payment bringing about anticompetitive effects depends upon its size, its scale in relation to the payor's anticipated future litigation costs, its independence from other services for which it might represent payment, and the lack of any other convincing justification. The existence and degree of any anticompetitive consequence may also vary as among industries. These complexities lead us to conclude that the FTC must prove its case as in other rule-of-reason cases.

To say this is not to require the courts to insist, contrary to what we have said, that the Commission need litigate the patent's validity, empirically demonstrate the virtues or vices of the patent system, present every possible supporting fact or refute every possible pro-defense theory. As a leading antitrust scholar has pointed out, " '[t]here is always something of a sliding scale in appraising reasonableness,'" and as such " 'the quality of proof required should vary with the circumstances.' " *California Dental, supra,* at 780 (quoting with approval 7 Areeda ¶ 1507, at 402 (1986)).

As in other areas of law, trial courts can structure antitrust litigation so as to avoid, on the one hand, the use of antitrust theories too abbreviated to permit proper analysis, and, on the other, consideration of every possible fact or theory irrespective of the minimal light it may shed on the basic question — that of the presence of significant unjustified anticompetitive consequences. See 7 *id.*, ¶ 1508c, at 438–440. We therefore leave to the lower courts the structuring of the present rule-of-reason antitrust litigation. We reverse the judgment of the Eleventh Circuit. And we remand the case for further proceedings consistent with this opinion.

It is so ordered.

JUSTICE ALITO took no part in the consideration or decision of this case.

CHIEF JUSTICE ROBERTS, with whom JUSTICE SCALIA and JUSTICE THOMAS join, dissenting.

*** A patent carves out an exception to the applicability of antitrust laws. The correct approach should therefore be to ask whether the settlement gives Solvay monopoly power beyond what the patent already gave it. The Court, however, departs from this approach, and would instead use antitrust law's amorphous rule of reason to inquire into the anticompetitive effects of such settlements. This novel approach is without support in any statute, and will discourage the settlement of patent litigation. I respectfully dissent. ***

The key, of course, is that the patent holder — when doing anything, including settling — must act within the scope of the patent. *** [U]nder our precedent, this is a fairly straight-forward case. Solvay paid a competitor to respect its patent — conduct which did not exceed the scope of its patent. No one alleges that there was sham litigation, or that Solvay's patent was obtained through fraud on the PTO. As in any settlement, Solvay gave its competitors something of value (money) and, in exchange, its competitors gave it something of value (dropping their legal claims).

In doing so, they put an end to litigation that had been dragging on for three years. Ordinarily, we would think this a good thing. ***

[N]one of the Court's reasons supports its conclusion that a patent holder, when settling a claim that its patent is invalid, is not immunized by the fact that it is acting within the scope of its patent. And I fear the Court's attempt to limit its holding to the context of patent settlements under Hatch–Waxman will not long hold. ***

The majority's rule will discourage settlement of patent litigation. Simply put, there would be no incentive to settle if, immediately after settling, the parties would have to litigate the same issue — the question of patent validity — as part of a defense against an antitrust suit. In that suit, the alleged infringer would be in the especially awkward position of being for the patent after being against it.

This is unfortunate because patent litigation is particularly complex, and particularly costly. ***

The majority today departs from the settled approach separating patent and antitrust law, weakens the protections afforded to innovators by patents, frustrates the public policy in favor of settling, and likely undermines the very policy it seeks to promote by forcing generics who step into the litigation ring to do so without the prospect of cash settlements. I would keep things as they were and not subject basic questions of patent law to an unbounded inquiry under antitrust law, with its treble damages and famously burdensome discovery. *See* 15 U.S.C. § 15; *Bell Atlantic Corp. v. Twombly*, 550 U.S. 544, 558–559 (2007). I respectfully dissent.

NOTES AND QUESTIONS

1. Do reverse settlement agreements resemble any of the categories of unreasonable restraint of trade explored earlier in this chapter? If so, which ones?

2. Before *Actavis*, circuit courts had dramatically differing views on the proper antitrust treatment for reverse settlement agreements. In *In re Cardizem CD Antitrust Litigation*, 332 F.3d 896 (6th Cir. 2003), the Sixth Circuit considered a reverse payment of $40 million made by a patented drug manufacturer to a potential manufacturer in exchange for the latter refraining from marketing its generic version of the patentee's drug even after it had received FDA approval. The court held the agreement to be "a classic example of a per se illegal restraint of trade." Other circuits had been more receptive to reverse payments. For example, in *Schering-Plough Corp. v. F.T.C.*, 402 F.3d 1056 (11th Cir. 2005), the Eleventh Circuit claimed "that neither the rule of reason nor the per se analysis is appropriate" to analyze reverse settlement agreements and instead held that "the proper analysis of antitrust liability requires an examination of: (1) the scope of the exclusionary potential of the patent; (2) the extent to which the agreements exceed that scope; and (3) the resulting anticompetitive effects." *Id.* at 1066. The court upheld the challenged reserve payment, expressing sympathy for patentholders while noting that they "should not be in a worse position, by virtue of the patent right, to negotiate and settle surrounding lawsuits." *Id.* at 1072. Similarly, in *In re Tamoxifen Citrate Antitrust Litigation*, 466 F.3d 187 (2d Cir. 2006), the Second Circuit upheld a reverse payment, reasoning that "'simply because a brand-name pharmaceutical company holding a patent paid its generic competitor money cannot be the sole basis for a violation of antitrust law,' unless the 'exclusionary effects of the agreement' exceed the 'scope of the patent's protection.'" *Id.* at 212 (citations omitted). In contrast, the Third Circuit rejected this "scope of the patent" approach because it creates an "almost unrebuttable presumption of patent validity," and thus "assumes away the question being litigated in the underlying patent suit . . . ." *In re K-Dur Antitrust Litigation*, 686 F.3d 197, 214 (3d Cir. 2012). Which position is more persuasive?

Sitting by designation as a district court judge, Judge Richard Posner asserted: "A ban on reverse-payment settlements would reduce the incentive to challenge patents by reducing the challenger's settlement options should he be sued for infringement, and so might well be thought anticompetitive." *Asahi Glass Co. v. Pentech Pharm., Inc.*, 289 F. Supp. 2d 986, 992 (N.D. Ill. 2003) (Posner, J.). Is Judge Posner correct? Would a per se rule against reverse-payment settlements reduce competition and innovation?

3. What do you think is the proper antitrust rule for reverse payment settlements? Per se legality? Per se illegality? Rule of reason? Quick look? If reverse payments were per se illegal, how might parties try to craft settlements in order to circumvent the per se rule?

The *Actavis* majority claimed to be applying rule of reason analysis. Does the Court's approach, however, resemble "quick look" analysis in any ways?

4. How do reverse payment settlements differ from traditional settlements? One significant difference is that the ordinary settlement is an output increasing event, making both patentee and licensee into producers. By contrast, a reverse payment settlement presumptively reduces output by preserving production only by the pioneer while raising its costs.

By granting the first generic entrant 180 days as the exclusive generic seller, the Hatch-Waxman Act creates temporary generic duopolies in which two firms can maximize their profits by jointly producing profit-maximizing output and charging the same supracompetitive price as a monopolist. Why does the Hatch-Waxman Act allow this dynamic to occur?

5. It appears unusual that a plaintiff would pay a defendant to settle a lawsuit. After all, if the plaintiff wants the litigation to end, it can seek to voluntarily dismiss its lawsuit. *See* Fed. R. Civ. Proc. 41(a). Are there legitimate — not anticompetitive — reasons why a patentholder would pay an accused infringer to settle?

6. Does a large settlement payment suggest that there is something wrong with the patent? Should the underlying patent receive judicial scrutiny or re-examination by the USPTO? See Christina Bohannan & Herbert Hovenkamp, Creation Without Restraint: Promoting Liberty and Rivalry in Innovation 93–96 (2012) (noting limitations on this approach); Gregory Dolin, *Reverse Settlements as Patent Invalidity Signals*, 24 Harv. J.L. & Tech. 281 (2011) (defending it).

7. For further reading, see Herbert Hovenkamp, Mark D. Janis, Mark A. Lemley & Christopher R. Leslie, IP and Antitrust § 15.3 (2d ed. Supp. 2013).

Antitrust Guidelines for the Licensing of Intellectual Property

Government Guidelines concerning the licensing of patents and other intellectual property rights take a generally benign attitude toward joint ventures that involve patent or copyright licensing. *Antitrust Guidelines for the Licensing of Intellectual Property* (1995), *available at* http://www.justice.gov/atr/public/guidelines/0558.htm. Under these Guidelines "the licensor and the licensee [of an intellectual property right] are deemed to be horizontal competitors only if they own or control technologies that are economic substitutes for each other or if they are competitors in a goods market other than through the use by the licensee of the licensed technology." Further, "[h]orizontal restraints in licensing arrangements that constitute price fixing, allocation of markets or customers, agreements to reduce output, and certain group boycotts may merit per se treatment." Beyond that, however, the rule of reason will be applied. The Guidelines then create a "safety zone" of reasonableness when the licensor and licensees collectively account for less than 20% of any market affected by the restraint. *Id.* at § 4.1.

If a joint activity does not fall within the safety zone, the Antitrust Division will first inquire whether the restraint has an anticompetitive effect. If so, it then asks whether "the restraint is reasonably necessary to achieve procompetitive benefits that outweigh those anticompetitive effects." *Id.* at § 4.2. Possible anticompetitive effects will be assessed by a structural inquiry similar to that described in the government's *2010 Horizontal Merger Guidelines*, at least if two or more of the parties are deemed to be competitors. (The *2010 Horizontal Merger Guidelines* are reprinted as Appendix A in this casebook.) By contrast, if the relationship between the licensor and licensee is vertical, "harm to competition from a restraint may occur if it forecloses access to, or increases competitors' costs of obtaining, important inputs (other than as a natural consequence of the licensee acquiring a licensed technology for its own use)." *See Intellectual Property Guidelines*, § 4.3.1:

> An example is a licensing arrangement with most of the established manufacturers in an industry preventing those manufacturers from using any other technology. The risk of foreclosing access or increasing competitors' costs is related to the fraction of the markets affected by the licensing restraint and to other characteristics of the input and output markets, such as concentration, difficulty of entry, and elasticities of supply and demand.

Licensing arrangements meriting particularly close attention under the rule of reason involve exclusivity, in the sense that the licensor (1) forbids the licensee from licensing others; (2) limits the uses that the licensee may make of the licensed technology; or (3) restrains the licensee in the use of competing technologies. The Guidelines indicate that (1) and (2) raise competitive concerns only if the licensor and licensees are actual or potential competitors absent the licensing arrangement itself. § 4.3.2. In all cases, if a threat to competition is found, the rule of reason inquiry requires an examination of efficiencies (§ 4.4) and less restrictive alternatives. On the latter, the Guidelines note that:

> The existence of practical and significantly less restrictive alternatives is relevant to a determination of whether a restraint is reasonably necessary. If it is clear that the parties could have achieved similar efficiencies by means that are significantly less restrictive, then the Department will not

give weight to the parties' efficiency claim. In making this assessment, however, the Department will not engage in a search for a theoretically least restrictive alternative that might be easier to construct in hindsight than in the practical prospective business situation faced by the parties.

Id.

The Department also identifies a category of licensing agreements that are subject to a "quick look" analysis, falling somewhere between per se and full rule of reason inquiry. *Id.* at § 4.5. "When the restraint is one that ordinarily warrants per se treatment, and a quick look at the claimed efficiencies reveals that the restraint is not reasonably necessary to achieve procompetitive efficiencies, the Department will likely challenge the restraint without further analysis."

Why do agreements involving intellectual property rights warrant special consideration under antitrust laws?

Chapter 5

VERTICAL RESTRICTIONS

I INTRABRAND DISTRIBUTIONAL RESTRAINTS

The preceding chapter considered agreements between competitors, or firms operating at the same level of activity in the same market. The antitrust concern there centered mainly on conduct which facilitated collusion among them. But restraints may also develop between firms at different levels in the production and distribution network. Agreements between a manufacturer and distributor, or between a wholesaler and retailer, or between any two sequential parties in a production-distribution chain, are characterized as "vertical."

Contractual arrangements between participants in the production-distribution chain may be similar to those discussed in the chapter on horizontal agreements. For example, a manufacturer may set the price at which the product will be distributed, or limit distributors to an exclusive territory, or allocate customers to distributors, thereby precluding the distributors from selling outside their designated area or to customers of another distributor. Still other vertical agreements may require distributors, wholesalers, or retailers to deal only in the products of a certain manufacturer, or may require those customers to take additional products if they want to purchase a particular product from the manufacturer.

Generally, the restraints discussed in this chapter can be classified as restrictions on production or distribution and restrictions foreclosing competition. Vertical agreements may take many forms, but different objectives and consequences may result, requiring distinctions to be drawn between vertical and horizontal restraints. The problems discussed in this chapter often come up in the context of franchise agreements, where the manufacturer desires to control the distribution of its products downstream.

[A] Rationales

The questions addressed in this chapter are whether vertical restraints should be condemned under the Sherman and Clayton Acts and, if so, under what standard they should be judged. The law of vertical restraints has been subject to significant reconsideration over the last several decades. Like horizontal agreements, vertical restraints may be used to facilitate horizontal collusion. The instigation for such a restraint might come from either a dealer cartel or manufacturer cartel. The vertical restraint may be used to promote price fixing or create barriers to entry that foreclose competition. Such consequences or objectives do not necessarily follow from a vertical agreement, however. If the effect or intent of a vertical agreement is to limit horizontal competition or foreclose competitors from the market, a restraint of trade can be demonstrated. But the vertical restraint may be designed instead to increase distributional efficiency and welfare in the intrabrand market so as to promote competition in the larger interbrand market.

One justification advanced for the use of vertical restraints is to permit manufacturers and dealers to avoid "free-rider" problems. Depending on the nature of the product, incentives may be necessary to encourage retail dealers to represent effectively the manufacturer's product. Restraints may be designed to encourage maintenance of product quality and promotion of the product at the vertical level. If distributional restraints are not enforced uniformly, distributors that adhere to restraints will incur costs associated with the restraints, while those that do not will have lower costs. With lower costs, the maverick distributor will be able to sell the product at a price below that of the cooperating distributor by taking a "free ride" on the promotion of the product by the cooperative distributor, thus reducing the incentive to adhere to the vertical restraint. The presence of the successful free-rider will cause the cooperative distributor to lose sales. The result may be that in the absence of an enforceable vertical restraint, the manufacturer will be unable to control the manner in which the product is marketed, sold, or serviced. This in turn may affect the image of the manufacturer's product and ultimately the effectiveness of the product. *See* HERBERT HOVENKAMP, FEDERAL ANTITRUST POLICY: THE LAW OF COMPETITION AND ITS PRACTICE, §§ 11.2–11.3 (4th ed. 2011); Richard A. Posner, *The Next Step in the Antitrust Treatment of Restricted Distribution: Per Se Legality*, 48 U. CHI. L. REV. 6 (1981); Lester Telser, *Why Should Manufacturers Want Fair Trade?*, 3 J.L. & ECON. 86 (1960).

The free rider problem suggests that the economic incentives of manufacturer and dealer are not always similar. While promotion of the product should benefit both manufacturer and dealer, how the product is promoted and serviced and the price at which it is sold are considerations over which the parties may have divergent viewpoints. Vertical restraints play a role in reconciling marketing techniques, with the result that distribution efficiencies may increase for the manufacturer while at the same time they may reduce intrabrand competition. In order to reconcile increased distributional efficiency with the risk of reduced competition, as the following cases indicate, courts have begun to apply a broader balancing analysis in determining the legality of certain vertical restraints, while maintaining *per se* rules for others.

As you explore the diverse approaches utilized by the courts, consider whether legal and economic policies support the distinctions drawn between vertical price and nonprice restraints. Consider the role that evidence of industry structure might play in determining the legality of the vertical restraint. Might the structure of the industry dictate whether the vertical restraint facilitates cartelization (collusion among competitors) at either the dealer or manufacturing level? Should the legality of the restraint vary depending on whether the restraint imposed is due to pressure from dealers who are interested in price coordination, or whether it is a genuine device designed to increase the manufacturer's distribution efficiency? Should it matter whether any resulting anticompetitive effects occur at the manufacturer level or retail level? Consider also what evidentiary relevancy there is to a market characterized by vertical restraints and substantial barriers to entry at the manufacturing level.

[B]   Resale Price Maintenance

[1]   Setting Vertical Minimum Prices

LEEGIN CREATIVE LEATHER PRODUCTS, INC. v. PSKS, INC., dba KAY'S KLOSET . . . KAY'S SHOES
551 U.S. 877 (2007)

JUSTICE KENNEDY delivered the opinion of the Court.

In *Dr. Miles Medical Co. v. John D. Park & Sons Co.*, 220 U.S. 373 (1911), the Court established the rule that it is *per se* illegal under § 1 of the Sherman Act, 15 U.S.C. § 1, for a manufacturer to agree with its distributor to set the minimum price the distributor can charge for the manufacturer's goods. The question presented by the instant case is whether the Court should overrule the *per se* rule and allow resale price maintenance agreements to be judged by the rule of reason, the usual standard applied to determine if there is a violation of § 1. The Court has abandoned the rule of *per se* illegality for other vertical restraints a manufacturer imposes on its distributors. Respected economic analysts, furthermore, conclude that vertical price restraints can have procompetitive effects. We now hold that *Dr. Miles* should be overruled and that vertical price restraints are to be judged by the rule of reason.

I

Petitioner, Leegin Creative Leather Products, Inc. (Leegin), designs, manufactures, and distributes leather goods and accessories. In 1991, Leegin began to sell belts under the brand name "Brighton." The Brighton brand has now expanded into a variety of women's fashion accessories. It is sold across the United States in over 5,000 retail establishments, for the most part independent, small boutiques and specialty stores. Leegin's president, Jerry Kohl, also has an interest in about 70 stores that sell Brighton products. Leegin asserts that, at least for its products, small retailers treat customers better, provide customers more services, and make their shopping experience more satisfactory than do larger, often impersonal retailers. Kohl explained: "[W]e want the consumers to get a different experience than they get in Sam's Club or in Wal-Mart. And you can't get that kind of experience or support or customer service from a store like Wal-Mart."

Respondent, PSKS, Inc. (PSKS), operates Kay's Kloset, a women's apparel store in Lewisville, Texas. Kay's Kloset buys from about 75 different manufacturers and at one time sold the Brighton brand. It first started purchasing Brighton goods from Leegin in 1995. Once it began selling the brand, the store promoted Brighton. For example, it ran Brighton advertisements and had Brighton days in the store. Kay's Kloset became the destination retailer in the area to buy Brighton products. Brighton was the store's most important brand and once accounted for 40 to 50 percent of its profits.

In 1997, Leegin instituted the "Brighton Retail Pricing and Promotion Policy." Following the policy, Leegin refused to sell to retailers that discounted Brighton goods below suggested prices. The policy contained an exception for products not selling well that the retailer did not plan on reordering. In the letter to retailers establishing the policy, Leegin stated:

> "In this age of mega stores like Macy's, Bloomingdales, May Co. and others, consumers are perplexed by promises of product quality and support of product which we believe is lacking in these large stores. Consumers are further confused by the ever popular sale, sale, sale, etc.

> "We, at Leegin, choose to break away from the pack by selling [at] specialty stores; specialty stores that can offer the customer great quality merchandise, superb service, and support the Brighton product 365 days a year on a consistent basis.

> "We realize that half the equation is Leegin producing great Brighton product and the other half is you, our retailer, creating great looking stores selling our products in a quality manner." *Ibid.*

Leegin adopted the policy to give its retailers sufficient margins to provide customers the service central to its distribution strategy. It also expressed concern that discounting harmed Brighton's brand image and reputation.

A year after instituting the pricing policy Leegin introduced a marketing strategy known as the "Heart Store Program." It offered retailers incentives to become Heart Stores, and, in exchange, retailers pledged, among other things, to sell at Leegin's suggested prices. Kay's Kloset became a Heart Store soon after Leegin created the program. After a Leegin employee visited the store and found it unattractive, the parties appear to have agreed that Kay's Kloset would not be a Heart Store beyond 1998. Despite losing this status, Kay's Kloset continued to increase its Brighton sales.

In December 2002, Leegin discovered Kay's Kloset had been marking down Brighton's entire line by 20 percent. Kay's Kloset contended it placed Brighton products on sale to compete with nearby retailers who also were undercutting Leegin's suggested prices. Leegin, nonetheless, requested that Kay's Kloset cease discounting. Its request refused, Leegin stopped selling to the store. The loss of the Brighton brand had a considerable negative impact on the store's revenue from sales.

. . . .

II

Section 1 of the Sherman Act prohibits "[e]very contract, combination in the form of trust or otherwise, or conspiracy, in restraint of trade or commerce among the several States." While § 1 could be interpreted to proscribe all contracts, *see, e.g.,* *Board of Trade of Chicago v. United States*, 246 U.S. 231, 238 (1918), the Court has never "taken a literal approach to [its] language," *Texaco Inc. v. Dagher*, 547 U.S. 1, 5 (2006). Rather, the Court has repeated time and again that § 1 "outlaw[s] only unreasonable restraints." *State Oil Co. v. Khan*, 522 U.S. 3, 10 (1997).

The rule of reason is the accepted standard for testing whether a practice restrains trade in violation of § 1. "Under this rule, the factfinder weighs all of the circumstances of a case in deciding whether a restrictive practice should be prohibited as imposing an unreasonable restraint on competition." *Continental T. V., Inc. v. GTE Sylvania Inc.*, 433 U.S. 36, 49 (1977). Appropriate factors to take into account include "specific information about the relevant business" and "the restraint's history, nature, and effect." Whether the businesses involved have market power is a further, significant consideration. In its design and function the rule distinguishes between restraints with anticompetitive effect that are harmful to the consumer and restraints stimulating competition that are in the consumer's best interest.

The rule of reason does not govern all restraints. Some types "are deemed unlawful *per se*." The *per se* rule, treating categories of restraints as necessarily illegal, eliminates the need to study the reasonableness of an individual restraint in light of the real market forces at work, *Business Electronics Corp. v. Sharp Electronics Corp.*, 485 U.S. 717, 723 (1988); and, it must be acknowledged, the *per se* rule can give clear guidance for certain conduct. Restraints that are *per se* unlawful include horizontal agreements among competitors to fix prices.

Resort to *per se* rules is confined to restraints, like those mentioned, "that would always or almost always tend to restrict competition and decrease output." To justify a *per se* prohibition a restraint must have "manifestly anticompetitive" effects, and "lack . . . any redeeming virtue. . . . "

As a consequence, the *per se* rule is appropriate only after courts have had considerable experience with the type of restraint at issue, see *Broadcast Music, Inc. v. Columbia Broadcasting System, Inc.*, 441 U.S. 1, 9 (1979), and only if courts can predict with confidence that it would be invalidated in all or almost all instances under the rule of reason, see *Arizona v. Maricopa County Medical Soc.*, 457 U.S. 332, 344 (1982). It should come as no surprise, then, that "we have expressed reluctance to adopt *per se* rules with regard to restraints imposed in the context of business relationships where the economic impact of certain practices is not immediately obvious." . . . And, as we have stated, a "departure from the rule-of-reason standard must be based upon demonstrable economic effect rather than . . . upon formalistic line drawing." *GTE Sylvania, supra*, at 58–59.

III

The Court has interpreted *Dr. Miles* as establishing a *per se* rule against a vertical agreement between a manufacturer and its distributor to set minimum resale prices. *See, e.g., Monsanto Co. v. Spray-Rite Service Corp.*, 465 U.S. 752, 761 (1984). In *Dr. Miles* the plaintiff, a manufacturer of medicines, sold its products only to distributors who agreed to resell them at set prices. The Court found the manufacturer's control of resale prices to be unlawful. It relied on the common-law rule that "a general restraint upon alienation is ordinarily invalid." 220 U.S., at 404–405. The Court then explained that the agreements would advantage the distributors, not the manufacturer, and were analogous to a combination among competing distributors, which the law treated as void. *Id.*, at 407–408.

The reasoning of the Court's more recent jurisprudence has rejected the rationales on which *Dr. Miles* was based. By relying on the common-law rule against restraints on alienation, *id.*, at 404–405, the Court justified its decision based on "formalistic" legal doctrine rather than "demonstrable economic effect," *GTE Sylvania, supra*, at 58–59. The Court in *Dr. Miles* relied on a treatise published in 1628, but failed to discuss in detail the business reasons that would motivate a manufacturer situated in 1911 to make use of vertical price restraints. Yet the Sherman Act's use of "restraint of trade" "invokes the common law itself, . . . not merely the static content that the common law had assigned to the term in 1890." *Business Electronics, supra*, at 732. The general restraint on alienation, especially in the age when then-Justice Hughes used the term, tended to evoke policy concerns extraneous to the question that controls here. Usually associated with land, not chattels, the rule arose from restrictions removing real property from the stream of commerce for generations. The Court should be cautious about putting dispositive weight on doctrines from antiquity but of slight relevance. We reaffirm that "the state of the common law 400 or even 100 years ago is irrelevant to the issue before us: the effect of the antitrust laws upon vertical distributional restraints in the American economy today." *GTE Sylvania*, 433 U.S., at 53, n. 21.

Dr. Miles, furthermore, treated vertical agreements a manufacturer makes with its distributors as analogous to a horizontal combination among competing distributors. See 220 U.S., at 407–408. In later cases, however, the Court rejected the approach of reliance on rules governing horizontal restraints when defining rules applicable to vertical ones. *See, e.g.*, *Business Electronics, supra*, at 734 (disclaiming the "notion of equivalence between the scope of horizontal *per se* illegality and that of vertical *per se* illegality"). . . . Our recent cases formulate antitrust principles in accordance with the appreciated differences in economic effect between vertical and horizontal agreements, differences the *Dr. Miles* Court failed to consider.

The reasons upon which *Dr. Miles* relied do not justify a *per se* rule. As a consequence, it is necessary to examine, in the first instance, the economic effects of vertical agreements to fix minimum resale prices, and to determine whether the *per se* rule is nonetheless appropriate. See *Business Electronics*, 485 U.S., at 726.

A

Though each side of the debate can find sources to support its position, it suffices to say here that economics literature is replete with procompetitive justifications for a manufacturer's use of resale price maintenance. *See, e.g.*, Brief for Economists as *Amici Curiae* 16 ("In the theoretical literature, it is essentially undisputed that minimum [resale price maintenance] can have procompetitive effects and that under a variety of market conditions it is unlikely to have anticompetitive effects"); Brief for United States as *Amicus Curiae* 9 ("[T]here is a widespread consensus that permitting a manufacturer to control the price at which its goods are sold may promote *inter* brand competition and consumer welfare in a variety of ways"); ABA Section of Antitrust Law, Antitrust Law and Economics of Product Distribution 76 (2006) ("[T]he bulk of the economic literature on [resale price maintenance] suggests that [it] is more likely to be used to enhance efficiency than for anticompetitive purposes"); *see also* H. Hovenkamp, The Antitrust Enterprise:

Principle and Execution 184–191 (2005) (hereinafter Hovenkamp); R. Bork, The Antitrust Paradox 288–291 (1978) (hereinafter Bork). Even those more skeptical of resale price maintenance acknowledge it can have procompetitive effects. *See, e.g.,* Brief for William S. Comanor et al. as *Amici Curiae* 3 ("[G]iven [the] diversity of effects [of resale price maintenance], one could reasonably take the position that a *rule of reason* rather than a *per se* approach is warranted"); F.M. Scherer & D. Ross, Industrial Market Structure and Economic Performance 558 (3d ed. 1990) (hereinafter Scherer & Ross) ("The overall balance between benefits and costs [of resale price maintenance] is probably close").

The few recent studies documenting the competitive effects of resale price maintenance also cast doubt on the conclusion that the practice meets the criteria for a *per se* rule. See T. Overstreet, Resale Price Maintenance: Economic Theories and Empirical Evidence 170 (1983) (hereinafter Overstreet) (noting that "[e]fficient uses of [resale price maintenance] are evidently not unusual or rare"); *see also* Ippolito, Resale Price Maintenance: Empirical Evidence From Litigation, 34 J. Law & Econ. 263, 292–293 (1991) (hereinafter Ippolito).

The justifications for vertical price restraints are similar to those for other vertical restraints. See *GTE Sylvania*, 433 U.S., at 54–57. Minimum resale price maintenance can stimulate interbrand competition-the competition among manufacturers selling different brands of the same type of product-by reducing intrabrand competition-the competition among retailers selling the same brand. See *id.*, at 51–52. The promotion of interbrand competition is important because "the primary purpose of the antitrust laws is to protect [this type of] competition." *Khan*, 522 U.S., at 15. A single manufacturer's use of vertical price restraints tends to eliminate intrabrand price competition; this in turn encourages retailers to invest in tangible or intangible services or promotional efforts that aid the manufacturer's position as against rival manufacturers. Resale price maintenance also has the potential to give consumers more options so that they can choose among low-price, low-service brands; high-price, high-service brands; and brands that fall in between.

Absent vertical price restraints, the retail services that enhance interbrand competition might be underprovided. This is because discounting retailers can free ride on retailers who furnish services and then capture some of the increased demand those services generate. *GTE Sylvania, supra*, at 55. Consumers might learn, for example, about the benefits of a manufacturer's product from a retailer that invests in fine showrooms, offers product demonstrations, or hires and trains knowledgeable employees. R. Posner, Antitrust Law 172–173 (2d ed. 2001) (hereinafter Posner). Or consumers might decide to buy the product because they see it in a retail establishment that has a reputation for selling high-quality merchandise. Marvel & McCafferty, Resale Price Maintenance and Quality Certification, 15 Rand J. Econ. 346, 347–349 (1984). If the consumer can then buy the product from a retailer that discounts because it has not spent capital providing services or developing a quality reputation, the high-service retailer will lose sales to the discounter, forcing it to cut back its services to a level lower than consumers would otherwise prefer. Minimum resale price maintenance alleviates the problem because it prevents the discounter from undercutting the service provider. With price competition decreased, the manufacturer's retailers compete among themselves over services.

Resale price maintenance, in addition, can increase interbrand competition by facilitating market entry for new firms and brands. "[N]ew manufacturers and manufacturers entering new markets can use the restrictions in order to induce competent and aggressive retailers to make the kind of investment of capital and labor that is often required in the distribution of products unknown to the consumer." *GTE Sylvania, supra,* at 55; see Marvel & McCafferty 349 (noting that reliance on a retailer's reputation "will decline as the manufacturer's brand becomes better known, so that [resale price maintenance] may be particularly important as a competitive device for new entrants"). New products and new brands are essential to a dynamic economy, and if markets can be penetrated by using resale price maintenance there is a procompetitive effect.

Resale price maintenance can also increase interbrand competition by encouraging retailer services that would not be provided even absent free riding. It may be difficult and inefficient for a manufacturer to make and enforce a contract with a retailer specifying the different services the retailer must perform. Offering the retailer a guaranteed margin and threatening termination if it does not live up to expectations may be the most efficient way to expand the manufacturer's market share by inducing the retailer's performance and allowing it to use its own initiative and experience in providing valuable services. See Mathewson & Winter, The Law and Economics of Resale Price Maintenance, 13 Rev. Indus. Org. 57, 74–75 (1998) (hereinafter Mathewson & Winter); Klein & Murphy, Vertical Restraints as Contract Enforcement Mechanisms, 31 J. Law & Econ. 265, 295 (1988); *see also* Deneckere, Marvel, & Peck, Demand Uncertainty, Inventories, and Resale Price Maintenance, 111 Q.J. Econ. 885, 911 (1996) (noting that resale price maintenance may be beneficial to motivate retailers to stock adequate inventories of a manufacturer's goods in the face of uncertain consumer demand).

B

While vertical agreements setting minimum resale prices can have procompetitive justifications, they may have anticompetitive effects in other cases; and unlawful price fixing, designed solely to obtain monopoly profits, is an ever present temptation. Resale price maintenance may, for example, facilitate a manufacturer cartel. See *Business Electronics,* 485 U.S., at 725. An unlawful cartel will seek to discover if some manufacturers are undercutting the cartel's fixed prices. Resale price maintenance could assist the cartel in identifying price-cutting manufacturers who benefit from the lower prices they offer. Resale price maintenance, furthermore, could discourage a manufacturer from cutting prices to retailers with the concomitant benefit of cheaper prices to consumers.

Vertical price restraints also "might be used to organize cartels at the retailer level." *Business Electronics, supra,* at 725–726. A group of retailers might collude to fix prices to consumers and then compel a manufacturer to aid the unlawful arrangement with resale price maintenance. In that instance the manufacturer does not establish the practice to stimulate services or to promote its brand but to give inefficient retailers higher profits. Retailers with better distribution systems and lower cost structures would be prevented from charging lower prices by the agreement. See Posner 172; Overstreet 13-19. Historical examples suggest this possibility is a legitimate concern. *See, e.g.*, Marvel & McCafferty, The Welfare Effects of Resale Price Maintenance, 28 J. Law & Econ. 363, 373 (1985) (hereinafter Marvel) (providing an example of the power of the National Association of Retail Druggists to compel manufacturers to use resale price maintenance); Hovenkamp 186 (suggesting that the retail druggists in *Dr. Miles* formed a cartel and used manufacturers to enforce it).

A horizontal cartel among competing manufacturers or competing retailers that decreases output or reduces competition in order to increase price is, and ought to be, *per se* unlawful. See *Texaco*, 547 U.S., at 5; *GTE Sylvania*, 433 U.S., at 58, n. 28. To the extent a vertical agreement setting minimum resale prices is entered upon to facilitate either type of cartel, it, too, would need to be held unlawful under the rule of reason. This type of agreement may also be useful evidence for a plaintiff attempting to prove the existence of a horizontal cartel.

Resale price maintenance, furthermore, can be abused by a powerful manufacturer or retailer. A dominant retailer, for example, might request resale price maintenance to forestall innovation in distribution that decreases costs. A manufacturer might consider it has little choice but to accommodate the retailer's demands for vertical price restraints if the manufacturer believes it needs access to the retailer's distribution network. See Overstreet 31; 8 P. Areeda & H. Hovenkamp, Antitrust Law 47 (2d ed. 2004) (hereinafter Areeda & Hovenkamp); cf. *Toys "R" Us, Inc. v. FTC*, 221 F.3d 928, 937–938 (C.A.7 2000). A manufacturer with market power, by comparison, might use resale price maintenance to give retailers an incentive not to sell the products of smaller rivals or new entrants. *See, e.g.*, Marvel 366–368. As should be evident, the potential anticompetitive consequences of vertical price restraints must not be ignored or underestimated.

C

Notwithstanding the risks of unlawful conduct, it cannot be stated with any degree of confidence that resale price maintenance "always or almost always tend[s] to restrict competition and decrease output." *Business Electronics, supra*, at 723 (internal quotation marks omitted). Vertical agreements establishing minimum resale prices can have either procompetitive or anticompetitive effects, depending upon the circumstances in which they are formed. And although the empirical evidence on the topic is limited, it does not suggest efficient uses of the agreements are infrequent or hypothetical. See Overstreet 170; *see also id.*, at 80 (noting that for the majority of enforcement actions brought by the Federal Trade Commission between 1965 and 1982, "the use of [resale price maintenance] was not likely motivated by collusive dealers who had successfully coerced their suppliers"); Ippolito 292 (reaching a similar conclusion). As the rule would proscribe a significant amount of procompetitive conduct, these agreements appear ill suited for *per se* condemnation.

Respondent contends, nonetheless, that vertical price restraints should be *per se* unlawful because of the administrative convenience of *per se* rules. *See, e.g.*, *GTE Sylvania, supra*, at 50, n. 16 (noting "*per se* rules tend to provide guidance to the business community and to minimize the burdens on litigants and the judicial system"). That argument suggests *per se* illegality is the rule rather than the exception. This misinterprets our antitrust law. *Per se* rules may decrease administrative costs, but that is only part of the equation. Those rules can be counterproductive. They can increase the total cost of the antitrust system by prohibiting procompetitive conduct the antitrust laws should encourage. See Easterbrook, Vertical Arrangements and the Rule of Reason, 53 Antitrust L.J. 135, 158 (1984). They also may increase litigation costs by promoting frivolous suits against legitimate practices. The Court has thus explained that administrative "advantages are not sufficient in themselves to justify the creation of *per se* rules," *GTE Sylvania*, 433 U.S., at 50, n. 16, and has relegated their use to restraints that are "manifestly anticompetitive," *id.*, at 49–50. Were the Court now to conclude that vertical price restraints should be *per se* illegal based on administrative costs, we would undermine, if not overrule, the traditional "demanding standards" for adopting *per se* rules. *Id.*, at 50. Any possible reduction in administrative costs cannot alone justify the *Dr. Miles* rule.

Respondent also argues the *per se* rule is justified because a vertical price restraint can lead to higher prices for the manufacturer's goods. *See also* Overstreet 160 (noting that "price surveys indicate that [resale price maintenance] in most cases increased the prices of products sold"). Respondent is mistaken in relying on pricing effects absent a further showing of anticompetitive conduct. Cf. *id.*, at 106 (explaining that price surveys "do not necessarily tell us anything conclusive about the welfare effects of [resale price maintenance] because the results are generally consistent with both procompetitive and anticompetitive theories"). For, as has been indicated already, the antitrust laws are designed primarily to protect interbrand competition, from which lower prices can later result. See *Khan*, 522 U.S., at 15. The Court, moreover, has evaluated other vertical restraints under the rule of reason even though prices can be increased in the course of promoting procompetitive effects. *See, e.g., Business Electronics*, 485 U.S., at 728. And resale price maintenance may reduce prices if manufacturers have resorted to costlier alternatives of controlling resale prices that are not *per se* unlawful. See *infra*, at 22–25; *see also* Marvel 371.

Respondent's argument, furthermore, overlooks that, in general, the interests of manufacturers and consumers are aligned with respect to retailer profit margins. The difference between the price a manufacturer charges retailers and the price retailers charge consumers represents part of the manufacturer's cost of distribution, which, like any other cost, the manufacturer usually desires to minimize. See *GTE Sylvania*, 433 U.S., at 56, n. 24; *see also id.*, at 56 ("Economists . . . have argued that manufacturers have an economic interest in maintaining as much intrabrand competition as is consistent with the efficient distribution of their products"). A manufacturer has no incentive to overcompensate retailers with unjustified margins. The retailers, not the manufacturer, gain from higher retail prices. The manufacturer often loses; interbrand competition reduces its competitiveness and market share because consumers will "substitute a different brand of the same product." *Id.*, at 52, n. 19; see *Business Electronics, supra*, at 725. As a general matter, therefore, a single manufacturer will desire to set minimum resale prices only if the "increase in demand resulting from enhanced service . . . will more than offset a negative impact on demand of a higher retail price." Mathewson & Winter 67.

The implications of respondent's position are far reaching. Many decisions a manufacturer makes and carries out through concerted action can lead to higher prices. A manufacturer might, for example, contract with different suppliers to obtain better inputs that improve product quality. Or it might hire an advertising agency to promote awareness of its goods. Yet no one would think these actions violate the Sherman Act because they lead to higher prices. The antitrust laws do not require manufacturers to produce generic goods that consumers do not know about or want. The manufacturer strives to improve its product quality or to promote its brand because it believes this conduct will lead to increased demand despite higher prices. The same can hold true for resale price maintenance.

Resale price maintenance, it is true, does have economic dangers. If the rule of reason were to apply to vertical price restraints, courts would have to be diligent in eliminating their anticompetitive uses from the market. This is a realistic objective, and certain factors are relevant to the inquiry. For example, the number of manufacturers that make use of the practice in a given industry can provide important instruction. When only a few manufacturers lacking market power adopt the practice, there is little likelihood it is facilitating a manufacturer cartel, for a cartel then can be undercut by rival manufacturers. See Overstreet 22; Bork 294. Likewise, a retailer cartel is unlikely when only a single manufacturer in a competitive market uses resale price maintenance. Interbrand competition would divert consumers to lower priced substitutes and eliminate any gains to retailers from their price-fixing agreement over a single brand. See Posner 172; Bork 292. Resale price maintenance should be subject to more careful scrutiny, by contrast, if many competing manufacturers adopt the practice. Cf. Scherer & Ross 558 (noting that "except when [resale price maintenance] spreads to cover the bulk of an industry's output, depriving consumers of a meaningful choice between high-service and low-price outlets, most [resale price maintenance arrangements] are probably innocuous"); Easterbrook 162 (suggesting that "every one of the potentially-anticompetitive outcomes of vertical arrangements depends on the uniformity of the practice").

The source of the restraint may also be an important consideration. If there is evidence retailers were the impetus for a vertical price restraint, there is a greater likelihood that the restraint facilitates a retailer cartel or supports a dominant, inefficient retailer. See Brief for William S. Comanor et al. as *Amici Curiae* 7–8. If, by contrast, a manufacturer adopted the policy independent of retailer pressure, the restraint is less likely to promote anticompetitive conduct. Cf. Posner 177 ("It makes all the difference whether minimum retail prices are imposed by the manufacturer in order to evoke point-of-sale services or by the dealers in order to obtain monopoly profits"). A manufacturer also has an incentive to protest inefficient retailer-induced price restraints because they can harm its competitive position.

As a final matter, that a dominant manufacturer or retailer can abuse resale price maintenance for anticompetitive purposes may not be a serious concern unless the relevant entity has market power. If a retailer lacks market power, manufacturers likely can sell their goods through rival retailers. *See also Business Electronics, supra,* at 727, n. 2 (noting "[r]etail market power is rare, because of the usual presence of interbrand competition and other dealers"). And if a manufacturer lacks market power, there is less likelihood it can use the practice to keep competitors away from distribution outlets.

The rule of reason is designed and used to eliminate anticompetitive transactions from the market. This standard principle applies to vertical price restraints. A party alleging injury from a vertical agreement setting minimum resale prices will have, as a general matter, the information and resources available to show the existence of the agreement and its scope of operation. As courts gain experience considering the effects of these restraints by applying the rule of reason over the course of decisions, they can establish the litigation structure to ensure the rule operates to eliminate anticompetitive restraints from the market and to provide more guidance to businesses. Courts can, for example, devise rules over time for offering proof, or even presumptions where justified, to make the rule of reason a fair and efficient way to prohibit anticompetitive restraints and to promote procompetitive ones.

For all of the foregoing reasons, we think that were the Court considering the issue as an original matter, the rule of reason, not a *per se* rule of unlawfulness, would be the appropriate standard to judge vertical price restraints.

IV

We do not write on a clean slate, for the decision in *Dr. Miles* is almost a century old. So there is an argument for its retention on the basis of *stare decisis* alone. Even if *Dr. Miles* established an erroneous rule, "[s]tare decisis reflects a policy judgment that in most matters it is more important that the applicable rule of law be settled than that it be settled right." *Khan*, 522 U.S., at 20. And concerns about maintaining settled law are strong when the question is one of statutory interpretation. *See, e.g., Hohn v. United States*, 524 U.S. 236, 251 (1998).

Stare decisis is not as significant in this case, however, because the issue before us is the scope of the Sherman Act. *Khan, supra*, at 20 ("[T]he general presumption that legislative changes should be left to Congress has less force with respect to the Sherman Act"). From the beginning the Court has treated the Sherman Act as a common-law statute. See *National Soc. of Professional Engineers v. United States*, 435 U.S. 679, 688 (1978); *see also Northwest Airlines, Inc. v. Transport Workers*, 451 U.S. 77, 98, n. 42 (1981) ("In antitrust, the federal courts . . . act more as common-law courts than in other areas governed by federal statute"). Just as the common law adapts to modern understanding and greater experience, so too does the Sherman Act's prohibition on "restraint[s] of trade" evolve to meet the dynamics of present economic conditions. The case-by-case adjudication contemplated by the rule of reason has implemented this common-law approach. See *National Soc. of Professional Engineers, supra*, at 688. Likewise, the boundaries of the doctrine of *per se* illegality should not be immovable. For "[i]t would make no sense to create out of the single term 'restraint of trade' a chronologically schizoid statute, in which a 'rule of reason' evolves with new circumstance and new wisdom, but a line of *per se* illegality remains forever fixed where it was." *Business Electronics*, 485 U.S., at 732.

A

Stare decisis, we conclude, does not compel our continued adherence to the *per se* rule against vertical price restraints. As discussed earlier, respected authorities in the economics literature suggest the *per se* rule is inappropriate, and there is now widespread agreement that resale price maintenance can have procompetitive effects. *See, e.g.*, Brief for Economists as *Amici Curiae* 16. It is also significant that both the Department of Justice and the Federal Trade Commission-the antitrust enforcement agencies with the ability to assess the long-term impacts of resale price maintenance-have recommended that this Court replace the *per se* rule with the traditional rule of reason. See Brief for United States as *Amicus Curiae* 6. In the antitrust context the fact that a decision has been "called into serious question" justifies our reevaluation of it. *Khan, supra*, at 21.

Other considerations reinforce the conclusion that *Dr. Miles* should be overturned. Of most relevance, "we have overruled our precedents when subsequent cases have undermined their doctrinal underpinnings." *Dickerson v. United States*, 530 U.S. 428, 443 (2000). The Court's treatment of vertical restraints has progressed away from *Dr. Miles'* strict approach. We have distanced ourselves from the opinion's rationales. See *supra*, at 7–8; *see also Khan, supra*, at 21 (overruling a case when "the views underlying [it had been] eroded by this Court's precedent") ; *Rodriguez de Quijas v. Shearson/American Express, Inc.*, 490 U.S. 477, 480–481 (1989) (same). This is unsurprising, for the case was decided not long after enactment of the Sherman Act when the Court had little experience with antitrust analysis. Only eight years after *Dr. Miles*, moreover, the Court reined in the decision by holding that a manufacturer can announce suggested resale prices and refuse to deal with distributors who do not follow them. *Colgate*, 250 U.S., at 307–308.

In more recent cases the Court, following a common-law approach, has continued to temper, limit, or overrule once strict prohibitions on vertical restraints. In 1977, the Court overturned the *per se* rule for vertical nonprice restraints, adopting the rule of reason in its stead. *GTE Sylvania*, 433 U.S., at 57–59 (overruling *United States v. Arnold, Schwinn & Co.*, 388 U.S. 365 (1967)); *see also* 433 U.S., at 58, n. 29 (noting "that the advantages of vertical restrictions should not be limited to the categories of new entrants and failing firms"). While the Court in a footnote in *GTE Sylvania* suggested that differences between vertical price and nonprice restraints could support different legal treatment, see 433 U.S., at 51, n. 18, the central part of the opinion relied on authorities and arguments that find unequal treatment "difficult to justify," *id.*, at 69–70 (White, J., concurring in judgment).

Continuing in this direction, in two cases in the 1980's the Court defined legal rules to limit the reach of *Dr. Miles* and to accommodate the doctrines enunciated in *GTE Sylvania* and *Colgate*. See *Business Electronics, supra*, at 726–728; *Monsanto*, 465 U.S., at 763–764.

. . . .

Most recently, in 1997, after examining the issue of vertical maximum price-fixing agreements in light of commentary and real experience, the Court overruled a 29-year-old precedent treating those agreements as *per se* illegal. *Khan*, 522 U.S., at 22 (overruling *Albrecht v. Herald Co.*, 390 U.S. 145 (1968)). It held instead that they should be evaluated under the traditional rule of reason. 522 U.S., at 22. Our continued limiting of the reach of the decision in *Dr. Miles* and our recent treatment of other vertical restraints justify the conclusion that *Dr. Miles* should not be retained.

The *Dr. Miles* rule is also inconsistent with a principled framework, for it makes little economic sense when analyzed with our other cases on vertical restraints. If we were to decide the procompetitive effects of resale price maintenance were insufficient to overrule *Dr. Miles*, then cases such as *Colgate* and *GTE Sylvania* themselves would be called into question. These later decisions, while they may result in less intrabrand competition, can be justified because they permit manufacturers to secure the procompetitive benefits associated with vertical price restraints through other methods. The other methods, however, could be less efficient for a particular manufacturer to establish and sustain. The end result hinders competition and consumer welfare because manufacturers are forced to engage in second-best alternatives and because consumers are required to shoulder the increased expense of the inferior practices.

. . .

There is yet another consideration. A manufacturer can impose territorial restrictions on distributors and allow only one distributor to sell its goods in a given region. Our cases have recognized, and the economics literature confirms, that these vertical nonprice restraints have impacts similar to those of vertical price restraints; both reduce intrabrand competition and can stimulate retailer services. *See, e.g.,* *Business Electronics, supra,* at 728; *Monsanto, supra,* at 762–763; *see also* Brief for Economists as *Amici Curiae* 17–18. Cf. Scherer & Ross 560 (noting that vertical nonprice restraints "can engender inefficiencies at least as serious as those imposed upon the consumer by resale price maintenance"); Steiner, How Manufacturers Deal with the Price-Cutting Retailer: When Are Vertical Restraints Efficient?, 65 Antitrust L.J. 407, 446–447 (1997) (indicating that "antitrust law should recognize that the consumer interest is often better served by [resale price maintenance]-contrary to its *per se* illegality and the rule-of-reason status of vertical nonprice restraints"). The same legal standard (*per se* unlawfulness) applies to horizontal market division and horizontal price fixing because both have similar economic effect. There is likewise little economic justification for the current differential treatment of vertical price and nonprice restraints. Furthermore, vertical nonprice restraints may prove less efficient for inducing desired services, and they reduce intrabrand competition more than vertical price restraints by eliminating both price and service competition. See Brief for Economists as *Amici Curiae* 17–18.

In sum, it is a flawed antitrust doctrine that serves the interests of lawyers — by creating legal distinctions that operate as traps for the unwary — more than the interests of consumers — by requiring manufacturers to choose second-best options to achieve sound business objectives.

. . . .

For these reasons the Court's decision in *Dr. Miles Medical Co. v. John D. Park*

& Sons Co., 220 U.S. 373 (1911), is now overruled. Vertical price restraints are to be judged according to the rule of reason.

JUSTICE BREYER, with whom JUSTICE STEVENS, JUSTICE SOUTER, and JUSTICE GINSBURG join, dissenting.

In *Dr. Miles*, this Court held that an agreement between a manufacturer of proprietary medicines and its dealers to fix the minimum price at which its medicines could be sold was "invalid . . . under the [Sherman Act, 15 U.S.C. § 1]." This Court has consistently read *Dr. Miles* as establishing a bright-line rule that agreements fixing minimum resale prices are *per se* illegal. *See, e.g., United States v. Trenton Potteries Co.*, 273 U.S. 392, 399–401 (1927); *NYNEX Corp. v. Discon, Inc.*, 525 U.S. 128, 133 (1998). That *per se* rule is one upon which the legal profession, business, and the public have relied for close to a century. Today the Court holds that courts must determine the lawfulness of minimum resale price maintenance by applying, not a bright-line *per se* rule, but a circumstance-specific "rule of reason." *Ante*, at 28. And in doing so it overturns *Dr. Miles*.

The Court justifies its departure from ordinary considerations of *stare decisis* by pointing to a set of arguments well known in the antitrust literature for close to half a century. Congress has repeatedly found in these arguments insufficient grounds for overturning the *per se* rule. *See, e.g.*, Hearings on H.R. 10527 et al. before the Subcommittee on Commerce and Finance of the House Committee on Interstate and Foreign Commerce, 85th Cong., 2d Sess., 74–76, 89, 99, 101–102, 192–195, 261–262 (1958). And, in my view, they do not warrant the Court's now overturning so well-established a legal precedent.

I

The Sherman Act seeks to maintain a marketplace free of anticompetitive practices, in particular those enforced by agreement among private firms. The law assumes that such a marketplace, free of private restrictions, will tend to bring about the lower prices, better products, and more efficient production processes that consumers typically desire. In determining the lawfulness of particular practices, courts often apply a "rule of reason." They examine both a practice's likely anticompetitive effects and its beneficial business justifications. . . .

Nonetheless, sometimes the likely anticompetitive consequences of a particular practice are so serious and the potential justifications so few (or, *e.g.*, so difficult to prove) that courts have departed from a pure "rule of reason" approach. And sometimes this Court has imposed a rule of *per se* unlawfulness-a rule that instructs courts to find the practice unlawful all (or nearly all) the time.

. . . .

The arguments focus on three sets of considerations, those involving: (1) potential anticompetitive effects, (2) potential benefits, and (3) administration. The difficulty arises out of the fact that the different sets of considerations point in different directions. . . .

On the one hand, agreements setting minimum resale prices may have serious anticompetitive consequences. *In respect to dealers:* Resale price maintenance agreements, rather like horizontal price agreements, can diminish or eliminate price competition among dealers of a single brand or (if practiced generally by manufacturers) among multibrand dealers. In doing so, they can prevent dealers from offering customers the lower prices that many customers prefer; they can prevent dealers from responding to changes in demand, say falling demand, by cutting prices; they can encourage dealers to substitute service, for price, competition, thereby threatening wastefully to attract too many resources into that portion of the industry; they can inhibit expansion by more efficient dealers whose lower prices might otherwise attract more customers, stifling the development of new, more efficient modes of retailing; and so forth. . . .

In respect to producers: Resale price maintenance agreements can help to reinforce the competition-inhibiting behavior of firms in concentrated industries. In such industries firms may tacitly collude, *i.e.,* observe each other's pricing behavior, each understanding that price cutting by one firm is likely to trigger price competition by all. . . . Where that is so, resale price maintenance can make it easier for each producer to identify (by observing retail markets) when a competitor has begun to cut prices. And a producer who cuts wholesale prices *without* lowering the minimum resale price will stand to gain little, if anything, in increased profits, because the dealer will be unable to stimulate increased consumer demand by passing along the producer's price cut to consumers. In either case, resale price maintenance agreements will tend to prevent price competition from "breaking out"; and they will thereby tend to stabilize producer prices. . . .

Those who express concern about the potential anticompetitive effects find empirical support in the behavior of prices before, and then after, Congress in 1975 repealed the Miller-Tydings Fair Trade Act, 50 Stat. 693, and the McGuire Act, 66 Stat. 631. Those Acts had permitted (but not required) individual States to enact "fair trade" laws authorizing minimum resale price maintenance. At the time of repeal minimum resale price maintenance was lawful in 36 States; it was unlawful in 14 States. See Hearings on S. 408 before the Subcommittee on Antitrust and Monopoly of the Senate Committee on the Judiciary, 94th Cong., 1st Sess., 173 (1975) (hereinafter Hearings on S. 408) (statement of Thomas E. Kauper, Assistant Attorney General, Antitrust Division). Comparing prices in the former States with prices in the latter States, the Department of Justice argued that minimum resale price maintenance had raised prices by 19% to 27%. See Hearings on H.R. 2384 before the Subcommittee on Monopolies and Commercial Law of the House Committee on the Judiciary, 94th Cong., 1st Sess., 122 (1975) (hereinafter Hearings on H.R. 2384) (statement of Keith I. Clearwaters, Deputy Assistant Attorney General, Antitrust Division).

After repeal, minimum resale price maintenance agreements were unlawful *per se* in every State. The Federal Trade Commission (FTC) staff, after studying numerous price surveys, wrote that collectively the surveys "indicate[d] that [resale price maintenance] in most cases increased the prices of products sold with [resale price maintenance]." Bureau of Economics Staff Report to the FTC, T. Overstreet, Resale Price Maintenance: Economic Theories and Empirical Evidence, 160 (1983) (hereinafter Overstreet). Most economists today agree that, in the words of a prominent antitrust treatise, "resale price maintenance tends to produce higher consumer prices than would otherwise be the case." 8 Areeda & Hovenkamp & 1604b, at 40 (finding "[t]he evidence . . . persuasive on this point"). *See also* Brief for William S. Comanor and Frederic M. Scherer as *Amici Curiae* 4 ("It is uniformly acknowledged that [resale price maintenance] and other vertical restraints lead to higher consumer prices").

On the other hand, those favoring resale price maintenance have long argued that resale price maintenance agreements can provide important consumer benefits. The majority lists two: First, such agreements can facilitate new entry. For example, a newly entering producer wishing to build a product name might be able to convince dealers to help it do so-if, but only if, the producer can assure those dealers that they will later recoup their investment. Without resale price maintenance, late-entering dealers might take advantage of the earlier investment and, through price competition, drive prices down to the point where the early dealers cannot recover what they spent. By assuring the initial dealers that such later price competition will not occur, resale price maintenance can encourage them to carry the new product, thereby helping the new producer succeed. See 8 Areeda & Hovenkamp ¶¶ 1617a, 1631b, at 193–196, 308. The result might be increased competition at the producer level, *i.e.*, greater *inter*-brand competition, that brings with it net consumer benefits.

Second, without resale price maintenance a producer might find its efforts to sell a product undermined by what resale price maintenance advocates call "free riding." Suppose a producer concludes that it can succeed only if dealers provide certain services, say, product demonstrations, high quality shops, advertising that creates a certain product image, and so forth. Without resale price maintenance, some dealers might take a "free ride" on the investment that others make in providing those services. Such a dealer would save money by not paying for those services and could consequently cut its own price and increase its own sales. Under these circumstances, dealers might prove unwilling to invest in the provision of necessary services. . . .

Moreover, where a producer and not a group of dealers seeks a resale price maintenance agreement, there is a special reason to believe some such benefits exist. That is because, other things being equal, producers should want to encourage price competition among their dealers. By doing so they will often increase profits by selling more of their product. See *Sylvania*, 433 U.S., at 56, n. 24; Bork 290. And that is so, even if the producer possesses sufficient market power to earn a super-normal profit. That is to say, other things being equal, the producer will benefit by charging his dealers a competitive (or even a higher-than-competitive) wholesale price while encouraging price competition among them. Hence, if the producer is the moving force, the producer must have some special reason for wanting resale price maintenance; and in the absence of, say, concentrated producer markets (where that special reason might consist of a desire to stabilize wholesale prices), that special reason may well reflect the special circumstances just described: new entry, "free riding," or variations on those themes.

The upshot is, as many economists suggest, sometimes resale price maintenance can prove harmful; sometimes it can bring benefits. . . . But before concluding that courts should consequently apply a rule of reason, I would ask such questions as, how often are harms or benefits likely to occur? How easy is it to separate the beneficial sheep from the antitrust goats?

Economic discussion, such as the studies the Court relies upon, can *help* provide answers to these questions, and in doing so, economics can, and should, inform antitrust law. But antitrust law cannot, and should not, precisely replicate economists' (sometimes conflicting) views. That is because law, unlike economics, is an administrative system the effects of which depend upon the content of rules and precedents only as they are applied by judges and juries in courts and by lawyers advising their clients. And that fact means that courts will often bring their own administrative judgment to bear, sometimes applying rules of *per se* unlawfulness to business practices even when those practices sometimes produce benefits. *See, e.g.*, F.M. Scherer & D. Ross, Industrial Market Structure and Economic Performance 335–339 (3d ed. 1990) (hereinafter Scherer & Ross). . . .

I have already described studies and analyses that suggest (though they cannot prove) that resale price maintenance can cause harms with some regularity-and certainly when dealers are the driving force. But what about benefits? How often, for example, will the benefits to which the Court points occur in practice? I can find no economic consensus on this point. There is a consensus in the literature that "free riding" takes place. But "free riding" often takes place in the economy without any legal effort to stop it. . . .

To be more specific, one can easily *imagine* a dealer who refuses to provide important presale services, say a detailed explanation of how a product works (or who fails to provide a proper atmosphere in which to sell expensive perfume or alligator billfolds), lest customers use that "free" service (or enjoy the psychological benefit arising when a high-priced retailer stocks a particular brand of billfold or handbag) and then buy from another dealer at a lower price. Sometimes this must happen in reality. But does it happen often? We do, after all, live in an economy where firms, despite *Dr. Miles'* *per se* rule, still sell complex technical equipment (as well as expensive perfume and alligator billfolds) to consumers.

All this is to say that the ultimate question is not whether, but *how much*, "free riding" of this sort takes place. And, after reading the briefs, I must answer that question with an uncertain "sometimes." . . .

How easily can courts identify instances in which the benefits are likely to outweigh potential harms? My own answer is, *not very easily*. For one thing, it is often difficult to identify *who*-producer or dealer-is the moving force behind any given resale price maintenance agreement. Suppose, for example, several large multibrand retailers all sell resale-price-maintained products. Suppose further that small producers set retail prices because they fear that, otherwise, the large retailers will favor (say, by allocating better shelf-space) the goods of other producers who practice resale price maintenance. Who 'initiated" this practice, the retailers hoping for considerable insulation from retail competition, or the producers, who simply seek to deal best with the circumstances they find? For another thing, as I just said, it is difficult to determine just when, and where, the "free riding" problem is serious enough to warrant legal protection.

. . . .

Are there special advantages to a bright-line rule? Without such a rule, it is often unfair, and consequently impractical, for enforcement officials to bring criminal proceedings. And since enforcement resources are limited, that loss may tempt some producers or dealers to enter into agreements that are, on balance, anticompetitive.

Given the uncertainties that surround key items in the overall balance sheet, particularly in respect to the "administrative" questions, I can concede to the majority that the problem is difficult. And, if forced to decide now, at most I might agree that the *per se* rule should be slightly modified to allow an exception for the more easily identifiable and temporary condition of "new entry." See Pitofsky 1495. But I am not now forced to decide this question. The question before us is not what should be the rule, starting from scratch. We here must decide whether to change a clear and simple price-related antitrust rule that the courts have applied for nearly a century.

II

We write, not on a blank slate, but on a slate that begins with *Dr. Miles* and goes on to list a century's worth of similar cases, massive amounts of advice that lawyers have provided their clients, and untold numbers of business decisions those clients have taken in reliance upon that advice. *See, e.g.*, *United States v. Bausch & Lomb Optical Co.*, 321 U.S. 707, 721 (1944); *Sylvania*, 433 U.S., at 51, n. 18 ("The *per se* illegality of [vertical] price restrictions has been established firmly for many years . . . "). Indeed a Westlaw search shows that *Dr. Miles* itself has been cited dozens of times in this Court and hundreds of times in lower courts. Those who wish this Court to change so well-established a legal precedent bear a heavy burden of proof. See *Illinois Brick Co. v. Illinois*, 431 U.S. 720, 736 (1977). . . . I am not aware of any case in which this Court has overturned so well-established a statutory precedent.

A

. . . .

The one arguable exception consists of the majority's claim that "even absent free riding," resale price maintenance "may be the most efficient way to expand the manufacturer's market share by inducing the retailer's performance and allowing it to use its own initiative and experience in providing valuable services." *Ante*, at 12. I cannot count this as an exception, however, because I do not understand how, in the absence of free-riding (and assuming competitiveness), an established producer would need resale price maintenance. Why, on these assumptions, would a dealer not "expand" its "market share" as best that dealer sees fit, obtaining appropriate payment from consumers in the process? There may be an answer to this question. But I have not seen it. And I do not think that we should place significant weight upon justifications that the parties do not explain with sufficient clarity for a generalist judge to understand.

. . . .

B

With the preceding discussion in mind, I would consult the list of factors that our case law indicates are relevant when we consider overruling an earlier case. Justice Scalia, writing separately in another of our cases this Term, well summarizes that law. See *Wisconsin Right to Life, Inc., ante*, at 19–21. (opinion concurring in part and concurring in judgment). And every relevant factor he mentions argues against overruling *Dr. Miles* here.

First, the Court applies *stare decisis* more "rigidly" in statutory than in constitutional cases. See *Glidden Co. v. Zdanok*, 370 U.S. 530, 543 (1962); *Illinois Brick Co.*, 431 U.S., at 736. This is a statutory case.

Second, the Court does sometimes overrule cases that it decided wrongly only a reasonably short time ago. As Justice Scalia put it, "[o]verruling a *constitutional* case decided just a few years earlier is far from unprecedented." *Wisconsin Right to Life, ante*, at 19 (emphasis added). We here overrule one *statutory* case, *Dr. Miles*, decided 100 years ago, and we overrule the cases that reaffirmed its *per se* rule in the intervening years. . . .

Third, the fact that a decision creates an "unworkable" legal regime argues in favor of overruling. See *Payne v. Tennessee*, 501 U.S. 808, 827–828 (1991); *Swift & Co. v. Wickham*, 382 U.S. 111, 116 (1965). Implementation of the *per se* rule, even with the complications attendant the exception allowed for in *United States v. Colgate & Co.*, 250 U.S. 300 (1919), has proved practical over the course of the last century, particularly when compared with the many complexities of litigating a case under the "rule of reason" regime. No one has shown how moving from the *Dr. Miles* regime to "rule of reason" analysis would make the legal regime governing minimum resale price maintenance more "administrable," *Wisconsin Right to Life, ante*, at 20 (opinion of Scalia, J.), particularly since *Colgate* would remain good law with respect to *unreasonable* price maintenance.

Fourth, the fact that a decision "unsettles" the law may argue in favor of overruling. See *Sylvania*, 433 U.S., at 47; *Wisconsin Right to Life, ante*, at 20–21 (opinion of Scalia, J.). The *per se* rule is well-settled law, as the Court itself has previously recognized. *Sylvania, supra*, at 51, n. 18. It is the majority's change here that will unsettle the law.

Fifth, the fact that a case involves property rights or contract rights, where reliance interests are involved, argues against overruling. *Payne, supra*, at 828. This case involves contract rights and perhaps property rights (consider shopping malls). And there has been considerable reliance upon the *per se* rule. As I have said, Congress relied upon the continued vitality of *Dr. Miles* when it repealed Miller-Tydings and McGuire. *Supra*, at 12–13. The Executive Branch argued for repeal on the assumption that *Dr. Miles* stated the law. *Ibid.* Moreover, whole sectors of the economy have come to rely upon the *per se* rule. A factory outlet store tells us that the rule "form[s] an essential part of the regulatory background against which [that firm] and many other discount retailers have financed, structured, and operated their businesses." Brief for Burlington Coat Factory Warehouse Corp. as *Amicus Curiae* 5. The Consumer Federation of America tells us that large low-price retailers would not exist without *Dr. Miles*; minimum resale price maintenance, "by stabilizing price levels and preventing low-price competition, erects a potentially insurmountable barrier to entry for such low-price innovators." Brief for Consumer Federation of America as *Amicus Curiae* 5, 7–9 (discussing, *inter alia*, comments by Wal-Mart's founder 25 years ago that relaxation of the *per se* ban on minimum resale price maintenance would be a " 'great danger' " to Wal-Mart's then-relatively-nascent business). . . . New distributors, including internet distributors, have similarly invested time, money, and labor in an effort to bring yet lower cost goods to Americans.

This Court's overruling of the *per se* rule jeopardizes this reliance, and more. What about malls built on the assumption that a discount distributor will remain an anchor tenant? What about home buyers who have taken a home's distance from such a mall into account? What about Americans, producers, distributors, and consumers, who have understandably assumed, at least for the last 30 years, that price competition is a legally guaranteed way of life? The majority denies none of this. It simply says that these "reliance interests . . . , like the reliance interests in *Khan*, cannot justify an inefficient rule." *Ante*, at 27. . . .

Sixth, the fact that a rule of law has become "embedded" in our "national culture" argues strongly against overruling. *Dickerson v. United States*, 530 U.S. 428, 443–444 (2000). The *per se* rule forbidding minimum resale price maintenance agreements has long been "embedded" in the law of antitrust. It involves price, the economy's " 'central nervous system.' " *National Soc. of Professional Engineers*, 435 U.S., at 692 (quoting *Socony-Vacuum Oil*, 310 U.S., at 226, n. 59). It reflects a basic antitrust assumption (that consumers often prefer lower prices to more service). It embodies a basic antitrust objective (providing consumers with a free choice about such matters). And it creates an easily administered and enforceable bright line, "Do not agree about price," that businesses as well as lawyers have long understood.

The only contrary *stare decisis* factor that the majority mentions consists of its claim that this Court has "[f]rom the beginning . . . treated the Sherman Act as a common-law statute," and has previously overruled antitrust precedent. *Ante*, at 20, 21–22. It points in support to *State Oil Co. v. Khan*, 522 U.S. 3 (1997), overruling *Albrecht v. Herald Co.*, 390 U.S. 145 (1968), in which this Court had held that *maximum* resale price agreements were unlawful *per se*, and to *Sylvania*, overruling *United States v. Arnold, Schwinn & Co.*, 388 U.S. 365 (1967), in which this Court had held that producer-imposed territorial limits were unlawful *per se*.

The Court decided *Khan*, however, 29 years after *Albrecht*-still a significant period, but nowhere close to the century *Dr. Miles* has stood. The Court specifically noted the *lack* of any significant reliance upon *Albrecht*, 522 U.S., at 18–19 (*Albrecht* has had "little or no relevance to ongoing enforcement of the Sherman Act"). *Albrecht* had far less support in traditional antitrust principles than did *Dr. Miles*. Compare, *e.g.*, 8 Areeda & Hovenkamp & 1632, at 316–328 (analyzing potential harms of minimum resale price maintenance), with *id.*, & 1637, at 352–361 (analyzing potential harms of maximum resale price maintenance). *See also, e.g.*, Pitofsky 1490, n. 17. And Congress had nowhere expressed support for *Albrecht's* rule. *Khan, supra*, at 19.

In *Sylvania*, the Court, in overruling *Schwinn*, explicitly distinguished *Dr. Miles* on the ground that while Congress had "recently . . . expressed its approval of a *per se* analysis of vertical price restrictions" by repealing the Miller-Tydings and McGuire Acts, "[n]o similar expression of congressional intent exists for nonprice restrictions." 433 U.S., at 51, n. 18. Moreover, the Court decided *Sylvania* only a decade after *Schwinn*. And it based its overruling on a generally perceived need to avoid "confusion" in the law, 433 U.S., at 47–49, a factor totally absent here.

The Court suggests that it is following "the common-law tradition." *Ante* at 26. But the common law would not have permitted overruling *Dr. Miles* in these circumstances. Common-law courts rarely overruled well-established earlier rules outright. Rather, they would over time issue decisions that gradually eroded the scope and effect of the rule in question, which might eventually lead the courts to put the rule to rest. One can argue that modifying the *per se* rule to make an exception, say, for new entry, see Pitofsky 1495, could prove consistent with this approach. To swallow up a century-old precedent, potentially affecting many billions of dollars of sales, is not. The reader should compare today's "common-law" decision with Justice Cardozo's decision in *Allegheny College v. National Chau tauqua Cty. Bank of Jamestown*, 246 N.Y. 369, 159 N.E. 173 (1927), and note a gradualism that does not characterize today's decision. . . .

In sum, every *stare decisis* concern this Court has ever mentioned counsels against overruling here. It is difficult for me to understand how one can believe both that (1) satisfying a set of *stare decisis* concerns justifies over-ruling a recent constitutional decision, *Wisconsin Right to Life, Inc., ante*, at 19–21 (Scalia, J., joined by Kennedy and Thomas, JJ., concurring in part and concurring in judgment), but (2) failing to satisfy any of those same concerns nonetheless permits overruling a longstanding statutory decision. Either those concerns are relevant or they are not.

*   *   *

The only safe predictions to make about today's decision are that it will likely raise the price of goods at retail and that it will create considerable legal turbulence as lower courts seek to develop workable principles. I do not believe that the majority has shown new or changed conditions sufficient to warrant overruling a decision of such long standing. All ordinary *stare decisis* considerations indicate the contrary. For these reasons, with respect, I dissent.

NOTES AND QUESTIONS

1.   The decision in *Dr. Miles Medical Co. v. John D. Park & Sons Co.*, 220 U.S. 373 (1911), which the Supreme Court's *Leegin* decision overruled, had condemned resale price maintenance categorically — today we would say under a "*per se*" rule, which means mainly that proof of market power or anticompetitive effects was not necessary. The Court reasoned:

> The basis of the argument appears to be that, as the manufacturer may make and sell, or not, as he chooses, he may affix conditions as to the use of the article or as to the prices at which purchasers may dispose of it. The propriety of the restraint is sought to be derived from the liberty of the

producer.

But because a manufacturer is not bound to make or sell, it does not follow that in case of sales actually made he may impose upon purchasers every sort of restriction. Thus a general restraint upon alienation is ordinarily invalid. "The right of alienation is one of the essential incidents of a right of general property in movables, and restraints upon alienation have been generally regarded as obnoxious to public policy, which is best subserved by great freedom of traffic in such things as pass from hand to hand. . . . "

The bill asserts the importance of a standard retail price and alleges generally that confusion and damage have resulted from sales at less than the prices fixed. But the advantage of established retail prices primarily concerns the dealers. The enlarged profits which would result from adherence to the established rates would go to them and not to the complainant. It is through the inability of the favored dealers to realize these profits, on account of the described competition, that the complainant works out its alleged injury. If there be an advantage to a manufacturer in the maintenance of fixed retail prices, the question remains whether it is one which he is entitled to secure by agreements restricting the freedom of trade on the part of dealers who own what they sell. As to this, the complainant can fare no better with its plan of identical contracts than could the dealers themselves if they formed a combination and endeavored to establish the same restrictions, and thus to achieve the same result, by agreement with each other. If the immediate advantage they would thus obtain would not be sufficient to sustain such a direct agreement, the asserted ulterior benefit to the complainant cannot be regarded as sufficient to support its system.

But agreements or combinations between dealers, having for their sole purpose the destruction of competition and the fixing of prices, are injurious to the public interest and void. They are not saved by the advantages which the participants expect to derive from the enhanced price to the consumer.

The complainant's plan falls within the principle which condemns contracts of this class. It, in effect, creates a combination for the prohibited purposes. No distinction can properly be made by reason of the particular character of the commodity in question. . . . Nor does the fact that the margin of freedom is reduced by the control of production make the protection of what remains, in such a case, a negligible matter. And where commodities have passed into the channels of trade and are owned by dealers, the validity of agreements to prevent competition and to maintain prices is not to be determined by the circumstance whether they were produced by several manufacturers or by one, or whether they were previously owned by one or by many. The complainant having sold its product at prices satisfactory to itself, the public is entitled to whatever advantage may be derived from competition in the subsequent traffic.

In dissent, Justice Holmes wrote:

There is no statute covering the case; there is no body of precedent that by ineluctable logic requires the conclusion to which the court has come. The conclusion is reached by extending a certain conception of public policy to a new sphere. On such matters we are in perilous country. I think that, at least, it is safe to say that the most enlightened judicial policy is to let people manage their own business in their own way, unless the ground for interference is very clear. What then is the ground upon which we interfere in the present case? Of course, it is not the interest of the producer. No one, I judge, cares for that. It hardly can be the interest of subordinate vendors, as there seems to be no particular reason for preferring them to the originator and first vendor of the product. Perhaps it may be assumed to be the interest of the consumers and the public. On that point I confess that I am in a minority as to larger issues than are concerned here. I think that we greatly exaggerate the value and importance to the public of competition in the production or distribution of an article (here it is only distribution), as fixing a fair price. What really fixes that is the competition of conflicting desires. We, none of us, can have as much as we want of all the things that we want. Therefore, we have to choose. As soon as the price of something that we want goes above the point at which we are willing to give up other things to have that, we cease to buy it and buy something else. Of course, I am speaking of things that we can get along without. There may be necessaries that sooner or later must be dealt with like short rations in a shipwreck, but they are not Dr. Miles's medicines. With regard to things like the latter it seems to me that the point of most profitable returns marks the equilibrium of social desires and determines the fair price in the only sense in which I can find meaning in those words. The Dr. Miles Medical Company knows better than we do what will enable it to do the best business. We must assume its retail price to be reasonable, for it is so alleged and the case is here on demurrer; so I see nothing to warrant my assuming that the public will not be served best by the company being allowed to carry out its plan. I cannot believe that in the long run the public will profit by this court permitting knaves to cut reasonable prices for some ulterior purpose of their own and thus to impair, if not to destroy, the production and sale of articles which it is assumed to be desirable that the public should be able to get.

Neither side of the *Dr. Miles* debate confronted the economic or other rationales for resale price maintenance and which might serve to make it reasonable. Both relied heavily on common law concepts pertaining to restraints on alienation. In that regard, the debate between the majority and the dissenters in *Leegin* is far more helpful.

2. The *Dr. Miles* rule of *per se* illegality for resale price maintenance was in effect for almost a century before *Leegin* overruled it. Congressional policy during the interval was all over the place. For a discussion of earlier congressional efforts to overrule the decision, see *Schwegmann Bros. v. Calvert Distillers Corp.*, 341 U.S. 384 (1951). On the "fair trade" political movement designed to permit states to authorize RPM, see Herbert Hovenkamp, *The Opening of American Law: Neoclassical Legal Thought*, 1870–1970, at Ch. 12 (2014). Congress responded in 1937 with the Miller-Tydings Fair Trade Amendment, ch. 690, 50 Stat. 693 (1937), which permitted states to authorize resale price maintenance agreements for branded commodities. State legislation thereafter was designed to insulate small businesses from price and marketing practices of large concerns that might be in a position, due to marketing economies, to offer products at discount. *See generally Old Dearborn Distrib. Co. v. Seagram-Distillers Corp.*, 299 U.S. 183 (1936) (upholding constitutionality of state fair trade laws). Minimum retail prices were approved under certain state "fair trade" laws so that small retail establishments might not face lower prices from larger, more efficient competitors. In those 46 states that adopted fair trade laws under the Miller-Tydings Act, the effect of *Dr. Miles* was suspended.

The suspension lasted almost 40 years. In 1975, Congress, dissatisfied with the competitive effects of the state fair trade laws, repealed its 1937 approval of the fair trade legislation. Consumer Goods Pricing Act, Pub. L. No. 94-145, 89 Stat. 801 (codified at 15 U.S.C. § 45 (amending 15 U.S.C. §§ 1, 45)). As a result, vertical price restrictions again came within the reach of *Dr. Miles* until it was overruled by *Leegin.*

3. Consider the economic consequences of *Dr. Miles.* Does RPM imposed by a manufacturer have the same competitive effects as RPM instituted at the behest of a dealer cartel? In terms of antitrust policy, should the law draw distinctions between RPM imposed by the manufacturer as a means of increasing distribution efficiency and RPM which has the effect of facilitating either a manufacturers 'or dealers' cartel? If a *per se* decisional process is utilized, could courts draw such a distinction? Can it necessarily be inferred from RPM supported by dealers that dealer collusion is present? Did Justice Hughes cite evidence *in his opinion* that would support a finding of dealer cartelization?

4. Some products such as books and CD music recordings have highly uncertain individual demand. A publisher might publish 100 titles per year, knowing in advance that on average only one-fourth of them will turn a profit. However, in most cases, it does not know in advance which titles will sell and which will be quickly sent to the remainder table or removed from the shelves. Retailers have every incentive to stock the proven sellers but not the failures, and this further exacerbates the tendency of less successful products to fail. In these circumstances resale price maintenance may operate as an inducement to the retailer to carry and display the publisher's full line, with the higher margin on the more successful titles offsetting the carrying costs of the less successful titles. In this case, territorial restraints are much less likely to succeed, for the distribution of books and recordings depend on relatively dense placement of stores. *See* Raymond Deneckere, Howard Marvel & James Peck, *Demand Uncertainty, Inventories, and Resale Price Maintenance*, 111 Q. J. Econ. 885 (1996); *see also* David A. Butz, *Vertical Price Controls with Uncertain Demand*, 40 J.L. & Econ. 433 (1997).

5. As *Leegin* suggests, when *Dr. Miles* was decided, the drug industry was plagued by collusion. Trade associations of drug wholesalers and retailers had entered into agreements for the purpose of maintaining retail prices of patent and proprietary medicines. These price agreements were communicated to the manufacturers with the admonition that they "desist from selling to aggressive cutters, or suppliers of cutters, when solicited to do so by the respective local [trade] associations." *Joyne v. Loder*, 149 F. 21, 25 (3d Cir. 1906). *See* Herbert Hovenkamp, Enterprise and American Law 1836–1937, ch. 25 (1991).

However, a fair amount of evidence suggests that RPM is not a very reliable way to facilitate collusion. Only a very small percentage of RPM prosecutions have involved collusion at either the dealer or supplier level. *See* Stanley I. Ornstein, *Resale Price Maintenance and Cartels*, 30 ANTITRUST BULL. 401 (1985). For a strongly stated contrary opinion, see 8 Phillip E. Areeda & Herbert Hovenkamp, Antitrust Law ¶ 1604 (3d ed. 2011).

6. A widely accepted "efficiency" explanation for resale price maintenance is that it is used by suppliers of products that require point-of-sale services in order to prevent "free riding." Free riding occurs when a "cut-rate" dealer underprices a high service dealer by reducing point of sale services, such as trained personnel to demonstrate a product, working displays, consultation about the customer's needs, and so on. The presence of the cut-rate dealers encourages customers to go to the high service dealers to obtain their "education," and then to the cut-rate dealers to make their purchase at a lower price. The high service dealers will be able to stay in business only by cutting services themselves so that they can match the cut-rate dealers' prices. Soon none of the dealers of the product will be offering the efficient amount of point-of-sale services, and the total number of sales will decline.

RPM forces *all* dealers to charge the same price. The (former) cut-rate dealer will no longer have a price advantage over the high service dealer, and will have to increase the number of services it provides if it is to continue making sales. As a result, the dealers will compete with each other, not by cutting price, but rather by offering increased point-of-sale services until the amount of these services rises to the optimal level. As a result, the number of sales can actually *increase*, even though the prevailing price is higher. *See* Lester Telser, *Why Should Manufacturers Want Fair Trade?*, 3 J.L. & ECON. 86 (1960). Does this mean that RPM is in the best interest of consumers? Not necessarily. *See* Frederic M. Scherer, *The Economics of Vertical Restraints*, 52 ANTITRUST L.J. 687 (1983); William Comanor, *Vertical Price-Fixing, Vertical Market Restrictions, and the New Antitrust Policy*, 98 HARV. L. REV. 983 (1985). Consider the illustration. P_1, which is equal to MC_1, is the dealers' marginal cost and the resale price when dealers' prices are unregulated and few point-of-sale services are offered. D_1 is the demand curve for the product at that price. Suppose now that the supplier imposes RPM at level "RPM" on the figure. The dealers will now all charge price RPM. They will compete for sales by increasing the number of point-of-sale services, education, more expensive show-rooms, etc., until their costs rise to MC_2, at which point they will once again be earning competitive returns. At the same time, however, the demand curve for the product will shift outward from D_1 to D_2, as demand increases in response to the increased number of point-of-sale services and other forms of dealer investment. Although MC_2 is higher than MC_1, output under RPM is actually higher than it was before RPM was in place, for the demand curve has shifted more than enough to make up the difference. Before RPM, the manufacturer sold O_1 of the product; now it sells O_2.

Figure 1

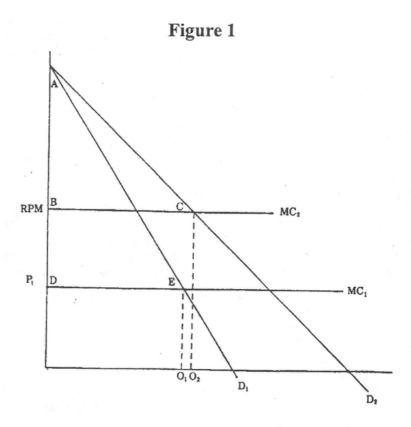

As a general rule, an output increase is a good sign that a practice is efficient. In fact, some writers virtually equate output increases with efficiency. *E.g.*, Frank H. Easterbrook, *Vertical Arrangements and the Rule of Reason*, 53 ANTITRUST L.J. 135 (1984). But the efficiency of a practice is generally equal to the amount of economic surplus that it creates — i.e., the sum of consumers' surplus and producers' surplus. In Figure 1, although output has increased under RPM, it appears that consumers' surplus has actually been reduced. Before RPM was in place, consumers' surplus (or the difference between the collective value that consumers place on a product and the amount they must pay for it; for a review, see Chapter 2) equalled triangle A-D-E. Under RPM, consumers' surplus is triangle A-B-C, which in this particular illustration is smaller than triangle A-D-E. Assuming the manufacturer is earning monopoly profits, its surplus is larger by the distance from O_1 to O_2 times the monopoly profits it is earning, but this may not be enough to offset the reduction in consumers' surplus. The dealers, which are in fierce competition with each other, are not earning a surplus, for they are competing away the higher retail price in increased point-of-sale services. As a result, RPM may be inefficient, *even* though it is being used to combat free riding, and even though supplier output is higher under RPM than it had been before.

Ever since Telser's seminal 1960 article cited above, advocates of the free-rider argument for RPM generally have assumed that demand curves D_1 (before RPM) and D_2 (under RPM) are parallel. This assumes that all customers place precisely the same value on the increased point-of-sale services that RPM produces. If demand curves D_1 and D_2 are parallel, RPM that increases output will also increase consumers' surplus. But as an empirical matter that assumption seems question able.

Consider the market for personal computers, for example. Some "marginal" consumers will have to be educated about why they need a computer, what kind of computer they need, how to operate it, and so on. Other people — perhaps business firms that already own half a dozen personal computers and want to purchase some more — already know exactly what they need, and for them the point-of-sale services are a waste of money. Figure 1 is drawn on the more realistic assumption that different consumers value point-of-sale services by different amounts, and that "marginal" consumers (those who place the lowest value on the product) are those whose surplus will increase the most from the point-of-sale services. That is, marginal consumers are those most in need of the educational and other services supplied by the dealer. Once this assumption is made, it can no longer be shown that any particular instance of RPM is efficient, even if it increases output. Some are and some are not.

Finally, note that consumers who do not place a high value on point-of-sale services can be forced to pay for them only if there are no lower priced alternatives to which they can turn. This would be true if (1) the manufacturer imposing RPM had substantial market power; or (2) all (or nearly all) manufacturers in the market were using RPM. These assumptions suggest that as a matter of economic efficiency, RPM ought to be evaluated under the rule of reason, instead of the current *per se* rule, and that a showing of market power would be important.

But for the availability of RPM, how can a manufacturer encourage its dealers to invest in product marketing, service, and sales? Assuming that the free-rider condition exists, if a manufacturer was not able to enforce RPM, wouldn't retail prices to the consumer be reduced, at least in the short run? What would you anticipate would be the long run effects of such a practice? Consider the effects on incentives that such market conduct might have. *See* E. THOMAS SULLIVAN & JEFFREY HARRISON, UNDERSTANDING ANTITRUST AND ITS ECONOMIC IMPLICATIONS, ch. 5 (5th ed. 2007); HERBERT HOVENKAMP, FEDERAL ANTITRUST POLICY, ch. 11 (4th ed. 2011); *see also* Richard A. Posner, *The Rule of Reason and the Economic Approach: Reflections on the* Sylvania *Decision*, 45 U. CHI. L. REV. 1 (1977).

7. How difficult will it be to maintain an RPM case under *Leegin*'s rule of reason? Since *Leegin*, one plaintiff has succeeded in proving a conspiracy of dealers to force their supplier to impose RPM on all dealers and to discipline the plaintiff for cutting prices — facts that are at least superficially similar to those of *Dr. Miles* itself. *See Toledo Mack Sales & Service, Inc. v. Mack Trucks, Inc.*, 530 F.3d 204 (3d Cir. 2008). The plaintiff alleged a conspiracy among Mack Truck dealers not to compete against one another in bidding for large truck sales. The court wrote:

> Because Toledo's evidence was sufficient to allow a jury to conclude that Mack entered into a competition-restricting agreement with its dealers, the only remaining question before us as to that agreement is whether, if proven, it violates § 1 of the Sherman Act. In contrast to horizontal price-fixing agreements between entities at the same level of a product's

distribution chain, the legality of a vertical agreement that imposes a restriction on the dealer's ability to sell the manufacturer's product is governed by the rule of reason. *Leegin*, 127 S. Ct. at 2725. The rule of reason analysis applies even when, as in this case, the plaintiff alleges that the purpose of the vertical agreement between a manufacturer and its dealers is to support illegal horizontal agreements between multiple dealers. *Id.* at 2717 ("A horizontal cartel among competing manufacturers or competing retailers that decreases output or reduces competition in order to increase price is, and ought to be, *per se* unlawful. To the extent a vertical agreement setting minimum resale prices is entered upon to facilitate either type of cartel, it, too, would need to be held unlawful *under the rule of reason.*") (citation omitted and emphasis added).

The court then found that such an agreement existed and was unlawful under the rule of reason. It summarized its rule of reason inquiry as requiring proof:

> (1) that the defendants contracted, combined or conspired among each other; (2) that the combination or conspiracy produced adverse, anti-competitive effects within the relevant product and geographic markets; (3) that the objects of and the conduct pursuant to that contract or conspiracy were illegal; and (4) that the plaintiffs were injured as a proximate result of that conspiracy.

The court observed that in *Leegin*, the Supreme Court had identified two additional issues that were relevant to the rule of reason inquiry:

> First, "[t]he source of the restraint may be an important consideration. If there is evidence retailers were the impetus for a vertical price restraint, there is a greater likelihood that the restraint facilitates a retailer cartel. . . . " 127 S. Ct. at 2719. Second, "that a dominant manufacturer or retailer can abuse resale price maintenance for anti-competitive purposes may not be a serious concern unless the relevant entity has market power." *Id.* at 2720.

The court then observed that an expert had testified that Mack "[has] market power in both the heavy duty vocational LCOE, as well as conventional straight truck markets, whether you look at the U.S. as a whole or the U.S., excluding the west." It did not give any details.

Cf. *Jacobs v. Tempur-Pedic Intern., Inc.*, 626 F.3d 1327 (11th Cir. 2010), which concluded in the wake of *Leegin* that a relevant market must be defined in a resale price maintenance case and the market in this instance included all mattresses, not just a narrower market of "foam" mattresses. Further, the fact that the manufacturer was engaged in dual distribution in that it owned some outlets while it franchised others, did not serve to transform the agreement into a per se unlawful price fixing conspiracy. And see *PSKS, Inc. v. Leegin Creative Leather Prods., Inc.*, 615 F.3d 412 (5th Cir. 2010), on remand from the Supreme Court's decision, which dismissed the RPM complaint after observing that the plaintiff had failed properly to allege a relevant market but had relied entirely on the per se rule that the Supreme Court overruled. The court also held that the defendant's Brighton brand could not constitute a relevant submarket.

[2] Consignment Contracts as Vertical Price Control Devices

Cases after *Dr. Miles* seem not to make the legality of RPM depend on whether the product was patented, trademarked, copyrighted, or semi-finished. *See, e.g., United States v. Univis Lens Co.*, 316 U.S. 241 (1942) (patented); *United States v. Sealy, Inc.*, 388 U.S. 350, 356 n.3 (1967) (trademark); *and see Bobbs-Merrill Co. v. Straus*, 210 U.S. 339 (1908) (copyright). But the question left open by *Dr. Miles* — whether the rule applied to a manufacturer that transferred the product through a consignment or agency relationship rather than an outright sale — was addressed in 1926 in *United States v. General Elec. Co.*, 272 U.S. 476 (1926). General Electric distributed lamps to wholesalers and dealers, which acted as agents for the company. Under the theory that these company agents were the first sellers of the product, General Electric attempted to control the price of the lamps as they were sold to customers. The Department of Justice challenged this arrangement as a contrived scheme to avoid *Dr. Miles*. The Supreme Court, speaking through Chief Justice Taft, disagreed.

> We are of opinion, therefore, that there is nothing as a matter of principle, or in the authorities, which requires us to hold that genuine contracts of agency like those before us, however comprehensive as a mass or whole in their effect, are violations of the Anti-Trust Act. The owner of an article, patented or otherwise, is not violating the common law or the Anti-Trust law, by seeking to dispose of his article directly to the consumer and fixing the price by which his agents transfer the title from him directly to such consumer.

272 U.S. at 488. As one would expect, after *General Electric*, the consignment contract became a favored method by which suppliers could control the product price through distribution to the retail seller. Under the consignment arrangement, dealers were considered agents of the manufacturer (consignor), who would retain title to the products until sold at retail. Not until 1964 did the Supreme Court reevaluate *General Electric* in light of the pervasive use of consignment contracts as a means to avoid the *Dr. Miles* proscription against RPM.

Then, in *Simpson v. Union Oil Co.*, 377 U.S. 13 (1964), the Supreme Court held that a franchise-wide use of consignment contracts would be treated for RPM purposes as an ordinary sale-plus-resale:

> We disagree with the Court of Appeals that there is no actionable wrong or damage if a Sherman Act violation is assumed. If the "consignment" agreement achieves resale price maintenance in violation of the Sherman Act, it and the lease are being used to injure interstate commerce by depriving independent dealers of the exercise of free judgment whether to become consignees at all, or remain consignees, and, in any event, to sell at competitive prices. The fact that a retailer can refuse to deal does not give the supplier immunity if the arrangement is one of those schemes condemned by the antitrust laws.

. . . .

Consignments perform an important function in trade and commerce, and their integrity has been recognized by many courts, including this one. Yet consignments, though useful in allocating risks between the parties and determining their rights *inter se*, do not necessarily control the rights of others, whether they be creditors or sovereigns. Thus the device has been extensively regulated by the States . . . .

. . . .

Dealers, like Simpson, are independent businessmen; and they have all or most of the indicia of entrepreneurs, except for price fixing. The risk of loss of the gasoline is on them, apart from acts of God. Their return is affected by the rise and fall in the market price, their commissions declining as retail prices drop. Practically the only power they have to be wholly independent businessmen, whose service depends on their own initiative and enterprise, is taken from them by the proviso that they must sell their gasoline at prices fixed by Union Oil. By reason of the lease and "consignment" agreement dealers are coercively laced into an arrangement under which their supplier is able to impose noncompetitive prices on thousands of persons whose prices otherwise might be competitive. The evil of this resale price maintenance program, like that of the requirements contracts held illegal . . . is its inexorable potentiality for and even certainty in destroying competition in retail sales of gasoline by these nominal "consignees" who are in reality small struggling competitors seeking retail gas customers. . . .

To allow Union Oil to achieve price fixing in this vast distribution system through this "consignment" device would be to make legality for antitrust purposes turn on clever draftsmanship. We refuse to let a matter so vital to a competitive system rest on such easy manipulation.

Query: How important is the distinction between a sale/resale and a consignment under the rule of reason adopted by the Supreme Court in *Leegin*? The important question is whether an instance of vertical price control results in reduced output and higher prices in a relevant market. What difference could it make whether the arrangement was one of resale or consignment?

One answer is that bona fide consignment agreements are legally classified as "agency" relationships, and such relationships are characteristic of decision making within a business firm, such as the relationship between a boss and an employee. Section 1 of the Sherman Act requires an agreement between two separate actors, and an "agreement" between two people within the same firm does not count. For example, if General Motors has a wholly owned automobile dealership in Kansas City, setting of that dealership's prices from the Detroit headquarters is not resale price maintenance. The law treats it as a unilateral act, for every firm has to be able to set its own prices. Consignment agreements occupy a position somewhere between outright sale and resale on one hand, and intrafirm decision making on the other.

The next decision involves a different aspect of the question of what counts as an "agreement" between separate actors.

[3]   Unilateral Refusals to Deal and the *Colgate* Doctrine

UNITED STATES v. COLGATE & CO.
250 U.S. 300 (1919)

JUSTICE MCREYNOLDS delivered the opinion of the Court.

The indictment runs only against Colgate & Company, a corporation engaged in manufacturing soap and toilet articles and selling them throughout the Union. It makes no reference to monopoly, and proceeds solely upon the theory of an unlawful combination. . . . [The indictment charges that].

"During the aforesaid period of time, within the said eastern district of Virginia and throughout the United States, the defendant knowingly and unlawfully created and engaged in a combination with said wholesale and retail dealers, in the eastern district of Virginia and throughout the United States, for the purpose and with the effect of procuring adherence on the part of such dealers (in reselling such products sold to them as aforesaid) to resale prices fixed by the defendant, and of preventing such dealers from reselling such products at lower prices, thus suppressing competition amongst such wholesale dealers, and amongst such retail dealers, in restraint of the aforesaid trade and commerce among the several States, in violation of the act entitled 'An Act to protect trade and commerce against unlawful restraints and monopolies,' approved July 2, 1890."

Following this is a summary of things done to carry out the purposes of the combination: Distribution among dealers of letters, telegrams, circulars and lists showing uniform prices to be charged; urging them to adhere to such prices and notices, stating that no sales would be made to those who did not; requests, often complied with, for information concerning dealers who had departed from specified prices; investigation and discovery of those not adhering thereto and placing their names upon "suspended lists"; requests to offending dealers for assurances and promises of future adherence to prices, which were often given; uniform refusals to sell to any who failed to give the same; sales to those who did; similar assurances and promises required of, and given by, other dealers followed by sales to them; unrestricted sales to dealers with established accounts who had observed specified prices, etc.

. . . .

Our problem is to ascertain, as accurately as may be, what interpretation the trial court placed upon the indictment — not to interpret it ourselves; and then to determine whether, so construed, it fairly charges violation of the Sherman Act. Counsel for the Government maintain, in effect, that, as so interpreted, the indictment adequately charges an unlawful combination (within the doctrine of *Dr. Miles Medical Co. v. Park & Sons Co.*, 220 U.S. 373) resulting from restrictive agreements between defendant and sundry dealers whereby the latter obligated themselves not to resell except at agreed prices. . . .

Considering all said in the opinion (notwithstanding some serious doubts) we are unable to accept the construction placed upon it by the Government. We cannot, *e.g.*, wholly disregard the statement that "[t]he retailer, after buying, could, if he chose, give away his purchase, or sell it at any price he saw fit, or not sell it at all; his course in these respects being affected only by the fact that he might by his action incur the displeasure of the manufacturer, who could refuse to make further sales to him, as he had the undoubted right to do." And we must conclude that, as interpreted below, the indictment does not charge Colgate & Company with selling its products to dealers under agreements which obligated the latter not to resell except at prices fixed by the company.

. . . .

The purpose of the Sherman Act is to prohibit monopolies, contracts and combinations which probably would unduly interfere with the free exercise of their rights by those engaged, or who wish to engage, in trade and commerce — in a word to preserve the right of freedom to trade. In the absence of any purpose to create or maintain a monopoly, the act does not restrict the long recognized right of trader or manufacturer engaged in an entirely private business, freely to exercise his own independent discretion as to parties with whom he will deal. And, of course, he may announce in advance the circumstances under which he will refuse to sell. . . .

Affirmed.

NOTES AND QUESTIONS

1. The *Colgate* doctrine retains some vitality even under a rule of reason for RPM. The difference is between unilateral and bilateral acts, and unilateral acts are generally governed by the much more permissible standards of Section 2 of the Sherman Act. Could unilaterally imposed resale price maintenance ever be an unlawful exclusionary practice? Who would it exclude? By contrast, agreed-upon RPM is analyzed under the Section 1 "restrain trade" standard.

2. Did the indictment in *Colgate* charge an agreement? What role did this omission play in the decision? Consider whether the Court could have inferred a tacit agreement from the price announcement and acquiescence. Recall the *Interstate Circuit* theory of prosecution discussed in Chapter 4.

3. *Colgate* implied that a manufacturer (or franchisor) could avoid the limitations of *Dr. Miles* by not entering into contracts to maintain vertical prices. As long as no maintenance agreement existed, the manufacturer could merely, though unilaterally, refuse to deal with a dealer who declined to adhere to the suggested price. In this limited manner, the manufacturer could attempt to influence pricing behavior of its dealers or franchisees. The line drawing seems finely tuned. Interestingly, Charles Evans Hughes, who wrote the majority opinion in *Dr. Miles*, was counsel for Colgate.

4. In *United States v. Parke, Davis & Co.*, 362 U.S. 29 (1960), a manufacturer informed wholesalers that their supply would be terminated if they sold for less than the announced wholesale price or if they dealt with retailers who resold for less than the manufacturer's suggested retail price. The Court declared that conduct to be outside *Colgate*'s protection. The Court reasoned that "an unlawful combination is not just as arises from a price maintenance agreement, express or implied, such a combination is also organized if the producer secures adherence to his prices by means which go beyond his mere declination to a customer who will not observe his announced policy."

Parke, Davis narrowed the channel through which a supplier could recommend vertical prices. How much affirmative action, in addition to an announcement of a price and a unilateral refusal to deal, is necessary to trigger a finding of per se illegality?

[4] Vertical Maximum Price Fixing

In *Albrecht v. Herald Co.*, 390 U.S. 145 (1968), a newspaper publisher attempted to set the *maximum* price at which independent carriers sold at retail. The Court held that a combination in restraint of trade existed when the newspaper combined with a subscription solicitor and route carrier to *coerce* the independent carrier into following the newspaper's suggested RPM. The Court reasoned as follows:

> If a combination arose when Parke Davis threatened its wholesalers with termination unless they put pressure on their retail customers, then there can be no doubt that a combination arose between [the newspaper and subscription solicitor and route carrier] to force petitioner to conform to the advertised retail price. When respondent learned that petitioner was overcharging, it hired Milne to solicit customers away from petitioner in order to get petitioner to reduce his price. It was through the efforts of Milne, as well as because of respondent's letter to petitioner's customers, that about 300 customers were obtained for Kroner. Milne's purpose was undoubtedly to earn its fee, but it was aware that the aim of the solicitation campaign was to force petitioner to lower his price. Kroner knew that respondent was giving him the customer list as part of a program to get petitioner to conform to the advertised price, and he knew that he might have to return the customers if petitioner ultimately complied with respondent's demands. He undertook to deliver papers at the suggested price and materially aided in the accomplishment of respondent's plan. Given the uncontradicted facts recited by the Court of Appeals, there was a combination within the meaning of § 1 between respondent, Milne, and Kroner, and the Court of Appeals erred in holding to the contrary.

Why would a manufacturer impose maximum resale price maintenance on its retail outlets? Actually, the explanation for that is far simpler than is the explanation for minimum RPM. If a retailer has any market power at all, it will be able to maximize its profits by reducing output below the competitive level. This monopoly pricing will generate a monopoly profit — but the profit will go to the retailer, not to the manufacturer. Any firm, even a monopolist, is best off if all other firms in the distribution chain are behaving competitively. This is easy to see intuitively if you look at backward integration. If a monopolist manufacturing aluminum must purchase its bauxite, a necessary ingredient, from another monopolist at $2.00 per pound, the monopolist will make less money than if it can purchase bauxite competitively at $1.50 per pound. Even the monopolist wants to deal on the market with people who behave like competitors. The same concept applies to forward integration: if the retail store is making a 25% monopoly profit, that is money that could be going into the hands of the manufacturer. *See* 3A Phillip E. Areeda & Herbert Hovenkamp, Antitrust Law, ch. 7D-1 (3d ed. 2008).

The extreme case is where the retailers are natural monopolists, as they were in *Albrecht*. A newspaper delivery route is a natural monopoly — it is far cheaper for one person to travel the route than it is for two to travel it and split the deliveries. The carriers in *Albrecht* had exclusive territories. 390 U.S. at 147. This gave the carriers an incentive to sell newspaper subscriptions at a monopoly price, with the result that circulation along the routes declined. The newspaper lost money from the carriers' exercise of monopoly power in two different ways: first, they lost money from reduced circulation; second, and much more significantly, they lost advertising revenues, because advertising rates are based on circulation. *See* Hovenkamp, *Vertical Integration by the Newspaper Monopolist*, 69 Iowa L. Rev. 451 (1984).

In 1997, the Supreme Court overruled *Albrecht*, holding that vertical, maximum price fixing should be evaluated under the rule of reason.

STATE OIL COMPANY v. KHAN
522 U.S. 3 (1997)

Justice O'Connor delivered the opinion of the Court.

I

Respondents, Barkat U. Khan and his corporation, entered into an agreement with petitioner, State Oil Company, to lease and operate a gas station and convenience store owned by State Oil. The agreement provided that respondents would obtain the station's gasoline supply from State Oil at a price equal to a suggested retail price set by State Oil, less a margin of 3.25 cents per gallon. Under the agreement, respondents could charge any amount for gasoline sold to the station's customers, but if the price charged was higher than State Oil's suggested retail price, the excess was to be rebated to State Oil. Respondents could sell gasoline for less than State Oil's suggested retail price, but any such decrease would reduce their 3.25 cents-per-gallon margin.

About a year after respondents began operating the gas station, they fell behind in lease payments. State Oil then gave notice of its intent to terminate the agreement and commenced a state court proceeding to evict respondents. At State Oil's request, the state court appointed a receiver to operate the gas station. The receiver operated the station for several months without being subject to the price restraints in respondents' agreement with State Oil. According to respondents, the receiver obtained an overall profit margin in excess of 3.25 cents per gallon by lowering the price of regular-grade gasoline and raising the price of premium grades.

Respondents sued State Oil . . . alleging in part that State Oil had engaged in price fixing in violation of § 1 of the Sherman Act by preventing respondents from raising or lowering retail gas prices. According to the complaint, but for the agreement with State Oil, respondents could have charged different prices based on the grades of gasoline, in the same way that the receiver had, thereby achieving increased sales and profits. State Oil responded that the agreement did not actually prevent respondents from setting gasoline prices, and that, in substance, respondents did not allege a violation of antitrust laws by their claim that State Oil's suggested retail price was not optimal. . . .

II

B

[O]ur reconsideration of *Albrecht*'s continuing validity is informed by several of our decisions, as well as a considerable body of scholarship discussing the effects of vertical restraints. Our analysis is also guided by our general view that the primary purpose of the antitrust laws is to protect interbrand competition. . . . "Low prices," we have explained, "benefit consumers regardless of how those prices are set, and so long as they are above predatory levels, they do not threaten competition." . . . Our interpretation of the Sherman Act also incorporates the notion that condemnation of practices resulting in lower prices to consumers is "especially costly" because "cutting prices in order to increase business often is the very essence of competition. . . . "

So informed, we find it difficult to maintain that vertically-imposed maximum prices could harm consumers or competition to the extent necessary to justify their per se invalidation. As Chief Judge Posner wrote for the Court of Appeals in this case:

> As for maximum resale price fixing, unless the supplier is a monopsonist he cannot squeeze his dealers' margins below a competitive level; the attempt to do so would just drive the dealers into the arms of a competing supplier. A supplier might, however, fix a maximum resale price in order to prevent his dealers from exploiting a monopoly position. . . . [S]uppose that State Oil, perhaps to encourage . . . dealer services . . . has spaced its dealers sufficiently far apart to limit competition among them (or even given each of them an exclusive territory); and suppose further that Union 76 is a sufficiently distinctive and popular brand to give the dealers in it at least a modicum of monopoly power. Then State Oil might want to place a ceiling on the dealers' resale prices in order to prevent them from exploiting that monopoly power fully. It would do this not out of disinterested malice, but in its commercial self-interest. The higher the price at which gasoline is resold, the smaller the volume sold, and so the lower the profit to the supplier if the higher profit per gallon at the higher price is being snared by the dealer. 93 F.3d, at 1362.

We recognize that the *Albrecht* decision presented a number of theoretical justifications for a per se rule against vertical maximum price fixing. But criticism of those premises abounds. The *Albrecht* decision was grounded in the fear that maximum price fixing by suppliers could interfere with dealer freedom. In response, as one commentator has pointed out, "the ban on maximum resale price limitations declared in *Albrecht* in the name of 'dealer freedom' has actually prompted many suppliers to integrate forward into distribution, thus eliminating the very independent trader for whom *Albrecht* professed solicitude." 7 P. Areeda, *Antitrust Law*, ¶ 1635, p. 395 (1989). For example, integration in the newspaper industry since *Albrecht* has given rise to litigation between independent distributors and publishers. See 3B P. Areeda & H. Hovenkamp, *Antitrust Law* ¶ 766i (3d ed. 2008).

The *Albrecht* Court also expressed the concern that maximum prices may be set too low for dealers to offer consumers essential or desired services. But such conduct, by driving away customers, would seem likely to harm manufacturers as well as dealers and consumers, making it unlikely that a supplier would set such a price as a matter of business judgment. In addition, *Albrecht* noted that vertical maximum price fixing could effectively channel distribution through large or specially-advantaged dealers. It is unclear, however, that a supplier would profit from limiting its market by excluding potential dealers. Further, although vertical maximum price fixing might limit the viability of inefficient dealers, that consequence is not necessarily harmful to competition and consumers.

Finally, *Albrecht* reflected the Court's fear that maximum price fixing could be used to disguise arrangements to fix minimum prices, 390 U.S., at 153, which remain illegal per se. Although we have acknowledged the possibility that maximum pricing might mask minimum pricing . . . we believe that such conduct as with the other concerns articulated in *Albrecht* can be appropriately recognized and punished under the rule of reason.

Not only are the potential injuries cited in *Albrecht* less serious than the Court imagined, the per se rule established therein could in fact exacerbate problems related to the unrestrained exercise of market power by monopolist-dealers. Indeed, both courts and antitrust scholars have noted that *Albrecht*'s rule may actually harm consumers and manufacturers. . . . Other commentators have also explained that *Albrecht*'s per se rule has even more potential for deleterious effect on competition after our decision in *GTE Sylvania*, because, now that vertical nonprice restrictions are not unlawful per se, the likelihood of dealer monopoly power is increased. . . . We do not intend to suggest that dealers generally possess sufficient market power to exploit a monopoly situation. Such retail market power may in fact be uncommon. . . . Nor do we hold that a ban on vertical maximum price fixing inevitably has anticompetitive consequences in the exclusive dealer context.

After reconsidering *Albrecht*'s rationale and the substantial criticism the decision has received, however, we conclude that there is insufficient economic justification for per se invalidation of vertical maximum price fixing. That is so not only because it is difficult to accept the assumptions underlying *Albrecht*, but also because *Albrecht* has little or no relevance to ongoing enforcement of the Sherman Act. . . . Moreover, neither the parties nor any of the amici curiae have called our attention to any cases in which enforcement efforts have been directed solely against the conduct encompassed by *Albrecht*'s per se rule.

* * *

C

Despite what Chief Judge Posner aptly described as *Albrecht's* "infirmities, [and] its increasingly wobbly, moth-eaten foundations," 93 F.3d, at 1363, there remains the question whether *Albrecht* deserves continuing respect under the doctrine of stare decisis. The Court of Appeals was correct in applying that principle despite disagreement with *Albrecht*, for it is this Court's prerogative alone to overrule one of its precedents.

We approach the reconsideration of decisions of this Court with the utmost caution. Stare decisis reflects "a policy judgment that 'in most matters it is more important that the applicable rule of law be settled than that it be settled right.' " *Agostini v. Felton*, 117 S. Ct. 1997, 2016 (1997) (quoting *Burnet v. Coronado Oil & Gas Co.*, 285 U.S. 393 (1932) (Brandeis, J., dissenting)). It "is the preferred course because it promotes the evenhanded, predictable, and consistent development of legal principles, fosters reliance on judicial decisions, and contributes to the actual and perceived integrity of the judicial process." *Payne v. Tennessee*, 501 U.S. 808 (1991). This Court has expressed its reluctance to overrule decisions involving statutory interpretation . . . and has acknowledged that stare decisis concerns are at their acme in cases involving property and contract rights. Both of those concerns are arguably relevant in this case.

But "[s]tare decisis is not an inexorable command." In the area of antitrust law, there is a competing interest, well-represented in this Court's decisions, in recognizing and adapting to changed circumstances and the lessons of accumulated experience. Thus, the general presumption that legislative changes should be left to Congress has less force with respect to the Sherman Act in light of the accepted view that Congress "expected the courts to give shape to the statute's broad mandate by drawing on common-law tradition." *National Soc. of Professional Engineers v. United States*, 435 U.S. 679 (1978). As we have explained, the term "restraint of trade," as used in § 1, also "invokes the common law itself, and not merely the static content that the common law had assigned to the term in 1890." Accordingly, this Court has reconsidered its decisions construing the Sherman Act when the theoretical underpinnings of those decisions are called into serious question.

Although we do not "lightly assume that the economic realities underlying earlier decisions have changed, or that earlier judicial perceptions of those realities were in error," we have noted that "different sorts of agreements" may amount to restraints of trade "in varying times and circumstances," and "[i]t would make no sense to create out of the single term 'restraint of trade' a chronologically schizoid statute, in which a 'rule of reason' evolves with new circumstances and new wisdom, but a line of per se illegality remains forever fixed where it was." *Business Electronics, supra*, at 731–732. Just as *Schwinn* was "the subject of continuing controversy and confusion" under the "great weight" of scholarly criticism, *Albrecht* has been widely criticized since its inception. With the views underlying *Albrecht* eroded by this Court's precedent, there is not much of that decision to salvage. . . .

Although the rule of *Albrecht* has been in effect for some time, the inquiry we must undertake requires considering " 'the effect of the antitrust laws upon vertical distributional restraints in the American economy today.' " As the Court noted in

ARCO, there has not been another case since *Albrecht* in which this Court has "confronted an unadulterated vertical, maximum-price-fixing arrangement." Now that we confront *Albrecht* directly, we find its conceptual foundations gravely weakened.

In overruling *Albrecht*, we of course do not hold that all vertical maximum price fixing is per se lawful. Instead, vertical maximum price fixing, like the majority of commercial arrangements subject to the antitrust laws, should be evaluated under the rule of reason. In our view, rule-of-reason analysis will effectively identify those situations in which vertical maximum price fixing amounts to anticompetitive conduct.

NOTES AND QUESTIONS

1. On remand, Khan did not pursue the question whether the maximum price-fixing was unlawful under the rule of reason and thus the Seventh Circuit ruled the claim was waived. 143 F.3d 362, 363 (7th Cir. 1998). Khan changed its theory to one of minimum resale price maintenance. The court found this argument to have no merit. *Id.* at 364. Judge Posner noted: "A supplier is free to charge any price he wants to his retailers. The fact that the higher that price is, the higher the retailer's price will have to be unless he is willing to sell below his cost has never been thought to be price-fixing." *Id.*

[5] Dealer Termination; Powerful Complaining Dealers

Vertical restraint issues typically are litigated after a dealer has been terminated, allegedly for noncompliance with the restraint. The antitrust litigation dockets are filled with complaints filed by dealers and distributors alleging wrongful termination or nonrenewal. While claims are brought frequently under tort or contract law, they often implicate antitrust laws as well. The terminated dealer generally asserts that the termination was caused by its failure to adhere to vertical restraints imposed by the manufacturer or supplier. The typical dealer termination case raises the same "characterization" issues discussed in this chapter, specifically whether the requisite "agreement" can be established, whether the agreement is horizontal or vertical in nature, and whether the agreement was for a "price" or "nonprice" reason. *See generally* PHILLIP E. AREEDA & HERBERT HOVENKAMP, 7 ANTITRUST LAW ¶¶ 1446, 1452–1460 (3d ed. 2010).

The *Colgate* doctrine is sometimes interposed as a defense to the dealer's charge that the termination amounts to a refusal to deal. The defense is available as long as the refusal to deal is unilateral and not in furtherance of conduct from which an "agreement" could be inferred or motivated by monopolistic purpose. When the decision to terminate is imposed by the supplier through an inducement or pressure from other dealers or franchisees, however, it will be scrutinized carefully in order to determine whether the termination was in fact unilateral.

Ever since the Supreme Court's *Colgate* decision, the lower courts have struggled with the issue of how to determine when manufacturer-imposed resale price maintenance (RPM) is "unilateral" conduct, unreachable under Section 1, or concerted behavior, which is illegal per se. The distinction has been faulted countless times, largely for being so artificial. Why should an announcement of future intent not to deal with price cutters be legal, while a mere telephone call to a dealer telling it that it will be terminated if it continues to cut price becomes illegal per se?

In recent years, commentators and some courts have begun to argue that *Colgate* or something like it can have a very important economic function after all. The agreement requirement can serve to distinguish situations in which RPM is consistent with the manufacturer's independent best interests from those when it is undertaken principally at the behest of dealers.

For example, suppose that a manufacturer is concerned about "free-riding" by some of its dealers, who might take advantage of the point-of-sale services or fixed-cost investments made by other dealers. Controlling free-riding is in the manufacturer's independent best interest, and it does not need a contract with Dealer A in order to have a motive to control the free-riding of Dealer B. In such a case the supplier's motive for imposing RPM may be quite "unilateral." To be sure, Dealer A would also be concerned about Dealer B's free-riding — *both* the manufacturer and Dealer A lose as a result. But if Dealer A complains about Dealer B's price-cutting and Dealer B is engaged in free-riding, then the complaint may serve the function of simply informing the manufacturer what Dealer B is doing. One could not infer from the fact of the complaint and the termination in response that there was an "agreement" between Dealer A and the manufacturer that Dealer A's prices would be maintained at a certain level.

What would you think of a rule that persistent free-riding by the terminated dealer (presumably the plaintiff) creates a presumption that the manufacturer was acting unilaterally?*See Lomar Whsle. Grocery, Inc. v. Dieter's Gourmet Foods, Inc.*, 824 F.2d 582 (8th Cir. 1987), *cert. denied*, 484 U.S. 1010 (1988), *and Valley Liquors, Inc. v. Renfield Importers, Ltd.*, 678 F.2d 742 (7th Cir. 1982), both suggesting that a desire to eliminate free-riders gives a supplier acting unilaterally a motive to terminate price cutters.

By contrast, RPM may be the product of dealer cartels or the influence of individual dealers who have a great deal of power in their respective retail markets. If Clancy's Department Store is the most prestigious store in Lansing, Michigan, and Clancy's tells the supplier that it will carry the supplier's product only if other Lansing dealers keep the price up, the supplier may be forced to impose RPM rather than risk losing Clancy's business. When Clancy's later complains about Dealer B's prices and the manufacturer terminates Dealer B, the inference is much stronger that there was a quid-pro-quo: that the manufacturer terminated Dealer B *in exchange for* Clancy's promise to continue selling the manufacturer's product. What would you think of a rule that if the complaining dealer is powerful and the defendant cannot show specific instances of free-riding, a presumption is created that the termination was the product of an agreement?*See McCabe's Furn. v. La-Z-Boy Chair Co.*, 798 F.2d 323 (8th Cir. 1986). The *Leegin* decision acknowledged that RPM at the behest of one or more powerful dealers could be unlawful even under the rule of reason.

The *Monsanto* decision, reprinted below, formulates a test for determining whether an agreement can be inferred from dealer complaints followed by a termination.

MONSANTO CO. v. SPRAY-RITE SERVICE CORP.
465 U.S. 752 (1984)

JUSTICE POWELL delivered the opinion of the Court.

This case presents a question as to the standard of proof required to find a vertical price-fixing conspiracy in violation of Section 1 of the Sherman Act.

Petitioner Monsanto Company manufactures chemical products, including agricultural herbicides. By the late 1960's, the time at issue in this case, its sales accounted for approximately 15% of the corn herbicide market and 3% of the soybean herbicide market. In the corn herbicide market, the market leader commanded a 70% share. In the soybean herbicide market, two other competitors each had between 30% and 40% of the market. Respondent Spray-Rite Service Corporation was engaged in the wholesale distribution of agricultural chemicals from 1955 to 1972. Spray-Rite was essentially a family business, whose owner and president, Donald Yapp, was also its sole salaried salesman. Spray-Rite was a discount operation, buying in large quantities and selling at a low margin.

In October 1968 Monsanto declined to renew Spray-Rite's distributorship. At that time, Spray-Rite was the tenth largest out of approximately 100 distributors of Monsanto's primary corn herbicide. Ninety percent of Spray-Rite's sales volume was devoted to herbicide sales, and 16% of its sales were of Monsanto products. After Monsanto's termination, Spray-Rite continued as a herbicide dealer until 1972. It was able to purchase some of Monsanto's products from other distributors, but not as much as it desired or as early in the season as it needed. . . .

Spray-Rite brought this action under Section 1 of the Sherman Act, 15 U.S.C. § 1. It alleged that Monsanto and some of its distributors conspired to fix the resale prices of Monsanto herbicides. Its complaint further alleged that Monsanto terminated Spray-Rite's distributorship, adopted compensation programs and shipping policies, and encouraged distributors to boycott Spray-Rite in furtherance of this conspiracy. Monsanto denied the allegations of conspiracy, and asserted that Spray-Rite's distributorship had been terminated because of its failure to hire trained salesmen and promote sales to dealers adequately.

The case was tried to a jury. The District Court instructed the jury that Monsanto's conduct was *per se* unlawful if it was in furtherance of a conspiracy to fix prices. In answers to special interrogatories, the jury found that the termination of Spray-Rite was pursuant to a conspiracy between Monsanto and one or more of its distributors to set resale prices. . . .

The Court of Appeals for the Seventh Circuit affirmed. 684 F.2d 1226 (1982). It held that there was sufficient evidence to satisfy Spray-Rite's burden of proving a conspiracy to set resale prices. The court stated that "proof of termination following competitor complaints is sufficient to support an inference of concerted action." Canvassing the testimony and exhibits that were before the jury, the court found evidence of numerous complaints from competing Monsanto distributors about

Spray-Rite's price-cutting practices. It also noted that there was testimony that a Monsanto official had said that Spray-Rite was terminated because of the price complaints.

In substance, the Court of Appeals held that an antitrust plaintiff can survive a motion for a directed verdict if it shows that a manufacturer terminated a price-cutting distributor in response to or following complaints by other distributors. This view brought the Seventh Circuit into direct conflict with a number of other Courts of Appeals. We reject the statement by the Court of Appeals for the Seventh Circuit of the standard of proof required to submit a case to the jury in distributor-termination litigation, but affirm the judgment under the standard we announce today.

. . . .

Monsanto does not dispute Spray-Rite's view that if the nonprice practices were proven to have been instituted as part of a price-fixing conspiracy, they would be subject to *per se* treatment. Instead, Monsanto argues that there was insufficient evidence to support the jury's finding that the nonprice practices were "created by Monsanto pursuant to" a price-fixing conspiracy. . . .

In view of Monsanto's concession that a proper finding that nonprice practices were part of a price-fixing conspiracy would suffice to subject the entire conspiracy to *per se* treatment, *Sylvania* is not applicable to this case. In that case only a nonprice restriction was challenged. *See* 433 U.S., at 51, n.18. Nothing in our decision today undercuts the holding of *Sylvania* that nonprice restrictions are to be judged under the rule of reason. In fact, the need to ensure the viability of *Sylvania* is an important consideration in our rejection of the Court of Appeal's standard of sufficiency of the evidence.

This Court has drawn two important distinctions that are at the center of this and any other distributor-termination case. First, there is the basic distinction between concerted and independent action — a distinction not always clearly drawn by parties and courts. Section 1 of the Sherman Act requires that there be a "contract, combination . . . or conspiracy" between the manufacturer and other distributors in order to establish a violation. 15 U.S.C. § 1. Independent action is not proscribed. A manufacturer of course generally has a right to deal, or refuse to deal, with whomever it likes, as long as it does so independently. *United States v. Colgate & Co.*, 250 U.S. 300, 307 (1919); *cf. United States v. Parke, Davis & Co.*, 362 U.S. 29 (1960). Under *Colgate*, the manufacturer can announce its resale prices in advance and refuse to deal with those who fail to comply. And a distributor is free to acquiesce in the manufacturer's demand in order to avoid termination.

The second important distinction in distributor-termination cases is that between concerted action to set prices and concerted action on nonprice restrictions. The former have been *per se* illegal since the early years of national antitrust enforcement. *See Dr. Miles Medical Co. v. John D. Park & Sons Co.*, 220 U.S. 373, 404–409 (1911). The latter are judged under the rule of reason, which requires a weighing of the relevant circumstances of a case to decide whether a restrictive practice constitutes an unreasonable restraint on competition. *See Continental T.V.,*

Inc. v. GTE Sylvania Inc., 433 U.S. 36 (1977).[1]

While these distinctions in theory are reasonably clear, often they are difficult to apply in practice. In *Sylvania* we emphasized that the legality of arguably anticompetitive conduct should be judged primarily by its "market impact." *See, e.g., id.,* at 51. But the economic effect of all of the conduct described above — unilateral and concerted vertical price-setting, agreements on price and nonprice restrictions — is in many, but not all, cases similar or identical. *See, e.g., Parke, Davis, supra,* at 43; note 7 *supra.* And judged from a distance, the conduct of the parties in the various situations can be indistinguishable. For example, the fact that a manufacturer and its distributors are in constant communication about prices and marketing strategy does not alone show that the distributors are not making independent pricing decisions. A manufacturer and its distributors have legitimate reasons to exchange information about the prices and the reception of their products in the market. Moreover, it is precisely in cases in which the manufacturer attempts to further a particular marketing strategy by means of agreements on often costly nonprice restrictions that it will have the most interest in the distributors' resale prices. The manufacturer often will want to ensure that its distributors earn sufficient profit to pay for programs such as hiring and training additional salesmen or demonstrating the technical features of the product, and will want to see that "free-riders" do not interfere. *See Sylvania, supra,* at 55. Thus, the manufacturer's strongly felt concern about resale prices does not necessarily mean that it has done more than the *Colgate* doctrine allows.

Nevertheless, it is of considerable importance that independent action by the manufacturer, and concerted action on nonprice restrictions, be distinguished from price-fixing agreements, since under present law the latter are subject to *per se* treatment and treble damages. On a claim of concerted price-fixing, the antitrust plaintiff must present evidence sufficient to carry its burden of proving that there was such an agreement. If an inference of such an agreement may be drawn from highly ambiguous evidence, there is a considerable danger that the doctrines enunciated in *Sylvania* and *Colgate* will be seriously eroded.

The flaw in the evidentiary standard adopted by the Court of Appeals in this case is that it disregards this danger. Permitting an agreement to be inferred merely from the existence of complaints, or even from the fact that termination came about

---

[1] [FN 7] The Solicitor General (by brief only) and several other amici suggest that we take this opportunity to reconsider whether "contract[s], combination[s] . . . or conspirac[ies]" to fix resale prices should always be unlawful. They argue that the economic effect of resale price maintenance is little different from agreements on nonprice restrictions. *See generally Continental T.V., Inc. v. GTE Sylvania Inc.,* 433 U.S. 36, 69–70 (1977) (White, J., concurring in the judgment) (citing sources); Baker, *Interconnected Problems of Doctrine and Economics in the Section One Labyrinth: Is Sylvania a Way Out?,* 67 Va. L. Rev. 1457, 1465–1466 (1981). They say that the economic objections to resale price maintenance that we discussed in *Sylvania* — such as that it facilitates horizontal cartels — can be met easily in the context of rule-of-reason analysis.

Certainly in this case we have no occasion to consider the merits of this argument. This case was tried on *per se* instructions to the jury. Neither party argued in the District Court that the rule of reason should apply to a vertical price-fixing conspiracy, nor raised the point on appeal. In fact, neither party before this Court presses the argument advanced by amici. We therefore decline to reach the question, and we decide the case in the context in which it was decided below and argued here.

"in response to" complaints, could deter or penalize perfectly legitimate conduct. As Monsanto points out, complaints about price-cutters "are natural — and from the manufacturer's perspective, unavoidable — reactions by distributors to the activities of their rivals." Such complaints, particularly where the manufacturer has imposed a costly set of nonprice restrictions, "arise in the normal course of business and do not indicate illegal concerted action." Moreover, distributors are an important source of information for manufacturers. In order to assure an efficient distribution system, manufacturers and distributors constantly must coordinate their activities to assure that their product will reach the consumer persuasively and efficiently. To bar a manufacturer from acting solely because the information upon which it acts originated as a price complaint would create an irrational dislocation in the market. *See* F. Warren-Boulton, Vertical Control of Markets 13, 164 (1978). In sum, "[t]o permit the inference of concerted action on the basis of receiving complaints alone and thus to expose the defendant to treble damage liability would both inhibit management's exercise of independent business judgment and emasculate the terms of the statute." *Edward J. Sweeney & Sons, Inc. v. Texaco, Inc.*, 637 F.2d 105, 111, n.2 (3d Cir. 1980), *cert. denied*, 451 U.S. 911 (1981).

Thus, something more than evidence of complaints is needed. There must be evidence that tends to exclude the possibility that the manufacturer and nonterminated distributors were acting independently. As Judge Aldisert has written, the antitrust plaintiff should present direct or circumstantial evidence that reasonably tends to prove that the manufacturer and others "had a conscious commitment to a common scheme designed to achieve an unlawful objective." *Edward J. Sweeney & Sons, supra*, at 111.

Applying this standard to the facts of this case, we believe there was sufficient evidence for the jury reasonably to have concluded that Monsanto and some of its distributors were parties to an "agreement" or "conspiracy" to maintain resale prices and terminate price-cutters. In fact there was substantial direct evidence of agreements to maintain prices. There was testimony from a Monsanto direct manager, for example, that Monsanto on at least two occasions in early 1969, about five months after Spray-Rite was terminated, approached price-cutting distributors and advised that if they did not maintain the suggested resale price, they would not receive adequate supplies of Monsanto's new corn herbicide. When one of the distributors did not assent, this information was referred to the Monsanto regional office, and it complained to the distributor's parent company. There was evidence that the parent instructed the subsidiary to comply, and the distributor informed Monsanto that it would charge the suggested price. Evidence of this kind plainly is relevant and persuasive as to a meeting of minds.

. . . .

If, as the courts below reasonably could have found, there was evidence of an agreement with one or more distributors to maintain prices, the remaining question is whether the termination of Spray-Rite was part of or pursuant to that agreement. It would be reasonable to find that it was, since it is necessary for competing distributors contemplating compliance with suggested prices to know that those who do not comply will be terminated. Moreover, there is some circumstantial evidence of such a link. Following the termination, there was a meeting between

Spray-Rite's president and a Monsanto official. There was testimony that the first thing the official mentioned was the many complaints Monsanto had received about Spray-Rite's prices. In addition, there was reliable testimony that Monsanto never discussed with Spray-Rite prior to the termination the distributorship criteria that were the alleged basis for the action. By contrast, a former Monsanto salesman for Spray-Rite's area testified that Monsanto representatives on several occasions in 1965–1966 approached Spray-Rite, informed the distributor of complaints from other distributors — including one major and influential one — and requested that prices be maintained. Later that same year, Spray-Rite's president testified, Monsanto officials made explicit threats to terminate Spray-Rite unless it raised its prices.

We conclude that the Court of Appeals applied an incorrect standard to the evidence in this case. The correct standard is that there must be evidence that tends to exclude the possibility of independent action by the manufacturer and distributor. That is, there must be direct or circumstantial evidence that reasonably tends to prove that the manufacturer and others had a conscious commitment to a common scheme designed to achieve an unlawful objective. Under this standard, the evidence in this case created a jury issue as to whether Spray-Rite was terminated pursuant to a price-fixing conspiracy between Monsanto and its distributors. The judgment of the court below is

Affirmed.

NOTES AND QUESTIONS

1. How much of *Monsanto* survives *Leegin*? Is it clear that Monsanto was imposing "price" rather than "nonprice" restraints? Under the rule established by the Supreme Court in *Continental T.V., Inc. v. GTE Sylvania, Inc.*, 433 U.S. 36 (1977), reprinted *infra*, Subsection C of this section, nonprice restraints receive rule of reason treatment even if they are the product of an "agreement" between the supplier and the dealer. However, does the fact that Dealer *A* was terminated by a supplier as a result of complaints from Dealer *B* about *A*'s price cutting imply that the supplier was imposing price restraints? How does a dealer violate vertical nonprice restraints — more often than not, by price cutting. The following argument comes from Hovenkamp, *Vertical Restrictions and Monopoly Power*, 64 B.U. L. Rev. 521 (1984):

> The Supreme Court's characterization notwithstanding, the facts of *Monsanto Co. v. Spray-Rite Service Corp.* suggest that the defendant had been imposing nonprice rather than price restraints. Spray-Rite was a wholesale distributor of Monsanto's products for eleven years, until Monsanto terminated Spray-Rite's distributorship. Spray-Rite argued that it was terminated because it was a price cutter and other dealers complained about the price cutting. Monsanto argued in return that Spray-Rite was terminated, not because it was a price cutter, but because it "fail[ed] to hire trained salesmen and adequately promote sales to dealers." The posture of this argument put the Court and the jury in the position of deciding that Spray-Rite was terminated for either a price reason or a nonprice reason, and both chose the former.

Actually, Spray Rite was a price cutter *because* it lacked adequately trained employees. It was able to charge less because it took advantage of information provided by the specialists hired by its competitors. When competing dealers complained, naturally they complained about the phenomenon that appeared to cause their injury: the price cutting, not the absence of skilled personnel.

Suppose that a manufacturer plagued with dealer free riding imposes a vertical territorial division. It gives Dealer A Massachusetts as an exclusive territory and Dealer B New Hampshire. Dealer B, however, persists in cheating by making unauthorized sales in Massachusetts. Dealer B probably can make these illicit sales in Massachusetts at a lower price than Dealer A because, unlike B, A bears the burden of promotional and post-sale service expenses in Massachusetts. Dealer B is likely to steal customers in Dealer A's territory only by underselling Dealer A there; customers in A's territory will not ordinarily buy from remote Dealer B, unless B offers them a lower price.

Although everything about this illustrated distribution practice suggests that it involves "nonprice" restraints, a court is likely to characterize the restrictions as pertaining to price. When Dealer A complains to the supplier that Dealer B has been violating the restrictions, A will complain about the territorial invasion and the price-cutting in the same sentence. Even though the supplier has said nothing about what price Dealer B may charge in B's own territory and would never discipline B for price cutting in B's territory, it will discipline B for invading A's territory and cutting prices there.

Most vertical restraints, whether characterized as "price" or "nonprice," are designed to combat free rider problems. A free rider, however, invariably *cuts price* by taking advantage of services provided by other dealers of the same product. In short, violations of *both* resale price maintenance and of nonprice restraints are evidenced by price cutting, and it is generally the price cutting that results in the competitor's complaint.

2. Consider the following: RPM can be used to: (1) facilitate horizontal price-fixing with other suppliers or manufacturers; (2) facilitate a dealer cartel, insulating retail dealers from price competition; or (3) provide higher dealer margins to support pre- and post-sale services to consumers, avoid free-riding, and maintain quality control over the product. In the first two categories, consumers are injured because output restrictions will increase price above competitive levels. In the third, consumers benefit through greater product services and stronger competition in the interbrand market. Thus an RPM can be either service-enhancing or collusive and restrictive in nature.

In a study of 203 reported private and government cases alleging RPM between 1976 and 1982, the FTC found that the collusion theory (either at the manufacturer or retail level) accounted for only 15% of the RPM cases filed, while the proefficiency, service-enhancing theories potentially explained a substantial percentage of the cases. Moreover, in 30% of the filed cases, the supplier was charged with maximum price fixing, the arrangement which attempts to put a ceiling on the price that can be charged at retail. And in 53% of the cases that reached a judicial decision (109/203), judgment was entered for the defendant. *See* FTC Bureau of Economics Staff Report, *Resale Price Maintenance* (Apr. 1, 1988).

3. In *Business Electronics v. Sharp Electronics*, 485 U.S. 717 (1988), the Supreme Court anticipated *Leegin* and restricted the reach of the *Dr. Miles* per se rule against RPM. The case involved an actual agreement between one dealer and the manufacturer to terminate the plaintiff, a rival dealer, because of the latter's price cutting. The Court held that the per se rule applied only if there was an express or implied agreement to set resale prices at a specific level. The Court drew extensive comparisons between the per se rule for resale price agreements, and the rule of reason applied for vertical nonprice restraints under *Continental T.V., Inc. v. GTE Sylvania*, 433 U.S. 36 (1977) (*see infra*). The Court held that the per se rule required a very explicit "price" agreement lest the ambiguity should effectively undermine the rule of reason for nonprice agreements by permitting any discipline of a price-cutting dealer to be treated as a "price" agreement:

> Any agreement between a manufacturer and a dealer to terminate another dealer who happens to have charged lower prices can be alleged to have been directed against the terminated dealer's "price cutting." In the vast majority of cases, it will be extremely difficult for the manufacturer to convince a jury that its motivation was to ensure adequate services, since price cutting and some measure of service cutting usually go hand in hand. Accordingly, a manufacturer that agrees to give one dealer an exclusive territory and terminates another dealer pursuant to that agreement, or even a manufacturer that agrees with one dealer to terminate another for failure to provide contractually-obligated services, exposes itself to th e highly plausible claim that its real motivation was to terminate a price cutter. Moreover, even vertical restraints that do not result in dealer termination, such as the initial granting of an exclusive territory or the requirement that certain services be provided, can be attacked as designed to allow existing dealers to charge higher prices. Manufacturers would be likely to forgo legitimate and competitively useful conduct rather than risk treble damages and perhaps even criminal penalties.

> We cannot avoid this difficulty by invalidating as illegal *per se* only those agreements imposing vertical restraints that contain the word "price," or that affect the "prices" charged by dealers. Such formalism was explicitly rejected in *GTE Sylvania*. As the above discussion indicates, all vertical restraints, including the exclusive territory agreement held not to be *per se* illegal in *GTE Sylvania*, have the potential to allow dealers to increase "prices" and can be characterized as intended to achieve just that. In fact, vertical nonprice restraints only accomplish the benefits identified in *GTE Sylvania* because they reduce intrabrand price competition to the point where the dealer's profit margin permits provision of the desired services. As we described it in *Monsanto:* "The manufacturer often will want to ensure that its distributors earn sufficient profit to pay for programs such as hiring and training additional salesmen or demonstrating the technical features of the product, and will want to see that 'free-riders' do not interfere." [*Sylvania,*] 465 U.S., at 762–763.

PROBLEM 5.1

Spree, Inc. is a manufacturer of clothing for teenagers, a very competitive market in which the key to success is convincing fashionable department stores to give the product display space. Products that do not receive prominent, glitzy displays do not sell, no matter how high their quality. Spree sells to several stores in Boston, one of which is Mack's Department Store, a high quality, eminently fashionable, high priced store that is all the rage among teens. A block away is Feline's Bargains Galore, an off-price retailer. Spree also sells to Feline's, which resells Spree clothing at about one-half the price that Mack's charges.

Mack's suddenly announces a policy to all its suppliers. It will give prominent floor space only to suppliers who either limit the distribution of their product in Boston to Mack's, or else who promise to pressure other stores to "keep their prices up." If the supplier fails to do this, Mack's will either (1) stop dealing in that supplier's product, or (2) move the product downstairs into "Mack's Bargain Basement," where clothing is piled indiscriminately on large tables and sold at substantial discounts. Two weeks after issuing this communication, Mack's writes Spree a letter, stating that henceforth it will sell Spree clothing only in its bargain basement. A week after that, Spree informs Feline's that it will no longer sell it Spree clothing.

Has there been an agreement under *Monsanto*? Should it be unlawful under the rule of reason? Is there any basis for a monopolization claim against Mack under section 2 of the Sherman Act?*See Burlington Coat Factory Warehouse v. Esprit de Corp.*, 769 F.2d 919 (2d Cir. 1985); *McCabe's Furn. v. La-Z-Boy Chair Co.*, 798 F.2d 323 (8th Cir. 1986).

PROBLEM 5.2

Zedco, Inc. manufactures small radios, which it places in boxes that are marked with suggested retail prices. Often the markings are prominent, saying such things as "Only $19.99," or "Manufacturer's Suggested Retail Price, $19.99." Zedco does not say anything to retailers about the prices they must charge for its radios. However, Zedco's warranty and some instructions are printed on the back of the box; as a result, if retailers take the product out of the box, it becomes much less attractive to consumers.

Blast, Inc. is a retailer of consumer electronics located in an area where rent is high and demand for consumer electronics is strong. Blast would like to sell Zedco's radios for more than the suggested retail price printed on Zedco's boxes. When it has tried that, however, it has encountered great consumer resistance and even outrage. Even relatively affluent customers feel "cheated" if they are asked to pay more than the preprinted price marked on the box.

Blast sues Zedco, claiming illegal maximum resale price maintenance, forbidden by Section 1 of the Sherman Act. Outcome under the rule of reason?*See* 8 Phillip E. Areeda & Herbert Hovenkamp, Antitrust Law & 1639d (3d ed. 2011).

PROBLEM 5.3

Parkway Gallery is an independent dealer of furniture. It sells its furniture at "deep discounts" in full-service retail stores in High Point and Boone, North Carolina. Along with other suppliers, it purchases a substantial amount of its furniture stock from Kittinger/Pennsylvania House Group. Pennsylvania House Group requires that the independent retailers dedicate a certain amount of floor space to display Pennsylvania House furniture and that each dealer participate in Pennsylvania House promotional programs and invest in local tabloids to advertise Pennsylvania House lines. Parkway receives about 100 customers a day, plus about 150 telephone inquiries and sales per day.

Other independent dealers complained to Pennsylvania House that they were losing sales to Parkway because of its deep discounts. Customers would visit stores of other dealers, but then buy at a discount from Parkway. Pennsylvania House responded by revising its retail marketing policy to prohibit dealers from soliciting or selling its furniture by mail or telephone order to consumers residing outside specified sales areas.

Before establishing the new policy, Pennsylvania House discussed its proposal with the complaining dealers at a single meeting attended by all of them, made a pledge to its dealer network that it would enforce the new policy against Parkway, found that a large number of its dealers were in agreement with the "aims and purpose of the policy," and obtained assurances from dealers that they would comply with the new policy. Several dealers even said that they would report Parkway violations to Pennsylvania House. After Parkway continued its practice of selling to customers outside its specified area through mail and telephone orders, it was terminated as a dealer by Pennsylvania House. Parkway seeks your advice. What result under *Monsanto*? Do these facts support the "something more" evidentiary standard established by *Monsanto*? Is there an "agreement" among the complaining dealers? If so, could it be characterized as a per se unlawful horizontal agreement? Price-fixing? Boycott?*See Toledo Mack Sales & Service, Inc. v. Mack Trucks, Inc.*, 530 F.3d 204 (3d Cir. 2008); *Watson Carpet & Floor Covering, Inc. v. Mohawk Indus., Inc.*, 648 F.3d 452 (6th Cir. 2011); *Parkway Gallery Furn. v. Kittinger/Pennsylvania House*, 878 F.2d 801 (4th Cir. 1989). *Cf. Bel Canto Design, Ltd. v. MSS HIFI, Inc.*, 2012 U.S. Dist. LEXIS 86628 (S.D.N.Y. June 20, 2012).

PROBLEM 5.4

Sedgwick, Inc. produces consumer electronics and has three dealers in Kansas City. Dealers A and B are full-service dealers who generally charge Sedgwick's suggested retail prices, subject to some downward deviation. C is a discounter. Independently of each other, A and B complain to Sedgwick about C's pricing, and each says words to this effect: "Make C raise its prices to the same level I am charging or else I am going to stop selling Sedgwick products." Soon thereafter, Sedgwick terminates C. Have the antitrust laws been violated? *See Ben Elfman & Sons v. Criterion Mills*, 774 F. Supp. 683, 684–685 (D. Mass. 1991); *LLC v. Jordan Reses Supply Co.*, 2011-2 Trade Cas. 77,583, 2010 U.S. Dist. LEXIS 88958 (E.D. La. Aug. 26, 2010).

[C] Territorial and Customer Restraints: From *White Motor* to *Sylvania*

The territorial and customer restraints considered in this section arise principally when a dealer and/or distributor of a manufacturer's product is given freedom from intrabrand competition within a particular geographic area or for trading with certain customers. Arguably, the restriction indicates that the manufacturer preferred to insulate its dealer from *intrabrand* competition so that the dealer could promote the manufacturer's product more competitively against the brand products of other manufacturers in the *interbrand* market. Such restrictions are usually contractual; the manufacturer agrees not to authorize other dealers in a given area and, in turn, the dealers agree not to compete outside the designated area. Customer restrictions are similarly drafted, restricting selling to certain customers. The dealer then is restricted from competing with other dealers (or the manufacturer) in that brand, according to territories or customers. These contractual arrangements are often associated with or found in a franchise arrangement. Because of the possible restrictions on competition, Section 1 of the Sherman Act is implicated.

As you study the following cases, consider the analysis used by the Court in the horizontal market division cases studied in Chapter 4, especially the *Sealy* and *Topco* decisions. In attempting to reconcile the varying approaches, consider the analysis by which courts characterize the relationship among the parties: whether they are in a seller-buyer, supplier-competitor, or franchisor-franchisee relationship; and how courts have evaluated those relationships within legal and economic standards.

The legal status of nonprice vertical restrictions was unclear up to 1963. The Department of Justice had long taken the position that vertical restraints were per se unlawful. The issue was addressed by the Supreme Court in *White Motor Co. v. United States*, 372 U.S. 253 (1963). The defendant, White Motor, manufactured trucks and truck components and contractually agreed with its dealers that the dealers would sell White Motor trucks only in certain designated areas, and then only to certain customers within the exclusive territory. These territorial and customer restrictions were challenged by the government as per se illegal. In reversing the trial court's summary judgment finding that the restrictions were unlawful, the Court stated:

> We are asked to extend the holding in *Timken Roller Bearing Co. v. United States* (which banned *horizontal* arrangements among competitors to divide territory) to a *vertical* arrangement by one manufacturer restricting the territory of his distributors or dealers. We intimate no view one way or the other on the legality of such an arrangement, for we believe that the applicable rule of law should be designed after a trial.

> This is the first case involving a territorial restriction in a *vertical* arrangement; and we know too little of the actual impact of both that restriction and the one respecting customers to reach a conclusion on the bare bones of the documentary evidence before us.

. . . .

Horizontal territorial limitations, like "[g]roup boycotts, or concerted refusals by traders to deal with other traders" are naked restraints of trade with no purpose except stifling of competition. A vertical territorial limitation may or may not have that purpose or effect. We do not know enough of the economic and business stuff out of which these arrangements emerge to be certain. They may be too dangerous to sanction or they may be allowable protections against aggressive competitors or the only practicable means a small company has for breaking into or staying in business and within the "rule of reason." We need to know more than we do about the actual impact of these arrangements on competition to decide whether they have such a "pernicious effect on competition and lack . . . any redeeming virtue" and therefore should be classified as *per se* violations of the Sherman Act.

. . . .

We conclude that the summary judgment, apart from the price-fixing phase of the case, was improperly employed in this suit. Apart from price fixing, we do not intimate any view on the merits. We only hold that the legality of the territorial and customer limitations should be determined only after a trial.

After remand, the parties entered into a consent decree, settling the suit, a part of which enjoined White Motor from engaging in the challenged restrictions.

Four years later, the Court was again confronted with the question of what legal standard to apply to vertical nonprice restraints. In *United States v. Arnold, Schwinn & Co.*, 388 U.S. 365 (1967), the Court, speaking through Justice Fortas, held that vertical (territory and dealer) restrictions by manufacturers require a different analysis "between the situation where the manufacturer parts with title, dominion, or risk with respect to the article, and where he completely retains ownership and risk of loss" *Id.* at 378–379. The Court concluded that "where a manufacturer *sells* products to his distributor subject to territorial [and customer] restrictions upon resale, a per se violation of the Sherman Act results." *Id.* at 379. Ten years later, the Court, in response to criticism of *Schwinn*, reviewed its per se rule for vertical restraints.

CONTINENTAL T.V., INC. v. GTE SYLVANIA, INC.
433 U.S. 36 (1977)

Justice Powell delivered the opinion of the Court.

Franchise agreements between manufacturers and retailers frequently include provisions barring the retailers from selling franchised products from locations other than those specified in the agreements. This case presents important questions concerning the appropriate antitrust analysis of these restrictions. . . .

I

Respondent GTE Sylvania Inc. (Sylvania) manufactures and sells television sets through its Home Entertainment Products Division. Prior to 1962, like most other television manufacturers, Sylvania sold its televisions to independent or company-owned distributors who in turn resold to a large and diverse group of retailers. Prompted by a decline in its market share to a relatively insignificant 1% to 2% of national television sales,[2] Sylvania conducted an intensive reassessment of its marketing strategy, and in 1962 adopted the franchise plan challenged here. Sylvania phased out its wholesale distributors and began to sell its televisions directly to a smaller and more select group of franchised retailers. An acknowledged purpose of the change was to decrease the number of competing Sylvania retailers in the hope of attracting the more aggressive and competent retailers thought necessary to the improvement of the company's market position.[3] To this end, Sylvania limited the number of franchises granted for any given area and required each franchisee to sell his Sylvania products only from the location or locations at which he was franchised.[4] A franchise did not constitute an exclusive territory, and Sylvania retained sole discretion to increase the number of retailers in an area in light of the success or failure of existing retailers in developing their market. The revised marketing strategy appears to have been successful during the period at issue here, for by 1965 Sylvania's share of national television sales had increased to approximately 5%, and the company ranked as the Nation's eighth largest manufacturer of color television sets.

This suit is the result of the rupture of a franchisor-franchisee relationship that had previously prospered under the revised Sylvania plan. Dissatisfied with its sales in the city of San Francisco, Sylvania decided in the spring of 1965 to franchise Young Brothers, an established San Francisco retailer of televisions, as an additional San Francisco retailer. The proposed location of the new franchise was approximately a mile from a retail outlet operated by petitioner Continental T.V., Inc. (Continental), one of the most successful Sylvania franchisees. Continental protested that the location of the new franchise violated Sylvania's marketing policy, but Sylvania persisted in its plans. Continental then canceled a large Sylvania order and placed a large order with Phillips, one of Sylvania's competitors.

During this same period, Continental expressed a desire to open a store in Sacramento, Cal., a desire Sylvania attributed at least in part to Continental's displeasure over the Young Brothers decision. Sylvania believed that the Sacramento market was adequately served by the existing Sylvania retailers and denied the request.[5] In the face of this denial, Continental advised Sylvania in early

---

[2] [FN 1] RCA at that time was the dominant firm with as much as 60% to 70% of national television sales in an industry with more than 100 manufacturers.

[3] [FN 2] The number of retailers selling Sylvania products declined significantly as a result of the change, but in 1965 there were at least two franchised Sylvania retailers in each metropolitan center of more than 100,000 population.

[4] [FN 3] Sylvania imposed no restrictions on the right of the franchisee to sell the products of competing manufacturers.

[5] [FN 6] Sylvania had achieved exceptional results in Sacramento, where its market share exceeded 15% in 1965.

September 1965, that it was in the process of moving Sylvania merchandise from its San Jose, Cal., warehouse to a new retail location that it had leased in Sacramento. Two weeks later, allegedly for unrelated reasons, Sylvania's credit department reduced Continental's credit line from $300,000 to $50,000. In response to the reduction in credit and the generally deteriorating relations with Sylvania, Continental withheld all payments owed to John P. Maguire & Co., Inc. (Maguire), the finance company that handled the credit arrangements between Sylvania and its retailers. Shortly thereafter, Sylvania terminated Continental's franchises, and Maguire filed this diversity action in the United States District Court for the Northern District of California seeking recovery of money owed and of secured merchandise held by Continental.

The antitrust issues before us originated in cross-claims brought by Continental against Sylvania and Maguire. Most important for our purposes was the claim that Sylvania had violated § 1 of the Sherman Act by entering into and enforcing franchise agreements that prohibited the sale of Sylvania products other than from specified locations.[6] At the close of evidence in the jury trial of Continental's claims, Sylvania requested the District Court to instruct the jury that its location restriction was illegal only if it unreasonably restrained or suppressed competition. Relying on this Court's decision in *Schwinn* the District Court rejected the proffered instruction in favor of the following one:

> "Therefore, if you find by a preponderance of the evidence that Sylvania entered into a contract, combination or conspiracy with one or more of its dealers pursuant to which Sylvania exercised dominion or control over the products sold to the dealer, after having parted with title and risk to the products, you must find any effort thereafter to restrict outlets or store locations from which its dealers resold the merchandise which they had purchased from Sylvania to be a violation of Section 1 of the Sherman Act, regardless of the reasonableness of the location restrictions."

In answers to special interrogatories, the jury found that Sylvania had engaged "in a contract, combination or conspiracy in restraint of trade in violation of the antitrust laws with respect to location restrictions alone," and assessed Continental's damages at $591,505, which was trebled pursuant to 15 U.S.C. § 15 to produce an award of $1,774,515.

On appeal, the Court of Appeals for the Ninth Circuit, sitting en banc, reversed by a divided vote. 537 F.2d 980 (1976). The court acknowledged that there is language in *Schwinn* that could be read to support the District Court's instruction but concluded that *Schwinn* was distinguishable on several grounds. Contrasting the nature of the restrictions, their competitive impact, and the market shares of the franchisers in the two cases, the court concluded that Sylvania's location restriction had less potential for competitive harm than the restrictions invalidated in *Schwinn* and thus should be judged under the "rule of reason" rather than the *per se* rule stated in *Schwinn*. The court found support for its position in the policies

---

[6] [FN 8] Although Sylvania contended in the District Court that its policy was unilaterally enforced, it now concedes that its location restriction involved understandings or agreements with the retailers.

of the Sherman Act and in the decisions of other federal courts involving nonprice vertical restrictions.[7]

. . . .

II

A

We turn first to Continental's contention that Sylvania's restriction on retail locations is a *per se* violation of § 1 of the Sherman Act as interpreted in *Schwinn*. . . .

In the present case, it is undisputed that title to the television sets passed from Sylvania to Continental. Thus, the *Schwinn per se* rule applies unless Sylvania's restriction on locations falls outside *Schwinn*'s prohibition against a manufacturer's attempting to restrict a "retailer's freedom as to where and to whom it will resell the products." *Id.*, at 378. As the Court of Appeals conceded, the language of *Schwinn* is clearly broad enough to apply to the present case. Unlike the Court of Appeals, however, we are unable to find a principled basis for distinguishing *Schwinn* from the case now before us.

Both Schwinn and Sylvania sought to reduce but not to eliminate competition among their respective retailers through the adoption of a franchise system. Although it was not one of the issues addressed by the District Court or presented on appeal by the Government, the Schwinn franchise plan included a location restriction similar to the one challenged here. These restrictions allowed Schwinn and Sylvania to regulate the amount of competition among their retailers by preventing a franchisee from selling franchised products from outlets other than the one covered by the franchise agreement. To exactly the same end, the Schwinn franchise plan included a companion restriction, apparently not found in the Sylvania plan, that prohibited franchised retailers from selling Schwinn products to nonfranchised retailers. In *Schwinn* the Court expressly held that this restriction was impermissible under the broad principle stated there. In intent and competitive impact, the retail-customer restriction in *Schwinn* is indistinguishable from the location restriction in the present case. In both cases the restrictions limited the freedom of the retailer to dispose of the purchased products as he desired. The fact that one restriction was addressed to territory and the other to customers is irrelevant to functional antitrust analysis and, indeed, to the language and broad thrust of the opinion in *Schwinn*. As Mr. Chief Justice Hughes stated in *Appalachian Coals, Inc. v. United States*, 288 U.S. 344, 360, 377 (1933): "Realities must dominate the judgment. . . . The Anti-Trust Act aims at substance."

---

[7] [FN 10] There were two major dissenting opinions. Judge Kilkenny argued that the present case is indistinguishable from *Schwinn* and that the jury had been correctly instructed. Agreeing with Judge Kilkenny's interpretation of *Schwinn*, Judge Browning stated that he found the interpretation responsive to and justified by the need to protect " 'individual traders from unnecessary restrictions upon their freedom of action.' " 537 F.2d, at 1021. See n. 21, *infra*.

III

Sylvania argues that if *Schwinn* cannot be distinguished, it should be reconsidered. Although *Schwinn* is supported by the principle of *stare decisis*, . . . we are convinced that the need for clarification of the law in this area justifies reconsideration. *Schwinn* itself was an abrupt and largely unexplained departure from *White Motor Co. v. United States*, 372 U.S. 253 (1963), where only four years earlier the Court had refused to endorse a *per se* rule for vertical restrictions. Since its announcement, *Schwinn* has been the subject of continuing controversy and confusion, both in the scholarly journals and in the federal courts. The great weight of scholarly opinion has been critical of the decision, and a number of the federal courts confronted with analogous vertical restrictions have sought to limit its reach. In our view, the experience of the past 10 years should be brought to bear on this subject of considerable commercial importance. . . .

The market impact of vertical restrictions is complex because of their potential for a simultaneous reduction of intrabrand competition and stimulation of interbrand competition. . . .

Vertical restrictions reduce intrabrand competition by limiting the number of sellers of a particular product competing for the business of a given group of buyers. Location restrictions have this effect because of practical constraints on the effective marketing area of retail outlets. Although intrabrand competition may be reduced, the ability of retailers to exploit the resulting market may be limited both by the ability of consumers to travel to other franchised locations and, perhaps more importantly, to purchase the competing products of other manufacturers. None of these key variables, however, is affected by the form of the transaction by which a manufacturer conveys his products to the retailers.

Vertical restrictions promote interbrand competition by allowing the manufacturer to achieve certain efficiencies in the distribution of his products. These "redeeming virtues" are implicit in every decision sustaining vertical restrictions under the rule of reason. Economists have identified a number of ways in which manufacturers can use such restrictions to compete more effectively against other manufacturers. . . . [8] For example, new manufacturers and manufacturers entering new markets can use the restrictions in order to induce competent and aggressive retailers to make the kind of investment of capital and labor that is often required in the distribution of products unknown to the consumer. Established manufacturers can use them to induce retailers to engage in promotional activities or to provide service and repair facilities necessary to the efficient marketing of

---

[8] [FN 23] Marketing efficiency is not the only legitimate reason for a manufacturer's desire to exert control over the manner in which his products are sold and serviced. As a result of statutory and common-law developments, society increasingly demands that manufacturers assume direct responsibility for the safety and quality of their products. For example, at the federal level, apart from more specialized requirements, manufacturers of consumer products have safety responsibilities under the Consumer Product Safety Act, 15 U.S.C. § 2051 *et seq.* (1970 ed., Supp. V), and obligations for warranties under the Consumer Product Warranties Act, 15 U.S.C. § 2301 *et seq.* (1970 ed., Supp. V). Similar obligations are imposed by state law. *See, e.g.*, Cal. Civ. Code Ann. § 1790 *et seq.* (West 1973). The legitimacy of these concerns has been recognized in cases involving vertical restrictions. *See, e.g.*, *Tripoli Co. v. Wella Corp.*, 425 F.2d 932 (3d Cir. 1970).

their products. Service and repair are vital for many products, such as automobiles and major household appliances. The availability and quality of such services affect a manufacturer's goodwill and the competitiveness of his product. Because of market imperfections such as the so-called "free rider" effect, these services might not be provided by retailers in a purely competitive situation, despite the fact that each retailer's benefit would be greater if all provided the services than if none did. . . .

Economists also have argued that manufacturers have an economic interest in maintaining as much intrabrand competition as is consistent with the efficient distribution of their products. Although the view that the manufacturer's interest necessarily corresponds with that of the public is not universally shared, even the leading critic of vertical restrictions concedes that *Schwinn's* distinction between sale and nonsale transactions is essentially unrelated to any relevant economic impact. Indeed, to the extent that the form of the transaction is related to interbrand benefits, the Court's distinction is inconsistent with its articulated concern for the ability of smaller firms to compete effectively with larger ones. Capital requirements and administrative expenses may prevent smaller firms from using the exception for nonsale transactions. . . . [9]

We revert to the standard articulated in *Northern Pac. R. Co.*, and reiterated in *White Motor*, for determining whether vertical restrictions must be "conclusively presumed to be unreasonable and therefore illegal without elaborate inquiry as to the precise harm they have caused or the business excuse for their use." 356 U.S., at 5. Such restrictions, in varying forms, are widely used in our free market economy. As indicated above, there is substantial scholarly and judicial authority supporting the economic utility. There is relatively little authority to the contrary.[10] Certainly, there has been no showing in this case, either generally or with respect to Sylvania's agreements, that vertical restrictions have or are likely to have a "pernicious effect on competition" or that they "lack . . . any redeeming virtue."[11] Accordingly, we conclude that the *per se* rule stated in *Schwinn* must be overruled. In so holding we do not foreclose the possibility that particular applications of

---

[9] [FN 26] We also note that *per se* rules in this area may work to the ultimate detriment of the small businessmen who operate as franchisees. To the extent that a *per se* rule prevents a firm from using the franchise system to achieve efficiencies that it perceives as important to its successful operation, the rule creates an incentive for vertical integration into the distribution system, thereby eliminating to that extent the role of independent businessmen.

[10] [FN 28] There may be occasional problems in differentiating vertical restrictions from horizontal restrictions originating in agreements among the retailers. There is no doubt that restrictions in the latter category would be illegal *per se*, *see, e.g., United States v. General Motors Corp.*, 384 U.S. 127 (1966); *United States v. Topco Associates, Inc.*, *supra*, but we do not regard the problems of proof as sufficiently great to justify a *per se* rule.

[11] [FN 29] The location restriction used by Sylvania was neither the least nor the most restrictive provision that it could have used. But we agree with the implicit judgment in *Schwinn* that a *per se* rule based on the nature of the restriction is, in general, undesirable. Although distinctions can be drawn among the frequently used restrictions, we are inclined to view them as differences of degree and form. . . . We are unable to perceive significant social gain from channeling transactions into one form or another. Finally, we agree with the Court in *Schwinn* that the advantages of vertical restrictions should not be limited to the categories of new entrants and failing firms. Sylvania was faltering, if not failing, and we think it would be unduly artificial to deny it the use of valuable competitive tools.

vertical restrictions might justify *per se* prohibition under *Northern Pac. R.. Co.* But we do make clear that departure from the rule-of-reason standard must be based upon demonstrable economic effect rather than — as in *Schwinn* — upon formalistic line drawing.

In sum, we conclude that the appropriate decision is to return to the rule of reason that governed vertical restrictions prior to *Schwinn.* When anticompetitive effects are shown to result from particular vertical restrictions they can be adequately policed under the rule of reason, the standard traditionally applied for the majority of anticompetitive practices challenged under § 1 of the Act. Accordingly, the decision of the Court of Appeals is *Affirmed.*

JUSTICE WHITE, concurring.

Although I agree with the majority that the location clause at issue in this case is not a *per se* violation of the Sherman Act and should be judged under the rule of reason, I cannot agree that this result requires the overruling of *United States v. Arnold, Schwinn & Co.*, 388 U.S. 365 (1967). In my view this case is distinguishable from *Schwinn* because there is less potential for restraint of intrabrand competition and more potential for stimulating interbrand competition. As to intrabrand competition, Sylvania, unlike Schwinn, did not restrict the customers to whom or the territories where its purchasers could sell. As to interbrand competition, Sylvania, unlike Schwinn, had an insignificant market share at the time it adopted its challenged distribution practice and enjoyed no consumer preference that would allow its retailers to charge a premium over other brands. . . .

One element of the system of interrelated vertical restraints invalidated in *Schwinn* was a retail-customer restriction prohibiting franchised retailers from selling Schwinn products to nonfranchised retailers. The Court rests its inability to distinguish *Schwinn* entirely on this retail-customer restriction, finding it "[i]n intent and competitive impact . . . indistinguishable from the location restriction in the present case," because "[i]n both cases the restrictions limited the freedom of the retailer to dispose of the purchased products as he desired." The customer restriction may well have, however, a very different "intent and competitive impact" than the location restriction: It prevents discount stores from getting the manufacturer's product and thus prevents intrabrand price competition. Suppose, for example, that interbrand competition is sufficiently weak that the franchised retailers are able to charge a price substantially above wholesale. Under a location restriction, these franchisers are free to sell to discount stores seeking to exploit the potential for sales at prices below the prevailing retail level. One of the franchised retailers may be tempted to lower its price and act in effect as a wholesaler for the discount house in order to share in the profits to be had from lowering prices and expanding volume.

Under a retail customer restriction, on the other hand, the franchised dealers cannot sell to discounters, who are cut off altogether from the manufacturer's product and the opportunity for intrabrand price competition. This was precisely the theory on which the Government successfully challenged Schwinn's customer restrictions in this Court. . . .

Just as there are significant differences between *Schwinn* and this case with respect to intrabrand competition, there are also significant differences with respect to interbrand competition. Unlike Schwinn, Sylvania clearly had no economic power in the generic product market. At the time they instituted their respective distribution policies, Schwinn was "the leading bicycle producer in the Nation," with a national market share of 22.5%, 388 U.S., at 368, 374, whereas Sylvania was a "faltering, if not failing" producer of television sets, with "a relatively insignificant 1% to 2%" share of the national market in which the dominant manufacturer had a 60% to 70% share. Moreover, the Schwinn brand name enjoyed superior consumer acceptance and commanded a premium price as, in the District Court's words, "the Cadillac of the bicycle industry." This premium gave Schwinn dealers a margin of protection from interbrand competition and created the possibilities for price cutting by discounters that the Government argued were forestalled by Schwinn's customer restrictions. Thus, judged by the criteria economists use to measure market power — product differentiation and market share — Schwinn enjoyed a substantially stronger position in the bicycle market than did Sylvania in the television market. This Court relied on Schwinn's market position as one reason not to apply the rule of reason to the vertical restraints challenged there. "Schwinn was not a newcomer, seeking to break into or stay in the bicycle business. It was not a 'failing company.' On the contrary, at the initiation of these practices, it was the leading bicycle producer in the Nation." 388 U.S., at 374. And the Court of Appeals below found "another significant distinction between our case and *Schwinn*" in Sylvania's "precarious market share," which "was so small when it adopted its locations practice that it was threatened with expulsion from the television market." 537 F.2d, at 991.

In my view there are at least two considerations, both relied upon by the majority to justify overruling *Schwinn*, that would provide a "principled basis" for instead refusing to extend *Schwinn* to a vertical restraint that is imposed by a "faltering" manufacturer with a "precarious" position in a generic product market dominated by another firm. The first is that, as the majority puts it, "when interbrand competition exists, as it does among television manufacturers, it provides a significant check on the exploitation of intrabrand market power because of the ability of consumers to substitute a different brand of the same product." Second is the view, argued forcefully in the economic literature cited by the majority, that the potential benefits of vertical restraints in promoting interbrand competition are particularly strong where the manufacturer imposing the restraints is seeking to enter a new market or to expand a small market share. The majority even recognizes that *Schwinn* "hinted" at an exception for new entrants and failing firms from its *per se* rule.

. . . .

NOTES AND QUESTIONS

1.   The majority held that the ancient rule against restraints on alienation did not justify the per se approach in the nonprice vertical restraint case — an approach that the Court tracked for resale price maintenance in its *Leegin* decision, *supra*. Was this conclusion a result of the *Schwinn* failure to identify an economic basis for

its distinction between sale and consignment transactions? Does an economic rationale exist for the *Schwinn* distinction? Consider Justice White's concurring opinion on this point. Consider whether there are societal values in protecting the exercise of discretion by independent businesses. Wasn't one of the goals of the Sherman Act the protection of unfettered decisionmaking by independent business persons? What role under *Sylvania* does dealer independence play in defining competition standards and in determining legality? If dealer independence does have a value to society apart from the effect on competition, can this noneconomic value be considered under the *Sylvania* analysis?

In considering whether *Sylvania* is hostile to the interest of small business, evaluate how *Sylvania* might protect the small business franchise. Consider the argument that but for the ability of a manufacturer to impose vertical restraints in promoting distributional efficiency, the manufacturer might be forced to integrate vertically, thereby eliminating the independent business entity. *See* Justice Douglas' opinions in *Simpson v. Union Oil Co.*, 377 U.S. 13 (1964), and *Standard Oil Co. v. United States (Standard Stations)*, 337 U.S. 293 (1949) (dissenting).

2.   Do you agree that *Sylvania* values economic efficiency as the principal goal of antitrust law? If so, how is efficiency defined? Is it limited to distribution economies?*Sylvania* indicates that courts are to weigh economic interests, policies, and factual variables in determining whether the "[v]ertical restriction [will] promote interbrand competition by allowing the manufacturer to achieve certain efficiencies." Consider what "objective benchmarks" the courts are to use in this analysis. Are the acceptable benchmarks limited to economic factors? Is the inquiry simply whether the benefits outweigh the adverse effects? Is there a suggestion in *Sylvania* that the balancing analysis inherent in the approved rule of reason standard is broader than that articulated in *Broadcast Music* and *NCAA* for horizontal restraints?

3.   Does *Sylvania*'s rule of reason require a structural analysis? If so, one may have to decide what amount of market power or level of market concentration is necessary to trigger illegality. Should it matter to the analysis whether a healthy interbrand market exists or whether the market is characterized by a monopoly or oligopoly? Perhaps the Court would apply a different approach if the vertical distributional restraint were imposed by a monopolist or an oligopolist. Moreover, the economic effect would vary depending on how many competitors engaged in the same vertical restraint or if the industry was characterized by other industry-wide vertical restraints.

What does the Court mean by harm to "intrabrand" competition? Does it mean that, as a result of the territorial division, Sylvania retailers might begin charging a higher retail price for Sylvania televisions? They could not do this unless Sylvania had market power in Sylvania televisions, could they? Should courts adopt a rule that vertical territorial restrictions are per se *legal* unless the defendant imposing the restraints has monopoly power?

4.   Does the Supreme Court's *Leegin* decision applying the rule of reason to resale price maintenance make judicial analysis of vertical price and nonprice restraints virtually identical? Or are there important differences remaining between the two? Consider the powerful dealer who insists on minimizing competition

with other dealers. Would such a dealer be more likely to (1) demand that a manufacturer impose minimum resale prices on competing dealers? Or (2) demand that the manufacturer not authorize another dealer within a specified distance from the powerful dealer? Either demand could serve the interests of the powerful dealer in maintaining high margins, to the detriment of both the manufacturer and consumers. Does *Leegin* make it more likely that the powerful dealer will insist on resale price maintenance, given that neither practice is now unlawful per se? Might the differences vary with the product? For example, a powerful automobile dealer might insist on territorial separation because car prices are individually negotiated and RPM would be more difficult to maintain. By contrast, a powerful dealer in clothing or shoes or small appliances might find RPM more attractive. *See* 8 PHILLIP E. AREEDA & HERBERT HOVENKAMP, ANTITRUST LAW ¶ 1604 (3d ed. 2011).

By the same token, what about the successful dealer who feels injured by a competing dealer's free riding. Is such a dealer more likely simply to request that the free riding competing dealer be terminated? If the free riding is serious enough, the manufacturer is likely to agree. Would it matter if we characterized this as a "price" or a "nonprice" restraint?

Finally, should the actions of a powerful dealer in inducing an anticompetitive vertical restraint be treated as an unlawful agreement in restraint of trade or as a unilateral exclusionary practice? Or to put the issue somewhat differently, should a challenge on this basis require proof that the complaining dealer is a dominant firm in its market, with enough market power to make it guilty of monopolization? There seems to be a trend in recent case law to treat exclusionary vertical practices as a form of monopolization under Section 2 of the Sherman Act. See the note in Chapter 6, as well as the *Microsoft* and *Dentsply* decisions reprinted there.

5. Five years after the Supreme Court handed down the opinion in *Sylvania* and 17 years after the litigation began, the Ninth Circuit Court of Appeals, on remand from the Supreme Court, concluded that "Sylvania's location clause was not an unreasonable restraint on trade." *Continental T.V., Inc. v. GTE Sylvania, Inc.,* 694 F.2d 1132, 1139–1140 (9th Cir. 1982). The court rejected Continental's argument that once it established a vertical restraint, the burden shifted to defendant to prove "reasonableness" of the restriction. Ruling that the burden of proof was on the plaintiff to demonstrate that the location clause was an unreasonable restraint of trade, the Ninth Circuit held that while Sylvania's location restrictions "harmed intrabrand competition to some extent, the restraint was neither overly restrictive nor adopted to prevent price-discounting." *Id.* at 1138.

In weighing the competitive effects in the interbrand market, the court adopted a market-structure analysis which considered the industry at the inception of the restrictive practice and at the time the challenged practice was enforced against Continental. In addition, the court examined other industry-wide restraints, and whether the imposition of the Sylvania location clause was encouraged by the retailers for the purpose of insulating them from price competition. The court concluded:

> We consider the television manufacturing industry at the time Sylvania adopted the location clause in question [1962] and at the time Sylvania enforced the restraint [1965] to prevent Continental from entering the

Sacramento market to sell Sylvania television sets. In both 1962 and 1965 there were other viable television manufacturers available to sell to any retailers, who wished to enter the Sacramento market, and their products were interchangeable with Sylvania's.

The precise restraints imposed by Sylvania and other manufacturers in the industry are also relevant to a determination of the effect Sylvania's location clause had on interbrand competition. . . . Sylvania did not prevent its retailers from handling competitor's products, and there is no evidence that any other manufacturer imposed such a restraint. A final consideration is that Sylvania did not adopt its distributorship arrangement at the request of other retailers. Rather, it independently determined that the restraint was necessary for Sylvania to remain competitive in the television industry.

694 F.2d at 1139. For commentary on *GTE Sylvania*, see *Robert* Pitofsky, *The* Sylvania *Case: Antitrust Analysis of Non-Price Vertical Restrictions*, 78 COLUM. L. REV. 1 (1978) (generally favoring per se illegality); *see also* Richard A. Posner, *The Next Step in the Antitrust Treatment of Restricted Distribution: Per Se Legality*, 48 U. CHI. L. REV. 6 (1981) (arguing that *Sylvania* does not go far enough and per se legality would be a better rule). *See also* 8 PHILLIP E. AREEDA & HERBERT HOVENKAMP, ANTITRUST LAW ¶¶ 1641–1649 (3d ed. 2011).

6. Since the *Sylvania* decision, the rule of reason has become, for all practical purposes, a rule of per se legality. Few courts have held a nonprice vertical restraint unlawful. *See Graphic Prods. Distribs. v. Itek Corp.*, 717 F.2d 1560 (11th Cir. 1983); *Eiberger v. Sony Corp.*, 622 F.2d 1068 (2d Cir. 1980). *But see Maris Distributing Co. v. Anheuser Busch, Inc.*, 302 F.3d 1207 (11th Cir. 2002). *See* Douglas H. Ginsburg, *Vertical Restraints: De Facto Legality Under the Rule of Reason*, 60 ANTITRUST L.J. 67 (1991) (observing that almost no plaintiffs have won vertical restraints cases post-*Sylvania*).

7. As Chapter 4 indicates, nonprice horizontal restraints, such as territorial and customer limitations between competitors, are illegal per se. Thus it is important in evaluating the evidence to determine whether the vertical restraint, though ostensibly imposed by the supplier, is in fact controlled or agreed upon by the dealers. *Cf. United States v. Apple, Inc.*, ___ F. Supp. 2d ___, 2013 U.S. Dist. LEXIS 96424 (S.D.N.Y. July 10, 2013) (agreement among publishers facilitated by Apple to impose higher resale prices on Amazon, Apple's rival in resale market, unlawful per se).

8. In *Toys "R" Us Inc. v. FTC*, 221 F.3d 928 (7th Cir. 2000), the Seventh Circuit upheld a Federal Trade Commission order that barred the retailer from attempting to restrict toy supplies to warehouse clubs. Toys R Us sells nearly 20% of all toys in the United States, and even manufacturing giants like Hasbro felt pressured to agree when the retailer requested that they not provide certain toys to warehouse clubs, which sold toys at discounts up to 30% of Toys R Us prices. There were at least 10 vertical agreements in effect. In addition, Toys R Us orchestrated a horizontal boycott of warehouse clubs by toy manufacturers, acting as a complaint clearinghouse, so toy manufacturers could be assured that their competitors were not cheating on the agreements. The FTC order bars Toys R Us from entering into such agreements. For additional discussion of the horizontal restraints involved in this case, see Chapter 4.

[1] Dual Distribution Systems — Vertical or Horizontal

A dual distribution system is one in which a manufacturer (supplier) functions at the same level in the market as its dealers at the same time it acts as a supplier. The manufacturer thus operates on two separate levels of competition, facing two separate competitive forces — one interbrand (on the manufacturing level) and the other intrabrand (on the distribution level). An example is when a franchisor-owned outlet competes with a franchisee-owned outlet in the same market. In analyzing such situations, courts have often considered whether the relationship between the franchisor and the independently owned franchisee should be characterized as horizontal, thus invoking a per se condemnation, or vertical, with the implication that *Sylvania's* rule of reason ought to control.

The issue has not been firmly decided by the Supreme Court. In *White Motor* and *Schwinn*, the Court implied that a dual distribution arrangement was vertical in nature. But in *Sylvania* the Court observed that "[t]here may be occasional problems in differentiating vertical restrictions from horizontal restrictions. . . . There is no doubt that restrictions in the latter category would be illegal per se." 433 U.S. at 58 n.28.

Compare further the Court's analysis in two cases. The manufacturer in *Schwinn* competed with its wholesale distributors for sales to retailers. The Court looked to the *source* of the restraints, and finding that they were imposed by the manufacturer, held that the restrictions were vertical. In *Sealy* and *Topco* (discussed in Chapter 4), the Court pierced the vertical veneer to find horizontal underpinnings. The resolution of the issue, to date, has been left to the lower federal courts. The Supreme Court has not spoken on the issue since its dictum in *Sylvania*. For a discussion of the analytical problems associated with this issue, see Liebeler, *Intrabrand "Cartels" Under GTE Sylvania*, 30 UCLA L. Rev. 1 (1982).

Due to the lack of guidance from the Court, the lower federal courts have adopted a variety of tests in determining whether a restraint is horizontal or vertical in the dual distributorship context. Once the court is able to characterize the conduct as either horizontal or vertical, the legal standard, whether per se or rule of reason, seems to follow automatically.

Several approaches have been employed by the lower courts during the characterization process. One approach could be labeled "the source of the restraint" rule. This analysis attempts to determine whether the restraint was initiated by competitors on the same level of the distribution chain or whether it was initiated primarily by the manufacturer for the purpose of achieving an efficient distribution system. *H & B Equip. Co. v. International Harvester Co.*, 577 F.2d 239 (5th Cir. 1978).

A second approach taken by the lower courts "focuses not on whether the vertical or horizontal aspects of the system predominate, but rather, on the actual competitive impact of the dual distribution system." *Krehl v. Baskin-Robbins Ice Cream Co.*, 664 F.2d 1348, 1356 (9th Cir. 1982). This functional economic analysis weighs the intrabrand restriction against the potential for enhancing interbrand competition, regardless of horizontal features.

In *International Logistics Group, Ltd. v. Chrysler Corp.*, 884 F.2d 904 (6th Cir. 1989), the Sixth Circuit held that a rule of reason analysis should apply to an automobile manufacturer's distribution practices regarding independent distributors and dealers. A division of Chrysler sold a Power Master engine at lower prices for the international export market than the domestic market. Plaintiffs purchased these engines "at overseas prices ostensibly for export and overseas resale." However, they did not export the engines but rather sold them for distribution in the domestic market at prices "substantially below Chrysler's prices to domestic dealers."

After Chrysler warned plaintiffs, who were independent distributors of Chrysler parts, not to resell in the domestic market parts purchased for the export market, Chrysler terminated plaintiffs for failure to comply.

The court held that Chrysler acted independently in establishing its marketing policies (pricing for particular markets), and that Chrysler announced that it "would reject all purchase orders from distributors who refused to comply with the marketing conditions." Thus, the court concluded that Chrysler's termination action was unilateral. Quoting Professor Areeda, the court reasoned that "there can be no conspiracy 'where the actor imposing the alleged restraint does not . . . need the acquiescence of the other party or any quid pro quo.' " *See also Cheatham's Furn. Co. v. La-Z-Boy Chair Co.*, 1990–1991 Trade Cases at & 68937 (E.D. Mo.) (termination of a dealer for failure to honor an explicit resale price maintenance scheme was lawful because there was no "agreement"). The court also concluded that Chrysler's marketing practices were directed at vertically related firms, notwithstanding that Chrysler was also a distributor. Do you agree with the court that Chrysler's marketing and distribution policies were vertical and nonprice in nature, thus warranting a rule of reason analysis? What argument could you advance to show horizontal competitive effects?

[D]   Exclusive Dealerships

One of the principal ways in which a dealer termination may occur is if the supplier decides to have its product marketed by only one dealer in the area. By definition, an "exclusive dealership" is a contractual arrangement whereby all but one dealer "in the same product of the same manufacturer are eliminated." *Packard Motor Car Co. v. Webster Motor Car Co.*, 243 F.2d 418 (D.C. Cir.), *cert. denied*, 355 U.S. 822 (1957). If the supplier unilaterally decides to sell to only one dealer in an area, there is no qualifying agreement and thus no Sherman Section 1 violation. But assuming that the supplier and designated dealer "agree" to an exclusive arrangement, is there any reason for thinking it illegal?

Consider the observation in *Schwinn* that:

> [A] manufacturer of a product . . . which [is] readily available in the market may select his customers, and for this purpose he may 'franchise' certain dealers to whom, alone, he will sell his goods. . . . If the restraint stops at that point — if nothing more is involved than vertical 'confinement'

of the manufacturer's own sales of the merchandise to selected dealers, and if competitive products are readily available to others, the restriction, on these facts alone, would not violate the Sherman Act.

388 U.S. at 376. Does this language indicate an approval of the exclusive dealership, or does it merely restate the *Colgate* doctrine?

In evaluating this vertical arrangement, weigh the competitive effects of such a distribution system. Is the exclusive arrangement as anticompetitive as a territorial restriction on a dealer? Does the restriction in fact run against the exclusive dealer, or is it simply a restriction on the supplier's right to deal with other distributors? If this is true, could not the exclusive dealer market the product in another area outside its own? The result would be that intrabrand competition would not be as restricted as the result under a territorial limitation. What incentives are there for a manufacturer to enter into such an exclusive dealership?

A manufacturer may desire to bring a new product on the market but fear that because of competition, the product will not be successful absent a vigorous promotion. If the manufacturer is permitted to extend an exclusive dealership in this product, the dealer, being free from intrabrand competition and free rider problems, will have the incentive to market aggressively the new product. If this argument is economically sound with regard to a new product, it also has application to the product where a substantial capital investment or other expenses must be incurred. The efficiency incentives for both the manufacturer and dealer seem clear, though intrabrand competition in the brand product is diminished.

Should it matter whether the manufacturer has to terminate existing dealers or merely promise not to license new dealers in establishing an exclusive dealership (franchise)? Do competitive effects differ between foreclosure of potential and existing competition? Is the presence of a horizontal restraint more likely in one situation than it is in the other?*See* LAWRENCE A. SULLIVAN, HANDBOOK OF THE LAW OF ANTITRUST 427–429 (1977).

The courts that have confronted these issues have often used a structural approach to inform their economic analysis of the competitive impact of the exclusive distribution system. The structure of the market and the market power of the individual firm that imposes the sole outlet arrangement have been considered relevant. The focus has been on whether a dominant firm with substantial market power ought to be permitted to establish an exclusive distribution system with the purpose and perhaps effect of further increasing its dominance in the manufacturing market. A related question is whether the market power of the exclusive dealer is relevant in evaluating the economic consequence of the exclusive dealership.

In an early but significant case, the District of Columbia Court of Appeals in *Packard Motor Car Co. v. Webster Motor Car Co.*, 243 F.2d 418 (D.C. Cir. 1957), held that an agreement between the Packard Motor Company and a Baltimore dealer to give it an exclusive contract to sell Packards in Baltimore and to terminate two other Packard dealers in the area was not a violation of the Sherman Act, either under Section 1 or Section 2. First, with regard to the monopolization charge under Section 2, the court said that because there were other cars "reasonably interchangeable by consumers," an exclusive franchise contract "for marketing Packards does not create a monopoly." Second, "[w]hen an exclusive dealership 'is not part and parcel of a scheme to monopolize and effective competition exists at both the seller and buyer levels, the arrangement has invariably been upheld as a reasonable restraint of trade . . . [and] virtually one of *per se* legality [under section 1].' "

Packard, of course, was a small manufacturer attempting to compete with large manufacturers. The court opined that "[t]o penalize the small manufacturer for competing in this way not only fails to promote the policy of the antitrust laws but defeats it." Moreover, the fact that one dealer requests the exclusive dealership with the consequence that others are eliminated does not make it illegal. "Since the immediate object of an exclusive dealership is to protect the dealer from competition in the manufacturer's product, it is likely to be the dealer who asks for it."

Note that the restraint in *Packard* was on the seller rather than the buyer. When the restraint is on the seller ("exclusive selling"), Section 3 of the Clayton Act does not apply. If the restraint is on the buyer, Section 3 of the Clayton Act applies, as well as Section 1 of the Sherman Act.

What are the competitive consequences of an exclusive dealership? If the purpose behind such a commercial transaction is to improve distribution efficiencies in the intrabrand market so as to promote interbrand competition, what competitive consequence would be expected if the surviving exclusive dealer was also the sole outlet for all other suppliers in that area? Consider the effect this would have on the interbrand market. Might the dealer's pressure on the manufacturer to grant it an exclusive franchise in this context amount to monopolization or an attempt to monopolize under Section 2 of the Sherman Act?*See* Chapter 6, *infra.* Should the *Packard Motor* rationale not apply whenever the manufacturer and/or the exclusive dealer possess market power in their respective markets?

In *Valley Liquors, Inc. v. Renfield Importers, Ltd.*, 678 F.2d 742 (7th Cir. 1982), the Seventh Circuit held that the burden is on the plaintiff "to show that the defendant has significant market power." The court opined that "[a] firm that has no market power is unlikely to adopt policies that disserve its consumers." Valley Liquors was a wholesale wine and liquor distributor; Renfield was one of its suppliers. Renfield terminated Valley as a distributor. Renfield had decided to adopt a system of restricted distribution whereby it would sell only to one or two wholesalers. "There [was] virtually no evidence concerning Renfield's motivation for the adoption of a more restricted distribution system and the concomitant realignment of wholesaler territories, except that it was a reaction to Renfield's disappointing sales." In addition, "unrebutted evidence [indicated] that Valley had been selling Renfield products at prices five percent below those charged by Renfield's other distributors." The Seventh Circuit affirmed the trial court's denial of a preliminary injunction. Here, the defendant's lack of market power "in the market subject to the challenged restraint appear[ed] decisive." H. HOVENKAMP, FEDERAL ANTITRUST POLICY § 11.6b (4th ed. 2011). *See also* Liebeler, *Intraband "Cartels" Under GTE Sylvanin*, 30 UCLA L. REV. 1, 10–13 (1982).

On remand from the appeal, the district court granted summary judgment for defendant Renfield. On the second appeal, the Seventh Circuit affirmed the district court, holding that plaintiff failed to rebut the defendant's summary judgment motion by failing to show a genuine factual issue on (1) whether there was a conspiracy between the importer and competing distributors to fix price and (2) whether the importer had sufficient market power to restrain trade. 822 F.2d 656 (7th Cir. 1987). The district court had found that Renfield's market share in metropolitan Chicago was less than 2% and in the state of Illinois or the rest of the county only 2–3%. *Id.* at 667.

In *Paddock v. Chicago Tribune*, 103 F.3d 42 (7th Cir. 1996), *cert. denied*, 520 U.S. 1265 (1997), the Seventh Circuit upheld a series of contracts under which various sellers of news and other services supplied exclusively one newspaper in a given area. For example, the New York Times News Service agreement gave the *Chicago Tribune* the exclusive right to New York Times News stores in the Chicago metropolitan area, thus denying that service to the *Tribune*'s competitors, such as the *Chicago Sun-Times* or the plaintiff *Chicago Daily Herald*. The court noted that "[e]xclusivity is one valuable feature the service offers, for a paper with exclusive rights to a service or feature is both more attractive to readers and more distinctive from its rivals."

The court also noted that the market for news services contained numerous providers and seemed to be quite competitive. Further, the contracts were of relatively short duration, and any newspaper could win an exclusive contract by offering the best deal:

> Competition-for-the-contract is a form of competition that antitrust laws protect rather than proscribe, and it is common. Every year or two, General Motors, Ford, and Chrysler invite tire manufacturers to bid for exclusive rights to have their tires used in the manufacturers' cars. Exclusive contracts make the market hard to enter in mid-year but cannot stifle competition over the longer run, and competition of this kind drives down the price of tires, to the ultimate benefit of consumers. Just so in the news business — if smaller newspapers are willing to bid with cash rather than legal talent. In the meantime, exclusive stories and features help the newspapers differentiate themselves, the better to compete with one another. A market in which every newspaper carried the same stories, columns, and cartoons would be a less vigorous market than the existing one. And a market in which the creators of intellectual property (such as the New York Times) could not decide how best to market it for maximum profit would be a market with less (or less interesting) intellectual property created in the first place.

While exclusivity might sometimes facilitate collusion, there was no allegation of any kind of forbearance by rivals. Further, while the local market for newspapers was reasonably concentrated, the national market for news services and other inputs seemed to be robustly competitive. This fact was particularly important because the allegation was of exclusive distributorships, not of exclusive dealing. The court continued:

> Despite the similarity in nomenclature, there is a difference. . . . An exclusive dealing contract obliges a firm to obtain its inputs from a single source. Each of the theaters [in *FTC v. Motion Picture Advertising Service Co.*, 344 U.S. 392 (1953)] was committed to one distributor for all of its ads. This was the genesis of the concern about foreclosure. A new advertising

distributor could not find outlets. An exclusive distributorship, by contrast, does not restrict entry at either level. None of the newspapers in Chicago (or anywhere else) has promised by contract to obtain all of its news from a single source — and the sources have not locked all of their output together (unlike the "block booking" involved in Loew's). A new entrant to the supplemental news service business could sell to every newspaper in the United States, if it chose to do so. Existing features syndicates sell to multiple firms in the same market (although most features go to one paper per city; this is the exclusive distribution aspect of the contracts). So vendors can and do sell news and features to multiple customers, and customers can and do buy news and features from multiple vendors. "Foreclosure" of the kind about which *Motion Picture Advertising Service* was concerned does not occur under exclusive distribution contracts.

The Supreme Court's decision in *American Needle, Inc. v. NFL*, 560 U.S. 183 (2010) (reprinted *supra*, Ch. 4), involved an exclusive trademark license, a practice akin to an exclusive dealership in which the owner of a trademark licenses a single firm to produce goods bearing its mark. In *American Needle*, the NFL had given an exclusive license to Reebok to produce caps and other headwear bearing the logos of individual NFL football teams. The issue in that case did not concern the legality of exclusive trademark licensing as such, but rather whether the NFL was a single entity or a combination of its individual teams. As a general matter, exclusive trademark licenses given unilaterally are lawful, and there are good reasons for this. Trademarks designate a good's origin and provide information about its quality. Customers might become confused if large numbers of firms could produce products bearing someone else's mark. 3 J. THOMAS MCCARTHY, MCCARTHY ON TRADEMARKS AND UNFAIR COMPETITION §§ 18.5–18.6 (4th ed. 2009). One way a trademark owner can create assurance about the products being produced bearing its mark is to limit the number of producers. But couldn't each team individually give an exclusive license to a manufacturer; that is, the marks of individual NFL teams are just as distinctive as the marks of, say, Microsoft and Apple, or General Motors and Ford, so why did exclusivity have to be "horizontal" as well as "vertical"?

PROBLEM 5.5

Hope Hospital had a policy of assisting patients at the hospital who were nearing discharge and who needed home health care by using independent nurses to assist and counsel patients in selecting an equipment supplier for their home needs. Vendors could not solicit in the hospital. Thereafter, Hope Hospital entered into a joint venture with a medical equipment vendor to supply this service. The previous hospital policy was changed when the hospital appointed an employee of the vendor, who had no health care training, as the patient equipment coordinator. This employee was named the exclusive agent to assist patients and to arrange equipment rentals. The coordinator referred patients to the joint venture medical equipment firm.

The self-employed nurses who previously served this function complained and in response the hospital policy was changed to permit the nurses to aid in making the patient assessment. But the nurses were encouraged to recommend the joint venture firm. As a result, 85% of the hospital's patients who needed home equipment received it from the joint venture firm.

If you were counsel for a competing vendor, what antitrust arguments would you make? What counter-arguments are available for Hope Hospital? Does a competing vendor suffer antitrust injury under the joint venture arrangement? Does a patient suffer antitrust injury?*See Key Enters. of Del., Inc. v. Venice Hosp.*, 919 F.2d 1550 (11th Cir. 1990).

II   INTERBRAND VERTICAL FORECLOSURE — MAINLY, EXCLUSIVE DEALING AND TYING

In addition to *intrabrand* distributional restraints on dealers, suppliers may attempt to foreclose interbrand competition through vertical restrictions on distributors and dealers. Competitors allegedly may be foreclosed from competing in a market through a supplier's exclusionary practices which restrict the buyer's ability to deal in the goods of the competitor of the supplier. It is alleged that the exclusionary practice might foreclose competition by means of a requirements contract between supplier and buyer.

The principal exclusionary distribution arrangements are exclusive dealing arrangements and tie-in sales. Both of these commercial arrangements have an effect on *interbrand* competition because the supplier's buyer is precluded by contract, either directly or indirectly, from purchasing from the supplier's competitors. In the exclusive dealing contract, the buyer explicitly or implicitly agrees to buy exclusively the products of the contracting supplier. In the second, the same result occurs because the buyer is forced to take all its requirements or a second product if it desires to buy the principal product, thereby precluding the buyer from purchasing the second product from a competitor of the seller. The competitive process and consumer welfare arguably are compromised because outlets for the supplier's competitors are denied and the consumer is limited in the range of choices.

The exclusive dealing contract discussed here differs from an exclusive dealership described previously in that the exclusive dealership contract is an output contract rather than a requirements contract. It restricts the ability of the *supplier* to supply competitors of the dealer. In contrast, exclusive dealing is a form of a requirements contract in that it places restrictions on the *dealer* as to with whom it can deal. A traditional requirements contract forced the buyer for a certain time period to purchase some or all of its product needs from the contracting supplier. An exclusive dealing contract would require the buyer to deal only in the goods of that supplier. The distinction between an output contract and requirements contract is not without legal significance.

The Clayton Act, adopted in 1914, places restrictions on requirements contracts but not output contracts. Consider Section 3 of the Act.

> It shall be unlawful for any person engaged in commerce, in the course of such commerce, to lease or make a sale or contract for sale of goods, wares, merchandise, machinery, supplies, or other commodities, whether

patented or unpatented, for use, consumption, or resale within the United States or any Territory thereof or the District of Columbia or any insular possession or other place under the jurisdiction of the United States, or fix a price charged therefor, or discount from, or rebate upon, such price, on the condition, agreement, or understanding that the lessee or purchaser thereof shall not use or deal in the goods, wares, merchandise, machinery, supplies, or other commodities of a competitor or competitors of the lessor or seller, where the effect of such lease, sale, or contract for sale or such condition, agreement, or understanding may be to substantially lessen competition or tend to create a monopoly in any line of commerce.

15 U.S.C. § 14. The statute condemns limitations on lessees or purchasers, but not on suppliers, sellers, or lessors. Thus, while the exclusive dealership will be scrutinized under Section 1 of the Sherman Act (but not the Clayton Act), the exclusive dealing contract or the buying arrangement will come within both the Sherman and the Clayton Acts if jurisdictional requirements are met. In light of the legislative history and interpretation of Section 3, the burden of proof is easier for the plaintiff to meet than under Section 1 of the Sherman Act. Note that Section 3 has a built-in standard of analysis: the conduct is unlawful if its effect "may be to substantially lessen competition or tend to create a monopoly in any line of commerce." The burden of proof under the statute is not the mere "possibility" of competitive injury, but one of "probability" that competition will be lessened. A further limitation on the application of these statutes to vertical arrangements that foreclose competition is that the Clayton Act does not apply to contracts for service, but only arrangements, including leases or sales, of "goods." The Sherman Act covers the vertical arrangement whether it involves goods or services.

[A] Exclusive Dealing Under the Rule of Reason

Efficiency considerations support a rule of reason analysis of exclusive dealing contracts because they are a form of partial vertical integration. Suppliers may be eager to enter exclusive dealing contracts as a means of obtaining assured outlets or markets for their products, as they attempt to recoup their investment with a reasonable profit. The predictability created by such a contract can enhance production and distribution efficiency, leading to increased competition. Moreover, by tying closely the buyer and supplier, the buyer's promotional efforts will center on the supplier's products, thereby creating increased dealer loyalty. This relationship may facilitate greater competitive assertiveness by the dealer on behalf of the supplier's product. Without this close contractual relationship, the supplier may be unwilling to risk investment in capital, innovation, and new products.

Conversely, buyers will be interested in obtaining a reliable source of supply to insulate themselves from market fluctuations, which can be achieved through an agreement with the supplier to furnish all or substantial portions of the buyer's needs. The exclusive dealing contract thus can minimize the transaction costs and diseconomies of both suppliers and buyers. The result may be that these parties are drawn through economic objectives toward long term requirements contracts as an alternative to complete vertical integration — a single integrated entity occupying multiple levels in the distribution chain. *See* Oliver E. Williamson, *Transaction-Cost Economics: The Governance of Contractual Relations*, 22 J.L. & ECON. 233 (1979); Ian R. MacNeil, *Contracts: Adjustment of Long-Term Economic Relations Under Classical, Neoclassical, and Relational Contract Law*, 72 Nw. U. L. REV. 854 (1978); Dennis Carlton, *Vertical Integration in Competitive Markets Under Uncertainty*, 27 J. INDUS. ECON. 189 (1979). But even if one accepts the efficiency underpinning as a basis for antitrust analysis, the exclusive dealing contract may be broader than necessary to achieve the planned economies and reasonable business practices, to the extent that it includes terms in excess of the time or conditions necessary to recoup the investment or enhance its distribution.

A growing body of economic literature argues that most exclusive dealing arrangements are efficient, and that exclusive dealing may be used to combat free rider problems, much the same way that vertical price and other nonprice restraints are used. For example, a manufacturer might use exclusive dealing to protect itself from "interbrand" free riding. Interbrand free riding occurs when a retailer is able to take advantage of amenities supplied by one manufacturer and apply them to products which originate from another manufacturer. Suppose, for example, that Exxon is a "full service" franchisor of gasoline stations, and supplies its independent franchisees (gasoline station operators) with a variety of things that make the station more attractive to the customer — "free" road maps, information services, and the big "Exxon" sign which the customer interprets as Exxon's guarantee of the quality of the products sold at that station.

Suppose, however, that the gasoline retailer also buys discounted off-brand gasoline and sells it at a substantially lower price from pumps adjacent to the Exxon gasoline pumps. Quite naturally, many of the amenities provided by Exxon will spill over to these pumps as well. Customers will drive into the station because it is a quality certified "Exxon" station, help themselves to a free road map, and buy the discount gasoline instead of Exxon's own brand. Exxon can protect itself from this problem by exclusive dealing — i.e., by insisting that the dealer who owns an Exxon franchise and holds itself out as an Exxon station operator sell nothing but Exxon gasoline. In such circumstances an exclusive dealing contract might also protect customers from fraud. For more on the recent literature concerning the economics of exclusive dealing, see H. Hovenkamp, Federal Antitrust Policy § 10.8 (4th ed. 2011).

Counterarguments to the efficiency objectives suggest that exclusive dealing arrangements tend to foreclose from markets competitors and potential competitors of the supplier. If effective, these contracts will deny existing competitors the opportunity to compete for business of the contracting buyer. The anticompetitive consequences would be increased if this contractual conduct occurred in a concentrated market, as opposed to the ideal market of unlimited demand. The exclusionary effect allegedly may create barriers to entry for new firms at the supplier's level. Moreover, if effective, the supplier allegedly may be able to use the exclusive dealing agreement as a means either to achieve a monopoly or maintain a monopoly position. Authority exists that even if the use of supply contracts and exclusive arrangements have economic justifications, they may nevertheless "be undertaken with unlawful intent and in the desire to achieve [a monopoly]." *United States v. Dairymen, Inc.*, 660 F.2d 192, 195 (6th Cir. 1981).

In any event, the conventional analysis suggests that exclusive dealing implicates the use of market power and leverage of that power at one level of competition (supplier level) to affect another level (buyer level) with the result that interbrand competition is diminished. *But see* R. POSNER, ANTITRUST LAW: AN ECONOMIC PERSPECTIVE 196–206 (1976). Thus, the exclusionary effects of exclusive dealings arguably must be weighed against the economies achieved through the contract's efficiency features. Because individual exclusive dealing contracts may have procompetitive aspects, and indeed may be in the buyer's best interest, courts, as the following section indicates, have been unwilling to apply the rule of per se illegality. *See generally* Steuer, *Exclusive Dealing in Distribution*, 69 CORNELL L. REV. 101 (1983).

Although the Antitrust Division of the Department of Justice has not set out a definite description of its approach toward enforcement against exclusive dealing, insight can be gained from some of the cases the Division has brought in the last few years. Arrangements of short or moderate duration are no longer protected from antitrust scrutiny, especially when imposed by companies with "significant market power." *Id.* at 26. Moreover, the Division is more willing now to look beyond the mere terms of the contract in deciding the scope of its exclusivity. *Id. See United States v. Microsoft*, 56 F.3d 1448 (D.C. Cir. 1995). *See also* Mary Lou Steptoe & Donna L. Wilson, *Developments in Exclusive Dealing*, 10 ANTITRUST 25 (1996) (reviewing the increased enforcement efforts of the Clinton administration with respect to exclusive dealing and analyzing the possible effects of the *Omega* verdict); Wanda Jane Rogers, Note, *Beyond Economic Theory: A Model for Analyzing the Antitrust Implications of Exclusive Dealing Arrangements*, 45 DUKE L.J. 1009, 1018–1025 (1996) (discussing the procompetitive and anticompetitive effects of exclusive dealing and commenting that courts today do not generally follow a strict "Chicago-school" efficiency approach but rather look to the actual marketplace effects of exclusive dealing arrangements).

Finally, a significant development observed in the following chapter is the increased use of Section 2 of the Sherman Act to pursue exclusive dealing and similar arrangements by dominant firms. See the related note in this chapter, *infra*.

Recall that as a prerequisite for Clayton Act coverage, a plaintiff must demonstrate that the challenged exclusive dealing arrangement arose from "a condition, agreement, or understanding" which has the effect of "substantially lessen[ing] competition or tend[ing] to create a monopoly in any line of commerce." This "concert of action" requirement under Section 3 of the Clayton Act, as under the Sherman Act, may not be established if the evidence demonstrates that the supplier merely, and unilaterally, refused to deal when the buyer would not consent to the exclusive dealing terms. On this element of the burden of proof, the *Colgate* doctrine arguably has continuing vitality. *See, e.g., Nelson Radio & Supply Co. v. Motorola, Inc.*, 200 F.2d 911 (5th Cir. 1952), *cert. denied*, 345 U.S. 925 (1953). In addition, the exceptions to the doctrine apply particularly when the evidence is susceptible to an inference of coercion or tacit understanding, leading to the conclusion that there has been a "meeting of the minds." Authority exists that even if the contract did not explicitly contain an exclusive dealing clause, it can be inferred from the "course of dealing" between the buyer and the seller. *Barnosky*

Oils, Inc. v. Union Oil Co., 665 F.2d 74, 86–87 (6th Cir. 1981). Finally, it should be noted that the allegations in the complaint must be drawn so that the court can at least infer a claim for relief from articulated anticompetitive effects in a defined market; otherwise dismissal may be appropriate. *See Gilbuilt Homes, Inc. v. Continental Homes*, 667 F.2d 209, 212 (1st Cir. 1981); *Perington Whsle., Inc. v. Burger King Corp.*, 631 F.2d 1369 (10th Cir. 1979).

In the leading case rejecting the per se characterization for exclusive dealing contracts, *Standard Oil Co. v. United States (Standard Stations)*, 337 U.S. 293, 305–306 (1949), Justice Frankfurter reasoned that while the rule of reason was the appropriate analysis to employ for determining the legality of such contracts, the Clayton Act did not require the broader-based weighing analysis embraced in *Chicago Board of Trade. Id.* at 313. A more focused analysis was adopted, designed to determine whether the contract substantially foreclosed competition. In addition to establishing the standard of legality under Section 3, *Standard Stations* set forth with clarity the economic rationale for the selection of the rule of reason decisional analysis. Over a decade later, the Court reaffirmed its rule of reason approach in *Tampa Elec. Co. v. Nashville Coal Co.*, 365 U.S. 320 (1961), but seemed to suggest a more wide-open analysis that placed a greater burden of proof on the plaintiff in establishing anticompetitiveness. The analysis also implied a less mechanical application of the relevant market structure factors.

Before considering *Tampa Elec.*, examine the facts and reasoning in *Standard Stations* which concerned the legality of exclusive supply contracts with independent retail dealers of gasoline.

The Standard Oil Co. was the largest seller of gasoline in the Western states. Its sales in 1946 amounted to 23%. Sales by company-owned service stations constituted 6.8% of the total, sales under exclusive dealing contracts with independent service stations amounted to 6.7% of the total, and the remainder of sales were to industrial users. Standard's six leading competitors in the retail service station market accounted for 42.5% of the market. The remaining retail sales were divided among more than 70 small competitors. Standard's major competitors all used similar exclusive dealing arrangements. In the Western states market, 5,937 independent dealers (16%) entered into exclusive supply contracts with Standard in 1947 which amounted to nearly $58 million worth of gasoline.

The Supreme Court, speaking through Justice Frankfurter, held that contracts, which affected $58 million of business, comprising 6.7% of the independent market, were enough from which an inference could be drawn that competition "has been or probably [would] be substantially lessened."

> The qualifying clause of § 3 is satisfied by proof that competition has been foreclosed in a substantial share of the line of commerce affected. It cannot be gainsaid that observance by a dealer of his requirements contract with Standard does effectively foreclose whatever opportunity there might be for competing suppliers to attract his patronage, and it is clear that the affected proportion of retail sales of petroleum products is substantial. In view of the widespread adoption of such contracts by Standard's competitors and the availability of alternative ways of obtaining an assured market, evidence that competitive activity has not actually declined is inconclusive.

Standard's use of the contracts creates just such a potential clog on competition as it was the purpose of § 3 to remove wherever, were it to become actual, it would impede a substantial amount of competitive activity.

Consider Justice Douglas' dissenting opinion, however:

> The economic theories which the Court has read into the Anti-Trust Laws have favored rather than discouraged monopoly. . . .

> It is common knowledge that a host of filling stations in the country are locally owned and operated. Others are owned and operated by the big oil companies. This case involves directly only the former. It pertains to requirements contracts that the oil companies make with these independents. It is plain that a filling station owner who is tied to an oil company for his supply of products is not an available customer for the products of other suppliers. The same is true of a filling station owner who purchases his inventory a year in advance. His demand is withdrawn from the market for the duration of the contract in the one case and for a year in the other. The result in each case is to lessen competition if the standard is day-to-day purchases. Whether it is a substantial lessening of competition within the meaning of the Anti-Trust Laws is a question of degree and may vary from industry to industry.

> The Court answers the question for the oil industry by a formula which under our decisions promises to wipe out large segments of independent filling station operators. The method of doing business under requirements contracts at least keeps the independents alive. They survive as small business units. The situation is not ideal from either their point of view or that of the nation. But the alternative which the Court offers is far worse from the point of view of both.

> The elimination of these requirements contracts sets the stage for Standard and the other oil companies to build service-station empires of their own. The opinion of the Court does more than set the stage for that development. It is an advisory opinion as well, stating to the oil companies how they can with impunity build their empires. The formula suggested by the Court is either the use of the "agency" device, which in practical effect means control of filling stations by the oil companies, . . . or the outright acquisition of them by subsidiary corporations or otherwise. . . . Under the approved judicial doctrine either of those devices means increasing the monopoly of the oil companies over the retail field.

> . . . .

> Today there is vigorous competition between the oil companies for the market. That competition has left some room for the survival of the independents. But when this inducement for their survival is taken away, we can expect that the oil companies will move in to supplant them with their own stations. There will still be competition between the oil companies. But there will be a tragic loss to the nation. The small, independent business man will be supplanted by clerks. Competition between suppliers of accessories (which is involved in this case) will diminish or cease

altogether. The oil companies will command an increasingly larger share of both the wholesale and the retail markets.

That is the likely result of today's decision. The requirements contract which is displaced is relatively innocuous as compared with the virulent growth of monopoly power which the Court encourages. The Court does not act unwittingly. It consciously pushes the oil industry in that direction. The Court approves what the Anti-Trust Laws were designed to prevent. It helps remake America in the image of the cartels.

TAMPA ELECTRIC CO. v. NASHVILLE COAL CO.
365 U.S. 320 (1961)

JUSTICE CLARK delivered the opinion of the Court.

We granted certiorari to review a declaratory judgment holding illegal under § 3 of the Clayton Act a requirements contract between the parties providing for the purchase by petitioner of all the coal it would require as boiler fuel at its Gannon Station in Tampa, Florida, over a 20-year period. Both the District Court and the Court of Appeals . . . agreed with respondents that the contract fell within the proscription of § 3 and therefore was illegal and unenforceable. We cannot agree that the contract suffers the claimed anti-trust illegality[12] and therefore, do not find it necessary to consider respondents' additional argument that such illegality is a defense to the action and a bar to enforceability.

The Facts

Petitioner Tampa Electric Company is a public utility located in Tampa, Florida. It produces and sells electric energy to a service area, including the city, extending from Tampa Bay eastward 60 miles to the center of the state, and some 30 miles in width. As of 1954 petitioner operated two electrical generating plants comprising a total of 11 individual generating units, all of which consumed oil in their burners. In 1955 Tampa Electric decided to expand its facilities by the construction of an additional generating plant to be comprised ultimately of six generating units, and to be known as the "Francis J. Gannon Station." Although every electrical generating plant in peninsular Florida burned oil at that time, Tampa Electric decided to try coal as boiler fuel in the first two units constructed at the Gannon Station. Accordingly, it contracted with the respondents to furnish the expected coal requirements for the units. The agreement, dated May 23, 1955, embraced Tampa Electric's "total requirements of fuel . . . for the operation of its first two units to be installed at the Gannon Station . . . not less than 225,000 tons of coal per unit per year," for a period of 20 years.

. . . .

The District Court . . . granted respondents' motion for summary judgment on

---

[12] [FN 2] In addition to their claim under § 3 of the Clayton Act, respondents argue the contract is illegal under the Sherman Act.

the sole ground that the undisputed facts, recited above, showed the contract to be a violation of § 3 of the Clayton Act. The Court of Appeals agreed. Neither court found it necessary to consider the applicability of the Sherman Act.

. . . .

Application of § 3 of the Clayton Act

In the almost half century since Congress adopted the Clayton Act, this Court has been called upon 10 times including the present, to pass upon questions arising under § 3. . . .

In practical application, even though a contract is found to be an exclusive-dealing arrangement, it does not violate the section unless the court believes it probable that performance of the contract will foreclose competition in a substantial share of the line of commerce affected. Following the guidelines of earlier decisions, certain considerations must be taken. *First*, the line of commerce, *i.e.*, the type of goods, wares, or merchandise, etc., involved must be determined, where it is in controversy, on the basis of the facts peculiar to the case. *Second*, the area of effective competition in the known line of commerce must be charted by careful selection of the market area in which the seller operates, and to which the purchaser can practicably turn for supplies. In short, the threatened foreclosure of competition must be in relation to the market affected. . . .

Third, and last, the competition foreclosed by the contract must be found to constitute a substantial share of the relevant market. That is to say, the opportunities for other traders to enter into or remain in that market must be significantly limited. . . .

To determine substantiality in a given case, it is necessary to weigh the probable effect of the contract on the relevant area of effective competition, taking into account the relative strength of the parties, the proportionate volume of commerce involved in relation to the total volume of commerce in the relevant market area, and the probable immediate and future effects which preemption of that share of the market might have on effective competition therein. It follows that a mere showing that the contract itself involves a substantial number of dollars is ordinarily of little consequence.

The Application of § 3 Here

In applying these considerations to the facts of the case before us, it appears clear that both the Court of Appeals and the District Court have not given the required effect to a controlling factor in the case — the relevant competitive market area. This omission, by itself, requires reversal, for, as we have pointed out, the relevant market is the prime factor in relation to which the ultimate question, whether the contract forecloses competition in a substantial share of the line of commerce involved, must be decided. . . .

Relevant Market of Effective Competition

Neither the Court of Appeals nor the District Court considered in detail the question of the relevant market. They do seem, however, to have been satisfied with inquiring only as to competition within "Peninsular Florida." It was noted that the total consumption of peninsular Florida was 700,000 tons of coal per year, about equal to the estimated 1959 requirements of Tampa Electric. It was also pointed out that coal accounted for less than 6% of the fuel consumed in the entire State. The District Court concluded that though the respondents were only one of 700 coal producers who could serve the same market, peninsular Florida, the contract for a period of 20 years excluded competitors from a substantial amount of trade. Respondents contend that the coal tonnage covered by the contract must be weighed against either the total consumption of coal in peninsular Florida, or all of Florida, or the Bituminous Coal Act area comprising peninsular Florida and the Georgia "finger," or, at most, all of Florida and Georgia. If the latter area were considered the relevant market, Tampa Electric's proposed requirements would be 18% of the tonnage sold therein. Tampa Electric says that both courts and respondents are in error, because the "700 coal producers who could serve" it, as recognized by the trial court and admitted by respondents, operated in the Appalachian coal area and that its contract requirements were less than 1% of the total marketed production of these producers; that the relevant effective area of competition was the area in which these producers operated, and in which they were willing to compete for the consumer potential.

We are persuaded that on the record in this case, neither peninsular Florida, nor the entire State of Florida, nor Florida and Georgia combined constituted the relevant market of effective competition. We do not believe that the pie will slice so thinly. By far the bulk of the overwhelming tonnage marketed from the same producing area as serves Tampa is sold outside of Georgia and Florida, and the producers were "eager" to sell more coal in those States. While the relevant competitive market is not ordinarily susceptible to a "metes and bounds" definition, . . . it is of course the area in which respondents and the other 700 producers effectively compete. The record shows that, like the respondents, they sold bituminous coal "suitable for [Tampa's] requirements," mined in parts of Pennsylvania, Virginia, West Virginia, Kentucky, Tennessee, Alabama, Ohio and Illinois. We take notice of the fact that the approximate total bituminous coal (and lignite) product in the year 1954 from the districts in which these 700 producers are located was 359,289,000 tons, of which some 290,567,000 tons were sold on the open market. Of the latter amount some 78,716,000 tons were sold to electric utilities. We also note that in 1954 Florida and Georgia combined consumed at least 2,304,000 tons, 1,100,000 of which were used by electric utilities, and the sources of which were mines located in no less than seven States. We take further notice that the production and marketing of bituminous coal (and lignite) from the same districts and assumedly equally available to Tampa on a commercially feasible basis, is currently on a par with prior years. In point of statistical fact, coal consumption in the combined Florida-Georgia area has increased significantly since 1954. In 1959 more than 3,775,000 tons were there consumed, 2,913,000 being used by electric utilities including, presumably, the coal used by the petitioner. The coal continued to come from at least seven States.[13]

From these statistics it clearly appears that the proportionate volume of the total relevant coal product as to which the challenged contract pre-empted competition, less than 1%, is, conservatively speaking, quite insubstantial. A more accurate figure, even assuming pre-emption to the extent of the maximum anticipated total requirements, 2,250,000 tons a year, would be.77%.

Effect on Competition in the Relevant Market

It may well be that in the context of antitrust legislation protracted requirements contracts are suspect, but they have not been declared illegal *per se.* Even though a single contract between single traders may fall within the initial broad proscription of the section, it must also suffer the qualifying disability, tendency to work a substantial — not remote — lessening of competition in the relevant competitive market. It is urged that the present contract pre-empts competition to the extent of purchases worth perhaps $128,000,000, and that this "is, of course, not insignificant or insubstantial." While $128,000,000 is a considerable sum of money, even in these days, the dollar volume, by itself, is not the test, as we have already pointed out.

The remaining determination, therefore, is whether the pre-emption of competition to the extent of the tonnage involved tends to substantially foreclose competition in the relevant coal market. We think not. That market sees an annual trade in excess of 250,000,000 tons of coal and over a billion dollars — multiplied by 20 years it runs into astronomical figures. There is here neither a seller with a dominant position . . . ; nor myriad outlets with substantial sales volume, coupled with an industry-wide practice of relying upon exclusive contracts, . . . ; nor a plainly restrictive tying arrangement. . . . On the contrary, we seem to have only that type of contract which "may well be of economic advantage to buyers as well as to sellers." *Standard Oil Co. v. United States*, [337 U.S. 293 (1949)], at p. 306. In the case of the buyer it "may assure supply," while on the part of the seller it "may make possible the substantial reduction of selling expenses, give protection against price fluctuations, and . . . offer the possibility of a predictable market." *Id.*, at 306–307. The 20-year period of the contract is singled out as the principal vice, but at least in the case of public utilities the assurance of a steady and ample supply of fuel is necessary in the public interest. Otherwise consumers are left unprotected against service failures owing to shutdowns; and increasingly unjustified costs might result in more burdensome rate structures eventually to be reflected in the consumer's bill. The compelling validity of such considerations has been recognized fully in the natural gas public utility field. This is not to say that utilities are immunized from Clayton Act proscriptions, but merely that, in judging the term of a requirements contract in relation to the substantiality of the foreclosure of competition, particularized considerations of the parties' operations are not irrelevant. In weighing the various factors, we have decided that in the competitive bituminous coal marketing area involved here the contract sued upon does not tend

---

[13] [FN 15] 1,787,000 tons from certain counties in West Virginia, Virginia, Kentucky, Tennessee, and North Carolina; 1,321,000 tons from counties in Alabama, Georgia and elsewhere in Tennessee; 665,000 tons from the western Kentucky fields; 2,000 tons from other counties in West Virginia and Virginia.

to foreclose a substantial volume of competition.

We need not discuss the respondents' further contention that the contract also violates § 1 and § 2 of the Sherman Act, for if it does not fall within the broader proscription of § 3 of the Clayton Act it follows that it is not forbidden by those of the former. . . .

Reversed.

NOTES AND QUESTIONS

1. How is the *Tampa Electric* "qualitative substantiality" test applied to the facts of that case under Section 3? Consider the Court's progression of analysis:

> "*First*, the line of commerce . . . involved must be determined, where it is in controversy, on the basis of the facts peculiar to the case. *Second*, the area of effective competition in the known line of commerce must be charted. . . .

Third, and last, the competition foreclosed by the contract must be found to constitute a substantial share of the relevant market. That is to say, the opportunities for other traders to enter into or remain in that market must be significantly limited. . . .

> To determine substantiality in a given case, it is necessary to weigh the probable effect of the contract on the relevant area of effective competition, taking into account the relative strength of the parties, the proportionate volume of commerce involved in relation to the total volume of commerce in the relevant market area, and the probable immediate and future effects which pre-emption of that share of the market might have on effective competition therein. It follows that a mere showing that the contract itself involves a substantial number of dollars is ordinarily of little consequence.

> . . . .

> There is here neither a seller with a dominant position in the market . . . nor myriad outlets with substantial sales volume, coupled with an industry-wide practice of relying upon exclusive contracts . . . nor a plainly restrictive tying arrangement. . . . On the contrary, we seem to have only that type of contract which "may well be of economic advantage to buyers as well as to sellers." . . . "

365 U.S. at 327–329, 334. Consider whether *Tampa Electric* makes prediction of the lawfulness of exclusive dealing less certain than the rule announced in *Standard Stations.* Is the presumptive illegality test (condemning any foreclosure that is more than de minimis) raised in *Standard Stations* operative after *Tampa Electric*? In utilizing that test, was the Court inferring competitive harm from a finding that commerce had been substantially affected? Is the effect now based on market share rather than dollar volume? Is it a relative test or an absolute one? *See, e.g., Magnus Petr. Co. v. Skelly Oil Co.*, 599 F.2d 196, 201–204 (7th Cir. 1979). Finally, consider where the line of legality is drawn between the *Tampa Electric* 1% and the *Standard Stations* 6.7%.

2. Note Justice Douglas' dissenting opinion in *Standard Stations*, briefly excerpted above. What did he mean when he stated that oil companies not permitted to engage in exclusive dealing would "build service-station empires of their own"? Justice Douglas was enough of an economist to know that vertical integration reduces the cost of doing business. The partial vertical integration facilitated by the requirements contracts in *Standard Stations* reduced transaction costs, gave the suppliers a chain of identifiable retail outlets, even though they did not own them, and added a great deal of predictability to a very erratic market. The cost reductions that can be achieved by vertical integration will benefit both monopolists and competitors. (See the discussion of the economics of vertical integration, *infra.*)

As a general rule, any firm is best off if other firms in the distribution chain are operating as efficiently as possible. In a competitive market, however, the consequences of not vertically integrating can be severe. If Standard Oil was a competitor — and the *Standard Stations* opinion suggests that it was — then it would lose market share to any firm able to deliver petroleum products at a lower cost. If a competitor saved money, either by means of a requirements contracts or else by building its own gasoline stations, Standard Oil would have little choice but to follow. The fact that the market in *Standard Stations* was probably competitive and that requirements contracts and other forms of vertical integration, such as outright ownership of retail stations, persisted is good evidence that the vertical integration was efficient.

In short, Justice Douglas put his finger on an issue that goes to the heart of antitrust policy: whom do the laws protect? Large firms in a competitive market might be "forced" by available economies to integrate vertically — with the result that independent retailers are either restrained or eliminated. The result in a competitive market will be lower prices for consumers. Thus, Justice Douglas' dissent forces us to choose sides: we must pick an antitrust policy that will protect either the independent gasoline retailers or else the preferences of the consumer. There are no easy answers — and no economic answers — to that question.

3. Should vertical integration by contract be treated any differently than vertical integration by merger? (See the discussion of vertical mergers, in Chapter 7.) What if Standard had purchased a set of independent retail stations instead of dealing with them by means of requirements contracts? The percentages of gasoline and other products "foreclosed" from the market would be the same. Some effects would be different. For example, the merger would last indefinitely, while the requirements contracts were periodic. Presumably, Standard would have even more control over retail stations that it owned than it did over independently owned stations that it controlled by contract. This need not always be the case, however. Certain franchise contracts between large firms and their independently owned franchisees are incredibly detailed — including such terms as how often lavatories must be cleaned and floors scrubbed and prescribing the uniforms that attendants must wear. *See Kypta v. McDonald's Corp.*, 671 F.2d 1282 (11th Cir.), *cert. denied*, 459 U.S. 857 (1982); *Principe v. McDonald's Corp.*, 631 F.2d 303 (4th Cir. 1980), *cert. denied*, 451 U.S. 970 (1981).

Traditionally, both the law of exclusive dealing and the law of vertical mergers have been predicated on a "foreclosure" theory. In fact, the traditional tests for legality in these two different areas of antitrust law have been remarkably similar. (See the discussion of vertical integration by merger in Chapter 7.) In 1984, the United States Department of Justice published a set of Guidelines that state the Justice Department's position on when certain mergers ought to be illegal. These Guidelines generally are far more lenient toward vertical mergers than much of the older Supreme Court case law suggests. The Guidelines suggest that the Department of Justice is not likely to challenge a vertical merger unless the firms involved have something like 25% or more of the relevant market. It remains to be seen whether the Guidelines for vertical mergers will have any effect on the law of exclusive dealing.

4. Consider the accuracy of this statement: The exclusive dealing cases define how markets are affected by full requirements contracts. Whether the market will be affected by a substantial lessening of competition within Section 3 of the Clayton Act is determined by a relative market factor analysis which weighs the "volume of commerce affected," "strength of the parties," and the "probable immediate and future effects which pre-emption of that share of the market might have on effective competition." Do you agree?*See Tampa Electric Co.*; ABA ANTITRUST SECTION, MONOGRAPH, VERTICAL RESTRICTIONS UPON BUYERS LIMITING PURCHASES OF GOODS FROM OTHERS 91 (1982).

5. In *Western Parcel Express v. United Parcel Service of America, Inc.*, 190 F.3d 974 (9th Cir. 1999), WPX claimed that UPS engaged in illegal exclusive dealing because it created insurmountable barriers to entry. The court rejected this contention because the contracts allowed a customer to terminate the contract for any reason with very little notice. The contracts also did not foreclose customers from contracting with other delivery service providers. The contracts were more like volume discount contracts, which provide pro-competitive effects. During the relevant time period, another competitor, RPS, had entered the market, weakening the claim that UPS had power to exclude competition. The court emphasized that a high market share alone does not raise an inference of monopoly power when there are low entry barriers.

In *Yaodi Hu v. Huey*, 2009-1 Trade Cas. 76,587, 2009 U.S. App. LEXIS 9224 (7th Cir. Apr. 16, 2009) (unpublished), the Seventh Circuit rejected an exclusive dealing challenge to a covenant in a commercial lease that prohibited the tenant from engaging in professional tax preparation services. The covenant had been inserted at the behest of a different tenant of the same landlord who was in the tax preparation business. However, the court found no allegations of impact in a relevant market:

> [A]ccording to his own allegations, the restrictive covenant in Huey's lease agreement . . . has not adversely affected the market for tax services in Chinatown. The lease agreement restricts the commercial activity of just one building — which Hu describes as "small" and only 45 feet long and three stories tall. It is difficult to see how a restrictive covenant that covers such a small area could adversely impact the entire Chinatown market.

Noncompetition agreements in both leases and employment contracts are often treated under the same principles as exclusive dealing contracts. In substance, the covenants often serve to limit the number of firms in a market with whom a vertically related party can deal. *See Harold Friedman, Inc. v. Thorofare Markets, Inc.*, 587 F.2d 127, 143–144 (3d Cir. 1978) (noting that the size of the area covered by the restrictive covenant in relation to the entire geographic market is relevant to the reasonableness analysis).

NOTE: EXCLUSIVE DEALING AND § 2 OF THE SHERMAN ACT

Exclusive dealing has traditionally been pursued under either § 1 of the Sherman Act or § 3 of the Clayton Act, both of which require an "agreement." But does the "agreement" requirement add much to the analysis. The practice generally benefits the dominant firm imposing it, not its dealers, who would presumably be better off if their supply market were competitive. Further, the competitive harm is exclusion of the dominant firm's rivals, not the rivals of its dealers. Some recent decisions have addressed exclusive dealing as a monopolization violation under § 2 of the Sherman Act. In that case the stricter structural requirements of the monopolization statute must be met, but § 2 is less categorical about the agreement requirement. The same reasoning generally applies to tying. *See, e.g., United States v. Dentsply Int'l, Inc.*, 399 F.3d 181 (3d Cir. 2005), *cert. denied*, 546 F.3d 1089 (2006), which condemned exclusive dealing arrangements under § 2. *See* 3B PHILLIP E. AREEDA & HERBERT HOVENKAMP, ANTITRUST LAW & 768 (3d ed. 2008). This might be a good time to read the *Dentsply* decision, which is reprinted in Chapter 6, *infra. See also United States v. Microsoft Corp.*, 253 F.3d 34 (D.C. Cir.), *cert. denied*, 534 U.S. 952 (2001), which applied § 2 to a series of practices that resembled both exclusive dealing and tying. The *Microsoft* court also rejected the defendant's argument that a failure to find liability under § 1 of the Sherman Act precluded liability under § 2. The court acknowledged that the "basic prudential concerns relevant to §§ 1 and 2 are admittedly the same." However, a monopolist's use of exclusive contracts, in certain circumstances, may give rise to a § 2 violation even though the contracts foreclose less than the roughly 40% or 50% share usually required in order to establish a § 1 violation.

In this case, plaintiffs allege that, by closing to rivals a substantial percentage of the available opportunities for browser distribution, Microsoft managed to preserve its monopoly in the market for operating systems. The IAPs [internet access providers] constitute one of the two major channels by which browsers can be distributed. Microsoft has exclusive deals with "fourteen of the top fifteen access providers in North America[, which] account for a large majority of all Internet access subscriptions in this part of the world." By ensuring that the "majority" of all IAP subscribers are offered IE either as the default browser or as the only browser, Microsoft's deals with the IAPs clearly have a significant effect in preserving its monopoly; they help keep usage of Navigator below the critical level necessary for Navigator or any other rival to pose a real threat to Microsoft's monopoly.

Other Section 2 decisions challenging arrangements that resemble exclusive dealing include *Geneva Pharmaceuticals Tech. Corp. v. Barr Labs, Inc.*, 386 F.3d 485 (2d Cir. 2004) (claim that defendant manufacturer of warfarin sodium entered into secret exclusive dealing agreement locking up only significant source of clathrate, an essential ingredient); *Defiance Hosp. v. Fauster-Cameron, Inc.*, 344 F. Supp. 2d 1097 (N.D. Ohio 2004) (denying summary judgment on plaintiff's claim that defendant monopolized market for anesthesiological services by refusing to supply anesthesiology support services to physicians who had not signed primary care contracts with the defendant); *JamSports and Entertainment, LLC v. Paradama Productions, Inc.*, 336 F. Supp. 2d 824 (N.D. Ill. 2004) (denying summary judgment on claim that racing promoter's claim that motorcycle association excluded it from market by threatening to terminate its relationship with stadiums that contracted with the plaintiff).

[B] Tying Arrangements

[1] Introduction: Economics of Tying

A contractual arrangement which conditions the sale or lease of one product on the purchase or lease of another from the same seller is characterized as a tie-in sale or tying arrangement. A related commercial transaction is a package licensing contract, where the lessee is required to take more than one copyrighted product or patent under a so-called "block" or "package" license. A third variation of the tying arrangement is the requirement that the buyer purchase the seller's full line of products if any are taken, though all products may not be desired. This practice is known as "full line forcing." The desired product is called the "tying" product, while the second required product is the "tied" product.

Three statutes govern the legality of the commercial practice of tying the sales of separate products. Sections 1 and 2 of the Sherman Act, Section 3 of the Clayton Act, and Section 5 of the FTC Act have application under certain circumstances as discussed in this subchapter. The Clayton Act is applicable, however, only when "goods" or commodities are involved; services which are tied are thus not covered under the Act.

The standard of legality under the Sherman and Clayton Acts has been distinguished in at least one principal Supreme Court decision, *Times-Picayune Pub'g Co. v. United States*, 345 U.S. 594 (1953). But the distinctions have been blurred subsequently in lower court decisions and it is presently unclear to what extent the burden of proof varies under the two statutes. *Compare Spartan Grain & Mill Co. v. Ayers*, 581 F.2d 419 (5th Cir. 1978), *cert. denied*, 444 U.S. 831 (1979), *with Sargent-Welch Scientific Co. v. Ventron Corp.*, 567 F.2d 701 (7th Cir. 1977), *cert. denied*, 439 U.S. 822 (1978). Under the FTC Act, on the other hand, the standard may be less restrictive. *FTC v. Texaco, Inc.*, 393 U.S. 223 (1968).

Traditionally, tie-ins were condemned because the forced purchase of the second product allegedly denied competitors of the seller access to the tied product market and because the tying contract forced the buyer to relinquish free choice over the purchasing decision. The underlying economic theory supporting this analysis centered on avoidance of monopoly power. This theory held that in order to prevent the seller from obtaining a monopoly in the tied product, it should be prevented from using its power or dominance in the tying product as a "lever" into the tied product market.

This leverage theory, which seeks to curtail "monopolistic exploitation," found acceptance in many Supreme Court opinions, beginning as early as 1917, and many of these classified ties as illegal *per se*. If the plaintiff could demonstrate that defendant possessed "sufficient economic power" in the tying product to force the purchase of a separate tied product, and if a "not insubstantial amount" of interstate commerce was affected, the burden of proof had been met and the tying arrangement would be declared per se illegal. No actual, specific anticompetitive effect was required to be established. The leverage theory itself supplied the projected exclusionary effect. *See generally* LAWRENCE A. SULLIVAN, HANDBOOK OF THE LAW OF ANTITRUST 431–463 (1977). Louis Kaplow, *Extension of Monopoly Power Through Leverage*, 85 COLUM. L. REV. 515 (1985). However, for an argument that the leverage theory deserves a second look, see Einer Elhauge, *Tying, Bundled Discounts, and the Death of the Single Monopoly Profit Theory*, 123 Harv. L. Rev. 397 (2009).

The leverage theory as a basis for tying arrangement analysis was first challenged in the late 1950s and more recently in the late 1970s. At first, the theory was attacked as being overinclusive. It did not consider whether the tying sale was the "only means of utilizing effectively a power already possessed." Moreover, it was urged that if "the tying seller is maximizing his return on the tying product and the same output of the tied product can still be produced . . . no additional or new monopoly effect should be assumed." Ward Bowman, *Tying Arrangements and the Leverage Problem*, 67 YALE L.J. 19, 20 (1957).

In general, the economic attack on the traditional "leverage" theory of tying arrangements has gone like this: profit-maximizing prices are final output prices. Assume, for example, that a firm has a monopoly in the bolt market but that the nut market is competitive. Most customers use a nut with a bolt and buy them in equal numbers. With respect to these customers the profit-maximizing price of the "package" — a nut and a bolt — is, say, 50 cents. If nuts are being sold at a competitive price of 10 cents, the monopolist in bolts will maximize his profits by selling bolts for 40 cents. But now suppose that the bolt monopolist uses a tying arrangement: he forces all purchasers of one of his bolts to take a nut from him as well. What price will he be able to charge for the nut? The answer is 10 cents, the competitive price. By charging the profit-maximizing price for the bolt, the bolt monopolist has already extracted all available monopoly profits from the bolt-nut package. If he attempts to use a tying arrangement to force customers to take their nuts from him at a price of, say, 15 cents, he will produce less, not more, monopoly profits.

Does this mean that the leverage theory of tying arrangements will never work? No, sometimes it does work — but only where there are other factors than the above facts include. For example, what if the nut market is cartelized and nuts which would have a competitive price of 10 cents are being sold by the cartel members for 20 cents. The cartel injures the bolt monopolist, because it reduces the profit-maximizing price for bolts (remember, the profit-maximizing price is 50 cents for the *package*). By manufacturing nuts himself and selling nuts and bolts as a package the bolt monopolist will be able to transfer the 10 cents in monopoly revenues away from the nut cartel and to himself. In this case the leverage theory may have some application.

Secondly, suppose that the price of bolts is regulated by the state. Suppose, for example, that the profit-maximizing price of a bolt-nut package is 50 cents, but that the bolt monopolist is required by law to charge only 20 cents for bolts. In this situation the bolt monopolist might be able to use the tying arrangement to force purchasers to take a nonprice-regulated product as a condition of taking the price-regulated product. In that case, by selling the nonregulated product at a monopoly price the seller could effectively circumvent the price regulation scheme. There is evidence that telephone companies have used such a scheme to avoid rate regulation. For example, if the lease rate for telephone lines is price-regulated, but equipment rentals are not, a telephone company might be able to "cheat" on the price regulation statute by requiring all lessees of its lines to lease their equipment from the company as well, and then charging a monopoly price for the equipment. *See Litton Sys. v. American Tel. & Tel. Co.*, 700 F.2d 785 (2d Cir. 1983), *cert. denied*, 464 U.S. 1073 (1984); *Phonetele, Inc. v. American Tel. & Tel. Co.*, 664 F.2d 716 (9th Cir. 1981), *cert. denied*, 459 U.S. 1145 (1983); Herbert Hovenkamp, *Tying Arrangements and Class Actions*, 36 VAND. L. REV. 213, 233–234 (1983).

Undoubtedly the most common purposes of certain types of tying arrangements, however, are price discrimination or "metering." Tying arrangements come in two general kinds: fixed proportion and variable proportion. In a fixed proportion tie-in, such as the bolt-and-nut arrangement described above, a purchaser takes one bolt with each nut, and vice-versa. Although price discrimination by means of such tie-ins is possible (see the discussion of block-booking, *infra*), variable proportion tying arrangements are much more conducive to price discrimination.

In a variable proportion arrangement, purchasers or lessees of the tying product use varying amounts of some tied product. For example, suppose that a lessor of mimeograph machines requires lessees to purchase all their mimeograph paper from the lessor. *See Henry v. A.B. Dick Co.*, 224 U.S. 1 (1912). People who use the mimeograph machine more will also consume more paper. By leasing the machine to all lessees at the same price and selling the paper at a supracompetitive price, the lessor might be doing one of two things. First, it might be using the paper to "meter" the more intense wear and tear and depreciation on the machine that results from high volume users. If the extra profit on a single sheet of mimeograph paper reflects precisely the costs in wear and tear on the machine that result from making a single copy, then the variable price of the "package" — the machine plus the paper — simply reflects the fact that high intensity users of the mimeograph machine impose greater costs on the lessor.

There is another possibility, however. It is likely that high intensity users of the mimeograph machine value the machine more highly than low intensity users value it. A tying arrangement can enable the lessor or seller of the machine to price discriminate — that is, to obtain a higher rate of profit from higher intensity users of the machine, who presumably are higher preference users as well. Assume for example that a lessor charges all lessees $100 per month for the mimeograph machine, which represents a rate of return on the machine of five percent. However, it requires all lessees to purchase their paper from the lessor as well, at two cents per sheet. This price represents a return of 25% on the paper. The overall rate of return will then be much larger from a lessee who makes 10,000 copies monthly than from a lessee who makes 500 copies monthly, even though both are paying the same basic rate for the machine. (See the discussion of the economics of price discrimination, *infra.*)

Why would a seller want to price discriminate by means of a tying arrangement in this way? First of all, in order to do it successfully the seller would need a certain amount of market power in the tying product. If the tying product were perfectly competitive, disadvantaged purchasers or lessees (those asked to pay the higher price) would go to a different seller or lessor. A seller with market power will price discriminate because by so doing it can make more money than it can by establishing a single profit-maximizing price. The best of all possible worlds for a seller is one in which it can sell a unit to each purchaser at precisely the amount that that purchaser values the unit. Price discrimination by variable proportion tying arrangements comes as close as any mechanism to approximating this kind of "perfect" price discrimination.

Second, price discrimination is often frustrated by arbitrage. For example, if a seller sells widgets to one set of customers at $1.00 and to another set of customers at 70 cents, sooner or later the favored customers will begin selling to the disfavored customers at some price between 70 cents and $1.00. Price discrimination by tying arrangements frustrates arbitrage because all sales of all products are made at the same price. Thirdly, and for the same reason, price discrimination undertaken by tie-ins avoids the Robinson-Patman Act, which is the federal antitrust statute that most commonly is used to condemn price discrimination. The Robinson-Patman Act applies only to sales in which the same or similar product is sold to two different purchasers at two different prices. When price discrimination is undertaken by tie-in, however, all sales are made at the same price per product. In the example above, all machines are leased at $100.00 per month and all sheets of paper are sold at two cents each. The mimeograph example would also fall outside the Robinson-Patman Act because the statute applies only to sales, not to leases.

Should tie-ins used to facilitate price discrimination be illegal? Economists and antitrust scholars are deeply divided on this question. On the one hand, variable proportion, price-discrimination tying arrangements enable a monopolist in the tying product to make even more money than it can make by charging its uniform profit-maximizing price to all purchasers. For this reason scholars who believe that wealth distribution is an important concern of antitrust policy would condemn such tying arrangements.

On the other hand, price discrimination often results in higher output, and thus less misallocation of resources, than unitary monopoly pricing does. Many people who believe that the antitrust laws should be concerned exclusively with allocative efficiency argue that price discrimination by tying arrangements ought to be legal. Courts have generally developed a unitary rule that purports to condemn all tying arrangements by the same test whether or not they are used to price discriminate.

For a discussion of these questions of tying arrangements and antitrust policy, see *IBM Corp. v. United States*, 298 U.S. 131 (1936) (goodwill defense discussed in early case); HERBERT HOVENKAMP, FEDERAL ANTITRUST POLICY, ch. 10 (4th ed. 2011); 9 PHILIP E. AREEDA & HERBERT HOVENKAMP, ANTITRUST LAW, ch. 17 (3d ed. 2012); RICHARD A. POSNER, ANTITRUST LAW (2d ed. 2001); ROBERT H. BORK, THE ANTITRUST PARADOX: A POLICY AT WAR WITH ITSELF 365–381 (1978); Burstein, *A Theory of Full-Line Forcing*, 55 NW. U. L. REV. 62 (1960); Ward Bowman, *Tying Arrangements and the Leverage Problem*, 67 YALE L.J. 19 (1957). For an analysis of current economic theories of tying see Erik N. Hovenkamp & Herbert Hovenkamp, Tying Arrangements (Oxford Handbook of International Competition Policy, 2013), available at http://papers.ssrn.com/sol3/papers.cfm?abstract_id=1999063.

The case for an "efficiency defense" in lawsuits alleging illegal tying arrangements is strong. The "defense" sometimes shows up, not as a rebuttal to a plaintiff's prima facie case, but rather as an argument that the plaintiff has failed to show that the defendant is selling or leasing distinct tying and tied "products." No general definition of a "product" for purposes of the law of tying arrangements has yet been produced. However, courts are increasingly inclined to view two items as a single "product" (thus precluding liability) if the combination results in certain efficiencies in production or distribution.

Consider the following analysis from Judge Posner in *Jack Walters & Sons Corp. v. Morton Bldg., Inc.*, 737 F.2d 698 (7th Cir. 1984):

> The problem is that there is no obvious way of deciding whether a product is a single product or an assemblage of components. The practice has been to classify a product as a single product if there are rather obvious economies of joint provision, as in the left-shoe-right-shoe example. . . . Although this approach seems to take what would otherwise be a matter of defense and make its absence a threshold requirement of the offense, it does serve to screen out many silly cases.

Judge Posner then concluded that a prefabricated building and the trademark given to the building by its manufacturer were a single "product" for purposes of the law of tying arrangements. To hold that a trademark and the product manufactured by the trademark's owner were separate "products," concluded Judge Posner, would virtually impose compulsory licensing of trademarks — at least on those firms who had some market power in the tying product. In such a case it could be illegal for someone who owned a trademark and manufactured a product under it to require those wanting the trademark to take the product as well. Would consumers be better off if IBM or Baskin-Robbins were forced to sell their trademarks to anyone who wanted to manufacture computers or ice cream?

For further discussion of efficiency and the "separate product" test in the law of tying arrangements, see Herbert Hovenkamp, Federal Antitrust Policy, ch. 10 (4th ed. 2011); E. Thomas Sullivan & Jeffrey Harrison, Understanding Antitrust and Its Economic Implications, ch. 5 (6th ed. 2013).

[2]   Development of Unique Per Se Rule for Tying Arrangements

Tying arrangements were first considered restraints of trade in patent cases. The Court in *Motion Picture Patents Co. v. Universal Film Mfg. Co.*, 243 U.S. 502 (1917), refused to sanction such a restriction in a patent infringement suit because it feared that it would lead to a monopoly. The leverage/monopoly theory found acceptance under antitrust laws quickly thereafter. Initially, the Court centered its Clayton Act analysis on whether the supplier had substantial market power or a dominant market position in the desired tying product market. *United Shoe Mach. Corp. v. United States*, 258 U.S. 451 (1922) (tying patented shoe manufacturing equipment to other related machines and supplies). Later the Court, in a Section 3 case involving the alleged protection of "good will" and "quality product" defense, spoke more clearly about the per se illegality of tie-in sale contracts. In *International Salt Co. v. United States*, 332 U.S. 392 (1947), the Court considered the legality of a tying arrangement which conditioned the lease of a patented salt machine on the purchase of the salt from the same lessor. Finding that these salt sale arrangements amounted to $500,000 annually, the Court concluded that a substantial amount of competition had been foreclosed and that it need not consider International's actual position in the tying product (salt machine) market. The Court held that when a substantial amount of commerce is affected by a tie-in contract, it is per se illegal under Section 3 of the Clayton Act:

> The volume of business affected by these contracts cannot be said to be insignificant or insubstantial and the tendency of the arrangement to accomplishment of monopoly seems obvious. Under the law (§ 3 of Clayton), agreements are forbidden which "tend to create a monopoly," and it is immaterial that the tendency is a creeping one rather than one that proceeds at full gallop; nor does the law await arrival of the goal before condemning the direction of the movement.

Id. at 396. On the validity of the "quality product" defense, the Court, without deciding the merits, held that International Salt failed to carry its burden that for the machine to operate properly it had to use the salt provided by the manufacturer of the machine.

Several years later the Court was called upon to apply the Sherman Act to a tying arrangement when a newspaper publisher sold advertising in the morning and afternoon papers as a single product: an advertiser could not buy advertising separately in *either* the morning or afternoon papers. In the course of its opinion, the Court drew distinctions between the burdens of proof under the Clayton and Sherman Acts.

TIMES-PICAYUNE PUBLISHING CO. v. UNITED STATES
345 U.S. 594 (1953)

JUSTICE CLARK delivered the opinion of the Court.

At issue is the legality under the Sherman Act of the Times-Picayune Publishing Company's contracts for the sale of newspaper classified and general display advertising space. The Company in New Orleans owns and publishes the morning Time-Picayune and the evening States. Buyers of space for general display and classified advertising in its publications may purchase only combined insertions appearing in both the morning and evening papers, and not in either separately.

. . . .

[T]he District Court at the outset denied the Government's motion for partial summary judgment [and] the case went to trial and eventuated in comprehensive and detailed findings of fact.

. . . .

On the basis of [its] findings, the District Judge held the unit contracts in violation of the Sherman Act. The contracts were viewed as tying arrangements which the Publishing Company because of the Times-Picayune's "monopoly position" could force upon advertisers. Postulating that contracts foreclosing competitors from a substantial part of the market restrain trade within the meaning of § 1 of the Act, and that effect on competition tests the reasonableness of a restraint, the court deemed a substantial percentage of advertising accounts in the New Orleans papers unlawfully "restrained." Further, a violation of § 2 was found: defendants by use of the unit plan "attempted to monopolize that segment of the afternoon newspaper general and classified advertising field which was represented by those advertisers who also required morning newspaper space and who could not because of budgetary limitations or financial inability purchase space in both afternoon newspapers."

. . . .

When the seller enjoys a monopolistic position in the market for the "tying" product, *or* if a substantial volume of commerce in the "tied" product is restrained, a tying arrangement violates the narrower standards expressed in § 3 of the Clayton Act because from either factor the requisite potential lessening of competition is inferred. And because for even a lawful monopolist it is "unreasonable, *per se*, to foreclose competitors from any substantial market," a tying arrangement is banned by § 1 of the Sherman Act whenever *both* conditions are met.

In this case, the rule of *International Salt* can apply only if both its ingredients are met. The Government at the outset elected to proceed not under the Clayton but the Sherman Act.[14]

. . . .

Once granted that the volume of commerce affected was not "insignificant or insubstantial," the Times-Picayune's market position becomes critical to the case. The District Court found that the Times-Picayune occupied a "dominant position"

---

[14] [FN 27] On oral argument here, the Government explanatorily referred to an early informal Federal Trade Commission opinion to the effect that advertising space was not a "commodity" within the meaning of § 2 of the Clayton Act. 81 Cong. Rec. App. 2336–2337. *Cf. Fleetway, Inc. v. Public Service Interstate Transp. Co.*, 3 Cir., 1934, 72 F.2d 761; *United States v. Investors Diversified Services*, D.C. 1951, 102 F. Supp. 645. We express no views on that statutory interpretation.

in New Orleans; the sole morning daily in the area, it led its competitors in circulation, number of pages and advertising linage. But every newspaper is a dual trader in separate though interdependent markets; it sells the paper's news and advertising content to its readers; in effect that readership is in turn sold to the buyers of advertising space. This case concerns solely one of these markets. The Publishing Company stands accused not of tying sales to its readers but only to buyers of general and classified space in its papers. For this reason, dominance in the advertising market, not in readership, must be decisive in gauging the legality of the Company's unit plan. . . .

We do not think that the Times-Picayune occupied a "dominant" position in the newspaper advertising market in New Orleans. Unlike other "tying" cases where patents or copyrights supplied the requisite market control, any equivalent market "dominance" in this case must rest on comparative marketing data. Excluding advertising placed through other communications media and including general and classified linage inserted in all New Orleans dailies, as we must since the record contains no evidence which could circumscribe a broader or narrower "market" defined by buyers' habits or mobility of demand, the Times-Picayune's sales of both general and classified linage over the years hovered around 40%. Obviously no magic inheres in numbers; "the relative effect of percentage command of a market varies with the setting in which that factor is placed." . . . If each of the New Orleans publications shared equally in the total volume of linage, the Times-Picayune would have sold 33 1/3%; in the absence of patent or copyright control, the small existing increment in the circumstances here disclosed cannot confer that market "dominance" which, in conjunction with a "not insubstantial" volume of trade in the "tied" product, would result in a Sherman Act offense under the rule of *International Salt.*

. . . Although advertising space in the Times-Picayune, as the sole morning daily, was doubtless essential to blanket coverage of the local newspaper readership, nothing in the record suggests that advertisers viewed the city's newspaper readers, morning or evening, as other than fungible customer potential. We must assume, therefore, that the readership "bought" by advertisers in the Times-Picayune was the selfsame "product" sold by the States. . . .

The factual departure from the "tying" cases then becomes manifest. The common core of the adjudicated unlawful tying arrangements is the forced purchase of a second distinct commodity with the desired purchase of a dominant "tying" product, resulting in economic harm to competition in the "tied" market. Here, however, two newspapers under single ownership at the same place, time, and terms sell indistinguishable products to advertisers; no dominant "tying" product exists (in fact, since space in neither the Times-Picayune nor the States can be bought alone, one may be viewed as "tying" as the other); no leverage in one market excludes sellers in the second, because for present purposes the products are identical and the market the same. . . .

The Publishing Company's advertising contracts must thus be tested under the Sherman Act's general prohibition on unreasonable restraints of trade. For purposes of § 1, "[a] restraint may be unreasonable either because a restraint otherwise reasonable is accompanied with a specific intent to accomplish a forbidden restraint or because it falls within the class of restraints that are illegal *per se.*" . . . Since the requisite intent is inferred whenever unlawful effects are found, and the rule of *International Salt* is out of the way, the contracts may yet be banned by § 1 if unreasonable restraint was either their object or effect. [O]ur inquiry to determine reasonableness under § 1 must focus on "the percentage of business controlled, the strength of the remaining competition [and] whether the action springs from business requirements or purpose to monopolize." . . .

. . . .

To be sure, economic statistics are easily susceptible to legerdemain, and only the organized context of all relevant factors can validly translate raw data into logical cause and effect. But we must take the record as we find it, and hack through the jungle as best we can. It may well be that any enhancement of the Times-Picayune's market position during the period of the assailed arrangements resulted from better service or lower prices, or was due to superior planning initiative or managerial skills; conversely, it is equally possible that but for the adoption of the unit contracts its market position might have turned for the worse. . . . [This] case has not met the *per se* criteria of Sherman Act § 1 from which proscribed effect automatically must be inferred. . . . Under the broad general policy directed by § 1 against unreasonable trade restraints, guilt cannot rest on speculation; the Government here has proved neither actual unlawful effects nor facts which radiate a potential for future harm.

[U]ncontradicted testimony suggests that unit insertions of classified ads substantially reduce the publisher's overhead costs. Approximately thirty separate operations are necessary to translate an advertiser's order into a published line of print. A reasonable price for a classified ad is necessarily low. And the Publishing Company processed about 2,300 classified ads for publication each day. Certainly a publisher's step to rationalize that operation do not bespeak a purposive quest for monopoly or restraint of trade.

Similarly, competitive business considerations apparently actuated the adoption of the unit rate for general display linage in 1950. At that time about 180 other publishers, the vast majority of morning-evening owners, had previously instituted similar unit plans. Doubtless, long-tolerated trade arrangements acquire no vested immunity under the Sherman Act; no prescriptive rights accrue by the prosecutor's delay. . . . In summary, neither unlawful effects nor aims are shown by the record.

Consequently, no Sherman Act violation has occurred unless the Publishing Company's refusal to sell advertising space except *en bloc*, viewed alone, constitutes a violation of the Act. [T]his Court's decisions have recognized individual refusals to sell as a general right, though "neither absolute nor exempt from regulation." . . . If accompanied by unlawful conduct or agreement, or conceived in monopolistic purpose or market control, even individual sellers' refusals to deal have transgressed the Act.

Reversed.

NORTHERN PACIFIC RAILWAY v. UNITED STATES
356 U.S. 1 (1958)

JUSTICE BLACK delivered the opinion of the Court.

In 1864 and 1870 Congress granted the predecessor of the Northern Pacific Railway Company approximately forty million acres of land in several Northwestern States and Territories to facilitate its construction of a railroad. . . . By 1949 the Railroad had sold about 37,000,000 acres of its holdings, but had reserved mineral rights in 6,500,000 of those acres. Most of the unsold land was leased for one purpose or another. In a large number of its sales contracts and most of its lease agreements the Railroad had inserted "preferential routing" clauses which compelled the grantee or lessee to ship over its lines all commodities produced or manufactured on the land, provided that its rates (and in some instances its service) were equal to those of competing carriers. Since many of the goods produced on the lands subject to these "preferential routing" provisions are shipped from one State to another the actual and potential amount of interstate commerce affected is substantial. Alternative means of transportation exist for a large portion of these shipments including the facilities of two other major railroad systems.

In 1949, the Government filed suit under § 4 of the Sherman Act seeking a declaration that the defendant's "preferential routing" agreements were unlawful as unreasonable restraints of trade under § 1 of that Act. After various pretrial proceedings the Government moved for summary judgment contending that on the undisputed facts it was entitled, as a matter of law, to the relief demanded. The district judge . . . granted the Government's motion. . . .

The Sherman Act was designed to be a comprehensive charter of economic liberty aimed at preserving free and unfettered competition as the rule of trade. It rests on the premise that the unrestrained interaction of competitive forces will yield the best allocation of our economic resources, the lowest prices, the highest quality and the greatest material progress, while at the same time providing an environment conducive to the preservation of our democratic political and social institutions. But even were that premise open to question, the policy unequivocally laid down by the Act is competition. And to this end it prohibits "Every contract, combination . . . or conspiracy, in restraint of trade or commerce among the several States." Although this prohibition is literally all-encompassing, the courts have construed it as precluding only those contracts or combinations which "unreasonably" restrain competition. . . .

However, there are certain agreements or practices which because of their pernicious effect on competition and lack of any redeeming virtue are conclusively presumed to be unreasonable and therefore illegal without elaborate inquiry as to the precise harm they have caused or the business excuse for their use. This principle of *per se* unreasonableness not only makes the type of restraints which are proscribed by the Sherman Act more certain to the benefit of everyone concerned, but it also avoids the necessity for an incredibly complicated and prolonged economic investigation into the entire history of the industry involved, as well as related industries, in an effort to determine at large whether a particular restraint has been unreasonable — an inquiry so often wholly fruitless when undertaken. Among the practices which the courts have heretofore deemed to be unlawful in and of themselves are price fixing, division of markets, group boycotts, and tying arrangements. . . .

For our purposes a tying arrangement may be defined as an agreement by a party to sell one product but only on the condition that the buyer also purchases a different (or tied) product, or at least agrees that he will not purchase that product from any other supplier. Where such conditions are successfully exacted competition on the merits with respect to the tied product is inevitably curbed. Indeed "tying agreements serve hardly any purpose beyond the suppression of competition." . . . They deny competitors free access to the market for the tied product, not because the party imposing the tying requirements has a better product or a lower price but because of his power or leverage in another market. At the same time buyers are forced to forego their free choice between competing products. For these reasons "tying agreements fare harshly under the laws forbidding restraints of trade." . . . They are unreasonable in and of themselves whenever a party has sufficient economic power with respect to the tying product to appreciably restrain free competition in the market for the tied product and a "not insubstantial" amount of interstate commerce is affected. . . . Of course where the seller has no control or dominance over the tying product so that it does not represent an effectual weapon to pressure buyers into taking the tied item any restraint of trade attributable to such tying arrangements would obviously be insignificant at most. As a simple example, if one of a dozen food stores in a community were to refuse to sell flour unless the buyer also took sugar it would hardly tend to restrain competition in sugar if its competitors were ready and able to sell flour by itself.

In this case we believe the district judge was clearly correct in entering summary judgment declaring the defendant's "preferential routing" clauses unlawful restraints of trade. We wholly agree that the undisputed facts established beyond any genuine question that the defendant possessed substantial economic power by virtue of its extensive landholdings which it used as leverage to induce large numbers of purchasers and lessees to give it preference, to the exclusion of its competitors, in carrying goods or produce from the land transferred to them. Nor can there be any real doubt that a "not insubstantial" amount of interstate commerce was and is affected by these restrictive provisions.

As pointed out before, the defendant was initially granted large acreages by Congress in the several Northwestern States through which its lines now run. This land was strategically located in checkerboard fashion amid private holdings and within economic distance of transportation facilities. Not only the testimony of various witnesses but common sense makes it evident that this particular land was often prized by those who purchased or leased it and was frequently essential to their business activities. In disposing of its holdings the defendant entered into contracts of sale or lease covering at least several million acres of land which included "preferential routing" clauses. The very existence of this host of tying arrangements is itself compelling evidence of the defendant's great power, at least where, as here, no other explanation has been offered for the existence of these restraints. The "preferential routing" clauses conferred no benefit on the purchasers or lessees. While they got the land they wanted by yielding their freedom to deal with competing carriers, the defendant makes no claim that it came any cheaper than if the restrictive clauses had been omitted. In fact any such price reduction in return for rail shipments would have quite plainly constituted an unlawful rebate to the shipper. So far as the Railroad was concerned its purpose obviously was to fence out competitors, to stifle competition. While this may have been exceedingly beneficial to its business, it is the very type of thing the Sherman Act condemns. In short, we are convinced that the essential prerequisites for treating the defendant's tying arrangements as unreasonable "*per se*" were conclusively established below and that the defendant has offered to prove nothing there or here which would alter this conclusion.

In our view *International Salt Co. . . .* is ample authority for affirming the judgment below. In that case the defendant refused to lease its salt-dispensing machines unless the lessee also agreed to purchase all the salt it used in the machines from the defendant. It was established that the defendant had made about 900 leases under such conditions and that in the year in question it had sold about $500,000 worth of salt for use in the leased machines. On that basis we affirmed unanimously a summary judgment finding the defendant guilty of violating § 1 of the Sherman Act. The Court ruled that it was "unreasonable, *per se*, to foreclose competitors from any substantial market" by tying arrangements. As we later analyzed the decision, "it was not established that equivalent machines were unobtainable, it was not indicated what proportion of the business of supplying such machines was controlled by defendant, and it was deemed irrelevant that there was no evidence as to the actual effect of the tying clauses upon competition." . . .

The defendant attempts to evade the force of *International Salt* on the ground that the tying product there was patented while here it is not. But we do not believe this distinction has, or should have, any significance. In arriving at its decision in *International Salt* the Court placed no reliance on the fact that a patent was involved nor did it give the slightest intimation that the outcome would have been any different if that had not been the case. If anything, the Court held the challenged tying arrangements unlawful *despite* the fact that the tying item was patented, not because of it. "By contracting to close this market for salt against competition, International has engaged in a restraint of trade for which its patents afford no immunity from the antitrust laws." . . .

While there is some language in the *Times-Picayune* opinion which speaks of "monopoly power" or "dominance" over the tying product as a necessary precondition for application of the rule of *per se* unreasonableness to tying arrangements, we do not construe this general language as requiring anything more than sufficient economic power to impose an appreciable restraint on free competition in the tied product (assuming all the time, of course, that a "not insubstantial" amount of interstate commerce is affected). . . .

The defendant contends that its "preferential routing" clauses are subject to so many exceptions and have been administered so leniently that they do not significantly restrain competition. It points out that these clauses permit the vendee or lessee to ship by competing carrier if its rates are lower (or in some instances if its service is better) than the defendant's. Of course if these restrictive provisions are merely harmless sieves with no tendency to restrain competition, as the defendant's argument seems to imply, it is hard to understand why it has expended so much effort in obtaining them in vast numbers and upholding their validity, or how they are of any benefit to anyone, even the defendant. But however that may be, the essential fact remains that these agreements are binding obligations held over the heads of vendees which deny defendant's competitors access to the fenced-off market on the same terms as the defendant. . . .

Affirmed.

[A dissent by JUSTICE HARLAN, joined by JUSTICES FRANKFURTER and WHITTAKER, is omitted.]

NOTES AND QUESTIONS

1. *Times-Picayune* held, inter alia, that one of the essential elements of an illegal tying arrangement was that there be two separate and distinct products. Opinions concerning how to apply the "two products" requirement have varied. The courts have considered the following factors: (1) physical characteristics; (2) business justification such as cost efficiencies; (3) end-usage; (4) whether the "challenged aggregation is an essential ingredient" of the product's success; (5) industry trade practices; and (6) whether the products are ever sold in separate markets. *See, e.g., Rosebrough Monument Co. v. Memorial Park Cem. Ass'n*, 666 F.2d 1130 (8th Cir. 1981), *cert. denied*, 457 U.S. 1111 (1982); *Hamro v. Shell Oil Co.*, 674 F.2d 784 (9th Cir. 1982); *United States v. Jerrold Elec. Corp.*, 187 F. Supp. 545 (E.D. Pa. 1960)365 U.S. 567 (1961).

Can you tell which of these factors Justice Clark relied on in the *Times-Picayune* case? Justice Clark must have been influenced by one fact that appears several times in the record: "unit" pricing (requiring identical advertisements in the morning and evening newspapers) permitted the newspaper to set type and establish the advertising layout for the two newspapers once a day instead of twice. For example, the single largest cost to the newspaper of running a classified advertisement was the cost of arranging the advertisements on a page and setting the type. Under the unit pricing plan the classified sections in the morning and evening newspapers were identical. This resulted in a very large cost savings to the newspaper, which was passed along to its customers. However, the unit pricing plan admitted no exceptions: it would work only if *all* advertisements were placed in both the morning and evening editions. *See* Record at 1127–1129, *Times-Picayune Pub'g Co. v. United States*, 345 U.S. 594 (1953); Herbert Hovenkamp, *Distributive Justice and the Antitrust Laws*, 51 GEO. WASH. L. REV. 1 (1982).

2. From *International Salt* through *Northern Pacific*, it seems that under a per se analysis, the plaintiff would be required to establish the following:

   (a) that two separate products were involved in the tie-in sale;

   (b) that defendant possessed sufficient economic power in the market of the tying product; and

   (c) that the amount of commerce affected in the tied product market was not insubstantial.

Some circuits have adopted a three-part per se test such as the one described above. *See, e.g., Siegel v. Chicken Delight, Inc.*, 448 F.2d 43, 47 (9th Cir. 1971), *cert. denied*, 405 U.S. 955 (1972). Other circuits have created more detailed tests. For instance, in 1980 the Second Circuit adopted the following test:

(a) There must be separate tying and tied products;

(b) There must be "evidence of actual coercion by the seller that in fact forced the buyer to accept the tied produce";

(c) The seller must possess "sufficient economic power in the tying product market to coerce purchaser acceptance of the tied product";

(d) There must be "anticompetitive effects in the tied market";

(e) There must be "involvement of a 'not insubstantial' amount of interstate commerce in the tied product market."

Yentsch v. Texaco, Inc., 630 F.2d 46, 56–57 (2d Cir. 1980). The Fifth Circuit currently uses a four element test. *Bob Maxfield, Inc. v. American Motors Corp.*, 637 F.2d 1033, 1037 (5th Cir. 1981).

3.   Is it clear after *Northern Pacific* that under the Clayton Act, a plaintiff need prove only the presence of *either* market dominance in the tying product *or* the involvement of a substantial amount of commerce in the tied product, but not both? Circuit courts generally have ignored Justice Clark's division in *Times-Picayune* and required both elements, regardless whether the action was brought under the Sherman Act or the Clayton Act. *Spartan Grain & Mill Co. v. Ayers*, 581 F.2d 419, 428 (5th Cir. 1978); *Moore v. Jas. H. Matthews & Co.*, 550 F.2d 1207, 1214 (9th Cir. 1977).

Does a rule that permits a plaintiff to recover without proving market power in the tying product make any sense? If the market for the tying product is perfectly competitive, then a seller would be powerless to impose an unwanted second product on the buyer, would it not? The buyer would simply purchase the tying product from a competitor who did not assess the requirement. What would explain a "tying arrangement" in a market in which the seller has no market power in the tying product? There might, of course, be a cartel, in which all the sellers of the tying product agreed to impose the tie-in — collectively, they would have market power.

The other explanation, however, is that the tie-in creates efficiency. In fact, if a package sale is cheaper than individual sales, a competitor may be forced to make the package sales in order to compete with other sellers. For example, it is probably far cheaper to sell shoes in pairs, because the demand for single shoes is very low in relation to the additional stocking, return, and inventory costs that selling single shoes would impose. As a result shoe stores almost universally require people to take a left shoe as a condition of purchasing a right shoe, or vice-versa, even where the shoe store involved clearly has no market power. A court would be likely to analyze such a tie-in by saying that a pair of shoes is a single product — but this simply states the result of the above economic analysis. Clearly there are certain customers — such as Captain Ahab — who would prefer to purchase right shoes alone.

Why did Northern Pacific tie the transportation requirements to its sales and leases of land? The traditional leverage argument that the Supreme Court relied on is problematic, because the tying arrangements contained "escape clauses": a lessee or purchaser of the land had to purchase his transportation requirements from Northern Pacific only if the price was no higher than the price offered by competitors. This seems inconsistent with the Supreme Court's conclusion that the railroad was using its market power in land to monopolize the shipping of freight as well.

Several explanations have been offered for the railroad's tying arrangements. One is that they were devices for avoiding price regulation of freight transportation. If the regulated price was artificially high the railroad might increase its volume by inducing land buyers to locate along the railroad by selling the land below its fair market value. By requiring these landowners to use Northern Pacific to ship their products, the railroad could increase its freight volume at the regulated price, which had a large amount of profit built into it. The increased volume of freight at the regulated price would more than compensate for the lower price at which the land was sold.

Another explanation is that the railroad was using the tie-in clauses to gather information about competing railroads that might be rate cutting. Under the arrangements any purchaser of land from Northern Pacific could be expected to ship his products by means of the Northern Pacific unless he was getting a lower price elsewhere. If a competing railroad seduced such a customer away by means of a secret rebate or other rate regulation avoidance scheme, Northern Pacific would know about it. Thus, the argument goes, the tie-ins made it easier for Northern Pacific to monitor the rate-setting practices of its competitors. For development of this argument, see Cummings & Ruther, *The Northern Pacific Case*, 22 J.L. & Econ. 329 (1979). The authors note that at the time there were several small railroads that were not rate regulated (the Northern Pacific was not one of them) and were not required by law to publish their rates. The tie-ins, the authors argue, made it easier for the Northern Pacific to gather information about the rate-setting practices of these small railroads. Periodically they would use this information to petition rate-making agencies for adjustments to their own rates.

Consider whether customers would have no preference between railroads, assuming that rates and service were equivalent. Would they object to a tie-in under these circumstances? The result might be that Northern Pacific would get all the rail business of its lessees, as long as it maintained rate and service parity, rather than a share of the business, probably determined at random.

4. In *Smugglers Notch Homeowners' Ass'n., Inc. v. Smugglers' Notch Management Co., Ltd.*, 2011 U.S. App. LEXIS 5180 (2d Cir. Mar. 15, 2011), the Second Circuit held that even though the vacation properties controlled by the defendant were "unique," this uniqueness alone was not sufficient to create an inference of market power for purposes of the antitrust law of tying arrangements; further, there was no "lock-in" under a Kodak theory when the homeowners were fully aware of defendant's policy of tying management services to its properties at the time of purchase.

5. *Palmyra Park Hosp., Inc. v. Phoebe Putney Memorial Hosp.*, 604 F.3d 1291 (11th Cir. 2010), accepted a claim that a defendant effectively tied hospital services by pressuring an insurer to offer more favorable reimbursement rates for hospitals that offered a broader array of services than the plaintiff's smaller hospital offered. There plaintiff also complained that the defendant insisted on higher reimbursement rates from the insurer for its "tying" services if the insurer accepted the plaintiff's hospital as a preferred provider with respect to its "tied" services.

[3] Modern Doctrine Tying Product Power and Anticompetitive Effects

JEFFERSON PARISH HOSPITAL DISTRICT NO. 2 v. HYDE
466 U.S. 2 (1984)

Justice Stevens delivered the opinion of the Court.

At issue in this case is the validity of an exclusive contract between a hospital and a firm of anesthesiologists. We must decide whether the contract gives rise to a *per se* violation of § 1 of the Sherman Act because every patient undergoing surgery at the hospital must use the services of one firm of anesthesiologists, and, if not, whether the contract is nevertheless illegal because it unreasonably restrains competition among anesthesiologists.

In July 1977, respondent Edwin G. Hyde, a board certified anesthesiologist, applied for admission to the medical staff of East Jefferson Hospital. The credentials committee and the medical staff executive committee recommended approval, but the hospital board denied the application because the hospital was a party to a contract providing that all anesthesiological services required by the hospital's patients would be performed by Roux & Associates, a professional medical corporation. Respondent then commenced this action seeking a declaratory judgment that the contract is unlawful and an injunction ordering petitioners to appoint him to the hospital staff.[15] After trial, the District Court denied relief, finding that the anticompetitive consequences of the Roux contract were minimal and outweighed by benefits in the form of improved patient care. 513 F. Supp. 532 (E.D. La. 1981)686 F.2d 286 (5th Cir. 1982). We granted certiorari and now reverse.

I

In February 1971, shortly before East Jefferson Hospital opened, it entered into an "Anesthesiology Agreement" with Roux & Associates ("Roux"), a firm that had recently been organized by Dr. Kermit Roux. The contract provided that any anesthesiologist designated by Roux would be admitted to the hospital's medical staff. The hospital agreed to provide the space, equipment, maintenance, and other supporting services necessary to operate the anesthesiology department. It also

---

[15] [FN 2] In addition to seeking relief under the Sherman Act, respondent's complaint alleged violations of 42 U.S.C. § 1983 and state law. The District Court rejected these claims. The Court of Appeals passed only on the Sherman Act Claim.

agreed to purchase all necessary drugs and other supplies. All nursing personnel required by the anesthesia department were to be supplied by the hospital, but Roux had the right to approve their selection and retention.[16] The hospital agreed to "restrict the use of its anesthesia department to Roux & Associates and [that] no other persons, parties or entities shall perform such services within the Hospital for the term of this contract."

The fees for anesthesiological services are billed separately to the patients by the hospital. They cover over the hospital's costs and the professional services provided by Roux. After a deduction of eight percent to provide a reserve for uncollectible accounts, the fees are divided equally between Roux and the hospital.

The 1971 contract provided for a one-year term automatically renewable for successive one-year periods unless either party elected to terminate. In 1976, a second written contract was executed containing most of the provisions of the 1971 agreement. Its term was five years and the clause excluding other anesthesiologists from the hospital was deleted; the hospital nevertheless continued to regard itself as committed to a closed anesthesiology department. Only Roux was permitted to practice anesthesiology at the hospital. At the time of trial the department included four anesthesiologists. The hospital usually employed 13 or 14 certified registered nurse anesthetists.[17]

The exclusive contract had an impact on two different segments of the economy: consumers of medical services, and providers of anesthesiological services. Any consumer of medical services who elects to have an operation performed at East Jefferson Hospital may not employ any anesthesiologist not associated with Roux. No anesthesiologists except those employed by Roux may practice at East Jefferson.

There are at least 20 hospitals in the New Orleans metropolitan area and about 70 percent of the patients living in Jefferson Parish go to hospitals other than East Jefferson. Because it regarded the entire New Orleans metropolitan area as the relevant geographic market in which hospitals compete, this evidence convinced he District Court that East Jefferson does not possess any significant "market power"; therefore it concluded that petitioners could not use the Roux contract to anticompetitive ends.[18] The same evidence led the Court of Appeals to draw a

---

[16] [FN 3] The contract required all of the physicians employed by Roux to confine their practice of anesthesiology to East Jefferson.

[17] [FN 6] Approximately 875 operations are performed at the hospital each month; as many as 12 of 13 operating rooms may be in use at one time.

[18] [FN 7] The District Court found:

> The impact on commerce resulting from the East Jefferson contract is minimal. The contract is restricted in effect to one hospital in an area containing at least twenty others providing the same surgical services. It would be a different situation if Dr. Roux had exclusive contracts in several hospitals in the relevant market. As pointed out by plaintiff, the majority of surgeons have privileges at more than one hospital in the area. They have the option of admitting their patients to another hospital where they can select the anesthesiologist of their choice. Similarly a patient can go to another hospital if he is not satisfied with the physicians available at East Jefferson.

513 F. Supp., at 541.

significant conclusion. Noting that 30 percent of the residents of the Parish go to East Jefferson Hospital, and that in fact "patients tend to choose hospitals by location rather than price or quality," the Court of Appeals concluded that the relevant geographic market was the East Bank of Jefferson Parish. The conclusion that East Jefferson Hospital possessed market power in that area was buttressed by the facts that the prevalence of health insurance eliminates a patient's incentive to compare costs, that the patient is not sufficiently informed to compare quality, and that family convenience tends to magnify the importance of location.

The Court of Appeals held that the case involves a "tying arrangement" because the "users of the hospital's operating rooms (the tying product) are also compelled to purchase the hospital's chosen anesthesia service (the tied product)." Having defined the relevant geographic market for the tying product as the East Bank of Jefferson Parish, the court held that the hospital possessed "sufficient market power in the tying market to coerce purchasers of the tied product." Since the purchase of the tied product constituted a "not insubstantial amount of interstate commerce," . . . the tying arrangement was therefore illegal *"per se."*

II

. . . It is far too late in the history of our antitrust jurisprudence to question the proposition that certain tying arrangements pose an unacceptable risk of stifling competition and therefore are unreasonable *"per se."* The rule was first enunciated in *International Salt Co. v. United States*, and has been endorsed by this Court many times since. The rule also reflects congressional policies underlying the antitrust laws. In enacting §3 of the Clayton Act, 15 U.S.C. §14, Congress expressed great concern about the anticompetitive character of tying arrangements. While this case does not arise under the Clayton Act, the congressional finding made therein concerning the competitive consequences of tying is illuminating, and must be respected.

It is clear, however, that every refusal to sell two products separately cannot be said to restrain competition. If each of the products may be purchased separately in a competitive market, one seller's decision to sell the two in a single package imposes no unreasonable restraint on either market, particularly if competing suppliers are free to sell either the entire package or its several parts. For example, we have written that "if one of a dozen food stores in a community were to refuse to sell flour unless the buyer also took sugar it would hardly tend to restrain competition if its competitors were ready and able to sell flour by itself." *Northern Pac. R. Co. v. United States*, 356 U.S. 1, 7 (1958). Buyers often find package sales attractive; a seller's decision to offer such packages can merely be an attempt to compete effectively — conduct that is entirely consistent with the Sherman Act.

Our cases have concluded that the essential characteristic of an invalid tying arrangement lies in the seller's exploitation of its control over the tying product to force the buyer into the purchase of a tied product that the buyer either did not want at all, or might have preferred to purchase elsewhere on different terms. When such "forcing" is present, competition on the merits in the market for the tied item is restrained and the Sherman Act is violated.

"Basic to the faith that a free economy best promotes the public weal is that goods must stand the cold test of competition; that the public, acting through the market's impersonal judgment, shall allocate the Nation's resources and thus direct the course its economic development will take. . . . By conditioning his sale of one commodity on the purchase of another, a seller coerces the abdication of buyers' independent judgment as to the "tied" product's merits and insulates it from the competitive stresses of the open market. But any intrinsic superiority of the "tied" product would convince freely choosing buyers to select it over others anyway." *Times-Picayune Publishing Co. v. United States*, 345 U.S. 594, 605 (1953).

Accordingly, we have condemned tying arrangements when the seller has some special ability — usually called "market power" — to force a purchaser to do something that he would not do in a competitive market.[19] When "forcing" occurs, our cases have found the tying arrangement to be unlawful.

Thus, the law draws a distinction between the exploitation of market power by merely enhancing the price of the tying product, on the one hand, and by attempting to impose restraints on competition in the market for a tied product, on the other. When the seller's power is just used to maximize its return in the tying product market, where presumably its product enjoys some justifiable advantage over its competitors, the competitive ideal of the Sherman Act is not necessarily compromised. But if that power is used to impair competition on the merits in another market, a potentially inferior product may be insulated from competitive pressures. This impairment could either harm existing competitors or create barriers to entry of new competitors in the market for the tied product . . . and can increase the social costs of market power by facilitating price discrimination, thereby increasing monopoly profits over what they would be absent the tie.[20] And from the standpoint of the consumer — whose interests the statute was especially intended to serve — the freedom to select the best bargain in the second market is impaired by his need to purchase the tying product, and perhaps by an inability to evaluate the true cost of either product when they are available only as a package.[21] In sum, to permit restraint of competition on the merits through tying arrangements would be, as we observed in *Fortner II*, to condone "the existence of power that a free market would not tolerate." 429 U.S., at 617 (footnote omitted).

Per se condemnation — condemnation without inquiry into actual market conditions — is only appropriate if the existence of forcing is probable. Thus, application of the *per se* rule focuses on the probability of anticompetitive consequences. Of course, as a threshold matter there must be a substantial potential for impact on competition in order to justify *per se* condemnation. If only

---

[19] [FN 20] This type of market power has sometimes been referred to as "leverage." Professors Areeda and Turner provide a definition that suits present purposes. " 'Leverage' is loosely defined here as a supplier's ability to induce his customer for one product to buy a second product from him that would not otherwise be purchased solely on the merit of that second product." V P. Areeda & D. Turner, Antitrust Law & 1134a at 202 (1980).

[20] [FN 23] Sales of the tied item can be used to measure demand for the tying item; purchasers with greater needs for the tied item make larger purchases and in effect must pay a higher price to obtain the tying item.

[21] [FN 24] Especially where market imperfections exist, purchasers may not be fully sensitive to the price or quality implications of a tying arrangement, and hence it may impede competition on the merits.

a single purchaser were "forced" with respect to the purchase of a tied item, the resultant impact on competition would not be sufficient to warrant the concern of antitrust law. It is for this reason that we have refused to condemn tying arrangements unless a substantial volume of commerce is foreclosed thereby. Similarly, when a purchaser is "forced" to buy a product he would not have otherwise bought even from another seller in the tied product market, there can be no adverse impact on competition because no portion of the market which would otherwise have been available to other sellers has been foreclosed.

Once this threshold is surmounted, *per se* prohibition is appropriate if anticompetitive forcing is likely. For example, if the government has granted the seller a patent or similar monopoly over a product, it is fair to presume that the inability to buy the product elsewhere gives the seller market power. *United States v. Loew's Inc.*, 371 U.S. 38, 45–47 (1962). Any effort to enlarge the scope of the patent monopoly by using the market power it confers to restrain competition in the market for a second product will undermine competition on the merits in that second market. Thus, the sale or lease of a patented item on condition that the buyer make all his purchases of a separate tied product from the patentee is unlawful.

The same strict rule is appropriate in situations in which the existence of market power is probable. When the seller's share of the market is high, or when the seller offers a unique product that competitors are not able to offer, the Court has held that the likelihood that market power exists and is being used to restrain competition in a separate market is sufficient to make *per se* condemnation appropriate. . . . When, however, the seller does not have either the degree or the kind of market power that enables him to force customers to purchase a second, unwanted product in order to obtain the tying product, an antitrust violation can be established only by evidence of and unreasonable restraint on competition in the relevant market.

In sum, any inquiry into the validity of a tying arrangement must focus on the market or markets in which the two products are sold, for that is where the anticompetitive forcing has its impact. Thus, in this case our analysis of the tying issue must focus on the hospital's sale of services to its patients, rather than its contractual arrangements with the providers of anesthesiological services. In making that analysis, we must consider whether petitioners are selling two separate products that may be tied together, and, if so, whether they have used their market power to force their patients to accept the tying arrangement.

III

The hospital has provided its patients with a package that includes the range of facilities and services required for a variety of surgical operations. At East Jefferson Hospital the package includes the services of the anesthesiologist.[22]

---

[22] [FN 28] It is essential to differentiate between the Roux contract and the legality of the contract between the hospital and its patients. The Roux contract is nothing more than an arrangement whereby Roux supplies all of the hospital's needs for anesthesiological services. That contract raises only an exclusive dealing question. The issue here is whether the hospital's insistence that its patients purchase

Petitioners argue that the package does not involve a tying arrangement at all — that they are merely providing a functionally integrated package of services. Therefore, petitioners contend that it is inappropriate to apply principles concerning tying arrangements to this case.

Our cases indicate, however, that the answer to the question whether one or two products are involved turns not on the functional relation between them, but rather on the character of the demand for the two items.[23] . . . These cases make it clear that a tying arrangement cannot exist unless two separate product markets have been linked. . . .

Unquestionably, the anesthesiological component of the package offered by the hospital could be provided separately and could be selected either by the individual patient or by one of the patient's doctors if the hospital did not insist on including anesthesiological services in the package it offers to its customers. As a matter of actual practice, anesthesiological services are billed separately from the hospital services petitioners provide. There was ample and uncontroverted testimony that patients or surgeons often request specific anesthesiologists to come to a hospital and provide anesthesia, and that the choice of an individual anesthesiologist separate from the choice of a hospital is particularly frequent in respondent's specialty, obstetric anesthesiology. The District Court found that "[t]he provision of anesthesia services is a medical service separate from the other services provided by the hospital." The Court of Appeals agreed with this finding, and went on to observe that "an anesthesiologist is normally selected by the surgeon, rather than the patient, based on familiarity gained through a working relationship. Obviously, the surgeons who practice at East Jefferson Hospital do not gain familiarity with any anesthesiologists other than Roux and Associates." The record amply supports the conclusion that consumers differentiate between anesthesiological services and the other hospital services provided by petitioners.[24]

Thus, the hospital's requirement that its patients obtain necessary anesthesiological services from Roux combined the purchase of two distinguishable services in a single transaction. Nevertheless, the fact that this case involves a required purchase of two services that would otherwise be purchased separately does not make the Roux contract illegal. As noted above, there is nothing inherently anticompetitive about packaged sales. Only if patients are forced to purchase Roux's

---

anesthesiological services from Roux creates a tying arrangement.

[23] [FN 30] The fact that anesthesiological services are functionally linked to the other services provided by the hospital is not in itself sufficient to remove the Roux contract from the realm of tying arrangements. We have often found arrangements involving functionally linked products at least one of which is useless without the other to be prohibited tying devices. See *Mercoid Corp. v. Mid-Continent Co.*, 320 U.S. 661 (1944) (heating system and stoker switch); *Morton Salt Co. v. Suppiger Co.*, 314 U.S. 488 (1942) (salt machine and salt). In fact, in some situations the functional link between the two items may enable the seller to maximize its monopoly return on the tying item as a means of charging a higher rent or purchase price to a larger user of the tying item.

[24] [FN 39] The record here shows that other hospitals often permit anesthesiological services to be purchased separately, that anesthesiologists are not fungible in that the services provided by each are not precisely the same, that anesthesiological services are billed separately, and that the hospital required purchases from Roux even though other anesthesiologists were available and Roux had no objection to their receiving staff privileges at East Jefferson. Therefore, the . . . analysis indicates that there was a tying arrangement here. . . .

services as a result of the hospital's market power would the arrangement have anticompetitive consequences. If no forcing is present, patients are free to enter a competing hospital and to use another anesthesiologist instead of Roux.[25] The fact that petitioner's patients are required to purchase two separate items is only the beginning of the appropriate inquiry.[26]

IV

The question remains whether this arrangement involves the use of market power to force patients to buy services they would not otherwise purchase. Respondent's only basis for invoking the *per se* rule against tying and thereby avoiding analysis of actual market conditions is by relying on the preference of persons residing in Jefferson Parish to go to East Jefferson, the closest hospital. A preference of this kind, however, is not necessarily probative of significant market power.

Seventy percent of the patients residing in Jefferson Parish enter hospitals other than East Jefferson. Thus East Jefferson's "dominance" over persons residing in Jefferson Parish is far from overwhelming.[27] The fact that a substantial majority of the parish's residents elect not to enter East Jefferson means that the geographic data does not establish the kind of dominant market position that obviates the need for further inquiry into actual competitive conditions. . . .

---

[25] [FN 41] An examination of the reason or reasons why petitioners denied respondent staff privileges will not provide the answer to the question whether the package of services they offered to their patients is an illegal tying arrangement. As a matter of antitrust law, petitioners may give their anesthesiology business to Roux because he is the best doctor available, because he is willing to work long hours, or because he is the son-in-law of the hospital administrator without violating the *per se* rule against tying. Without evidence that petitioners are using market power to force Roux upon patients there is no basis to view the arrangement as unreasonably restraining competition whatever the reasons for its creation. Conversely, with such evidence, the per se rule against tying may apply. Thus, we reject the view of the District Court that the legality of an arrangement of this kind turns on whether it was adopted for the purpose of improving patient care.

[26] [FN 42] Petitioners argue and the District Court found that the exclusive contract had what it characterized as procompetitive justifications in that an exclusive contract ensures 24-hour anesthesiology coverage, enables flexible scheduling, and facilitates work routine, professional standards and maintenance of equipment. The Court of Appeals held these findings to be clearly erroneous since the exclusive contract was not necessary to achieve these ends. Roux was willing to provide 24-hour coverage even without an exclusive contract and the credentials committee of the hospital could impose standards for staff privileges that would ensure staff would comply with the demands of scheduling, maintenance, and professional standards. In the past, we have refused to tolerate manifestly anticompetitive conduct simply because the health care industry is involved. . . . Petitioners seek no special solicitude. We have also uniformly rejected similar "goodwill" defenses for tying arrangements, finding that the use of contractual quality specifications are generally sufficient to protect quality without the use of a tying arrangement. Since the District Court made no finding as to why contractual quality specifications would not protect the hospital, there is no basis for departing from our prior cases here.

[27] [FN 43] In fact its position in this market is not dissimilar from the market share at issue in *Times-Picayune*, which the Court found insufficient as a basis for inferring market power. *See* 345 U.S., at 611–613. Moreover, in other antitrust contexts this Court has found that market shares comparable to the present here do not create an unacceptable likelihood of anticompetitive conduct. *See United States v. Connecticut National Bank*, 418 U.S. 656 (1974); *United States v. DuPont & Co.*, 351 U.S. 377 (1956).

Tying arrangements need only be condemned if they restrain competition on the merits by forcing purchases that would not otherwise be made. A lack of price or quality competition does not create this type of forcing. If consumers lack price consciousness, that fact will not force them to take an anesthesiologist whose services they do not want — their indifference to price will have no impact on their willingness or ability to go to another hospital where they can utilize the services of the anesthesiologist of their choice. Similarly, if consumers cannot evaluate the quality of anesthesiological services, it follows that they are indifferent between certified anesthesiologists even in the absence of a tying arrangement — such an arrangement cannot be said to have foreclosed a choice that would have otherwise been made "on the merits."

Thus, neither of the "market imperfections" relied upon by the Court of Appeals forces consumers to take anesthesiological services they would not select in the absence of a tie. It is safe to assume that every patient undergoing a surgical operation needs the services of an anesthesiologist; at least this record contains no evidence that the hospital "forced" any such services on unwilling patients. The record therefore does not provide a basis for applying the *per se* rule against tying to this arrangement.

V

In order to prevail in the absence of *per se* liability, respondent has the burden of proving that the Roux contract violated the Sherman Act because it unreasonably restrained competition. That burden necessarily involves an inquiry into the actual effect of the exclusive contract on competition among anesthesiologists. This competition takes place in a market that has not been defined. The market is not necessarily the same as the market in which hospitals compete in offering services to patients; it may encompass competition among anesthesiologists for exclusive contracts such as the Roux contract and might be statewide or merely local.[28] There is, however, insufficient evidence in this record to provide a basis for finding that the Roux contract, as it actually operates in the market, has unreasonably restrained competition. The record sheds little light on how this arrangement affected consumer demand for separate arrangements with a specific anesthesiologist.[29] The evidence indicates that some surgeons and patients preferred respondent's services to those of Roux, but there is no evidence that any patient who was sophisticated enough to know the difference between two anesthesiologists was not also able to go

---

[28] [FN 48] While there was some rather impressionistic testimony that the prevalence of exclusive contracts tended to discourage young doctors from entering the market, the evidence was equivocal and neither the District Court nor the Court of Appeals made any findings concerning the contract's effect on entry barriers. Respondent does not press the point before this Court. It is possible that under some circumstances an exclusive contract could raise entry barriers since anesthesiologists could not compete for the contract without raising the capital necessary to run a hospital-wide operation. However, since the hospital has provided most of the capital for the exclusive contractor in this case, that problem does not appear to be present.

[29] [FN 49] While it is true that purchasers may not be fully sensitive to the price or quality implications of a tying arrangement, so that competition may be impeded, this depends on an empirical demonstration concerning the effect of the arrangement on price or quality, and the record reveals little if anything about the effect of this arrangement on the market for anesthesiological services.

to a hospital that would provide him with the anesthesiologist of his choice.

In sum, all that the record established is that the choice of anesthesiologists at East Jefferson has been limited to one of the four doctors who are associated with Roux and therefore have staff privileges. Even if Roux did not have an exclusive contract, the range of alternatives open to the patient would be severely limited by the nature of the transaction and the hospital's unquestioned right to exercise some control over the identity and the number of doctors to whom it accords staff privileges. If respondent is admitted to the staff of East Jefferson, the range of choice will be enlarged from four to five doctors, but the most significant restraints on the patient's freedom to select a specific anesthesiologist will nevertheless remain.[30] Without a showing of actual adverse effect on competition, respondent cannot make out a case under the antitrust laws, and no such showing has been made.

VI

Petitioners' closed policy may raise questions of medical ethics, and may have inconvenienced some patients who would prefer to have their anesthesia administered by someone other than a member of Roux & Associates, but it does not have the obviously unreasonable impact on purchasers that has characterized the tying arrangements that this Court has branded unlawful. There is no evidence that the price, the quality, or the supply or demand for either the "tying product' ' or the "tied product" involved in this case has been adversely affected by the exclusive contract between Roux and the hospital. It may well be true that the contract made it necessary for Dr. Hyde and others to practice elsewhere, rather than at East Jefferson. But there has been no showing that the market as a whole has been affected at all by the contract. Indeed, as we previously noted, the record tells us very little about the market for the services of anesthesiologists. Yet that is the market in which the exclusive contract has had its principal impact. There is simply no showing here of the kind of restraint in competition that is prohibited by the Sherman Act. Accordingly, the judgment of the Court of Appeals is reversed and the case is remanded to that court for further proceedings consistent with this opinion.

JUSTICE POWELL, and JUSTICE REHNQUIST join, concurring in the judgment.

. . . .

---

[30] [FN 52] The record simply tells us little if anything about the effect of this arrangement on price or quality of anesthesiological services. As to price, the arrangement did not lead to an increase in the price charged to the patient. As to quality, the record indicates little more than that there have never been any complaints about the quality of Roux's services, and no contention that his services are in any respect inferior to those of respondent. Moreover, the self interest of the hospital, as well as the ethical and professional norms under which it operates, presumably protect the quality of anesthesiological services.

I

Some of our earlier cases did indeed declare that tying arrangements serve "hardly any purpose beyond the suppression of competition." *Standard Oil Co. of California v. United States*, 337 U.S. 293, 305–306 (1949) (dictum). However, this declaration was not taken literally even by the cases that purported to rely upon it. In practice, a tie has been illegal only if the seller is shown to have "sufficient economic power with respect to the tying product to appreciably restrain free competition in the market for the tied product. . . . " *Northern Pacific R. Co.*, [356 U.S. 1,] at 6. Without "control or dominance over the tying product," the seller could not use the tying products as "an effectual weapon to pressure buyers into taking the tied item," so that any restraint of trade would be "insignificant." The Court has never been willing to say of tying arrangements, as it has of price-fixing, division of markets and other agreements subject to *per se* analysis, that they are always illegal, without proof of market power or anticompetitive effect.

The "*per se*" doctrine in tying cases has thus always required an elaborate inquiry into the economic effects of the tying arrangement.[31] As a result, tying doctrine incurs the costs of rule of reason approach without achieving its benefits: the doctrine calls for the extensive and time-consuming economic analysis characteristic of the rule of reason, but then may be interpreted to prohibit arrangements that economic analysis would show to be beneficial. Moreover, the per se label in the tying context has generated more confusion than coherent law because it appears to invite lower courts to omit the analysis of economic circumstances of the tie that has always been a necessary element of tying analysis.

The time has therefore come to abandon the "*per se*" label and refocus the inquiry on the adverse economic effects, and the potential economic benefits, that the tie may have. The law of tie-ins will thus be brought into accord with the law applicable to all other allegedly anticompetitive economic arrangements, except those few horizontal or quasi-horizontal restraints that can be said to have no economic justification whatsoever. This change will rationalize rather than abandon tie-in doctrine as it is already applied.

II

Our prior opinions indicate that the purpose of tying law has been to identify and control those tie-ins that have a demonstrable exclusionary impact in the tied product market, or that abet the harmful exercise of market power that the seller possesses in the tying product market. Under the rule of reason tying arrangements should be disapproved only in such instances.

Market power in the tying product may be acquired legitimately (*e.g.*, through the grant of a patent) or illegitimately (*e.g.*, as a result of unlawful monopolization). In either event, exploitation of consumers in the market for the tying product is a possibility that exists and that may be regulated under § 2 of the Sherman Act without reference to any tying arrangements that the seller may have developed.

---

[31] [FN 1] This inquiry has been required in analyzing both the prima facie case and affirmative defenses. . . .

The existence of a tied product normally does not increase the profit that the seller with market power can extract from sales of the tying product. A seller with a monopoly on flour, for example, cannot increase the profit it can extract from flour consumers simply by forcing them to buy sugar along with their flour. Counterintuitive though that assertion may seem, it is easily demonstrated and widely accepted. *See, e.g.*, R. Bork, The Antitrust Paradox 372–374 (1978); P. Areeda, Antitrust Analysis 735 (3d ed. 1981).

Tying may be economically harmful primarily in the rare cases where power in the market for the tying product is used to create additional market power in the market for the tied product. The antitrust law is properly concerned with tying when, for example, the flour monopolist threatens to use its market power to acquire additional power in the sugar market, perhaps by driving out competing sellers of sugar, or by making it more difficult for new sellers to enter the sugar market. But such extension of market power is unlikely, or poses no threat of economic harm, unless the two markets in question and the nature of the two products tied satisfy three threshold criteria.

. . . .

First, the seller must have power in the tying product market. Absent such power tying cannot conceivably have any adverse impact in the tied-product market, and can be only procompetitive in the tying-product market. If the seller of flour has no market power over flour, it will gain none by insisting that its buyers take some sugar as well.

Second, there must be a substantial threat that the tying seller will acquire market power in the tied-product market. No such threat exists if the tied-product market is occupied by many stable sellers who are not likely to be driven out by the tying, or if entry barriers in the tied product market are low. If, for example, there is an active and vibrant market for sugar — one with numerous sellers and buyers who do not deal in flour — the flour monopolist's tying of sugar to flour need not be declared unlawful. If, on the other hand, the tying arrangement is likely to erect significant barriers to entry into the tied-product market, the tie remains suspect.

Third, there must be a coherent economic basis for treating the tying and tied products as distinct. All but the simplest products can be broken down into two or more components that are "tied together" in the final sale. Unless it is to be illegal to sell cars with engines or cameras with lenses, this analysis must be guided by some limiting principle. For products to be treated as distinct, the tied product must, at a minimum, be one that some consumers might wish to purchase separately without also purchasing the tying product.[32] When the tied product has no use other than in conjunction with the tying product, a seller of the tying product can acquire no additional market power by selling the two products together. If sugar is useless to consumers except when used with flour, the flour seller's market

---

[32] [FN 8] Whether the tying product is one that consumers might wish to purchase without the tied product should be irrelevant. Once it is conceded that the seller has market power over the tying product it follows that the seller can sell the tying product on non competitive terms. The injury to consumers does not depend on whether the seller chooses to charge a super-competitive price, or charges a competitive price but insists that consumers also buy a product that they do not want.

power is projected into the sugar market whether or not the two products are actually sold together; the flour seller can exploit what market power it has over flour with or without the tie. The flour seller will therefore have little incentive to monopolize the sugar market unless it can produce and distribute sugar more cheaply than other sugar sellers. And in this unusual case, where flour is monopolized and sugar is useful only when used with flour, consumers will suffer no further economic injury by the monopolization of the sugar market.

Even when the tied product does have a use separate from the tying product, it makes little sense to label a package as two products without also considering the economic justifications for the sale of the package as a unit. When the economic advantages of joint packaging are substantial the package is not appropriately viewed as two products, and that should be the end of the tying inquiry. . . . [33]

These three conditions — market power in the tying product, a substantial threat of market power in the tied product, and a coherent economic basis for treating the products as distinct — are only threshold requirements. Under the Rule of Reason a tie-in may prove acceptable even when all three are met. Tie-ins may entail economic benefits as well as economic harms, and if the threshold requirements are met these benefits should enter the Rule of Reason balance.

"Tie-ins . . . may facilitate new entry into fields where established sellers have wedded their customers to them by ties of habit and custom. *Brown Shoe Co. v. United States*, 370 U.S. 294 330 (1962). . . . They may permit clandestine price cutting in products which otherwise would have no price competition at all because of fear of retaliation from the few other producers dealing in the market. They may protect the reputation of the tying product if failure to use the tied product in conjunction with it may cause it to misfunction: [citing *Pick Mfg. Co. v. General Motors Corp.*, 80 F.2d 641 (7th Cir. 1935), *aff'd*, 299 U.S. 3 (1936)]. . . . And, if the tied and tying products are functionally related, they may reduce costs through economies of joint production and distribution." *Fortner I*, 394 U.S., at 514 n. 9 (justice white, dissenting).

The ultimate decision whether a tie-in is illegal under the antitrust laws should depend upon the demonstrated economic effects of the challenged agreement. It may, for example, be entirely innocuous that the seller exploits its control over the tying product to "force" the buyer to purchase the tied product. For when the seller exerts market power only in the tying product market, it makes no difference to him or his customers whether he exploits that power by raising the price of the tying product or by "forcing" customers to buy a tied product. On the other hand, tying may make the provision of packages of goods and services more efficient. A tie-in

---

[33] [FN 10] The examination of the economic advantages of tying may properly be conducted as part of the Rule of Reason analysis, rather than at the threshold of the tying inquiry. This approach is consistent with this Court's occasional references to the problem. The Court has not heretofore had occasion to set forth any general criteria for determining when two apparently separate products are components of a single product for tying analysis. . . . [The] cases indicate that consideration of whether a buyer might prefer to purchase one component without the other is one of the factors in tying analysis and, more generally, that economic analysis rather than mere conventional separability into different markets should determine whether one or two products are involved in the alleged tie.

should be condemned only when its anticompetitive impact outweighs its contribution to efficiency.

III

Application of these criteria to the case at hand is straightforward.

Although the issue is in doubt, we may assume that the Hospital does have market power in the provision of hospital services in its area. . . .

Second, in light of the Hospital's presumed market power, we may also assume that there is a substantial threat that East Jefferson will acquire market power over the provision of anesthesiological services in its market. By tying the sale of anesthesia to the sale of other hospital services the Hospital can drive out other sellers of those services who might otherwise operate in the local market. The Hospital may thus gain local market power in the provision of anesthesiology: anesthesiological services offered in the Hospital's market, narrowly defined, will be purchased only from Roux, under the Hospital's auspices.

But the third threshold condition for giving closer scrutiny to a tying arrangement is not satisfied here: there is no sound economic reason for treating surgery and anesthesia as separate services. Patients are interested in purchasing anesthesia only in conjunction with hospital services, so the Hospital can acquire no additional market power by selling the two services together. Accordingly, the link between the Hospital's services and anesthesia administered by Roux will affect neither the amount of anesthesia provided nor the combined price of anesthesia and surgery for those who choose to become the Hospital's patients. In these circumstances, anesthesia and surgical services should probably not be characterized as distinct products for tying purposes.

Even if they are, the tying should not be considered a violation of § 1 of the Sherman Act because tying here cannot increase the seller's already absolute power over the volume of production of the tied product, which is an inevitable consequence of the fact that very few patients will choose to undergo surgery without receiving anesthesia. The Hospital-Roux contract therefore has little potential to harm the patients. On the other side of the balance, the District Court found, and the Court of Appeals did not dispute, that the tie-in conferred significant benefits upon the hospital and the patients that it served.

The tie-in improves patient care and permits more efficient hospital operation in a number of ways. From the viewpoint of hospital management, the tie-in ensures 24-hour anesthesiology coverage, aids in standardization of procedures and efficient use of equipment, facilitates flexible scheduling of operations, and permits the hospital more effectively to monitor the quality of anesthesiological services. Further, the tying arrangement is advantageous to patients because, as the District Court found, the closed anesthesiology department places upon the hospital, rather than the individual patient, responsibility to select the physician who is to provide anesthesiological services. The hospital also assumes the responsibility that the anesthesiologist will be available, will be acceptable to the surgeon, and will provide suitable care to the patient. In assuming these responsibilities — responsibilities that a seriously ill patient frequently may be unable to discharge — the hospital provides a valuable service to its patients. And there is no indication that patients were dissatisfied with the quality of anesthesiology that was provided at the hospital or that patients wished to enjoy the services of anesthesiologists other than those that the hospital employed. Given this evidence of the advantages and effectiveness of the closed anesthesiology department, it is not surprising that, as the District Court found, such arrangements are accepted practice in the majority of hospitals of New Orleans and in health care industry generally. Such an arrangement, that has little anti-competitive effect and achieves substantial benefits in the provision of care to patients, is hardly one that the antitrust law should condemn. This conclusion reaffirms our threshold determination that the joint provision of hospital services and anesthesiology should not be viewed as involving a tie between distinct products, and therefore should require no additional scrutiny under the antitrust law.

IV

Whether or not the Hospital-Roux contract is characterized as a tie between distinct products, the contract unquestionably does constitute exclusive dealing. Exclusive dealing arrangements are independently subject to scrutiny under § 1 of the Sherman Act, and are also analyzed under the Rule of Reason. *Tampa Electric Co. v. Nashville Coal Co.*, 365 U.S. 32, 333–335 (1961).

The Hospital-Roux arrangement could conceivably have an adverse effect on horizontal competition among anesthesiologists, or among hospitals. Dr. Hyde, who competes with the Roux anesthesiologists, and other hospitals in the area, who compete with East Jefferson, may have grounds to complain that the exclusive contract stifles horizontal competition and therefore has an adverse, albeit indirect, impact on consumer welfare even if it is not a tie.

. . . .

At issue here is an exclusive dealing arrangement between a firm of four anesthesiologists and one relatively small hospital. There is no suggestion that East Jefferson Hospital is likely to create a "bottleneck" in the availability of anesthesiologists that might deprive other hospitals of access to needed anesthesiological services, or that the Roux associates have unreasonably narrowed the range of choices available to other anesthesiologists in search of a hospital or patients that will buy their services. A firm of four anesthesiologists represents only a very small fraction of the total number of anesthesiologists whose services are available for hire by other hospitals, and East Jefferson is one among numerous hospitals buying such services. Even without engaging in a detailed analysis of the size of the relevant markets we may readily conclude that there is no likelihood that the exclusive dealing arrangement challenged here will either unreasonably enhance the Hospital's market position relative to other hospitals, or unreasonably permit Roux to acquire power relative to other anesthesiologists. Accordingly, this exclusive dealing arrangement must be sustained under the Rule of Reason.

V

. . . Since anesthesia is a service useful to consumers only when purchased in conjunction with hospital services, the arrangement is not properly characterized as a tie between distinct products. It threatens no additional economic harm to consumers beyond that already made possible by any market power that the Hospital may possess. The fact that anesthesia is used only together with other hospital services is sufficient, standing alone, to insulate from attack the Hospital's decision to tie the two types of service.

Whether or not this case involves tying of distinct products, the Hospital-Roux contract is subject to scrutiny under the Rule of Reason as an exclusive dealing arrangement. Plainly, however, the arrangement forecloses only a small fraction of the markets in which anesthesiologists may sell their services, and a still smaller fraction of the market in which hospitals may secure anesthesiological services. The contract therefore survives scrutiny under the Rule of Reason.

NOTES AND QUESTIONS

1. For many years economists and other antitrust commentators have been urging the Supreme Court to abolish the notion that tying arrangements are governed by a per se rule. The Court refused the invitation. However, the four participants in Justice O'Connor's concurring opinion were more than ready to jettison the per se label for tying arrangements.

What sense does it make to say that tying arrangements are governed by a per se rule when courts in fact (1) require a showing of market power in the tying product; (2) more often than not require some kind of showing of an anticompetitive *effect* in the tied product market; and (3) often hold that tying arrangements are legal — in fact, in most of the cases? Do tying arrangements fall within that category of practices that are almost always harmful to consumers, and therefore can be condemned without extensive analysis of their actual economic effects?

The economic criticism of the per se rule against tying arrangements is summarized in HERBERT HOVENKAMP, FEDERAL ANTITRUST POLICY, §§ 10.2–10.4 (4th ed. 2011).

2. What does the *Hyde* decision do to the market power requirement in tie-in cases? In *Fortner I* a simple showing that the tying product was "unique" was sufficient to create a presumption of market power. In *Hyde*, however, the defendant's market share was about 30%. How many Supreme Court tie-in cases from the 1960's and earlier were in fact overruled by *Hyde*?

3. At oral argument, the Supreme Court was told that the contract at issue in *Hyde* was not a tying arrangement at all, but rather an exclusive dealing arrangement. Four Justices agreed. Distinguishing tying arrangements from exclusive dealing contracts can be very difficult. Nevertheless, the two practices are governed by very different legal tests. Reconsider the arrangement at issue in the *Standard Stations* case, noted *supra*. Is it obvious that the case involved exclusive dealing rather than tying? What if Standard required individual stations to sell nothing but its gasoline as a condition of receiving the right to bear the Standard name? In *Krehl v. Baskin-Robbins Ice Cream Co.*, 664 F.2d 1348 (9th Cir. 1982), the defendant was charged with requiring all its franchisees (Baskin-Robbins ice cream stores) to sell exclusively the defendant's ice cream. The case was characterized as a tying arrangement, however, in which the tying product was the Baskin-Robbins trademark and method of doing business, and the tied product was the ice cream.

4. What do you think of Justice O'Connor's argument that only a single "product," for the purposes of the law of tie-ins, was involved in the *Hyde* case? Justice O'Connor concluded that "[f]or products to be treated as distinct, the tied product must, at a minimum, be one that some consumers might wish to purchase separately without also purchasing the tying product." Suppose that a manufacturer of stereo equipment made buyers of its phonographic turntables agree to purchase all their phonographic records from it as well. A single "product" under Justice O'Connor's test?

PROBLEM 5.6

Yale University requires all freshmen and sophomores to live in on-campus dormitories. Sally Smart wants to live in an apartment her first two years at Yale. A friend of hers attends Yale Law School and tells her, after taking the antitrust class at Yale Law School, that Yale may be illegally tying the dormitory requirement to an education at Yale and the award of a Yale degree. Is this a Section 1 violation? Analyze the elements of the alleged tying arrangement. Does Yale have market power under a tying analysis? *See Hack v. Yale College*, 237 F.3d 81 (2d Cir. 2000), *cert. denied*, 534 U.S. 888 (2001).

EASTMAN KODAK CO. v. IMAGE TECHNICAL SERVICES, INC.
504 U.S. 451 (1992)

JUSTICE BLACKMUN delivered the opinion of the Court.

This is yet another case that concerns the standard for summary judgment in an antitrust controversy. The principal issue here is whether a defendant's lack of market power in the primary equipment market precludes — as a matter of law — the possibility of market power in derivative aftermarkets.

Petitioner Eastman Kodak Company manufactures and sells photocopiers and micrographic equipment. Kodak also sells service and replacement parts for its equipment. Respondents are 18 independent service organizations (ISOs) that in the early 1980s began servicing Kodak copying and micrographic equipment. Kodak subsequently adopted policies to limit the availability of parts to ISOs and to make it more difficult for ISOs to compete with Kodak in servicing Kodak equipment.

Respondents instituted this action . . . alleging that Kodak's policies were unlawful under both §§ 1 and 2 of the Sherman Act, 15 U.S.C. §§ 1 and 2. After truncated discovery, the District Court granted summary judgment for Kodak. The Court of Appeals for the Ninth Circuit reversed. The appellate court found that the respondents had presented sufficient evidence to raise a genuine issue concerning Kodak's market power in the service and parts markets. . . .

I

A

Because this case comes to us on petitioner Kodak's motion for summary judgment, "[t]he evidence of [respondents] is to be believed, and all justifiable inferences are to be drawn in [their] favor." . . .

Kodak manufactures and sells complex business machines — as relevant here, high-volume photocopier and micrographics equipment. Kodak equipment is unique; micrographic software programs that operate on Kodak machines, for example, are not compatible with competitors' machines. Kodak parts are not compatible with other manufacturers' equipment, and vice versa. Kodak equipment, although expensive when new, has little resale value.

Kodak provides service and parts for its machines to its customers. It produces some of the parts itself; the rest are made to order for Kodak by independent original-equipment manufacturers (OEMs). Kodak does not sell a complete system of original equipment, lifetime service, and lifetime parts for a single price. Instead, Kodak provides service after the initial warranty period either through annual service contracts, which include all necessary parts, or on a per-call basis. It charges, through negotiations and bidding, different prices for equipment, service, and parts for different customers. Kodak provides 80% to 95% of the service for Kodak machines.

Beginning in the early 1980s, ISOs began repairing and servicing Kodak equipment. They also sold parts and reconditioned and sold used Kodak equipment. Their customers were federal, state, and local government agencies, banks, insurance companies, industrial enterprises, and providers of specialized copy and microfilming services. ISOs provide service at a price substantially lower than Kodak does. Some customers found that the ISO service was of higher quality.

Some of the ISOs' customers purchase their own parts and hire ISOs only for service. Others choose ISOs to supply both service and parts. ISOs keep an inventory of parts, purchased from Kodak or other sources, primarily the OEMs.

In 1985 and 1986, Kodak implemented a policy of selling replacement parts for micrographic and copying machines only to buyers of Kodak equipment who use Kodak service or repair their own machines.

As part of the same policy, Kodak sought to limit ISO access to other sources of Kodak parts. Kodak and the OEMs agreed that the OEMs would not sell parts that fit Kodak equipment to anyone other than Kodak. Kodak also pressured Kodak equipment owners and independent parts distributors not to sell Kodak parts to ISOs. In addition, Kodak took steps to restrict the availability of used machines.

Kodak intended, through these policies, to make it more difficult for ISOs to sell service for Kodak machines. It succeeded. ISOs were unable to obtain parts from reliable sources and many were forced out of business, while others lost substantial revenue. Customers were forced to switch to Kodak service even though they preferred ISO service.

B

In 1987, the ISOs filed the present action in the District Court alleging *inter alia*, that Kodak had unlawfully tied the sale of service for Kodak machines to the sale of parts, in violation of § 1 of the Sherman Act, and had unlawfully monopolized and attempted to monopolize the sale of service for Kodak machines, in violation of § 2 of that Act.

Kodak filed a motion for summary judgment before respondents had initiated discovery. The District Court permitted respondents to file one set of interrogatories and one set of requests for production of documents, and to take six depositions. Without a hearing, the District Court granted summary judgment in favor of Kodak.

As to the § 1 claim, the court found that respondents had provided no evidence of a tying arrangement between Kodak equipment and service or parts. The court, however, did not address respondents' § 1 claim that is at issue here. Respondents allege a tying arrangement not between Kodak *equipment* and service, but between Kodak *parts* and service. As to the § 2 claim, the District Court concluded that although Kodak had a "natural monopoly over the market for parts its sells under its name," a unilateral refusal to sell those parts to ISOs did not violate § 2.

The Court of Appeals for the Ninth Circuit, by a divided vote, reversed. 903 F.2d 612 (1990). With respect to the § 1 claim, the court first found that whether service or parts were distinct markets and whether a tying arrangement existed between them were disputed issues of fact. Having found that a tying arrangement might exist, the Court of Appeals considered a question not decided by the District Court: was there "an issue of material fact as to whether Kodak has sufficient economic power in the tying product market [parts] to restrain competition appreciably in the tied product market [service]." The court agreed with Kodak that competition in the equipment market might prevent Kodak from possessing power in the parts market, but refused to uphold the District Court's grant of summary judgment "on this theoretical basis" because "market imperfections can keep economic theories about how consumers will act from mirroring reality." Noting that the District Court had not considered the market power issue, and that the record was not fully developed through discovery, the court declined to require respondents to conduct market analysis or to pinpoint specific imperfections in order to withstand summary judgment. "It is enough that [respondents] have presented evidence of actual events from which a reasonable trier of fact could conclude that . . . competition in the [equipment] market does not, in reality, curb Kodak's power in the parts market."

The court then considered the three business justifications Kodak proffered for its restrictive parts policy: (1) to guard against inadequate service, (2) to lower inventory costs, and (3) to prevent ISOs from free-riding on Kodak's investment in the copier and micrographic industry. The court then concluded that the trier of fact might find the product quality and inventory reasons to be pretextual and that there was a less restrictive alternative for achieving Kodak's quality-related goals. The court also found Kodak's third justification, preventing ISOs from profiting on Kodak's investments in the equipment markets, legally insufficient. As to the § 2 claim, the Court of Appeals concluded that sufficient evidence existed to support a finding that Kodak's implementation of its parts policy was "anticompetitive" and "exclusionary" and "involved a specific intent to monopolize." . . . It held that the ISOs had come forward with sufficient evidence, for summary judgment purposes, to disprove Kodak's business justifications. . . .

II

A tying arrangement is "an agreement by a party to sell one product but only on the condition that the buyer also purchases a different (or tied) product, or at least agrees that he will not purchase that product from any other supplier." *Northern Pacific R. Co. v. United States*, 356 U.S. 1, 5–6 (1958). Such an arrangement violates § 1 of the Sherman Act if the seller has "appreciable economic power" in the tying product market and if the arrangement affects a substantial volume of commerce in the tied market. *Fortner Enterprises, Inc. v. United States Steel Corp.*, 394 U.S. 495, 503 (1969).

Kodak did not dispute that its arrangement affects a substantial volume of interstate commerce. It, however, did challenge whether its activities constituted a "tying arrangement" and whether Kodak exercised "appreciable economic power" in the tying market. We consider these issues in turn.

A

For the respondents to defeat a motion for summary judgment on their claim of a tying arrangement, a reasonable trier of fact must be able to find, first, that service and parts are two distinct products, and, second, that Kodak has tied the sale of the two products.

For service and parts to be considered two distinct products, there must be sufficient consumer demand so that it is efficient for a firm to provide service separately from parts. *Jefferson Parish Hospital Dist. No. 2 v. Hyde*, 466 U.S. 2, 21–22 (1984). Evidence in the record indicates that service and parts have been sold separately in the past and still are sold separately to self-service equipment owners. Indeed, the development of the entire high-technology service industry is evidence of the efficiency of a separate market for service.

Kodak insists that because there is no demand for parts separate from service, there cannot be separate markets for service and parts. By that logic, we would be forced to conclude that there can never be separate markets, for example, for cameras and film, computers and software, or automobiles and tires. That is an assumption we are unwilling to make. "We have often found arrangements involving functionally linked products at least one of which is useless without the other to be prohibited tying devices." *Jefferson Parish*, 466 U.S., at 19, n. 30.

Kodak's assertion also appears to be incorrect as a factual matter. At least some consumers would purchase service without parts, because some service does not require parts, and some consumers, those who self-service for example, would purchase parts without service. Enough doubt is cast on Kodak's claim of a unified market that it should be resolved by the trier of fact.

Finally, respondents have presented sufficient evidence of a tie between service and parts. The record indicates that Kodak would sell parts to third parties only if they agreed not to buy service from ISOs.[34]

B

Having found sufficient evidence of a tying arrangement, we consider the other necessary feature of an illegal tying arrangement: appreciable economic power in the tying market. Market power is the power "to force a purchaser to do something that he would not do in a competitive market." *Jefferson Parish*, 466 U.S. at 14. It has been defined as "the ability of a single seller to raise price and restrict output." *Fortner Inc.*, 394 U.S. at 503; *United States v. E.I. du Pont de Nemours & Co.*, 351 U.S. 377, 391 (1956). The existence of such power ordinarily is inferred from the seller's possession of a predominant share of the market. *Jefferson Parish*, 466 U.S. at 17; *United States v. Grinnell Corp.*, 384 U.S. 563, 571 (1966); *Times-Picayune Publishing Co. v. United States*, 345 U.S. 594, 611–13 (1953).

1

Respondents contend that Kodak has more than sufficient power in the parts market to force unwanted purchases of the tied market, service. Respondents provide evidence that certain parts are available exclusively through Kodak. Respondents also assert that Kodak has control over the availability of parts it does not manufacture. According to respondents' evidence, Kodak prohibited independent manufacturers from selling Kodak parts to ISOs, pressured Kodak equipment owners and independent parts distributors to deny ISOs the purchase of Kodak parts, and taken [*sic*] steps to restrict the availability of used machines.

Respondents also allege that Kodak's control over the parts market has excluded service competition, boosted service prices, and forced unwilling consumption of Kodak service. Respondents offer evidence that consumers have switched to Kodak service even though they preferred ISO service, that Kodak service was of higher price and lower quality than the preferred ISO service, and that ISOs were driven out of business by Kodak's policies. Under our prior precedents, this evidence would be sufficient to entitle respondents to a trial on their claim of market power.

2

Kodak counters that even if it concedes monopoly *share* of the relevant parts market, it cannot actually exercise the necessary market *power* for a Sherman Act violation. This is so, according to Kodak, because competition exists in the equipment market. Kodak argues that it could not have the ability to raise prices of service and parts above the level that would be charged in a competitive market because any increase in profits from a higher price in the aftermarkets at least would be offset by a corresponding loss in profits from lower equipment sales as consumers began purchasing equipment with more attractive service costs.

---

[34] [FN 8] In a footnote, Kodak contends that this practice is only a unilateral refusal to deal, which does not violate the antitrust laws. Assuming, *arguendo*, that Kodak's refusal to sell parts to any company providing service can be characterized as a unilateral refusal to deal, its alleged sale of parts to third parties on condition that they buy service from Kodak is not.

Kodak does not present any actual data on the equipment, service, or parts markets. Instead, it argues the adoption of a substantive legal rule that "equipment competition precludes any finding of monopoly power in derivative aftermarkets." Kodak argues that such a rule would satisfy its burden as the moving party of showing "that there is no genuine issue as to any material fact" on the market power issue.

Legal presumptions that rest on formalistic distinctions rather than actual market realities are generally disfavored in antitrust law. This Court has preferred to resolve antitrust claims on a case-by-case basis, focusing on the "particular facts disclosed by the record." In determining the existence of market power, and specifically the "responsiveness of the sales of one product to price changes of the other," this Court has examined closely the economic reality of the market at issue.

Kodak contends that there is no need to examine the facts when the issue is market power in the aftermarkets. A legal presumption against a finding of market power is warranted in this situation, according to Kodak, because the existence of market power in the service and parts markets absent power in the equipment market "simply makes no economic sense," and the absence of a legal presumption would deter procompetitive behavior.

Kodak analogizes this case to *Matsushita* where a group of American corporations that manufactured or sold consumer electronic products alleged that their 21 Japanese counterparts were engaging in a 20-year conspiracy to price below cost in the United States in the hope of expanding their market share sometime in the future. After several years of detailed discovery, the defendants moved for summary judgment. Because the defendants had every incentive not to engage in the alleged conduct which required them to sustain losses for decades with no foreseeable profits, the Court found an "absence of any rational motive to conspire." In that context, the Court determined that the plaintiffs' theory of predatory pricing makes no practical sense, was "speculative" and was not "reasonable." Accordingly, the Court held that a reasonable jury could not return a verdict for the plaintiffs and that summary judgment would be appropriate against them unless they came forward with more persuasive evidence to support their theory.

The Court's requirement in *Matsushita* that the plaintiffs' claims make economic sense did not introduce a special burden on plaintiffs facing summary judgment in antitrust cases. The Court did not hold that if the moving party enunciates *any* economic theory supporting its behavior, regardless of its accuracy in reflecting the actual market, it is entitled to summary judgment. *Matsushita* demands only that the nonmoving party's inferences be reasonable in order to reach the jury, a requirement that was not invented, but merely articulated, in that decision. If the plaintiff's theory is economically senseless, no reasonable jury could find in its favor, and summary judgment should be granted.

Kodak, then, bears a substantial burden in showing that it is entitled to summary judgment. It must show that despite evidence of increased prices and excluded competition, an inference of market power is unreasonable. To determine whether Kodak has met that burden, we must unravel the factual assumptions underlying its proposed rule that lack of power in the equipment market necessarily precludes power in the aftermarkets.

The extent to which one market prevents exploitation of another market depends on the extent to which consumers will change their consumption of one product in response to a price change in another, *i.e.*, the "cross-elasticity of demand." See *du Pont*, 351 U.S. at 400;[35] Kodak's proposed rule rests on a factual assumption about the cross-elasticity of demand in the equipment and aftermarkets: "If Kodak raised its parts or service prices above competitive levels, potential customers would simply stop buying Kodak equipment. Perhaps Kodak would be able to increase short term profits through such a strategy, but at a devastating cost to its long term interests."[36] Kodak argues that the Court should accept, as a matter of law, this "basic economic realit[y]," that competition in the equipment market necessarily prevents market power in the aftermarkets.

Even if Kodak could not raise the price of service and parts one cent without losing equipment sales, that fact would not disprove market power in the aftermarkets. The sales of even a monopolist are reduced when it sells goods at a monopoly price, but the higher price more than compensates for the loss in sales. Kodak's claim that charging more for service and parts would be "a short-run game," is based on the false dichotomy that there are only two prices that can be charged — a competitive price or a ruinous one. But there could easily be a middle, optimum price at which the increased revenues from the higher-priced sales of service and parts would more than compensate for the lower revenues from lost equipment sales. The fact that the equipment market imposes a restraint on prices in the aftermarkets by no means disproves the existence of power in those markets. ("[T]he existence of significant substitution in the event of *further* price increases or even at the *current* price does not tell us whether the defendant *already* exercises significant market power") (emphasis in original). Thus, contrary to Kodak's assertion, there is no immutable physical law — no "basic economic reality" — insisting that competition in the equipment market cannot coexist with market power in the aftermarkets.

We next consider the more narrowly drawn question: Does Kodak's theory describe actual market behavior so accurately that respondents' assertion of Kodak

---

[35] [FN 15] What constrains the defendant's ability to raise prices in the service market is "the elasticity of demand faced by the defendant — the degree to which its sales fall . . . as its price rises." P. Areeda & L. Kaplow, Antitrust Analysis & 342(c) (4th ed. 1988).

Courts have considered the relationship between price in one market and demand in another in defining the relevant market. Because market power is often inferred from market share, market definition generally determines the result of the case. Pitofsky, *New Definitions of Relevant Market and the Assault on Antitrust*, 90 Colum. L. Rev. 1805, 1806–13 (1990). Kodak chose to focus on market power directly rather than arguing that the relationship between equipment and service and parts is such that the three should be included in the same market definition. Whether considered in the conceptual category of "market definition" or "market power," the ultimate inquiry is the same — whet her competition in the equipment market will significantly restrain power in the service and parts markets.

[36] [FN 16] The United States as *Amicus Curiae* in support of Kodak echoes this argument: "The ISOs' claims are implausible because Kodak lacks market power in the markets for its copier and micrographic equipment. Buyers of such equipment regard an increase in the price of parts or service as an increase in the price of the equipment, and sellers recognize that the revenues from its sales of parts and services are attributable to sales of the equipment. In such circumstances, it is not apparent how an equipment manufacturer such as Kodak could exercise power in the aftermarkets for parts and service." Brief for United States as *Amicus Curiae* 8.

market power in the aftermarkets, if not impossible, is at least unreasonable?[37]

To review Kodak's theory, it contends that higher service prices will lead to a disastrous drop in equipment sales. Presumably, the theory's corollary is to the effect that low service prices lead to a dramatic increase in equipment sales. According to the theory, one would have expected Kodak to take advantage of lower-priced ISO service as an opportunity to expand equipment sales. Instead, Kodak adopted a restrictive sales policy consciously designed to eliminate the lower-priced ISO service, an act that would be expected to devastate either Kodak's equipment sales or Kodak's faith in its theory. Yet, according to the record, it has done neither. Service prices have risen for Kodak customers, but there is no evidence or assertion that Kodak's equipment sales have dropped.

Kodak and the United States attempt to reconcile Kodak's theory with the contrary actual results by describing a "marketing strategy of spreading over time the total cost to the buyer of Kodak equipment." In other words, Kodak could charge subcompetitive prices for equipment and make up the difference with supracompetitive prices for service, resulting in an overall competitive price. This pricing strategy would provide an explanation for the theory"s descriptive failings — if Kodak in fact had adopted it. But Kodak never has asserted that it prices its equipment or parts subcompetitively and recoups its profits through service. Instead, it claims that it prices its equipment comparably to its competitors, and intends that both its equipment sales and service divisions be profitable. Moreover, this hypothetical pricing strategy is inconsistent with Kodak's policy toward its self-service customers. If Kodak were underpricing its equipment, hoping to lock in customers and recover its losses in the service market, it could not afford to sell customers parts without service. In sum, Kodak's theory does not explain the actual market behavior revealed in the record.

Respondents offer a forceful reason why Kodak's theory, although perhaps intuitively appealing, may not accurately explain the behavior of the primary and derivative markets for complex durable goods: the existence of significant information and switching costs. These costs could create a less responsive connection between service and parts prices and equipment sales.

For the service-market price to affect equipment demand, consumers must inform themselves of the total cost of the "package" — equipment, service and parts — at the time of purchase; that is, consumers must engage in accurate lifecycle

---

[37] [FN 18] Although Kodak repeatedly relies on *Continental T.V.* as support for its factual assertion that the equipment market will prevent exploitation of the service and parts markets, the case is inapposite. In *Continental T.V.*, the Court found that a manufacturer's policy restricting the number of retailers that were permitted to sell its product could have a procompetitive effect. See 433 U.S. at 55. The Court also noted that any negative effect of exploitation of the intrabrand market (the competition between retailers of the same product) would be checked by competition in the interbrand market (competition over the same generic product) because consumers would substitute a different brand of the same product. Unlike *Continental T.V.*, this case does not concern vertical relationships between parties on different levels of the same distribution chain. In the relevant market, service, Kodak and the ISOs are direct competitors; their relationship is horizontal. The interbrand competition at issue here is competition over the provision of service. Despite petitioner's best effort, repeating the mantra "interbrand competition" does not transform this case into one over an agreement the manufacturer has with its dealers that would fall under the rubric of *Continental T.V.*

pricing. Lifecycle pricing of complex, durable equipment is difficult and costly. In order to arrive at an accurate price, a consumer must acquire a substantial amount of raw data and undertake sophisticated analysis. The necessary information would include data on price, quality, and availability of products needed to operate, upgrade, or enhance the initial equipment, as well as service and repair costs, including estimates of breakdown frequency, nature of repairs, price of service and parts, length of "down-time" and losses incurred from down-time.

Much of this information is difficult — some of it is impossible — to acquire at the time of purchase. During the life of a product, companies may change the service and parts prices, and develop products with more advanced features, a decreased need for repair, or new warranties. In addition, the information is likely to be customer-specific; lifecycle costs will vary from customer to customer with the type of equipment, degrees of equipment use, and costs of down-time.

Kodak acknowledges the cost of information, but suggests, again without evidentiary support, that customer information needs will be satisfied by competitors in the equipment markets. It is a question of fact, however, whether competitors would provide the necessary information. . . .

In sum, there is a question of fact whether information costs and switching costs foil the simple assumption that the equipment and service markets act as pure complements to one another.

We conclude, then, that Kodak has failed to demonstrate that respondents' inference of market power in the service and parts markets is unreasonable, and that, consequently, Kodak is entitled to summary judgment. It is clearly reasonable to infer that Kodak has market power to raise prices and drive out competition in the aftermarkets, since respondents offer direct evidence that Kodak did so. It is also plausible, as discussed above, to infer that Kodak chose to gain immediate profits by exerting that market power where locked-in customers, high information costs, and discriminatory pricing limited and perhaps eliminated any long-term loss. Viewing the evidence in the light most favorable to respondents, their allegations of market power "mak[e] . . . economic sense." Cf. *Matsushita*, 475 U.S. at 587.

Nor are we persuaded by Kodak's contention that it is entitled to a legal presumption on the lack of market power because, as in *Matsushita*, there is a significant risk of deterring procompetitive conduct. Plaintiffs in *Matsushita* attempted to prove the antitrust conspiracy "through evidence of rebates and other price-cutting activities." Because cutting prices to increase business is "the very essence of competition," the Court was concerned that mistaken inferences would be "especially costly," and would "chill the very conduct the antitrust laws were designed to protect." But the facts in this case are just the opposite. The alleged conduct — higher service prices and market foreclosure — is facially anticompetitive and exactly the harm that antitrust laws aim to prevent. In this situation, *Matsushita* does not create any presumption in favor of summary judgment for the defendant. . . .

We need not decide whether Kodak's behavior has any procompetitive effects and, if so, whether they outweigh the anticompetitive effects. We note only that

Kodak's service and parts policy is simply not one that appears always or almost always to enhance competition, and therefore to warrant a legal presumption without any evidence of its actual economic impact. In this case, when we weigh the risk of deterring procompetitive behavior by proceeding to trial against the risk that illegal behavior go unpunished, the balance tips against summary judgment. Cf. *Matsushita*, 475 U.S. at 594–95.

For the foregoing reasons, we hold that Kodak has not met the requirements of Federal Rule of Civil Procedure 56(c). We therefore affirm the denial of summary judgment on respondents' § 1 claim.

III

Respondents also claim that they have presented genuine issues for trial as to whether Kodak has monopolized or attempted to monopolize the service and parts markets in violation of § 2 of the Sherman Act. "The offense of monopoly under § 2 of the Sherman Act has two elements: (1) the possession of monopoly power in the relevant market and (2) the willful acquisition or maintenance of that power as distinguished from growth or development as a consequence of a superior product, business acumen, or historic accident." *United States v. Grinnell Corp.*, 384 U.S. at 570–71.

A

The existence of the first element, possession of monopoly power is easily resolved. As has been noted, respondents have presented a triable claim that service and parts are separate markets, and that Kodak has the "power to control prices or exclude competition" in service and parts. *Du Pont*, 351 U.S. at 391. Monopoly power under § 2 requires, of course, something greater than market power under § 1. See *Fortner*, 394 U.S. at 502. Respondents' evidence that Kodak controls nearly 100% of the parts market and 80% to 95% of the service market, with no readily available substitutes, is, however, sufficient to survive summary judgment under the more stringent monopoly standard of § 2. See *National Collegiate Athletic Assn. v. Board of Regents of Univ. of Okla.*, 468 U.S. 85, 112 (1984). *Cf. United States v. Grinnell Corp.*, 384 U.S. at 571 (87% of the market is a monopoly); *American Tobacco Co. v. United States*, 328 U.S. 781, 797 (1946) (over 2/3 of the market is a monopoly).

Kodak also contends that, as a matter of law, a single brand of a product or service can never be a relevant market under the Sherman Act. We disagree. The relevant market for antitrust purposes is determined by the choices available to Kodak equipment owners. See *Jefferson Parish*, 466 U.S. at 19. Because service and parts for Kodak equipment are not interchangeable with other manufacturers' service and parts, the relevant market from the Kodak-equipment owner's perspective is composed of only those companies that service Kodak machines. See *du Pont*, 351 U.S. at 404 (the "market is composed of products that have reasonable interchangeability"). This Court's prior cases support the proposition that in some instances one brand of a product can constitute a separate market. See *National Collegiate Athletic Assn.*, 468 U.S. at 101–02, 111–12 (1984); *International Boxing*

Club of New York, Inc. v. United States, 358 U.S. 242, 249–52 (1959); *International Business Machines Corp. v. United States*, 298 U.S. 131 (1936). The proper market definition in this case can be determined only after a factual inquiry into the "commercial realities" faced by consumers. *United States v. Grinnell Corp.*, 384 U.S. at 572.

B

The second element of a § 2 claim is the use of monopoly power "to foreclose competition, to gain a competitive advantage, or to destroy a competitor." *United States v. Griffith*, 334 U.S. 100, 107 (1948). If Kodak adopted its parts and service policies as part of a scheme of willful acquisition or maintenance of monopoly power, it will have violated § 2. *Grinnell Corp.*, 384 U.S. at 570–71; *United States v. Aluminum Co. of America*, 148 F.2d 416, 432 (2d Cir. 1945); *Aspen Skiing Co. v. Aspen Highlands Skiing Corp.*, 472 U.S. 585, 600–05 (1985).

As recounted at length above, respondents have presented evidence that Kodak took exclusionary action to maintain its parts monopoly and used its control over parts to strengthen its monopoly share of the Kodak service market. Liability turns, then, on whether "valid business reasons" can explain Kodak's actions. *Aspen Skiing Co.*, 472 U.S. at 605; *United States v. Aluminum Co. of America*, 148 F.2d at 432. Kodak contends that it has three valid business justifications for its actions: "(1) to promote interbrand equipment competition by allowing Kodak to stress the quality of its service; (2) to improve asset management by reducing Kodak's inventory costs; and (3) to prevent ISOs from free riding on Kodak's capital investment in equipment, parts and service." Factual questions exist, however, about the validity and sufficiency of each claimed justification, making summary judgment inappropriate.

Kodak first asserts that by preventing customers from using ISOs "it [can] best maintain high quality service for its sophisticated equipment" and avoid being "blamed for an equipment malfunction, even if the problem is the result of improper diagnosis, maintenance or repair by an ISO." Respondents have offered evidence that ISOs provide quality service and are preferred by some Kodak equipment owners. This is sufficient to raise a genuine issue of fact. See *International Business Machines Corp. v. United States*, 298 U.S. at 139–40 (rejecting IBM's claim that it had to control the cards used in its machines to avoid "injury to the reputation of the machines and the goodwill of" IBM in the absence of proof that other companies could not make quality cards); *International Salt Co. v. United States*, 332 U.S. 392, 397–98 (1947) (rejecting International Salt's claim that it had to control the supply of salt to protect its leased machines in the absence of proof that competitors could not supply salt of equal quality).

Moreover, there are other reasons to question Kodak's proffered motive of commitment to quality service; its quality justification appears inconsistent with its thesis that consumers are knowledgeable enough to lifecycle price, and its self-service policy. Kodak claims the exclusive-service contract is warranted because customers would otherwise blame Kodak equipment for breakdowns resulting from inferior ISO service. Thus, Kodak simultaneously claims that its customers are sophisticated enough to make complex and subtle lifecycle-pricing decisions, and yet too obtuse to distinguish which breakdowns are due to bad equipment and which are due to bad service. Kodak has failed to offer any reason why informational sophistication should be present in one circumstance and absent in the other. In addition, because self-service customers are just as likely as others to blame Kodak equipment for breakdowns resulting from (their own) inferior service, Kodak's willingness to allow self-service casts doubt on its quality claim. In sum, we agree with the Court of Appeals that respondents "have presented evidence from which a reasonable trier of fact could conclude that Kodak's first reason is pretextual." 903 F.2d at 618.

There is also a triable issue of fact on Kodak's second justification — controlling inventory costs. As respondents argue, Kodak's actions appear inconsistent with any need to control inventory costs. Presumably, the inventory of parts needed to repair Kodak machines turns only on breakdown rates, and those rates should be the same whether Kodak or ISOs perform the repair. More importantly, the justification fails to explain respondents' evidence that Kodak forced OEMs, equipment owners, and parts brokers not to sell parts to ISOs, actions that would have no effect on Kodak's inventory costs.

Nor does Kodak's final justification entitle it to summary judgment on respondents' § 2 claim. Kodak claims that its policies prevent ISOs from "exploit[ing] the investment Kodak has made in product development, manufacturing and equipment sales in order to take away Kodak's service revenues." Kodak does not dispute that respondents invest substantially in the service market, with training of repair workers and investment in parts inventory. Instead, according to Kodak, the ISOs are free-riding because they have failed to enter the equipment and parts markets. This understanding of free-riding has no support in our caselaw.[38] To the contrary, as the Court of Appeals noted, one of the evils proscribed by the antitrust laws is the creation of entry barriers to potential competitors by requiring them to enter two markets simultaneously. *Jefferson Parish*, 466 U.S. at 14; *Fortner*, 394 U.S. at 509.

None of Kodak's asserted business justifications, then, are sufficient to prove that Kodak is "entitled to a judgment as a matter of law" on respondents' § 2 claim. Fed. Rule Civ. Proc. 56(c).

IV

In the end, of course, Kodak's arguments may prove to be correct. It may be that its parts, service, and equipment are components of one unified market, or that the equipment market does not discipline the aftermarkets so that all three are priced

---

[38] [FN 33] Kodak claims that both *Continental T.V.* and *Monsanto* support its free-rider argument. Neither is applicable. In both *Continental T.V.*, 433 U.S. at 55, and *Monsanto*, 465 U.S. at 762–63, the Court accepted free-riding as a justification because without restrictions a manufacturer would not be able to induce competent and aggressive retailers to make the kind of investment of capital and labor necessary to distribute the product. In *Continental T.V.* the relevant market level was retail sale of televisions and in *Monsanto* retail sale of herbicides. Some retailers were investing in those markets; others were not, relying, instead, on the investment of the other retailers. To be applicable to this case, the ISOs would have to be relying on Kodak's investment in the service market; that, however, is not Kodak's argument.

competitively overall, or that any anticompetitive effects of Kodak's behavior are outweighed by its competitive effects. But we cannot reach these conclusions as a matter of law on a record this sparse. Accordingly, the judgment of the Court of Appeals denying summary judgment is affirmed.

It is so ordered.

JUSTICE SCALIA, with whom JUSTICE O'CONNOR and JUSTICE THOMAS join, dissenting.

. . . .

The Court today finds in the typical manufacturer's inherent power over its own brand of equipment — over the sale of distinctive repair parts for that equipment, for example — the sort of "monopoly power" sufficient to bring the sledgehammer of § 2 into play. And, not surprisingly in light of that insight, it readily labels single-brand power over aftermarket products "monopoly power" sufficient to permit an antitrust plaintiff to invoke the *per se* rule against tying. In my opinion, this makes no economic sense. The holding that market power can be found on the present record causes these venerable rules of selective proscription to extend well beyond the point where the reasoning that supports them leaves off. Moreover, because the sort of power condemned by the Court today is possessed by every manufacturer of durable goods with distinctive parts, the Court's opinion threatens to release a torrent of litigation and a flood of commercial intimidation that will do much more harm than good to enforcement of the antitrust laws and to genuine competition. . . .

II

On appeal in the Ninth Circuit, respondents, having waived their "rule of reason" claim, were limited to arguing that the record, construed in the light most favorable to them, supported application of the *per se* tying prohibition to Kodak's restrictive parts and service policy. As the Court observes, in order to survive Kodak's motion for summary judgment on this claim, respondents bore the burden of proffering evidence on which a reasonable trier of fact could conclude that Kodak possesses power in the market for the alleged "tying" product. . . .

In the absence of the interbrand power, a seller's predominant or monopoly share of its single-brand derivative markets does not connote the power to raise derivative market prices *generally* by reducing quantity. As Kodak and its principal *amicus*, the United States, point out, a rational consumer considering the purchase of Kodak equipment will inevitably factor into his purchasing decision the expected cost of aftermarket support. "[B]oth the price of the equipment and the price of parts and service over the life of the equipment are expenditures that are necessary to obtain copying and micrographic services." If Kodak set generally supracompetitive prices for either spare parts or repair services without making an offsetting reduction in the price of its machines, rational consumers would simply turn to Kodak's competitors for photocopying and micrographic systems. True, there are — as the Court notes — the occasional irrational consumers that consider only the hardware cost at the time of purchase (a category that regrettably includes the Federal

Government, whose "purchasing system," we are told, assigns foremarket purchases and aftermarket purchases to different entities). But we have never before premised the application of antitrust doctrine on the lowest common denominator of consumer.

The Court attempts to counter this theoretical point with theory of its own. It says that there are "information costs" — the costs and inconvenience to the consumer of acquiring and processing life-cycle pricing data for Kodak machines — that "could create a less responsive connection between service and parts prices and equipment sales." But this truism about the functioning of markets for sophisticated equipment cannot create "market power" of concern to the antitrust laws where otherwise there is none. "Information costs," or, more accurately, gaps in the availability and quality of consumer information, pervade real-world markets; and because consumers generally make do with "rough cut" judgments about price in such circumstances, in virtually any market there are zones within which otherwise competitive suppliers may overprice their products without losing appreciable market share. We have never suggested that the principal players in a market with such commonplace informational deficiencies (and, thus, bands of apparent consumer pricing indifference) exercise market power in any sense relevant to the antitrust laws. "While [such] factors may generate 'market power' in some abstract sense, they do not generate the kind of market power that justifies condemnation of tying." *Jefferson Parish Hospital Dist. No. 2 v. Hyde*, 466 U.S. at 27. . . .

We have never before accepted the thesis the Court today embraces: that a seller's inherent control over the unique parts for its own brand amounts to "market power" of a character sufficient to permit invocation of the *per se* rule against tying. . . .

I would instead evaluate the aftermarket tie alleged in this case under the rule of reason, where the tie's *actual* anticompetitive effect in the tied product market, together with its potential economic benefits, can be fully captured in the analysis, *see, e.g., Jefferson Parish Hospital Dist. No. 2 v. Hyde*, 466 U.S. at 41 (O'Connor, J., concurring in judgment). Disposition of this case does not require such an examination, however, as respondents apparently waived any rule-of-reason claim they may have had in the District Court. I would thus reverse the Ninth Circuit's judgment on the tying claim outright.

III

These considerations apply equally to respondents' § 2 claims. An antitrust defendant lacking relevant "market power" sufficient to permit invocation of the *per se* prohibition against tying *a fortiori* lacks the monopoly power that warrants heightened scrutiny of his allegedly exclusionary behavior. Without even so much as asking whether the purposes of § 2 are implicated here, the Court points to Kodak's control of "100% of the parts market and 80% to 95% of the service market," markets with "no readily available substitutes," and finds that the proffer of such statistics is sufficient to fend off summary judgment. But this showing could easily be made . . . with respect to virtually any manufacturer of differentiated products requiring aftermarket support. By permitting antitrust plaintiffs to invoke § 2 simply upon the unexceptional demonstration that a manufacturer controls the supplies of its single-branded merchandise, the Court transforms § 2 from a specialized mechanism for responding to extraordinary agglomerations (or threatened agglomerations) of economic power to an all-purpose remedy against run-of-the-mill business torts.

In my view, if the interbrand market is vibrant, it is simply not necessary to enlist § 2's machinery to police a seller's intrabrand restraints. In such circumstances, the interbrand market functions as an infinitely more efficient and more precise corrective to such behavior, rewarding the seller whose intrabrand restraints enhance consumer welfare while punishing the seller whose control of the aftermarkets is viewed unfavorably by interbrand consumers. See *Business Electronics Corp.*, *supra*, at 725. Because this case comes to us on the assumption that Kodak is without such interbrand power, I believe we are compelled to reverse the judgment of the Court of Appeals. I respectfully dissent.

NOTES AND QUESTIONS

1. Does *Kodak* alter the approach taken in *Matsushita* regarding the burden of pleading and proof for a motion for summary judgment? How does the Court distinguish the moving party's burden in *Kodak* from that announced in *Matsushita*? What summary judgment standard applies when there is ambiguous evidence in the pretrial record?

2. Consider *Kodak*'s discussion of the plaintiff's burden of showing a tying arrangement violation. Does it differ from that articulated in Justice Stevens' opinion in *Jefferson Parish*, or is it closer to the analysis of Justice O'Connor's concurrence? After *Kodak*, is there still a *per se* rule for tying claims? If so, why did the majority not use the *per se* language?

3. Do you agree with Justice Scalia that the determinative question is Kodak's lack of market power in the interbrand equipment market? Is the lack of market power enough to discipline Kodak's pricing conduct in the derivative aftermarkets of service and parts? Is the majority's point simply that it is a fact question to be decided at trial whether, if Kodak raises prices too high for the aftermarkets of parts and service, customers will not continue to buy Kodak machines? Or, is the factual issue at trial whether, when a defendant lacks market power in the interbrand market, its opportunistic conduct can still violate Section 1 if it exercises market power over its own parts or service because certain customers are "locked-in" to the manufacturer's equipment?*See* Herbert Hovenkamp, *Market Power in Aftermarkets: Antitrust Policy and the Kodak Case*, 40 UCLA L. Rev. 1447 (1993).

4. The majority opinion in *Kodak* restricts a broad interpretation of *Matsushita*'s summary judgment standard at least where the plaintiff's economic theory of antitrust enforcement — use of dominant market power to create a tying arrangement in the intrabrand market — can be shown to have an anticompetitive, exclusionary effect. The Court seemed to return to the traditional summary judgment standard when, in the Court's opinion, the enforcement theory is not economically implausible.

5. With regard to market power, as discussed in Chapter 6, note the Court's holding: it is not economically implausible for a firm to have the use of market power in an intrabrand (parts and service) market, even when there is competition and a lack of market power in the interbrand market (equipment). Thus, *Matsushita* does not apply. Importantly, the Court holds that a single brand of a product or service can be a relevant, separate market under the Sherman Act. This, of course, is highly relevant under both Sections 1 and 2 of the Sherman Act where market power is then determined within the defined market. See discussion in Chapter 6.

6. *Kodak* rests, in the main, on a controversial analysis that relates market power to the economics of switching costs and imperfect information by consumers. The costs of switching to new products and the costs of less than perfect information may make the defendants' market power more inelastic and consumers less mobile. Does *Kodak*'s switching and information costs analysis turn Section 1 or 2 into a consumer protection statute that can be triggered whenever the market does not signal, nor the seller furnish, complete product information? Does it signal that false or deceptive advertising can be an antitrust violation?

7. Any suggestion that *Kodak* signalled a return to *Poller*-like hostility toward summary judgment in predation cases was undermined by the Supreme Court's decision a year later in *Brooke Group Ltd. v. Brown & Williamson Tobacco Corp.*, 509 U.S. 209 (1993). That decision, which involved a judgment notwithstanding the verdict rather than summary judgment, indicated that the plaintiff's burden in predatory pricing cases is very high. Unless the evidence is extremely strong that predation is profitable, summary disposition is apparently appropriate. The decision is reprinted in Chapter 6.

8. The cases are largely in agreement that there can be no *Kodak*-style lock-in if one purchases the tying product and tied product at the same time. *See, e.g.*, *Digital Equipment Corp v. Uniq Digital Technologies, Inc.*, 73 F.3d 756 (7th Cir. 1996) (rejecting an expansive reading of *Kodak*; no "lock-in" when a computer and its operating system are purchased by the customer at the same time); *Lee v. Life Ins. Co. of North America*, 23 F.3d 14 (1st Cir. 1994) (same; distinguishing *Kodak*'s "derivative after market analysis"); *Virtual Maintenance, Inc. v. Prime Computer, Inc.*, 11 F.3d 660 (6th Cir. 1993) (reviewing on remand after *Kodak*, an earlier decision on a tying claim).

In *Kodak*, you will recall, the Court concluded that aftermarket power might exist even though Kodak had no power in the primary market because poorly informed customers might purchase a copier not knowing about subsequent repair costs, and thus be "locked in," since it would ordinarily be cheaper to pay a monopoly price for parts rather than discard the copier and purchase a different brand. Both the *Digital* and *Lee* cases noted the obvious fact that the lock-in theory applies only if there is a time gap between the decision to buy the copier and the need for repair parts. Thus, in *Digital*, a computer purchaser could not be locked in to an operating system when both had to be purchased at the same time; and in *Lee*, a student registered in a certain college could not be locked in to a certain brand of student health insurance when the decision to register and information about mandatory health insurance were given to the student simultaneously. In such cases, power in the primary market must be established by the usual criteria.

See *Xerox Corp. v. Media Sciences, Inc.*, 660 F. Supp. 2d 535, 547–548 (S.D.N.Y. 2009), which found insufficient evidence of lock-in based on the complaint of single customer that he was "stuck" with a Xerox printer and forced to buy its overpriced cartridges. Many other customers had switched or threatened to switch in light of Xerox's high cost per page, and per page printing costs were widely disseminated. The court observed:

> Insofar as ignorant customers are concerned, *Kodak* teaches that the relevant question is whether some feature of the market prevents knowledgeable customers who would otherwise constrain the exercise of an alleged monopolist's economic power from performing this checking function. . . . MSI, however, has not presented any evidence from which a reasonable trier of fact could infer that this has occurred in the ink-stick aftermarket. In contrast to *Kodak*, there is no evidence that a "substantial amount of raw data' is necessary to estimate the lifecycle costs of a Xerox printer, that information concerning ink-stick prices is not readily available, or that Xerox discriminates in price between sophisticated and unsophisticated customers. To the contrary, Xerox has submitted substantial evidence that lifecycle pricing information is readily available, and that it competes with other OEMs on a cost-per-page basis. MSI dismisses this evidence, arguing that cost-per-page is only part of a printer's lifecycle cost. But even assuming that variable usage patterns and repair costs introduce some uncertainty into customers' lifecycle pricing, the Court fails to see how this is relevant under *Kodak*. The information deficit that worried the Court arose from Kodak's anti-competitive business practices, not the common human inability to predict the future with certainty.

Upon remand of *Kodak* by the Supreme Court, the district court jury found for the ISOs on the attempt to monopolize theory, but not on the tying arrangement theory, which the plaintiffs had dropped. The judge entered a 10 year permanent injunction requiring Kodak to sell "all parts" to the plaintiffs. The Ninth Circuit affirmed. *Image Technical Services, Inc. v. Eastman Kodak Co.*, 125 F.3d 1195 (9th Cir. 1997), *cert. denied*, 523 U.S. 1094 (1998). That decision is discussed in Chapter 6.

9. In *SMS Systems Maintenance Services, Inc. v. Digital Equipment Corp.*, 188 F.3d 11 (1st Cir. 1999), the First Circuit did not find an antitrust violation in a product warranty. In 1994, DEC, a computer hardware manufacturer, began offering three-year warranties on its mid-range servers, which was uncommon at the time. SMS accused DEC of using the warranty to create an aftermarket monopoly that would put ISOs out of business. The aftermarket was not the relevant market because there was no showing that DEC could assert raw power in the aftermarket without regard for commercial consequences in the foremarket. DEC successfully argued that purchasers are keenly aware of the warranty terms, distinguishing it from the high information costs discussed in *Kodak*. Further, they purchase the computer and the warranty at the same time, and are thus not "locked in" to the warranty by virtue of a previous computer purchase. The court treated a warranty as a tool of competition, implying that its obvious commercial justification would require a very strong showing of market power and anticompetitive effects to prove its illegality.

In *United States v. International Business Machines Corp. v. Independent Service Network International*, 163 F.3d 737 (2d Cir. 1998), the Second Circuit held that without a showing of actual tying, or at least a determination that future tying was likely, IBM should be released from a prior consent decree. The ability to achieve an illegal tie alone is not a violation of antitrust laws, the court observed:

> IBM and the government entered a consent decree in 1956 requiring IBM to sell parts and provide training to outside firms in the markets for supplies and services on IBM machines. Subsequently, the government determined that the termination of the remaining provisions of the decree would be in the public interest. ISNI, an association of independent servicers of IBM products, was allowed to intervene to appeal the granting of the motion to terminate the remaining provisions of the decree. ISNI alleged that IBM would, in the future, stop selling parts to ISOs and would tie the computers to maintenance, using its monopoly on spare parts as leverage. The Second Circuit held that market power alone is not enough to cause antitrust concern. There must be some action taken, or some action likely to be taken, that is anticompetitive in nature before the court will intervene.

10. The lower courts are divided on how *Kodak*'s theory of aftermarket liability without market power in the primary market affects tying claims by franchisees. In *Collins v. International Dairy Queen, Inc.*, 939 F. Supp. 875 (M.D. Ga. 1996), the plaintiff alleged that the Dairy Queen franchise indeed possesses market power in the national market for ice cream franchises, given its 91.3% market share. Although Dairy Queen argued that the relevant market should be fast food franchises, where it has a mere 2.5% market share, the court held that the franchisee had at least presented evidence that "would not foreclose a rational trier of fact from finding in their favor on the question of the proper definition of the relevant tying market. . . . " The court also held that the franchisee stated a claim for tying under *Kodak* because it alleged that the franchisor did not disclose adequately the scope of the tying arrangement and the extent to which it would deny franchisees the right to use cheaper comparable products. The court also noted that franchisees could face dangers similar to the information and switching costs present in *Kodak*. (One of the co-authors of this casebook served as an advisor in this case.)

A settlement of *International Dairy Queen* was approved by the United States District Court for the Middle District of Georgia in March 2000. The $50 million settlement allows franchisees to obtain products from suppliers other than International Dairy Queen, Inc., and American Dairy Queen Corp.

By contrast, in *Queen City Pizza, Inc. v. Domino's Pizza, Inc.*, 922 F. Supp. 1055 (E.D. Pa. 1996), *aff'd*, 124 F.3d 430 (3d Cir. 1997), the court held that one franchise cannot constitute a relevant market for tying purposes. Furthermore, the court stated that *Kodak* could never apply to franchises because any claims by franchisees that franchisors did not disclose adequately the terms of the franchise agreement are strictly matters of contract law. In the words of the *Queen City* court:

> The important economic distinction that must be made is between pre-
> and post-contract economic power. Precontract, competition among fran-

chisors (such as McDonald's or Kentucky Fried Chicken) to sign up franchisees prevents [a single franchisor] from exercising any economic power in setting contract terms with potential franchisees. [The franchisor], although it possesses a trademark, does not possess any economic power in the market in which it operates — the fast food franchising (or perhaps, more generally, the franchising) market. Postcontract, on the other hand, a franchisor can use the threat of termination to "hold up" a franchisee that has made a specific investment in the marketing arrangement. However, this potential economic power has nothing to do with market power, ultimate consumers' welfare, or antitrust.

The court then concluded that:

> The economic power [the defendant] possesses results not from the unique nature of the product or from its market share in the fast food franchise business, but from the franchise agreement. And as recognized above, allegations of wrongdoing in the post-contractual setting implicate principles of contract, and are not the concern of the antitrust laws.

Accord *Rick-Mik Enterp., Inc. v. Equilon Enterprises, LLC*, 532 F.3d 963 (9th Cir. 2008), which refused to find that contract lock-in created market power so as to condemn a gasoline refiner's tie of credit card services.

Which of these decisions is correct? A relevant market is a grouping of sales such that customers cannot easily switch to something else in response to a price increase in that grouping. A contract, of course, has a roughly similar effect. When a contract obligates the purchaser to take a stipulated good at a certain price, the purchaser cannot readily switch away if the contract subsequently becomes unfavorable in comparison with alternative opportunities elsewhere. Switching would place the purchaser in breach of the contract.

Indeed, most long-term purchase contracts have this type of "lock-in" effect. For example, if *A* contracts to sell *B* 100 tons of coal per year for 10 years at $10 per ton, both *A* and *B* are "locked in" in the sense that (1) *A* is obliged to continue providing the coal at $10 even if the market price moves higher; and (2) *B* is obliged to take the coal and pay $10 even if the market price moves lower. The more open ended the contract, or the more issues it leaves unresolved, the more harmful might be the future consequences of such lock-in. Consider this example: *L* and *T* enter into a lease agreement for a commercial building, providing for a 20-year lease and rental rates that increase by five percent annually. Suppose that after *T* has established itself, the rental market goes into decline and actual market rates decrease or else increase by much less than five percent per year. The unfortunate *T* must pay a higher-than-market rate, however, because it is "locked-in" to the lease terms. Even if *T* could break the contract without penalty, it would lose any investment made in that particular location; thus the contract imposes "switching costs" that may effectively force *T* to pay the higher lease rate rather than moving to a building with a lower cost.

But clearly any legal problems that arise from *T*'s injury are problems of contract law and negotiation, not antitrust problems. This is true even if the unfavorable lease forces *T* to pay "monopoly" rental rates for an extended period. Perhaps *T* did not foresee that rental rates would not increase as rapidly as the lease provided; perhaps information from which to make this prediction was not available at the time. For example, perhaps an unanticipated downturn in business depressed local rental rates, leaving only T to pay the higher rates stipulated in its agreement with L.

Further, not every instance of unfavorable contract lock-in results from unforeseen changes in market circumstances. Some contract buyers may be locked in to high contract prices because of fraud or misrepresentation by the sellers. For example, the landlord in the hypothetical lease might have misrepresented the building's value, understated its cost of operation, or overstated the traffic flow. Once again, the result of such misrepresentations might well be that the tenant under such a lease ends up paying more than the market value of the lease in question. But again, any lawsuit that the tenant might bring against the misrepresenting landlord would be in contract law, the law of landlord-tenant relations, or perhaps the law of fraud or misrepresentation; it would not be antitrust law.

This conclusion rests, in part, on the fact that the contractually defined grouping of sales covered by such a contract does not become an antitrust "relevant market" simply because the contract forces the buyer to pay more than the market price. To be sure, the lease requiring the tenant to pay more than market value has characteristics that resemble those of a relevant antitrust market. *First*, any price greater than the price that would be charged under competition might be seen as a "monopoly" price. *Second*, the contract imposes significant "switching costs" on the buyer/lessee in that he cannot abandon the lease without breaching the contract or perhaps losing any investment he has made in the leased premises. Thus we might say that the single building covered by the lease is a "relevant market" that has become monopolized by the landlord's misrepresentations.

But this conclusion would be incorrect for several reasons of both principle and policy. *First*, an economic market is a grouping of sales such that *general market circumstances* make consumer substitution very difficult. Numerous things may make it difficult for any particular buyer to substitute one product for another. For example, the fact that I own a pair of shoes accommodating only 24-inch strings means that I am "locked in" to shoestrings of that length, but that hardly establishes a relevant market for 24-inch shoestrings.

Second, given the ubiquity of contractual lock-in as described above, finding a "relevant market" on such a basis would turn antitrust into an engine for resolving contract disputes generally, and perhaps even for intervening in perfectly valid contracts where circumstances turned out to be less favorable than a buyer (or seller) predicted. The contracting system encourages market participants to take rational risks at the time of contracting. Antitrust intervention providing *ex post* "fixes" for contracts that have become unfavorable to one party or the other would not only exceed antitrust's mission, it would also undermine the market for assessing risks by providing post-hoc relief for those who lost, thus reducing or destroying the incentives for those who win as well. But the entrepreneurial market depends on parties' willingness to take risks.

Finally, who is injured by the tying arrangements in these cases? For example, in *Queen City, supra*, the plaintiffs alleged a relevant market of "pizza dough sold to Domino's Pizza franchisees." But pizza dough is made of flour, salt, water, and some other common ingredients. Not even a large pizza firm like Domino's would have a significant share of the market for these ingredients. In that case, what would happen if Domino's began charging its franchisees more money for its own pizza dough? Presumably, they would have higher costs and would respond by making less pizza. But if the pizza market is competitive, other pizza makers such as Pizza Hut, Godfathers, and thousands of independents would simply make more. Consumers would not be injured at all.

Other courts have tried to limit *Kodak* in other ways. For example, *PSI Repair Services v. Honeywell*, 104 F.3d 811 (6th Cir.), *cert. denied*, 520 U.S. 1265 (1997), concluded that a parts/aftermarket "lock-in" did not create significant power where the defendant had refused from the first inception of sales to provide aftermarket parts to independents. By contrast, Kodak had instituted the policy after having sold parts to ISOs for some time; as a result, there was a significant group of customers who had purchased a Kodak machine at a time when ISOs had been able to obtain aftermarket parts, and continued to use this equipment after Kodak changed its policy to one of not selling the parts to ISOs. As the court later explained:

> By changing its policy after its customers were "locked in," Kodak took advantage of the fact that its customers lacked the information to anticipate this change. Therefore, it was Kodak's own actions that increased its customers' information costs. In our view, this was the evil condemned by the Court and the reason for the Court's extensive discussion of information costs. . . . Put another way, the Court rejected the premise that imperfect consumer information resulting from basic market imperfections [rather than the contrivance of the defendant] could be used as a basis to infer market power for purposes of the Sherman Act. . . . Accepting PSI's argument would expose many manufacturers of durable, expensive equipment to potential antitrust liability for having inherent power over the aftermarkets of their products, a result certainly not intended by *Kodak*.

The Seventh Circuit came substantially to the same conclusion in *Digital Equip. Corp. v. Uniq Digital Techs.*, 73 F.3d 756, 763 (7th Cir. 1996). *See also Maris Distributing Co. v. Anheuser-Busch, Inc.*, 302 F.3d 1207 (11th Cir. 2002).

11. The VisaCheck/MasterMoney litigation involved a contractual arrangement between VisaCheck/MasterMoney issuers and retailers that requires retail stores to accept Visa and Mastercard debit cards if they also accept Visa and Mastercard credit cards. Visa and Mastercard charge retailers higher fees for debit card transactions than competing debit card issuers, and prohibit retailers from requesting that customers use a different payment system other than the debit card. The retail store plaintiffs allege that this is tying in violation of Section 1 of the Sherman Act. *See In re VisaCheck/MasterMoney Antitrust Litig.*, 192 F.R.D. 68 (E.D.N.Y 2000), *aff'd*, 280 F.3d 124 (2d Cir. 2001), *cert. denied*, 536 U.S. 917 (2002).

* * *

The *Microsoft* Litigation

Microsoft Corp. was accused in *United States v. Microsoft*, 980 F. Supp. 537 (D.C. Cir. 1997), of acting in violation of a consent decree forbidding it from tying the sales of "other products" to the sales of its hugely successful personal computers. A decree was entered in 1995, barring the company from becoming party to any license agreement that is conditioned, either expressly or impliedly, upon the licensing of any separate product. Microsoft was not prohibited, however, from developing new integrated products. The conflict concerned the company's Internet browser (the tied product); the question was whether it is an integrated or separate product capable of being tied to sales of Windows 95 (the tying product). The Antitrust Division, and the court, feared that Microsoft was using the browser to gain an unfair advantage on Netscape, its main competition in providing internet services. The district court ordered a preliminary injunction pending discovery. On appeal, the United States Court of Appeals for the District of Columbia held that the preliminary injunction was issued without adequate notice to Microsoft in light of the entered consent decree. On the issue of tying the operating system to the Internet browser, the court issued an opinion on when a technological integration of products is legal, holding that Microsoft's technological bundling of the Internet browser with the Windows 95 did not violate the consent decree. The court analogized the term "integrated product" as used in the consent decree to the established tying law's requirement that there be separate products. The court reserved the question whether the bundling violated Section 1 or 2 of the Sherman Act.

UNITED STATES v. MICROSOFT CORP.
147 F.3d 935 (D.C. Cir. 1998)

JUDGE WILLIAMS.

. . . .

We think that an "integrated product" is most reasonably understood as a product that combines functionalities (which may also be marketed separately and operated together) in a way that offers advantages unavailable if the functionalities are bought separately and combined by the purchaser.

The point of the test is twofold and may be illustrated by its application to the paradigm case of the Novell complaint and the subsequent release of Windows 95. First, "integration" suggests a degree of unity, something beyond merely placing disks in the same box. If an OEM or end user (referred to generally as "the purchaser") could buy separate products and combine them himself to produce the "integrated product," then the integration looks like a sham. If Microsoft had simply placed the disks for Windows 3.11 and MS-DOS in one package and covered it with a single license agreement, it would have offered purchasers nothing they could not get by buying the separate products and combining them on their own.

Windows 95, by contrast, unites the two functionalities in a way that purchasers could not; it is not simply a graphical user interface running on top of MS-DOS. Windows 95 is integrated in the sense that the two functionalities — DOS and graphical interface — do not exist separately: the code that is required to produce one also produces the other. Of course one can imagine that code being sold on two different disks, one containing all the code necessary for an operating system, the other with all the code necessary for a graphical interface. But as the code in the two would largely overlap, it would be odd to speak of either containing a discrete functionality. Rather, each would represent a disabled version of Windows 95. The customer could then "repair" each by installing them both on a single computer, but in such a case it would not be meaningful to speak of the customer "combining" two products. Windows 95 is an example of what Professor Areeda calls "physical or technological interlinkage that the customer cannot perform." X P. Areeda, E. Elhauge, & H. Hovenkamp, *Antitrust Law* ¶ 1746b at 227, 228 (3d ed. 2011).

So the combination offered by the manufacturer must be different from what the purchaser could create from the separate products on his own. The second point is that it must also be better in some respect; there should be some technological value to integration. Manufacturers can stick products together in ways that purchasers cannot without the link serving any purpose but an anticompetitive one. The concept of integration should exclude a case where the manufacturer has done nothing more than to metaphorically "bolt" two products together . . . X Areeda, *Antitrust Law* ¶ 1746 at 227 (discussing literal bolting). Thus if there is no suggestion that the product is superior to the purchaser's combination in some respect, it cannot be deemed integrated.

It might seem difficult to put the two elements discussed above together. If purchasers cannot combine the two functionalities to make Windows 95, it might seem that there is nothing to test Windows 95 against in search of the required superiority. But purchasers can combine the functionalities in their stand-alone incarnations. They can install MS-DOS and Windows 3.11. The test for the integration of Windows 95 then comes down to the question of whether its integrated design offers benefits when compared to a purchaser's combination of corresponding stand-alone functionalities. The decree's evident embrace of Windows 95 as a permissible single product can be taken as manifesting the parties' agreement that it met this test.

The short answer is thus that integration may be considered genuine if it is beneficial when compared to a purchaser combination. But we do not propose that in making this inquiry the court should embark on product design assessment. In antitrust law, from which this whole proceeding springs, the courts have recognized the limits of their institutional competence and have on that ground rejected theories of "technological tying." A court's evaluation of a claim of integration must be narrow and deferential. As the Fifth Circuit put it, "[S]uch a violation must be limited to those instances where the technological factor tying the hardware to the software has been designed for the purpose of tying the products, rather than to achieve some technologically beneficial result. Any other conclusion would enmesh the courts in a technical inquiry into the justifiability of product innovations." *Response of Carolina, Inc. v. Leasco Response, Inc.*, 537 F.2d 1307, 1330 (5th Cir. 1976).

In fact, Microsoft did, in negotiations, suggest such an understanding of "integrated." In response to . . . [a] statement of concern about tying, it asserted its right to "continue to develop integrated products like [Windows 95] that provide technological benefits to end users." Microsoft later withdrew this qualifying phrase, in order, it claims, to avoid the application of "vague or subjective criteria" — though why the absence of criteria should cure a vagueness problem is unclear. But we do not think that removing the phrase can drain the word "integrated" of all meaning, and we do not accept the suggestion that . . . the Department bargained for an "integrated products" proviso so boundless as to swallow § IV(E)(i). Significantly, Microsoft assured the Department . . . that the elimination of the qualifying phrase "did not represent a substantive change."

We believe this understanding is consistent with tying law. The Court in *Eastman Kodak Co. v. Image Tech. Servs.*, 504 U.S. 451, for example, found parts and service separate products because sufficient consumer demand existed to make separate provision efficient. See *id.* at 462. But we doubt that it would have subjected a self-repairing copier to the same analysis; i.e., the separate markets for parts and service would not suggest that such an innovation was really a tie-in. (The separate opinion, we take it, makes roughly the same point by its observation about digital cameras. See Sep. Op. at 3–4.) Similarly, Professor Areeda argues that new products integrating functionalities in a useful way should be considered single products regardless of market structure. See X Areeda, *Antitrust Law* ¶ 1746b.

We emphasize that this analysis does not require a court to find that an integrated product is superior to its stand-alone rivals. See *ILC Peripherals Leasing Corp. v. International Business Machines Corp.*, 458 F. Supp. 423, 439 (N.D. Cal. 1978) ("Where there is a difference of opinion as to the advantages of two alternatives which can both be defended from an engineering standpoint, the court will not allow itself to be enmeshed 'in a technical inquiry into the justifiability of product innovations.' ") (quoting *Leasco*, 537 F.2d at 1330), *aff'd per curiam sub nom. Memorex Corp. v. IBM Corp.*, 636 F.2d 1188 (9th Cir. 1980). We do not read § IV(E)(i) to "put[] judges and juries in the unwelcome position of designing computers." IX Areeda, Antitrust Law ¶ 1700j at 15 (1991). The question is not whether the integration is a net plus but merely whether there is a plausible claim that it brings some advantage. Whether or not this is the appropriate test for antitrust law generally, we believe it is the only sensible reading of [the consent decree].

On the facts before us, Microsoft has clearly met the burden of ascribing facially plausible benefits to its integrated design as compared to an operating system combined with a stand-alone browser such as Netscape's Navigator. Incorporating browsing functionality into the operating system allows applications to avail themselves of that functionality without starting up a separate browser application. Further, components . . . provide system services not directly related to Web browsing, enhancing the functionality of a wide variety of applications. Finally, . . . technologies are used to upgrade some aspects of the operating system unrelated to Web browsing. For example, they are used to let users customize their "Start" menus, making favored applications more readily available. They also make possible "thumbnail" previews of files on the computer's hard drive, using the HTML reader to display a richer view of the files' contents. Even the Department apparently concedes that integration of functionality into the operating system can bring benefits; responding to a comment on the proposed 1994 consent decree (which the Department published in the Federal Register as required by the Tunney Act), it stated that "a broad injunction against such behavior generally would not be consistent with the public interest." 59 Fed. Reg. 59426, 59428 (Nov. 17, 1994).

The conclusion that integration brings benefits does not end the inquiry we have traced out. It is also necessary that there be some reason Microsoft, rather than the OEMs or end users, must bring the functionalities together. See X Areeda, Elhauge & Hovenk amp, *Antitrust Law* ¶ 1746b at 227; ¶ 1747 at 229. Some more subtleties emerge at this stage, parallel to those encountered in determining the integrated status of Windows 95. Microsoft provides OEMs with IE 4 on a separate CD-ROM (a fact to which the Department attaches great significance). It might seem, superficially, that the OEM is just as capable as Microsoft of combining the browser and the operating system.

. . . .

What, then, counts as the combination that brings together the two functionalities? Since neither fully exists separately, we think the only sensible answer is that the act of combination is the creation of the design that knits the two together. . . . The factual conclusion is, of course, subject to reexamination on a more complete record. On the facts before us, however, we are inclined to conclude that the Windows 95/IE package is a genuine integration; consequently, [the consent decree] does not bar Microsoft from offering it as one product.

NOTE

Do you agree with the court when it finds on analogy between "integrated products" and the separate products requirement? Didn't *Jefferson Parish* observe that the separate products test does not turn on the "functional relation" between two products, but rather on the history of separate sales and the efficiency of offering one product rather than two?*See* Herbert Hovenkamp, *IP Ties and Microsoft's Role of Reason*, 47 ANTITRUST BULL. 369, 408 (2002). *But see* J. Gregory Sidak, *An Antitrust Rule for Software Integration*, 18 YALE J. REG. 1 (2001).

One source of Microsoft's economic power is said to be network "externalities," or situations where the value of a good increases as a larger number of people use it. In the case of computer operating systems most people value not merely performance for its own sake but also compatibility with as large a number of other users as possible. The presence of network externalities may entail that the firm that initially acquires a large installed base can maintain its position even when superior products come along. People value technical superiority, but they value compatibility with everyone else even more. If that is so, Microsoft might be able continually to fold one version of its operating system into the next by gradual improvements and assurances that new versions will be fully compatible with existing versions. For an excellent discussion of the complex issues, see M. Lemley & D. McGowan, *Legal Implications of Network Economic Effects*, 86 Cal. L. Rev. 479 (1998). Network externalities may explain how a firm can have durable market power in a rapidly changing industry such as computer software. They also suggest why practices such as bundling or exclusive dealing, which may have only modest effects in other industries, can completely exclude even superior rivals in an industry subject to network externalities.

In May 1998, shortly before the Windows 95 *Microsoft* decision discussed above was issued, the Department and 18 states filed complaints against Microsoft regarding Windows 98 alleging, among other issues, unlawful exclusive dealing arrangements and an unlawful tying of the Internet browser to the Windows software.

In the more recent case dealing with the Windows 98 operating system, District Court Judge Thomas Penfield Jackson found that Microsoft's combination of Windows and Internet Explorer did constitute an illegal tying arrangement. He found that the products were indeed separate products, and that consumers were forced to "pay" for the tied product even if the price of the product was zero. Judge Jackson found that Microsoft had not engaged under Section 1 of the Sherman Act, in illegal exclusive dealing because the competitor, Netscape, had many other channels available through which to distribute its product. *United States v. Microsoft Corp.*, 87 F. Supp. 2d 30 (D.D.C. 2000).

The Court of Appeals reversed again. It remanded the finding of liability to the district court with a new judge presiding, stating that the tying arrangement allegation must be considered under a rule of reason, and not per se, analysis. In reaching its conclusion, the court appeared to give weight to the *Jefferson Parish* separate products test, but stated, as Justice O'Connor had, that the analysis could not stop there. Bundling two products could result in efficiencies; moreover, the "consumer demand" test that *Jefferson Parish* had advocated could have the effect of chilling technological innovation. Primarily, the Court of Appeals was concerned that the kind of tying arrangement the *Microsoft* case presented was "unlike any the Supreme Court had[d] considered." The court concluded that the per se test was inappropriate because Microsoft had designed its browser and operating system to be integrated physically and technologically, and had presented an efficiency business justification for the integration.

UNITED STATES v. MICROSOFT CORP.
253 F.3d 34 (D.C. Cir.)534 U.S. 952 (2001)

Per Curiam

IV. TYING

. . . The District Court concluded that Microsoft's contractual and technological bundling of the IE web browser (the "tied" product) with its Windows operating system ("OS") (the "tying" product) resulted in a tying arrangement that was per se unlawful. We hold that the rule of reason, rather than per se analysis, should govern the legality of tying arrangements involving platform software products. . . .

The key District Court findings are that (1) Microsoft required licensees of Windows 95 and 98 also to license IE as a bundle at a single price, (2) Microsoft refused to allow OEMs to uninstall or remove IE from the Windows desktop, (3) Microsoft designed Windows 98 in a way that withheld from consumers the ability to remove IE by use of the Add/Remove Programs utility, and (4) Microsoft designed Windows 98 to override the user's choice of default web browser in certain circumstances. . . . Although the District Court also found that Microsoft commingled operating system-only and browser-only routines in the same library files, it did not include this as a basis for tying liability despite plaintiffs' request that it do so. . . .

Microsoft does not dispute that it bound Windows and IE in the four ways the District Court cited. Instead it argues that Windows (the tying good) and IE browsers (the tied good) are not "separate products," . . . .

The first case to give content to the separate-products test was *Jefferson Parish*, 466 U.S. 2. That case addressed a tying arrangement in which a hospital conditioned surgical care at its facility on the purchase of anesthesiological services from an affiliated medical group. The facts were a challenge for casual separate-products analysis because the tied service — anesthesia — was neither intuitively distinct from nor intuitively contained within the tying service — surgical care. A further complication was that, soon after the Court enunciated the per se rule for tying liability in *International Salt Co. v. United States*, 332 U.S. 392, 396 (1947), and *Northern Pacific Railway Co. v. United States*, 356 U.S. 1, 5–7 (1958), new economic research began to cast doubt on the assumption, voiced by the Court when it established the rule, that " 'tying agreements serve hardly any purpose beyond the suppression of competition,' " *id.* at 6.

The *Jefferson Parish* Court resolved the matter in two steps. First, it clarified that "the answer to the question whether one or two products are involved" does not turn "on the functional relation between them. . . . " In other words, the mere fact that two items are complements, that "one . . . is useless without the other," *id.*, does not make them a single "product" for purposes of tying law. . . . Second, reasoning that the "definitional question [whether two distinguishable products are involved] depends on whether the arrangement may have the type of competitive consequences addressed by the rule [against tying]," the Court decreed that "no tying arrangement can exist unless there is a sufficient demand for the purchase of anesthesiological services separate from hospital services to identify a distinct product market in which it is efficient to offer anesthesiological services separately from hospital service. . . . "

To understand the logic behind the Court's consumer demand test, consider first the postulated harms from tying. The core concern is that tying prevents goods from competing directly for consumer choice on their merits, i.e., being selected as a result of "buyers' independent judgment," . . . With a tie, a buyer's "freedom to select the best bargain in the second market [could be] impaired by his need to purchase the tying product, and perhaps by an inability to evaluate the true cost of either product. . . . " Direct competition on the merits of the tied product is foreclosed when the tying product either is sold only in a bundle with the tied product or, though offered separately, is sold at a bundled price, so that the buyer pays the same price whether he takes the tied product or not. . . .

But not all ties are bad. Bundling obviously saves distribution and consumer transaction costs. 9 Areeda, Antitrust Law ¶ 1703g2 (1991). This is likely to be true, to take some examples from the computer industry, with the integration of math co-processors and memory into microprocessor chips and the inclusion of spell checkers in word processors. . . . Indeed, if there were no efficiencies from a tie (including economizing on consumer transaction costs such as the time and effort involved in choice), we would expect distinct consumer demand for each individual component of every good. . . .

Before concluding our exegesis of *Jefferson Parish*'s separate-products test, we should clarify two things. First, *Jefferson Parish* does not endorse a direct inquiry into the efficiencies of a bundle. Rather, it proposes easy-to-administer proxies for net efficiency. In describing the separate-products test we discuss efficiencies only to explain the rationale behind the consumer demand inquiry. . . .

Second, the separate-products test is not a one-sided inquiry into the cost savings from a bundle. Although *Jefferson Parish* acknowledged that prior lower court cases looked at cost-savings to decide separate products, the Court conspicuously did not adopt that approach in its disposition of tying arrangement before it. Instead it chose proxies that balance costs savings against reduction in consumer choice.

. . . [T]here is merit to Microsoft's broader argument that *Jefferson Parish*'s consumer demand test would "chill innovation to the detriment of consumers by preventing firms from integrating into their products new functionality previously provided by standalone products — and hence, by definition, subject to separate consumer demand."

In light of the monopoly maintenance section, obviously, we do not find that Microsoft's integration is welfare-enhancing or that it should be absolved of tying liability. Rather, we heed Microsoft's warning that the separate-products element of the per se rule may not give newly integrated products a fair shake.

The Supreme Court has warned that " '[i]t is only after considerable experience with certain business relationships that courts classify them as per se violations. . . . ' " *Broadcast Music*, 441 U.S. at 9. . . . Yet the sort of tying arrangement attacked here is unlike any the Supreme Court has considered. . . .

In none of [the earlier Supreme Court] cases was the tied good physically and technologically integrated with the tying good. Nor did the defendants ever argue that their tie improved the value of the tying product to users and to makers of complementary goods. In those cases where the defendant claimed that use of the tied good made the tying good more valuable to users, the Court ruled that the same result could be achieved via quality standards for substitutes of the tied good. . . . Here Microsoft argues that IE and Windows are an integrated physical product and that the bundling of IE APIs with Windows makes the latter a better applications platform for third-party software. It is unclear how the benefits from IE APIs could be achieved by quality standards for different browser manufacturers. We do not pass judgment on Microsoft's claims regarding the benefits from integration of its APIs. We merely note that these and other novel, purported efficiencies suggest that judicial "experience" provides little basis for believing that, "because of their pernicious effect on competition and lack of any redeeming virtue," a software firm's decisions to sell multiple functionalities as a package should be "conclusively presumed to be unreasonable and therefore illegal without elaborate inquiry as to the precise harm they have caused or the business excuse for their use." . . .

. . . The failure of the separate-products test to screen out certain cases of productive integration is particularly troubling in platform software markets such as that in which the defendant competes. Not only is integration common in such markets, but it is common among firms without market power. We have already reviewed evidence that nearly all competitive OS vendors also bundle browsers. Moreover, plaintiffs do not dispute that OS vendors can and do incorporate basic internet plumbing and other useful functionality into their OSs. . . .

. . . [B]ecause of the pervasively innovative character of platform software markets, tying in such markets may produce efficiencies that courts have not previously encountered and thus the Supreme Court had not factored into the per se rule as originally conceived. For example, the bundling of a browser with OSs enables an independent software developer to count on the presence of the browser's APIs, if any, on consumers' machines and thus to omit them from its own package. . . .

We do not have enough empirical evidence regarding the effect of Microsoft's practice on the amount of consumer surplus created or consumer choice foreclosed by the integration of added functionality into platform software to exercise sensible judgment regarding that entire class of behavior.

Our judgment regarding the comparative merits of the per se rule and the rule of reason is confined to the tying arrangement before us, where the tying product is software whose major purpose is to serve as a platform for third-party applications and the tied product is complementary software functionality. While our reasoning may at times appear to have broader force, we do not have the confidence to speak to facts outside the record. . . .

Should plaintiffs choose to pursue a tying claim under the rule of reason, we note the following for the benefit of the trial court:

> . . . [O]n remand, plaintiffs must show that Microsoft's conduct unreason-ably restrained competition. Meeting that burden "involves an inquiry into the actual effect" of Microsoft's conduct on competition in the tied good market, *Jefferson Parish*, 466 U.S. at 29, the putative market for browsers. [*However, given its loss on market power questions of the browser attempt claim the court forbad the government from relying on any theory that required the definition of a browser market and a showing of high entry barriers there — ed.*]

NOTES AND QUESTIONS

1. Was the Circuit Court justified in creating a special rule of reason for a tie, but limited to a particular market (computer software)?*See* Herbert Hovenkamp, *IP Ties and the Microsoft Rule of Reason*, 47 ANTITRUST BULL. 369 (2002). Do you think the Court was following the majority opinion in *Jefferson Parish* or was it more aligned with the concurring opinion authored by Justice O'Connor in *Jefferson*

Parish? Does the Court read out of Section 1 a per se test for tying in computer software markets? Why this particular market? Under prior, existing Supreme Court tying law, do you think Microsoft's tie was per se unlawful? On remand, how should the district court apply the rule of reason test? What does it entail according to the D.C. Circuit?

2. While the case was on remand, the U.S. government and nine states settled the case with Microsoft. As part of the settlement, the government dropped the tying claim. However, most of the conduct alleged under the tying claim was condemned and found illegal under the monopolization claim under Section 2. For a discussion of the tying conduct held to be illegal under Section 2, see Chapter 6.

3. For *Microsoft*'s discussion of the government's charges of exclusive dealing under Section 2 of the Sherman Act regarding both a monopoly maintenance claim and an attempt to monopolize claim, see Chapter 6, *infra*.

4. Technological tying, or "tech ties" refers to situation where two products are bound together, not by a contract, but rather by some design feature that prevents them from being used separately. Because they are commonly treated as unilateral acts they are usually analyzed under § 2 of the Sherman Act, and are covered extensively in Chapter 6. For examples, see *Allied Orthopedic Appliances, Inc. v. Tyco Health Care Group LP*, 592 F.3d 991 (9th Cir. 2010) (rejecting challenge to defendant's redesign of pulse oximetry monitor so as to make it incompatible with the plaintiff's disposable sensors; but plaintiff did not rely on a tying theory; *see id.* at 996); *HDC Med., Inc. Plaintiff v. Minntech Corp.*, 411 F. Supp. 2d 1096, 1100–1101 (D. Minn. 2006), *aff'd*, 474 F.3d 543 (8th Cir. 2007) (defendant did not tie two components of kidney dialysis equipment together simply because its software for using the first machine was incompatible with a rival's complementary machine; in this case there was other software available that could operate with the two machines together).

[4]   Tying and Intellectual Property

ILLINOIS TOOL WORKS, INC. v. INDEPENDENT INK, INC.
547 U.S. 28 (2006)

JUSTICE STEVENS delivered the opinion of the Court.

In *Jefferson Parish Hospital Dist. No. 2 v. Hyde*, 466 U.S. 2 (1984), we repeated the well-settled proposition that "if the Government has granted the seller a patent or similar monopoly over a product, it is fair to presume that the inability to buy the product elsewhere gives the seller market power." *Id.*, at 16. This presumption of market power, applicable in the antitrust context when a seller conditions its sale of a patented product (the "tying" product) on the purchase of a second product (the "tied" product), has its foundation in the judicially created patent misuse doctrine. See *United States v. Loew's Inc.*, 371 U.S. 38, 46 (1962). In 1988, Congress substantially undermined that foundation, amending the Patent Act to eliminate the market power presumption in patent misuse cases. See 102 Stat. 4674, codified at 35 U.S.C. § 271(d). The question presented to us today is whether the presumption of market power in a patented product should survive as a matter of antitrust law despite its demise in patent law. We conclude that the mere fact that a tying product is patented does not support such a presumption.

I

Petitioners, Trident, Inc., and its parent, Illinois Tool Works Inc., manufacture and market printing systems that include three relevant components: (1) a patented piezoelectric impulse ink jet printhead; (2) a patented ink container, consisting of a bottle and valved cap, which attaches to the printhead; and (3) specially designed, but unpatented, ink. Petitioners sell their systems to original equipment manufacturers (OEMs) who are licensed to incorporate the printheads and containers into printers that are in turn sold to companies for use in printing barcodes on cartons and packaging materials. The OEMs agree that they will purchase their ink exclusively from petitioners, and that neither they nor their customers will refill the patented containers with ink of any kind.

Respondent, Independent Ink, Inc., has developed an ink with the same chemical composition as the ink sold by petitioners. After an infringement action brought by Trident against Independent was dismissed for lack of personal jurisdiction, Independent filed suit against Trident seeking a judgment of noninfringement and invalidity of Trident's patents.[39] In an amended complaint, it alleged that petitioners are engaged in illegal tying and monopolization in violation of §§ 1 and 2 of the Sherman Act. 15 U.S.C. §§ 1, 2.

After discovery, the District Court granted petitioners' motion for summary judgment on the Sherman Act claims. *Independent Ink, Inc. v. Trident, Inc.*, 210 F. Supp. 2d 1155, 1177 (C.D. Cal. 2002). It rejected respondent's submission that petitioners "necessarily have market power in the market for the tying product as a matter of law solely by virtue of the patent on their printhead system, thereby rendering [the] tying arrangements *per se* violations of the antitrust laws." *Id.*, at 1159. Finding that respondent had submitted no affirmative evidence defining the relevant market or establishing petitioners' power within it, the court concluded that respondent could not prevail on either antitrust claim. *Id.*, at 1167, 1173, 1177. The parties settled their other claims, and respondent appealed.

After a careful review of the "long history of Supreme Court consideration of the legality of tying arrangements," 396 F.3d 1342, 1346 (2005), the Court of Appeals for the Federal Circuit reversed the District Court's decision as to respondent's § 1 claim, *id.*, at 1354. Placing special reliance on our decisions in *International Salt Co. v. United States*, 332 U.S. 392 (1947), and *Loew's*, 371 U.S. 38, as well as our *Jefferson Parish* dictum, and after taking note of the academic criticism of those cases, it concluded that the "fundamental error" in petitioners' submission was its disregard of "the duty of a court of appeals to follow the precedents of the Supreme Court until the Court itself chooses to expressly overrule them." 396 F.3d at 1351. We granted certiorari to undertake a fresh examination of the history of both the judicial and legislative appraisals of tying arrangements. Our review is informed by

---

[39] [FN 1] Illinois Tool did not acquire Trident until February 19, 1999, approximately six months after this action commenced.

extensive scholarly comment and a change in position by the administrative agencies charged with enforcement of the antitrust laws.

II

American courts first encountered tying arrangements in the course of patent infringement litigation. See, e.g., *Heaton-Peninsular Button-Fastener Co. v. Eureka Specialty Co.*, 77 F. 288 (6th Cir. 1896). Such a case came before this Court in *Henry v. A.B. Dick Co.*, 224 U.S. 1 (1912), in which, as in the case we decide today, unpatented ink was the product that was "tied" to the use of a patented product through the use of a licensing agreement. Without commenting on the tying arrangement, the Court held that use of a competitor's ink in violation of a condition of the agreement — that the rotary mimeograph " 'may be used only with the stencil, paper, ink and other supplies made by A.B. Dick Co.' " — constituted infringement of the patent on the machine. *Id.*, at 25–26. Chief Justice White dissented, explaining his disagreement with the Court's approval of a practice that he regarded as an "attempt to increase the scope of the monopoly granted by a patent . . . which tend[s] to increase monopoly and to burden the public in the exercise of their common rights." *Id.*, at 70. Two years later, Congress endorsed Chief Justice White's disapproval of tying arrangements, enacting § 3 of the Clayton Act. See 38 Stat. 731 (applying to "patented or unpatented" products); see also *Motion Picture Patents Co. v. Universal Film Mfg. Co.*, 243 U.S. 502, 517–518 (1917) (explaining that, in light of § 3 of the Clayton Act, *A.B. Dick* "must be regarded as overruled"). And in this Court's subsequent cases reviewing the legality of tying arrangements we, too, embraced Chief Justice White's disapproval of those arrangements. See, e.g., *Standard Oil Co. of Cal. v. United States*, 337 U.S. 293, 305–306 (1949); *Mercoid Corp. v. Mid-Continent Investment Co.*, 320 U.S. 661, 664–665 (1944).

In the years since *A.B. Dick*, four different rules of law have supported challenges to tying arrangements. They have been condemned as improper extensions of the patent monopoly under the patent misuse doctrine, as unfair methods of competition under § 5 of the Federal Trade Commission Act, 15 U.S.C. § 45, as contracts tending to create a monopoly under § 3 of the Clayton Act, 15 U.S.C. § 13a, and as contracts in restraint of trade under § 1 of the Sherman Act.[40] In all of those instances, the justification for the challenge rested on either an assumption or a showing that the defendant's position of power in the market for the tying product was being used to restrain competition in the market for the tied product. As we explained in *Jefferson Parish*, 466 U.S., at 12, "[o]ur cases have concluded that the essential characteristic of an invalid tying arrangement lies in the seller's exploitation of its control over the tying product to force the buyer into the purchase of a tied product that the buyer either did not want at all, or might have preferred to purchase elsewhere on different terms."

---

40 [FN 2] See, *e.g., Jefferson Parish Hospital Dist. No. 2 v. Hyde*, 466 U.S. 2, 9 (1984) (Sherman Act); *Times-Picayune Publishing Co. v. United States*, 345 U.S. 594, 609 (1953) (Federal Trade Commission Act); *International Salt Co. v. United States*, 332 U.S. 392, 395–396 (1947) (Clayton Act and Sherman Act); *Morton Salt Co. v. G.S. Suppiger Co.*, 314 U.S. 488, 494 (1942) (patent misuse); *Motion Picture Patents Co. v. Universal Film Mfg. Co.*, 243 U.S. 502, 516 (1917) (same).

Over the years, however, this Court's strong disapproval of tying arrangements has substantially diminished. Rather than relying on assumptions, in its more recent opinions the Court has required a showing of market power in the tying product. Our early opinions consistently assumed that "[t]ying arrangements serve hardly any purpose beyond the suppression of competition." *Standard Oil Co.*, 337 U.S., at 305–306. In 1962, in *Loew's*, 371 U.S., at 47–48, the Court relied on this assumption despite evidence of significant competition in the market for the tying product. And as recently as 1969, Justice Black, writing for the majority, relied on the assumption as support for the proposition "that, at least when certain prerequisites are met, arrangements of this kind are illegal in and of themselves, and no specific showing of unreasonable competitive effect is required." *Fortner Enterprises, Inc. v. United States Steel Corp.*, 394 U.S. 495, 498–499*(Fortner I)*. Explaining the Court's decision to allow the suit to proceed to trial, he stated that "decisions rejecting the need for proof of truly dominant power over the tying product have all been based on a recognition that because tying arrangements generally serve no legitimate business purpose that cannot be achieved in some less restrictive way, the presence of any appreciable restraint on competition provides a sufficient reason for invalidating the tie." *Id.*, at 503.

Reflecting a changing view of tying arrangements, four Justices dissented in *Fortner I*, arguing that the challenged "tie" — the extension of a $2 million line of credit on condition that the borrower purchase prefabricated houses from the defendant — might well have served a legitimate purpose. *Id.*, at 510 (opinion of White, J.); *id.*, at 520 (opinion of Fortas, J.). In his opinion, Justice White noted that promotional tie-ins may provide "uniquely advantageous deals" to purchasers. *Id.*, at 519. And Justice Fortas concluded that the arrangement was best characterized as "a sale of a single product with the incidental provision of financing." *Id.*, at 522.

The dissenters' view that tying arrangements may well be procompetitive ultimately prevailed; indeed, it did so in the very same lawsuit. After the Court remanded the suit in *Fortner I*, a bench trial resulted in judgment for the plaintiff, and the case eventually made its way back to this Court. Upon return, we unanimously held that the plaintiff's failure of proof on the issue of market power was fatal to its case — the plaintiff had proved "nothing more than a willingness to provide cheap financing in order to sell expensive houses." *United States Steel Corp. v. Fortner Enterprises, Inc.*, 429 U.S. 610, 622 (1977)*(Fortner II)*.

The assumption that "[t]ying arrangements serve hardly any purpose beyond the suppression of competition," rejected in *Fortner II*, has not been endorsed in any opinion since. Instead, it was again rejected just seven years later in *Jefferson Parish*, where, as in *Fortner II*, we unanimously reversed a Court of Appeals judgment holding that an alleged tying arrangement constituted a *per se* violation of § 1 of the Sherman Act. 466 U.S., at 5. Like the product at issue in the *Fortner* cases, the tying product in *Jefferson Parish* — hospital services — was unpatented, and our holding again rested on the conclusion that the plaintiff had failed to prove sufficient power in the tying product market to restrain competition in the market for the tied product — services of anesthesiologists. 466 U.S., at 28–29.

In rejecting the application of a *per se* rule that all tying arrangements constitute antitrust violations, we explained:

> "[W]e have condemned tying arrangements when the seller has some special ability — usually called 'market power' — to force a purchaser to do something that he would not do in a competitive market. . . .

> . . . .

> "*Per se* condemnation — condemnation without inquiry into actual market conditions — is only appropriate if the existence of forcing is probable. Thus, application of the *per se* rule focuses on the probability of anticompetitive consequences. . . .

> "For example, if the Government has granted the seller a patent or similar monopoly over a product, it is fair to presume that the inability to buy the product elsewhere gives the seller market power.

> *United States v. Loew's Inc.*, 371 U.S., at 45–47. Any effort to enlarge the scope of the patent monopoly by using the market power it confers to restrain competition in the market for a second product will undermine competition on the merits in that second market. Thus, the sale or lease of a patented item on condition that the buyer make all his purchases of a separate tied product from the patentee is unlawful." *Id.*, at 13–16 (footnote omitted).

Notably, nothing in our opinion suggested a rebuttable presumption of market power applicable to tying arrangements involving a patent on the tying good. Instead, it described the rule that a contract to sell a patented product on condition that the purchaser buy unpatented goods exclusively from the patentee is a *per se* violation of § 1 of the Sherman Act.

Justice O'Connor wrote separately in *Jefferson Parish*, concurring in the judgment on the ground that the case did not involve a true tying arrangement because, in her view, surgical services and anesthesia were not separate products. 466 U.S., at 43. In her opinion, she questioned not only the propriety of treating any tying arrangement as a *per se* violation of the Sherman Act, *id.*, at 35, but also the validity of the presumption that a patent always gives the patentee significant market power, observing that the presumption was actually a product of our patent misuse cases rather than our antitrust jurisprudence, *id.*, at 37–38, n. 7. It is that presumption, a vestige of the Court's historical distrust of tying arrangements, that we address squarely today.

III

Justice O'Connor was, of course, correct in her assertion that the presumption that a patent confers market power arose outside the antitrust context as part of the patent misuse doctrine. That doctrine had its origins in *Motion Picture Patents Co. v. Universal Film Mfg. Co.*, 243 U.S. 502 (1917), which found no support in the patent laws for the proposition that a patentee may "prescribe by notice attached to a patented machine the conditions of its use and the supplies which must be used in the operation of it, under pain of infringement of the patent," *id.*, at 509. Although *Motion Picture Patents Co.* simply narrowed the scope of possible patent infringement claims, it formed the basis for the Court's subsequent decisions creating a patent misuse defense to infringement claims when a patentee uses its patent "as the effective means of restraining competition with its sale of an unpatented article." *Morton Salt Co. v. G.S. Suppiger Co.*, 314 U.S. 488, 490 (1942); see also, *e.g.*, *Carbice Corp. of America v. American Patents Development Corp.*, 283 U.S. 27, 31 (1931).

Without any analysis of actual market conditions, these patent misuse decisions assumed that, by tying the purchase of unpatented goods to the sale of the patented good, the patentee was "restraining competition," *Morton Salt*, 314 U.S., at 490, or "secur[ing] a limited monopoly of an unpatented material," *Mercoid*, 320 U.S., at 664; see also *Carbice*, 283 U.S., at 31–32. In other words, these decisions presumed "[t]he requisite economic power" over the tying product such that the patentee could "extend [its] economic control to unpatented products." *Loew's*, 371 U.S., at 45–46.

The presumption that a patent confers market power migrated from patent law to antitrust law in *International Salt Co. v. United States*, 332 U.S. 392 (1947). In that case, we affirmed a District Court decision holding that leases of patented machines requiring the lessees to use the defendant's unpatented salt products violated § 1 of the Sherman Act and § 3 of the Clayton Act as a matter of law. *Id.*, at 396. Although the Court's opinion does not discuss market power or the patent misuse doctrine, it assumes that "[t]he volume of business affected by these contracts cannot be said to be insignificant or insubstantial and the tendency of the arrangement to accomplishment of monopoly seems obvious." *Ibid.*

The assumption that tying contracts "ten[d] . . . to accomplishment of monopoly" can be traced to the Government's brief in *International Salt*, which relied heavily on our earlier patent misuse decision in *Morton Salt*. The Government described *Morton Salt* as "present[ing] a factual situation almost identical with the instant case," and it asserted that "although the Court in that case did not find it necessary to decide whether the antitrust laws were violated, its language, its reasoning, and its citations indicate that the policy underlying the decision was the same as that of the Sherman Act." Brief for United States in *International Salt Co. v. United States*, O.T. 1947, No. 46, p. 19 (United States Brief). Building on its assertion that *International Salt* was logically indistinguishable from *Morton Salt*, the Government argued that this Court should place tying arrangements involving patented products in the category of *per se* violations of the Sherman Act. United States Brief 26–33.

Our opinion in *International Salt* clearly shows that we accepted the Government's invitation to import the presumption of market power in a patented product into our antitrust jurisprudence. While we cited *Morton Salt* only for the narrower proposition that the defendant's patents did not confer any right to restrain competition in unpatented salt or afford the defendant any immunity from the antitrust laws, *International Salt*, 332 U.S., at 395–396, given the fact that the defendant was selling its unpatented salt at competitive prices, *id.*, at 396–397, the rule adopted in *International Salt* necessarily accepted the Government's submission that the earlier patent misuse cases supported the broader proposition "that this type of restraint is unlawful on its face under the Sherman Act," United States Brief 12.

Indeed, later in the same Term we cited *International Salt* for the proposition that the license of "a patented device on condition that unpatented materials be employed in conjunction with the patented device" is an example of a restraint that is "illegal *per se.*" *United States v. Columbia Steel Co.*, 334 U.S. 495, 522–523, and n. 22 (1948). And in subsequent cases we have repeatedly grounded the presumption of market power over a patented device in *International Salt.* See, *e.g., Loew's,* 371 U.S., at 45–46; *Times-Picayune Publishing Co. v. United States,* 345 U.S. 594, 608 (1953); *Standard Oil Co.,* 337 U.S., at 304.

IV

Although the patent misuse doctrine and our antitrust jurisprudence became intertwined in *International Salt,* subsequent events initiated their untwining. This process has ultimately led to today's reexamination of the presumption of *per se* illegality of a tying arrangement involving a patented product, the first case since 1947 in which we have granted review to consider the presumption's continuing validity.

Three years before we decided *International Salt,* this Court had expanded the scope of the patent misuse doctrine to include not only supplies or materials used by a patented device, but also tying arrangements involving a combination patent and "unpatented material or [a] device [that] is itself an integral part of the structure embodying the patent." *Mercoid,* 320 U.S., at 665; see also *Dawson Chemical Co. v. Rohm & Haas Co.,* 448 U.S. 176, 188–198 (1980) (describing in detail *Mercoid* and the cases leading up to it). In reaching this conclusion, the Court explained that it could see "no difference in principle" between cases involving elements essential to the inventive character of the patent and elements peripheral to it; both, in the Court's view, were attempts to "expan [d] the patent beyond the legitimate scope of its monopoly." *Mercoid,* 320 U.S., at 665.

Shortly thereafter, Congress codified the patent laws for the first time. At least partly in response to our *Mercoid* decision, Congress included a provision in its codification that excluded some conduct, such as a tying arrangement involving the sale of a patented product tied to an "essential" or "nonstaple" product that has no use except as part of the patented product or method, from the scope of the patent misuse doctrine. § 271(d); see also *Dawson,* 448 U.S., at 214. Thus, at the same time that our antitrust jurisprudence continued to rely on the assumption that "tying arrangements generally serve no legitimate business purpose," *Fortner I,* 394 U.S., at 503, Congress began chipping away at the assumption in the patent misuse context from whence it came.

It is Congress' most recent narrowing of the patent misuse defense, however, that is directly relevant to this case. Four years after our decision in *Jefferson Parish* repeated the patent-equals-market-power presumption, 466 U.S., at 16, Congress amended the Patent Code to eliminate that presumption in the patent misuse context, 102 Stat. 4674. The relevant provision reads:

"(d) No patent owner otherwise entitled to relief for infringement or contributory infringement of a patent shall be denied relief or deemed guilty of misuse or illegal extension of the patent right by reason of his having done one or more of the following: . . . (5) conditioned the license of any rights to the patent or the sale of the patented product on the acquisition of a license to rights in another patent or purchase of a separate product, *unless, in view of the circumstances, the patent owner has market power in the relevant market for the patent or patented product on which the license or sale is conditioned.*" 35 U.S.C. § 271(d)(5) (emphasis added).

The italicized clause makes it clear that Congress did not intend the mere existence of a patent to constitute the requisite "market power." Indeed, fairly read, it provides that without proof that Trident had market power in the relevant market, its conduct at issue in this case was neither "misuse" nor an "illegal extension of the patent right."

While the 1988 amendment does not expressly refer to the antitrust laws, it certainly invites a reappraisal of the *per se* rule announced in *International Salt*.[41] A rule denying a patentee the right to enjoin an infringer is significantly less severe than a rule that makes the conduct at issue a federal crime punishable by up to 10 years in prison. See 15 U.S.C. § 1. It would be absurd to assume that Congress intended to provide that the use of a patent that merited punishment as a felony would not constitute "misuse." Moreover, given the fact that the patent misuse doctrine provided the basis for the market power presumption, it would be anomalous to preserve the presumption in antitrust after Congress has eliminated its foundation. *Cf.* 10 P. Areeda, H. Hovenkamp, & E. Elhauge, Antitrust Law ¶ 1737c (2d ed. 2004) (hereinafter Areeda).

After considering the congressional judgment reflected in the 1988 amendment, we conclude that tying arrangements involving patented products should be evaluated under the standards applied in cases like *Fortner II* and *Jefferson Parish* rather than under the *per se* rule applied in *Morton Salt* and *Loew's*. While some such arrangements are still unlawful, such as those that are the product of a true monopoly or a marketwide conspiracy, see, *e.g., United States v. Paramount Pictures, Inc.*, 334 U.S. 131, 145–146 (1948), that conclusion must be supported by proof of power in the relevant market rather than by a mere presumption thereof.[42]

V

Rather than arguing that we should retain the rule of *per se* illegality, respondent contends that we should endorse a rebuttable presumption that patentees possess

---

[41] [FN 3] While our opinions have made clear that such an invitation is not necessary with respect to cases arising under the Sherman Act, see *State Oil Co. v. Khan*, 522 U.S. 3, 20 (1997), it is certainly sufficient to warrant reevaluation of our precedent, *id.*, at 21 ("[T]his Court has reconsidered its decisions construing the Sherman Act when the theoretical underpinnings of those decisions are called into serious question").

[42] [FN 4] Our imposition of this requirement accords with the vast majority of academic literature on the subject. See, *e.g.*, 10 Areeda & 1737a ("[T]here is no economic basis for inferring any amount of market power from the mere fact that the defendant holds a valid patent"); Burchfiel, Patent Misuse and Antitrust Reform: "Blessed be the Tie?" 4 Harv. J.L. & Tech. 1, 57, and n. 340 (noting that the market power presumption has been extensively criticized and citing sources); 1 H. Hovenkamp, M. Janis, & M. Lemley, IP and Antitrust § 4.2a (2005 Supp.) ("[C]overage of one's product with an intellectual property right does not confer a monopoly"); W. Landes & R. Posner, The Economic Structure of Intellectual Property Law 374 (2003).

market power when they condition the purchase of the patented product on an agreement to buy unpatented goods exclusively from the patentee. Respondent recognizes that a large number of valid patents have little, if any, commercial significance, but submits that those that are used to impose tying arrangements on unwilling purchasers likely do exert significant market power. Hence, in respondent's view, the presumption would have no impact on patents of only slight value and would be justified, subject to being rebutted by evidence offered by the patentee, in cases in which the patent has sufficient value to enable the patentee to insist on acceptance of the tie.

Respondent also offers a narrower alternative, suggesting that we differentiate between tying arrangements involving the simultaneous purchase of two products that are arguably two components of a single product — such as the provision of surgical services and anesthesiology in the same operation, *Jefferson Parish*, 466 U.S., at 43 (O'Connor, J., concurring in judgment), or the licensing of one copyrighted film on condition that the licensee take a package of several films in the same transaction, *Loew's*, 371 U.S. 38 — and a tying arrangement involving the purchase of unpatented goods over a period of time, a so-called "requirements tie." According to respondent, we should recognize a presumption of market power when faced with the latter type of arrangements because they provide a means for charging large volume purchasers a higher royalty for use of the patent than small purchasers must pay, a form of discrimination that "is strong evidence of market power." Brief for Respondent 27; see generally *Jefferson Parish*, 466 U.S., at 15, n. 23 (discussing price discrimination of this sort and citing sources).

The opinion that imported the "patent equals market power" presumption into our antitrust jurisprudence, however, provides no support for respondent's proposed alternative. In *International Salt*, it was the existence of the patent on the tying product, rather than the use of a requirements tie, that led the Court to presume market power. 332 U.S., at 395 ("The appellant's patents confer a limited monopoly of the invention they reward"). Moreover, the requirements tie in that case did not involve any price discrimination between large volume and small volume purchasers or evidence of noncompetitive pricing. Instead, the leases at issue provided that if any competitor offered salt, the tied product, at a lower price, "the lessee should be free to buy in the open market, unless appellant would furnish the salt at an equal price." *Id.*, at 396.

As we have already noted, the vast majority of academic literature recognizes that a patent does not necessarily confer market power. Similarly, while price discrimination may provide evidence of market power, particularly if buttressed by evidence that the patentee has charged an above-market price for the tied package, it is generally recognized that it also occurs in fully competitive markets, see, *e.g.*, Baumol & Swanson, The New Economy and Ubiquitous Competitive Price Discrimination: Identifying Defensible Criteria of Market Power, 70 Antitrust L.J. 661, 666 (2003); 9 Areeda ¶ 1711; Landes & Posner 374–375. We are not persuaded that the combination of these two factors should give rise to a presumption of market power when neither is sufficient to do so standing alone. Rather, the lesson to be learned from *International Salt* and the academic commentary is the same: Many tying arrangements, even those involving patents and requirements ties, are fully consistent with a free, competitive market. For this reason, we reject both respondent's proposed rebuttable presumption and their narrower alternative.

It is no doubt the virtual consensus among economists that has persuaded the enforcement agencies to reject the position that the Government took when it supported the *per se* rule that the Court adopted in the 1940's. In antitrust guidelines issued jointly by the Department of Justice and the Federal Trade Commission in 1995, the enforcement agencies stated that in the exercise of their prosecutorial discretion they "will not presume that a patent, copyright, or trade secret necessarily confers market power upon its owner." U.S. Dept. of Justice and FTC, Antitrust Guidelines for the Licensing of Intellectual Property § 2.2 (Apr. 6, 1995), available at http://www.usdoj.gov/atr/ public/guidelines/. While that choice is not binding on the Court, it would be unusual for the Judiciary to replace the normal rule of lenity that is applied in criminal cases with a rule of severity for a special category of antitrust cases.

Congress, the antitrust enforcement agencies, and most economists have all reached the conclusion that a patent does not necessarily confer market power upon the patentee. Today, we reach the same conclusion, and therefore hold that, in all cases involving a tying arrangement, the plaintiff must prove that the defendant has market power in the tying product.

VI

In this case, respondent reasonably relied on our prior opinions in moving for summary judgment without offering evidence defining the relevant market or proving that petitioners possess power within it. When the case returns to the District Court, respondent should therefore be given a fair opportunity to develop and introduce evidence on that issue, as well as any other issues that are relevant to its remaining § 1 claims. Accordingly, the judgment of the Court of Appeals is vacated, and the case is remanded for further proceedings consistent with this opinion.

NOTES AND QUESTIONS

1. How much of the per se tying rule remains under the Supreme Court's decision? Suppose that tying product market power is established by conventional market power criteria, or by *Kodak*-style lock-in?

2. *Package licensing, blanket licensing, and block booking.* Package licensing, blanket licensing, and block-booking are intellectual property licensing devices under which IP rights are bundled together. While these arrangements are often analogized to patent ties, they differ in that both the "tying product" and the "tied product" are intellectual property rights — usually but not necessarily licenses sold independently of any product, and usually but not necessarily licenses of the same species. In the classical patent tie, as in the *Illinois Tool Works* case, the tying product is typically a product to which one or more patent licenses are attached, such as a mimeograph machine or film projector. The tied product is typically unpatented staple products.

Of course, if the licensee requests a package of patents and the patentee complies, neither patent misuse nor antitrust concerns are raised. But if the patentee refuses to license a particular patent unless the licensee accepts an entire "package," or if the patentee's royalty scale makes package licensing far cheaper than single patent licensing, then both patent misuse and antitrust become relevant. "Mandatory" package licensing such as this includes "block-booking" in the case of motion pictures, as in *Loew's*, and blanket licensing of copyrighted music or other performances. The patent or group of patents that the licensee desires becomes the "tying" product, while the unwanted patents forced upon the licensee by the package sale are the "tied" product. In block booking, the desired film, television show, or other copyrighted product is the equivalent of the tying product, while the undesired ones are the tied product. In many of the cases the distinction between "tying" and "tied" product is really not all that important. What the licensee wants is some smaller bundle than the bundle that the licensor insists that it take.

The pervasive question that arises in such cases is where is the competitive harm, because typically no one is being foreclosed. For example, suppose that I own five patents on related microprocessor technology. You build microprocessors and would like to license three of my patents. I tell you that I license them only as a group of five and that the license fee is $10 per microprocessor. You object, stating that you are willing to pay $6 and use only three of the patents. Clearly, we are just disputing the size of the package and the price. There is no more competitive harm than if the owner of a 100 acre farm refuses to subdivide it and sell you only one acre, or if the grocer refuses to split a carton of a dozen eggs. The only way a court could provide meaningful relief is if it (1) forced the seller to break up the package; *and* (2) stipulated the price that the seller must charge. See, e.g., *BMI, Inc. v. Moor-Law, Inc.*, 527 F. Supp. 758, 767–768, 212 U.S.P.Q. 873 (D. Del. 1981), where the court refused to break up a blanket license for juke box songs so that the plaintiff, the Triple Nickel Saloon, could license only country and western songs. The court held that the licensor's library of songs, which included everything from classical music to country and western to rap, constituted a "single product" for purposes of tying law. Significantly, there was no foreclosure. The Triple Nickel did not want *someone else's* classical music. It did not want classical music at all; as a result, no rival seller was being excluded from the market.

3. Recall from the discussion above that variable proportion tying arrangements are often used to facilitate price discrimination. It has been suggested that block-booking — a form of fixed proportion tie-in — can be used for the same purpose. Suppose, for example, that two different television stations, which cater to two different audiences, place different values on different kinds of films. Station *A* values a license to show *Casablanca* at $7000, while it values a license for *I Was a Teenage Werewolf* at only $4000. On the other hand, station *B* values the license for *Casablanca* at only $5000, while it values the license for *Werewolf* at $6000. Assuming that the licensor must charge both stations the same price, it can do one of the following three things:

> (a) It can charge $7000 for *Casablanca* and $6000 for *Werewolf.* In this case it will license *Casablanca* once (to station *A*) and *Werewolf* once (to station *B*). Total revenues will be $13,000.

(b) It can charge $5000 for *Casablanca* and $4000 for *Werewolf.* In this case both stations will take both films and the total revenues will be $18,000.

(c) It can "package" the two films together and sell the package at $11,000. In this case both stations will take the package and the total revenues will be $22,000.

See George J. Stigler, *United States v. Loew's, Inc.: A Note on Block-Booking,* 1963 Sup. Ct. Rev. 152, 152–154 (1963); Richard Markovits, *Tie-Ins, Reciprocity, and the Leverage Theory,* 76 YALE L.J. 1397, 1406–1408 (1967).

Whether such block-booking is "price discrimination" depends on the meaning of the term. The ratio of price to marginal cost for the *package* is the same for both stations, assuming that both stations impose the same costs on the seller, so no price discrimination exists from the seller's viewpoint. On the other hand, the ratio of marginal cost to what each station believes it is paying for each individual film is different for station *A* than station *B*. Economists have been content to call this "simulated price discrimination."

4. The case for inferring market power from the existence of other forms of intellectual property is generally even weaker than it is for patents. Previously the Supreme Court had held that sufficient market power to condemn a tying arrangement could be inferred from a copyright. *See United States v. Loew's, Inc.,* 371 U.S. 38, 45 (1962). In *ITW,* the Supreme Court overruled dicta in *Loew's* stating that a patent confers sufficient power, but said nothing about the decision's actual holding — the "block booking" of motion pictures that the case condemned involved products that were copyrighted but not patented, and the Supreme Court stated its presumption for copyrights as well. The Supreme Court has never held that a trademark would confer sufficient power to condemn a tie, but a few lower courts did. *See, e.g., Siegel v. Chicken Delight, Inc.,* 448 F.2d 43 (9th Cir. 1971), *cert. denied,* 405 U.S. 955 (1972); *Photovest Corp v. Fotomat Corp.,* 606 F.2d 704 (7th Cir. 1979), *cert. denied,* 445 U.S. 917 (1980).

Without citing *Photovest,* in *Sheridan v. Marathon Petroleum Co., LLC,* 530 F.3d 590 (7th Cir. 2008), the Seventh Circuit held that Marathon oil company's trademark was not sufficient to give it sufficient market power to condemn its tie of credit card processing services to a Marathon franchise. Judge Posner observed that Marathon accounted for only 4.3% of domestic gasoline sales. He then added:

> Marathon does of course have a "monopoly" of Marathon franchises. But "Marathon" is not a market; it is a trademark; and a trademark does not confer a monopoly; all it does is prevent a competitor from attaching the same name to his product. "Not even the most zealous antitrust hawk has ever argued that Amoco gasoline, Mobil gasoline, and Shell gasoline" — or, we interject, Marathon gasoline — "are three [with Marathon, four] separate product markets." . . . The complaint does not allege that there are any local gasoline markets in which Marathon has monopoly (or market) power. No market share statistics for Marathon either locally or nationally are given, and there is no information in the complaint that would enable local shares to be calculated.

What is true is that a firm selling under conditions of "monopolistic competition" — the situation in which minor product differences (or the kind of locational advantage that a local store, such as a barber shop, might enjoy in competing for some customers) limit the substitutability of otherwise very similar products — will want to trademark its brand in order to distinguish it from its competitors' brands. But the exploitation of the slight monopoly power thereby enabled does not do enough harm to the economy to warrant trundling out the heavy artillery of federal antitrust law. And anyway in this case monopolistic competition is not alleged either. So we are given no reason to doubt that if Marathon raises the price of using the Marathon name above the competitive level by raising the price of the credit card processing service that it offers, competing oil companies will nullify its price increase simply by keeping their own wholesale gasoline prices at the existing level. The complaint does not allege that Marathon is colluding with the other oil companies to raise the price of credit card processing.

In *Paramount Pictures Corp. v. Johnson Broadcasting, Inc.*, 432 F. Supp. 2d 707 (S.D. Tex. 2006), the court concluded that *ITW* upset the presumption for copyright as well. However, it denied summary judgment on the plaintiff's challenge to block booking of television shows, holding that two courtroom shows involving disputes between actual litigants, "Judge Judy" and "Judge Joe Brown," could have been sufficiently unique to confer market power on the shows' owner. Do you agree with that holding? How difficult would it be for a television producer wishing to emulate one of these shows to find a retired judge and assemble the other needed inputs? In any event, would not such shows compete with many other forms of entertainment, on television as well as elsewhere?

Cf. Rick-Mik Enterp., Inc. v. Equilon Enterprises, LLC, 532 F.3d 963 (9th Cir. 2008), which also dismissed a .claim that a large petroleum refiner (a joint venture covering the Shell and Texaco brands) unlawfully forced its dealer to accept its credit card processing services. The court held:

> Nor is Rick-Mik's complaint saved by the allegation that "Shell and Texaco-branded gasolines are protected by various trademarks, copyrights and patents providing EQUILON [the joint venture] sufficient economic power over Plaintiffs in connection with its tying products to appreciably restrain competition in the tied product market." Even construing that allegation as one alleging market power in the gasoline franchise market as opposed to the gasoline retail market, it lacks the factual specificity required "to raise a right to relief above the speculative level." *See Twombly*, 127 S. Ct. at 1965. Because intellectual property rights are no longer presumed to confer market power, *see Illinois Toolworks Inc.*, 547 U.S. at 42–43, Rick-Mik's conclusory allegation that Equilon's intellectual property rights nonetheless do confer market power, unaccompanied by supporting facts, is insufficient.

5. *Patent Misuse.* The *Illinois Tool Works* decision speaks a great deal about the defense of patent "misuse," which created a defense to a patent infringement action if the defendant could show that the patentee had "misused" the patent, often by tying. The defense is still recognized and is often asserted, although it is seldom recognized. Further, a controversy exists about whether the misuse defense should be defined by antitrust principles, or whether it should reach more broadly to practices that might not be anticompetitive in the antitrust sense but that might violate patent (or copyright) policy for other reasons. *See* Christina Bohannan, *IP Misuse as Foreclosure*, 96 Iowa L. Rev. 475 (2011), *available at* http://papers.ssrn.com/sol3/papers.cfm?abstract_id=1474407:

> Although courts generally agree that the misuse doctrine relates to the use of IP licenses and other arrangements to obtain rights "beyond the scope" of a statutory IP right, the doctrine lacks coherence and certitude in determining the types of practices that should be condemned and why. Perhaps as a result, much of the case law has embraced an antitrust standard for misuse, which may be coherent but is less faithful to the core IP values of promoting innovation and protecting access to the public domain. The result is a schizophrenic doctrine that vacillates between IP and antitrust law.[43]

> The misuse doctrine evolved first in patent law. The classic case involved the tying of patented and unpatented goods — that is, the seller's requirement that one could not purchase or lease the patented product without also taking unpatented products or services as well.[44] Several courts held that such tying violated federal patent policy by attempting to expand the statutory monopoly to include a second product not covered by the patent claims. Since then, misuse has expanded into other practices and into copyright law. Courts have considered the doctrine's applicability to a variety of practices including tying, package licensing of related patented or copyrighted goods, restraints on a licensee's ability to produce competing technologies, and requiring royalty payments beyond the expiration of the patent or copyright term.

> From the beginning, courts have stated that the purpose of the misuse doctrine is to provide a remedy against attempts to expand the IP holder's statutory "monopoly." Although some of these early cases indicated that such an expansion of the IP "monopoly" is a concern of antitrust law,[45] they

---

[43] On the divide between antitrust and IP approaches to misuse generally, see Christina Bohannan and Herbert Hovenkamp, Creation Without Restraint: Promoting Liberty and Rivalry in Innovation (N.Y.: Oxford Univ. Press, 2011).

[44] *E.g., Henry v. A.B. Dick Co.*, 224 U.S. 1 (1912) (pre-misuse case in which maker of patented mimeograph machine tied stencils, paper, and ink); *Motion Picture Patents Company v. Universal Film Manufacturing Company (MPPC)*, 243 U.S. 502 (1917) (pre-misuse case involving tying of patented film projector and unpatented film); *Carbice Corp. v. American Patents Dev. Corp.*, 283 U.S. 27 (1931) (pre-misuse case involving tying of patented refrigeration box and dry ice; pre-misuse); *Leitch Mfg. Co. v. Barber Co.*, 302 U.S. 458, 461–463 (1938) (pre-misuse case involving tying of patented process for installing asphalt emulsion on roads to the unpatented emulsion); *Morton Salt Co. v. G.S. Suppiger Co.*, 314 U.S. 488 (1942) (first case articulating modern misuse doctrine and applying it to tie of patented salt injection machine to unpatented salt).

[45] *See, e.g., MPPC*, 243 U.S. 502, 517 (noting relevance of Clayton Act's anti-tying provision, 15 U.S.C. § 14 (2006), which had been passed in 1914, and which "confirmed" its resolution of the case). *See also Mercoid Corp. v. Mid-Continent Inv. Co.*, 320 U.S. 680, 684 (1944) (*Mercoid II*) ("the legality of any

relied primarily on federal IP policy to justify the doctrine. Over time, however, courts have begun to judge many cases of alleged misuse by antitrust standards, probably because antitrust law provides courts with a well-developed set of rules by which to judge the complexities of effects on competition. This merger of antitrust and misuse has provoked a great deal of confusion and criticism. The relationship between misuse and antitrust is not well understood, and it is unclear why IP misuse should be defined as a breach of antitrust policy rather than as a breach of intellectual property policy. After all, misuse is a creature of IP law. In addition, antitrust law does not reach all of the conduct that has been deemed to constitute misuse.

The incoherence in misuse doctrine is particularly problematic given the nature and severity of the penalty. Misuse is not an affirmative cause of action but, subject to a few exceptions, is raised as a defense in an IP infringement claim. Thus, the doctrine benefits primarily infringers, including infringers who have not been injured in any way by the misuse but instead argue that the IP holder has misused the IP right against others.[46] Moreover, a finding of misuse can be devastating for a patent or copyright holder. If misuse is found, the patent or copyright is rendered unenforceable until the misuse is "purged."[47] There is a serious question, therefore, as to whether the benefits of remedying misuse outweigh the costs of foregoing patent enforcement. As a result, some scholars believe that assertions of misuse should be, as one has put it, "safe, legal, and rare."[48]

. . . The dominant view over the past few decades has been that patent misuse occurs only when the patentee's conduct — a tying arrangement or license restriction or other practice — violates the antitrust laws. Under the antitrust model of misuse, the defendant must prove that the patented product has market power in the relevant market for the product, and that the patent holder's conduct or restriction tends to exclude rivals from the market or prevent them from entering it. . . .

Congress incorporated this approach, to some extent, in the Patent Misuse Reform Act of 1988, 35 U.S.C. § 271(d), which provides that a patent holder cannot be guilty of misuse for tying an unpatented product to a patented one unless there is market power in the patented product:

(d) No patent owner otherwise entitled to relief for infringement or contributory infringement of a patent shall be denied relief or deemed

---

attempt to bring unpatented goods within the protection of the patent is measured by the anti-trust laws not by the patent law").

[46] *See, e.g., Morton Salt Co. v. G.S. Suppiger Co.*, 314 U.S. 488 (1942) (infringement defendant was a competing maker of salt injection machines, and was not injured by the salt tie).

[47] *See, e.g., B.B. Chem. Co. v. Ellis*, 314 U.S. 495, 498 (1942) (patentee could resume enforcement of patent once misuse was purged). *See also U.S. Gypsum v. National Gypsum Co.*, 352 U.S. 457 (1957) (patentee may not recover royalties for period during which misuse continued prior to when it was purged); *Practice Mgm't Information Corp. v. American Medical Ass'n*, 121 F.3d 516, 520 n.9 (9th Cir. 1997) ("Copyright misuse does not invalidate a copyright, but precludes its enforcement during the period of misuse.").

[48] *See* Thomas F. Cotter, *Misuse*, 44 Hous. L. Rev. 901, 903 (2007).

guilty of misuse or illegal extension of the patent right by reason of his having done one or more of the following: . . . (5) conditioned the license of any rights to the patent or the sale of the patented product on the acquisition of a license to rights in another patent or purchase of a separate product, unless, in view of the circumstances, the patent owner has market power in the relevant market for the patent or patented product on which the license or sale is conditioned.

Nevertheless, the case law is somewhat mixed. In some decisions the Federal Circuit Court of Appeals appears to have adopted an antitrust standard for misuse.[49] Others have suggested that misuse has a somewhat broader reach. For example, in its recent decision in *Monsanto Co. v. Scruggs*, the majority concluded that "[p]atent misuse is . . . a broader wrong than [an] antitrust violation."[50] It stated that the "policy of the patent misuse doctrine is 'to prevent a patentee from using the patent to obtain market benefit beyond that which inures in the statutory patent right.'" Thus, in order for misuse to occur, one must "impermissibly broaden[ ] the scope of the patent grant with anticompetitive effect."

In *Princo Corp. v. ITC*, 616 F.3d 1318 (Fed. Cir. 2010)131 S. Ct. 2480 (2011), the Federal Circuit held that an alleged agreement among two joint venture partners not to license a patent for inchoate technology did not constitute patent misuse. Philips and Sony held patents used in the development of rewritable compact disc (CD) technology which they pooled and jointly licensed to manufacturers. In the course of developing this technology the firms encountered a particular problem of encoding position information on a disc so that the writer would put new data in the correct place. Philips developed an analog solution to this problem, covered by the "Raaymakers" patents, while Sony developed a digital solution covered by the "Lagadec" patent. The Lagadec system was found to be unstable and prone to error, so the two firms agreed to employ the Raaymakers technology, which they then incorporated into standards recorded in the "Orange Book" used for achieving compatibility in the manufacturing of devices for reading and writing CDs. While the Orange Book standards did not employ the Lagadec digital approach, one claim of the Lagadec patent conflicted with, and thus "blocked" at least one Orange Book standard; as a result, a license to use the Lagadec patent had to be incorporated into the Orange Book package.

The court properly rejected Princo's tying-like claim that including the Lagadec patent in the package license agreement constituted patent misuse. Princo claimed that it was required to take unwanted patents in the Philips/Sony package as a

---

[49] *See, e.g., Windsurfing Intl. v. AMF*, 782 F.2d 995, 1001–1009 & n.2 (Fed. Cir. 1986) ("To sustain a misuse defense involving a licensing arrangement not held to have been per se anticompetitive by the Supreme Court, a factual determination must reveal that the overall effect of the license tends to restrain competition unlawfully in an appropriately defined relevant market."). *See also Virginia Panel Corp. v. Mac Panel Co.*, 133 F.3d 860, 868 (Fed. Cir. 1997) (misuse occurs when patent holder has "impermissibly broadened the physical or temporal scope of the patent grant with anticompetitive effect"); *Mallinckrodt v. Medipart, Inc.*, 976 F.2d 700, 703–704, 708 (Fed. Cir. 1992) (suggesting that misuse largely tracks antitrust although it might occasionally reach more broadly).

[50] *Monsanto Co. v. Scruggs*, 459 F.3d 1328, 1339 (Fed. Cir. 2006). *See also Monsanto Co. v. McFarling*, 363 F.3d 1336, 1341 (Fed. Cir. 2004) (not misuse for developer of patented genetically modified seed to prevent farmers from planting second generation seeds).

condition of getting the patent that it wanted.[51] As a general proposition, however, blocking patents must be licensed together. Otherwise the licensee will not be able to practice one without infringing the other. As a result, if the Lagadec patent did indeed block other patents contained in the Orange Book package, then it had to be included in the package license.[52]

The Federal Circuit panel had unanimously agreed that tying the Lagadec patent to the Orange Book package was not misuse, given that the patents in question were "blocking." If one patent cannot be used without another, then it cannot be unlawful to license them together. However, the initial three-judge panel had found misuse in one of Princo's allegations — namely, that Philips and Sony had agreed with each other to suppress the Lagadec digital technology and use license provisions that forbad licensees or others to develop competing digital technology that relied on the Lagadec method. The claim was that Sony and Philips, having licensed analog technology for production, but also having a patent on digital technology, agreed with each other that they would (1) not use the digital technology in their license package, and (2) not permit any other firm to develop digital technology that infringed the Lagadec patent claims.

In vacating the panel's decision the Federal Circuit en banc assumed that such an agreement "to suppress the technology embodied in Sony's Lagadec patent" existed, but concluded that this was "not the type of conduct that could give rise to the defense of patent misuse." It concluded that the provision in § 271(d) stating that it is not misuse to refuse to license a patent extended to concerted as well as unilateral refusals to license. But is that conclusion justified, particularly in light of the very strong distinction that antitrust policy makes between unilateral and concerted refusals to deal? The Federal Circuit made no distinction between naked and ancillary refusals. Given the Supreme Court's view in *Illinois Tool Works* that an important purpose of the 1988 Patent Misuse Reform Act was to bring misuse and antitrust more closely in alignment with one another, this would suggest continued harsher treatment for concerted refusals than for unilateral refusals.

The en banc court concluded that, even if there had been a concerted refusal to license a patent, the challenger could not pursue it because the technology covered by the patent was inchoate and it would be highly speculative to conclude that it would ever have turned into anything. The majority stated:

> What Princo had to demonstrate was that there was a "reasonable probability" that the Lagadec technology, if available for licensing, would have matured into a competitive force in the storage technology market. It was not enough that there was some speculative possibility that Lagadec could have overcome the barriers to its technical feasibility and commercial success and become the basis for competing disc technology. The Commission found that Princo failed to show that the Lagadec technology had technical or commercial prospects that could enable it to compete with the Orange Book technology. Those findings wholly undermine Princo's con-

---

[51] On why requiring purchasers to take an unwanted tied product is not anticompetitive, see ¶ 1724b.

[52] *See* 563 F.3d 1301 (Fed. Cir. 2009).

tention that this is a case in which the patents in suit have been used as part of an overall horizontal agreement with the effect of keeping a viable competitor out of the relevant market.

But doesn't that confuse the antitrust standard with the misuse standard, which emanates from patent policy rather than antitrust policy? Shouldn't patent policy be concerned with a restraint that might prevent competition down the road, even if antitrust law's requirements of harm and causation cannot be met? In any event, if the Lagadec patent had no commercial "prospects," then an agreement to restrain the development of the technology it described would not have been necessary. Further, such an agreement has no obvious utility except to forestall the development of as yet nascent technology by others. *See* Christina Bohannan & Herbert Hovenkamp, *Concerted Refusals to License Intellectual Property Rights*, 1 Harv. Bus. L. Rev. Online 21 (2011), *available at* http://papers.ssrn.com/sol3/papers.cfm?abstract_id=1710531.

> On the role of tying and misuse doctrine in information technologies, particularly in networked industries, see Christina Bohannan & Herbert Hovenkamp, Creation Without Restraint: Promoting Liberty and Rivalry in Innovation, ch. 2 (New York: Oxford Univ. Press, 2012).

[5] Full Line Forcing, Full System Contracts, and Franchise Arrangements

When a supplier requires a dealer to purchase a complete line of related products, though less is desired, the vertical arrangement is known as full line forcing. Although the dealer is not generally explicitly forbidden from stocking the products of the supplier's competitors, the practical effect of the full system contract may inhibit the dealer from carrying competing lines of merchandise. Thus the consequences of full line forcing may be to foreclose the market to competitors or potential competitors of the seller that insists on the full system contract, and to deny the dealer freedom to choose from whom it will purchase its products and parts. The competitive effect, therefore, may be similar to the typical tying arrangement and exclusive dealing restriction.

The same efficiency justifications discussed previously in this chapter have application to full line contracts. Economies may be achieved in production, distribution, and marketing of certain products jointly, rather than individually. Moreover, cost economies may enable the manufacturer and supplier to charge less for the full line of products than the sum of individually priced products. In addition, the supplier may believe that in order to maintain its brand image and "good will" reputation it is necessary that its dealers carry its full line of products, particularly its components or parts.

While full line forcing is a form of tying arrangement, a strict per se analysis has generally not been applied. Several reasons suggest this conclusion. In addition to the emerging efficiency analysis, which permits business justification for the tie-in to be explored, it is not always clear whether separate products are involved, as is required under *Times-Picayune* and *Fortner.* Products must be defined and distinguished as separate items, rather than merely the aggregation of one or a whole system or unit of components. In the franchise context the "two product" requirement was discussed in *Siegel v. Chicken Delight, Inc.*, 448 F.2d 43 (9th Cir. 1971), *cert. denied*, 405 U.S. 955 (1972), and *Principe v. McDonald's Corp.*, 631 F.2d 303 (4th Cir. 1980), with differing results. Consider the following courts' resolution of the "two product" problem.

UNITED STATES v. JERROLD ELECTRONICS CORP.
187 F. Supp. 545 (E.D. Pa. 1960), *aff'd per curiam*, 365 U.S. 567 (1961)

JUDGE VAN DUSEN.

[Defendant sold television antenna systems and in doing so refused to sell separately the components or individual items of the system. The complete system and components were sold only on the condition that the purchaser also enter into a service contract with Jerrold.]

The difficult question raised by the defendants is whether this should be treated as a case of tying the sale of one product to the sale of another product or merely as the sale of a single product. It is apparent that, as a general rule, a manufacturer cannot be forced to deal in the minimum product that could be sold or is usually sold. On the other hand, it is equally clear that one cannot circumvent the anti-trust laws simply by claiming that he is selling a single product. The facts must be examined to ascertain whether or not there are legitimate reasons for selling normally separate items in a combined form to dispel any inferences that it is really a disguised tie-in.

There are several facts presented in this record which tend to show that a community television antenna system cannot properly be characterized as a single product. Others who entered the community antenna field offered all of the equipment necessary for a complete system, but none of them sold their gear exclusively as a single package as did Jerrold. The record also establishes that the number of pieces in each system varied considerably so that hardly any two versions of the alleged product were the same. Furthermore, the customer was charged for each item of equipment and not a lump sum for the total system. Finally, while Jerrold had cable and antennas to sell which were manufactured by other concerns, it only required that the electronic equipment in the system be bought from it.

In rebuttal, it must first be noted that the attitude of other manufacturers, while relevant, is hardly conclusive. Equally significant is the fact that the record indicates that some customers were interested in contracting for an installed system and not in building their own. Secondly, it was the job the system was designed to accomplish which dictated that each system be "custom made" in the sense that there were variations in the type and amount of equipment in each system. This, in turn, explains determining cost on a piece by piece, rather than a lump sum, basis. Finally, while the non-electronic equipment could be ordered from other sources and the system would be useless without the antenna and connecting cable, it is generally agreed that the electronic equipment is the most vital element in the system and Jerrold was still in charge of assembling all of the equipment into a functioning system.

Balancing these considerations only, the defendants' position would seem to be highly questionable. The several deviations from the normal situation one would expect to find become particularly suspect when viewed in the context of Jerrold's market leverage resulting from its highly regarded head end equipment. There is a further factor, however, which, in the court's opinion, makes Jerrold's decision to sell only full systems reasonable. There was a sound business reason for Jerrold to adopt this policy. Jerrold's decision was intimately associated with its belief that a service contract was essential. This court has already determined that, in view of the condition of Jerrold, the equipment, and the potential customers, the defendants' policy of insisting on a service contract was reasonable at its inception. Jerrold could not render the service it promised and deemed necessary if the customer could purchase any kind of equipment he desired. The limited knowledge and instability of equipment made specifications an impractical, if not impossible, alternative. Furthermore, Jerrold's policy could not have been carried out if separate items of its equipment were made available to existing systems or any other customer because the demand was so great that this equipment would find its way to a new system. Thus, the court concludes that Jerrold's policy of full system sales was a necessary adjunct to its policy of compulsory service and was reasonably regarded as a product as long as the conditions which dictated the use of the service contract continued to exist. As the circumstances changed and the need for compulsory service contracts disappeared, the economic reasons for exclusively selling complete systems were eliminated. Absent these economic reasons, the court feels that a full system was not an appropriate sales unit. The defendants have the burden not only of establishing the initial existence of the facts necessary to support their claim but also their continuing existence in view of the fact that it is not disputed that the conditions did change. The defendants have not satisfied this latter burden. It has already been noted that on the present record it would be a matter of speculation to determine how long the conditions justifying Jerrold's policy remained in effect.

The defendants also assert a further justification for its policy insofar as it applied to systems using a large quantity of non-Jerrold equipment. Jerrold spent considerable time and effort in developing its head end equipment. As a result, its equipment was considered the best available and an asset to any system, since it affected the quality of the initial signal which would be transmitted through the rest of the system. The head-end equipment, while intricate, did not represent a large portion of the investment in a system because only a few items were involved. The real profit in a system came from the sale of the amplifiers, since a large number were involved. Jerrold felt that other companies who had not invested time and money into the development of satisfactory head-end equipment sought to take advantage of it by competing with it as to the amplifiers, but relying on Jerrold's head end equipment to make the system successful. [It] resented these other companies "picking our brains" and competing for the real source of profit. Jerrold, therefore, felt justified in recovering its substantial investment in the development of superior head end equipment by using it to preserve for itself a share of the more lucrative market for amplifiers. While the court is sympathetic with Jerrold's predicament, it does not feel that it provides sufficient justification for the use of a tying arrangement. If the demand for Jerrold's equipment was so great, it could recover its investment by raising its prices. Admittedly, the return would not be as great, but it provides sufficient protection to serve as a more reasonable and less restrictive alternative to a tying arrangement.

The court concludes that the defendants' policy of selling full systems only was lawful at its inception but constituted a violation of § 1 of the Sherman Act and § 3 of the Clayton Act during part of the time it was in effect.

PROBLEM 5.7

Sterling Electric, Inc. manufactures electric motors and replacement parts for the motors. Easy Startup, Inc. is a distributor of Sterling brand electric motors and parts.

Easy Startup has been a Sterling distributor for several years but it also carries other brands of electric motors and parts. From 1985 through 1989, Easy Startup was the largest distributor of Sterling parts but only fifth nationally in Sterling electric motors. Easy Startup purchased $100,000 of Sterling electric motors in 1985–1987, $75,000 in 1987–1988, and $110,000 in 1989. Its corresponding purchases of parts were larger: $300,000 for 1985–1987 and $350,000 for 1987–1989. During this period of time Sterling had annual sales over $10 million.

In 1987, Sterling instituted a new distribution program. It required each of its nonexclusive distributors, like Easy Startup, to buy a minimum amount of its electric motors if the distributors wanted to continue to sell the Sterling parts. Under the contract with its distributors, Sterling had the right to terminate the distributors for failure to buy the agreed minimum quantities of electric motors.

Sterling warned Easy Startup that if it did not purchase more of the Sterling electric motors, it risked termination as a Sterling distributor. Thereafter in 1989 Easy Startup, fearing the loss of access to Sterling motors, steered its customers toward the Sterling electric motors even though Easy Startup normally would have recommended other brands of motors. As a result, Sterling motor sales increased. Nevertheless, in late 1989, Sterling terminated Easy Startup as a parts and motor distributor because Easy Startup had not purchased (and sold) a sufficient number of the electric motors.

Easy Startup decides to sue Sterling for the termination. Sterling concedes that it has 100% dominance in the parts market for its own electric motors; that is, Sterling's parts cannot be used on any other brands of electric motors and no other manufacturer makes parts compatible with and usable in the Sterling electric motor. Sterling, however, has only 12% market share in the market for electric motors parts and 5% market share in the market for electric motors. Other potential evidence suggests that there are economic barriers to entry into the market for parts compatible with Sterling motors because the demand for Sterling parts will accommodate only one manufacturer. Further evidence indicates that a large number of Sterling distributors had entered into the same minimum quantities requirements contract as did Easy Startup.

    1. As counsel for Easy Startup, what antitrust arguments would you advance to show that there was a per se or rule of reason violation of section 1 of the Sherman Act and section 3 of the Clayton Act?

2. As counsel for defendant Sterling, what counter-arguments would you raise that no antitrust violations are present? *See Parts & Elec. Motors, Inc. v. Sterling Elec., Inc.*, 826 F.2d 712 (7th Cir. 1987).

NOTE

1. In *Smith Mach. Co. v. Hesston Corp.*, 878 F.2d 1290 (10th Cir. 1989), the court held that a per se analysis was inappropriate for a supplier's requirement that a farm equipment retailer wanting to sell the supplier's balers and windrowers also must sell its tractors. The court characterized this requirement as a nonprice vertical restraint that was subject to a rule of reason analysis. Under the reasonableness test, the court found the full line forcing lawful because the retailer was not prohibited from carrying competing equipment lines and the effect was that the forcing actually enhanced interbrand competition by making the manufacturer's tractor available for sale. No output reduction would occur, the court concluded, and at worst there would be only a substitution of one tractor for another. For the plaintiff to establish a violation, it would have to show that the forcing restricted the marketing of the competitor's products by limiting competition in the consumer market. "[F]oreclosure of choice to an ultimate consumer appears to be the principal key to a tie that is illegal per se." *Id.* at 1297.

2. Suppose a manufacturer requires a dealer to carry two complementary products, but that customers are free to take either product separately. Unlawful tying? In *Roy B. Taylor Sales, Inc. v. Hollymatic Corp.*, 28 F.3d 1379 (5th Cir. 1994), the plaintiff dealer in restaurant equipment was required to stock the defendant's hamburger patty paper as a condition of carrying its hamburger patty machines. But the same condition was not imposed upon the plaintiff's customers: *they* were free to purchase the machine with or without the paper. If the vice of the tying arrangement is foreclosure of alternate makers of patty paper, then there was no foreclosure, was there? Is there any other way such an arrangement could injure competition? The *Roy B. Taylor* arrangement is a form of full line forcing and illustrates why the practice rarely excludes anyone. The manufacturer wants the dealer to carry the full line, be it automobiles, kitchen appliances, or clothing. But retail customers get to pick and choose and take only what they want.

PROBLEM 5.8

Mozart is an independent auto parts distributor and manufacturer. Mercedes-Benz is an automobile and automotive parts manufacturer. Mercedes-Benz operates in the United States through 400 franchised dealerships. Each dealer must enter a franchise contract which, in part, states:

> Dealer shall neither sell or offer to sell for use in connection with Mercedes-Benz cars nor use in the repair or servicing of Mercedes-Benz passenger cars any parts other than genuine Mercedes-Benz parts or parts expressly approved by the U.S. distributor if such parts are necessary to the mechanical operation of such passenger cars.

Mozart contends that the above contract is a tying arrangement that is per se unlawful because Mercedes-Benz is tying the Mercedes parts to the passenger car and its trademark, and that Mercedes-Benz and the dealers have conspired to boycott independent replacement parts distributors.

1. (a) Consider whether a quality control and goodwill defense by Mercedes-Benz would be a valid business justification for the exclusive dealing and tying contracts with the dealers.

(b) Are less restrictive alternatives available to protect Mercedes-Benz's reputation? If there are, does this fact make the contractual arrangement a violation of the Sherman and Clayton Acts?

2. Consider also whether Mozart has standing to raise the antitrust issues. *See Mozart Co. v. Mercedes-Benz of N. Am., Inc.*, 833 F.2d 1342 (9th Cir. 1987).

[6] The Unwanted Tied Product

The general theory of tying is that it forecloses rivals in the tied product market who would like to compete for the defendant's trade in that product. For example, the plaintiff in *JeffersonParish* was a rival anesthesiologist excluded by the tie, and the plaintiffs in *Kodak* were rival service firms who wanted to maintain Kodak's photocopiers. But what if the defendant ties something that buyers do not want at all, from anyone? In that case no one has been foreclosed by the tie. For example, suppose that in an effort to unload my spoiling peaches, I require that all purchasers of my apples take a like number of peaches. Presumably there is no foreclosure. The customer's injury is not that he or she is denied the opportunity to purchase rotten peaches from a different vendor, but rather that the customer does not want the peaches at all! How much more could I charge for my apples if I threw in the spoiling peaches? If the answer is zero, wouldn't I be better off simply throwing the peaches away? See *Bafus/Dudley v. Aspen Realty, Inc.*, 2008-1 Trade Cas. 76012, 2007 U.S. Dist. LEXIS 88228, 2008 U.S. Dist. LEXIS 23166 (D. Idaho Mar. 24, 2008), *subsequent appeal at Blough v. Holland Realty, Inc.*, 574 F.3d 1084 (9th Cir. 2009), which dismissed an antitrust claim that the defendant real estate developer tied a brokerage fee for an unbuilt house to lots it was selling when the plaintiffs did not want a house at all. See also *Blough v. Holland Realty, Inc.*, 574 F.3d 1084 (9th Cir. 2009), which rejected a claim that buyers of undeveloped residential lots were required to pay commissions for services that they did not want.

BRANTLEY v. NBC UNIVERSAL, INC.
675 F.3d 1192 (9th Cir. 2012)

Iᴋᴜᴛᴀ, Cɪʀᴄᴜɪᴛ Jᴜᴅɢᴇ:

Plaintiffs allege that Programmers' practice of selling multi-channel cable packages violates Section 1 of the Sherman Act, 15 U.S.C. § 1. In essence, plaintiffs seek to compel programmers and distributors of television programming to sell each cable channel separately, thereby permitting plaintiffs to purchase only those channels that they wish to purchase, rather than paying for multi-channel packages, as occurs under current market practice. Plaintiffs appeal the dismissal with prejudice of their complaint for failure to state a claim. We affirm.

The television programming industry can be divided into upstream and down-stream markets. In the upstream market, programmers such as NBC Universal and Fox Entertainment Group own television programs (such as "Law and Order") and television channels (such as NBC's Bravo and MSNBC, and Fox Entertainment Group's Fox News Channel and FX) and sell them wholesale to distributors. In the downstream retail market, distributors such as Time Warner and Echostar sell the programming channels to consumers.

According to plaintiffs' third amended complaint, Programmers have two categories of programming channels: "must-have" channels with high demand and a large number of viewers, and a group of less desirable, low-demand channels with low viewership. Plaintiffs allege that "[e]ach programmer defendant, because of its full or partial ownership of a broadcast channel and its ownership or control of multiple important cable channels, has a high degree of market power vis-a-vis all distributors," and that Programmers exploit this market power by requiring distributors, "as a condition to purchasing each programmer's broadcast channel and its 'must have' cable channels," to "also acquire and resell to consumers all the rest of the cable channels owned or controlled by each programmer" and "agree they will not offer unbundled [i.e., individual] cable channels to consumers." "As a consequence," plaintiffs contend, "distributors can offer consumers only prepackaged tiers of cable channels which consist of each programmer's entire offering of channels." . . .

The district court dismissed plaintiffs' first amended complaint without prejudice on the ground that plaintiffs failed to show that their alleged injuries were caused by an injury to competition. In their second amended complaint, plaintiffs alleged that Programmers' practice of selling packaged cable channels foreclosed independent programmers from entering and competing in the upstream market for programming channels. The district court subsequently denied defendants' motion to dismiss, holding that plaintiffs had adequately pleaded injury to competition.

After preliminary discovery efforts on the question whether the Programmers' practices had excluded independent programmers from the upstream market, the plaintiffs decided to abandon this approach.[53] Pursuant to a stipulation among the parties, plaintiffs filed their third amended complaint, which deleted all allegations that the Programmers and Distributors' contractual practices foreclosed independent programmers from participating in the upstream market, along with a motion requesting the court to rule that plaintiffs did not have to allege foreclosure in the upstream market in order to defeat a motion to dismiss . . . . The district court entered an order on October 15, 2009 granting Programmers and Distributors' motion to dismiss the third amended complaint with prejudice because plaintiffs failed to allege any cognizable injury to competition. The district court also denied plaintiffs' motion to rule on the question whether allegations of foreclosed competition are required to state a Section 1 claim. Plaintiffs timely appeal. . . .

---

[53] [FN 5] Programmers and Distributors claim that plaintiffs decided to discontinue discovery after preliminary review showed there was no evidence to support their claim that the packaging of channels foreclosed competition in the upstream market.

The parties do not dispute that the rule of reason applies in this case, and the pleading requirements for a rule of reason case therefore apply.[54]

. . . In order to plead injury to competition . . . sufficiently to withstand a motion to dismiss, "a section one claimant may not merely recite the bare legal conclusion that competition has been restrained unreasonably."*Les Shockley Racing, Inc. v. Nat'l Hot Rod Ass'n*, 884 F.2d 504, 507–08 (9th Cir.1989). "Rather, a claimant must, at a minimum, sketch the outline of [the injury to competition] with allegations of supporting factual detail." Such allegations must "raise a reasonable expectation that discovery will reveal evidence of" an injury to competition. *Bell Atl. Corp. v. Twombly*, 550 U.S. 544, 556 (2007). . . .

Courts have also concluded that agreements between firms operating at different levels of a given product market (referred to as "vertical agreements"), such as agreements between a supplier and a distributor, may or may not cause an injury to competition. Vertical agreements that foreclose competitors from entering or competing in a market can injure competition by reducing the competitive threat those competitors would pose. Some types of vertical agreements can also injure competition by facilitating horizontal collusion. . . .

The complaint in this case focuses on a type of vertical agreement that creates a restraint known as "tying." Tying is defined as an arrangement where a supplier agrees to sell a buyer a product (the tying product), but "only on the condition that the buyer also purchases a different (or tied) product . . . ."*N. Pac. Ry. Co. v. United States*, 356 U.S. 1, 5, 78 S. Ct. 514, 2 L. Ed. 2d 545 (1958). The potential injury to competition threatened by this practice is that the tying arrangement will either "harm existing competitors or create barriers to entry of new competitors in the market for the tied product,"*Jefferson Parish Hosp. Dist. No. 2 v. Hyde*, 466 U.S. 2, 14 (1984); *Cascade*, 515 F.3d at 912, or will "force buyers into giving up the purchase of substitutes for the tied product,"*United States v. Loew's*, 371 U.S. 38, 45 (1962), *abrogated in part on other grounds by Ill. Tool Works*, 547 U.S. 28.

But courts distinguish between tying arrangements in which a company exploits its market power by attempting "to impose restraints on competition in the market for a tied product" (which may threaten an injury to competition) and arrangements that let a company exploit its market power "by merely enhancing the price of the tying product" (which does not). *Jefferson Parish*, 466 U.S. at 14. . . .

. . . . As the Supreme Court has noted, "when a purchaser is 'forced' to buy a product he would not have otherwise bought even from another seller in the tied product market, there can be no adverse impact on competition because no portion of the market which would otherwise have been available to other sellers has been

---

[54] [FN 7] In the case of "tying" claims, a per se rule is applied in some circumstances. A tying arrangement will constitute a per se violation of the Sherman Act if the plaintiff proves "(1) that the defendant tied together the sale of two distinct products or services; (2) that the defendant possesses enough economic power in the tying product market to coerce its customers into purchasing the tied product; and (3) that the tying arrangement affects a not insubstantial volume of commerce in the tied product market."*Cascade Health Solutions v. PeaceHealth*, 515 F.3d 883, 913 (9th Cir. 2008) (quoting *Paladin Assocs., Inc. v. Mont. Power Co.*, 328 F.3d 1145, 1159 (9th Cir. 2003)) (internal quotation marks omitted). The parties have disclaimed any contention that the tying practices in this case are per se antitrust violations.

foreclosed."*Jefferson Parish*, 466 U.S. at 16 . . . .

Therefore, a plaintiff bringing a rule of reason tying case cannot succeed . . . merely by alleging the existence of a tying arrangement, because such an arrangement is consistent with pro-competitive behavior. . . .

There is no dispute that the complaint alleges the existence of a tying arrangement. In fact, according to the plaintiffs' complaint, the Programmer-Distributor agreements at issue consist of two separate tying arrangements. First, in the upstream market, each Programmer requires each Distributor that wishes to purchase that Programmer's high-demand channels (the tying product) to purchase all of that Programmer's low-demand channels (the tied product) as well.[55] Second, in the downstream market, Distributors sell consumers cable channels only in packages consisting of each Programmer's entire offering of channels. Thus, consumers, like Distributors, are allegedly required to purchase each Programmer's low-demand channels, which they do not want (the tied product), in order to gain access to that Programmer's high-demand channels, which they do want (the tying product).

But as explained above, tying arrangements, without more, do not necessarily threaten an injury to competition. Therefore, the complaint's allegations regarding the two separate tying arrangements do not, by themselves, constitute a sufficient allegation of injury to competition. Rather, plaintiffs must also allege facts showing that an injury to competition flows from these tying arrangements. We conclude that such allegations are not present in the complaint.

First, it is clear that the complaint does not allege the types of injuries to competition that are typically alleged to flow from tying arrangements. The complaint does not allege that Programmers' practice of selling "must-have" and low-demand channels in packages excludes other sellers of low-demand channels from the market, or that this practice raises barriers to entry into the programming market.[56] Nor do the plaintiffs allege that the tying arrangement here causes consumers to forego the purchase of substitutes for the tied product. *Loew's*, 371 U.S. at 45, 83 S. Ct. 97. Nothing in the complaint indicates that the arrangement between the Programmers and Distributors forces Distributors or consumers to forego the purchase of alternative low-demand channels. Indeed, Plaintiffs disavow any intent to allege that the practices engaged in by Programmers and Distributors foreclosed rivals from entering or participating in the upstream or downstream markets. *Cf. Jefferson Parish*, 466 U.S. at 14, 104 S. Ct. 1551; *Cascade*, 515 F.3d at 912 ("Tying arrangements are forbidden on the theory that, if the seller has market power over the tying product, the seller can leverage this market power through tying arrangements to exclude other sellers of the tied product."). Nor does the complaint allege that the tying arrangements pose a threat to competition because they facilitate horizontal collusion.

---

[55] [FN 8] We assume for purposes of this opinion, without deciding, that high-demand and low-demand channels are actually separate products, and do not address the question whether it is more apt to view each Programmer's block of channels as a single product, which would preclude any argument that there was an illegal tying arrangement.

[56] [FN 9] Thus, there is effectively "zero foreclosure" of competitors.

Instead of identifying such standard-issue threats to competition, the complaint alleges that the injury to competition stems from Programmers' requirement that channels must be sold to consumers in packages. According to the complaint, the required sale of multi-channel packages harms consumers by (1) limiting the manner in which Distributors compete with one another in that Distributors are unable to offer a la carte programming, which results in (2) reducing consumer choice, and (3) increasing prices. These assertions do not sufficiently allege an injury to competition for purposes of stating a Section 1 claim. First, because Section 1 does not proscribe all contracts that limit the freedom of the contracting parties, a statement that parties have entered into a contract that limits some freedom of action (in this case, by circumscribing the distributors' ability to offer smaller packages or channels on an unbundled basis) is not sufficient to allege an injury to competition.[57]

Second, allegations that an agreement has the effect of reducing consumers' choices or increasing prices to consumers does not sufficiently allege an injury to competition. Both effects are fully consistent with a free, competitive market. . . .

Plaintiffs disagree, and argue that under the rule in *Loew's*, 371 U.S. 38, and *Ross v. Bank of America, N.A.* (USA), 524 F.3d 217 (2d Cir. 2008), they have sufficiently alleged an injury to competition by alleging that the agreements have the effect of reducing choice and increasing prices. This argument is unavailing. In *Loew's*, the United States brought antitrust actions against six major film distributors, alleging that the defendants had conditioned the license or sale of one or more feature films upon the acceptance by television stations of a package or block containing one or more unwanted or inferior films. The Court observed that the restraint injured competition because the movie studios' block booking forced the television stations to forego purchases of movies from other distributors. The relevant injury in *Loew's* was to competition, not to the ultimate consumers, because the challenged practice forced television stations to forego the purchase of other movies, and therefore created barriers to entry for competing movie owners. *Cf. Jefferson Parish*, 466 U.S. at 14. Here, Plaintiffs have not alleged that the contracts between Programmers and Distributors forced either Distributors or consumers to forego the purchase of other low-demand channels (a result analogous to the competitive injury in *Loew's*), but only that consumers could not purchase programs a la carte and they did not want all of the channels they were required to buy from Distributors. "[C]ompelling the purchase of unwanted products" is not itself an injury to competition. We have explained why this is so:

> In order to obtain desired product A, let us suppose, the defendant's customer is forced to take product B, which it does not want, cannot use, and would not have purchased from anyone. This is typically the equivalent of a higher price for product A. From the viewpoint of the defendant seller, its revenue on product A consists of the A price plus the excess of the B price over B's cost to the seller. From the viewpoint of the customer, the

---

[57] [FN 10] A rule to the contrary could cast doubt on whether musicians would be free to sell their hit singles only as a part of a full album, or writers to sell a collection of short stories. Indeed, such a rule would call into question whether Programmers and Distributors could sell cable channels at all, since such channels are themselves packages of separate television programs.

cost of obtaining the desired product A is the nominal A price plus the excess of the B price over its salvage value. This has nothing to do with gaining power in the B market or upsetting competition there.

Blough, 574 F.3d at 1089–90 (quoting IX Phillip E. Areeda & Herbert Hovenkamp, *Antitrust Law* ¶ 1724b, at 270 (2004 & Supp. 2009)); *see also Jefferson Parish*, 466 U.S. at 14 ("When the seller's power is just used to maximize its return in the tying product market, where presumably its product enjoys some justifiable advantage over its competitors, the competitive ideal of the Sherman Act is not necessarily compromised."). Nor does plaintiffs' citation to Ross support their argument; that case involved allegations of horizontal collusion, which has not been alleged by plaintiffs in this case, and pertained to standing, not injury to competition.

Plaintiffs also contend that because most or all Programmers and Distributors engage in the challenged practice, we should hold that in the aggregate, the practice constitutes an injury to competition. We cannot rule out the possibility that competition could be injured or reduced due to a widely applied practice that harms consumers. *See Leegin*, 551 U.S. at 897 (indicating that vertical restraints, such as resale price maintenance, "should be subject to more careful scrutiny" if the practice is adopted by many competitors). But the plaintiffs here have not alleged in their complaint how competition (rather than consumers) is injured by the widespread practice of packaging low- and high-demand channels. The complaint did not allege that Programmers' sale of cable channels in packages has any effect on other programmers' efforts to produce competitive programming channels or on Distributors' competition as to cost and quality of service. Nor is there any allegation that any programmer's decision to offer its channels only in packages constrained other programmers from offering their channels individually if that practice was competitively advantageous. In sum, the complaint does not include any allegation of injury to competition, as opposed to injuries to the plaintiffs.

Injury to competition must be alleged to state a violation of Sherman Act § 1. Kendall, 518 F.3d at 1047. Plaintiffs' complaint does not allege facts that "raise a reasonable expectation that discovery will reveal evidence of" injury to competition. *Twombly*, 550 U.S. at 566, 127 S. Ct. 1955. Thus, plaintiffs' complaint did not allege facts that, taken as true, "state a claim to relief that is plausible on its face." *Id.* at 570, 127 S. Ct. 1955. Dismissal was proper.

Affirmed.

NOTE AND QUESTIONS

Why did the plaintiffs plead their tying case only under the rule of reason? Foreclosure of competitors is not an articulated requirement of the per se tying rule? Does the Ninth Circuit's decision effectively require foreclosure in all tying cases, even those brought under the per se rule?

Chapter 6

MONOPOLY STRUCTURE, POWER, AND CONDUCT

INTRODUCTION

"Market power" is the ability of a firm to obtain higher profits by reducing output and selling at a higher price. "Monopolization," the central concern of this chapter, is illegal conduct by which a single firm seeks either to obtain or to retain market power.

I THE PROBLEM OF MONOPOLY

UNITED STATES v. AMERICAN CAN CO.
230 F. 859 (D. Md. 1916), *appeal dismissed*, 256 U.S. 706 (1921)

JUDGE ROSE.

The United States, hereinafter called the "government," brings this proceeding under the fourth section of the Anti-Trust Act of July 2, 1890. It says that the American Can Company, a New Jersey corporation, was formed and has since been maintained in violation of the first and second sections of that statute. [The United States sought dissolution of the company.] . . . The government says the defendant, by its size, its wealth, and its power, exerts a great influence upon the entire trade in cans, and that this influence, in some very important respects . . . is so great that it may, without straining words, be said to dominate the market.

The defendant answers its size is not a crime. The government replies, in substance: "True, provided such size is the result of natural and legitimate growth, but not when it is the outcome of unlawful means used for the very purpose of securing a control of the market. In the latter case, so long as the control continues, the illegal purpose is still in process of execution, and, if nothing short of dissolving the defendant into a number of smaller companies will completely emancipate the trade, the court must decree such dissolution."

. . . .

. . . It is quite possible that in an industry like can making, as it was carried on in the closing years of the last century by more than 100 separate concerns, no union, however desirable from the standpoint of either the can makers or the public, could have been brought about except by the efforts of some individuals who thought they could make a quick and large profit for themselves by uniting the various plants under one management, no matter what the immediate or even the ultimate results of such union might prove to be. If that be so, those who think the result desirable will hold that promoters' profits and the extravagant sums required to induce so many independent manufacturers to sell out were a part of the inevitable price of achieving a useful purpose. Unfortunately, under such circumstances the cost of getting rid of competition sometimes proves almost as great as that of letting it alone. To pass from the general to the particular: The men who really brought about the organization of the defendant do not appear to have been more than five in number, and only one of them, Edwin Norton, was a can maker. He did practically all the work of persuading, inducing, or coercing the can makers to sell out. He and his brothers had been for a number of years the largest and doubtless the most generally known manufacturers of cans in the country, as he was certainly one of the most active and aggressive. The factories of his firm had probably the best equipment of labor saving machinery. Certainly in this respect they were surpassed by none. . . . The idea of forming a can combine seems to have occurred to him more than once, although the record appears to indicate that the scheme which was actually carried through originated, not with him, but with the defendant William H. Moore and his partner and brother, the defendant J. Hobart Moore. . . .

The record shows that in the latter part of 1899 Norton was commissioned by the Moores to get options on can-making plants, and then, or later, on plants for making can-making machinery, as well. He set about this mission promptly, and apparently had little difficulty in getting many of the desired options. . . .

. . . .

How were so large a proportion of the can makers induced to sell? Fear of what would happen to them, if they did not, unquestionably had more or less influence with a good many of them. There is some testimony that Norton told some of them that if they did not sell out they would be put out. The record does not affirmatively show that such threats were frequently made. They were not required. Apart from anything he said, apprehension was quite general that the only choice was between going out or being driven out. The country was at that time familiar with stories of the fate of those who in other lines of business had refused liberal offers from combinations previously formed. The records of the so-called Anti-Trust cases have since shown that some of these tales were not without foundation in fact. What was most feared was that a can maker who did not go into the combine would have difficulty in getting tin plate, the raw material of his business. The concern to which the defendant the American Steel & Tin Plate Company succeeded, and which, together with that successor, will be called the "Tin Plate Company," had been then recently organized. Prominent among those who officiated at its birth were the Moore Bros., Reid, and Leeds. Norton and others spoke as if the relations between the proposed can company and the new Tin Plate Company would be very close. . . .

. . . .

It is to be borne in mind that, for reasons already stated, few of the can makers were, or could have supposed themselves to have been, even moderately equipped to carry on a competitive struggle with a rival possessed of many times their capital. Some of them who were financially stronger than most of the others were elderly men, or were in poor health, or for other reasons were loath to venture upon so perilous a warfare. . . .

. . . .

As a rule, the prices paid were liberal, not only to the verge of extravagance, but in cases almost beyond the limits of prodigality. If Norton sometimes showed the can makers that there was steel in his scabbard, his hands always dropped gold. The record does not disclose a single case in which the price named in the option did not exceed the value of all the tangible property transferred. The amounts paid appear to have ranged all the way from 1 1/2 to 25 times the sum which would have sufficed to have replaced the property sold with brand new articles of the same kind. Before agreeing on the figures to be inserted in an option, Norton does not appear to have taken the trouble either to make, or to cause to be made, any inspection or appraisement of the plant to be transferred. Under such circumstances, the ratio between the real value and the price named depended more upon the nerve or the impudence of the seller, than upon any estimate of his property's probable worth to the new combination.

. . . .

With very few exceptions, all the options contained a clause which bound the sellers, in the event that it was accepted, not to engage for 15 years in can making within 3,000 miles of Chicago. Where the seller was a corporation, its principal officers personally bound themselves by like covenants. In some few instances, can makers declined so to restrict their freedom, and still their plants were bought. Nevertheless, the promoters obviously attached considerable importance to securing such covenants. It is in evidence that the owners of one plant struck it out from the first option they signed. Afterwards, they were induced to give another with it in, but in return were allowed to raise their price from $300,000 to $700,000.

. . . .

Much can-making machinery, more or less in use as late as 1900 had never been patented, or, if it had been, the patents on it had expired. A great many of these machines were of such simple construction that they could be made in almost any fairly equipped machine shop. To secure control of all such would have been impossible. Some of the most modern machines, those by which a large part of the work formerly done by hand was performed automatically, were, however, covered by patents. If these patents could be secured and arrangements made with the few machine shops in the country which were then equipped for turning out machinery of that class, competition in can making and can selling would be greatly hampered. Indeed, if the possibility of competitors obtaining such machinery could be cut off for a comparatively limited period, possibly even for a year or two, the can company which acquired a number of plants equipped with such machinery, and which could obtain more of it from the manufacturers, could, if its operations otherwise were wisely carried on, secure a domination of the market, which could not be seriously shaken for years to come. The record shows that the defendant did acquire such control. . . . It sought for six years to close to its competitors the machine shops which really counted. The largest manufacturer of automatic machinery for can-making purposes was the E. W. Bliss Company. For the sum of $25,000 a quarter, that company agreed that for six years it would not make certain can-making machinery for anybody other than the defendant. . . . From the Adriance Machine Company defendant agreed it would annually for six years take $75,000 worth of machinery. That amount represented the full capacity of the machine company. To the Ferracute Machine Company, in return for exclusive privileges, the defendant guaranteed a profit of $10,000 a year for six years. Defendant induced the Bliss Company to break contracts which the latter had already made to furnish such machinery, and, when the injured parties sued the Bliss Company for damages thus resulting, the defendant paid both the expense of defending the suits and the substantial judgments some of the aggrieved parties recovered.

. . . The record amply justifies the assertion that for a year or two after defendant's formation it was practically impossible for any competitor to obtain the most modern, up-to-date, automatic machinery, and that the difficulties in the way of getting such machinery were not altogether removed until the expiration of the six years for which the defendant had bound up the leading manufacturers of such machinery.

. . . .

The record does not disclose whether the promoters of the defendant really had reason to believe that they would be able practically to shut off the supply of tin plate from their competitors, as Norton in 1900 and early in 1901 was at least willing that the trade should think. As already stated, none of the promoters have seen fit to tell their story under oath. As it turned out, all the Tin Plate Company was willing to do was to bind itself to sell its tin plate to defendant at a certain fixed figure, below the price at which it sold to any one else. This preferential discount or rebate amounted, when the published list price of tin plate was $3.50 a base box, to about 64 cents on the quantity of plate required to make 1,000 3-pound packers' cans. This difference, the record shows, was far from negligible. In a close competitive struggle it might well have proved a decisive factor.

The defendant began to shut up plants [as] soon as it got possession of them. It kept on shutting them up until by April 21, 1903, it was operating only 36 can factories, and 3 machine shops, and it then proposed to close 5 more of the former and 1 or 2 of the latter. There has been a good deal of profitless dispute as to the proper term to describe what was done. What the government terms "dismantling" the defendant prefers to speak of as "transferring" or "concentrating." What actually took place is clear enough, whatever one may choose to call it. Two-thirds of the plants bought were abandoned within two years of their purchase. Many of them were never operated by the defendant at all, and others were closed after a few weeks or a few months. Where they had any machinery for which use could be found at some other of defendant's plants, such machinery was transferred to the place where it could be used, which might be a few blocks away in the same city or hundreds of miles off in another state. Where it was possible that a piece of machinery might some day be of some use, although there was no immediate call for it, it was sent to some abandoned factory building to be there stored until it was wanted, or until it became clear that it never would be. Such machines, and there appear to have been many of them, as were too obsolete for economical use, were broken up and their fragments sold as junk. . . .

. . . .

What happened shows that prices were put up to a point which made it apparently profitable for outsiders to start making cans with any antiquated or crude machinery they could find in old lumber rooms or which they could have made for them in a hurry, or even to resume can making by hand. The evidence on these points is absolutely conclusive. Can making became attractive. Any number of people began to make cans, or, at least, began to try to make them. Perhaps in some cases the prices which had been paid for can shops made them hope that if they could get a can shop they would be able to sell out at a figure which would make them comfortable for the rest of their days. At first, the defendant seems to have thought it would try to buy them out, and it bought a few of them, as already has been mentioned; but in a few weeks, if not in a few days, it became plain that such policy was impossible. In the first place, its money was gone. . . . There were too many new shops to buy them all, and, as it has turned out, it was easy enough to start some more. The real remedy would have been to reduce the price of cans. If defendant had not been under the necessity of realizing large and quick profits, doubtless it would have done so. Its mere cost of operation, excluding any allowance for capital investment, must have been below that of many of its poorly equipped competitors, who then rushed into the field. But, if prices had been reduced, the idea that there was a speedy fortune to be made by defendant's stockholders would have been too speedily dispelled. Other devices were resorted to. The attempt to keep up the price of cans was persisted in. In an effort to do so, the defendant itself sent brokers into the market and bought some millions of cans from its rivals. Some of these were very badly made, as was to be expected from new shops, equipped with wretched machinery and hastily rushed into business. These cans were stored for a while, and ultimately such of them as were salable at all were sold for what they would bring. Possibly these purchases did keep up the price longer than would otherwise have been the case.

. . . .

Thus far consideration has been chiefly given to the government's charges against the defendant. Some of these have been held not well founded. It has been said that others are made out.

Defendant has directed much of the nine volumes of testimony it has offered, to show that whatever criticisms might be made as to the way in which it was formed, and to certain of its isolated acts since, it has on the whole served the can trade well, and that its dissolution would do harm and not good. There is no room for question that since 1901 there have been many improvements, not only in can making, but in can selling and in can delivery as well, and that these improvements are greatly appreciated by all who buy cans from can makers. There is the usual difficulty, in such cases, in telling how much of these good things are because of that which defendant has done and how much would have come about if defendant had never been thought of.

By 1904, if not earlier, the defendant had definitely abandoned the policy of charging prices which to the consumer seemed unduly high. It is natural, nevertheless, to ask whether since that time prices have been lower or higher than they would have been had it never come into being. The record does not give any certain answer to this question. A great many consumers of cans testified that the price has tended downward. Up to the time of the closing of the evidence in this case, that was generally true. There were fluctuations, and the downward trend was slight; but there was such a trend. A comparison of the price of tin plate and of cans from 1897 to 1913 shows that the prices of the latter for 1911, 1912, and 1913 were just about the same as they were in 1897, 1898, and 1899, when allowance is made for the difference in the cost of the former. The margin between the cost of the tin plate and the selling price of the cans seems to have been as great when, as now, cans were made and sold at prices fixed by the defendant, as it was when they were made and sold by its numberless predecessors in the business. The cans have been better, in that they have been more uniformly well made. With the machinery now in use there is no reason to think it costs appreciably more to make good than bad cans. The manufacturing cost is now less than it was before defendant's formation. It is true that each laborer employed now receives more wages than he did then, but so great has been the improvement in machinery that the actual labor cost per thousand cans is now materially less than it was 15 years ago. Moreover, as a result of better methods of manufacture, much less solder is now used, and a net saving of some importance is thereby effected. A reduction in the price of cans does not appear to be among the benefits the defendant has conferred upon the trade.

Defendant takes some credit to itself for bringing about a standardization in packers' cans, so that a No. 1, a No. 2, or a No. 3 can, of any one of the recognized types of openings, is now precisely the same, no matter from what shop it comes. A good deal of progress in this direction had been made before defendant was organized. The first effect, not of its formation, but of the policy adopted by it in its earlier history, was probably to retard rather than to accelerate this tendency. The prices it quoted brought about, as has been seen, an opening or reopening of a number of shops poorly fitted to make good cans. The owners of such establishments probably gave little thought to standardization or to any similar problem. Subsequently, the influence and example of defendant made greatly for uniformity. It is, however, probable that, even if it had never come into being, the pressure from the canners and other sources would . . . have resulted in the general establishment of the standards now in use. It is very possible that it would have taken longer than it did.

Defendant makes good cans. It has always done so, at least after the first few months of its existence. The impression produced by the testimony is that it has been more uniformly successful in so doing than perhaps any of its competitors. . . . It is its policy to spare no trouble nor, within reasonable limits, expense to meet its customers' wishes. It is therefore not surprising that some users of certain sorts of general line cans feel that it can be safely depended on to make what they want. Some of them have reason to believe, or to know, that not every one of its competitors can be, and, as they are not certain that any of them can, it gets the business at the same or even a little higher price. . . .

The defendant claims, with much reason, to have been the first of the can makers systematically and scientifically to study canners' problems, with a view to discovering the causes of damage to and deterioration in canned goods. It says it has done more in that direction than any of its competitors, or all of them together. A number of years ago the defendant established a laboratory for the investigation of such matters. It has always been ready and willing to use the resources of this laboratory to aid canners, without expense to the latter and whether they bought their cans from it or not. When, some years ago, the National Canners' Association made up its mind that it would like to establish and maintain a well-equipped and efficiently managed laboratory at Washington, the defendant, and for that matter its principal competitors, furthered the project by contributing liberally, apparently in some rough proportion to the number of packers' cans sold by each.

. . . .

. . . The defendant has many shops, most of its competitors but one. The probability of its delivery of cans being altogether prevented by a factory accident is therefore almost negligible. Prompt delivery at short notice cannot, however, be assured unless the can factory is near the place of consumption. If there is a long railroad journey between, accidents and mistakes on the lines may postpone the arrival of cans which have been shipped in due season. The testimony shows that for this reason users of cans often prefer to deal with a neighboring factory, whether of the defendant or one of its competitors, in preference to buying cheaper elsewhere. The defendant has always given special attention to insuring prompt deliveries, and apparently has been rather unusually successful in so doing. Moreover, it stands ready to do its best to furnish cans on the shortest notice to any one who wants a carload or many carloads, and at its published prices. The failure of prompt delivery from one of its factories, or from a factory of one of its competitors, is no longer by any means so serious a matter as such an event formerly might have been. From one or the other of its shops the defendant is usually able in brief space to place the cans where they are needed. No concern which had not a number of plants and ample resources, both in men and money, could have done what the defendant has accomplished in protecting can users against serious delays in delivery. Perhaps this has been its most valuable service to the trade.

. . . .

One who sells only one-half of the cans that are sold does not, of course, possess a monopoly in the same sense as he would if he sold all or nearly all of them. Yet he may have more power over the industry than it is well for any one concern to possess. No one can say with any certainty that anybody would be better off if defendant had never, in any way, restrained or controlled absolutely free competition in cans. All that can be argued is that, in view of the declared policy of Congress, the legal presumption must be that which was done was against the public weal.

If it be true that size and power, apart from the way in which they were acquired, or the purpose with which they are used, do not offend against the law, it is equally true that one of the designs of the framers of the Anti-Trust Act was to prevent the concentration in a few hands of control over great industries. They preferred a social and industrial state in which there should be many independent producers. Size and power are themselves facts some of whose consequences do not depend upon the way in which they were created or in which they are used. It is easy to conceive that they might be acquired honestly and used as fairly as men who are in business for the legitimate purpose of making money for themselves and their associates could be expected to use them, human nature being what it is, and for all that constitute a public danger, or at all events give rise to difficult social, industrial and political problems. . . .

The problem presented by size and power is one of such far-reaching difficulty that Congress has said, while it does not see how to deal with them when acquired in the legitimate expansion of a lawful business, it will prevent their illegitimate and unnatural acquirement by any attempt to restrain trade or monopolize industry. Perhaps the framers of the Anti-Trust Act believed that, if such illegitimate attempts were effectively prevented, the occasions on which it would become necessary to deal with size and power otherwise brought about would be so few and so long postponed that it might never be necessary to deal with them at all. In administering the anti-trust acts, a number of great and powerful offenders against them have been dissolved. So far as is possible to judge, the consuming public has not as yet greatly profited by their dissolution. It is perhaps not likely that any benefit could have been expected until in the slow course of time the ownership of the newly created corporations gradually drifts into different hands. In most of the cases in which dissolution has been decreed, the defendants had, not long before proceedings against them were instituted, done things which evidenced their continued intent to dominate and restrain trade by the use of methods which interfered more or less seriously with the reasonable freedom of their customers or their competitors.

As has been shown, defendant for a number of years past has done nothing of the sort. While it had its origin in unlawful acts and thereby acquired a power which may be harmful, and the acquisition of which in any event was contrary to the policy of Congress as embodied in the statute, it has for some time past used that power, on the whole, rather for weal than for woe. In this case, if a dissolution be decreed, it will have as its sole reason the carrying out of the policy of Congress that a trading or industrial corporation shall not, by an attempt to restrain or monopolize trade, become so powerful that it exerts an influence on the industry far greater than that of any of its competitors. . . .

. . . .

Defendant once sought to emancipate itself from restraints of competition. Its power is great, but, as has already been pointed out, is limited by a large volume of actual competition and to a still greater extent by the potential competition, from the possibility of which in the present state of the industry it cannot escape. Those in the trade are satisfied with it. They do not want it dissolved. Whether its dissolution would profit any one is doubtful. The first and immediate effect would almost certainly be the reverse, whatever larger good might in the end come from it.

I am frankly reluctant to destroy so finely adjusted an industrial machine as the record shows defendant to be. Yet the government, too, has its rights, and has thus far been properly insistent upon them. . . .

The government recognizes that the situation which existed before defendant was formed cannot be restored. What it principally fears is that the defendant will, to the public prejudice, hereafter dangerously use the strength which it gained by its original lawbreaking. Defendant's reply, that in that event it will be time enough for the government to act, does not fully meet the case. If this petition be dismissed upon its merits and without qualification, defendant might be entitled to claim in any future proceeding that nothing here in issue may be there used against it. . . .

Under the circumstances, would it not be better simply to retain the bill, without at present decreeing a dissolution, but reserving the right to do so whenever, if ever, it shall be made to appear to the court that the size and power of the defendant, brought about as they originally were, are being used to the injury of the public, or whenever such size and power, without being intentionally so used, have given to the defendant a dominance and control over the industry, or some portion of it, so great as to make dissolution or other restraining decree of the court expedient. It is, of course, not suggested that this court should or could undertake the regulation of defendant's business. Courts have no such power and no fitness for its exercise. What is proposed is in default of a better way of dealing with a somewhat unusual and very difficult condition. It is to be hoped that, before any occasion to act upon the power reserved shall arise, Congress will substitute some other method than dissolution for dealing with the problems which arise when a single corporation absorbs a large part of the country's productive capacity in any one line.

NOTES AND QUESTIONS

1. Note the acts that the American Can Company was alleged to have committed: it threatened to drive its competitors out of business (how might it accomplish this?); it threatened to prevent can makers who did not join the "combination" from obtaining needed raw materials, such as tin plate; it bought out its rivals, often paying many times the value of the purchased company, and always paying more than the company was worth; when it purchased the plants of rivals, it required the rivals to promise not to compete in the industry for 15 years; it bought up the patents for can-making machinery; it forced the makers of can-making machinery to agree not to sell machinery to competitors. What do these practices have in common? Are all of them equally harmful?

The allegations that American Can entered contracts with vertically related firms that exclude rivals unnecessarily have reappeared many times in antitrust. Consider the following from *United States v. Microsoft*, 56 F.3d 1448, 1451 (D.C. Cir. 1995): "The key anticompetitive practice against which the [government's antitrust] complaint is aimed is Microsoft's use of contract terms requiring original equipment manufacturers ("OEMs") to pay Microsoft a royalty for each computer the OEM sells containing a particular microprocessor . . . whether or not the OEM has included a Microsoft operating system with that computer. The practical effect of such "per processor licenses," it is alleged, is to deter OEMs from using competing operating systems during the life of their contracts with Microsoft. The complaint further charges that Microsoft has exacerbated the anticompetitive effect of the per processor licenses by executing long-term contracts with major OEMs . . . ."

Thus, the government alleged, if a computer maker wanted to put a competing operating system, such as IBM's OS/2 system, on one of its computers, it would have to pay twice: once to IBM for the right to IBM's system, and a second time to Microsoft under the "per processor" license requiring the manufacturer to pay to have Microsoft Windows installed on every computer it made, whether or not it was actually installed.

2. How plausible is the court's reasoning that American Can could have driven some of its competitors out of business, but chose instead to buy them out, sometimes paying them as much as 25 times the value of their assets? Would it not have been much cheaper simply to drive the competitors into bankruptcy? See the discussion of predatory pricing, *infra*.

3. Notice some of American Can's defenses: after the monopoly was created, cans became much cheaper and were generally of a higher quality; the new megacompany was able to engage in substantial research and development; the new company paid employees higher wages than the older, smaller companies did; because of the unified manufacturing process permitted by a single large manufacturer, can sizes and shapes were more standardized than they had been before; the defendant's size and financial security made the can market much less convulsive than it had been before the monopoly was created: buyers of the defendant's cans could generally get them when they wanted them, without having to worry about manufacturing delays or suppliers going out of business. These and other alleged advantages of the can monopoly gave the court some pause. The judge was "reluctant to destroy so finely adjusted an industrial machine." Do you suppose that these improvements in the quality and delivery of cans occurred because of, or in spite of, the existence of a monopoly? Would some of them have happened even in the absence of a dominant firm in the market? Is there any reason to believe that monopolists pay higher wages than competitors? Is that question relevant in an antitrust case? The argument that a monopolist can "standardize" the output in a market is certainly plausible, but couldn't the same result be obtained in a less offensive way?

What about the argument that the monopolized market was more predictable for canneries because the small competitors had a tendency to go out of business? Nothing guarantees a supplier's financial stability more than an abundance of monopoly profits. Should that ever be a defense in a monopolization case?

4. Monopolists have often attempted to defend their monopolies by arguing that the monopoly undertook research and development that would not have occurred in an industry made up of smaller, competitive firms. In fact, monopolists in this position have made two, quite different arguments: (1) only a very large firm can afford to undertake research and development or exploration in certain areas in which such activities are very expensive; and (2) only monopoly profits give a firm enough money to finance such research — that is, firms in competition are forced to reduce expenses and will cut out expenditures for research. Do both arguments strike you as equally plausible? Does the fact that the monopolist has extra money mean that the monopolist will spend it on research rather than on yachts or caviar? The answer, most likely, is that the monopolist will spend the money on research if it thinks the research is a good investment — that is, if it produces a profitable return. But if that is the case, would not the competitor do it as well?

The first argument is a little more convincing. There may be circumstances when certain kinds of research or exploration require large amounts of capital, and only relatively large firms will be able to finance it. However, is this an argument for monopoly? Wouldn't a joint venture have the same social benefits but pose fewer social evils? See the discussion of research joint ventures, *supra*.

5.   One of the consequences of American Can's monopoly price increase was that the market became flooded with new entrants, many of which were so inefficient that they would not have survived in a competitive market. It became profitable to make cans with "any antiquated or crude machinery [the new entrants] could find in old lumber rooms . . . or even to resume can making by hand." These fringe firms are the bane of every monopolist's existence. One way to deal with them, as the opinion notes, is to reduce price to the point that production for the inefficient fringe is unprofitable; however, that costs the monopolist part of its monopoly profits. The American Can Company took a second, ill-advised route. It bought up the cans from the inefficient producers, paying them a profitable price. This strategy was calculated to invite even more firms into the market, for they would have a guaranteed outlet for their product. The third alternative is to drive the fringe firms out of business in such a way that no new firms will dare to enter the market.

NOTE: THE ECONOMICS OF MONOPOLIZATION

Monopoly is not necessarily bad. In certain industries, such as delivery of electric power to consumers, monopoly has traditionally been regarded as the most efficient way to serve the public. Once a single set of electric cables is in place, it can service an entire city. It would be very costly to have two, three, or more sets of electric wires running through a city, and to give two or more electric companies the eminent domain power to run their wires across private property. For these reasons, electric utilities are generally considered to be "natural" monopolies — that is, firms that can deliver their services optimally if they are permitted to have a monopoly within a certain market. In general, an industry is a natural monopoly if the most efficient size of a plant or installation in that industry will satisfy 100% of the entire profitable demand in that market. The other side of the coin, however, is that such natural monopolies are generally price-regulated by a state, municipality, or some other governmental body.

In industries that are not natural monopolies, most people in market economies believe that monopoly is bad and competition good. Antitrust lawyers and economists generally agree about this, although different groups do so for different reasons. There are both noneconomic and economic arguments against monopoly. The noneconomic arguments focus on the tendency of monopoly to concentrate large amounts of power in the hands of a few private owners, and on the fact that monopoly pricing transfers wealth away from consumers (who must pay more for monopolized products) and toward monopoly producers (who are able to charge monopoly prices). The economic arguments, by contrast, focus on the tendency of monopoly to cause inefficiency in the production and distribution of goods and services. These inefficiencies result from two aspects of monopoly: monopoly pricing and monopolistic conduct.

At this time you might find it helpful to review the discussion of monopoly in Chapter 2. Figure 1 illustrates the demand, marginal cost, and marginal revenue curves for a firm with substantial market power. A firm with no market power would take the market price as given and produce at the rate at which its marginal cost curve crosses the market demand curve. That would be price P_c and output Q_c in Figure 1. A firm with market power, however, will not take the market price as given; rather, it will reduce its output to the point at which its marginal cost and marginal revenue curves intersect. At that point, one further unit of production would generate greater expenses than income. This is the monopolist's profit-maximizing price, and it is represented on the graph by P_m. The profit-maximizing output that will generate that price is Q_m.

Figure 1

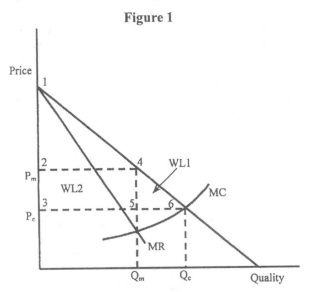

The large triangle 1-3-6 in Figure 1 represents the "consumers' surplus" generated by a competitive market. Competitive markets maximize consumers' surplus, and there is a positive correlation between consumers' surplus and consumer welfare. Consumers' surplus is the difference between the amount that a particular consumer is willing to pay for a product and the price the consumer must actually pay for it. If a consumer values a product at $1.50 but is able to purchase it at a competitive price of $1.00, the transaction generates a consumers' surplus of 50 cents. If the same consumer must pay a monopoly price of $1.20, there will still be a consumer's surplus, but it will be reduced to 30 cents. The triangle 1-3-6 illustrates the size of the consumers' surplus generated in the entire market, represented by Figure 1, if the market were competitive.

Monopoly pricing at P_m with monopoly output at Q_m reduces the size of the consumers' surplus to an area represented by triangle 1-2-4. Rectangle 2-3-5-4 represents lost consumers' surplus that the monopolist has been able to turn into "producers' surplus." Producer's surplus is the amount by which a producer's price exceeds the competitive price. If the competitive price of a widget is $1.00 (which includes a reasonable profit, sufficient to attract new capital into the industry), but a seller with market power is able to sell the widget for $1.20, the transaction has generated a producers' surplus of 20 cents. Rectangle 2-3-5-4 therefore represents, at least in part, a wealth transfer away from consumers and toward producers.

However, as we shall see later, to describe rectangle 2-3-5-4 as a wealth "transfer" is an oversimplification.

What about triangle 4-5-6, which is also lost producers' surplus? Triangle 4-5-6 represents the traditional "deadweight" loss caused by monopoly. The potential purchasers located along the demand curve between points 4 and 6 would have been willing to pay the competitive price for a widget, but at the monopoly price, they refuse to buy and purchase something else instead. These purchasers therefore lose the producers' surplus they would have obtained by buying widgets in a competitive market; however, their loss does not become a gain to the monopolist, for the monopolist cannot earn money from sales that it does not make. Triangle 4-5-6 represents resources that are misallocated, or wasted, because of the monopolization.

Monopoly therefore does two things at the same time: it transfers wealth away from consumers and to the monopolist, and it causes a certain amount of deadweight loss because of inefficient buyer substitutions. Both of these reasons have been used at one time or another to support the antitrust laws against monopolization.

Now let us take another look at rectangle 2-3-5-4, which we described above as a transfer of wealth from consumers to the monopolist. Suppose that a producer is currently manufacturing widgets and selling them in a competitive market and making $50,000 per year in profits. However, the producer discovers that by driving its closest rival out of business, it could price monopolistically and obtain profits of $60,000. How much is it worth to the producer to drive out the rival?

The answer, quite clearly, is $10,000. That is, the ability to obtain (or to retain) market power is valuable, and a profit-maximizing seller will therefore spend money in order to obtain or keep it. In fact, if market power is worth $10,000 a year to a seller, the seller will be willing to spend almost any amount of money less than $10,000 in order to acquire and keep the market power. *See* RICHARD POSNER, ANTITRUST LAW 12–25 (2d ed. 2001). This money can be spent in a variety of ways. For example, it might be spent in research and development that will make the producer more efficient than its rivals. On the other hand, the producer might spend the money sabotaging its rival's plants or making false advertisements about its own products. The first of these ways is probably socially beneficial, but the second two are almost certainly socially harmful.

In short, rectangle 2-3-5-4 does not necessarily represent a transfer of wealth from consumers to the monopolist. To the extent that the monopolist has spent extra funds in order to acquire the market power, 2-3-5-4 represents money that does not accrue to the monopolist either. Furthermore, if that money has been spent in socially inefficient ways, such as industrial sabotage or predatory pricing, much of rectangle 2-3-5-4 is also pure social, deadweight loss.

Figure 1 thus suggests that monopoly can be inefficient from a purely economic standpoint for two different reasons. Triangle 4-5-6 represents inefficiency caused by inefficient monopoly *pricing*. However, at least a part of rectangle 2-3-5-4 can represent inefficiency caused by inefficient monopoly *conduct* — i.e., resources inefficiently spent by the monopolist in attaining or retaining its position.

But there is a third social cost of monopolization that Figure 1 simply fails to illustrate: the social cost of the resources *of competitors* or others, which might be inefficiently lost by the monopolist's attempt to attain or retain a dominant position. Consider the Supreme Court's decision in *Allied Tube & Conduit Corp. v. Indian Head, Inc.*, 486 U.S. 492 (1988), reprinted in Chapter 9, as an example. Suppose that a cartel of manufacturers of steel conduit corrupts a standard-setting organization by "packing" one of its meetings and forces the passage of a rule keeping plastic conduit off the market. The result is that the steel cartel continues to make monopoly profits on its conduit. Triangle 4-5-6 in Figure 1 represents the social cost of the output reduction that results from the perpetuation of this monopoly. Part of rectangle 2-3-5-4 represents the social cost of the means by which the cartel protected its monopoly — resources inefficiently spent. But what of the social cost of the years of lost research the plaintiff spent in developing a superior product, plastic conduit, that now cannot reach the market? That loss is not even accounted for by Figure 1. It could be far larger than either triangle 4-5-6 or rectangle 2-3-5-4. Although rectangle 2-3-5-4 represents the most the putative monopolist is willing to spend in the creation or maintenance of a monopoly, there is no necessary limit to the size of the inefficient losses it might impose on competitors. Many forms of monopolization, such as predatory pricing, fraudulent petitions to the government, and patent fraud deny competitors the opportunity to use efficiently resources that are already consumed. This is a social cost of monopoly that antitrust, with its prominent concern with the socially costly processes by which monopoly is acquired, must take into account as well. *See* Herbert Hovenkamp, *Antitrust's Protected Classes*, 88 MICH. L. REV. 1 (1989); Herbert Hovenkamp, *Antitrust Policy and the Social Cost of Monopoly*, 78 IOWA L. REV. 371 (1993).

UNITED STATES v. ALUMINUM CO. OF AMERICA
148 F.2d 416 (2d Cir. 1945)

[In 1912, the United States had brought a monopolization action against the Aluminum Company of America (Alcoa) and obtained a consent decree. In 1937, the United States sued for additional relief, including dissolution of the company. The trial court found for the defendant. 44 F. Supp. 97 (S.D.N.Y. 1941). The Expediting Act permitted a direct appeal to the U.S. Supreme Court, but four Justices disqualified themselves. The statutory quorum is six Justices. Congress responded with a statute providing that in such cases, the court of last resort should be made up of the three most senior judges of the appropriate court of appeals. As a result, the *Alcoa* case is traditionally considered to have as much authority as a Supreme Court opinion.]

JUDGE HAND.

"Alcoa" is a corporation, organized under the laws of Pennsylvania on September 18, 1888. . . . It has always been engaged in the production and sale of "ingot" aluminum, and since 1895 also in the fabrication of the metal into many finished and semi-finished articles. It has proliferated into a great number of subsidiaries, created at various times between the years 1900 and 1929, as the business expanded. Aluminum is a chemical element; it is never found in a free state, being always in chemical combination with oxygen. One form of this combination is known as alumina; and for practical purposes the most available material from which alumina can be extracted is an ore, called, "bauxite." . . .

The extraction of aluminum from alumina requires a very large amount of electrical energy. . . . Beginning at least as early as 1895, "Alcoa" secured such power from several companies by contracts, containing in at least three instances, covenants binding the power companies not to sell or let power to anyone else for the manufacture of aluminum. "Alcoa" — either itself or by a subsidiary — also entered into four successive "cartels" with foreign manufacturers of aluminum by which, in exchange for certain limitations upon its import into foreign countries, it secured covenants from the foreign producers, either not to import into the United States at all, or to do so under restrictions, which in some cases involved the fixing of prices. These "cartels" and restrictive covenants and certain other practices were the subject of a suit filed by the United States against "Alcoa" on May 16, 1912, in which a decree was entered by consent on June 7, 1912, declaring several of these covenants unlawful and enjoining their performance; and also declaring invalid other restrictive covenants obtained before 1903 relating to the sale of alumina. . . .

None of the foregoing facts are in dispute, and the most important question in the case is whether the monopoly in "Alcoa's" production of "virgin" ingot, secured by the two patents until 1909, and in part perpetuated between 1909 and 1912 by the unlawful practices, forbidden by the decree of 1912, continued for the ensuing twenty-eight years; and whether, if it did, it was unlawful under § 2 of the Sherman Act, 15 U.S.C.A. § 2. It is undisputed that throughout this period "Alcoa" continued to be the single producer of "virgin" ingot in the United States; and the plaintiff argues that this without more was enough to make it an unlawful monopoly. It also takes an alternative position: that in any event during this period "Alcoa" consistently pursued unlawful exclusionary practices, which made its dominant position certainly unlawful, even though it would not have been, had it been retained only by "natural growth." Finally, it asserts that many of these practices were of themselves unlawful, as contracts in restraint of trade under § 1 of the Act, 15 U.S.C.A. § 1. "Alcoa's" position is that the fact that it alone continued to make "virgin" ingot in this country did not, and does not, give it a monopoly of the market; that it was always subject to the competition of imported "virgin" ingot, and of what is called "secondary" ingot; and that even if it had not been, its monopoly would not have been retained by unlawful means, but would have been the result of a growth which the Act does not forbid, even when it results in a monopoly. . . .

From 1902 onward until 1928 "Alcoa" was making ingot in Canada through a wholly owned subsidiary; so much of this as it imported into the United States it is proper to include with what it produced here. In the year 1912 the sum of these two items represented nearly ninety-one per cent of the total amount of "virgin" ingot available for sale in this country. This percentage varied year by year up to and including 1938: in 1913 it was about seventy-two per cent; in 1921 about sixty-eight per cent; in 1922 about seventy-two per cent; with these exceptions it was always over eighty per cent of the total and for the last five years 1934–1938 inclusive it averaged over ninety per cent. The effect of such a proportion of the production upon the market we reserve for the time being, for it will be necessary first to consider the nature and uses of "secondary" ingot, the name by which the industry knows ingot made from aluminum scrap. This is of two sorts, though for our purposes it is not important to distinguish between them. One of these is the clippings and trimmings of "sheet" aluminum, when patterns are cut out of it, as a suit is cut from a bolt of cloth. The chemical composition of these is obviously the same as that of the "sheet" from which they come; and, although they are likely to accumulate dust or other dirt in the factory, this may be removed by well known processes. If a record of the original composition of the "sheet" has been preserved, this scrap may be remelted into new ingot, and used again for the same purpose.

. . .

Nevertheless, there is an appreciable "sales resistance" even to this kind of scrap, and for some uses (airplanes and cables among them), fabricators absolutely insist upon "virgin": just why is not altogether clear. The other source of scrap is aluminum which has once been fabricated and the article, after being used, is discarded and sent to the junk heap . . . as for example, cooking utensils, like kettles and pans, and the pistons or crank cases of motorcars. These are made with a substantial alloy and to restore the metal to its original purity costs more than it is worth. However, if the alloy is known both in quality and amount, scrap, when remelted, can be used again for the same purpose as before. In spite of this, as in the case of clippings and trimmings, the industry will ordinarily not accept ingot so salvaged upon the same terms as "virgin." There are some seventeen companies which scavenge scrap of all sorts, clean it, remelt it, test it for its composition, make it into ingots and sell it regularly to the trade. There is in all these salvage operations some inevitable waste of actual material; not only does a certain amount of aluminum escape altogether, but in the salvaging process itself some is skimmed off as scum and thrown away. The judge found that the return of fabricated products to the market as "secondary" varied from five to twenty-five years, depending upon the article; but he did not, and no doubt could not, find how many times the cycle could be repeated before the metal was finally used up.

There are various ways of computing "Alcoa's" control of the aluminum market — as distinct from its production — depending upon what one regards as competing in that market. The judge figured its share — during the years 1929-1938, inclusive — as only about thirty-three per cent; to do so he included "secondary," and excluded that part of "Alcoa's" own production which it fabricated and did not therefore sell as ingot. If, on the other hand, "Alcoa's" total production, fabricated and sold, be included, and balanced against the sum of imported "virgin" and "secondary," its share of the market was in the neighborhood of sixty-four per cent for that period. The percentage we have already mentioned — over ninety — results only if we both include all "Alcoa's" production and exclude "secondary." That percentage is enough to constitute a monopoly; it is doubtful whether sixty or sixty-four per cent would be enough; and certainly thirty-three per cent is not. Hence it is necessary to settle what he shall treat as competing in the ingot market. That part of its production which "Alcoa" itself fabricates, does not of course ever reach the market as ingot; and we recognize that it is only when a restriction of production either inevitably affects prices, or is intended to do so, that it violates § 1 of the Act. However, even though we were to assume that a monopoly is unlawful under § 2 only in case it controls prices, the ingot fabricated by "Alcoa," necessarily had a direct effect upon the ingot market. All ingot — with trifling exceptions — is used to fabricate intermediate, or end, products; and therefore all intermediate, or end, products which "Alcoa" fabricates and sells, pro tanto reduce the demand for ingot itself. . . . We cannot therefore agree that the computation of the percentage of "Alcoa's" control over the ingot market should not include the whole of its ingot production.

As to "secondary," as we have said, for certain purposes the industry will not accept it at all; but for those for which it will, the difference in price is ordinarily not very great; the judge found that it was between one and two cents a pound, hardly enough margin on which to base a monopoly. Indeed, there are times when all differential disappears, and "secondary" will actually sell at a higher price: i.e. when there is a supply available which contains just the alloy that a fabricator needs for the article which he proposes to make. Taking the industry as a whole, we can say nothing more definite than that, although "secondary" does not compete at all in some uses, (whether because of "sales resistance" only, or because of actual metallurgical inferiority), for most purposes it competes upon a substantial equality with "virgin." On these facts the judge found that "every pound of secondary or scrap aluminum which is sold in commerce displaces a pound of virgin aluminum which otherwise would, or might have been, sold." We agree: so far as "secondary" supplies the demand of such fabricators as will accept it, it increases the amount of "virgin" which must seek sale elsewhere; and it therefore results that the supply of that part of the demand which will accept only "virgin" becomes greater in proportion as "secondary" drives away "virgin" from the demand which will accept "secondary." (This is indeed the same argument which we used a moment ago to include in the supply that part of "virgin" which "Alcoa" fabricates; it is not apparent to us why the judge did not think it applicable to that item as well.) At any given moment therefore "secondary" competes with "virgin" in the ingot market; further, it can, and probably does, set a limit or "ceiling" beyond which the price of "virgin" cannot go, for the cost of its production will in the end depend only upon the expense of scavenging and reconditioning. It might seem for this reason that in estimating "Alcoa's" control over the ingot market, we ought to include the supply of "secondary," as the judge did. Indeed, it may be thought a paradox to say that anyone has the monopoly of a market in which at all times he must meet a competition that limits his price. We shall show that it is not.

In the case of a monopoly of any commodity which does not disappear in use and which can be salvaged, the supply seeking sale at any moment will be made up of two components: (1) the part which the putative monopolist can immediately produce and sell; and (2) the part which has been, or can be, reclaimed out of what he has produced and sold in the past. By hypothesis he presently controls the first of these components; the second he has controlled in the past, although he no longer does. During the period when he did control the second, if he was aware of his interest, he was guided, not alone by its effect at that time upon the market, but by his knowledge that some part of it was likely to be reclaimed and seek the future market. That consideration will to some extent always affect his production until he decides to abandon the business, or for some other reason ceases to be concerned with the future market. Thus, in the case at bar "Alcoa" always knew that the future supply of ingot would be made up in part of what it produced at the time, and, if it was as far-sighted as it proclaims itself, that consideration must have had its share in determining how much to produce. How accurately it could forecast the effect of present production upon the future market is another matter. Experience, no doubt, would help; but it makes no difference that it had to guess; it is enough that it had an inducement to make the best guess it could, and that it would regulate that part of the future supply, so far as it should turn out to have guessed right. The competition of "secondary" must therefore be disregarded, as soon as we consider the position of "Alcoa" over a period of years; it was as much within "Alcoa's" control as was the production of the "virgin" from which it had been derived. . . .

We conclude therefore that "Alcoa's" control over the ingot market must be reckoned at over ninety per cent; that being the proportion which its production bears to imported "virgin" ingot. If the fraction which it did not supply were the produce of domestic manufacture there could be no doubt that this percentage gave it a monopoly — lawful or unlawful, as the case might be. The producer of so large a proportion of the supply has complete control within certain limits. It is true that, if by raising the price he reduces the amount which can be marketed — as always, or almost always, happens — he may invite the expansion of the small producers who will try to fill the place left open; nevertheless, not only is there an inevitable lag in this, but the large producer is in a strong position to check such competition; and, indeed, if he has retained his old plant and personnel, he can inevitably do so. There are indeed limits to his power; substitutes are available for almost all commodities, and to raise the price enough is to evoke them. . . . Moreover, it is difficult and expensive to keep idle any part of a plant or of personnel; and any drastic contraction of the market will offer increasing temptation to the small producers to expand. But these limitations also exist when a single producer occupies the whole market: even then, his hold will depend upon his moderation in exerting his immediate power.

The case at bar is however different, because, for aught that appears there may well have been a practically unlimited supply of imports as the price of ingot rose. Assuming that there was no agreement between "Alcoa" and foreign producers not to import, they sold what could bear the handicap of the tariff and the cost of transportation. For the period of eighteen years — 1920–1937 — they sold at times a little above "Alcoa's" prices, at times a little under; but there was substantially no gross difference between what they received and what they would have received, had they sold uniformly at "Alcoa's" prices. While the record is silent, we may therefore assume — the plaintiff having the burden — that, had "Alcoa" raised its prices, more ingot would have been imported. Thus there is a distinction between domestic and foreign competition: the first is limited in quantity, and can increase only by an increase in plant and personnel; the second is of producers who, we must assume, produce much more than they import, and whom a rise in price will presumably induce immediately to divert to the American market what they have been selling elsewhere. It is entirely consistent with the evidence that it was the threat of greater foreign imports which kept "Alcoa's" prices where they were, and prevented it from exploiting its advantage as sole domestic producer; indeed, it is hard to resist the conclusion that potential imports did put a "ceiling" upon those prices. Nevertheless, within the limits afforded by the tariff and the cost of transportation, "Alcoa" was free to raise its prices as it chose, since it was free from domestic competition, save as it drew other metals into the market as substitutes.

Was this a monopoly within the meaning of § 2? The judge found that, over the whole half century of its existence, "Alcoa's" profits upon capital invested, after payment of income taxes, had been only about ten per cent, and, although the plaintiff puts this figure a little higher, the difference is negligible. . . . This assumed, it would be hard to say that "Alcoa" had made exorbitant profits on ingot, if it is proper to allocate the profit upon the whole business proportionately among all its products — ingot, and fabrications from ingot. A profit of ten per cent in such an industry, dependent, in part at any rate, upon continued tariff protection, and subject to the vicissitudes of new demands, to the obsolescence of plant and process — which can never be accurately gauged in advance — to the chance that substitutes may at any moment be discovered which will reduce the demand, and to the other hazards which attend all industry; a profit of ten per cent, so conditioned, could hardly be considered extortionate.

There are however, two answers to any such excuse; and the first is that the profit on ingot was not necessarily the same as the profit of the business as a whole, and that we have no means of allocating its proper share to ingot. It is true that the mill cost appears; but obviously it would be unfair to "Alcoa" to take, as the measure of its profit on ingot, the difference between selling price and mill cost; and yet we have nothing else. It may be retorted that it was for the plaintiff to prove what was the profit upon ingot in accordance with the general burden of proof. We think not. Having proved that "Alcoa" had a monopoly of the domestic ingot market, the plaintiff had gone far enough; if it was an excuse, that "Alcoa" had not abused its power, it lay upon "Alcoa" to prove that it had not. But the whole issue is irrelevant anyway, for it is no excuse for "monopolizing" a market that the monopoly has not been used to extract from the consumer more than a "fair" profit. The Act has wider purposes. Indeed, even though we disregarded all but economic considerations, it would by no means follow that such concentration of producing power is to be desired, when it has not been used extortionately. Many people believe that possession of unchallenged economic power deadens initiative, discourages thrift and depresses energy; that immunity from competition is a narcotic, and rivalry is a stimulant, to industrial progress; that the spur of constant stress is necessary to counteract an inevitable disposition to let well enough alone. Such people believe that competitors, versed in the craft as no consumer can be, will be quick to detect opportunities for saving and new shifts in production, and be eager to profit by them. In any event the mere fact that a producer, having command of the domestic market, has not been able to make more than a "fair" profit, is no evidence that a "fair" profit could not have been made at lower prices. *United States v. Corn Products Refining Co.*, *supra*, 1014, 1015 (234 F. 964). True, it might have been thought adequate to condemn only those monopolies which could not show that they had exercised the highest possible ingenuity, had adopted every possible economy, had anticipated every conceivable improvement, stimulated every possible demand. No doubt, that would be one way of dealing with the matter, although it would imply constant scrutiny and constant supervision, such as courts are unable to provide. Be that as it may, that was not the way that Congress chose; it did not condone "good trusts" and condemn "bad" ones; it forbad all. Moreover, in so doing it was not necessarily actuated by economic motives alone. It is possible, because of its indirect social or moral effect, to prefer a system of small producers, each dependent for his success upon his own skill and character, to one in which the great mass of those engaged must accept the direction of a few. These considerations, which we have suggested only as possible purposes of the Act, we think the decisions prove to have been in fact its purposes.

It is settled, at least as to § 1, that there are some contracts restricting competition which are unlawful, no matter how beneficent they may be. . . . Starting, however, with the authoritative premise that all contracts fixing prices are unconditionally prohibited, the only possible difference between them and a monopoly is that while a monopoly necessarily involves an equal, or even greater, power to fix prices, its mere existence might be thought not to constitute an exercise of that power. That distinction is nevertheless purely formal; it would be valid only so long as the monopoly remained wholly inert; it would disappear as soon as the monopoly began to operate; for, when it did — that is, as soon as it began to sell at all — it must sell at some price and the only price at which it could sell is a price which it itself fixed. Thereafter the power and its exercise must needs coalesce. Indeed it would be absurd to condemn such contracts unconditionally, and not to extend the condemnation to monopolies; for the contracts are only steps toward that entire control which monopoly confers: they are really partial monopolies.

But we are not left to deductive reasoning. Although in many settings it may be proper to weigh the extent and effect of restrictions in a contract against its industrial or commercial advantages, this is never to be done when the contract is made with intent to set up a monopoly. . . .

We have been speaking only of the economic reasons which forbid monopoly; but, as we have already implied, there are others, based upon the belief that great industrial consolidations are inherently undesirable, regardless of their economic results. In the debates in Congress Senator Sherman himself . . . showed that among the purposes of Congress in 1890 was a desire to put an end to great aggregations of capital because of the helplessness of the individual before them. . . . That Congress is still of the same mind appears in the Surplus Property Act of 1944, 50 U.S.C.A. Appendix § 1611 et seq., and the Small Business Mobilization Act, 50 U.S.C.A. Appendix § 1101 et seq. Not only does § 2(d) of the first declare it to be one aim of that statute to "preserve the competitive position of small business concerns," but § 18 is given over to directions designed to "preserve and strengthen" their position. . . . Throughout the history of these statutes it has been constantly assumed that one of their purposes was to perpetuate and preserve, for its own sake and in spite of possible cost, an organization of industry in small units which can effectively compete with each other. We hold that "Alcoa's" monopoly of ingot was of the kind covered by § 2.

It does not follow because "Alcoa" had such a monopoly, that it "monopolized" the ingot market: it may not have achieved monopoly; monopoly may have been thrust upon it. If it had been a combination of existing smelters which united the whole industry and controlled the production of all aluminum ingot, it would certainly have "monopolized" the market. In several decisions the Supreme Court has decreed the dissolution of such combinations, although they had engaged in no unlawful trade practices. . . . We may start therefore with the premise that to have combined ninety per cent of the producers of ingot would have been to "monopolize" the ingot market; and, so far as concerns the public interest, it can make no difference whether an existing competition is put an end to, or whether prospective competition is prevented. The Clayton Act itself speaks in that alternative: "to injure, destroy, or prevent competition." Nevertheless, it is unquestionably true that from the very outset the courts have at least kept in reserve the possibility that the origin of a monopoly may be critical in determining its legality; and for this they had warrant in some of the congressional debates which accompanied the passage of the Act. . . . This notion has usually been expressed by saying that size does not determine guilt; that there must be some "exclusion" of competitors; that the growth must be something else than "natural" or "normal"; that there must be a "wrongful intent," or some other specific intent; or that some "unduly" coercive means must be used. At times there has been emphasis upon the use of the active verb, "monopolize," as the judge noted in the case at bar. . . . What engendered these compunctions is reasonably plain; persons may unwittingly find themselves in possession of a monopoly, automatically so to say: that is, without having intended either to put an end to existing competition, or to prevent competition from arising when none had existed; they may become monopolists by force of accident. Since the Act makes "monopolizing" a crime, as well as a civil wrong, it would be not only unfair, but presumably contrary to the intent of Congress, to include such instances. A market may, for example, be so limited that it is impossible to produce at all and meet the cost of production except by a plant large enough to supply the whole demand. Or there may be changes in taste or in cost which drive out all but one purveyor. A single producer may be the survivor out of a group of active competitors, merely by virtue of his superior skill, foresight and industry. In such cases a strong argument can be made that, although, the result may expose the public to the evils of monopoly, the Act does not mean to condemn the resultant of those very forces which it is its prime object to foster: finis opus coronat. The successful competitor, having been urged to compete, must not be turned upon when he wins. . . . Cardozo, J., in *United States v. Swift & Co.*, 286 U.S. 106, said, "Mere size . . . is not an offense against the Sherman Act unless magnified to the point at which it amounts to a monopoly . . . but size carries with it an opportunity for abuse that is not to be ignored when the opportunity is proved to have been utilized in the past." "Alcoa's" size was "magnified" to make it a "monopoly"; indeed, it has never been anything else; and its size, not only offered it an "opportunity for abuse," but it "utilized" its size for "abuse," as can easily be shown.

It would completely misconstrue "Alcoa's" position in 1940 to hold that it was the passive beneficiary of a monopoly, following upon an involuntary elimination of competitors by automatically operative economic forces. Already in 1909, when its last lawful monopoly ended, it sought to strengthen its position by unlawful practices, and these concededly continued until 1912. In that year it had two plants in New York, at which it produced less than 42 million pounds of ingot; in 1934 it had five plants (the original two, enlarged; one in Tennessee; one in North Carolina; one in Washington), and its production had risen to about 327 million pounds, an increase of almost eight-fold. Meanwhile not a pound of ingot had been produced by anyone else in the United States. This increase and this continued and undisturbed control did not fall undesigned into "Alcoa's" lap; obviously it could not have done so. It could only have resulted, as it did result, from a persistent determination to maintain the control, with which it found itself vested in 1912. There were at least one or two abortive attempts to enter the industry, but "Alcoa" effectively anticipated and forestalled all competition, and succeeded in holding the field alone. True, it stimulated demand and opened new uses for the metal, but not without making sure that it could supply what it had evoked. There is no dispute as to this; "Alcoa" avows it as evidence of the skill, energy and initiative with which it has always conducted its business; as a reason why, having won its way by fair means, it should be commended, and not dismembered. We need charge it with no moral derelictions after 1912; we may assume that all it claims for itself is true. The only question is whether it falls within the exception established in favor of those who do not seek, but cannot avoid, the control of a market. It seems to us that that question scarcely survives its statement. It was not inevitable that it should always anticipate increases in the demand for ingot and be prepared to supply them. Nothing compelled it to keep doubling and redoubling its capacity before others entered the field. It insists that it never excluded competitors; but we can think of no more effective exclusion than progressively to embrace each new opportunity as it opened, and to face every newcomer with new capacity already geared into a great organization, having the advantage of experience, trade connections and the elite of personnel. Only in case we interpret "exclusion" as limited to maneuvres not honestly industrial, but actuated solely by a desire to prevent competition, can such a course, indefatigably pursued, be deemed not "exclusionary." So to limit it would in our judgment emasculate the Act; would permit just such consolidations as it was designed to prevent.

"Alcoa" answers that it positively assisted competitors, instead of discouraging them. That may be true as to fabricators of ingot; but what of that? They were its market for ingot, and it is charged only with a monopoly of ingot. . . .

We disregard any question of "intent." Relatively early in the history of the Act — 1905 — Holmes, J., in *Swift & Co. v. United States*, 196 U.S. 375, explained this aspect of the Act in a passage often quoted. Although the primary evil was monopoly, the Act also covered preliminary steps, which, if continued, would lead to it. These may do no harm of themselves; but, if they are initial moves in a plan or scheme which, carried out, will result in monopoly, they are dangerous and the law will nip them in the bud. For this reason conduct falling short of monopoly, is not illegal unless it is part of a plan to monopolize, or to gain such other control of a market as is equally forbidden. To make it so, the plaintiff must prove what in the criminal law is known as a "specific intent"; an intent which goes beyond the mere intent to do the act. By far the greatest part of the fabulous record piled up in the case at bar, was concerned with proving such an intent. The plaintiff was seeking to show that many transactions, neutral on their face, were not in fact necessary to the development of "Alcoa's" business, and had no motive except to exclude others and perpetuate its hold upon the ingot market. Upon that effort success depended in case the plaintiff failed to satisfy the court that it was unnecessary under § 2 to convict "Alcoa" of practices unlawful of themselves. The plaintiff has so satisfied us, and the issue of intent ceases to have any importance; no intent is relevant except that which is relevant to any liability, criminal or civil: i.e. an intent to bring about the forbidden act. . . . In order to fall within § 2, the monopolist must have both the power to monopolize, and the intent to monopolize. To read [Swift & Co.] as demanding any 'specific,' intent, makes nonsense of it, for no monopolist monopolizes unconscious of what he is doing. So here, "Alcoa" meant to keep, and did keep, that complete and exclusive hold upon the ingot market with which it started. That was to "monopolize" that market, however innocently it otherwise proceeded. So far as the judgment held that it was not within § 2, it must be reversed.

As we have said, the plaintiff also sought to convict "Alcoa" of practices in which it engaged, not because they were necessary to the development of its business, but only in order to suppress competitors. Since we are holding that "Alcoa" "monopolized" the ingot market in 1940, regardless of such practices, these issues might be moot, if it inevitably followed from our holding that "Alcoa" must be dissolved. It could be argued that the new companies which would then emerge, should not be charged in retrospect with their predecessor's illegal conduct; but should be entitled to start without the handicap of injunctions, based upon its past. Possibly that would be true, except that conditions have so changed since the case was closed, that, as will appear, it by no means follows, because "Alcoa" had a monopoly in 1940, that it will have one when final judgment is entered after the war. That judgment may leave it intact as a competing unit among other competing units, and the plaintiff might argue, and undoubtedly will, that, if it was in the past guilty of practices, aimed at "monopolizing" the ingot market, it would be proper and necessary to enjoin their resumption, even though it no longer will have a monopoly. For this reason it appears to us that the issues are not altogether moot. . . .

. . . .

The plaintiff describes as the "Price Squeeze" a practice by which, it says, "Alcoa" intended to put out of business the manufacturers of aluminum "sheet" who were its competitors; for "Alcoa" was itself a large — in fact much the largest — maker of that product, and had been the first to introduce it many years before the period in question. . . . The plaintiff says that the "squeeze" had been in operation for a long time before the year 1925, and that by means of it "Alcoa" had succeeded in eliminating four out of the eight companies which competed with it.

. . . .

The plaintiff's theory is that "Alcoa" consistently sold ingot at so high a price that the "sheet rollers," who were forced to buy from it, could not pay the expenses of "rolling" the "sheet" and make a living profit out of the price at which "Alcoa" itself sold "sheet." To establish this the plaintiff asks us to take "Alcoa's" costs of "rolling" as a fair measure of its competitors' costs, and to assume that they had to meet "Alcoa's" price for all grades of "sheet," and could not buy ingot elsewhere. It seems to us altogether reasonable, in the absence of proof to the contrary, to suppose that "Alcoa's" "rolling" costs were not higher than those of other "sheet rollers"; and, although it is true that theoretically, imported "virgin" was always available, for the reasons we have already given when we were discussing the monopoly in ingot, we think that it could at best be had at very little less than "Alcoa's" prices. As for "secondary," there were a number of uses for "sheet" for which the trade would not accept such of it as was available in the years in question. Besides, the "spread" between suitable grades of "secondary" and "virgin" was also very small. . . .

. . . That it was unlawful to set the price of "sheet" so low and hold the price of ingot so high, seems to us unquestionable, provided, as we have held, that on this record the price of ingot must be regarded as higher than a "fair price." True, this was only a consequence of "Alcoa's" control over the price of ingot, and perhaps it ought not to be considered as a separate wrong; moreover, we do not use it as part of the reasoning by which we conclude that the monopoly was unlawful. But it was at least an unlawful exercise of "Alcoa's" power after it had been put on notice by the "sheet rollers" complaints; and this is true, even though we assent to the judge's finding that it was not part of an attempt to monopolize the "sheet" market. . . .

Nearly five years have passed since the evidence was closed; during that time the aluminum industry, like most other industries, has been revolutionized by the nation's efforts in a great crisis. That alone would make it impossible to dispose of the action upon the basis of the record as we have it; and so both sides agree; both appeal to us to take "judicial notice" of what has taken place meanwhile, though they differ as to what should be the result. The plaintiff wishes us to enter a judgment that "Alcoa" shall be dissolved, and that we shall direct it presently to submit a plan, whose execution, however, is to be deferred until after the war. . . . On the other hand, "Alcoa" argues that, when we look at the changes that have taken place — particularly the enormous capacity of plaintiff's aluminum plants — it appears that, even though we should conclude that it had "monopolized" the ingot industry up to 1941, the plaintiff now has in its hands the means to prevent any possible "monopolization" of the industry after the war, which it may use as it wills. . . .

[W]e refuse to take "notice" of facts relevant to the correctness of the findings; but we do take "notice" of those relevant to remedies.

After doing so, it is impossible to say what will be "Alcoa's" position in the industry after the war. The plaintiff has leased to it all its new plants and the leases do not expire until 1947 and 1948, though they may be surrendered earlier. No one can now forecast in the remotest way what will be the form of the industry after the plaintiff has disposed of these plants, upon their surrender. It may be able to transfer all of them to persons who can effectively compete with "Alcoa"; it may be able to transfer some; conceivably, it may be unable to dispose of any. The measure of its success will be at least one condition upon the propriety of dissolution, and upon the form which it should take, if there is to be any. It is as idle for the plaintiff to assume that dissolution will be proper, as it is for "Alcoa" to assume that it will not be; and it would be particularly fatuous to prepare a plan now, even if we could be sure that eventually some form of dissolution will be proper. Dissolution is not a penalty but a remedy; if the industry will not need it for its protection, it will be a disservice to break up an aggregation which has for so long demonstrated its efficiency. The need for such a remedy will be for the district court in the first instance, and there is a peculiar propriety in our saying nothing to control its decision, because the appeal from any judgment which it may enter, will perhaps be justiciable only by the Supreme Court, if there are then six justices qualified to sit.

NOTES AND QUESTIONS

1.   Contrast the "bad acts" committed by Alcoa with those committed by the American Can Company. Is it just as obvious that Alcoa's bad acts were socially harmful? What about the "price squeeze," by which Alcoa allegedly monopolized the ingot market by (1) selling independent fabricators' ingot at a relatively high price

and (2) pricing its own fabrications fairly low, with the result that the independent fabricators could not obtain a sufficient markup to earn a profit? Why would Alcoa bother with a "price squeeze?" Alcoa could lawfully stop selling any ingot at all to the fabricators, could it not? The alleged "price squeeze" may have been the result of nothing more than Alcoa's efficiency: its costs in fabricating its own aluminum were lower than the combined costs of selling and shipping ingot to others, plus their fabrication costs. See the *Linkline* decision reprinted *infra*.

2. The *Alcoa* opinion developed the modern two-stage definition of the offense of monopolization under Section 2 of the Sherman Act. First, the court must determine whether the defendant has "monopoly power" — that is, sufficient market power to "dominate" an industry. If the answer is no, then the defendant is not guilty. If the answer is yes, however, the court must additionally determine whether the defendant is an "innocent" monopolist whose dominance was "thrust upon" it by its own skill or efficiency, or whether it engaged in anticompetitive or monopolistic acts.

3. Consider Judge Hand's notion that expanding capacity to meet anticipated demand is "exclusionary." How can this be so? In order to price monopolistically, a monopolist must limit output. One often suggested possibility is that Alcoa could build a plant larger than it actually needed to meet either current or foreseeable demand. It could then set a price higher than the competitive level but not so high as to encourage immediate entry. A firm contemplating entry would see that Alcoa had substantial excess capacity and could reduce price and enlarge output at any time. The firm would also know that its own start-up costs would be high. It would look for another industry where there was not so much excess capacity. This combination of excess capacity plus so-called "limit" pricing has frequently been alleged of monopolists who appeared not to be restricting output. See the *du Pont* (titanium dioxide) case, reprinted *infra*, where the Federal Trade Commission dismissed a case that was not all that different from *Alcoa*. One problem with the theory is that it requires the alleged monopolist to maintain a great deal of unused productive capacity. This can be very expensive. The monopoly profits generated by the scheme must be large enough to offset this cost, but not so large as to encourage a potential competitor to enter the industry.

4. Judge Hand concluded in *Alcoa* that "throughout the history of [the antitrust laws] it has been constantly assumed that one of their purposes was to perpetuate and preserve, for its own sake and in spite of possible cost, an organization of industry in small units." Assumed by whom, do you suppose? Judge Hand did not cite a single Supreme Court opinion for that proposition, although he did suggest that it is explicit in the legislative history of the Sherman Act. For an argument that Hand's interpretation of the legislative history was wrong, see Robert Bork, *Legislative Intent and the Policy of the Sherman Act*, 9 J.L. & ECON. 7 (1966); *cf.* Robert H. Lande, *Wealth Transfers as the Original and Primary Concern of Antitrust: The Efficiency Interpretation Challenged*, 34 HASTINGS L.J. 65 (1982).

5. Judge Hand noted that Alcoa's profits were not inordinately high for a firm of its size. Would you expect a firm guilty of monopolization to have higher-than-normal rates of profit? Should the absence of high profitability be evidence that a firm is not a monopolist? It is possible that a firm engaged in illegal monopolization does not have particularly high profits because it incurs large expenses in maintaining its monopoly power. *See* RICHARD POSNER, ANTITRUST LAW 15–17 (2d ed. 2001). In fact, measuring market power from accounting rates of return is extraordinarily difficult, and some believe that it is conceptually impossible. *See* 2B PHILLIP AREEDA & HERBERT HOVENKAMP, ANTITRUST LAW ¶ 520 (4th ed. 2014).

6. *The Dilemma of the Durable Goods Monopolist.* As Judge Hand noted, Alcoa faced competition from its own aluminum — reclaimed and sold as "secondary" on the aluminum market. The monopolist of durable goods — goods that last a long time and can be reused by people other than the original purchasers — has one big problem. The more it sells, the more of its own product is out there in competition.

If a good is "perfectly durable" — i.e., if the demand curve for the "used — good is identical to the demand curve for the new good because consumers are indifferent as between them — then the monopolist will simply lose its monopoly position. Can you think of such a good? Land is probably the best example. All of it is very old, none (except a little in Holland) is being manufactured, and old land is just as good as new land. Suppose that a land monopolist owned an entire island, consisting of 100 lots. As soon as it sold the first lot, its market share would decline to 99%; when it had sold 50 lots, its market share would be only 50%. In short, in the very process of profiting from its monopoly, the land monopolist will have destroyed it.

To take a simple illustration of the durable goods monopolist's dilemma, suppose that a baby buggy is used by parents of a new baby for precisely one year, and that the life of a baby buggy is 10 years. Assume further that customers are indifferent between new baby buggies and used baby buggies, provided they are less than 10 years old. Each year, 10 couples have babies and need a buggy. Finally, suppose that the cost of making a baby buggy is $100, but that the use of a baby buggy for one year is worth $50 to every customer. After one year, parents place no value on the baby buggy for their own use; they either store it in the attic, where it is worthless, or sell it for the best price they can get.

What will the customers in the first year be willing to pay for the baby buggy? One would think that the buggy is worth $500 — $50 per customer multiplied by 10 consecutive customers. But the first customer will not be willing to pay $500 because he knows that the second year there will be competition in the baby buggy market. There will be 10 new sets of parents needing buggies and 10 used baby buggies on the market. But there will also be the output of new baby buggies by the manufacturer. What will the price be the second year? The manufacturer will presumably not sell them for less than their $100 production cost. But the very first year competition may easily drive the price in this market down to the competitive level. The second year the situation will be even worse. A wise customer will probably not be willing to pay much more than $150 for the buggy —$50 for the one year's use, and $100 for a reasonable estimate of the selling price at the end of the first year. In this particular case, instead of getting the $400 in available monopoly profits from its durable good, the monopolist gets only $50.

But suppose that the durable goods monopolist rents, rather than sells, its baby buggies. Because each customer values the buggy at $50, it will charge $50 per year for nine years. The tenth year it will sell the buggy for $50 to the final customer, and then the buggy will be worn out. In this case, the monopolist will be able to earn

$400 in monopoly profits from each buggy. This undoubtedly explains why United Shoe Machinery, Xerox, IBM, and other durable goods monopolists who were able to do so rented, rather than sold, their products. *See also Hawaii Hous. Auth. v. Midkiff*, 467 U.S. 229 (1984), in which an apparent land cartel in Hawaii leased rather than sold its property. Once the monopolist has lost its monopoly position, of course, customer preference will dictate whether it sells or rents its output.

Alcoa sold both raw and fabricated aluminum. The transaction costs of renting aluminum kitchen utensils, aircraft and automobile parts, and building materials would be extremely high, and customers would place a much lower value on such parts if they could not purchase them. Alcoa's monopoly position was saved by the fact that aluminum is only an imperfectly durable good. Only part of it could be reused, and many customers either found second-hand aluminum unacceptable or were willing to pay a premium for new aluminum. The monopolist of an imperfectly durable good can continue to enjoy some monopoly profits. Can you see why?

Another way that the durable goods monopolist might obtain more than the competitive price is to make a credible commitment to make less of the good than would clear the market at a competitive price. For example, what if the baby buggy manufacturer in the above illustration could make a credible promise to its customers that it was going to manufacture buggies for exactly one year and then go out of business. In that case, it should be able to obtain the full $500 for its buggies. Consider the artist who promises to make only 50 copies of a particular lithograph and then destroy the plate. Shouldn't the price be higher than if the artist made an unlimited number of copies?

See Barak Y. Orbach, *The Durapolist Puzzle: Monopoly Power in Durable-Goods Markets*, 21 YALE J. ON REG. 67 (2004); John Shepard Wiley Jr., Eric Rasmusen, & J. Mark Ramseyer, *The Leasing Monopolist*, 37 UCLA L. REV. 693 (1990); David Malueg & John Solow, *On Requiring the Durable Goods Monopolist to Sell*, 25 ECON. LETTERS 283 (1987); Ronald Coase, *Durability and Monopoly*, 15 J.L. & ECON. 143 (1972); Dennis Carlton & Robert Gertner, *Market Power and Mergers in Durable-Good Industries*, 32 J.L. & ECON. S203 (1989) (arguing that mergers should be of much less concern in durable goods industries); Luke Froeb, *Evaluating Mergers in Durable Goods Industries*, 34 ANTITRUST BULL. 99 (1989) (in many markets durability limits market power).

UNITED STATES v. UNITED SHOE MACHINERY CORP.
110 F. Supp. 295 (D. Mass. 1953), *aff'd per curiam*, 347 U.S. 521 (1954)

JUDGE WYZANSKI.

[The United States sued to restrain violations of Section 2 of the Sherman Act.]

Stripped to its essentials, the 52 page complaint charged, *first*, that since 1912 United had been "monopolizing interstate trade and commerce in the shoe machinery industry of the United States" . . . .

. . . .

There are 18 major processes for the manufacturing of shoes by machine. Some machine types are used only in one process, but others are used in several; and the relationship of machine types to one another may be competitive or sequential. The approximately 1460 shoe manufacturers themselves are highly competitive in many respects, including their choice of processes and other technological aspects of production. Their total demand for machine services . . . constitutes an identifiable market which is a "part of the trade or commerce among the several States."

United, the largest source of supply, is a corporation lineally descended from a combination of constituent companies, adjudged lawful by the Supreme Court of the United States in 1918. It now has assets rising slightly over 100 million dollars and employment rolls of around 6,000. In recent years it has earned before federal taxes 9 to 13.5 million dollars annually.

. . . United at the present time is supplying over 75%, and probably 85%, of the current demand in the American shoe machinery market, as heretofore defined. This is somewhat less than the share it was supplying in 1915. . . .

Although at the turn of the century, United's patents covered the fundamentals of shoe machinery manufacture, those fundamental patents have expired. Current patents cover for the most part only minor developments, so that it is possible to "invent around" them, to use the words of United's chief competitor. However, the aggregation of patents does to some extent block potential competition. It furnishes a trading advantage. It leads inventors to offer their ideas to United, on the general principle that new complicated machines embody numerous patents. And it serves as a hedge or insurance for United against unforeseen competitive developments.

. . . .

In supplying its complicated machines to shoe manufacturers, United, like its more important American competitors, has followed the practice of never selling, but only leasing. Leasing has been traditional in the shoe machinery field since the Civil War. So far as this record indicates, there is virtually no expressed dissatisfaction from consumers respecting that system; and Compo, United's principal competitor, endorses and uses it. Under the system, entry into shoe manufacture has been easy. The rates charged for all customers have been uniform. The machines supplied have performed excellently. United has, without separate charge, promptly and efficiently supplied repair service and many kinds of other service useful to shoe manufacturers. These services have been particularly important, because in the shoe manufacturing industry a whole line of production can be adversely affected, and valuable time lost, if some of the important machines go out of function, and because machine breakdowns have serious labor and consumer repercussions. The cost to the average shoe manufacturer of its machines and services supplied to him has been less than 2% of the wholesale price of his shoes.

However, United's leases, in the context of the present shoe machinery market, have created barriers to the entry by competitors into the shoe machinery field.

First, the complex of obligations and rights accruing under United's leasing system in operation deter a shoe manufacturer from disposing of a United machine and acquiring a competitor's machine. He is deterred more than if he owned that same United machine, or if he held it on a short lease carrying simple rental provisions and a reasonable charge for cancellation before the end of the term. The lessee is now held closely to United by the combined effect of the 10 year term, the requirement that if he has work available he must use the machine to full capacity, and by the return charge which can in practice, through the right of deduction fund, be reduced to insignificance if he keeps this and other United machines to the end of the periods for which he leased them.

Second, when a lessee desires to replace a United machine, United gives him more favorable terms if the replacement is by another United machine than if it is by a competitive machine.

Third, United's practice of offering to repair, without separate charges, its leased machines, has had the effect that there are no independent service organizations to repair complicated machines. In turn, this has had the effect that the manufacturer of a complicated machine must either offer repair service with his machine, or must face the obstacle of marketing his machine to customers who know that repair service will be difficult to provide.

Through its success with its principal and more complicated machines, United has been able to market more successfully its other machines, whether offered only for sale, or on optional sale or lease terms. In ascending order of importance, the reasons for United's success with these simpler types are these. These other, usually more simple, machines are technologically related to the complex leased machines to which they are auxiliary or preparatory. Having business relations with, and a host of contacts with, shoe factories, United seems to many of them the most efficient, normal, and above all, convenient supplier.

Finally, United has promoted the sale of these simple machine types by the sort of price discrimination between machine types, about to be stated.

Although maintaining the same nominal terms for each customer, United has followed, as between machine types, a discriminatory pricing policy. [E]xamples of this policy can be found in the wide, and relatively permanent, variations in the rates of return United secures upon its long line of machine types. United's own internal documents reveal that these sharp and relatively durable differentials are traceable, at least in large part, to United's policy of fixing a higher rate of return where competition is of minor significance, and a lower rate of return where competition is of major significance. . . .

     . . . .

In *Aluminum* [148 F.2d 416] Judge Hand, perhaps because he was cabined by the findings of the District Court, did not rest his judgment on the corporation's coercive or immoral practices. Instead, adopting an economic approach, he defined the appropriate market, found that Alcoa supplied 90% of it, determined that this control constituted a monopoly, and ruled that since Alcoa established this monopoly by its voluntary actions, such as building new plants, though, it was assumed, not by moral derelictions, it had "monopolized" in violation of § 2. Judge Hand reserved the issue as to whether an enterprise could be said to "monopolize" if its control was purely the result of technological, production, distribution, or like objective factors, not dictated by the enterprise, but thrust upon it by the economic character of the industry; and he also reserved the question as to control achieved solely "by virtue of . . . superior skill, foresight and industry." At the same time, he emphasized that an enterprise had "monopolized" if, regardless of its intent, it had achieved a monopoly by manoeuvres which, though "honestly industrial," were not economically inevitable, but were rather the result of the firm's free choice of business policies.

. . . .

[R]ecent authorities [suggest] at least three different, but cognate, approaches. The approach which has the least sweeping implications really antedates the decision in *Aluminum*. But it deserves restatement. An enterprise has monopolized in violation of § 2 of the Sherman Act if it has acquired or maintained a power to exclude others as a result of using an unreasonable "restraint of trade" in violation of § 1 of the Sherman Act. *See United States v. Columbia Steel Co.*, 334 U.S. 495, 525; *see also United States v. Griffith*, 334 U.S. 100.

A more inclusive approach was adopted by Mr. Justice Douglas in *United States v. Griffith*, 334 U.S. 100. He stated that to prove a violation of § 2 it was not always necessary to show a violation of § 1. And he concluded that an enterprise has monopolized in violation of § 2 if it (a) has the power to exclude competition, and (b) has exercised it, or has the purpose to exercise it. The least that this conclusion means is that it is a violation of § 2 for one having effective control of the market to use, or plan to use, any exclusionary practice, even though it is not a technical restraint of trade. But the conclusion may go further.

Indeed the way in which Mr. Justice Douglas used the terms "monopoly power" and "effective market control," and cited *Aluminum* suggests that he endorses a third and broader approach, which originated with Judge Hand. It will be recalled that Judge Hand said that one who has acquired an overwhelming share of the market "monopolizes" whenever he does business, apparently even if there is no showing that his business involves any exclusionary practice. But this doctrine is softened by Judge Hand's suggestion that the defendant may escape statutory liability if it bears the burden of proving that it owes its monopoly solely to superior skill, superior products, natural advantages, (including accessibility to raw materials or markets), economic or technological efficiency, (including scientific research), low margins of profit maintained permanently and without discrimination, or licenses conferred by, and used within, the limits of law, (including patents on one's own inventions, or franchises granted directly to the enterprise by a public authority).

In the case at bar, the Government contends that the evidence satisfies each of the three approaches to § 2 of the Sherman Act, so that it does not matter which one is taken. . . .

This Court finds it unnecessary to choose between the second and third approaches. For, taken as a whole, the evidence satisfies the tests laid down in both *Griffith* and *Aluminum*. The facts show that (1) defendant has, and exercises, such overwhelming strength in the shoe machinery market that it controls that market, (2) this strength excludes some potential, and limits some actual, competition, and (3) this strength is not attributable solely to defendant's ability, economies of scale, research, natural advantages, and adaptation to inevitable economic laws.

In estimating defendant's strength, this Court gives some weight to the 75 plus percentage of the shoe machinery market which United serves. But the Court considers other factors as well. In the relatively static shoe machinery market where there are no sudden changes in the style of machines or in the volume of demand, United has a network of long-term, complicated leases with over 90% of the shoe factories. These leases assure closer and more frequent contacts between United and its customers than would exist if United were a seller and its customers were buyers. Beyond this general quality, these leases are so drawn and so applied as to strengthen United's power to exclude competitors. Moreover, United offers a long line of machine types, while no competitor offers more than a short line. Since in some parts of its line United faces no important competition, United has the power to discriminate, by wide differentials and over long periods of time, in the rate of return it procures from different machine types. Furthermore, being by far the largest company in the field, with by far the largest resources in dollars, in patents, in facilities, and in knowledge, United has a marked capacity to attract offers of inventions, inventors' services, and shoe machinery businesses. And, finally, there is no substantial substitute competition from a vigorous secondhand market in shoe machinery.

To combat United's market control, a competitor must be prepared with knowledge of shoemaking, engineering skill, capacity to invent around patents, and financial resources sufficient to bear the expense of long developmental and experimental processes. The competitor must be prepared for consumers' resistance founded on their long-term, satisfactory relations with United, and on the cost to them of surrendering United's leases. Also, the competitor must be prepared to give, or point to the source of, repair and other services, and to the source of supplies for machine parts, expendable parts, and the like. Indeed, perhaps a competitor who aims at any large scale success must also be prepared to lease his machines. These considerations would all affect *potential* competition, and have not been without their effect on *actual* competition.

Not only does the evidence show United has control of the market, but also the evidence does not show that the control is due entirely to excusable causes. The three principal sources of United's power have been the original constitution of the company, the superiority of United's products and services, and the leasing system. The first two of these are plainly beyond reproach. The original constitution of United in 1899 was judicially approved in *United States v. United Shoe Machinery Company of New Jersey*, 247 U.S. 32. It is no longer open to question, and must be regarded as protected by the doctrine of *res judicata*, which is the equivalent of a legal license. Likewise beyond criticism is the high quality of United's products, its understanding of the techniques of shoemaking and the needs of shoe manufacturers, its efficient design and improvement of machines, and its prompt and knowledgeable service. These have illustrated in manifold ways that "superior skill, foresight and industry" of which Judge Hand spoke in *Aluminum.*

But United's control does not rest solely on its original constitution, its ability, its research, or its economies of scale. There are other barriers to competition, and these barriers were erected by United's own business policies. Much of United's market power is traceable to the magnetic ties inherent in its system of leasing, and not selling, its more important machines. The lease-only system of distributing complicated machines has many "partnership" aspects, and it has exclusionary features such as the 10-year term, the full capacity clause, the return charges, and the failure to segregate service charges from machine charges. Moreover, the leasing system has aided United in maintaining a pricing system which discriminates between machine types. . . .

In one sense, the leasing system and the miscellaneous activities just referred to (except United's purchases in the secondhand market) were natural and normal, for they were, in Judge Hand's words, "honestly industrial." They are the sort of activities which would be engaged in by other honorable firms. And, to a large extent, the leasing practices conform to long-standing traditions in the shoe machinery business. Yet, they are not practices which can be properly described as the inevitable consequences of ability, natural forces, or law. They represent something more than the use of accessible resources, the process of invention and innovation, and the employment of those techniques of employment, financing, production, and distribution, which a competitive society must foster. They are contracts, arrangements, and policies which, instead of encouraging competition based on pure merit, further the dominance of a particular firm. In this sense, they are unnatural barriers; they unnecessarily exclude actual and potential competition; they restrict a free market. While the law allows many enterprises to use such practices, the Sherman Act is now construed by superior courts to forbid the continuance of effective market control based in part upon such practices. . . .

So far, nothing in this opinion has been said of defendant's *intent* in regard to its power and practices in the shoe machinery market. This point can be readily disposed of by reference once more to Aluminum. Defendant intended to engage in the leasing practices and pricing policies which maintained its market power. That is all the intent which the law requires when both the complaint and the judgment rest on a charge of "monopolizing," not merely "attempting to monopolize." Defendant having willed the means, has willed the end.

. . . .

Where a defendant has monopolized commerce in violation of § 2, the principal objects of the decrees are to extirpate practices that have caused or may hereafter cause monopolization, and to restore workable competition in the market.

. . . Concentrations of power, no matter how beneficently they appear to have acted, nor what advantages they seem to possess, are inherently dangerous. Their good behavior in the past may not be continued; and if their strength were hereafter grasped by presumptuous hands, there would be no automatic check and balance from equal forces in the industrial market. . . . Dispersal of private economic power is thus one of the ways to preserve the system of private enterprise. . . .

. . . .

Judges . . . do not *ex officio* have economic or political training. Their prophecies as to the economic future are not guided by unusually subtle judgment. They are not so representative as other branches of the government. The recommendations they receive from government prosecutors do not always reflect the overall approach of even the executive branch of the government, sometimes not indeed the seasoned and fairly informed judgment of the head of the Department of Justice.

Hearings in court do not usually give the remote judge as sound a feeling for the realities of a situation as other procedures do. . . .

. . . .

In the light of these general considerations, it is now meet to consider the principal problems respecting a proposed decree. . . .

The Government's proposal that the Court dissolve United into three separate manufacturing companies is unrealistic. United conducts all machine manufacture at one plant in Beverly, with one set of jigs and tools, one foundry, one laboratory for machinery problems, one managerial staff, and one labor force. It takes no Solomon to see that this organism cannot be cut into three equal and viable parts.

. . . .

On the whole, therefore, the suggested remedy of dissolution is rejected.

From the opinion on defendant's violations it follows that some form of relief regarding defendant's leases and leasing practices is proper and necessary.

. . . .

Although leasing should not now be abolished by judicial decree, the Court agrees with the Government that the leases should be purged of their restrictive features. In the decree filed herewith, the term of the lease is shortened, the full capacity clause is eliminated, the discriminatory commutative charges are removed, and United is required to segregate its charges for machines from its charges for repair service. For the most part, the decree speaks plainly enough upon these points. Yet, on two matters, a further word is in order.

The decree does not prohibit United from rendering service, because, in the Court's view, the rendition of service, if separately charged for, has no exclusionary effects. Moreover, the rendition of service by United will keep its research and manufacturing divisions abreast of technological problems in the shoe manufacturing industry; and this will be an economic advantage of the type fostered by the Sherman Act. . . .

The Court also agrees with the Government that if United chooses to continue to lease any machine type, it must offer that type of machine also for sale. The principal merit of this proposal does not lie in its primary impact, that is, in its effect in widening the choices open to owners of shoe factories. For present purposes it may be assumed that the anti-trust laws are not designed, chiefly, if at all, to give a customer choice as to the selling methods by which his supplier offers that supplier's own products. The merit of the Government's proposal is in its secondary impact. Insofar as United's machines are sold rather than leased, they will ultimately, in many cases, reach a second-hand market. From that market, United will face a type of substitute competition which will gradually weaken the prohibited market power which it now exercises. Moreover, from that market, or from United itself, a competitor of United can acquire a United machine in order to study it, to copy its unpatented features, and to experiment with improvements in, or alterations of, the machine. Thus, in another and more direct way, United's market power will be diminished.

. . . .

A . . . possible objection to the decree is that it confers upon United's competitors the unearned opportunity to copy the unpatented features of United's machines. These competitors get a free ride.

In reply, it might be enough to say that there does not appear to be any federal or local, statutory or common law, principle protecting United's interest in these unpatented features. That is, the decree takes from United nothing which the policy of our law protects. A further answer is that if the creation of a sales alternative to leasing is, as this Court believes, necessary to dissipate United's monopoly power, the Court should not withhold its decree because its effect is to allow competitors to copy United's designs.

. . . .

NOTES AND QUESTIONS

1. Judge Wyzanski identified the defendant's lease-only policy as an exclusionary practice because the long-term leases tended to limit the ability of potential competitors to enter the market. Is this plausible? Suppose the useful life of a machine is 15 years. The defendant could not lease a machine for longer than its lifespan, could it? A purchaser of the machine would operate it for its full lifespan, or until it became obsolete. The lessee's holding period would likely be shorter, unless the lessee was obligated to continue using the machine even after it became obsolete. In that case, United would have to charge less money for the machine.

Judge Wyzanski also noted that the lease-only policy had the effect of foreclosing the market in second-hand machines, for United could always take them back when the lease expired. In this way, United allegedly avoided the problem that Alcoa had faced of competing with its own "secondary" aluminum. The argument depends on several assumptions. One is that a shoe machine is still usable enough to "compete" in the market after the first owner is through with it. If it is, then why did the first owner get rid of it? Because it is obsolete? That argument won't work, unless we posit that United was afraid of competing with its own outdated machines. Perhaps if the shoe manufacturer went out of business? Isn't there a better explanation for United's wanting control over the reversions in its machines? The same reason that United leased them to begin with: so that it could maintain them itself and not have a number of machines bearing its name breaking down. Another possibility is that United Shoe Machinery's lease-only policy was designed to maximize its revenues, given the fact that shoe machinery is a durable good. See the note following the *Alcoa* decision, *supra*, on monopoly and durability.

2. *Price discrimination.* Judge Wyzanski identifies price discrimination as one of the defendant's exclusionary practices. Wyzanski found that United obtained a high rate of return from machines in which it had a monopoly, but a lower rate from machines in which it faced competition. In other words, United probably charged its profit-maximizing price for each machine. But why would that practice be exclusionary? Perhaps Judge Wyzanski believed United was using its high prices in its monopoly products to "subsidize" lower prices in the competitive products, thereby driving the competitors out of business. As we shall see in the section on predatory

pricing, *infra*, however, such an explanation is not likely. What if United were ordered by the court to obtain the same rate of return from all its machines? It could then sell or lease all of them at the monopoly price, in which case, it would lose its market in the more competitive machines, and perhaps even cede a monopoly to someone else. Otherwise, it could charge the competitive price in all of its markets, which would be even more "exclusionary" because then there would be no supra competitive profits to attract new entrants.

3.   Although price discrimination is not an "exclusionary" practice, it is evidence of market power. Assuming that the rate of return on the low-priced machines was profitable, the rate of return on the higher-priced machines must have been monopolistic. As the discussion of price discrimination, *infra*, suggests, only a seller with market power can engage in systematic price discrimination. However, the amount of power need not be very large; indeed most sellers in product-differentiated markets can usually engage in at least some price discrimination. *See* 3 Phillip E. Areeda & Herbert Hovenkamp, Antitrust Law ¶ 721 (3d ed. 2008).

4.   Judge Wyzanski took note of the fact that the case law suggested a variety of tests for illegal monopolization. The "classic" test was developed in *Standard Oil Co. v. United States*, 221 U.S. 1 (1911), and *United States v. American Tobacco Co.*, 221 U.S. 106 (1911). Under Judge Wyzanski's reading of that test, Section 2 of the Sherman Act is violated if a company acquires or maintains a monopoly by means which themselves violate Section 1. Cases involving mergers to monopoly would clearly fall within the definition. Section 1, however, requires a "combination" (at least initially) of two or more firms. If a firm has never merged and has never otherwise conspired with a second party to violate Section 1, then the firm could not be guilty of illegal monopolization either. But Judge Wyzanski read *Standard Oil* and *American Tobacco* too narrowly. In both of them, the Supreme Court made clear that Section 2 of the Sherman Act was designed to supplement Section 1 by reaching single-firm conduct that falls outside of Section 1 because of the combination or conspiracy requirement, and which results in the creation of a monopoly.

5.   Judge Wyzanski's second suggested test for monopolization has come to resemble the current formulation. It comes from the Supreme Court's decision in *United States v. Griffith*, 334 U.S. 100, 106–107 (1948), where the Court concluded:

> Section 1 [of the Sherman Act] covers contracts, combinations, or conspiracies in restraint of trade. Section 2 is not restricted to conspiracies or combinations to monopolize but also makes it a crime for any person to monopolize or to attempt to monopolize any part of . . . commerce. So it is that monopoly power, whether lawfully or unlawfully acquired, may itself constitute an evil and stand condemned under § 2 even though it remains unexercised. For § 2 of the Act is aimed, *inter alia*, at the acquisition or retention of effective market control. Hence the existence of power "to exclude competition when it is desired to do so" is itself a violation of § 2, provided it is coupled with the purpose or intent to exercise that power. . . . It follows . . . that the use of monopoly power, however lawfully acquired, to foreclose competition, to gain a competitive advantage, or to destroy a competitor, is unlawful.

6. Judge Wyzanski cited both Justice Douglas and Judge Hand for the suggestion that a company with a large market power should be guilty of monopolization whenever it "does business." At various times in the history of the antitrust laws, commentators have debated so-called "no fault" or "no conduct" monopolization. Perhaps the most famous proposal was made in Carl Kaysen & Donald TURNER, ANTITRUST POLICY: AN ECONOMIC AND LEGAL ANALYSIS 111, 265–272 (1959), which argued that "excessive" market power, without more, should be illegal. Under the Kaysen and Turner proposal, illegal market power would be conclusively presumed if for five or more years one company had 50% or more of the annual sales in the relevant market, or if four or fewer companies had 80% or more of the sales. The proposal would have permitted affirmative defenses of economies of scale, ownership and legal use of valid patents, or superior products and extraordinary efficiency. How would United Shoe Machinery have fared under the proposed statute?

In the past, "no fault" monopoly statutes have been proposed to Congress several times, but there has been no legislation. *See* Yale Brozen, *The Concentration-Collusion Doctrine*, 46 ANTITRUST L.J. 826 (1977); *Materials Presented to the National Commission for the Review of Antitrust Laws and Procedures*, 48 ANTITRUST L.J. 845 (1979). At present, none appears likely.

II   THE MODERN MONOPOLIZATION OFFENSE: POWER

[A]   Market Power, Barriers to Entry, and the Relevant Market

Today we can state the test for illegal monopolization in a single sentence: a defendant (1) must have a large amount of market power; and (2) it must have engaged in certain monopolistic, or anticompetitive, acts.

The verbal formulation of that test has not changed for more than a half century. That stability, however, belies the great deal of flux that has existed in judicial interpretation of Section 2 of the Sherman Act. First, our notion of market power is much more technical today than it was at the time *Alcoa* was decided. Secondly, judges in the 1970s and 1980s have examined much more critically those practices that are alleged to be monopolistic. For example, Judge Hand believed it was illegal monopolization for a firm with market power to enlarge its plant to meet an anticipated increase in demand for its product; few courts today would agree. *See, e.g., Dial A Car, Inc. v. Transportation, Inc.*, 82 F.3d 484, 486 (D.C. Cir. 1996) (not unlawful for cab company to expand its service so as to compete with existing limousine companies: the expansion "would appear to be fostering competition, rather than reducing it").

One of the reasons for this shift in the definition of monopolistic or anticompetitive acts has been a major change in the fundamental ideology of the federal antitrust laws. Alcoa could expand its output of aluminum only by finding new uses for it (i.e., expanding the market) or else by lowering the price. Consumers were better off because of these activities. By expanding its plant, however, Alcoa prevented competitors from entering the market: as the market grew, Alcoa was always there, ready to supply the full demand, allegedly at a low enough price that it was unprofitable for competitors to enter the market. In short, while Alcoa's expansion program benefitted consumers of aluminum, it injured competitors, or at least prevented potential competitors from entering the market. When Judge Hand looked at the "injuries" caused by the defendant's acts, he concentrated largely on injuries that accrued to competitors or potential competitors of the defendant. The same was true in the *American Can* case: most of American Can's judicially recognized "victims" were competitors. Today, on the other hand, the circuit courts are more likely to look at the effects that the alleged monopolization has on consumers rather than competitors. *See* the *Berkey Photo* and *California Computer Products* cases, *infra*, this chapter.

In an often-quoted passage in *Alcoa*, Judge Hand attempted to define a "monopoly" under the Sherman Act. Hand observed that Alcoa dominated over 90% of America's aluminum market. He concluded: "That percentage is enough to constitute a monopoly; it is doubtful whether sixty or sixty-four per cent would be enough; and certainly thirty-three per cent is not." Judge Hand found a very high correlation — perhaps even an identification — between the defendant's percentage of a certain market and the existence of a monopoly. This seems logical because the historical definition of a monopoly at common law was a legal right to 100% of a certain market.

But large market share is not the evil that the Sherman Act condemns. Rather, the evil is that, perhaps *because* it has a large percentage, it is able to charge more than a competitive price for the monopolized product. "Market power" is the ability to raise price by reducing output. Today we measure market power as the ratio of the profit-maximizing price for a seller's output to the seller's marginal cost at that rate of output. A seller whose marginal cost of producing a widget is $1.00, but who can maximize its profits by selling the widget at $1.02 has a small amount of market power. A seller whose marginal cost is $1.00 but whose profit-maximizing price is $1.75 has a great deal of market power. (In perfect competition, prices are driven to marginal cost. In that case, a seller's marginal cost and its profit-maximizing price would be the same. If the seller attempted to charge more than marginal cost, and it was not more efficient than its rivals, it would lose all its sales to competitors.) The Lerner Index measures market power this way, by the expression:

P-MC

P

Where:

P = the firm's profit-maximizing price, which we generally assume is the price that the firm is charging at any given time

MC = the firm's marginal cost

The formula is easy to use if true marginal cost is known. For example, in a competitive market, price equals marginal cost, so the value of the Index is zero. If a firm's price is double its marginal cost, say P = 2 and MC = 1, then the index value is 1/2, or 0.5, suggesting significant market power.

Market power expressed as the ratio of a seller's marginal cost to its profit-maximizing price, is a function of the elasticity of demand for the seller's output. The more elastic the demand for a certain product, the more customers will opt away when the product's price goes up, and the less will be the ability of a seller to sell at a supra competitive level.

It is easy to quantify the relationship that exists between elasticity of demand and market power.

Market power, defined as the ratio of the monopoly price (the profit-maximizing price) and the competitive price (marginal cost), varies with firm elasticity of demand by the following formula:

$$\frac{P_m}{P_c} = \frac{e}{e-1}$$

Where:

P_m = the profit-maximizing price of the product

P_c = the competitive price of the product (marginal cost)

P_e = the price elasticity of demand facing the seller

For derivation of the formula, plus analysis of some of its uses and limitations, see William Landes & Richard Posner, *Market Power in Antitrust Cases*, 94 HARV. L. REV. 937 (1981); HERBERT HOVENKAMP, FEDERAL ANTITRUST POLICY § 3.1 (4th ed. 2011).

However, don't let the equation fool you into thinking that there are easy answers to the question of market power. The formula simply tells us that there is a fixed relationship between the amount consumers as a group are willing to pay for a particular seller's product and the amount that the seller can charge for it. That statement is a tautology. To be able to express the ability of a firm to charge a monopoly price as a function of firm elasticity of demand does us little good in the courtroom unless it is easier to determine elasticity of demand facing a firm than it is to estimate monopoly power from market share. Most often it is not. The same thing is true of the Lerner Index itself. Our ability to measure market power under the Index is no better than our ability to measure marginal cost, and direct measurement of marginal cost in antitrust cases has not yet met with much success.

As a result, market share percentages continue to dominate judicial estimates of market power. In fact, our intuition tells us that someone who has a very large market share, other things being equal, has more ability to control price than someone whose market share is very small. If someone with 1% share of the market for a certain product attempts unilaterally to raise the price of the product, consumers are likely to have dozens of other places to which they can turn for the same product. The result will be that the seller will lose its customers.

By contrast, if a seller produces 90% of a certain product, then it is more likely to get away with the price increase. The producers who control the remaining 10% of the market will not be able to service all the monopolist's customers, and many of those customers will have to decide either to pay the higher price or not to buy at all. In fact, the producers holding the remaining 10% of the market may find it profitable to raise their own prices to a level equal with or slightly lower than the price charged by the monopolist. The monopolist's high price will therefore provide the fringe competitors with an "umbrella" that will enable them to obtain monopoly profits as well.

This intuitive relationship between market power and market share can also be demonstrated mathematically, although the equation for market power contains more variables than market share alone. *See* William Landes & Richard Posner, *Market Power in Antitrust Cases*, 94 HARV. L. REV. 937, 944–948 (1981). For alternative mechanisms for measuring market power, see 2B PHILLIP AREEDA, HERBERT HOVENKAMP & JOHN SOLOW, Antitrust Law ¶¶ 515–521 (4th ed. 2014). Today the law of antitrust recognizes that market power and not market share is the evil that the antitrust laws govern, but that the correlation between market power and market share permits courts to use market share as a limited proxy or surrogate for market power.

As a general rule, therefore, courts begin their analysis in monopolization cases by determining the defendant's market share. In order to do this, the court must define a certain "relevant" market. The relevant market consists of two parts, the product market and the geographic market. Clearly, a defendant who has market power does not have market power in every product, but only in the particular product that it sells. But how does one define the relevant "product"? Are Ford automobiles and Chevrolet automobiles the same product? Color televisions and black and white televisions? Secondly, it is clear that someone who has market power does not have it everywhere. The owner of the only movie theater in Ozona, Texas, may have substantial market power in Ozona — but how about 20 miles away? In Dallas? In New York City?

In determining market share, the court generally does three things. First, it identifies the "product" that is alleged to be monopolized. In the *Alcoa* case, Judge Hand decided that the relevant product was virgin ingot manufactured and sold in the United States and foreign-produced ingot actually sold in the United States. Second, the court determines a relevant geographic market. In *Alcoa*, Judge Hand decided that the market was the entire United States. Finally, the court computes a "market share" expressed as the defendant's output of the relevant product in the relevant market, divided by the total output of the relevant product in the relevant market. Judge Hand decided that Alcoa's market share was about 90%.

As the *Alcoa* decision indicates, identifying a relevant product or geographic market can be difficult enough. However, our analysis of market power is made even more complex because market share is not a perfect expression of market power. Courts express the imperfection of the relationship in various ways — frequently by saying that a very high market share creates an "inference" of market power that can be rebutted if the defendant can show that it is not able to control output or price in the market. In fact, market power is a function of three different values: the defendant's market share, the elasticity of demand in the entire market, and the cross-elasticity of supply of competing or potentially competing firms. Can a seller with a very small percentage of the market ever control the market output or price? *See Dimmitt Agri Indus., Inc. v. CPC Int'l, Inc.*, 679 F.2d 516 (5th Cir. 1982).

Suppose that Alcoa does in fact have 90% of the market share of aluminum but that consumer preferences for aluminum track the costs of producing it very closely. If the market price of aluminum rises by even a small amount, droves of customers will stop buying aluminum and substitute away. In such a case, it seems clear, Alcoa would not have power to control the price of aluminum, even though its market share is very high. In short, the more elastic the demand for the allegedly monopolized product when it is priced at marginal cost, the less market power the defendant has. For a more detailed and more technical analysis of the relationship between market power and demand elasticities, see Landes & Posner, *supra*, at pp. 945–948.

Secondly, suppose that Alcoa does in fact produce 90% of the virgin aluminum currently sold in the United States, but that there are dozens of underutilized steel mills that could shift over to the production of aluminum at very low cost. If the market price of aluminum rises by even a small amount, it will be profitable for these steel companies to shift to production of aluminum. Alcoa's market share will then drop and the enlarged production of aluminum in the country will force prices back down. In that case, it seems equally clear that Alcoa's control over the price of aluminum is small. The same thing would be true if Alcoa had competitors actually making aluminum, but these competitors were operating at far below their capacity. Suppose, for example, that Alcoa is currently manufacturing 7 million tons of aluminum per year and that it has competitors in the United States who manufacture 3 million tons per year. Suppose, in addition, that these competitors actually have plants large enough to manufacture 7 million tons of aluminum themselves, but they have not been doing so because the price of aluminum has not been high enough. If the price goes up, however, they will have an incentive to enlarge their production. This unused productive capacity limits Alcoa's control over the price of aluminum.

The presence of unused capacity in the industry, or the existence of firms that could easily shift to production of the product, is called the elasticity of supply in the market. The greater the elasticity of supply, the less control a particular producer has over the market price. Both elasticity of demand and elasticity of supply therefore limit the ability of a producer — even a producer with a very large market share — to raise its prices to a supra competitive level. The two elasticities are often unrelated to each other. That is, high elasticity of demand does not entail high elasticity of supply, or vice-versa. Suppose, for example, that one firm has a 90% share of the current production of tissue paper. However, the production of corrugated paper for heavy boxes is carried on by dozens of small competitors. The *demand* for tissue paper might be very inelastic. Furthermore, the cross-elasticity of demand between tissue paper and corrugated paper is probably very low, that is, the price of tissue paper would have to go very high before many customers would find corrugated paper to be an attractive substitute. But suppose additionally that at the *production* end the same plants that produce corrugated paper can, simply by making a few minor alterations, shift their equipment over to manufacturing tissue paper instead. How should we measure this? Should we say that the relevant "product" is tissue paper and corrugated paper together, or that the two are separate products? What appears clearly to be two different products on the demand side (for example, cookbooks and telephone directories) may in fact seem much more similar on the supply side (if a printer can costlessly shift over from producing cookbooks to producing telephone directories).

The concept of elasticity of supply also suggests that when we identify a defendant's percentage of a relevant market, we consider the industry's production *capacity*, not merely the amount that it is actually producing. As a general matter, it is much cheaper for a competitor to increase its output in an already existing plant than it is to build an additional plant, or for a new competitor to enter the field. Thus the existence of large amounts of excess capacity in times of slack demand can seriously distort our picture of market power, particularly if one lucky competitor is less affected by the declining demand than others are. For example, if market demand for steel drops from 90% of plant capacity to 40%, but that decrease affects certain plants much more severely than it does others, the favored plants may have a misleading percentage of output in the market which suggests that they have far more market power than they really do. Unfortunately, however, the theoretical superiority of capacity is not the only relevant consideration. Plant capacity is extraordinarily difficult to measure. Many plants can produce far more than they currently do, but only at higher costs. On the other hand, current output figures are readily available. Virtually all courts continue to use output, rather than capacity, in measuring market share. *See* 2B Phillip Areeda, Herbert Hovenkamp & John Solow, Antitrust Law, ch. 5 (3d ed. 2007).

Now let us return to one of Judge Hand's conclusions in *Alcoa*. In computing the defendant's market share, Judge Hand included foreign aluminum actually imported into the United States. However, he did not include aluminum that was manufactured and sold abroad, and he did not include excess capacity of aluminum-producing foreign plants. Was Judge Hand correct?

Judge Hand correctly noted that foreign producers operate under certain cost disadvantages; for example, they must pay transportation and tariff costs which do not have to be paid by a domestic producer. Some foreign products are at such a high cost disadvantage that none of them are imported. Sand and gravel are good examples. In such situations, we should exclude all foreign production as well as foreign capacity from the market definition. However, the fact that *some* foreign aluminum was imported into the United States indicates that it is profitable to import aluminum, cost disadvantages notwithstanding. If it is profitable to import a small amount, why would it not be profitable to import more? One answer is that there might not only be a tariff on imports, but also an absolute quota. In that case, only the maximum amount of foreign aluminum allowed to be imported under the quota ought to be included in the market. But if there is no quota, then doesn't *all* foreign aluminum actually compete with domestic aluminum? This analysis assumes that the marginal cost curve to the foreign producers is flat — that is, it would cost them no more per unit to import additional aluminum into the United States than it is costing them to import what is already coming in. If there were only one foreign producer, it would have an upward sloping marginal cost curve, just as Alcoa does. However, in a competitive market, where plants are tending to their most efficient output level and new entry is relatively easy and common, the marginal cost for the industry as a whole remains flat. In this case, wouldn't any attempt by Alcoa to raise its prices encourage foreign producers to enlarge their American imports? *See* Landes & Posner, *Market Power, supra,* at 964–968.

One other problem of market definition that Judge Hand faced deserves attention. Alcoa sold much of its aluminum as ingot to other firms for fabrication, and it was accused of monopolizing the ingot market. But Alcoa also fabricated some aluminum itself. Should the ingot which Alcoa itself fabricated be included in the relevant market? Judge Hand was correct to include it. Ingot which is transferred from Alcoa's "ingot division" to its "fabricating division" passes through the distribution chain to consumers just as much as ingot which is sold to independent fabricators. The fact that Alcoa is vertically integrated has no impact on market definition.

In the *American Can* case, printed before *Alcoa,* the court concluded that cans made by canners who used the cans themselves ought not be included in the relevant market. The judge reasoned that a bread combination would be illegal "in spite of the fact that in that city one-half or two-thirds or even three-quarters of the bread consumed was actually baked in the kitchens of private families." *United States v. American Can Co.,* 230 F. 859, 899 (D. Md. 1916). Is that argument convincing? Apparently not, for the judge then made an observation that contradicted his conclusion: "Yet the fact that one-third of the cans used in the country are made by the people who use them is one of great significance. It shows that any considerable rise in the price of cans . . . would probably lead to two things . . .": (1) self-makers would begin to sell them; and (2) other canners would begin making their own. *Id.*

The relationship between market power, market share, and supply and demand elasticities has plagued the federal courts ever since *Alcoa* was decided. The case that follows is one of the Supreme Court's most significant statements of the relationship between demand elasticities and a defendant's power over price.

Finally, one observation must be made that is commonplace for economists but sometimes trips up noneconomist judges: the things to be grouped inside a relevant market must, to a significant degree, be *substitutes* for each other. That is, to conclude that a grouping of sales constitutes a relevant market is to conclude both (1) that the things inside the grouping do not face significant competition from the things outside the grouping; and (2) that the things inside the grouping *do* compete with each other. Consider the Ninth Circuit's *Kodak* decision, which held that a group of non-substitutable repair parts for photocopiers constituted a single relevant market:

> Consideration of the "commercial realities" in the markets for Kodak parts compels the use of an "all parts" market theory. The "commercial reality" faced by service providers and equipment owners is that a service provider must have ready access to all parts to compete in the service market. As the relevant market for service "from the Kodak equipment owner's perspective is composed of only those companies that service Kodak machines," id., the relevant market for parts from the equipment owners' and service providers' perspective is composed of "all parts" that are designed to meet Kodak photocopier and micrographics equipment specifications. The makers of these parts "if unified by a monopolist or a

hypothetical cartel, would have market power in dealing with" ISOs and end users.

Image Technical Services v. Eastman Kodak Co., 125 F.3d 1195, 1203–1204 (9th Cir. 1997).

Clearly, the court has confused complements with substitutes. Granted, a photocopier needs all of its parts in order to function, just as an automobile needs both an engine and a oil filter, and computer operations require both hardware and software. But that does not mean that there is an "engine/oil filter" market or a "hardware/software" market. As the court observes, there is a "commercial reality" linking the various parts in a photocopier. But the reality in this case is precisely the opposite from the one that groups parts into a single market. When goods are substitutes for each other, and thus within the same market, their prices move up and down together. For example, if Alcoa's aluminum is a substitute for Reynold's aluminum, then the two prices will move in the same direction as the market price for aluminum rises and falls. By contrast, the prices of complementary goods move in opposite directions. For example, if the price of engines should increase dramatically, people would buy fewer cars and, as a result, demand for oil filters would fall, thus reducing their price. Combining complements into a "relevant market" undermines the entire market power inquiry because it becomes impossible to determine whether the defendant has market power in any specific parts. For example, a firm might make 70% of 100 different parts, but grouping them together deprives the fact finder of the ability to determine whether this means 70% of each of the 100 parts (which would indicate market power in all of them if other requirements were met), or whether it means 100% of some parts and lower numbers right down to zero for others.

To illustrate, consider whether four gasoline stations on the same intersection are the same relevant market for antitrust purposes. Clearly, it is not because the motorist needs to stop at all four of them. Quite the contrary, the reason they compete with each other, and thus belong in the same relevant market, is that the motorist does *not* need to stop at all four of them; as a result, they must compete with each other on price or services.

And what do you think of the Ninth Circuit's conclusion that "all parts" are a relevant market because if the makers of all these parts were unified by a monopolist or cartel, they would be able to charge monopoly prices? Suppose three firms in the aggregate make 80% of the glass plates that go on top of a photocopier and 85% of the rubber wheels that go at the bottom. If they got together, they could fix the price of both the glass plates and the wheels. But does this entail that there is a relevant "glass plate/rubber wheel" market? The court was paraphrasing (incorrectly) the government's *1992 Horizontal Merger Guidelines* § 1.0 (which have since been replaced by the *2010 Horizontal Merger Guidelines*, reprinted as Appendix A); *see* 2B Phillip Areeda, Herbert Hovenkamp & John Solow, Antitrust Law ¶ 530a (3d ed. 2007). The Ninth Circuit used the hypothetical cartel analogy correctly in *Rebel Oil Co. v. Atlantic Richfield Co.*, 51 F.3d 1421, 1436 (9th Cir. 1995), when it concluded that self-service and full-service gasoline were in the same relevant market because a cartel of self-service providers could not increase price significantly without losing sales to full-service providers. That is, one asks whether the entire grouping of transactions inside the proposed market faces competition from some grouping of sales outside the proposed market. As the 2010 Merger Guidelines point out, the sine qua non for grouping things into a relevant market is "demand substitution." *Guidelines, supra,* at § 4. Faced with a merger of the above firms, the Guidelines require the government to look separately at the glass plate and rubber wheel markets, and assess the firms' respective market position in each.

PROBLEM 6.1

The intersection of Hayes Street and Rose Street has gasoline stations on three of its four corners. Beyond this, the nearest gasoline station is 30 miles away. Stations A and B have accused Station C of monopolization by predatory pricing and other exclusionary practices. The parties have stipulated that the relevant geographic market includes only these three stations. The evidence shows the following. Over the relevant time period, C has sold 2000 gallons of gasoline daily. A and B have each sold 500 gallons daily. In addition, C has eight pumps, while A and B each have six pumps. Each pump will generally accommodate 40 cars daily with no waiting, and a car purchases, on average, 10 gallons. What is C's market share? What is the relevant unit of output? What factors are relevant to determining C's market power?

UNITED STATES v. E.I. DU PONT DE NEMOURS & CO.
351 U.S. 377 (1956)

JUSTICE REED delivered the opinion of the Court.

The United States brought this civil action . . . against E. I. du Pont de Nemours and Company. The complaint, filed December 13, 1947, . . . charged du Pont with monopolizing . . . interstate commerce in cellophane . . . in violation of § 2 of the Sherman Act. Relief by injunction was sought against defendant and its officers, forbidding monopolizing or attempting to monopolize interstate trade in cellophane. The prayer also sought action to dissipate the effect of the monopolization by divestiture or other steps.

. . . .

During the period that is relevant to this action, du Pont produced almost 75% of the cellophane sold in the United States, and cellophane constituted less than 20% of all "flexible packaging material" sales. . . .

The Government contends that, by so dominating cellophane production, du Pont monopolized a "part of the trade or commerce" in violation of § 2. Respondent agrees that cellophane is a product which constitutes "a 'part' of commerce within the meaning of Section 2." But it contends that the prohibition of § 2 against monopolization is not violated because it does not have the power to control the price of cellophane or to exclude competitors from the market in which cellophane is sold. The court below found that the "relevant market for determining the extent of du Pont's market control is the market for flexible packaging materials," and that competition from those other materials prevented du Pont from possessing monopoly powers in its sales of cellophane.

The Government asserts that cellophane and other wrapping materials are neither substantially fungible nor like priced. For these reasons, it argues that the market for other wrappings is distinct from the market for cellophane and that the competition afforded cellophane by other wrappings is not strong enough to be considered in determining whether du Pont has monopoly powers. Market delimitation is necessary under du Pont's theory to determine whether an alleged monopolist violates § 2. The ultimate consideration in such a determination is whether the defendants control the price and competition in the market for such part of trade or commerce as they are charged with monopolizing. Every manufacturer is the sole producer of the particular commodity it makes but its control in the above sense of the relevant market depends upon the availability of alternative commodities for buyers: i.e., whether there is a cross-elasticity of demand between cellophane and the other wrappings. This interchangeability is largely gauged by the purchase of competing products for similar uses considering the price, characteristics and adaptability of the competing commodities. The court below found that the flexible wrappings afforded such alternatives. . . .

. . . For consideration of the issue as to monopolization, a general summary of the development of cellophane is useful.

In the early 1900's, Jacques Brandenberger, a Swiss chemist, attempted to make tablecloths impervious to dirt by spraying them with liquid viscose (a cellulose solution available in quantity from wood pulp) and by coagulating this coating. His idea failed, but he noted that the coating peeled off in a transparent film. This first "cellophane" was thick, hard, and not perfectly transparent, but Brandenberger apparently foresaw commercial possibilities in his discovery. By 1908 he developed the first machine for the manufacture of transparent sheets of regenerated cellulose. The 1908 product was not satisfactory, but by 1912 Brandenberger was making a saleable thin flexible film used in gas masks. He obtained patents to cover the machinery and the essential ideas of his process. . . .

In 1917 Brandenberger assigned his patents to La Cellophane Societe Anonyme and joined that organization. . . .

In 1923 du Pont organized with La Cellophane an American company for the manufacture of plain cellophane.

. . . .

An important factor in the growth of cellophane production and sales was the perfection of moistureproof cellophane, a superior product of du Pont research and patented by that company through a 1927 application. Plain cellophane has little resistance to the passage of moisture vapor. Moistureproof cellophane has a composition added which keeps moisture in and out of the packed commodity. This patented type of cellophane has had a demand with much more rapid growth than the plain.

In 1931 Sylvania began the manufacture of moistureproof cellophane under its own patents. After negotiations over patent rights, du Pont in 1933 licensed Sylvania to manufacture and sell moistureproof cellophane produced under the du Pont patents at a royalty of 2% of sales.

. . . .

If cellophane is the "market" that du Pont is found to dominate, it may be assumed it does have monopoly power over that "market." Monopoly power is the power to control prices or exclude competition. It seems apparent that du Pont's power to set the price of cellophane has been limited only by the competition afforded by other flexible packaging materials. Moreover, it may be practically impossible for anyone to commence manufacturing cellophane without full access to du Pont's technique. However, du Pont has no power to prevent competition from other wrapping materials. The trial court consequently had to determine whether competition from the other wrappings prevented du Pont from possessing monopoly power in violation of § 2. . . .

If a large number of buyers and sellers deal freely in a standardized product, such as salt or wheat, we have complete or pure competition. Patents, on the other hand, furnish the most familiar type of classic monopoly. As the producers of a standardized product bring about significant differentiations of quality, design, or packaging in the product that permit differences of use, competition becomes to a greater or less degree incomplete and the producer's power over price and competition greater over his article and its use, according to the differentiation he is able to create and maintain. A retail seller may have in one sense a monopoly on certain trade because of location, as an isolated country store or filling station, or because no one else makes a product of just the quality or attractiveness of his product, as for example in cigarettes. Thus one can theorize that we have monopolistic competition in every nonstandardized commodity with each manufacturer having power over the price and production of his own product. However, this power that, let us say, automobile or soft-drink manufacturers have over their trademarked products is not the power that makes an illegal monopoly. Illegal power must be appraised in terms of the competitive market for the product.

Determination of the competitive market for commodities depends on how different from one another are the offered commodities in character or use, how far buyers will go to substitute one commodity for another. For example, one can think of building materials as in commodity competition but one could hardly say that brick competed with steel or wood or cement or stone in the meaning of Sherman Act litigation; the products are too different. This is the interindustry competition emphasized by some economists. On the other hand, there are certain differences in the formulae for soft drinks but one can hardly say that each one is an illegal monopoly. Whatever the market may be, we hold that control of price or competition establishes the existence of monopoly power under § 2. Section 2 requires the application of a reasonable approach in determining the existence of monopoly power. . . .

. . . The Government argues:

We do not here urge that in *no* circumstances may competition of substitutes negative possession of monopolistic power over trade in a product. The decisions make it clear at the least that the courts will not consider substitutes other than those which are substantially fungible with the monopolized product and sell at substantially the same price.

But where there are market alternatives that buyers may readily use for their purposes, illegal monopoly does not exist merely because the product said to be monopolized differs from others. If it were not so, only physically identical products would be a part of the market. To accept the Government's argument, we would have to conclude that the manufacturers of plain as well as moistureproof cellophane were monopolists, and so with films such as Pliofilm, foil, glassine, polyethylene, and Saran, for each of these wrapping materials is distinguishable. These were all exhibits in the case. New wrappings appear, generally similar to cellophane: is each a monopoly? What is called for is an appraisal of the "cross-elasticity" of demand in the trade. . . . In considering what is the relevant market for determining the control of price and competition, no more definite rule can be declared than that commodities reasonably interchangeable by consumers for the same purposes make up that "part of the trade or commerce," monopolization of which may be illegal. As respects flexible packaging materials, the market geographically is nationwide.

Industrial activities cannot be confined to trim categories. Illegal monopolies under § 2 may well exist over limited products in narrow fields where competition is eliminated. That does not settle the issue here. In determining the market under the Sherman Act, it is the use or uses to which the commodity is put that control. The selling price between commodities with similar uses and different characteristics may vary, so that the cheaper product can drive out the more expensive. Or, the superior quality of higher priced articles may make dominant the more desirable. Cellophane costs more than many competing products and less than a few. But whatever the price, there are various flexible wrapping materials that are bought by manufacturers for packaging their goods in their own plants or are sold to converters who shape and print them for use in the packaging of the commodities to be wrapped.

Cellophane differs from other flexible packaging materials. From some it differs more than from others. . . .

It may be admitted that cellophane combines the desirable elements of transparency, strength and cheapness more definitely than any of the others. Comparative characteristics have been noted thus:

> Moistureproof cellophane is highly transparent, tears readily but has high bursting strength, is highly impervious to moisture and gases, and is resistant to grease and oils. Heat sealable, printable, and adapted to use on wrapping machines, it makes an excellent packaging material for both display and protection of commodities.

> Other flexible wrapping materials fall into four major categories: (1) opaque nonmoistureproof wrapping *paper* designed primarily for convenience and protection in handling packages; (2) moistureproof *films* of varying degrees of transparency designed primarily either to protect, or to display and protect, the products they encompass; (3) nonmoistureproof transparent *films* designed primarily to display and to some extent protect, but which obviously do a poor protecting job where exclusion or retention of moisture is important; and (4) moistureproof *materials* other than films of varying degrees of transparency (foils and paper products) designed to protect and display.

But, despite cellophane's advantages, it has to meet competition from other materials in every one of its uses. . . . Food products are the chief outlet, with cigarettes next. The Government makes no challenge . . . that cellophane furnishes less than 7% of wrappings for bakery products, 25% for candy, 32% for snacks, 35% for meats and poultry, 27% for crackers and biscuits, 47% for fresh produce, and 34% for frozen foods. Seventy-five to eighty percent of cigarettes are wrapped in cellophane. Thus, cellophane shares the packaging market with others. The overall result is that cellophane accounts for 17.9% of flexible wrapping materials, measured by the wrapping surface.

Moreover a very considerable degree of functional interchangeability exists between these products. . . . It will be noted that except as to permeability to gases, cellophane has no qualities that are not possessed by a number of other materials. Meat will do as an example of interchangeability. Although du Pont's sales to the meat industry have reached 19,000,000 pounds annually, nearly 35%, this volume is attributed "to the rise of self-service retailing of fresh meat." In fact, since the popularity of self-service meats, du Pont has lost "a considerable proportion" of this packaging business to Pliofilm. Pliofilm is more expensive than cellophane, but its superior physical characteristics apparently offset cellophane's price advantage. While retailers shift continually between the two, the trial court found that Pliofilm is increasing its share of the business. One further example is worth noting. Before World War II, du Pont cellophane wrapped between 5 and 10% of baked and smoked meats. The peak year was 1933. Thereafter du Pont was unable to meet the competition of Sylvania and of greaseproof paper. Its sales declined and the 1933 volume was not reached again until 1947. It will be noted that greaseproof paper, glassine, waxed paper, foil and Pliofilm are used as well as cellophane. [The Court notes the competition and the] advantages that have caused the more expensive Pliofilm to increase its proportion of the business.

An element for consideration as to cross-elasticity of demand between products is the responsiveness of the sales of one product to price changes of the other. If a slight decrease in the price of cellophane causes a considerable number of customers of other flexible wrappings to switch to cellophane, it would be an indication that a high cross-elasticity of demand exists between them; that the products compete in the same market. The court below held that the "[g]reat sensitivity of customers in the flexible packaging markets to price or quality changes" prevented du Pont from possessing monopoly control over price. The record sustains these findings.

We conclude that cellophane's interchangeability with the other materials mentioned suffices to make it a part of this flexible packaging material market.

The Government stresses the fact that the variation in price between cellophane and other materials demonstrates they are noncompetitive. As these products are all flexible wrapping materials, it seems reasonable to consider, as was done at the trial, their comparative cost to the consumer in terms of square area. . . . Cellophane costs two or three times as much, surface measure, as its chief competitors for the flexible wrapping market, glassine and greaseproof papers. Other forms of cellulose wrappings and those from other chemical or mineral substances, with the exception of aluminum foil, are more expensive. . . . The wrapping is a relatively small proportion of the entire cost of the article. Different producers need different qualities in wrappings and their need may vary from time to time as their products undergo change. But the necessity for flexible wrappings is the central and unchanging demand. We cannot say that these differences in cost gave du Pont monopoly power over prices in view of the findings of fact on that subject.

On the findings of the District Court, its judgment is

Affirmed.

CHIEF JUSTICE WARREN's dissenting opinion is omitted.

NOTE: CROSS-ELASTICITY OF DEMAND

Is the concept of cross-elasticity of demand developed in the *du Pont* case an aid in defining the relevant product market? Or is it a mechanism for measuring the elasticity of demand for a given product? Or is it a hybrid? Is there any difference between saying that the relevant product is "cellophane" but the elasticity of demand for the product is very high, or saying that the relevant product is "flexible packaging materials" and the elasticity of demand is low? It makes no difference. Market share and market power vary directly with one another. Elasticity of demand and market power, however, vary inversely.

Cross-elasticity of demand is simply a way of measuring what consumers will do when a seller attempts to raise the price of something. A certain number will substitute away. Whether what they buy instead is the same "product" or a different "product" is a purely semantic question, although many courts have failed to recognize this. The fundamental question in antitrust is not how to identify the product being monopolized, but how to determine whether the defendant has the power to charge more than a competitive price.

What does the concept of cross-elasticity of demand contribute to analysis of market power? Mainly, it reminds us that when we define a seller's share of the market we must consider close substitutes as part of our product definition.

Did the court in *du Pont* apply the concept of cross-elasticity of demand correctly? Probably not. The court found that du Pont had very little power over the price of cellophane because there were many substitutes for cellophane as a packaging material, and if du Pont attempted to raise the price of cellophane many customers would buy one of these substitutes instead. In short, there was high cross-elasticity of demand. Is that analysis complete?

Suppose that there is a competitively produced product known as Widgets, which are sold at $1.00 each. Now a bright inventor develops the Flidget, which does everything a Widget can do, but which can be produced and sold for 80 cents. The inventor patents the Flidget and becomes its only producer. At what price will the inventor sell Flidgets?

The inventor will sell Flidgets at the profit maximizing price, and the profit maximizing price might very well be something like 99 cents. If Widgets and Flidgets are interchangeable in consumers' eyes, then the inventor will probably not be able to charge more than $1.00 for Flidgets because then customers would stay with Widgets. But unless there are a large number of potential customers who will not buy Widgets at $1.00 but who would buy Flidgets at a lower price, the profit-maximizing price of Flidgets would not be substantially less than $1.00. At a price of 99 cents, most former Widget customers would buy Flidgets instead, up to the capacity of the inventor to make them.

Now suppose the Flidget producer is accused of monopolization. It defends by arguing that the "cross-elasticity of demand" between Flidgets and Widgets is very high, so Widgets ought to be included in the relevant market. After all, Flidgets are currently being sold at 99 cents, and if the producer raises its price by as little as 2 cents it will lose most of its customers. Is the argument persuasive? Clearly not. The reason is simple. The profit-maximizing price of any product lies in the high elasticity region of its demand curve. When a producer with market power seeks out its profit-maximizing price, it asks "how much can I charge before too many customers will substitute away for something else?" The producer tries to get as close to this edge as possible without going over.

As a result, high cross-elasticity of demand at the current market price for a product is not persuasive evidence that the producer has no market power. It *is* evidence, however, that the producer is charging its profit-maximizing price. In order to know whether the producer has market power, we need to know whether its profit-maximizing price is substantially higher than its marginal cost. But the only way we can know that is by determining the defendant's marginal cost. If we know marginal cost, there is no need to rely on market definition, for we can compute market power directly by looking at the difference between marginal cost and the price at which the product is being sold.

Du Pont's high rate of profit during the period of alleged monopolization suggests (although not very reliably) that the Supreme Court's analysis was incorrect. There was high cross-elasticity of demand between du Pont's cellophane at the current price and other packaging materials; however, the current price of cellophane was a very profitable (monopoly) price.

Today we speak of the "*Cellophane* fallacy" as concluding from observed high cross-elasticity of demand at current market prices that the defendant lacks power, while ignoring the possibility that the firm is already charging a monopoly price. Although the fallacy is well known by economists, courts continue to commit it. *See, e.g., Cable Holdings of Ga. v. Home Video*, 825 F.2d 1559, 1563 (11th Cir. 1987) (relevant market included not only cable television but also broadcast television and videocassette recordings). Some judges have noted that they are "cognizant of the Cellophane fallacy which cautions that '[the] existence of significant substitution in the event of further price increases or even at the current price does not tell us whether the defendant *already* exercises significant market power.'" *ZF Meritor, LLC v. Eaton Corp.*, 769 F. Supp. 2d 684 (D. Del. 2011), *aff'd*, 696 F.3d 254 (3d Cir. 2012) (quoting *Eastman Kodak Co. v. Image Tech. Serv. Inc.*, 504 U.S. 451, 471 (1992) (internal quotation omitted) (emphasis in original)).

This still does not mean du Pont was an illegal monopolist. It means only that it probably had sufficient market power to meet the first element of the monopolization test. Is there evidence in the opinion that du Pont's activities would have satisfied the conduct element as well?

If the monopolist employs the same technology as its rivals and apparently has the same costs, then, observed substitution may indicate that other firms are in the market. But in many monopoly cases, the monopolist has a unique technology, patents, or other characteristics that presumably give it a cost advantage over rivals. As in the *Cellophane* case itself, where DuPont enjoyed both a unique technology and historical patent rights, asking the question whether the defendant can impose a yet further price increase from competitive levels is incorrect. This suggests that in monopolization cases in particular, the observed cross-elasticity methodology must not be used uncritically, and alternative indicia of market power should be explored. *See* Gregory J. Werden, *Market Delineation Under the Merger Guidelines: Monopoly Cases and Alternative Approaches*, 16 Rev. Ind. Org. 211 (2000); Lawrence J. White, *Market Definition in Monopolization Cases: A Paradigm is Missing (2005), in* Issues in Competition Law and Policy (Wayne D. Collins ed., 2008). *See also* Thomas G. Krattenmaker, Robert H. Lande & Steven Salop, *Monopoly Power and Market Power in Antitrust Law*, 76 Geo. L. Rev. 241 (1987); Dennis W. Carlton, *Market Definition: Use and Abuse*, 3 Competition Pol'y Int'l. 1 (2007) (explaining why measurement of market power is significantly more difficult in Section 2 cases than in merger cases); 2B Phillip E. Areeda & Herbert Hovenkamp, Antitrust Law ¶ 539 (4th ed. 2014); Louis Kaplow, *Why (Ever) Define Markets?*, 124 Harv. L. Rev. 437 (2010).

REBEL OIL CO. v. ATLANTIC RICHFIELD CO.,
51 F.3d 1421 (9th Cir. 1995)

Beezer, Circuit Judge:

This case presents three antitrust claims arising from the defendant's conduct in the retail gasoline market in Las Vegas, Nevada. The plaintiffs contend that the defendant engaged in predatory pricing between 1985 and 1989, selling self-serve, cash-only gasoline below marginal cost. The plaintiffs claim that the alleged predatory pricing was an attempt by the defendant to monopolize the market, in violation of Sherman Act § 2. . . .

The plaintiffs, Rebel Oil Co., Inc., and Auto Flite Oil Co., Inc. (collectively "Rebel"), are retail marketers of gasoline in Las Vegas who sell only self-serve, cash-only gasoline. Rebel operates 16 retail stations under various gasoline brand names. Nine stations operate under the "Rebel" brand name, six stations operate under the "Unocal" brand name and one operates under the "Texaco" brand name. In addition to its retail sales, Rebel is one of the several wholesale marketers who ship gasoline via the Cal-Nev pipeline and sell to retail marketers.

The defendant, Atlantic Richfield Co. ("ARCO"), is a retail and wholesale marketer of gasoline in Las Vegas, as well as a major driller and refiner of crude oil in Los Angeles. ARCO supplies gasoline to 53 retail stations in Las Vegas bearing the "ARCO" brand name. These stations sell only self-serve, cash-only gasoline. . . .

In opposing ARCO's motion for summary judgment, and in supporting its own cross motion, Rebel submitted circumstantial evidence to the district court purporting to show that ARCO possessed market power. We must determine whether this circumstantial evidence was sufficient to create a genuine triable issue with regard to market power in the Sherman Act § 2 claim.

We begin with the issue of market definition. . . . Market definition is crucial. Without a definition of the relevant market, it is impossible to determine market share.

There are two possible definitions of the market in the present case. Rebel contends the relevant market includes all retail sales of gasoline in Las Vegas, except for sales of full-serve gasoline. This is the market in which ARCO exclusively operates. ARCO disputes Rebel's narrow market definition. ARCO contends the market is broader, consisting of all sales of retail gasoline in Las Vegas, including full-serve gasoline.

The dispute between Rebel and ARCO focused on cross-elasticity of demand: whether consumers view the products as substitutes for each other. If consumers view the products as substitutes, the products are part of the same market. Rebel's expert concluded that self-serve, cash-only gasoline and full-serve gasoline are not substitutes. He stated that consumers of full-serve gasoline base their purchase strictly on the availability of services, for which they pay a premium. Likewise, self-serve, cash-only gasoline consumers do not consider full-serve gasoline as a substitute, he said, because they will always buy the lower cost gasoline, even if the premium for full-service is less than the cost of the service.

The district court accepted ARCO's position, concluding that both self-serve, cash-only gasoline and full-serve gasoline should be included in the relevant market. ARCO introduced affidavits from an expert who said the two products were correlated in price, indicating that the products are substitutes for each other. . . .

Our independent review of Rebel's expert affidavits compels the conclusion that it would be unreasonable for a juror to infer from those affidavits that full-serve sales of gasoline should be excluded from the relevant market. Rebel's expert relied on "demand elasticity" — that is, whether a price rise in self-serve, cash-only gasoline would cause self-serve consumers to shift their demand to full-serve gasoline. A price differential between two products may reflect a low cross-elasticity of demand, if the higher priced product offers additional service for which consumers are willing to pay a premium.

But defining a market on the basis of demand considerations alone is erroneous. A reasonable market definition must also be based on "supply elasticity." Supply elasticity measures the responsiveness of producers to price increases. If producers of product X can readily shift their production facilities to produce product Y, then the sales of both should be included in the relevant market. The affidavit of Rebel's expert fails to account for the fact that sellers of full-serve gasoline can easily convert their full-serve pumps, at virtually no cost, into self-serve, cash-only pumps, expanding output and thus constraining any attempt by ARCO to charge supracompetitive prices for self-serve gasoline. The ease by which marketers can convert their full-serve facilities to increase their output of self-serve gasoline requires that full-serve sales be part of the relevant market; it is immaterial that consumers do not regard the products as substitutes, that a price differential exists, or that the prices are not closely correlated.

NOTES AND QUESTIONS

1. Did the *Rebel Oil* court rely on elasticity of demand, elasticity of supply, or both, as the basis for its definition of the relevant product market?

2. Elasticity of supply has played an increasing role in circuit court determination of market power since the mid-1970s. Frequently, courts use a different term, such as "supply substitutability," or "substitutability in production." See, e.g., *Twin City Sportservice, Inc. v. Charles O. Finley & Co.*, 512 F.2d 1264 (9th Cir. 1975), where the issue was whether the defendant monopolized the market in concession services at major league baseball stadiums. The court held that there was a high degree of "substitutability of production" between concessions at major league baseball stadiums and concessions at other entertainment events. Therefore, the market alleged to be monopolized was drawn too narrowly. See *Science Prods. Co. v. Chevron Chem. Co.*, 384 F. Supp. 793 (N.D. Ill. 1974), where the plaintiff alleged that the defendant had monopolized the market for, inter alia, garden insecticides. The Court held that the market must be defined more broadly to include household insecticides as well:

> Household insecticides share the same chemical components and manufacturing facilities with insecticides labeled and intended for outdoor use. Once a manufacturer enters the lawn and garden chemical field, it can easily expand its product line to include household insecticides.

> Significantly, both [plaintiff and defendant] manufacture and market products falling into every category including household insecticides. Although some producers of household insecticides tend to concentrate their sales in grocery and drug stores, in general, most distributors and retailers of lawn and garden chemicals also handle household insecticides. Moreover, [the plaintiff] has been unable to point to a single manufacturer which makes any distinction in its organization or personnel based upon products sold for use inside and outside the home.

> [The plaintiff's] argument that household insecticides are lower in toxicity than products intended for outdoor use is equally specious. Most household insecticides are packaged in aerosol form and therefore in final diluted form. By contrast, many outdoor insecticides are packaged in concentrated form and must be diluted with water before they can safely be used.

384 F. Supp. at 800.

3. In *U.S. Anchor Manufacturing., Inc. v. Rule Industries, Inc.*, 7 F.3d 986 (11th Cir. 1993), the Eleventh Circuit quoted an FTC opinion to establish the importance of cross-elasticity analysis and the relevant factors for performing the analysis:

> Reliable measures of supply and demand elasticities provide the most accurate estimates of relevant markets. However, it is ordinarily quite

difficult to measure cross-elasticities of supply and demand accurately. Therefore, it is usually necessary to consider other factors that can serve as useful surrogates for cross-elasticity data . . . . In the case of product market definition, these factors may include

> whether the products and services have sufficiently distinctive uses and characteristics; whether industry firms routinely monitor each other's actions and calculate and adjust their own prices (at least in part) on the basis of other firms' prices; the extent to which consumers consider various categories of sellers . . . as substitutes; and whether a sizeable price disparity between different types of . . . sellers . . . persists over time for equivalent amounts of comparable goods and services.

Id. at 995 (quoting International Tel. & Tel. Corp., 104 F.T.C. 208, 409 (1984)) (internal quotations omitted) (ellipses in original).

Applying these factors to the facts of *du Pont*, what is the relevant product market?

4. Once market share has been computed, should very small shares be dispositive of the issue of market power? In *Broadway Delivery Corp. v. United Parcel Serv. of Am.*, 651 F.2d 122 (2d Cir. 1981), the trial judge had instructed a jury that, "[i]f you find that the defendants possessed less than 50% of the relevant market, you don't have to go any further on a monopolization claim. Possession of less than 50% of the market fails to establish monopoly power." The Second Circuit held this instruction to be erroneous, for the jury was "entitled to assess monopoly power on the record as a whole." The Court concluded:

> The extent to which market characteristics should be explained to the jury in a particular case will vary with the nature of the underlying facts and the expert testimony. Sometimes, but not inevitably, it will be useful to suggest that a market share below 50% is rarely evidence of monopoly power, a share between 50% and 70% can occasionally show monopoly power, and a share above 70% is usually strong evidence of monopoly power. But when the evidence presents a fair jury issue of monopoly power, the jury should not be told that it must find monopoly power lacking below a specified share or existing above a specified share. Of course, cases may arise where the parties' dispute concerning market definition creates a jury issue on monopoly power only if one side's market definition, usually the plaintiff's, is established. In such circumstances a jury can be instructed to find for the defendant if the plaintiff fails to prove its definition of the relevant market. Alternatively, a jury could be instructed to answer a special interrogatory concerning market definition, which would permit the trial judge to direct a verdict for the defendant if the plaintiff failed to prevail on its market definition. On the other hand, in some cases, there may be a genuine issue as to monopoly power in the market as defined by either party, in which event the market share under either definition would not be conclusive. However the instruction is phrased, it should not deflect the jury's attention from indicia of monopoly power other than market share.

651 F.2d at 129–130.

Under the Second Circuit's analysis, when would a defendant's motion for directed verdict or summary judgment on the basis of small market share be appropriate? What if the plaintiff had successfully defined a relevant market, but the pleadings clearly established that the defendant's market share was 25%? See *Energex Lighting Indus. v. NAPLC*, 656 F. Supp. 914 (S.D.N.Y. 1987), where the court followed *Broadway Delivery* in holding that a 25% market share could support a monopolization offense, where the number of competitors in the market had declined from eleven to four. Why should that make a difference?

The Fifth Circuit apparently disagrees with the Second. In *Dimmitt Agri Indus. v. CPC Int'l*, 679 F.2d 516 (5th Cir. 1982), the record established that the defendant's market share ranged from 21%–27% of one relevant market (starch) and 16% of another (corn syrup). The jury found that the defendant illegally monopolized. The Fifth Circuit reversed the judgment for the plaintiff, finding no case "in which monopolization was found on the basis of such meager evidence and despite undisputed proof of market shares significantly below 50 percent." However, the court found "considerable support for the proposition that low market shares, if undisputed, make monopolization an impossibility as a matter of law." It then held that market shares in the range of 16%–25% "are insufficient — at least absent other compelling structural evidence — as a matter of law to support monopolization." What kind of "structural evidence" did the court have in mind? Evidence that the market was very highly concentrated? This would suggest that the defendant was not the largest firm in the market. What if the defendant had 25% of the market, two other firms had 20% each, and smaller firms made up the balance?

5. In *Eastman Kodak Co. v. Image Tech. Servs.*, 504 U.S. 451 (1992), the Supreme Court refused to grant the defendant summary judgment against the plaintiff's claim that there could be a relevant market for Kodak brand replacement parts for Kodak photocopiers, notwithstanding the fact that the photocopier market itself was competitive. The decision is reprinted, *supra*, Chapter 4. As it turned out, however, Kodak manufactured only some 30% of "Kodak parts." On remand, the Ninth Circuit noted that courts generally require a 65% market share to create an inference of market power, but then found that inference met by the following facts:

(1) [Kodak's] own manufacture of Kodak parts (30%); (2) its control of original-equipment manufacturers' sale of Kodak parts to ISOs through tooling clauses (20–25%), engineering clauses and other proprietary arrangements (exact percentage unknown); and (3) its discouragement of self-servicing and resale of parts by end users.

Image Technical Services v. Eastman Kodak Co., 125 F.3d 1195, 1203–1204 (9th Cir. 1997).

PROBLEM 6.2

When Zyrex, a manufacturer of high technology photocopiers, refuses to sell repair parts for its photocopiers, Independent Service Organizations (ISOs) who repair these machines in competition with Zyrex allege that the defendant is attempting to use its market dominance in the photocopier market to create a secondary monopoly in the market for "servicing of Zyrex photocopy machines." The defendant disputes that servicing of its own brand of photocopiers is a relevant market. Describe how each of the following facts would be relevant to your answer: (1) customers who already own a Zyrex photocopier require a technician who is trained to service their brand; (2) the ISOs as firms actually service multiple brands of photocopiers, and the same individual technicians are typically trained to service two or more different brands; and (3) in response to a relatively high frequency of repair calls for Zyrex machines, the ISOs can retrain a technician currently servicing Alpha or Beta brand photocopiers in about three weeks. *Cf. Independent Service Organizations Antitrust Litigation*, 964 F. Supp. 1469 (D. Kan. 1997).

PROBLEM 6.3

Biffco, a manufacturer of kitchen sponges, is accused of terminating its dealers, predatory pricing, and other exclusionary practices. It appears that Biffco's market share of a nationwide market for kitchen sponges is only 20%. But the plaintiff offers an expert economist who will testify that Biffco has "power over price." The expert will testify that if Biffco wished, it could charge more than it is currently charging without losing more than a trivial number of sales. Is the testimony probative? Should the jury be permitted to consider it as "alternative" evidence of substantial market power? *See Valley Liquors, Inc. v. Renfield Importers, Ltd.*, 822 F.2d 656 (7th Cir. 1987).

PROBLEM 6.4

Smalltime, Inc., a now-defunct hardware store, alleges illegal monopolization against a competitor, Bonanza Co., in a market for "the retail sale of building, plumbing, and electrical supplies for use primarily by home remodelers and do-it-yourselfers." Upon inspection, it turns out that Bonanza sells 1% of the region's building supplies, 1.5% of its electrical supplies, and 0.5% of its plumbing supplies. However, it is one of only two stores in the region that carries all three types of supplies, and it is the only one that advertises primarily to do-it-yourself home remodelers. How should the market be defined? *See Westman Commun. Co. v. Hobart Int'l*, 796 F.2d 1216 (10th Cir. 1986); *Thurman Indus. v. Pay'N'Pak Stores*, 709 F. Supp. 985, 1987-1 Trade Cas. ¶ 67,591 (W.D. Wash. 1987). *Contra JBL Enters. v. Jhirmack Enters.*, 698 F.2d 1011, 1016–1017 (9th Cir. 1983). *See also* Ian Ayres, *Rationalizing Antitrust Cluster Markets*, 95 YALE L.J. 109 (1985).

PROBLEM 6.5

Lexington Power Company is an electric company charged with violating the antitrust laws in the wholesaling of electric power. Many other firms in the area also wholesale electric power, and can reach the same geographic areas that Lexington can. However, Lexington's power generation plant is very old and cost much less money to build than its competitors' new plants. When Lexington's plant wears out — perhaps in 10 more years — it will have to build a more expensive plant as well. The plaintiff alleges that the antiquated, low-cost plant gives Lexington a cost advantage so substantial that Lexington's plant itself should be found to be a relevant market. In that case, of course, Lexington would have monopoly power. Should the plaintiff's argument prevail? *See Town of Concord v. Boston Edison Co.*, 915 F.2d 17 (1st Cir. 1990).

NOTE: BARRIERS TO ENTRY IN MONOPOLIZATION CASES

The principal concern of the antitrust laws today is with practices that facilitate the creation or preservation of market power. Firms like to charge more than their economic costs, and the result is lower output and higher prices for consumers. But even a firm with a very large market share cannot earn monopoly returns if new firms can easily and quickly begin producing and selling the same product. Ordinarily, we expect new investors to look for places where the rate of return is highest, and monopoly prices attract new investment. The new investment will result in higher output, and eventually prices will be driven back to the competitive level.

The successful monopolist must therefore be protected by "barriers to entry." *See Ball Mem. Hosp. v. Mutual Hosp. Ins. Co.*, 784 F.2d 1325, 1335 (7th Cir. 1986), concluding that even a health insurer with a very large market share could not have substantial market power because insurers deal in money and risk — and both of these products can easily be duplicated:

> The insurance industry is not like the steel industry, in which a firm must take years to build a costly plant before having anything to sell. The "productive asset" of the insurance business is money, which may be supplied on a moment's notice, plus the ability to spread risk, which many firms possess and which has no geographic boundary.

Although economists agree that the concept of barriers to entry is important in antitrust analysis, widespread disagreement about definitions continues to divide them. Today the two most influential definitions of entry barriers are what might be called the Bainian definition that a barrier to entry is some factor in a market that permits incumbent firms to earn monopoly prices (i.e., prices above marginal cost) without attracting new entry. *See* J. BAIN, BARRIERS TO NEW COMPETITION 3 (1956). The alternative is a much narrower definition, developed by economist George Stigler and used principally by the Chicago School, that an entry barrier is "a cost of producing (at some or every rate of output) which must be borne by firms which seek to enter an industry but is not borne by firms already in the industry." G. STIGLER, THE ORGANIZATION OF INDUSTRY 67 (1968). In the *United Shoe Machinery* case, Judge Wyzanski identified USM's array of patents as a barrier to entry, for any potential entrant into shoe machinery manufacturing would have to invent around them or else purchase a license from USM. This would put the new entrant at a cost disadvantage. Does this qualify as a "barrier to entry" under Bain's definition? Under Stigler's definition?

The differences between these two concepts of entry barriers can be substantial. For example, under the Bainian definition, economies of scale are a barrier to entry. The fact that firms with high outputs have lower costs than firms with low outputs tends to discourage entry. The new entrant will necessarily have a lower output than established firms and will therefore have higher costs. Incumbent firms should be able to charge a price slightly less than the anticipated costs of the new entrant, even though these prices are well above their own costs. Under the Stigler definition, however, there is no cost of entering the market which must be incurred by new firms that was not incurred by incumbent firms. Each of them faced the same situation at the time it entered; so there are no entry barriers.

Another important difference between the Bainian and Stiglerian approaches to entry barriers is that the Bainian approach focuses on the market as it exists and considers whether the incumbents can charge supra competitive prices while yet discouraging entry. The Chicago School, by contrast, tends to look at the process by which firms enter the market, and finds no significant entry barriers if the process is the same for newcomers as it was for established firms.

Undoubtedly the most effective kind of barrier to entry is a monopoly restriction from the government. If a firm can persuade a state or local government to give it a monopoly, say, of all the taxicab business from Downtown Chicago to O'Hare Airport, then it will have created for itself the perfect barrier to entry, under both the Bainian and Stiglerian definitions. Antitrust controls of such barriers to entry are taken up in Chapter 9, principally under the *Noerr-Pennington* and "state action" doctrines.

At times, the Federal Trade Commission has been more receptive of the Stigler approach to entry barriers. Its *Echlin Manufacturing* merger decision defined barriers to entry as "additional long-run costs that must be incurred by an entrant relative to the long-run costs faced by incumbent firms." The Commission then continued:

> The only meaningful way to compare the risks and costs incurred by the two firms [i.e., the established firm and the prospective or new entrant] is to apply the same yardstick to each by viewing each of them at the time of its own entry. . . . The incumbent firm's apparently lower costs may merely reflect compensation for the risk it incurred in entering the market. The potential entrant(s apparently higher costs will decline to that of the incumbent firm if its attempted entry is successful.

Echlin Mfg., 3 Trade Reg. Rep. ¶ 22268, at 22301–22302 (F.T.C. 1985). The Commission explicitly rejected the notion that the risk of failure faced by a prospective entrant was a qualifying barrier to entry, even though that risk was substantially higher than it was for an established firm.

Perhaps the most generalized "cost" that must be faced by prospective firms is risk. For the established business already earning high profits, the risk of failure is relatively small. For the prospective entrant who has not yet built a plant, the risk of failure is much, much higher. An investment of $100,000,000 "costs" much more in the presence of high risk. This probably explains why it is much easier for, say, Ford Motor Company to build a new $100,000,000 automobile plant in response to increased auto demand than it is for a new company to build the same plant and start manufacturing cars. Under the rationale of *Echlin Manufacturing*, risk should not be considered a qualifying entry barrier. Thus, the firm that has already survived the risk is entitled to indefinite monopoly profits — i.e., profits sufficiently high to deter others from undergoing the same risk — assuming that the incumbent firm has market power and that there are not other entry barriers in the market. Does this analysis seem sound? Should risk be a factor when determining entry barriers? If so, how should it be quantified?

But risk alone is not really a barrier to entry even under the Bainian definition. Even if entry is expensive and the probability of failure is high, it will probably occur unless a significant amount of startup costs cannot be recovered in the event of failure. For example, suppose that you want to enter the parcel delivery business which is extremely risky because the incumbent firms are very well established. Your chances of success are only 70%. But assume that your only investment is a fleet of trucks which will cost $100,000,000, and that if your business fails, you will immediately be able to resell the entire fleet of trucks for exactly what you paid for it. In that case, you face high entry costs *and* a high risk that the business will fail — but the costs of failure are precisely zero. You get all your money back if the business goes under. This suggests that a true barrier to entry is an *unrecoverable,* or "sunk," cost that must borne by the prospective entrant.

It seems as if a barrier to entry must meet three requirements. First, there must be some relatively high cost that the prospective entrant must bear. Second, there must be a significant risk of failure. Third, a significant percentage of these costs must be "sunk," or unrecoverable, in the event of failure. In its *Echlin Manufacturing* decision, *supra,* the FTC noted that the extent of "sunk" costs in the market at issue, the assembly of carburetor repair kits from parts manufactured by others, was very small. As a result, entry barriers were not substantial.

Does this analysis tell us anything about where we might expect to find barriers to entry? It suggests that barriers to entry are most likely to exist in industries that use large amounts of durable (why durable?), expensive, and specialized equipment. Once a steel mill is built, for example, it cannot easily be converted into apartment buildings or even a glass factory. If a steel mill is expensive and can be used only for manufacturing steel, then the consequences of failure in the steel industry can be rather high.

But the analysis also suggests that barriers to entry exist in some less likely places. The costs of many kinds of goods or services are "sunk" because the good or service is used up as soon as it is delivered. A good example of this is advertising. If the incumbents in a market have used advertising to produce strong customer brand loyalties, then a prospective entrant will have to match them. The new entrant may have to finance an expensive pre-production advertising campaign, as well as an expensive promotional campaign after production has started. Once the advertising has been purchased and delivered, it cannot be sold to someone else. *See* A. Jacquemin, The New Industrial Organization: Market Forces and Strategic Behavior 100 (1987); Mensch & Freeman, *Efficiency and Image: Advertising as an Antitrust Issue,* 1990 Duke L.J. 321.

Determining the appropriate role of barriers to entry in antitrust analysis has turned out to be a perplexing problem. The problem arises because a particularly significant "barrier to entry" is efficiency itself, particularly under the Bainian definition. Suppose, for example, that economies of scale are such that the most efficient size for a Smidget plant is one that produces 75% of the relevant market for Smidgets when they are sold at a competitive price. The firm that operates that plant might control 75% of the relevant market, or even more. Any new entrant would begin with a market share of substantially less than 75% and would thus be at a distinct cost disadvantage to the incumbent. Such economies of scale have frequently been described as a "barrier to entry." *E.g.*, J. BAIN, BARRIERS TO NEW COMPETITION, ch. 1 (1956).

But if we are willing to recognize economies of scale as a barrier to entry, do we also want to say that the erection of barriers to entry is an anticompetitive practice which, when undertaken by a firm with substantial market power, violates the Sherman Act? Should it be illegal for a producer with market power to erect a plant of the most efficient size? The concept of "barriers to entry" is a useful part of antitrust analysis, but we must keep in mind that high entry barriers are not necessarily an antitrust violation. Mainly, they add plausibility to the plaintiff's story that a particular act was anticompetitive because it was calculated to create or maintain a monopoly. At various times, a host of things have been suggested as monopolistic barriers to entry: advertising, patents, vertical integration, tying arrangements, and product differentiation. All of these have in common that they may make it harder for potential competitors to enter a market. Unfortunately, that is about the only thing they have in common. What is worse, each of them can be used in socially beneficial ways that antitrust should be loathe to condemn. The antitrust tribunal has the difficult task of distinguishing the efficient from the inefficient uses.

For differing views of the role of entry barriers in antitrust analysis, see Robert H. Bork, *The Antitrust Paradox: A Policy at War with Itself* 310–329 (1978, rev. ed. 1993); FREDERIC M. SCHERER & DAVID ROSS, INDUSTRIAL MARKET STRUCTURE AND ECONOMIC PERFORMANCE 386–404 (3d ed. 1990).

Finally, consider the relationship between barriers to entry and market definition. Suppose that Firm A produces a large share of the market for Widgets, but, in response to any price increase above the competitive level, Smidget producers, who are competitive, will begin producing Widgets as well. In such a case, one might wish to define the market as Widgets, but say that entry barriers are very low; or one might define the relevant market to include both Widgets and Smidgets. Which approach is correct?

Sometimes it makes little difference. A finding of low entry barriers may compensate for an excessively narrow market definition. However, a finding of high barriers will not compensate for a market definition that is too broad, for the court may determine that the broadly defined market is competitive, and then the height of entry barriers becomes irrelevant, at least in monopolization and merger cases. One important distinction must be kept in mind. Market definition encompasses only the productive assets of firms already in existence that are capable of competing with the firm under consideration. By contrast, entry barrier analysis looks both at the productive assets of firms capable of shifting into competition with the firm under consideration, and firms that are not yet in existence, but which may enter in response to higher prices. The Justice Department Merger Guidelines, which are discussed at length in the following chapter, generally include existing firms capable of switching production to the product under consideration in the same relevant market; they generally reserve the concept of entry barriers for firms that may come into existence in response to high prices.

[B]   The Geographic Market

UNITED STATES v. GRINNELL CORP.
384 U.S. 563 (1966)

Justice Douglas delivered the opinion of the Court.

. . . .

Grinnell manufactures plumbing supplies and fire sprinkler systems. It also owns 76% of the stock of ADT [American District Telegraph Co.], 89% of the stock of AFA [American Fire Alarm Co.], and 100% of the stock of [Holmes Electric Protective Co.]. ADT provides both burglary and fire protection services; Holmes provides burglary services alone; AFA supplies only fire protection service. Each offers a central station service under which hazard-detecting devices installed on the protected premises automatically transmit an electric signal to a central station. The central station is manned 24 hours a day. Upon receipt of a signal, the central station, where appropriate, dispatches guards to the protected premises and notifies the police or fire department direct. There are other forms of protective services. But the record shows that subscribers to accredited central station service (*i.e.,* that approved by the insurance underwriters) receive reductions in their insurance premiums that are substantially greater than the reduction received by the users of other kinds of protection service. . . . ADT, Holmes, and AFA are the three largest companies in the business in terms of revenue: ADT (with 121 central stations in 115 cities) has 73% of the business; Holmes (with 12 central stations in three large cities) has 12.5%; AFA (with three central stations in three large cities) has 2%. Thus the three companies that Grinnell controls have over 87% of the business.

Over the years ADT purchased the stock or assets of 27 companies engaged in the business of providing burglar or fire alarm services. Holmes acquired the stock or assets of three burglar alarm companies in New York City using a central station. Of these 30, the officials of seven agreed not to engage in the protective service business in the area for periods ranging from five years to permanently. After Grinnell acquired control of the other defendants, the latter continued in their attempts to acquire central station companies — offers being made to at least eight companies between the years 1955 and 1961, including four of the five largest nondefendant companies in the business. When the present suit was filed, each of those defendants had outstanding an offer to purchase one of the four largest nondefendant companies. . . .

ADT over the years reduced its minimum basic rates to meet competition and renewed contracts at substantially increased rates in cities where it had a monopoly of accredited central station service. ADT threatened retaliation against firms that contemplated inaugurating central station service. And the record indicates that, in contemplating opening a new central station, ADT officials frequently stressed that such action would deter their competitors from opening a new station in that area.

. . . .

The offense of monopoly under § 2 of the Sherman Act has two elements: (1) the possession of monopoly power in the relevant market and (2) the willful acquisition or maintenance of that power as distinguished from growth or development as a consequence of a superior product, business acumen, or historic accident. We shall see that this second ingredient presents no major problem here, as what was done in building the empire was done plainly and explicitly for a single purpose. In *United States v. du Pont & Co.*, 351 U.S. 377, 391, we defined monopoly power as "the power to control prices or exclude competition." The existence of such power ordinarily may be inferred from the predominant share of the market. . . . In the present case, 87% of the accredited central station service business leaves no doubt that the congeries of these defendants have monopoly power — power which, as our discussion of the record indicates, they did not hesitate to wield — if that business is the relevant market. The only remaining question therefore is, what is the relevant market?

In case of a product it may be of such a character that substitute products must also be considered, as customers may turn to them if there is a slight increase in the price of the main product. That is the teaching of the *du Pont* case, *viz.*, that commodities reasonably interchangeable make up that "part" of trade or commerce which § 2 protects against monopoly power.

The District Court treated the entire accredited central station service business as a single market and we think it was justified in so doing. Defendants argue that the different central station services offered are so diverse that they cannot under *du Pont* be lumped together to make up the relevant market. For example, burglar alarm services are not interchangeable with fire alarm services. They further urge that *du Pont* requires that protective services other than those of the central station variety be included in the market definition.

But there is here a single use, *i.e.*, the protection of property, through a central station that receives signals. It is that service, accredited, that is unique and that competes with all the other forms of property protection. We see no barrier to combining in a single market a number of different products or services where that combination reflects commercial realities. To repeat, there is here a single basic service — the protection of property through use of a central service station — that must be compared with all other forms of property protection.

. . . The defendants have not made out a case for fragmentizing the types of services into lesser units.

Burglar alarm service is in a sense different from fire alarm service; from waterflow alarms; and so on. But it would be unrealistic on this record to break down the market into the various kinds of central station protective services that are available. Central station companies recognize that to compete effectively, they must offer all or nearly all types of service. The different forms of accredited central station service are provided from a single office and customers utilize different services in combination. . . .

There are, to be sure, substitutes for the accredited central station service. But none of them appears to operate on the same level as the central station service so as to meet the interchangeability test of the *du Pont* case. Nonautomatic and automatic local alarm systems appear on this record to have marked differences, not the low degree of differentiation required of substitute services as well as substitute articles.

Watchman service is far more costly and less reliable. Systems that set off an audible alarm at the site of a fire or burglary are cheaper but often less reliable. . . .

Defendants earnestly urge that despite these differences, they face competition from these other modes of protection. They seem to us seriously to overstate the degree of competition, but we recognize that (as the District Court found) they "do not have unfettered power to control the price of their services . . . due to the fringe competition of other alarm or watchmen services." What defendants overlook is that the high degree of differentiation between central station protection and the other forms means that for many customers, only central station protection will do. . . .

We also agree with the District Court that the geographic market for the accredited central station service is national. The activities of an individual station are in a sense local as it serves, ordinarily, only that area which is within a radius of 25 miles. But the record amply supports the conclusion that the business of providing such a service is operated on a national level. There is national planning. The agreements we have discussed covered activities in many States. The inspection, certification and rate-making is largely by national insurers. The appellant ADT has a national schedule of prices, rates, and terms, though the rates may be varied to meet local conditions. It deals with multistate businesses on the basis of nationwide contracts. The manufacturing business of ADT is interstate. The fact that Holmes is more nearly local than the others does not save it, for it is part and parcel of the combine presided over and controlled by Grinnell.

As the District Court found, the relevant market for determining whether the defendants have monopoly power is not the several local areas which the individual stations serve, but the broader national market that reflects the reality of the way in which they built and conduct their business.

Justice Fortas, with whom Justice Stewart joins, dissenting.

The geographical market is defined as nationwide. But the need and the service are intensely local. . . . Protection must be provided on the spot. It must be furnished by local personnel able to bring help to the scene within minutes. Even the central stations can provide service only within a 25-mile radius. Where the tenants of the premises turn to central stations for this service, they must make their contracts locally with the central station and purchase their services from it on the basis of local conditions.

But because these defendants, the trial court found, are connected by stock ownership, interlocking management and some degree of national corporate direction, and because there is some national participation in selling as well as national financing, advertising, purchasing of equipment, and the like, the court concluded that the competitive area to be considered is national. This Court now affirms that conclusion.

This is a non sequitur. It is not permissible to seize upon the nationwide scope of defendants' operation and to bootstrap a geographical definition of the market from this. . . . The central issue is where does a potential buyer look for potential suppliers of the service — what is the geographical area in which the buyer has, or, in the absence of monopoly, would have, a real choice as to price and alternative facilities? This depends upon the facts of the market place, taking into account such economic factors as the distance over which supplies and services may be feasibly furnished, consistently with cost and functional efficiency.

. . . .

Here, there can be no doubt that the correct geographic market is local. The services at issue are intensely local: they can be furnished only locally. The business as it is done is local — not nationwide. If, as might well be the case on this record, defendants were found to have violated the Sherman Act in a number of these local areas, a proper decree, directed to those markets, as well as to general corporate features relevant to the condemned practices, could be fashioned. On the other hand, a gross definition of the market as nationwide leads to a gross, nationwide decree which does not address itself to the realities of the market place. . . .

. . . .

NOTES AND QUESTIONS

1. How do you measure the relevant geographic market when the seller is a nationwide company with retail outlets in all states, but the buyer looks for alternatives only within her own city or community? Suppose that a company owns shoe stores in 50 cities and towns across the United States. In some of these cities it operates the only shoe store, but in others it is in intense competition. How would the company price its shoes? Clearly, absent a restraint on price discrimination it would price in each city at the profit-maximizing level. If it had a monopoly in City A and the profit-maximizing price there was $50, it would charge $50. On the other hand, if City B were competitive, it might charge a competitive price of $40. If it attempted to charge $50 in B, it would lose its sales, even though it has a monopoly elsewhere. Should the fact that the company makes all its pricing decisions at central headquarters make any difference?

Does your analysis of the relevant geographic market change if you look at elasticity of supply rather than demand? The supply of accredited central station protective service outlets was controlled by three or four large companies, each of whom did business in several states. Presumably it would be easier for one of these companies to inaugurate service into a new city than it would be for a newcomer to enter the industry.

One argument for a national rather than local markets in *Grinnell* is the doctrine of potential competition (see the discussion, *infra*). Perhaps the market for central station protective services could be structured to contain three or four national companies bidding for the business in each city. In that case, even though each city contained only one current provider of the service, there would always be other established companies available to come in should the incumbent attempt to charge monopoly prices. In other words, although on the demand side the business was entirely local, on the supply side, firms established in the business were very likely entrants. The creation of a multiplicity of national companies could increase considerably the elasticity of supply in the market.

Might there be other reasons, however, for concluding that the market ought to be nationwide rather than local? For example, because Grinnell is a national company, might it not be able to use its market power in some cities to exact a kind of monopolistic "leverage" in other cities? For example, might it use its monopoly profits from a monopoly city to subsidize predatory pricing in a different city? Even if it could do so, would that be a basis for saying that it is monopolizing the market in both cities?

2.   Suppose firm P sells 90% of the widgets in a four-state region. The only other firm selling in the region is Q, which is much larger than P, but which is located one thousand miles away from the nearest point in the four-state region. How should P's market share be calculated? To say that P has 90% of the market would seem to overstate its share. If P attempted to raise prices further, Q could presumably divert more widgets into the four-state region. Should it make a difference if P is currently charging a monopoly price? *See* 2A Phillip Areeda, Herbert Hovenkamp & John Solow, Antitrust Law, ch. 5C-E (4th ed. 2014). Another possibility is to include Q's total production, or perhaps its productive capacity, rather than merely the amount Q actually imports into the four-state region. By the same token, however, that may understate P's market power because Q may not be able to shift all its production into the four-state region. Suppose that part of Q's output is committed under long-term contracts, while the rest is not? Suppose, further, that Q's output is similar enough to P's to be included in the same product market, but the products of the two firms are quite different from each other, and there are some customers who strongly prefer P's widgets over Q's, and vice-versa? *See* Louis Kaplow, *The Accuracy of Traditional Market Power Analysis and a Direct Adjustment Alternative*, 95 Harv. L. Rev. 1817 (1982).

3.   It is important not to confuse a geographic market for antitrust purposes with a "sales area," or area in which a firm services most customers. The sales area considers the extent to which customers are willing to travel *to* the defendant in order to buy its product. The relevant geographic market, by contrast, considers the extent to which customers are willing to travel *away* from the defendant in order to avoid its product. Consider this example: Smallville is a town of 900 families located 15 miles outside Metropolis. It has a single small grocery store, frequented almost exclusively by Smallville residents. Of these residents, 400 families do their regular shopping in Smallville, while 500 families drive to Metropolis, where there are several large stores and prices are generally lower. Is Smallville a relevant market for retail groceries? Probably not. The "sales area" of Smallville Grocery is indeed Smallville. That is, if one took the address of every Smallville Grocery customer for a week, virtually all would report that they came from Smallville. But that fact is quite irrelevant to determining the relevant antitrust market. We want to know the extent to which people living in Smallville can go *elsewhere*, such as Metropolis, in order to avoid Smallville Grocery's high prices.

In *Bathke v. Casey's General Stores*, 64 F.3d 340 (8th Cir. 1995), the court followed this reasoning. It rejected the plaintiff's argument that the geographic market for retail sales of self-service gasoline were equal to the defendant's "trade area," which was said to be an area from one to three miles around each store. Whether or not most of the defendant's sales were made to buyers from that area, there may have been numerous other customers within that area who purchased gasoline elsewhere. In this case, census data showed that some one-half of the employed people who lived in the proposed markets actually held jobs in other towns well outside the trade area, and could presumably have purchased gasoline where they worked.

4. The Elzinga-Hogarty test for geographic markets suggests that a geographic area is a relevant geographic market if the average of production inside the area shipped outside, and of production outside the area consumed inside, is less than 10%. Under the common formulation, a cross-over of less than 10% is deemed a "strong" market, while a cross-over greater than 10% but less than 25% is deemed a "weak" market. The case law discussing the issue has generally stated a preference for the "strong" version of this test. *See* Kenneth G. Elzinga & Thomas F. Hogarty, *The Problem of Geographic Market Delineation in Antimerger Suits*, 18 Antitrust Bull. 45 (1973); subsequently revised in Kenneth G. Elzinga & Thomas F. Hogarty, *The Problem of Geographic Market Delineation Revisited: The Case of Coal*, 23 Antitrust Bull. 1 (1978).

The logic of Elzinga-Hogarty is that one can relate the ability of a firm to charge a monopoly price in a particular area to the number of sales that "cross the boundary" from that area to somewhere else in either direction. The test has been used extensively in merger cases, where the question is whether a merger might lead to a *further* price increase from current prices; but not much in monopolization cases. Do you see why? Is the test subject to the *Cellophane* fallacy? Perhaps the amount of boundary crossing is high because a local firm is already charging its monopoly price.

III THE MODERN MONOPOLIZATION OFFENSE: CONDUCT

The offense of monopolization under Section 2 of the Sherman Act requires not only that the defendant have market power but also that it "exercise" that power. The exercise of monopoly power does not refer to monopolistic pricing, however, but rather to the creation or preservation of market power by means that we consider anticompetitive. It is not illegal for a firm to have a large amount of market power, and it is not illegal for a firm with market power to charge its profit-maximizing price, even if that price is far higher than the firm's costs. The more profitable the monopoly is, however, the more attractive the market becomes to other potential producers and sellers. People with money to invest look for high returns, and monopolized markets frequently provide them. The monopolist would prefer that these people invest their money somewhere else, and sometimes it will take certain actions to encourage them to do so. These "exclusionary practices" are the activities which, when combined with market power, yield the offense of monopolization.

It is impossible to edit cases in such a way as to separate issues of market power from issues of conduct. The opinions that appeared above, such as *Alcoa* and

Grinnell, mentioned certain anticompetitive acts in the process of discussing market power. The cases that follow necessarily include analysis of market power in their discussion of conduct. Nevertheless, the following cases are particularly good examples of the kinds of conduct that courts over the years have come to regard as "exclusionary," and which, when combined with market power, will form the offense of monopolization.

Section Two of the Sherman Act provides, in relevant part: "Every person who shall monopolize, or attempt to monopolize, or combine or conspire with any other person or persons, to monopolize any part of the trade or commerce among the several States, or with foreign nations, shall be deemed guilty of a felony . . . ." 15 U.S.C. § 2. Thus, there are three separate causes of action: monopolization, attempted monopolization, and conspiracies to monopolize. Each of these causes of action has its own elements that a plaintiff must prove in order to establish liability.

As you have read, the Supreme Court in *Grinnell* created a two-element test for illegal monopolization: "(1) the possession of monopoly power in the relevant market and (2) the willful acquisition or maintenance of that power as distinguished from growth or development as a consequence of a superior product, business acumen, or historic accident." *United States v. Grinnell Corp.*, 384 U.S. 563, 570–571 (1966). The second element is often referred to as the monopoly conduct requirement. This Part focuses on that conduct element.

In *Spectrum Sports, Inc. v. McQuillan*, 506 U.S. 447 (1993), the Supreme Court fashioned a three-element test for attempted monopolization. The Court held that "to demonstrate attempted monopolization a plaintiff must prove (1) that the defendant has engaged in predatory or anticompetitive conduct with (2) a specific intent to monopolize and (3) a dangerous probability of achieving monopoly power." *Id.* at 456 (1993). The intricacies of these elements — and the relationship between the *Grinnell* test and *Spectrum Sports* test — are discussed in Part IV of this chapter. At this point, however, it is worth noting that the first element of the *Spectrum Sports* test for attempted monopolization is equivalent to the second element of the *Grinnell* test for illegal monopolization. Monopoly conduct under *Grinnell* is the same as "predatory or anticompetitive conduct" under *Spectrum Sports*, and vice-versa. Thus, all of the alleged anticompetitive conduct discussed in the cases in this Part apply to the conduct element of both of these Section 2 causes of action.

[A]   Innovation and Exclusion

BERKEY PHOTO, INC. v. EASTMAN KODAK CO.
603 F.2d 263 (2d Cir. 1979)

JUDGE KAUFMAN

This action, one of the largest and most significant private antitrust suits in history, was brought by Berkey Photo, Inc., a far smaller but still prominent participant in the industry. Berkey competes with Kodak in providing photofinishing services — the conversion of exposed film into finished prints, slides, or movies.

Until 1978, Berkey sold cameras as well. It does not manufacture film, but it does purchase Kodak film for resale to its customers, and it also buys photofinishing equipment and supplies, including color print paper, from Kodak.

. . . In this action, Berkey claims that every aspect of the association has been infected by Kodak's monopoly power in the film, color print paper, and camera markets, willfully acquired, maintained, and exercised in violation of § 2 of the Sherman Act, 15 U.S.C. § 2 . . . Berkey alleges that these violations caused it to lose sales in the camera and photofinishing markets and to pay excessive prices to Kodak for film, color print paper, and photofinishing equipment. . . .

. . . .

The principal markets relevant here, each nationwide in scope, are amateur conventional still cameras, conventional photographic film, photofinishing services, photofinishing equipment, and color print paper. The numerous technological interactions among the products and services constituting these markets are manifest. To take an obvious example, not only are both camera and film required to produce a snapshot, but the two must be in compatible "formats." This means that the film must be cut to the right size and spooled in a roll or cartridge that will fit the camera mechanism. . . .

The "amateur conventional still camera" market now consists almost entirely of the so-called 110 and 126 instant-loading cameras. These are the direct descendants of the popular "box" cameras, the best-known of which was Kodak's so-called "Brownie." Small, simple, and relatively inexpensive, cameras of this type are designed for the mass market rather than for the serious photographer.

Kodak has long been the dominant firm in the market thus defined. Between 1954 and 1973 it never enjoyed less than 61% of the annual unit sales, nor less than 64% of the dollar volume, and in the peak year of 1964, Kodak cameras accounted for 90% of market revenues. Much of this success is no doubt due to the firm's history of innovation. In 1963 Kodak first marketed the 126 "Instamatic" instant-loading camera, and in 1972 it came out with the much smaller 110 "Pocket Instamatic." Not only are these cameras small and light, but they employ film packaged in cartridges that can simply be dropped in the back of the camera, thus obviating the need to load and position a roll manually. Their introduction triggered successive revolutions in the industry. Annual amateur still camera sales in the United States averaged 3.9 million units between 1954 and 1963, with little annual variation. In the first full year after Kodak's introduction of the 126, industry sales leaped 22%, and they took an even larger quantum jump when the 110 came to market. Other camera manufacturers, including Berkey, copied both these inventions but for several months after each introduction anyone desiring to purchase a camera in the new format was perforce remitted to Kodak.

Berkey has been a camera manufacturer since its 1966 acquisition of the Keystone Camera Company, a producer of movie cameras and equipment. In 1968 Berkey began to sell amateur still cameras made by other firms, and the following year the Keystone Division commenced manufacturing such cameras itself. From 1970 to 1977, Berkey accounted for 8.2% of the sales in the camera market in the United States, reaching a peak of 10.2% in 1976. In 1978, Berkey sold its camera division and thus abandoned this market.

The relevant market for photographic film comprises color print, color slide, color movie, and black-and-white film. Kodak's grip on this market is even stronger than its hold on cameras. Since 1952, its annual sales have always exceeded 82% of the nationwide volume on a unit basis, and 88% in revenues. Foreign competition has recently made some inroads into Kodak's monopoly, but the Rochester firm concedes that it dominated film sales throughout the period relevant to this case.
. . .

Kodak's monopoly in the film market is particularly important to this case, because the jury accepted Berkey's contention, noted above, that it had been used to disadvantage rivals in cameras, photofinishing, photofinishing equipment, and other markets. Of special relevance to this finding is the color print film segment of the industry, which Kodak has dominated since it introduced "Kodacolor," the first amateur color print film, in 1942. In 1963, when Kodak announced the 126 Instamatic camera, it also brought out a new, faster color print film — Kodacolor X — which was initially available to amateur photographers only in the 126 format. Nine years later, Kodak repeated this pattern with the simultaneous introduction of the 110 Pocket Instamatic and Kodacolor II film. For more than a year, Kodacolor II was made only for 110 cameras, and Kodak has never made any other color print film in the 110 size.

Before 1954, Kodak's Color Print and Processing Laboratories (CP&P) had a nearly absolute monopoly of color photofinishing maintained by a variety of practices. Accounting for over 95% of color film sales, Kodak sold every roll with an advance charge for processing included. Consumers had little choice but to purchase Kodak film, and in so doing they acquired the right to have that film developed and printed by CP&P at no further charge. Since few customers would duplicate their costs to procure the services of a non-Kodak photofinisher, Kodak was able to parlay its film monopoly to achieve equivalent market power in photofinishing.

This film/processing "tie-in" attracted the attention of the Justice Department, and in 1954 a consent decree changed the structure of the color photofinishing market drastically. Kodak was forbidden to link photofinishing to film sales, and it agreed to make its processing technology, chemicals, and paper available to rivals at reasonable rates. As a result, CP&P's share of the market plummeted from 96% in 1954 to 69% two years later, and it has declined sharply ever since. In 1970, CP&P accounted for but 17% of the market, and by 1976 its share reached a low of 10%. There are now approximately 600 independent photofinishers in the United States.

. . . .

Although the 1954 decree steadily loosened Kodak's grip in photofinishing, it did not immediately affect the firm's control of color paper. For more than a decade, the independent photofinishers that sprang up after the decree was entered looked only to Kodak for their paper supplies.

. . . Kodak's control of the film and color paper markets clearly reached the level of a monopoly. And, while the issue is a much closer one, it appears that the evidence was sufficient for the jury to find that Kodak possessed such power in the camera market as well. But our inquiry into Kodak's liability cannot end there.

> [W]hile proclaiming vigorously that monopoly power is the evil at which § 2 is aimed, courts have declined to take what would have appeared to be the next logical step — declaring monopolies unlawful *per se* unless specifically authorized by law. To understand the reason for this, one must comprehend the fundamental tension — one might almost say the paradox — that is near the heart of 2. This tension creates much of the confusion surrounding § 2. It makes the cryptic *Alcoa* opinion a litigant's wishing well, into which, it sometimes seems, one may peer and find nearly anything he wishes.

> . . . .

In *Alcoa* the crosscurrents and pulls and tugs of § 2 law were reconciled by noting that, although the firm controlled the aluminum ingot market, "it may not have achieved monopoly; monopoly may have been thrust upon it." In examining this language, which would condemn a monopolist unless it is "the passive beneficiary of a monopoly," we perceive Hand the philosopher. As an operative rule of law, however, the "thrust upon" phrase does not suffice. It has been criticized by scholars, and the Supreme Court appears to have abandoned it. *Grinnell* instructs that after possession of monopoly power is found, the second element of the § 2 offense is "the willful acquisition or maintenance of that power as distinguished from growth or development as a consequence of a superior product, business acumen, or historic accident."

This formulation appears to square with the understanding of the draftsmen of the Sherman Act that § 2 does not condemn one "who merely by superior skill and intelligence . . . got the whole business because nobody could do it as well." Thus the statement in *Alcoa* that even well-behaved monopolies are forbidden by § 2 must be read carefully in context. Its rightful meaning is that, if monopoly power has been acquired or maintained through improper means, the fact that the power has not been used to extract improper benefits provides no succor to the monopolist.

But the law's hostility to monopoly power extends beyond the means of its acquisition. Even if that power has been legitimately acquired, the monopolist may not wield it to prevent or impede competition. Once a firm gains a measure of monopoly power, whether by its own superior competitive skill or because of such actions as restrictive combinations with others, it may discover that the power is capable of being maintained and augmented merely by using it. That is, a firm that has achieved dominance of a market might find its control sufficient to preserve and even extend its market share by excluding or preventing competition. A variety of techniques may be employed to achieve this end — predatory pricing, lease-only policies, and exclusive buying arrangements, to list a few.

. . . A firm that has lawfully acquired a monopoly position is not barred from taking advantage of scale economies by constructing, for example, a large and efficient factory. These benefits are a consequence of size and not an exercise of power over the market. Nevertheless, many anticompetitive actions are possible or effective only if taken by a firm that dominates its smaller rivals. . . .

In sum, although the principles announced by the § 2 cases often appear to conflict, this much is clear. The mere possession of monopoly power does not *ipso facto* condemn a market participant. But, to avoid the proscriptions of § 2, the firm must refrain at all times from conduct directed at smothering competition. This doctrine has two branches. Unlawfully acquired power remains anathema even when kept dormant. And it is no less true that a firm with a legitimately achieved monopoly may not wield the resulting power to tighten its hold on the market.

It is clear that a firm may not employ its market position as a lever to create — or attempt to create — a monopoly in another market. Kodak, in the period relevant to this suit, was never close to gaining control of the markets for photofinishing equipment or services and could not be held to have attempted to monopolize them. Berkey nevertheless contends that Kodak illicitly gained an advantage in these areas by leveraging its power over film and cameras. Accordingly, we must determine whether a firm violates § 2 by using its monopoly power in one market to gain a competitive advantage in another, albeit without an attempt to monopolize the second market. We hold, as did the lower court, that it does.

This conclusion appears to be an inexorable interpretation of the antitrust laws. We tolerate the existence of monopoly power, we repeat, only insofar as necessary to preserve competitive incentives and to be fair to the firm that has attained its position innocently. There is no reason to allow the exercise of such power to the detriment of competition, in either the controlled market or any other. That the competition in the leveraged market may not be destroyed but merely distorted does not make it more palatable. Social and economic effects of an extension of monopoly power militate against such conduct. . . .

Accordingly, the use of monopoly power attained in one market to gain a competitive advantage in another is a violation of § 2, even if there has not been an attempt to monopolize the second market. It is the use of economic power that creates the liability. But, as we have indicated, a large firm does not violate § 2 simply by reaping the competitive rewards attributable to its efficient size, nor does an integrated business offend the Sherman Act whenever one of its departments benefits from association with a division possessing a monopoly in its own market. So long as we allow a firm to compete in several fields, we must expect it to seek the competitive advantages of its broad-based activity — more efficient production, greater ability to develop complementary products, reduced transaction costs, and so forth. These are gains that accrue to any integrated firm, regardless of its market share, and they cannot by themselves be considered uses of monopoly power.

We turn now to the events surrounding Kodak's introduction of the 110 photographic system in 1972. . . .

. . . On March 16, 1972, amid great fanfare, the system was announced. Finally, said Kodak, there was a "little camera that takes big pictures." Kodacolor II was "a remarkable new film" — indeed, the best color negative film Kodak had ever manufactured. There had long been other small cameras, Kodak explained: "But they weren't like these. Now there are films fine enough, and sharp enough, to give you big, sharp pictures from a very small negative." In accord with Kodak's 1967 plan, Kodacolor II was sold only in the 110 format for eighteen months after introduction. It remains the only 110-size color print film Kodak has ever sold.

As Kodak had hoped, the 110 system proved to be a dramatic success. In 1972 — the system's first year — the company sold 2,984,000 Pocket Instamatics, more than 50% of its sales in the amateur conventional still camera market. The new camera thus accounted in large part for a sharp increase in total market sales, from 6.2 million units in 1971 to 8.2 million in 1972. Rival manufacturers hastened to market their own 110 cameras, but Kodak stood alone until Argus made its first shipment of the "Carefree 110" around Christmas 1972. . . .

Berkey's Keystone division was a late entrant in the 110 sweepstakes, joining the competition only in late 1973. Moreover, because of hasty design, the original models suffered from latent defects, and sales that year were a paltry 42,000. With interest in the 126 dwindling, Keystone thus suffered a net decline of 118,000 unit sales in 1973. The following year, however, it recovered strongly, in large part because improvements in its pocket cameras helped it sell 406,000 units, 7% of all 110s sold that year.

Berkey contends that the introduction of the 110 system was both an attempt to monopolize and actual monopolization of the camera market. It also alleges that the marketing of the new camera constituted an impermissible leveraging of Kodak's film monopoly into the two photofinishing markets, services and equipment. . . .

It will be useful at the outset to present the arguments on which Berkey asks us to uphold its verdict:

(1) Kodak, a film and camera monopolist, was in a position to set industry standards. Rivals could not compete effectively without offering products similar to Kodak's. Moreover, Kodak persistently refused to make film available for most formats other than those in which it made cameras. Since cameras are worthless without film, this policy effectively prevented other manufacturers from introducing cameras in new formats. Because of its dominant position astride two markets, and by use of its film monopoly to distort the camera market, Kodak forfeited its own right to reap profits from such innovations without providing its rivals with sufficient advance information to enable them to enter the market with copies of the new product on the day of Kodak's introduction. . . .

(2) The simultaneous introduction of the 110 camera and Kodacolor II film, together with a campaign advertising the two jointly, enabled Kodak to garner more camera sales than if it had merely scaled down Kodacolor X to fit the new camera. The jury could conclude that Kodacolor II was an inferior product and not technologically necessary for the success of the 110. In any event, Kodak's film monopoly prevented any other camera manufacturer from marketing such a film-camera "system" and the joint introduction was therefore anticompetitive.

(3) For eighteen months after its introduction, Kodacolor II was available only in the 110 format. Thus it followed that any consumer wishing to use Kodak's "remarkable new film" had to buy a 110 camera. Since Kodak was the leading — and at first the only — manufacturer of such devices, its camera sales were boosted at the expense of its competitors.

For the reasons explained below, we do not believe any of these contentions is sufficient on the facts of this case to justify an award of damages to Berkey. . . .

As Judge Frankel indicated, and as Berkey concedes, a firm may normally keep its innovations secret from its rivals as long as it wishes, forcing them to catch up on the strength of their own efforts after the new product is introduced. It is the possibility of success in the marketplace, attributable to superior performance, that provides the incentives on which the proper functioning of our competitive economy rests. If a firm that has engaged in the risks and expenses of research and development were required in all circumstances to share with its rivals the benefits of those endeavors, this incentive would very likely be vitiated.

Withholding from others advance knowledge of one's new products, therefore, ordinarily constitutes valid competitive conduct. Because, as we have already indicated, a monopolist is permitted, and indeed encouraged, by § 2 to compete aggressively on the merits, any success that it may achieve through "the process of invention and innovation" is clearly tolerated by the antitrust laws.

. . . A significant vice of the theory propounded by Berkey lies in the uncertainty of its application. Berkey does not contend, in the colorful phrase of Judge Frankel, that "Kodak has to live in a goldfish bowl," disclosing every innovation to the world at large. However predictable in its application, such an extreme rule would be insupportable. Rather, Berkey postulates that Kodak had a duty to disclose limited types of information to certain competitors under specific circumstances. But it is difficult to comprehend how a major corporation, accustomed though it is to making business decisions with antitrust considerations in mind, could possess the omniscience to anticipate all the instances in which a jury might one day in the future retrospectively conclude that predisclosure was warranted. And it is equally difficult to discern workable guidelines that a court might set forth to aid the firm's decision. For example, how detailed must the information conveyed be? And how far must research have progressed before it is "ripe" for disclosure? These inherent uncertainties would have an inevitable chilling effect on innovation. They go far, we believe, towards explaining why no court has ever imposed the duty Berkey seeks to create here.

An antitrust plaintiff urging a predisclosure rule, therefore, bears a heavy burden in justifying his request. Berkey recognizes the weight of this burden. It contends that it has been met. Kodak is not a monolithic monopolist, acting in a single market. Rather, its camera monopoly was supported by its activity as a film manufacturer. Berkey therefore argues that by not disclosing the new format in which it was manufacturing film, Kodak unlawfully enhanced its power in the camera market. Indeed, Kodak not only participates in but monopolizes the film industry. The jury could easily have found that, when Kodak introduced a new film format, rival camera makers would be foreclosed from a substantial segment of the market until they were able to manufacture cameras in the new format. Accordingly, Berkey contended that Kodak illegitimately used its monopoly power in film to gain a competitive advantage in cameras. Thus Berkey insists that the jury was properly permitted to consider whether, on balance, the failure to predisclose the new format was exclusionary. We disagree.

We note that this aspect of Berkey's claim is in large measure independent of the fact that a new film, Kodacolor II, was introduced simultaneously with the new format. It is primarily introduction of the format itself — the size of the film and the cartridge in which it is packaged — of which Berkey complains. Indeed, at oral argument counsel for Berkey contended that predisclosure would have been required even had Kodak merely cut down Kodacolor X to fit the new 110 camera and cartridge.

We do not perceive, however, how Kodak's introduction of a new format was rendered an unlawful act of monopolization in the camera market because the firm also manufactured film to fit the cameras. The 110 system was in substantial part a camera development. . . . Indeed, Berkey not only argues that a new film was not necessary to introduce the new pocket cameras; it also concedes that the early models of its own 110 cameras, brought to market some eighteen months after it first learned of the new format, suffered because of the haste with which they were designed.

Clearly, then, the policy considerations militating against predisclosure requirements for monolithic monopolists are equally applicable here. The first firm, even a monopolist, to design a new camera format has a right to the lead time that follows from its success. The mere fact that Kodak manufactured film in the new format as well, so that its customers would not be offered worthless cameras, could not deprive it of that reward. Nor is this conclusion altered because Kodak not only participated in but dominated the film market. Kodak's ability to pioneer formats does not depend on it possessing a film monopoly. Had the firm possessed a much smaller share of the film market, it would nevertheless have been able to manufacture sufficient quantities of 110-size film — either Kodacolor X or Kodacolor II — to bring the new camera to market. It is apparent, therefore, that the ability to introduce the new format without predisclosure was solely a benefit of integration and not, without more, a use of Kodak's power in the film market to gain a competitive advantage in cameras. . . .

Our analysis, however, must proceed beyond the conclusion that introduction of film to meet Kodak's new camera format was not in itself an exercise of the company's monopoly power in film. Berkey contends that Kodak in the past used its film monopoly to stifle format innovations by any other camera manufacturer. Accordingly, it argues that Kodak was barred from reaping the benefits of such developments without making predisclosure to allow its rivals to share from the beginning in the rewards.

There is, indeed, little doubt that the jury could have found that Kodak, by refusing to make film available on economical terms, obstructed sales of cameras in competing formats. Thus, Kodak has never supplied film to fit the Minox, a small camera that uses a cartridge similar to that of the Instamatics and that has been on the market since the 1930s, or similar cameras by Minolta and Mamiya that were also introduced before the Kodak 126. . . .

We accept the proposition that it is improper, in the absence of a valid business policy, for a firm with monopoly power in one market to gain a competitive advantage in another by refusing to sell a rival the monopolized goods or services he needs to compete effectively in the second market. . . . Moreover, as indicated by our discussion of § 2 principles, such a use of power would be illegal regardless of whether the film monopoly were legally or illegally acquired. . . .

But Berkey did not sue Kodak then for its refusal to sell film, and it concedes that it is not now claiming a right to damages on this basis. Rather, it contends that Kodak's past offenses created a continuing duty to disclose its new formats to competing camera manufacturers, and that its violation of that obligation supports the jury's verdict. [W]e decline to recognize such a duty. . . .

Berkey's claims regarding the introduction of the 110 camera are not limited to its asserted right to predisclosure. The Pocket Instamatic not only initiated a new camera format, it was also promoted together with a new film. As we noted earlier, the view was expressed at Kodak that "[w]ithout a new film, the [camera] program is not a new advertisable system." Responding in large measure to this perception, Kodak hastened research and development of Kodacolor II so that it could be brought to market at the same time as the 110 system. Based on such evidence, and the earlier joint introduction of Kodacolor X and the 126 camera, the jury could readily have found that the simultaneous release of Kodacolor II and the Pocket Instamatic was part of a plan by which Kodak sought to use its combined film and camera capabilities to bolster faltering camera sales. Berkey contends that this program of selling was anticompetitive and therefore violated § 2. We disagree.

It is important to identify the precise harm Berkey claims to have suffered from this conduct. It cannot complain of a product introduction *simpliciter* for the same reason it could not demand predisclosure of the new format: any firm, even a monopolist, may generally bring its products to market whenever and however it chooses. Rather, Berkey's argument is more subtle. It claims that by marketing the Pocket Instamatics in a system with a widely advertised new film, Kodak gained camera sales at Berkey's expense. And, because Kodacolor II was not necessary to produce satisfactory 110 photographs and in fact suffered from several deficiencies, these gains were unlawful.

It may be conceded that, by advertising Kodacolor II as a "remarkable new film" capable of yielding "big, sharp pictures from a very small negative," Kodak sold more 110 cameras than it would have done had it merely marketed Kodacolor X in 110-size cartridges. The quality of the end product — a developed snapshot — is at least as dependent upon the characteristics of the film as upon those of the camera. It is perfectly plausible that some customers bought the Kodak 110 camera who would have purchased a competitor's camera in another format had Kodacolor II not been available and widely advertised as capable of producing "big, sharp pictures" from the tiny Pocket Instamatic. Moreover, there was also sufficient evidence for the jury to conclude that a new film was not necessary to bring the new cameras to market. . . .

But necessity is a slippery concept. Indeed, the two scientists, Zwick and Groet, conceded that improvements in the quality of Kodacolor X would be "most welcome." Even if the 110 camera would produce adequate snapshots with Kodacolor X, it would be difficult to fault Kodak for attempting to design a film that could provide better results. The attempt to develop superior products is, as we have explained, an essential element of lawful competition. Kodak could not have violated § 2 merely by introducing the 110 camera with an improved film.

Accordingly, much of the evidence at trial concerned the dispute over the relative merits of Kodacolor II and Kodacolor X. There was ample evidence that for some months following the 110 introduction, Kodacolor II was inferior to its predecessor in several respects. Most notably, it degenerated more quickly than Kodacolor X, so that its shelf life was shorter. It is undisputed, however, that the grain of Kodacolor II, though not as fine as Kodak had hoped, was better than that of the older film.

In this context, therefore, the question of product quality has little meaning. A product that commends itself to many users because superior in certain respects may be rendered unsatisfactory to others by flaws they considered fatal. . . .

It is evident, then, that in such circumstances no one can determine with any reasonable assurance whether one product is "superior" to another. Preference is a matter of individual taste. The only question that can be answered is whether there is sufficient demand for a particular product to make its production worthwhile, and the response, so long as the free choice of consumers is preserved, can only be inferred from the reaction of the market. . . .

We conclude, therefore, that Kodak did not contravene the Sherman Act merely by introducing Kodacolor II simultaneously with the Pocket Instamatic and advertising the advantages of the new film for taking pictures with a small camera.

There is another aspect to Berkey's claim that introduction of Kodacolor II simultaneously with the Pocket Instamatic camera was anticompetitive. For eighteen months after the 110 system introduction, Kodacolor II was available only in the 110 format. Since Kodak was the first to have the 110s on the market, Berkey asserts it lost camera sales because consumers who wished to use the "remarkable new film" would be compelled to buy a Kodak camera. This facet of the claim, of course, is not dependent on a showing that Kodacolor II was inferior in any respect to Kodacolor X. Quite the opposite is true. The argument is that, since consumers were led to believe that Kodacolor II was superior to Kodacolor X, they were more likely to buy a Kodak 110, rather than a Berkey camera, so that the new film could be used.

. . . We shall assume *arguendo* that Kodak violated § 2 of the Sherman Act if its decision to restrict Kodacolor II to the 110 format was not justified by the nature of the film but was motivated by a desire to impede competition in the manufacture of cameras capable of using the new film. This might well supply the element of coercion we found lacking in the previous section. We shall assume also that there was sufficient evidence for the jury to conclude that the initial decision to market Kodacolor II exclusively in the 110 format during its introductory period was indeed taken for anticompetitive purposes.

But to prevail, Berkey must prove more, for injury is an element of a private treble damages action. Berkey must, therefore, demonstrate that some consumers who would have bought a Berkey camera were dissuaded from doing so because Kodacolor II was available only in the 110 format. This it has failed to establish. The record is totally devoid of evidence that Kodak or its retailers actually attempted to persuade customers to purchase the Pocket Instamatic because it was the only camera that could use Kodacolor II, or that, in fact, any consumers did choose the 110 in order to utilize the finer-grained film. . . .

To summarize our conclusions on the 110 camera claims, we hold:

1. Kodak was under no obligation to predisclose information of its new film and format to its camera-making competitors.

2. It is no basis for antitrust liability that Kodacolor II, despite certain deficiencies compared to Kodacolor X, may have encouraged sales of the 110 camera.

3. Finally, although the restriction of Kodacolor II to the 110 format may have been unjustified, there was no evidence that Berkey was injured by this course of action.

CALIFORNIA COMPUTER PRODUCTS v. IBM CORP.
613 F.2d 727 (9th Cir. 1979)

JUDGE CHOY.

[The plaintiff was a manufacturer of peripheral products for computers, such as disk drives and memory units. It commonly "reverse engineered" IBM peripheral products and manufactured similar peripherals compatible with IBM mainframe computers and Central Processing Units (CPUs). Under pre-1970s technology such peripheral units were commonly connected to CPUs by cables, and it was possible to buy different units from different manufacturers, as long as they were compatible with each other. In 1971, however, IBM introduced a new line of computers which integrated disk drive and memory functions into the CPU itself. As a result, anyone who purchased such a CPU from IBM was obliged to take the IBM disk drive and memory units as well, for they were all part of the same physical unit in the new line of machines. The plaintiffs claimed that the defendant's new design was illegal monopolization in violation of Section 2 of the Sherman Act.]

CalComp characterized these design changes as "technological manipulation" which did not improve performance. It also complained of the fact that the newly integrated functions were priced below their non-integrated counterparts. But as we have stated, price and performance are inseparable parts of any competitive offering; and equivalent function at lower cost certainly represents a superior product from the buyer's point of view. The evidence at trial was uncontroverted that integration was a cost-saving step, consistent with industry trends, which enabled IBM effectively to reduce prices for equivalent functions. Moreover, there was substantial evidence as well that in the case of Models 145, 158 and 168 the integration of control and memory functions also represented a performance improvement.

One of CalComp's witnesses stated: "I think in general the manufacturer will try and minimize his costs and where he integrates the control unit the assumption must be that he is achieving a lower cost solution." Other of CalComp's evidence showed that among the reasons a separate control unit is more expensive than integrated control circuitry are that the former requires its own cabinet, frames, power supply, additional cabling and electronics. According to an IBM witness, the monolithic systems technology that preceded the 145 — 2319A system required a large standalone controller, whereas the new generation technology represented by the 145 — 2319A system produced a comparable control function "which was in the area of ten times smaller. . . . [Y]ou could now put that into the 145 system, utilizing its frames and its covers and then passing on the advantages of that to the customer in a price reduction." CalComp's Chairman stated that as a result of integration, the customer uses less floor space which "tends to be relatively expensive in a computer room."

IBM, assuming it was a monopolist, had the right to redesign its products to make them more attractive to buyers — whether by reason of lower manufacturing cost and price or improved performance. It was under no duty to help CalComp or other peripheral equipment manufacturers survive or expand.

Affirmed.

NOTES AND QUESTIONS

1. *Berkey Photo* was decided by Judge Learned Hand's court, which had decided the *Alcoa* case 35 years earlier. How much of *Alcoa* remains?

2. Should a manufacturer with substantial market power ever have a duty to predisclose a new product to competitors?

3. Any new invention injures competitors of the inventor. Should a new invention ever be the basis of a monopolization claim? For an argument that sometimes technological innovation can itself be predatory, and should then be condemned, see Janusz Ordover & Robert Willig, *An Economic Definition of Predation: Pricing and Product Innovation*, 91 YALE L.J. 8 (1981); for a response, see Gregory Sidak, *Debunking Predatory Innovation*, 83 COLUM. L. REV. 1121 (1983).

In general, we reward innovation by giving the innovator monopoly profits. That is the express policy of the patent laws. Kodak and IBM were innovators, but Berkey Photo and California Computer Products were free riders. They made money by copying the products of their competitors. Should firms have a right, protected by the law against monopolization, to copy someone else's innovations? What if the antitrust laws held that as soon as someone developed a new product everyone had a legal right of access to the new technology? What would happen to the incentive to innovate?

4. What of California Computer's allegation that IBM's new line of integrated computers, which eliminated part of the separate market for peripheral products, was nothing more than "'technological manipulation' which did not improve performance"? Suppose that the new, integrated machines were really inferior to the older, separate ones, but IBM introduced the new ones simply to destroy the independent market for peripheral devices. Why would consumers buy them? Could such a plan be profitable to IBM? Would it have to stop manufacturing its older line of computers? What if one or more other firms also manufactured computers similar to the older, superior units?

In 1969, the government also brought its own case against IBM, arguing that in the 1960s, IBM introduced an entire computer line, the System/360, as "fighting machines." The Antitrust Division alleged that (1) the machines were announced long before IBM was ready to ship them, (2) their capabilities were exaggerated, and (3) they were priced at less than cost. Assuming these three allegations were true, which should be antitrust violations? For discussion of the case by authors sympathetic with the defendant, see Franlin M. Fisher, John J. McGowan & Joan E. Greenwood, Folded, Spindled, and Mutilated: Economic Analysis and U.S. v. IBM (1983). For discussion from the government's perspective, see Richard T. DeLamarter, Big Blue: IBM's Use and Abuse of Power (1986). The government's case was voluntarily dismissed in 1982.

5.   Courts have sometimes upheld verdicts finding the redesign of a product to constitute exclusionary conduct for Section 2 purposes. *See, e.g., C.R. Bard, Inc. v. M3 Systems, Inc.,* 157 F.3d 1340 (Fed. Cir. 1998). Bard manufactured a patented biopsy gun, which injected a biopsy needle into body tissue in order to extract a tissue sample that could be tested in a laboratory. Although its biopsy gun — sold under the trademarked name "Biopty gun" — was patented, the replacement needles used with the gun were not. M3 Systems made replacement needles. M3 Systems alleged that Bard violated Section 2 of the Sherman Act by, among other anticompetitive acts, modifying its biopsy gun to accept only Bard needles. The jury found for M3 Systems on this antitrust claim and Bard appealed, arguing that it was entitled to judgment as a matter of law. Writing for the majority on a split panel, Judge Bryson opined:

> The jury considered evidence that Bard modified its Biopty gun to prevent its competitors' non-infringing, flangeless needles from being used in Bard's guns. By special verdicts, the jury found that there was a relevant product market for replacement needles for fully automated reusable *biopsy guns*, that Bard had monopoly power in that market, and that it had acquired or maintained its monopoly power in that market through restrictive or exclusionary conduct.

> In order to prevail on its claim of an antitrust violation based on Bard's modification of its Biopty gun to prevent the use of competing replacement needles, M3 was required to prove that Bard made a change in its Biopty gun for predatory reasons, i.e., for the purpose of injuring competitors in the replacement needle market, rather than for improving the operation of the gun. [c.o.] . . . While the evidence of Bard's market power was in dispute, the jury specifically found that Bard enjoyed monopoly power in the market for replacement needles. The evidence was sufficient to support the jury's verdict on that point and also to support the jury's conclusion that Bard maintained its monopoly position by exclusionary conduct, to wit, modifying its patented gun in order to exclude competing replacement needles.

> The dissent on this issue starts from the premise that the modification to Bard's Biopty gun was an "improvement" and argues from that premise that to hold Bard liable for the modification would have the "pernicious" effect of penalizing innovators for making improvements to their products. The dissent's premise, however, is contrary to the jury's verdict, which was supported by the evidence. Although Bard contended at trial that it modified its Biopty gun to make it easier to load and unload, there was substantial evidence that Bard's real reasons for modifying the gun were to

raise the cost of entry to potential makers of replacement needles, to make doctors apprehensive about using non-Bard needles, and to preclude the use of "copycat" needles. One internal Bard document showed that the gun modifications had no effect on gun or needle performance; another internal document showed that the use of non-Bard needles in the gun "could not possibly result in injury to either the patient or the physician." In view of that evidence, the jury could reasonably conclude that Bard's modifications to its guns constituted "restrictive or exclusionary conduct" in a market over which it had monopoly power.

Id. at 1382.

The courts in *Bard* and *California Computers* reached different conclusions on whether the challenged product design was predatory. Why? *See also Allied Orthopedic Appliances Inc. v. Tyco Health Care Group LP*, 592 F.3d 991 (9th Cir. 2010) (design change could not be unlawful if the redesigned product was an improvement; rejecting plaintiff's argument that court should balance positive effects from redesign against amount of harm done to rival).

6.   For many years, an automobile manufacturer has been manufacturing cars equipped with a particular dashboard design that accommodates a car radio. The manufacturer also makes car radios, which it sells as "factory installed" or "dealer installed." However, several small competing companies manufacture radios that will fit into the dashboard as well. These competing radios are commonly sold at a lower price than radios produced by the automobile manufacturer itself.

One year, without warning, the automobile manufacturer changes its dashboard design to make installation of radios by competitors more difficult. Worse yet, the dashboard design now changes every year with the year-end model change, and each year the competing radio manufacturers must alter the design of their radio installation kits in order to fit the new dashboard design. Because automobile models are kept secret by auto manufacturers until they are displayed for sale, the competing radio manufacturers lose sales during the lucrative period immediately after new car models are introduced because it takes them several months to design and produce an installation kit that will fit the new models.

Suppose further that the yearly design changes are purely aesthetic; that is, there is no evidence that they improve the performance of the automobile radio. Has the automobile manufacturer violated the antitrust laws? *See Automatic Radio Mfg. Co. v. Ford Motor Co.*, 272 F. Supp. 744 (D. Mass. 1967), *aff'd*, 390 F.2d 113 (1st Cir. 1968).

7.   Many physical tie-ins are actually price discrimination devices. For example, if Kodak charged a monopoly price for the film in its newly developed camera-film package, a photographer who used 30 rolls of film per month (and presumably placed a high value on the camera) would yield higher profits to Kodak than a photographer who used only 3 rolls per year. For the use of tying arrangements as price discrimination devices, see Chapter 5, *supra*.

8.   *Berkey Photo* breathed new life into the "leverage" theory of Section 2 with its statement that "the use of monopoly power attained in one market to gain a competitive advantage in another is a violation of § 2, even if there has not been an

attempt to monopolize the second market." The formula was developed by the Supreme Court in *United States v. Griffith*, 334 U.S. 100 (1948), which found it unlawful for theater owners to use their dominant position in one set of cities to achieve a competitive advantage in other cities, even if they did not intend to acquire monopolies in the second set of cities. One problem with the theory is that it does not seem to be covered by the language of the Sherman Act. First, the defendant is not being accused of monopolizing the towns where it already has a monopoly. Second, it is neither monopolizing nor attempting to monopolize the second set of towns. Since *Berkey Photo*, numerous courts have considered leverage claims and, not surprisingly, have been divided on the basic issue. *See, e.g., Lantec v. Novell*, 306 F.3d 1003, 1022 n.11 (10th Cir. 2002) (recognizing split in Circuits on whether there is a viable leveraging claim, but refusing to decide issue); *Eleven Line, Inc. v. North Tex. State Soccer Ass'n, Inc.*, 213 F.3d 198, 206 n.16 (5th Cir. 2000) (recognizing circuit split); *Covad Communications Co. v. BellSouth Corp.*, 299 F.3d 1272 (11th Cir. 2002) (recognizing leveraging claim); *Kerasotes Mich. Theatres v. Nat'l Amusements*, 854 F.2d 135 (6th Cir. 1988) (defendant, who was a dominant exhibitor in many areas but not Flint, Michigan, could have used monopoly power in other areas to gain a competitive advantage in Flint, in violation of Section 2); *Alaska Airlines v. United Airlines*, 948 F.2d 536 (9th Cir. 1991) (rejecting the theory).

The Supreme Court seemed to have approved a leverage claim, at least in dicta, in its 1992 *Kodak* decision:

> The Court has held many times that power gained through some natural and legal advantage such as a patent, copyright, or business acumen can give rise to liability if "a seller exploits his dominant position in one market to expand his empire into the next."

Eastman Kodak Co. v. Image Tech. Servs., 504 U.S. 451, 479 n.29 (1992). But then the Court made a sharp about-face a year later in its *Spectrum Sports* decision, reprinted below:

> § 2 makes the conduct of a single firm unlawful only when it actually monopolizes or dangerously threatens to do so. The concern that § 2 might be applied so as to further anticompetitive ends is plainly not met by inquiring only whether the defendant has engaged in "unfair" or "predatory" tactics.

Spectrum Sports v. McQuillan, 506 U.S. 447, 448 (1993).

Speaking of the leveraging doctrine, which it described as "dicta" in previous Second Circuit opinions, the Second Circuit said the following in *Virgin Atlantic Airways v. British Airways PLC*, 257 F.3d 256, 272 (2d Cir. 2001):

> Were we to allow pursuit of a monopoly leveraging claim, Virgin would need to submit proof that British Airways: (1) possessed monopoly power in one market; (2) used that power to gain a competitive advantage over Virgin in another distinct market; and (3) caused injury by such anticompetitive conduct.

The court then concluded that "[i]t is unnecessary for us to decide, as a matter of law, the viability of a claim for monopoly leveraging as described in *Berkey Photo*.

. . ." because the plaintiff could not prove the claim even as *Berkey* defined it.

The Supreme Court has apparently now laid monopoly leveraging claims to rest once and for all. *Verizon Communications, Inc. v. Law Offices of Curtis Trinko, LLP*, 540 U.S. 398 (2004). The Court held that no Section 2 action can be maintained unless there is a "dangerous probability of success" in monopolizing the second market. As a result, monopoly leveraging can exist *only* where the requirements for the attempt to monopolize offense have been satisfied, which is simply to say that a free standing monopoly leveraging claim no longer exists. Further, the Supreme Court observed that even the monopoly leveraging theory "presupposes anticompetitive conduct," and the Court had already rejected the plaintiff's proposition that a unilateral refusal to deal was qualifying anticompetitive conduct. In general, the offense of attempt to monopolize offense has more severe conduct requirements than the substantive monopolization offense. The Supreme Court decision is reprinted *infra*.

In *Schor v. Abbott Laboratories*, 457 F.3d 608, 611–612, 614 (7th Cir. 2006), the Seventh Circuit rejected a monopoly "leveraging" claim that the defendant priced a combination of two AIDS drugs in such a way — a very high price for one and a very low price for the other — as to make it impossible for a rival to sell the second drug.

> The problem with "monopoly leveraging" as an antitrust theory is that the practice cannot increase a monopolist's profits. Abbott has (we must assume) a monopoly, but a monopolist can take its monopoly profit just once. It can collect a monopoly profit for ritonavir and allow a competitive market to continue in other products. Or, by reducing the price of ritonavir, it can induce customers to buy more from it. But it can't do both. Suppose the competitive price of ritonavir would be $2 per 100 mg, and that the monopoly price is $7; suppose further that the competitive price of some other protease inhibitor such as saquinavir is $3 per 400 mg. Without ritonavir, the patient must take 3,600 mg of saquinavir daily, at a price of $27; take 100 mg of ritonavir with each 800 mg of saquinavir, however, and the cost falls to $26 (1,600 mg of saquinavir plus 200 mg of ritonavir) even with ritonavir at the monopoly price. If Abbott offered Kaletra at $24 for a daily dose, that would knock saquinavir out of the market — but Abbott would make less money than if it had charged the monopoly price for ritonavir alone. If it then raised the price of Kaletra to $28 (say), the producer of saquinavir would bring that drug back to market — and Abbott would lose money from reduced sales even if it did not, for it would now be charging an (implicit) price of $8 per dose of ritonavir, or *more* than the profit-maximizing, monopoly price.

> The basic point is that a firm that monopolizes some essential component of a treatment (or product or service) can extract the whole monopoly profit by charging a suitable price for the component alone. If the monopolist gets control of another component as well and tries to jack up the price of that item, the effect is the same as setting an excessive price for the monopolized component. The monopolist can take its profit just once; an effort to do more makes it worse off and is self-deterring.

The court also rejected Schor's argument that patents created a special situation permitting broader monopoly leveraging claims. On the contrary:

> Abbott's patents do more to support its position than to assist Schor. Recall that the patents cover not only ritonavir administered by itself but also ritonavir administered in combination with another protease inhibitor. Abbott therefore could take control of the market in combination treatments until the patents expire. A patent does not permit its owner to condition use of the patented product on the surrender of a monopoly in some other unpatented product. But the product "ritonavir in combination with another protease inhibitor" is patented to Abbott, which therefore is entitled to monopolize the combination. Yet it has not done so — doubtless because, as we have explained, Abbott's profits are highest when the price of other protease inhibitors is lowest, and Abbott therefore has a powerful incentive to encourage competition among other producers rather than monopolize the market for all protease inhibitors. It would make little sense to use the antitrust laws to condemn Abbott for a strategy (a) that it has not in fact pursued; (b) that would disserve its own interests; and (c) that the patents entitle Abbott to pursue if it chooses.

On whether § 5 of the Federal Trade Commission Act, whose 'unfair methods of competition' language does not seem to foreclose monopoly leveraging claims, see Herbert Hovenkamp, *The Federal Trade Commission and the Sherman Act*, 62 FLA. L. REV. 871 (2010).

UNITED STATES v. MICROSOFT CORP.
253 F.3d 34 (D.C. Cir. 2001)

PER CURIAM:

. . . The action against Microsoft arose pursuant to a complaint filed by the United States and separate complaints filed by individual States. The District Court determined that Microsoft had maintained a monopoly in the market for Intel-compatible PC operating systems in violation of § 2; attempted to gain a monopoly in the market for internet browsers in violation of § 2; and illegally tied two purportedly separate products, Windows and Internet Explorer ("IE"), in violation of § 1. *United States v. Microsoft Corp.*, 87 F. Supp. 2d 30 (D.D.C. 2000) ("Conclusions of Law"). The District Court then found that the same facts that established liability under §§ 1 and 2 of the Sherman Act mandated findings of liability under analogous state law antitrust provisions. *Id.* To remedy the Sherman Act violations, the District Court issued a Final Judgment requiring Microsoft to submit a proposed plan of divestiture, with the company to be split into an operating systems business and an applications business. *United States v. Microsoft Corp.*, 97 F. Supp. 2d 59, 64–65 (D.D.C. 2000) ("Final Judgment"). . . .

. . . we find that some but not all of Microsoft's liability challenges have merit. . . .

I. INTRODUCTION

In July 1994, officials at the Department of Justice ("DOJ"), on behalf of the United States, filed suit against Microsoft, charging the company with, among other things, unlawfully maintaining a monopoly in the operating system market through anticompetitive terms in its licensing and software developer agreements. The parties subsequently entered into a consent decree, thus avoiding a trial on the merits. *See United States v. Microsoft Corp.*, 56 F.3d 1448 (D.C. Cir. 1995) ("*Microsoft I*"). Three years later, the Justice Department filed a civil contempt action against Microsoft for allegedly violating one of the decree's provisions. On appeal from a grant of a preliminary injunction, this court held that Microsoft's technological bundling of IE 3.0 and 4.0 with Windows 95 did not violate the relevant provision of the consent decree. *United States v. Microsoft Corp.*, 147 F.3d 935 (D.C. Cir. 1998) ("*Microsoft II*"). We expressly reserved the question whether such bundling might independently violate §§ 1 or 2 of the Sherman Act. *Id.* at 950 n.14.

On May 18, 1998, shortly before issuance of the *Microsoft II* decision, the United States and a group of State plaintiffs filed separate (and soon thereafter consolidated) complaints, asserting antitrust violations by Microsoft and seeking preliminary and permanent injunctions against the company's allegedly unlawful conduct. . . . Relying almost exclusively on Microsoft's varied efforts to unseat Netscape Navigator as the preeminent internet browser, plaintiffs charged four distinct violations of the Sherman Act: (1) unlawful exclusive dealing arrangements in violation of § 1; (2) unlawful tying of IE to Windows 95 and Windows 98 in violation of § 1; (3) unlawful maintenance of a monopoly in the PC operating system market in violation of § 2; and (4) unlawful attempted monopolization of the internet browser market in violation of § 2. The States also brought pendent claims charging Microsoft with violations of various State antitrust laws.

The District Court scheduled the case on a "fast track." The hearing on the preliminary injunction and the trial on the merits were consolidated pursuant to FED. R. CIV. P. 65(a)(2). The trial was then scheduled to commence on September 8, 1998, less than four months after the complaints had been filed. In a series of pretrial orders, the District Court limited each side to a maximum of 12 trial witnesses plus two rebuttal witnesses. It required that all trial witnesses' direct testimony be submitted to the court in the form of written declarations. The District Court also made allowances for the use of deposition testimony at trial to prove subordinate or predicate issues. Following the grant of three brief continuances, the trial started on October 19, 1998.

After a 76-day bench trial, the District Court issued its Findings of Fact. *United States v. Microsoft Corp.*, 84 F. Supp. 2d 9 (D.D.C. 1999) ("Findings of Fact"). This triggered two independent courses of action. First, the District Court established a schedule for briefing on possible legal conclusions, inviting Professor Lawrence Lessig to participate as amicus curiae. Second, the District Court referred the case to mediation to afford the parties an opportunity to settle their differences. The Honorable Richard A. Posner, Chief Judge of the United States Court of Appeals for the Seventh Circuit, was appointed to serve as mediator. The parties concurred in the referral to mediation and in the choice of mediator.

Mediation failed after nearly four months of settlement talks between the parties. On April 3, 2000, with the parties' briefs having been submitted and considered, the District Court issued its conclusions of law. The District Court found Microsoft liable on the § 1 tying and § 2 monopoly maintenance and attempted monopolization claims, while ruling that there was insufficient evidence to support a § 1 exclusive dealing violation. . . .

. . . [J]ust over six years have passed since Microsoft engaged in the first conduct plaintiffs allege to be anticompetitive. As the record in this case indicates, six years seems like an eternity in the computer industry. By the time a court can assess liability, firms, products, and the marketplace are likely to have changed dramatically. This, in turn, threatens enormous practical difficulties for courts considering the appropriate measure of relief in equitable enforcement actions, both in crafting injunctive remedies in the first instance and reviewing those remedies in the second. Conduct remedies may be unavailing in such cases, because innovation to a large degree has already rendered the anticompetitive conduct obsolete (although by no means harmless). And broader structural remedies present their own set of problems, including how a court goes about restoring competition to a dramatically changed, and constantly changing, marketplace. . . .

We [also] decide this case against a backdrop of significant debate amongst academics and practitioners over the extent to which "old economy" § 2 monopolization doctrines should apply to firms competing in dynamic technological markets characterized by network effects. In markets characterized by network effects, one product or standard tends towards dominance, because "the utility that a user derives from consumption of the good increases with the number of other agents consuming the good." Michael L. Katz & Carl Shapiro, *Network Externalities, Competition, and Compatibility*, 75 Am. Econ. Rev. 424, 424 (1985). For example, "[a]n individual consumer's demand to use (and hence her benefit from) the telephone network . . . increases with the number of other users on the network whom she can call or from whom she can receive calls." Howard A. Shelanski & J. Gregory Sidak, *Antitrust Divestiture in Network Industries*, 68 U. Chi. L. Rev. 1, 8 (2001). Once a product or standard achieves wide acceptance, it becomes more or less entrenched. Competition in such industries is "for the field" rather than "within the field." *See* H. Demsetz, *Why Regulate Utilities?*, 11 J.L. & Econ. 55, 57 & n.7 (1968) (emphasis omitted). . . .

With this backdrop in mind, we turn to the specific challenges raised in Microsoft's appeal.

II. MONOPOLIZATION

. . . We begin by considering whether Microsoft possesses monopoly power, and finding that it does, we turn to the question whether it maintained this power through anticompetitive means. Agreeing with the District Court that the company behaved anticompetitively, see *infra* Section II.B, and that these actions contributed to the maintenance of its monopoly power, see *infra* Section II.C, we affirm the court's finding of liability for monopolization.

A. Monopoly Power

While merely possessing monopoly power is not itself an antitrust violation, see *Northeastern Tel. Co. v. AT & T*, 651 F.2d 76, 84–85 (2d Cir. 1981), it is a necessary element of a monopolization charge, see *Grinnell*, 384 U.S. at 570. . . .

The District Court [defined] . . . the market as Intel-compatible PC operating systems, [and] found that Microsoft has a greater than 95% share. It also found the company's market position protected by a substantial entry barrier.

Microsoft argues that the District Court incorrectly defined the relevant market. It also claims that there is no barrier to entry in that market. Alternatively, Microsoft argues that because the software industry is uniquely dynamic, direct proof, rather than circumstantial evidence, more appropriately indicates whether it possesses monopoly power. Rejecting each argument, we uphold the District Court's finding of monopoly power in its entirety.

. . . Microsoft argues that the District Court improperly excluded three types of [competing] products: non-Intel compatible operating systems (primarily Apple's Macintosh operating system, Mac OS), operating systems for non-PC devices (such as handheld computers and portal websites), and "middleware" products, which are not operating systems at all.

We begin with Mac OS. Microsoft's argument that Mac OS should have been included in the relevant market suffers from a flaw that infects many of the company's monopoly power claims: the company fails to challenge the District Court's factual findings, or to argue that these findings do not support the court's conclusions. The District Court found that consumers would not switch from Windows to Mac OS in response to a substantial price increase because of the costs of acquiring the new hardware needed to run Mac OS (an Apple computer and peripherals) and compatible software applications, as well as because of the effort involved in learning the new system and transferring files to its format. The court also found the Apple system less appealing to consumers because it costs considerably more and supports fewer applications. . . .

Microsoft's challenge to the District Court's exclusion of non-PC based competitors, such as information appliances (handheld devices, etc.) and portal websites that host server-based software applications, suffers from the same defect: the company fails to challenge the District Court's key factual findings. In particular, the District Court found that because information appliances fall far short of performing all of the functions of a PC, most consumers will buy them only as a supplement to their PCs. . . .

This brings us to Microsoft's main challenge to the District Court's market definition: the exclusion of middleware. Because of the importance of middleware to this case, we pause to explain what it is and how it relates to the issue before us.

Operating systems perform many functions, including allocating computer memory and controlling peripherals such as printers and keyboards. Operating systems also function as platforms for software applications. They do this by "exposing" — i.e., making available to software developers-routines or protocols that perform certain widely-used functions. These are known as Application

Programming Interfaces, or "APIs." For example, Windows contains an API that enables users to draw a box on the screen. Software developers wishing to include that function in an application need not duplicate it in their own code. Instead, they can "call" — i.e., use-the Windows API.

Every operating system has different APIs. Accordingly, a developer who writes an application for one operating system and wishes to sell the application to users of another must modify, or "port," the application to the second operating system. . . .

"Middleware" refers to software products that expose their own APIs. Because of this, a middleware product written for Windows could take over some or all of Windows's valuable platform functions-that is, developers might begin to rely upon APIs exposed by the middleware for basic routines rather than relying upon the API set included in Windows. If middleware were written for multiple operating systems, its impact could be even greater. The more developers could rely upon APIs exposed by such middleware, the less expensive porting to different operating systems would be. Ultimately, if developers could write applications relying exclusively on APIs exposed by middleware, their applications would run on any operating system on which the middleware was also present. . . .

Microsoft argues that, because middleware could usurp the operating system's platform function and might eventually take over other operating system functions (for instance, by controlling peripherals), the District Court erred in excluding Navigator and Java from the relevant market. The District Court found, however, that neither Navigator, Java, nor any other middleware product could now, or would soon, expose enough APIs to serve as a platform for popular applications, much less take over all operating system functions. Again, Microsoft fails to challenge these findings, instead simply asserting middleware's "potential" as a competitor. The test of reasonable interchangeability, however, required the District Court to consider only substitutes that constrain pricing in the reasonably foreseeable future. . . .

Having thus properly defined the relevant market, the District Court found that Windows accounts for a greater than 95% share. The court also found that even if Mac OS were included, Microsoft's share would exceed 80%. . . .

[In considering entry barriers] the court focused not only on Microsoft's present market share, but also on the structural barrier that protects the company's future position. That barrier-the "applications barrier to entry"-stems from two characteristics of the software market: (1) most consumers prefer operating systems for which a large number of applications have already been written; and (2) most developers prefer to write for operating systems that already have a substantial consumer base. This "chicken-and-egg" situation ensures that applications will continue to be written for the already dominant Windows, which in turn ensures that consumers will continue to prefer it over other operating systems. . . .

Of course, were middleware to succeed, it would erode the applications barrier to entry. Because applications written for multiple operating systems could run on any operating system on which the middleware product was present with little, if any, porting, the operating system market would become competitive. But as the District Court found, middleware will not expose a sufficient number of APIs to erode the applications barrier to entry in the foreseeable future. . . .

B. Anticompetitive Conduct

. . . [A]fter concluding that Microsoft had monopoly power, the District Court held that Microsoft had violated § 2 by engaging in a variety of exclusionary acts (not including predatory pricing), to maintain its monopoly by preventing the effective distribution and use of products that might threaten that monopoly. Specifically, the District Court held Microsoft liable for: (1) the way in which it integrated IE into Windows; (2) its various dealings with Original Equipment Manufacturers ("OEMs"), Internet Access Providers ("IAPs"), Internet Content Providers ("ICPs"), Independent Software Vendors ("ISVs"), and Apple Computer; (3) its efforts to contain and to subvert Java technologies; and (4) its course of conduct as a whole. Upon appeal, Microsoft argues that it did not engage in any exclusionary conduct. . . .

From a century of case law on monopolization under § 2, . . . several principles . . . emerge. *First*, to be condemned as exclusionary, a monopolist's act must have an "anticompetitive effect." That is, it must harm the competitive process and thereby harm consumers. In contrast, harm to one or more competitors will not suffice. . . .

Second, . . . the Government . . . must demonstrate that the monopolist's conduct harmed competition, not just a competitor.

Third, if a plaintiff successfully establishes a prima facie case under § 2 by demonstrating anticompetitive effect, then the monopolist may proffer a "procompetitive justification" for its conduct. . . . If the monopolist asserts a procompetitive justification — a nonpretextual claim that its conduct is indeed a form of competition on the merits because it involves, for example, greater efficiency or enhanced consumer appeal-then the burden shifts back to the plaintiff to rebut that claim. . . .

Fourth, if the monopolist's procompetitive justification stands unrebutted, then the plaintiff must demonstrate that the anticompetitive harm of the conduct outweighs the procompetitive benefit. . . .

Finally, in considering whether the monopolist's conduct on balance harms competition and is therefore condemned as exclusionary for purposes of § 2, our focus is upon the effect of that conduct, not upon the intent behind it. Evidence of the intent behind the conduct of a monopolist is relevant only to the extent it helps us understand the likely effect of the monopolist's conduct.

With these principles in mind, we now consider Microsoft's objections to the District Court's holding that Microsoft violated § 2 of the Sherman Act in a variety of ways.

1. Licenses Issued to Original Equipment Manufacturers

The District Court condemned a number of provisions in Microsoft's agreements licensing Windows to OEMs, because it found that Microsoft's imposition of those provisions (like many of Microsoft's other actions at issue in this case) serves to reduce usage share of Netscape's browser and, hence, protect Microsoft's operating system monopoly. The reason market share in the browser market affects market power in the operating system market is complex, and warrants some explanation.

Browser usage share is important because . . . a browser (or any middleware product, for that matter) must have a critical mass of users in order to attract software developers to write applications relying upon the APIs it exposes, and away from the APIs exposed by Windows. Applications written to a particular browser's APIs, however, would run on any computer with that browser, regardless of the underlying operating system. "The overwhelming majority of consumers will only use a PC operating system for which there already exists a large and varied set of . . . applications, and for which it seems relatively certain that new types of applications and new versions of existing applications will continue to be marketed. . . ." If a consumer could have access to the applications he desired-regardless of the operating system he uses-simply by installing a particular browser on his computer, then he would no longer feel compelled to select Windows in order to have access to those applications; he could select an operating system other than Windows based solely upon its quality and price. In other words, the market for operating systems would be competitive.

Therefore, Microsoft's efforts to gain market share in one market (browsers) served to meet the threat to Microsoft's monopoly in another market (operating systems) by keeping rival browsers from gaining the critical mass of users necessary to attract developer attention away from Windows as the platform for software development. . . .

In evaluating the restrictions in Microsoft's agreements licensing Windows to OEMs, we first consider whether plaintiffs have made out a prima facie case by demonstrating that the restrictions have an anticompetitive effect. In the next subsection, we conclude that plaintiffs have met this burden as to all the restrictions. We then consider Microsoft's proffered justifications for the restrictions and, for the most part, hold those justifications insufficient. . . .

The restrictions Microsoft places upon Original Equipment Manufacturers are of particular importance in determining browser usage share because having an OEM pre-install a browser on a computer is one of the two most cost-effective methods by far of distributing browsing software. (The other is bundling the browser with internet access software distributed by an IAP.) The District Court found that the restrictions Microsoft imposed in licensing Windows to OEMs prevented many OEMs from distributing browsers other than IE. In particular, the District Court condemned the license provisions prohibiting the OEMs from: (1) removing any desktop icons, folders, or "Start" menu entries; (2) altering the initial boot sequence; and (3) otherwise altering the appearance of the Windows desktop.

The District Court concluded that the first license restriction — the prohibition upon the removal of desktop icons, folders, and Start menu entries — thwarts the distribution of a rival browser by preventing OEMs from removing visible means of user access to IE. The OEMs cannot practically install a second browser in addition to IE, the court found, in part because "[p]re-installing more than one product in a given category . . . can significantly increase an OEM's support costs, for the redundancy can lead to confusion among novice users."

. . . [T]estimony . . . supports the District Court's finding that fear of such confusion deters many OEMs from pre-installing multiple browsers. . . . Most telling, in presentations to OEMs, Microsoft itself represented that having only one icon in a particular category would be "less confusing for endusers."

The second license provision at issue prohibits OEMs from modifying the initial boot sequence — the process that occurs the first time a consumer turns on the computer. Prior to the imposition of that restriction, "among the programs that many OEMs inserted into the boot sequence were Internet sign-up procedures that encouraged users to choose from a list of IAPs assembled by the OEM." Microsoft's prohibition on any alteration of the boot sequence thus prevents OEMs from using that process to promote the services of IAPs, many of which-at least at the time Microsoft imposed the restriction-used Navigator rather than IE in their internet access software. . . . Because this prohibition has a substantial effect in protecting Microsoft's market power, and does so through a means other than competition on the merits, it is anticompetitive. . . .

Finally, Microsoft . . . prohibits OEMs from causing any user interface other than the Windows desktop to launch automatically. . . .

Microsoft argues that the license restrictions are legally justified because, in imposing them, Microsoft is simply "exercising its rights as the holder of valid copyrights." . . .

Microsoft's primary copyright argument borders upon the frivolous. The company claims an absolute and unfettered right to use its intellectual property as it wishes: "[I]f intellectual property rights have been lawfully acquired," it says, then "their subsequent exercise cannot give rise to antitrust liability." Appellant's Opening Br. at 105. That is no more correct than the proposition that use of one's personal property, such as a baseball bat, cannot give rise to tort liability. As the Federal Circuit succinctly stated: "Intellectual property rights do not confer a privilege to violate the antitrust laws." *In re Indep. Serv. Orgs. Antitrust Litig.*, 203 F.3d 1322, 1325 (Fed. Cir. 2000). . . .

The only license restriction Microsoft seriously defends as necessary to prevent a "substantial alteration" of its copyrighted work is the prohibition on OEMs automatically launching a substitute user interface upon completion of the boot process. . . . We agree that a shell that automatically prevents the Windows desktop from ever being seen by the user is a drastic alteration of Microsoft's copyrighted work, and outweighs the marginal anticompetitive effect of prohibiting the OEMs from substituting a different interface automatically upon completion of the initial boot process. We therefore hold that this particular restriction is not an exclusionary practice that violates § 2 of the Sherman Act. . . .

In sum, we hold that with the exception of the one restriction prohibiting automatically launched alternative interfaces, all the OEM license restrictions at issue represent uses of Microsoft(s market power to protect its monopoly, unredeemed by any legitimate justification. The restrictions therefore violate § 2 of the Sherman Act.

2. Integration of IE and Windows

Although Microsoft's license restrictions have a significant effect in closing rival browsers out of one of the two primary channels of distribution, the District Court found that "Microsoft's executives believed . . . its contractual restrictions placed on OEMs would not be sufficient in themselves to reverse the direction of Navigator's usage share. Consequently, in late 1995 or early 1996, Microsoft set out to bind [IE] more tightly to Windows 95 as a technical matter." . . .

Although the District Court . . . broadly condemned Microsoft's decision to bind "Internet Explorer to Windows with . . . technological shackles," its findings of fact in support of that conclusion center upon three specific actions Microsoft took to weld IE to Windows: excluding IE from the "Add/Remove Programs" utility; designing Windows so as in certain circumstances to override the user's choice of a default browser other than IE; and commingling code related to browsing and other code in the same files, so that any attempt to delete the files containing IE would, at the same time, cripple the operating system. As with the license restrictions, we consider first whether the suspect actions had an anticompetitive effect, and then whether Microsoft has provided a procompetitive justification for them.

As a general rule, courts are properly very skeptical about claims that competition has been harmed by a dominant firm's product design changes. . . . In a competitive market, firms routinely innovate in the hope of appealing to consumers, sometimes in the process making their products incompatible with those of rivals; the imposition of liability when a monopolist does the same thing will inevitably deter a certain amount of innovation. This is all the more true in a market, such as this one, in which the product itself is rapidly changing. Judicial deference to product innovation, however, does not mean that a monopolist's product design decisions are per se lawful. . . .

The District Court first condemned as anticompetitive Microsoft's decision to exclude IE from the "Add/Remove Programs" utility in Windows 98. . . . This change reduces the usage share of rival browsers not by making Microsoft's own browser more attractive to consumers but, rather, by discouraging OEMs from distributing rival products. Because Microsoft's conduct, through something other than competition on the merits, has the effect of significantly reducing usage of rivals' products and hence protecting its own operating system monopoly, it is anticompetitive; we defer for the moment the question whether it is nonetheless justified.

Second, the District Court found that Microsoft designed Windows 98 "so that using Navigator on Windows 98 would have unpleasant consequences for users" by, in some circumstances, overriding the user's choice of a browser other than IE as his or her default browser. Plaintiffs argue that this override harms the competitive process by deterring consumers from using a browser other than IE even though they might prefer to do so, thereby reducing rival browsers' usage share and, hence, the ability of rival browsers to draw developer attention away from the APIs exposed by Windows. . . .

Finally, the District Court condemned Microsoft's decision to bind IE to Windows 98 "by placing code specific to Web browsing in the same files as code that provided operating system functions." Putting code supplying browsing functionality into a file with code supplying operating system functionality "ensure[s] that the deletion of any file containing browsing-specific routines would also delete vital operating system routines and thus cripple Windows. . . ."

Microsoft proffers no justification for two of the three challenged actions that it took in integrating IE into Windows-excluding IE from the Add/Remove Programs utility and commingling browser and operating system code . . . Plaintiffs plainly made out a prima facie case of harm to competition in the operating system market by demonstrating that Microsoft's actions increased its browser usage share and thus protected its operating system monopoly from a middleware threat and, for its part, Microsoft failed to meet its burden of showing that its conduct serves a purpose other than protecting its operating system monopoly. Accordingly, we hold that Microsoft's exclusion of IE from the Add/Remove Programs utility and its commingling of browser and operating system code constitute exclusionary conduct, in violation of § 2.

As for the other challenged act that Microsoft took in integrating IE into Windows — causing Windows to override the user's choice of a default browser in certain circumstances-Microsoft . . . claims that it was necessary to design Windows to override the user's preferences when he or she invokes one of "a few" out "of the nearly 30 means of accessing the Internet." According to Microsoft:

> The Windows 98 Help system and Windows Update feature depend on ActiveX controls not supported by Navigator, and the now-discontinued Channel Bar utilized Microsoft's Channel Definition Format, which Navigator also did not support. Lastly, Windows 98 does not invoke Navigator if a user accesses the Internet through "My Computer" or "Windows Explorer" because doing so would defeat one of the purposes of those features-enabling users to move seamlessly from local storage devices to the Web in the same browsing window.

The plaintiff bears the burden not only of rebutting a proffered justification but also of demonstrating that the anticompetitive effect of the challenged action outweighs it. In the District Court, plaintiffs appear to have done neither, . . . Microsoft may not be held liable for this aspect of its product design.

3. Agreements with Internet Access Providers

The District Court also condemned as exclusionary Microsoft's agreements with various IAPs. The IAPs include both Internet Service Providers, which offer consumers internet access, and Online Services ("OLSs") such as America Online ("AOL"), which offer proprietary content in addition to internet access and other services. . . .

The District Court condemned Microsoft's actions in (1) offering IE free of charge to IAPs and (2) offering IAPs a bounty for each customer the IAP signs up for service using the IE browser. In effect, the court concluded that Microsoft is acting to preserve its monopoly by offering IE to IAPs at an attractive price. Similarly, the District Court held Microsoft liable for (3) developing the IE Access Kit ("IEAK"), a software package that allows an IAP to "create a distinctive identity for its service in as little as a few hours by customizing the [IE] title bar, icon, start and search pages," and (4) offering the IEAK to IAPs free of charge, on the ground that those acts, too, helped Microsoft preserve its monopoly. Finally, the District Court found that (5) Microsoft agreed to provide easy access to IAPs' services from the Windows desktop in return for the IAPs' agreement to promote IE exclusively and to keep shipments of internet access software using Navigator under a specific percentage, typically 25%. We address the first four items — Microsoft's inducements — and then its exclusive agreements with IAPs.

. . . [T]he antitrust laws do not condemn even a monopolist for offering its product at an attractive price, and we therefore have no warrant to condemn Microsoft for offering either IE or the IEAK free of charge or even at a negative price. . . .

We turn now to Microsoft's deals with IAPs concerning desktop placement. . . . The most significant of the OLS deals is with AOL, which, when the deal was reached, "accounted for a substantial portion of all existing Internet access subscriptions and . . . attracted a very large percentage of new IAP subscribers." Under that agreement Microsoft puts the AOL icon in the OLS folder on the Windows desktop and AOL does not promote any non-Microsoft browser, nor provide software using any non-Microsoft browser except at the customer's request, and even then AOL will not supply more than 15% of its subscribers with a browser other than IE.

. . . [C]ourts considering antitrust challenges to exclusive contracts have taken care to identify the share of the market foreclosed. . . . Though what is "significant" may vary depending upon the antitrust provision under which an exclusive deal is challenged, it is clear that in all cases the plaintiff must both define the relevant market and prove the degree of foreclosure. This is a prudential requirement; exclusivity provisions in contracts may serve many useful purposes. *See, e.g., Omega Envtl., Inc. v. Gilbarco, Inc.*, 127 F.3d 1157, 1162 (9th Cir. 1997) ("There are, however, well-recognized economic benefits to exclusive dealing arrangements, including the enhancement of interbrand competition."); *Barry Wright Corp. v. ITT Grinnell Corp.*, 724 F.2d 227, 236 (1st Cir. 1983) (Breyer, J.) ("[V]irtually every contract to buy 'forecloses' or 'excludes' alternative sellers from some portion of the market, namely the portion consisting of what was bought.") . . .

[*Plaintiffs did not appeal the district court's holding that the foreclosure percentages were too small to warrant condemnation of exclusive dealing under § 1 of the Sherman Act. — ed.*]

Turning to § 2, the court stated: "the fact that Microsoft's arrangements with various [IAPs and other] firms did not foreclose enough of the relevant market to constitute a § 1 violation in no way detracts from the Court's assignment of liability for the same arrangements under § 2. . . . [A]ll of Microsoft's agreements, including the non-exclusive ones, severely restricted Netscape's access to those distribution channels leading most efficiently to the acquisition of browser usage share."

On appeal Microsoft argues that "courts have applied the same standard to alleged exclusive dealing agreements under both Section 1 and Section 2," and it argues that the District Court's holding of no liability under § 1 necessarily precludes holding it liable under § 2. . . . . [We] reject Microsoft's contention.

. . . In this case, plaintiffs allege that, by closing to rivals a substantial percentage of the available opportunities for browser distribution, Microsoft managed to preserve its monopoly in the market for operating systems. The IAPs constitute one of the two major channels by which browsers can be distributed. Microsoft has exclusive deals with "fourteen of the top fifteen access providers in North America[, which] account for a large majority of all Internet access subscriptions in this part of the world." By ensuring that the "majority" of all IAP subscribers are offered IE either as the default browser or as the only browser, Microsoft's deals with the IAPs clearly have a significant effect in preserving its monopoly; they help keep usage of Navigator below the critical level necessary for Navigator or any other rival to pose a real threat to Microsoft's monopoly.

4. Dealings with . . . Apple Computer

. . . [Microsoft] "Office" is a suite of business productivity applications that Microsoft has ported to [Apple's] Mac OS. The District Court found that "ninety percent of Mac OS users running a suite of office productivity applications [use] Microsoft's Mac Office." Further, the District Court found that:

> In 1997, Apple's business was in steep decline, and many doubted that the company would survive much longer. . . . [M]any ISVs questioned the wisdom of continuing to spend time and money developing applications for the Mac OS. Had Microsoft announced in the midst of this atmosphere that it was ceasing to develop new versions of Mac Office, a great number of ISVs, customers, developers, and investors would have interpreted the announcement as Apple's death notice.

. . . In June 1997 Microsoft Chairman Bill Gates determined that the company's negotiations with Apple " 'have not been going well at all. . . . Apple let us down on the browser by making Netscape the standard install.' Gates then reported that he had already called Apple's CEO . . . to ask 'how we should announce the cancellation of Mac Office. . . .' " The District Court further found that, within a month of Gates' call, Apple and Microsoft had reached an agreement pursuant to which

> Microsoft's primary obligation is to continue releasing up-to-date versions of Mac Office for at least five years. . . . [and] Apple has agreed . . . to "bundle the most current version of [IE] . . . with [Mac OS]" . . . [and to] "make [IE] the default [browser]" . . . Navigator is not installed on the computer hard drive during the default installation, which is the type of installation most users elect to employ . . . [The] Agreement further provides that . . . Apple may not position icons for non-Microsoft browsing software on the desktop of new Macintosh PC systems or Mac OS upgrades.

The agreement also prohibits Apple from encouraging users to substitute another browser for IE, and states that Apple will "encourage its employees to use [IE]."

This exclusive deal between Microsoft and Apple has a substantial effect upon the distribution of rival browsers. If a browser developer ports its product to a second operating system, such as the Mac OS, it can continue to display a common set of APIs. Thus, usage share, not the underlying operating system, is the primary determinant of the platform challenge a browser may pose. Pre-installation of a browser (which can be accomplished either by including the browser with the operating system or by the OEM installing the browser) is one of the two most important methods of browser distribution, and Apple had a not insignificant share of worldwide sales of operating systems. . . . See Conclusions of Law, at 42 (citing Findings of Fact § 356) ("By extracting from Apple terms that significantly diminished the usage of Navigator on the Mac OS, Microsoft helped to ensure that developers would not view Navigator as truly cross-platform middleware.").

Microsoft offers no procompetitive justification for the exclusive dealing arrangement. . . . Accordingly, we hold that the exclusive deal with Apple is exclusionary, in violation of § 2 of the Sherman Act.

5. Java

[Java is a set of software technologies developed by Sun Microsystems that enables software written to Java to run on virtually any computer operating system. Microsoft feared that development of Java would "commoditize" the operating system — making all of them compatible with one another — and thus force Microsoft to compete on the basis of price and features rather than relying on its large installed base. The "Java Virtual Machine" (JVM) is the portion of Java installed on the user's computer which acts as receptor for Java programs.— ed.]

The District Court held that Microsoft engaged in exclusionary conduct by developing and promoting its own JVM. . . . The JVM developed by Microsoft allows Java applications to run faster on Windows than does Sun's JVM, but a Java application designed to work with Microsoft's JVM does not work with Sun's JVM and vice versa. . . . As explained above, however, a monopolist does not violate the antitrust laws simply by developing a product that is incompatible with those of its rivals. . . . In order to violate the antitrust laws, the incompatible product must have an anticompetitive effect that outweighs any procompetitive justification for the design. Microsoft's JVM is not only incompatible with Sun's, it allows Java applications to run faster on Windows than does Sun's JVM. . . . Therefore, we reverse the District Court's imposition of liability for Microsoft's development and promotion of its JVM. . . .

To the extent Microsoft's First Wave Agreements with the ISVs conditioned receipt of Windows technical information upon the ISVs' agreement to promote Microsoft's JVM exclusively, they raise a different competitive concern. The District Court found that, although not literally exclusive, the deals were exclusive in practice because they required developers to make Microsoft's JVM the default in the software they developed.

. . . Moreover, Microsoft's exclusive deals with the leading ISVs took place against a backdrop of foreclosure: the District Court found that "[w]hen Netscape announced in May 1995 [prior to Microsoft's execution of the First Wave Agreements] that it would include with every copy of Navigator a copy of a Windows JVM that complied with Sun's standards, it appeared that Sun's Java implementation would achieve the necessary ubiquity on Windows." As discussed above, however, Microsoft undertook a number of anticompetitive actions that seriously reduced the distribution of Navigator, and the District Court found that those actions thereby seriously impeded distribution of Sun's JVM. Because Microsoft's agreements foreclosed a substantial portion of the field for JVM distribution and because, in so doing, they protected Microsoft's monopoly from a middleware threat, they are anticompetitive.

Microsoft offered no procompetitive justification. . . .

Microsoft's "Java implementation" included, in addition to a JVM, a set of software development tools it created to assist ISVs in designing Java applications. The District Court found that, not only were these tools incompatible with Sun's cross-platform aspirations for Java-no violation, to be sure-but Microsoft deceived Java developers regarding the Windows-specific nature of the tools. . . . That is, developers who relied upon Microsoft's public commitment to cooperate with Sun and who used Microsoft's tools to develop what Microsoft led them to believe were cross-platform applications ended up producing applications that would run only on the Windows operating system.

. . . Microsoft documents confirm that Microsoft intended to deceive Java developers, and predicted that the effect of its actions would be to generate Windows-dependent Java applications that their developers believed would be cross-platform; these documents also indicate that Microsoft's ultimate objective was to thwart Java's threat to Microsoft's monopoly in the market for operating systems. One Microsoft document, for example, states as a strategic goal: "Kill cross-platform Java by grow[ing] the polluted Java market." . . .

Microsoft's conduct related to its Java developer tools served to protect its monopoly of the operating system in a manner not attributable either to the superiority of the operating system or to the acumen of its makers, and therefore was anticompetitive. Unsurprisingly, Microsoft offers no procompetitive explanation for its campaign to deceive developers. Accordingly, we conclude this conduct is exclusionary, in violation of § 2 of the Sherman Act. . . .

The District Court held that Microsoft also acted unlawfully with respect to Java by using its "monopoly power to prevent firms such as Intel from aiding in the creation of cross-platform interfaces." In 1995 Intel was in the process of developing a high performance, Windows-compatible JVM. Microsoft wanted Intel to abandon that effort because a fast, cross-platform JVM would threaten Microsoft's monopoly in the operating system market. At an August 1995 meeting, Microsoft's Gates told Intel that its "cooperation with Sun and Netscape to develop a Java runtime environment . . . was one of the issues threatening to undermine cooperation between Intel and Microsoft."

Intel nonetheless continued to undertake initiatives related to Java. By 1996 "Intel had developed a JVM designed to run well . . . while complying with Sun's cross-platform standards." In April of that year, Microsoft again urged Intel not to help Sun by distributing Intel's fast, Sun-compliant JVM. And Microsoft threatened

Intel that if it did not stop aiding Sun on the multimedia front, then Microsoft would refuse to distribute Intel technologies bundled with Windows.

Intel finally capitulated in 1997, after Microsoft delivered the coup de grace.

> [O]ne of Intel's competitors, called AMD, solicited support from Microsoft for its "3DX" technology. . . . Microsoft's Allchin asked Gates whether Microsoft should support 3DX, despite the fact that Intel would oppose it. Gates responded: "If Intel has a real problem with us supporting this then they will have to stop supporting Java Multimedia the way they are. I would gladly give up supporting this if they would back off from their work on JAVA."

Microsoft's internal documents and deposition testimony confirm both the anticompetitive effect and intent of its actions. . . .

Microsoft does not deny the facts found by the District Court, nor does it offer any procompetitive justification for pressuring Intel not to support cross-platform Java. Microsoft lamely characterizes its threat to Intel as "advice." The District Court, however, found that Microsoft's "advice" to Intel to stop aiding cross-platform Java was backed by the threat of retaliation, and this conclusion is supported by the evidence cited above. Therefore we affirm the conclusion that Microsoft's threats to Intel were exclusionary, in violation of § 2 of the Sherman Act.

C. Causation

As a final parry, Microsoft urges this court to reverse on the monopoly maintenance claim, because plaintiffs never established a causal link between Microsoft's anticompetitive conduct, in particular its foreclosure of Netscape's and Java's distribution channels, and the maintenance of Microsoft's operating system monopoly. . . . We disagree.

Microsoft points to no case, and we can find none, standing for the proposition that, as to § 2 liability in an equitable enforcement action, plaintiffs must present direct proof that a defendant's continued monopoly power is precisely attributable to its anticompetitive conduct. As its lone authority, Microsoft cites the following passage from Professor Areeda's antitrust treatise: "The plaintiff has the burden of pleading, introducing evidence, and presumably proving by a preponderance of the evidence that reprehensible behavior has contributed significantly to the . . . maintenance of the monopoly." 3 Phillip E. Areeda & Herbert Hovenkamp, Antitrust Law ¶ 650c, at 69 (1996).

But, with respect to actions seeking injunctive relief, the authors of that treatise also recognize the need for courts to infer "causation" from the fact that a defendant has engaged in anticompetitive conduct that "reasonably appear[s] capable of making a significant contribution to . . . maintaining monopoly power." *Id.* § 651c. . . . To require that § 2 liability turn on a plaintiff's ability or inability to reconstruct the hypothetical marketplace absent a defendant's anticompetitive conduct would only encourage monopolists to take more and earlier anticompetitive action.

We may infer causation when exclusionary conduct is aimed at producers of nascent competitive technologies as well as when it is aimed at producers of established substitutes. Admittedly, in the former case there is added uncertainty, inasmuch as nascent threats are merely potential substitutes. But the underlying proof problem is the same — neither plaintiffs nor the court can confidently reconstruct a product's hypothetical technological development in a world absent the defendant(s exclusionary conduct.

[T]he question in this case is not whether Java or Navigator would actually have developed into viable platform substitutes, but (1) whether as a general matter the exclusion of nascent threats is the type of conduct that is reasonably capable of contributing significantly to a defendant's continued monopoly power and (2) whether Java and Navigator reasonably constituted nascent threats at the time Microsoft engaged in the anticompetitive conduct at issue. . . .

Microsoft's concerns over causation have more purchase in connection with the appropriate remedy issue, i.e., whether the court should impose a structural remedy or merely enjoin the offensive conduct at issue. As we point out later in this opinion, divestiture is a remedy that is imposed only with great caution, in part because its long-term efficacy is rarely certain. . . . See 3 Areeda & Hovenkamp, Antitrust Law ¶ 653b, at 91–92 ("[M]ore extensive equitable relief, particularly remedies such as divestiture designed to eliminate the monopoly altogether, raise more serious questions and require a clearer indication of a significant causal connection between the conduct and creation or maintenance of the market power."). But these queries go to questions of remedy, not liability.

III. ATTEMPTED MONOPOLIZATION

[The court reversed the district court's finding that Microsoft unlawfully attempted to monopolize the web "browser" market, mainly because (1) the relevant product market was never properly defined; and (2) entry barriers into this market were not shown to be high. — ed.]

IV. TYING

[The court's discussion of tying is reprinted in Chapter Five, supra.]

V. REMEDY

[T]he District Court's remedies decree must be vacated for three independent reasons: (1) the court failed to hold a remedies-specific evidentiary hearing when there were disputed facts; (2) the court failed to provide adequate reasons for its decreed remedies; and (3) this Court has revised the scope of Microsoft's liability and it is impossible to determine to what extent that should affect the remedies provisions. . . .

It is a cardinal principle of our system of justice that factual disputes must be heard in open court and resolved through trial-like evidentiary proceedings. Any other course would be contrary "to the spirit which imbues our judicial tribunals prohibiting decision without hearing." *Sims v. Greene*, 161 F.2d 87, 88 (3d Cir. 1947).

. . .

This rule is no less applicable in antitrust cases. The Supreme Court "has recognized that a 'full exploration of facts is usually necessary in order (for the District Court) properly to draw (an antitrust) decree' so as 'to prevent future violations and eradicate existing evils.' " *United States v. Ward Baking Co.*, 376 U.S. 327, 330–31 (1964) (quoting *Associated Press v. United States*, 326 U.S. 1, 22 (1945)). Hence a remedies decree must be vacated whenever there is "a bona fide disagreement concerning substantive items of relief which could be resolved only by trial." *Id.* at 334; . . .

Despite plaintiffs' protestations, there can be no serious doubt that the parties disputed a number of facts during the remedies phase. In two separate offers of proof, Microsoft identified 23 witnesses who, had they been permitted to testify, would have challenged a wide range of plaintiffs' factual representations, including the feasibility of dividing Microsoft, the likely impact on consumers, and the effect of divestiture on shareholders. . . .

We vacate the District Court's remedies decree for the additional reason that the court has failed to provide an adequate explanation for the relief it ordered. The Supreme Court has explained that a remedies decree in an antitrust case must seek to "unfetter a market from anticompetitive conduct," *Ford Motor Co.*, 405 U.S. at 577, to "terminate the illegal monopoly, deny to the defendant the fruits of its statutory violation, and ensure that there remain no practices likely to result in monopolization in the future," *United States v. United Shoe Mach. Corp.*, 391 U.S. 244, 250 (1968). . . .

The District Court has not explained how its remedies decree would accomplish those objectives. . . . Nowhere did the District Court discuss the objectives the Supreme Court deems relevant. . . .

Quite apart from its procedural difficulties, we vacate the District Court's final judgment in its entirety for the additional, independent reason that we have modified the underlying bases of liability. Of the three antitrust violations originally identified by the District Court, one is no longer viable: attempted monopolization of the browser market in violation of Sherman Act § 2. One will be remanded for liability proceedings under a different legal standard: unlawful tying in violation of § 1. Only liability for the § 2 monopoly maintenance violation has been affirmed — and even that we have revised. . . . [W]e cannot presume that a District Court would exercise its discretion to fashion the same remedy where the erroneous grounds of liability were stripped from its consideration.

In short, we must vacate the remedies decree in its entirety and remand the case for a new determination. This court has drastically altered the District Court's conclusions on liability. On remand, the District Court, after affording the parties a proper opportunity to be heard, can fashion an appropriate remedy for Microsoft's antitrust violations. . . .

On remand, the District Court must reconsider whether the use of the structural remedy of divestiture is appropriate with respect to Microsoft, which argues that it is a unitary company. By and large, cases upon which plaintiffs rely in arguing for the split of Microsoft have involved the dissolution of entities formed by mergers and acquisitions. On the contrary, the Supreme Court has clarified that divestiture "has traditionally been the remedy for Sherman Act violations whose heart is intercorporate combination and control," *du Pont*, 366 U.S. at 329 (emphasis added), and that "[c]omplete divestiture is particularly appropriate where asset or stock acquisitions violate the antitrust laws," *Ford Motor Co.*, 405 U.S. at 573 (emphasis added).

One apparent reason why courts have not ordered the dissolution of unitary companies is logistical difficulty. As the court explained in *United States v. ALCOA*, 91 F. Supp. 333, 416 (S.D.N.Y. 1950), a "corporation, designed to operate effectively as a single entity, cannot readily be dismembered of parts of its various operations without a marked loss of efficiency." A corporation that has expanded by acquiring its competitors often has preexisting internal lines of division along which it may more easily be split than a corporation that has expanded from natural growth.

. . . . Microsoft's Offer of Proof in response to the court's denial of an evidentiary hearing included proffered testimony from its President and CEO Steve Ballmer that the company "is, and always has been, a unified company without free-standing business units. . . ."

In devising an appropriate remedy, the District Court also should consider whether plaintiffs have established a sufficient causal connection between Microsoft's anticompetitive conduct and its dominant position in the OS market. "Mere existence of an exclusionary act does not itself justify full feasible relief against the monopolist to create maximum competition." 3 Areeda & Hovenkamp, Antitrust Law § 650a. Rather, structural relief, which is "designed to eliminate the monopoly altogether . . . require[s] a clearer indication of a significant causal connection between the conduct and creation or maintenance of the market power." *Id.* § 653b, at 91–92. Absent such causation, the antitrust defendant's unlawful behavior should be remedied by "an injunction against continuation of that conduct." *Id.* § 650a. . . . If the court on remand is unconvinced of the causal connection between Microsoft's exclusionary conduct and the company's position in the OS market, it may well conclude that divestiture is not an appropriate remedy. . . .

NOTES AND QUESTIONS

1. The D.C. Circuit suggests that competition in the market for a "network" product such as Windows is "for the field" rather than "in the field." But is that necessarily true? Many networks are structured in such a way as to have multiple, competing providers. Perhaps the most famous example is the telephone system, an elaborate network requiring complete interconnectivity among its various users. Until the early 1980s, this network was controlled by a single firm, AT&T, but that company — not the network — was broken up; and today literally hundreds of firms participate in the operation of this giant network, many in competition with one another. *See United States v. AT&T*, 552 F. Supp. 131 (D.D.C. 1982), *aff'd mem. sub nom. Maryland v. U.S.*, 460 U.S. 1001 (1983). Other networks run by competing firms include real-estate multiple listing services, bank credit card networks such as Visa, ATM networks, and sports leagues. Is there any reason that the network for computer operating systems cannot be organized in the same way?

2. Would you characterize Microsoft's conduct as pro- or anti-innovative? Do any liability elements strike you as using the antitrust laws to chill "legitimate" innovation? Aren't some of them blatantly anti-innovative, such as the pressure on Intel to force it not to develop chip technology to run Java applications better?

3. Compare the list of anticompetitive acts found unlawful in *Microsoft* with the list in *Alcoa, United Shoe Machinery,* or *Image Tech. v. Kodak.* Is Microsoft a more flagrant violator, or less? Has the court done a better job of explaining how the practices are anticompetitive? Are you convinced by all of the explanations?

4. Computer operating systems are said to be subject to "positive network externalities," which means that they become more valuable to a particular user as the system has a larger number of other users. The classic example of the positive network externality is the telephone system. Even the highest tech telephone is virtually worthless as long as it cannot be connected to anyone else. As soon as the phone can be connected to at least one other subscriber it acquires value, and the value to each user increases as the number of other subscribers increases. As a result, a system with a large number of subscribers is always more desirable to a new subscriber than a system with few subscribers, assuming that the two systems cannot be hooked together.

The sources of network externalities for Windows or any computer operating system are manifold, but mainly they include (1) users' needs for compatibility and interchange with other users, and (2) software developers' need to develop for a large number of users. An operating system with a large installed base will always be more attractive to both users and software developers than an equally good operating system with a smaller installed base.

Netscape and Sun Microsystem's Java threatened to take out Microsoft's advantage by interconnecting multiple operating systems with each other, thus taking out the network advantage. An illustration that may help you think of the problem is a country with two telephone systems that cannot be connected together. One system has older technology but has been around longer and has 100,000 subscribers. The newer system has superior technology but only 100 subscribers. Notwithstanding its inferior technology, the large installed base gives the older firm a very significant advantage over the new firm because consumers place a very high value on being interconnected with as many other people as possible. As a result, the larger system has less incentive to improve its technology or cut its price.

But now suppose that someone develops a switch that enables the two systems to be connected together, so that a subscriber to one system can readily talk to people on the other system, and vice versa. The network advantages can now be aggregated across the two systems; or to say it another way, there is no unique advantage to being on one system or the other. Now consumers will be able to choose a telephone on the basis of other factors, such as who has the better technology, price, or service.

Netscape, enhanced by Java, threatened to produce the "switch" that would connect multiple operating systems, thus destroying Microsoft's significant network advantage over rival systems and permitting people to base their purchasing decisions on factors such as price or quality. Bill Gates expressed the fear that these programs would "commoditize" the operating system market. In particular, Java's "write once, run anywhere" strategy threatened to make different operating systems completely compatible on both the user end and the software writing end. *See United States v. Microsoft*, 65 F. Supp. 2d 1, 21 (D.D.C. 1999) (findings of fact 74–77). The result would be the emergence of a traditional product-differentiated market in which one could choose a Microsoft or non-Microsoft operating system based entirely on price, features, speed, support, and so on. Compatibility with other users would not be a factor.

The government's theory is that Microsoft did everything in its power to keep this switch from being deployed, and thus to preserve the inability of the different systems to become interconnected.

5.   The standard for a remedy that the D.C. Circuit adopts is quite severe. It must:

> seek to "unfetter a market from anticompetitive conduct," to "terminate the illegal monopoly, deny to the defendant the fruits of its statutory violation, and ensure that there remain no practices likely to result in monopolization in the future. . . ."

Is any purely conduct remedy likely to accomplish this? *See* E. Thomas Sullivan, *The Jurisprudence of Antitrust Divestiture: The Road Less Traveled*, 86 MINN. L. REV. 565 (2002).

In the final portion of the opinion, which is omitted, the D.C. Circuit chastised the district judge for several extra-judicial statements which created the appearance of bias, although it found no actual bias. It remanded the case for re-assignment to a different judge, who approved a conduct-only remedy agreed to by Microsoft and the federal government, but over the objections of some states. Very briefly, the decree (1) bars Microsoft from retaliating against computer manufacturers or software developers who choose to support non-Microsoft products that compete with Microsoft products; (2) requires Microsoft to disclose more coding information to software developers so that they will be freer to develop products for non-Microsoft platforms; (3) provides for an independent three-member panel that will supervise various aspects of Microsoft's business; and (4) provides for continuing court jurisdiction over disputes that might arise concerning Microsoft's compliance. Finally, the agreement permitted Microsoft to continue to integrate Internet Explorer into its operating system, even though that practice had been found unlawful. The opinions discussing the decree are long and complex. However, the court issued a readable "executive summary" which can be found at *State of New York v. Microsoft Corp.*, 231 F. Supp. 2d 203 (D.D.C. 2002); or at several Internet sites. The decree was approved by the D.C. Circuit in *Massachusetts v. Microsoft Corp.*, 373 F.3d 1199 (D.C. Cir. 2004). Most provisions of the decree were set to expire in 2007, but were extended until late 2009. At that time, the states may seek a re-evaluation and portions of the decree could be extended by three additional years.

There have also been many private lawsuits pending against Microsoft. Under the doctrine of offensive collateral estoppel, a plaintiff challenging conduct that was condemned in this case will probably not need to re-prove the violation; however, it will still have to prove injury, causation, and damages (Chapter 3). Federal lawsuits by indirect purchasers, which include people who purchased pre-installed versions of Windows through their computer vendor, will be governed by the indirect purchaser rule, which is explained in Chapter 3.

6. European Union Competition law recognizes a broader set of duties upon dominant firms than United States antitrust law does. In its 2007 *Microsoft* decision, the European Court of First Instance held that this duty extended to the mandatory provision of protocols that would make alternative server operating systems more compatible with the Windows operating system. Case T-201/04, *Microsoft Corp.* CFI (Sept. 17, 2007), at ¶¶ 41, 560–561. The Court concluded:

> • It is normal practice for operators in the industry to disclose to third parties the information which will facilitate interoperability with their products and Microsoft itself had followed that practice until it was sufficiently established on the work group server operating systems market. . . .

> • Microsoft's refusal prevented its competitors from developing work group server operating systems capable of attaining a sufficient degree of interoperability with the Windows domain architecture, with the consequence that consumers' purchasing decisions in respect of work group server operating systems were channeled towards Microsoft's products. . . .

> • Microsoft's competitors would not be able to clone or reproduce its products solely by having access to the interoperability information covered by the contested decision . . . the information at issue does not extend to implementation details or to other features of Microsoft's source code. . . .

> • Microsoft's argument that it will have less incentive to develop a given technology if it is required to make that technology available to its competitors is of no relevance . . . where the issue to be decided is the impact of the refusal to supply on the incentive for Microsoft's competitors to innovate and not on Microsoft's incentives to innovate.

The Court held that the protocols were "indispensable" for firms seeking to compete with Microsoft in the server market.

The Court also condemned Microsoft's technological tie of its Media Player software by commingling the code into the Windows operating system:

> Microsoft's argument that the integration of Windows Media Player in the Windows operating system was dictated by technical reasons is scarcely credible in the light of the content of certain of its own internal communications. Thus . . . the integration of Windows Media Player in Windows was primarily designed to make Windows Media Player more competitive with RealPlayer by presenting it as a constituent part of Windows and not as application software that might be compared with RealPlayer.

> The Commission was correct to find . . . that software developers who wrote applications that relied on a media player had incentives to write

foremost to Windows Media Player.

Specifically, the Court found:

> • Because of the bundling, Microsoft's competitors are . . . at a disadvantage even if their products are inherently better than Windows Media Player;

> •Microsoft shields itself from effective competition from vendors of potentially more efficient media players who could challenge its position, and thus reduces the talent and capital invested in innovation of media players;

> • [B]y means of the bundling, Microsoft sends signals which deter innovation in any technologies in which it might conceivably take an interest and which it might tie with Windows in the future.

[B] Monopolization and the Intellectual Property Laws (Mainly Patent and Copyright)

The federal patent and copyright laws respond to the Constitutional authorization to Congress to "promote the Progress of Science and useful Arts, by securing for limited Times to . . . Inventors the exclusive Right to . . . their Writings and Discoveries." U.S. Const. art. I, § 8, cl. 8. Under the patent laws, the owner of a patent has a 20-year "monopoly" on the right to manufacture and sell the patented product. 35 U.S.C. § 154.

But patents can be abused, and sometimes the abuses violate Section 2's prohibition of monopolization and attempts to monopolize. One important caveat is in order. Both the offenses of monopolization and of attempted monopolization require a showing that the defendant has or may have monopoly power in some relevant market. Although we sometimes call the right created by a patent a "monopoly," the great majority of patents do not confer substantial market power in a relevant market. (In fact, the majority of patents are commercial failures and confer no market power whatsoever.) As a result, in a monopolization or attempt case alleging patent abuse, the plaintiff must still prove a relevant market. That market is not necessarily the product defined by any particular patent. The Supreme Court recognized this in *Walker Process* in 1965:

> To establish monopolization or attempt to monopolize a part of trade or commerce under § 2 of the Sherman Act, it would then be necessary to appraise the exclusionary power of the illegal patent claim in terms of the relevant market for the product involved. Without a definition of that market there is no way to measure [the defendant's] ability to lessen or destroy competition. It may be that the [patented] device . . . does not comprise a relevant market. There may be effective substitutes for the devices which do not infringe the patent. This is a matter of proof.

Walker Process Equip., Inc. v. Food Mach. & Chem. Corp., 382 U.S. 172, 177–178 (1965).

Assuming, then, that market power or the threat of it in a relevant market can be shown, under what circumstances might patent abuses violate Section 2?

[1] Improprieties in Procurement or Enforcement of an Invalid Patent

In *Walker Process, supra*, the Supreme Court held that a "knowing" and "wilful" misrepresentation to the patent office, permitting the antitrust defendant to obtain an invalid patent, and the subsequent enforcement of that patent could constitute monopoly conduct. A showing that the patent is valid generally undermines the plaintiff's claim. *See Brunswick Corp. v. Riegel Textile Corp.*, 752 F.2d 261 (7th Cir. 1984). The antitrust plaintiff still must prove the other elements of an antitrust claim.

The more common situation involves a firm which knows that its patent is invalid but nevertheless sues or threatens to sue rivals for infringement. Such infringement actions raise a problem: people have a constitutional right to go to court to assert their legal rights. On the other hand, "sham" litigation is not protected, and asserting a right in court that one knowingly does not have can constitute a "sham." These issues are taken up more fully in the discussion of the *Noerr-Pennington* doctrine in Chapter 9. In general, courts have addressed this problem by holding that a patent infringement lawsuit can be shown to be a sham attempt to enforce an invalid patent only if the antitrust plaintiff presents "clear and convincing" evidence that the antitrust defendant knew that its patent claim was invalid and was bringing it only to create or perpetuate a monopoly. *Handgards v. Ethicon (Handgards I)*, 601 F.2d 986 (9th Cir. 1979) ("Patentees must be permitted to test the validity of their patents in court through actions against alleged infringers. . . . On the other hand, infringement actions initiated and conducted in bad faith contribute nothing to the furtherance of the policies of either the patent law or the antitrust law."); *See also CVD v. Raytheon Co.*, 769 F.2d 842 (1st Cir. 1985) (applying a similar rule to a "sham" lawsuit to enforce a trade secret).

In *NobelPharma v. Implant Innovations*, 141 F.3d 1059 (Fed. Cir. 1998), the court decided that future decisions on "sham" patent claims would be decided under the law of the Federal Circuit rather than the court from which the appeal was taken. It then held that a patentee who had knowingly and intentionally failed to disclose important information to the Patent Office that might have undermined the patent, and knew of this fact when it later sued to enforce the patent against a rival, could be held liable under the *Walker Process* doctrine.

In *Unitherm Food Sys., Inc. v. Swift-Eckrich, Inc.*, 375 F.3d 1341, 1358 (Fed. Cir. 2004), the court concluded that a *Walker Process* claim that the defendant violated Section 2 of the Sherman Act by filing an infringement action based on a patent that had been fraudulently obtained needed to plead the fraud according to the general common law elements:

(1) a representation of a material fact, (2) the falsity of that representation, (3) the intent to deceive or, at least, a state of mind so reckless as to the consequences that it is held to be the equivalent of intent (scienter), (4) a justifiable reliance upon the misrepresentation by the party deceived

which induces him to act thereon, and (5) injury to the party deceived as a result of his reliance on the misrepresentation.

But a misrepresentation of material fact alone could be enough to invalidate a patent, even though elements (3), (4), and (5) could not be shown. Suppose a firm files a patent infringement suit when it knows that the patent cannot be enforced because the patentee lied on its patent application. Should the conduct requirement for Section 2 of the Sherman Act require more?

The *Unitherm* court ultimately rejected the antitrust claim for failure to show a relevant market. On the "intent to deceive" requirement, the court required "a state of mind so reckless as to the consequences that it is held to be the equivalent of intent" will suffice to show fraud. *Id.* at 1358. Once again, however, suppose that the patentee did not have this intent at the time it made its patent application, but subsequently learns that the application contained false statements rendering the patent unenforceable. Ignoring these, it files a patent infringement suit against a rival anyway. Should there be *Walker Process* liability?

See Erbe Elektromedizin GmbH v. Canady Tech., LLC, 629 F.3d 1278 (Fed. Cir. 2010) (rejecting antitrust claim when the patentee's lawsuit was not objectively baseless even though patent had been found to be invalid; invalidity turned on a technical issue of patent claim construction, and reasonable persons could have differed on the issue); *Kaiser Found. Health Plan, Inc. v. Abbott Labs., Inc.*, 552 F.3d 1033 (9th Cir. 2009) (patent applicant's failure to disclose to PTO (a) a judicial decision that there had been prior sales that would have violated the on-sale bar; and (b) an English translation of a Japanese document that revealed prior art could have amounted to fraud in procurement of the patent sufficient to support a later *Walker Process* claim). See also *Ritz Camera & Image, LLC v. SanDisk Corp.*, 700 F.3d 503 (Fed. Cir. 2012), which held that consumers had standing to bring a *Walker Process* cause of action because by enforcing a fraudulently procured patent, a monopolist can charge higher prices to consumers. Query: would the plaintiffs in such a case have to prove that the patent is invalid? Cf. the Supreme Court's *Actavis* decision reprinted in Chapter 4, holding that a horizontal agreement settling a patent dispute could be found unlawful under the antitrust laws without a finding on patent validity.

[2] Patent "Hold up"

In *Rambus, Inc.*, 522 F.3d 456, 2006 WL 2330117 (FTC, Aug. 2, 2006), *rev'd*, 522 F.3d 456 (D.C. Cir. 2008), the FTC concluded that Rambus, a producer of technology for computer memory chips, violated Section 5 of the Federal Trade Commission Act by engaging in exclusionary conduct that violated Section 2 of the Sherman Act. The conduct involved Rambus' manipulation of information about its IP rights while participating in a standard setting process. Rambus itself did not manufacture memory chips, but rather researched and developed technology which it patented to others.

Rambus was a member of the Joint Electronic Device Engineering Council ("JEDEC"), a standard setting organization (SSO). As the FTC summarized the allegations, while actively participating in JEDEC standard setting discussions, Rambus refused to disclose the existence of its patents and applications, which deprived JEDEC members of critical information as they worked to evaluate potential standards. Rambus took additional actions that misled members to believe that Rambus was not seeking patents that would cover implementations of the standards under consideration by JEDEC. Rambus also went a step further: through its participation in JEDEC, Rambus gained information about the pending standard, and then amended its patent applications to ensure that subsequently issued patents would cover the ultimate standard. Through its successful strategy, Rambus was able to conceal its patents and patent applications until after the standards were adopted and the market was locked in. Only then did Rambus reveal its patents — through patent infringement lawsuits against JEDEC members who practiced the standard.

The result, according to the FTC complaint, was anticompetitive exclusion resulting in:

> increased royalties; increased prices for memory products compliant with JEDEC standards; decreased incentives to produce memory using JEDEC-compliant memory technology; and decreased incentives to participate in, and rely on, standard-setting organizations and activities.

> The Commission defined anticompetitive exclusionary conduct as "conduct other than competition on the merits — or other than restraints reasonably 'necessary' to competition on the merits — that reasonably appear[s] capable of making a significant contribution to creating or maintaining monopoly power." The Commission also concluded that intentional deception of a standard setting organization in order to acquire patents to shared technology was not competition on the merits. The opinion also noted that, given the FTC's broader role in consumer protection, it had developed "special expertise" in the recognition of deceptive conduct.

In reversing, the D.C. Circuit observed:

> Even if deception raises the price secured by a seller, but does so without harming competition, it is beyond the antitrust laws' reach. Cases that recognize deception as exclusionary hinge, therefore, on whether the conduct impaired rivals in a manner tending to bring about or protect a defendant's monopoly power. In Microsoft, for example, we found *Microsoft* engaged in anticompetitive conduct when it tricked independent software developers into believing that its software development tools could be used to design crossplatform Java applications when, in fact, they produced Windows-specific ones. The deceit had caused "developers who were opting for portability over performance . . . unwittingly [to write] Java applications that [ran] only on Windows." The focus of our antitrust scrutiny, therefore, was properly placed on the resulting harms to competition rather than the deception itself.

> . . . JEDEC lost only an opportunity to secure a RAND commitment from Rambus. But loss of such a commitment is not a harm to competition from alternative technologies in the relevant markets. "[A]n antitrust plaintiff must establish that the standard-setting organization would not

have adopted the standard in question but for the misrepresentation or omission." Indeed, had JEDEC limited Rambus to reasonable royalties and required it to provide licenses on a nondiscriminatory basis, we would expect less competition from alternative technologies, not more; high prices and constrained output tend to attract competitors, not to repel them.

The court concluded that if JEDEC would have adopted Rambus' technology anyway, but for the deception, although perhaps at a lower royalty rate, then the deception did not injure competition. As a result, the Commission failed to demonstrate that Rambus' conduct was exclusionary, as Section 2 required.

The court also faulted JEDEC's own disclosure requirements, finding nothing pertaining to potential patent amendments of the kind that Rambus had made. In fact, "JEDEC's patent disclosure policies suffered from a 'staggering lack of defining details.'" Beginning with the observation that unpublished continuing patent applications are trade secrets, the court observed:

> One would expect that disclosure expectations ostensibly requiring competitors to share information that they would otherwise vigorously protect as trade secrets would provide clear guidance and define clearly what, when, how, and to whom the members must disclose. This need for clarity seems especially acute where disclosure of those trade secrets itself implicates antitrust concerns; JEDEC involved, after all, collaboration by competitors. In any event, the more vague and muddled a particular expectation of disclosure, the more difficult it should be for the Commission to ascribe competitive harm to its breach.

In contrast to the D.C. Circuit's approach, the Third Circuit in *Broadcom Corp. v. Qualcomm Inc.*, 501 F.3d 297 (3d Cir. 2007), held that a patent holder's deceptive conduct before a private standards-determining organization ("SDO") could provide the basis for a monopolization or attempted monopolization claim under § 2 of the Sherman Act. In *Broadcom*, the antitrust plaintiff alleged that the defendant deceived the relevant SDO by committing to license its technology on fair, reasonable, and non-discriminatory ("FRAND") terms and then, after the standard that incorporated the defendant's technology had been adopted and lock-in had occurred, demanding non-FRAND royalties. The Third Circuit held: "that (1) in a consensus-oriented private standard-setting environment, (2) a patent holder's intentionally false promise to license essential proprietary technology on FRAND terms, (3) coupled with an SDO's reliance on that promise when including the technology in a standard, and (4) the patent holder's subsequent breach of that promise, is actionable anticompetitive conduct. This holding follows directly from established principles of antitrust law and represents the emerging view of enforcement authorities and commentators, alike. Deception in a consensus-driven private standard-setting environment harms the competitive process by obscuring the costs of including proprietary technology in a standard and increasing the likelihood that patent rights will confer monopoly power on the patent holder." *Id.* at 314.

For more on Rambus and decisions raising similar issues, see 3 PHILLIP E. AREEDA & HERBERT HOVENKAMP, ANTITRUST LAW ¶ 712 (3d ed. 2008). On the relationship between intellectual property and the antitrust laws, see Christina

Bohannan & Herbert Hovenkamp, *IP and Antitrust: Reformation and Harm*, 51 B.C. L. Rev. 905 (2010).

PROBLEM 6.6

Firm *A* has developed an important new process which it is about to patent. The patent, once created, will give Firm *A* an effective monopoly over the process, which is more efficient than any alternative. In the final stages of development, Firm *B* hires away a key Firm *A* employee and quickly obtains enough information to file for the patent. Firm *A* sues, claiming that the "theft" of the patent, and the attendant monopoly, is an antitrust violation. Outcome? *See Brunswick Corp. v. Riegel Textile Corp.*, 752 F.2d 261 (7th Cir. 1984); *compare Fishman v. Estate of Wirtz*, 807 F.2d 520 (7th Cir. 1986), especially at 563–564 (Easterbrook, J., dissenting). Alternatively, suppose that *A* claims that the "theft" of the employee is illegal monopolization? *See Midwest Radio Co. v. Forum Pub'g Co.*, 942 F.2d 1294 (8th Cir. 1991).

[3] Refusal to License IP Rights

INDEPENDENT SERVICE ORGANIZATIONS ANTITRUST LITIGATION
203 F.3d 1322 (Fed. Cir. 2000)

MAYER, CHIEF JUDGE.

CSU, L.L.C. appeals the judgment of the United States District Court for the District of Kansas, dismissing on summary judgment CSU's claims that Xerox's refusal to sell patented parts and copyrighted manuals and to license copyrighted software violate the antitrust laws. . . .

Xerox manufactures, sells, and services high-volume copiers. Beginning in 1984, it established a policy of not selling parts unique to its series 10 copiers to independent service organizations ("ISOs"), including CSU, unless they were also end-users of the copiers. . . .

To maintain its existing business of servicing Xerox equipment, CSU used parts cannibalized from used Xerox equipment, parts obtained from other ISOs, and parts purchased through a limited number of its customers. . . . CSU . . . filed this suit alleging that Xerox violated the Sherman Act by setting the prices on its patented parts much higher for ISOs than for end-users to force ISOs to raise their prices. This would eliminate ISOs in general and CSU in particular as competitors in the relevant service markets for high speed copiers and printers.

Xerox counterclaimed for patent and copyright infringement and contested CSU's antitrust claims as relying on injury solely caused by Xerox's lawful refusal to sell or license patented parts and copyrighted software. Xerox also claimed that CSU could not assert a patent or copyright misuse defense to Xerox's infringement counterclaims based on Xerox's refusal to deal.

The district court granted summary judgment to Xerox dismissing CSU's antitrust claims and holding that if a patent or copyright is lawfully acquired, the patent or copyright holder's unilateral refusal to sell or license its patented invention or copyrighted expression is not unlawful exclusionary conduct under the antitrust laws, even if the refusal to deal impacts competition in more than one market. The court also held, in both the patent and copyright contexts, that the right holder's intent in refusing to deal and any other alleged exclusionary acts committed by the right holder are irrelevant to antitrust law. This appeal followed.

. . . .

As a general proposition, when reviewing a district court's judgment involving federal antitrust law, we are guided by the law of the regional circuit in which that district court sits, in this case the Tenth Circuit. *See Nobelpharma AB v. Implant Innovations, Inc.*, 141 F.3d 1059, 1068 (Fed. Cir. 1998). We apply our own law, not regional circuit law, to resolve issues that clearly involve our exclusive jurisdiction. *See Pro-Mold & Tool Co. v. Great Lakes Plastics, Inc.*, 75 F.3d 1568, 1574–75 (Fed. Cir. 1996). "Whether conduct in procuring or enforcing a patent is sufficient to strip a patentee of its immunity from the antitrust laws is to be decided as a question of Federal Circuit law." *Nobelpharma*, 141 F.3d at 1068. . . . The district court's grant of summary judgment as to CSU's antitrust claims arising from Xerox's refusal to sell its patented parts is therefore reviewed as a matter of Federal Circuit law, while consideration of the antitrust claim based on Xerox's refusal to sell or license its copyrighted manuals and software is under Tenth Circuit law.

Intellectual property rights do not confer a privilege to violate the antitrust laws. *See Intergraph Corp. v. Intel Corp.*, 195 F.3d 1346, 1362 (Fed. Cir. 1999). "But it is also correct that the antitrust laws do not negate the patentee's right to exclude others from patent property." "The commercial advantage gained by new technology and its statutory protection by patent do not convert the possessor thereof into a prohibited monopolist." *Abbott Lab. v. Brennan*, 952 F.2d 1346, 1354 (Fed. Cir. 1991). "The patent right must be 'coupled with violations of § 2', and the elements of violation of 15 U.S.C. § 2 must be met." *Id.* "Determination of whether the patentee meets the Sherman Act elements of monopolization or attempt to monopolize is governed by the rules of application of the antitrust laws to market participants, with due consideration to the exclusivity that inheres in the patent grant." . . .

A patent alone does not demonstrate market power. The United States Department of Justice and Federal Trade Commission have issued guidance that, even where it exists, such "market power does not 'impose on the intellectual property owner an obligation to license the use of that property to others.' " *Intergraph*, 195 F.3d at 1362, 52 USPQ2d at 1652 (citing United States Department of Justice and Federal Trade Comm'n Antitrust Guidelines for the Licensing of Intellectual Property 4 (1995)). There is "no reported case in which a court ha[s] imposed antitrust liability for a unilateral refusal to sell or license a patent. . . ." *Id.* (citing *Image Technical Servs. v. Eastman Kodak Co.*, 125 F.3d 1195, 1216 (9th Cir. 1997)). The patentee's right to exclude is further supported by section 271(d) of the Patent Act which states, in pertinent part, that "[n]o patent owner otherwise entitled to relief . . . shall be denied relief or deemed guilty of misuse or illegal extension of the patent right by reason of his having . . . (4) refused to license or use any rights to the patent . . ." 35 U.S.C. § 271(d) (1999).

The patentee's right to exclude, however, is not without limit. As we recently observed in *Glass Equipment Development Inc. v. Besten, Inc.*, a patent owner who brings suit to enforce the statutory right to exclude others from making, using, or selling the claimed invention is exempt from the antitrust laws, even though such a suit may have an anticompetitive effect, unless the infringement defendant proves one of two conditions. 174 F.3d 1337, 1343 (Fed. Cir. 1999) (citing *Nobelpharma*, 141 F.3d at 1068). First, he may prove that the asserted patent was obtained through knowing and willful fraud within the meaning of *Walker Process Equipment, Inc. v. Food Machinery & Chemical Corp.*, 382 U.S. 172, 177 (1965). Or he may demonstrate that the infringement suit was a mere sham to cover what is actually no more than an attempt to interfere directly with the business relationships of a competitor. *See id.* (citing *Eastern R.R. Presidents Conference v. Noerr Motor Freight, Inc.*, 365 U.S. 127, 144 (1961)). Here, CSU makes no claim that Xerox obtained its patents through fraud in the Patent and Trademark Office; the Walker Process analysis is not implicated.

"[I]rrespective of the patent applicant's conduct before the [Patent and Trademark Office], an antitrust claim can also be based on [an] allegation that a suit is baseless; in order to prove that a suit was within Noerr's 'sham' exception to immunity, [see *Noerr*, 365 U.S. at 144], an antitrust plaintiff must prove that the suit was both objectively baseless and subjectively motivated by a desire to impose collateral, anti-competitive injury rather than to obtain a justifiable legal remedy." *Nobelpharma*, 141 F.3d at 1071. "Accordingly, if a suit is not objectively baseless, an antitrust defendant's subjective motivation is immaterial." CSU has alleged that Xerox misused its patents but has not claimed that Xerox's patent infringement counterclaims were shams.

To support its argument that Xerox illegally sought to leverage its presumably legitimate dominance in the equipment and parts market into dominance in the service market, CSU relies on a footnote in *Eastman Kodak Co. v. Image Technical Services, Inc.*, 504 U.S. 451, 480 n.29 (1992), that "[t]he Court has held many times that power gained through some natural and legal advantage such as a patent, . . . can give rise to liability if 'a seller exploits his dominant position in one market to expand his empire into the next.' " Notably, *Kodak* was a tying case when it came before the Supreme Court, and no patents had been asserted in defense of the antitrust claims against Kodak. Conversely, there are no claims in this case of illegally tying the sale of Xerox's patented parts to unpatented products. Therefore, the issue was not resolved by the Kodak language cited by CSU. Properly viewed within the framework of a tying case, the footnote can be interpreted as restating the undisputed premise that the patent holder cannot use his statutory right to refuse to sell patented parts to gain a monopoly in a market beyond the scope of the patent. *See, e.g., Atari Games Corp. v. Nintendo of Am., Inc.*, 897 F.2d 1572, 1576 (Fed. Cir. 1990) ("[A] patent owner may not take the property right granted by a patent and use it to extend his power in the marketplace improperly, i.e. beyond the limits of what Congress intended to give in the patent laws.").

The cited language from *Kodak* does nothing to limit the right of the patentee to refuse to sell or license in markets within the scope of the statutory patent grant.

In fact, we have expressly held that, absent exceptional circumstances, a patent may confer the right to exclude competition altogether in more than one antitrust market. *See B. Braun Med., Inc. v. Abbott Lab.*, 124 F.3d 1419, 1427 n.4 (Fed. Cir. 1997) (patentee had right to exclude competition in both the market for patented valves and the market for extension sets incorporating patented valves).

CSU further relies on the Ninth Circuit's holding on remand in *Image Technical Services* ["*Kodak*"] that " 'while exclusionary conduct can include a monopolist's unilateral refusal to license a [patent] or to sell its patented . . . work, a monopolist's 'desire to exclude others from its [protected] work is a presumptively valid business justification for any immediate harm to consumers.' " 125 F.3d at 1218 (citing *Data General Corp. v. Grumman Sys. Support Corp.*, 36 F.3d 1147, 1187 (1st Cir. 1994)). By that case, the Ninth Circuit adopted a rebuttable presumption that the exercise of the statutory right to exclude provides a valid business justification for consumer harm, but then excused as harmless the district court's error in failing to give any instruction on the effect of intellectual property rights on the application of the antitrust laws. It concluded that the jury must have rejected the presumptively valid business justification as pretextual. *See id.* This logic requires an evaluation of the patentee's subjective motivation for refusing to sell or license its patented products for pretext. We decline to follow *Image Technical Services*.

We have held that "if a [patent infringement] suit is not objectively baseless, an antitrust defendant's subjective motivation is immaterial." Nobelpharma, 141 F.3d at 1072. We see no more reason to inquire into the subjective motivation of Xerox in refusing to sell or license its patented works than we found in evaluating the subjective motivation of a patentee in bringing suit to enforce that same right. In the absence of any indication of illegal tying, fraud in the Patent and Trademark Office, or sham litigation, the patent holder may enforce the statutory right to exclude others from making, using, or selling the claimed invention free from liability under the antitrust laws. We therefore will not inquire into his subjective motivation for exerting his statutory rights, even though his refusal to sell or license his patented invention may have an anticompetitive effect, so long as that anticompetitive effect is not illegally extended beyond the statutory patent grant. It is the infringement defendant and not the patentee that bears the burden to show that one of these exceptional situations exists and, in the absence of such proof, we will not inquire into the patentee's motivations for asserting his statutory right to exclude. Even in cases where the infringement defendant has met this burden, which CSU has not, he must then also prove the elements of the Sherman Act violation.

We answer the threshold question of whether Xerox's refusal to sell its patented parts exceeds the scope of the patent grant in the negative. Therefore, our inquiry is at an end. Xerox was under no obligation to sell or license its patented parts and did not violate the antitrust laws by refusing to do so.

. . . .

The Copyright Act expressly grants a copyright owner the exclusive right to distribute the protected work by "transfer of ownership, or by rental, lease, or lending." 17 U.S.C. § 106(3) (1996). "[T]he owner of the copyright, if [it] pleases, may refrain from vending or licensing and content [itself] with simply exercising the right to exclude others from using [its] property." *Data General*, 36 F.3d at 1186 (citing *Fox Film Corp. v. Doyal*, 286 U.S. 123, 127 (1932)).

The Supreme Court has made clear that the property right granted by copyright law cannot be used with impunity to extend power in the marketplace beyond what Congress intended. *See United States v. Loew's, Inc.*, 371 U.S. 38, 47–48 (1962) (block booking of copyrighted motion pictures is illegal tying in violation of Sherman Act). The Court has not, however, directly addressed the antitrust implications of a unilateral refusal to sell or license copyrighted expression.

. . . The Fourth Circuit has rejected a claim of illegal tying, supported only by evidence of a unilateral decision to license copyrighted diagnostic software to some but not to others. *See Service & Training, Inc. v. Data General Corp.*, 963 F.2d 680, 686 (4th Cir. 1992). In reaching this conclusion, the court recognized the copyright owner's exclusive right to "sell, rent, lease, lend, or otherwise distribute copies of a copyrighted work," *id.* (citing 17 U.S.C. § 106(3)), and concluded that "Section 1 of the Sherman Act does not entitle 'a purchaser . . . to buy a product that the seller does not wish to offer for sale.' "

Perhaps the most extensive analysis of the effect of a unilateral refusal to license copyrighted expression was conducted by the First Circuit in *Data General Corp. v. Grumman Systems Support Corp.*, 36 F.3d 1147. There, the court noted that the limited copyright monopoly is based on Congress' empirical assumption that the right to "exclude others from using their works creates a system of incentives that promotes consumer welfare in the long term by encouraging investment in the creation of desirable artistic and functional works of expression. . . . We cannot require antitrust defendants to prove and reprove the merits of this legislative assumption in every case where a refusal to license a copyrighted work comes under attack." The court went on to establish as a legal standard that "while exclusionary conduct can include a monopolist's unilateral refusal to license a copyright, an author's desire to exclude others from use of its copyrighted work is a presumptively valid business justification for any immediate harm to consumers." The burden to overcome this presumption was firmly placed on the antitrust plaintiff. The court gave no weight to evidence showing knowledge that developing a proprietary position would help to maintain a monopoly in the service market in the face of contrary evidence of the defendant's desire to develop state-of-the-art diagnostic software to enhance its service and consumer benefit.

As discussed above, the Ninth Circuit adopted a modified version of this *Data General* standard. Both courts agreed that the presumption could be rebutted by evidence that "the monopolist acquired the protection of the intellectual property laws in an unlawful manner." *Image Technical Servs.*, 125 F.3d at 1219. The Ninth Circuit, however, extended the possible means of rebutting the presumption to include evidence that the defense and exploitation of the copyright grant was merely a pretextual business justification to mask anticompetitive conduct. *See id.* The hazards of this approach are evident in both the path taken and the outcome reached. The jury in that case was instructed to examine each proffered business justification for pretext, and no weight was given to the intellectual property rights in the instructions. This permitted the jury to second guess the subjective motivation of the copyright holder in asserting its statutory rights to exclude under the copyright laws without properly weighing the presumption of legitimacy in asserting its rights under the copyright laws. While concluding that the failure to weigh the intellectual property rights was an abuse of discretion, the Ninth Circuit nevertheless held the error harmless because it thought the jury must have rejected the presumptive validity of asserting the copyrights as pretextual. This is in reality a significant departure from the First Circuit's central premise that rebutting the presumption would be an uphill battle and would only be appropriate in those rare cases in which imposing antitrust liability is unlikely to frustrate the objectives of the Copyright Act. *See Data General*, 36 F.3d at 1187 n.64, 1188.

We believe the First Circuit's approach is more consistent with both the antitrust and the copyright laws and is the standard that would most likely be followed by the Tenth Circuit in considering the effect of Xerox's unilateral right to refuse to license or sell copyrighted manuals and diagnostic software on liability under the antitrust laws. We therefore reject CSU's invitation to examine Xerox's subjective motivation in asserting its right to exclude under the copyright laws for pretext, in the absence of any evidence that the copyrights were obtained by unlawful means or were used to gain monopoly power beyond the statutory copyright granted by Congress. In the absence of such definitive rebuttal evidence, Xerox's refusal to sell or license its copyrighted works was squarely within the rights granted by Congress to the copyright holder and did not constitute a violation of the antitrust laws.

Accordingly, the judgment of the United States District Court for the District of Kansas is affirmed.

NOTES AND QUESTIONS

1. Consider the proposition: "the antitrust laws never require the owner of a patent, acting unilaterally and unconditionally, to license it." Is the proposition absolutely true? Or are further qualifications necessary? How about conditional refusals, such as "I'll license my patented photocopier to you only if you agree to use my (unpatented) paper"? Or "I'll give you license to use my patented hard drive in your computer only if you agree to purchase hard drives exclusively from me"? Clearly these enjoy no automatic antitrust immunity. Section 3 of the Clayton Act, 15 U.S.C. § 14, applies its prohibitions of tying and exclusive dealing to goods "whether patented or unpatented." *Cf.* § 271(d) of the Patent Act:

> No patent owner otherwise entitled to relief . . . shall be denied relief or deemed guilty of misuse or illegal extension of the patent right by reason of his having . . . (4) refused to license or use any rights to the patent.

35 U.S.C. § 271(d) (2002). Note that this provision does not expressly create a Sherman Act immunity; rather, it states that a refusal to license is neither "misuse" or "illegal extension of the patent right." If patent "misuse" is defined by antitrust principles, then of course the provision contains a complete antitrust immunity as well. But how about the language "or illegal extension of the patent right." Isn't that designed to cover all "extensions," such as those traditionally condemned under the antitrust laws?

In *Image Technical Services v. Eastman Kodak Co.*, 125 F.3d 1195, 1216 (9th Cir. 1997), the Ninth Circuit adopted an alternative formulation that the *Independent*

Service Organizations court rejected — namely, that a refusal to license a patent could be unlawful depending on the patentee's intent. If the patentee simply intends to protect its intellectual property rights, the refusal is lawful. However, if the patentee intends to create a monopoly in a secondary market (for example, by refusing to license a patented part in order to create a monopoly in the service market for installing such parts), then the refusal to license is unlawful. Is that distinction defensible? Is it even meaningful? As the Federal Circuit observes, a patent does not simply cover a "market." It covers a wide variety of uses in markets that may have little relation to one another. If I refuse to license to you my patented electric polishing machine, that may restrict your efforts to (1) resell my machine to others; (2) make polished furniture; or (3) go into the business of polishing furniture that people already own. What if I intend to do all three things? Am I simply seeking to protect my patent? Or am I seeking to create a monopoly in a "secondary" market? Given that intent issues often survive summary judgment and go to a jury, does this mean that under the Ninth Circuit's rule, a refusal to license a patent invites an antitrust trial to determine the defendant's intent?

2. If a patentee can always refuse to license, does it follow automatically that the patentee can also charge any price it wants for the patented article?

[4] Patent Accumulation

Suppose a dominant firm maintains a policy of buying up every patent that comes along in its market area. Some of these it uses; others it does not use. Its principal purpose is to make it very difficult for potential competitors to enter the same market. Suppose, for example, that the dominant firm has established patents for Process A, and is currently earning monopoly profits for goods produced under that process. A small firm now develops and patents Process B, which can do the same thing as Process A at about the same cost. As a basic proposition, Process B is worth more money to the dominant firm than it is to a competitor. If the dominant firm acquires Process B, it will maintain its monopoly. If a competitor acquires Process B, the two firms will compete away the monopoly returns. As a result, the dominant firm is likely to be the highest bidder for Process B, which it will then purchase and retire, refusing to license it to anyone else. *See* Richard J. Gilbert & David M.G. Newberry, *Preemptive Patenting and the Persistence of Monopoly*, 72 AM. ECON. REV. 514 (1982).

The Supreme Court has not been particularly helpful on the question of antitrust liability for patent accumulation. In *Transparent-Wrap Mach. Corp. v. Stokes & Smith Co.*, 329 U.S. 637, 646–647 (1947), it suggested that one

> who acquires two patents acquires a double monopoly. As patents are added to patents a whole industry may be regimented. The owner of a basic patent might thus perpetuate his control over an industry long after the basic patent expired. Competitors might be eliminated and an industrial monopoly perfected and maintained.

But only three years later the Court concluded in *Automatic Radio Mfg. Co. v. Hazeltine Res., Inc.*, 339 U.S. 827, 834 (1950), that the "mere accumulation of patents, no matter how many," is not a Sherman Act violation. In the *SCM* case, *supra*, the court echoed the latter view, holding that "where a patent has been lawfully acquired, subsequent conduct permissible under the patent laws cannot trigger any liability under the antitrust laws." 645 F.2d 1195, at 1206.

[C]   Predatory Pricing and Related Practices

Predatory pricing is the offense of driving rivals out of business by selling products at less than their cost, with the expectation of charging a monopoly price in the future when the rivals have either left the market or have been cajoled into raising their own prices. The formulation of an administrable test for predatory pricing has occupied center stage in attempted monopolization cases since the mid-1970s. On the one hand, low prices are an important goal of the antitrust laws. Any test designed to make selling at a low price illegal must employ a great deal of caution, or else the antitrust laws will end up subverting the very ends they were designed to achieve. On the other hand, few people have doubted that there are times when sellers attempt to create a monopoly by temporarily charging below-cost prices.

When *Standard Oil Co. v. United States*, 221 U.S. 1 (1911), was decided, Progressive Era lawyers generally believed that predatory pricing was easy to pull off, relatively common, and that it represented an important means by which certain large monopolies such as the Standard Oil Company had come into existence. Some scholars have argued that Standard generally eliminated rivals from the market by buying them out, not by predating them into bankruptcy. *See* John McGee, *Predatory Price Cutting: The Standard Oil (N.J.) Case*, 1 J.L. & Econ. 137 (1958); *but see* Christopher R. Leslie, *Revisiting the Revisionist History of Standard Oil*, 85 S. Cal. L. Rev. 573 (2012) (refuting McGee's claims); Elizabeth Granitz & Benjamin Klein, *Monopolization by "Raising Rivals' Costs": The Standard Oil Case*, 39 J.L. & Econ. 1 (1996) (arguing that, while Standard may not have used below-cost pricing, it did employ other anticompetitive strategies).

Whether or not Standard used predatory pricing, the popular feeling that price predation was one of the most serious industrial evils of the time inspired Progressive Era lawmakers to devote a great deal of attention to it. Many Progressives were outraged with the rule of reason announced in the *Standard* case. Ignoring the fact that the Supreme Court condemned Standard Oil on virtually every count, critics of Chief Justice White's opinion alleged that the rule of reason would eviscerate the Sherman Act. All three major political parties (Democratic, Republican, and Progressive (Bull Moose)) in the 1912 Presidential election promised stronger antitrust laws. Woodrow Wilson's Democratic administration followed through with the Clayton Act, which was enacted in 1914. Section 2 of the Clayton Act (15 U.S.C. § 13) was concerned with predatory pricing. Today predatory pricing can be condemned under Section 1 of the Sherman Act (if done pursuant to a conspiracy), Section 2 of the Sherman Act, and Section 2 of the Clayton Act, although the statutes have traditionally employed different requirements.

Built into Section 2 of the Clayton Act was its framer's theory about how predatory pricing worked. Today we know that theory as the "subsidy" theory of predatory pricing. Under the theory, giant trusts like the Standard Oil Company were able to predate smaller rivals out of the market because the trusts operated in many geographic markets, while the smaller rivals operated in only one. The framers of Section 2 of the Clayton Act believed that the giant companies would engage in below-cost selling in a market in which they had rivals, until the rivals were driven from business. They would finance this below-cost selling by raising their prices in other areas where their monopoly position was already secure. By this means they could use a monopoly in one area to leverage a monopoly in a second area. Section 2 of the Clayton Act was designed to reach this perceived practice by making it illegal for the giant companies to charge two different prices in two different markets where the effect of such "discriminatory" pricing was to injure competition.

Today, cases applying Section 2 of the Clayton Act to predatory pricing are known as "primary-line" price discrimination cases. In 1936, Section 2 of the Clayton Act was modified and broadened substantially by the Robinson-Patman amendments to include "secondary-line" injuries, which are injuries that accrue not to the seller's competitors but to its customers. Secondary-line application of the statute is covered in Chapter 8. Today we refer to Section 2 of the Clayton Act in its entirety as the Robinson-Patman Act, even though predatory pricing is governed by the original 1914 language.

Whether we analyze predatory pricing under the Sherman Act or the Robinson-Patman Act, it is best understood as conduct by which the defendant pays certain higher costs today in order to reap the benefit of supra competitive monopoly profits tomorrow.

[1] Structural Prerequisites for a Predatory Pricing Claim — "Recoupment"

BROOKE GROUP LTD. v. BROWN & WILLIAMSON TOBACCO CORP.
509 U.S. 209 (1993)

JUSTICE KENNEDY delivered the opinion of the Court.

This case stems from a market struggle that erupted in the domestic cigarette industry in the mid-1980's. Petitioner Brooke Group, Inc., whom we, like the parties to the case, refer to as Liggett because of its former corporate name, charges that to counter its innovative development of generic cigarettes, respondent Brown & Williamson Tobacco Corporation introduced its own line of generic cigarettes in an unlawful effort to stifle price competition in the economy segment of the national cigarette market. Liggett contends that Brown & Williamson cut prices on generic cigarettes below cost and offered discriminatory volume rebates to wholesalers to force Liggett to raise its own generic cigarette prices and introduce oligopoly pricing in the economy segment. We hold that Brown & Williamson is entitled to judgment as a matter of law.

I

In 1980, Liggett pioneered the development of the economy segment of the national cigarette market by introducing a line of "black and white" generic cigarettes. The economy segment of the market, sometimes called the generic segment, is characterized by its bargain prices and comprises a variety of different products: black and whites, which are true generics sold in plain white packages with simple black lettering describing their contents; private label generics, which carry the trade dress of a specific purchaser, usually a retail chain; branded generics, which carry a brand name but which, like black and whites and private label generics, are sold at a deep discount and with little or no advertising; and "Value-25s," packages of 25 cigarettes that are sold to the consumer some 12.5% below the cost of a normal 20-cigarette pack. By 1984, when Brown & Williamson entered the generic segment and set in motion the series of events giving rise to this suit, Liggett's black and whites represented 97% of the generic segment, which in turn accounted for a little more than 4% of domestic cigarette sales. Prior to Liggett's introduction of black and whites in 1980, sales of generic cigarettes amounted to less than 1% of the domestic cigarette market.

. . . Cigarette manufacturing has long been one of America's most concentrated industries, . . . and for decades, production has been dominated by six firms: R.J. Reynolds, Philip Morris, American Brands, Lorillard, and the two litigants involved here, Liggett and Brown & Williamson. R.J. Reynolds and Philip Morris, the two industry leaders, enjoyed respective market shares of about 28% and 40% at the time of trial. Brown & Williamson ran a distant third, its market share never exceeding 12% at any time relevant to this dispute. Liggett's share of the market was even less, from a low of just over 2% in 1980 to a high of just over 5% in 1984.

The cigarette industry also has long been one of America's most profitable, in part because for many years there was no significant price competition among the rival firms. . . . List prices for cigarettes increased in lock-step, twice a year, for a number of years, irrespective of the rate of inflation, changes in the costs of production, or shifts in consumer demand. Substantial evidence suggests that in recent decades, the industry reaped the benefits of prices above a competitive level.
. . .

By 1980, however, broad market trends were working against the industry. Overall demand for cigarettes in the United States was declining, and no immediate prospect of recovery existed. As industry volume shrank, all firms developed substantial excess capacity. This decline in demand, coupled with the effects of nonprice competition, had a severe negative impact on Liggett. Once a major force in the industry, with market shares in excess of 20%, Liggett's market share had declined by 1980 to a little over 2%. With this meager share of the market, Liggett was on the verge of going out of business.

At the urging of a distributor, Liggett took an unusual step to revive its prospects: It developed a line of black and white generic cigarettes. When introduced in 1980, black and whites were offered to consumers at a list price roughly 30% lower than the list price of full-priced, branded cigarettes. They were also promoted at the wholesale level by means of rebates that increased with the volume of cigarettes ordered. Black and white cigarettes thus represented a new marketing category. The category's principal competitive characteristic was low price. Liggett's black and whites were an immediate and considerable success, growing from a fraction of a percent of the market at their introduction to over 4% of the total cigarette market by early 1984.

As the market for Liggett's generic cigarettes expanded, the other cigarette companies found themselves unable to ignore the economy segment. In general, the growth of generics came at the expense of the other firms' profitable sales of branded cigarettes. Brown & Williamson was hardest hit, because many of Brown & Williamson's brands were favored by consumers who were sensitive to changes in cigarette prices. Although Brown & Williamson sold only 11.4% of the market's branded cigarettes, 20% of the converts to Liggett's black and whites had switched from a Brown & Williamson brand. Losing volume and profits in its branded products, Brown & Williamson determined to enter the generic segment of the cigarette market. In July 1983, Brown & Williamson had begun selling Value-25s, and in the spring of 1984, it introduced its own black and white cigarette.

Brown & Williamson was neither the first nor the only cigarette company to recognize the threat posed by Liggett's black and whites and to respond in the economy segment. R.J. Reynolds had also introduced a Value-25 in 1983. And before Brown & Williamson introduced its own black and whites, R.J. Reynolds had repriced its "Doral" branded cigarette at generic levels. . . .

Brown & Williamson's entry was an even graver threat to Liggett's dominance of the generic category. Unlike R.J. Reynolds' Doral, Brown & Williamson's product was also a black and white and so would be in direct competition with Liggett's product at the wholesale level and on the retail shelf. Because Liggett's and Brown & Williamson's black and whites were more or less fungible, wholesalers had little incentive to carry more than one line. And unlike R.J. Reynolds, Brown & Williamson not only matched Liggett's prices but beat them. . . .

. . . This precipitated a price war at the wholesale level, in which Liggett five times attempted to beat the rebates offered by Brown & Williamson. At the end of each round, Brown & Williamson maintained a real advantage over Liggett's prices. Although it is undisputed that Brown & Williamson's original net price for its black and whites was above its costs, Liggett contends that by the end of the rebate war, Brown & Williamson was selling its black and whites at a loss. . . . Liggett's second response was to file a lawsuit. . . .

. . . Liggett alleged that Brown & Williamson's volume rebates to wholesalers amounted to price discrimination that had a reasonable possibility of injuring competition, in violation of § 2(a). Liggett claimed that Brown & Williamson's discriminatory volume rebates were integral to a scheme of predatory pricing, in which Brown & Williamson reduced its net prices for generic cigarettes below average variable costs. According to Liggett, these below-cost prices were not promotional but were intended to pressure it to raise its list prices on generic cigarettes, so that the percentage price difference between generic and branded cigarettes would narrow. Liggett explained that it would have been unable to reduce its wholesale rebates without losing substantial market share to Brown & Williamson; its only choice, if it wished to avoid prolonged losses on its principal product line, was to raise retail prices. The resulting reduction in the list price gap, it was said, would restrain the growth of the economy segment and preserve Brown & Williamson's supra competitive profits on its branded cigarettes. . . .

After a 115-day trial involving almost 3,000 exhibits and over a score of witnesses, the jury returned a verdict in favor of Liggett, finding on the special verdict form that Brown & Williamson had engaged in price discrimination that had a reasonable possibility of injuring competition in the domestic cigarette market as a whole. The jury awarded Liggett $49.6 million in damages, which the District Court trebled to $148.8 million. After reviewing the record, however, the District Court held that Brown & Williamson was entitled to judgment as a matter of law on three separate grounds: lack of injury to competition, lack of antitrust injury to Liggett, and lack of a causal link between the discriminatory rebates and Liggett's alleged injury. . . .

The United States Court of Appeals for the Fourth Circuit affirmed. *Liggett Group, Inc. v. Brown & Williamson Tobacco Corp.*, 964 F.2d 335 (1992). The Court of Appeals held that the dynamic of conscious parallelism among oligopolists could not produce competitive injury in a predatory pricing setting, which necessarily involves a price cut by one of the oligopolists. . . . In the Court of Appeals' view, "[t]o rely on the characteristics of an oligopoly to assure recoupment of losses from a predatory pricing scheme after one oligopolist has made a competitive move is . . . economically irrational." . . .

II

A

. . . By its terms, the Robinson-Patman Act condemns price discrimination only to the extent that it threatens to injure competition. . . . Liggett contends that Brown & Williamson's discriminatory volume rebates to wholesalers threatened substantial competitive injury by furthering a predatory pricing scheme designed to purge competition from the economy segment of the cigarette market.

This type of injury, which harms direct competitors of the discriminating seller, is known as primary-line injury. . . . We last addressed primary line injury over 25 years ago, in *Utah Pie Co. v. Continental Baking Co.*, 386 U.S. 685 (1967). In *Utah Pie*, we reviewed the sufficiency of the evidence supporting jury verdicts against three national pie companies that had engaged in a variety of predatory practices in the market for frozen pies in Salt Lake City, with the intent to drive a local pie manufacturer out of business. We reversed the Court of Appeals and held that the evidence presented was adequate to permit a jury to find a likelihood of injury to competition.

Utah Pie has often been interpreted to permit liability for primary-line price discrimination on a mere showing that the defendant intended to harm competition or produced a declining price structure. The case has been criticized on the grounds that such low standards of competitive injury are at odds with the antitrust laws' traditional concern for consumer welfare and price competition. *See* Bowman, *Restraint of Trade by the Supreme Court: The Utah Pie Case*, 77 Yale L.J. 70 (1967); R. Posner, *Antitrust Law: An Economic Perspective* 193–194 (1976); L. Sullivan,

Antitrust 687 (1977); 3 P. Areeda & D. Turner, *Antitrust Law* § 720c (1978) (hereinafter Areeda & Turner); R. Bork, *The Antitrust Paradox* 386–387 (1978); H. Hovenkamp, Economics and Federal Antitrust Law 188–189 (1985). We do not regard the *Utah Pie* case itself as having the full significance attributed to it by its detractors. *Utah Pie* was an early judicial inquiry in this area and did not purport to set forth explicit, general standards for establishing a violation of the Robinson-Patman Act. As the law has been explored since *Utah Pie*, it has become evident that primary-line competitive injury under the Robinson-Patman Act is of the same general character as the injury inflicted by predatory pricing schemes actionable under § 2 of the Sherman Act. . . . There are, to be sure, differences between the two statutes. For example, we interpret § 2 of the Sherman Act to condemn predatory pricing when it poses "a dangerous probability of actual monopolization," *Spectrum Sports, Inc. v. McQuillan*, [506 U.S. 447 (1993)], whereas the Robinson-Patman Act requires only that there be "a reasonable possibility" of substantial injury to competition before its protections are triggered. *Falls City Industries, Inc. v. Vanco Beverage, Inc.*, 460 U.S. 428, 434 (1983). But whatever additional flexibility the Robinson-Patman Act standard may imply, the essence of the claim under either statute is the same: A business rival has priced its products in an unfair manner with an object to eliminate or retard competition and thereby gain and exercise control over prices in the relevant market.

Accordingly, whether the claim alleges predatory pricing under § 2 of the Sherman Act or primary-line price discrimination under the Robinson-Patman Act, two prerequisites to recovery remain the same. First, a plaintiff seeking to establish competitive injury resulting from a rival's low prices must prove that the prices complained of are below an appropriate measure of its rival's costs.[1] . . . [W]e have rejected elsewhere the notion that above-cost prices that are below general market levels or the costs of a firm's competitors inflict injury to competition cognizable under the antitrust laws. See *Atlantic Richfield Co. v. USA Petroleum Co.*, 495 U.S. 328, 340 (1990). "Low prices benefit consumers regardless of how those prices are set, and so long as they are above predatory levels, they do not threaten competition. . . . We have adhered to this principle regardless of the type of antitrust claim involved." *Ibid.* As a general rule, the exclusionary effect of prices above a relevant measure of cost either reflects the lower cost structure of the alleged predator, and so represents competition on the merits, or is beyond the practical ability of a judicial tribunal to control without courting intolerable risks of chilling legitimate price-cutting. . . .

Even in an oligopolistic market, when a firm drops its prices to a competitive level to demonstrate to a maverick the unprofitability of straying from the group, it would be illogical to condemn the price cut: The antitrust laws then would be an obstacle to the chain of events most conducive to a breakdown of oligopoly pricing and the onset of competition. Even if the ultimate effect of the cut is to induce or reestablish supra competitive pricing, discouraging a price cut and forcing firms to maintain supra competitive prices, thus depriving consumers of the benefits of lower

---

[1] [FN 1] Because the parties in this case agree that the relevant measure of cost is average variable cost, however, we again decline to resolve the conflict among the lower courts over the appropriate measure of cost. See Cargill, Inc. v. Montfort of Colorado, Inc., 479 U.S. 104, 117–118, n. 12 (1986); Matsushita Elec. Industrial Co. v. Zenith Radio Corp., 475 U.S. 574, 585, n. 8 (1986).

prices in the interim, does not constitute sound antitrust policy. . . .

The second prerequisite to holding a competitor liable under the antitrust laws for charging low prices is a demonstration that the competitor had a reasonable prospect, or, under § 2 of the Sherman Act, a dangerous probability, of recouping its investment in below-cost prices. See *Matsushita, supra,* at 589; *Cargill, supra,* at 119, n.15. "For the investment to be rational, the [predator] must have a reasonable expectation of recovering, in the form of later monopoly profits, more than the losses suffered." Recoupment is the ultimate object of an unlawful predatory pricing scheme; it is the means by which a predator profits from predation. Without it, predatory pricing produces lower aggregate prices in the market, and consumer welfare is enhanced. Although unsuccessful predatory pricing may encourage some inefficient substitution toward the product being sold at less than its cost, unsuccessful predation is in general a boon to consumers.

That below-cost pricing may impose painful losses on its target is of no moment to the antitrust laws if competition is not injured. . . . Even an act of pure malice by one business competitor against another does not, without more, state a claim under the federal antitrust laws. . . .

For recoupment to occur, below-cost pricing must be capable, as a threshold matter, of producing the intended effects on the firm's rivals, whether driving them from the market, or, as was alleged to be the goal here, causing them to raise their prices to supra competitive levels within a disciplined oligopoly. This requires an understanding of the extent and duration of the alleged predation, the relative financial strength of the predator and its intended victim, and their respective incentives and will. . . .

If circumstances indicate that below-cost pricing could likely produce its intended effect on the target, there is still the further question whether it would likely injure competition in the relevant market. The plaintiff must demonstrate that there is a likelihood that the predatory scheme alleged would cause a rise in prices above a competitive level that would be sufficient to compensate for the amounts expended on the predation, including the time value of the money invested in it. . . .

Evidence of below-cost pricing is not alone sufficient to permit an inference of probable recoupment and injury to competition. Determining whether recoupment of predatory losses is likely requires an estimate of the cost of the alleged predation and a close analysis of both the scheme alleged by the plaintiff and the structure and conditions of the relevant market. *Cf., e.g.,* Elzinga & Mills, *Testing for Predation: Is Recoupment Feasible?,* 34 Antitrust Bull. 869 (1989) (constructing one possible model for evaluating recoupment). If market circumstances or deficiencies in proof would bar a reasonable jury from finding that the scheme alleged would likely result in sustained supra competitive pricing, the plaintiff's case has failed. In certain situations — for example, where the market is highly diffuse and competitive, or where new entry is easy, or the defendant lacks adequate excess capacity to absorb the market shares of his rivals and cannot quickly create or purchase new capacity — summary disposition of the case is appropriate. . . .

These prerequisites to recovery are not easy to establish, but they are not artificial obstacles to recovery; rather, they are essential components of real market injury. As we have said in the Sherman Act context, "predatory pricing schemes are rarely tried, and even more rarely successful," *Matsushita, supra,* at 589, and the costs of an erroneous finding of liability are high. . . .

B

Liggett does not allege that Brown & Williamson sought to drive it from the market but that Brown & Williamson sought to preserve supra competitive profits on branded cigarettes by pressuring Liggett to raise its generic cigarette prices through a process of tacit collusion with the other cigarette companies. . . .

In *Matsushita*, we remarked upon the general implausibility of predatory pricing. *Matsushita* observed that such schemes are even more improbable when they require coordinated action among several firms. . . . In order to succeed, the conspirators must agree on how to allocate present losses and future gains among the firms involved, and each firm must resist powerful incentives to cheat on whatever agreement is reached.

However unlikely predatory pricing by multiple firms may be when they conspire, it is even less likely when, as here, there is no express coordination. Firms that seek to recoup predatory losses through the conscious parallelism of oligopoly must rely on uncertain and ambiguous signals to achieve concerted action. The signals are subject to misinterpretation and are a blunt and imprecise means of ensuring smooth cooperation, especially in the context of changing or unprecedented market circumstances. This anticompetitive minuet is most difficult to compose and to perform, even for a disciplined oligopoly.

. . . Liggett suggests that these considerations led the Court of Appeals to rule out its theory of recovery as a matter of law. . . .

To the extent that the Court of Appeals may have held that the interdependent pricing of an oligopoly may never provide a means for achieving recoupment and so may not form the basis of a primary-line injury claim, we disagree. A predatory pricing scheme designed to preserve or create a stable oligopoly, if successful, can injure consumers in the same way, and to the same extent, as one designed to bring about a monopoly. However unlikely that possibility may be as a general matter, when the realities of the market and the record facts indicate that it has occurred and was likely to have succeeded, theory will not stand in the way of liability. See *Eastman Kodak Co. v. Image Technical Services, Inc.*, 504 U.S. 451 (1992).

The Robinson-Patman Act, which amended § 2 of the original Clayton Act, suggests no exclusion from coverage when primary-line injury occurs in an oligopoly setting. Unlike the provisions of the Sherman Act, which speak only of various forms of express agreement and monopoly, the Robinson-Patman Act is phrased in broader, disjunctive terms, prohibiting price discrimination "where the effect of such discrimination may be substantially to lessen competition or tend to create a monopoly." . . . We decline to create a per se rule of nonliability for predatory price discrimination when recoupment is alleged to take place through supra competitive oligopoly pricing.

III

Although Liggett's theory of liability, as an abstract matter, is within the reach of the statute, we agree with the Court of Appeals and the District Court that Liggett was not entitled to submit its case to the jury. . . .

A

Liggett's theory of competitive injury through oligopolistic price coordination depends upon a complex chain of cause and effect: Brown & Williamson would enter the generic segment with list prices matching Liggett's but with massive, discriminatory volume rebates directed at Liggett's biggest wholesalers; as a result, the net price of Brown & Williamson's generics would be below its costs; Liggett would suffer losses trying to defend its market share and wholesale customer base by matching Brown & Williamson's rebates; to avoid further losses, Liggett would raise its list prices on generics or acquiesce in price leadership by Brown & Williamson; higher list prices to consumers would shrink the percentage gap in retail price between generic and branded cigarettes; and this narrowing of the gap would make generics less appealing to the consumer, thus slowing the growth of the economy segment and reducing cannibalization of branded sales and their associated supra competitive profits.

Although Brown & Williamson's entry into the generic segment could be regarded as procompetitive in intent as well as effect, the record contains sufficient evidence from which a reasonable jury could conclude that Brown & Williamson envisioned or intended this anticompetitive course of events. . . . There is also sufficient evidence in the record from which a reasonable jury could conclude that for a period of approximately 18 months, Brown & Williamson's prices on its generic cigarettes were below its costs, and that this below-cost pricing imposed losses on Liggett that Liggett was unwilling to sustain. . . . Liggett has failed to demonstrate competitive injury as a matter of law, however, because its proof is flawed in a critical respect: The evidence is inadequate to show that in pursuing this scheme, Brown & Williamson had a reasonable prospect of recovering its losses from below-cost pricing through slowing the growth of generics. . . .

. . . Recoupment through supra competitive pricing in the economy segment of the cigarette market is an indispensable aspect of Liggett's own proffered theory, because a slowing of growth in the economy segment, even if it results from an increase in generic prices, is not itself anticompetitive. Only if those higher prices are a product of nonmarket forces has competition suffered. If prices rise in response to an excess of demand over supply, or segment growth slows as patterns of consumer preference become stable, the market is functioning in a competitive manner. Because relying on tacit coordination among oligopolists as a means of recouping losses from predatory pricing is "highly speculative," Areeda & Hovenkamp, [Antitrust Law] ¶ 711.2c, competent evidence is necessary to allow a reasonable inference that it poses an authentic threat to competition. The evidence in this case is insufficient to demonstrate the danger of Brown & Williamson's alleged scheme.

B

Based on Liggett's theory of the case and the record it created, there are two means by which one might infer that Brown & Williamson had a reasonable prospect of producing sustained supra competitive pricing in the generic segment adequate to recoup its predatory losses: first, if generic output or price information indicates that oligopolistic price coordination in fact produced supra competitive prices in the generic segment; or second, if evidence about the market and Brown & Williamson's conduct indicate that the alleged scheme was likely to have brought about tacit coordination and oligopoly pricing in the generic segment, even if it did not actually do so.

1

In this case, the price and output data do not support a reasonable inference that Brown & Williamson and the other cigarette companies elevated prices above a competitive level for generic cigarettes. supra competitive pricing entails a restriction in output. . . . In the present setting, in which output expanded at a rapid rate following Brown & Williamson's alleged predation, output in the generic segment can only have been restricted in the sense that it expanded at a slower rate than it would have absent Brown & Williamson's intervention. Such a counterfactual proposition is difficult to prove in the best of circumstances; here, the record evidence does not permit a reasonable inference that output would have been greater without Brown & Williamson's entry into the generic segment.

Following Brown & Williamson's entry, the rate at which generic cigarettes were capturing market share did not slow; indeed, the average rate of growth doubled. . . .

In arguing that Brown & Williamson was able to exert market power and raise generic prices above a competitive level in the generic category through tacit price coordination with the other cigarette manufacturers, Liggett places its principal reliance on direct evidence of price behavior. This evidence demonstrates that the list prices on all cigarettes, generic and branded alike, rose to a significant degree during the late 1980's. . . .

A reasonable jury, however, could not have drawn the inferences Liggett proposes. All of Liggett's data is based upon the list prices of various categories of cigarettes. Yet the jury had before it undisputed evidence that during the period in question, list prices were not the actual prices paid by consumers. As the market became unsettled in the mid-1980s, the cigarette companies invested substantial sums in promotional schemes, including coupons, stickers, and give-aways, that reduced the actual cost of cigarettes to consumers below list prices. . . .

Even on its own terms, the list price data relied upon by Liggett to demonstrate a narrowing of the price differential between generic and full-priced branded cigarettes could not support the conclusion that supra competitive pricing had been introduced into the generic segment. . . .

2

Not only does the evidence fail to show actual supra competitive pricing in the generic segment, it also does not demonstrate its likelihood. At the time Brown & Williamson entered the generic segment, the cigarette industry as a whole faced declining demand and possessed substantial excess capacity. . . . The only means by which Brown & Williamson is alleged to have established oligopoly pricing in the face of these unusual competitive pressures is through tacit price coordination with the other cigarette firms. Yet the situation facing the cigarette companies in the 1980's would have made such tacit coordination unmanageable. Tacit coordination is facilitated by a stable market environment, fungible products, and a small number of variables upon which the firms seeking to coordinate their pricing may focus. . . .

The larger number of product types and pricing variables also decreased the probability of effective parallel pricing. . . . With respect to each product, the net price in the market was determined not only by list prices, but also by a wide variety of discounts and promotions to consumers, and by rebates to wholesalers. In order to coordinate in an effective manner and eliminate price competition, the cigarette companies would have been required, without communicating, to establish parallel practices with respect to each of these variables, many of which, like consumer stickers or coupons, were difficult to monitor. . . .

Liggett argues that the means by which Brown & Williamson signaled its anticompetitive intent to its rivals was through its pricing structure. According to Liggett, maintaining existing list prices while offering substantial rebates to wholesalers was a signal to the other cigarette firms that Brown & Williamson did not intend to attract additional smokers to the generic segment by its entry. But a reasonable jury could not conclude that this pricing structure eliminated or rendered insignificant the risk that the other firms might misunderstand Brown & Williamson's entry as a competitive move. . . . Without effective signaling, it is difficult to see how the alleged predation could have had a reasonable chance of success through oligopoly pricing. . . .

. . . We hold that the evidence cannot support a finding that Brown & Williamson's alleged scheme was likely to result in oligopolistic price coordination and sustained supra competitive pricing in the generic segment of the national cigarette market. Without this, Brown & Williamson had no reasonable prospect of recouping its predatory losses and could not inflict the injury to competition the antitrust laws prohibit. The judgment of the Court of Appeals is

Affirmed.

Justice Stevens, with whom Justice White and Justice Blackmun join, dissenting.

. . . .

[The Sherman Act and the Clayton Act, as amended by the Robinson-Patman Act] differ significantly with respect to one element of the violation, the competitive consequences of predatory conduct. . . . Section 2 of the Sherman Act . . . may be violated when there is a "dangerous probability" that an attempt to achieve monopoly power will succeed. The Clayton Act goes beyond the "dangerous probability" standard to cover price discrimination "where the effect of such discrimination may be to substantially lessen competition or tend to create a monopoly in any line of commerce."

. . . The Robinson-Patman Act was designed to reach discriminations "in their incipiency, before the harm to competition is effected. It is enough that they 'may' have the proscribed effect."

. . . Perhaps the Court's most significant error is the assumption that seems to pervade much of the final sections of its opinion: that Liggett had the burden of proving either the actuality of supra competitive pricing, or the actuality of tacit collusion. . . . In my opinion, the jury was entitled to infer from the succession of price increases after 1985 . . . that B & W's below-cost pricing actually produced supra competitive prices, with the help of tacit collusion among the players. But even if that were not so clear, the jury would surely be entitled to infer that B & W's predatory plan, in which it invested millions of dollars for the purpose of achieving an admittedly anticompetitive result, carried a "reasonable possibility" of injuring competition.

Accordingly, I respectfully dissent.

NOTES AND QUESTIONS

1.   Of what relevance was the fact that the defendant engaged in price "discrimination," as the Robinson-Patman Act defines it? The requirement effectively means that bona fide predatory pricing intended to perpetuate an oligopoly could be defeated if the predator was simply careful to charge the same predatory price to everyone. The Robinson-Patman Act requires not only that the defendant charge two different prices but that the high- and low-priced goods be "of like grade and quality." *See* Chapter 9, § I[C], *infra*. That requirement often runs contrary to the logic of predatory pricing. For example, in *Brooke*, the plaintiff alleged that the defendant's generic and premium cigarettes were "of like grade and quality," thus making the requirement. However, the logic of predatory price discrimination is that the defendant *isolates* buyers of the low price good and prices predatorily only to them, thus making predation less expensive than if it had to charge the predatory price to everyone. If the two classes of cigarettes really were similar, then large numbers of customers buying premium cigarettes would switch to generics, thus undermining the predation scheme.

2.   Some circuit decisions have opined that the standard for predatory pricing under the Sherman and Robinson-Patman Acts should be the same. *See, e.g., A. A. Poultry Farms v. Rose Acre Farms*, 881 F.2d 1396 (7th Cir. 1989). In *Brooke*, the Supreme Court did not follow that course. Rather, it held that, while the concern of the Sherman Act is with predatory pricing that creates monopoly, the Robinson-Patman Act may be additionally concerned with predation that creates or perpetuates oligopoly.

A. A. Poultry dealt with a different distinction, however. Several lower courts had held that while Sherman Act predatory pricing requires a "dangerous probability of success" in creating a monopoly, Robinson-Patman predation could be proven under a much lighter standard, such as price cutting to below cost with specific intent to harm a rival. This standard originated in the Supreme Court's decision in *Utah Pie Co. v. Continental Baking Co.*, 386 U.S. 685 (1967), where the Court condemned differential price cuts by three national companies in competition with a local company that had the dominant market share. As the *Brooke* case points out, *Utah Pie* has been among the most castigated of Supreme Court antitrust opinions. Its critics have argued that the effect of *Utah Pie* was to prohibit large, but locally nondominant firms from engaging in aggressive price competition against rivals, even if the rivals were larger than the price cutter and there was absolutely no chance that the market would be monopolized. The *Brooke* Court purports to distinguish rather than overrule *Utah Pie*, but the argument is hollow. At the beginning of the complaint period, the plaintiff's (Utah Pie's) market share was 66.5%. The market shares of the defendants were: Carnation, 10.3%; Continental, 1.3%; and Pet, 16.4%. By the end of the complaint period, the plaintiff's share had dropped to 45.3%, but it was still making a profit. Pet's share had risen to 29.4%. The other two defendants were much smaller. 386 U.S. at 692 n.7. The evidence showed vigorous price competition and widely varying market shares over a period of three or four years. Further, the three defendants actively competed against each other as well as the plaintiff.

3. *Brooke* implicitly overrules several circuit decisions that permit evidence of intent as a substitute for structural evidence in Robinson-Patman Act predatory pricing claims. *See, e.g., Henry v. Chloride, Inc.*, 809 F.2d 1334 (8th Cir. 1987) (requiring below cost prices but recognizing a possible violation upon a showing of price cut plus specific intent to harm a rival). *Accord Double H Plastics v. Sonoco Prods.*, 732 F.2d 351 (3d Cir. 1984).

4. What is the significance of *Brooke*'s conclusion that supracompetitive pricing during the recoupment period "entails" a reduction in output? In the actual case, output during the alleged "recoupment" period was higher than during the period just before predation began. In that set of circumstances, the Court concluded, "output in the generic segment can only have been restricted in the sense that it expanded at a slower rate than it would have absent [the defendant's] intervention." The Court then concluded that this was a "counterfactual" proposition, "difficult to prove in the best of circumstances." 509 U.S. at 233.

What does this mean? That predatory pricing can never be proven in a case where overall market output during the claimed recoupment period is higher than it had been before the alleged predation began? In the "classic" predation story, the market is competitive with an output of, say, 100 units. Then the predator drops price dramatically, and output necessarily rises, perhaps to 125 units. After rivals have been destroyed or disciplined, the market then becomes a monopoly (Sherman Act) or "disciplined oligopoly" (Robinson-Patman Act) with an output of, say, 80 units. By contrast, a "recoupment" output of 110 units would indicate that the price cut was profitable because it produced more sales, not because it was predatory.

Consider a blanket rule that below-cost pricing is per se lawful if market output during the alleged recoupment period is higher than output during the period immediately before predation began. Does such a rule go too far? Suppose that the market was already an oligopoly before alleged predation began, as in *Brooke*, and that the purpose of the price cutting was simply to discipline a firm that was no longer adhering to the oligopoly.

5. In *Spirit Airlines, Inc. v. Northwest Airlines, Inc.*, 431 F.3d 917 (6th Cir. 2005), the Sixth Circuit found recoupment plausible and denied summary judgment on a predatory pricing claim. The court concluded that access to airport gate space could be a significant barrier to entry into the passenger airline market, particularly in light of tight control of airports by local governments, quoting an expert's report:

> While route schedules and pricing for the airline industry have been largely deregulated for over 20 years, many other aspects of the industry are still highly regulated. Perhaps the most important regulation comes from local governments, which own and manage the airports in their region and therefore control key bottlenecks to airport service: access to boarding gates and runways. Most local airport commissions allocate gates without a formal market mechanism. . . .

Id. at 928.

In addition, existing airlines in many cases obtained access to gate space at more favorable terms than new entrants could obtain access, giving an entry cost advantage to the incumbents. Later, the court observed that Northwest controlled 64 of the 86 gates (78%) available at the Detroit-Metro Airport, under long-term leases. In this particular instance, the plaintiff Spirit had to pay $100,000 to access a gate, as well as 25% higher landing fees than airlines with long-term leases. The court observed that such dominance was the product of the hub-and-spoke transfer system used by major carriers, which created dominant shares at many airport; plus local government policies that were not sufficiently attentive to competitive concerns. The court went on to quote a law review note:

> Economists studying networks have demonstrated that . . . adopting a hub-and-spoke structure is an effective means of entry deterrence. Part of this deterrence stems from the market power that hubbing creates on flights that originate or terminate at the hub. Since the hubbing airline typically controls a large proportion of the flights in and out of its hub airport, it can raise fares on those flights without fear of competitive entry. Furthermore, an airline's dominant presence at its hub may allow it to exert veto power over any plans to expand the airport's capacity, which further limits the possibility of competitive entry and its attendant check on market power. According to some scholars, having a large network also enables legacy airlines to price predatorily on routes served by entrants, thereby causing the entrant to expend cash reserves and exit the market while the incumbent experiences an economy of scope in the value of reputation for fierceness as a deterrent to other entrants in other markets or in the future.

Id. at 947.

The Sixth Circuit concluded that the proper benchmark for measuring recoupment in airline predatory pricing case is the profits that the defendant would have earned had the rival low-price carrier stayed in the market. The court noted that the plaintiff's expert had concluded that the defendant could very likely recoup its predation investment "within months" after the rival's exit from the market. The court concluded:

> The trier of fact could reasonably find that Northwest recouped any losses from its predatory pricing quickly after Spirit left these routes. Here, Spirit's expert proof shows that Northwest recovered its losses within months of Spirit's exit from the market. In addition, upon Spirit's exit, Northwest increased its prices on these routes to a multiple of seven from its prices during Spirit's presence. These facts could also lead a reasonable juror to conclude that a competitive injury occurred in this market, namely, air travelers' payment of higher prices by consumers for air travel on these routes.
>
> After Spirit's exit, Northwest also dropped flights notwithstanding the increased customer demand of "price-sensitive travelers" for those routes. The significant adverse competitive impact from Northwest's conduct could reasonably be found to be those Detroit consumers who were leisure travelers to Boston and Philadelphia and who lost a choice of airlines. These consumers suffered not only a reduction in the supply of flights to these cities, but to travel these routes, had to pay an almost seven-fold price increase. With the "very high" barriers to entry, the consumers for this route likely would not have any viable alternatives to Northwest airlines for the foreseeable future.

Id. at 950–51.

6. In one important post-*Brooke* decision, the Ninth Circuit held that structural characteristics of the Las Vegas market for retail gasoline necessitated summary judgment on a Sherman Act predatory pricing claim but not on a Robinson-Patman Act claim. *Rebel Oil Co. v. Atlantic Richfield Co (ARCO)*, 51 F.3d 1421, 1434 (9th Cir. 1995). The Sherman Act claim failed because it showed that two rivals of defendant ARCO, Texaco, and Southland could readily expand their output of gasoline, thus undermining any attempt by ARCO to effect a monopoly marketwide output reduction. *Id.* at 1441. But while the Sherman Act claim required the defendant to destroy or significantly disable these rivals, the Robinson-Patman oligopoly claim required the defendant to do no more than get the rivals to see that restraining their own output and adhering to an oligopoly price structure was in their own best interests. As the court explained:

> The economic forces at work in an oligopoly are very different than in a monopoly. A predator is able to establish and maintain supra competitive prices in an oligopoly by making it too painful for its existing competitors to challenge its prices, and thus, "disciplining" them. This distinction between oligopolistic and monopolistic practices is crucial to the survival of Rebel's price discrimination claim. Read in the most favorable light, Rebel's evidence tends to indicate that no new competition can enter the market to challenge ARCO, and that the existing competition, while it may be able to challenge ARCO, lacks the will to do so.

Id. at 1448.

As a general matter, convincing a smaller rival that it is in its own best interest to play the oligopoly game and thus make good profits is far easier than predating that rival into destruction. Indeed, after one or two brief "defections" from the oligopoly, followed by a period of predatory pricing-imposed losses, the maverick firm might learn that cutting price is not a profitable activity and adhere to the oligopoly.

7.   In *Wallace v. IBM Corp.*, 467 F.3d 1104 (7th Cir. 2006), the Seventh Circuit held that IBM's participation along with Red Hat, Novell, and others in the provision of free, open-source operating system software (Linux) did not constitute predatory pricing. Under the "General Public License" (GPL) distributed by the Free Software Foundation, participants were permitted to use the licensed operating system without charge, and were also free to introduce variations in the software as derivative works, provided that the derivative works themselves were also freely useable by others without charge. While the software itself must be free, commercial producers were free to charge for the media on which it was contained, and also for technical support. The plaintiff wanted to compete with his own operating system, which apparently was not yet on the market, and intended either to write his own program from scratch or else to employ a GPL version of Linux. However, he could not compete with the "free" price of the GPL software and claimed predatory pricing.

As the court observed in rejecting this claim, predatory pricing requires more than a predatory period of below-cost prices. It also requires rival exit from the market and then a recoupment period of monopoly prices. In this case, the GPL required by its terms that the royalty-free license arrangement exist forever. As a result, recoupment was not in prospect. The court also noted that Linux variations claimed only a small portion of the operating system software market, and that new proprietary operating systems were still entering.

In all events it seems very unlikely that IBM and others who program variations into Linux software are pricing "below cost." While the code itself must be made available to customers without charge, firms may charge whatever the market will bear for complementary services such as installation and maintenance. Whether the price of a package of complementary goods is predatory generally depends on the price of the bundle, not of each individual component in it. For example, one who typesets, prints, and binds *Moby Dick* and sells copies for $10 apiece is not engaged in predatory pricing of the text simply because the text itself is in the public domain. The only relevant price is the one for the finished book, and the printer is in fact being compensated for the costs of assembly, production, and distribution.

8.   The law of the European Union does not require "recoupment" when the defendant's prices are below average variable cost or an equivalent measure. *See* Case C-333/94P, *Tetra Pak Int'l SA v. Comm'n*, 1996 E.C.R. I-5951; Case T-340/03, *France T, l, com v. Commission* (Jan. 30, 2007) (First Instance). The European tribunals reason that prices below variable costs are "irrational," except for their tendency to eliminate competition. Because the only plausible purpose for such pricing is anticompetitive, the conduct can be condemned without a showing that it would be profitable to the defendant.

In fact, a strict recoupment requirement places severe burdens on a plaintiff. Estimating the costs of predation requires a prediction about (a) how deep the price cuts must be; (b) how long it will take for the cuts to discipline rivals; and (c) how many units will have to be sold at the predatory price. Then, recoupment requires an estimate of how profitable a future period of monopoly prices will be before new entry erodes them. For a critique of the *Brooke* requirement and an argument that United States antitrust law would be better off if it simply required monopoly power in a well-defined market protected by high entry barriers, and rivals that have only limited ability to expand output, see 3A PHILLIP E. AREEDA & HERBERT HOVENKAMP, ANTITRUST LAW ¶¶ 726d5, 728 (3d ed. 2008).

NOTE: WHEN IS PREDATORY PRICING RATIONAL?

Not all markets are conducive to predatory pricing. Consider some of the pitfalls. First of all, it is illegal and can yield substantial damages, and there is at least some risk that the predator will be caught: no one is more likely to file an antitrust lawsuit than a competitor who has been driven out of business by prices that it has been unable to meet.

But legality aside, there are substantial economic difficulties facing any predator. Consider a manufacturer of swidgets, who is in competition with an equally efficient rival. The current (competitive) price of swidgets is $1.00. Suppose the manufacturer decides to destroy its competitor by selling swidgets at 80 cents. First of all, the manufacturer will have to increase its output substantially and many of the victim's customers will flock to the predator. The predator will have to have sufficient output to satisfy all of them. Worse yet, if the market has an average elasticity of demand, when the price of swidgets goes down by 20%, the demand for swidgets will increase by 20% or 25%. In other words, the predator will have to sell additional swidgets (at 20 cents loss per swidget) not only to customers stolen from the victim, but also to new customers who enter the market at the lower price. In order to do all of this, the predator may have to build a large amount of plant capacity that it does not intend to use permanently — for later, when the rival has been dispatched, the predator intends to charge a monopoly price (say, $1.20), and then demand for swidgets will drop. (The decrease in demand must, of course, be discounted by the amount that capacity in the market will be reduced by the victim's exit.) The predator can attempt to minimize its losses by targeting its below-cost pricing to current customers of its rivals, as Standard Oil did by creating bogus shell companies that charged predatory prices only to customers of selected competing oil companies. *See* Christopher R. Leslie, *Revisiting the Revisionist History of Standard Oil*, 85 S. CAL. L. REV. 573 (2012).

What is the purpose of all this? The predator intends to incur all these losses now because it believes that future gains from monopoly pricing will more than offset the losses. First of all, we must consider the time-value of money. The predator sustains the losses immediately; the gains from expected monopoly pricing may be a year or even several years away. These dollars must be discounted to their present value. Secondly, what will happen when the predator eliminates its rival and raises the price to its monopolistic level? The supra competitive profits will attract new entrants into the market and the predator will have to lower its price all over again.

Furthermore, the predator must consider what will become of the victim's plant. When a firm goes into bankruptcy, it does not necessarily cease production. Sometimes it can reorganize; other times it can sell its plant and equipment to an existing company or a new entrant into the market. These possibilities are generally out of the predator's control. If the victim's plant remains in production, the entire predation scheme will be frustrated.

It seems clear that before predatory pricing can be expected to succeed, certain prerequisites must be met. For example, barriers to entry in the market must be high enough that the predator can expect a relatively stable period of monopoly returns after the predation has done its work.

Even more importantly, the predator must have a relatively large market share. Consider a market with 10 firms, each with a 10% market share. Suppose that firm *A* tries to predate against firm *D*. When *A* lowers its price, it will attract customers not only from *D*, but from all other competitors as well, and these competitors control 90% of the market. If *A* doubles its own output (selling every unit at a loss), the result will be to deprive each competitor of a little over 10% of its own sales — hardly enough to drive most firms out of business. And this does not even include the new customers who will enter the market at *A*'s predatory price! Furthermore, suppose that *A* actually succeeded in driving *D* out of business. The concentration in the market would decrease from 10 firms to 9, and presumably the remaining 9 firms would share the defunct firm's customers. In that case, *A*'s market share would rise from 10% to 11%. It would hardly be a monopolist.

If *A* has 90% of the market, however, while a single rival has 10%, then the picture is much different. Now a 10% output increase by *A* (ignoring customers who enter the market at the predatory price) will almost wipe out firm *B*. In short, before predatory pricing is likely to succeed, the market must be relatively concentrated and conducive to monopolization; secondly, the putative predator must have a relatively large market share in relation to its intended victim. For further discussion of the market structures conducive to predatory pricing, see Paul Joskow & Alvin Klevorick, *A Framework for Analyzing Predatory Pricing Policy*, 89 Yale L.J. 213 (1979).

Some commentators have gone so far as to argue that predatory pricing is *never* rational. *See* Frank H. Easterbrook, *Predatory Strategies and Counterstrategies*, 48 U. Chi. L. Rev. 263 (1981); Robert H. Bork, The Antitrust Paradox: A Policy at War with Itself 148–156 (1978). Others are less sure. They note, for example, that if there are legal or economic constraints on new entry into a market, or if the victim has substantially higher capital costs than the predator, predatory pricing might be plausible. Furthermore, predatory pricing might have high strategic values: it might be used, at relatively lower cost, merely to "discipline" rivals rather than drive them out of business. By so punishing one rival in one market, a predator could also "send a message" to other rivals in other markets. *See* 3A Phillip E. Areeda & Herbert Hovenkamp, Antitrust Law § 727 (3d ed. 2008). Finally, information about costs in an industry is generally more readily available to incumbents than it is to potential new entrants. If a potential entrant has imperfect information about an incumbent's true costs, the challenger might view a predatory price as reflecting lower (but uncertain) costs and conclude that entry would be risky and unprofitable. *See* STEVEN C. SALOP, STRATEGY, PREDATION, AND ANTITRUST ANALYSIS 19–22 (1981). By engaging in predatory pricing, a monopolist can acquire a reputation for aggression that may deter entry if the monopolist successfully communicates that any entry will be greeted with another round of below-cost pricing. *See* Christopher R. Leslie, *Rationality Analysis in Antitrust*, 158 U. PA. L. REV. 261 (2010).

The *Brooke* decision, *supra*, is not the first instance where the Supreme Court insisted that structural indicators be evaluated carefully in cases claiming predatory pricing. In *Cargill, Inc. v. Monfort of Colo., Inc.*, 479 U.S. 104, 119 n.15 (1986), the plaintiff charged that a merger might facilitate predatory pricing, the Supreme Court suggested that predation was unlikely, given that the defendant's share of market output was only 21% and its share of market capacity only 28.4%. Further, the defendant operated at nearly full capacity, thus making predation more expensive, since it would have to build additional plant capacity in order to enlarge output during the predatory period. In both *Cargill* and *Matsushita Elec. Indus. Co. v. Zenith Radio Corp.*, 475 U.S. 574 (1986), the Court noted that "without barriers to entry it would presumably be impossible to maintain supra competitive prices for an extended time." *Matsushita*, 475 U.S. at 591–592 n.15; *Cargill, id.* The *Cargill* court also noted:

> In evaluating entry barriers in the context of a predatory pricing claim, . . . a court should focus on whether significant entry barriers would exist *after* the merged firm had eliminated some of its rivals, because at that point the remaining firms would begin to charge supra competitive prices, and the barriers that existed during competitive conditions might well prove insignificant. In this case, for example, although costs of entry into the current competitive market may be high, if Excel [the defendant] and others in fact succeeded in driving competitors out of the market, the facilities of the bankrupt competitors would then be available, and the record shows, without apparent contradiction, that shut-down plants could be producing efficiently in a matter of months and that equipment and a labor force could readily be obtained.

Id. The *Cargill* case is reprinted in Chapter 3, *supra*.

Because most courts deal with predatory pricing as an attempt to monopolize, they examine structural issues under the rubric of "dangerous probability of success" in creating a monopoly, or dominant firm. For example, see *International Distrib. Centers v. Walsh Trucking Co.*, 812 F.2d 786, 788 (2d Cir. 1987), which rejected the plaintiff's argument that "there can be a dangerous probability that a market will be monopolized where one firm in the market has the specific intent to drive a competitor from the market and has engaged in arguably tortious activity to achieve that objective but does not have significant market power and will not possess such power even if the competitor is driven out of business." The court found entry into the market (shipping of clothing on hangers in trucks) to be extremely easy and noted that new shippers had entered the business even during the alleged predation period. It concluded that it "need not inquire" whether the defendant's prices were below its "reasonably anticipated marginal costs." See also *Shoppin' Bag of Pueblo v. Dillon Cos.*, 783 F.2d 159 (10th Cir. 1986), approving a jury verdict for the defendant where its market share was less than 38%.

The Seventh Circuit has concluded that unlawful predatory pricing under the Sherman Act is "highly unlikely unless the defendant already has monopoly power." *American Acad. Suppliers v. Beckley-Cardy*, 922 F.2d 1317, 1319 (7th Cir. 1991) (summary judgment for defendant). Likewise, the Fourth Circuit holds:

> (1) claims of less than 30% market shares should presumptively be rejected;

> (2) claims involving between 30% and 50% shares should usually be rejected, except when conduct is very likely to achieve monopoly or when conduct is invidious, but not so much so as to make the defendant per se liable; (3) claims involving greater than 50% share should be treated as attempts at monopolization when the other elements for attempted monopolization are also satisfied.

M&M Med. Supplies & Serv. v. Pleasant Valley Hosp., 981 F.2d 160, 168 (4th Cir. 1992) (en banc).

PROBLEM 6.7

For many years, Autosound, Inc. has manufactured a highly successful radio sound system that included only an AM/FM receiver. It manufactures about 80% of all such systems. Its only competitor is Car Stereo, Inc., which has the remaining 20%. In recent years, the market for car stereo systems having only a radio has declined substantially, for most purchasers prefer a system containing a radio integrated with a cassette tape or even CD player.

Autosound develops a new, integrated AM/FM-cassette-CD system and decides to exit from the market for radio-only car stereos. However, at the time it makes this decision it is stuck with very large inventories of the old system. Autosound decides that these inventories must be cleared out within one year, so it drops the price of the old system dramatically — even lower than the direct cost of parts plus assembly labor. Car Stereo's sales of its competing product plummet, and it sues Autosound, charging predatory pricing. Result? *See Olympia Equip. Leasing Co. v. Western Union Tel. Co.*, 797 F.2d 370 (7th Cir. 1986).

PROBLEM 6.8

For many years, AAA Towing has had an exclusive contract with the City of Metropolis to provide towing services for stalled and illegally parked vehicles. Each year this towing franchise is put up for competitive bidding, but no one bids against AAA Towing. Two years ago, AAA Towing won with a bid of $60 per tow.

Last year, a newcomer, Rainbow Towing, decided to bid against AAA towing, believing it could do the job profitably for much less. Rainbow bid $52 per tow. But when the bids were opened AAA Towing had bid $40, and it retained the franchise. The following year no one bid against AAA, and its bid was $65.

Rainbow believes that the low bid in the single year in which AAA faced competition was predatory. It files suit, arguing that AAA engaged in predatory pricing in order to retain its franchise monopoly. What economic issues should be investigated? Is it significant that: (1) AAA's franchise with Metropolis is exclusive? *See National Reporting Co. v. Alderson Reporting Co.*, 763 F.2d 1020 (8th Cir. 1985); (2) AAA dropped its bid sharply when there was competition, but raised it again when there was none? *See Instructional Sys. Dev. v. Aetna Cas.*, 817 F.2d 639 (10th Cir. 1987).

NOTE: PREDATORY PRICING AND THE ROBINSON-PATMAN ACT

The Robinson-Patman Act, 15 U.S.C. § 13, makes it illegal for someone to sell the same product at two different prices where the effect is to injure "competition" as the statute defines it. The Robinson-Patman Act is commonly called a "price discrimination" statute. That term is a misnomer. Price discrimination occurs when two different sales are made at two different rates of return — that is, when the ratio of price to marginal cost is different in the two sales. The Robinson-Patman Act tags as "discriminatory," however, any two sales made at two different prices. For a fuller discussion of the difference, see Herbert Hovenkamp, Federal Antitrust POLICY, ch. 14 (4th ed. 2011); E. THOMAS SULLIVAN & JEFFREY HARRISON, UNDERSTANDING ANTITRUST AND ITS ECONOMIC IMPLICATIONS, ch. 8 (5th ed. 2007).

The offense that the framers of the Robinson-Patman Act had in mind was "geographic price-cutting," a particular form of predatory pricing. The framers believed that a large and powerful seller could "finance" predatory pricing by engaging in price discrimination. Their theory went like this: suppose that *A* and *B* are competitors in a certain market. *B* operates in only this market, but *A* is large and operates in other markets as well, and has monopoly power in some of these markets. *A* attempts to drive *B* out of business so that *A* can also acquire a monopoly in the market shared with *B*. *A* does this by pricing its output below cost in *B*'s market. Meanwhile, however, *A* raises its price in other markets, where it has monopoly power, and uses these increased revenues to pay for the predatory pricing in the market shared with *B*.

Generally speaking, *A*'s scheme is implausible. First of all, if *A* is a rational businessperson and there are no legal or physical restraints on price discrimination, *A* is already selling its output in each market at the profit-maximizing price. *A* cannot simply raise its price in some markets in order to subsidize predatory pricing in a different market. If *A* raised its price in its monopoly markets to more than the profit-maximizing level, it would produce less, not more, net revenue.

One answer to the above objection, of course, is that the Robinson-Patman Act *is* a law against selling the same product in two different markets at two different prices. As a result, *A* may not be selling its output in each market at the profit-maximizing price for that market. Because of the Robinson-Patman Act, *A* may be selling at its profit-maximizing price for all markets taken together, but if it could segregate the markets and avoid the law it could obtain higher profits by selling at higher prices in some of them. For example, suppose that A sells in three different markets, Detroit, Atlanta, and Salt Lake City. It has monopoly power in Detroit and Atlanta but faces competition in Salt Lake City. The profit-maximizing monopoly price in Detroit and Atlanta, considered by themselves, would be $1.00. Because of competition, however, A's profit-maximizing price in Salt Lake City is 90 cents. If A prices at more than 90 cents in Salt Lake City, most of A's customers there will turn to A's rivals.

If A is legally prohibited from selling its output at different prices in different markets, A must choose either to sell in all three markets at 90 cents, in all three markets at $1.00, or in all three markets at some price between 90 cents and $1.00. Under some circumstances it might be profit-maximizing to sell in all three markets at 90 cents, particularly if Salt Lake City (the competitive market) were much larger than the two monopoly markets.

Suppose that A decided that its profit-maximizing price in the three markets taken together is 90 cents, and it has been selling at that price. Now A decides to drive B, its competitor in Salt Lake City, out of business by lowering its price there to 80 cents. Once B has been dispatched, A can raise its price in all three markets. Absent any legal sanction, A might in fact be able to price its output in Detroit and Atlanta at $1.00 and obtain more revenue because the profit-maximizing price in each of those markets considered alone is $1.00. The Robinson-Patman Act, however, will require A to reduce its price to 80 cents in all three markets.

In short, the statute *can* make predatory pricing more expensive for a seller who operates in many markets but wants to predate only in one. It will have to lower its price in all markets simultaneously. Furthermore, predatory pricing is relatively easy to conceal. One can identify it today only by looking at complex cost figures that may be in the exclusive control of the predator. Under the prevailing judicial tests, predatory pricing is a function either of the alleged predator's marginal costs, or else of its average variable costs. Both are likely to be information generally unavailable to competitors. The former is additionally very difficult to determine even if cost information is made available. See the discussion of the Areeda-Turner test for predatory pricing, *infra*.

In most cases, however, price differences are not so easy to conceal, although sometimes they can be kept secret. *See O. Hommel Co. v. Ferro Corp.*, 659 F.2d 340 (3d Cir. 1981).

Thus the Robinson-Patman Act can sometimes make price predation by certain sellers (particularly those that operate in more markets than their victims) much more expensive. The statute might require such a predator to lower its prices in all markets, not merely the predated market. By contrast, if the predator decides to cut prices only in the predated market, the activity will be easier to discover and condemn.

However, the effect of a law against differential pricing in different geographic markets is not as simple as the above illustration suggests. To be sure, the primary-line application of the Robinson-Patman Act may make predatory pricing more expensive. Ironically, however, the statute makes *competitive* pricing in Salt Lake City in the above illustration more expensive too, for exactly the same reason.

Suppose, for example, that *A* has had a monopoly in all three markets for some time and has enjoyed supra competitive profits from making sales in all three markets at $1.00 each. Now *B* enters Salt Lake City and begins price-cutting to a competitive price of 90 cents. The Robinson-Patman Act may put *A* to the difficult choice of dropping its price to 90 cents in *all three markets* in order to preserve its position in Salt Lake City, or else simply closing its outlets in Salt Lake City, effectively conceding a monopoly to *B*. The latter option may indeed be more attractive, particularly if the Salt Lake City market is relatively small. In short, a statute prohibiting geographic price differences is just as likely to prohibit competitive pricing as it is to prohibit predatory pricing. Which of the two it does more often depends on which of the two (competitive or predatory pricing) occurs more often. Today, courts are inclined to think that predatory pricing is extraordinarily difficult to accomplish and that it occurs only infrequently. If that is true, it is likely that the Robinson-Patman Act condemns more instances of competitive pricing than of predatory pricing.

One solution to this dilemma is to interpret the Robinson-Patman Act in such a way as to condemn differential pricing when it is predatory, but tolerate it when it is competitive. How does one tell whether a particular instance of differential pricing is competitive or predatory? In general, one must determine if the sales in the market alleged to be predatory are made below cost and with the reasonable expectation that they will dispatch competitors from the market or discipline them in order to permit the predator to price monopolistically later.

This determination is identical with the determination that courts make today in cases alleging predatory pricing under Section 2 of the Sherman Act. The reason for this similarity of analysis seems clear: the presence or absence of differential pricing or price discrimination in a different geographic market is *absolutely irrelevant* to the question whether a seller is engaging in predatory pricing in a particular market. Although a law against differential pricing makes both predation and intense competition in a single market more expensive for a firm that sells the same product in other markets as well, the presence of differential pricing is of absolutely no help to a court in distinguishing whether the pricing in the low-priced market is predatory or competitive. In order to determine if pricing in the low-priced market is predatory, the court must analyze the relationship between the defendant's prices and its costs in that market. Pricing in the low-priced market is predatory if the only reasonable explanation for the pricing is that the defendant is selling at below cost today in order to drive competitors from the market so that it can price monopolistically tomorrow.

Lower courts have treated predatory pricing claims brought under the Robinson-Patman Act in virtually the same way that predatory pricing is analyzed as an attempt to monopolize under Section 2 of the Sherman Act. *See, e.g., A. A. Poultry Farms v. Rose Acre Farms*, 881 F.2d 1396 (7th Cir. 1989) (applying the same test under both statutes). *Brooke Group Ltd. v. Brown & Williamson Tobacco Corp.*, reprinted *supra*, illustrates both the similarities and the differences between predatory pricing analysis under the Sherman Act and the Robinson-Patman Act.

[2] Identifying the Predatory Price

The *Brooke* decision makes clear that predatory pricing claims can be sustained only under narrowly defined structural conditions that involve either monopoly or oligopoly, high entry barriers, and thus the prospect of a sustained "recoupment" period following the predatory campaign. But the *offense* of predatory pricing consists of the defendant's intentional selection of a particular price for its value in excluding, disciplining, or destroying competition. Identifying that price has been the subject of considerable judicial dispute. The *Brooke* decision provided a little guidance by its dicta suggesting that the defendant's price must be "below an appropriate measure of its rival's costs," and then elaborating:

> [W]e have rejected elsewhere the notion that above-cost prices that are below general market levels or the costs of a firm's competitors inflict injury to competition cognizable under the antitrust laws. See *Atlantic Richfield Co. v. USA Petroleum Co.*, 495 U.S. 328, 340 (1990). "Low prices benefit consumers regardless of how those prices are set, and so long as they are above predatory levels, they do not threaten competition. . . . We have adhered to this principle regardless of the type of antitrust claim involved." *Ibid.* As a general rule, the exclusionary effect of prices above a relevant measure of cost either reflects the lower cost structure of the alleged predator, and so represents competition on the merits, or is beyond the practical ability of a judicial tribunal to control without courting intolerable risks of chilling legitimate price-cutting.

One of the major doctrinal developments in antitrust has been the proposal of the Areeda-Turner test for predatory pricing and its consideration by various federal circuit courts. The Supreme Court has not yet approved the test, and the Circuit courts, while generally applying it, disagree about many details.

The orthodox statement of the Areeda-Turner test is as follows:

(1) With respect to a monopolist's general (non-discriminatory) pricing in the market in which he has monopoly power:

(A) A short-run profit-maximizing . . . price is non-predatory. . . .

(B) A price at or above full cost is non-predatory. . . .

(C) A price at or above reasonably anticipated short-run marginal cost is non-predatory. . . .

(D) Unless at or above full cost, a price below reasonably anticipated short-run marginal cost is predatory, and the monopolist may not defend on the grounds that his price was "promotional" or merely met an equally low price of a competitor.

(2) Recognizing that marginal cost data are often unavailable, we conclude that:

(A) A price at or above reasonably anticipated average variable cost should be presumed lawful.

(B) A price below reasonably anticipated average variable cost should be conclusively presumed unlawful.

3A P. AREEDA & H. HOVENKAMP, ANTITRUST LAW ¶¶ 724c, 735, 739–740 (3d ed. 2008).

Areeda and Turner reasoned this way: over the long run no firm will stay in business unless it can recover its total costs. Total costs include *fixed* costs (such as plant, property taxes, and most kinds of equipment), which do not vary with output; and *variable* costs (such as most labor costs, raw materials, and utilities) which do vary with output. In order to recover its total costs, a firm must price each unit of its output at average total cost, or "average cost." Average cost is total cost divided by the number of units of output.

Although we would expect a profit-seeking firm to price its output at or above average cost over the long run, there are occasions when firms must sell their output at less than average cost. Sometimes they need money quickly; sometimes they are stuck with excess inventory that may spoil or become obsolete. In short, a price below average total cost can be profit-maximizing (or loss-minimizing) in the short run. For that reason, a rule that condemned pricing at below average total cost would make competitive behavior illegal, and might cause extreme waste of valuable resources. Suppose, for example, that there were a legal rule that forbade a farmer from selling ripe peaches, or a car dealer from selling year-end models, at a reduced price merely because the lower price would be less than the average total cost of producing the product.

But what about pricing at below short-run marginal cost? Short-run marginal cost is the cost incurred by a seller in producing and selling one additional unit of output. Because fixed costs are costs that do not vary with changes in output, short-run marginal cost is a function of variable costs alone. To sell a unit at less than short-run marginal cost is to obtain less money for it than the cost of producing it or — if it is already produced — of bringing it to market. In short, a sale at less than short-run marginal cost produces losses in *both* the short run and the long run. Areeda and Turner conclude that a price below short-run marginal cost is never reasonable unless it can be explained only as an attempt to drive rivals out of business so that the seller can charge a higher (monopoly) price later.

As a result, Areeda and Turner label a price below short-run marginal cost as "predatory." They observe, however, that marginal cost is an artificial concept thrown about largely by economists. Marginal cost measures an incremental change in producer output, but this amount itself varies at differing rates of output. Few businesses have comprehensive knowledge of marginal costs at any particular level of output, and it is virtually impossible to establish in litigation. The same thing is not true of average variable cost, however. Once we have identified certain costs — such as labor and raw materials — as "variable" over a certain period of time, then we can compute average variable cost simply by dividing the sum of those costs by the output during the same time period. Accountants can generally give testimony about a firm's average variable costs, but not about its marginal costs. Areeda and Turner therefore propose using average variable cost as a surrogate for short-run marginal cost. Thus they conclude that a price reasonably anticipated to be above average variable cost should be considered lawful, while a price below reasonably anticipated average variable cost should be conclusively presumed unlawful.

Figure 2

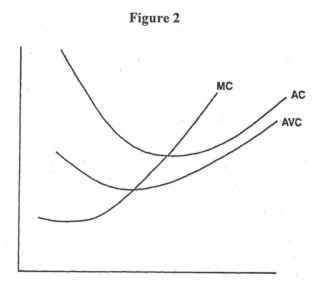

Figure 2 illustrates what is perhaps the greatest problem of the Areeda-Turner average variable cost test. At high levels of output (and predatory pricing generally occurs at high levels of output), marginal cost and average variable cost tend to diverge, with marginal cost higher than average variable cost. The result is that the Areeda-Turner test may excuse many instances of actual price predation. In fact, if a predator knows that its jurisdiction has adopted the Areeda-Turner test, it can compute its average variable costs and add to the sales price, thereby engaging in legal predatory pricing — because such pricing at high levels of output would probably be lower than the seller's short-run marginal costs. *See* HERBERT HOV-ENKAMP, FEDERAL ANTITRUST POLICY § 8.3a (4th ed. 2011). For this reason, one commentator has described the Areeda-Turner rule as a "defendant's paradise." *See* Oliver E. Williamson, *Predatory Pricing: A Strategic and Welfare Analysis*, 87 YALE L.J. 284, 305 (1977). Judge Richard A. Posner describes the Areeda-Turner test for predatory pricing as "toothless." *See* RICHARD POSNER, ANTITRUST LAW 219 (2d ed. 2001).

Some courts, such as the Ninth Circuit in the *Inglis* case, have responded to this difficulty in the Areeda-Turner test by accepting the basic Areeda-Turner cost paradigm but minimizing the use to which they put it. In *Inglis*, for example, the Ninth Circuit changed the conclusive presumptions of the Areeda-Turner test into rebuttable presumptions that invited consideration, at least in part, of the defendant's subjective intent. To be sure, such a modification comes with its own difficulties; most importantly, evaluation of subjective intent — the so-called smoking gun — is precisely the kind of thing that Areeda and Turner want to avoid. Their test is designed to enable a court to identify price predation by looking purely at pricing behavior. On the other hand, the Areeda-Turner test runs afoul of the criticism that although it may measure something more accurately than the older subjective tests, the thing that it measures is not really predatory pricing.

In spite of conceptual problems, no one has come up with a better test than average variable cost, and it has its supporters even among economists. *See, e.g.,* William Baumol, *Predation and the Logic of the Average Variable Cost Test*, 39 J.L. & ECON. 49, 72 (1996) (average variable cost "is really the pertinent criterion, and not merely an inferior proxy for marginal cost").

NOTES AND QUESTIONS

1. The Areeda-Turner test is a very difficult one for plaintiffs to meet and few have been successful under its orthodox formulation. Among the few victories — and both in courts that have very considerably modified the Areeda-Turner formulation — are *U.S. Philips Corp. v. Windmere Corp.*, 861 F.2d 695 (Fed. Cir. 1988); *D&S Redi-Mix v. Sierra Redi-Mix & Contr'g Co.*, 692 F.2d 1245 (9th Cir. 1982).

Many circuits have accepted the Areeda-Turner test for predatory pricing without substantial qualification. For example, *Northeastern Tel. Co. v. AT&T*, 651 F.2d 76, 88 (2d Cir. 1981): "We agree with Areeda and Turner that in the general case at least, the relationship between a firm's prices and its marginal costs provides the best single determinant of predatory pricing." *National Ass'n of Regulatory Util. Comm'rs v. Federal Commun. Comm'n*, 525 F.2d 630, 638 n.34 (D.C. Cir. 1976); *International Air Indus. v. American Excelsior Co.*, 517 F.2d 714, 724 (5th Cir. 1975).

2. One of the disappointments of the Areeda-Turner test is the difficulty that courts have had in computing average variable cost. The premise of the test is that in most cases, marginal cost is the correct measure of predation, but that average variable cost is a useful surrogate because it is usually close enough and it is much easier to compute. Theoretically, variable costs change with changes in output over a defined time period, while fixed costs do not. But the time period must be defined, and excess capacity does quirky things with cost measurement. For example, if a baker's oven is designed to hold 100 loaves of bread, it may cost no more in fuel to bake 100 loaves than to bake 50. As a result, when increasing from 50 to 100 loaves, the baker encounters no fuel cost increase, and this would suggest that fuel is a fixed cost. However, as soon as the baker goes to 101 loaves it will have to run the oven twice (or get a second oven), and this suggests that fuel and perhaps even the oven are variable costs. In *Inglis, supra*, the Ninth Circuit approached the problem this way:

> It is true, of course, that the fixed production costs of a firm are those costs that do not vary with output and that would remain even if the firm discontinued production. Likewise, variable costs, as the term suggests, are those costs that do vary with output and that the firm is likely to be most concerned with when contemplating a change in price and consequent changes in output. However, to determine whether particular costs are variable, one must evaluate the relationship of the prospective change in output to that level of output which presently exists. For example, some production decisions of great magnitude may entail the substantial retirement or expansion, as the case may be, of productive capacity, in which case costs typically considered fixed become variable. At the other extreme,

small expansions of output may entail no change in costs, such as labor or transportation, that are considered typically variable.

In predatory pricing cases the relevant changes in output will be those attributable to the price reduction alleged to be predatory. The reduction of price in such a case no doubt will have resulted in an expansion of output to "clear the market," *i.e.*, to satisfy the increased demand generated by the price reduction. It is those costs that change as a result of the expanded output that appropriately are considered to be variable. Thus, the first step in determining average variable cost in a predatory pricing case will generally be to compare the costs of production before and after the price reduction. The variable costs would then be those expenses that increased as a result of the output expansion attributable to the price reduction. If the new price is below the average of these costs per unit of output there is good reason, as we have said, to infer that the price reduction was predatory. . . .

It follows that the determination of which costs are variable and which fixed will vary with the facts of each case. Moreover, cost categories are solely for the purpose of providing aid in answering the ultimate question: Did the justification for the defendant's price depend upon its anticipated destructive effect on competition or was the price justified as a reasonably calculated means of maximizing profits, minimizing losses, or achieving some other legitimate end? Accordingly, we hold that the determination of fixed and variable costs is a matter for the jury under appropriate instructions.

By contrast, the Areeda-Turner formulation would treat the difference between fixed and variable costs much more categorically, and make it a question of law. Specifically, it would include in fixed costs only (1) capital costs, which include interest on debt and the opportunity cost of equity capital attributable to investment in land, plant, and equipment; (2) property and other taxes unaffected by output; and (3) depreciation on plant. With respect to equipment, the Areeda-Turner formulation would consider "use" depreciation — such as that of a truck that has a generally known life expectancy of, say, 200,000 miles — a variable cost as well. If a piece of equipment does not depreciate with use, its costs would be considered fixed. *See* 3A PHILLIP AREEDA & HERBERT HOVENKAMP, ANTITRUST LAW ¶ 740d (3d ed. 2008).

3. *"Incremental" vs. "fully allocated" costs in predatory pricing cases.* An average cost figure is "fully allocated" when it includes all costs that are encountered in a single firm or plant, however loosely connected to the product under analysis. Consider, for example, a very small store that sells only two items, gasoline and milk. The milk requires a dairy refrigerator and the gasoline requires a tank. Suppose that the current fixed costs of each is $10 a month, that the store sells 100 gallons of each product monthly, that it buys each product for $1 per gallon, and that these are its only costs. The firm then "breaks even" by charging $1.10 for each unit of each product. If the store substitutes an improved refrigerator whose fixed costs are $20 per month, with no change in sales, the fully allocated cost (total cost of all inputs divided by all units sold of both products) is now $1.15 per month. The $1.10

price for gasoline now appears to be "below cost."

But this fully allocated cost measure ignores the process by which any firm makes investment decisions. The firm contemplating a new refrigerator asks whether the *incremental* cost of the new equipment will be offset by the anticipated incremental revenue that the new equipment will produce. The new dairy refrigerator may be needed to replace an ailing refrigerator; or perhaps the firm contemplates higher milk volume. A legal rule attributing part of the refrigerator cost to gasoline could perversely force the perfectly competitive firm to maintain artificially high gasoline prices.

Suppose that the store in the previous illustration added a small display case containing cigars and was later accused of predation on that product. The display case is set on empty space that was not previously used. A fully allocated average total cost test would include not only the case itself but also a pro rata share of the property taxes, mortgage payment, payment for the gasoline tanks, and refrigerator. But these costs were already being paid by sales of other products and do not increase simply because the store adds cigars to previously unused space. When the store manager considers the profitability of adding cigars, she does not compute a pro rata share of these costs; rather, she considers whether the anticipated additional ("incremental") revenue that the cigars promise to bring in will be sufficient to cover the incremental costs.

Courts taking fixed costs into account using an average total cost test or a long-run incremental cost test have generally concluded that the proper measure of fixed costs is not fully allocated costs, but rather "incremental" costs. The relevant question is how much *additional* fixed cost does the firm encounter in the sale or expansion of sales of the particular product deemed to be predatory. *See, e.g., MCI Communic. Corp. v. AT&T*, 708 F.2d 1081, 1118 (7th Cir. 1983) ("average total cost" for predatory pricing must refer to "average incremental cost"; fully allocated cost measure arbitrary and incorrect); *Southern Pacific Commun. Co. v. AT&T*, 556 F. Supp. 825, 922 (D.D.C. 1982), *aff'd*, 740 F.2d 980, 1004 (D.C. Cir. 1984) ("unlike the concept of average total cost, which has sound economic underpinnings when defined as average incremental cost, the allocation methods used to compute fully distributed cost are inherently arbitrary and have no economic basis"); *William Inglis & Sons Baking Co. v. Continental Baking Co.*, 942 F.2d 1332, 1336 & n.6 (9th Cir. 1991) (may consider only costs "uniquely incurred" in the addition of a new product or output increase in the allegedly predated product).

Consider this example: a major airline has a plane with 100 seats and a flight costs $10,000, or $100 per seat. It sells 60 "full coach" class seats for $200 each, but also sells 40 "supersaver" tickets at $70 each. A competitor in the business of offering discount charter flights sues the airline, claiming predatory pricing in the supersaver seats. What result? *See International Travel Arrangers v. Northwest Airlines*, 991 F.2d 1389, 1396 (8th Cir. 1993).

PROBLEM 6.9

Fuel for ovens is ordinarily considered a variable cost. Suppose that Breadco has ovens capable of producing 10,000 loaves of bread per day, but they are currently producing only 6,000. At that rate of output, fuel costs $120, or 2 cents per loaf. Breadco then has the opportunity to supply Super Foods, a large supermarket, with 4,000 loaves daily, provided the price is right, and it wins the bid with a price significantly lower than the amount it charges other customers of its bread. Breadco is charged with predatory pricing by a competing bidder for the Super Foods contract.

It takes exactly the same amount of fuel to run a full oven as one that is only 60% full. How should fuel costs be attributed to the sales to Super Foods? Are the costs zero, given that Breadco can increase output from 6,000 to 10,000 loaves without using additional fuel? Or must fuel costs be averaged over the entire output, yielding average variable costs of 1.2 cents per loaf? *See Marsann Co. v. Brammall*, 788 F.2d 611 (9th Cir. 1986), especially at 614 n.2.

PROBLEM 6.10

Gourmet grocery sells 750 items in its medium-sized store. Two or three of them, such as milk and bread, are heavily promoted and used to get shoppers inside the door, where they presumably will purchase more. Frequently, the promotional prices, widely advertised in the newspapers, are lower than average variable cost. Mom'n'Pop Grocery down the street depends heavily on milk and bread sales for its profits, and it charges predatory pricing on those two items. Gourmet defends by saying that the relevant issue is not whether Gourmet has sold milk and bread at a price lower than AVC; rather, the question is whether Gourmet's entire product line in the aggregate is sold at prices below AVC. Who is correct? *See Lomar Wholesale Grocery, Inc. v. Dieter's Gourmet Foods, Inc.*, 824 F.2d 582 (8th Cir. 1987).

Alternatively, Northwest Airlines offers a wide variety of fares on its scheduled flights. The lowest, or "supersaver," fares are substantially below average variable cost. A small regional airline charges predation on those fares. Northwest argues that the relevant question is not whether the "supersaver" fares are lower than AVC, but whether each scheduled flight as a whole produces revenues in excess of AVC. Who is correct? *See International Travel Arrangers v. NWA (Northwest Airlines)*, 991 F.2d 1389 (8th Cir. 1993).

[3] Predatory Buying

WEYERHAEUSER CO. v. ROSS-SIMMONS HARDWOOD LUMBER CO., INC.
549 U.S. 312 (2007)

JUSTICE THOMAS delivered the opinion of the Court.

Respondent Ross-Simmons, a sawmill, sued petitioner Weyerhaeuser, alleging that Weyerhaeuser drove it out of business by bidding up the price of sawlogs to a level that prevented Ross-Simmons from being profitable. A jury returned a verdict in favor of Ross-Simmons on its monopolization claim, and the Ninth Circuit affirmed. We granted certiorari to decide whether the test we applied to claims of predatory pricing in *Brooke Group Ltd. v. Brown & Williamson Tobacco Corp.*, 509

U.S. 209 (1993), also applies to claims of predatory bidding. We hold that it does. Accordingly, we vacate the judgment of the Court of Appeals.

Ross-Simmons began operating a hardwood-lumber sawmill in Longview, Washington, in 1962. Weyerhaeuser entered the Northwestern hardwood-lumber market in 1980 by acquiring an existing lumber company. Weyerhaeuser gradually increased the scope of its hardwood-lumber operation, and it now owns six hardwood sawmills in the region. By 2001, Weyerhaeuser's mills were acquiring approximately 65 percent of the alder logs available for sale in the region.

From 1990 to 2000, Weyerhaeuser made more than $75 million in capital investments in its hardwood mills in the Pacific Northwest. During this period, production increased at every Northwestern hardwood mill that Weyerhaeuser owned. In addition to increasing production, Weyerhaeuser used "state-of-the-art technology," including sawing equipment, to increase the amount of lumber recovered from every log. By contrast, Ross-Simmons appears to have engaged in little efficiency-enhancing investment.

Logs represent up to 75 percent of a sawmill's total costs. And from 1998 to 2001, the price of alder sawlogs increased while prices for finished hardwood lumber fell. These divergent trends in input and output prices cut into the mills' profit margins, and Ross-Simmons suffered heavy losses during this time. Saddled with several million dollars in debt, Ross-Simmons shut down its mill completely in May 2001.

Ross-Simmons blamed Weyerhaeuser for driving it out of business by bidding up input costs, and it filed an antitrust suit against Weyerhaeuser for monopolization and attempted monopolization under § 2 of the Sherman Act. Ross-Simmons alleged that, among other anticompetitive acts, Weyerhaeuser had used "its dominant position in the alder sawlog market to drive up the prices for alder sawlogs to levels that severely reduced or eliminated the profit margins of Weyerhaeuser's alder sawmill competition." Proceeding in part on this "predatory-bidding" theory, Ross-Simmons argued that Weyerhaeuser had overpaid for alder sawlogs to cause sawlog prices to rise to artificially high levels as part of a plan to drive Ross-Simmons out of business. As proof that this practice had occurred, Ross-Simmons pointed to Weyerhaeuser's large share of the alder purchasing market, rising alder sawlog prices during the alleged predation period, and Weyerhaeuser's declining profits during that same period.

Prior to trial, Weyerhaeuser moved for summary judgment on Ross-Simmons' predatory-bidding theory. The District Court denied the motion. At the close of the 9-day trial, Weyerhaeuser moved for judgment as a matter of law, or alternatively, for a new trial. The motions were based in part on Weyerhaeuser's argument that Ross-Simmons had not satisfied the standard this Court set forth in *Brooke Group*, *supra*. The District Court denied Weyerhaeuser's motion. The District Court also rejected proposed predatory-bidding jury instructions that incorporated elements of the *Brooke Group* test. Ultimately, the District Court instructed the jury that Ross-Simmons could prove that Weyerhaeuser's bidding practices were anticompetitive acts if the jury concluded that Weyerhaeuser "purchased more logs than it needed, or paid a higher price for logs than necessary, in order to prevent [Ross-Simmons] from obtaining the logs they needed at a fair price." Finding that Ross-Simmons had proved its claim for monopolization, the jury returned a $26 million verdict against Weyerhaeuser. The verdict was trebled to approximately $79 million.

Weyerhaeuser appealed to the Court of Appeals for the Ninth Circuit. There, Weyerhaeuser argued that *Brooke Group's* standard for claims of predatory pricing should also apply to claims of predatory bidding. The Ninth Circuit disagreed and affirmed the verdict against Weyerhaeuser.

The Court of Appeals reasoned that "buy-side predatory bidding" and "sell-side predatory pricing," though similar, are materially different in that predatory bidding does not necessarily benefit consumers or stimulate competition in the way that predatory pricing does. Concluding that "the concerns that led the *Brooke Group* Court to establish a high standard of liability in the predatory-pricing context do not carry over to this predatory bidding context with the same force," the Court of Appeals declined to apply *Brooke Group* to Ross-Simmons' claims of predatory bidding. . . .

II

In *Brooke Group*, we considered what a plaintiff must show in order to succeed on a claim of predatory pricing under § 2 of the Sherman Act.[2] In a typical predatory-pricing scheme, the predator reduces the sale price of its product (its output) to below cost, hoping to drive competitors out of business. Then, with competition vanquished, the predator raises output prices to a supra competitive level. For the scheme to make economic sense, the losses suffered from pricing goods below cost must be recouped (with interest) during the supra competitive-pricing stage of the scheme. Recognizing this economic reality, we established two prerequisites to recovery on claims of predatory pricing. "First, a plaintiff seeking to establish competitive injury resulting from a rival's low prices must prove that the prices complained of are below an appropriate measure of its rival's costs." Second, a plaintiff must demonstrate that "the competitor had . . . a dangerous probabil- it[y] of recouping its investment in below-cost prices."

The first prong of the test-requiring that prices be below cost-is necessary because "[a]s a general rule, the exclusionary effect of prices above a relevant measure of cost either reflects the lower cost structure of the alleged predator, and so represents competition on the merits, or is beyond the practical ability of a judicial tribunal to control." We were particularly wary of allowing recovery for above-cost price cutting because allowing such claims could, perversely, "chil[l] legitimate price cutting," which directly benefits consumers. . . . Thus, we specifi- cally declined to allow plaintiffs to recover for above-cost price cutting, concluding that "discouraging a price cut and . . . depriving consumers of the benefits of lower prices . . . does not constitute sound antitrust policy."

The second prong of the *Brooke Group* test-requiring that there be a dangerous

---

[2] [FN 1] *Brooke Group* dealt with a claim under the Robinson-Patman Act, but as we observed, "primary-line competitive injury under the Robinson-Patman Act is of the same general character as the injury inflicted by predatory pricing schemes actionable under § 2 of the Sherman Act." Because of this similarity, the standard adopted in *Brooke Group* applies to predatory-pricing claims under § 2 of the Sherman Act.

probability of recoupment of losses-is necessary because, without a dangerous probability of recoupment, it is highly unlikely that a firm would engage in predatory pricing. As the Court explained in *Matsushita [Elec. Industrial Co. v. Zenith Radio Corp.*, 475 U.S. 574, 588–589 (1986)], a firm engaged in a predatory-pricing scheme makes an investment-the losses suffered plus the profits that would have been realized absent the scheme-at the initial, below-cost-selling phase. For that investment to be rational, a firm must reasonably expect to recoup in the long run at least its original investment with supra competitive profits. Without such a reasonable expectation, a rational firm would not willingly suffer definite, short-run losses. Recognizing the centrality of recoupment to a predatory-pricing scheme, we required predatory-pricing plaintiffs to "demonstrate that there is a likelihood that the predatory scheme alleged would cause a rise in prices above a competitive level that would be sufficient to compensate for the amounts expended on the predation, including the time value of the money invested in it."

We described the two parts of the *Brooke Group* test as "essential components of real market injury" that were "not easy to establish." We also reiterated that the costs of erroneous findings of predatory-pricing liability were quite high because " '[t]he mechanism by which a firm engages in predatory pricing-lowering prices-is the same mechanism by which a firm stimulates competition,' " and therefore, mistaken findings of liability would "chill the very conduct the antitrust laws are designed to protect."

III

Predatory bidding, which Ross-Simmons alleges in this case, involves the exercise of market power on the buy side or input side of a market. In a predatory-bidding scheme, a purchaser of inputs "bids up the market price of a critical input to such high levels that rival buyers cannot survive (or compete as vigorously) and, as a result, the predating buyer acquires (or maintains or increases its) monopsony power." Kirkwood, Buyer Power and Exclusionary Conduct, 72 Antitrust L.J. 625, 652 (2005) (hereinafter Kirkwood). Monopsony power is market power on the buy side of the market. Blair & Harrison, Antitrust Policy and Monopsony, 76 Cornell L. Rev. 297 (1991). As such, a monopsony is to the buy side of the market what a monopoly is to the sell side and is sometimes colloquially called a "buyer's monopoly." Piraino, A Proposed Antitrust Approach to Buyers' Competitive Conduct, 56 Hastings L.J. 1121, 1125 (2005).

A predatory bidder ultimately aims to exercise the monopsony power gained from bidding up input prices. To that end, once the predatory bidder has caused competing buyers to exit the market for purchasing inputs, it will seek to "restrict its input purchases below the competitive level," thus "reduc[ing] the unit price for the remaining input[s] it purchases." Salop, Anticompetitive Overbuying by Power Buyers, 72 Antitrust L.J. 669, 672 (2005). The reduction in input prices will lead to "a significant cost saving that more than offsets the profit[s] that would have been earned on the output." If all goes as planned, the predatory bidder will reap monopsonistic profits that will offset any losses suffered in bidding up input prices. (In this case, the plaintiff was the defendant's competitor in the input-purchasing market. Thus, this case does not present a situation of suppliers suing a monopsonist buyer under § 2 of the Sherman Act, nor does it present a risk of significantly increased concentration in the market in which the monopsonist sells, *i.e.*, the market for finished lumber.)

IV

A

Predatory-pricing and predatory-bidding claims are analytically similar. See Hovenkamp, The Law of Exclusionary Pricing, 2 Competition Policy Int'l, No. 1, pp. 21, 35 (Spring 2006). This similarity results from the close theoretical connection between monopoly and monopsony. *Khan v. State Oil Co.*, 93 F.3d 1358, 1361 (7th Cir. 1996) ("[M]onopsony pricing . . . is analytically the same as monopoly or cartel pricing and [is] so treated by the law"), vacated and remanded on other grounds, 522 U.S. 3 (1997). . . . The kinship between monopoly and monopsony suggests that similar legal standards should apply to claims of monopolization and to claims of monopsonization.

Tracking the economic similarity between monopoly and monopsony, predatory-pricing plaintiffs and predatory-bidding plaintiffs make strikingly similar allegations. A predatory-pricing plaintiff alleges that a predator cut prices to drive the plaintiff out of business and, thereby, to reap monopoly profits from the output market. In parallel fashion, a predatory-bidding plaintiff alleges that a predator raised prices for a key input to drive the plaintiff out of business and, thereby, to reap monopsony profits in the input market. Both claims involve the deliberate use of unilateral pricing measures for anticompetitive purposes.[3] And both claims logically require firms to incur short-term losses on the chance that they might reap supra competitive profits in the future.

B

More importantly, predatory bidding mirrors predatory pricing in respects that we deemed significant to our analysis in *Brooke Group*. In *Brooke Group*, we noted that " 'predatory pricing schemes are rarely tried, and even more rarely successful.' " 509 U.S. at 226. . . . Predatory pricing requires a firm to suffer certain losses in the short term on the chance of reaping supra competitive profits in the future. A rational business will rarely make this sacrifice. The same reasoning applies to predatory bidding. A predatory-bidding scheme requires a buyer of inputs to suffer losses today on the chance that it will reap supra competitive profits in the future. For this reason, "[s]uccessful monopsony predation is probably as unlikely as

---

[3] [FN 3] Predatory bidding on inputs is not analytically different from predatory overbuying of inputs. Both practices fall under the rubric of monopsony predation and involve an input purchaser's use of input prices in an attempt to exclude rival input purchasers. The economic effect of the practices is identical: input prices rise. In a predatory-bidding scheme, the purchaser causes prices to rise by offering to pay more for inputs. In a predatory-overbuying scheme, the purchaser causes prices to rise by demanding more of the input. Either way, input prices increase. Our use of the term "predatory bidding" is not meant to suggest that different legal treatment is appropriate for the economically identical practice of "predatory overbuying."

successful monopoly predation." R. Blair & J. Harrison, Monopsony 66 (1993).

And like the predatory conduct alleged in *Brooke Group*, actions taken in a predatory-bidding scheme are often "the very essence of competition." 509 U.S. at 226. . . . Just as sellers use output prices to compete for purchasers, buyers use bid prices to compete for scarce inputs. There are myriad legitimate reasons-ranging from benign to affirmatively procompetitive-why a buyer might bid up input prices. A firm might bid up inputs as a result of miscalculation of its input needs or as a response to increased consumer demand for its outputs. A more efficient firm might bid up input prices to acquire more inputs as a part of a procompetitive strategy to gain market share in the output market. A firm that has adopted an input-intensive production process might bid up inputs to acquire the inputs necessary for its process. Or a firm might bid up input prices to acquire excess inputs as a hedge against the risk of future rises in input costs or future input shortages. See Salop 682–683; Kirkwood 655. There is nothing illicit about these bidding decisions. Indeed, this sort of high bidding is essential to competition and innovation on the buy side of the market.

Brooke *Group* also noted that a failed predatory-pricing scheme may benefit consumers. The potential benefit results from the difficulty an aspiring predator faces in recouping losses suffered from below-cost pricing. Without successful recoupment, "predatory pricing produces lower aggregate prices in the market, and consumer welfare is enhanced." Failed predatory-bidding schemes can also, but will not necessarily, benefit consumers. See Salop 677–678. In the first stage of a predatory-bidding scheme, the predator's high bidding will likely lead to its acquisition of more inputs. Usually, the acquisition of more inputs leads to the manufacture of more outputs. And increases in output generally result in lower prices to consumers. Thus, a failed predatory-bidding scheme can be a "boon to consumers" in the same way that we considered a predatory-pricing scheme to be.

C

The general theoretical similarities of monopoly and monopsony combined with the theoretical and practical similarities of predatory pricing and predatory bidding convince us that our two-pronged *Brooke Group* test should apply to predatory-bidding claims.

The first prong of *Brooke Group's* test requires little adaptation for the predatory-bidding context. A plaintiff must prove that the alleged predatory bidding led to below-cost pricing of the predator's outputs. That is, the predator's bidding on the buy side must have caused the cost of the relevant output to rise above the revenues generated in the sale of those outputs. As with predatory pricing, the exclusionary effect of higher bidding that does not result in below-cost output pricing "is beyond the practical ability of a judicial tribunal to control without courting intolerable risks of chilling legitimate" procompetitive conduct. Given the multitude of procompetitive ends served by higher bidding for inputs, the risk of chilling procompetitive behavior with too lax a liability standard is as serious here as it was in *Brooke Group*. Consequently, only higher bidding that leads to below-cost pricing in the relevant output market will suffice as a basis for liability for predatory bidding.

A predatory-bidding plaintiff also must prove that the defendant has a dangerous probability of recouping the losses incurred in bidding up input prices through the exercise of monopsony power. Absent proof of likely recoupment, a strategy of predatory bidding makes no economic sense because it would involve short-term losses with no likelihood of offsetting long-term gains. As with predatory pricing, making a showing on the recoupment prong will require "a close analysis of both the scheme alleged by the plaintiff and the structure and conditions of the relevant market."

Ross-Simmons has conceded that it has not satisfied the *Brooke Group* standard. Therefore, its predatory-bidding theory of liability cannot support the jury's verdict.

V

For these reasons, we vacate the judgment of the Court of Appeals and remand the case for further proceedings consistent with this opinion.

It is so ordered.

[4]   Anticompetitive Discounting Practices, Including Package Discounts

CASCADE HEALTH SOLUTIONS v. PEACEHEALTH
515 F.3d 883 (9th Cir. 2008)

Before: Ronald M. Gould, Richard A. Paez, and Johnnie B. Rawlinson, Circuit Judges.

Gould, Circuit Judge:

McKenzie-Willamette Hospital ("McKenzie") filed a complaint in the district court against PeaceHealth asserting seven claims for relief. Five of the claims arose under the federal antitrust laws: . . . After a two-and-a-half-week trial, the jury rendered a verdict in favor of PeaceHealth on McKenzie's claims of monopolization, conspiracy to monopolize, and exclusive dealing. However, the jury found in favor of McKenzie on McKenzie's claims of attempted monopolization, price discrimination, and tortious interference. The jury awarded McKenzie $5.4 million in damages, which the district court trebled for a final award of $16.2 million. The district court also awarded McKenzie $1,583,185.57 in attorneys' fees, costs, and expenses. . . .

McKenzie and PeaceHealth are the only two providers of hospital care in Lane County, Oregon. The jury found and, for the purposes of this appeal, the parties do not dispute, that the relevant market in this case is the market for primary and secondary acute care hospital services in Lane County. Primary and secondary acute care hospital services are common medical services like setting a broken bone and performing a tonsillectomy. Some hospitals also provide what the parties call "tertiary care," which includes more complex services like invasive cardiovascular surgery and intensive neonatal care.

In Lane County, PeaceHealth operates three hospitals while McKenzie operates one. McKenzie's sole endeavor is McKenzie-Willamette Hospital, a 114-bed hospital that offers primary and secondary acute care in Springfield, Oregon. McKenzie does not provide tertiary care. In the time period leading up to and including this litigation, McKenzie had been suffering financial losses, and, as a result, merged with Triad Hospitals, Inc., so that it could add tertiary services to its menu of care.

The largest of PeaceHealth's three facilities is Sacred Heart Hospital, a 432-bed operation that offers primary, secondary, and tertiary care in Eugene, Oregon. PeaceHealth also operates Peace Harbor Hospital, a 21-bed hospital in Florence, Oregon and Cottage Grove Hospital Lane County, PeaceHealth has a 90% market share of tertiary neonatal services, a 93% market share of tertiary cardiovascular services, and a roughly 75% market share of primary and secondary care services.

To understand the antitrust issues in this case, it is necessary to appreciate the structure of the market in which this case arises. The market for hospital services and medical care is complex. However, based on the record, there appear to be three major participants in the market for hospital services: hospitals, insurers, and patients. Hospitals, like those operated by PeaceHealth and McKenzie, provide services to patients and sell services to insurers. Insurers are usually commercial health insurance companies that seek to buy medical services from hospitals on the best terms possible. The insurers in turn sell insurance services to patients and employers. . . .

In the transaction between a hospital that sells care services and an insurer that buys care services, the price agreed upon is often referred to as a "reimbursement rate." For example, in a hospital-insurer contract, the agreed upon price might be "a 90% reimbursement rate." A 90% reimbursement rate price means that, when the insurer must purchase services from the hospital, the insurer gets a 10% discount off the hospital's regular price, also called the charge master or list price. It follows that hospitals prefer high reimbursement rates and insurers prefer low reimbursement rates, as each group pursues its own economic interest.

. . . On McKenzie's monopolization and attempted monopolization claims, McKenzie's primary theory was that PeaceHealth engaged in anticompetitive conduct by offering insurers "bundled" or "package" discounts. McKenzie asserted that PeaceHealth offered insurers discounts of 35% to 40% on tertiary services if the insurers made PeaceHealth their sole preferred provider for all services — primary, secondary, and tertiary. McKenzie introduced evidence of a few specific instances of PeaceHealth's bundled discounting practices.

For example, in 2001, PeaceHealth was the only preferred provider of hospital care under the preferred provider plan ("PPP") of Regence BlueCross BlueShield of Oregon ("Regence").[4] At that time, Regence was paying PeaceHealth a 76% reimbursement rate for all of PeaceHealth's medical services, including primary, secondary, and tertiary services. Around that time, pursuant to McKenzie's request, Regence considered adding McKenzie to the PPP as a preferred provider of

---

[4] [FN 2] In a preferred provider plan, health care providers contract with an insurer to provide health care to the insurer's customers. The insurer's customers pay much higher prices if they obtain services from providers other than those with whom their insurer has contracted.

primary and secondary services. When Regence's contract with PeaceHealth came up for its annual renewal, Regence solicited two proposals from PeaceHealth. Under one proposal, PeaceHealth would remain the only preferred provider. Under the other proposal, McKenzie would be added as a preferred provider. PeaceHealth offered an 85% reimbursement rate for all services if it remained Regence's sole preferred provider of primary, secondary, and tertiary services, and a 90% reimbursement rate if McKenzie was added as a preferred provider of primary and secondary services. Regence thereafter declined to include McKenzie as a preferred provider. . . .

Bundling is the practice of offering, for a single price, two or more goods or services that could be sold separately. A bundled discount occurs when a firm sells a bundle of goods or services for a lower price than the seller charges for the goods or services purchased individually. *See* Daniel A. Crane, *Mixed Bundling, Profit Sacrifice, and Consumer Welfare*, 55 Emory L.J. 423, 425 (2006); David S. Evans & Michael Salinger, *Why Do Firms Bundle and Tie?*, 22 Yale J. on Reg. 37, 41 (2005); Thomas A. Lambert, *Evaluating Bundled Discounts*, 89 Minn. L. Rev. 1688, 1693 (2005). As discussed above, PeaceHealth offered bundled discounts to Regence and other insurers in this case. Specifically, PeaceHealth offered insurers discounts if the insurers made PeaceHealth their exclusive preferred provider for primary, secondary, and tertiary care.

Bundled discounts are pervasive, and examples abound. Season tickets, fast food value meals, all-in-one home theater systems-all are bundled discounts. Like individual consumers, institutional purchasers seek and obtain bundled discounts, too. *See, e.g., LePage's Inc. v. 3M*, 324 F.3d 141, 154 (3d Cir. 2003) (en banc) (involving rebates offered by 3M to retailers who purchased 3M's full line of health care, home care, home improvement, stationary, retail auto, and "Leisure Time" products) . . . .

Bundled discounts generally benefit buyers because the discounts allow the buyer to get more for less. Lambert, *supra*, 89 Minn. L. Rev. at 1726 (suggesting that bundled discounts always provide some immediate consumer benefit in the form of lower prices); 3 Phillip E. Areeda & Herbert Hovenkamp, Antitrust Law ¶ 749b at 324 (Supp. 2006) (explaining that "[t]he great majority of discounting practices are procompetitive" and "reflect hard bargaining"). Bundling can also result in savings to the seller because it usually costs a firm less to sell multiple products to one customer at the same time than it does to sell the products individually.

Not surprisingly, the Supreme Court has instructed that, because of the benefits that flow to consumers from discounted prices, price cutting is a practice the antitrust laws aim to promote. *See Matsushita Elec. Indus. Co. v. Zenith Radio Corp.*, 475 U.S. 574, 594 (1986) ("[C]utting prices in order to increase business often is the very essence of competition."). Consistent with that principle, we should not be too quick to condemn price-reducing bundled discounts as anticompetitive, lest we end up with a rule that discourages legitimate price competition. *See Barry Wright Corp. v. ITT Grinnell Corp.*, 724 F.2d 227, 234 (1st Cir. 1983) (Breyer, J.).

However, it is possible, at least in theory, for a firm to use a bundled discount to exclude an equally or more efficient competitor and thereby reduce consumer welfare in the long run. *See* Richard A. Posner, *Antitrust Law* 236 (2d ed. 2001); Barry Nalebuff, *Exclusionary Bundling*, 50 Antitrust Bull. 321, 321 (2005). For example, a competitor who sells only a single product in the bundle (and who produces that single product at a lower cost than the defendant) might not be able to match profitably the price created by the multi-product bundled discount. *See Ortho Diagnostic Sys., Inc. v. Abbott Labs., Inc.*, 920 F. Supp. 455, 467 (S.D.N.Y. 1996). This is true even if the post-discount prices for both the entire bundle and each product in the bundle are above the seller's cost. *See Ortho*, 920 F. Supp. at 467 (noting that "a firm that enjoys a monopoly on one or more of a group of complementary products, but which faces competition on others, can price all of its products above average variable cost and yet still drive an equally efficient competitor out of the market"). Judge Kaplan's opinion in *Ortho* provides an example of such a situation:

> Assume for the sake of simplicity that the case involved the sale of two hair products, shampoo and conditioner, the latter made only by A and the former by both A and B. Assume as well that both must be used to wash one's hair. Assume further that A's average variable cost for conditioner is $2.50, that its average variable cost for shampoo is $1.50, and that B's average variable cost for shampoo is $1.25. B therefore is the more efficient producer of shampoo. Finally, assume that A prices conditioner and shampoo at $5 and $3, respectively, if bought separately but at $3 and $2.25 if bought as part of a package. Absent the package pricing, A's price for both products is $8. B therefore must price its shampoo at or below $3 in order to compete effectively with A, given that the customer will be paying A $5 for conditioner irrespective of which shampoo supplier it chooses. With the package pricing, the customer can purchase both products from A for $5.25, a price above the sum of A's average variable cost for both products. In order for B to compete, however, it must persuade the customer to buy B's shampoo while purchasing its conditioner from A for $5. In order to do that, B cannot charge more than $0.25 for shampoo, as the customer otherwise will find A's package cheaper than buying conditioner from A and shampoo from B. On these assumptions, A would force B out of the shampoo market, notwithstanding that B is the more efficient producer of shampoo, without pricing either of A's products below average variable cost.

. . . In this case, the district court based its jury instruction regarding the anticompetitive effect of bundled discounting on the Third Circuit's en banc decision in *LePage's Inc. v. 3M*, 324 F.3d 141 (3d Cir. 2003) (en banc). In that case, the plaintiff, LePage's, was the market leader in sales of "private label" (i.e., store brand) transparent tape. . . . LePage's alleged that 3M's multitiered bundled rebate structure was anticompetitive. The bundled rebate structure offered progressively higher rebates when customers increased purchases across 3M's different product lines — discounts LePage's could not offer because it did not sell the same diverse array of products as 3M.

. . . 3M argued that its bundled rebate structure was legal as a matter of law because it never priced below cost. 3M relied heavily on the United States Supreme Court's decision in *Brooke Group Ltd. v. Brown & Williamson Tobacco Corp.*, 509 U.S. 209 (1993). In *Brooke Group*, a primary-line price discrimination case brought under the Robinson-Patman Act, the Supreme Court held that, in a single product predatory pricing case, a plaintiff must prove (1) that its rival's low prices were below an appropriate measure of its rival's costs and (2) that its rival "had a reasonable prospect, or, under § 2 of the Sherman Act, a dangerous probability, of recouping its investment in below-cost prices." . . . The Third Circuit, in a 7-3 en banc decision, refused to apply Brooke Group's below-cost pricing requirement to bundled discounting.

The Third Circuit first distinguished *Brooke Group* by noting that the defendant in that case was an oligopolist while 3M was a monopolist. The court reasoned that while *Brooke Group'* s requirement of below-cost pricing with a probability of recoupment is appropriate when the defendant is an oligopolist who still faces competition when it tries to recoup the losses it suffered during the predation period, below-cost pricing and a probability of recoupment should not be required when the defendant is a monopolist whose behavior will be unconstrained by the market after it eliminates its lone rival. The court in *LePage's* also noted that the plaintiff in *Brooke Group* simply challenged the defendant's pricing practices, not bundling accomplished through discounting. The court reasoned that *Brooke Group* did not require below-cost pricing for any pricing practice to be deemed exclusionary.

The court noted that "[t]he principal anticompetitive effect of bundled rebates as offered by 3M is that when offered by a monopolist they may foreclose portions of the market to a potential competitor who does not manufacture an equally diverse group of products and who therefore cannot make a comparable offer." *Id.* at 155. The Third Circuit concluded that the jury could reasonably have found that 3M used its monopoly in transparent tape along with its extensive catalog of other products to exclude LePage's from the market and that 3M did not present any adequate business justification for its bundled discounting program. The court thus affirmed the jury verdict in LePage's favor, even though LePage's economist testified that LePage's was not as efficient a tape producer as 3M . . . .

As the bipartisan Antitrust Modernization Commission ("AMC") noted, the fundamental problem with the LePage's standard is that it does not consider whether the bundled discounts constitute competition on the merits, but simply concludes that all bundled discounts offered by a monopolist are anticompetitive with respect to its competitors who do not manufacture an equally diverse product line. Antitrust Modernization Comm'n, Report and Recommendations 97 (2007) [hereinafter AMC Report]. The *LePage's* standard, the AMC noted, asks the jury to consider whether the plaintiff has been excluded from the market, but does not require the jury to consider whether the plaintiff was at least as efficient of a producer as the defendant. . . . Thus, the *LePage's* standard could protect a less efficient competitor at the expense of consumer welfare. As Judge Greenberg explained in his *LePage's* dissent, the Third Circuit's standard "risks curtailing price competition and a method of pricing beneficial to customers because the bundled rebates effectively lowered [the seller's] costs."

The AMC also lamented that *LePage's* "offers no clear standards by which firms can assess whether their bundled rebates are likely to pass antitrust muster." *AMC Report, supra,* at 94. The Commission noted that efficiencies, and not schemes to acquire or maintain monopoly power, likely explain the use of bundled discounts because many firms without market power offer them. *Id.* at 95. The AMC thus proposed a three-part test that it believed would protect procompetitive bundled discounts from antitrust scrutiny. The AMC proposed that:

> Courts should adopt a three-part test to determine whether bundled discounts or rebates violate Section 2 of the Sherman Act. To prove a violation of Section 2, a plaintiff should be required to show each one of the following elements (as well as other elements of a Section 2 claim): (1) after allocating all discounts and rebates attributable to the entire bundle of products to the competitive product, the defendant sold the competitive product below its incremental cost for the competitive product; (2) the defendant is likely to recoup these short-term losses; and (3) the bundled discount or rebate program has had or is likely to have an adverse effect on competition.

The AMC reasoned that the first element would (1) subject bundled discounts to antitrust scrutiny only if they could exclude a hypothetical equally efficient competitor and (2) provide sufficient clarity for businesses to determine whether their bundled discounting practices run afoul of § 2. The AMC concluded that the three-part test would, as a whole, bring the law on bundled discounting in line with the Supreme Court's reasoning in *Brooke Group. Id.*

Observers have commented that, in some respects, bundled discounts are similar to both predatory pricing and tying. *See* Nalebuff, *supra*, 50 Antitrust Bull. at 365; Daniel L. Rubinfeld, *3M's Bundled Rebates: An Economic Perspective*, 72 U. Chi. L. Rev. 243, 252–56 (2005). . . . However, "[o]ne difference between traditional tying by contract and tying via package discounts is that the traditional tying contract typically forces the buyer to accept both products, as well as the cost savings." 3 Areeda & Hovenkamp, *supra*, ¶ 749b2 at 332 (Supp. 2006). Conversely, "the package discount gives the buyer the choice of accepting the cost savings by purchasing the package, or foregoing the savings by purchasing the products separately." *Id.* The package discount thus does not constrain the buyer's choice as much as the traditional tie. For that reason, the late-Professor Areeda and Professor Hovenkamp suggest that "[a] variation of the requirement that prices be 'below cost' is essential for the plaintiff to establish one particular element of unlawful bundled discounting-namely, that there was actually 'tying'-that is, that the purchaser was actually 'coerced' (in this case, by lower prices) into taking the tied-up package."

. . . Given the endemic nature of bundled discounts in many spheres of normal economic activity, we decline to endorse the Third Circuit's definition of when bundled discounts constitute the exclusionary conduct proscribed by § 2 of the Sherman Act. Instead, we think the course safer for consumers and our competitive economy to hold that bundled discounts may not be considered exclusionary conduct within the meaning of § 2 of the Sherman Act unless the discounts resemble the behavior that the Supreme Court in *Brooke Group* identified as predatory. Accordingly, we hold that the exclusionary conduct element of a claim arising under § 2 of the Sherman Act cannot be satisfied by reference to bundled discounts unless the discounts result in prices that are below an appropriate measure of the defendant's costs.

The next question we must address is how we define the appropriate measure of the defendant's costs in bundled discounting cases and how we determine whether discounted prices fall below that mark. Defining the appropriate measure of costs in a bundled discounting case is more complex than in a single product case. In a single product case, we may simply ask whether the defendant has priced its product below its incremental cost of producing that product because a rival that produces the same product as efficiently as the defendant should be able to match any price at or above the defendant's cost. However, as we discussed above, a defendant offering a bundled discount, without pricing below cost either the individual products in the bundle or the bundle as a whole, can, in some cases, exclude a rival who produces one of the products in the bundle equally or more efficiently than the defendant. . . .

PeaceHealth and some amici urge us to adopt a rule they term the "aggregate discount" rule. This rule condemns bundled discounts as anticompetitive only in the narrow cases in which the discounted price of the entire bundle does not exceed the bundling firm's incremental cost to produce the entire bundle. PeaceHealth and amici argue that support for such a rule can be found in the Supreme Court's single product predation cases. . . .

We are not persuaded that those cases require us to adopt an aggregate discount rule in multi-product discounting cases. As we discussed above, bundled discounts present one potential threat to consumer welfare that single product discounts do not: A competitor who produces fewer products than the defendant but produces the competitive product at or below the defendant's cost to produce that product may nevertheless be excluded from the market because the competitor cannot match the discount the defendant offers over its numerous product lines. This possibility exists even when the defendant's prices are above cost for each individual product and for the bundle as a whole. . . .

Additionally, as commentators have pointed out, *Brooke Group's* safe harbor for above-cost discounting in the single product discount context is not based on a theory that above-cost pricing strategies can never be anticompetitive, but rather on a cost-benefit rejection of a more nuanced rule. 3 Areeda & Hovenkamp, *supra*, ¶ 749b at 324 (Supp. 2006); Lambert, *supra*, 89 Minn. L. Rev. at 1704 . . .; *see also Verizon Commc'ns Inc. v. Law Offices of Curtis v. Trinko, LLP*, 540 U.S. 398, 414 (2004) (explaining that while above-cost predatory pricing schemes may exist, they are " 'beyond the practical ability of a judicial tribunal to control' " (quoting *Brooke Group*, 509 U.S. at 223). That is, the safe harbor rests on the premise that "any consumer benefit created by a rule that permits inquiry into above-cost, single-product discounts, but allows judicial condemnation of those deemed legitimately exclusionary, would likely be outweighed by the consumer harm occasioned by overdeterring nonexclusionary discounts." Lambert, *supra*, 89 Minn. L. Rev. at 1705 . . .; 3 Areeda & Hovenkamp, *supra*, ¶ 749b at 324 (Supp. 2006) (noting that "our measurement tools are too imprecise to evaluate [above-cost discounting] strategies without creating an intolerable risk of chilling competitive behavior"). So, in adopting an appropriate cost-based test for bundled discounting cases, we should not adopt an aggregate discount rule without inquiring whether a rule exists that is more likely to identify anticompetitive bundled discounting practices while at the same time resulting in little harm to competition.

The first potential alternative cost-based standard we consider derives from the district court's opinion in *Ortho*. This standard deems a bundled discount exclusionary if the plaintiff can show that it was an equally efficient producer of the competitive product, but the defendant's bundled discount made it impossible for the plaintiff to continue to produce profitably the competitive product. As the district court in Ortho phrased the standard: a plaintiff basing a § 2 claim on an anticompetitive bundled discount "must allege and prove either that (a) the monopolist has priced below its average variable cost or (b) the plaintiff is at least as efficient a producer of the competitive product as the defendant, but that the defendant's pricing makes it unprofitable for the plaintiff to continue to produce." Under this standard, above-cost prices are not per se legal. Instead, this standard treats below-cost prices as simply one beacon for identifying discounts that create the risk of excluding firms that are as efficient as the defendant-the unique anticompetitive risk posed by bundled discounts. Under *Ortho*'s standard, an above-cost discount can still be anticompetitive if a plaintiff proves it is as efficient a producer as the defendant, but is excluded because the defendant sells in more product markets than the plaintiff and can "spread the total discount over all those product lines and . . . force competitors to provide the entire dollar amount of the discount on a smaller collection of products." Lambert, *supra*, 89 Minn. L. Rev. at 1728. As compared to the discount aggregation rule, Ortho's approach does a better job of identifying bundled discounts that threaten harm to competition.

However, one downside of *Ortho*'s standard is that it does not provide adequate guidance to sellers who wish to offer procompetitive bundled discounts because the standard looks to the costs of the actual plaintiff. A potential defendant who is considering offering a bundled discount will likely not have access to information about its competitors' costs, thus making it hard for that potential discounter, under the Ortho standard, to determine whether the discount it wishes to offer complies with the antitrust laws. Also, the *Ortho* standard, which asks whether the actual plaintiff is as efficient a producer as the defendant, could require multiple suits to determine the legality of a single bundled discount. While it might turn out that the plaintiff in one particular case is not as efficient a producer of the competitive product as the defendant, another rival might be. This second rival would have to bring another suit under the Ortho approach. We decline to adopt a rule that might encourage more antitrust litigation than is reasonably necessary to ferret out anticompetitive practices. . . .

Instead, as our cost-based rule, we adopt what amici refer to as a "discount attribution" standard. Under this standard, the full amount of the discounts given by the defendant on the bundle are allocated to the competitive product or products. If the resulting price of the competitive product or products is below the defendant's incremental cost to produce them, the trier of fact may find that the bundled discount is exclusionary for the purpose of § 2. This standard makes the defendant's bundled discounts legal unless the discounts have the potential to exclude a hypothetical equally efficient producer of the competitive product. . . .

In their leading treatise on antitrust law, Professors Areeda and Hovenkamp support an approach that focuses on whether a bundled discount excludes a hypothetical equally efficient rival. Rejecting *Ortho*'s "actual plaintiff" standard, they explain:

> [W]e would not require a showing that the actual plaintiff be equally efficient. The relevant question is not necessarily whether a particular plaintiff was equally efficient, but whether the challenged bundling practices would have excluded an equally efficient rival, without reasonable justification. This rule is preferable on grounds of both administrability and principle. On the first, proving whether a hypothetical equally efficient rival is excluded by a multiproduct discount is typically quite manageable. By contrast, proof that the plaintiff is equally efficient can be quite difficult, particularly in cases where the defendant produces a larger product line than the plaintiff and there are joint costs.
>
> A requirement that the bundling practice be sufficiently severe so as to exclude an equally efficient single-product rival, and without an adequate business justification, seems to strike about the right balance between permitting aggressive pricing while prohibiting conduct that can only be characterized as anticompetitive. Requiring the defendant's pricing policies to protect the trade of higher cost rivals is overly solicitous of small firms and denies customers the benefits of the defendant's lower costs. Further, if the practice will exclude an equally efficient rival, then it will exclude whether or not the rival is equally efficient in fact.

3 Areeda & Hovenkamp, *supra*, ¶ 749a at 322–23 (Supp. 2006). . . . Judge Posner's work on antitrust law also supports an approach that asks whether a bundled discount excludes a hypothetical equally efficient rival, stating that the acts of a monopolist should be deemed exclusionary if "the challenged practice is likely in the circumstances to exclude from the defendant's market an equally or more efficient competitor."

Areeda and Hovenkamp also support using a discount attribution approach to determine if a bundled discount is exclusionary. They state:

> To see whether a package price is "exclusionary" . . . one simply attributes the entire discount on all products in the package to the product for which exclusion is claimed. If the resulting price is less than the defendant's cost, then the package discount is exclusionary as against a rival who makes only one of the two goods in the package.

3 Areeda & Hovenkamp, *supra*, ¶ 749b2 at 335–36 (Supp. 2006) (footnotes omitted); *accord* Nalebuff, *supra*, 50 Antitrust Bull. at 328. . . .

The discount attribution standard provides clear guidance for sellers that engage in bundled discounting practices. A seller can easily ascertain its own prices and costs of production and calculate whether its discounting practices run afoul of the rule we have outlined. . . . Unlike under the *Ortho* standard, under the discount attribution standard a bundled discounter need not fret over and predict or determine its rivals' cost structure. *See* Nalebuff, *supra*, 50 Antitrust Bull. at 330.

We are aware that liability under the discount attribution standard has the potential to sweep more broadly than under the aggregate discount rule or the *Ortho* standard. However, there is limited judicial experience with bundled discounts, and academic inquiry into the competitive effects of bundled discounts is only beginning. By comparison, the Supreme Court's decision in *Brooke Group* (prefaced by the Court's discussion of predatory pricing in *Matsushita*, 475 U.S. at 588–91) marked the culmination of nearly twenty years of scholarly and judicial analysis of the feasibility and competitive effects of single product predatory pricing schemes. *Cf.* 3 Areeda & Hovenkamp, *supra*, ¶ 749b at 323 (Supp. 2006) ("[T]he theory of anticompetitive discounting is in much the same position as the theory of predatory pricing was in the 1970s: no shortage of theories, but a frightening inability of courts to assess them."). The cost-based standard we adopt will allow courts the experience they need to divine the prevalence and competitive effects of bundled discounts and will allow these difficult issues to further percolate in the lower courts. . . .

To summarize, the primary anticompetitive danger posed by a multi-product bundled discount is that such a discount can exclude a rival is who is equally efficient at producing the competitive product simply because the rival does not sell as many products as the bundled discounter. Thus, a plaintiff who challenges a package discount as anticompetitive must prove that, when the full amount of the discounts given by the defendant is allocated to the competitive product or products, the resulting price of the competitive product or products is below the defendant's incremental cost to produce them. This requirement ensures that the only bundled discounts condemned as exclusionary are those that would exclude an equally efficient producer of the competitive product or products.

The next issue before us is the appropriate measure of incremental costs in a bundled discounting case. In single product predatory pricing cases, the appropriate measure of incremental costs is an open question in this circuit. *See Rebel Oil Co. v. Atl. Richfield Co.*, 146 F.3d 1088, 1092 (9th Cir. 1998). The Supreme Court has likewise refused to decide the matter. *See Brooke Group*, 509 U.S. at 222 n.1, *Cargill*, 479 U.S. at 118 n.12.

As our cases and the relevant academic literature thoroughly discuss, firms face both fixed costs-costs that a firm must bear regardless of the amount of output-and variable costs-costs that change with the amount of output. The sum of fixed and variable costs is a firm's total cost. Marginal cost is the increase to total cost that occurs as a result of producing one additional unit of output. Average cost is the sum of fixed costs and total variable costs, divided by the amount of output. In their oft-cited 1975 law review article, Professors Areeda and Turner concluded that the optimal measure of a firm's cost in a predatory pricing case is marginal cost-the cost to produce one additional unit and the price that would obtain in the market under conditions of perfect competition. *See* Phillip Areeda & Donald F. Turner, Predatory Pricing and Related Practices Under Section 2 of the Sherman Act, 88 Harv. L. Rev. 697, 712, 716 (1975). However, Professors Areeda and Turner also recognized that "[t]he incremental cost of making and selling the last unit cannot readily be inferred from conventional business accounts, which typically go no further than showing observed average variable cost." *Id.* at 716. Thus, the professors adopted average variable cost as a surrogate for marginal cost. *Id.* A number of circuits have adopted the Areeda-Turner formulation and concluded that prices below average variable cost can indicate predation. *See, e.g., Stearns Airport Equip. Co. v. FMC Corp.,* 170 F.3d 518, 532 (5th Cir. 1999); *Morgan v. Ponder,* 892 F.2d 1355, 1360 (8th Cir. 1989); *Barry Wright,* 724 F.2d at 236; *Ne. Tel. Co. v. AT & T Co.,* 651 F.2d 76, 87–88 (2d Cir. 1981).[5]

Likewise, "we have approved the use of marginal or average variable cost statistics in proving predation." *See William Inglis & Sons Baking Co. v. ITT Cont'l Baking Co.,* 668 F.2d 1014, 1033 (9th Cir. 1981). We have also held that a plaintiff can establish a prima facie case of predatory pricing by proving that the defendant's prices were below average variable cost. *Id.* at 1036. We see no reason to depart from these principles in the bundled discounting context, and we hold that the appropriate measure of costs for our cost-based standard is average variable cost.

In summary, we hold the following: To prove that a bundled discount was exclusionary or predatory for the purposes of a monopolization or attempted monopolization claim under § 2 of the Sherman Act, the plaintiff must establish that, after allocating the discount given by the defendant on the entire bundle of products to the competitive product or products, the defendant sold the competitive product or products below its average variable cost of producing them. The district court's jury instruction on the attempted monopolization claim, which built on the holding of LePage's that we have rejected, thus contained an error of law.

NOTES AND QUESTIONS

1. Although judicial experience with package discounts is still limited, the conduct itself has been likened to two seemingly quite different practices that have produced hundreds of judicial decisions — namely, tying and predatory pricing. Tying is unlawful when the defendant "ties" two products together, thereby requiring the buyer to purchase its tied product rather than a rival's. Thus the injury is to competition in the tied product market. Tying requires that the two goods be "tied together," but it does not require that the goods be priced at below cost. Nor must the tying plaintiff prove "recoupment," or that the costs of the defendant's tying program will be recovered in some later period of monopoly pricing. Of course, prices are relevant to exclusionary effect: if the defendant ties but also charges too high a price, rivals will be able to compete for sales in both the tying and the tied products.

By contrast, the plaintiff in a predatory pricing case need not show that two or

---

[5] [FN 19] At least one circuit has held that average total cost, not average variable cost, is the appropriate baseline for determining predation. *See McGahee v. N. Propane Gas Co.,* 858 F.2d 1487, 1500 (11th Cir. 1988). However, such an approach is inconsistent with the Supreme Court's instruction in Brooke Group that predatory prices are those below " 'some measure of *incremental* cost.' " *Brooke Group,* 509 U.S. at 223 (quoting *Cargill,* 479 U.S. at 117–18 n.12) (emphasis added). As the Antitrust Law treatise explains:

> In the ordinary case a predator increases output out of existing facilities, cutting the price to predatory levels. For this reason the Supreme Court has emphasized that predators must have excess capacity from which to produce the increased output. But in that case, the only "incremental" cost of the predation is variable costs.

3 Areeda & Hovenkamp, *supra,* ¶ 741c at 444 (2d ed. 2002) (footnote omitted).

more different products were linked or tied together. However, it must show prices below an appropriate measure of cost and provide proof that the defendant could reasonably expect that its investment in predatory pricing would be recouped during a subsequent period of monopoly prices.

Many plaintiffs have brought these cases emphasizing their "tying" character, sometimes even requesting the court to apply a variation of tying's per se rule. *See, e.g., SmithKline Corp. v. Eli Lilly & Co.*, 427 F. Supp. 1089, 1114 (E.D. Pa. 1976), *aff'd*, 575 F.2d 1056 (3d Cir. 1978). In contrast, defendants have maintained that package discounting should be lawful per se unless the discount forces prices below the defendant's costs — i.e., they have used a predatory pricing analogy. *See, e.g.,* the defendant's petition for certiorari in *LePage's, Inc. v. 3M Corp.*, 324 F.3d 141 (3d Cir. 2003) (en banc).

Package discounts bear some characteristics of both predatory pricing and tying. Indeed, they are best analyzed by a model that draws a little from each area. A variation of the requirement that prices be "below cost" is essential for the plaintiff to establish one particular element of unlawful bundled discounting — namely, that the purchaser was actually "coerced" (in this case, by lower prices) into taking the tied-up package. In the case of tying arrangements, this requirement comes in numerous variations, ranging from the express tying contract requiring the buyer to take the tied product as a condition of getting the tying product, to "implied" contracts, and to technological ties and package discounts.

In addition to showing the existence of a "tie," however, the plaintiff must also show other anticompetitive effects normally associated with tying or exclusive dealing assessed under the rule of reason, as well as the absence of numerous defenses.

An important difference between traditional tying by contract and tying via package discounts is that the traditional tying contract typically forces the buyer to purchase both products. By contrast, the package discount gives the buyer the choice of accepting the cost savings by purchasing the package, or foregoing the savings by purchasing the products separately. For example, suppose that one dozen decongestant capsules sell at a price of $3 for the pills plus $2 for packaging. One dozen cough suppressant capsules also sell for $3 plus $2 for packaging. However, the packaging costs are no higher when the two chemicals are mixed together and distributed in the same packaging. By employing traditional tying, the seller would achieve the packaging cost savings but require all purchasers to take the combined capsules at a price of $3 + $3 + $2, or $8. Alternatively, the seller could offer the decongestant alone for $5, the cough suppressant alone for $5, or the package for $8, a $2 savings. The package discount does not constrain consumer choice as much as the outright tie, for it gives the buyer the option of foregoing the discount if he or she wants only one of the items in the package.

2. The Antitrust Modernization Commission was created by Congress to report on the state of United States antitrust law and make recommendations. Its website, including the full text of its report is *available at* http://govinfo.library.unt.edu/amc/report_recommendation/toc.htm. The Commission contained four members appointed by President George W. Bush, four appointed by the House, and four appointed by the Senate. At this writing, it remains to be seen how influential the Commission's Report will be.

The Commission's Report found bundled discounts by monopolists to be particularly problematic. Its three-part test first adopted the "attribution" test used in *PeaceHealth*, asking whether when all discounts are attributed to the competitive product (the one on which exclusion is claimed) the price of that product falls below cost. Second, the AMC required the plaintiff to show that losses incurred during the period of discounting could be recouped, roughly similar to the requirement assessed in *Brooke Group*. Finally, the plaintiff must show an adverse impact on competition.

In a footnote in *PeaceHealth*, the Ninth Circuit rejected the Commission's recoupment requirement:

> . . . The second element proposed by the AMC is that there is a dangerous probability that the defendant will recoup its investment in the bundled discounting program. AMC Report, *supra*, at 99. This requirement, adopted from Brooke Group, is imported from the single product predatory pricing context, but we think imported incorrectly. We do not believe that the recoupment requirement from single product cases translates to multi-product discounting cases. Single-product predatory pricing, unlike bundling, necessarily involves a loss for the defendant. For a period of time, the defendant must sell below its cost, with the intent to eliminate its competitors so that, when its competition is eliminated, the defendant can charge supra competitive prices, recouping its losses and potentially more. By contrast, as discussed above, exclusionary bundling does not necessarily involve any loss of profits for the bundled discounter. See Nalebuff, *supra*, 50 Antitrust Bull. at 327. As the example from Ortho illustrates, a bundled discounter can exclude its rivals who do not sell as many product lines even when the bundle as a whole, and the individual products within it, are priced above the discounter's incremental cost to produce them. The trier of fact can identify cases that present this possibility for anticompetitive exclusion by applying the discount attribution standard outlined above. Under that standard, the ultimate question is whether the bundled discount would exclude an equally efficient rival. But because discounts on all products in the bundle have been allocated to the competitive product in issue, a conclusion of below-cost sales under the discount attribution standard may occur in some cases even where there is not an actual loss because the bundle is sold at a price exceeding incremental cost. In such a case, we do not think it is analytically helpful to think in terms of recoupment of a loss that did not occur.

See Erik N. Hovenkamp & Herbert Hovenkamp, *The Exclusionary Bundled Discounts and the Antitrust Modernization Commission*, 53 Antitrust Bull. 517 (2008).

3. *Quantity and Market Share Discounts.* In *Concord Boat Corp. v. Brunswick Corp.*, 207 F.3d 1039 (8th Cir. 2000), the Eighth Circuit entered judgment as a matter of law for Brunswick, which was accused of monopolizing the market for stern drive boat motors by giving discounts that depended on the percentage of motors that boat builders purchased from Brunswick. The discounts reached a 3–5% maximum when a boat builder purchased 70% or more of its motors from Brunswick. The plaintiff purchasers claimed that these discounts so completely locked boat builders into Brunswick motors that its overall price was approximately 16% or more above the competitive price. In rejecting the theory, the court said:

> The boat builders argue that the discount programs . . . were part of a deliberate plan to exclude competitors from the stern drive engine market, and that this exclusion enabled Brunswick to charge supra competitive high prices for its engines. . . . They also allege that Brunswick attempted to erect and maintain barriers to entry and to place its customers in "golden handcuffs," such that boat builders and dealers had no choice but to purchase engines from it.

> The Supreme Court "has urged great caution and a skeptical eye when dealing with unfair pricing claims." . . . This is because "[l]ow prices benefit consumers regardless of how those prices are set, and so long as they are above predatory levels, they do not threaten competition. Hence, they cannot give rise to antitrust injury." *Atlantic Richfield Co. v. USA Petroleum Co.*, 495 U.S. 328, 340 (1990) (rejecting Section 1 claim that a maximum price fixing conspiracy caused antitrust injury when the prices were fixed above a predatory level). In the absence of predatory prices, any losses caused by pricing "cannot be said to stem from an anticompetitive aspect of the defendant's conduct. It is in the interest of competition to permit dominant firms to engage in vigorous competition, including price competition." *Id.* at 340–41 (emphasis in original) (internal quotations and citations omitted).

> Because cutting prices in order to increase business often is the very essence of competition, which antitrust laws were designed to encourage, it "is beyond the practical ability of a judicial tribunal to control [above cost discounting] without courting intolerable risks of chilling legitimate price cutting." *Brooke Group Ltd.*, 509 U.S. at 223. . . . If a firm has discounted prices to a level that remains above the firm's average variable cost, "the plaintiff must overcome a strong presumption of legality by showing other factors indicating that the price charged is anticompetitive." . . . This is because a firm's ability to offer above cost discounts is attributable to "the lower cost structure of the alleged predator, and so represents competition on the merits . . . ."

No one argues in this case that Brunswick's discounts drove the engine price below cost, and Brunswick contends that its discounts were therefore per se lawful. The district court questioned Brunswick's per se legality theory because the boat builders' claim was that Brunswick's conduct as a whole, including the discounts and acquisitions, enabled it to "charge[] anticompetitive high prices for its engines." *Concord Boat Corp.*, 21 F. Supp. 2d at 929. The court examined several cases that had "rejected the argument that any pricing practice that leads to above costs prices is per se lawful under the antitrust laws." *Id.* (emphasis in original); *see LePage's Inc. v. 3M*, 1997 U.S. Dist. LEXIS 18501 (E.D. Pa. Nov. 14, 1997) (bundling discounts on several products purchased together); *SmithKline Corp. v.*

Eli Lilly & Co., 575 F.2d 1056 (3d Cir. 1978) (pricing scheme linking monopolistic product with another competitive product violated Section 2); *Ortho Diagnostic Sys., Inc. v. Abbott Labs., Inc.*, 920 F. Supp. 455, 467 (S.D.N.Y. 1996) (refusing to dismiss Section 2 bundling claims even though defendant not accused of pricing below cost because "average variable cost is the controlling standard in this Circuit [only for] single product cases"). The cases examined by the district court all involve bundling or tying, however, which "cannot exist unless two separate product markets have been linked. . . . Because only one product, stern drive engines, is at issue here and there are no allegations of tying or bundling with another product, we do not find these cases persuasive."

In *Allied Orthopedic Appliances Inc. v. Tyco Health Care Group LP*, 592 F.3d 991 (9th Cir. 2010), the Ninth Circuit rejected another challenge to a discount pricing program. The product in question was pulse oximetry devices which collect information about a hospital patient's heart and blood oxygen and transmits this information to a screen. Tyco pioneered technology that made it less costly for hospitals to upgrade and add additional features to their pulse oximetry systems. Tyco sold these devices to hospitals principally through group purchasing organizations (GPOs), and many of the sales were "sole source," which means that Tyco's product was the only one on the GPO contract. The pricing was also subject to market share, or "loyalty," discounts which gave purchasers a lower price if they agreed to purchase a specified minimum percentage of their pulse oximetry needs from Tyco. However, hospitals were not required to purchase exclusively from Tyco and, for that matter, were not required to purchase exclusively through the GPO contract at all. They were free to purchase elsewhere, although they could lose Tyco's discount if they purchased more than a specified percentage elsewhere. Finally, even Tyco's fully discounted prices were not alleged to be below cost; to the contrary, the plaintiffs were purchasers seeking damages for overcharges on the theory that the prices contained an element of monopoly markup.

Tyco had at least two rivals, Masimo and GE, and at least one of these was selling generic sensors at a lower price than Tyco's price. The plaintiff's expert:

> postulated that if a hospital chose to purchase a competitor's monitor, that hospital could lose Tyco's discounts on the sensors it continued to need for its installed base of Tyco monitors. Nonetheless, even such a hospital could simply begin to purchase less expensive generic sensors for its remaining Tyco monitors. We thus agree with the district court that on the facts of this case, something more than the discount itself is necessary to prove that Tyco's market-share discount agreements forced customers to purchase its sensors rather than generics.

Id. at 997.

In sum, "any customer subject to one of Tyco's market-share discount agreements could choose at anytime to forego the discount offered by Tyco and purchase from a generic competitor," and this fact substantially negated the foreclosure claim.

The court also distinguished its earlier decision in *Masimo Corp. v. Tyco Health Care Group, L.P.*, 2009 U.S. App. LEXIS 23765 (9th Cir. Oct. 28, 2009), which had condemned some market-share and sole-source arrangements under the Sherman Act. In that case, however, the facts were that a particular Tyco patent was still in effect that effectively required customers to purchase Tyco sensors for their installed base of Tyco monitors. This fact had given Tyco additional tying-like leverage and served to justify the lower court's conclusion of illegality. But the patent had since expired and the monitors and sensors were not technologically independent of one another.

See also Doe v. Abbott Labs., 571 F.3d 930 (9th Cir. 2009), which rejected a bundled discount claim as applied to a "cocktail" of aid's drugs. Once again, prices were not shown to be below cost. Abbott increased the price of a stand-alone drug some fivefold but kept its price lower when used in a cocktail with another of its drugs. This made it very difficult for rivals who made an equivalent to the second drug to compete. However, Abbott was willing to sell the stand-alone drug; thus there was no refusal to deal. Further, all relevant prices were above cost. The court found this practice to be the "functional equivalent" of the price squeeze that the Supreme Court refused to condemn in *Pac. Bell Tel. Co. v. LinkLine Communs., Inc.*, 555 U.S. 438 (2009), reprinted in your casebook. Do you agree? *Compare Safeway, Inc. v. Abbott Labs.*, 761 F. Supp. 2d 874 (N.D. Cal. 2011) (denying motion for summary judgment on facts similar to those in the *Doe* case, but pursued as a bundled discount under attribution test).

In *ZF Meritor, LLC v. Eaton Corp.*, 696 F.3d 254 (3d Cir. 2012), the defendant, a monopolist in the market for heavy-duty transmissions, imposed long-term agreements ("LTAs") on truck manufacturers (original equipment manufacturers or "OEMs"). These contracts included conditional rebate provisions, under which each buyer would only receive rebates if it purchased a specified percentage of its requirements from the defendant. These percentages were as high as 97.5%. These provisions resulted in de facto exclusivity. The jury returned a verdict in favor of the plaintiffs. On appeal, the defendant argued that because its prices were above cost, its pricing policies could not violate Section 2 of the Sherman Act. The Third Circuit debated whether the plaintiffs' allegations were "subject to the price-cost test or the 'rule of reason' applicable to exclusive dealing claims." *Id.* at 268. The majority of the panel held:

> a plaintiff's characterization of its claim as an exclusive dealing claim does not take the price-cost test off the table. Indeed, contracts in which discounts are linked to purchase (volume or market share) targets are frequently challenged as de facto exclusive dealing arrangements on the grounds that the discounts induce customers to deal exclusively with the firm offering the rebates. Hovenkamp ¶ 1807a, at 132. However, when price is the clearly predominant mechanism of exclusion, the price-cost test tells us that, so long as the price is above-cost, the procompetitive justifications for, and the benefits of, lowering prices far outweigh any potential anticompetitive effects.

Id. at 275.

> Here, in contrast to . . . *Brooke Group*, Plaintiffs did not rely solely on the exclusionary effect of [the defendant's] prices, and instead highlighted a number of anticompetitive provisions in the LTAs. Plaintiffs alleged that

[the defendant] used its position as a supplier of necessary products to persuade OEMs to enter into agreements imposing de facto purchase requirements of roughly 90% for at least five years, and that [the defendant] worked in concert with the OEMs to block customer access to Plaintiffs' products, thereby ensuring that Plaintiffs would be unable to build enough market share to pose any threat to [the defendant's] monopoly. Therefore, because price itself was not the clearly predominant mechanism of exclusion, the price-cost test cases are inapposite, and the rule of reason is the proper framework within which to evaluate Plaintiffs' claims.

Id. at 277.

Although the Supreme Court has created a safe harbor for above-cost discounting, it has not established a per se rule of non-liability under the antitrust laws for all contractual practices that involve above-cost pricing.

Id. at 278 (citing *Cascade Health Solutions*).

Writing in dissent, Judge Greenberg argued:

although the price-cost test may not bar a claim of exclusive dealing challenging a defendant's above-cost pricing practices, regardless of how a plaintiff casts its claim or the non-price elements of the pricing practices that the plaintiff identifies as the exclusionary conduct, where a plaintiff attacks a defendant's pricing practices — and to be clear that is what the market-share rebate programs at issue here are — the fact that defendant's prices were above-cost must be a high barrier to the plaintiff's success. Accordingly, I believe that we must apply the *Brooke Group* price-cost test to the present case and give that test persuasive effect in the context of our broader analysis under the antitrust laws at issue.

Id. at 311–12.

. . . I believe that it is evident that the Supreme Court's reasoning with respect to above-costs pricing applies to a plaintiff's challenge to a defendant's pricing practices even if the plaintiff claims that the non-price aspects of the defendant's practices were the actual exclusionary tactics.

Id. at 320.

Which approach do you think is most appropriate?

4. The Federal Trade Commission brought a monopolization case against Intel, accusing it of using market share discounts and related pricing practices as well as some strategic product redesigns in order to exclude its principal rival, AMD. The FTC's complaint acknowledged that it was using § 5 of the Federal Trade Commission Act to reach conduct that might not have been reachable under § 2 of the Sherman Act. The FTC accused Intel of using discounts that were conditioned on a computer maker's purchase of a large share of its processor needs from Intel, and also making design changes in its chips and interfaces that made its rival's microprocessors perform more poorly than its own. In 2010 the parties entered a consent order, which prohibited Intel from:

6. Condition[ing] any Benefit to a Customer or End User, either formally or informally, directly or indirectly, upon a Customer's purchase or sale of (a) Mainstream Microprocessors and (b) Computer Product Chipsets in a fixed proportion where, if the entire value of the Benefit were attributed to the Mainstream Microprocessors or Computer Product Chipsets included in the bundle, the selling price of those Mainstream Microprocessors or Computer Product Chipsets, as the case may be, would be below Respondent's Consent Order Cost.

7. provide[ing] to a Customer or End User a discount as a flat or lump-sum payment of monies or any other item(s) of pecuniary value based upon a Customer's sales or purchases of Respondent's Relevant Products or Computer Product Chipsets reaching a specified threshold (in units, revenues, or any other measure) or otherwise reducing the price of one unit of Respondent's Relevant Products because of the purchase or sale of an additional unit of that product; provided, however, that Respondent may offer a discount or other items of pecuniary value based upon sales or purchases beyond a specified threshold. By way of example, Respondent may offer or provide a discount of X% on all sales in excess of Y units, but it may not offer or provide a discount of X% on all units if sales exceed Y units.

Finally, the consent decree provided that Intel:

shall not make any engineering or design change to a Relevant Product if that change (1) degrades the performance of a Relevant Product sold by a competitor of Respondent and (2) does not provide an actual benefit to the Relevant Product sold by Respondent, including without limitation any improvement in performance, operation, cost, manufacturability, reliability, compatibility, or ability to operate or enhance the operation of another product; provided, however, that any degradation of the performance of a competing product shall not itself be deemed to be a benefit to the Relevant Product sold by Respondent. Respondent shall have the burden of demonstrating that any engineering or design change at issue complies with . . . this Order.

Paragraph 7 depended on a claim that because of its popularity among computer users, manufacturers could not avoid using Intel chips for a substantial portion of their computers, and competition would thus be effective for only the more "marginal" sales. For example, for any given computer model Intel might effectively have a lock on, say, 70% of sales but would compete with AMD for the other 30%. This creates a situation similar to one involving bundled discounts where the rival makes only one of the two products. For example, the dominant firm might condition its discount on a buyer's purchasing 90% of its needs from the dominant firm, putting the discount on all the units. In that case a rival wishing to compete for the 20% excess above the "locked in" 70% would have to match not only the price on the incremental 20% but also the foregone discount on the first 70%. Under the consent decree, if Intel wishes to offer a discount to buyers who will take more than 70% of its chips from Intel, it can make the discount apply to the excess but it cannot apply the discount to all of the units.

The consent decree is available on the FTC's website, at http://www.ftc.gov/os/adjpro/d9341/101102inteldo.pdf.

5. *Nonprice Competition and Business Torts as Antitrust Violations.* In *Conwood Corp. v. U.S. Tobacco Co.*, 290 F.3d 768 (6th Cir. 2002), the Sixth Circuit affirmed the largest damages award in antitrust history ($1.05 billion) for an amalgamation of actions that included both procompetitive and tortious conduct. The product was moist snuff, a tobacco product that was traditionally sold through individualized racks that each manufacturer provided for its own brands. The defendant had developed integrated racks that held the brands of all firms and that took up less space than individual racks required. In some cases, retailers requested these integrated racks and the defendant supplied them, or in other cases installed them after obtaining the retailers' permission. In yet other cases, however, it substituted the racks without permission, an act that may have been tortious under state law. The defendant also gave modest rebates to retailers in exchange for sales information, and an expert (although no retailers themselves) testified that the defendant sometimes supplied misleading information to retailers about rivals' sales in order to get them to carry more of the defendant's brands.

The Sixth Circuit held that the jury was entitled to assign liability and damages to this amalgamation of activity, without distinguishing between rack replacements that were tortious and those that were requested or permitted by retailers. The court also concluded that it was unlawful for the defendant to "suggest that retailers carry fewer products, particularly competitor's products," and to "suggest that stores carry its slower moving products instead of better selling competitor products."

The court also rejected a line of cases holding that before conduct can be condemned under Section 2, the plaintiff's expert must provide some basis for "disaggregating" the effects of unlawful conduct from the effects of lawful conduct or other market factors that the defendant could not control. For example, if the plaintiff's market growth was slowed by (A) unlawful acts, (B) lawful acts, and (C) other factors, such as new product introductions by other rivals, then the expert's damages study must be capable of showing the amount of damages attributable to (A) alone. In this particular case, the expert had not done so, but had merely offered two damage estimates based on two hypothetical growth projections — a higher number based on the premise that the plaintiff would have grown by about eight additional market share points but for the violation, and a lower number premised on growth of about five additional points. The jury was instructed to consider only unlawful conduct in awarding damages, and it split the difference. The court concluded that it was reasonable to infer that the jury had determined for itself which part of the plaintiff's injury resulted from unlawful conduct, and which resulted from lawful conduct or other market factors, and the amount of damages to be attributed to each.

Contrast the approach taken by the Ninth Circuit in *Image Technical Services v. Eastman Kodak Co.*, 125 F.3d 1195, 1224 (9th Cir. 1997):

> The [plaintiffs] must segregate damages attributable to lawful competition from damages attributable to Kodak's monopolizing conduct. A failure to do so contravenes the command of the Clayton Act. Although the district

court instructed the jury to award only those damages arising from Kodak's monopolization of the service market, the ISOs point to no basis in the record for quantifying lost sales of used equipment caused by Kodak's service monopoly.

Suppose you were advising a manufacturer in Detroit (in the Sixth Circuit) who just developed an innovative display that retailers were likely to prefer over existing displays, but rivals were likely to object because the display contained advertising for your client? Would you advise him to pursue placing the display with retailers, or just to drop it? Suppose your client operated in Minneapolis (in the Eighth Circuit, where *Brunswick, supra,* was decided)? Suppose your client operated in both cities?

[D] Vertical Integration, Refusals to Deal and Exclusionary Contracting

When a manufacturer with monopoly power integrates vertically — perhaps by purchasing its own distributorship or retail outlets — we generally presume that it does so to lower its costs. By obtaining its own retail outlets, a manufacturer can reduce the risks, uncertainties, and transaction costs of the market, and it can control the way its product is sold. Vertical integration often enables firms to provide better products or services, at lower prices.

When the monopolist integrates vertically, however, courts have traditionally perceived substantial threats to competition. They have noted, for example, that by acquiring or building its own retail stores, a monopolist in manufacturing can acquire a second monopoly at the retail level. The law of vertical mergers is concerned in large part with the problem of vertical integration when one of the firms involved has or threatens to have market power. When the monopolist integrates vertically, not by acquiring an existing company but by creating its own retail stores or distribution systems, the antimerger laws do not apply. The question then becomes whether vertical integration by a monopolist violates Section 2 of the Sherman Act.

Although it is true that a monopolist can use vertical integration to create a second monopoly, it is unlikely that it will be able to enlarge its monopoly profits this way. When a retail customer purchases a product, the customer is interested only in the total price, not in the amount of mark-up at each level in the distribution system for that product. A monopolist at any single stage in a distribution scheme should be able to extract all the monopoly profits available from a product, provided that the other stages in the distribution scheme are competitive.

That last proviso is important. Suppose that a manufacturing monopolist believes that the independent retail stores selling its product have formed a cartel. By refusing to sell to these stores and setting up its own stores instead, the manufacturing monopolist might be able to transfer the retail stores' cartel profits to itself.

In general, however, the same reasons that make vertical integration efficient for firms in competition are also likely to increase the efficiency of monopolists. The monopolist has an interest in seeing that its product is distributed as efficiently as possible, just as much as a competitive producer does. If the profit-maximizing retail price of a Widget is $1.00, it is to the monopolist's advantage to sell through retail stores that add a mark-up of 20 cents rather than stores that add a mark-up of 30 cents. Likewise, the monopolist is better off buying from low-cost sources of supply than from high-cost sources. As a general rule, all producers, whether competitors or monopolists, are best off if the other links in the distribution chain for their particular product are operating at optimal efficiency.

In the middle of the twentieth century, courts were generally very hostile toward integration and often used Section 2 to condemn such practices as an automobile dealer's termination of dealerships and switch to self distribution. *See, e.g., Mt. Lebanon Motors, Inc. v. Chrysler Corp.*, 283 F. Supp. 453 (W.D. Pa. 1968), *aff'd per curiam*, 417 F.2d 622 (3d Cir. 1969). Frequently, the thinking was that a firm could "monopolize" something simply by taking over the distribution of its own product.

Most such decisions rest on serious misunderstandings about the nature of distribution. Manufacturers of complex products requiring point of sale services or other forms of dealer investment commonly limit distribution to selected distributors under franchise contracts imposing extensive controls on franchise performance; or they integrate forward into one or more stages of distribution where the costs of "policing" franchise performance are substantial. In other cases, economies of scale may dictate only one or a limited number of distributors in various local markets, and integration may be employed to prevent monopoly pricing at the local level.

In all these respects, the interests of consumers in efficient, low-priced distribution coincide with those of the manufacturer whether the latter is a monopolist or not. As the Second Circuit observed:

> [A] complaint pleading that a defendant expanded vertically and as a result, decided to discontinue doing business with its erstwhile trading partners at the next level down, does not plead an actionable refusal to deal. Such allegations are equally consistent with the idea that the monopolist expected to perform the second level service more efficiently than the old trading partners and thus undertook the vertical integration for a valid business reason, rather than for an anticompetitive one.

Port Dock & Stone Corp. v. Oldcastle Northeast, Inc., 507 F.3d 117 (2d Cir. 2007).

[1] The Monopolist's Refusal to Deal and the Essential Facility Doctrine

ASPEN SKIING CO. v. ASPEN HIGHLANDS SKIING CORP.
472 U.S. 585 (1985)

JUSTICE STEVENS delivered the opinion for the Court.

In a private treble damages action, the jury found that petitioner Aspen Skiing Company (Ski Co.) had monopolized the market for downhill skiing services in

Aspen, Colorado. The question presented is whether that finding is erroneous as a matter of law because it rests on an assumption that a firm with monopoly power has a duty to cooperate with its smaller rivals in a marketing arrangement in order to avoid violating § 2 of the Sherman Act.

I

Aspen is a destination ski resort with a reputation for "super powder," "a wide range of runs," and an "active night life," including "some of the best restaurants in North America." . . . Between 1945 and 1960, private investors independently developed three major facilities for downhill skiing: Aspen Mountain (Ajax), Aspen Highlands (Highlands), and Buttermilk. A fourth mountain, Snowmass, opened in 1967. . . .

Between 1958 and 1964, three independent companies operated Ajax, Highlands, and Buttermilk. In the early years, each company offered its own day or half-day tickets for use of its mountain. . . . In 1962, however, the three competitors also introduced an interchangeable ticket. . . . The 6-day, all-Aspen ticket provided convenience to the vast majority of skiers who visited the resort for weekly periods, but preferred to remain flexible about what mountain they might ski each day during the visit. . . . It also emphasized the unusual variety in ski mountains available in Aspen. . . .

In 1964, Buttermilk was purchased by Ski Co., but the interchangeable ticket program continued. . . . Lift operators at Highlands monitored usage of the ticket in the 1971–1972 season by recording the ticket numbers of persons going onto the slopes of that mountain. Highlands officials periodically met with Ski Co. officials to review the figures recorded at Highlands, and to distribute revenues based on that count. . . .

. . . .

In the next four seasons, Ski Co. and Highlands used surveys to allocate the revenues from the 4-area, 6-day ticket. Highlands' share of the revenues from the ticket was 17.5% in 1973–1974, 18.5% in 1974–1975, 16.8% in 1975–1976, and 13.2% in 1976–1977. During these four seasons, Ski Co. did not offer its own 3-area, multi-day ticket in competition with the all-Aspen ticket. By 1977, multi-area tickets accounted for nearly 35% the total market. . . . Holders of multi-area passes also accounted for additional daily ticket sales to persons skiing with them.

. . . [F]or the 1977–1978 season, Ski Co. offered to continue the all-Aspen ticket only if Highlands would accept a 13.2% fixed share of the ticket's revenues.

Although that had been Highlands' share of the ticket revenues in 1976–1977, Highlands contended that that season was an inaccurate measure of its market performance since it had been marked by unfavorable weather and an unusually low number of visiting skiers. Moreover, Highlands wanted to continued to divide revenues on the basis of actual usage, as that method of distribution allowed it to compete for the daily loyalties of the skiers who had purchased the tickets. . . . Fearing that the alternative might be no interchangeable ticket at all, and hoping to persuade Ski Co. to reinstate the usage division of revenues, Highlands eventually accepted a fixed percentage of 15% for the 1977-1978 season. . . . No survey was made during that season of actual usage of the 4-area ticket at the two competitors' mountains.

In March 1978, the Ski Co. management recommended to the Board of Directors that the 4-area ticket be discontinued for the 1978-1979 season. The Board decided to offer Highlands a 4-area ticket provided that Highlands would agree to receive a 12.5% fixed percentage of the revenue — considerably below Highlands' historical average based on usage. . . . Later in the 1978-1979 season, a member of Ski Co.'s Board of Directors candidly informed a Highlands' official that he had advocated making Highlands "an offer that [it] could not accept." . . . Ski Co. refused to consider any counterproposals, and Highlands finally rejected the offer of the fixed percentage.

As far as Ski Co. was concerned, the all-Aspen ticket was dead. In its place Ski Co. offered the 3-area, 6-day ticket featuring only its mountains. In an effort to promote this ticket, Ski Co. embarked on a national advertising campaign that strongly implied to people who were unfamiliar with Aspen that Ajax, Buttermilk, and Snowmass were the only ski mountains in the area. For example, Ski Co. had a sign changed in the Aspen Airways waiting room at Stapleton Airport in Denver. The old sign had a picture of the four mountains in Aspen touting "Four Big Mountains" whereas the new sign retained the picture but referred only to three.
. . .

Ski Co. took additional actions that made it extremely difficult for Highlands to market its own multi-area package to replace the joint offering. Ski Co. discontinued the 3-day, 3-area pass for the 1978-1979 season, and also refused to sell Highlands any lift tickets, either at the tour operator's discount or at retail. . . . Highlands finally developed an alternative product, the "Adventure Pack," which consisted of a 3-day pass at Highlands and three vouchers, each equal to the price of a daily lift ticket at a Ski Co. mountain. The vouchers were guaranteed by funds on deposit in an Aspen bank, and were redeemed by Aspen merchants at full value. . . . Ski Co., however, refused to accept them. . . .

Without a convenient all-Aspen ticket, Highlands basically "becomes a day ski area in a destination resort." . . . Highlands' share of the market for downhill skiing services in Aspen declined steadily after the 4-area ticket based on usage was abolished in 1977: from 20.5% in 1976–1977, to 15.7% in 1977–1978, to 13.1% in 1978–1979, to 12.5% in 1979–1980, to 11% in 1980–1981. . . .

II

In 1979, Highlands filed a complaint in the United States District Court for the District of Colorado naming Ski Co. as a defendant. Among various claims, the complaint alleged that Ski Co. had monopolized the market for downhill skiing services at Aspen in violation of § 2 of the Sherman Act, and prayed for treble damages. The case was tried to a jury which rendered a verdict finding Ski Co. guilty of the § 2 violation and calculating Highlands' actual damages at $2.5 million.
. . .

In her instructions to the jury, the District Judge explained that the offense of monopolization under § 2 of the Sherman Act has two elements: (1) the possession of monopoly power in a relevant market, and (2) the willful acquisition, maintenance, or use of that power by anticompetitive or exclusionary means or for anticompetitive or exclusionary purposes. . . . Although the first element was vigorously disputed at the trial and in the Court of Appeals, in this Court Ski Co. does not challenge the jury's special verdict finding that it possessed monopoly power. Nor does Ski Co. criticize the trial court's instructions to the jury concerning the second element of the § 2 offense.

On this element, the jury was instructed that it had to consider whether "Aspen Skiing Corporation willfully acquired, maintained, or used that power by anti-competitive or exclusionary means or for anti-competitive or exclusionary purposes." . . . The instructions elaborated:

> [A] firm that has lawfully acquired a monopoly position is not barred from taking advantage of scale economies by constructing a large and efficient factory. These benefits are a consequence of size and not an exercise of monopoly power. Nor is a corporation which possesses monopoly power under a duty to cooperate with its business rivals. Also a company which possesses monopoly power and which refuses to enter into a joint operating agreement with a competitor or otherwise refuses to deal with a competitor in some manner does not violate Section 2 if valid business reasons exist for that refusal.

> In other words, if there were legitimate business reasons for the refusal, then the defendant, even if he is found to possess monopoly power in a relevant market, has not violated the law. We are concerned with conduct which unnecessarily excludes or handicaps competitors. This is conduct which does not benefit consumers by making a better product or service available — or in other ways — and instead has the effect of impairing competition. . . ."

The jury answered a specific interrogatory finding the second element of the offense as defined in these instructions.

. . . The District Court . . . entered a judgment awarding Highlands treble damages of $7,500,000, costs and attorney's fees. . . .

The Court of Appeals affirmed in all respects. . . .

. . . .

III

In this Court, Ski Co. contends that even a firm with monopoly power has no duty to engage in joint marketing with a competitor, that a violation of § 2 cannot be established without evidence of substantial exclusionary conduct, and that none of its activities can be characterized as exclusionary. It also contends that the Court of Appeals incorrectly relied on the "essential facilities" doctrine and that an "anti-competitive intent" does not transform nonexclusionary conduct into monopolization. In response, Highlands submits that, given the evidence in the record, it is not necessary to rely on the "essential facilities" doctrine in order to affirm the judgment. . . .

"The central message of the Sherman Act is that a business entity must find new customers and higher profits through internal expansion — that is, by competing successfully rather than by arranging treaties with its competitors." *United States v. Citizens & Southern National Bank*, 422 U.S. 86, 116 (1975). Ski Co., therefore, is surely correct in submitting that even a firm with monopoly power has no general duty to engage in a joint marketing program with a competitor. Ski Co. is quite wrong, however, in suggesting that the judgment in this case rests on any such proposition of law. For the trial court unambiguously instructed the jury that a firm possessing monopoly power has no duty to cooperate with its business rivals. . . .

The absence of an unqualified duty to cooperate does not mean that every time a firm declines to participate in a particular cooperative venture, that decision may not have evidentiary significance, or that it may not give rise to liability in certain circumstances. The absence of a duty to transact business with another firm is, in some respects, merely the counterpart of the independent businessman's cherished right to select his customers and his associates. The high value that we have placed on the right to refuse to deal with other firms does not mean that the right is unqualified.

In *Lorain Journal v. United States*, 342 U.S. 143 (1951), we squarely held that this right was not unqualified. Between 1933 and 1948 the publisher of the Lorain Journal, a newspaper, was the only local business disseminating news and advertising in that Ohio town. In 1948, a small radio station was established in a nearby community. In an effort to destroy its small competitor, and thereby regain its "pre-1948 substantial monopoly over the mass dissemination of all news and advertising," the Journal refused to sell advertising to persons that patronized the radio station. . . .

In holding that this conduct violated § 2 of the Sherman Act, the Court dispatched the same argument raised by the monopolist here:

> "The publisher claims a right as a private business concern to select its customers and to refuse to accept advertisements from whomever it pleases. We do not dispute that general right. "But the word 'right' is one of the most deceptive of pitfalls; it is so easy to slip from a qualified meaning in the premise to an unqualified one in the conclusion. Most rights are qualified." . . ."

The Court approved the entry of an injunction ordering the Journal to print the advertisements of the customers of its small competitor.

In *Lorain Journal*, the violation of § 2 was an "attempt to monopolize," rather than monopolization, but the question of intent is relevant to both offenses. In the former case it is necessary to prove a "specific intent" to accomplish the forbidden objective — as Judge Hand explained, "an intent which goes beyond the mere intent to do the act." *United States v. Aluminum Co. of America*, 148 F.2d 416, 432 (2d Cir. 1945). In the latter case evidence of intent is merely relevant to the question whether the challenged conduct is fairly characterized as "exclusionary" or "anticompetitive" — to use the words in the trial court's instructions — or "predatory," to use a word that scholars seem to favor. Whichever label is used, there is agreement on the proposition that "no monopolist monopolizes unconscious of what he is doing." As Judge Bork stated more recently: "Improper exclusion (exclusion not the result of superior efficiency) is always deliberately intended."

The qualification on the right of a monopolist to deal with whom he pleases is not so narrow that it encompasses no more than the circumstances of *Lorain Journal.* In the actual case that we must decide, the monopolist did not merely reject a novel offer to participate in a cooperative venture that had been proposed by a competitor. Rather, the monopolist elected to make an important change in a pattern of distribution that had originated in a competitive market and had persisted for several years. The all-Aspen, 6-day ticket with revenues allocated on the basis of usage was first developed when three independent companies operated three different ski mountains in the Aspen area. . . . It continued to provide a desirable option for skiers when the market was enlarged to include four mountains, and when the character of the market was changed by Ski Co.'s acquisition of monopoly power. Moreover, since the record discloses that interchangeable tickets are used in other multi-mountain areas which apparently are competitive, it seems appropriate to infer that such tickets satisfy consumer demand in free competitive markets.

Ski Co.'s decision to terminate the all-Aspen ticket was thus a decision by a monopolist to make an important change in the character of the market.

Moreover, we must assume that the jury followed the court's instructions. The jury must, therefore, have drawn a distinction "between practices which tend to exclude or restrict competition on the one hand, and the success of a business which reflects only a superior product, a well-run business, or luck, on the other." . . . Since the jury was unambiguously instructed that Ski Co.'s refusal to deal with Highlands "does not violate § 2 if valid business reasons exist for that refusal," . . . we must assume that the jury concluded that there were no valid business reasons for the refusal. The question then is whether that conclusion finds support in the record.

IV

The question whether Ski Co.'s conduct may properly be characterized as exclusionary cannot be answered by simply considering its effect on Highlands. In addition, it is relevant to consider its impact on consumers and whether it has impaired competition in an unnecessarily restrictive way. If a firm has been "attempting to exclude rivals on some basis other than efficiency," it is fair to characterize its behavior as predatory. It is, accordingly, appropriate to examine the effect of the challenged pattern of conduct on consumers, on Ski Co.'s smaller rival, and on Ski Co. itself.

Superior Quality of the All-Aspen Ticket

The average Aspen visitor "is a well-educated, relatively affluent, experienced skier who has skied a number of times in the past. . . ." . . . Over 80% of the skiers visiting the resort each year have been there before — 40% of these repeat visitors have skied Aspen at least five times. . . . Over the years, they developed a strong demand for the 6-day, all-Aspen ticket in its various refinements. Most experienced skiers quite logically prefer to purchase their tickets at once for the whole period that they will spend at the resort; they can then spend more time on the slopes and enjoying the amenities and less time standing in ticket lines. The 4-area attribute of the ticket allowed the skier to purchase his 6-day ticket in advance while reserving the right to decide in his own time and for his own reasons which mountain he would ski on each day. It provided convenience and flexibility, and expanded the vistas and the number of challenging runs available to him during the week's vacation.

. . . [T]he actual record of competition between a 3-area ticket and the all-Aspen ticket in the years after 1967 indicated that skiers demonstrably preferred four mountains to three. . . . Highlands' expert marketing witness testified that many of the skiers who come to Aspen want to ski the four mountains, and the abolition of the 4-area pass made it more difficult to satisfy that ambition. . . . A consumer survey undertaken in the 1979–1980 season indicated that 53.7% of the respondents wanted to ski Highlands, but would not; 39.9% said that they would not be skiing at the mountain of their choice because their ticket would not permit it. . . .

Ski Co.'s Business Justification

Perhaps most significant, however, is the evidence relating to Ski Co. itself, for Ski Co. did not persuade the jury that its conduct was justified by any normal business purpose. Ski Co. was apparently willing to forgo daily ticket sales both to skiers who sought to exchange the coupons contained in Highlands' Adventure Pack, and to those who would have purchased Ski Co. daily lift tickets from Highlands if Highlands had been permitted to purchase them in bulk. The jury may well have concluded that Ski Co. elected to forgo these short run benefits because it was more interested in reducing competition in the Aspen market over the long run by harming its smaller competitor.

That conclusion is strongly supported by Ski Co.'s failure to offer any efficiency justification whatever for its pattern of conduct. In defending the decision to terminate the jointly offered ticket, Ski Co. claimed that usage could not be properly monitored. The evidence, however, established that Ski Co. itself monitored the use of the 3-area passes based on a count taken by lift operators, and distributed the revenues among its mountains on that basis. Ski Co. contended that coupons were administratively cumbersome, and that the survey takers had been disruptive and their work inaccurate. Coupons, however, were no more burdensome than the credit cards accepted at Ski Co. ticket windows. . . . Moreover, in other markets Ski Co. itself participated in interchangeable lift tickets using coupons. . . . As for the survey, its own manager testified that the problems were much overemphasized by Ski Co. officials, and were mostly resolved as they arose. . . . Ski Co.'s explanation for the rejection of Highlands' offer to hire — at its own expense — a reputable national accounting firm to audit usage of the 4-area tickets at Highlands' mountain, was that there was no way to "control" the audit. . . .

In the end, Ski Co. was pressed to justify its pattern of conduct on a desire to disassociate itself from — what it considered — the inferior skiing services offered at Highlands. . . . The all-Aspen ticket based on usage, however, allowed consumers to make their own choice on these matters of quality. Ski Co.'s purported concern for the relative quality of Highlands' product was supported in the record by little more than vague insinuations, and was sharply contested by numerous witnesses. Moreover, Ski Co. admitted that it was willing to associate with what it considered to be inferior products in other markets. . . .

Although Ski Co.'s pattern of conduct may not have been as " 'bold, relentless, and predatory' " as the publisher's actions in *Lorain Journal,* the record in this case comfortably supports an inference that the monopolist made a deliberate effort to discourage its customers from doing business with its smaller rival. The sale of its 3-area, 6-day ticket, particularly when it was discounted below the daily ticket price, deterred the ticket holders from skiing at Highlands. The refusal to accept the Adventure Pack coupons in exchange for daily tickets was apparently motivated entirely by a decision to avoid providing any benefit to Highlands even though accepting the coupons would have entailed no cost to Ski Co. itself, would have provided it with immediate benefits, and would have satisfied its potential customers. Thus the evidence supports an inference that Ski Co. was not motivated by efficiency concerns and that it was willing to sacrifice short run benefits and consumer good will in exchange for a perceived long-run impact on its smaller rival.

Because we are satisfied that the evidence in the record, construed most favorably in support of Highlands' position, is adequate to support the verdict under the instructions given by the trial court, the judgment of the Court of Appeals is

Affirmed.

JUSTICE WHITE took no part in the decision of this case.

NOTES AND QUESTIONS

1. *Raising Rivals' Costs.* The Supreme Court occasionally characterized the *Aspen* defendant's activities as "predatory." But Ski Co. almost certainly did not engage in predatory pricing — i.e., undergoing short-run losses in order to reap long-run monopoly gains. (Predatory pricing is discussed earlier in this chapter.) Rather, Ski Co.'s activities may be an example of strategic raising of a rival's costs in order to earn higher profits. Ski Co.'s refusal to participate with Highlands in a joint ticket arrangement was "costly" to Ski Co. But it was even more costly to Highlands. To put it another way, Highlands benefitted much more from the Ski Co.-Highlands joint venture than Ski Co. did. By ceasing the venture, the costs to both Ski Co. and Highlands of filling their slopes and lodges rose, but Highlands' costs rose more. The result was that Ski Co. was able to charge a higher premium over its costs, assuming that it was a monopolist.

The dominant firm or firms in an industry may sometimes select a strategy that is calculated, not so much to exclude firms from a market, but rather to ensure that smaller firms or new entrants will have higher costs than those of the dominant firm. *See* ABA, NON-PRICE PREDATION UNDER SECTION TWO OF THE SHERMAN ACT (E. Thomas Sullivan ed., ABA Monograph #18, 1991); Thomas Krattenmaker & Steven Salop, *Anticompetitive Exclusion: Raising Rivals' Cost to Achieve Power Over Price,* 96 YALE L.J. 209 (1986); Steven Salop & David Scheffman, *Raising Rivals' Costs,* 73 AM. ECON. REV. 267 (1983); Steven Salop & David Scheffman, *Cost-Raising Strategies,* 36 J. INDUS. ECON. 19 (1987).

What kind of things might a monopoly firm do in order to raise its rivals' costs? Consider the following:

(1) The dominant firm is capital intensive, while the smaller competitors are labor intensive. The entire industry is unionized. The dominant firm agrees to a contract giving workers a considerable wage increase, and the smaller firms are forced to follow. Although the dominant firm's costs rise, the costs of the smaller firms rise even more, and the result is that the dominant firm can raise price by a greater margin over its costs. *See* Oliver Williamson, *Wage Rates as a Barrier to Entry: the Pennington Case in Perspective*, 82 Q.J. Econ. 85 (1968).

(2) The dominant firm litigates against its smaller rival on patent issues, whether or not the litigation is well-founded. Although the litigation costs the dominant firm and its rival the same amount, the rival has a smaller output over which the litigation costs can be distributed. Its fixed costs (why fixed?) rise by a greater amount than do those of the dominant firm. *See* Herbert Hovenkamp, *Antitrust Policy After Chicago*, 84 Mich. L. Rev. 213, 274–80 (1985).

(3) The dominant firm or firms petition a regulatory agency for rules, compliance with which is subject to substantial economies of scale. For example, a dominant firm with a plant capable of producing 100,000 units monthly has four competitors whose plants can produce 20,000 units monthly each. It successfully petitions an agency for the mandatory installation of safety devices that cost $1,000,000 per plant, regardless of size. Once again, the relative fixed costs of the smaller firms rise much more than for the dominant firm. *See* Steven Salop, David Scheffman & Warren Schwartz, "A Bidding Analysis of Special Interest Regulation: Raising Rivals' Costs in a Rent Seeking Society," in *The Political Economy of Regulation: Private Interests in the Regulatory Process* 102 (R. Rogowsky & B. Yandle, eds. 1984).

(4) The dominant firm in an industry which uses electricity in the production process purchases from several electric utilities a promise that they will not sell electricity to the dominant firm's rivals. *See* Eric Rasmusen, Mark Ramseyer, & John Shepard Wiley, *Naked Exclusion*, 81 Am. Econ. Rev. 1137 (1991); Thomas Krattenmaker & Steven Salop, *Anticompetitive Exclusion: Raising Rivals' Costs to Achieve Power Over Price*, 96 Yale L.J. 209 (1986).

What can antitrust policy do about such strategies? In some cases, such as (4), the answer is relatively easy. A "naked" agreement under which Firm A extracts a promise that a utility will not deal with Firm A's competitors is illegal per se. The answers to (1), (2), and (3) are far more difficult. Strategies (2) and (3) in particular may involve activity protected by each person's right to petition the government. *See* Chapter 9. The labor contract in (1) may not be protected activity. What kind of evidence would be required to show that a dominant firm's agreement to a new wage contract was anticompetitive?

To date, courts have been slow to condemn activity as monopolistic merely because it raised a rival's costs (in *Aspen*, the Supreme Court condemned the activity, but did not cite the strategy of raising rivals' costs). In *Ball Mem. Hosp. v. Mutual Hosp. Ins. Co.*, 784 F.2d 1325, 1340 (7th Cir. 1986), the Seventh Circuit refused to condemn alleged monopolization by a health insurer on such a theory. The plaintiffs charged that Blue Shield's Preferred Provider Organization plan (PPO), under which Blue Shield set stringent limits on the amount it reimbursed hospitals for certain medical procedures, raised rivals' costs because it forced hospitals to shift costs to other insured patients. The theory was that the PPO actually reimbursed hospitals less than the cost of providing a particular insured medical procedure. The hospital could then break even only by increasing the price for the same procedure to other patients, who would then make claims against their insurers. As a result, the costs of other health insurers would rise as Blue Shield's costs declined.

In rejecting this argument, the court found it sufficient that Blue Shield had been found not to have substantial market power. In the absence of market power, such a scheme could not succeed, for the hospitals would not tolerate it. The court refused to assess any standard that required Blue Shield to show that its low reimbursement rates were "cost-justified," particularly when it held no monopoly power. Such a requirement would force the district courts to become "little versions of the Office of Price Administration."

By contrast, *Reazin v. Blue Cross & Blue Shield of Kan.*, 899 F.2d 951 (10th Cir. 1990), found that Blue Cross violated § 2 when it terminated its provider agreement with a hospital because the hospital had established an independent, competing mechanism for providing prepaid health care. Under the policy change, the plaintiff hospital would not receive reimbursements directly from Blue Cross, but its patients would have to pay their bills and seek reimbursement. The result was alleged to be that patients would shift from the plaintiff hospital to other hospitals, and this would raise the plaintiff hospital's cost of doing business.

2. The *Aspen* Court made much of the fact that the defendant could not produce a satisfactory business justification for its decision to stop cooperating with the plaintiff. In *Olympia Equip. Leasing Co. v. Western Union Tel. Co.*, 797 F.2d 370 (7th Cir. 1986), the court distinguished *Aspen*, and found an adequate business justification for the defendant's actions. Western Union had sold both telex equipment and telex communications services in "bundled" packages, but decided to withdraw from the telex equipment market when deregulation led to competition there. It encouraged others, including the plaintiff, to help it liquidate its inventory of terminals, even providing sales help and customer contacts. But later, Western Union decided to sell more of its own terminals, and encouraged its salesmen to sell more terminals themselves instead of referring the sales to the plaintiff. Western Union's sales of its terminals then rose dramatically, while those of the plaintiff fell to nothing and it went out of business. In declining to find monopolization, the Seventh Circuit said:

> Today it is clear that a firm with lawful monopoly power has no general duty to help its competitors, whether by holding a price umbrella over their heads or by otherwise pulling its competitive punches. . . .

If a monopolist does extend a helping hand, though not required to do so, and later withdraws it as happened in this case, does he incur antitrust liability? We think not. Conceivably he may be liable in tort or contract law, under theories of equitable or promissory estoppel or implied contract . . . , or by analogy to the common law tort rule that though there is no duty to help a bystander in distress, once help is extended it may not be withdrawn. . . . But the controlling consideration in an antitrust case is antitrust policy rather than common law analogies. Since Western Union had no duty to encourage the entry of new firms into the equipment market, the law would be perverse if it made Western Union's encouraging gestures the fulcrum of an antitrust violation. Then no firm would dare to attempt a graceful exit from a market in which it was a major seller. . . . Refusing to act as your competitor's sales agent is not an unnatural practice engaged in only by firms bent on monopolization.

The court found that the defendant's decision to sell its terminals in competition with the plaintiff was quite justified by its desire to exit the market more quickly. Perhaps more to the point, as the court noted in a later opinion denying a rehearing, the offense of monopolization consists of acts calculated to create or preserve the monopolist's position in the market. Here, the defendant was trying to *exit* from the market as effectively as possible. Such conduct cannot conceivably be calculated to create or preserve a monopoly, even though, in this case, it injured a rival. In distinguishing *Aspen*, Judge Posner noted that Western Union changed a previous course of cooperation with the defendant "not because its monopoly power had grown but because it wasn't getting out [of the market] fast enough!" *Olympia Equipment Leasing Co. v. Western Union Telegraph Co.*, 802 F.2d 217, 219 (7th Cir. 1986).

3.   In *Aspen*, the relevant market was defined as "downhill skiing in Aspen, Colorado," and the Supreme Court approved a jury verdict forcing the defendant to continue in a marketing and sales joint venture for an "All-Aspen" skiing ticket. But suppose the plaintiff had asked for *everything* in the relevant market: ski lodges, lifts, ski rentals — in sum, everything one needs except the labor to be set up in the business of providing skiing services. In *Image Technical Servs. v. Kodak*, 125 F.3d 1195, 1203 (9th Cir. 1997), the Ninth Circuit concluded that once a relevant market was defined for "all Kodak parts," Kodak had a duty under Section 2 of the Sherman Act to provide every single input in the market, including both parts that Kodak made and parts it had to buy from others, and whether or not the parts were available from alternative sources. All the plaintiffs had to supply for themselves was their labor, and presumably office space and trucks. Does anything in *Aspen* restrict its holding to things the plaintiff really needed or were capable of being monopolized? Or would the Supreme Court have forced Ski Co. to share its rental equipment and ski lodge as well?

4.   *Aspen* involved a defendant who participated in a joint venture with the plaintiff and then terminated the venture without a good business reason for doing so. But should it be a Section 2 violation for a dominant firm never to agree to enter into a venture in the first place? In *SmileCare Dental Group v. Delta Dental Plan*, 88 F.3d 780 (9th Cir. 1996), the plaintiff alleged that the defendant violated Section 2 by refusing to cooperate with it in the joint provision of a full coverage dental

insurance plan under which the defendant would sell the first 80% of coverage and the plaintiff would sell the remaining, or supplemental, 20%:

> Unlike the defendant skiing company in *Aspen*, Delta Dental did not discontinue a marketing arrangement with SmileCare. Delta Dental's copayment plan pre-existed SmileCare's supplemental plan and the parties have never cooperated to supply the market with a new or better product.

Id. at 786.

5. Sometimes monopolists may integrate vertically, whether or not integration is economically efficient, in order to avoid a group of antitrust decisions condemning refusals to deal by monopolists. As a basic premise, a firm is free to deal or refuse to deal with any other firm as it pleases. In *Eastman Kodak Co. v. Southern Photo Materials Co.*, 273 U.S. 359 (1927), however, the Supreme Court held that it could be illegal monopolization for a firm with monopoly power to refuse to deal with a firm in a different link of the distribution scheme if the monopolist's purpose was to extend its monopoly. Likewise, in *Otter Tail Power Co. v. United States*, 410 U.S. 366 (1973), the Court held it to be illegal monopolization for a large electric utility to refuse to "wheel" (i.e., transmit) power to community delivery systems if its purpose was to maintain a monopoly of such delivery systems. In *Eastman Kodak Co. v. Image Tech. Servs.*, 504 U.S. 451 (1992), the Court held that a firm could "monopolize" a market for its own brand of photocopier by refusing to provide repair parts to independent service technicians. The decision is reprinted in Chapter 5. The Ninth Circuit subsequently approved a finding of unlawful monopolization. *Image Technical Services v. Eastman Kodak Co.*, 125 F.3d 1195, 1203–1204 (9th Cir. 1997).

6. Even the monopolist is ordinarily free to bargain for the best price — i.e., to pay as little as it can for its inputs, and to sell at the highest price possible. *See Kartell v. Blue Shield of Mass., Inc.*, 749 F.2d 922 (1st Cir. 1984), holding that it was legal for Blue Shield as health insurer to purchase medical services on behalf of its insureds and to stipulate the maximum price it was willing to pay, even assuming it was a monopolist:

> Once one accepts that . . . Blue Shield in essence "buys" medical services for the account of others, the reasoning . . . indicates that the ban on balance billing is permissible. . . . Suppose a father buys toys for his son — toys the son picks out. Or suppose a landlord hires a painter to paint his tenant's apartment, to the tenant's specifications. Is it not obviously lawful for the father (the landlord) to make clear to the seller that the father (landlord) is in charge and will pay the bill? Why can he not then forbid the seller to charge the child (the tenant) anything over and above what the father (landlord) pays — at least if the seller wants the buyer's business?
>
> . . . The relevant antitrust facts are that Blue Shield pays the bill and seeks to set the amount of the charge.

7. In *Weiss v. York Hosp.*, 745 F.2d 786 (3d Cir. 1984), the court dismissed monopolization charges brought by a doctor of osteopathy (DO) who claimed that the defendant hospital illegally denied staff privileges to DOs. The defendant accounted for 80% of inpatient care in its service area, which was sufficient to give it monopoly power; however, the plaintiff's complaint faltered for failure to explain how the defendant's denial could be anticompetitive:

> York, like any hospital, would maximize its revenues by giving staff privileges to every qualified doctor who applied. Hospitals are in the business of providing facilities (rooms and equipment) and support staff (nurses, administrators, etc.). These resources are fixed in the short run, and the hospital maximizes its revenues by encouraging competition for its hospital beds and operating rooms. Since only physicians with staff privileges can admit and treat patients, York can maximize competition for its facilities by granting staff privileges to every qualified doctor who applies. Excluding DOs on the other hand is likely to weaken York's monopoly position in the long run, since a potential rival . . . would have an incentive to provide competing services for the DOs excluded from York.

Id. at 828

This tended to support the defendant's theory that it had adequate professional or medical reasons for denying staff privileges to DOs.

PROBLEM 6.11

Dogs'n'Cats, Inc., is a dominant manufacturer of pet supplies for sale in retail stores. Dogs'n'Cats relies on independent distributors to wholesale its supplies to various retail chain stores. Dogs'n'Cats' goal is to have every retail chain in the United States stock its pet supplies exclusively. One of the distributors is Petco. When a chain store complained to Petco about the relatively high cost of Dogs'n'Cats products, Petco began looking about for alternatives and found an Asian supplier, Animals, Inc., which manufactured pet products of equal quality but sold them at a much lower wholesale price. Petco began giving its stores the option of purchasing either Dogs'n'Cats or Animals, Inc., pet supplies. Several chose the latter. Dogs'n'Cats immediately (1) terminated Petco's distributorship and (2) announced that hereafter it would deal only with distributors who sold its supplies exclusively. Has Dogs'n'Cats violated the Sherman Act? *See General Indus. Corp. v. Hartz Mountain Corp.*, 810 F.2d 795 (8th Cir. 1987).

PROBLEM 6.12

Molar Insurance is the nation's dominant provider of dental insurance, most of which is marketed to employers for inclusion in employee benefit packages. Molar's "standard" dental protection policy includes 80% coverage for most dental procedures, requiring the patient to pick up the remaining 20% of his or her dental services out-of-pocket. Bicuspid Underwriting is a new insurance company entering the dental insurance field for the first time. It innovates and offers "complementary" dental insurance that will pick up the remaining 20% of Molar insured's costs. Thus, an employer who purchases both Molar's and Bicuspid's plans can offer 100% coverage. However, Molar not only refuses to cooperate with Bicuspid in marketing the plan, but also excludes from its coverage any procedures performed on a patient who is also covered by the Bicuspid complementary dental plan. Molar cites a "moral hazard" problem as its business justification: the impact of 100% coverage is that patients will use dental services more, thus increasing the costs and therefore the premiums of Molar's insureds. Under *Aspen*, has Molar violated Section 2? *See SmileCare Dental Group v. Delta Dental Plan*, 88 F.3d 780 (9th Cir. 1996).

NOTE: THE ESSENTIAL FACILITY DOCTRINE

In *Aspen*, the Supreme Court referred to the "essential facilities" doctrine, but did not decide the case on that basis. Several lower courts have addressed the doctrine. Briefly, the doctrine makes it illegal for the person operating a properly defined "essential facility" to deny access to someone else. The courts are hopelessly confused about what constitutes an "essential facility," and under what circumstances the controller of an essential facility has a right to deny access. The "essential facility" doctrine originated in Supreme Court decisions that really involved concerted refusals to deal, attacked principally under Section 1 of the Sherman Act. For example, in *United States v. Terminal R.R. Ass'n*, 224 U.S. 383 (1912), the Court held that toll bridges and cargo transfer facilities on the Mississippi River operated as a joint venture by several railroads had to be shared with other railroads who needed these facilities in order to move their cargo. *Associated Press v. United States*, 326 U.S. 1 (1945), then held that a news gathering agency operated as a joint venture had to be opened to nonmembers on nondiscriminatory terms. Finally, *Otter Tail Power Co. v. United States*, 410 U.S. 366 (1973), held that a public utility acting unilaterally could not refuse to transfer, or "wheel," power for the use of smaller power companies.

The formulation of the "essential facility" doctrine has been left to the lower courts. In *Hecht v. Pro-Football, Inc.*, 570 F.2d 982 (D.C. Cir. 1977), the court characterized an "essential facility" as something which (1) is essential to the plaintiff's competitive survival; (2) cannot practically be duplicated; (3) can be used by the plaintiff without interference with the defendant's use. The court additionally suggested that in order to show a duty to share an essential facility, the plaintiff must show that the defendant's denial was anticompetitively motivated, or that competition would be improved if access was granted. *Id.* at 992–993.

In *Fishman v. Estate of Wirtz*, 807 F.2d 520 (7th Cir. 1986), the Seventh Circuit applied the essential facility doctrine to a public sports stadium which had "a strategic dominance over the market for indoor team sports arenas in Chicago," and which "could charge much higher prices than the other arenas without causing its patrons to switch." The denial of the stadium lease to a group of investors constituted a per se illegal boycott and monopolization, the court found. In a strident dissent, Judge Easterbrook found that the sports arena was not even a relevant market, for there were plenty of substitutes in the Chicago area.

At the very least, it seems, an "essential facility" must constitute a relevant market. Otherwise, the controller of the facility (assuming that it did not control all other sources of output as well) could not charge monopoly prices. *See Illinois Bell Tel. Co. v. Haines & Co.*, 905 F.2d 1081 (7th Cir. 1990) (alleged essential facility must dominate properly defined relevant market). Further, even the dominant firm has no *general* duty to share its production capacity or anything else with a rival. *See Olympia Equip. Leasing Co. v. Western Union Tel. Co.*, 797 F.2d 370, 376 (7th Cir. 1986): "Today it is clear that a firm with lawful monopoly power has no general duty to help its competitors, whether by holding a price umbrella over their heads or by otherwise pulling its competitive punches."

One trend in the case law is to find essentiality under circumstances where (1) the facility is owned or somehow subsidized by the government; or (2) the controller of the essential facility is a public utility with an exclusive right created by the government. For example, the football stadium found to be an essential facility in *Hecht v. Pro-Football, supra*, was owned by the government. The duty of a regulated public utility to deal with others comes from the early common law, and the antitrust laws may do no more than carry it out. *See* Hovenkamp, *Regulatory Conflict in the Gilded Age: Federalism and the Railroad Problem*, 88 YALE L.J. 1017 (1988). The Government lawsuit against AT&T, which ended up in the divestiture of the telephone monopoly, was predicated in large part on an essential facility doctrine. The theory of the case was that once competition in long distance communications became technically feasible, AT&T had a duty to share access to the local telephone networks with others. *United States v. AT&T*, 552 F. Supp. 131 (D.D.C. 1982), *aff'd mem. sub nom. Maryland v. United States*, 460 U.S. 1001 (1983).

In a case from the same period brought by a competitor, the court characterized the local telephone exchanges as an "essential facility":

> AT&T had complete control over the local distribution facilities that MCI required. The interconnections were essential for MCI to offer [long distance] service. The facilities in question met the criteria of "essential facilities" in that MCI could not duplicate Bell's local facilities. Given present technology, local telephone service is generally regarded as a natural monopoly and is regulated as such. It would not be economically feasible for MCI to duplicate Bell's local distribution facilities (involving millions of miles of cable and lines to individual homes and businesses), and regulatory authorization could not be obtained for such an uneconomical duplication.

MCI Commun. Corp. v. AT&T, 708 F.2d 1081 (7th Cir. 1983). How does the following decision fit into this framework?

On the essential facility doctrine, see Marina Lao, *Networks, Access, and "Essential Facilities": From Terminal Railroad to Microsoft*, 62 SMU L. REV. 557 (2009); Brett Frischmann & Spencer Weber Waller, *Revitalizing Essential Facilities*, 75 ANTITRUST L.J. 1 (2008); Spencer Weber Waller, *Areeda, Epithets, and Essential Facilities*, 2008 WIS. L. REV. 359 (2008); Robert Pitofsky, Donna Patterson & Jonathan Hooks, *The Essential Facilities Doctrine Under U.S. Antitrust Law*, 70 ANTITRUST L.J. 443 (2002); Phillip Areeda, *Essential Facilities: An Epithet in Need of Limiting Principles*, 58 ANTITRUST L.J. 841 (1990).

VERIZON COMMUNICATIONS, INC. v. LAW OFFICES OF CURTIS v. TRINKO, LLP
540 U.S. 398 (2004)

Justice Scalia delivered the opinion of the Court.

The Telecommunications Act of 1996, Pub. L. 104-104, 110 Stat. 56, imposes certain duties upon incumbent local telephone companies in order to facilitate market entry by competitors, and establishes a complex regime for monitoring and enforcement. In this case we consider whether a complaint alleging breach of the incumbent's duty under the 1996 Act to share its network with competitors states a claim under § 2 of the Sherman Act, 26 Stat. 209.

I

Petitioner Verizon Communications Inc. is the incumbent local exchange carrier (LEC) serving New York State. Before the 1996 Act, Verizon, like other incumbent LECs, enjoyed an exclusive franchise within its local service area. The 1996 Act sought to "uproo[t]" the incumbent LECs' monopoly and to introduce competition in its place. Central to the scheme of the Act is the incumbent lecs' obligation under 47 U.S.C. § 251(c) to share its network with competitors, including provision of access to individual elements of the network on an "unbundled" basis. § 251(c)(3). New entrants, so-called competitive LECs, resell these unbundled network elements (UNEs), recombined with each other or with elements belonging to the LECs.

Verizon, like other incumbent LECs, has taken two significant steps within the Act's framework in the direction of increased competition. First, Verizon has signed interconnection agreements with rivals such as AT & T, as it is obliged to do under § 252, detailing the terms on which it will make its network elements available. (Because Verizon and AT & T could not agree upon terms, the open issues were subjected to compulsory arbitration under §§ 252(b) and (c).) In 1997, the state regulator, New York's Public Service Commission (PSC), approved Verizon's interconnection agreement with AT & T.

Second, Verizon has taken advantage of the opportunity provided by the 1996 Act for incumbent LECs to enter the long-distance market (from which they had long been excluded). That required Verizon to satisfy, among other things, a 14-item checklist of statutory requirements, which includes compliance with the Act's network-sharing duties. §§ 271(d)(3)(A) and (c)(2)(B). Checklist item two, for example, includes "nondiscriminatory access to network elements in accordance with the requirements" of § 251(c)(3). . . .

In late 1999, competitive LECs complained to regulators that . . . Verizon [was violating its] obligation to provide access. . . . The PSC and FCC opened parallel investigations, which led to a series of orders by the PSC and a consent decree with the FCC. Under the FCC consent decree, Verizon undertook to make a "voluntary contribution" to the U.S. Treasury in the amount of $3 million, 15 FCC Rcd. 5415, 5421, ¶ 16 (2000); under the PSC orders, Verizon incurred liability to the competitive

LECs in the amount of $10 million. Under the consent decree and orders, Verizon was subjected to new performance measurements and new reporting requirements to the FCC and PSC, with additional penalties for continued noncompliance.

Respondent Law Offices of Curtis v. Trinko, LLP, a New York City law firm, was a local telephone service customer of AT & T. The day after Verizon entered its consent decree with the FCC, respondent filed a complaint in the District Court for the Southern District of New York, on behalf of itself and a class of similarly situated customers. The complaint, as later amended, alleged that Verizon had filled rivals' orders on a discriminatory basis as part of an anticompetitive scheme to discourage customers from becoming or remaining customers of competitive LECs, thus impeding the competitive LECs' ability to enter and compete in the market for local telephone service. According to the complaint, Verizon "has filled orders of [competitive LEC] customers after filling those for its own local phone service, has failed to fill in a timely manner, or not at all, a substantial number of orders for [competitive LEC] customers . . . , and has systematically failed to inform [competitive LECs] of the status of their customers' orders." . . . The complaint sought damages and injunctive relief for violation of § 2 of the Sherman Act, 15 U.S.C. § 2, pursuant to the remedy provisions of §§ 4 and 16 of the Clayton Act. The complaint also alleged violations of the 1996 Act, § 202(a) of the Communications Act of 1934, 48 Stat. 1064, as amended, 47 U.S.C. § 151 et seq., and state law.

The District Court dismissed the complaint in its entirety. As to the antitrust portion, it concluded that respondent's allegations of deficient assistance to rivals failed to satisfy the requirements of § 2. The Court of Appeals for the Second Circuit reinstated the complaint in part, including the antitrust claim. 305 F.3d 89, 113 (2002). We granted certiorari, limited to the question whether the Court of Appeals erred in reversing the District Court's dismissal of respondent's antitrust claims.

II

To decide this case, we must first determine what effect (if any) the 1996 Act has upon the application of traditional antitrust principles. The Act imposes a large number of duties upon incumbent LECs — above and beyond those basic responsibilities it imposes upon all carriers, such as assuring number portability and providing access to rights-of-way, see 47 U.S.C. §§ 251(b)(2), (4). Under the sharing duties of § 251(c), incumbent LECs are required to offer three kinds of access. Already noted, and perhaps most intrusive, is the duty to offer access to UNEs on "just, reasonable, and nondiscriminatory" terms, § 251(c)(3), a phrase that the FCC has interpreted to mean a price reflecting long-run incremental cost. See *Verizon Communications Inc. v. FCC*, 535 U.S., at 495–496. A rival can interconnect its own facilities with those of the incumbent LEC, or it can simply purchase services at wholesale from the incumbent and resell them to consumers. See §§ 251(c)(2), (4). The Act also imposes upon incumbents the duty to allow physical "collocation" — that is, to permit a competitor to locate and install its equipment on the incumbent's premises — which makes feasible interconnection and access to UNEs.

That Congress created these duties, however, does not automatically lead to the conclusion that they can be enforced by means of an antitrust claim. Indeed, a detailed regulatory scheme such as that created by the 1996 Act ordinarily raises the question whether the regulated entities are not shielded from antitrust scrutiny altogether by the doctrine of implied immunity. *See, e.g., United States v. National Assn. of Securities Dealers, Inc.*, 422 U.S. 694 (1975); *Gordon v. New York Stock Exchange, Inc.*, 422 U.S. 659 (1975). In some respects the enforcement scheme set up by the 1996 Act is a good candidate for implication of antitrust immunity, to avoid the real possibility of judgments conflicting with the agency's regulatory scheme "that might be voiced by courts exercising jurisdiction under the antitrust laws." *United States v. National Assn. of Securities Dealers, Inc., supra*, at 734.

Congress, however, precluded that interpretation. Section 601(b)(1) of the 1996 Act is an antitrust-specific saving clause providing that "nothing in this Act or the amendments made by this Act shall be construed to modify, impair, or supersede the applicability of any of the antitrust laws." 110 Stat. 143, 47 U.S.C. § 152, note. This bars a finding of implied immunity. . . .

But just as the 1996 Act preserves claims that satisfy existing antitrust standards, it does not create new claims that go beyond existing antitrust standards; that would be equally inconsistent with the saving clause's mandate that nothing in the Act "modify, impair, or supersede the applicability" of the antitrust laws. We turn, then, to whether the activity of which respondent complains violates preexisting antitrust standards.

III

The complaint alleges that Verizon denied interconnection services to rivals in order to limit entry. If that allegation states an antitrust claim at all, it does so under § 2 of the Sherman Act, 15 U.S.C. § 2, which declares that a firm shall not "monopolize" or "attempt to monopolize." It is settled law that this offense requires, in addition to the possession of monopoly power in the relevant market, "the willful acquisition or maintenance of that power as distinguished from growth or development as a consequence of a superior product, business acumen, or historic accident." *United States v. Grinnell Corp.*, 384 U.S. 563, 570–571 (1966). The mere possession of monopoly power, and the concomitant charging of monopoly prices, is not only not unlawful; it is an important element of the free-market system. The opportunity to charge monopoly prices — at least for a short period — is what attracts "business acumen" in the first place; it induces risk taking that produces innovation and economic growth. To safeguard the incentive to innovate, the possession of monopoly power will not be found unlawful unless it is accompanied by an element of anticompetitive *conduct*.

Firms may acquire monopoly power by establishing an infrastructure that renders them uniquely suited to serve their customers. Compelling such firms to share the source of their advantage is in some tension with the underlying purpose of antitrust law, since it may lessen the incentive for the monopolist, the rival, or both to invest in those economically beneficial facilities. Enforced sharing also requires antitrust courts to act as central planners, identifying the proper price, quantity, and other terms of dealing — a role for which they are ill-suited. Moreover, compelling negotiation between competitors may facilitate the supreme evil of antitrust: collusion. Thus, as a general matter, the Sherman Act "does not restrict the long recognized right of [a] trader or manufacturer engaged in an entirely private business, freely to exercise his own independent discretion as to parties with whom he will deal." *United States v. Colgate & Co.*, 250 U.S. 300, 307 (1919).

However, "[t]he high value that we have placed on the right to refuse to deal with other firms does not mean that the right is unqualified." *Aspen Skiing Co. v. Aspen Highlands Skiing Corp.*, 472 U.S. 585, 601 (1985). Under certain circumstances, a refusal to cooperate with rivals can constitute anticompetitive conduct and violate § 2. We have been very cautious in recognizing such exceptions, because of the uncertain virtue of forced sharing and the difficulty of identifying and remedying anticompetitive conduct by a single firm. The question before us today is whether the allegations of respondent's complaint fit within existing exceptions or provide a basis, under traditional antitrust principles, for recognizing a new one.

The leading case for § 2 liability based on refusal to cooperate with a rival, and the case upon which respondent understandably places greatest reliance, is *Aspen Skiing, supra*. The Aspen ski area consisted of four mountain areas. The defendant, who owned three of those areas, and the plaintiff, who owned the fourth, had cooperated for years in the issuance of a joint, multiple-day, all-area ski ticket. After repeatedly demanding an increased share of the proceeds, the defendant canceled the joint ticket. The plaintiff, concerned that skiers would bypass its mountain without some joint offering, tried a variety of increasingly desperate measures to re-create the joint ticket, even to the point of in effect offering to buy the defendant's tickets at retail price. The defendant refused even that. We upheld a jury verdict for the plaintiff, reasoning that "[t]he jury may well have concluded that [the defendant] elected to forgo these short-run benefits because it was more interested in reducing competition . . . over the long run by harming its smaller competitor."

Aspen Skiing is at or near the outer boundary of § 2 liability. The Court there found significance in the defendant's decision to cease participation in a cooperative venture. See *id.*, at 608, 610–611. The unilateral termination of a voluntary (*and thus presumably profitable*) course of dealing suggested a willingness to forsake short-term profits to achieve an anticompetitive end. Similarly, the defendant's unwillingness to renew the ticket *even if compensated at retail price* revealed a distinctly anticompetitive bent.

The refusal to deal alleged in the present case does not fit within the limited exception recognized in *Aspen Skiing*. The complaint does not allege that Verizon voluntarily engaged in a course of dealing with its rivals, or would ever have done so absent statutory compulsion. Here, therefore, the defendant's prior conduct sheds no light upon the motivation of its refusal to deal — upon whether its regulatory lapses were prompted not by competitive zeal but by anticompetitive malice. The contrast between the cases is heightened by the difference in pricing behavior. In *Aspen Skiing*, the defendant turned down a proposal to sell at its own retail price, suggesting a calculation that its future monopoly retail price would be higher. Verizon's reluctance to interconnect at the cost-based rate of compensation available under § 251(c)(3) tells us nothing about dreams of monopoly.

The specific nature of what the 1996 Act compels makes this case different from *Aspen Skiing* in a more fundamental way. In *Aspen Skiing*, what the defendant refused to provide to its competitor was a product that it already sold at retail — to oversimplify slightly, lift tickets representing a bundle of services to skiers. Similarly, in *Otter Tail Power Co. v. United States*, 410 U.S. 366 (1973), another case relied upon by respondent, the defendant was already in the business of providing a service to certain customers (power transmission over its network), and refused to provide the same service to certain other customers. In the present case, by contrast, the services allegedly withheld are not otherwise marketed or available to the public. The sharing obligation imposed by the 1996 Act created "something brand new" — "the wholesale market for leasing network elements." *Verizon Communications Inc. v. FCC*, 535 U.S., at 528. The unbundled elements offered pursuant to § 251(c)(3) exist only deep within the bowels of Verizon; they are brought out on compulsion of the 1996 Act and offered not to consumers but to rivals, and at considerable expense and effort. New systems must be designed and implemented simply to make that access possible — indeed, it is the failure of one of those systems that prompted the present complaint.[6]

We conclude that Verizon's alleged insufficient assistance in the provision of service to rivals is not a recognized antitrust claim under this Court's existing refusal-to-deal precedents. This conclusion would be unchanged even if we considered to be established law the "essential facilities" doctrine crafted by some lower courts, under which the Court of Appeals concluded respondent's allegations might state a claim. See generally Areeda, Essential Facilities: An Epithet in Need of Limiting Principles, 58 Antitrust L.J. 841 (1989). We have never recognized such a doctrine, see *Aspen Skiing Co.*, 472 U.S., at 611, n.44; *AT & T Corp. v. Iowa Utilities Bd.*, 525 U.S., at 428 (opinion of Breyer, J.), and we find no need either to recognize it or to repudiate it here. It suffices for present purposes to note that the indispensable requirement for invoking the doctrine is the unavailability of access to the "essential facilities"; where access exists, the doctrine serves no purpose. Thus, it is said that "essential facility claims should . . . be denied where a state or federal agency has effective power to compel sharing and to regulate its scope and terms." P. Areeda & H. Hovenkamp, Antitrust Law, p. 150, ¶ 773e (2003 Supp.). Respondent believes that the existence of sharing duties under the 1996 Act supports its case. We think the opposite: The 1996 Act's extensive provision for access makes it unnecessary to impose a judicial doctrine of forced access. To the extent respondent's "essential facilities" argument is distinct from its general § 2 argument, we reject it.

IV

Finally, we do not believe that traditional antitrust principles justify adding the present case to the few existing exceptions from the proposition that there is no

---

[6] [FN 3] Respondent also relies upon United States v. Terminal Railroad Assn. of St. Louis, 224 U.S. 383 (1912), and Associated Press v. United States, 326 U.S. 1 (1945). These cases involved concerted action, which presents greater anticompetitive concerns and is amenable to a remedy that does not require judicial estimation of free-market forces: simply requiring that the outsider be granted nondiscriminatory admission to the club.

duty to aid competitors. Antitrust analysis must always be attuned to the particular structure and circumstances of the industry at issue. Part of that attention to economic context is an awareness of the significance of regulation. As we have noted, "careful account must be taken of the pervasive federal and state regulation characteristic of the industry." *United States v. Citizens & Southern Nat. Bank*, 422 U.S. 86, 91 (1975); *see also* IA P. Areeda & H. Hovenkamp, Antitrust Law, p. 12, ¶ 240c3 (2d ed. 2000). "[A]ntitrust analysis must sensitively recognize and reflect the distinctive economic and legal setting of the regulated industry to which it applies." *Concord v. Boston Edison Co.*, 915 F.2d 17, 22 (C.A.1 1990) (Breyer, C.J.) (internal quotation marks omitted).

One factor of particular importance is the existence of a regulatory structure designed to deter and remedy anticompetitive harm. Where such a structure exists, the additional benefit to competition provided by antitrust enforcement will tend to be small, and it will be less plausible that the antitrust laws contemplate such additional scrutiny. Where, by contrast, "[t]here is nothing built into the regulatory scheme which performs the antitrust function," *Silver v. New York Stock Exchange*, 373 U.S. 341 (1963), the benefits of antitrust are worth its sometimes considerable disadvantages. Just as regulatory context may in other cases serve as a basis for implied immunity, *see, e.g.*, *United States v. National Assn. of Securities Dealers, Inc.*, 422 U.S., at 730–735, it may also be a consideration in deciding whether to recognize an expansion of the contours of § 2.

The regulatory framework that exists in this case demonstrates how, in certain circumstances, "regulation significantly diminishes the likelihood of major antitrust harm." *Concord v. Boston Edison Co., supra*, at 25. Consider, for example, the statutory restrictions upon Verizon's entry into the potentially lucrative market for long-distance service. To be allowed to enter the long-distance market in the first place, an incumbent LEC must be on good behavior in its local market. Authorization by the FCC requires state-by-state satisfaction of § 271's competitive checklist, which as we have noted includes the nondiscriminatory provision of access to UNEs. Section 271 applications to provide long-distance service have now been approved for incumbent LECs in 47 States and the District of Columbia.

The FCC's § 271 authorization order for Verizon to provide long-distance service in New York discussed at great length Verizon's commitments to provide access to UNEs, including the provision of OSS. In re Application by Bell Atlantic New York for Authorization Under Section 271 of the Communications Act To Provide In-Region, InterLATA Service in the State of New York, 15 FCC Rcd. 3953, 3989-4077, ¶¶ 82-228 (1999) (Memorandum Opinion and Order). Those commitments are enforceable by the FCC through continuing oversight; a failure to meet an authorization condition can result in an order that the deficiency be corrected, in the imposition of penalties, or in the suspension or revocation of long-distance approval. Verizon also subjected itself to oversight by the PSC under a so-called "Performance Assurance Plan" (PAP). See In re New York Telephone Co., 197 P.U.R. 4th 266, 280–281 (N.Y.P.S.C., 1999) (Order Adopting the Amended PAP) (hereinafter PAP Order). The PAP, which by its terms became binding upon FCC approval, provides specific financial penalties in the event of Verizon's failure to achieve detailed performance requirements. . . .

The regulatory response to the OSS failure complained of in respondent's suit provides a vivid example of how the regulatory regime operates. When several competitive LECs complained about deficiencies in Verizon's servicing of orders, the FCC and PSC responded. The FCC soon concluded that Verizon was in breach of its sharing duties under § 251(c), imposed a substantial fine, and set up sophisticated measurements to gauge remediation, with weekly reporting requirements and specific penalties for failure. The PSC found Verizon in violation of the PAP even earlier, and imposed additional financial penalties and measurements with *daily* reporting requirements. In short, the regime was an effective steward of the antitrust function.

Against the slight benefits of antitrust intervention here, we must weigh a realistic assessment of its costs. Under the best of circumstances, applying the requirements of § 2 "can be difficult" because "the means of illicit exclusion, like the means of legitimate competition, are myriad." *United States v. Microsoft Corp.*, 253 F.3d 34, 58 (C.A.D.C. 2001) (en banc) (per curiam). Mistaken inferences and the resulting false condemnations "are especially costly, because they chill the very conduct the antitrust laws are designed to protect." *Matsushita Elec. Industrial Co. v. Zenith Radio Corp.*, 475 U.S. 574, 594 (1986). The cost of false positives counsels against an undue expansion of § 2 liability. One false-positive risk is that an incumbent LEC's failure to provide a service with sufficient alacrity might have nothing to do with exclusion. Allegations of violations of § 251(c)(3) duties are difficult for antitrust courts to evaluate, not only because they are highly technical, but also because they are likely to be extremely numerous, given the incessant, complex, and constantly changing interaction of competitive and incumbent LECs implementing the sharing and interconnection obligations. . . .

Even if the problem of false positives did not exist, conduct consisting of anticompetitive violations of § 251 may be, as we have concluded with respect to above-cost predatory pricing schemes, "beyond the practical ability of a judicial tribunal to control." *Brooke Group Ltd. v. Brown & Williamson Tobacco Corp.*, 509 U.S. 209, 223 (1993). Effective remediation of violations of regulatory sharing requirements will ordinarily require continuing supervision of a highly detailed decree. We think that Professor Areeda got it exactly right: "No court should impose a duty to deal that it cannot explain or adequately and reasonably supervise. The problem should be deemed irremedia[ble] by antitrust law when compulsory access requires the court to assume the day-to-day controls characteristic of a regulatory agency." Areeda, 58 Antitrust L. J., at 853. In this case, respondent has requested an equitable decree to "[p]reliminarily and permanently enjoi[n] [Verizon] from providing access to the local loop market . . . to [rivals] on terms and conditions that are not as favorable" as those that Verizon enjoys. An antitrust court is unlikely to be an effective day-to-day enforcer of these detailed sharing obligations.[7]

---

[7] [FN 4] The Court of Appeals also thought that respondent's complaint might state a claim under a "monopoly leveraging" theory (a theory barely discussed by respondent, see Brief for Respondent 24, n.10). We disagree. To the extent the Court of Appeals dispensed with a requirement that there be a "dangerous probability of success" in monopolizing a second market, it erred, Spectrum Sports, Inc. v. McQuillan, 506 U.S. 447, 459 (1993). In any event, leveraging presupposes anticompetitive conduct, which in this case could only be the refusal-to-deal claim we have rejected.

The 1996 Act is in an important respect much more ambitious than the antitrust laws. It attempts *"to eliminate the monopolies* enjoyed by the inheritors of AT & T's local franchises." *Verizon Communications Inc. v. FCC,* 535 U.S., at 476 (emphasis added). Section 2 of the Sherman Act, by contrast, seeks merely to prevent *unlawful monopolization.* It would be a serious mistake to conflate the two goals. The Sherman Act is indeed the "Magna Carta of free enterprise," *United States v. Topco Associates, Inc.,* 405 U.S. 596, 610 (1972), but it does not give judges *carte blanche* to insist that a monopolist alter its way of doing business whenever some other approach might yield greater competition. We conclude that respondent's complaint fails to state a claim under the Sherman Act.

Accordingly, the judgment of the Court of Appeals is reversed, and the case is remanded for further proceedings consistent with this opinion.

It is so ordered.

[In a concurring opinion, which is omitted, Justice Stevens, joined by Souter & Thomas, JJ., would have reversed the Second Circuit on grounds of standing.]

NOTES AND QUESTIONS

1.   The Supreme Court did not purport to overrule *Aspen,* but merely regarded it as being at the "outer boundary" of Section 2 liability. But how much of *Aspen* remains. And does anything remain of the essential facility doctrine? How would you argue a unilateral refusal to deal case under Section 2 if you were the plaintiff's lawyer?

2.   *Trinko* may overrule or seriously qualify other court decisions that granted relatively broad duties to deal. For example, several decisions appear to hold that a firm must share its inputs with a rival even though it is not in the general business of selling these things to customers. *See, e.g., Consolidated Gas Co. of Fla. v. City Gas Co. of Fla.,* 665 F. Supp. 1493 (S.D. Fla. 1987), *aff'd,* 880 F.2d 297 (11th Cir.)889 F.2d 264 (11th Cir. 1989), *on reh'g,* 912 F.2d 1262 (11th Cir. 1990), *rev'd per curiam on nonantitrust grounds,* 499 U.S. 915 (1991) (refusal to share gas pipeline); *Delaware & Hudson Ry. Co. v. Consolidated Rail Corp.,* 902 F.2d 174 (2d Cir. 1990) (refusal to share track with rival railroad, as opposed to transporting the latter's cargo). See also *Evic Class Action Litigation (Farina v. UPS),* 2002 U.S. Dist. LEXIS 14049 (S.D.N.Y. July 30, 2002), which held that UPS's software for tracking packages could be an essential facility that must be shared with rival shippers.

And what about cases holding that a private plaintiff requesting compulsory sharing does not need to show that it actually needs access to the defendant's assets. For example, in *Eastman Kodak Co. v. Image Technical Services, Inc.,* 125 F.3d 1195, 1209–1212 (9th Cir. 1997), the Ninth Circuit held that a firm had a duty to sell its aftermarket parts to rival repair firms even though only a small portion of the parts were unavailable from alternative sources.

3.   In *Aspen Skiing,* the Court found it "unnecessary to consider" the essential facility doctrine. It based liability on a general Section 2 duty to deal. However, the lower courts have fashioned a quite distinctive "essential facility" doctrine, with the

result that plaintiffs have two bites at the apple: they can show either an *Aspen*-style refusal to deal or an essential facility violation. Is there any reason after *Trinko* for thinking that there are two doctrines of unilateral refusal to deal?

4. In *Christy Sports, LLC v. Deer Valley Resort Co.*, 555 F.3d 1188 (10th Cir. 2009), the court held that a dominant ski resort developer did not violate § 2 by entering the ski rental business for itself and enforcing a restrictive covenant that forbad an existing commercial lessee operating on the defendant's property from doing so. The court noted that if it refused to enforce the agreement it would effectively be forcing the defendant to lease space for a competing business on its own property.

5. *Refusal to Purchase from a Rival? United National Maintenance, Inc. v. San Diego Convention Center Corp., Inc.*, 2010 U.S. Dist. LEXIS 78322 (S.D. Cal. Aug. 2, 2010), sustained a complaint that the San Diego Convention Center violated the Sherman Act by insisting that it do its own clean-up after trade shows rather than purchasing the plaintiff's independent cleaning service. The plaintiff had previously been under a cleaning services contract with the defendant, but lost that contract when the convention center switched to self-cleaning. Rather than refusal to supply a rival, the case involves a refusal to *purchase* from a rival. Should the antitrust laws ever require a firm with monopoly power to purchase an input from someone else, when it would prefer to produce that input internally? For example, should Microsoft have an antitrust obligation to contract out with computer programming firms rather than simply hiring its own programmers? Does *Aspen* require a different outcome in a case such as this, where the plaintiff had previously performed cleaning services for the defendant and was then terminated when the defendant switched to self-cleaning?

[2] Exclusionary Contracting by the Monopolist

UNITED STATES v. DENTSPLY INTERNATIONAL, INC.
399 F.3d 181 (3d Cir. 2005)

WEIS, CIRCUIT JUDGE.

In this antitrust case we conclude that an exclusivity policy imposed by a manufacturer on its dealers violates Section 2 of the Sherman Act. . . .

The Government alleged that Defendant, Dentsply International, Inc., acted unlawfully to maintain a monopoly in violation of Section 2 of the Sherman Act, 15 U.S.C. § 2; entered into illegal restrictive dealing agreements prohibited by Section 3 of the Clayton Act, 15 U.S.C. § 14; and used unlawful agreements in restraint of interstate trade in violation of Section 1 of the Sherman Act, 15 U.S.C. § 1. After a bench trial, the District Court denied the injunctive relief sought by the Government and entered judgment for defendant.

In its comprehensive opinion, the District Court found the following facts. Dentsply International, Inc. is a Delaware Corporation with its principal place of business in York, Pennsylvania. It manufactures artificial teeth for use in dentures and other restorative appliances and sells them to dental products dealers. The dealers, in turn, supply the teeth and various other materials to dental laboratories, which fabricate dentures for sale to dentists.

The relevant market is the sale of prefabricated artificial teeth in the United States.

Because of advances in dental medicine, artificial tooth manufacturing is marked by a low or no-growth potential. Dentsply has long dominated the industry consisting of 12–13 manufacturers and enjoys a 75%–80% market share on a revenue basis, 67% on a unit basis, and is about 15 times larger than its next closest competitor. . . .

Dealers sell to dental laboratories a full range of metals, porcelains, acrylics, waxes, and other materials required to fabricate fixed or removal restorations. Dealers maintain large inventories of artificial teeth and carry thousands of products, other than teeth, made by hundreds of different manufacturers. Dentsply supplies $400 million of products other than teeth to its network of 23 dealers.

There are hundreds of dealers who compete on the basis of price and service among themselves, as well as with manufacturers who sell directly to laboratories. The dealer field has experienced significant consolidation with several large national and regional firms emerging.

For more than fifteen years, Dentsply has operated under a policy that discouraged its dealers from adding competitors' teeth to their lines of products. In 1993, Dentsply adopted "Dealer Criterion 6." It provides that in order to effectively promote Dentsply-York products, authorized dealers "may not add further tooth lines to their product offering." Dentsply operates on a purchase order basis with its distributors and, therefore, the relationship is essentially terminable at will. Dealer Criterion 6 was enforced against dealers with the exception of those who had carried competing products before 1993 and were "grandfathered" for sales of those products. Dentsply rebuffed attempts by those particular distributors to expand their lines of competing products beyond the grandfathered ones. . . .

16,000 dental laboratories fabricate restorations and a subset of 7,000 provide dentures. The laboratories compete with each other on the basis of price and service. Patients and dentists value fast service, particularly in the case of lost or damaged dentures. When laboratories' inventories cannot supply the necessary teeth, dealers may fill orders for walk-ins or use over-night express mail as does Dentsply, which dropped-shipped some 60% of orders from dealers.

Dealers have been dissatisfied with Dealer Criterion 6, but, at least in the recent past, none of them have given up the popular Dentsply teeth to take on a competitive line. Dentsply at one time considered selling directly to the laboratories, but abandoned the concept because of fear that dealers would retaliate by refusing to buy its other dental products. . . .

Dentsply has had a reputation for aggressive price increases in the market and has created a high price umbrella. Its artificial tooth business is characterized as a "cash cow" whose profits are diverted to other operations of the company. A report in 1996 stated its profits from teeth since 1990 had increased 32% from $16.8 million to $22.2 million.

The District Court found that Dentsply's business justification for Dealer Criterion 6 was pretextual and designed expressly to exclude its rivals from access to dealers. The Court however concluded that other dealers were available and direct sales to laboratories was a viable method of doing business. Moreover, it concluded that Dentsply had not created a market with supra competitive pricing, dealers were free to leave the network at any time, and the Government failed to prove that Dentsply's actions "have been or could be successful in preventing 'new or potential competitors from gaining a foothold in the market.' " Accordingly, the Court concluded that the Government had failed to establish violations of Section 3 of the Clayton Act and Sections 1 or 2 of the Sherman Act.

The Government appealed, contending that a monopolist that prevents rivals from distributing through established dealers has maintained its monopoly by acting with predatory intent and violates Section 2. Additionally, the Government asserts that the maintenance of a 75%–80% market share, establishment of a price umbrella, repeated aggressive price increases and exclusion of competitors from a major source of distribution, show that Dentsply possesses monopoly power, despite the fact that rivals are not entirely excluded from the market and some of their prices are higher. The Government did not appeal the rulings under Section 1 of the Sherman Act or Section 3 of the Clayton Act.

Dentsply argues that rivals had obtained a share of the relevant market, that there are no artificially high prices and that competitors have access to all laboratories through existing or readily convertible systems. In addition, Dentsply asserts that its success is due to its leadership in promotion and marketing and not the imposition of Dealer Criterion 6.

To run afoul of Section 2, a defendant must be guilty of illegal conduct "to foreclose competition, gain a competitive advantage, or to destroy a competitor." *Lorain Journal Co. v. United States*, 342 U.S. 143 (1951). Behavior that otherwise might comply with antitrust law may be impermissibly exclusionary when practiced by a monopolist. As we said in *LePage's, Inc. v. 3M*, 324 F.3d 141, 151–52 (3d Cir. 2003), "a monopolist is not free to take certain actions that a company in a competitive (or even oligopolistic) market may take, because there is no market constraint on a monopolist's behavior." 3 Areeda & Turner, *Antitrust Law* ¶ 813, at 300–02 (1978).

Although not illegal in themselves, exclusive dealing arrangements can be an improper means of maintaining a monopoly. *United States v. Grinnell Corp.*, 384 U.S. 563 (1966). A prerequisite for such a violation is a finding that monopoly power exists. In addition, the exclusionary conduct must have an anti-competitive effect. If those elements are established, the monopolist still retains a defense of business justification.

Unlawful maintenance of a monopoly is demonstrated by proof that a defendant has engaged in anti-competitive conduct that reasonably appears to be a significant contribution to maintaining monopoly power. *United States v. Microsoft*, 253 F.3d 34, 79 (D.C. Cir. 2001); 3 Phillip E. Areeda & Herbert Hovenkamp, Antitrust Law, ¶ 651c, at 78 (1996). Predatory or exclusionary practices in themselves are not sufficient. There must be proof that competition, not merely competitors, has been harmed.

III. MONOPOLY POWER

The concept of monopoly is distinct from monopoly power, which has been defined as the ability "to control prices or exclude competition." *Grinnell*, 384 U.S. at 571; *see also United States v. E.I. du Pont de Nemours and Co.*, 351 U.S. 377 (1956). However, because such evidence is "only rarely available, courts more typically examine market structure in search of circumstantial evidence of monopoly power." *Microsoft*, 253 F.3d at 51. Thus, the existence of monopoly power may be inferred from a predominant share of the market. . . .

A less than predominant share of the market combined with other relevant factors may suffice to demonstrate monopoly power. *Fineman v. Armstrong World Indus.*, 980 F.2d 171, 201 (3d Cir. 1992). Absent other pertinent factors, a share significantly larger than 55% has been required to established prima facie market power. *Id.* at 201. Other germane factors include the size and strength of competing firms, freedom of entry, pricing trends and practices in the industry, ability of consumers to substitute comparable goods, and consumer demand.

. . . . The District Court found the market to be "the sale of prefabricated artificial teeth in the United States." Further, the Court found that "[t]he manufacturers participating in the United States artificial tooth market historically have distributed their teeth into the market in one of three ways: (1) directly to dental labs; (2) through dental dealers; or (3) through a hybrid system combining manufacturer direct sales and dental dealers." The Court also found that the "labs are the relevant consumers for prefabricated artificial teeth."

There is no dispute that the laboratories are the ultimate consumers because they buy the teeth at the point in the process where they are incorporated into another product. Dentsply points out that its representatives concentrate their efforts at the laboratories as well as at dental schools and dentists.

During oral argument, Dentsply's counsel said, "the dealers are not the market . . . [t]he market is the dental labs that consume the product." Emphasizing the importance of end users, Dentsply argues that the District Court understood the relevant market to be the sales of artificial teeth to dental laboratories in the United States. Although the Court used the word "market" in a number of differing contexts, the findings demonstrate that the relevant market is not as narrow as Dentsply would have it. . . . [T]he Court said that Dentsply "has had a persistently high market share between 75% and 80% on a revenue basis, in the artificial tooth market." Dentsply sells only to dealers and the narrow definition of market that it urges upon us would be completely inconsistent with that finding of the District Court. . . .

Dentsply's apparent belief that a relevant market cannot include sales both to the final consumer and a middleman is refuted in the closely analogous case of *Allen-Myland, Inc. v. IBM Corp.*, 33 F.3d 194 (3d Cir. 1994). In that case, IBM sold mainframe computers directly to the ultimate consumers and also sold to companies that leased computers to ultimate users. We concluded that the relevant market encompassed the sales directly to consumers as well as those to leasing companies. ". . . to the extent that leasing companies deal in used, non-IBM mainframes that have not already been counted in the sales market, these machines belong in the relevant market for large-scale mainframe computers."

To resolve any doubt, therefore, we hold that the relevant market here is the sale of artificial teeth in the United States both to laboratories and to the dental dealers.

Dentsply's share of the market is more than adequate to establish a prima facie case of power. In addition, Dentsply has held its dominant share for more than ten years and has fought aggressively to maintain that imbalance. One court has commented that, "[i]n evaluating monopoly power, it is not market share that counts, but the ability to *maintain* market share." *United States v. Syufy Enters.*, 903 F.2d 659, 665–66 (9th Cir. 1990).

The District Court found that it could infer monopoly power because of the predominant market share, but despite that factor, concluded that Dentsply's tactics did not preclude competition from marketing their products directly to the dental laboratories. "Dentsply does not have the power to exclude competitors from the ultimate consumer."

Moreover, the Court determined that failure of Dentsply's two main rivals, Vident and Ivoclar, to obtain significant market shares resulted from their own business decisions to concentrate on other product lines, rather than implement active sales efforts for teeth.

The District Court's evaluation of Ivoclar and Vident business practices as a cause of their failure to secure more of the market is not persuasive. The reality is that over a period of years, because of Dentsply's domination of dealers, direct sales have not been a practical alternative for most manufacturers. It has not been so much the competitors' less than enthusiastic efforts at competition that produced paltry results, as it is the blocking of access to the key dealers. This is the part of the real market that is denied to the rivals.

The apparent lack of aggressiveness by competitors is not a matter of apathy, but a reflection of the effectiveness of Dentsply's exclusionary policy. Although its rivals could theoretically convince a dealer to buy their products and drop Dentsply's line, that has not occurred. In *United States v. Visa U.S.A.*, 344 F.3d at 229, 240 (2d Cir. 2003), the Court of Appeals held that similar evidence indicated that defendants·had excluded their rivals from the marketplace and thus demonstrated monopoly power.

The Supreme Court on more than one occasion has emphasized that economic realities rather than a formalistic approach must govern review of antitrust activity. "Legal presumptions that rest on formalistic distinctions rather than actual market realities are generally disfavored in antitrust law . . . in determining the existence of market power . . . this Court has examined closely the economic reality of the market at issue." *Eastman Kodak Co. v. Image Technical Servs., Inc.*, 504 U.S. 451, 466–67 (1992). . . .

The realities of the artificial tooth market were candidly expressed by two former managerial employees of Dentsply when they explained their rules of engagement. One testified that Dealer Criterion 6 was designed to "block competitive distribution points." He continued, "Do not allow competition to achieve toeholds in dealers; tie up dealers; do not 'free up' key players."

Another former manager said:

You don't want your competition with your distributors, you don't want to give the distributors an opportunity to sell a competitive product. And you don't want to give your end user, the customer, meaning a laboratory and/or a dentist, a choice. He has to buy Dentsply teeth. That's the only thing that's available. The only place you can get it is through the distributor and the only one that the distributor is selling is Dentsply teeth. That's your objective.

These are clear expressions of a plan to maintain monopolistic power.

The District Court detailed some ten separate incidents in which Dentsply required agreement by new as well as long-standing dealers not to handle competitors' teeth. For example, when the DLDS firm considered adding two other tooth lines because of customers' demand, Dentsply threatened to sever access not only to its teeth, but to other dental products as well. DLDS yielded to that pressure. The termination of Trinity Dental, which had previously sold Dentsply products other than teeth, was a similar instance. When Trinity wanted to add teeth to its line for the first time and chose a competitor, Dentsply refused to supply other dental products. . . .

The factual pattern here is quite similar to that in *LePage's, Inc. v. 3M*, 324 F.3d 141 (3d Cir. 2003). There, a manufacturer of transparent tape locked up high volume distribution channels by means of substantial discounts on a range of its other products. *LePage's*, 324 F.3d at 144, 160–62. We concluded that the use of exclusive dealing and bundled rebates to the detriment of the rival manufacturer violated Section 2. Similarly, in *Microsoft*, the Court of Appeals for the D.C. Circuit concluded that, through the use of exclusive contracts with key dealers, a manufacturer foreclosed competitors from a substantial percentage of the available opportunities for product distribution. *See Microsoft*, 253 F.3d at 70–71.

The evidence in this case demonstrates that for a considerable time, through the use of Dealer Criterion 6 Dentsply has been able to exclude competitors from the dealers' network, a narrow, but heavily traveled channel to the dental laboratories.

An increase in pricing is another factor used in evaluating existence of market power. Although in this case the evidence of exclusion is stronger than that of Dentsply's control of prices, testimony about suspect pricing is also found in this record.

The District Court found that Dentsply had a reputation for aggressive price increases in the market. It is noteworthy that experts for both parties testified that were Dealer Criterion 6 abolished, prices would fall. A former sales manager for Dentsply agreed that the company's share of the market would diminish should Dealer Criterion 6 no longer be in effect. In 1993, Dentsply's regional sales manager complained, "[w]e need to moderate our increases — twice a year for the last few years was not good." Large scale distributors observed that Dentsply's policy created a high price umbrella.

Although Dentsply's prices fall between those of Ivoclar and Vita's premium tooth lines, Dentsply did not reduce its prices when competitors elected not to follow its increases. Dentsply's profit margins have been growing over the years. The picture is one of a manufacturer that sets prices with little concern for its competitors, "something a firm without a monopoly would have been unable to do." *Microsoft*, 253 F.3d at 58. The results have been favorable to Dentsply, but of no benefit to consumers. . . . .

IV. ANTI-COMPETITIVE EFFECTS

Having demonstrated that Dentsply possessed market power, the Government must also establish the second element of a Section 2 claim, that the power was used "to foreclose competition." *United States v. Griffith*, 334 U.S. 100, 107 (1948). Assessing anti-competitive effect is important in evaluating a challenge to a violation of Section 2. Under that Section of the Sherman Act, it is not necessary that all competition be removed from the market. The test is not total foreclosure, but whether the challenged practices bar a substantial number of rivals or severely restrict the market's ambit. *LePage's*, 324 F.3d at 159–60; *Microsoft*, 253 F.3d at 69.

A leading treatise explains,

> A set of strategically planned exclusive dealing contracts may slow the rival's expansion by requiring it to develop alternative outlets for its products or rely at least temporarily on inferior or more expensive outlets. Consumer injury results from the delay that the dominant firm imposes on the smaller rival's growth.

Herbert Hovenkamp, Antitrust Law ¶ 1802c, at 64 (2d ed. 2002).

By ensuring that the key dealers offer Dentsply teeth either as the only or dominant choice, Dealer Criterion 6 has a significant effect in preserving Dentsply's monopoly. It helps keep sales of competing teeth below the critical level necessary for any rival to pose a real threat to Dentsply's market share. As such, Dealer Criterion 6 is a solid pillar of harm to competition. . . .

Benefits of Dealers

Dentsply has always sold its teeth through dealers. Vita sells through Vident, its exclusive distributor and domestic affiliate, but has a mere 3% of the market. Ivoclar had some relationship with dealers in the past, but its direct relationship with laboratories yields only a 5% share. . . .

The record is replete with evidence of benefits provided by dealers. For example, they provide laboratories the benefit of "one stop-shopping" and extensive credit services. Because dealers typically carry the products of multiple manufacturers, a laboratory can order, with a single phone call to a dealer, products from multiple sources. Without dealers, in most instances laboratories would have to place individual calls to each manufacturer, expend the time, and pay multiple shipping charges to fill the same orders.

The dealer-provided reduction in transaction costs and time represents a substantial benefit, one that the District Court minimized when it characterized "one stop shopping" as merely the ability to order from a single manufacturer all the materials necessary for crown, bridge and denture construction. Although a laboratory can call a manufacturer directly and purchase any product made by it, the laboratory is unable to procure from that source products made by its competitors. Thus, purchasing through dealers, which as a class traditionally carries the products of multiple vendors, surmounts this shortcoming, as well as offers other advantages.

Buying through dealers also enables laboratories to take advantage of obtaining discounts. Because they engage in price competition to gain laboratories' business, dealers often discount manufacturers' suggested laboratory price for artificial teeth. There is no finding on this record that manufacturers offer similar discounts.

Another service dealers perform is taking back tooth returns. Artificial teeth and denture returns are quite common in dentistry. Approximately 30% of all laboratory tooth purchases are returned for exchange or credit. The District Court disregarded this benefit on the ground that all manufacturers except Vita accept tooth returns. However, in equating dealer and manufacturer returns, the District Court overlooked the fact that using dealers, rather than manufacturers, enables laboratories to consolidate their returns. In a single shipment to a dealer, a laboratory can return the products of a number of manufacturers, and so economize on shipping, time, and transaction costs.

Conversely, when returning products directly to manufacturers, a laboratory must ship each vendor's product separately and must track each exchange individually. Consolidating returns yields savings of time, effort, and costs.

Dealers also provide benefits to manufacturers, perhaps the most obvious of which is efficiency of scale. Using select high-volume dealers, as opposed to directly selling to hundreds if not thousands of laboratories, greatly reduces the manufacturer's distribution costs and credit risks. Dentsply, for example, currently sells to twenty three dealers. If it were instead to sell directly to individual laboratories, Dentsply would incur significantly higher transaction costs, extension of credit burdens, and credit risks.

Although a laboratory that buys directly from a manufacturer may be able to avoid the marginal costs associated with "middleman" dealers, any savings must be weighed against the benefits, savings, and convenience offered by dealers.

In addition, dealers provide manufacturers more marketplace exposure and sales representative coverage than manufacturers are able to generate on their own. Increased exposure and sales coverage traditionally lead to greater sales.

"Viability" of Direct Sales

The benefits that dealers provide manufacturers help make dealers the preferred distribution channels — in effect, the "gateways" — to the artificial teeth market. Nonetheless, the District Court found that selling direct is a "viable" method of distributing artificial teeth. But we are convinced that it is "viable" only in the sense that it is "possible," not that it is practical or feasible in the market as it exists and functions. The District Court's conclusion of "viability" runs counter to the facts and is clearly erroneous.

It is true that Dentsply's competitors can sell directly to the dental laboratories and an insignificant number do. The undeniable reality, however, is that dealers have a controlling degree of access to the laboratories. The long-entrenched Dentsply dealer network with its ties to the laboratories makes it impracticable for a manufacturer to rely on direct distribution to the laboratories in any significant amount. *See United States v. Visa U.S.A.*, 344 F.3d 229, 240 (2d Cir. 2003).

That some manufacturers resort to direct sales and are even able to stay in business by selling directly is insufficient proof that direct selling is an effective means of competition. The proper inquiry is not whether direct sales enable a competitor to "survive" but rather whether direct selling "poses a real threat" to defendant's monopoly. *See Microsoft*, 253 F.3d at 71. The minuscule 5% and 3% market shares eked out by direct-selling manufacturers Ivoclar and Vita, Dentsply's "primary competitors," FF26, 36, 239, reveal that direct selling poses little threat to Dentsply.

Efficacy of Dealer Criterion 6

Although the parties to the sales transactions consider the exclusionary arrangements to be agreements, they are technically only a series of independent sales. Dentsply sells teeth to the dealers on an individual transaction basis and essentially the arrangement is "at-will." Nevertheless, the economic elements involved — the large share of the market held by Dentsply and its conduct excluding competing manufacturers — realistically make the arrangements here as effective as those in written contracts. *See Monsanto Co. v. Spray-Rite Serv. Corp.*, 465 U.S. 752, 764 n.9 (1984).

Given the circumstances present in this case, there is no ground to doubt the effectiveness of the exclusive dealing arrangement. . . .

Limitation of Choice

An additional anti-competitive effect is seen in the exclusionary practice here that limits the choices of products open to dental laboratories, the ultimate users. A dealer locked into the Dentsply line is unable to heed a request for a different manufacturers' product and, from the standpoint of convenience, that inability to some extent impairs the laboratory's choice in the marketplace.

As an example, current and potential customers requested Atlanta Dental to carry Vita teeth. Although these customers could have ordered the Vita teeth from Vident in California, Atlanta Dental's tooth department manager believed that they were interested in a local source. Atlanta Dental chose not to add the Vita line after being advised that doing so would cut off access to Dentsply teeth, which constituted over 90% of its tooth sales revenue. . . .

Barriers to Entry

Entrants into the marketplace must confront Dentsply's power over the dealers. The District Court's theory that any new or existing manufacturer may "steal" a Dentsply dealer by offering a superior product at a lower price, *see Omega Environmental, Inc. v. Gilbarco*, 127 F.3d 1157 (9th Cir. 1997), simply has not proved to be realistic. To the contrary, purloining efforts have been thwarted by

Dentsply's longtime, vigorous and successful enforcement actions. The paltry penetration in the market by competitors over the years has been a refutation of theory by tangible and measurable results in the real world.

The levels of sales that competitors could project in wooing dealers were minuscule compared to Dentsply's, whose long-standing relationships with these dealers included sales of other dental products. . . .

The dominant position of Dentsply dealers as a gateway to the laboratories was confirmed by potential entrants to the market. The president of Ivoclar testified that his company was unsuccessful in its approach to the two large national dealers and other regional dealers. He pointed out that it is more efficient to sell through dealers and, in addition, they offered an entre to future customers by promotions in the dental schools.

Dealer Criterion 6 created a strong economic incentive for dealers to reject competing lines in favor of Dentsply's teeth. As in *LePage's*, the rivals simply could not provide dealers with a comparable economic incentive to switch. Moreover, the record demonstrates that Dentsply added Darby as a dealer "to block Vita from a key competitive distribution point." According to a Dentsply executive, the "key issue" was "Vita's potential distribution system." He explained that Vita was "having a tough time getting teeth out to customers. One of their key weaknesses is their distribution system."

Teeth are an important part of a denture, but they are but one component. The dealers are dependent on serving all of the laboratories' needs and must carry as many components as practicable. The artificial teeth business cannot realistically be evaluated in isolation from the rest of the dental fabrication industry.

A leading treatise provides a helpful analogy to this situation:

> [S]uppose that mens's bow ties cannot efficiently be sold in stores that deal exclusively in bow ties or even ties generally; rather, they must be sold in department stores where clerks can spread their efforts over numerous products and the ties can be sold in conjunction with shirts and suits. Suppose further that a dominant bow tie manufacturer should impose exclusive dealing on a town's only three department stores. In this case the rival bow tie maker cannot easily enter. Setting up another department store is an unneeded and a very large investment in proportion to its own production, which we assume is only bow ties, but any store that offers less will be an inefficient and costly seller of bow ties. As a result, such exclusive dealing could either exclude the nondominant bow tie maker or else raise its costs in comparison to the costs of the dominant firm. While the department stores might prefer to sell the ties of multiple manufacturers, if faced with an "all-or-nothing" choice they may accede to the dominant firm's wish for exclusive dealing.

Herbert Hovenkamp, Antitrust Law ¶ 1802e3, at 78–79 (2d ed. 2002).

Criterion 6 imposes an "all-or-nothing" choice on the dealers. The fact that dealers have chosen not to drop Dentsply teeth in favor of a rival's brand demonstrates that they have acceded to heavy economic pressure.

This case does not involve a dynamic, volatile market like that in *Microsoft*, 253 F.3d at 70, or a proven alternative distribution channel. The mere existence of other avenues of distribution is insufficient without an assessment of their overall significance to the market. The economic impact of an exclusive dealing arrangement is amplified in the stagnant, no growth context of the artificial tooth field. . . .

Dentsply's grip on its 23 authorized dealers effectively choked off the market for artificial teeth, leaving only a small sliver for competitors. The District Court erred when it minimized that situation and focused on a theoretical feasibility of success through direct access to the dental labs. While we may assume that Dentsply won its preeminent position by fair competition, that fact does not permit maintenance of its monopoly by unfair practices. We conclude that on this record, the Government established that Dentsply's exclusionary policies and particularly Dealer Criterion 6 violated Section 2.

V. BUSINESS JUSTIFICATION

As noted earlier, even if a company exerts monopoly power, it may defend its practices by establishing a business justification. The Government, having demonstrated harm to competition, the burden shifts to Dentsply to show that Dealer Criterion 6 promotes a sufficiently pro-competitive objective. *United States v. Brown Univ.*, 5 F.3d 658, 669 (3d Cir. 1993). Significantly, Dentsply has not done so. The District Court found that "Dentsply's asserted justifications for its exclusionary policies are inconsistent with its announced reason for the exclusionary policies, its conduct enforcing the policy, its rival suppliers' actions, and dealers' behavior in the marketplace."

Some of the dealers opposed Dentsply's policy as exerting too much control over the products they may sell, but the grandfathered dealers were no less efficient than the exclusive ones, nor was there any difference in promotional support. Nor was there any evidence of existence of any substantial variation in the level of service provided by exclusive and grandfathered dealers to the laboratories.

The record amply supports the District Court's conclusion that Dentsply's alleged justification was pretextual and did not excuse its exclusionary practices.

VI. AVAILABILITY OF SHERMAN ACT SECTION 2 RELIEF

One point remains. Relying on *dicta* in *Tampa Electric Co. v. Nashville Coal Co.*, 365 U.S. 320 (1961), the District Court said that because it had found no liability under the stricter standards of Section 3 of the Clayton Act, it followed that there was no violation of Section 2 of the Sherman Act. However, as we explained in *LePage's v. 3M*, 324 F.3d at 157 n.10, a finding in favor of the defendant under Section 1 of the Sherman Act and Section 3 of the Clayton Act, did not "preclude the application of evidence of . . . exclusive dealing to support the [Section] 2 claim." All of the evidence in the record here applies to the Section 2 claim and, as in *LePage's*, a finding of liability under Section 2 supports a judgment against defendant. . . .

Accordingly, for the reasons set forth above, we will reverse the judgment in favor of Dentsply and remand the case to the District Court with directions to grant injunctive relief requested by the Government and for such other proceedings as are consistent with this opinion.

NOTES AND QUESTIONS

1. In *NicSand, Inc. v. 3M Co.*, 507 F.3d 442 (6th Cir. 2007), the Sixth Circuit dismissed a Section 2 complaint in which a previously dominant supplier of automotive abrasives lost most of its business to the defendant, 3M, who lured away customers (large retailers) by making large upfront payments in exchange for exclusive commitments. The retailers themselves apparently preferred exclusive contracts, wishing to sell only a single supplier's abrasives at any given time. There appeared to be no allegation that the impact of the upfront payment was to drive the overall price of the abrasives below cost. Indeed, the plaintiff itself had enjoyed very high margins when it controlled the business.

In such a case, the upfront payment operates much like a "slotting" fee, which forces the seller to bear a portion of the risk of poor sales of the product. A large upfront fee is effectively a mechanism for "purchasing" the retailer's shelf space, and generates a positive payoff if the volume of subsequent sales is sufficiently large. If it is not so large, then part of the loss occasioned by poor business is absorbed by the seller as well as the buyer. In any event, the gravamen of the challenge was not to the exclusivity, for the plaintiff had also had exclusive arrangements with the retailers prior to its loss of business. Rather, it was to the large upfront payments by which the defendant had stolen the business. Without a claim of prices below cost, the plaintiff could complain only that it had lost a competitive bidding battle.

2. In *Barry Wright Corp. v. ITT Grinnell Corp.*, 724 F.2d 227 (1st Cir. 1983), the First Circuit rejected a claim of market preemption violating § 2. The author was then-Judge Breyer before he was appointed to the Supreme Court. Grinnell, accounting for about half the purchases in the market, contracted to buy roughly its requirements for three years from dominant firm Pacific — an exclusionary practice creating an illegal monopoly, according to the plaintiff Barry, a would-be new entrant. The court found the challenged arrangements reasonable because (1) "Grinnell did not actually promise to buy all its requirements from Pacific; it entered into a contract for a fixed dollar amount." This left Grinnell free to buy small and increasingly larger amounts from Barry should they have become available. (2) The Grinnell-Pacific contract was not a single three-year agreement but a succession of shorter-term contracts. (3) The lag between new entry and product availability meant that Grinnell's purchase of a year or two's worth of the product from Pacific did not significantly reduce its opportunity to make advance contracts to buy from new entrants. (4) There were legitimate business reasons for the challenged contracts: stable supply and favorable price for Grinnell and employment of excess capacity and efficient production planning for Pacific. (5) "Grinnell is not a small firm that Pacific could likely bully into accepting a contract that might foreclose new competition. . . . To the contrary, it was Grinnell, not Pacific, that sought" the challenged contract extensions. Indeed, Grinnell had financed Barrys efforts to enter in order to have an alternative source and would hardly have contracted with Pacific in a way that would significantly interfere with new entry.

3. Other Section 2 decisions challenging arrangements that resemble exclusive dealing include *Geneva Pharmaceuticals Tech. Corp. v. Barr Labs, Inc.*, 386 F.3d 485 (2d Cir. 2004) (claim that defendant manufacturer of warfarin sodium entered into secret exclusive dealing agreement locking up only significant source of clathrate, an essential ingredient. Here, the plaintiffs successfully stated a claim in their assertion that the defendant deceived them into thinking that clathrate would be available, while secretly negotiating with the dominant supplier of clathrate for an exclusive agreement. On this issue, the court found several questions of fact as to the willingness and ability of alternative suppliers to enter the market and/or supply the plaintiff, and denied summary judgment on the issue; *id.* at 503–504); *Defiance Hosp. v. Fauster-Cameron, Inc.*, 344 F. Supp. 2d 1097 (N.D. Ohio 2004) (denying summary judgment on plaintiff's claim that defendant monopolized market for anesthesiological services by refusing to supply anesthesiology support services to physicians who had not signed primary care contracts with the defendant); *JamSports and Entertainment, LLC v. Paradama Productions, Inc.*, 336 F. Supp. 2d 824 (N.D. Ill. 2004) (denying summary judgment on claim that racing promoter's claim that motorcycle association excluded it from market by threatening to terminate its relationship with stadiums that contracted with the plaintiff).

NOTE: TYING AND EXCLUSIVE DEALING BY THE MONOPOLIST

Both tying and exclusive dealing are analyzed under Section 1 of the Sherman Act and Section 3 of the Clayton Act. As such they are treated as multilateral conduct and covered under the law of interbrand restraints. See the previous Chapter. Further, those statutes are more aggressive than Section 2 of the Sherman Act, and may condemn these practices on market shares in the vicinity of 40%. So why would anyone want to apply Section 2, with its more stringent monopoly power requirement?

The principal reasons are (1) certain conduct might resemble tying or exclusive dealing but be imposed unilaterally so that the "agreement" requirement cannot be met; or (2) certain conduct may not fall within the technical limits of tying or exclusive dealing but is anticompetitive and thus falls within the much more general definition of "monopolizing" conduct. More fundamentally, exclusive dealing and tying are "unilateral" in the sense that they are typically imposed on buyers who would prefer dealer freedom. That is, we condemn them at all because we count them as "exclusionary" practices directed at rivals, not at customers. In other areas, such as the law of predatory pricing, we treat the conduct as unilateral even though one cannot engage in predatory pricing without agreements with customers. As a result, Section 2 may be a conceptually superior tool than Section 1 is for assessing these two practices.

The technical requirements of tying law were developed for non-monopolists. Indeed, until recently, many firms found liable for illegal tying were non-dominant firms with relatively modest market shares. Tying law's technical requirements were developed largely because the so-called per se rule against tying has a significant potential to over-reach, particularly when applied to nondominant firms.

For example, tying law's "separate products" test serves a valuable screening function to assure that only irregular market practices are condemned. In such cases, illegality was presumed even though market power and foreclosure were too low to warrant a reasonable inference of competitive harm — a defect subsequently corrected in case law that took the market power requirement more seriously. Rightly or wrongly, in that earlier regime, the "separate product" requirement served to distinguish the unusual practice that seemed to run counter to ordinary market practices, and from which an inference of anticompetitive results might be drawn notwithstanding the defendant's lack of significant market control.

When the defendant is a dominant firm, however, this special screening function is largely unnecessary and the more general standards of Section 2 become relevant. Rule of reason challenges to bundling behavior assess a much stricter power requirement; but dispense with the technical requirements that attach only to per se ties.

Thus, when the monopolist bundles the product in which it has monopoly power, the technicalities of the separate product requirement give way to the more open-ended Section 2 inquiry whether a practice injures competition unnecessarily. For example, courts might be reluctant to find that significantly integrated software components are "separate products" for the purpose of tying law. But failing to find separate products is not dispositive of antitrust liability when the defendant is a monopolist. The "separate products" requirement is unique to tying law under Section 1 of the Sherman Act or Section 3 of the Clayton Act.

While the standard for a Section 2 violation is significantly stricter in its power assessment, it is broader and less categorical in its definition of proscribed conduct. The usual formulation is that the monopolist violates Section 2 when its practices unreasonably create, maintain, or enhance its monopoly power. For that reason, mandatory bundling by the monopolist may be unlawful even if the items in the bundled package would not constitute separate products. Rather, the question is whether, viewing the monopolist's conduct as a whole, it has unreasonably maintained or enhanced its monopoly position.

The trend in case law has been to apply Section 2 rather than Section 1 of the Sherman Act or Section 3 of the Clayton Act to exclusive dealing or related claims when the defendant is also a monopolist. For example, in *Microsoft*, the D.C. Circuit rejected Microsoft's argument that a failure to find liability under Section 1 of the Sherman Act precluded liability under Section 2. The court acknowledged that the "basic prudential concerns relevant to §§ 1 and 2 are admittedly the same." However:

> [A] monopolist's use of exclusive contracts, in certain circumstances, may give rise to a § 2 violation even though the contracts foreclose less than the roughly 40% or 50% share usually required in order to establish a § 1 violation.

> In this case, plaintiffs allege that, by closing to rivals a substantial percentage of the available opportunities for browser distribution, Microsoft managed to preserve its monopoly in the market for operating systems. The IAPs [internet access providers] constitute one of the two

major channels by which browsers can be distributed. Microsoft has exclusive deals with "fourteen of the top fifteen access providers in North America[, which] account for a large majority of all Internet access subscriptions in this part of the world." By ensuring that the "majority" of all IAP subscribers are offered IE either as the default browser or as the only browser, Microsoft's deals with the IAPs clearly have a significant effect in preserving its monopoly; they help keep usage of Navigator below the critical level necessary for Navigator or any other rival to pose a real threat to Microsoft's monopoly.

United States v. Microsoft Corp., 253 F.3d 34 (D.C. Cir. 2001).

[3]   Vertical Integration and the Price "Squeeze"

PACIFIC BELL TELEPHONE CO. v. LINKLINE COMMUNICATIONS, INC.
555 U.S. 438 (2009)

CHIEF JUSTICE ROBERTS DELIVERED THE OPINION OF THE COURT.

The plaintiffs in this case, respondents here, allege that a competitor subjected them to a "price squeeze" in violation of § 2 of the Sherman Act. They assert that such a claim can arise when a vertically integrated firm sells inputs at wholesale and also sells finished goods or services at retail. If that firm has power in the wholesale market, it can simultaneously raise the wholesale price of inputs and cut the retail price of the finished good. This will have the effect of "squeezing" the profit margins of any competitors in the retail market. Those firms will have to pay more for the inputs they need; at the same time, they will have to cut their retail prices to match the other firm's prices. The question before us is whether such a price-squeeze claim may be brought under § 2 of the Sherman Act when the defendant is under no antitrust obligation to sell the inputs to the plaintiff in the first place. We hold that no such claim may be brought.

I

This case involves the market for digital subscriber line (DSL) service, which is a method of connecting to the Internet at high speeds over telephone lines. AT & T owns much of the infrastructure and facilities needed to provide DSL service in California. In particular, AT & T controls most of what is known as the "last mile" — the lines that connect homes and businesses to the telephone network. Competing DSL providers must generally obtain access to AT & T's facilities in order to serve their customers.

Until recently, the Federal Communications Commission (FCC) required incumbent phone companies such as AT & T to sell transmission service to independent DSL providers, under the theory that this would spur competition. . . . In 2005, the Commission largely abandoned this forced-sharing requirement in light of the emergence of a competitive market beyond DSL for high-speed Internet service; DSL now faces robust competition from cable companies and wireless and satellite services. As a condition for a recent merger, however, AT & T remains bound by the mandatory interconnection requirements, and is obligated to provide wholesale "DSL transport" service to independent firms at a price no greater than the retail price of AT & T's DSL service. *In re AT & T Inc. and BellSouth Corp.*, 22 FCC Rcd. 5662, 5814 (2007).

The plaintiffs are four independent Internet service providers (ISPs) that compete with AT & T in the retail DSL market. Plaintiffs do not own all the facilities needed to supply their customers with this service. They instead lease DSL transport service from AT & T pursuant to the merger conditions described above. AT & T thus participates in the DSL market at both the wholesale and retail levels; it provides plaintiffs and other independent ISPs with wholesale DSL transport service, and it also sells DSL service directly to consumers at retail.

In July 2003, the plaintiffs brought suit in District Court, alleging that AT & T violated § 2 of the Sherman Act, 15 U.S.C. § 2, by monopolizing the DSL market in California. The complaint alleges that AT & T refused to deal with the plaintiffs, denied the plaintiffs access to essential facilities, and engaged in a "price squeeze." Specifically, plaintiffs contend that AT & T squeezed their profit margins by setting a high wholesale price for DSL transport and a low retail price for DSL Internet service. This maneuver allegedly "exclude[d] and unreasonably impede[d] competition," thus allowing AT & T to "preserve and maintain its monopoly control of DSL access to the Internet."

In *Verizon Communications Inc. v. Law Offices of Curtis V. Trinko, LLP*, 540 U.S. 398 (2004), we held that a firm with no antitrust duty to deal with its rivals at all is under no obligation to provide those rivals with a "sufficient" level of service. . . .

As a general rule, businesses are free to choose the parties with whom they will deal, as well as the prices, terms, and conditions of that dealing. See *United States v. Colgate & Co.*, 250 U.S. 300, 307 (1919). But there are rare instances in which a dominant firm may incur antitrust liability for purely unilateral conduct. For example, we have ruled that firms may not charge "predatory" prices-below-cost prices that drive rivals out of the market and allow the monopolist to raise its prices later and recoup its losses. *Brooke Group*, 509 U.S., at 222-224. Here, however, the complaint at issue does not contain allegations meeting those requirements.

There are also limited circumstances in which a firm's unilateral refusal to deal with its rivals can give rise to antitrust liability. See *Aspen Skiing Co. v. Aspen Highlands Skiing Corp.*, 472 U.S. 585, 608–611 (1985). Here, however, the District Court held that AT & T had no such antitrust duty to deal with its competitor, and this holding was not challenged on appeal.

The challenge here focuses on retail prices — where there is no predatory pricing — and the terms of dealing — where there is no duty to deal. Plaintiffs' price-squeeze claims challenge a different type of unilateral conduct in which a firm "squeezes" the profit margins of its competitors. This requires the defendant to be operating in two markets, a wholesale ("upstream") market and a retail ("downstream") market. A firm with market power in the upstream market can squeeze its downstream competitors by raising the wholesale price of inputs while cutting its own retail prices. This will raise competitors' costs (because they will have to pay more for their inputs) and lower their revenues (because they will have to match the dominant firm's low retail price). Price-squeeze plaintiffs assert that defendants must leave them a "fair" or "adequate" margin between the wholesale price and the retail price. In this case, we consider whether a plaintiff can state a price-squeeze claim when the defendant has no obligation under the antitrust laws to deal with the plaintiff at wholesale.

A straightforward application of our recent decision in *Trinko* forecloses any challenge to AT & T's wholesale prices. In *Trinko*, Verizon was required by statute to lease its network elements to competing firms at wholesale rates. The plaintiff — a customer of one of Verizon's rivals — asserted that Verizon denied its competitors access to interconnection support services, making it difficult for those competitors to fill their customers' orders. The complaint alleged that this conduct in the upstream market violated § 2 of the Sherman Act by impeding the ability of independent carriers to compete in the downstream market for local telephone service.

We held that the plaintiff's claims were not actionable under § 2. Given that Verizon had no antitrust duty to deal with its rivals at all, we concluded that "Verizon's al-leged insufficient assistance in the provision of service to rivals" did not violate the Sherman Act. *Trinko* thus makes clear that if a firm has no antitrust duty to deal with its competitors at wholesale, it certainly has no duty to deal under terms and conditions that the rivals find commercially advantageous.

In this case, as in *Trinko*, the defendant has no antitrust duty to deal with its rivals at wholesale; any such duty arises only from FCC regulations, not from the Sherman Act. There is no meaningful distinction between the "insufficient assistance" claims we rejected in *Trinko* and the plaintiffs' price-squeeze claims in the instant case. The *Trinko* plaintiffs challenged the quality of Verizon's interconnection service, while this case involves a challenge to AT & T's pricing structure. But for antitrust purposes, there is no reason to distinguish between price and nonprice components of a transaction. See, e.g., *American Telephone & Telegraph Co. v. Central Office Telephone, Inc.*, 524 U.S. 214, 223 (1998) ("Any claim for excessive rates can be couched as a claim for inadequate services and vice versa"). The nub of the complaint in both *Trinko* and this case is identical-the plaintiffs alleged that the defendants (upstream monopolists) abused their power in the wholesale market to prevent rival firms from competing effectively in the retail market. *Trinko* holds that such claims are not cognizable under the Sherman Act in the absence of an antitrust duty to deal.

The District Court and the Court of Appeals did not regard *Trinko* as controlling because that case did not directly address price-squeeze claims. This is technically true, but the reasoning of *Trinko* applies with equal force to price-squeeze claims. AT & T could have squeezed its competitors' profits just as effectively by providing poor-quality interconnection service to the plaintiffs, as Verizon allegedly did in *Trinko*. But a firm with no duty to deal in the wholesale market has no obligation to deal under terms and conditions favorable to its competitors. If AT & T had simply stopped providing DSL transport service to the plaintiffs, it would not have run afoul of the Sherman Act. Under these circumstances, AT & T was not required to offer this service at the wholesale prices the plaintiffs would have preferred.

The other component of a price-squeeze claim is the assertion that the defendant's retail prices are "too low." Here too plaintiffs' claims find no support in our existing antitrust doctrine. "[C]utting prices in order to increase business often is the very essence of competition." *Matsushita Elec. Industrial Co. v. Zenith Radio Corp.*, 475 U.S. 574, 594, 106 S.Ct. 1348, 89 L.Ed.2d 538 (1986). In cases seeking to impose antitrust liability for prices that are too low, mistaken inferences are "especially costly, because they chill the very conduct the antitrust laws are designed to protect." *Ibid.*; see also *Brooke Group*, 509 U.S. at 226; *Cargill, Inc. v. Monfort of Colo., Inc.*, 479 U.S. 104, 121–122, n. 17 (1986). To avoid chilling aggressive price competition, we have carefully limited the circumstances under which plaintiffs can state a Sherman Act claim by alleging that prices are too low. Specifically, to prevail on a predatory pricing claim, a plaintiff must demonstrate that: (1) "the prices complained of are below an appropriate measure of its rival's costs"; and (2) there is a "dangerous probability" that the defendant will be able to recoup its "investment" in below-cost prices. *Brooke Group, supra*, at 222–224, 113 S. Ct. 2578. "Low prices benefit consumers regardless of how those prices are set, and so long as they are above predatory levels, they do not threaten competition." *Atlantic Richfield Co. v. USA Petroleum Co.*, 495 U.S. 328, 340 (1990).

In the complaint at issue in this interlocutory appeal, there is no allegation that AT & T's conduct met either of the *Brooke Group* requirements. Recognizing a price-squeeze claim where the defendant's retail price remains above cost would invite the precise harm we sought to avoid in *Brooke Group*: Firms might raise their retail prices or refrain from aggressive price competition to avoid potential antitrust liability. See 509 U.S., at 223 ("As a general rule, the exclusionary effect of prices above a relevant measure of cost either reflects the lower cost structure of the alleged predator, and so represents competition on the merits, or is beyond the practical ability of a judicial tribunal to control without courting intolerable risks of chilling legitimate price cutting").

Plaintiffs' price-squeeze claim, looking to the relation between retail and wholesale prices, is thus nothing more than an amalgamation of a meritless claim at the retail level and a meritless claim at the wholesale level. If there is no duty to deal at the wholesale level and no predatory pricing at the retail level, then a firm is certainly not required to price both of these services in a manner that preserves its rivals' profit margins. Institutional concerns also counsel against recognition of such claims. We have repeatedly emphasized the importance of clear rules in antitrust law. Courts are ill suited "to act as central planners, identifying the proper price, quantity, and other terms of dealing." *Trinko*, 540 U.S. at 408. " 'No court should impose a duty to deal that it cannot explain or adequately and reasonably supervise. The problem should be deemed irremedia[ble] by antitrust law when compulsory access requires the court to assume the day-to-day controls characteristic of a regulatory agency.' " *Id.*, at 415 (quoting Areeda, *Essential Facilities: An Epithet in Need of Limiting Principles*, 58 Antitrust L.J. 841, 853 (1989)); see also *Town of Concord v. Boston Edison Co.*, 915 F.2d 17, 25 (C.A.1 1990) (Breyer, C.J.) ("[A]ntitrust courts normally avoid direct price administration, relying on rules and remedies . . . that are easier to administer").

It is difficult enough for courts to identify and remedy an alleged anticompetitive practice at one level, such as predatory pricing in retail markets or a violation of the duty-to-deal doctrine at the wholesale level. See *Brooke Group, supra,* at 225 (predation claims "requir[e] an understanding of the extent and duration of the alleged predation, the relative financial strength of the predator and its intended victim, and their respective incentives and will"); *Trinko, supra,* at 408. Recognizing price-squeeze claims would require courts simultaneously to police both the wholesale and retail prices to ensure that rival firms are not being squeezed. And courts would be aiming at a moving target, since it is the interaction between these two prices that may result in a squeeze.

Perhaps most troubling, firms that seek to avoid price-squeeze liability will have no safe harbor for their pricing practices. See *Town of Concord, supra,* at 22 (antitrust rules "must be clear enough for lawyers to explain them to clients"). At least in the predatory pricing context, firms know they will not incur liability as long as their retail prices are above cost. *Brooke Group, supra,* at 223. No such guidance is available for price-squeeze claims. See, e.g., 3B P. Areeda & H. Hovenkamp, Antitrust Law ¶ 767c, p. 138 (3d ed. 2008) ("[A]ntitrust faces a severe problem not only in recognizing any § 2 [price-squeeze] offense, but also in formulating a suitable remedy").

The most commonly articulated standard for price squeezes is that the defendant must leave its rivals a "fair" or "adequate" margin between the wholesale price and the retail price. See *Town of Concord, supra,* at 23–25; *Alcoa,* 148 F.2d 416, 437–438 (C.A.2 1945). One of our colleagues has highlighted the flaws of this test in Socratic fashion:

> "[H]ow is a judge or jury to determine a 'fair price?' Is it the price charged by other suppliers of the primary product? None exist. Is it the price that competition 'would have set' were the primary level not monopolized? How can the court determine this price without examining costs and demands, indeed without acting like a rate-setting regulatory agency, the rate-setting proceedings of which often last for several years? Further, how is the court to decide the proper size of the price 'gap?' Must it be large enough for all independent competing firms to make a 'living profit,' no matter how inefficient they may be? . . . And how should the court respond when costs or demands change over time, as they inevitably will?" *Town of Concord, supra,* at 25.

Some amici respond to these concerns by proposing a "transfer price test" for identifying an unlawful price squeeze: A price squeeze should be presumed if the upstream monopolist could not have made a profit by selling at its retail rates if it purchased inputs at its own wholesale rates. Whether or not that test is administrable, it lacks any grounding in our antitrust jurisprudence. An upstream monopolist with no duty to deal is free to charge whatever wholesale price it would like; antitrust law does not forbid lawfully obtained monopolies from charging monopoly prices. . . .

Amici assert that there are circumstances in which price squeezes may harm competition. For example, they assert that price squeezes may raise entry barriers that fortify the upstream monopolist's position; they also contend that price squeezes may impair nonprice competition and innovation in the downstream market by driving independent firms out of business.

The problem, however, is that amici have not identified any independent competitive harm caused by price squeezes above and beyond the harm that would result from a duty-to-deal violation at the wholesale level or predatory pricing at the retail level. See 3A P. Areeda & H. Hovenkamp, Antitrust Law ¶ 767c, p. 126 (2d ed. 2002) ("[I]t is difficult to see any competitive significance [of a price squeeze] apart from the consequences of vertical integration itself"). To the extent a monopolist violates one of these doctrines, the plaintiffs have a remedy under existing law. We do not need to endorse a new theory of liability to prevent such harm.

Lastly, as mentioned above, plaintiffs have asked us for leave to amend their complaint to bring a *Brooke Group* predatory pricing claim. We need not decide whether leave to amend should be granted. Our grant of certiorari was limited to the question whether price-squeeze claims are cognizable in the absence of an antitrust duty to deal.

. . .

It is for the District Court on remand to consider whether the amended complaint states a claim upon which relief may be granted. . . . Even if the amended complaint is further amended to add a Brooke Group claim, it may not survive a motion to dismiss. For if AT & T can bankrupt the plaintiffs by refusing to deal altogether, the plaintiffs must demonstrate why the law prevents AT & T from putting them out of business by pricing them out of the market. Nevertheless, such questions are for the District Court to decide in the first instance. . . .

The judgment of the Court of Appeals is reversed, and the case is remanded for further proceedings consistent with this opinion.

It is so ordered.

[A concurring opinion by JUSTICE BREYER, joined by JUSTICES STEVENS, SOUTER, and GINSBURG, is omitted.]

NOTES AND QUESTIONS

1. Is it entirely fair to say that the price squeeze in *Linkline* is nothing more than an amalgamation of a "meritless" refusal to deal claim at the wholesale level, and a "meritless" predatory pricing claim at the retail level? Isn't the whole point that one can assess the conduct only by looking at the two together.

2. Judge Hand's price squeeze test in the *Aluminum Co.* (*Alcoa*) decision, reprinted supra this chapter, is sometimes presented as if it had been based merely on some notion of "fairness." In fact, however, Judge Hand had employed a cost-based test, which was: Did the defendant set the wholesale price to rivals so high in relation to its own retail price that Alcoa itself could not have earned a profit on the spread between the two? *See United States v. Alcoa*, 148 F.2d 416, 436–437 (2d Cir. 1945):

The plaintiff's theory is that "Alcoa" consistently sold ingot at so high a price that the "sheet rollers," who were forced to buy from it, could not pay the expenses of "rolling" the "sheet" and make a living profit out of the price at which "Alcoa" itself sold "sheet." To establish this the plaintiff asks us to take "Alcoa's" costs of "rolling" as a fair measure of its competitors' costs, and to assume that they had to meet "Alcoa's" price for all grades of "sheet," and could not buy in-got elsewhere. It seems to us altogether reasonable, in the absence of proof to the contrary, to suppose that "Alcoa's" "rolling" costs were not higher than those of other "sheet rollers."

3. High fixed costs create more room for a squeeze in which the independent firm can cover its variable costs but not its fixed costs. A typical attribute of industries with high fixed costs is that a vertically integrated firm can profitably increase output by engaging in price discrimination, and this can lead to situations in which a large firm actually charges a lower "retail" price to its own customers than it charges its rival for the requisite input. For example, suppose I am a vertically integrated firm with a monopoly in an upstream market for Alpha, an input into the production of Beta, which is sold downstream to consumers. A rival wishes to buy Alpha from me. Because the inputs used in producing Beta are not homogenous, this rival invests in the specific production technologies required to make Beta from my Alpha. Suppose that every unit of Beta is sold downstream for $100, and that it costs $20 to fabricate Beta from Alpha. I sell Alpha to my rival for $70, which includes a $20 markup. At this price my rival earns a $10 profit on each unit of Beta sold downstream. However, I learn that I can profit by offering a quantity discount of 10 units of Beta for $650. This package price of $65 per unit is $5 less than the price I charge my rival for Alpha. However, it is profitable for me because I still earn a profit of $150 on the bundle; I have simply used this bundle as a way of appealing to large-scale consumers that were not otherwise willing to buy my product. At this per-unit price level my rival clearly faces a price-squeeze, yet I have every reason to impose it. The squeeze (which exists only with respect to customers of 10 or more units) is merely the result of an independently profitable price discrimination strategy. It is profitable without regard to any injury that might accrue to my rival.

Controlling price discrimination in regulated industries subject to high fixed costs is a highly complex regulatory task. On the one hand, price discrimination in such cases clearly increases output and thus enables the regulated firm to charge less to everyone. That is, price discrimination enables a seller in such an industry to capture additional sales in a range where the contribution of a price to fixed cost is quite low but nevertheless positive. On the other hand, price discrimination often entails that the marginal sale is made at a much lower price than much more inframarginal sales to long-term customers. *See* Erik N. Hovenkamp & Herbert Hovenkamp, *The Viability of Antitrust Price Squeeze Claims*, 51 ARIZ. L. REV. 273 (2009).

4. Suppose the monopolist wishes to stop supplying an input to its rival and could lawfully do so immediately; or perhaps it plans to do so in the foreseeable future when its own downstream capacity has increased. However, the rival has a costly, dedicated facility with many useful years remaining. The dominant firm might then pursue a strategy of squeezing the rival's margins so that they cover only variable costs, in effect appropriating its fixed cost investment. While the dominant firm could do this by cutting its downstream price, the more promising strategy would very likely be to raise the upstream transfer price. This allows the integrated firm to keep the downstream price at its profit-maximizing level, which may or may not change after the rival exits the market. During the time that this squeeze occurs the dominant firm would in effect be obtaining the use of the rivals fixed cost assets without paying for them. Eventually, of course, the smaller firm would go into bankruptcy or exit the market by some other means.

Assuming that the refusal to deal and "instant" termination of the smaller firm were legal to begin with, is there any incremental consumer harm that might serve to turn this price squeeze into an antitrust violation? Of course, there might be harm to the creditors or shareholders of the smaller firm, but this is hardly clear. An abrupt refusal to deal might result in the immediate closure of the plant and have the same effect or worse on shareholders and creditors. But in any event consumer injury would not obviously be any more severe when the small firm died a gradual death by squeezing rather than a sudden death caused by a refusal to deal. Two decisions which appear to recognize this theory are *Bonjorno v. Kaiser Aluminum & Chem. Corp.*, 752 F.2d 802, 808–11 (3d Cir. 1984); *Columbia Metal Culvert Co. v. Kaiser Aluminum & Chem. Corp.*, 579 F.2d 20, 24 (3d Cir. 1978).

IV THE OFFENSE OF ATTEMPT TO MONOPOLIZE

The offense of "attempt" to monopolize is explicit in Section 2 of the Sherman Act, which condemns "[e]very person who shall monopolize or attempt to monopolize." Nevertheless, the word "attempt" had a rich common law meaning at the time the Sherman Act was passed, and much of that legacy has been assimilated into the statutory offense of attempt to monopolize. Consider the following seminal definition from Justice Holmes, whose understanding of the common law attempt offense was as sophisticated as that of any legal scholar:

> It is suggested that the several acts charged [in the complaint] are lawful and that intent can make no difference. But they are bound together as the parts of a single plan. The plan may make the parts unlawful. The [Sherman Act] gives this proceeding against combinations in restraint of commerce among the States and against attempts to monopolize the same. Intent is almost essential to such a combination and is essential to such an attempt. Where acts are not sufficient in themselves to produce a result which the law seeks to prevent — for instance, the monopoly,— but require further acts in addition to the mere forces of nature to bring that result to pass, an intent to bring it to pass is necessary in order to produce a dangerous probability that it will happen. But when that intent and the consequent dangerous probability exist, this statute, like many others and like the common law in some cases, directs itself against that dangerous probability as well as against the completed result.

Swift & Co. v. United States, 196 U.S. 375, 396 (1905).

TOPS MARKETS, INC. v. QUALITY MARKETS, INC.,
142 F.3d 90 (2d Cir. 1998)

CARDAMONE, CIRCUIT JUDGE:

. . . The corporate parties to this action include: plaintiff Tops Markets, a New York corporation engaged in the retail supermarket business, operating 53 supermarkets and 87 convenience stores in western New York; defendant Penn Traffic Company (Penn), which owns and operates 267 supermarkets and 15 discount department stores throughout New York, Pennsylvania, Ohio and West Virginia; defendant Quality Markets (Quality), a New York corporation that is a division of Penn and competes with Tops by operating supermarkets in western New York and western Pennsylvania; and defendant Sunrise Properties (Sunrise), a Pennsylvania corporation and wholly-owned subsidiary of Penn that owns and develops commercial real estate for Penn and its divisions. Quality, Penn and Sunrise together comprise the "Quality defendants." The remaining party is defendant James V. Paige, Jr., a Jamestown, New York, real estate developer.

A. The Relevant Market

For purposes of reviewing the grant of summary judgment in this antitrust appeal, the relevant geographical market is that to which the parties stipulated: an area in the southeastern portion of Chautauqua County, New York, extending approximately seven to ten miles in all directions from the city of Jamestown. The area includes 17 municipalities and is populated by approximately 75,000 people. The parties also stipulated that the relevant product market consists of the retail sale by "supermarkets" of predominantly food items, together with general household merchandise. A "supermarket" is defined as a retail store with at least 7,500 square feet of retail space that sells a full range of perishable and non-perishable food items and general household merchandise.

The Jamestown market recently has undergone dramatic changes. In 1992 Quality owned five of the nine supermarkets in the geographical market. Of the remaining four supermarkets, "Bells" and "Super Duper" each owned and operated two. In January 1993 Quality acquired and within one year closed both "Bells" stores. In April 1995 it purchased both "Super Duper" stores and immediately shut them both as well. In May 1995 Wegmans, a Quality competitor, successfully opened a large 100,000 square foot supermarket in the Jamestown market area.

B. The Disputed Act: The Washington Street Site

Tops owned a supermarket in the Jamestown market until 1984 when it voluntarily terminated operations there. Seven years later, in 1991, it resolved to re-enter the Jamestown market and commissioned studies to evaluate the feasibility and profitability of numerous potential sites for a new store location. These studies determined certain property located on Washington Street in Jamestown (the Washington Street site) was the most suitable spot for a supermarket. The Washington Street site consisted of several parcels of land, four of which were owned by defendant Paige.

Paige agreed to sell his four parcels to Tops. Under the terms of a March 13, 1992 contract, Paige undertook to transfer title to Tops for $475,000. The parties set December 15, 1992 as the date for closing, subject to change only by their mutual agreement. The contract also called for Paige to obtain options to purchase the remaining parcels he did not own at the Washington Street site, giving him until March 15, 1992 to comply with this requirement. The contract specified that if Paige failed to acquire these additional parcels, Tops could elect unilaterally to terminate the agreement.

When Quality discovered Tops' intention to re-enter the Jamestown market at the Washington Street site, it expressed an interest in acquiring two of Paige's Washington site parcels. Paige and Sunrise subsequently entered into a "Back-Up" agreement on June 30, 1992 under which Sunrise would acquire for $225,000 two non-contiguous parcels lacking any frontage on Washington Street. The contract of sale was made expressly contingent upon the termination of Paige's prior contract with Tops.

Sunrise and Paige restructured their contract on November 4, 1992 to grant Sunrise the option to purchase the same two parcels for a total purchase price (i.e., the sum of the option price and the "strike price") of $360,000. This arrangement again was amended on January 27, 1993 to increase the total purchase price to $765,000. Also included was a right of repurchase by Paige within one year after the deed to the property was conveyed to Sunrise. Any repurchase however, would be subject to a deed restriction limiting the property to uses other than a supermarket. On the same day that the second amendment was prepared, Paige notified Sunrise that his contract with Tops had terminated. Sunrise thereafter exercised its option and did acquire title to the two Washington Street parcels in April 1993. This lawsuit followed.

Plaintiff eventually acquired the entire Washington Street site when the Jamestown Urban Renewal Agency, exercising its power of eminent domain, condemned the property and later sold it to Tops. Tops opened a superstore at the site on April 19, 1997.

C. Prior Proceedings

Plaintiff filed the present action in the Western District of New York in April 1993 to recover damages from the Quality defendants and Paige for their alleged violations of §§ 1 and 2 of the Sherman Antitrust Act, 15 U.S.C. §§ 1 & 2. . . . Defendants moved for summary judgment with respect to all of plaintiff's causes of action. . . . With respect to the § 2 cause of action, it further ruled that Tops failed to demonstrate Quality had either the requisite market power or potential market power to sustain a monopolization or attempted monopolization claim respectively. Plaintiff urges on appeal that dismissing its Sherman Act causes of action was error.

. . .

DISCUSSION . . .

II. The Sherman Act, § 2

Section 2 of the Sherman Act . . . forbids both monopolization and attempted monopolization. We address each offense in turn.

A. Completed Monopolization

To establish a § 2 violation for completed monopolization, a plaintiff must produce evidence sufficient to prove the defendant: (1) possessed monopoly power in the relevant market; and (2) willfully acquired or maintained that power. *See United States v. Grinnell Corp.*, 384 U.S. 563, 570–71 (1966). The second element is distinct from business growth or development as a consequence of superior product, business acumen or historic accident. *See Grinnell Corp.*, 384 U.S. at 571.

The district court granted summary judgment in favor of defendants regarding Tops' claim for completed monopolization. It held, as a matter of law, without even addressing the issue of defendants' conduct, that Quality lacked the requisite monopoly power. We must therefore carefully consider whether the relevant evidence created an issue of fact for the jury regarding monopoly power.

Monopoly power, also referred to as market power, is "the power to control prices or exclude competition." *United States v. E.I. du Pont de Nemours & Co.*, 351 U.S. 377, 391 (1956). It may be proven directly by evidence of the control of prices or the exclusion of competition, or it may be inferred from one firm's large percentage share of the relevant market. . . .

Tops . . . presented evidence of Quality's high market share in the Jamestown market to establish indirectly Quality's monopoly power. While market share is not the functional equivalent of monopoly power, it nevertheless is highly relevant to the determination of monopoly power. A court may infer monopoly power from a high market share.

A court will draw an inference of monopoly power only after full consideration of the relationship between market share and other relevant market characteristics. These characteristics include the "strength of the competition, the probable development of the industry, the barriers to entry, the nature of the anticompetitive conduct and the elasticity of consumer demand."

In the case at hand, Tops presented evidence that Quality's share of the total sales of food items and general household merchandise by Jamestown area supermarkets always exceeded 72 percent. At the time Quality contracted with Paige in 1992 to purchase the Washington Street property, Quality's market share stood at roughly 73 percent. After its acquisition and closing of the "Bells" and "Super Duper" stores and the opening of the Wegmans store, Quality's share steadied at 74 percent in 1995.

Tops asks us to infer Quality's monopoly power from these statistics. We have held that a market share of over 70 percent is usually "strong evidence" of monopoly power. *See Broadway Delivery*, 651 F.2d at 129 ("Sometimes, but not inevitably, it will be useful to suggest that a market share below 50% is rarely evidence of monopoly power, a share between 50% and 70% can occasionally show monopoly power, and a share above 70% is usually strong evidence of monopoly power."). Nonetheless, such evidence does not conclusively establish Quality's monopoly power.

At this juncture, either plaintiff or defendants may introduce evidence regarding these other market factors to determine whether Quality possessed monopoly power. *See* 2A Phillip E. Areeda & Herbert Hovenkamp, *Antitrust Law*, ¶ 532a, at 161 (1995) ("[T]he courts generally allow the defendant to rebut inferences of market power by showing easy entry conditions."). The Quality defendants point to several facts in the record suggesting there are no barriers to entry, and Tops failed to produce any further evidence to rebut this assertion. Tops alleges that site availability in the Jamestown market was extremely limited, but offers no proof demonstrating what geographic barriers inhibit a competitor's ability to enter that market. Instead, the record suggests that undeveloped land on which to locate a supermarket has been available at all relevant times throughout the market area. As already noted, Wegmans, a major competitor of Quality, opened a 100,000 square foot store at a different site in 1995 and quickly gained a respectable share of the market. Even Tops' own contemporaneous market studies indicate that Quality did not have such a strong market position as to enable it to exclude competitors. According to these studies, competitors, like Tops and Wegmans, could readily enter the Jamestown market at any number of available sites and successfully compete for supermarket sales.

We agree with Judge Elfvin's conclusion that as a matter of law, despite evidence of Quality's high market share, consideration of other relevant factors does not support a conclusion that Quality did, in fact, possess monopoly power. We cannot be blinded by market share figures and ignore marketplace realities, such as the relative ease of competitive entry. . . .

On this record we can draw no reasonable inference other than that Quality lacks monopoly power. Despite its high market share, no other evidence — such as barriers to entry, the elasticity of demand, or the nature of defendant's conduct — supports the conclusion that Quality can control prices or exclude competition and in fact, Wegmans' quick garnishment of such high market share dispositively refutes such a conclusion. Thus, absent a showing of Quality's monopoly power, Tops' claim for completed monopolization was properly dismissed.

B. Attempted Monopolization

To establish a claim for attempted monopolization, a plaintiff must prove: "(1) that the defendant has engaged in predatory or anticompetitive conduct with (2) a specific intent to monopolize and (3) a dangerous probability of achieving monopoly power." *Spectrum Sports, Inc. v. McQuillan*, 506 U.S. 447, 456 (1993). In the discussion that follows we deal first with anticompetitive conduct, second with a dangerous probability of achieving monopoly power and, third, with defendants' intent.

1. Anticompetitive Conduct

A factfinder could reasonably find that the Quality defendants' and Paige's conduct was anticompetitive. For purposes of this summary judgment motion, we assume that a valid contract existed between Paige and Tops for the sale of the Washington Street site; the Quality defendants interfered with that contract and induced Paige to breach it; and Paige then sold to Sunrise the land targeted by Tops for its store site. The plain effect of this conduct was to prevent Tops, a Quality competitor, from entering the Jamestown market at the Washington site.

2. Dangerous Probability of Success

The district court determined, again as a matter of law, that there was no proof of a dangerous probability that Quality would achieve monopoly power and therefore dismissed the attempted monopolization claim. We think, to the contrary, that a factfinder could reasonably find that Quality was close to achieving monopoly power. Critical to deciding the dangerous probability prong of plaintiff's attempted monopolization claim is defendant's economic power in the relevant market. *See Spectrum Sports*, 506 U.S. at 458–59. Attempted monopolization requires some degree of market power. In considering the likelihood of achieving monopoly power, we employ the same concept of market power as that used in a completed monopolization claim, i.e., one which considers the defendant's relevant market share in light of other market characteristics, including barriers to entry.

Despite the similar approaches, a lesser degree of market power may establish an attempted monopolization claim than that necessary to establish a completed monopolization claim. That Tops failed to demonstrate the monopoly power required to prove the offense of completed monopolization therefore does not, a fortiori, lead to the conclusion that it failed to make a sufficient showing with respect to its attempted monopolization cause of action.

In view of the lowered quantum of proof requirement, the minimum threshold of evidence Tops must adduce to survive summary judgment on its attempted monopolization claim is reduced. While concededly, Tops proffered only Quality's market share figures as evidence of a dangerous probability of success, those figures demonstrate that Quality possessed a market share exceeding 72 percent when it purchased the Washington Street parcels. Holding such a large market share percentage at the time when defendants took other anticompetitive actions is sufficient, in our mind, to create a genuine factual issue as to whether there was a dangerous probability that Quality would achieve monopoly power. *See U.S. Anchor Mfg., Inc. v. Rule Indus., Inc.*, 7 F.3d 986, 999 (11th Cir.1993); *McGahee v. Northern Propane Gas Co.*, 858 F.2d 1487, 1506 (11th Cir.1988) (finding that a 60 or 65 percent market share is sufficiently large to create a genuine issue of material fact as to whether there was a dangerous probability of success); *see also H.L. Hayden Co.*, 879 F.2d at 1017 (holding a dangerous probability of monopoly may exist where a party possesses a significant market share at the time it undertakes the challenged anticompetitive conduct); 3A Phillip E. Areeda & Herbert Hovenkamp, Antitrust Law, ¶ 801a, at 301 (1996) (suggesting it is reasonable to presume substantial market power when defendant's share of relevant market exceeds 70-75 percent for the five years preceding the complaint).

We recognize that the Quality defendants point to the lack of barriers to entry, and that we found such evidence dispositive in our previous discussion of market power regarding a completed monopolization claim. Yet, with respect to an attempted monopolization claim, such evidence is insufficient to support summary judgment in defendants' favor. Because plaintiff's quantum of proof is lower in this context, defendants' evidence serves only to raise questions of fact for trial. Whereas Tops' proof of market share alone — even when countered with evidence of easy market access — failed to show as a matter of law that Quality actually possessed market power, it could nevertheless support a finding that Quality had a dangerous probability of achieving market power. Plaintiff's attempted monopolization claim therefore survives summary judgment on this point.

Consequently, on remand, the jury should be instructed to consider the impact of other market characteristics, particularly the barriers to entry, on this high market share to determine whether a dangerous probability, in fact, existed. A jury may also properly consider Quality's subsequent decline in market share attributable to the entry and growth of a competitor. *See* 3A Phillip E. Areeda & Herbert Hovenkamp, *Antitrust Law*, ¶ 807el, at 358 (1996).

3. Specific Intent

Although the completed offense of monopolization requires only a general intent, "a specific intent to destroy competition or build monopoly is essential to guilt for the mere attempt." *Times-Picayune Publ'g Co. v. United States*, 345 U.S. 594, 626 (1953). An examination of the record would permit a reasonable factfinder to find that the Quality defendants intended to acquire monopoly power.

To begin with, defendants' intent can be derived from their words. Defendants' officials frequently affirmed their stated goal of preventing Tops from entering the Jamestown market. For example, John Dixon, then-president of Quality and current President and C.E.O. of Penn, stated that one reason why the Quality defendants purchased the Washington Street parcels was to prevent Tops from competing at that site. Gary Hirsh, Chairman of the Board at Penn, echoed this sentiment. After purchasing the disputed parcels, the Quality defendants announced at a press conference they would not allow the property to be used by a competing supermarket company. In fact, the "Second Amendment Agreement" between the Quality defendants and Paige is strong evidence of the Quality defendants' aim of preventing a supermarket from opening at the Washington Street site by requiring, if Paige repurchases the property, that he would preclude the development of a supermarket on the transferred parcels.

Second, a factfinder could also reasonably infer a specific intent to destroy competition from the Quality defendants' conduct. *See Northeastern Tel. Co. v. American Tel. & Tel. Co.*, 651 F.2d 76, 85 (2d Cir. 1981) (explaining that proof of unlawful conduct may imply specific intent). The Quality defendants purchased for above-market value two non-contiguous land parcels with no street frontage, which are, by themselves, essentially undevelopable.[8] A jury could find this conduct was

---

[8] [FN 1] Quality originally agreed to pay $225,000 and then later bought the two parcels for a total

not motivated by a valid business justification. *See Aspen Skiing Co. v. Aspen Highlands Skiing Corp.*, 472 U.S. 585, 605 (1985). The Quality defendants obviously could have chosen a more profitable location for a possible convenience store, but were willing to pay a very substantial premium for land on Washington Street in an attempt to exclude Tops from entering the Jamestown market. *Cf. Consolidated Rail*, 902 F.2d at 178–79 (finding that defendant monopolist's pursuit of non-profit-maximizing market behavior supports a showing of willful acquisition of monopoly power for a completed monopolization claim); *Berkey Photo, Inc. v. Eastman Kodak Co.*, 603 F.2d 263, 291 (2d Cir. 1979) (finding that a monopolist's use of monopoly power to act in a manner "that a firm would have found substantially less effective, or even counterproductive, if it lacked market control" demonstrates a willful acquisition of monopoly power for a completed monopolization claim).

. . . .

CONCLUSION

Accordingly, for the foregoing reasons, we affirm the district court's dismissal of the . . . § 2 claim for completed monopolization. We vacate the dismissal of the § 2 claim for attempted monopolization, and remand that cause of action to the district court for further proceedings consistent with this opinion. . . .

NOTES AND QUESTIONS

1. The Supreme Court laid out the modern 3-element test for attempted monopolization in *Spectrum Sports, Inc. v. McQuillan*, 506 U.S. 447 (1993). In doing so, the Court rejected a Ninth Circuit rule that provided that evidence of predatory conduct could satisfy both the specific intent and dangerous probability elements of the attempted monopolization, without defining a relevant market or proving the defendant's market power. The Ninth Circuit rule also permitted an "inference of dangerous probability . . . from a showing of intent." *Id.* at 457. The Supreme Court rejected this, holding "dangerous probability of success requires proof of more than intent alone." *Id.* at 457–58.

2. The third prong of the attempted monopolization test (that the defendant has "a dangerous probability of achieving monopoly power") is similar to the first prong of *Grinnell* test (that the defendant possesses monopoly power in a relevant market). "To demonstrate that there is a dangerous probability that the defendant will achieve monopoly power, . . . "a plaintiff must: (1) define the relevant market, (2) show that the defendant owns a dominant share of that market, and (3) show that there are significant barriers to entry and show that existing competitors lack the capacity to increase their output in the short run." *East Portland Imaging Center, P.C. v. Providence Health System-Oregon*, 2008 U.S. App. LEXIS 10984, at *3–*5 (9th Cir. May 7th, 2008) (quoting *Rebel Oil Co., Inc. v. Atl. Richfield Co.*, 51 F.3d 1421, 1434 (9th Cir. 1995)). This is the same process used to determine whether a defendant possesses monopoly power. The primary difference between the third prong of *Spectrum Sports* and the first prong of *Grinnell* is that the former is easier

---

price of $765,000. Tops had been willing to pay $475,000 for all four of Paige's Washington site parcels.

to satisfy because the market share requirement for actual monopolization is higher than the market share requirement for attempted monopolization. *Rebel Oil, supra,* at 1438 ("the minimum showing of market share required in an attempt case is a lower quantum than the minimum showing required in an actual monopolization case"). For either cause of action, however, in addition to sufficiently high market share, courts require the plaintiff to prove that barriers to entry exist. AD/SAT v. Associated Press, 181 F.3d 216, 226–227 (2d Cir. 1999).

The Second Circuit in *Tops Market* held that the defendant was entitled to summary judgment on the plaintiff's claim of actual monopolization because the plaintiff could not prove the presence of barriers to entry. Yet the court allowed the plaintiff's attempted monopolization claim to proceed to trial. If there are no barriers to entry, can there be a dangerous probability that the defendant will monopolize the market? The *Tops Market* court noted that "on remand, the jury should be instructed to consider the impact of other market characteristics, particularly the barriers to entry, on this high market share to determine whether a dangerous probability, in fact, existed." Do you see any inconsistencies with the court's rulings on the actual monopolization and attempted monopolization claims?

3. The traditional statement of the attempt offense comes from Justice Holmes's formulation in the *Swift* case, *supra*. It requires the plaintiff to prove three things: (1) the defendant's specific intent to monopolize; (2) some kind of anticompetitive conduct; and (3) a "dangerous probability" that the defendant would have acquired monopoly power. Courts agree that the attempt offense includes these elements. When they interpret the elements, however, all agreement stops. The differences among the circuits go to a wide range of issues: Must the intent be subjective, or can it be measured objectively? Must there actually be an intent to monopolize the market (that is, to acquire sufficient market power to engage in monopoly pricing), or must there be merely an intent to engage in conduct that satisfies the conduct requirement of the attempt offense? Will conduct, not sufficient to make one a monopolist, nevertheless convict one of attempt to monopolize? Does proof of a "dangerous probability" of success require a showing that the defendant already has "substantial" market power, or are the power requirements substantially less than they are for monopolization?

One theme underlies the caution that many courts have expressed about using the attempt offense too expansively: the Sherman Act is not a broad statute designed to cover all unfair business practices. Principled use of the statute requires courts to distinguish those questionable business practices that pose a great danger of giving sellers monopoly power from those that do not.

The "intent" requirement in attempt cases reflects in large part the ideology of the various antitrust schools. Economists and Chicago school analysts, for example, are uncomfortable about measuring subjective intent and would prefer to discern intent from pricing behavior. Courts sometimes follow their lead, at least to the point of holding that bad intent cannot be inferred from conduct that has an alternative "legitimate" business explanation. *See Knutson v. Daily Review,* 548 F.2d 795, 814 (9th Cir. 1976). For discussion of the problem of subjective intent in predatory pricing cases, generally concluding that courts would do well to avoid considering it, see 3A P. Areeda & H. Hovenkamp, Antitrust Law ¶ 728 (3d ed.

2008). Courts and commentators generally agree about one thing: the mere "intent" to injure one's rivals by producing a better product at a lower (but nevertheless profitable) price should never violate the antitrust laws. To turn efficiency into an antitrust violation would subvert the most fundamental goal of the antitrust laws, for efficiency is the heart of the competitive process.

Once a relevant market is defined, what is required to establish a "dangerous probability" that the defendant would achieve monopoly power in that market? Must the plaintiff show that the defendant already has some market power, or that it, in some other way, "dominates" the defined market? Here the case law varies considerably with the kind of conduct at issue. For example, *Lorain Journal Co. v. United States*, 342 U.S. 143 (1951), discussed at some length in the *Aspen* decision, *supra*, condemned a newspaper's policy of not selling advertising to those who also purchased advertising from a competing radio station. Such a claim is plausible only if the newspaper has a large market share. If it did not, a merchant who wanted to advertise in both newspaper and radio would have purchased its newspaper advertising from someone else, unless Lorain Journal compensated the merchant by the amount it valued the radio advertising. By contrast, an attempt to monopolize involving fraudulent patent procurement or badly motivated litigation (see Chapter 9) might be plausible on a much smaller market share. As you might expect, market *share* requirements vary widely in attempt cases. *See, e.g., Ford v. Stroup*, 1997-1 Trade Cas. 71838, 1997 U.S. App. LEXIS 8692 (6th Cir. Apr. 23, 1997), (unpublished) (radiologist group's 50–55% share insufficient where entry barriers were not shown to be high; showing of absence of historical entry insufficient when market appeared to be competitive; although a new entrant required an expensive linear accelerator, at least three local facilities having such equipment would have been available to a new entrant); *Springfield Terminal Rwy. Co. v. Canadian Pacific Limited*, 133 F.3d 103 (1st Cir. 1997) (10% insufficient); *United States v. Empire Gas Corp.*, *supra* (47–50% insufficient); *Twin City Sportservice, Inc. v. Charles O. Finley & Co.*, 676 F.2d 1291 (9th Cir. 1982) (24% sufficient).

4. In *United States v. American Airlines, Inc.*, 743 F.2d 1114 (5th Cir. 1984), the court held that a government complaint stated a claim of attempted monopolization against an airline company accused of attempting to fix prices. The government produced evidence that the president of American (Crandall) called the president of Braniff Airlines (Putnam) and had the following conversation:

Crandall: I think it's dumb as hell . . . to sit here and pound the **** out of each other and neither one of us making a ******* dime.

Putnam: Well —

Crandall: . . . We can, we can both live here and there ain't no room for Delta. But there's, ah, no reason that I can see, all right, to put both companies out of business.

Putnam: But if you're going to overlay every route of American's on top of ours, on top of every route that Braniff has — I can't just sit here and allow you to bury us without giving our best effort.

Crandall: Oh, sure, but Eastern and Delta do the same thing. . . .

Putnam: Do you have a suggestion for me?

Crandall: Yes. I have a suggestion for you. Raise your ****** fares twenty percent. I'll raise mine the next morning.

. . .

Putnam: We can't talk about pricing.

Crandall: Oh bull****, Howard. We can talk about any ****** thing we want to talk about.

Putnam, unknown to Crandall, was taping the entire conversation. He turned the tape over to the Department of Justice, which then accused American Airlines of an attempt to monopolize.

The defendant argued, inter alia, that a mere solicitation could not constitute an illegal attempt, and that under the circumstances of this case, the attempt would require an actual agreement between the two firms to control price and output. The trial court agreed and dismissed the complaint for failure to state a claim.

In reversing, the Fifth Circuit concluded that if Putnam had accepted Crandall's offer to fix prices, "the two airlines, at the moment of acceptance, would have acquired monopoly power. At the same moment, the offense of joint monopolization would have been complete." The court observed that the fact of Crandall's specific intent to monopolize was beyond dispute. Furthermore, Crandall's proposal (a joint price increase by the two dominant firms in the market) was "the most proximate to the commission of the completed offense that Crandall was capable of committing. Considering the alleged market share of American and Braniff, the barriers to entry by other airlines, and the authority of Crandall and Putnam, the complaint sufficiently alleged that Crandall's proposal had a dangerous probability of success."

Finally, the court added:

> [The defendant further argues] that price fixing is an offense under section 1 of the Sherman Act and since the government charges that Crandall sought to have American and Braniff fix prices, the government's complaint in reality seeks to have us write an attempt provision into section 1. This argument is meritless. Appellees confuse the section 1 offense of price fixing with the power to control price following acquisition of monopoly power under section 2. Under the facts alleged in the complaint, Crandall wanted both to obtain joint monopoly power and to engage in price fixing. That he was not able to price fix and thus, has no liability under section 1, has no effect on whether his unsuccessful efforts to monopolize constitute attempted monopolization.

Id. at 1122.

Query: The court seems reluctant to "write an attempt provision into section 1" of the Sherman Act. Why should it be? Didn't Holmes simply write the common-law attempt provision into section 2? Or does the fact that section 2 recognizes "attempt to monopolize" *explicitly* suggest that an attempt should not be *implied* with respect to section 1, where it is not made explicit? The Justice Department apparently draws the line by concluding that an *agreement* to fix prices or divide markets constitutes a criminal offense, while an unaccepted solicitation, as in *American Airlines*, is only a civil violation. Joel Klein, Antitrust Division Head, News Conference, May 18, 1998 (explaining why an alleged but unaccepted offer from Microsoft to Netscape to divide the internet browser market would not be treated as a criminal offense).

NOTE: CONSPIRACY TO MONOPOLIZE

Section 2 of the Sherman Act condemns not only monopolization and attempts to monopolize, but also "[e]very person who shall . . . combine or conspire with any other person or persons, to monopolize. . . ." There is little separate case law on the offense of conspiracy to monopolize because any imaginable multi-party "conspiracy" to monopolize would also constitute a combination in restraint of trade under Section 1, where the burden of proof is generally much lighter. Most judicial statements of the conspiracy offense come in cases in which the defendants' conduct is also analyzed under Section 1 of the Sherman Act. *See Todorov v. DCH Healthcare Auth.*, 921 F.2d 1438, 1460 n.35 (11th Cir. 1991); *Hudson Valley Asbestos v. Tougher Heating & Plumbing Co.*, 510 F.2d 1140 (2d Cir. 1975). See also *International Distrib. Centers v. Walsh Trucking Co.*, 812 F.2d 786 (2d Cir. 1987), concluding that the conspiracy offense required proof that the alleged conspirators had a specific intent to monopolize, not merely an intent to do the alleged act. Further, a qualifying "agreement" must be proven. *See Seagood Trading Corp. v. Jerrico, Inc.*, 924 F.2d 1555 (11th Cir. 1991) (summary judgment for defendant where there was insufficient evidence of agreement). However, a plaintiff may not have to define a relevant market. *Key Enters. of Del., Inc. v. Venice Hosp.*, 919 F.2d 1550, 1564 (11th Cir. 1990).

NOTE: INDUSTRIAL CONCENTRATION AND NON-DOMINANT FIRMS: FROM MONOPOLIZATION TO MERGER POLICY

One effect of the "substantial" market power requirement required for monopolization or attempt cases is that Section 2 of the Sherman Act fails to reach situations where markets perform anticompetitively but there is no dominant firm guilty of unlawful exclusionary practices. For example, in *Dimmitt Agri. Indus. v. CPC Int'l.*, 679 F.2d 516 (5th Cir. 1982), the court refused to condemn the practices of a firm that was clearly the price "leader" in a well disciplined oligopoly, but whose own market share was too small to make it guilty of monopolization or attempt. The court concluded:

> We do not dispute Dimmitt's [the plaintiff's] contention that its memoranda evidence, weighed with all reasonable inferences drawn in favor of the jury verdict, supports the conclusion that during 1971-72 CPC [the defendant] exercised a significant degree of control over price.

> We conclude, however, that this conduct evidence alone is insufficient to overcome the presumption against monopoly power implied by CPC's indisputably low market shares in the two relevant undifferentiated products, corn syrup and cornstarch. Dimmitt's structural evidence is

consistent with the proposition that the corn wet milling industry is only an oligopoly, with CPC as its price leader. If so, CPC's market power is dependent upon joint action by at least some of its rivals. While we realize that any degree of market power tends to cause economic harm, such as high prices, low output, and underutilized capacity, an interpretation of the completed monopolization offense, to embrace *any* degree of market power, would complicate enforcement, overwhelm the enforcement machinery, and deter arguably legitimate conduct.

See also Brooke Group Ltd. v. Brown & Williamson Tobacco Corp., 509 U.S. 209 (1993), reprinted *supra* (refusing to condemn predatory pricing in a "lockstep" oligopoly where the defendant's market share was only 12%). Likewise, in *Kellogg*, 99 F.T.C. 8 (1982), the Federal Trade Commission refused to recognize a doctrine of "shared monopoly," alleging that the major ready-to-eat breakfast cereal companies had a tacit understanding that they would introduce large numbers of brands in order to dominate grocer shelf space, thus permitting them to raise price to oligopoly levels. *See* HERBERT HOVENKAMP, FEDERAL ANTITRUST POLICY §§ 4.2–4.6 (4th ed. 2011); George Hay, *Oligopoly, Shared Monopoly, and Antitrust Law*, 67 CORNELL L. REV. 439 (1982); Richard Schmalensee, *Entry Deterrence in the Ready-to-Eat Breakfast Cereal Industry*, 9 BELL J. ECON. 305 (1976).

The *Brooke, Dimmitt*, and *Kellogg* decisions suggest a perplexing problem about antitrust policy in highly concentrated markets that do not have a single dominant firm. The first question is *whether* something must be done about apparently unilateral exclusionary practices in such markets (concerted practices are dealt with somewhat more easily under Section 1 of the Sherman Act). The second question is: Given an affirmative answer to question one, what is the appropriate method or statute that antitrust policy makers should use?

On the first question, economists have debated the problem of industrial concentration for several decades, and the end of the debate is not in sight. The traditional, centrist view is frequently expressed as the "structure-conduct-performance" paradigm, and holds that highly concentrated markets naturally yield exclusionary and collusive conduct first, and anticompetitive performance second. Thus, the failure of a market to perform competitively is principally one of market structure. Dominance by a single firm may yield an anticompetitive structure, but so might moderately high market shares, in the order of 20% or 25%, held by three or four firms. What determines market concentration? Economies of scale contribute a little, but cannot fully explain very large market shares. Many of the determinants of market share are "stochastic," or random. Thus, high market concentration — because it results in poor performance — is most generally a bad thing. *See* F.M. SCHERER & DAVID ROSS, INDUSTRIAL MARKET STRUCTURE AND ECONOMIC PERFORMANCE, ch. 4 (3d ed. 1990); LEONARD WEISS, *The Concentration-Profits Relationship and Antitrust, in* INDUSTRIAL CONCENTRATION: THE NEW LEARNING 184–233 (H. Goldschmid, H. Mann & J. Weston eds., 1974). *See also* Richard Schmalensee, *Do Markets Differ Much?*, 75 AM. ECON. REV. 341 (1985). For a good survey, see James W. Meehan, Jr. & Robert J. Larner, *The Structural School, Its Critics, and Its Progeny: An Assessment, in* ECONOMICS AND ANTITRUST POLICY 182 (Robert J. Larner & James W. Meehan, Jr. eds., Quorum 1989).

In response, the Chicago School has completely rejected the structure-conduct-performance paradigm, arguing that it states the relationship backwards. *See* Herbert Hovenkamp, *The Rationalization of Antitrust*, 116 HARV. L. REV. 917 (2003). Performance comes first. Firms grow large because they are innovative and industrious. A firm comes up with a new process or a new product that decreases its costs or makes its offering more attractive in consumers' eyes than the offerings of competitors. As a result, that firm's market share grows very large. In fact, other firms may never catch up. High concentration may be a result of aggressive competition rather than a cause of poor performance. *See* John McGee, *Efficiency and Economies of Size* and Harold Demsetz, *Two Systems of Belief About Monopoly*, both in INDUSTRIAL CONCENTRATION: THE NEW LEARNING, *supra*, at 55 and 164; Harold Demsetz, *Industrial Structure, Market Rivalry, and Public Policy*, 16 J.L. & ECON. 1 (1973); Sam Peltzman, *The Gains and Losses from Industrial Concentration*, 20 J.L. & ECON. 229 (1977).

Most of the empirical studies have found correlations between poor industry performance (measured as high price/cost margins) and concentration, but fail to distinguish between high profits in concentrated industries that are a "result" of high concentration and those that are the result of lower costs, higher relative product demand, or some other form of competitive superiority. In this respect, both the centrist and the Chicago School theories seem to be deficient. *See* Roger Clarke, Stephen Davies & Michael Waterson, *The Profitability-Concentration Relation: Market Power or Efficiency?*, 32 J. INDUS. ECON. 435 (1984).

Other scholarship is inclined to regard both views as half-truths. High concentration may often be the result of competitive prowess, but it may also result in an indefinite period of monopoly returns for the winners. *See* Almarin Phillips, *Market Concentration and Performance: A Survey of the Evidence*, 61 NOTRE DAME L. REV. 1099 (1986). In such cases, a value judgment must be made about whether the monopoly profits are too high a reward for innovative behavior, whether workable solutions to the problem are available, and whether a court is capable of administering these. Some neoclassicists, particularly members of the Chicago School, believe that any policy of forced deconcentration will destroy incentives to innovate. Why bother to innovate and capture a large share of a market if a court will later take it all away from you? The social cost of such a destruction of incentives is likely to be greater than the social value of any efficiencies that result from deconcentration. *E.g.*, Frank Easterbrook, *On Identifying Exclusionary Conduct*, 61 NOTRE DAME L. REV. 972 (1986).

On the modern Harvard and Chicago approaches respecting the relationship between structure and performance, see HERBERT HOVENKAMP, THE ANTITRUST ENTERPRISE: PRINCIPLE AND EXECUTION 31–56 (2005).

The second question — the proper antitrust policy for dealing with the concentration problem — is just as vexing. Because of its requirement of substantial market power held by a single firm, Section 2 of the Sherman Act is not an appropriate vehicle for dealing with high market concentration in the absence of a clearly dominant firm. Likewise, Section 1 works only when there is a more or less explicit "agreement" among the firms. The principal antitrust device for dealing with industrial concentration has been merger policy under Section 7 of the Clayton

Act, which historically has accepted the structure-conduct-performance paradigm and was thus directed toward preventing a certain kind of industrial concentration: that which results from combination rather than internal growth. In the last 15 or 20 years, this reliance on market structure has been relaxed considerably, and merger policy has increasingly looked at non-structural factors. However, as the subsequent chapter illustrates, a concentrated market structure is still an essential prerequisite to merger illegality.

Chapter 7

MERGERS AND ACQUISITIONS

INTRODUCTION

Often a firm finds it profitable to expand business by increasing output or moving into a new market or a new distributional level. One way the firm can do this is by new entry — by building a new plant, for example, or by constructing its own chain of retail stores. Another way is by acquisition of a second firm that is already operating in the expansion market. Antitrust policymakers have generally regarded entry or output expansion by acquisition with more suspicion than so-called "de novo" entry. When a company enters a market de novo, it generally increases the capacity in the targeted market, and the result may be higher output and lower prices. When a firm expands by acquisition, however, increased output is not as likely and the possibilities for monopolization, collusion, or other anticompetitive practices may be greater. The law of mergers and acquisitions addresses these concerns. We begin with expansion through merger into a vertically related market.

I VERTICAL INTEGRATION THROUGH MERGER

UNITED STATES v. COLUMBIA STEEL CO
334 U.S. 495 (1948)

JUSTICE REED delivered the opinion of the Court.

The United States brings this suit under § 4 of the Sherman Act to enjoin United States Steel Corporation and its subsidiaries from purchasing the assets of the largest independent steel fabricator on the West Coast on the ground that such acquisition would violate §§ 1 and 2 of the Sherman Act. The complaint, filed on February 24, 1947, charged that if the contract of sale between United States Steel and Consolidated Steel Corporation were carried out, competition in the sale of rolled steel products and in fabricated steel products would be restrained. . . .

. . . .

The steel production involved in this case may be spoken of as being divided into two stages: the production of rolled steel products and their fabrication into finished steel products. Rolled steel products consist of steel plates, shapes, sheets, bars, and other unfinished steel products and are in turn made from ingots by means of rolling mills. The steel fabrication involved herein may also be divided into structural fabrication and plate fabrication. Fabricated structural steel products consist of building framework, bridges, transmission towers, and similar permanent structures, and are made primarily from rolled steel shapes, although plates and other rolled steel products may also be employed. Fabricated plate products, on the other hand, consist of pressure vessels, tanks, welded pipe, and similar products made principally from rolled steel plates, although shapes and bars are also occasionally used. . . .

The theory of the United States in bringing this suit is that the acquisition of Consolidated constitutes an illegal restraint of interstate commerce because all manufacturers except United States Steel will be excluded from the business of supplying Consolidated's requirements of rolled steel products. . . .

. . . Over the ten-year period from 1937 to 1946 Consolidated purchased over two million tons of rolled steel products, including the abnormally high wartime requirements. Whatever amount of rolled steel products Consolidated uses in the future will be supplied insofar as possible from other subsidiaries of United States Steel, and other producers of rolled steel products will lose Consolidated as a prospective customer.

The parties are in sharp dispute as to the size and nature of the market for rolled steel products with which Consolidated's consumption is to be compared. The appellees argue that rolled steel products are sold on a national scale, and that for the major producers the entire United States should be regarded as the market. Viewed from this standpoint, Consolidated's requirements are an insignificant fraction of the total market, less than 1/2 of 1%. The government argues that the market must be more narrowly drawn, and that the relevant market to be considered is the eleven state area in which Consolidated sells its products, and further that in that area by considering only the consumption of structural and plate fabricators a violation of the Sherman Act has been established. If all sales of rolled steel products in the Consolidated market are considered, Consolidated's purchases of two million tons represent a little more than 3% of the total of 60 million tons. . . . If the comparable market is construed even more narrowly, and is restricted to the consumption of plates and shapes in the Consolidated market, figures for 1937 indicate that Consolidated's consumption of plates and shapes was 13% of the total. . . .

The government realizes the force of appellees' argument that rolled steel products are sold on a national scale, and attempts to demonstrate that during the non-war years 80% of Consolidated's requirements were produced on the West Coast; Consolidated resorts to data not in the record to demonstrate that in fact only 26% of Consolidated's rolled steel purchases were produced in plants located in the Consolidated market area. Whether we accept the government's or Consolidated's figures, however, they are of little value in determining the extent to which West Coast fabricators will purchase rolled steel products in the eastern market in the future, since the construction of new plants at Geneva and Fontana and the creation of new basing points on the West Coast will presumably give West Coast rolled steel producers a far larger share of the West Coast fabricating market than before the war.

Another difficulty is that the record furnishes little indication as to the propriety of considering plates and shapes as a market distinct from other rolled steel products. If rolled steel producers can make other products as easily as plates and shapes, then the effect of the removal of Consolidated's demand for plates and shapes must be measured not against the market for plates and shapes alone, but for all comparable rolled products. The record suggests, but does not conclusively indicate, that rolled steel producers can make other products interchangeably with shapes and plates, and that therefore we should not measure the potential injury to competition by considering the total demand for shapes and plates alone, but rather compare Consolidated's demand for rolled steel products with the demand for all comparable rolled steel products in the Consolidated marketing area.

. . . We recognize the difficulty of laying down a rule as to what areas or products are competitive, one with another. In this case and on this record we have circumstances that strongly indicate to us that rolled steel production and consumption in the Consolidated marketing area is the competitive area and product for consideration.

. . . .

. . . A restraint may be unreasonable either because a restraint otherwise reasonable is accompanied with a specific intent to accomplish a forbidden restraint or because it falls within the class of restraints that are illegal *per se*. . . .

A subsidiary will in all probability deal only with its parent for goods the parent can furnish. That fact, however, does not make the acquisition invalid. . . .

The legality of the acquisition by United States Steel of a market outlet for its rolled steel through the purchase of the manufacturing facilities of Consolidated depends not merely upon the fact of that acquired control but also upon many other factors. Exclusive dealings for rolled steel between Consolidated and United States Steel, brought about by vertical integration or otherwise, are not illegal, at any rate until the effect of such control is to unreasonably restrict the opportunities of competitors to market their product. . . .

It seems clear to us that vertical integration, as such without more, cannot be held violative of the Sherman Act. It is an indefinite term without explicit meaning. Even in the iron industry, where could a line be drawn — at the end of mining the ore, the production of the pig iron or steel ingots, when the rolling mill operation is completed, fabrication on order or at some stage of manufacture into standard merchandise? No answer would be possible and therefore the extent of permissible integration must be governed, as other factors in Sherman Act violations, by the other circumstances of individual cases. Technological advances may easily require a basic industry plant to expand its processes into semi-finished or finished goods so as to produce desired articles in greater volume and with less expense.

. . . .

[W]e conclude that the so-called vertical integration resulting from the acquisition of Consolidated does not unreasonably restrict the opportunities of the competitor producers of rolled steel to market their product. We accept as the relevant competitive market the total demand for rolled steel products in the eleven-state area; over the past ten years Consolidated has accounted for only 3% of that demand, and if expectations as to the development of the western steel industry are realized, Consolidated's proportion may be expected to be lower than that figure in the future. . . .

. . . .

Affirmed.

NOTES AND QUESTIONS

1. A firm is "vertically integrated" whenever it does or makes for itself something it would otherwise purchase in the marketplace. A pizza parlor with its own delivery truck is vertically integrated as is a shoe store owner who washes her own store windows. Obviously, therefore, any notion that there might be a per se rule against vertical integration must be taken with several bags of salt.

2. When will a firm perform or make for itself something it would otherwise purchase? A profit-maximizing firm will generally do so when self-production or self-service is cheaper than purchase of the product or service from others. *See* R. Coase, *The Nature of the Firm*, 4 Economica, New Series 386 (1937). In perfect competition, efficiency-creating vertical integration by one firm will have to be matched by the firm's competitors, or else the competitors will lose market share to the more efficient firm. As more firms become vertically integrated, competition among the vertically integrated firms will transfer the benefits of the newly-created efficiency to consumers. Clearly, vertical integration by one firm can injure competitors who cannot integrate vertically themselves, or who cannot do so immediately. Under what circumstances, however, can vertical integration injure consumers?

3. Is the "Rule of Reason" for mergers developed in *Columbia Steel* the same as the rule of reason developed for horizontal restraint cases?

4. The *Columbia Steel* case was brought under the Sherman Act. Section 7 of the Clayton Act, which forbids mergers, had been passed in 1914, but it applied only to acquisitions of the *stock* of another corporation. The *Columbia Steel* case involved an acquisition of another company's physical assets. Early in the century, asset acquisitions were a preferred form of merger for two reasons. First, the original Clayton Act did not reach them; second, stock acquisitions often ran afoul of state corporate law provisions. *See* H. HOVENKAMP, ENTERPRISE AND AMERICAN LAW, 1836-1937, ch. 20 (1991).

As originally passed, Section 7 of the Clayton Act also seemed not to apply to vertical acquisitions; it spoke of mergers that eliminated competition "between" the merging firms — that is, mergers of competitors. However, the Supreme Court disagreed in the following case and applied the "policy" of the act to a vertical transaction. One result of the government's defeat in *Columbia Steel* was increased political momentum for expansion of Section 7 to include vertical acquisitions as well. The statute was expanded in 1950, to make clear that it applied both to asset acquisitions and to vertical mergers.

The *du Pont* case, reprinted below, was brought under Section 7 of the Clayton Act, albeit before the 1950 amendments. Can you tell the difference in the legal standard?

UNITED STATES v. E.I. DU PONT DE NEMOURS & CO
353 U.S. 586 (1957)

Justice Brennan delivered the opinion of the Court.

. . . The complaint alleged a violation of § 7 of the [Clayton] Act resulting from the purchase by E. I. du Pont de Nemours and Company in 1917-1919 of a 23% stock interest in General Motors Corporation. . . .

The primary issue is whether du Pont's commanding position as General Motors' supplier of automotive finishes and fabrics was achieved on competitive merit alone, or because its acquisition of the General Motors' stock, and the consequent close intercompany relationship, led to the insulation of most of the General Motors' market from free competition, with the resultant likelihood, at the time of suit, of the creation of a monopoly of a line of commerce.

. . . .

Section 7 is designed to arrest . . . in their incipiency restraints . . . in a relevant market which, as a reasonable probability, appear at the time of suit likely to result from the acquisition by one corporation of all or any part of the stock of any other corporation. The section is violated whether or not actual restraints or monopolies, or the substantial lessening of competition, have occurred or are intended. . . .

. . . .

We hold that any acquisition by one corporation of all or any part of the stock of another corporation, competitor or not, is within the reach of the section whenever the reasonable likelihood appears that the acquisition will result in a restraint of commerce or in the creation of a monopoly of any line of commerce. Thus, although du Pont and General Motors are not competitors, a violation of the section has occurred if, as a result of the acquisition, there was at the time of suit a reasonable likelihood of a monopoly of any line of commerce. . . .

Appellees argue that there exists no basis for a finding of a probable restraint or monopoly within the meaning of § 7 because the total General Motors market for finishes and fabrics constituted only a negligible percentage of the total market for these materials for all uses, including automotive uses. It is stated in the General Motors brief that in 1947 du Pont's finish sales to General Motors constituted 3.5% of all sales of finishes to industrial users, and that its fabrics sales to General Motors comprised 1.6% of the total market for the type of fabric used by the automobile industry.

Determination of the relevant market is a necessary predicate to a finding of a violation of the Clayton Act because the threatened monopoly must be one which will substantially lessen competition "within the area of effective competition." Substantiality can be determined only in terms of the market affected. The record shows that automotive finishes and fabrics have sufficient peculiar characteristics and uses to constitute them products sufficiently distinct from all other finishes and fabrics to make them a "line of commerce" within the meaning of the Clayton

Act. . . . Thus, the bounds of the relevant market for the purposes of this case are not coextensive with the total market for finishes and fabrics, but are coextensive with the automobile industry, the relevant market for automotive finishes and fabrics.

The market affected must be substantial. Moreover, in order to establish a violation of § 7 the Government must prove a likelihood that competition may be "foreclosed in a substantial share of . . . [that market]." Both requirements are satisfied in this case. The substantiality of a relevant market comprising the automobile industry is undisputed. The substantiality of General Motors' share of that market is fully established in the evidence.

General Motors is the colossus of the giant automobile industry. It accounts annually for upwards of two-fifths of the total sales of automotive vehicles in the Nation. . . . Expressed in percentages, du Pont supplied 67% of General Motors' requirements for finishes in 1946 and 68% in 1947. In fabrics du Pont supplied 52.3% of requirements in 1946, and 38.5% in 1947. Because General Motors accounts for almost one-half of the automobile industry's annual sales, its requirements for automotive finishes and fabrics must represent approximately one-half of the relevant market for these materials. Because the record clearly shows that quantitatively and percentagewise du Pont supplies the largest part of General Motors' requirements, we must conclude that du Pont has a substantial share of the relevant market.

. . . .

The du Pont Company's commanding position as a General Motors supplier was not achieved until shortly after its purchase of a sizable block of General Motors stock in 1917. At that time its production for the automobile industry and its sales to General Motors were relatively insignificant. General Motors then produced only about 11% of the total automobile production and its requirements, while relatively substantial, were far short of the proportions they assumed as it forged ahead to its present place in the industry.

. . . .

. . . [T]hat the purchase [of General Motors stock] would result in du Pont's obtaining a new and substantial market, was echoed in the Company's 1917 and 1918 annual reports to stockholders. In the 1917 report appears: "Though this is a new line of activity, it is one of great promise and one that seems to be well suited to the character of our organization. *The motor companies are very large consumers of our Fabrikoid and Pyralin as well as paints and varnishes.*" (Emphasis added.) The 1918 report says: "The consumption of paints, varnishes and fabrikoid in the manufacture of automobiles gives another common interest."

. . . .

In less than four years, by August 1921, Lammot du Pont, then a du Pont vice-president and later Chairman of the Board of General Motors, in response to a query from Pierre S. du Pont, then Chairman of the Board of both du Pont and General Motors, "whether General Motors was taking its entire requirements of du Pont products from du Pont," was able to reply that four of General Motors' eight operating divisions bought from du Pont their entire requirements of paints and varnishes, five their entire requirements of Fabrikoid, four their entire requirements of rubber cloth, and seven their entire requirements of Pyralin and celluloid. . . .

. . . .

Competitors did obtain higher percentages of the General Motors business in later years, although never high enough at any time substantially to affect the dollar amount of du Pont's sales. Indeed, it appears likely that General Motors probably turned to outside sources of supply at least in part because its requirements outstripped du Pont's production, when General Motors' proportion of total automobile sales grew greater and the company took its place as the sales leader of the automobile industry. For example, an undisputed Government exhibit shows that General Motors took 93% of du Pont's automobile Duco production in 1941 and 83% in 1947. . . .

We agree with the trial court that considerations of price, quality and service were not overlooked by either du Pont or General Motors. Pride in its products and its high financial stake in General Motors' success would naturally lead du Pont to try to supply the best. But the wisdom of this business judgment cannot obscure the fact, plainly revealed by the record, that du Pont purposely employed its stock to pry open the General Motors market to entrench itself as the primary supplier of General Motors' requirements for automotive finishes and fabrics.

. . . .

The statutory policy of fostering free competition is obviously furthered when no supplier has an advantage over his competitors from an acquisition of his customer's stock likely to have the effects condemned by the statute. We repeat, that the test of a violation of § 7 is whether, at the time of suit, there is a reasonable probability that the acquisition is likely to result in the condemned restraints. The conclusion upon this record is inescapable that such likelihood was proved as to this acquisition. The fire that was kindled in 1917 continues to smolder. It burned briskly to forge the ties that bind the General Motors market to du Pont, and if it has quieted down, it remains hot, and, from past performance, is likely at any time to blaze and make the fusion complete.[1]

JUSTICE BURTON, whom JUSTICE FRANKFURTER joins, dissenting.

. . . [E]ven assuming the correctness of the Court's conclusion that du Pont's competitors have been or will be foreclosed from General Motors' paint and fabric trade, it is still necessary to resolve one more issue in favor of the Government in order to reverse the District Court. It is necessary to hold that the Government proved that this foreclosure involves a substantial share of the relevant market and that it significantly limits the competitive opportunities of others trading in that market.

---

[1] [FN 36] The potency of the influence of du Pont's 23% stock interest is greater today because of the diffusion of the remaining shares which, in 1947, were held by 436,510 stockholders; 92% owned no more than 100 shares each, and 60% owned no more than 25 shares each. 126 F. Supp., at 244.

The Court holds that the relevant market in this case is the automotive market for finishes and fabrics, and not the total industrial market for these products. The Court reaches that conclusion because in its view "automotive finishes and fabrics have sufficient peculiar characteristics and uses to constitute them products sufficiently distinct from all other finishes and fabrics. . . . " We are not told what these "peculiar characteristics" are. Nothing is said about finishes other than that Duco represented an important contribution to the process of manufacturing automobiles. Nothing is said about fabrics other than that sales to the automobile industry are made by means of bids rather than fixed price schedules. . . .

[T]he types of fabrics used for automobile trim and convertible tops — imitation leather and coated fabrics — are used in the manufacture of innumerable products, such as luggage, furniture, railroad upholstery, books, brief cases, baby carriages, hassocks, bicycle saddles, sporting goods, footwear, belts and table mats. In 1947, General Motors purchased about $9,454,000 of imitation leather and coated fabrics. Of this amount, $3,639,000 was purchased from du Pont (38.5%) and $5,815,000 from over 50 du Pont competitors. Since du Pont produced about 10% of the national market for these products in 1946, 1947 and 1948, and since only 20% of its sales were to the automobile industry, the du Pont sales to the automobile industry constituted only about 2% of the total market. The Court ignores the record by treating this small fraction of the total market as a market of distinct products.

. . . .

NOTES AND QUESTIONS

1. In deciding that the relevant market foreclosed by the vertical merger was the market for automobile finishes and fabrics, the Court looked almost exclusively at elasticity of demand. Once made, automotive finishes and fabrics were not particularly useful for manufacturers of other products, such as appliances or furniture. The Court virtually ignored elasticity of supply. The Court conceded that the fabrics used by the automotive industry were of the same "type" as the fabrics used by other large purchasers of fabrics. If the only difference between fabrics used for automobile seat covers and fabrics used for, say, sofas was that the two were cut into different shapes, the cross-elasticity of supply would be very high. In that case, the Court erred in its market definition, and Justice Burton's dissent has the better argument. A fabrics manufacturer "foreclosed" from General Motors as a customer could search out a wide variety of alternative customers.

2. Suppose that General Motors could buy better finishes at a lower price from one of du Pont's competitors. Would it be reasonable for du Pont to force General Motors to buy from itself anyway?

3. Private antitrust damages actions under Section 4 of the Clayton Act are governed by a four-year statute of limitation. Criminal antitrust prosecutions are generally governed by a five-year statute, and when the government sues for damages for its own injuries, it is generally held to the four-year statute. There is, however, no statute of limitation for civil actions brought by either the government or private parties seeking injunctive relief (although the doctrine of laches may apply).

Does this mean that a firm that acquires another firm is liable forever? In *du Pont*, the acquisition occurred in 1917. The action was brought in 1949. At the time the acquisition occurred, General Motors manufactured only 11% of American automobile production, and the effects of the acquisition were not substantial. Should General Motors' growth, after the merger occurred, to a size that the Court was willing to recognize as harmful, be relevant to the legality of the merger? Do you suppose the Court was influenced by the fact that the two companies were still distinct from each other? Suppose that in 1917, General Motors had acquired a fabrics and finishes company and completely integrated that company's operations with its own. Should the government be given an injunction requiring divestiture in such circumstances, when the fabrics and finishes company has completely lost its separate identity? The government might argue that the doctrine of laches should not apply, especially if it was only in recent years that the defendant acquired a large enough market share to make the acquisition anticompetitive. In *du Pont*, the Court said that the anticompetitive effects of the acquisition are to be measured "at the time of suit." In 1975, it reiterated that policy. *See United States v. ITT Continental Baking Co.*, 420 U.S. 223 (1975).

NOTE: THE ECONOMICS OF VERTICAL MERGERS

Since the early 1980s, the number of vertical merger challenges has dropped dramatically, in large part because most of the fears of reduced competition now seem far fetched or at least greatly exaggerated. For example, courts suggested that a company with a monopoly at one distributional level (such as the manufacturing of taxicabs) could "leverage" a second monopoly at a different distributional level (the operating of taxicabs), and thus turn one monopoly into two. Secondly, courts have suggested that by vertical integration, a firm can "foreclose" rivals by restricting their markets or source of supply. For example, if a chain of shoe stores acquired a shoe manufacturer, and after the merger, the manufacturer refused to sell to competing, independent shoe stores, those competitors would have a more difficult time obtaining shoes. Likewise, if a manufacturer bought many of the retail stores in a particular area, competing manufacturers might find it more difficult to find a market for their products. Thirdly, courts have suggested, as the Supreme Court did in *Yellow Cab*, that a firm could make more money by "forcing" its own subsidiary to sell to it at a lower price.

Most of these theories have either vanished or else they play a very reduced role in vertical merger analysis today. The implausibility of a firm's making money by buying from itself at a lower price or selling to itself at a higher price seems obvious. One exception might be where a firm acquires less than 100% ownership in a firm at a different distributional level, but nevertheless acquires enough to control decision making in the acquired firm. For example, there was evidence in the *du Pont* (GM) case, reprinted *supra*, that du Pont influenced General Motors' decision to buy du Pont products even though du Pont owned only 23% of General Motors' common stock. In that case, du Pont might find it profitable to instruct General Motors to do something not in its own interest, such as purchasing materials from du Pont at a supra competitive price. Although du Pont's gains would be offset by General Motors' losses, du Pont would suffer only 23% of those losses, while the other General Motors stockholders would suffer the balance.

The leverage and foreclosure theories have appeared frequently in decisions involving both vertical mergers and other kinds of vertical restrictions. For example, *see Heatransfer Corp. v. Volkswagenwerk, A.G.*, 553 F.2d 964 (5th Cir. 1977), *cert. denied*, 434 U.S. 1087 (1978) (involving both a vertical merger and a tying arrangement). But both theories have come under broad attack by economists, and courts rely on them less than they once did. Economists commonly argue, for example, that someone with a monopoly at one level of a distributional chain can extract all the monopoly profits available in that chain; the seller cannot enlarge its monopoly profits by acquiring a second monopoly at a different level of distribution. End-use consumers generally pay a single price for a product, and if there is a monopoly mark-up along the distributional chain, they are indifferent to (and probably do not even know) whether that monopoly mark-up occurred at the retail level, the distributor level, or the manufacturing level.

Secondly, economists generally note that in markets that are even modestly competitive, vertical acquisitions cannot really "foreclose" anyone from the market. Unless someone controls nearly all the sources of supply or outlets, the effect of a vertical acquisition is not foreclosure but a certain amount of reshuffling in the market, and a subsequent new alignment of purchasers and sellers among those firms that are not vertically integrated. For example, if a manufacturer with 20% of a market acquires a retail chain with 10% of the market, the effect may be that the two firms will deal with each other. However, no one will necessarily be foreclosed. Competitors of the newly integrated retailer may switch orders from the acquiring manufacturer to a manufacturer who formerly sold to the acquired retailer. In turn, those competitors of the acquiring manufacturer will have enhanced economic incentive to attract orders from stores that formerly bought from the acquiring manufacturer. The ratio of independent sellers to independent buyers may well be the same as it was before the acquisition, even if there is a somewhat different alignment of buyers and sellers. For a general discussion of these theories, see 4A P. AREEDA & H. HOVENKAMP, ANTITRUST LAW ¶¶ 1003-13 (3d. ed. 2009); H. HOVENKAMP, FEDERAL ANTITRUST POLICY, ch. 9 (4th ed. 2011).

There are other alleged evils of vertical integration that are more controversial, although virtually all of these require that one of the two firms involved have a substantial amount of market power, or at least a very large market share. For example, it is often said that vertical integration by a monopolist creates "barriers to entry" by requiring a potential new entrant to enter the market at two levels instead of one. For example, if a monopolist in the manufacture of aluminum owns all its own fabricators, then anyone seeking to enter the market at the fabrication level will also have to build its own aluminum plant. Likewise, anyone seeking to enter at the aluminum manufacturing level may have to establish its own fabricating plants.

One answer to the barriers to entry argument is that the vertical integration creates a barrier to entry only if it results in lower cost production of the same product than independent levels of operation would entail. For example, suppose that an independent manufacturer of aluminum has costs of $1.00 per unit, while an independent fabricator has costs of 40 cents per unit. If the vertically integrated firm has total costs of $1.40 per unit for both manufacturing and fabricating, then it is profitable for independent manufacturers and independent fabricators to continue to enter the two separate production levels. However, if because of vertical integration the integrated firm can reduce its costs to $1.35, then the nonintegrated firms will have a difficult time competing unless they can also enter the market at both levels. In short, vertical integration may indeed force potential competitors to enter the market at two levels instead of one — but it is likely to do so only if the vertically integrated operation is more efficient than independent operations are.

It has also been said that vertical integration by a firm with market power can make price discrimination easier, or can hide it from the public and from customers (and law enforcement agents). For example, suppose that a manufacturer makes smidgets and has a large share of the market. Smidgets can be sold in two kinds of stores — discount stores and boutiques. However, smidgets command widely different prices in those two stores. The smidget manufacturer knows that boutique owners are willing to pay $5.00 each for smidgets, but the discount stores will pay only $4.00 each. Both prices are profitable to the smidget manufacturer. Ideally, the manufacturer would like to make each set of sales at the profit-maximizing price for that particular set — that is, it would like to sell to the boutiques at $5.00 and to the discount stores at $4.00. However, two things make this difficult. One is arbitrage: eventually, the store owners will find out what is happening and the discount store owners will begin reselling smidgets to boutique owners at some price greater than $4.00 but less than $5.00. If that happens, the manufacturer will lose its most profitable sales. The other problem is the Robinson-Patman Act, which may prevent this form of differential pricing. (*See* Chapter 8, *infra.*) Suppose, however, that the smidget manufacturer acquires the boutiques. It will then be able to internalize the sales to the boutiques and take advantage of the higher retail price that smidgets command there. At the same time, it will continue making sales to discount stores at $4.00.

Although vertical integration may facilitate price discrimination, does that mean it is bad? Unquestionably, the manufacturer of smidgets makes more money by price discriminating, or else the manufacturer would not do it. However, it is not at all clear that consumers are worse off. In fact, they may be better off because the availability of price discrimination may encourage the manufacturer to produce more smidgets than it would otherwise. Whether or not it would depends on what its nondiscriminatory profit-maximizing price would be. For example, if the smidget manufacturer decided (when it did not own the boutiques) that it could maximize its profits by selling only to the boutiques at $5.00, and forgetting about the discount stores, then the price discrimination that resulted from the acquisition of the boutiques would make the discount stores and their customers better off: now they can have smidgets too. By contrast, if the smidget manufacturer could previously maximize its profits by selling to both the discount stores and boutiques at $4.00, then the effect of the vertical merger will be to make the boutique's customers worse off, while the discount store's customers are no better off. In short, once we accept that the smidget manufacturer has market power, it is difficult to tell whether price discrimination is socially preferable to nondiscriminatory pricing.

In general, long-term systematic price discrimination is impossible for a seller without market power. If the seller faces substantial competition, then disfavored purchasers (those asked to pay the higher price) will simply buy from a competitor. Of course, it might be socially preferable that the smidget manufacturer not have market power in the first place, but that is not an option that is before us now. For further development of the theory that vertical integration can facilitate or disguise price discrimination, see 3A P. AREEDA & H. HOVENKAMP, ANTITRUST LAW ¶ 756b5 (3d ed. 2007); O. WILLIAMSON, MARKETS AND HIERARCHIES 82–131 (1975); THE NATURE OF THE FIRM: ORIGINS, EVOLUTION, AND DEVELOPMENT (O. Williamson & S. Winter eds., 1991).

Another theory of vertical integration is that under certain circumstances it may facilitate horizontal price fixing. For example, one of the most difficult aspects of maintaining a cartel is detection of cheating by cartel members. A member of a manufacturing cartel who wanted to cheat could offer retailers secret rebates if they bought the cartel member's product. By contrast, retail prices are public and are easily policed. If the members of a cartel agree to sell their output only through their own retail stores, cheating will be easier to detect.

The vast majority of vertical acquisitions probably cannot be explained on any of these theories. Most firms integrate vertically in order to reduce costs. Probably the most significant of these are the transaction costs that accrue from the use of the market system itself. As a general rule, a firm can maximize its own profits by dealing with other firms in the distribution chain that are maximally efficient. For example, the aluminum manufacturer is best off if it can obtain bauxite or iron ore at the lowest possible cost. It is likewise better off if it can pay a lower price for transportation services for its finished product. In order to obtain goods or services that are best suited to itself, and at the lowest possible price, a firm may spend a great deal of money in searching for a suitable provider, and additional sums in negotiating a suitable contract. Then it must rely on the other party to the contract to be a stable and financially sound business partner. Firms generally have less information about the financial stability of other firms than they have about themselves; as a result, trusting the financial security of someone else involves more risk than trusting oneself. Often a firm can avoid these costs and risks by obtaining its own source of supply, its own means of transportation, or its own resale outlets.

A firm can also reduce its cost by vertically integrating if another link in the distribution chain is either monopolized or cartelized. For example, suppose that a manufacturer of wash machines purchases electric motors which cost $50 to produce, but are sold to the wash machine manufacturer for $70 because the motor manufacturers are engaged in a successful cartel. In this case, the wash machine manufacturer could profit by obtaining its own producer of electric motors: by so doing it could transfer the $20 in monopoly profits away from the cartel and to itself. In fact, even if the wash machine manufacturer were itself a monopolist, it would be better off producing its own motors than it would be paying a monopoly price for them. Likewise, consumers would be better off, for when the monopolist's costs go down, its profit-maximizing price declines as well.

Figure 1

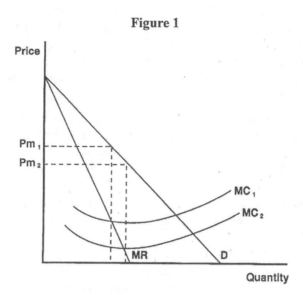

In general, a monopolist who has lower costs will have a lower profit-maximizing price. If the monopolist's marginal cost drops from MC1 to MC2, its profit-maximizing price — determined by the intersection of the marginal cost curve and the marginal revenue curve — will drop from Pm1 to Pm2. As a result, if one monopolist vertically integrates with another monopolist, the integrated firm's profit-maximizing price will be lower than if each firm independently charged its own profit-maximizing price. 3A P. AREEDA & H. HOVENKAMP, ANTITRUST LAW ¶ 758 (3d ed. 2008).

Government regulations can also make it cheaper for firms to integrate vertically. For example, when a firm buys or sells a certain good or service, that transaction may have to be accounted for on a tax return. However, if the firm integrates and eliminates the market transaction, then there may not be a purchase or sale that the tax laws recognize. Likewise, many regulations regarding pricing, information disclosure, production restrictions, and market environment apply to exchanges between independent parties, but not to internal exchanges.

There are literally hundreds of ways that firms can lower their costs or provide better service by integrating vertically. Some of these cost savings come out of avoidance of the unregulated market, others come out of mechanisms by which integrated firms can avoid governmental regulations. In general, the kinds of particular costs savings available vary greatly from one industry to another — but most industries can find ways to reduce some costs by engaging in a certain amount of vertical integration.

To be sure, many of these forms of vertical integration are not carried out by merger but by new entry. However, whether or not there is a merger may be economically irrelevant to the cost savings that can result (although it may be relevant to the impact of the integration on the existing market). For this reason, most economists are inclined to treat all instances of vertical integration, whether by merger or by contract, as more-or-less similar. Thus, for example, the economist might treat exclusive dealing, franchise tie-ins, and vertical acquisitions as different mechanisms for getting the same result, and as creating roughly equivalent risks of harm and possibilities for good. Largely because of their historical development and statutory structure, however, the antitrust laws view these practices as quite different from each other.

The antitrust literature on vertical integration and vertical mergers is vast. Interested readers might look at 4A P. AREEDA & H. HOVENKAMP, ANTITRUST LAW, ch. 10 (3d ed. 2009); F. M. SCHERER & D. ROSS, INDUSTRIAL MARKET STRUCTURE AND ECONOMIC PERFORMANCE, chs. 3 and 4 (3d ed. 1990); R. BLAIR & D. KASERMAN, ANTITRUST ECONOMICS, chs. 11 & 12 (2d ed. 2008); H. HOVENKAMP, FEDERAL ANTITRUST POLICY, ch. 9 (4th ed. 2011); E.T. SULLIVAN & J. HARRISON, UNDERSTANDING ANTITRUST AND ITS ECONOMIC IMPLICATIONS, chs. 6 and 7 (5th ed. 2008).

SILICON GRAPHICS
5 Trade Reg. Rep. ¶ 23,838 (1995)
Federal Trade Commission

Complaint

. . . Respondent Silicon Graphics, Inc. ("SGI"). designs and supplies a family of workstation, server and supercomputer systems. SGI develops and markets, among other things, computer hardware incorporating interactive three-dimensional ("3D") graphics, digital media and multiprocessor supercomputing technologies

Alias Research Inc. ("Alias") . . . is a leading producer of workstation-based, 3D and two-dimensional ("2D") computer graphics software, for professional entertainment and industrial customers. Users of Alias' products in the entertainment industry create 3D computer graphic special effects, which may be output to a variety of media, including film and video for use in movies, television, interactive computer games, and other forms of presentation. . . .

Wavefront Technologies, Inc. ("Wavefront") . . . is a full-line producer of workstation-based, 3D and 2D computer graphics software, for professional entertainment and industrial customers. Users of Wavefront's products in the entertainment industry create 3D computer graphic special effects, which may be output to a variety of media, including film and video for use in movies, television, interactive computer games, and other forms of presentation. . . .

One relevant line of commerce in which to analyze the effects of the proposed acquisitions is the development, production and sale of entertainment graphics workstations. Entertainment graphics workstations generally are UNIX-based computers with high-speed graphic capability and suitable for use with entertainment graphics software. Personal computers, including Intel-based PCs and Apple MacIntosh computers, are not adequate substitutes for entertainment graphics workstations as platforms for running entertainment graphics software.

Another relevant line of commerce in which to analyze the effects of the proposed acquisitions is the development, production and sale of entertainment graphics software. . . .

The entertainment graphics workstation market is extremely concentrated. SGI is the dominant provider of entertainment graphics workstations, with over 90% of the market. Although various other companies manufacture workstations, most entertainment graphics software was developed for use on SGI workstations and is available only for SGI workstations.

The entertainment graphics software market is highly concentrated and rapidly growing. Alias and Wavefront are two of the three leading developers and sellers of entertainment graphics software. Alias and Wavefront compete principally with SoftImage Inc., a subsidiary of Microsoft Corp. . . .

Prior to the acquisitions described in Paragraph 5, SGI maintained an open software interface for its entertainment graphics workstations, sponsored independent software developer programs, and shared with developers of entertainment graphics software advance information concerning new SGI products to facilitate and promote competitive development of entertainment graphics software. . . .

Entry into the entertainment graphics workstation market would not be timely, likely, or sufficient in its magnitude, character, and scope to deter or counteract anticompetitive effects of the acquisitions in the entertainment graphics workstation market. Other manufacturers of computer workstations have graphic engines for their computers that are technically capable of running entertainment graphics software provided a version of the software is written for use with the workstation and its graphic engine. However, without the possibility of having Alias or Wavefront entertainment graphics software developed for those workstations, entry would be unlikely. Marketing a technically comparable or even an improved combination of non-SGI workstations with entertainment graphics software other than that of Alias or Wavefront would be difficult, time consuming and not likely to occur because of the extensive installed user base of SGI workstations with Alias, Wavefront and SoftImage entertainment graphics software.

Entry into the market for the development and sale of entertainment graphics software would not be timely, likely, or sufficient in its magnitude, character, and scope to deter or counteract anticompetitive effects of the acquisitions in the entertainment graphics software market. Developing an entertainment graphics software suite similar to those of Alias and Wavefront is time consuming and unlikely to occur because of extensive installed user bases trained on and using the Alias and Wavefront software programs on SGI entertainment graphics workstations. Combining smaller software developers' niche programs or making smaller producers of entertainment graphics software significant competitors to Alias and Wavefront would be difficult, time consuming and not likely to occur because of the extensive installed user base of SGI workstations with Alias, Wavefront, and SoftImage entertainment graphics software. . . .

[These] acquisitions . . . , if consummated, may, individually or in combination, substantially lessen competition and tend to create a monopoly in the relevant markets in violation of Section 7 of the Clayton Act, 15 U.S.C. § 18, and Section 5 of the FTC Act, 15 U.S.C. § 45, in the following ways, among others:

"a. They may foreclose workstation producers other than SGI from significant, independent sources of entertainment graphics software, reducing competition in the manufacture and sale of entertainment graphics workstations;

b. They may increase costs to workstation producers other than SGI for obtaining entertainment graphics software for their workstation platforms, reducing competition in the manufacture and sale of entertainment graphics workstations;

c. They will facilitate SGI's unilateral exercise of market power in entertainment graphics workstations through price discrimination;

d. They may enable SGI to gain proprietary, competitively sensitive information pertaining to other workstation producers if such workstation producers are able to get Alias or Wavefront entertainment graphics software ported to their workstations, reducing competition in the manufacture and sale of entertainment graphics workstations;

e. They will eliminate Alias and Wavefront as substantial independent competitors, eliminate actual, direct and substantial competition between Alias and Wavefront, and increase the level of concentration in the entertainment graphics software market;

f. They will increase barriers to entry into the relevant markets and make two-level entry necessary;

g. They may foreclose, or increase costs to, competitors to Alias and Wavefront in the entertainment graphics software market in developing software for use in connection with future entertainment graphics workstation products developed by SGI, reducing competition in the development, manufacture and sale of entertainment graphics software;

h. They may cause consumers to pay higher prices for entertainment graphics software and for entertainment graphics workstations;

i. They may reduce innovation competition among producers of entertainment graphics software and among producers of entertainment graphics workstations."

NOTES AND QUESTIONS

1. Silicon Graphics agreed to a consent order requiring it (1) to ensure the continued compatibility of software developed by its newly acquired subsidiaries with the hardware of rivals; and (2) to maintain an "open architecture" policy of publicizing technical information about its own hardware, so that rival manufacturers of graphics software would be able to write products for Silicon Graphics computers and operating systems. *Silicon Graphics*, 120 F.T.C. 928, Dkt. No. C-3626, Nov. 14, 1995.

2. In *Time-Warner*, 5 Trade Reg. Rep. ¶ 24,104 (consent decree, FTC, 1996), the FTC challenged a major cable television system operator's (Time-Warner's) acquisition of a major television programmer (Turner Communications). One of the theories of the complaint was that the acquisition would increase the costs of rival programmers by denying them access to a sufficient number of cable systems. The fixed costs of television programming are very high, but licensing an additional cable system to broadcast an existing program costs very little. As a result, programming is cost effective only if it can be sold to a large number of systems. One claim was that post-acquisition Time-Warner would put Turner's Cable News Network (CNN) on its cable systems exclusively, thus excluding infant rivals such as FoxNews, a competing 24-hour cable news program. The result would be that not enough independent cable systems would remain to enable FoxNews to have sufficient revenue to maintain its program. Time-Warner also entered into a consent decree.

3. In *Fruehauf Corp. v. FTC*, 603 F.2d 345 (2d Cir. 1979), the court refused to enforce an FTC order condemning a truck trailer manufacturer's acquisition of a firm that manufactured wheels and braking devices for such trailers. The court observed:

> Although it has been suggested that a significant percentage of market foreclosure, standing alone, might constitute a sufficient 'clog on competition' to amount to a violation of § 7 without more, . . . no such *per se* rule has been adopted, except where the share of the market foreclosed reaches monopoly proportions.
>
> . . . A showing of some probable anticompetitive impact is still essential (e.g., promotion of a trend toward integration; reduction in number of potential market competitors; entrenchment of a large supplier or purchaser; increase in barriers to entry).

The main theory of the FTC's complaint was that in times of shortages of wheels and brakes, Fruehauf would give itself preferred treatment over rival purchasers. The court found no evidence that this would occur, but even if it did, would it be anticompetitive? *See* 4A P. Areeda & H. Hovenkamp, Antitrust Law ¶ 1003b4 (3d ed. 2009):

> Integrated firms may well prefer their own outlets if there is a permanent fall in supply — for example, the decline of an exhaustible resource. In that case, second level output must also decline, and the number of efficient surviving — firms may fall below the number needed for effective competition. But integration is not harmful in that situation and might be beneficial. Assume, for example, that there are five integrated and five unintegrated firms at the — level, all of minimum efficient size. If the A supply declines, some — firms will be eliminated. If the decline is substantial enough, the number may fall to, say, five firms. But all the vertical integration does is to make it probable that the survivors will be integrated firms. If the number of survivors is too few for competitive pricing, it is socially preferable (or at least no worse) that they be integrated.

4. 4. Suppose that a large purchaser of a certain product acquires a supplier. As a result, the purchaser buys exclusively from its new subsidiary, and no longer purchases from *A*, a competing supplier. Should *A* have a damage action for the lost sales under Section 7 of the Clayton Act? *See Alberta Gas Chems. v. E.I. du Pont de Nemours & Co.*, 826 F.2d 1235, 1244–1246 (3d Cir. 1987):

> A vertically integrated firm seeking to increase profits will engage in self-dealing if the supplying division's output cannot be more profitably sold elsewhere, or is not more costly or inferior than the product of outside suppliers. . . . Because of post-merger efficiencies allowing it to purchase the acquiring company's output at a better price than in the marketplace, the acquired company's purchasing costs would fall — a procompetitive benefit capable of being passed on via lower prices for its products. . . .

> Injuries to competitors of this nature should not be compensable under the antitrust laws because they do not flow from the anticompetitive effects of a merger. Far from being caused by any post-merger market power, the competitor's losses would spring from the efficient aspects of the merger. . . .

> If the merger were considered unlawful for reasons other than foreclosure of sales, the question then would become whether damages from the foreclosure flowed from the illegal act. . . . [P]laintiff must establish that its harm was caused by that which makes the action unlawful. Assuming the merger violated the antitrust laws because it concentrated economic power in the production of methanol — as Alberta [the plaintiff] asserts — any resulting foreclosure from this concentration is but an incident of, and not a result of, the unlawful act.

NOTE: MERGER GUIDELINES AND VERTICAL MERGERS

In 1968, the Justice Department first issued Guidelines describing its standards for challenging mergers under Section 7 of the Clayton Act. These Guidelines were completely rewritten in 1982 and revised again in 1984. In 1992 they were revised much more substantially and issued jointly by the Antitrust Division and the Federal Trade Commission. The latest significant revision occurred in 2010.[2] The 1992 and also the 2010 Guidelines, which are reprinted in Appendix A, pertain only to horizontal mergers, however. In analyzing a vertical merger, these agencies will presumably rely on the market definition, entry barriers, and efficiencies sections of the 2010 Guidelines. The Antitrust Division will then apply the substantive analysis contained in the 1984 Guidelines. The discussion below briefly contrasts the old 1968 Guidelines with the 1984 Guidelines as they pertain to vertical mergers.

The 1968 Guidelines identified vertical mergers as suspicious largely on the basis of the market shares of the merging firms. For example, they provided that the Justice Department would "ordinarily challenge a merger or a series of mergers between a supplying firm, accounting for approximately 10% or more of the sales in its market, and one or more purchasing firms, accounting in toto for approximately 6% or more of the total purchases in that market, unless it clearly

---

[2] One of the co-authors of this casebook (Shelanski) was also one of the six drafters of the 2010 Guidelines.

appears that there are no significant barriers to entry into the business of the purchasing firm or firms." In general, the 1968 Guidelines perceived barriers to entry as the greatest potential danger from vertical mergers, although it recognized that barriers to entry resulting from economies of scale are "not questionable as such." The 1968 Guidelines, also perceived certain vertical mergers as creating the danger of a "supply squeeze." Under the supply squeeze theory, a producer could injure its competitors by acquiring an important source of a scarce or technologically complex essential product.

The 1984 Guidelines, for vertical mergers are more explicit and technical than the 1968 Guidelines, and see few occasions for condemning them. First, discussion of the "supply squeeze" has all but disappeared. On the danger that a vertical merger might raise entry barriers, the 1984 Guidelines, state the following:

> In certain circumstances, the vertical integration resulting from vertical mergers could create competitively objectionable barriers to entry. Stated generally, three conditions are necessary (but not sufficient) for this problem to exist. First, the degree of vertical integration between the two markets must be so extensive that entrants to one market (the 'primary market') also would have to enter the other market (the 'secondary market') simultaneously. Second, the requirement of entry at the secondary level must make entry at the primary level significantly more difficult and less likely to occur. Finally, the structure and other characteristics of the primary market must be otherwise so conducive to non-competitive performance that the increased difficulty of entry is likely to affect its performance. The following standards state the criteria by which the Department will determine whether these conditions are satisfied.

> If there is sufficient unintegrated capacity in the secondary market, new entrants to the primary market would not have to enter both markets simultaneously. The Department is unlikely to challenge a merger on this ground where post-merger sales (purchases) by unintegrated firms in the secondary market would be sufficient to service two minimum-efficient-scale plants in the primary market. When the other conditions are satisfied, the Department is increasingly likely to challenge a merger as the unintegrated capacity declines below this level.

> The relevant question is whether the need for simultaneous entry to the secondary market gives rise to a substantial incremental difficulty as compared to entry into the primary market alone. If entry at the secondary level is easy in absolute terms, the requirement of simultaneous entry to that market is unlikely adversely to affect entry to the primary market. . . .

> When entry is not possible under those conditions, the Department is increasingly concerned about vertical mergers as the difficulty of entering the secondary market increases. The Department, however, will invoke this theory only where the need for secondary market entry significantly increases the costs (which may take the form of risks) of primary market entry. . . .

Economies of scale in the secondary market may constitute an additional barrier to entry to the primary market in some situations requiring two-level entry. The problem could arise if the capacities of minimum-efficient-scale plants in the primary and secondary markets differ significantly. For example, if the capacity of a minimum-efficient-scale plant in the secondary market were significantly greater than the needs of a minimum-efficient-scale plant in the primary market, entrants would have to choose between inefficient operation at the secondary level (because of operating an efficient plant at an inefficient output or because of operating an inefficiently small plant) or a larger than necessary scale at the primary level. Either of these effects could cause a significant increase in the operating costs of the entering firm.

1984 Guidelines, § 4.21.

The Guidelines also note that a vertical merger might be used to facilitate collusion at the retail level:

> The elimination by vertical merger of a particularly disruptive buyer in a downstream market may facilitate collusion in the upstream market. If upstream firms view sales to a particular buyer as sufficiently important, they may deviate from the terms of a collusive agreement in an effort to secure that business, thereby disrupting the operation of the agreement. The merger of such a buyer with an upstream firm may eliminate that rivalry, making it easier for the upstream firms to collude effectively. Adverse competitive consequences are unlikely unless the upstream market is generally conducive to collusion and the disruptive firm is significantly more attractive to sellers than the other firms in its market.

> The Department is unlikely to challenge a merger on this ground unless (1) overall concentration of the upstream market is 1800 HHI or above (a somewhat lower concentration will suffice if one or more of the factors discussed in Section 3.4 indicate that effective collusion is particularly likely), and (2) the allegedly disruptive firm differs substantially in volume of purchases or other relevant characteristics from the other firms in its market. Where the stated thresholds are met or exceeded, the Department's decision whether to challenge a merger on this ground will depend upon an individual evaluation of its likely competitive effect.

1984 Guidelines, § 4.22.

Finally, the 1984 Guidelines note "evasion of rate regulation" as an anticompetitive rationale for some vertical mergers. Recall the discussion of the *Yellow Cab* case at the beginning of this chapter. The Guidelines state:

> Non-horizontal mergers may be used by monopoly public utilities subject to rate regulation as a tool for circumventing that regulation. The clearest example is the acquisition by a regulated utility of a supplier of its fixed or variable inputs. After the merger, the utility would be selling to itself and might be able arbitrarily to inflate the prices of internal transactions. Regulators may have great difficulty in policing these prac-

tices, particularly if there is no independent market for the product (or service) purchased from the affiliate.

As a result, inflated prices could be passed along to consumers as 'legitimate' costs. . . .

1984 Guidelines, § 4.23.

NOTES AND QUESTIONS

1. The acronym "HHI" used in the 1984 Guidelines stands for Herfindahl-Hirschman Index, which is a measure of industrial concentration commonly used by economists and now incorporated into the Guidelines. The HHI and its use are discussed more fully in the Guidelines for horizontal mergers, discussed *infra*. For purposes of understanding the part of the Guidelines dealing with vertical mergers, you should know that a concentration of approximately 1800 HHI (the relevant threshold for a concentrated market in the older guidelines, since raised in the 2010 Guidelines to be discussed below) would be achieved by any of the following markets: (1) a market with two firms of slightly less than 30% share each, and several very small firms; (2) a market containing two firms, each with 25% of the market, and five firms each with 10% of the market; and (3) a market having one firm with 30% of the market, two having 20% each, and several firms having about 5% of the market each.

2. The concern of the Guidelines as applied to vertical mergers is whether the merger will contribute to some kind of horizontal restraint of trade, particularly whether it will facilitate collusion. If there is not such a perceived danger, it appears that the Justice Department will not challenge the acquisition, regardless of existing case law. The "foreclosure" theory is all but forgotten. Is it a usurpation of legislative authority for the executive branch to refuse to challenge an acquisition that existing case law suggests is illegal? *See* Easterbrook, *Is There a Ratchet in Antitrust Law?*, 60 TEX. L. REV. 705 (1982).

3. The Guidelines recognize that price-regulated firms such as electric utilities have a special incentive to integrate vertically into a market that is not price-regulated: the price-regulated firm could charge itself a high price from its subsidiary and use this inflated price to increase its rate base. An example might be an electric utility that acquires its own coal-producing firm. The one problem with the utility's scheme, however, is that coal is bought and sold daily at public prices, and if the utility attempts to charge itself a high price for its own coal, the excessive price will be apparent to the rate-making authority. One way the utility might get around this problem, suggests the Guidelines, is by acquiring *all* the available coal and selling it to all buyers at the same inflated price, so that the price appears to be normal. Is this plausible? Would it make a difference if the product was plutonium fuel, which is used only by nuclear power plants?

II MERGERS OF COMPETITORS

The great majority of merger enforcement activity involves mergers between firms that already compete with each other in one or more markets. We turn next to the development of law and policy direct at such consolidation among horizontal competitors.

[A] The Development of Horizontal Merger Law Under the Sherman Act

NORTHERN SECURITIES CO. v. UNITED STATES
193 U.S. 197 (1904)

[The defendant was a holding company which acquired two large, parallel railroads that ran through the northern United States — the Great Northern Railway and the Northern Pacific Railway. The two lines competed for long hauls, although substantially less so for short ones. The United States charged that the formation of the holding company violated Section 1 of the Sherman Act.]

JUSTICE HARLAN delivered the opinion of the Court.

. . . Necessarily by this combination or arrangement the holding company in the fullest sense dominates the situation in the interest of those who were stockholders of the constituent companies; as much so, for every practical purpose, as if it had been itself a railroad corporation which had built, owned, and operated both lines for the exclusive benefit of its stockholders. Necessarily, also, the constituent companies ceased, under such a combination, to be in active competition for trade and commerce along their respective lines, and have become, practically, one powerful consolidated corporation, by the name of a holding corporation, the principal, if not the sole, object for the formation of which was to carry out the purpose of the original combination, under which competition between the constituent companies would cease. Those who were stockholders of the Great Northern and Northern Pacific and became stockholders in the holding company are now interested in preventing all competition between the two lines, and, as owners of stock or of certificates of stock in the holding company, they will see to it that no competition is tolerated. . . . This combination is, within the meaning of the act, a "trust;" but if not, it is a *combination in restraint of interstate and international commerce;* and that is enough to bring it under the condemnation of the act. The mere existence of such a combination, and the power acquired by the holding company as its trustee, constitute a menace to, and a restraint upon, that freedom of commerce which Congress intended to recognize and protect, and which the public is entitled to have protected. If such combination be not destroyed, all the advantages that would naturally come to the public under the operation of the general laws of competition, as between the Great Northern and Northern Pacific Railway Companies, will be lost, and the entire commerce of the immense territory in the northern part of the United States between the Great Lakes and the Pacific at Puget Sound will be at the mercy of a single holding corporation, organized in a state distant from the people of that territory.

. . . .

[T]o vitiate a combination such as the act of Congress condemns, it need not be shown that the combination, in fact, results or will result, in a total suppression of trade or in a complete monopoly, but it is only essential to show that, by its necessary operation, it tends to restrain interstate or international trade or commerce or tends to create a monopoly in such trade or commerce and to deprive the public of the advantages that flow from free competition.

. . . .

JUSTICE HOLMES, with whom concurred THE CHIEF JUSTICE, JUSTICE WHITE and JUSTICE PECKHAM, dissenting.

. . . .

Great cases, like hard cases, make bad law. For great cases are called great, not by reason of their real importance in shaping the law of the future, but because of some accident of immediate overwhelming interest which appeals to the feelings and distorts the judgment. These immediate interests exercise a kind of hydraulic pressure which makes what previously was clear seem doubtful, and before which even well settled principles of law will bend. What we have to do in this case is to find the meaning of some not very difficult words. . . .

. . . .

The first section [of the Sherman Act] makes "Every contract, combination in the form of trust or otherwise, or conspiracy in restraint of trade or commerce among the several states, or with foreign nations" a misdemeanor, punishable by fine, imprisonment, or both. Much trouble is made by substituting other phrases assumed to be equivalent, which then are reasoned from as if they were in the act. The court below argued as if maintaining competition were the expressed object of the act. The act says nothing about competition. I stick to the exact words used. The words hit two classes of cases, and only two, — Contracts in restraint of trade and combinations or conspiracies in restraint of trade, — and we have to consider what these respectively are. Contracts in restraint of trade are dealt with and defined by the common law. They are contracts with a stranger to the contractor's business (although, in some cases, carrying on a similar one), which wholly or partially restrict the freedom of the contractor in carrying on that business as otherwise he would. The objection of the common law to them was, primarily, on the contractor's own account. The notion of monopoly did not come in unless the contract covered the whole of England. Of course, this objection did not apply to partnerships or other forms, if there were any, of substituting a community of interest where there had been competition. There was no objection to such combinations merely as in restraint of trade or otherwise unless they amounted to a monopoly. Contracts in restraint of trade, I repeat, were contracts with strangers to the contractor's business, and the trade restrained was the contractor's own.

Combinations or conspiracies in restraint of trade, on the other hand, were combinations to keep strangers to the agreement out of the business. The objection to them was not an objection to their effect upon the parties making the contract, the members of the combination or firm, but an objection to their intended effect upon strangers to the firm and their supposed consequent effect upon the public at large. In other words, they were regarded as contrary to public policy because they monopolized, or attempted to monopolize, some portion of the trade or commerce of the realm. All that is added to the first section by § 2 is that like penalties are imposed upon every single person who, without combination, monopolizes, or attempts to monopolize, commerce among the states; and that the liability is extended to attempting to monopolize any part of such trade or commerce. It is more important as an aid to the construction of § 1 than it is on its own account. It shows that whatever is criminal when done by way of combination is equally criminal if done by a single man. That I am right in my interpretation of words of § 1 is shown by the words "in the form of trust or otherwise." The prohibition was suggested by the trusts, the objection to which, as everyone knows, was not the union of former competitors, but the sinister power exercised or supposed to be exercised by the combination in keeping rivals out of the business and ruining those who already were in. It was the ferocious extreme of competition with others, not the cessation of competition among the partners, that was the evil feared. . . .

I assume that the Minnesota charter of the Great Northern, and the Wisconsin charter of the Northern Pacific, both are valid. Suppose that, before either road was built, Minnesota, as part of a system of transportation between the states, had created a railroad company authorized singly to build all the lines in the states now actually built, owned, or controlled by either of the two existing companies. I take it that that charter would have been just as good as the present one, even if the statutes which we are considering had been in force. In whatever sense it would have created a monopoly, the present charter does. It would have been a large one, but the act of Congress makes no discrimination according to size. Size has nothing to do with the matter. A monopoly of "any part" of commerce among the states is unlawful. The supposed company would have owned lines that might have been competing; probably the present one does. But the act of Congress will not be construed to mean the universal disintegration of society into single men, each at war with all the rest, or even the prevention of all further combinations for a common end.

. . . [I]t has occurred to me that it might be that when a combination reached a certain size it might have attributed to it more of the character of a monopoly merely by virtue of its size than would be attributed to a smaller one. I am quite clear that it is only in connection with monopolies that size could play any part. But my answer has been indicated already. In the first place, size, in the case of railroads, is an inevitable incident; and if it were an objection under the act, the Great Northern and the Northern Pacific already were too great and encountered the law. In the next place, in the case of railroads it is evident that the size of the combination is reached for other ends than those which would make them monopolies. The combinations are not formed for the purpose of excluding others from the field. Finally, even a small railroad will have the same tendency to exclude others from its narrow area that great ones have to exclude others from the greater one, and the statute attacks the small monopolies as well as the great. . . .

. . . .

A partnership is not a contract or combination in restraint of trade between the partners unless the well known words are to be given a new meaning, invented for the purposes of this act. It is true that the suppression of competition was referred to in *United States v. Trans-Missouri Freight Ass'n* but, as I have said, that was in connection with a contract with a stranger to the defendant's business, — a true contract in restraint of trade. To suppress competition in that way is one thing; to suppress it by fusion is another. The law, I repeat, says nothing about competition, and only prevents its suppression by contracts or combinations in restraint of trade, and such contracts or combinations derive their character as restraining trade from other features than the suppression of competition alone. To see whether I am wrong, the illustrations put in the argument are of use. If I am, then a partnership between two stage drivers who had been competitors in driving across a state line, or two merchants once engaged in rival commerce among the states, whether made after or before the act, if now continued, is a crime. For, again I repeat, if the restraint on the freedom of the members of a combination, caused by their entering into partnership, is a restraint of trade, every such combination, as well the small as the great, is within the act.

NOTES AND QUESTIONS

1. In a concurring opinion, Justice Brewer argued as follows: "It must also be remembered that under present conditions a single railroad is, if not a legal, largely a practical, monopoly, and the arrangement by which the control of these two competing roads was merged in a single corporation broadens and extends such monopoly." 193 U.S. at 363. Are you persuaded? If the only electric utility in Minneapolis acquires the only electric utility in St. Paul, has the monopoly been "broadened and extended"?

2. In his dissent in *Northern Securities*, Justice Holmes attempted to restrict the phrase "contract in restraint of trade" to its common law meaning, referring mainly to noncompetition covenants or boycotts, and thus implicitly taking sides in the early debate over how far the Sherman Act's prohibitions went beyond the common law restraints of trade.

3. One of Holmes's arguments goes something like this: if one company from the beginning had built both lines consolidated into the Northern Securities holding company, the company would clearly have been legal. Why should it make a difference that the lines were originally built by two different companies and later consolidated?

One answer might be that if the lines really were in competition, and if railroads are natural monopolies, then no reasonable corporation would have built both lines. However, once the two lines were built, there was excess capacity that would eventually drive one of the lines into bankruptcy. In fact, the Northern Pacific Company had gone bankrupt before the consolidation occurred. One way to eliminate the "ruinous" competition caused by the excess capacity was for the two firms to merge. *See* Hovenkamp, *Regulatory Conflict in the Gilded Age: Federalism and the Railroad Problem*, 88 YALE L.J. 1017 (1988).

But that is not an entirely satisfactory answer to Justice Holmes's question, is it? He could have asked the same question with respect to an industry that was not a natural monopoly. In most merger cases, it is clear that the defendant could legally have achieved its size by internal growth. However, because the size came about by merger, it runs afoul of the antitrust laws. Is there any reason to believe that a company created by internal growth is more efficient or preferable in some other way than an identical company that has attained its size by merger? Is the latter company more likely to have market power?

4. The *Northern Securities* merger was part of the greatest merger movement in American history, which occurred during the decade 1895–1905. Why did so many mergers occur after, rather than before, the passage of the Sherman Act? One possibility is that economies of scale made business consolidations efficient, that the Sherman Act prevented "loose" consolidations by contract among competing companies, and so they merged as an alternative. *See* A.D. CHANDLER, JR., THE VISIBLE HAND: THE MANAGERIAL REVOLUTION IN AMERICAN BUSINESS, 315–344 (1977). Another argument is that the Sherman Act's prohibition of agreements among competitors was merely an excuse for firms to achieve anticompetitive market positions by merger rather than by contract. *See* N.R. LAMOREAUX, THE GREAT MERGER MOVEMENT IN AMERICAN BUSINESS, 1895-1904 (1985); H. HOVENKAMP, ENTER-PRISE, *supra*, at ch. 20. As Professor Lamoreaux noted, only a few of the consolidations of this period succeeded. Most were defeated, not by the federal antitrust laws, but by new competition. What does this suggest about the efficiency of these mergers?

UNITED STATES v. COLUMBIA STEEL CO
334 U.S. 495 (1948)

[The United States sought to enjoin United States Steel Co. from acquiring certain assets of Consolidated Steel Corp. United States Steel produced about one-third of the national output of rolled steel. Consolidated purchased rolled steel and fabricated it into various steel products. United States Steel also fabricated steel, in competition with Consolidated. Thus, the merger was both vertical and horizontal. The Supreme Court's analysis of the vertical aspects appears *supra*. Until it was amended in 1950, Section 7 of the Clayton Act applied only to stock acquisitions, not to asset acquisitions; so this case was brought under Sections 1 and 2 of the Sherman Act.]

JUSTICE REED delivered the opinion of the Court.

We turn first to the field of fabricated structural steel products. As in the case of rolled steel, the appellees claim that structural fabricators sell on a national scale, and that Consolidated's production must be measured against all structural fabricators. An index of the position of Consolidated as a structural fabricator is shown by its bookings for the period 1937-1942, as reported by the American Institute of Steel Construction. During that period total bookings in the entire country were nearly 10,000,000 tons, of which Consolidated's share was only 84,533 tons. The government argues that competition is to be measured with reference to the eleven-state area in which Consolidated sells its products. Viewed on that basis, total bookings for the limited area for the six-year period were 1,665,698, of which United States Steel's share was 17% and Consolidated's 5%. The government claims that Consolidated has become a more important factor since that period, and alleges that bookings for 1946 in the Consolidated market were divided among 90 fabricators, of which United States Steel had 13% and Consolidated and Bethlehem Steel each had 11%. The next largest structural fabricators had 9%, 6% and 3% of the total. . . . The figures on which the government relies demonstrate that at least in the past competition in structural steel products has been conducted on a national scale. Five out of the ten structural fabricators having the largest sales in the Consolidated market perform their fabrication operations outside the area, including United States Steel and Bethlehem Steel. Purchasers of fabricated structural products have been able to secure bids from fabricators throughout the country, and therefore statistics showing the share of United States Steel and Consolidated in the total consumption of fabricated structural products in any prescribed area are of little probative value in ascertaining the extent to which consumers of these products would be injured through elimination of competition between the two companies. . . .

Apart from the question of the geographical size of the market, the appellees urge that the bookings for fabricated structural steel products are of little significance because Consolidated and United States Steel make different types of structural steel products. In view of the fact that structural steel jobs are fabricated on an individual basis, it is difficult to compare the output of United States Steel with that of Consolidated, but the appellees argue that in general Consolidated does only light and medium fabrication, whereas United States Steel does heavy fabrication. The appellees support their argument with an elaborate statistical analysis of bids by the two companies. Those figures show that Consolidated and United States Steel submitted bids for the same project in a very small number of instances.[3]

Such figures are not conclusive of lack of competition; the government suggests that knowledge that one party has submitted a bid may discourage others from bidding. The government has introduced very little evidence, however, to show that in fact the types of structural steel products sold by Consolidated are similar to those sold by United States Steel. The appellees further urge that only a small proportion of Consolidated's business fell in the category of structural steel products, and that as to plate fabrication and miscellaneous work there was no competition with United States Steel whatsoever. The trial court found on this issue that 16% of Consolidated's business was in structural steel products and 70% in plate fabrication. On the basis of the statistics here summarized, the trial court

---

[3] [FN 13] During the ten-year period ending in 1946 United States Steel bid on 2,409 jobs in the Consolidated area and was successful in 839. Consolidated bid on 6,377 jobs and was successful in 2,390. There were only 166 jobs, however, on which both companies bid. Forty of these jobs on which both companies bid were awarded to United States Steel, 35 were awarded to Consolidated, and 91 were awarded to competitors. . . .

The above figures indicate that Consolidated customarily bid on lighter types of work; the average tonnage for Consolidated's bids was 90 tons, whereas the average tonnage for United States Steel was 528 tons. The 166 jobs on which both companies submitted bids were considerably larger in volume, averaging 737 tons.

found that competition between the two companies in the manufacture and sale of fabricated structural steel products was not substantial.

. . . .

The United States makes the point that the acquisition of Consolidated would preclude and restrain substantial potential competition in the production and sale of other steel products than fabricated structural steel and pipe. Force is added to this contention by the fact, adverted to above, that United States Steel does no plate fabrication while Consolidated does. By plate fabrication Consolidated produces many articles not now produced by United States Steel. We mention, as examples, boilers, gas tanks, smoke stacks, storage tanks and barges. Attention is also called to the war activities of Consolidated in steel shipbuilding as indicative of its potentialities as a competitor. We have noted, that this construction was under government direction and financing. We agree that any acquisition of fabricating equipment eliminates some potential competition from anyone who might own or acquire such facilities. We agree, too, with the government's position that potential competition from producers of presently non-competitive articles as well as the possibility that acquired facilities may be used in the future for the production of new articles in competition with others may be taken into consideration in weighing the effect of any acquisition of assets on restraint of trade.

The government's argument, however, takes us into highly speculative situations. Steel ship construction for war purposes was an enterprise undertaken at government expense. We know of nothing from the record that would lead Consolidated or United States Steel to branch out into the peace-time steel ship industry at their own risk. The necessary yards have been sold. It is true that United States Steel might go into plate fabrication. The record shows nothing as to production or demand in the Consolidated trade area for plate fabricated articles. Nothing appears as to the number of producers of such goods in that territory. What we have said in other places in this opinion as to the growing steel industry in this area is pertinent here. Eastern fabricators will find it difficult to meet competition from western fabricators in the western market. Cheaper western rolled steel and freight rates are a handicap to eastern fabricators. Looking at the situation here presented, we are unwilling to hold that possibilities of interference with future competition are serious enough to justify us in declaring that this contract will bring about unlawful restraint.

We conclude that in this case the government has failed to prove that the elimination of competition between Consolidated and the structural fabricating subsidiaries of United States Steel constitutes an unreasonable restraint. . . .

NOTES AND QUESTIONS

1. In *Columbia Steel*, as in *Northern Securities*, the Supreme Court was faced with the fact that most "horizontal" mergers are not perfectly horizontal. The railroads in *Northern Securities* were not perfect competitors because they passed through different cities, and for many customers, there was no competitive choice at all. Likewise, the Supreme Court noted in *Columbia Steel* that United States Steel fabricated heavy projects, while Consolidated tended to fabricate lighter ones. The question of proper market definition in merger cases is even more difficult than it is in monopolization cases because in merger cases, we must look at two or more firms simultaneously, rather than one at a time.

In general, defendants in monopolization cases try to argue that the relevant geographic and product markets are actually larger than the plaintiff is alleging. By making the market larger, the defendant's market share becomes smaller. In merger cases, defendants sometimes argue that relevant market is larger than alleged because smaller market shares decrease the likelihood that the court will find an illegal merger. However, sometimes in a merger case, it is to the defendant's advantage to argue that certain relevant markets are actually smaller than the plaintiff alleges; this raises the possibility that the acquiring company and the acquired company actually are located in different markets, so their merger would not be a merger of competitors at all.

In *Columbia Steel*, the defendants tried to do both things. With respect to the geographic market, they alleged that the market was the entire United States, not merely the American West. This would give both companies a much smaller share in the relevant geographic market. On the other hand, they also argued that the market for "fabricated steel" was too large — that in fact it should have been divided into "heavy fabricated steel" and "light fabricated steel." The adoption of such an argument may have yielded the conclusion that the two companies were not competitors, but in fact produced two different products.

2. In footnote 13 of its opinion, the Court noted that United States Steel bid on approximately 2,400 jobs, while Consolidated bid on about 6,400 jobs. Each was successful about one-third of the time. However, both companies bid on the same job only 166 times. What does this tell you about the extent of the competition between the two firms? Should the relevant product market have been defined as the market for the product involved in those 166 bids? Should one consider the projects the two companies actually built or the ones they bid for, in measuring the competition between them?

3. The Supreme Court termed as "highly speculative" any argument that, although the two firms were not currently competitors, they might be at some future time, but the merger prevented that possibility. Do you regard that argument as speculative?

4. *Columbia Steel* was held to its facts and the Supreme Court resurrected the *Northern Securities* case in *United States v. First Nat'l Bank & Trust Co. of Lexington*, 376 U.S. 665 (1964). The United States sued under Sections 1 and 2 of the Sherman Act to enjoin a horizontal merger between two Fayette County, Kentucky, banks. First National, one of the merging partners, was the largest bank in the county, with about 40% of deposits. Security Trust, the other partner, was the fourth largest, with about 12% of deposits. The post-merger bank had more than half the county's assets, deposits, loans, and trust assets. The government brought suit under the Sherman Act because at the time, it was unsure whether Section 7 of the Clayton Act applied to bank mergers. (In the *Philadelphia Bank* case, reprinted *infra*, the Court held that Section 7 did apply to banks, but that decision was reached after the *Lexington* case had been brought.) In *Lexington*, the Supreme Court cited *Northern Securities* "for the proposition that where merging

companies are major competitive factors in a relevant market, the elimination of significant competition between them, by merger or consolidation, itself constitutes a violation of § 1 of the Sherman Act." It has been widely suggested that the *Lexington* case made the Sherman Act just as expansive as Section 7 of the Clayton Act in reaching anticompetitive mergers in their incipiency. This could have proved useful to attack certain mergers because before 1980, Section 7 of the Clayton Act applied only to transactions that were actually in the flow of interstate commerce, not to transactions that merely "affected" interstate commerce. In addition, before 1980, Section 7 applied only to corporations, not to natural persons or unincorporated associations. Since the 1980 amendments, however, the subject-matter jurisdiction of Section 7 is probably as great as that of the Sherman Act. *See United States v. Rockford Memorial Corp.*, 898 F.2d 1278 (7th Cir.), *cert. denied*, 498 U.S. 920 (1990), which concluded that mergers should be analyzed by the same standard under both statutes. The court characterized the "defendants' argument that section 7 prevents *probable* restraints and section 1 *actual* ones" as "word play." The court found unpersuasive the argument that earlier Supreme Court decisions had condemned large horizontal mergers under Clayton Section 7 without a finding that the merger was likely to reduce competition in the post-merger market. Today, both statutes have the same concern: both would condemn "mergers that are likely to 'hurt consumers, as by making it easier for the firms in the market to collude. . . .' "

[B] Horizontal Mergers Under Section 7 of the Clayton Act and Its 1950 Amendments

The Clayton Act was passed in 1914, largely because Congress feared that the "Rule of Reason" developed in *Standard Oil Co. v. United States* would eviscerate the Sherman Act. Congress wanted to make it absolutely clear that certain specific practices, such as the anticompetitive acquisition of competitors, were illegal. Thus, while the language of the Sherman Act is cast very broadly, the Clayton Act is quite specific. The original Section 7 of the Clayton Act condemned a corporation's acquisition of "the whole or any part of the stock" of another corporation if the effect was "to substantially lessen competition between the corporation whose stock is so acquired and the corporation making the acquisition."

As enacted in 1914, Section 7 of the Clayton Act proved not to be effective in combating mergers. It suffered from three difficulties that were corrected in 1950 by the Celler-Kefauver Amendments to the Act. The first was the split infinitive. In 1950, the Act was amended to read "substantially to lessen competition." Second, the 1914 statute applied to acquisitions of stock, but not to acquisitions of assets. A corporation could avoid the statute simply by purchasing all the property and goodwill of another corporation and leaving the empty shell. *See Thatcher Mfg. Co. v. FTC*, 272 U.S. 554 (1926). The merger in the *Columbia Steel* case, *supra*, was an asset acquisition, not a stock acquisition. Third, as enacted in 1914, Section 7 applied only to acquisitions that lessened competition "between" the acquiring and acquired firms. Horizontal mergers eliminate competition "between" the two parties to the merger. Vertical mergers do not, however. If they lessen competition at all, it is competition between the post-merger firm and other businesses that were not parties to the merger. In the *du Pont* (GM) case, the Supreme Court applied old Section 7 to a vertical merger. The action had been brought in 1949, before the Celler-Kefauver Amendments were passed. It was decided afterwards, however, and the court applied the "policy" of the new statute. Since 1950, there have been three significant amendments to Section 7. In 1976, Congress added § 7A, which requires advance notification and a waiting period for mergers of a specified minimum size. The Antitrust Improvements Act (1980) made the reach of Section 7 under the Commerce Clause equal to the reach of the Sherman Act. Formerly the Sherman Act had been interpreted to reach all activities "in or affecting" interstate commerce, but Section 7 had been held to reach activities only "in the flow" of interstate commerce. *See United States v. American Bldg. Maint. Indus.*, 422 U.S. 271 (1975). The Improvements Act also replaced the word "corporation" in the old statute with the word "person," so that the statute now covers unincorporated business associations as well as corporations.

The most significant effect of the Celler-Kefauver Amendments to Section 7 came not from the changes in the language of the statute but from the extensive legislative history. Both houses of Congress appeared to be alarmed by the "rising tide" of industrial concentration. Their fear, however, was not that concentrated firms would be able to charge supra competitive prices to consumers, but that mergers were enabling some firms to sell products more cheaply than their nonmerging competitors. As a result, many small businesses were either being "gobbled up" by larger companies or else driven into bankruptcy. *See* Hovenkamp, *Derek Bok and the Merger of Law and Economics*, 21 J.L. Reform 515 (1988). The following decision is the Supreme Court's first response to the concerns articulated by Congress when it passed the Celler-Kefauver Amendments in 1950.

BROWN SHOE CO. v. UNITED STATES
370 U.S. 294 (1962)

Chief Justice Warren delivered the opinion of the Court.

In the District Court, the Government contended that the effect of the merger of Brown — the third largest seller of shoes by dollar volume in the United States, a leading manufacturer of men's, women's, and children's shoes, and a retailer with over 1,230 owned, operated or controlled retail outlets — and Kinney — the eighth largest company, by dollar volume, among those primarily engaged in selling shoes, itself a large manufacturer of shoes, and a retailer with over 350 retail outlets — "may be substantially to lessen competition or to tend to create a monopoly" by eliminating actual or potential competition in the production of shoes for the national wholesale shoe market and in the sale of shoes at retail in the Nation. . . . The Government argued that the "line of commerce" affected by this merger is "footwear," or alternatively, that the "line[s]" are "men's," "women's," and "children's" shoes, separately considered, and that the "section of the country," within which the anticompetitive effect of the merger is to be judged, is the Nation as a whole, or alternatively, each separate city or city and its immediate surrounding area in which the parties sell shoes at retail.

In the District Court, Brown contended that the merger would be shown not to endanger competition if the "line[s] of commerce" and the "section[s] of the country" were properly determined. Brown urged that not only were the age and sex of the intended customers to be considered in determining the relevant line of commerce, but that differences in grade of material, quality of workmanship, price, and customer use of shoes resulted in establishing different lines of commerce. While agreeing with the Government that, with regard to manufacturing, the relevant geographic market for assessing the effect of the merger upon competition is the country as a whole, Brown contended that with regard to retailing, the market must vary with economic reality from the central business district of a large city to a "standard metropolitan area" for a smaller community. Brown further contended that, both at the manufacturing level and at the retail level, the shoe industry enjoyed healthy competition and that the vigor of this competition would not, in any event, be diminished by the proposed merger because Kinney manufactured less than 0.5% and retailed less than 2% of the Nation's shoes.

[The Court traced the legislative history of the 1950 amendments to Section 7 of the Clayton Act. It noted that Congress was concerned, not merely with the fact that the original statute applied only to stock acquisitions, but that it had not been successful in averting the trend toward industrial concentration.]

The dominant theme pervading congressional consideration of the 1950 amendments was a fear of what was considered to be a rising tide of economic concentration in the American economy. Apprehension in this regard was bolstered by the publication in 1948 of the Federal Trade Commission's study on corporate mergers. Statistics from this and other current studies were cited as evidence of the danger to the American economy in unchecked corporate expansions through mergers. Other considerations cited in support of the bill were the desirability of retaining "local control" over industry and the protection of small businesses. Throughout the recorded discussion may be found examples of Congress' fear not only of accelerated concentration of economic power on economic grounds, but also of the threat to other values a trend toward concentration was thought to pose.

What were some of the factors, relevant to a judgment as to the validity of a given merger, specifically discussed by Congress in redrafting § 7?

First, there is no doubt that Congress did wish to "plug the loophole" and to include within the coverage of the Act the acquisition of assets no less than the acquisition of stock.

Second, by the deletion of the "acquiring-acquired" language in the original text, it hoped to make plain that § 7 applied not only to mergers between actual competitors, but also to vertical and conglomerate mergers whose effect may tend to lessen competition in any line of commerce in any section of the country.

Third, it is apparent that a keystone in the erection of a barrier to what Congress saw was the rising tide of economic concentration, was its provision of authority for arresting mergers at a time when the trend to a lessening of competition in a line of commerce was still in its incipiency. Congress saw the process of concentration in American business as a dynamic force; it sought to assure the Federal Trade Commission and the courts the power to brake this force at its outset and before it gathered momentum.

Fourth, and closely related to the third, Congress rejected, as inappropriate to the problem it sought to remedy, the application to § 7 cases of the standards for judging the legality of business combinations adopted by the courts in dealing with cases arising under the Sherman Act, and which may have been applied to some early cases arising under original § 7.

Fifth, at the same time that it sought to create an effective tool for preventing all mergers having demonstrable anticompetitive effects, Congress recognized the stimulation to competition that might flow from particular mergers. When concern as to the Act's breadth was expressed, supporters of the amendments indicated that it would not impede, for example, a merger between two small companies to enable the combination to compete more effectively with larger corporations dominating the relevant market, nor a merger between a corporation which is financially healthy and a failing one which no longer can be a vital competitive factor in the market. The deletion of the word "community" in the original Act's description of the relevant geographic market is another illustration of Congress' desire to indicate that its concern was with the adverse effects of a given merger on competition only in an economically significant "section" of the country. Taken as a whole, the legislative history illuminates congressional concern with the protection of *competition*, not *competitors*, and its desire to restrain mergers only to the extent that such combinations may tend to lessen competition.

Sixth, Congress neither adopted nor rejected specifically any particular tests for measuring the relevant markets, either as defined in terms of product or in terms of geographic locus of competition, within which the anticompetitive effects of a merger were to be judged. Nor did it adopt a definition of the word "substantially," whether in quantitative terms of sales or assets or market shares or in designated qualitative terms, by which a merger's effects on competition were to be measured.

Seventh, while providing no definite quantitative or qualitative tests by which enforcement agencies could gauge the effects of a given merger to determine whether it may "substantially" lessen competition or tend toward monopoly , Congress indicated plainly that a merger had to be functionally viewed, in the context of its particular industry. That is, whether the consolidation was to take place in an industry that was fragmented rather than concentrated, that had seen a recent trend toward domination by a few leaders or had remained fairly consistent in its distribution of market shares among the participating companies, that had experienced easy access to markets by suppliers and easy access to suppliers by buyers or had witnessed foreclosure of business, that had witnessed the ready entry of new competition or the erection of barriers to prospective entrants, all were aspects, varying in importance with the merger under consideration, which would properly be taken into account.

Eighth, Congress used the words "*may be* substantially to lessen competition" (emphasis supplied), to indicate that its concern was with probabilities, not certainties. . . .

     . . . .

     . . . [T]he proper definition of the market is a "necessary predicate" to an examination of the competition that may be affected by the horizontal aspects of the merger. The acquisition of Kinney by Brown resulted in a horizontal combination at both the manufacturing and retailing levels of their businesses. Although the District Court found that the merger of Brown's and Kinney's *manufacturing* facilities was economically too insignificant to come within the prohibitions of the Clayton Act, the Government has not appealed from this portion of the lower court's decision. Therefore, we have no occasion to express our views with respect to that finding. On the other hand, appellant does contest the District Court's finding that the merger of the companies' *retail* outlets may tend substantially to lessen competition.

[The Court decided that the relevant lines of commerce (product markets) were men's shoes, women's shoes, and children's shoes.]

. . . [A]lthough the geographic market in some instances may encompass the entire Nation, under other circumstances it may be as small as a single metropolitan area. . . . The fact that two merging firms have competed directly on the horizontal level in but a fraction of the geographic markets in which either has operated, does not, in itself, place their merger outside the scope of § 7. That section speaks of "any . . . section of the country," and if anticompetitive effects of a merger are probable in "any" significant market, the merger — at least to that extent — is proscribed.[4]

The parties do not dispute the findings of the District Court that the Nation as a whole is the relevant geographic market for measuring the anticompetitive effects of the merger viewed vertically or of the horizontal merger of Brown's and Kinney's manufacturing facilities. As to the retail level, however, they disagree.

The District Court found that the effects of this aspect of the merger must be analyzed in every city with a population exceeding 10,000 and its immediate contiguous surrounding territory in which both Brown and Kinney sold shoes at retail through stores they either owned or controlled. By this definition of the geographic market, less than one-half of all the cities in which either Brown or Kinney sold shoes through such outlets are represented. The appellant recognizes that if the District Court's characterization of the relevant market is proper, the number of markets in which both Brown and Kinney have outlets is sufficiently numerous so that the validity of the entire merger is properly judged by testing its effects in those markets. However, it is appellant's contention that the areas of effective competition in shoe retailing were improperly defined by the District Court. It claims that such areas should, in some cases, be defined so as to include only the central business districts of large cities, and in others, so as to encompass the "standard metropolitan areas" within which smaller communities are found. It argues that any test failing to distinguish between these competitive situations is improper.

We believe, however, that the record fully supports the District Court's findings that shoe stores in the outskirts of cities compete effectively with stores in central

---

[4] [FN 65] To illustrate: If two retailers, one operating primarily in the eastern half of the Nation, and the other operating largely in the West, competed in but two mid-Western cities, the fact that the latter outlets represented but a small share of each company's business would not immunize the merger in those markets in which competition might be adversely affected. On the other hand, that fact would, of course, be properly considered in determining the equitable relief to be decreed. . . .

downtown areas, and that while there is undoubtedly some commercial intercourse between smaller communities within a single "standard metropolitan area," the most intense and important competition in retail sales will be confined to stores within the particular communities in such an area and their immediate environs.

We therefore agree that the District Court properly defined the relevant geographic markets in which to analyze this merger as those cities with a population exceeding 10,000 and their environs in which both Brown and Kinney retailed shoes through their own outlets. Such markets are large enough to include the downtown shops and suburban shopping centers in areas contiguous to the city, which are the important competitive factors, and yet are small enough to exclude stores beyond the immediate environs of the city, which are of little competitive significance.

. . . .

. . . [I]n 32 separate cities, ranging in size and location from Topeka, Kansas, to Batavia, New York, and Hobbs, New Mexico, the combined share of Brown and Kinney sales of women's shoes (by unit volume) exceeded 20%. In 31 cities — some the same as those used in measuring the effect of the merger in the women's line — the combined share of children's shoes sales exceeded 20%; in 6 cities their share exceeded 40%. In Dodge City, Kansas, their combined share of the market for women's shoes was over 57%; their share of the children's shoe market in that city was 49%. In the 7 cities in which Brown's and Kinney's combined shares of the market for women's shoes were greatest (ranging from 33–57%) each of the parties alone, prior to the merger, had captured substantial portions of those markets (ranging from 13–34%); the merger intensified this existing concentration. In 118 separate cities the combined shares of the market of Brown and Kinney in the sale of one of the relevant lines of commerce exceeded 5%. In 47 cities, their share exceeded 5% in all three lines.

The market share which companies may control by merging is one of the most important factors to be considered when determining the probable effects of the combination on effective competition in the relevant market. In an industry as fragmented as shoe retailing, the control of substantial shares of the trade in a city may have important effects on competition. If a merger achieving 5% control were now approved, we might be required to approve future merger efforts by Brown's competitors seeking similar market shares. The oligopoly Congress sought to avoid would then be furthered and it would be difficult to dissolve the combinations previously approved. Furthermore, in this fragmented industry, even if the combination controls but a small share of a particular market, the fact that this share is held by a large national chain can adversely affect competition. Testimony in the record from numerous independent retailers, based on their actual experience in the market, demonstrates that a strong, national chain of stores can insulate selected outlets from the vagaries of competition in particular locations and that the large chains can set and alter styles in footwear to an extent that renders the independents unable to maintain competitive inventories. A third significant aspect of this merger is that it creates a large national chain which is integrated with a manufacturing operation. The retail outlets of integrated companies, by eliminating wholesalers and by increasing the volume of purchases from the manufacturing division of the enterprise, can market their own brands at prices below those of competing independent retailers. Of course, some of the results of large integrated or chain operations are beneficial to consumers. Their expansion is not rendered unlawful by the mere fact that small independent stores may be adversely affected. It is competition, not competitors, which the Act protects. But we cannot fail to recognize Congress' desire to promote competition through the protection of viable, small, locally owned businesses. Congress appreciated that occasional higher costs and prices might result from the maintenance of fragmented industries and markets. It resolved these competing considerations in favor of decentralization. We must give effect to that decision.

Other factors to be considered in evaluating the probable effects of a merger in the relevant market lend additional support to the District Court's conclusion that this merger may substantially lessen competition. One such factor is the history of tendency toward concentration in the industry. As we have previously pointed out, the shoe industry has, in recent years, been a prime example of such a trend. Most combinations have been between manufacturers and retailers, as each of the larger producers has sought to capture an increasing number of assured outlets for its wares. Although these mergers have been primarily vertical in their aim and effect, to the extent that they have brought ever greater numbers of retail outlets within fewer and fewer hands, they have had an additional important impact on the horizontal plane. By the merger in this case, the largest single group of retail stores still independent of one of the large manufacturers was absorbed into an already substantial aggregation of more or less controlled retail outlets. As a result of this merger, Brown moved into second place nationally in terms of retail stores directly owned. Including the stores on its franchise plan, the merger placed under Brown's control almost 1,600 shoe outlets, or about 7.2% of the Nation's retail "shoe stores" as defined by the Census Bureau, and 2.3% of the Nation's total retail shoe outlets. We cannot avoid the mandate of Congress that tendencies toward concentration in industry are to be curbed in their incipiency, particularly when those tendencies are being accelerated through giant steps striding across a hundred cities at a time. In the light of the trends in this industry we agree with the Government and the court below that this is an appropriate place at which to call a halt.

At the same time appellant has presented no mitigating factors, such as the business failure or the inadequate resources of one of the parties that may have prevented it from maintaining its competitive position, nor a demonstrated need for combination to enable small companies to enter into a more meaningful competition with those dominating the relevant markets. On the basis of the record before us, we believe the Government sustained its burden of proof. . . .

NOTES AND QUESTIONS

1. How did the Supreme Court deal with the lower court's finding that the Brown-Kinney merger created certain efficiencies that would enable the post-merger firm to charge a lower price than before? At one time or another, both courts and commentators have taken three different positions on the relationship between efficiency and the legality of a merger:

(a) mergers should be analyzed in terms of their effect on market power, and efficiency considerations are irrelevant;

(b) mergers that create substantial efficiencies should be legal, or there should be at least a limited "efficiency defense" in certain merger cases;

(c) mergers should be condemned *because* they create efficiencies, even if the merger produces no foreseeable effects on the market power of the post-merger firm or increases the likelihood of collusion in the industry.

Does the *Brown Shoe* opinion leave any doubt about the Supreme Court's view in 1962? Perhaps this passage from the District Court's opinion will help:

[I]ndependent retailers of shoes are having a harder and harder time in competing with company-owned and company-controlled retail outlets. National advertising by large concerns has increased their brand name acceptability and retail stores handling the brand named shoes have a definite advertising advantage. Company-owned and company-controlled retail stores have definite advantages . . . in advertising, insurance, inventory control . . . and price control. These advantages result in lower prices or in higher quality for the same price and the independent retailer can no longer compete in the low and medium-priced fields and has been driven to concentrate his business in the higher-priced, higher-quality type of shoes — and, the higher the price, the smaller the market. He has been placed in this position, not by choice, but by necessity.

179 F. Supp. at 738 (E.D. Mo. 1959). In fact, the theory under which the government brought the *Brown Shoe* case was not that the Brown-Kinney merger would permit the post-merger firm to price monopolistically or that it would encourage collusion in the industry. Rather, the theory was that, because of efficiencies created by the merger, competitors would either be driven out of business or else they would be forced to merge themselves so that they could compete. This argument forced the defendants to argue that the merger did *not* create any efficiencies and that the post-merger firm would not be able to charge lower prices or produce shoes of a higher quality for the same price. Brief for Petitioner 193–199.

Was the government's (and the court's) theory that the Brown merger was bad because it created efficiencies wrong? That theory came under severe criticism in the late 1970s and 1980s. *See, e.g.*, R. BORK, THE ANTITRUST PARADOX: A POLICY AT WAR WITH ITSELF, 198–216 (1978; rev. ed. 1993). However, the government's theory was quite consistent with the legislative history of the 1950 amendments to Section 7 of the Clayton Act. In 1950, the issue foremost on the minds of Congress was not consumer welfare and encouragement of efficiency in the production of goods and services. Rather, it was the protection of small, independent businesses that were being injured by larger, more efficient firms. If it is quite clear that Congress had a particular policy in mind when it passed a statute, should judges (or antitrust scholars) ignore Congressional intent and interpret the statute in a different way, even if the different way is in the best interest of consumers? *See* Hovenkamp, *Antitrust Policy After Chicago*, 84 MICH. L. REV. 213, 249–255 (1985).

2.   The Supreme Court argued that if it approved the Brown Shoe merger now, it "might be required" to approve other mergers of similar size companies later, although by then the industry would be much more concentrated and the risks of collusion much higher. Suppose the court approved a merger today which yielded a

10% market share to the post-merger firm, in a market with dozens of competitors. Ten years from now, when the number of competitors in the market has been reduced to five or six, the Court is asked to approve another merger yielding a 10% market share for that post-merger firm. Would fairness, justice, due process, equal protection, or anything else "require" the Supreme Court to approve the second merger? Probably not, if the second proposed merger would have measurable effects on competition in the market, while the first merger did not.

The Supreme Court's "domino theory" argument may have been based not on some concept of fairness, however, but on a particular economic policy. As long as all the competitors in an industry are small, all of them operate under the same set of economic disadvantages. However, if a merger of two of them generates substantial economies, then smaller competitors will immediately be placed at a disadvantage and they will have to merge in order to stay in business. To permit them to go out of business would leave the industry even more concentrated than permitting the merger to go ahead, so the court would have to permit the future mergers as well.

The argument makes sense if one accepts the premise that mergers ought to be condemned because they create efficiency. A wave of mergers in a particular market generally tells us that larger size generates substantial economies in that market. Once one set of firms has achieved these economies, other firms must achieve them (either by merger or by internal growth) or they will not be able to compete. In an unrestrained market, the firms will gravitate toward the most efficient size and when most of them have reached that size, the "wave" of mergers will cease. This is undoubtedly what the Court was observing when it noted a "tendency toward concentration" in the shoe industry.

3. Suppose that the merger between Brown and Kinney had actually been consummated. A few years later a private business person, formerly an independent shoe seller, alleges that she was driven out of business as a result of the illegal merger. Because of the merger, the plaintiff argues, the Brown-Kinney shoe store across the street from her own store was able to sell higher quality shoes at a lower price than she was able to sell them. Should the private entrepreneur have a cause of action for damages? *See Brunswick Corp. v. Pueblo Bowl-O-Mat, Inc.*, reprinted in Chapter 3, *supra*.

UNITED STATES v. PHILADELPHIA NATIONAL BANK
374 U.S. 321 (1963)

JUSTICE BRENNAN delivered the opinion of the Court.

The United States, appellant here, brought this civil action . . . to enjoin a proposed merger of the Philadelphia National Bank (PNB) and Girard Trust Corn Exchange Bank (Girard). . . . The complaint charged violations of § 1 of the Sherman Act, and § 7 of the Clayton Act. . . . We hold that the merger of appellees is forbidden by § 7 of the Clayton Act and so must be enjoined; we need not, and therefore do not, reach the further question of alleged violation of § 1 of the Sherman Act. . . .

The Philadelphia National Bank and Girard Trust Corn Exchange Bank are, respectively, the second and third largest of the 42 commercial banks with head offices in the Philadelphia metropolitan area, which consists of the City of Philadelphia and its three contiguous counties in Pennsylvania. The home county of both banks is the city itself; Pennsylvania law, however, permits branching into the counties contiguous to the home county, and both banks have offices throughout the four-county area. PNB, a national bank, has assets of over $1,000,000,000, making it (as of 1959) the twenty-first largest bank in the Nation. Girard, a state bank, is a member of the FRS [Federal Reserve System] and is insured by the FDIC; it has assets of about $750,000,000. Were the proposed merger to be consummated, the resulting bank would be the largest in the four-county area, with (approximately) 36% of the area banks' total assets, 36% of deposits, and 34% of net loans. It and the second largest (First Pennsylvania Bank and Trust Company, now the largest) would have between them 59% of the total assets, 58% of deposits, and 58% of the net loans, while after the merger the four largest banks in the area would have 78% of total assets, 77% of deposits, and 78% of net loans.

The present size of both PNB and Girard is in part the result of mergers. Indeed, the trend toward concentration is noticeable in the Philadelphia area generally, in which the number of commercial banks has declined from 108 in 1947 to the present 42. Since 1950, PNB has acquired nine formerly independent banks and Girard six; and these acquisitions have accounted for 59% and 85% of the respective banks' asset growth during the period, 63% and 91% of their deposit growth, and 12% and 37% of their loan growth. During this period, the seven largest banks in the area increased their combined share of the area's total commercial bank resources from about 61% to about 90%.

. . . .

The Government's case in the District Court relied chiefly on statistical evidence bearing upon market structure and on testimony by economists and bankers to the effect that, notwithstanding the intensive governmental regulation of banking, there was a substantial area for the free play of competitive forces; that concentration of commercial banking, which the proposed merger would increase, was inimical to that free play; that the principal anticompetitive effect of the merger would be felt in the area in which the banks had their offices, thus making the four-county metropolitan area the relevant geographical market; and that commercial banking was the relevant product market. The defendants, in addition to offering contrary evidence on these points, attempted to show business justifications for the merger. They conceded that both banks were economically strong and had sound management, but offered the testimony of bankers to show that the resulting bank, with its greater prestige and increased lending limit, would be better able to compete with large out-of-state (particularly New York) banks, would attract new business to Philadelphia, and in general would promote the economic development of the metropolitan area.

We have no difficulty in determining the "line of commerce" (relevant product or services market) and "section of the country" (relevant geographical market) in which to appraise the probable competitive effects of appellees' proposed merger. We agree with the District Court that the cluster of products (various kinds of credit) and services (such as checking accounts and trust administration) denoted by the term "commercial banking," composes a distinct line of commerce. Some commercial banking products or services are so distinctive that they are entirely free of effective competition from products or services of other financial institutions; the checking account is in this category. Others enjoy such cost advantages as to be insulated within a broad range from substitutes furnished by other institutions. For example, commercial banks compete with small-loan companies in the personal-loan market; but the small-loan companies' rates are invariably much higher than the banks', in part, it seems, because the companies' working capital consists in substantial part of bank loans. Finally, there are banking facilities which, although in terms of cost and price they are freely competitive with the facilities provided by other financial institutions, nevertheless enjoy a settled consumer preference, insulating them, to a marked degree, from competition; this seems to be the case with savings deposits. In sum, it is clear that commercial banking is a market "sufficiently inclusive to be meaningful in terms of trade realities."

We part company with the District Court on the determination of the appropriate "section of the country." The proper question to be asked in this case is not where the parties to the merger do business or even where they compete, but where, within the area of competitive overlap, the effect of the merger on competition will be direct and immediate. This depends upon "the geographic structure of supplier-customer relations." . . .

We recognize that the area in which appellees have their offices does not delineate with perfect accuracy an appropriate "section of the country" in which to appraise the effect of the merger upon competition. Large borrowers and large depositors, the record shows, may find it practical to do a large part of their banking business outside their home community; very small borrowers and depositors may, as a practical matter, be confined to bank offices in their immediate neighborhood; and customers of intermediate size, it would appear, deal with banks within an area intermediate between these extremes. So also, some banking services are evidently more local in nature than others. But that in banking the relevant geographical market is a function of each separate customer's economic scale means simply that a workable compromise must be found: some fair intermediate delineation which avoids the indefensible extremes of drawing the market either so expansively as to make the effect of the merger upon competition seem insignificant, because only the very largest bank customers are taken into account in defining the market, or so narrowly as to place appellees in different markets, because only the smallest customers are considered. We think that the four-county Philadelphia metropolitan area, which state law apparently recognizes as a meaningful banking community in allowing Philadelphia banks to branch within it, and which would seem roughly to delineate the area in which bank customers that are neither very large nor very small find it practical to do their banking business, is a more appropriate "section of the country" in which to appraise the instant merger than any larger or smaller or different area. . . .

We noted in *Brown Shoe* that "[t]he dominant theme pervading congressional consideration of the 1950 amendments [to § 7] was a fear of what was considered to be a rising tide of economic concentration in the American economy." This intense congressional concern with the trend toward concentration warrants dispensing, in certain cases, with elaborate proof of market structure, market behavior, or probable anticompetitive effects. Specifically, we think that a merger which produces a firm controlling an undue percentage share of the relevant market, and results in a significant increase in the concentration of firms in that market, is so inherently likely to lessen competition substantially that it must be enjoined in the absence of evidence clearly showing that the merger is not likely to have such anticompetitive effects.

Such a test lightens the burden of proving illegality only with respect to mergers whose size makes them inherently suspect in light of Congress' design in § 7 to prevent undue concentration. Furthermore, the test is fully consonant with economic theory. That "[c]ompetition is likely to be greatest when there are many sellers, none of which has any significant market share," is common ground among most economists, and was undoubtedly a premise of congressional reasoning about the antimerger statute.

The merger of appellees will result in a single bank's controlling at least 30% of the commercial banking business in the four-county Philadelphia metropolitan area. Without attempting to specify the smallest market share which would still be considered to threaten undue concentration, we are clear that 30% presents that threat. Further, whereas presently the two largest banks in the area (First Pennsylvania and PNB) control between them approximately 44% of the area's commercial banking business, the two largest after the merger (PNB-Girard and First Pennsylvania) will control 59%. Plainly, we think, this increase of more than 33% in concentration must be regarded as significant.

Our conclusion that these percentages raise an inference that the effect of the contemplated merger of appellees may be substantially to lessen competition is not an arbitrary one, although neither the terms of § 7 nor the legislative history suggests that any particular percentage share was deemed critical. The House Report states that the tests of illegality under amended § 7 "are intended to be similar to those which the courts have applied in interpreting the same language as used in other sections of the Clayton Act." Accordingly, we have relied upon decisions under these other sections in applying § 7. In *Standard Oil Co. v. United States*, 337 U.S. 293, this Court held violative of § 3 of the Clayton Act exclusive contracts whereby the defendant company, which accounted for 23% of the sales in the relevant market and, together with six other firms, accounted for 65% of such sales, maintained control over outlets through which approximately 7% of the sales were made. . . . In the instant case, by way of comparison, the four largest banks after the merger will foreclose 78% of the relevant market. . . . Doubtless these cases turned to some extent upon whether "by the nature of the market there is room for newcomers." But they remain highly suggestive in the present context, for as we noted in *Brown Shoe* integration by merger is more suspect than integration by contract, because of the greater permanence of the former. The market share and market concentration figures in the contract-integration cases, taken together with scholarly opinion support, we believe, the inference we draw in the instant case from the figures disclosed by the record. . . .

[I]t is suggested that the increased lending limit of the resulting bank will enable it to compete with the large out-of-state banks, particularly the New York banks, for very large loans. We reject this application of the concept of "countervailing power." If anticompetitive effects in one market could be justified by procompetitive consequences in another, the logical upshot would be that every firm in an industry could, without violating § 7, embark on a series of mergers that would make it in the end as large as the industry leader. . . .

NOTES AND QUESTIONS

1. What do you make of the Court's argument that the same market share percentages that trigger liability in a vertical integration-exclusive dealing case ought to suggest liability in a horizontal merger case? Are the issues similar enough to justify this inference?

2. Market power, as you may recall, is a function of both the elasticity of demand in a certain market and the elasticity of supply. What would be the effect of a law that limited the number of banks in a particular community, or that made it very difficult for a new bank to enter? Wouldn't such a law reduce the elasticity of supply in the market? And wouldn't that reduction tend to increase the market power of the banks already in the market?

3. The Supreme Court concluded that a merger between firms controlling an "undue percentage" of a market and which results in a "significant increase" in concentration is "inherently likely to lessen competition." Is this a virtual per se rule banning mergers, once specified market concentration and shares have been reached? Or is it merely a description of the burden a plaintiff must carry in order to establish a prima facie case of illegality in a concentrated market? What if the merger occurred in an unconcentrated market? Would the Court then revert to the *Brown Shoe* test? If so, then doesn't the rule of *Philadelphia Bank* require the defendant to have an "undue" market share?

4. *Philadelphia Bank* involved neither a stock acquisition nor an asset acquisition but a consolidation of two banks into one. At the time *Philadelphia Bank* was decided, it was widely believed that Section 7 did not apply to such mergers involving banks. Congress was not pleased with the holding in *Philadelphia Bank* and responded with the Bank Merger Act of 1966. The statute generally exempted bank mergers consummated before the date of the *Philadelphia Bank* decision, and those consummated before the date the statute was passed if they had not yet been challenged by the government. Clayton Act standards continue to apply, however, to bank mergers or consolidations undertaken after the effective date of the statute, and the Clayton Act is incorporated by reference into the Bank Merger Act. The Bank Merger Act additionally provides that the Justice Department can attack a bank merger only during a 30-day period immediately following approval of the merger by the relevant banking authorities (the identity of the authorities depends on the source of the post-merger bank's charter).

Additionally, the Bank Merger Act permits one of the defenses that was raised unsuccessfully in *Philadelphia Bank:* that the merger will not be illegal if the court finds "that the anticompetitive effects [of the consolidation] are clearly outweighed in the public interest by the probable effect of the transaction in meeting the convenience and needs of the community served." 12 U.S.C. § 1828(c) (1987). The

Supreme Court has not been particularly tolerant of this defense. *See United States v. First City Nat'l Bank*, 386 U.S. 361 (1967), where the Court remanded for more fact-finding on the competitive benefits of the merger once it was found to be prima facie illegal under a traditional Section 7 approach.

5. In *United States v. Von's Grocery Co.*, 384 U.S. 270 (1966), the Supreme Court condemned a merger between the third and sixth ranked grocery chains in Los Angeles, with an aggregate market share of 7.5%. At the time of the merger, Los Angeles had 96 grocery chains with two or more stores, and an additional 3500 single store operations. Further, entry was easy. Is there any theory under which such a merger could lead to higher retail prices? Justice Stewart (joined by Justice Harlan) dissented, complaining that the majority was using Section 7 to "roll back the supermarket revolution" with an opinion that was nothing more than a "requiem for the so-called 'Mom and Pop' grocery stores" that had become "economically and technologically obsolete."

PROBLEM 7.1

Electro and Conductro are two producers of electric cable, which comes in four kinds, insulated and bare aluminum cable, and insulated and bare copper cable. The copper cable costs much more than the aluminum cable, but there are certain places, such as in homes and underground, where only copper can be used. High tension lines are commonly made of aluminum.

The manufacture of bare aluminum cable requires exactly the same equipment as the manufacture of bare copper cable. Once a firm has the machinery, it can make either kind of cable interchangeably. Likewise, the cable is distributed through the same channels, both ending up in independently owned wholesale and retail electric supply outlets.

The manufacturing difference between insulated and bare cable is another matter. Putting insulation on cable requires expensive, sophisticated machinery, and not all cable manufacturers have it.

At the time Electro proposed to acquire all of the assets of Conductro, the market shares of the two firms with respect to each of the above types of cable were as follows:

Electro	Conductro	
Insulated aluminum cable	11.0%	5.0%
Bare aluminum cable	32.0%	0.3%
Bare and insulated aluminum cable	27.8%	1.3%
All insulated cable	0.3%	1.3%
All four types of cable combined	1.8%	1.4%

Which of these are relevant "lines of commerce" for purposes of Section 7? Under *Brown Shoe* and *Philadelphia Bank*, is the merger illegal? *See United States v. Aluminum Co. of Am. (Rome Cable)*, 377 U.S. 271 (1964). Note particularly the dissent.

UNITED STATES v. GENERAL DYNAMICS CORP
415 U.S. 486 (1974)

JUSTICE STEWART delivered the opinion of the Court.

On September 22, 1967, the Government commenced this suit . . . challenging as violative of § 7 of the Clayton Act, the acquisition of the stock of United Electric Coal Companies by Material Service Corp. and its successor, General Dynamics Corp. . . .

At the time of the acquisition involved here, Material Service Corp. was a large midwest producer and supplier of building materials, concrete, limestone, and coal. All of its coal production was from deep-shaft mines operated by it or its affiliate, appellee Freeman Coal Mining Corp., and production from these operations amounted to 6.9 million tons of coal in 1959 and 8.4 million tons in 1967. In 1954, Material Service began to acquire the stock of United Electric Coal Companies. United Electric at all relevant times operated only strip or open-pit mines in Illinois and Kentucky; at the time of trial in 1970 a number of its mines had closed and its operations had been reduced to four mines in Illinois and none in Kentucky. In 1959, it produced 3.6 million tons of coal, and by 1967, it had increased this output to 5.7 million tons. Material Service's purchase of United Electric stock continued until 1959. At this point Material's holdings amounted to more than 34% of United Electric's outstanding shares and — all parties are now agreed on this point — Material had effective control of United Electric. . . .

Some months after this takeover, Material Service was itself acquired by the appellee General Dynamics Corp., a large diversified corporation, much of its revenues coming from sales of aircraft, communications, and marine products to Government agencies. . . .

The thrust of the Government's complaint was that the acquisition . . . substantially lessened competition in the production and sale of coal in either or both of two geographic markets. It contended that a relevant "section of the country" within the meaning of § 7 was, alternatively, the State of Illinois or the Eastern Interior Coal Province Sales Area, the latter . . . comprising Illinois and Indiana, and parts of Kentucky, Tennessee, Iowa, Minnesota, Wisconsin, and Missouri. . . .

As to the relevant product market, the court found that coal faced strong and direct competition from other sources of energy such as oil, natural gas, nuclear energy, and geothermal power which created a cross-elasticity of demand among those various fuels. As a result, it concluded that coal, by itself, was not a permissible product market and that the "energy market" was the sole "line of commerce" in which anticompetitive effects could properly be canvassed.

Similarly, the District Court rejected the Government's proposed geographic markets on the ground that they were "based essentially on past and present production statistics and do not relate to actual coal consumption patterns." The court found that a realistic geographic market should be defined in terms of transportation arteries and freight charges that determined the cost of delivered coal to purchasers and thus the competitive position of various coal producers. . . . In lieu of the State of Illinois or the Eastern Interior Coal Province Sales Area, the court accordingly found the relevant geographic market to be 10 smaller areas. . . .

[T]he District Court found that the evidence did not support the Government's contention that the 1959 acquisition of United Electric substantially lessened competition in any product or geographic market. . . .

The Government sought to prove a violation of § 7 of the Clayton Act principally through statistics showing that within certain geographic markets the coal industry was concentrated among a small number of large producers; that this concentration was increasing; and that the acquisition of United Electric would materially enlarge the market share of the acquiring company and thereby contribute to the trend toward concentration.

The concentration of the coal market in Illinois and, alternatively, in the Eastern Interior Coal Province was demonstrated by a table of the shares of the largest two, four, and 10 coal-producing firms in each of these areas for both 1957 and 1967 that revealed the following:

	Eastern Interior Coal Province		Illinois	
	1957	1967	1957	1967
Top 2 firms	29.6	48.6	37.8	52.9
Top 4 firms	43.0	62.9	54.5	75.2
Top 10 firms	65.5	91.4	84.0	98.0

These statistics, the Government argued, showed not only that the coal industry was concentrated among a small number of leading producers, but that the trend had been toward increasing concentration. Furthermore, the undisputed fact that the number of coal-producing firms in Illinois decreased almost 73% during the period of 1957 to 1967 from 144 to 39 was claimed to be indicative of the same trend. The acquisition of United Electric by Material Service resulted in increased concentration of coal sales among the leading producers in the areas chosen by the Government, as shown by the following table:

	1959			1967		
	Share of top 2 but for merger	Share of top 2 given merger	Percent increase	Share of top 2 but for merger	Share of top 2 given merger	Percent increase
Province	33.1	37.9	14.5	45.0	48.6	8.0
Illinois	36.6	44.3	22.4	44.0	52.9	20.2

In prior decisions involving horizontal mergers between competitors, this Court has found prima facie violations of § 7 of the Clayton Act from aggregate statistics of the sort relied on by the United States in this case. . . .

The effect of adopting this approach to a determination of a "substantial" lessening of competition is to allow the Government to rest its case on a showing of even small increases of market share or market concentration in those industries or markets where concentration is already great or has been recently increasing, since "if concentration is already great, the importance of preventing even slight increases in concentration and so preserving the possibility of eventual deconcentration is correspondingly great."

While the statistical showing proffered by the Government in this case, the accuracy of which was not discredited by the District Court or contested by the appellees, would under this approach have sufficed to support a finding of "undue concentration" in the absence of other considerations, the question before us is whether the District Court was justified in finding that other pertinent factors affecting the coal industry and the business of the appellees mandated a conclusion that no substantial lessening of competition occurred or was threatened by the acquisition of United Electric. We are satisfied that the court's ultimate finding was not in error.

. . . .

Much of the District Court's opinion was devoted to a description of the changes that have affected the coal industry since World War II. . . . *First*, it found that coal had become increasingly less able to compete with other sources of energy in many segments of the energy market. Following the War the industry entirely lost its largest single purchaser of coal — the railroads — and faced increasingly stiffer competition from oil and natural gas as sources of energy for industrial and residential uses. Because of these changes in consumption patterns, coal's share of the energy resources consumed in this country fell from 78.4% in 1920 to 21.4% in 1968. The court reviewed evidence attributing this decline not only to the changing relative economies of alternative fuels and to new distribution and consumption patterns, but also to more recent concern with the effect of coal use on the environment and consequent regulation of the extent and means of such coal consumption.

Second, the court found that to a growing extent since 1954, the electric utility industry has become the mainstay of coal consumption. While electric utilities consumed only 15.76% of the coal produced nationally in 1947, their share of total consumption increased every year thereafter, and in 1968 amounted to more than 59% of all the coal consumed throughout the Nation.

Third, and most significantly, the court found that to an increasing degree, nearly all coal sold to utilities is transferred under long-term requirements contracts, under which coal producers promise to meet utilities' coal consumption requirements for a fixed period of time, and at predetermined prices. The court described the mutual benefits accruing to both producers and consumers of coal from such long-term contracts in the following terms:

> "This major investment [in electric utility equipment] can be jeopardized by a disruption in the supply of coal. Utilities are, therefore, concerned with assuring the supply of coal to such a plant over its life. In addition, utilities desire to establish in advance, as closely as possible, what fuel costs will be for the life of the plant. For these reasons, utilities typically arrange

> long-term contracts for all or at least a major portion of the total fuel requirements for the life of the plant. . . . "

These developments in the patterns of coal distribution and consumption, the District Court found, have limited the amounts of coal immediately available for "spot" purchases on the open market, since "[t]he growing practice by coal producers of expanding mine capacity only to meet long-term contractual commitments and the gradual disappearance of the small truck mines has tended to limit the production capacity available for spot sales."

Because of these fundamental changes in the structure of the market for coal, the District Court was justified in viewing the statistics relied on by the Government as insufficient to sustain its case. Evidence of past production does not, as a matter of logic, necessarily give a proper picture of a company's future ability to compete. . . .

. . . The focus of competition in a given time frame is not on the disposition of coal already produced but on the procurement of new long-term supply contracts. In this situation, a company's past ability to produce is of limited significance, since it is in a position to offer for sale neither its past production nor the bulk of the coal it is presently capable of producing, which is typically already committed under a long-term supply contract. A more significant indicator of a company's power effectively to compete with other companies lies in the state of a company's uncommitted reserves of recoverable coal. A company with relatively large supplies of coal which are not already under contract to a consumer will have a more important influence upon competition in the contemporaneous negotiation of supply contracts than a firm with small reserves, even though the latter may presently produce a greater tonnage of coal. In a market where the availability and price of coal are set by long-term contracts rather than immediate or short-term purchases and sales, reserves rather than past production are the best measure of a company's ability to compete.

The testimony and exhibits in the District Court revealed that United Electric's coal reserve prospects were "unpromising." United's relative position of strength in reserves was considerably weaker than its past and current ability to produce. While United ranked fifth among Illinois coal producers in terms of annual production, it was 10th in reserve holdings, and controlled less than 1% of the reserves held by coal producers in Illinois, Indiana, and western Kentucky. Many of the reserves held by United had already been depleted at the time of trial, forcing the closing of some of United's midwest mines. Even more significantly, the District Court found that of the 52,033,304 tons of currently minable reserves in Illinois, Indiana, and Kentucky controlled by United, only four million tons had not already been committed under long-term contracts. United was found to be facing the future with relatively depleted resources at its disposal, and with the vast majority of those resources already committed under contracts allowing no further adjustment in price. In addition, the District Court found that "United Electric has neither the possibility of acquiring more [reserves] nor the ability to develop deep coal reserves," and thus was not in a position to increase its reserves to replace those already depleted or committed.

. . . .

In addition to contending that the District Court erred in finding that the acquisition of United Electric would not substantially lessen competition, the Government urges us to review the court's determinations of the proper product and geographic markets. . . .

While under normal circumstances a delineation of proper geographic and product markets is a necessary precondition to assessment of the probabilities of a substantial effect on competition within them, in this case we nevertheless affirm the District Court's judgment without reaching these questions. By determining that the amount and availability of usable reserves, and not the past annual production figures relied on by the Government, were the proper indicators of future ability to compete, the District Court wholly rejected the Government's prima facie case. Irrespective of the markets within which the acquiring and the acquired company might by viewed as competitors for purposes of this § 7 suit, the Government's statistical presentation simply did not establish that a substantial lessening of competition was likely to occur in any market. . . . Since we agree with the District Court that the Government's reliance on production statistics in the context of this case was insufficient, it follows that the judgment before us may be affirmed without reaching the issues of geographic and product markets.

NOTES AND QUESTIONS

1. Are deep-mined and strip-mined coal the same "line of commerce" for purposes of Section 7 of the Clayton Act — that is, was the merger in *General Dynamics* really a horizontal merger? What if customers made no distinction between the two kinds of coal? What if it was much cheaper to produce strip-mined coal than deep-mined coal? How do you evaluate the fact that it takes an entirely different set of equipment to mine deep coal than it takes to strip mine?

2. In *General Dynamics*, the district court decided that the relevant market was not coal but "energy." It based this conclusion on the fact that the cross-elasticity of demand between coal and alternative sources of energy such as natural gas, oil, nuclear, and geothermal power was very high. Did the court make the same error that the Supreme Court made in *du Pont* (cellophane)? Probably not. There were many coal producers (39 in the Eastern Interior Coal Province alone), which would suggest that coal was selling at a competitive price. At that competitive price, the cross-elasticity of demand between coal and other energy sources was very high. This would suggest that even were coal to come under the control of a monopolist, the monopolist would be held to the competitive price by competition from alternative energy sources.

3. Does the *General Dynamics* case discard any "per se" rule against mergers that may have been developed in the *Philadelphia Bank* case? By suggesting that in "prior decisions," the Supreme Court had found "prima facie violations" based on statistical evidence of concentration, was the Court overruling *Philadelphia Bank*? A few recent decisions have suggested that the *Philadelphia Bank* presumption either no longer applies or else must be considerably weakened. As a result, market concentration becomes little more than one of many factors that the court must consider. Barriers to entry have become *at least* as important as market concentration in merger analysis. *See, e.g., United States v. Baker Hughes*, 908 F.2d 981,

991–992 (D.C. Cir. 1990), in which the court approved a merger even though the post-merger HHI exceeded 4000. It then noted:

> [A] defendant seeking to rebut a presumption of anticompetitive effect must show that the *prima facie* case inaccurately predicts the relevant transaction's probable effect on future competition. The more compelling the *prima facie* case, the more evidence the defendant must present to rebut it successfully. A defendant can make the required showing by affirmatively showing why a given transaction is unlikely to substantially lessen competition, or by discrediting the data underlying the initial presumption in the government's favor.

However,

> [i]mposing a heavy burden of production on a defendant would be particularly anomalous where, as here, it is easy to establish a *prima facie* case. The government, after all, can carry its initial burden of production simply by presenting market concentration statistics. To allow the government virtually to rest its case at that point, leaving the defendant to prove the core of the dispute, would grossly inflate the role of statistics in actions brought under section 7. The Herfindahl-Hirschman Index cannot guarantee litigation victories.

908 F.2d at 991–992. Is the latter paragraph consistent with *Philadelphia Bank*? With *General Dynamics*?

4. In earlier cases, the Supreme Court tended to view long-term requirements contracts as enhancing the market power of the selling firm, by enabling it to "foreclose" a certain market. *See, e.g., Standard Oil of Cal. v. United States*, 337 U.S. 293 (1949) (*Standard Stations*). In *General Dynamics*, however, the Court viewed the coal companies as victims of their own requirements contracts. In the Court's eyes, sale of coal under requirements contracts did "not represent the exercise of competitive power but rather the obligation to fulfill previously negotiated contracts at a previously fixed price." Is the situation in *General Dynamics* that much different, or has the Court's attitude toward vertical integration by contract changed?

5. Suppose that a company is currently producing 10% of the coal being produced in some market, but it has only 2% of the reserves in that market. It merges with another company that is currently producing 10% of the coal but that owns only 2% of the reserves. What are the relevant percentages for determining each party's share of the relevant market? The answer to that question is more complex than first appears. If coal reserves are large enough to satisfy the demand for coal for the next 1,000 years, then a company with 2% of the reserves might go on producing 10% of production for a long time. By contrast, if reserves are being rapidly depleted and are likely to run out within the next few decades, then a company with 10% of current output but only 2% of the reserves is in trouble and will have to reduce production or find additional reserves in the near future. As a result, there cannot be a general rule that one must look at either reserves or at current output in determining relevant market shares of nonrenewable natural resources. Sand, for example, may be a nonrenewable natural resource. However, an electronics company that made silicon chips from sand and owned .001% of the world's sand would probably have sufficient sand to corner 100% of the silicon chip market for the next 1,000 years.

6. How would the Supreme Court treat a merger of two coal companies that have very small shares of current output (say, 2–3%), but very large shares of available reserves (say, 25% each)?

NOTE: PARTIAL ACQUISITIONS

Section 7 of the Clayton Act applies to the acquisition of the "whole or any part" of the stock or assets of another firm. When the Supreme Court decided *General Dynamics*, Material Service Corp. had acquired 34% of the outstanding shares of United Electric. In the vertical acquisition at issue in the *du Pont* (GM) case, du Pont owned 23% of General Motors' outstanding common stock. No one disputed that these acquisitions were not covered by the statute because they involved less than all or even half of the acquired firm's equity. Clearly, under the literal language of the statute, if a firm purchases a single share of another firm's stock, Section 7 could be applied. Because Section 7 applies to asset acquisitions as well, presumably if du Pont had purchased a single General Motors truck for delivery purposes, it would come within the statute. After all, a truck is part of the "assets" of General Motors. How broadly must the statute be read?

One answer to the problem of defining an appropriate lower limit to partial acquisitions for Section 7 purposes is that an acquisition is not illegal unless it substantially lessens competition or "tends to" create a monopoly. However, the determination that a particular acquisition lessens competition requires a great deal of sophisticated economic analysis. Would it not be far better to have some threshold below which a partial stock or asset acquisition would be considered per se legal? After all, every firm that deals with other firms (and all firms do) is involved daily in asset acquisitions.

One such threshold is explicit in the statute. Section 7 creates an exception for "persons purchasing . . . stock solely for investment and not using the same by voting or otherwise to bring about . . . the substantial lessening of competition." How does one determine whether a particular stock purchase was "solely for investment"? The courts have been consistent about one thing: if the purchase has any anticompetitive effect, then it will not be considered "solely for investment," regardless of the intent of the purchasing party. *See Gulf & W. Indus. v. Great Atl. & Pac. Tea Co.*, 476 F.2d 687, 693 (2d Cir. 1973). The result is that the "solely for investment" exception is no exception at all. Any stock purchase may be challenged on the grounds that it may substantially lessen competition or tend to create a monopoly, and if it does so, the investment exception will not provide a defense.

It is also no answer that we need not worry about stock acquisitions unless the stock purchaser acquires enough shares to control the corporation in which it is a shareholder. First of all, how many shares must one purchase in order to "control" a corporation? To control everything, perhaps one needs 51% of the shares. But a large shareholder with substantially less than 51% can have considerable influence on a firm's decision making. The 23% interest in the *du Pont* case, for example, was enough. In *General Dynamics*, the parties agreed that the 34% acquisition was enough to give the acquiring firm "effective control."

But to focus on "control" provides an incomplete answer because ownership affects people's attitudes in other ways. The extreme case is ownership of the stock of a competitor. Suppose that corporations *A*, *B*, and *C* are all intense competitors in a certain market. The competitive game being what it is, each of them would like nothing better than to drive one of the other two (or perhaps both) out of business. Now suppose that *A* acquires 10% of the shares of *B*. Suppose further that *B* has several larger shareholders, and there is no plausible way that *A*, with its 10% ownership, can control *B*'s operations. *A*'s purchase of *B* may be intended "solely" for investment. For example, *A* as a competitor of *B* might have good knowledge about *B*'s financial stability, or about the expanding market for the product that both *A* and *B* manufacture. As a result, *A* might conclude that *B*'s shares are a good investment. Clearly, however, the "competition" between *A* and *B* has taken on a new characteristic. It is clear that *A* now has a large stake in *B*'s survival and profitability. Will *A* and *B* continue to compete just as strongly as they did before? Might *C* have some cause for concern about *A*'s stock acquisition of *B*?

The problems presented by partial acquisitions of assets are generally different than those presented by partial stock acquisitions. For example, if *A* purchased an unused plant or fleet of trucks from its competitor *B*, that purchase would not give *A* a continuing interest in *B*'s welfare. In fact, a very substantial asset acquisition might not affect competition at all. Suppose for example that *A* and *B* were the only competitors in a market and that *A* operated two plants and *B* three. Then *A* purchases one of *B*'s plants. The result is that now *A* operates three plants and *B* two. Under what circumstances could such a transaction lessen competition?

Market efficiency considerations urge relatively free exchange of productive assets between competitors. Relatively technical industries in particular are apt to employ a great deal of specialized equipment that has little use in other markets. If a company is not using a large, specialized plant or piece of equipment and puts it on the market, the highest bidder (or perhaps the only bidders) for the asset are often competitors. A rule that forbade too many such transactions could cause a great amount of social waste.

On the other hand, it is clear that when a company purchases a plant from a competitor, there is a danger of precisely the kind of anticompetitive results that amended Section 7 was designed to prevent. Presumably, such a sale will not take place unless the plant is more valuable to the buyer than it is to the seller, and that suggests that the buyer may produce more from it than the seller would produce if the seller kept the plant. Under what circumstances would the purchase of a plant give the new owner more market power to raise prices by *reducing* output? It is possible, of course, that the purchaser of the plant does not intend to use it, but is buying it in order to remove it from the market — i.e., so that neither the seller nor some other competitor could use it either. Is this a plausible scheme for creating market power?

If *A*'s rival operates only one plant, and *A* purchases it, and the rival exits from the market, the transaction is likely to be just as anticompetitive as a merger between the two firms. This was a common mechanism by which firms avoided application of Section 7 of the Clayton Act before its 1950 amendments. Because the statute then applied only to stock acquisitions, a firm could purchase nearly all the assets of a corporation and leave nothing behind except the corporate charter.

In general, courts have not developed any easy threshold for determining when a partial stock or asset acquisition raises an issue under Section 7. Unless a claim is implausible on its face, the plaintiff will generally be given an opportunity to show that any partial stock or asset acquisition may substantially lessen competition or tend to create a monopoly. For an excellent discussion of the problem of partial acquisitions, see 5 P. AREEDA & H. HOVENKAMP, ANTITRUST LAW ¶¶ 1202–1204 (3d ed. 2009).

[1] The Horizontal Merger Guidelines

The Justice Department first issued Guidelines describing its standards for challenging mergers under Section 7 of the Clayton Act in 1968. To take account of changes in the economic theory and enforcement policies of the Department's Antitrust Division and of legal developments like General Dynamics, the Justice Department completely revised the Guidelines in 1982 and again in 1984. The Justice Department and the Federal Trade Commission teamed up to revise the Guidelines much more substantially in 1992 and then collaborated on another significant revision in 2010. The 2010 Guidelines describe the standards that the two antitrust enforcement agencies will today apply in analyzing horizontal mergers. The 2010 Guidelines are reprinted in this book as Appendix A, *infra*. Vertical and conglomerate (potential competition) mergers continue to be analyzed under older Guidelines printed in 1984. It is important to remember that the merger Guidelines are merely guidelines, designed to aid firms in predicting Justice Department's response to prospective acquisitions. The courts are not bound by them except to the extent that an appellate court adopts the Guidelines' position as the law.

First, the guidelines established a method for determining the relevant markets for analyzing a merger, and a measure of market concentration from which the agencies would draw initial presumptions about the likely effects of the merger. Second, the Guidelines discuss how the agencies would analyze the likelihood that a transaction would harm the market through increased collusion (coordinated effects) or monopolization (unilateral effects). The 1992 Guidelines had been particularly important in signaling greater focus on the latter than had previously existed. Third, the Guidelines set forth how the enforcement agencies would think about the market entry that might offset any anticompetitive effects from a given merger. And finally, the Guidelines discussed conditions under which the agencies might consider the "failing firm" or "exiting assets" defenses for a transaction, and the conditions under which agencies would credit efficiencies achieved by a merger in their review of the transaction.

This set of structural presumptions, effects analyses, and defenses came to define a standard pattern for reviewing mergers under the Guidelines. Typically, the agencies would define relevant product and geographic markets, assess the concentration of those markets to draw a presumption about whether the transaction would have anticompetitive effects, and then put together evidence from which to predict that coordinated or unilateral effects would in fact occur and not be offset by reasonably near-term market entry. The merging parties would then counter with their own evidence on relevant market and effects, but also raise efficiencies or other defenses of the transaction. The modern Guidelines therefore fit very closely with the *General Dynamics* analysis of moving beyond market share statistics alone to evidence of likely effects.

NOTE: MARKET DEFINITION AND MARKET CONCENTRATION UNDER THE GUIDELINES: THE HYPOTHETICAL MONOPOLIST TEST AND THE HERFINDAHL-HIRSCHMAN INDEX

Market definition has a central role in merger review under the Guidelines, even if the Guidelines' emphasis on market definition has diminished somewhat over time (as we will discuss below in the note on the 2010 Guidelines). The Guidelines use two important tools in defining the markets relevant for evaluating the effects of a merger: the "hypothetical monopolist test" and the "small but significant but non-transitory increase in price (SSNIP)" benchmark. The following section and examples from Section 4.1 of the 2010 Guidelines (reprinted in Appendix A of this casebook) explain:

> The Agencies employ the hypothetical monopolist test to evaluate whether groups of products in candidate markets are sufficiently broad to constitute relevant antitrust markets. The Agencies use the hypothetical monopolist test to identify a set of products that are reasonably inter-changeable with a product sold by one of the merging firms.

> The hypothetical monopolist test requires that a product market contain enough substitute products so that it could be subject to post-merger exercise of market power significantly exceeding that existing absent the merger. Specifically, the test requires that a hypothetical profit-maximizing firm, not subject to price regulation, that was the only present and future seller of those products ("hypothetical monopolist") likely would impose at least a small but significant and non-transitory increase in price ("SSNIP") on at least one product in the market, including at least one product sold by one of the merging firms. For the purpose of analyzing this issue, the terms of sale of products outside the candidate market are held constant. The SSNIP is employed solely as a methodological tool for performing the hypothetical monopolist test; it is not a tolerance level for price increases resulting from a merger.

> Groups of products may satisfy the hypothetical monopolist test without including the full range of substitutes from which customers choose. The hypothetical monopolist test may identify a group of products as a relevant market even if customers would substitute significantly to products outside that group in response to a price increase.

Example 5: Products A and B are being tested as a candidate market. Each sells for $100, has an incremental cost of $60, and sells 1200 units. For every dollar increase in the price of Product A, for any given price of Product B, Product A loses twenty units of sales to products outside the candidate market and ten units of sales to Product B, and likewise for Product B. Under these conditions, economic analysis shows that a hypothetical profit-maximizing monopolist controlling Products A and B would raise both of their prices by ten percent, to $110. Therefore, Products A and B satisfy the hypothetical monopolist test using a five percent SSNIP, and indeed for any SSNIP size up to ten percent. This is true even though two-thirds of the sales lost by one product when it raises its price are diverted to products outside the relevant market.

When applying the hypothetical monopolist test to define a market around a product offered by one of the merging firms, if the market includes a second product, the Agencies will normally also include a third product if that third product is a closer substitute for the first product than is the second product. The third product is a closer substitute if, in response to a SSNIP on the first product, greater revenues are diverted to the third product than to the second product.

Example 6: In Example 5, suppose that half of the unit sales lost by Product A when it raises its price are diverted to Product C, which also has a price of $100, while one-third are diverted to Product B. Product C is a closer substitute for Product A than is Product B. Thus Product C will normally be included in the relevant market, even though Products A and B together satisfy the hypothetical monopolist test.

The hypothetical monopolist test ensures that markets are not defined too narrowly, but it does not lead to a single relevant market. The Agencies may evaluate a merger in any relevant market satisfying the test, guided by the overarching principle that the purpose of defining the market and measuring market shares is to illuminate the evaluation of competitive effects. Because the relative competitive significance of more distant substitutes is apt to be overstated by their share of sales, when the Agencies rely on market shares and concentration, they usually do so in the smallest relevant market satisfying the hypothetical monopolist test.

Example 7: In Example 4, including cars in the market will lead to misleadingly small market shares for motorcycle producers. Unless motorcycles fail the hypothetical monopolist test, the Agencies would not include cars in the market in analyzing this motorcycle merger.

As the above section from the Guidelines shows, the antitrust agencies will use the hypothetical monopolist test to define markets in a manner most likely to capture the actual competitive effects of a merger. Of course, the definition of the market through the hypothetical monopolist and SSNIP tests says nothing about the *actual* structures of the relevant markets at issue in the merger. Market definition, therefore, is followed by a determination of the actual structures and levels of concentration in those markets.

For more than a half century, economists have been using "indexes" to measure the relative sizes or concentration of firms in a particular market. The 1968 Merger Guidelines issued by the Antitrust Division selected the Four-Firm Concentration Ratio (CR4) as an index for merger policy. The CR4, which is nothing more than the sum of the market shares of the four largest firms in the market, came to have a powerful influence on judicial treatment of mergers. It is still a commonly used index in antitrust litigation.

One of the most dramatic changes in the 1982/84 Merger Guidelines, continued to the 2010 Guidelines, is the abandonment of the CR4 in favor of the Herfindahl-Hirschman Index (HHI). The HHI consists of the sums of the squares of the market shares of all participants in the market.

There are important differences between the CR4 and the HHI. The most obvious have to do with use of data and scope of conclusions. On the one hand, the CR4 is easier to use than the HHI, for the CR4 requires market share information only about the four largest firms (although information about a few other firms may be necessary in order to determine which four are the largest). By contrast, the HHI requires market share information about every firm in the market, except perhaps for very small firms, whose impact on the HHI is very small. For this same reason, however, the HHI purports to "say" more about market concentration than the CR4. Because the data used in generating the HHI covers the entire market, the conclusion may be somehow more valid than a conclusion drawn from an examination of only four firms.

The HHI always responds to a particular merger in the same way. For example, a merger of a 10% firm and a 5% firm will always increase the HHI by 100. The effect of such a merger on the CR4 depends on how the two firms were ranked. If both firms were among the top four, they will become one and the CR4 will increase by the size of what had been the fifth firm. If neither firm was among the top four, the CR4 will remain unchanged, unless the post-merger firm becomes one of the top four. If the 10% firm was among the top four but the 5% firm was not, the CR4 will increase by five. Is the HHI's consistency superior? Probably not. The CR4 may be telling us that mergers by firms whose absolute size is the same, but whose relative size in relation to the rest of the market is greater, pose a greater anticompetitive threat.

The HHI is much more sensitive to errors in market share measurement, at least if a very large firm is measured incorrectly. This is so because the squaring of market shares tends to exaggerate such errors. For example, if a 35% firm is incorrectly measured as 40%, the CR4 increases by only five. The HHI will increase by 375. This makes accurate market definition particularly important when the HHI is used.

But there is a deeper differences between the two indexes: the HHI is much more sensitive than the CR4 to disparities *among* the sizes of the largest firms. In other words, the HHI captures the size distribution of firms' shares of the relevant market. For example, a market whose four largest firms each have 10% shares and one whose largest firm has a 37% share and whose second, third, and fourth firms have 1% each have the same CR4: 40. But the first market has an HHI of 400 (plus a 100 or 200 to account for other firms), while the second market has an HHI of 1,370 (plus 60 or 70 to account for other firms).

Why the large difference? The HHI is predicated on a "market dominance" model that weighs large firms very heavily into the calculus. For this reason, the choice of the HHI as a concentration index for the Merger Guidelines strikes some people as peculiar given that one of the central concerns of the Guidelines is coordination — i.e., increased post-merger ability of firms in the relevant market to facilitate express or tacit collusion (oligopoly). Is such collusion more likely to occur when a market is dominated by three or four firms of roughly equal size, or when it has one large firm and several smaller ones? That may depend on the type of collusion. Express collusion may work best when firms have more-or-less equal market shares and similar cost functions (which are more likely when the firms are about the same size). Certain forms of oligopoly "price leadership," by contrast, may work best when there is a single dominant firm large enough to discipline price-cutting rivals. Depending on the anticompetitive threat posed by a particular industry, the CR4 may actually predict performance more reliably. At least one study has found the CR4 to be superior in this as well as other respects. *See* Kwoka, *The Effect of Market Share Distribution on Industry Performance*, 61 REV. ECON. & STATISTICS 101 (1979). For a summary of findings comparing the two indexes, see 4 P. Areeda & H. Hovenkamp, Antitrust Law ¶¶ 930–931 (3d ed. 2009); Kwoka, *The Herfindahl Index in Theory and Practice*, 30 ANTITRUST BULL. 915 (1985).

This discussion should suggest to you that the CR4 and the HHI are alternative but not "equivalent" indexes. In a general sense, they both respond to increases in concentration, but at the margin they do so in very different ways. For example, an HHI reading of 1,000 can describe markets with CR4's ranging from 33.5 to 62. An HHI of 1,800 can describe markets with CR4's from 44.73 to 84.48. *See* Weinstock, *Some Little-Known Properties of the Herfindahl-Hirschman Index: Problems of Translation and Specification*, 29 ANTITRUST BULL. 705, 707 (1984).

Finally, and most importantly, there is no single "correct" index. A particular index is based on a particular theory about the relationship between structure and competition. There are a variety of such theories and they often conflict with each other. Furthermore, the CR4 may work better in some markets, while the HHI may be superior in others.

PROBLEM 7.2

Nine firms currently manufacture billups. Last year, the billup revenue of each of the firms was as follows: Firm A = \$8,000,000; Firm B = \$5,500,000; Firm C = \$5,000,000; Firm D = \$4,000,000; Firm E = \$3,000,000; Firm F = \$1,500,000; Firm G = \$1,000,000; Firm H = \$1,000,000; Firm I = \$1,000,000. Billups are undifferentiated, unbranded products, and all the firms have more-or-less the same costs. In response to a "small but significant and nontransitory increase in price," it would take at least four years for a new firm to begin manufacturing billups, but firms G, H, and I all have fairly substantial excess capacity. Customers have no good substitutes for billups. The firms are widely dispersed spatially, and transportation costs are relatively high. There is no known history of collusion or other anticompetitive behavior in the market, and it currently appears to be performing competitively. Firm C proposes to acquire Firm H. Analyze the merger under the DOJ Guidelines.

NOTE: THE 2010 HORIZONTAL MERGER GUIDELINES: KEY CHANGES AND INNOVATIONS

The 2010 Guidelines reflect more than slight revisions to the 1992 Horizontal Merger Guidelines, which had last been very modestly revised in 1997 to include a new efficiencies section; the new Guidelines incorporate important organizational and conceptual changes designed to better reflect how the agencies in practice evaluate whether a merger, in the words of Section 7 of the Clayton Act, "may substantially lessen competition."

Whereas the 1992 Guidelines contained six sections, the 2010 Guidelines contain 13 separate sections. Part of this difference reflects simple reorganization of topics into their own sections, but part lies in the addition and expansion of several topics. The 2010 Guidelines go from: (1) overview; to (2) evidence of adverse competitive effects; to (3) targeted customers and price discrimination; to (4) market definition; to (5) market participants, market shares, and market concentration; to (6) unilateral effects; to (7) coordinated effects; to (8) powerful buyers; to (9) entry; to (10) efficiencies; to (11) failure and exiting assets; to (12) mergers of competing buyers; to (13) partial acquisitions.

Note the relative placement of the market definition and adverse competitive effects sections in the two sets of Guidelines. Whereas the 1992 Guidelines began with market definition, the 2010 Guidelines begin with competitive effects and only later reach the issue of market definition. This reversal was deliberate and signals an emphasis on evidence of a merger's effects rather than on the often-formalistic exercise of market definition. The 2010 Guidelines expressly state at the beginning of Section 4.0:

> [t]he Agencies' analysis need not start with market definition. Some of the analytical tools used by the Agencies to assess competitive effects do not rely on market definition, although evaluation of competitive alternatives available to customers is always necessary at some point in the analysis.
>
> Evidence of competitive effects can inform market definition, just as market definition can be informative regarding competitive effects. For example, evidence that a reduction in the number of significant rivals offering a group of products causes prices for those products to rise significantly can itself establish that those products form a relevant market. Such evidence also may more directly predict the competitive effects of a merger, reducing the role of inferences from market definition and market shares.
>
> Where analysis suggests alternative and reasonably plausible candidate markets, and where the resulting market shares lead to very different inferences regarding competitive effects, it is particularly valuable to examine more direct forms of evidence concerning those effects.

The above passage marks an important change in the centrality of market definition in the agencies' analysis of mergers. This change has both practical and theoretical motivations. On the practical side, it is designed to show that the central issue in merger review is to determine competitive effects and that disputes over the precise location of market boundaries should not become unnecessary hurdles or distractions in that inquiry. On the more theoretical side, the change reflects the recognition that most mergers involve products that are to varying degrees imperfect substitutes for each other, in product markets that are "differentiated" in the degree to which consumer demand for any two products overlaps. Some products in a potential relevant market might be close substitutes and some more distant substitutes. Trying to draw a bright-line boundary around "the" relevant market is not a very promising or helpful enterprise. For that reason, the 2010 Guidelines explain that the agencies will use a variety of tools and evidence, of which market definition and concentration are included but neither exclusive nor necessarily primary.

The agencies nonetheless make clear that market definition, the SSNIP test, and market concentration all still play a very important role in merger analysis. The 2010 Guidelines do not abandon the tools or framework of the1992 Guidelines. The 2010 Guidelines retain the Herfindahl-Hirschman Index ("HHI") for measuring market concentration, although in Section 5.3 they do explain and adjust the thresholds as follows:

> Based on their experience, the Agencies generally classify markets into three types:
>
> - Unconcentrated Markets: HHI below 1500
>
> - Moderately Concentrated Markets: HHI between 1500 and 2500
>
> - Highly Concentrated Markets: HHI above 2500
>
> - *Small Change in Concentration:* Mergers involving an increase in the HHI of less than 100 points are unlikely to have adverse competitive effects and ordinarily require no further analysis.
>
> - *Unconcentrated Markets:* Mergers resulting in unconcentrated markets are unlikely to have adverse competitive effects and ordinarily require no further analysis.
>
> - *Moderately Concentrated Markets:* Mergers resulting in moderately concentrated markets that involve an increase in the HHI of more than 100 points potentially raise significant competitive concerns and often warrant scrutiny.
>
> - *Highly Concentrated Markets.* Mergers resulting in highly concentrated markets that involve an increase in the HHI of between 100 points and 200 points potentially raise significant competitive concerns and often warrant scrutiny. Mergers resulting in highly concentrated markets that involve an increase in the HHI of more than 200 points will be presumed to be likely to enhance market power. The presumption may be rebutted by persuasive evidence showing that the merger is unlikely to enhance market power.

The purpose of these thresholds is not to provide a rigid screen to separate acceptable mergers from anticompetitive transactions, although high levels of concentration do raise concerns. Rather, they provide one way to identify those mergers for which it is particularly important to examine whether other competitive factors confirm, reinforce, or would counteract the potentially harmful effects of increased concentration. The higher the post-merger HHI and the increase in the HHI, the greater is the likelihood that the Agencies will request additional information to conduct their analysis.

The 2010 Guidelines not only adjust the thresholds upward from their 1992 levels to bring them more into line with actual enforcement patterns, but also state more clearly what merging parties should expect if their transaction creates certain threshold levels of market concentration. Notably, the 2010 Guidelines state more clearly that the HHI thresholds should be read more as an indicator of whether the parties can expect a "second request" for information from the agencies than as a screen for whether or not the merger will ultimately receive approval.

Earlier in this note we mentioned differentiated product markets and why the use of tools other than market definition to assess competitive effects is particularly important in such markets. Section 6 of the 2010 Guidelines addresses "unilateral effects" from mergers, as discussed *infra*, and explains what some of those additional analytical tools might be. The 2010 Guidelines recognize that in differentiated product markets, the rate at which demand for one product "diverts" to another product as the price on the first product rises is a critical piece of information when assessing the competitive effects of a merger of the producers of the two products. Section 6 of the 2010 Guidelines builds on Section 2.2 of the 1992 Guidelines to present a much more developed analysis of unilateral effects, reflecting the growing importance of such effects in the agencies' merger investigations. Importantly, however, the 2010 Guidelines make clear in Section 1 that despite their expanded development of certain analytic tools for unilateral effects, "merger analysis does not consist of uniform application of a single methodology. Rather, it is a fact-specific process through which the Agencies . . . apply a range of analytic tools to the reasonably available and reliable evidence to evaluate competitive concerns in a limited period of time."

The 2010 Guidelines similarly expand on the 1992 Guidelines' treatment of other key topics such as coordinated effects (Section 7), innovation (Section 6.4), entry (Section 9), and mergers that create monopsony power through the consolidation of competing buyers (Section 12).

How the 2010 Guidelines will actually affect merger review and how, in turn, the courts will respond to the revised guidelines remains to be seen. As of this writing, no specific aspect of the 2010 Guidelines has been addressed by any court. Because the 2010 Guidelines are likely to be tested in court as they have been in effect longer, we encourage readers to study them and to compare them with the 1992 Guidelines in order better to understand the future direction of merger enforcement. Would any of the cases discussed in Chapter 7 that were decided under the 1992 Guidelines come out differently, or be analyzed differently, under the 2010 Guidelines? If so, how and why?

The 2010 Guidelines neither abandon market definition and structural analysis nor impose some new method of analysis that presumptively trumps conventional tools for evaluating a merger's potential competitive effects. The 2010 Guidelines do, however, make clear that the antitrust agencies do and will sometimes use analytic tools that do not depend on reviewing agency's having already defined the relevant market. As Section 6.1 of the 2010 Guidelines discusses, for example, in some cases there might be enough evidence to show (1) that two merging firms previously would have attracted customers from each other if one or the other of them had tried to raise price by 5–10% (i.e., impose a SSNIP), and (2) that by merging, the combined firm would recapture a sufficient proportion of the customers it previously would have diverted to turn an unprofitable per-merger price increase into a profitable post-merger price increase. Where the relevant data on margins and diversion ratios exists, the calculation of the upward pricing pressure that the merger could create can be made without knowing the specific boundaries or structure of the relevant market.

Continuing with the above example, one might ask whether it won't always be true that a merged entity will recapture some of the customers that would have been diverted to rivals had one of the firms tried to raise its price before the merger. For example, if 2 of 10 competing firms were to merge, multiplying the proportion of customers that the first merging firm would have lost to the second pre-merger times the margin the second firm earns on sales to its newly gained customers yields a quantity that the merged firm would recapture. Does that mean the merger is anticompetitive? Not unless the calculation showed enough recapture to make a SSNIP profitable, and not unless the other evidence in the case showed that the other eight firms in the market would for some reason be incapable of disciplining such a price increase. In other words, the merger would be unlikely under the facts given to be anticompetitive. Just as the HHI threshold of 1800 for a concentrated market under the 1992 Guidelines did not imply that any merger that significantly raised the HHI above that level would be challenged, the tools receiving expanded emphasis and development in the 2010 Guidelines will not be rigidly applied.

In *The 2010 Horizontal Merger Guidelines: From Hedgehog to Fox in Forty Years*, 77 Antitrust L.J. 701 (2010), Carl Shapiro, who as then-Deputy Assistant Attorney General for Economic Analysis at the Department of Justice was instrumental in drafting the 2010 Guidelines, explains further how the agencies intend to apply the 2010 Guidelines' analytical tools. In particular, Shapiro addresses the additional complexity some may perceive in the increased emphasis on analysis of competitive effects over market definition as the focus and objective of merger review:

> [T]he supposed simplicity and predictability based on market definition and market concentration was more apparent than real. Market definition is often disputed. In many merger investigations, such as the *Staples* or *Whole Foods* cases, the merging parties assert a broad market in which they argue that the post-merger HHI or the change in HHI is small, but the Agencies respond that the hypothetical monopolist test properly leads to a narrower market. Unfortunately, completely eliminating any uncertainty about the results of the hypothetical monopolist test is not possible. It is inherent in the need to measure "reasonable" interchangeability. Some of this uncertainty can be reduced, however, when one focuses on competitive effects rather than the line-drawing exercise of market definition. Furthermore, placing greater weight on market concentration does not eliminate uncertainty. The 1992 Guidelines state: "Where the postmerger

HHI exceeds 1800, it will be presumed that mergers producing an increase in the HHI of more than 100 points are likely to create or enhance market power or facilitate its exercise." Merger enforcement data show that this presumption has frequently been overcome. Few would favor giving the business community greater certainty by making this presumption irrebuttable.

[The] tradeoff between simple bright lines and accuracy is inherent in the antitrust review of proposed horizontal mergers. This fundamental tradeoff has been a consideration going back to *Philadelphia National Bank* and the 1968 Guidelines. The 1968 Guidelines are anything but flexible, but I doubt the business community would welcome a return to those Guidelines. Accounting for the real-world business conditions in which a merger takes place is worthwhile, even if doing so means that some simplicity must be sacrificed to achieve greater accuracy in merger enforcement.

NOTES AND QUESTIONS

1. How would some of the big 1960 s merger cases decided by the Supreme Court fare under the new merger Guidelines? For some, the answer is clear, assuming one accepts the market definitions adopted in those cases. In *Von's*, for example, Von's Grocery commanded 4.7% of the market, Shopping Bag 4.2% of the market, and the top four firms before the merger controlled about 25% of the market. This suggests a pre-merger HHI of less than 300 and a post-merger HHI of about 40 points higher. The *Von's* merger would certainly not be challenged under the new Guidelines.

The situation in *Brown Shoe* is a little more complex. The district court found that the merger of Brown's and Kinney's manufacturing plants was not illegal, and that finding was not challenged on appeal. Brown manufactured about 4% of the nation's shoes and Kinney about 0.5%. The 24 largest shoe manufacturers in the United States manufactured about 35% of the shoes. This certainly indicates that the industry was very diffuse.

Both the district court and the Supreme Court condemned the merger at the retail level, however. At the retail level, the relevant markets were found to be citywide, consisting of cities (including their suburbs) having a population of more than 10,000 and including one or more Brown retail stores and one or more Kinney retail stores. The Supreme Court condemned the merger in all such cities. However, the court's opinion reveals that the combined retail market shares of Brown and Kinney exceeded 20% in only 30 or so cities. It exceeded 30% in only a dozen cities, and 40% in only six cities. Although the opinion does not provide enough information to compute the HHI in each city, it is unlikely that the merger would be challenged in more than a dozen or so cities, even though there were well over 100 cities in which both Brown and Kinney operated retail stores. Under the "fix it first" rule that the agencies often employ, the merger would probably be permitted to proceed, but only after the company sold off the offending stores in those cities in which the post-merger concentration was too great.

2. How workable is a litigation strategy of defining a relevant market by hypothesizing a "small but significant and nontransitory increase in price," and then considering the number of customer defections and extent of entry by competitors? How accurately do you suppose an economist can "hypothesize" a "small but significant" increase — say, 5% — in the price of typewriters and predict how many typewriter customers will refuse to buy? Is this form of analysis any more accurate than the kind undertaken in *Brown Shoe* or *Philadelphia Bank*? For critiques, see Stigler & Sherwin, *The Extent of the Market*, 28 J.L. & ECON. 555, 582 (1985); Scheffman, *Merger Policy and Enforcement at the Federal Trade Commission: The Economist's View*, 54 ANTITRUST L.J. 117, 119 (1985); Harris & Jorde, *Market Definition in the Merger Guidelines: Implications for Antitrust Enforcement*, 71 CAL. L. REV. 464, 481 (1983).

4. *Facilitation of Collusion.* Notice the not-so-subtle shift in the focus of merger policy as expressed in the Guidelines. Traditionally, American merger policy was concerned with the merger that created the very large single firm. The earliest cases involved mergers that created dominant firms. But even in the 1960s, the most frequently articulated concern was single-firm dominance. That concern was often unrealistic, given a standard that condemned mergers creating market shares of as little as 5%.

One important difference between a focus on single-firm dominance and a focus on collusion is the perceived impact of the merger on competitors. Both single large firms and cartels can charge monopoly prices, but single large firms are probably more effective at exclusionary practices because it is difficult for a cartel to orchestrate them while disguising their concerted action. The Supreme Court made this observation in *Matsushita Elec. Indus. Co. v. Zenith Radio Corp.*, 475 U.S. 574, 590 (1986), when it opined that predatory pricing by a group of firms acting in concert was highly unlikely.

Thus, an important result of the Guidelines is that concern about injury to competitors has virtually dropped out of merger policy. Is this consistent with the legislative history of the Clayton Act? With the 1950 Amendments? (*See* the *Brown Shoe* case, *supra.*) Collusion, when it occurs, benefits rivals.

A more subtle shift between the 1982/1984 Guidelines and the 1992 and 2010 Guidelines is that, while both sets are concerned with facilitation of collusion, the 1992 Guidelines speak of "coordinated interaction" rather than collusion and the 2010 Guidelines speak even more broadly of "parallel accommodating conduct." Why are these differences important? Because the term "collusion" suggests price fixing, while "coordinated interaction" refers to *both* explicit price fixing and tacit oligopoly behavior, and "parallel accommodating conduct" may encompass purely individual firm conduct undertaken in anticipation of, but not coordination with, the conduct of rivals Many of the market conditions that make collusion easier also facilitate oligopolistic behavior — e.g., a small number of firms, high entry barriers, and homogenous products. The Guidelines' new usage suggests an increased role for "game theory" in future merger analysis. The relevant game theory deals with a firm's rational responses to the behavior of other firms when they are unable to reach an explicit "agreement." Often game theory suggests collusion-like outcomes that can be more stable than cartels, and hence are more likely to be socially damaging. *See* H. HOVENKAMP, FEDERAL ANTITRUST POLICY § 4.2 (4th ed. 2011).

5. In 1987, the National Association of Attorneys General (NAAG) of the 50 states adopted an alternative set of Guidelines for horizontal mergers. These Guidelines were substantially revised in 1993. The Guidelines were designed to apply to decisions by state attorneys general to enforce Section 7 of the Clayton Act, an authority which they have been held to have. *Georgia v. Pennsylvania R.R.*, 324 U.S. 439 (1945). However, the Guidelines also apply to decisions by state attorneys general to enforce the state merger statutes of their own respective states. At least tacitly, the Supreme Court has approved state challenges to mergers under federal law under standards that are inconsistent with the standards employed by the federal enforcement agencies. In *California v. American Stores Co.*, 495 U.S. 271 (1990), the Court held that a private person (in this case, the State of California, which is a "private" enforcer of the federal antitrust laws) may obtain divesture in a merger case. Importantly, the California challenge to the merger came after the Federal Trade Commission had already approved it.

The principal differences between the federal Guidelines and the Guidelines of the state attorneys general are in basic ideology and market definition. The state Guidelines argue that the purpose of merger enforcement is not necessarily to make markets more efficient, but rather to prevent wealth transfers from consumers to suppliers. As a result, they would presumably challenge any merger that threatened to yield a price increase, whether or not it produced compensating efficiencies. Respecting market definition, the state attorneys general reject the federal government's "five per cent" rule and simply look from the consumers' perspective to the range of products that consumers in general consider to be adequate substitutes. "A comparably priced substitute will be deemed suitable and thereby expand the product market definition if, and only if, considered suitable by customers accounting for 75% of the purchases."

See Harris & Jorde, *Antitrust Market Definition: An Integrated Approach*, 72 CAL. L. REV. 1 (1984), upon which the NAAG Guidelines relied for their relevant market analysis. *See also* Barnes, *Federal and State Philosophies in the Antitrust Law of Mergers*, 56 GEO. WASH. L. REV. 263 (1988).

Why would political officials representing the states be more concerned about mergers than those representing the federal government?

6. The *"Cellophane" Fallacy in the Federal Merger Guidelines.* The *Cellophane* fallacy, you may recall from Chapter 6, is the error of concluding that a firm is not a monopolist because it cannot profitably raise prices higher than the current level. In the *du Pont* (Cellophane) case, reprinted in Chapter 6, the Supreme Court concluded that cellophane was not a relevant market capable of being monopolized, for if du Pont increased cellophane prices by only a small amount, large numbers of customers would substitute waxed paper, glassine, or some other flexible packaging material. Quite possibly, however, this high cross-elasticity of demand existed between cellophane and its substitutes because du Pont was already charging its profit-maximizing price for cellophane, and could not profitably charge more.

The Merger Guidelines do something quite similar to what the Supreme Court did in the *du Pont* case. The Guidelines define markets in merger cases by beginning with the output of the merging firm, starting with current market prices, and then asking how many customers will walk away or how many new firms will enter in response to a "small but significant and nontransitory increase in price," often around 5%.

But what if the market is already subject to collusion? The effect may be that too large a market will be drawn. For example, the dominant firm in the market for electronic watches, which are cheap to produce, might face its principal competition from manufacturers of mechanical watches, which cost more to produce. As a result, the dominant electronic watch maker — with a share of the electronic watch market of, say, 80% — is able to charge prices well above its marginal costs. The mechanical watch makers have plenty of capacity but they have high costs. The smaller competing electronic watch makers have roughly the same costs as the dominant firm, but they do not have the additional capacity and will not have it for several years. The dominant maker of electronic watches may set its price very close to the price currently charged by the mechanical watch makers. In this market, by beginning with current market prices and then positing a "small but significant and nontransitory" price increase, the Department of Justice is likely to end up grouping the electronic and mechanical watches into the same market. The result is that it might permit the dominant electronic watch manufacturer to purchase its largest rival. If the market were correctly identified as electronic watches, the merger would be challenged.

Is the possible *Cellophane* fallacy in the Merger Guidelines a drafting error? Probably not, for two reasons. First of all, use of current market prices as a predicate for delineating markets is essential in any "quick look" market definition scheme (in fact, it may be essential in *all* market definition schemes). Current market prices are all that we have to go by. For example, if we knew what the competitive price (marginal cost) was, we could already see how much market power is being exercised in the market by comparing the competitive and actual prices. The *Cellophane* fallacy consists not in using current market prices as a basis for delineating markets, but in not understanding the limitations that such a use imposes.

Second, and more problematic, is the Antitrust Division's argument that the purpose of Section 7 is to condemn mergers that enhance or enlarge market power beyond the present level, not to minimize the amount of market power already being exercised. *See* Baxter, *Responding to the Reaction: The Draftsman's View*, 71 CAL. L. REV. 618, 623 and n.35 (1983). If collusion or monopoly pricing is already occurring in a market, as this argument goes, a merger among two of the participants will not make competition any worse than it already is, so the merger will not "lessen" competition.

But isn't this view somewhat naive about cartel behavior? Markets are functional, dynamic creatures. For many cartels, the biggest threat is not new entry by outsiders (which the Guidelines take into account in their discussion of entry barriers), but rather "cheating" by cartel members. Cartel cheating is unlikely to show up in the "prevailing market price" that the Antitrust Division uses under the Guidelines for one very good reason: the cheating, in order to be pulled off, must be disguised from fellow cartel members. If the cheater can hide it from fellow cartel members, he or she can probably hide it from the Antitrust Division as well. Perhaps the most direct form of cheating is secret rebates paid to buyers who choose a particular cartel member. But such rebates are probably not common today because they signal to customers that the market is cartelized. In a competitive, unregulated market, we do not expect sellers to say "the price of widgets is $10, but if you buy them from me I will secretly give you $2 back for each one you purchase." Rather, the cheating takes more subtle forms that do not show up in the price at all — principally, the provision of extra services. Manufacturers engaged in collusion may provide advertising services, delivery services, investment in retail stores, or may even redesign the product, or at least install add-ons, in order to convince a customer to purchase from them rather than a different cartel member. The result, of course, is that although the cartel price remains high, many of the profits are frittered away. A merger among cartel members in such a case can then facilitate collusion, not by increasing the prevailing price, but rather by decreasing the amount of such costly extras. The cartel with the costly extras is bad, but the cartel without them is worse. Such a merger facilitates collusion even though the prevailing market price does not change by one cent.

The same thing is generally true of tacit collusion, or oligopoly behavior. There is ample reason today for thinking that firms in oligopolized markets are quite inflexible about competing on price, but much more willing to compete by offering — often on a discriminatory basis — various kinds of services. A merger in such a market may likewise not affect prevailing prices very much, but may enable the firms in the market to avoid some of this service competition.

In short, a merger in a concentrated market where the dominant firms already have substantial power can make the market far more stable, even though it has little short run impact on the dominant firms' profit maximizing price. When mergers shrink, a concentrated market from five firms to four, or from six firms to five, collusion becomes easier to manage, the chance of detection by customers or enforcers is diminished, and long run stability becomes easier to achieve. Analysis of market power in merger cases should look very carefully at markets where the *Cellophane* fallacy is a possibility for the simple reason that these are markets that have demonstrated a capacity to perform anticompetitively at the current level of concentration; they are likely to become even more anticompetitive at higher concentration levels.

7. The 1984 Guidelines had stated that the relevant question for determining market boundaries was whether a single firm that controlled all sales in a provisional market could profitably impose a "small but significant and non-transitory" increase in price. The 2010 Guidelines (see Appendix A of this casebook) state the question differently, as "whether a hypothetical profit-maximizing firm . . . that was the only present and future producer or seller of those products in that area likely would impose at least a 'small but significant and nontransitory' increase in price. . . . " § 1.0. This difference becomes important when a 5% price increase would not be profitable to a monopolist or cartel but a much larger price increase would be.

For example, suppose a cartel of sellers *A*, *B*, and *C* is currently charging $1.00 per unit. It sells to two classes of buyers: a "high elasticity" class that is very sensitive at the current price level and will shift to different suppliers X, Y, and Z if the price rises above $1.02; a "low elasticity" class that does not have an adequate substitute for the product and is willing to pay any price up to $1.40. The former class accounts for 10 sales per period and the latter accounts for 90. This is a common situation. For example, an automobile maker may consider a heavy steel part as an adequate substitute for an aluminum part, but an aircraft maker would not.

In this case, assuming zero costs, a 5% price increase would be unprofitable to cartel ABC: pre-increase revenue is $100.00. If cartel ABC increases the price to $1.05, it will sell 90 units and total revenue will be $94.50. Further, this 5% price increase is unprofitable *because* the high elasticity customers shifted their purchases to X, Y, and Z; so the apparent result is that X, Y, and Z must be included in the relevant market.

However, if cartel ABC should raise its price to $1.40, the firms will also lose precisely the same 10 sales, but total revenue would go from $100.00 to 90 * $1.40, or $126.00, making this 40% price increase quite profitable. As a result, inclusion of X, Y, and Z in the market would be a serious error, and might result in approval of a merger involving A, B, or C, depending on their relative sizes compared to X, Y, and Z.

The new Guidelines correctly delineate the relevant market as the output of A, B, and C, excluding X, Y, and Z, on the principle that the profit-maximizing price increase for an ABC cartel is 5% *or more*.

Although this approach is technically more correct, it is more difficult to produce the relevant data. The economic expert must consider not only the profitability of a price increase of 5% above current levels, but of all possible price increases of 5% or more. As the hypothesized price increase departs further from current prices, estimates about customer responses become increasingly speculative.

8. Data released by the Federal Trade Commission on its merger enforcement activity revealed a fairly significant disparity between the thresholds stated in the 1992 Merger Guidelines and the actual practice of that government agency. *See* FTC, *Merger Challenges Data, Fiscal Years 1999–2003, available at* www.ftc.gov. The FTC rarely challenged mergers where the post-merger HHI fell below 2000, unless they involved the largest firms in the market. It has not challenged very many mergers where the post-merger HHI falls below 2400, unless the merger increased the HHI by 300 points or more. Mergers where the post-merger HHI falls between 1000 and 1800 are rarely challenged. The petroleum industry was one exception, where government practice seems to follow the Guidelines more closely. For historical perspective, see David Scheffman, Malcolm Coate & Louis Silvia, *20 Years of Merger Guidelines Enforcement at the FTC: an Economic Perspective, available at* www.usdoj.gov/atr/hmerger/11255.pdf. The authors note, for example, that price discrimination is relatively common in the petroleum industry, thus explaining what appears to be more aggressive merger enforcement there.

[2] Judicial Responses to the Merger Guidelines

FTC v. STAPLES, INC.

United States District Court, Dist. of Columbia, 970 F. Supp. 1066

(D.D.C. 1997)

THOMAS F. HOGAN, DISTRICT JUDGE.

Plaintiff, the Federal Trade Commission ("FTC" or "Commission"), seeks a preliminary injunction pursuant to Section 13(b) of the Federal Trade Commission Act, 15 U.S.C. § 53(b), to enjoin the consummation of any acquisition by defendant Staples, Inc., of defendant Office Depot, Inc. . . .

Defendants are both corporations which sell office products — including office supplies, business machines, computers and furniture — through retail stores, commonly described as office supply superstores, as well as through direct mail delivery and contract stationer operations. Staples is the second largest office superstore chain in the United States with approximately 550 retail stores located in 28 states and the District of Columbia, primarily in the Northeast and California. In 1996 Staples' revenues from those stores were approximately $4 billion through all operations. Office Depot, the largest office superstore chain, operates over 500 retail office supply superstores that are located in 38 states and the District of Columbia, primarily in the South and Midwest. Office Depot's 1996 sales were approximately $6.1 billion. OfficeMax, Inc., is the only other office supply superstore firm in the United States. . . .

Whenever the Commission has reason to believe that a corporation is violating, or is about to violate, Section 7 of the Clayton Act, the FTC may seek a preliminary injunction to prevent a merger pending the Commission's administrative adjudication of the merger's legality. . . . However, in a suit for preliminary relief, the FTC is not required to prove, nor is the Court required to find, that the proposed merger would in fact violate Section 7. . . . Federal Trade Commission Act, 15 U.S.C. § 53(b), provides that "[u]pon a proper showing that, weighing the equities and considering the Commission's likelihood of ultimate success, such action would be in the public interest. . . . " Courts have interpreted this to mean that a court must engage in a two-part analysis in determining whether to grant an injunction. . . . (1) First, the Court must determine the Commission's likelihood of success on the merits in its case under Section 7 of the Clayton Act, and (2) Second, the Court must balance the equities. *See FTC v. Freeman Hospital*, 69 F.3d 260, 267 (8th Cir. 1995). . . .

Likelihood of success on the merits in cases such as this means the likelihood that the Commission will succeed in proving, after a full administrative trial on the merits, that the effect of a merger between Staples and Office Depot "may be substantially to lessen competition, or to tend to create a monopoly" in violation of Section 7 of the Clayton Act. . . . It is not enough for the FTC to show merely that it has a "fair and tenable chance" of ultimate success on the merits as has been argued and rejected in other cases. *See FTC v. Freeman Hospital*, 69 F.3d 260, 267 (8th Cir. 1995). . . . However, the FTC need not prove to a certainty that the merger will have an anti-competitive effect. That is a question left to the Commission after a full administrative hearing. Instead, in a suit for a preliminary injunction, the government need only show that there is a "reasonable probability" that the challenged transaction will substantially impair competition. . . .

One of the few issues about which the parties to this case do not disagree is that metropolitan areas are the appropriate geographic markets for analyzing the competitive effects of the proposed merger. A geographic market is that geographic area "to which consumers can practically turn for alternative sources of the product and in which the antitrust defendant faces competition." *Morgenstern v. Wilson*, 29 F.3d 1291, 1296 (8th Cir. 1994), *cert. denied*, 513 U.S. 1150 (1995). In its first amended complaint, the FTC identified forty-two such metropolitan areas as well as future areas which could suffer anti-competitive effects from the proposed merger. Defendants have not challenged the FTC's geographic market definition in this proceeding. Therefore, the Court will accept the relevant geographic markets identified by the Commission.

In contrast to the parties' agreement with respect to the relevant geographic market, the Commission and the defendants sharply disagree with respect to the appropriate definition of the relevant product market or line of commerce. . . . The Commission defines the relevant product market as "the sale of consumable office supplies through office superstores," with "consumable" meaning products that consumers buy recurrently, i.e., items which "get used up" or discarded. For example, under the Commission's definition, "consumable office supplies" would not include capital goods such as computers, fax machines, and other business machines or office furniture, but does include such products as paper, pens, file folders, post-it notes, computer disks, and toner cartridges. The defendants characterize the FTC's product market definition as "contrived" with no basis in law or fact, and counter that the appropriate product market within which to assess the likely competitive consequences of a Staples-Office Depot combination is simply the overall sale of office products, of which a combined Staples-Office Depot accounted for 5.5% of total sales in North America in 1996. . . .

The consumable office products at issue here are identical whether they are sold by Staples or Office Depot or another seller of office supplies. A legal pad sold by Staples or Office Depot is "functionally interchangeable" with a legal pad sold by Wal-Mart. A post-it note sold by Staples or Office Depot is "functionally interchangeable" with a post-it note sold by Viking or Quill. . . .

The Court recognizes that it is difficult to overcome the first blush or initial gut reaction of many people to the definition of the relevant product market as the sale of consumable office supplies through office supply superstores. The products in question are undeniably the same no matter who sells them, and no one denies that many different types of retailers sell these products. After all, a combined Staples-Office Depot would only have a 5.5% share of the overall market in consumable office supplies. Therefore, it is logical to conclude that, of course, all these retailers compete, and that if a combined Staples-Office Depot raised prices after the merger, or at least did not lower them as much as they would have as separate companies, that consumers, with such a plethora of options, would shop elsewhere. . . . However, the mere fact that a firm may be termed a competitor in the overall marketplace does not necessarily require that it be included in the relevant product market for antitrust purposes. The Supreme Court has recognized that within a broad market, "well-defined submarkets may exist which, in themselves, constitute product markets for antitrust purposes." *Brown Shoe*. . . . There is a possibility, therefore, that the sale of consumable office supplies by office superstores may qualify as a submarket within a larger market of retailers of office supplies in general. . . .

[T]he FTC presented evidence comparing Staples' prices in geographic markets where Staples is the only office superstore, to markets where Staples competes with Office Depot or OfficeMax, or both. Based on the FTC's calculations, in markets where Staples faces no office superstore competition at all, something which was termed a one firm market during the hearing, prices are 13% higher than in three firm markets where it competes with both Office Depot and OfficeMax. The data which underly this conclusion make it compelling evidence. . . . Similarly, the evidence showed that Office Depot's prices are significantly higher — well over 5% higher, in Depot-only markets than they are in three firm markets. . . .

There is similar evidence with respect to the defendants' behavior when faced with entry of another competitor. The evidence shows that the defendants change their price zones[5] when faced with entry of another superstore, but do not do so for other retailers. For example, Staples changed its price zone for Cincinnati to a lower priced zone when Office Depot and OfficeMax entered that area. . . . There are numerous additional examples of zones being changed and prices falling as a result of superstore entry. There is no evidence that zones change and prices fall when another non-superstore retailer enters a geographic market.

Though individually the FTC's evidence can be criticized for looking at only brief snapshots in time or for considering only a limited number of [areas], taken together, however, the Court finds this evidence a compelling showing that a small but significant increase in Staples' prices will not cause a significant number of consumers to turn to non-superstore alternatives for purchasing their consumable office supplies. Despite the high degree of functional interchangeability between consumable office supplies sold by the office superstores and other retailers of office supplies, the evidence presented by the Commission shows that even where Staples and Office Depot charge higher prices, certain consumers do not go elsewhere for their supplies. This further demonstrates that the sale of office supplies by non-superstore retailers are not responsive to the higher prices charged by Staples and Office Depot in the one firm markets. This indicates a low cross-elasticity of demand between the consumable office supplies sold by the superstores and those sold by other sellers. . . .

When assessing key trends and making long range plans, Staples and Office Depot focus on the plans of other superstores. In addition, when determining whether to enter a new metropolitan area, both Staples and Office Depot evaluate the extent of office superstore competition in the market and the number of office superstores the market can support. When selecting sites and markets for new

---

[5] [The record showed that the merger participants placed each store into a pre-designated price "zone" depending on the identity and amount of competition it faced in that area —ed.]

store openings, defendants repeatedly refer to markets without office superstores as "non-competitive," even when the new store is adjacent to or near a warehouse club, consumer electronics store, or a mass merchandiser such as Wal-Mart. In a monthly report entitled "Competitor Store Opening/Closing Report" which Office Depot circulates to its Executive Committee, Office Depot notes all competitor store closings and openings, but the only competitors referred to for its United States stores are Staples and OfficeMax. . . .

After accepting the Commission's definition of the relevant product market, the Court next must consider the probable effect of a merger between Staples and Office Depot in the geographic markets previously identified. One way to do this is to examine the concentration statistics and HHIs within the geographic markets. If the relevant product market is defined as the sale of consumable office supplies through office supply superstores, the HHIs in many of the geographic markets are at problematic levels even before the merger. Currently, the least concentrated market is that of Grand Rapids-Muskegon-Holland, Michigan, with an HHI of 3,597, while the most concentrated is Washington, D.C. with an HHI of 6,944. In contrast, after a merger of Staples and Office Depot, the least concentrated area would be Kalamazoo-Battle Creek, Michigan, with an HHI of 5,003, and many areas would have HHIs of 10,000. The average increase in HHI caused by the merger would be 2,715 points. The concentration statistics show that a merged Staples-Office Depot would have a dominant market share in 42 geographic markets across the country. The combined shares of Staples and Office Depot in the office superstore market would be 100% in 15 metropolitan areas. It is in these markets the post-merger HHI would be 10,000. In 27 other metropolitan areas, where the number of office superstore competitors would drop from three to two, the post-merger market shares would range from 45% to 94%, with post-merger HHIs ranging from 5,003 to 9,049. Even the lowest of these HHIs indicates a "highly concentrated" market. . . .

Barriers to Entry

The defendants argued during the hearing and in their briefs that the rapid growth in overall office supply sales has encouraged and will continue to encourage expansion and entry. One reason for this, according to Dr. Hausman's declaration, is that entry is more attractive when an industry is growing, because new entrants can establish themselves without having to take all of their sales away from existing competitors. In addition, the defendants' impressive retailing expert, Professor Maurice Segall, testified at the hearing that there are "no barriers to entry in retailing," and defendants pointed to the fact that all office superstore entrants have entered within the last 11 years. . . .

There are problems with the defendants' evidence, however, that prevent the Court from finding in this case that entry into the market by new competitors or expansion into the market by existing firms would likely avert the anti-competitive effects from Staples' acquisition of Office Depot. For example, while it is true that all office superstore entrants have entered within the last 11 years, the recent trend for office superstores has actually been toward exiting the market rather than entering. Over the past few years, the number of office superstore chains has dramatically dropped from twenty-three to three. All but Staples, Office Depot, and OfficeMax have either closed or been acquired. The failed office superstore entrants include very large, well-known retail establishments such as Kmart, Montgomery Ward, Ames, and Zayres. A new office superstore would need to open a large number of stores nationally in order to achieve the purchasing and distribution economies of scale enjoyed by the three existing firms. Sunk costs would be extremely high. Economies of scale at the local level, such as in the costs of advertizing and distribution, would also be difficult for a new superstore entrant to achieve since the three existing firms have saturated many important local markets. For example, according to the defendants' own saturation analyses, Staples estimates that there is room for less than two additional superstores in the Washington, D.C. area and Office Depot estimates that there is room for only two more superstores in Tampa, Florida. . . .

For the reasons discussed above, the Court finds it extremely unlikely that a new office superstore will enter the market and thereby avert the anti-competitive effects from Staples' acquisition of Office Depot. . . .

Efficiencies

Whether an efficiencies defense showing that the intended merger would create significant efficiencies in the relevant market, thereby offsetting any anti-competitive effects, may be used by a defendant to rebut the government's prima facie case is not entirely clear. The newly revised efficiencies section of the Merger Guidelines recognizes that, "mergers have the potential to generate significant efficiencies by permitting a better utilization of existing assets, enabling the combined firm to achieve lower costs in producing a given quality and quantity than either firm could have achieved without the proposed transaction." See Merger Guidelines § 4. This coincides with the view of some courts that "whether an acquisition would yield significant efficiencies in the relevant market is an important consideration in predicting whether the acquisition would substantially lessen competition. . . . [T]herefore, . . . an efficiency defense to the government's prima facie case in section 7 challenges is appropriate in certain circumstances." *FTC v. University Health*, 938 F.2d 1206, 1222 (11th Cir. 1991). The Supreme Court, however, in *FTC v. Procter & Gamble Co.*, 386 U.S. 568, 579, 87 S. Ct. 1224, 1230, 18 L. Ed. 2d 303 (1967), stated that "[p]ossible economics cannot be used as a defense to illegality in section 7 merger cases." There has been great disagreement regarding the meaning of this precedent and whether an efficiencies defense is permitted. Compare *RSR Corp. v. FTC*, 602 F.2d 1317, 1325 (9th Cir. 1979)445 U.S. 927 (1980) with *University Health*, 938 F.2d at 1222 (recognizing the defense). . . . Assuming that it is a viable defense, however, the Court cannot find in this case that the defendants' efficiencies evidence rebuts the presumption that the merger may substantially lessen competition or shows that the Commission's evidence gives an inaccurate prediction of the proposed acquisition's probable effect.

The Court agrees with the defendants that where, as here, the merger has not yet been consummated, it is impossible to quantify precisely the efficiencies that it will generate. In addition, the Court recognizes a difference between efficiencies which are merely speculative and those which are based on a prediction backed by sound business judgment. Nor does the Court believe that the defendants must prove their efficiencies by "clear and convincing evidence" in order for those efficiencies to be considered by the Court. That would saddle Section 7 defendants with the nearly impossible task of rebutting a possibility with a certainty, a burden which was rejected in *United States v. Baker Hughes, Inc.*, 908 F.2d 981, 992 (D.C. Cir. 1990). Instead, like all rebuttal evidence in Section 7 cases, the defendants must simply rebut the presumption that the merger will substantially lessen competition by showing that the Commission's evidence gives an inaccurate prediction of the proposed acquisition's probable effect. See id. at 991. Defendants, however, must do this with credible evidence, and the Court with respect to this issue did not find the defendants' evidence to be credible.

Defendants submitted an "Efficiencies Analysis" which predicated that the combined company would achieve savings of between $4.9 and $6.5 billion over the next five years. In addition, the defendants argued that the merger would also generate dynamic efficiencies. For example, defendants argued that as suppliers become more efficient due to their increased sales volume to the combined Staples-Office Depot, they would be able to lower prices to their other retailers. Moreover, defendants argued that two-thirds of the savings realized by the combined company would be passed along to consumers.

. . . [T]he cost savings estimate of $4.947 billion over five years which was submitted to the Court exceeds by almost 500% the figures presented to the two Boards of Directors in September 1996, when the Boards approved the transaction. The cost savings claims submitted to the Court are also substantially greater than those represented in the defendants' Joint Proxy Statement/Prospectus "reflecting the best currently available estimate of management," and filed with the Securities and Exchange Commission on January 23, 1997. . . .

There are additional examples of projected savings, such as the projected savings on employee health insurance, which are not merger specific, but the Court need not discuss every example here. However, in addition to the non-merger specific projected savings, Mr. Painter also revealed problems with the defendants' methodology in making some of the projections. For example, in calculating the projected cost savings from vendors, Staples estimated cost savings for a selected group of vendors, and then extrapolated these estimated savings to all other vendors. Mr. Painter testified that, although Hewlett Packard is Staples' single largest vendor, it was not one of the vendors used for the savings estimate. In addition, the evidence shows that Staples was not confident that it could improve its buying from Hewlett Packard. Yet, Staples' purchases and sales of Hewlett Packard products were included in the "all other" vendor group, and defendants , thereby, attributed cost savings in the amount of $207 million to Hewlett Packard even though Staples' personnel did not believe that they could, in fact, achieve cost savings from Hewlett Packard.

In addition to the problems that the Court has with the efficiencies estimates themselves, the Court also finds that the defendants' projected pass through rate — the amount of the projected savings that the combined company expects to pass on to customers in the form of lower prices — is unrealistic. The Court has no doubt that a portion of any efficiencies achieved through a merger of the defendants would be passed on to customers. Staples and Office Depot have a proven track record of achieving cost savings through efficiencies, and then passing those savings to customers in the form of lower prices. However, in this case the defendants have projected a pass through rate of two-thirds of the savings while the evidence shows that, historically, Staples has passed through only 15-17%. Based on the above evidence, the Court cannot find that the defendants have rebutted the presumption that the merger will substantially lessen competition by showing that, because of the efficiencies which will result from the merger, the Commission's evidence gives an inaccurate prediction of the proposed acquisition's probable effect.

[The court then concluded that the private losses from temporary prohibition of the merger failed to outweigh the threat of public injury if it occurred; thus, the equities favored granting the preliminary injunction.]

NOTES AND QUESTIONS

1.   The defendants subsequently scrapped their merger plans.

2.   *Submarkets in Merger Cases.* Ever since *Brown Shoe Co. v. United States*, 370 U.S. 294 (1962), so-called "submarkets" have played an important role in merger litigation. As *Brown Shoe* explained:

> The outer boundaries of a product market are determined by the reasonable interchangeability of use or the cross-elasticity of demand between the product itself and substitutes for it. However, within this broad market, well-defined submarkets may exist which, in themselves, constitute product markets for antitrust purposes. The boundaries of such a submarket may be determined by examining such practical indicia as industry or public recognition of the submarket as a separate economic entity, the product's peculiar characteristics and uses, unique production facilities, distinct customers, distinct prices, sensitivity to price changes, and specialized vendors.

Id. at 325–326.

At this time, you should reread the note on submarkets in monopolization cases, reprinted *supra* Chapter 6, following the *Aspen* decision. As that discussion observes, the concept of a "submarket" is contradictory to the existence of a larger market. To say that a grouping of sales is a "market" implies a high degree of consumption or production substitutability among them. To say that some segment of this grouping constitutes a "submarket" is to say that there is not sufficiently high substitutability between the market sales inside the submarket and the market sales outside the submarket. In short, if a grouping of sales is really a "market," it can logically contain no submarket. Antitrust would be far better off had we never heard of submarkets.

3.   Do submarkets survive as a concept under the 2010 Merger Guidelines? Consider the smallest market principle articulated in Section 4 of the current Guidelines. Doesn't that principle effectively do away with the unhelpful notion of submarkets?

4. How would *Staples* come out under the 2010 Guidelines? Are the new Guidelines more or less hospitable to the FTC's analysis in *Staples* than were the 1992 Guidelines that were in place when the case was decided? In what ways?

5. In a 2007 enforcement action against the merger of Whole Foods Market and Wild Oats Markets, the Federal Trade Commission tried to define the market as "premium natural and organic" (PNO) supermarkets. The FTC's theory was similar to that in Staples, in that the Commission tried to show that other kinds of supermarkets, despite carrying some competitive products and facing low barriers to entry to competition against PNO supermarkets, failed to provide meaningful competition in the PNO market. In this case the district court ruled against the FTC, finding that PNO markets did in fact regard non-PNO markets as competitors and that non-PNO markets had repositioned themselves to compete against the PNO stores. The district court also found that grocery consumers were price-sensitive and regularly "cross-shopped" among a variety of supermarkets for their goods. *FTC v. Whole Foods Mkt., Inc.*, 502 F. Supp. 2d 1 (D.D.C. 2007). Unlike in *Staples*, where the merging parties' prices were higher in geographic markets without a competing office superstore, in Whole Foods the court found the merging parties' prices to be constrained by conventional supermarkets even without a competing PNO supermarket in a given geographic market. *Id.* The court therefore concluded that although PNO supermarkets were differentiated from non-PNO supermarkets, they were not sufficiently so to constitute a relevant market unto themselves. *Id.* The FTC, however, prevailed on appeal, successfully making a case for a narrower market definition than the district court had been willing to credit. *FTC v. Whole Foods Markets*, 548 F.3d 1028 (D.C. Cir. 2008).

HOSPITAL CORP. OF AMERICA v. FTC
807 F.2d 1381 (7th Cir. 1986), *cert. denied*, 481 U.S. 1038 (1987)

POSNER, CIRCUIT JUDGE.

Hospital Corporation of America, the largest proprietary hospital chain in the United States, asks us to set aside the decision by the Federal Trade Commission that it violated section 7 of the Clayton Act by the acquisition in 1981 and 1982 of two corporations, Hospital Affiliates International, Inc. and Health Care Corporation. Before these acquisitions (which cost Hospital Corporation almost $700 million), Hospital Corporation had owned one hospital in Chattanooga, Tennessee. The acquisitions gave it ownership of two more. In addition, pursuant to the terms of the acquisitions it assumed contracts, both with four-year terms, that Hospital Affiliates International had made to manage two other Chattanooga- area hospitals. So after the acquisitions Hospital Corporation owned or managed 5 of the 11 hospitals in the area. . . .

If all the hospitals brought under common ownership or control by the two challenged acquisitions are treated as a single entity, the acquisitions raised Hospital Corporation's market share in the Chattanooga area from 14 percent to 26 percent. This made it the second largest provider of hospital services in a highly concentrated market where the four largest firms together had a 91 percent market share compared to 79 percent before the acquisitions. . . .

. . . .

When an economic approach is taken in a section 7 case, the ultimate issue is whether the challenged acquisition is likely to facilitate collusion. In this perspective the acquisition of a competitor has no economic significance in itself; the worry is that it may enable the acquiring firm to cooperate (or cooperate better) with other leading competitors on reducing or limiting output, thereby pushing up the market price. . . .

The acquisitions reduced the number of competing hospitals in the Chattanooga market from 11 to 7. . . .

The reduction in the number of competitors is significant in assessing the competitive vitality of the Chattanooga hospital market. The fewer competitors there are in a market, the easier it is for them to coordinate their pricing without committing detectable violations of section 1 of the Sherman Act, which forbids price fixing. This would not be very important if the four competitors eliminated by the acquisitions in this case had been insignificant, but they were not; they accounted in the aggregate for 12 percent of the sales of the market. As a result of the acquisitions the four largest firms came to control virtually the whole market, and the problem of coordination was therefore reduced to one of coordination among these four.

Moreover, both the ability of the remaining firms to expand their output should the big four reduce their own output in order to raise the market price (and, by expanding, to offset the leading firms' restriction of their own output), and the ability of outsiders to come in and build completely new hospitals, are reduced by Tennessee's certificate-of-need law. Any addition to hospital capacity must be approved by a state agency. . . . Should the leading hospitals in Chattanooga collude, a natural consequence would be the creation of excess hospital capacity, for the higher prices resulting from collusion would drive some patients to shorten their hospital stays and others to postpone or reject elective surgery. If a noncolluding hospital wanted to expand its capacity so that it could serve patients driven off by the high prices charged by the colluding hospitals, the colluders would have not only a strong incentive to oppose the grant of a certificate of need but also substantial evidence with which to oppose it — the excess capacity (in the market considered as a whole) created by their own collusive efforts. At least the certificate of need law would enable them to delay any competitive sally by a noncolluding competitor. . . .

All this would be of little moment if, in the event that hospital prices in Chattanooga rose above the competitive level, persons desiring hospital services in Chattanooga would switch to hospitals in other cities, or to nonhospital providers of medical care. But this would mean that the Chattanooga hospital market, which is to say the set of hospital-services providers to which consumers in Chattanooga can feasibly turn, includes hospitals in other cities plus nonhospital providers both in Chattanooga and elsewhere; and we do not understand Hospital Corporation to be challenging the Commission's market definition, which is limited to hospital providers in Chattanooga. Anyway, these competitive alternatives are not important enough to deprive the market shares statistics of competitive significance. Going to another city is out of the question in medical emergencies; and even when an operation or some other hospital service can be deferred, the patient's doctor will not (at least not for reasons of price) send the patient to another city, where the doctor is unlikely to have hospital privileges. Finally, although hospitals increasingly are providing services on an out-patient basis, thus competing with nonhospital providers of the same services (tests, minor surgical procedures, etc.), most hospital services cannot be provided by nonhospital providers; as to these, hospitals have no competition from other providers of medical care. . . .

All these considerations, taken together, supported — we do not say they compelled — the Commission's conclusion that the challenged acquisitions are likely to foster collusive practices, harmful to consumers, in the Chattanooga hospital market. Section 7 does not require proof that a merger or other acquisition has caused higher prices in the affected market. All that is necessary is that the merger create an appreciable danger of such consequences in the future. . . .

But of course we cannot just consider the evidence that supports the Commission's prediction. We must consider all the evidence in the record. We must therefore consider the significance of the facts, pressed on us by Hospital Corporation, that hospital services are complex and heterogeneous, that the sellers in this market are themselves heterogeneous because of differences in the services provided by the different hospitals and differences in the corporate character of the hospitals (some are publicly owned, some are proprietary, and some are private but nonprofit), that the hospital industry is undergoing rapid technological and economic change, that the payors for most hospital services (Blue Cross and other insurance companies, and the federal government) are large and knowledgeable, and that the FTC's investigation which led to this proceeding was touched off by a complaint from a competitor of Hospital Corporation. Most of these facts do detract from a conclusion that collusion in this market is a serious danger, but it was for the Commission — it is not for us — to determine their weight.

The first fact is the least impressive. It is true that hospitals provide a variety of different services many of which are "customized" for the individual patient, but the degree to which this is true seems no greater than in other markets. Although collusion is more difficult the more heterogeneous the output of the colluding firms, there is no established threshold of complexity beyond which it is infeasible and Hospital Corporation made no serious effort to show that hospital services are more complex than products and services in other markets, such as steel, building materials and transportation, which collusion has been frequent.

The heterogeneity of the sellers has two aspects: the hospitals in Chattanooga offer different mixtures of services; and they have different types of ownership — private for-profit ("proprietary"), private not-for-profit, public. The significance of these features is unclear. Concerning the first, if one assumes that collusion is practiced on a service-by-service basis, the fact that hospitals provide different mixtures of service seems irrelevant to the feasibility of collusion. True, since different types of service may not be substitutable — open-heart surgery is not a substitute for setting a broken leg — specialized hospitals might not compete with one another. But that is not Hospital Corporation's argument. Its argument is that the different mixture of services in the different hospitals would make it difficult for their owners to fix prices of competing services, and this we don't understand.

Different ownership structures might reduce the likelihood of collusion but this possibility is conjectural and the Commission was not required to give it conclusive weight. . . . Nonprofit status affects the method of financing the enterprise (substituting a combination of gift and debt financing for equity and debt financing) and the form in which profits (in the sense of the difference between revenue and costs) are distributed, and it may make management somewhat less beady-eyed in trying to control costs. But no one has shown that it makes the enterprise unwilling to cooperate in reducing competition — which most enterprises dislike and which nonprofit enterprises may dislike on ideological as well as selfish grounds. . . .

. . . .

Hospital Corporation's most telling point is that the impetus for the Commission's complaint came from a competitor — a large nonprofit hospital in Chattanooga. A rational competitor would not complain just because it thought that Hospital Corporation's acquisitions would facilitate collusion. Whether the competitor chose to join a cartel or stay out of it, it would be better off if the cartel were formed than if it were not formed. For the cartel would enable this seller to raise its price, whether or not to the cartel level. By staying out of the cartel and by pricing just below the cartel price, the competitor might, as we noted earlier, do even better than by joining the cartel.

The hospital that complained to the Commission must have thought that the acquisitions would lead to lower rather than higher prices — which would benefit consumers, and hence, under contemporary principles of antitrust law, would support the view that the acquisitions were lawful. But this is just one firm's opinion. It was not binding on the Commission, which having weighed all the relevant facts concluded that the acquisitions had made collusion in this market significantly more likely than before. Since, moreover, the complainant was a nonprofit hospital, in attributing the complaint to fear of lower prices Hospital Corporation is contradicting its argument that the non-profit sector of the hospital industry does not obey the laws of economic self-interest.

. . . .

The Commission's order is affirmed and enforced. 15 U.S.C. § 21(c).

NOTES AND QUESTIONS

1. The *Hospital* case generally looks at much simpler indicia of injury to competition than the Merger Guidelines suggest. *See also FTC v. Elders Grain,* 868 F.2d 901 (7th Cir. 1989), where the court dwelt mainly on the fact that the merger would reduce the number of large firms in the market from six to five, thus facilitating collusion. The court concluded:

> The penalties for price-fixing are now substantial, but they are brought into play only where sellers actually agree on price or output or other dimensions of competition; and if conditions are ripe, sellers may not have to communicate or otherwise collude overtly in order to coordinate their price and output decisions; at least they may not have to collude in a readily detectable manner.

Contrast this with the approach of the Federal Trade Commission in *B.F. Goodrich Co.*, 5 Trade Reg. Rep. (CCH) ¶ 22,519 (F.T.C. 1988), which required the fact finder to estimate the increased likelihood of collusion that might result from a merger by determining whether there were

> (1) relatively high barriers or impediments to entry; (2) a relatively high level of concentration; (3) a low level of product differentiation, and a low level of geographic differentiation occasioned by transportation cost differences; (4) a relatively inelastic demand for industry output at competitive price levels; (5) insignificant intra-industry differences in cost functions; (6) a large number of small buyers; (7) a high degree of transaction frequency and visibility; and (8) relatively stable and predictable demand and supply conditions.

Which approach seems best calculated to produce accurate merger decisions?

2. *Entry Barriers Under the Merger Guidelines.* The 2010 Horizontal Merger Guidelines, §§ 9.0 *et seq.*, contain an elaborate discussion of barriers to entry, which are market conditions that tend to preclude competitors from entering the market even when prices are higher than the competitive level. The elaborate discussion is actually a corrective of a very spare statement in the 1984 Guidelines saying simply that mergers would not be challenged "if entry . . . is so easy that existing competitors could not succeed in raising price. . . . " The Government then lost some cases in which entry appeared easy even though the markets were concentrated. *See, e.g., United States v. Waste Management*, 743 F.2d 976, 981 (2d Cir. 1984); *United States v. Country Lake Foods*, 754 F. Supp. 669, 678 (D. Minn. 1990).

The Guidelines define low entry barriers in terms of *timeliness, likelihood,* and *sufficiency* of entry. Entry is considered to be "timely" only if it can "achieve significant market impact" within a two-year period following the post-merger price increase. Entry is considered to be "likely" only if it would have been profitable at pre-merger levels. Obviously, entry is not likely to occur unless it is profitable to the entrant. If not profitable at pre-merger price levels, moreover, entry cannot protect consumers by maintaining or restoring pre-merger prices. In making this calculation, the Guidelines adopt the criterion of "minimum viable scale" entry. The government first determines the minimum scale of production necessary for the new entrant's profitability at pre-merger prices. It then considers whether adding that volume of production to the market would drive prices below pre-merger levels. If not, entry will be considered likely. Finally, entry is considered "sufficient" only if the new entrant would have adequate access to needed inputs so that its output will be able to restore prices to pre-merger levels. This may not occur if incumbents control all or most of some essential input.

In sum, when analyzing a merger in a concentrated market, the government will consider whether entry is likely to occur within two years after the merger, and if such entry will be sufficient to drive prices back to pre-merger levels.

In addition, a merger is less likely to be anticompetitive if smaller firms in the market are able to increase their own output significantly in response to a post-merger price increase. In *State of New York v. Kraft General Foods*, 926 F. Supp. 321 (S.D.N.Y. 1995), the court refused to enjoin a merger of two major ready-to-eat breakfast cereal companies. During the preceding few years, private label brands had grown from less than 5% to more than 9% of the relevant market. The evidence suggested they would grow even more if the post-merger firm attempted to raise prices. But query: is this relaxed attitude consistent with the theory that mergers are unlawful because they tend to facilitate collusion or oligopoly coordination? At a certain concentration level, might it not be in the smaller firms' interest to participate in the cartel rather than grow their market shares?

3. In *FTC v. Arch Coal, Inc.*, 329 F. Supp. 2d 109 (D.D.C. 2004), the court rejected the FTC's request for a preliminary injunction against a merger of two coal producers. The court concluded that the government made out a prima facie case of illegality when the HHI based on coal reserves was 2103 and the HHI increase resulting from the merger was 49. Nevertheless,

> ". . . it is important to note that this case is not one in which the post-merger increase in HHI produces an overwhelming statistical case for the likely creation or enhancement of anticompetitive market power. Indeed, the single best available measure of market concentration — reserves — produces an increase in HHI of only 49, which is actually below the level for significant concern in the highly concentrated SPRB market. [That is, coal produced in the Southern Powder River Basin (SPRB) of Wyoming — Eds.] The measure plaintiffs urge — loadout capacity — only produces an HHI increase of 224. Such HHI increases are far below those typical of antitrust challenges brought by the FTC and DOJ. For example, in Heinz the HHI increase was 510 based on a pre-merger HHI of 4775. *See* 246 F.3d at 716. In *Baker Hughes* the HHI increase was 1425, from 2878 pre-merger to 4303 post-merger. *See* 908 F.2d at 983 n. 3. In *Staples* the average HHI increase in the several markets under consideration was 2715. See 970 F. Supp. at 1082. And in *FTC v. Libbey, Inc.*, 211 F. Supp. 2d 34, 51 (D.D.C.2002), the impact of the original merger agreement (used by the court for its analysis) was an HHI increase of 1052. All of these levels of HHI increase dwarf even the highest increase arguably present here. [FN12] Indeed, between 1999 and 2003, only twenty-six merger challenges out of 1,263 (two percent) occurred in markets with comparable concentration levels to those argued here. *See* DX 0833 (Federal Trade Comm'n & United States Dep't of Justice, *Merger Challenges Data, Fiscal Years 1999-2003* (Dec. 18, 2003)).

The district court also faulted the FTC's "novel theory" that after the merger the major firms in the market would limit their output so that demand would push prices higher. However, the court suggested, previous cases involved challenges to mergers based on the increased risk of price coordination.

Is the court correct? Most cartels coordinate output rather than price. Indeed, in orthodox noncooperative oligopoly, the theory upon which the government's Merger Guidelines are based, output is the variable that the firms select. As a result, there is nothing novel about the theory that following a merger the firms would find it easier to coordinate output. The court then found that while there was adequate structural evidence that the markets were conducive to coordinated interaction, in fact there was relatively little history of such interaction. Although there was considerable discussion among firms of the need to keep production down, the court found no production decreases that did not have non-collusive explanations, and it found no effort to discipline firms who bid aggressively. As the court concluded, "[t]he structure and dynamics of the SPRB market may permit coordination, but do not make coordination likely." For example, the market placed great emphasis on sealed competitive bids and confidentiality, which the court believed made coordinated interaction less likely. Most of the sales were short term, and changes in the market were difficult to predict. Further,

> Tacit agreement would also be difficult to coordinate in this marketplace because the terms of agreement would be hard to communicate between producers, even though tacit agreement only requires producers to adopt a uniform strategy that is consistent with less aggressive competition. Moreover, there is no effective mechanism in the SPRB to discipline any producer that would deviate from the terms of coordination. Plaintiffs' economic expert posited no theory for punitive discipline among producers. Due to the nature of the confidential bidding and contracting process that gives producers incentives to submit aggressive bids to capture long term contracts, cheating would not be detected until well after the fact, if ever, and any punishment would come well after the fact as well. Such delays in detection or punishment generally mean that deviations are likely and that coordinated interaction is unlikely to succeed.

The court also noted that there was a fringe of producers who were likely to expand output in response to a price increase.

The court then denied a preliminary injunction, with these observations:

> Among the conclusions reasonably drawn from an examination of the record evidence relating to the operation of the SPRB coal market are the following. Although the tacit coordination on production by major SPRB producers feared by the FTC is feasible, and some producers have indicated an interest in greater production discipline in the market, the SPRB has been (and remains) a competitive market with no historical evidence of actual express or tacit anticompetitive coordination. Production in the SPRB has increased steadily over the past decade. Neither the 2001 price spike (which is explained by factors other than tacit coordination to limit production) nor occasional mine closures in 1999 and 2000 (which are explained by legitimate, independent business reasons) constitute evidence of anticompetitive coordination among SPRB coal producers. When Arch made statements in 2000 supporting production discipline in the SPRB and thereafter curtailed its coal production, other coal producers did not adopt Arch's approach, and instead continued to produce and sell coal at incremental cost. The absence of evidence of tacit coordination to limit production is fully consistent with the structure and dynamics of the SPRB market, in which sufficient supply and pricing information to facilitate coordination is generally not available, and which is dependent upon an extremely competitive sealed bid contracting process. These features of the SPRB market make tacit agreement difficult to coordinate and demon-

strate both that it would be hard to identify deviations from any agreement to limit production and that there is no effective mechanism in the SPRB to discipline producers who deviate from the terms of coordination.

In *United States v. Oracle Corp.*, 331 F. Supp. 2d 1098 (N.D. Cal. 2004), the court rejected the government's contention that the merger of two large software database providers would lessen competition under a unilateral effects theory. In the process it spoke somewhat critically of the unilateral effects theory as set forth in the Merger Guidelines:

> Although the Guidelines' discussion . . . may be a helpful start, the factors described therein are not sufficient to describe a unilateral effects claim. First, the Guidelines' discussion, at least in section 2.21, emphasizes only the relative closeness of a buyer's first and second choices. But the relative closeness of the buyer's other choices must also be considered in analyzing the potential for price increases. The Guidelines later acknowledge as much in section 2.212, which recognizes that if a buyer's other options include "an equally competitive seller not formerly considered, then the merger is not likely to lead to a unilateral elevation of prices." Accordingly, a plaintiff must prove not only that the merging firms produce close substitutes but also that other options available to the buyer are so different that the merging firms likely will not be constrained from acting anticompetitively.

> . . . it appears that four factors make up a differentiated products unilateral effects claim. First, the products controlled by the merging firms must be differentiated. Products are differentiated if no "perfect" substitutes exist for the products controlled by the merging firms. Second, the products controlled by the merging firms must be close substitutes. Products are close substitutes if a substantial number of the customers of one firm would turn to the other in response to a price increase. Third, other products must be sufficiently different from the products controlled by the merging firms that a merger would make a small but significant and non-transitory price increase profitable for the merging firms. Finally, repositioning by the non-merging firms must be unlikely. In other words, a plaintiff must demonstrate that the non-merging firms are unlikely to introduce products sufficiently similar to the products controlled by the merging firms to eliminate any significant market power created by the merger.

Finally, "[i]n a unilateral effects case, a plaintiff is attempting to prove that the merging parties could unilaterally increase prices. Accordingly, a plaintiff must demonstrate that the merging parties would enjoy a post-merger monopoly or dominant position, at least in a 'localized competition' space."

The court also noted some conceptual problems in market definition in unilateral effects merger cases:

> A closer look at product differentiation demonstrates further difficulties in defining the relevant market in differentiated product unilateral effects cases. Price is one, but only one, of many ways in which to differentiate a

product. A market of homogeneous goods can be seen as a market in which sellers have only one dimension in which to differentiate their product. One expects sellers in such a market to "differentiate" their products by lowering the price until price equals marginal cost. On the other hand, a differentiated product "market" is a market in which sellers compete along more dimensions than price. As a result, products competing against one another in a differentiated product market may have widely different prices. That products with widely different prices may, in fact, be in the same market complicates market definition considerably.

The court also faulted the government's market definition analysis and rejected its proposed market definitions as too narrow. As a result, the court concluded, it could not "conduct a burden-shifting statistical analysis under *Philadelphia Nat Bank*, much less hold that plaintiffs are entitled to . . . a presumption" of illegality. Nor could the court apply the HHI concentration methodology as outlined in the Guidelines. However, the court did permit the government to show anticompetitive effects by direct evidence, even in the absence of a good market definition. No evidence was presented of coordinated effects. Rather, the government relied mainly on a unilateral effects test focusing on "localized" competition between Oracle and Peoplesoft, the two merger partners. But the court found this unpersuasive, noting that the third firm SAP, seemed to have a significant position in the United States and to offer significant competition to the merging firms. The court concluded:

> The court finds that the plaintiffs have wholly failed to prove the fundamental aspect of a unilateral effects case-they have failed to show a "node" or an area of localized competition between Oracle and PeopleSoft. In other words, plaintiffs have failed to prove that there are a significant number of customers (the "node") who regard Oracle and PeopleSoft as their first and second choices. If plaintiffs had made such a showing, then the court could analyze the potential for exercise of monopoly power over this "node" by a post-merger Oracle or the ability of SAP or Lawson to reposition itself within the node in order to constrain such an exercise of monopoly power.

Further, ". . . plaintiffs' evidence was devoid of any thorough econometric analysis such as diversion ratios showing recapture effects. Both the *Kraft Gen Foods* and *Swedish Match* courts, the only other courts explicitly to address unilateral effects, based their rulings in part upon econometric evidence submitted by the parties. *Kraft Gen. Foods*, 926 F. Supp. at 356 (relying on econometric evidence of the cross-price elasticity of demand between Post cereal brands and Nabisco brands); *Swedish Match*, 131 F. Supp. 2d at 169 (relying upon the diversion ratio between two brands of loose leaf tobacco)."

The court also stated some misgivings about what it saw as undue structuralism in the 1992 Horizontal Merger Guidelines:

> The Guidelines adopt a structural approach for addressing unilateral effects claims that closely mirrors traditional structural analysis. *See* Guidelines §2.211. The biggest weakness in the Guidelines' approach appears to be its strong reliance on particular market share concentrations.

Under the Guidelines, anticompetitive effects are presumed "[w]here market concentration data fall outside the safeharbor regions of Section 1.5, the merging firms have a combined market share of at least thirty-five percent, and where data on product attributes and relative product appeal show that a significant share of purchasers of one merging firm's product regard the other as their second choice," unless "rival sellers likely would replace any localized competition lost through the merger by repositioning their product lines. *Id.* at §2.211, 2.212.

NOTE: AN EFFICIENCY DEFENSE IN MERGER CASES?

The *Staples* court, *supra*, considered, but ultimately rejected, the defendant's claim that the challenged merger generated significant efficiencies that would offset any anticompetitive effects. The court concluded (1) the defendants greatly exaggerated the scope of "merger-specific" efficiencies — that is, efficiencies uniquely attributable to the merger that could not be achieved by other means; and (2) there was little evidence that these efficiencies, even if realized, would be "passed on" to consumers.

Courts have had a difficult time determining the proper role that efficiency considerations should play in merger law. Today, few people doubt that mergers can create substantial efficiencies. The transactional efficiencies that can be created by vertical mergers are discussed *supra*. In the *Brown Shoe* case, both the district court and the Supreme Court noted that the post-merger Brown-Kinney firm would be more efficient than the two companies had been before the merger, and more efficient than many of their competitors. In his dissent in *Von's*, Justice Stewart observed that the "supermarket revolution" was making small, independent grocery stores "economically and technologically obsolete."

Nevertheless, despite an outpouring of literature, an "efficiency defense" has never played a significant role in merger cases. In *Brown Shoe*, the Supreme Court condemned the merger *because* it produced certain efficiencies that would injure competitors of the post-merger firm, although they would benefit consumers. Leading representatives of the Chicago School of antitrust believe that there should not be a general efficiency defense in merger cases. *See* R. Bork, The Antitrust Paradox: A Policy at War with Itself, 124 (1978); R. Posner, Antitrust Law 133 (2d ed. 2001). Both former Judge Bork and Judge Posner conclude that there should be no efficiency defense because relevant efficiencies simply cannot be measured in litigation. It is relatively easy to conclude in a generalized way that vertical integration saves the cost of contracting, but it is very difficult to compute the amount of the savings. Likewise, it is often obvious that horizontal mergers can create certain multi-plant economies, but it is very difficult to determine in litigation how much these economies will reduce the cost of production. An "efficiency defense" would have to begin with a merger that is prima facie illegal (or otherwise the defense is unnecessary) and then attempt to balance the potential for inefficiency created by the increased market power of the merging firms against the efficiency created by the merger. Neither of those things is particularly easy to measure; balancing them against each other can be extraordinarily difficult. However, several commentators have argued for an efficiency defense in merger cases. *See* Williamson, *Economies as an Antitrust Defense Revisited*, 125 U. PA. L. REV. 699 (1977); Fisher & Lande, *Efficiency Considerations in Merger Enforcement*, 71 CAL. L. REV. 1580 (1983); Muris, *The Efficiency Defense Under Section 7 of the Clayton Act*, 30 CASE W. RES. L. REV. 381 (1980).

At the same time, the view that mergers in general produce substantial efficiencies has come under broad attack, with several authors finding that firms who have experienced recent mergers actually perform more poorly than other firms in the same market. *See* D. RAVENSCRAFT AND F.M. SCHERER, MERGERS, SELL-OFFS, AND ECONOMIC EFFICIENCY (1987); D. RAVENSCRAFT AND F.M. SCHERER, THE LONG-RUN PERFORMANCE OF MERGERS AND TAKEOVERS, 17–18 (1986). Assuming these authors are correct, should such a discovery affect merger policy? Won't the market itself discipline firms for transacting unprofitable mergers?

The entire notion of an "efficiencies defense" raises an additional problem that has as much to do with the political ideology of antitrust as with its economic content. To the economist, all efficiency gains are good ones, regardless of where they go. Is that necessarily true for antitrust policy? Some people have argued that efficiency should be the exclusive goal of antitrust policy. *See, e.g.*, R. POSNER, ANTITRUST LAW (2d ed. 2001). Suppose that two competing firms, each with 30% of the blivet market, should merge. Such a merger would be prima facie illegal under the new merger guidelines. Before the merger, the market behaved fairly competitively, the marginal cost of producing blivets was $1.00 and they sold for $1.05. After the merger, however, the post-merger firm has substantial market power and is able to reduce the output of blivets to a level lower than the pre-merger output had been. It now sells blivets at a profit-maximizing price of $1.10. Should it be a defense that the merger has enabled the firm to reduce the marginal cost of manufacturing blivets to 90 cents? In that case, the merger has produced a great deal of efficiency, but most of the efficiency shows up as increased profits for the post-merger firm. Consumers pay a higher price after the merger than they did before. Pure economic analysis suggests that we balance the efficiency gains from the merger against the efficiency losses that result from the increase in market power. If the gains exceed the losses, the merger is efficient. The economist is not concerned with the identity of the people who benefit from the increase in efficiency, for that is a purely distributive question.

Nevertheless, this distributive question may be very important to antitrust policy. The antitrust laws are democratically passed statutes. Their legislative histories are peppered with concerns for fairness, wealth distribution, and protection for small businesses or consumers. On the other hand, there is little evidence that any member of Congress believed that all efficiency gains were good ones, regardless of who pocketed them. *See* Hovenkamp, *Antitrust's Protected Classes*, 88 MICH. L. REV. 1 (1989).

Thus, one controversial issue in merger policy is whether firms asserting the efficiency defense must show that the resulting efficiencies will be "passed on" to consumers. Several courts have suggested such a requirement. *See FTC v. University Health*, 938 F.2d 1206, 1222–1223 (11th Cir. 1991) (defendant asserting efficiency defense "must demonstrate that the intended acquisition would result in significant economies and that these economies ultimately would benefit competition and, hence, consumers"); *United States v. United Tote*, 768 F. Supp. 1074, 1084–1085 (D. Del. 1991) (rejecting efficiency defense in part because there was "no guarantee that these benefits will be passed along" to consumers); *American Medical Int'l*, 104 F.T.C. 1, 213–220 (1984) (similar).

But is the requirement realistic? First, contrary to popular belief, in a competitive market, efficiencies are *never* passed on, at least not in the short run. Take the example of two farmers who merge, enabling the larger post-merger farm to use less equipment and labor per acre. While the larger farm has lower costs, its corn is sold in a competitive market and the farm's output is much too small to have any impact on the market price. The post-merger farmer responds to the cost reduction by producing more, but *not* by charging less than the market price. *See* P. Yde & M. Vita, *Merger Efficiencies: Reconsidering the "Passing-on" Requirement*, 64 ANTITRUST L.J. 735 (1996); G. Werden, *An Economic Perspective on the Analysis of Merger Efficiencies*, 11 ANTITRUST 12 (1997).

Of course, if *all* farmers could take advantage of these efficiencies, competition would drive the price down and efficiency gains would be substantially passed on to consumers. But that would be an extraordinarily rare case: for example, suppose a market contained 50 perfectly competitive firms and they paired off in mergers to create 25 firms that were still in perfect competition but had lower costs.

In contrast to the perfectly competitive farmers, the firm with market power (whether previously held or acquired by the merger) responds to reduced costs by lowering its price, but not to the same extent as the efficiency gains. This, of course, is the case that concerns merger policy. A requirement that efficiency gains be *entirely* passed on would eviscerate the efficiency defense.

A weaker but more realistic requirement is not that efficiencies be entirely passed on, but that they offer cost reductions sufficient to offset any likely price increases. As a result, the merger will not produce higher prices. For example, if a merger is likely to result in a five percent price increase when efficiencies are ignored, the amount of efficiencies passed through to consumers must be roughly five percent as well, with the result that market output remains just as high as it was before the merger, and prices just as low.

A similar statement is contained in the horizontal merger guidelines issued by the state attorneys general:

> [E]fficiencies will only be considered when the merging parties can demonstrate by clear and convincing evidence that the merger will lead to significant efficiencies. Moreover, the merging parties must demonstrate that the efficiencies will ensure that consumer prices will not increase despite any increase in market power due to the merger. In highly concentrated markets, even a merger which produces efficiencies will tend to create or enhance market power and will likely increase consumer prices.

Horizontal Merger Guidelines of the National Association of Attorneys General § 5.3 (1993).

One interesting conclusion of the efficiency analysis is that if one considers only economic welfare, a small efficiency gain is sufficient to offset a significant increase in market power. In such a case, a merger that produced an actual price increase would be regarded as efficient if the efficiency gains equalled or exceeded the economic losses that result from inefficient monopoly pricing. However, if one considers wealth transfers from consumers as the relevant policy criterion, then it takes a very large efficiency gain to offset relatively modest gains in market power. *See* Fisher, Johnson & Lande, *Price Effects of Horizontal Mergers*, 77 Cal. L. Rev. 777 (1989).

Does this mean that the potential of mergers to create certain efficiencies is irrelevant? No it does not. If we totally ignored the efficiencies created by mergers, and operated from the assumption that the only economic effect that can come from mergers is increased market power, we could have a per se rule against all mergers. The per se rule is built on the premise that certain practices are highly likely to have bad consequences, and almost certain not to have any good ones. We do not have a per se rule against mergers, however, and today, most mergers are approved by the Justice Department or simply ignored. We recognize the potential of mergers to create efficiencies by a rule that condemns mergers only when their potential to create market power or to permit its exercise is apparent.

Many of the mergers found illegal under current law create substantial efficiencies. They are nevertheless condemned because no court is capable of balancing the increase in market power or the potential for its exercise against the economies achieved, and then determining whether the post-merger firm is more likely to raise its prices or lower them. Judges must find ways to simplify. When a merger involves companies having a small share of the market, we can infer that the potential for increased market power is simply not present; therefore, the merger must be calculated to increase the efficiency of the post-merger firm. By contrast, if the merger involves firms sufficiently large that the impact on market power is real, then the dangers are too great — in spite of possible economies that are incapable of measurement. In that case we condemn the merger rather than take the risk.

FEDERAL TRADE COMM'N v. H.J. HEINZ CO.
246 F.3d 708 (D.C. Cir. 2001)

Karen LeCraft Henderson, Circuit Judge.

On February 28, 2000, H.J. Heinz Company (Heinz) and Milnot Holding Corporation (Beech-Nut) entered into a merger agreement. The Federal Trade Commission (Commission or FTC) sought a preliminary injunction pursuant to section 13(b) of the Federal Trade Commission Act (FTCA), 15 U.S.C. § 53(b), to enjoin the consummation of the merger. . . . The district court denied the preliminary injunction and the FTC appealed to this court. For the reasons set forth below, we reverse the district court and remand for entry of a preliminary injunction against Heinz and Beech-Nut.

I. BACKGROUND

Four million infants in the United States consume 80 million cases of jarred baby food annually, representing a domestic market of $865 million to $1 billion. The baby food market is dominated by three firms, Gerber Products Company (Gerber), Heinz and Beech-Nut. Gerber, the industry leader, enjoys a 65 per cent market share while Heinz and Beech-Nut come in second and third, with a 17.4 per cent and a 15.4 per cent share respectively. The district court found that Gerber enjoys unparalleled brand recognition with a brand loyalty greater than any other product sold in the United States. Gerber's products are found in over 90 per cent of all American supermarkets.

By contrast, Heinz is sold in approximately 40 per cent of all supermarkets. Its sales are nationwide but concentrated in northern New England, the Southeast and Deep South and the Midwest. Despite its second-place domestic market share, Heinz is the largest producer of baby food in the world with $1 billion in sales worldwide. Its domestic baby food products with annual net sales of $103 million are manufactured at its Pittsburgh, Pennsylvania plant, which was updated in 1991 at a cost of $120 million. The plant operates at 40 per cent of its production capacity and produces 12 million cases of baby food annually. Its baby food line includes about 130 SKUs (stock keeping units), that is, product varieties (*e.g.*, strained carrots, apple sauce, etc.). Heinz lacks Gerber's brand recognition; it markets itself as a "value brand" with a shelf price several cents below Gerber's.

Beech-Nut has a market share (15.4%) comparable to that of Heinz (17.4%), with $138.7 million in annual sales of baby food, of which 72 per cent is jarred baby food. Its jarred baby food line consists of 128 SKUs. Beech-Nut manufactures all of its baby food in Canajoharie, New York at a manufacturing plant that was built in 1907 and began manufacturing baby food in 1931. Beech-Nut maintains price parity with Gerber, selling at about one penny less. It markets its product as a premium brand. Consumers generally view its product as comparable in quality to Gerber's. Beech-Nut is carried in approximately 45 per cent of all grocery stores. Although its sales are nationwide, they are concentrated in New York, New Jersey, California and Florida.

At the wholesale level Heinz and Beech-Nut both make lump-sum payments called "fixed trade spending" (also known as "slotting fees" or "pay-to-stay" arrangements) to grocery stores to obtain shelf placement. Gerber, with its strong name recognition and brand loyalty, does not make such pay-to-stay payments. The other type of wholesale trade spending is "variable trade spending," which typically consists of manufacturers' discounts and allowances to supermarkets to create retail price differentials that entice the consumer to purchase their product instead of a competitor's. . . .

II. ANALYSIS

. . . . In *United States v. Baker Hughes Inc.*, 908 F.2d 981, 982–83 (D.C. Cir.1990), we explained the analytical approach by which the government establishes a section 7 violation. First the government must show that the merger would produce "a firm controlling an undue percentage share of the relevant market, and [would] result[] in a significant increase in the concentration of firms in that market." *Philadelphia Nat'l Bank*, 374 U.S. at 363, 83 S. Ct. 1715. Such a showing establishes a "presumption" that the merger will substantially lessen competition. *See Baker Hughes*, 908 F.2d at 982. To rebut the presumption, the defendants must produce evidence that "show[s] that the market-share statistics [give] an inaccurate account of the [merger's] probable effects on competition" in the relevant market. *United States v. Citizens & S. Nat'l Bank*, 422 U.S. 86, 120, 95 S. Ct. 2099, 45 L. Ed. 2d 41 (1975). "If the defendant successfully rebuts the presumption [of illegality], the burden of producing additional evidence of anticompetitive effect shifts to the government, and merges with the ultimate burden of persuasion, which remains with the government at all times." *Baker Hughes Inc.*, 908 F.2d at 983. . . . Accordingly, we look at the FTC's prima facie case and the defendants' rebuttal evidence.

a. Prima Facie Case

. . . Sufficiently large HHI figures establish the FTC's prima facie case that a merger is anti-competitive. *See Baker Hughes*, 908 F.2d at 982–83 & n.3; *PPG*, 798 F.2d at 1503. The district court found that the pre-merger HHI "score for the baby food industry is 4775"-indicative of a highly concentrated industry. *H.J. Heinz*, 116 F. Supp. 2d at 196; *see PPG*, 798 F.2d at 1503; Horizontal Merger Guidelines, *supra*, § 1.51. The merger of Heinz and Beech-Nut will increase the HHI by 510 points. This creates, by a wide margin, a presumption that the merger will lessen competition in the domestic jarred baby food market. *See* Horizontal Merger Guidelines, *supra*, § 1.51 (stating that HHI increase of more than 100 points, where post-merger HHI exceeds 1800, is "presumed . . . likely to create or enhance market power or facilitate its exercise"). . . . Here, the FTC's market concentration statistics are bolstered by the indisputable fact that the merger will eliminate competition between the two merging parties at the wholesale level, where they are currently the only competitors for what the district court described as the "second position on the supermarket shelves." *H.J. Heinz*, 116 F. Supp. 2d at 196. Heinz's own documents recognize the wholesale competition and anticipate that the merger will end it. Indeed, those documents disclose that Heinz considered three options to end the vigorous wholesale competition with Beech-Nut: two involved innovative measures while the third entailed the acquisition of Beech-Nut. Heinz chose the third, and least pro-competitive, of the options.

Finally, the anticompetitive effect of the merger is further enhanced by high barriers to market entry. The district court found that there had been no significant entries in the baby food market in decades and that new entry was "difficult and improbable." *H.J. Heinz*, 116 F. Supp. 2d at 196. This finding largely eliminates the possibility that the reduced competition caused by the merger will be ameliorated by new competition from outsiders and further strengthens the FTC's case.

As far as we can determine, no court has ever approved a merger to duopoly under similar circumstances.

b. Rebuttal Arguments

In response to the FTC's prima facie showing, the appellees make three rebuttal arguments, which the district court accepted in reaching its conclusion that the merger was not likely to lessen competition substantially. For the reasons discussed below, these arguments fail and thus were not a proper basis for denying the FTC injunctive relief.

1. Extent of Pre-Merger Competition

The appellees first contend, and the district court agreed, that Heinz and Beech-Nut do not really compete against each other at the retail level. Consumers do not regard the products of the two companies as substitutes, the appellees claim, and generally only one of the two brands is available on any given store's shelves. Hence, they argue, there is little competitive loss from the merger.

This argument has a number of flaws which render clearly erroneous the court's finding that Heinz and Beech-Nut have not engaged in significant pre-merger competition. First, in accepting the appellees' argument that Heinz and Beech-Nut do not compete, the district court failed to address the record evidence that the two do in fact price against each other, and that, where both are present in the same areas, they depress each other's prices as well as those of Gerber even though they are virtually never all found in the same store. This evidence undermines the district court's factual finding.

Second, the district court's finding is inconsistent with its conclusion that there is a single, national market for jarred baby food in the United States. The Supreme Court has explained that "[t]he outer boundaries of a product market are determined by the reasonable interchangeability of use [by consumers] or the cross-elasticity of demand between the product itself and substitutes for it." *Brown Shoe*, 370 U.S. at 325, 82 S. Ct. 1502; *see also United States v. E.I. du Pont de Nemours & Co.*, 351 U.S. 377, 395, 76 S. Ct. 994, 100 L. Ed. 1264 (1956). The definition of product market thus "focuses solely on demand substitution factors," *i.e.*, that consumers regard the products as substitutes. By defining the relevant product market generically as jarred baby food, the district court concluded that in areas where Heinz's and Beech-Nut's products are both sold, consumers will switch between them in response to a "small but significant and nontransitory increase in price (SSNIP)." Horizontal Merger Guidelines, *supra*, § 1.11; *H.J. Heinz*, 116 F. Supp. 2d at 195. The district court never explained this inherent inconsistency in its logic nor could counsel for the appellees explain it at oral argument.

Third, and perhaps most important, the court's conclusion concerning pre-merger competition does not take into account the indisputable fact that the merger will eliminate competition at the wholesale level between the only two competitors for the "second shelf" position. Competition between Heinz and Beech-Nut to gain accounts at the wholesale level is fierce with each contest concluding in a winner-take-all result. The district court regarded this loss of competition as irrelevant because the FTC did not establish to its satisfaction that wholesale competition ultimately benefitted consumers through lower retail prices. The district court concluded that fixed trade spending did not affect consumer prices and that "the FTC's assertion that the proposed merger will affect variable trade spending levels and consumer prices is . . . at best, inconclusive." *H.J. Heinz*, 116 F. Supp. 2d at 197. Although the court noted the FTC's examples of consumer benefit through couponing initiatives, the court held that it was "impossible to conclude with any certainty that the consumer benefit from such couponing initiatives would be lost in the merger."

In rejecting the FTC's argument regarding the loss of wholesale competition, the court committed two legal errors. First, as the appellees conceded at oral argument, no court has ever held that a reduction in competition for wholesale purchasers is not relevant unless the plaintiff can prove impact at the consumer level. *See Hospital Corp. of Am. v. FTC*, 807 F.2d 1381, 1389 (7th Cir.1986) ("Section 7 does not require proof that a merger or other acquisition has caused higher prices in the affected market. All that is necessary is that the merger create an appreciable danger of [collusive practices] in the future. A predictive judgment, necessarily probabilistic and judgmental rather than demonstrable, is called for.") (citation omitted). Second, it is, in any event, not the FTC's burden to prove such an impact with "certainty." To the contrary, the antitrust laws assume that a retailer faced with an increase in the cost of one of its inventory items "will try so far as competition allows to pass that cost on to its customers in the form of a higher price for its product." *In re Brand Name Prescription Drugs Antitrust Litig.*, 123 F.3d 599, 605 (7th Cir.1997), *reh'g and suggestion for reh'g en banc denied* (Oct. 8, 1997). . . .

2. Post-Merger Efficiencies

The appellees' second attempt to rebut the FTC's prima facie showing is their contention that the anticompetitive effects of the merger will be offset by efficiencies resulting from the union of the two companies, efficiencies which they assert will be used to compete more effectively against Gerber. It is true that a merger's primary benefit to the economy is its potential to generate efficiencies. *See generally* 4A Phillip E. Areeda, Herbert Hovenkamp & John L. Solow, *Antitrust Law* ¶ 970 at 22–25 (1998). As the Merger Guidelines now recognize, efficiencies "can enhance the merged firm's ability and incentive to compete, which may result in lower prices, improved quality, or new products." Horizontal Merger Guidelines, *supra*, § 4.

Although the Supreme Court has not sanctioned the use of the efficiencies defense in a section 7 case, *see Procter & Gamble Co.*, 386 U.S. at 580, 87 S. Ct. 1224, the trend among lower courts is to recognize the defense. *See, e.g., FTC v. Tenet Health Care Corp.*, 186 F.3d 1045, 1054 (8th Cir.1999), *reh'g and reh'g en banc denied* (Oct. 6, 1999); *University Health*, 938 F.2d at 1222; *FTC v. Cardinal Health, Inc.*, 12 F. Supp. 2d 34, 61 (D.D.C. 1998); *Staples*, 970 F. Supp. at 1088–89; *see also* ABA Antitrust Section, *Mergers and Acquisitions: Understanding the Antitrust Issues* 152 (2000) ("The majority of courts have considered efficiencies as a means to rebut the government's prima facie case that a merger will lead to restricted output or increased prices. These courts, however, generally have found inadequate proof of efficiencies to sustain a rebuttal of the government's case."). In 1997 the Department of Justice and the FTC revised their Horizontal Merger Guidelines to recognize that "mergers have the potential to generate significant efficiencies by permitting a better utilization of existing assets, enabling the combined firm to achieve lower costs in producing a given quantity and quality than either firm could have achieved without the proposed transaction." Horizontal Merger Guidelines, *supra*, § 4.

Nevertheless, the high market concentration levels present in this case require, in rebuttal, proof of extraordinary efficiencies, which the appellees failed to supply. *See University Health*, 938 F.2d at 1223 ("[A] defendant who seeks to overcome a presumption that a proposed acquisition would substantially lessen competition must demonstrate that the intended acquisition would result in significant economies and that these economies ultimately would benefit competition and, hence, consumers."); Horizontal Merger Guidelines, *supra*, § 4 (stating that "[e]fficiencies almost never justify a merger to monopoly or near-monopoly"); 4A Areeda, *et al., Antitrust Law* ¶ 971f, at 44 (requiring "extraordinary" efficiencies where the "HHI is well above 1800 and the HHI increase is well above 100"). Moreover, given the high concentration levels, the court must undertake a rigorous analysis of the kinds of efficiencies being urged by the parties in order to ensure that those "efficiencies" represent more than mere speculation and promises about post-merger behavior. The district court did not undertake that analysis here.

In support of its conclusion that post-merger efficiencies will outweigh the merger's anticompetitive effects, the district court found that the consolidation of baby food production in Heinz's under-utilized Pittsburgh plant "will achieve substantial cost savings in salaries and operating costs." *H.J. Heinz*, 116 F. Supp. 2d at 199. The court also credited the appellees' promise of improved product quality as a result of recipe consolidation. The only cost reduction the court quantified as a percentage of pre-merger costs, however, was the so called "variable conversion cost": the cost of processing the volume of baby food now processed by Beech-Nut. The court accepted the appellees' claim that this cost would be reduced by 43% if the Beech-Nut production were shifted to Heinz's plant, *see* JA 4619, a reduction the appellees' expert characterized as "extraordinary."

The district court's analysis falls short of the findings necessary for a successful efficiencies defense in the circumstances of this case. We mention only three of the most important deficiencies here. First, "variable conversion cost" is only a percentage of the total variable manufacturing cost. A large percentage reduction in only a small portion of the company's overall variable manufacturing cost does not necessarily translate into a significant cost advantage to the merger. Thus, for cost reduction to be relevant, we must at least consider the percentage of Beech-Nut's total variable manufacturing cost that would be reduced as a consequence of the merger. At oral argument, the appellees' counsel agreed. Oral Arg. Tr. at 43. This correction immediately cuts the asserted efficiency gain in half since, according to the appellees' evidence, using total variable manufacturing cost as the measure cuts the cost savings from 43% to 22.3%.

Second, the percentage reduction in *Beech-Nut's* cost is still not the relevant figure. After the merger, the two entities will be combined, and to determine whether the merged entity will be a significantly more efficient competitor, cost reductions must be measured across the new entity's combined production-not just across the pre-merger output of Beech-Nut. *See* 4A Areeda, *et al., supra*, ¶ 976d at 93–94. The district court, however, did not consider the cost reduction over the merged firm's combined output. At oral argument the appellees' counsel was unable to suggest a formula that could be used for determining that cost reduction.

Finally, and as the district court recognized, the asserted efficiencies must be "merger-specific" to be cognizable as a defense. *H.J. Heinz*, 116 F. Supp. 2d at 198–99; *see* Horizontal Merger Guidelines, *supra*, § 4; 4A Areeda, *et al., supra*, ¶ 973, at 49–62. That is, they must be efficiencies that cannot be achieved by either company alone because, if they can, the merger's asserted benefits can be achieved without the concomitant loss of a competitor. *See generally* 4A Areeda, *et al., supra*, ¶ 973. Yet the district court never explained why Heinz could not achieve the kind of efficiencies urged without merger. As noted, the principal merger benefit asserted for Heinz is the acquisition of Beech-Nut's better recipes, which will allegedly make its product more attractive and permit expanded sales at prices lower than those charged by Beech-Nut, which produces at an inefficient plant. Yet, neither the district court nor the appellees addressed the question whether Heinz could obtain the benefit of better recipes by investing more money in product development and promotion-say, by an amount less than the amount Heinz would spend to acquire Beech-Nut. At oral argument, Heinz's counsel agreed that the taste of Heinz's products was not so bad that no amount of money could improve the brand's consumer appeal. That being the case, the question is how much Heinz would have to spend to make its product equivalent to the Beech-Nut product and hence whether Heinz could achieve the efficiencies of merger without eliminating Beech-Nut as a competitor. The district court, however, undertook no inquiry in this regard. In short, the district court failed to make the kind of factual determinations necessary to render the appellees' efficiency defense sufficiently concrete to offset the FTC's prima facie showing.

3. Innovation

The appellees claim next that the merger is required to enable Heinz to innovate, and thus to improve its competitive position against Gerber. Heinz and Beech-Nut asserted, and the district court found, that without the merger the two firms are unable to launch new products to compete with Gerber because they lack a sufficient shelf presence or ACV. *See H.J. Heinz*, 116 F. Supp. 2d at 199–200. This kind of defense is often a speculative proposition. *See* 4A Areeda, *et al., supra*, ¶ 975g (noting "truly formidable" proof problems in determining innovation economies). In this case, given the old-economy nature of the industry as well as Heinz's position as the world's largest baby food manufacturer, it is a particularly difficult defense to prove. The court below accepted the appellees' argument principally on the basis of their expert's testimony that new product launches are cost-effective only when a firm's ACV is 70% or greater (Heinz's is presently 40%; Beech-Nut's is 45%). That testimony, in turn, was based on a graph that plotted revenue against ACV. According to the expert, the graph showed that only four out of 27 new products launched in 1995 had been successful-all for companies with an ACV of 70% or greater.

The chart, however, does not establish this proposition and the court's consequent finding that the merger is necessary for innovation is thus unsupported and clearly erroneous. All the chart plotted was revenue against ACV and hence all it showed was the unsurprising fact that the greater a company's ACV, the greater the revenue it received. Because the graph did not plot the profitability (or any measure of "cost-effectiveness"), there is no way to know whether the expert's claim-that a 70% ACV is required for a launch to be "successful" in an economic sense-is true. Moreover, the number of data points on the chart were few; they were limited to launches in a single year; and they involved launches of all new grocery products rather than of baby food alone. Assessing such data's statistical significance in establishing the proposition at issue, *i.e.*, the necessity of 70% ACV penetration, is thus highly speculative. The district court did not even address the question of the data's statistical significance and the appellees' counsel could offer no help at oral argument. . . . In the absence of reliable and significant evidence that the merger will permit innovation that otherwise could not be accomplished, the district court had no basis to conclude that the FTC's showing was rebutted by an innovation defense.

Moreover, Heinz's insistence on a 70-plus ACV before it brings a new product to market may be largely to persuade the court to recognize promotional economies as a defense. Heinz argues that to profitably launch a new product, it must have nationwide market penetration to recoup the money spent on advertising and promotion. It wants to spread advertising costs out among as many product units as possible, thereby lowering the advertising cost per unit. It does not want to "waste" promotional expenditures in markets where its products are not on the shelf or where they are on only a few shelves. For example, in a metropolitan area in which Heinz has a 75 per cent ACV, every dollar spent on advertising is two or three times more "effective" than in a market in which it has only a 25 per cent ACV. As one authority notes, however, "[t]he case for recognizing a defense based on promotional economies is relatively weak." 4A Areeda, *et al., supra,* ¶ 975f, at 77. The district court accepted Heinz's claim that it could not introduce new products without at least a 70 per cent ACV because it would be unable to adequately diffuse its advertising and promotional expenditures. But the court failed to determine whether substantial promotional scale economies exist now and, if they do, whether Heinz and Beech-Nut "for that reason operate at a substantial competitive disadvantage in the market or markets in which they sell" or whether there are effective alternatives to merger by which the disadvantage can be overcome. *Id.* at ¶ 975f2, at 78.

4. Structural Barriers to Collusion

In a footnote the district court dismissed the likelihood of collusion derived from the FTC's market concentration data. "[S]tructural market barriers to collusion" in the retail market for jarred baby food, the court said, rebut the normal presumption that increases in concentration will increase the likelihood of tacit collusion. *H.J. Heinz,* 116 F. Supp. 2d at 198 n.7. The court's sole citation, however, was to testimony by the appellees' expert, Jonathan B. Baker, a former Director of the Bureau of Economics at the FTC, who testified that in order to coordinate successfully, firms must solve "cartel problems" such as reaching a consensus on price and market share and deterring each other from deviating from that consensus by either lowering price or increasing production. He opined that after the merger the merged entity would want to expand its market share at Gerber's expense, thereby decreasing the likelihood of consensus on price and market share.

In his report, Baker elaborated on his theory, explaining that the efficiencies created by the merger will give the merged firm the ability and incentive to take on Gerber in price and product improvements. He also predicted that policing and monitoring of any agreement would be more difficult than it is now, due in part to a time lag in the ability of one firm to detect price cuts by another. But the district court made no finding that any of these "cartel problems" are so much greater in the baby food industry than in other industries that they rebut the normal presumption. In fact, Baker's testimony about "time lag" is refuted by the record which reflects that supermarket prices are available from industry-wide scanner data within 4–8 weeks. His testimony is further undermined by the record evidence of past price leadership in the baby food industry.

The combination of a concentrated market and barriers to entry is a recipe for price coordination. *See University Health,* 938 F.2d at 1218 n.24 ("Significant market concentration makes it 'easier for firms in the market to collude, expressly or tacitly, and thereby force price above or farther above the competitive level.'" (citation omitted)). "[W]here rivals are few, firms will be able to coordinate their behavior, either by overt collusion or implicit understanding, in order to restrict output and achieve profits above competitive levels." *PPG,* 798 F.2d at 1503. The creation of a durable duopoly affords both the opportunity and incentive for both firms to coordinate to increase prices. The district court recognized this when it questioned Baker on whether the merged entity will, up to a point, expand its market share but "then [with Gerber will] find a nice equilibrium and they'll all get along together." Tacit coordination:

> "is feared by antitrust policy even more than express collusion, for tacit coordination, even when observed, cannot easily be controlled directly by the antitrust laws. It is a central object of merger policy to obstruct the creation or reinforcement by merger of such oligopolistic market structures in which tacit coordination can occur."

4 Phillip E. Areeda, Herbert Hovenkamp & John L. Solow, *Antitrust Law* ¶ 901 b2, at 9 (rev. ed.1998). Because the district court failed to specify any "structural market barriers to collusion" that are unique to the baby food industry, its conclusion that the ordinary presumption of collusion in a merger to duopoly was rebutted is clearly erroneous. . . .

III. CONCLUSION

It is important to emphasize the posture of this case. We do not decide whether the FTC will ultimately prove its case or whether the defendants' claimed efficiencies will carry the day. Our task is to review the district court's order to determine whether, under section 13(b), preliminary injunctive relief would be in the public interest. We have considered the FTC's likelihood of success on the merits. We have weighed the equities. We conclude that the FTC has raised serious and substantial questions. We also conclude that the public equities weigh in favor of preliminary injunctive relief and therefore that a preliminary injunction would be in the public interest. Accordingly, we reverse the district court's denial of preliminary injunctive relief and remand the case for entry of a preliminary injunction pursuant to section 13(b) of the Federal Trade Commission Act.

So ordered.

PROBLEM 7.3

Personal compact disc players are high-tech devices that are manufactured in a market that is highly product-differentiated and highly concentrated. World output is controlled by three firms, one of which is Japanese and two of which are American. Kasawa, the Japanese firm, makes a high quality player that commands a high price. Last year, its revenues from personal compact disc player sales were $125,000,000, and it sold about 250,000 units. Sound, Inc., is the larger of the two American firms, manufacturing a medium quality player that commands a lower price. Last year, it sold about 125,000 units, for total revenues of $50,000,000. Sonic, the second American company, makes a low quality unit that sells for the lowest price. Last year, it sold about 100,000 units, for total revenues of $30,000,000.

None of the three firms manufacture components for personal compact disc players. They merely assemble them, and assembly does not require any particular skills. The components are traded freely in an unrestricted market. Sound now proposes to acquire Sonic. Analyze the proposed merger.

NOTE: "UNILATERAL" ANTITCOMPETITIVE EFFECTS OF HORIZONTAL MERGERS

One important change in the 1992 Guidelines and carried over to the 2010 Guidelines is the notion that mergers in product-differentiated markets may enable certain firms to increase prices *unilaterally*. The theory originated in a famous article by Harold Hotelling. Hotelling, *Stability in Competition*, 39 ECON. J. 41 (1929).

Consider a row of hot dog vendors arrayed 50 yards apart across a beach. The hot dogs and the vendor-stands are physically identical but the differentiation applies to the variable distances that bathers must walk in order to reach a hot dog stand. Assume further that the pre-merger price of each vendor is a dollar, and that bathers, who are the potential customers, are willing to pay as much as two dollars less one cent for each yard they must walk. Thus, when all vendors charge the same price, the customers maximize their value by walking to the closest vendor, but they would be willing to walk to any vendor who is as far as 100 yards away. The 100-yard remote vendor produces value to the customer of precisely the hot dog's cost, and no customer will walk to a vendor who is 101 yards or further away. The vendors are called $A, B, C, D \ldots N$.

FIGURE A

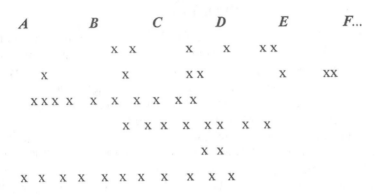

In this setting, a potential customer would be willing to purchase a hot dog from as many as five vendors. For example, if a potential customer were sunbathing precisely at the location of vendor *D*, then vendors *C* and *E* would be 50 yards away in either direction, and vendors *B* and *F* would be 100 yards away in either direction. Ordinarily, the customer would prefer to purchase from *D*, which gives her value of $2.00 for a price of $1.00. Because she must walk 50 yards to either *C* or *E*, these vendors give her value of $1.50 ($2.00—50 cents for 50 yards) for $1.00; and vendors *B* and *F* give her value of $1.00 ($2.00—$1.00 for 100 yards) for her $1.00, thus depriving her of all consumers' surplus, but nevertheless leaving her willing to purchase a hot dog.

Also observe that each of the vendors has a range of "captured" or preferred customers of 50 yards, or 25 yards on either side, which is half way to the next vendor. That is, a customer located 20 yards to the left of vendor *B* would be 30 yards from vendor *A*. To that customer, vendor *B* could charge a price as much as 10 cents higher than vendor *A* and still make the sale. However, the vendors are unable to price discriminate; they must charge the same price to all. In this "equilibrium" situation, they all charge a price of $1.00.

Suppose that vendors *C* and *D* should merge, while leaving their stands (or "plants") in the same location. The two vendors together will be able to charge a significantly higher price than they were when they were competing. For example, considering the customers sunbathing between *C* and *D*, the new firm *CD* has at least a 50-cent (50-yard) advantage over vendors *B* and *E*, both of which are at least 50 yards more remote. Considering this group of customers alone, *CD* could increase its price to $1.50 without losing any of them to either *B* or *E*. And further, the range of customers located between former *C* and *D* is a full 50 yards, the same as the range of individual firms' preferred customers before the merger. In sum, this merger would very likely facilitate a significant price increase, perhaps by as much as 30 or 40 cents.

Also, observe that the significant increase in power occurs only because the *CD* merger united two firms that were *adjacent* in the beach or hot dog market. If two remote firms, such as *A* and *E* had merged, leaving three competitors between them, these price effects would not occur.

While greatly simplified and highly artificial, this illustration nevertheless makes an important point. In product differentiated markets, mergers between firms making "adjacent," or similar, product variations can have a much more significant anticompetitive effect than mergers between firms making more remote products. The differentiations can apply to both spatial location, as in the hot dog vendor illustration, and to product specification or design, as in the case of manufacturers selling products that compete with each other (such as BMW and Oldsmobile) but are nevertheless distinctive in consumers' minds.

Note also that the competitive effects of the hot dog vendor merger would quickly be dissipated if individual hot dog vendors could cheaply and quickly relocate their stands — for example, if all were mobile carts that could be moved at the vendor's will. In that case, when firms C and D merged and attempted a price increase of, say, 30 percent, we would expect firms A, B, E, F, and perhaps others, to move their carts closer into the CD territory in order to participate in these price increases. The effect would be to drive the prices back down towards the $1.00 level. Thus, the threat of such a merger to produce anticompetitive results depends on the inability of other firms to respond by innovating or relocating *into* that portion of the market that has now become more competitive as a result of the merger.

Before a merger of adjacent sellers can be anticompetitive, the product differentiation in question must be "significant," going to fairly fundamental differences in product design, manufacturing costs, technology, or use of inputs. While most markets exhibit some degree of product differentiation, not all product differentiation is significant. For example, today even agricultural products are subject to branding, such as Chiquita and Del Monte bananas. Other products, such as ready-to-eat breakfast cereals, seem far more different on first appearance than they are in fact. While Kellogg's Frosted Flakes and Post's Alphabits might appear quite distinctive, they are in fact made with common ingredients and common technology, with equipment that can be reconfigured to extrude different shapes or designs. And, of course, they are promoted differently. Leaving aside intellectual property rights, a firm making one could quite easily switch its production facilities to the manufacturing of the other. To this extent, costs are more-or-less the same and collusion might be quite possible.

As the hot dog vendor illustration suggests, a merger in a product-differentiated market is more likely to result in a unilateral price increase as:

> (1) the products of the two merger participants are more similar to one another;

> (2) the products of the two merger participants are more different from the products produced by nonparticipants; and

> (3) nonparticipants are unable to alter or reconfigure their products to make them more nearly like the products of the merger participants.

To the extent that such a merger enables the post-merger firm profitably to assess a significant price increase without losing sales to other firms, we would say that the merger facilitates the emergence of a new grouping of sales in which the merging firms have either a monopoly or else a dominant share.

In *United States v. Interstate Bakers Corp.*, 1996-1 Trade Cas. ¶ 71,272 (N.D. Ill. 1995), the court approved a consent decree requiring the merging wholesale bakers, Interstate and Continental, to divest certain brand labels:

> The Complaint alleges that Interstate's acquisition of Continental would likely lead to an increase in price charged to consumers for white pan bread. Following the acquisition, Interstate likely would unilaterally raise the price of its own brands. . . . Because Interstate and Continental's brands are perceived by consumers as close substitutes, Interstate could pursue such a pricing strategy without losing so much in sales to competing white pan bread brands or to private labels that the price increase would be unprofitable. Interstate could, for instance, profitably impose a significant increase in the price of Wonder white pan bread, because a substantial portion of any sales lost for that product would be recaptured by increased sales of Interstate's other brands.

> Because many consumers consider Interstate and Continental brands to be closer substitutes than most other branded or private label white breads, the competitive discipline provided by rivals after the acquisition would be insufficient to prevent Interstate from significantly increasing the prices now being charged for Interstate and Continental branded white pan bread. Moreover, in response to Interstate's price increases, competing bakers would likely increase their prices of white pan bread.

For more on unilateral anticompetitive effects of horizontal mergers, see 4 P. AREEDA, H. HOVENKAMP, & J. SOLOW, ANTITRUST LAW ¶ 914 (3d ed. 2009); Baker, *Contemporary Empirical Merger Analysis*, 5 GEO. MASON L. REV. 347 (1997); Baker, *Unilateral Competitive Effects Theories in Merger Analysis*, 11 ANTITRUST 21 (1997); Shapiro, *Mergers with Differentiated Products*, 10 ANTITRUST 23, 24 (1996). *See also* Vellturo, *Evaluating Mergers with Differentiated Products*, 11 Antitrust 16 (Spring, 1997). As Vellturo notes, often the data necessary to estimate the rate at which customers respond to a price increase in product A by switching to product B are more readily obtained than the data necessary to measure a relevant market and compute overall demand effects. To that extent, such analysis can be more reliable than traditional market concentration analysis.

NOTE: MERGERS AND INNOVATION

In recent years there has been increasing focus on the relationship between mergers and technological innovation. There are two principal ways in which innovation and merger enforcement may affect each other. First, technological change might change the relationship between the pre-merger marketplace and the effects of a merger. For example, pre-merger market shares are often used as indicators of market power that form the basis of predictions about a merger's effects on the relevant market. But future innovation by a rival could displace a firm that by the traditional measure of current market share looks dominant at the time its merger is being considered. The effect of innovation on future market conditions and, hence, on the inferences one can draw from current market structure might be called "the innovation impact criterion." *See* Katz & Shelanski, *Mergers and Innovation*, 74 ANTITRUST L.J. 1, 12 (2007). Second, a merger might affect innovation itself by altering, for better or worse, the incentives of the merging parties to invest in developing and deploying new technology. One might call this "the innovation incentives criterion." *Id.*

Should antitrust enforcement take account of technological innovation and, if so, how should it do so? Both questions have been controversial. One school of thought has applied the work of Austrian economist Joseph Schumpeter, who argued in the middle of the last century that large firms with market power were more likely to innovate. *See, e.g.*, J. SCHUMPETER, CAPITALISM, SOCIALISM, AND DEMOCRACY, chs. 7-8 (1942). Present-day "Schumpeterians" argue that merger enforcement becomes less warranted when innovation is taken into account because a firm's accumulation of market power is, first, a normal part of the innovation cycle and, second, likely to be temporary because competitive innovators strive to displace the dominant incumbents through a process of "creative destruction." *Id. See also* EVANS & SCHMALENSEE, SOME ECONOMIC ASPECTS OF ANTITRUST ANALYSIS IN DYNAMICALLY COMPETITIVE INDUSTRIES, 2 INNOVATION POLICY AND THE ECONOMY (Jaffee et al. eds., 2002); Pleatsikis & Teece, *The Analysis of Market Definition and Market Power in the Context of Rapid Innovation*, 19 INT'L J. INDUS. ORG. 665 (2001); ANTITRUST, INNOVATION, AND COMPETITIVENESS (T. Jorde & D. Teece, eds., 1992).

A contrary school of thought often cites the work of American Economist Kenneth Arrow for the proposition that competition is a better motivator of innovation than are concentration and market power. ARROW, Economic Welfare and the Allocation of Resources for Invention, in THE RATE AND DIRECTION OF INVENTIVE ACTIVITY (R. Nelson, ed., 1962). The implication is that antitrust should not retreat systematically in the face of innovation, but should instead enforce competition to preserve innovation and find ways to adapt the existing framework for competition analysis to the objective of innovation. *See, e.g.*, Gilbert & Sunshine, *Incorporating Dynamic Efficiency Concerns in Merger Analysis: The Use of Innovation Markets*, 63 ANTITRUST L.J. 569 (1995).

The empirical and theoretical data on the relationship between market structure and innovation are sufficiently ambiguous to ensure that the debate over the correct posture of antitrust toward innovation will not be easily settled. *See, e.g.*, Katz & Shelanski, *supra*. There seems, however, to be broad consensus on three points: first, that the existing framework for antitrust can with some modification accommodate innovation as a policy criterion — the argument is over what those modifications should be; second, that the conventional presumptions that tie increased competition to increased economic welfare might not always apply where innovation, as opposed to more static price and output considerations; and third, that innovation is too important for antitrust to ignore.

The debate over antitrust and innovation is not purely an academic one. In a number of cases, the Justice Department and the FTC have paid close attention to both the effect of innovation on the analysis of competitive effects and to the potential effects of a proposed merger on innovation. The Justice Department challenged a merger partly on innovation grounds in 1993 after concluding that ZF Friedrichshafen's acquisition of General Motors' Allison Division would bring 85 percent of the world's production of heavy truck and bus transmissions into a single firm. *U.S. v. General Motors Corp.*, Civ. No. 93-530 (D. Del., Nov. 16, 1993), 6 Trade Reg. Rep. (CCH) ¶ 45,093. Although ZF and GM largely operated in distinct geographical markets, the Justice Department concluded that even consumers in markets whose structure would not be affected by the transaction would be harmed by the merger's reduction of innovation incentives for the merging firms. *Id.* The parties abandoned the transaction in the face of the Department's challenge.

In a case that similarly focused on a merger's innovation incentives effect, the FTC in 2004 reached a different conclusion in the merger between Genzyme and Novazyme, two biotechnology companies. Genzyme and Novazyme were the only two companies engaged in the development of therapies for Pompe Disease, a rare and fatal enzyme-replacement disorder. Their merger therefore represented a concentration to monopoly in the relevant market. In a post-consumation review (because the merger was below the threshold required for pre-notification) the FTC approved the merger. *Closing Letter, Investigation of Genzyme Corporation Acquisition of Novazyme Pharmaceuticals, Inc.*, FCT File No. 021 0026 (Jan. 13, 2004), *available at* http://www.ftc.gov//os/2004/01/040113genzyme.pdf. What is most important about this case is that the FTC appears for the first time to have based a merger decision solely on innovation considerations. In GM-ZF and the many other decisions through the 1990s innovation was a factor, but not necessarily a determinative one because conventional price and output considerations were also central in those mergers. In *Genzyme-Novazyme*, Chairman Muris wrote that the merger's effects on future innovation were the sole consideration in the case. *Closing Statement of Chairman Timothy J. Muris in the Matter of Genzyme Corporation/Novazyme Pharmaceuticals, Inc.*, FTC File No. 021 0026 (Jan. 13, 2004), *available at* http://www.ftc.gov//os/2004/01/murisgenzymestmt.pdf. He then tried to set out some principles for when and how antitrust authorities should factor innovation concerns into enforcement decisions. *Id.* Notably, he argued that a merger's effects on innovation should only be considered when the universe of potential innovators was small and clearly identified. He then argued that the relationship between competition and innovation incentives should be analyzed on the facts of each case and without any presumptions about the relationship between market structure and innovation. *Id.* With this case, innovation has moved to center stage in merger review.

The FTC's *Genzyme* decision set the stage for future enforcement actions in technologically dynamic markets, a subject that the 2010 Guidelines addressed more directly than had previous Guideline versions. Examples of how the 2010 Guidelines approach evolved and might be implemented can be found in the FTC's treatment of the proposed mergers of Thoratec and HeartWare, and Google and AdMob, to be discussed next.

The FTC's 2004 review of Genzyme's acquisition of Novazyme focused on "whether the merged firm was likely to have a reduced incentive to invest in R&D, and also whether it was likely to have the ability to conduct R&D more successfully." Statement of Chairman Timothy J. Muris in the Matter of Genzyme Corporation/Novazyme Pharmaceuticals, Inc. (2004, p. 6), *available at* http://www.ftc.gov/os/2004/01/murisgenzymestmt.pdf. The same questions arose when Thoratec proposed to acquire HeartWare in July 2009 and when Google set out to acquire AdMob in early 2010. While the 2010 Guidelines had not yet been issued when those investigations were undertaken, the analysis the Commission used in each case is consistent with and thus illustrative of the approach the 2010 Guidelines later adopted. Thoratec made the only FDA-approved left ventricular assist device (LVAD) on the market. LVADs are surgically implantable blood pumps that sustain patients who suffer from end-stage heart failure. HeartWare was a potential entrant whose LVAD product was well into the FDA approval process and promised several advantages over Thoratec's LVAD. A potential benefit of the merger was that Thoratec's experience and distribution channels might help overcome remaining regulatory and marketing hurdles and enable the merged firm to get HeartWare's innovation to patients sooner than would an independent HeartWare. Against this potential efficiency benefit was the issue that Chairman Muris identified in *Genzyme*: Would Thoratec have as strong an incentive as would an independent HeartWare to bring the innovation to market? Weighing the evidence, the Commission issued a complaint to block the merger, which the parties abandoned.

The Complaint alleged that competition from HeartWare had already forced Thoratec to innovate (*see* paragraph 4), that no other firms working to develop LVADs posed as strong a competitive threat to Thoratec as HeartWare (*see* paragraph 18), and that upon receiving FDA approval HeartWare would take significant market share from Thoratec (*see* paragraph 21). [The public version of the Complaint in the Matter of Thoratec Corporation and HeartWare International, Inc. can be found at http://www.ftc.gov/os/adjpro/d9339/090730thorateadmincmpt. pdf.] Taken together, these allegations lead to the conclusion that by purchasing HeartWare, Thoratec would face less competitive pressure to bring the new product to market. With information about the prices, margins, and likely diversion ratio, one can quantify this effect and compare the pre- and post-merger incentives to bring HeartWare's product to market.

The fundamental economics are described in § 6.4 of the 2010 Horizontal Merger Guidelines. If introduced, the innovation will take customers from the incumbent's pre-existing product, and this "cannibalization" effect discourages the incumbent from introducing the new product. Suppose that firm 1 produces product A and that a rival, firm 2, is developing innovation B, which will compete with A. If introduced, product B will draw a fraction d of its sales from customers who would otherwise buy A (thus d is the diversion ratio). Let MA be the profit margin that firm 1 earns on incremental sales of A, and let MB be the profit margin that (for simplicity) either firm would earn on sales of B once introduced.

Firm 2's profit from introducing B and selling Q units exceeds its cost, C_2, of product introduction if $M_B Q \geq C_2$. But if the firms have merged and no other entry is imminent, the merged firm will find it profitable to introduce B only if [MB - d M_A] Q $\geq C_M$, where C_M is the merged firm's cost of product introduction. If $d M_A$ is not much less than MB, then the merged firm may well find the introduction much less profitable than would an independent firm 2, even if the merged firm's cost of introduction is considerably lower. This example illustrates how a merger can dramatically affect the incentives to introduce an innovative product.

To elaborate a bit, the reduced innovation incentive comes from the fact that, if a monopolist innovates, it will take customers from its own pre-existing product (assuming constant demand for the relevant product).[6] This cannibalization effect, whereby innovation consumes the monopolist's own pre-existing profits, is a deterrent to innovation and narrows the conditions under which the monopolist will invest in a next-generation product. A monopolist might still innovate if it can expand demand by improving the product, reduce costs to improve per-unit profits, or reduce demand elasticity in order to charge a higher per-unit price. A monopolist will generally not, however, undertake all innovations that a new entrant or a firm facing competition would find it profitable to invest in, and therein lies a potential cost in allowing mergers that eliminate or substantially reduce competition where innovation is important.

To see this more clearly, suppose that firm 1 that produces product A and a struggling rival, firm 2, that also sells A but is losing the market to firm 1. To combat its slide, firm 2 is developing product B, an innovation that will compete to some degree with A and benefit consumers. Should the government allow the merger of firms 1 and 2? On one hand there is the risk that firm 2 will fail; on the other hand is the risk of unnecessarily removing an innovative competitor and perhaps its innovative product or technology from the marketplace. How likely is that counter-vailing risk? One way to answer the question is to ask whether after the acquisition firm 1 will have incentive to consider developing B, and how those incentives will compare to those of an independent firm 2.

A simple numerical condition helps to illustrate the above comparison. Assume that half of product B's sales would have gone to product A had B not been available. Assume that the firms' margin on B is 10, that firm 1's margin on A is 10, and that the output of B is 1000. In that case, then firm 2 earns 10x1000 = $10,000 from introducing B, which is above zero and, therefore, sufficient to induce the innovation in B. From the same sales, firm 1 would earn 10x1000 - 0.5(1000x10) = $5000, because firm 1 has to account for its lost sales of A in deciding whether to introduce B into the market. Firm 1 has exactly half the economic incentive to introduce B, but will still earn enough to make innovation in B profitable. But what if the costs of B are higher than the costs of A or the price of B must be lower than the price for A? It is not at all unlikely that the margin on B (MB) is less than the margin on A (MA) when the forward-looking costs of further development and marketing of B are taken into account. Suppose, for example, that MA=10 but that MB is only 4. Firm 2 will still introduce B into the market because it will earn 4x1000 = $4000, which is greater than the threshold requirement of 0. But firm 1 will earn only 4x1000 - 0.5(10x1000) = -1000. The threshold condition for firm 1 to introduce B fails and the merged firm will not introduce product B.

---

[6] Kenneth Arrow made this observation in a famous debate with Joseph Schumpeter over whether monopoly or competition was more conducive to innovation. *See* JOSEPH A. SHUMPETER, CAPITALISM, SOCIALISM AND DEMOCRACY 101–106 (1942); Kenneth J. Arrow, *Economic Welfare and the Allocation of Resources for Invention, in* ESSAYS IN THE THEORY OF RISK-BEARING 144, 157 (3d ed. 1976) (1962). The debate and its consequences for antitrust policy are developed in CHRISTINA BOHANNAN & HERBERT HOVENKAMP, CREATION WITHOUT RESTRAINT: PROMOTING LIBERTY AND RIVALRY IN INNOVATION, ch. 1 (2011); Jonathan Baker, *Beyond Schumpeter and Arrow: How Antitrust Fosters Innovation*, 74 ANTITRUST L.J. 575, 586 (2007).

The above example, which can be generalized with some additional complexity beyond the case of merger to monopoly, demonstrates how a transaction can lead to very different pre- and post-merger probabilities of the introduction of an innovative product. Firms claiming the need for an emergency merger, as in the above example, will emphasize the greater capability of firm 1 than of the struggling firm 2 to introduce the new product. But incentives, not just capability, must be considered, and claims about capability should not obscure a transaction's effects on incentives to exercise that capability.

It is certainly the case that the type of analysis described above will not be possible in all or even many cases. But experience has shown that it is possible in some cases. It therefore provides a tool for the agencies to use in appropriate circumstances, as does Muris's approach in *Genzyme*.

That each innovation analysis must be tailored to the facts of the particular transaction was highlighted by a different case the FTC examined in the past year: Google's acquisition of AdMob, which shows how the presence of an additional competitor can change the analysis. [See the FTC's closing statement in the matter at http://www.ftc.gov/os/closings/100521google-admobstmt.pdf.] AdMob was in some respects the leading mobile advertising network, and Google was a significant and particularly fast-growing rival. Mobile advertising networks place advertising and thus monetize many applications for mobile platforms — notably, Apple's iPhone. Initially, there was concern that the merger would reduce future competition in the terms that mobile ad networks offered to advertisers and applications developers, and that Google would reduce its R&D in mobile advertising once it had AdMob's technology. During the course of the investigation, however, staff learned that Apple itself was about to enter mobile advertising. Apple was not just a potentially powerful entrant into mobile advertising, but also was the owner of the dominant mobile platform on which consumers use applications that show ads. Apple therefore had the ability, and had announced its intention, to manage its platform in a way that would provide its proprietary mobile advertising service with advantages that were unavailable to unaffiliated mobile ad networks. This set of circumstances made the merging firms' current market positions and historic trajectories poor predictors of their future competitive significance. The FTC closed its investigation and allowed Google to acquire AdMob.

NOTE: MARKET DEFINITION AND COMPETITIVE EFFECTS AFTER THE 2010 GUIDELINES

As of this writing, courts have had few occasions to opine on mergers under the 2010 Guidelines. The agencies, for their part, have been applying the principles of the 2010 revisions. One good example is the FTC's pending complaint against the merger of Ardagh Group and Saint-Gobain Containers, Inc. That FTC applies the smallest market principle from the 2010 Guidelines to allege a glass-only market for certain containers and in certain geographic markets. http://www.ftc.gov/os/adjpro/d9356/130701ardaghcmpt.pdf. In two cases, the federal district courts have addressed issues of market definition and competitive effects under the 2010 Guidelines, with significantly differing degrees of deftness.

FTC v. LUNDBECK, INC.
650 F.3d 1236 (8th Cir. 2011)

BENTON, CIRCUIT JUDGE.

The Federal Trade Commission and Minnesota (collectively the FTC) sued Lundbeck, Inc., alleging its acquisition of the drug NeoProfen violated the Federal Trade Commission Act, the Sherman Act, the Clayton Act, the Minnesota Antitrust Law of 1971, and unjustly enriched Lundbeck. After a bench trial, the district court ruled for Lundbeck based on the FTC's failure to identify a relevant market.

Patent ductus arteriosus (PDA) is a life-threatening heart condition that primarily affects low-birth-weight, usually premature, babies. There are two primary treatments: pharmacological and surgical. Pharmacological treatment (a drug) is the first-line treatment; surgical ligation is considered after other treatments are ineffective. Approximately 30,000 cases of PDA are treated with drugs in the U.S. yearly.

When this case was brought, there were two FDA-approved drugs for PDA: Indocin IV and NeoProfen. (In 2010, two generic alternatives to Indocin IV were introduced by Bedford Laboratories and APP Pharmaceuticals, LLC.) Indocin IV-an off-patent, injectable drug with the active ingredient indomethacin-has been FDA-approved for PDA since 1985. NeoProfen-a patented injectable drug with the active ingredient ibuprofen lysine-has been FDA-approved for PDA since 2006. Because their active ingredients differ, Indocin IV and NeoProfen are not bioequivalents and have different side effects.

Lundbeck purchased the rights to Indocin IV from Merck & Co. in 2005, and the rights to NeoProfen from Abbott Laboratories in 2006 (before it was put on the market). Until generics appeared in 2010, Lundbeck owned all the drugs for PDA.

When Lundbeck purchased Indocin IV, Merck charged $77.77 per treatment. Lundbeck immediately raised the price of Indocin IV. Two days after acquiring the rights to NeoProfen, Lundbeck raised the price thirteen-fold. By 2008, the price of Indocin IV settled at $1614.44. When Lundbeck introduced NeoProfen in 2006, it charged $1450 per NeoProfen treatment, and its price eventually settled at $1522.50.

Both Indocin IV and NeoProfen are hospital-based drugs dispensed and used in inpatient care. Most hospitals assemble a formulary-a list of recommended drugs-to streamline purchasing. The formulary-listed drugs are chosen by pharmacy and therapeutics committees who often seek input from specialist physicians. Some hospitals use closed formularies (special approval is required to prescribe non-listed drugs). Others apply open formularies (physicians can prescribe non-listed drugs at their discretion). Hospitals use inclusion in the formulary to extract better prices from sellers of clinically-substitutable drugs.

After a bench trial, the district court determined that the FTC did not meet its burden to prove that Indocin IV and NeoProfen were in the same product market and thus failed to identify a relevant market.

"The determination of the relevant market is an issue for the trier of fact." *Ryko Mfg. Co. v. Eden Servs.*, 823 F.2d 1215, 1232 (8th Cir. 1987). After a bench trial, this court reviews for clear error the district court's fact-findings supporting its ultimate determination of the existence of a relevant market. If the district court's fact-findings are "plausible in light of the record viewed in its entirety," they must be affirmed, regardless of how this court might have weighed the evidence in the first instance.

The FTC argues that this court should review the district court's judgment de novo because the court "applied an incorrect legal standard" by failing to "examin[e] all the pertinent factors" determining a relevant market. Contrary to the FTC's argument, the district court examined the pertinent factors determining a relevant market, including the "readiness and ability of consumers to turn to reasonable alternatives to the product in question." *Empire Gas Corp.*, 537 F.2d at 303. Though cloaked as a legal argument, the FTC really challenges the district court's weighing of the relevant market factors, which this court reviews for clear error.

To prevail, the FTC bears the burden of identifying a relevant market. The parties agree that the geographic market is the United States, but dispute the product market.

The outer boundaries of a product market can be identified by the reasonable interchangeability, or cross-elasticity of demand, between the product and possible substitutes for it. *Brown Shoe Co. v. United States*, 370 U.S. 294, 325, 82 S. Ct. 1502, 8 L. Ed. 2d 510 (1962). Determining a product market requires identifying the choices available to consumers, focusing on "whether consumers will shift from one product to the other in response to changes in their relative cost." *SuperTurf, Inc. v. Monsanto Co.*, 660 F.2d 1275, 1278 (8th Cir. 1981); *see also Horizontal Merger Guidelines § 1, 57 Fed. Reg. 41552 (1992)* ("Market definition focuses solely on demand substitution factors-i.e., possible consumer responses.").

In its fact-findings, the district court credited the testimony of five clinical pharmacists, representing approximately 43 hospitals throughout the country. The pharmacists uniformly stated that while they make drug recommendations, the neonatologists decide which drug a patient receives. The court also credited the testimony of seven neonatologists who said that treatment decisions are based solely on perceived clinical advantages/disadvantages of Indocin IV versus NeoProfen. The neonatologists' preferences differed (some prescribe Indocin IV, others NeoProfen), but each echoed the same concept: The relative price of the drugs does not factor into the choice of drug treatment. The court was not persuaded by the testimony of one neonatologist (cited often by the FTC and its experts), who believed the drugs to be equally safe, implying he was comfortable using either one for PDA.

Based on this evidence, the court determined that the neonatologists "ultimately determine the demand for Indocin IV and Neoprofen," and that these treatment decisions are made "without regard to price." Thus, an increase in the price of Indocin IV would not drive a hospital to purchase NeoProfen, and vice versa. Considering these facts, as well as testimony by Lundbeck's expert whom the court found "persuasive," the court ruled that there is low cross-elasticity of demand between Indocin IV and Neoprofen, and thus the drugs are not in the same product market. *See H.J., Inc. v. International Tel. & Tel. Corp.*, 867 F.2d 1531, 1538, 1540 (8th Cir. 1989) (holding that cross-price elasticity is essential to market definition. Plaintiff did not identify a relevant market because it offered only "casual statements, not made as part of a serious market analysis" and there was "no market data concerning sales . . . nor was there any testimony describing the degree of cross-elasticity").

The FTC contends that the district court relied too much on the testimony of the neonatologists, and ignored evidence demonstrating that Indocin IV and NeoProfen are in the same product market. Challenging the court's reliance on the neonatologists' testimony, the FTC argues that the hospitals, not the neonatologists, are the consumers, and the hospitals would switch between Indocin IV and NeoProfen based on price differences. The FTC offers no evidence that hospitals would disregard the preferences of the neonatologists and make purchasing decisions based on price. The district court did not err in finding more persuasive the testimony of the pharmacists and most neonatologists, compared to the one neonatologist favorable to the FTC.

According to the FTC, the district court (and the neonatologists) ignored the fact that Indocin IV and NeoProfen are practicable alternatives, relying instead on stated consumer preference. In fact, the practicable alternatives here are clear, were the subject of testimony by the neonatologists, and were considered by the district court. When the case was tried, Indocin IV and NeoProfen were the two drug treatments available for PDA. Aware of the drug options — the "practicable alternatives" — the neonatologists preferred one treatment or the other (without regard for cost), which the court credited as persuasive evidence of low cross-elasticity.

In a variation of the "practicable alternatives" argument, the FTC asserts that functionally similar products must be in the same product market. To the contrary, functionally similar products may be in separate product markets, depending on the facts of the case. *Compare Henry v. Chloride, Inc.*, 809 F.2d 1334, 1342–43 (8th Cir. 1987) (batteries sold through route-truck distribution was a separate market from identical batteries sold through warehouses), *United States v. Archer-Daniels-Midland Comp.*, 866 F.2d 242, 248 (8th Cir. 1988) (functionally interchangeable sweeteners were separate product markets because "a small change in the price of [one] would have little or no effect on the demand for [the other]"), *Geneva Pharms. Tech. Corp. v. Barr Labs. Inc.*, 386 F.3d 485, 496 (2d Cir. 2004) (bioequivalent, functionally-interchangeable branded and generic drugs were in separate product markets), *and SmithKline Corp. v. Eli Lilly & Co.*, 575 F.2d 1056, 1064 (3d Cir. 1978) (despite a certain degree of functional interchangeability among antibiotics, specific class of antibiotics was separate product market based on court's finding that there was a lack of price sensitivity and cross-elasticity of demand), *with HDC Med., Inc.*, 474 F.3d at 547–48 (rejecting argument that dialyzers with identical uses can be separated into two product markets based solely on a price differential), *and H.J., Inc.*, 867 F.2d at 1538–40 (holding that a new product and the product it was meant to supercede were in same product market because competitor did not produce evidence sufficient to establish low cross-elasticity of demand).

Further attacking the district court's reliance on consumer preference, the FTC argues that the court ignored the ability of marginal customers to constrain prices. Whether there are enough marginal consumers to constrain prices is a factual question that requires analyzing consumer-demand and profit-margins. *See Tenet Health Care Corp.*, 186 F.3d at 1050–51, 1054 (marginal consumer substitution and profit-margins must be supported with more than "common sense." This court pointed to the "compelling and essentially unrefuted [critical loss analysis] evidence that the switch to another [product] by a small percentage of [consumers] would constrain a price increase" as evidence of marginal consumer's ability to constrain prices in a broader geographic market); *see also United States v. Engelhard Corp.*, 126 F.3d 1302, 1306 (11th Cir. 1997) (requiring evidence in order to evaluate the possibility that losing marginal customers responsible for high-margin purchases may constrain prices). The FTC offered testimony of one expert explaining that "marginal customers"-neonatologists who are ambivalent between prescribing Indocin IV or NeoProfen-may constrain prices on either drug. Although not addressing this testimony in its fact-findings, the district court did state that it generally found the FTC expert unpersuasive. *See Fox v. Dannenberg*, 906 F.2d 1253, 1256 (8th Cir. 1990) ("The question of the expert's credibility and the weight to be accorded the expert testimony are ultimately for the trier of fact to determine."). Critically, the district court did credit Lundbeck's expert who stated that the number of neonatologists willing to switch between the drugs based on price was insufficient to exercise price constraint. *See Pioneer Hi-Bred Int'l v. Holden Found. Seeds, Inc.*, 35 F.3d 1226, 1238 (8th Cir. 1994) ("[This court] will not disturb the district court's decision to credit the reasonable testimony of one of two competing experts."). Lundbeck's expert was clear that even those neonatologists who might be willing to switch in response to a price difference would do so only if there was a very significant price decrease, indicating that the level of cross-elasticity was low.

Finally, the FTC contends that the district court ignored its own findings about Lundbeck's internal documents, claiming they indicate Indocin IV and NeoProfen are in the same market. True, industry recognition is a factor in a product market definition. *See Brown Shoe Co.*, 370 U.S. at 325 (a submarket may be identified by a number of a factors, including industry or public recognition of its separate economic character). It is not, however, dispositive. *See C.R. Bard, Inc.*, 642 F.3d at 614, 617 (holding that a hospital did not identify a relevant market even though there was evidence of industry recognition). According to Lundbeck's internal documents, it anticipated that a dramatic price increase of Indocin IV would draw generic competitors into the market. As a result, it ceased promoting Indocin IV, focusing instead on increasing the market share of NeoProfen-as a superior PDA treatment. The FTC argues that this business strategy-to market NeoProfen as better than Indocin IV-means that Lundbeck viewed NeoProfen as a direct competitor to Indocin IV, and thus the drugs must be in the same product market. However, Lundbeck's strategy to discontinue promoting Indocin IV in favor of NeoProfen can also be interpreted to mean that while Indocin IV was vulnerable to generics, NeoProfen was not, and thus the products are not interchangeable. If there are two permissible views of evidence, the factfinder's choice between them is not clearly erroneous. *Anderson*, 470 U.S. at 574.

The judgment is affirmed.

KOPF, DISTRICT JUDGE, concurring.

When defining the product market, and considering the issue of cross-elasticity of demand, the district court relied heavily upon the testimony of doctors that they would use Indocin or NeoProfen without regard to price. Admittedly, those doctors had no responsibility to pay for the drugs or otherwise concern themselves with cost. Thus, the doctors had scant incentive to conserve the scarce resources that would be devoted to paying for the medication. Why the able and experienced trial judge relied upon the doctors' testimony so heavily is perplexing. In an antitrust case, it seems odd to define a product market based upon the actions of actors who eschew rational economic considerations. *See, e.g., F.T.C. v. Tenet Health Care Corp.*, 186 F.3d 1045, 1054 & n.14 (8th Cir. 1999) (observing that "market participants are not always in the best position to assess the market long term" and that is particularly so where their testimony is "contrary to the payers' economic interests and thus is suspect"). That oddity seems especially strange where, as here, there is no real dispute that (1) both drugs are effective when used to treat the illness about which the doctors testified and (2) internal records from the defendant raise an odor of predation.

The foregoing having been said, the standard of review carries the day in this case as it does in so many others. As a result, I fully concur in Judge Benton's excellent opinion.

NOTES AND QUESTIONS

1. This case raises a number of interesting conceptual and evidentiary issues. The district court had before it documentary evidence showing the two products to be each other's closest competitor and showing them to be functional substitutes. But the district court found the record to lack rigorous evidence of cross-elasticity of demand. The court appeared to hold that the latter was necessary for the FTC to prove the two products were in the same relevant market. The case is perplexing because it was clear from the record that Indocin and NeoProfen were, while not bio-equivalent, functionally interchangeable for the treatment of PDA. How then, did the court conclude that the two products were not in the same relevant market?

2. One concern with the district court's analysis is that the judge appeared to be looking for evidence that upon imposition of a SSNIP on one of the products, most doctors would shift to the now less expensive product. There are two problems with this analysis. The first is, as the concurring judge pointed out, the doctors did not bear the cost of the drugs and were therefore unlikely to be the right economic actors to look to for responsiveness to price changes. A second, fundamental problem with the district court's analysis is that the products at issue here, while functionally interchangeable, were biologically distinct. In differentiated product markets price increases will be disciplined by marginal consumers; indeed, in this case it appears that before the merger those marginal customers were sufficient to discipline pricing, as evidenced by the very high post-merger price increase. The district court appears to have missed this point in letting the testimony of just five doctors drive its decision, without recognizing that the actions of the marginal rather than average consumers are most important in differentiated product

markets. *See* Herbert Hovenkamp, Mergers, Market Dominance, and the Lundbeck Case (2011), http://papers.ssrn.com/sol3/papers.cfm?abstract_id=1968151.

3.   While the district court opinion has fundamental conceptual flaws that allowed a clearly anticompetitive consolidation to stand, the FTC's position also raises questions. The agency argued that functionally interchangeable products must be included in the same market, an argument that the Court of Appeals soundly rejected. The citations in the opinion excerpted above show that there can be many cases in which functionally interchangeable products should *not* be in the same market. Consider the *Staples* case, in which the relevant market was consumable office supplies sold by office superstores. The paper sold by Staples was functionally interchangeable with paper sold at the local stationery store, but were rightly not in the same market. What limiting principle is there on the FTC's "functional interchangeability"? How narrowly should function be defined? How interchangeable should the products have to be? Whereas insistence on rigorous proof of high cross-elasticity of demand might be unrealistic in some cases, resort to the concept of "functional interchangeability" could be so malleable as to greatly weaken antitrust enforcement because most merging firms could point to other firms whose products were at least to some degree "functionally interchangeable" even if not sufficiently so to discipline price increases.

4.   The H&R Block case, excerpted below, provided an interesting contrast to *Lundbeck* in its treatment of market definition.

U.S. v. H&R BLOCK, INC.
833 F. Supp. 2d 36 (D.D.C. 2011)

Beryl A. Howell, United States District Judge.

The United States, through the Antitrust Division of the Department of Justice (the "DOJ," the "government," or the "plaintiff"), filed this action on May 23, 2011. The DOJ seeks to enjoin Defendant H&R Block, Inc. from acquiring Defendant 2SS Holdings, Inc. ("TaxACT"), which sells digital do-it-yourself tax preparation products marketed under the brand name TaxACT.

[A]pproximately 140 million Americans filed tax returns with the IRS in 2010. Broadly speaking, there are three methods for preparing a tax return. The "pen and paper" or "manual" method includes preparation by hand and with free, electronically fillable forms available on the IRS website. A second method, known as "assisted" preparation, involves hiring a tax professional - typically either a certified public accountant ("CPA") or a specialist at a retail tax store. HRB operates the largest retail tax store chain in the United States. The companies Jackson-Hewitt and Liberty Tax Service also operate well-known retail tax stores. Finally, many taxpayers now prepare their returns using digital do-it-yourself tax preparation products ("DDIY"), such as the popular software product "TurboTax." DDIY preparation is becoming increasingly popular and an estimated 35 to 40 million taxpayers used DDIY in 2010.

The three most popular DDIY providers are HRB, TaxACT, and Intuit, the maker of TurboTax. According to IRS data, these three firms accounted for approximately 90 percent of the DDIY-prepared federal returns filed in tax season 2010. The proposed acquisition challenged in this case would combine HRB and TaxACT, the second and third most popular providers of DDIY products, respectively. According to the government, this combination would result in an effective duopoly between HRB and Intuit in the DDIY market, in which the next nearest competitor will have an approximately 3 percent market share, and most other competitors will have less than a 1 percent share. The government also alleges that unilateral anticompetitive effects would result from the elimination of head-to-head competition between the merging parties.

Thus, the DOJ alleges that because the proposed acquisition would reduce competition in the DDIY industry by eliminating head-to-head competition between the merging parties and by making anticompetitive coordination between the two major remaining market participants substantially more likely, the proposed acquisition violates Section 7 of the Clayton Act, 15 U.S.C. § 18. Accordingly, the government seeks a permanent injunction blocking HRB from acquiring TaxACT.

On August 1, 2011, the DOJ filed a motion for preliminary injunction against the merger, which was fully briefed by August 18, 2011. The parties subsequently agreed to forego the preliminary injunction phase and proceed directly to a trial on the merits of this action.

The government's motion to enjoin HRB's acquisition of TaxACT is presently before the Court. For the reasons explained in this opinion, the Court grants the government's motion.

C. The History of TaxACT and the Proposed Transaction

Over the years, TaxACT has emphasized high-quality free product offerings as part of its business strategy. TaxACT initially offered a DDIY tax preparation product that made it free to prepare and print a federal tax return, but TaxACT charged a fee for electronic filing ("e-filing") or preparation of a state tax return. Thus, from the beginning, TaxACT's business strategy relied on promoting "free" or "freemium" products, in which a basic part of the service is offered for free and add-ons and extra features are sold for a price.4 As Mr. Dunn put it, "Free is an integral part of the value model. And the beauty of it is it has universal appeal. Everybody likes something for free."

Currently, TaxACT's free product offering allows customers to prepare, print, and e-file a federal tax return completely for free. TaxACT's "Deluxe" edition, which costs $9.95, contains additional features, such as the ability to import data from a return filed the prior year through TaxACT. Customers who use TaxACT to prepare a state tax return in addition to a federal return pay either $14.95 for the state return in combination with the free federal product or $17.95 for the state return in combination with the "Deluxe" federal product. TaxACT's prices have generally remained unchanged for the past decade.

D. Free Products And The Free File Alliance

The evolution of TaxACT's free product offerings and the other free offerings in the DDIY market is important for understanding the claims in this case. The players in the DDIY market offer various "free" tax preparation products, but the features and functionality offered in these free products vary significantly, as do the ways in which these free products are ultimately combined with paid products to earn revenue. While the availability of some types of free product offers has long been a feature of the DDIY market, a spike in free offerings occurred during the last decade in parallel with the growth of e-filing.

As a matter of public policy, the IRS actively promotes e-filing because it has an interest in efficient and accessible tax return preparation and filing.

The IRS determined that the most effective and efficient way to accomplish its goal of promoting access to free online tax preparation and filing options was to partner with a consortium of companies in the electronic tax preparation and filing industry. In 2002, this consortium of companies formed Free File Alliance, LLC ("FFA") in order to partner with the IRS on this initiative to promote free filing. HRB, TaxACT, and Intuit are all members of the FFA, as are approximately fifteen smaller companies. On October 30, 2002, the IRS and the FFA entered into a "Free On-Line Electronic Tax Filing Agreement" to provide free online tax return preparation and filing to individual taxpayers. Pursuant to this agreement, members of the FFA would offer free, online tax preparation and filing services to taxpayers, and the IRS would provide taxpayers with links to those free services through a web page, hosted at irs.gov and accessible through another government website. HRB, TaxACT, and Intuit were among the original members to make free offers through the FFA.

In tax year 2005, in response to restrictions that the IRS imposed on the scope of offers that could be made through the FFA, TaxACT became the first DDIY company to offer all tax payers a free DDIY product for preparation of federal returns directly on its website. Today, free offers in various forms are an entrenched part of the DDIY market.

II. STANDARD OF REVIEW

"*Section 7* of the Clayton Act, *15 U.S.C. § 18*, prohibits a corporation from acquiring 'the whole or any part of the assets of another [corporation] engaged also in commerce or in any activity affecting commerce, where in any line of commerce or in any activity affecting commerce in any section of the country, the effect of such acquisition may be substantially to lessen competition, or to tend to create a monopoly." *United States v. Sungard Data Sys., Inc.*, 172 F. Supp. 2d 172, 180 (D.D.C. 2001) (quoting 15 U.S.C. § 18). "The United States is authorized by *Section 15* of the Clayton Act to seek an injunction to block a pending acquisition." *Id.* (citing 15 U.S.C. § 25). "The United States has the ultimate burden of proving a *Section 7* violation by a preponderance of the evidence." *Id.*

"As this Circuit explained in *Heinz*, 246 F.3d at 715, the decision in *United States v. Baker Hughes Inc.*, 908 F.2d 981, 285 U.S. App. D.C. 222 (D.C. Cir. 1990), sets forth the analytical approach for establishing a Section 7 violation." *Sungard*, 172 F.

Supp. 2d at 180. "The basic outline of a section 7 horizontal acquisition case is familiar. By showing that a transaction will lead to undue concentration in the market for a particular product in a particular geographic area, the government establishes a presumption that the transaction will substantially lessen competition." *Baker Hughes*, 908 F.2d at 982. To establish this presumption, the government must "show that the merger would produce 'a firm controlling an undue percentage share of the relevant market, and [would] result [ ] in a significant increase in the concentration of firms in that market.'" *Heinz*, 246 F.3d at 715 (quoting *United States v. Philadelphia Nat'l Bank*, 374 U.S. 321, 363, 83 S. Ct. 1715, 10 L. Ed. 2d 915 (1963)) (alterations in original). Once the government has established this presumption, the burden shifts to the defendants to rebut the presumption by "show[ing] that the market-share statistics give an inaccurate account of the merger's probable effects on competition in the relevant market." *Heinz*, 246 F.3d at 715 (internal quotation omitted). "'If the defendant successfully rebuts the presumption [of illegality], the burden of producing additional evidence of anticompetitive effect shifts to the government, and merges with the ultimate burden of persuasion, which remains with the government at all times.'" *Id.* (quoting *Baker Hughes*, 908 F.2d at 983). Ultimately, "[t]he Supreme Court has adopted a totality-of-the-circumstances approach to the statute, weighing a variety of factors to determine the effects of particular transactions on competition." *Baker Hughes*, 908 F.2d at 984.

III. DISCUSSION

A. The Relevant Product Market

"Merger analysis begins with defining the relevant product market." *FTC v. Swedish Match*, 131 F. Supp. 2d 151, 156 (D.D.C. 2000) (citing *Brown Shoe*, 370 U.S. 294, 324, 82 S. Ct. 1502, 8 L. Ed. 2d 510 (1962)). "Defining the relevant market is critical in an antitrust case because the legality of the proposed merger[] in question almost always depends upon the market power of the parties involved." *Id.* (quoting *FTC v. Cardinal Health, Inc.*, 12 F. Supp. 2d 34, 45 (D.D.C. 1998)). Indeed, the relevant market definition is often "the key to the ultimate resolution of this type of case because of the relative implications of market power." *Id.*

The government argues that the relevant market in this case consists of all DDIY products, but does not include assisted tax preparation or pen-and-paper. Under this view of the market, the acquisition in this case would result in a DDIY market that is dominated by two large players — H&R Block and Intuit — that together control approximately 90 percent of the market share, with the remaining 10 percent of the market divided amongst a plethora of smaller companies. In contrast, the defendants argue for a broader market that includes all tax preparation methods ("all methods"), comprised of DDIY, assisted, and pen-and-paper. Under this view of the market, the market concentration effects of this acquisition would be much smaller and would not lead to a situation in which two firms control 90 percent of the market. This broader view of the market rests primarily on the premise that providers of all methods of tax preparation compete with each other for the patronage of the same pool of customers — U.S. taxpayers. After carefully considering the evidence and arguments presented by all parties, the Court has concluded that the relevant market in this case is, as the DOJ contends, the market for digital do-it-yourself tax preparation products.

A "relevant product market" is a term of art in antitrust analysis. The Supreme Court has set forth the general rule for defining a relevant product market: "The outer boundaries of a product market are determined by the reasonable inter-changeability of use [by consumers] or the cross-elasticity of demand between the product itself and substitutes for it." *Brown Shoe*, 370 U.S. at 325; *see also United States v. E.I. du Pont de Nemours & Co.*, 351 U.S. 377, 395 (1956). In other words, courts look at "whether two products can be used for the same purpose, and, if so, whether and to what extent purchasers are willing to substitute one for the other." *FTC v. Staples, Inc.*, 970 F. Supp. 1066, 1074 (D.D.C. 1997) (citation omitted).

An analytical method often used by courts to define a relevant market is to ask hypothetically whether it would be profitable to have a monopoly over a given set of substitutable products. If so, those products may constitute a relevant market. *See* 5C Phillip E. Areeda & Herbert Hovenkamp, Antitrust Law (hereinafter, "Areeda & Hovenkamp"), ¶ 530a, at 226 (3d ed. 2007) ("[A] market can be seen as the array of producers of substitute products that could control price if united in a hypothetical cartel or as a hypothetical monopoly."). This approach — sometimes called the "hypothetical monopolist test" — is endorsed by the Horizontal Merger Guidelines issued by the DOJ and Federal Trade Commission. *See Fed. Trade Comm'n & U.S. Dep't of Justice Horizontal Merger Guidelines* (2010) (hereinafter, "Merger Guidelines"), § 4.1.1. In the merger context, this inquiry boils down to whether "a hypothetical profit-maximizing firm, not subject to price regulation, that was the only present and future seller of those products . . . likely would impose at least a small but significant and non-transitory increase in price ("SSNIP") on at least one product in the market, including at least one product sold by one of the merging firms." *Id.* The "small but significant and non-transitory increase in price," or SSNIP, is typically assumed to be five percent or more. *Id.* § 4.1.2.

Thus, the question here is whether it would be hypothetically useful to have a monopoly over all DDIY tax preparation products because the monopolist could then profitably raise prices for those products by five percent or more; or whether, to the contrary, there would be no reason to monopolize all DDIY tax preparation products because substitution and price competition with other methods of tax preparation would restrain any potential DDIY monopolist from profitably raising prices. In other words, would enough DDIY users switch to the assisted or pen-and-paper methods of tax preparation in response to a five-to-ten percent increase in DDIY prices to make such a price increase unprofitable?

In evaluating the relevant product market here, the Court considers business documents from the defendants and others, the testimony of the fact witnesses, and the analyses of the parties' expert economists. This evidence demonstrates that DDIY is the relevant product market in this case.

1. The Defendants' Documents Show That DDIY Is The Relevant Product Market.

When determining the relevant product market, courts often pay close attention to the defendants' ordinary course of business documents. *See, e.g., Staples*, 970 F. Supp. at 1076; *CCC Holdings*, 605 F. Supp. 2d at 41–42. The government argues that the defendants' ordinary course of business documents in this case "conclusively demonstrate that competition with other [DDIY] firms drive Defendants' pricing decisions, quality improvements, and corporate strategy" for their own DDIY products — thus supporting the government's view of the relevant market. The defendants contend that the government has relied on "select, 'out-of-context' snippets from documents," and that the documents as a whole support the defendants' view that the relevant product market is all methods of tax preparation. The Court finds that the documentary evidence in this case supports the conclusion that DDIY is the relevant product market.

Internal TaxACT documents establish that TaxACT has viewed DDIY offerings by HRB and TurboTax as its primary competitors, that it has tracked their marketing, product offerings, and pricing, and that it has determined its own pricing and business strategy in relation to those companies' DDIY products. Confidential memoranda prepared by TaxACT's investment bankers for potential private equity buyers of TaxACT identify HRB and TurboTax as TaxACT's primary competitors in a DDIY market. These documents also recognize that TaxACT's strategy for competing with Intuit and HRB is to offer a lower price for what it deems a superior product.

While, as defendants point out, parts of these TaxACT documents also discuss the broader tax preparation industry, these documents make clear that TaxACT's own view — and that conveyed by its investment bankers to potential buyers — is that the company primarily competes in a DDIY market against Intuit and HRB and that it develops its pricing and business strategy with that market and those competitors in mind. These documents are strong evidence that DDIY is the relevant product market. *See Whole Foods*, 548 F.3d at 1045 *(Tatel, J.)* ("[E]vidence of industry or public recognition of the submarket as a separate economic unit matters because we assume that economic actors usually have accurate perceptions of economic realities.") (internal quotation omitted).

2. The Relevant Product Market Does Not Include Assisted Tax Preparation Or Manual Preparation.

It is beyond debate — and conceded by the plaintiff — that all methods of tax preparation are, to some degree, in competition. All tax preparation methods provide taxpayers with a means to perform the task of completing a tax return, but each method is starkly different. Thus, while providers of all tax preparation methods may compete at some level, this "does not necessarily require that [they] be included in the relevant product market for antitrust purposes." *Staples*, 970 F. Supp. at 1075. DDIY tax preparation products differ from manual tax preparation and assisted tax preparation products in a number of meaningful ways. As compared to manual and assisted methods, DDIY products involve different technology, price, convenience level, time investment, mental effort and type of interaction by the consumer. Taken together, these different attributes make the consumer experience of using DDIY products quite distinct from other methods of tax preparation. *See Whole Foods*, 548 F.3d at 1037–38 *(Brown, J.)* (noting that a "product's peculiar characteristics and uses" and "distinct prices" may distinguish a relevant market) (citing *Brown Shoe*, 370 U.S. at 325). The question for this court is whether DDIY and other methods of tax preparation are "reasonably interchangeable" so that it would not be profitable to have a monopoly over only DDIY products.

a. Assisted Tax Preparation Is Not In The Relevant Product Market.

Apart from the analysis of their economic expert, the defendants' main argument for inclusion of assisted tax preparation in the relevant market is that DDIY and assisted companies compete for customers. As evidence for this point, the defendants emphasize that Intuit's marketing efforts have targeted HRB's assisted customers. While the evidence does show that companies in the DDIY and assisted markets all generally compete with each other for the same overall pool of potential customers — U.S. taxpayers — that fact does not necessarily mean that DDIY and assisted must be viewed as part of the same relevant product market. DDIY provides customers with tax preparation services through an entirely different method, technology, and user experience than assisted preparation. As Judge Tatel explained in *Whole Foods:*

> [W]hen the automobile was first invented, competing auto manufacturers obviously took customers primarily from companies selling horses and buggies, not from other auto manufacturers, but that hardly shows that cars and horse-drawn carriages should be treated as the same product market. That Whole Foods and Wild Oats have attracted many customers away from conventional grocery stores by offering extensive selections of natural and organic products thus tells us nothing about whether Whole Foods and Wild Oats should be treated as operating in the same market as conventional grocery stores. Indeed, courts have often found that sufficiently innovative retailers can constitute a distinct product market even when they take customers from existing retailers.

Whole Foods, 548 F.3d at 1048; *see also Staples*, 970 F. Supp. at 1074–80 (finding a distinct market of office supply superstores despite competition from mail-order catalogues and stores carrying a broader range of merchandise).

The key question for the Court is whether DDIY and assisted products are sufficiently close substitutes to constrain any anticompetitive DDIY pricing after the proposed merger. Evidence of the absence of close price competition between DDIY and assisted products makes clear that the answer to that question is no — and that DDIY is the relevant product market here. *See Swedish Match*, 131 F. Supp. 2d at 165 ("Distinct pricing is also a consideration" in determining the relevant product market) (citing *Brown Shoe*, 370 U.S. at 325). Significantly, despite some DDIY efforts to capture tax store customers, none of the major DDIY competitors sets their prices based on consideration of assisted prices. Indeed, there are quite significant price disparities between the average prices of DDIY and assisted products. The average price of TurboTax, the most popular DDIY brand is approximately $55. The average price of HRB's DDIY products is approximately $25. Overall, the DDIY industry average price is $44.13. In contrast, the typical price of an assisted tax return is significantly higher, in the range of $150-200. A 10 percent or even 20 percent price increase in the average price of DDIY would only move the average price up to $48.54 or $52.96, respectively — still substantially below the average price of assisted tax products. The overall lack of evidence of price competition between DDIY and assisted products supports the conclusion that DDIY is a separate relevant product market for evaluating this transaction, despite the fact that DDIY and assisted firms target their marketing efforts at the same pool of customers.

b. Manual Tax Preparation Is Not In The Relevant Product Market.

The defendants also argue that manual tax preparation, or pen-and-paper, should be included in the relevant product market. At the outset, the Court notes that pen-and-paper is not a "product" at all; it is the task of filling out a tax return by oneself without any interactive assistance. Even so, the defendants argue pen-and-paper should be included in the relevant product market because it acts as a "significant competitive constraint" on DDIY. The defendants' argument relies primarily on two factors. First, the defendants' cite the results of a 2011 email survey of TaxACT customers. For reasons detailed in the following section, the Court declines to rely on this email survey. Second, the defendants point to documents and testimony indicating that TaxACT has considered possible diversion to pen-and-paper in setting its prices.

The Court finds that pen-and-paper is not part of the relevant market because it does not believe a sufficient number of consumers would switch to pen-and-paper in response to a small, but significant increase in DDIY prices. The possibility of preparing one's own tax return necessarily constrains the prices of other methods of preparation at some level. For example, if the price of DDIY and assisted products were raised to $1 million per tax return, surely all but the most well-heeled taxpayers would switch to pen-and-paper. Yet, at the more practical price increase levels that trigger antitrust concern — the typical five to ten percent price increase of the SSNIP test — pen-and-paper preparation is unlikely to provide a meaningful restraint for DDIY products, which currently sell for an average price of $44.13.

The government well illustrated the overly broad nature of defendants' proposed relevant market by posing to the defendants' expert the hypothetical question of whether "sitting at home and drinking chicken soup [would be] part of the market for [manufactured] cold remedies?" The defendants' expert responded that the real "question is if the price of cold medicines went up sufficiently, would people turn to chicken soup?" As an initial matter, in contrast to the defendants' expert, the Court doubts that it would ever be legally appropriate to define a relevant product market that included manufactured cold remedies and ordinary chicken soup. This conclusion flows from the deep functional differences between those products. Setting that issue aside, however, a price has increased "sufficiently" to trigger antitrust concern at the level of a five to ten percent small, but significant non-transitory increase in price. Just as chicken soup is unlikely to constrain the price of manufactured cold remedies sufficiently, the Court concludes that a SSNIP in DDIY would not be constrained by people turning to pen-and-paper.

The main case the defendants rely on to show that "self-supply" substitutes should be included in the relevant market involved a consumer market consisting of vertically integrated companies and explicitly distinguished cases, such as this one, involving markets of individual consumers. In *United States v. Sungard Data Systems, Inc.*, Judge Huvelle found that disaster recovery computer systems developed internally by companies were in the same relevant product market as shared data recovery systems provided by outside vendors. *Sungard*, 172 F. Supp. 2d at 187–89. The *Sungard* court, however, distinguished the case before it — which involved vertical integration — from the situation in *Heinz*, the case involving the market for jarred baby food, because "homemade baby food is not an aspect of vertical integration . . . [and] individual consumers cannot vertically integrate by producing a product that they would otherwise have to purchase." *Id. at 187 n.15.* In finding that in-house computer systems were included in its relevant product market, the *Sungard* court cited the following example from Areeda & Hovenkamp ¶ 535e regarding vertical integration:

> If iron ore is the relevant market and if shares are best measured there by sales, then internally used ore — so-called captive output — is part of the ore market even though it is not sold as such.
>
> In measuring the market power of a defendant selling iron ore, the ore used internally by other firms constrains the defendant's ability to profit by raising ore prices to monopoly levels. The higher ore price may induce an integrated firm to expand its ore production — to supply others in direct competition with the alleged monopolist or to expand its own steel production and thereby reduce the demand of other steel makers for ore, or both. Hence, captive output constrains the defendant regardless of whether integrated firms sell their ore to other steel makers previously purchasing from the defendant. In sum, the integrated firm's ore output belongs in the market.

Id. at 186 n.14. This rationale for including "self-supply" in a relevant product market does not appear to apply to the DDIY market in which the consumers are individuals and not also potential traders or producers.

While some diversion from DDIY to manual filing may occur in response to a SSNIP, the Court finds that it would likely be limited and marginal. The functional experience of using a DDIY product is meaningfully different from the self-service task of filling out tax forms independently. Manual completion of a tax return requires different tools, effort, resources, and time investment by a consumer than use of either DDIY or assisted methods.

Indeed, the pen-and-paper method, in which the consumer essentially relies on his or her own labor to prepare a tax return, is perhaps most analogous to walking as opposed to purchasing a ride on any means of transportation. In sum, filling out a tax return manually is not reasonably interchangeable with DDIY products that effectively fill out the tax return with data input provided by the consumer.

B. Likely Effect on Competition

1. The Plaintiff's Prima Facie Case

Having defined the relevant market as DDIY tax preparation products, "the Court must next consider the likely effects of the proposed acquisition on competition within that market." *Swedish Match*, 131 F. Supp. 2d at 166. The government must now make out its prima facie case by showing "that the merger would produce 'a firm controlling an undue percentage share of the relevant market, and [would] result[ ] in a significant increase in the concentration of firms in that market.'" *Heinz*, 246 F.3d at 715 (quoting *Philadelphia Nat'l Bank*, 374 U.S. at 363). "Such a showing establishes a 'presumption' that the merger will substantially lessen competition." *Id.*

"Market concentration, or the lack thereof, is often measured by the Herfindahl-Hirschmann Index ('HHI')." *Id. at 716*. "The HHI is calculated by totaling the squares of the market shares of every firm in the relevant market. For example, a market with ten firms having market shares of 20%, 17%, 13%, 12%, 10%, 10%, 8%, 5%, 3%, and 2% has an HHI of 1304 ($20^2 + 17^2 + 13^2 + 12^2 + 10^2 + 10^2 + 8^2 + 5^2 + 3^2 + 2^2$)." *Id.* at 715 n.9. Sufficiently large HHI figures establish the government's prima facie case that a merger is anticompetitive. *Id.* Under the Horizontal Merger Guidelines, markets with an HHI above 2500 are considered "highly concentrated" and mergers "resulting in highly concentrated markets that involve an increase in the HHI of more than 200 points will be presumed to be likely to enhance market power." Merger Guidelines § 5.3.

In this case, market concentration as measured by HHI is currently 4,291, indicating a highly concentrated market under the Merger Guidelines. The most recent measures of market share show Intuit with 62.2 percent of the market, HRB with 15.6 percent, and TaxACT with 12.8 percent. These market share calculations are based on data provided by the IRS for federal tax filings for 2010, the most recent data available.

The proposed acquisition in this case would give the combined firm a 28.4 percent market share and will increase the HHI by approximately 400, resulting in a post-acquisition HHI of 4,691. These HHI levels are high enough to create a presumption of anticompetitive effects. *See, e.g., Heinz*, 246 F.3d at 716 (three-firm to two-firm merger that would have increased HHI by 510 points from 4,775 created presumption of anticompetitive effects by a "wide margin"); *Swedish Match*, 131 F. Supp. 2d at 166–67 (60 percent market share and 4,733 HHI established presumption). Accordingly, the government has established a prima facie case of anticompetitive effects.

"Upon the showing of a *prima facie* case, the burden shifts to defendants to show that traditional economic theories of the competitive effects of market concentration are not an accurate indicator of the merger's probable effect on competition in these markets or that the procompetitive effects of the merger are likely to outweigh any potential anticompetitive effects." *CCC Holdings*, 605 F. Supp. 2d at 46. "The courts have not established a clear standard that the merging parties must meet in order to rebut a prima facie case, other than to advise that '[t]he more compelling the prima facie case, the more evidence the defendant must present to rebut [the presumption] successfully.'" *Id.* at 46–47 (quoting *Baker Hughes*, 908 F.2d at 991). Even in cases where the government has made a strong prima facie showing:

> [i]mposing a heavy burden of production on a defendant would be particularly anomalous where, as here, it is easy to establish a prima facie case. The government, after all, can carry its initial burden of production simply by presenting market concentration statistics. To allow the government virtually to rest its case at that point, leaving the defendant to prove the core of the dispute, would grossly inflate the role of statistics in actions brought under section 7. The Herfindahl-Hirschman Index cannot guarantee litigation victories.

Baker Hughes, 908 F.2d at 992. Thus, ultimately,"[t]he Supreme Court has adopted a totality-of-the-circumstances approach to the [Clayton Act], weighing a variety of factors to determine the effects of particular transactions on competition." *Id.* at 984. With these observations in mind, the Court will evaluate the parties' evidence and arguments about the likely effect of the transaction on competition in the DDIY market.

2. Defendants' Rebuttal Arguments

a. Barriers to Entry

Defendants argue that the likelihood of expansion by existing DDIY companies besides Intuit, HRB, and TaxACT will offset any potential anticompetitive effects from the merger. Courts have held that likely entry or expansion by other competitors can counteract anticompetitive effects that would otherwise be expected. *See Heinz*, 246 F.3d at 717 n.13 ("Barriers to entry are important in evaluating whether market concentration statistics accurately reflect the pre- and likely post-merger competitive picture."); *Baker Hughes*, 908 F.2d at 987 ("In the absence of significant barriers, a company probably cannot maintain supracompetitive pricing for any length of time."). According to the Merger Guidelines, entry or expansion must be "timely, likely, and sufficient in its magnitude, character, and scope to deter or counteract the competitive effects of concern." Merger Guidelines § 9; *see also CCC Holdings*, 605 F. Supp. 2d at 47; *United States v. Visa USA, Inc.*, 163 F. Supp. 2d 322, 342 (S.D.N.Y. 2001) (entry must be "timely, likely, and [of a] sufficient scale to deter or counteract any anticompetitive restraints"). "Determining whether there is ease of entry hinges upon an analysis of barriers to new firms entering the market or existing firms expanding into new regions of the market." *CCC Holdings*, 605 F. Supp. 2d at 47 (quoting *FTC v. Cardinal Health, Inc.*, 12 F. Supp. 2d 34, 55 (D.D.C. 1998)). In this case, the parties essentially agree that the proper focus of this inquiry is on the likelihood of expansion by existing competitors rather than new entry into the market. Since the government has established its prima facie case, the defendants carry the burden to show that ease of expansion is sufficient "to fill the competitive void that will result if [defendants are] permitted to purchase" their acquisition target. *Swedish Match*, 131 F. Supp. 2d at 169.

In describing the competitive landscape, the defendants note there are 18 companies offering various DDIY products through the FFA. Most of these companies are very small-time operators, however. The defendants acknowledge this fact, but nevertheless contend that the companies "TaxSlayer and TaxHawk are the two largest and most poised to replicate the scale and strength of TaxACT." Witnesses from TaxSlayer and TaxHawk were the only witnesses from other DDIY companies to testify at the hearing. As such, the Court's ease of expansion analysis will focus on whether these two competitors are poised to expand in a way that is "timely, likely, and sufficient in its magnitude, character, and scope to deter or counteract" any potential anticompetitive effects resulting from the merger.

TaxHawk runs five different websites, including FreeTaxUSA.com, that all market the same underlying DDIY product. TaxHawk was founded in 2001, three years after TaxACT, although it has a significantly smaller market share of 3.2 percent. TaxHawk's vice-president and co-founder, Mr. Dane Kimber, testified that the company has the technical infrastructure to grow by five to seven times the number of customers in any given year. TaxHawk's marketing strategy relies substantially on search engine advertising and search term optimization, including by using the FreeTaxUSA.com domain name, which contains the keywords "free" and "tax." Despite having been in business for a decade, its products are functionally more limited than those of Intuit, HRB, and TaxACT in various ways. Although TaxHawk services the forms that cover most taxpayers, its program does not service all federal forms, it excludes two states' forms in their entirety, and it does not service city income tax forms for major cities that have income taxes — notably, New York City. In fact, Mr. Kimber testified that the company would likely need another decade before its DDIY products could fully support all the tax forms. The reason is that TaxHawk is what Mr. Kimber "like[s] to call . . . a 'lifestyle' company. We like the lifestyle we have as owners. We want our employees to have a life, if you will. I do feel we have the expertise to [expand functionality] more rapidly, but we choose not to." Mr. Kimber also testified that TaxHawk had suddenly experienced an unprecedented growth rate of over 60 percent since April 2011, but that the company had not done any analysis to attempt to explain this unanticipated (and presumably welcome) growth.

TaxHawk's relaxed attitude toward its business stands in stark contrast to the entrepreneurial verve that was apparent throughout the testimony of Mr. Dunn and that has been rewarded by the impressive growth of TaxACT over the years. In short, TaxHawk is a very different company from TaxACT. TaxHawk is a small company that has developed a string of search-engine-optimized DDIY websites, which deliver a sufficient income stream to sustain its owners' comfortable lifestyle, without requiring maximal effort on their part. While TaxHawk's decision to prioritize a relaxed lifestyle over robust competition and innovation is certainly a valid one, expansion from TaxHawk that would allow it to compete "on the same playing field" as the merged company appears unlikely. *Chicago Bridge & Iron Co. N.V. v. FTC*, 534 F.3d 410, 430 (5th Cir. 2008).

After TaxHawk, TaxSlayer is the next largest DDIY competitor, with a 2.7 percent market share.

TaxSlayer's stable market share despite its (significant) marketing expenditure as a proportion of revenue points to what the government considers the key barrier to entry in this market — the importance of reputation and brand in driving consumer behavior in purchasing DDIY products. Simply put, tax returns are highly personal documents that carry significant financial and legal consequences for consumers. Consumers, therefore, must trust and have confidence in their tax service provider. As one of TaxACT's bankers put it a confidential memorandum, "[t]ax filers must have confidence that sensitive data is being handled with care and that returns are processed in a secure, error-free and timely manner."

Building a reputation that a significant number of consumers will trust requires time and money. As HRB's former CEO noted, it takes millions of dollars and lots of time to develop a brand. TaxACT's offering memoranda also point to the difficulty in building a brand in the industry as a barrier to competition. In the DDIY industry, the Big Three incumbent players spend millions on marketing and advertising each year to build and maintain their brands, dwarfing the combined spending of the smaller companies. For example, in tax year 2009, Intuit, HRB, and TaxACT collectively spent approximately (over $100 million) on marketing and advertising. By contrast, (TaxSlayer and TaxHawk spent a significantly smaller amount).

In support of their argument that TaxSlayer and TaxHawk are poised to expand in response to a price increase, the defendants emphasize that these companies "are at about the same position in terms of customer base as TaxACT was in 2002, which was the year before it did the Free For All [offer on] the FFA." The government points out, however, that there are two flaws in this comparison, even assuming that TaxSlayer and TaxHawk were TaxACT's competitive equals. First, while these companies may have a similar number of customers to TaxACT in 2002 in absolute terms, TaxACT's market share at 8 percent was already significantly larger than the market shares of these firms today, despite the fact that TaxACT had been in the market for fewer years.

Second, the DDIY market has matured considerably since 2002, in parallel with the general ripening of various online industries during the past decade. Notably, the pool of pen-and-paper customers has dwindled as DDIY preparation has grown. Thus, the "low hanging fruit" of DDIY customer acquisition may have been plucked. This trend suggests existing market shares may become further entrenched and that growing market share may be even harder, especially because there are barriers to switching from one DDIY product to another. For example, the hearing evidence showed that it is difficult to import prior-year tax return data across DDIY brands. If a taxpayer uses, say, TurboTax or TaxACT in one year, then when the taxpayer returns the next year, the program can automatically import the prior year's data, which is not only convenient but can also help the taxpayer identify useful tax information, such as carry forwards and available deductions. Currently, it is not possible to import much of this data if the taxpayer switches to a competitor's product. *Id.* Thus, this feature lends a "stickiness" to each particular DDIY product once a customer has used it.

Upon consideration of all of the evidence relating to barriers to entry or expansion, the Court cannot find that expansion is likely to avert anticompetitive effects from the transaction. The Court will next consider whether the evidence supports a likelihood of coordinated or unilateral anticompetitive effects from the merger.

b. Coordinated Effects

Merger law "rests upon the theory that, where rivals are few, firms will be able to coordinate their behavior, either by overt collusion or implicit understanding in order to restrict output and achieve profits above competitive levels." *CCC Holdings*, 605 F. Supp. 2d at 60 (quoting *Heinz*, 246 F.3d at 715). The government argues that the "elimination of TaxACT, one of the 'Big 3' Digital DIY firms" will facilitate tacit coordination between Intuit and HRB. "Whether a merger will make coordinated interaction more likely depends on whether market conditions, on the whole, are conducive to reaching terms of coordination and detecting and punishing deviations from those terms." *CCC Holdings*, 605 F. Supp. 2d at 60 (internal quotation omitted). Since the government has established its prima facie case, the burden is on the defendants to produce evidence of "structural market barriers to collusion" specific to this industry that would defeat the "ordinary presumption of collusion" that attaches to a merger in a highly concentrated market. *See Heinz*, 246 F.3d at 725.

The defendants argue the primary reason that coordinated effects will be unlikely is that Intuit will have no incentive to compete any less vigorously post-merger. The defendants assert that the competition between Intuit and HRB's retail stores would be "fundamentally nullified if Intuit decided to reduce the competitiveness of TurboTax." Further, defendants contend that Intuit has no incentive to reduce the competitiveness of its free product because it views its free product as a critical driver of new customers. Therefore, the defendants conclude that if HRB does not compete as aggressively as possible with its post-merger products, it will lose customers to Intuit.

The most compelling evidence the defendants marshal in support of these arguments consists of documents and testimony indicating that Intuit engaged in a series of "war games" designed to anticipate and defuse new competitive threats that might emerge from HRB post-merger. The documents and testimony do indicate that Intuit and HRB will continue to compete for taxpayers' patronage after the merger — indeed, in the DDIY market, they would be the only major competitors. This conclusion, however, is not necessarily inconsistent with some coordination. As the Merger Guidelines explain, coordinated interaction involves a range of conduct, including unspoken understandings about *how* firms will compete or refrain from competing. *See* Merger Guidelines § 7.

In this case, the government contends that coordination would likely take the form of mutual recognition that neither firm has an interest in an overall "race to free" in which high-quality tax preparation software is provided for free or very low prices. Indeed, the government points to an outline created as part of the Intuit "war games" regarding post-merger competition with HRB that also indicates an Intuit employee's perception that part of HRB's post-merger strategy would be to "not escalate free war: Make free the starting point not the end point for customers."[30] Since, as defendants point out, DDIY companies have found "free" offers to be a useful marketing tool, it is unlikely that free offers would be eliminated. Rather, the government argues, it is more likely that HRB and Intuit may find it "in their mutual interest to reduce the quality of their free offerings . . . offer a lower quality free product and maintain higher prices for paid products . . . ."

The government points to a highly persuasive historical act of cooperation between HRB and Intuit that supports this theory. *Cf.* Merger Guidelines § 7.2 ("[M]arket conditions are conducive to coordinated interaction if firms representing a substantial share in the relevant market appear to have previously engaged in express collusion."). After TaxACT launched its free-for-all offer in the FFA, Intuit proposed that the firms in the market limit their free FFA offers, a move which TaxACT opposed and which Mr. Dunn believed was an illegal restraint on trade. HRB, Intuit, and others then joined together and successfully lobbied the IRS for limitations on the scope of the free offers through the FFA — limitations that remain in place today. This action illustrates how the pricing incentives of HRB and Intuit differ from those of TaxACT and it also shows that HRB and Intuit, although otherwise competitors, are capable of acting in concert to protect their common interests.

c. Unilateral Effects

A merger is likely to have unilateral anticompetitive effect if the acquiring firm will have the incentive to raise prices or reduce quality after the acquisition, independent of competitive responses from other firms. *See Swedish Match*, 131 F. Supp. 2d at 169; Merger Guidelines § 6 ("The elimination of competition between two firms that results from their merger may alone constitute a substantial lessening of competition."). "The extent of direct competition between the products sold by the merging parties is central to the evaluation of unilateral price effects." Merger Guidelines § 6.1. As Judge Collyer in *CCC Holdings* explained:

> Unilateral effects in a differentiated product market are likely to be profitable under the following conditions: (1) the products must be differentiated; (2) the products controlled by the *merging* firms must be close substitutes, *i.e.*, "a substantial number of the customers of one firm would turn to the other in response to a price increase"; (3) other products must be sufficiently different from the products offered by the merging firms that a merger would make a small but significant and non-transitory price increase profitable for the merging firm; and (4) repositioning must be unlikely.

605 F. Supp. 2d at 68 (citing *Oracle*, 331 F. Supp. 2d at 1117–18). Since the Court has already found that the preponderance of the evidence shows a reasonable likelihood of coordinated effects, the Court need not reach the issue of unilateral effects. *See id.* at 67. The Court will discuss it, however, since there has been substantial argument on this topic and the Court's findings regarding unilateral effects bolster the conclusion that this proposed merger would violate Section 7 of the Clayton Act. As with coordinated effects, since the government has established its prima facie case, the burden is on the defendants to produce evidence showing that the presumption of anticompetitive effects that attaches to a merger in a highly

concentrated market is unfounded, but the ultimate burden of proof remains with the government.

i. Elimination of Direct Competition Between the Merging Parties

The government argues that unilateral effects are likely because the merger will eliminate head-to-head competition between HRB and TaxACT that has benefited taxpaying American consumers. Much of the evidence indicating direct competition between HRB and TaxACT is discussed above in relation to the market definition. *See supra* Section III.A. The government emphasizes that HRB has lowered its DDIY prices to better compete with free online products, the category pioneered by TaxACT, and has directly considered TaxACT's prices in setting its own prices. HRB has also determined the nature of its free offerings in response to competitive activity from TaxACT. The government also points to HRB documents that appear to acknowledge that TaxACT has put downward pressure on HRB's pricing ability. From all of this evidence, and the additional evidence discussed in this opinion, it is clear that HRB and TaxACT are head-to-head competitors.

ii. Pledge to Maintain TaxACT's Current Prices

Defendants press a few different arguments against a finding of likely unilateral anticompetitive effects. First, the defendants have pledged to maintain TaxACT's current prices for three years. While the Court has no reason to doubt that defendants would honor their promise, this type of guarantee cannot rebut a likelihood of anticompetitive effects in this case. *See Cardinal Health, 12 F. Supp. 2d at 64* (finding that "even with such guarantees [to maintain prices], the mergers would likely result in anti-competitive prices."). Even if TaxACT's list price remains the same, the merged firm could accomplish what amounts to a price increase through other means. For example, instead of raising TaxACT's prices, it could limit the functionality of TaxACT's products, reserving special features or innovations for higher priced, HRB-branded products. The merged firm could also limit the availability of TaxACT to consumers by marketing it more selectively and less vigorously. Indeed, the defendants concede that one immediate effect of the merger will be the removal of TaxACT from the IRS-sponsored FFA website, a marketing channel whose importance the defendants themselves emphasize in their argument regarding barriers to expansion.

iii. Value Versus Premium Market Segments

Second, defendants argue that HRB and TaxACT are not particularly close competitors. The defendants contend that HRB and TaxACT largely compete in distinct segments of the market — with HRB in the higher-priced, "premium" segment and TaxACT in the lower-priced, "value" segment. The defendants also argue that there can be no unilateral effects because the evidence shows that both TaxACT and HRB are closer competitors to TurboTax than to each other.

The fact that Intuit may be the closest competitor for both HRB and TaxACT also does not necessarily prevent a finding of unilateral effects for this merger. *See* Areeda & Hovenkamp, ¶ 914, 77–80 (explaining that the merging parties need not be the closest rivals for there to be unilateral anticompetitive effects); *see also* Commentary on the Horizontal Merger Guidelines (2006) at 28 ("A merger may produce significant unilateral effects even though a non-merging product is the 'closest' substitute for every merging product . . . ."). Using a simple estimate of diversion based on market share would indeed suggest that HRB and TaxACT are each other's second closest rivals after Intuit.

iv. Merged Company's Combined Market Share

Another argument that the defendants present against a likelihood of unilateral effects is that, in their view, unilateral effects cannot be demonstrated where the combined firm's market share does not surpass a certain threshold. The defendants point out that in *Oracle*, the court stated that "[a] presumption of anticompetitive effects from a combined share of 35% in a differentiated products market is unwarranted. Indeed, the opposite is likely true." 331 F. Supp. 2d at 1123. The *Oracle* court stated that "[t]o prevail on a differentiated products unilateral effects claim, a plaintiff must prove a relevant market in which the merging parties would have essentially a monopoly or dominant position." *Id.* Some commentators have criticized this standard, however, because "impermissible price increases . . . can be achieved on far lower market shares" than *Oracle*'s standard evidently requires. Areeda & Hovenkamp ¶ 914, at 84. Indeed, Judge Brown's subsequent opinion from this Circuit in *Whole Foods* implied that a market definition itself may not even be required for proving a Section 7 violation based on unilateral effects. *See Whole Foods*, 548 F.3d at 1036. In a footnote, Judge Brown explained that "a merger between two close competitors can sometimes raise antitrust concerns due to unilateral effects in highly differentiated markets. In such a situation, it might not be necessary to understand the market definition to conclude a preliminary injunction should issue." *Id.* at n.1 (citation omitted). The Court therefore declines the defendants' invitation, in reliance on *Oracle*, to impose a market share threshold for proving a unilateral effects claim.

d. Post-Merger Efficiencies

One of the key benefits of a merger to the economy is its potential to generate efficiencies. *See Heinz*, 246 F.3d at 720. As the Merger Guidelines recognize, merger-generated efficiencies can "enhance the merged firm's ability and incentive to compete, which may result in lower prices, improved quality, enhanced service, or new products." Merger Guidelines § 10. Courts have recognized that a showing of sufficient efficiencies may rebut the government's showing of likely anticompetitive effects. *Heinz*, 246 F.3d at 720. High market concentration levels require "proof of extraordinary efficiencies," however, and courts "generally have found inadequate proof of efficiencies to sustain a rebuttal of the government's case." *Id.* (citation omitted).

"[T]he court must undertake a rigorous analysis of the kinds of efficiencies being urged by the parties in order to ensure that those 'efficiencies' represent more than mere speculation and promises about post-merger behavior." *Id.* at 721. As the Merger Guidelines explain, "[c]ognizable efficiencies are merger-specific efficiencies that have been verified and do not arise from anticompetitive reductions in output or service." Merger Guidelines § 10. Efficiencies are inherently "difficult to verify and quantify" and "it is incumbent upon the merging firms to substantiate efficiency claims" so that it is possible to "verify by reasonable means the likelihood and magnitude of each asserted efficiency, how and when each would be achieved (and any costs of doing so), how each would enhance the merged firm's ability and incentive to compete, and why each would be merger-specific." *Id.* In other words, a "cognizable" efficiency claim must represent a type of cost saving that could not be achieved without the merger and the estimate of the predicted saving must be reasonably verifiable by an independent party.

The defendants claim that "H&R Block's primary motivation for the TaxACT acquisition is to achieve significant synergies that will enable H&R Block to provide better products at a lower price and to compete more effectively." The defendants predict that they will achieve over $(redacted) million in annual efficiencies in 10 different areas. *Id.* at 24–25.

Dr. Mark E. Zmijewski, an expert witness for the government, analyzed the defendants' alleged efficiencies and concluded that — with the exception of (one efficiency related to eliminating third-party contracts) — the proposed efficiencies identified by the defendants are either not merger-specific or not verifiable.

The Court agrees with Dr. Zmijewski that the defendants have not demonstrated that their claimed efficiencies are merger-specific. If a company could achieve certain cost savings without any merger at all, then those stand-alone cost savings cannot be credited as merger-specific efficiencies. The defendants must show that their "efficiencies . . . cannot be achieved by either company alone because, if they can, the merger's asserted benefits can be achieved without the concomitant loss of a competitor." *Heinz,* 246 F.3d at 722. For example, if HRB's (redacted) are not running in the most efficient, cost-effective manner, it is hard to see why a merger with TaxACT is necessary to improve their cost structure. The reasons HRB claims it has higher (redacted) costs than TaxACT include (1) that TaxACT has lower labor costs in Cedar Rapids than HRB has in Kansas City and (2) that TaxACT is simply more cost conscious. Plainly, then, HRB could therefore achieve at least some of the (redacted) cost savings on its own — by relocating (redacted) and taking a more cost conscious attitude toward them. Likewise, the efficiencies related to bringing HRB's outsourced (redacted) functions in-house are unlikely to be wholly merger-specific.

Similarly, the defendants' IT-related efficiencies, which account for the largest efficiency claims, are not entirely merger-specific either. Both TaxACT and HRB witnesses testified that (redacted) — suggesting that the platform consolidation would result in at least some merger-specific efficiencies. One way in which (redacted). Thus, the IT consolidation efficiency actually can be thought of as entailing two distinct consolidations: (1) (redacted) and (2) HRB's platform will be merged with TaxACT's platform. Yet the claimed IT efficiency is not discounted for whatever savings HRB could obtain by (performing the first consolidation) on its own — an option the company considered in the past but did not adopt — and the defendants did not present evidence explaining why, as a technical matter, (performing the first consolidation) would not be feasible or, in fact, would not be more feasible than (the double consolidation). The IT efficiencies also apparently account for cost reductions associated with TaxACT's more cost-conscious culture and practices.

Even if the efficiencies were entirely merger-specific, many of them are also not independently verifiable. As Dr. Zmijewski explained, for the various efficiencies that involve the activities now performed by HRB or its vendors that are proposed to be transferred to TaxACT, TaxACT's predicted cost figures for taking over these activities were not based on an analysis of facts that could be verified by a third party. Instead, TaxACT based its cost estimates on management judgments. By comparison, HRB's estimated costs for the relevant activities were rooted in accounting and planning documents prepared in the ordinary course of business.

The testimony at the hearing confirmed that TaxACT's recurring cost estimates were largely premised on its managers experiential judgment about likely costs, rather than a detailed analysis of historical accounting data. While reliance on the estimation and judgment of experienced executives about costs may be perfectly sensible as a business matter, the lack of a verifiable method of factual analysis resulting in the cost estimates renders them not cognizable by the Court. If this were not so, then the efficiencies defense might well swallow the whole of Section 7 of the Clayton Act because management would be able to present large efficiencies based on its own judgment and the Court would be hard pressed to find otherwise. The difficulty in substantiating efficiency claims in a verifiable way is one reason why courts "generally have found inadequate proof of efficiencies to sustain a rebuttal of the government's case." *Heinz*, 246 F.3d at 720 (citation omitted); *see also Staples*, 970 F. Supp. at 1089 (finding "defendants failed to produce the necessary documentation for verification" of efficiencies).

Particular scrutiny of HRB's efficiencies claims is also warranted in light of HRB's historical acquisitions. In 2006, HRB acquired a software company called TaxWorks, which was renamed "RedGear." For the RedGear acquisition, which was much smaller in scale than the proposed TaxACT deal, HRB projected a total of $(redacted) million in efficiencies over three years. HRB failed to achieve these (efficiencies) (redacted). *Id.* In this case, the efficiency estimates are much more aggressive, in that defendants are claiming approximately $(redacted) million in efficiencies for 2013 and $(redacted) million in annual savings going forward thereafter, as opposed to $(redacted) million over three years. While HRB has attempted to learn from the mistakes of the RedGear acquisition, *id.* at 85–87, the Court finds that this history only underscores the need for any claimed efficiencies to be independently verifiable in order to constitute evidence that can rebut the government's presumption of anticompetitive effects.

Considering all of the evidence regarding efficiencies, the Court finds that most of the defendants' claimed efficiencies are not cognizable because the defendants have not demonstrated that they are merger-specific and verifiable.[7]

---

[7] [FN 44] In addition, the defendants have not addressed how much of the claimed efficiencies would be passed through to consumers. *See Staples*, 970 F. Supp. at 1090 (analyzing projected pass-through rate for claimed efficiencies).

IV. CONCLUSION

The Court concludes that the proposed merger between HRB and TaxACT violates Section 7 of the Clayton Act because it is reasonably likely to cause anticompetitive effects. The law of this Circuit supports this conclusion. In *Heinz*, the Court of Appeals reversed a district court's denial of a preliminary injunction against a merger involving the second- and third-largest jarred baby food companies. 246 F.3d at 711–12. After noting the high barriers to entry and high HHI figures that characterized the market, the D.C. Circuit observed that "[a]s far as we can determine, no court has ever approved a merger to duopoly under similar circumstances." *Id.* at 717. The situation in this case is similar. The government established a prima facie case indicating that anticompetitive effects are likely to result from the merger. The defendants have not made a showing of evidence that rebuts the presumption of anticompetitive effects by demonstrating that the government's market share statistics give an inaccurate account of the merger's probable effects on competition in the relevant market. To the contrary, the totality of the evidence confirms that anticompetitive effects are a likely result of the merger, which would give H&R Block and Intuit control over 90 percent of the market for digital do-it-yourself tax preparation products.

Accordingly, the Court will enjoin H&R Block's proposed acquisition of TaxACT. An appropriate Order will accompany this Memorandum Opinion.

NOTES AND QUESTIONS

1.   What test or tests does the court use to determine the relevant product market? The court states that "[t]he outer boundaries of a product market are determined by the reasonable interchangeability of use [by consumers] or the cross-elasticity of demand between the product itself and substitutes for it." Are the "reasonable interchangeability of use" and "the cross-elasticity of demand" synonyms? Alternatives? What are the pros and cons of each formulation, and when might one use one or the other? Had the district court in *Lundbeck* applied the same formulation, would that case have come out as it did?

2.   On what grounds does the court conclude that paid preparation by an accountant or other expert is not in the same product market as DDIY tax preparation? What kind of evidence did the court find persuasive?

3.   How does the government shift the burden of proof to the merging parties in this case? Note the court's discussion of the HHIs: the court says that the government has established a prima facie case of anticompetitive harm that shifts the burden to defendants to show why harm and concentration do not correlate in this particular case. At first blush, this sounds like exactly the sort mere statistical showing that the Court in *General Dynamics* said could not suffice for the government to win. The district court goes on, however, to say that the HHI statistics should not be able to guarantee a government victory, so the burden on defendants is not a heavy one. What does this mean? If the defendant does not put on any evidence on its behalf would the government be able to win by a mere showing of concentration without further evidence of harmful effects? Is that consistent with *General Dynamics*?

4. The coordinated and unilateral effects analyses in this opinion track the 2010 *Guidelines* quite closely. The decision focuses on coordinated effects, looking at the prospects for express collusion in light of the parties' past conduct. It does not really address the possibility of conscious parallelism raised in the 2010 *Guidelines*. Even though the court found coordinated effects sufficient to block the transaction, it went on to examine the unilateral effects. In so doing, the court appeared much more hospitable to unilateral effects than did the district court in *Oracle*, expressly declining to impose a minimum market share threshold for the finding of unilateral effects. Of interest in this regard was the court's favorable reference to Judge Brown's opinion in *Whole Foods*, in which Judge Brown indicated that market definition might not be necessary in all unilateral effects cases.

5. The court rejected the parties' efficiencies justifications for the merger on grounds that they were neither merger specific nor sufficiently verifiable. In footnote 44 the court also noted that the parties had not shown how much of the efficiency savings would be passed through to consumers. Does this mean that even had the efficiencies been merger specific and verifiable the merging firms would have to show pass through? Should pass through of efficiencies be required?

The attempted merger between AT&T and T-Mobile. The biggest merger attempted in recent years was AT&T's $39 billion dollar bid for rival wireless carrier T-Mobile. The parties scuttled the deal in December 2011 in the face of a suit by the Justice Department to block the transaction. The Justice Department had argued in its complaint that the merger would lead to anticompetitive effects in the market for nationwide mobile telecommunications services generally, as well as more specifically in the provision of such services to enterprise and government customers. DOJ Complaint at ¶¶ 12–14. While the merger was newsworthy and was the subject of much discussion and investigation, it did not present or novel legal issues or create any new law. To the extent it is legally interesting, it is because it showed that the government would take on a major transaction in a changing, high-technology market and that it would demand credible evidence that the transaction's alleged benefits — expanding wireless broadband services — would be substantial, merger specific, and likely to occur. The DOJ clearly was not persuaded of any efficiency gains from the merger, DOJ Complaint at ¶ 46, where as the Department was quite convinced of the merger's anticompetitive effects. DOJ Complaint at ¶¶ 27–44. There was, however, an interesting procedural wrinkle in the investigation of the merger. Shortly before AT&T dropped its bid altogether, it had withdrawn its application to the FCC for the relevant license transfers. Such license applications are the vehicle through with the FCC gains jurisdiction to review telecommunications mergers and the Commission had been well into its investigation when it allowed AT&T and T-Mobile to withdraw. The withdrawal was ostensibly to allow the merging parties to focus on their pending court battle with the Justice Department without simultaneously dealing with the FCC's investigation. Despite the application withdrawal, the FCC nonetheless released a substantial report in November 2011 detailing its concerns with the transaction. Notably, the Commission was concerned about the loss of an independent and aggressive competitor, T-Mobile, from the wireless marketplace, thought that AT&T would build mobile broadband networks even absent the merger, and concluded that the transaction would lead to substantial job losses. It was unusual for the FCC to release such a report without a transaction pending before it, and some might question whether it was fair for the agency to do so. The Commission was probably signaling, however, that regardless of whether AT&T prevailed in court against the DOJ, the merging parties would have another tough battle at the FCC. The matter became moot less than a month later when AT&T gave up the fight and paid T-Mobile a substantial break-up fee consisting of billions in cash as well as spectrum.

NOTE: GOVERNMENT GUIDELINES ON MERGER REMEDIES

In the fall of 2004 the Antitrust Division of the Department of Justice initially issued a *Policy Guide to Merger Remedies*. These Guidelines were substantially revised in 2011 and can be found at http://www.justice.gov/atr/public/guidelines/272350.pdf, The revised Guidelines observe:

- The Division's central goal is preserving competition, not determining outcomes or picking winners and losers. Thus, decree provisions should preserve competition generally rather than protect or favor particular competitors. The Division will accept merger remedies that protect the competitive landscape by effectively preserving competition without removing the incentive for individual firms to compete. A remedy carefully tailored to the competitive harm is the best way to ensure effective relief.

- Effective merger remedies typically include structural or conduct provisions. Each can be used to preserve competition in the appropriate factual circumstances. . . . [I]n some cases an effective remedy may call for a combination of different types of relief. In other cases, an effective remedy may be unavailable. In that circumstance, the Division will seek to block the merger.

One significant change between the 2004 remedies Guidelines and the 2011 revision is that the later Guidelines are more favorably inclined to permit conduct provisions to be used rather than structural provisions.

III   MERGERS OF POTENTIAL COMPETITORS

UNITED STATES v. SIDNEY W. WINSLOW
227 U.S. 202 (1913)

JUSTICE HOLMES delivered the opinion of the Court.

This is a writ of error to determine whether two counts in an indictment . . . charge offenses under the Sherman Act. . . .

The facts alleged are as follows: For the last twenty-five years practically all the shoes worn in the United States have been made by the help of machines, grouped as lasting machines, welt-sewing machines and outsole-stitching machines, heeling machines and metallic fastening machines. . . . Before and up to February 7, 1899, the defendants Winslow, Hurd and Brown, through the Consolidated and McKay Lasting Machine Company, under letters patent, made sixty per cent of all the lasting machines made in the United States; the defendants Barbour and Howe, through the Goodyear Shoe Machinery Company, in like manner made eighty per cent of all the welt-sewing machines and outsole-stitching machines, and ten per cent of all the lasting machines; and the defendant Storrow, through the McKay Shoe Manufacturing Company, made seventy per cent of all the heeling machines and eighty per cent of all the metallic fastening machines made in the United States. . . .

On February 7, 1899, the three groups of defendants above named, up to that time separate, organized the United Shoe Machinery Company and turned over to that company the stocks and business of the several corporations that they respectively controlled. The new company now makes all the machines that had been made in different places, at a single new factory at Beverly, Massachusetts, and directly, or through subsidiary companies, carries on all the commerce among the States that had been carried on independently by the constituent companies before. . . . The defendants are alleged to have done the acts recited with intent unreasonably to extend their monopolies, rights and control over commerce among the States; to enhance the value of the same at the expense of the public, and to discourage others from inventing and manufacturing machines for the work done by those of the defendants. The organization of the new company and the turning over of the stocks and business to it are alleged to constitute a breach of the Sherman Act.

. . . .

. . . On the face of it the combination was simply an effort after greater efficiency. The business of the several groups that combined, as it existed before the combination, is assumed to have been legal. The machines are patented, making them is a monopoly in any case, the exclusion of competitors from the use of them is of the very essence of the right conferred by the patents, and it may be assumed that the success of the several groups was due to their patents having been the best. As . . . they did not compete with one another, it is hard to see why the collective business should be any worse than its component parts. It is said that from seventy to eighty per cent of all the shoe machinery business was put into a single hand. This is inaccurate, since the machines in question are not alleged to be types of all the machines used in making shoes, and since the defendants' share in commerce among the States does not appear. But taking it as true we can see no greater objection to one corporation manufacturing seventy per cent of three noncompeting groups of patented machines collectively used for making a single product than to three corporations making the same proportion of one group each. The disintegration aimed at by the statute does not extend to reducing all manufacture to isolated units of the lowest degree. It is as lawful for one corporation to make every part of a steam engine and to put the machine together as it would be for one to make the boilers and another to make the wheels. . . .

NOTES AND QUESTIONS

1. Justice Holmes's short opinion amounts to little more than a rhetorical question: when two people who do not compete with each other merge, how much competition do they eliminate? Clearly, in Holmes's mind, none.

Justice Holmes never considered the possibility that a manufacturer of lasting machines might someday want to expand its business to include heeling machines, and that its experience in the lasting machine business might give it some expertise and goodwill that would make its entry into the heeling machine business easier. In short, Justice Holmes never considered the fact that, although the defendants were not actual competitors, they were *potential* competitors. Each of them was a likely entrant into the businesses run by the others.

The entire notion of potential competition must be considered carefully. Few people may be actual competitors in any practical sense, but *everyone* is a "potential" competitor with everyone else. The relevant question for merger policy is how much does a particular person "potentially compete" with someone else?

In large part, this is a question of cross-elasticity of supply. If a seller attempts to raise its prices, the higher profits will attract new entry into the seller's market. This new entry may come from persons operating in the same geographic market but manufacturing a slightly different product, or it may come from someone manufacturing the same product but in a different geographic market. The new entry may, of course, come from someone who is presently not manufacturing anything in any market. If a particular merger eliminates the most likely entrant into a market, the reduction in cross-elasticity of supply can be far more substantial than if it eliminates someone who was really not likely to enter. In general, the greater the reduction in the cross-elasticity of supply generated by a merger (or by any other exclusionary practice, for that matter), the greater will be the increase in market power of those persons operating in the relevant market. At the outer limit, a person manufacturing 100% of a certain product may have no market power because a minuscule price increase would invite large-scale entry by someone sitting on the "edge" of the market. The elimination of that potential entrant by merger could greatly increase the market power of the post-merger firm. The theory illustrates that market power is a function not only of market share, but also of demand and supply elasticities. If a firm making 70% of the heeling machines in the country (the relevant market) merges with a firm that makes 70% of the lasting machines, the post-merger firm's market share is exactly the same as it was before the merger: 70% of the heeling machines and 70% of the lasting machines. Nevertheless, if each of the firms had been a potential entrant into the business of the other, the increase in market power could be substantial.

2. The other side of the story, of course, is that after the merger, the newly formed United Shoe Machinery Company consolidated all its operations into a single plant and was able to offer a full line of shoe machinery and related products to people who wanted to manufacture shoes. The efficiencies produced by a potential competition merger can be just as large as the efficiencies produced by a horizontal or vertical merger, particularly if the merger partners produce complementary products, as they did in the *Sidney Winslow* case. As Justice Holmes observes, it is as lawful for one corporation to manufacture an entire steam engine

as it is for a group of corporations to make each individual part — and it is probably a lot cheaper.

UNITED STATES v. CONTINENTAL CAN CO
378 U.S. 441 (1964)

JUSTICE WHITE delivered the opinion of the Court.

In 1956, Continental Can Company, the Nation's second largest producer of metal containers, acquired all of the assets, business and good will of Hazel-Atlas Glass Company, the Nation's third largest producer of glass containers, in exchange for 999,140 shares of Continental's common stock and the assumption by Continental of all the liabilities of Hazel-Atlas. The Government brought this action seeking a judgment that the acquisition violated § 7 of the Clayton Act and requesting an appropriate divestiture order. Trying the case without a jury, the District Court found that the Government had failed to prove reasonable probability of anticompetitive effect in any line of commerce, and accordingly dismissed the complaint at the close of the Government's case. . . .

The industries with which this case is principally concerned are . . . the metal can industry, the glass container industry and the plastic container industry, each producing one basic type of container made of metal, glass, and plastic, respectively.

Continental Can is a New York corporation organized in 1913 to acquire all the assets of three metal container manufacturers. Since 1913 Continental has acquired 21 domestic metal container companies as well as numerous others engaged in the packaging business, including producers of flexible packaging; a manufacturer of polyethylene bottles and similar plastic containers; 14 producers of paper containers and paperboard; four companies making closures for glass containers; and one — Hazel-Atlas — producing glass containers. In 1955, the year prior to the present merger, Continental, with assets of $382 million, was the second largest company in the metal container field, shipping approximately 33% of all such containers sold in the United States. It and the largest producer, American Can Company, accounted for approximately 71% of all metal container shipments. National Can Company, the third largest, shipped approximately 5%, with the remaining 24% of the market being divided among 75 to 90 other firms.

. . . .

Hazel-Atlas was a West Virginia corporation which in 1955 had net sales in excess of $79 million and assets of more than $37 million. Prior to the absorption of Hazel-Atlas into Continental the pattern of dominance among a few firms in the glass container industry was similar to that which prevailed in the metal container field. Hazel-Atlas, with approximately 9.6% of the glass container shipments in 1955, was third. Owens-Illinois Glass Company had 34.2% and Anchor-Hocking Glass Company 11.6%, with the remaining 44.6% being divided among at least 39 other firms.

. . . .

We deal first with the relevant market. It is not disputed here, and the District

Court held, that the geographical market is the entire United States. As for the product market, the court found, as was conceded by the parties, that the can industry and the glass container industry were relevant lines of commerce. Beyond these two product markets, however, the Government urged the recognition of various other lines of commerce, some of them defined in terms of the end uses for which tin and glass containers were in substantial competition. These end-use claims were containers for the beer industry, containers for the soft drink industry, containers for the canning industry, containers for the toiletry and cosmetic industry, containers for the medicine and health industry, and containers for the household and chemical industry.

. . . The court, nevertheless, with one exception — containers for beer — rejected the Government's claim that existing competition between metal and glass containers had resulted in the end-use product markets urged by the Government: "The fact that there is inter-industry or inter-product competition between metal, glass and plastic containers is not determinative of the metes and bounds of a relevant product market." In the trial court's view, the Government failed to make "appropriate distinctions . . . between inter-industry or overall commodity competition and the type of competition between products with reasonable interchangeability of use and cross-elasticity of demand which has Clayton Act significance." The interindustry competition, concededly present, did not remove this merger from the category of the conglomerate combination, "in which one company in two separate industries combined with another in a third industry for the purpose of establishing a diversified line of products."

. . . The District Court's findings having established the existence of three product markets — metal containers, glass containers and metal and glass beer containers — the disputed issue on which that court erred is whether the admitted competition between metal and glass containers for uses other than packaging beer was of the type and quality deserving of § 7 protection and therefore the basis for defining a relevant product market. In resolving this issue we are instructed on the one hand that "[f]or every product, substitutes exist. But a relevant market cannot meaningfully encompass that infinite range." On the other hand it is improper "to require that products be fungible to be considered in the relevant market." In defining the product market between these terminal extremes, we must recognize meaningful competition where it is found to exist. Though the "outer boundaries of a product market are determined by the reasonable interchangeability of use or the cross-elasticity of demand between the product itself and substitutes for it," there may be "within this broad market, well-defined submarkets . . . which, in themselves, constitute product markets for antitrust purposes." . . .

It is quite true that glass and metal containers have different characteristics which may disqualify one or the other, at least in their present form, from this or that particular use; that the machinery necessary to pack in glass is different from that employed when cans are used; that a particular user of cans or glass may pack in only one or the other container and does not shift back and forth from day to day as price and other factors might make desirable; and that the competition between metal and glass containers is different from the competition between the can companies themselves or between the products of the different glass companies. These are relevant and important considerations but they are not sufficient to obscure the competitive relationships which this record so compellingly reveals.

Baby food was at one time packed entirely in metal cans. Hazel-Atlas played a significant role in inducing the shift to glass as the dominant container by designing "what has become the typical baby food jar." According to Continental's estimate, 80% of the Nation's baby food now moves in glass containers. Continental has not been satisfied with this contemporary dominance by glass, however, and has made intensive efforts to increase its share of the business at the expense of glass. In 1954, two years before the merger, the Director of Market Research and Promotion for the Glass Container Manufacturers Institute concluded, largely on the basis of Continental's efforts to secure more baby food business, that "the can industry is beginning to fight back more aggressively in this field where it is losing ground to glass." In cooperation with some of the baby food companies Continental carried out what it called a Baby Food Depth Survey in New York and Los Angeles to discover specific reasons for the preference of glass-packed baby food. Largely in response to this and other in-depth surveys, advertising campaigns were conducted which were designed to overcome mothers' prejudices against metal containers.

In the soft drink business, a field which has been, and is, predominantly glass territory, the court recognized that the metal can industry had "[a]fter considerable initial difficulty . . . developed a can strong enough to resist the pressures generated by carbonated beverages" and "made strenuous efforts to promote the use of metal cans for carbonated beverages as against glass bottles." Continental has been a major factor in this rivalry. It studied the results of market tests to determine the extent to which metal cans could "penetrate this tremendous market," and its advertising has centered around the advantages of cans over glass as soft drink containers, emphasizing such features as convenience in stacking and storing, freedom from breakage and lower distribution costs resulting from the lighter weight of cans.

The District Court found that "[a]lthough at one time almost all packaged beer was sold in bottles, in a relatively short period the beer can made great headway and may well have become the dominant beer container." Regardless of which industry may have the upper hand at a given moment, however, an intense competitive battle on behalf of the beer can and the beer bottle is being waged both by the industry trade associations and by individual container manufacturers. . . .

In the food canning, toiletry and cosmetic, medicine and health, and household and chemical industries the existence of vigorous competition was also recognized below. In the case of food it was noted that one type of container has supplanted the other in the packing of some products and that in some instances similar products are packaged in two or more different types of containers. In the other industries "glass container, plastic container and metal container manufacturers are each seeking to promote their lines of containers at the expense of other lines, . . . all are attempting to improve their products or to develop new ones so as to have a wider customer appeal," the result being that "manufacturers from time to time may shift a product from one type of container to another."

In the light of this record and these findings, we think the District Court employed an unduly narrow construction of the "competition" protected by § 7 and of "reasonable interchangeability of use or the cross-elasticity of demand" in judging the facts of this case. . . .

. . . In our view there is and has been a rather general confrontation between metal and glass containers and competition between them for the same end uses which is insistent, continuous, effective and quantity wise very substantial. Metal has replaced glass and glass has replaced metal as the leading container for some important uses; both are used for other purposes; each is trying to expand its share of the market at the expense of the other; and each is attempting to preempt for itself every use for which its product is physically suitable, even though some such uses have traditionally been regarded as the exclusive domain of the competing industry. . . .

Moreover, price is only one factor in a user's choice between one container or the other. That there are price differentials between the two products or that the demand for one is not particularly or immediately responsive to changes in the price of the other are relevant matters but not determinative of the product market issue. Whether a packager will use glass or cans may depend not only on the price of the package but also upon other equally important considerations. The consumer, for example, may begin to prefer one type of container over the other and the manufacturer of baby food cans may therefore find that his problem is the housewife rather than the packer or the price of his cans. This may not be price competition but it is nevertheless meaningful competition between interchangeable containers.

. . . .

Based on the evidence thus far revealed by this record we hold that the interindustry competition between glass and metal containers is sufficient to warrant treating as a relevant product market the combined glass and metal container industries and all end uses for which they compete. . . .

. . . .

Continental occupied a dominant position in the metal can industry. It shipped 33% of the metal cans shipped by the industry and together with American shipped about 71% of the industry total. Continental's share amounted to 13 billion metal containers out of a total of 40 billion and its $433 million gross sales of metal containers amounted to 31.4% of the industry's total gross of $1,380,000,000. Continental's total assets were $382 million, its net sales and operating revenues $666 million. . . .

Continental's major position in the relevant product market — the combined metal and glass container industries — prior to the merger is undeniable. Of the 59 billion containers shipped in 1955 by the metal (39¾ billion) and glass (19 billion) industries, Continental shipped 21.9%, to a great extent dispersed among all of the end uses for which glass and metal compete. Of the six largest firms in the product market, it ranked second.

When Continental acquired Hazel-Atlas it added significantly to its position in the relevant line of commerce. Hazel-Atlas was the third largest glass container manufacturer in an industry in which the three top companies controlled 55.4% of the total shipments of glass containers. Hazel-Atlas' share was 9.6%, which amounted to 1,857,000,000 glass containers out of a total of 19 1 / 3 billion industrial total. . . .

. . . It is not at all self-evident that the lack of current competition between Continental and Hazel-Atlas for some important end uses of metal and glass containers significantly diminished the adverse effect of the merger on competition. Continental might have concluded that it could effectively insulate itself from competition by acquiring a major firm not presently directing its market acquisition efforts toward the same end uses as Continental, but possessing the potential to do so. Two examples will illustrate. Both soft drinks and baby food are currently packed predominantly in glass, but Continental has engaged in vigorous and imaginative promotional activities attempting to overcome consumer preferences for glass and secure a larger share of these two markets for its tin cans. Hazel-Atlas was not at the time of the merger a significant producer of either of these containers, but with comparatively little difficulty, if it were an independent firm making independent business judgments, it could have developed its soft drink and baby food capacity. The acquisition of Hazel-Atlas by a company engaged in such intense efforts to effect a diversion of business from glass to metal in both of these lines cannot help but diminish the likelihood of Hazel-Atlas realizing its potential as a significant competitor in either line. . . . It would make little sense for one entity within the Continental empire to be busily engaged in persuading the public of metal's superiority over glass for a given end use, while the other is making plans to increase the Nation's total glass container output for that same end use. Thus, the fact that Continental and Hazel-Atlas were not substantial competitors of each other for certain end uses at the time of the merger may actually enhance the long-run tendency of the merger to lessen competition.

NOTES AND QUESTIONS

1. Are a manufacturer of glass bottles and a manufacturer of metal cans "actual" competitors, "potential" competitors — or is this simply a question of degree? Suppose that brewers are absolutely indifferent whether their beer is placed in bottles or in cans, provided that the two sell for the same price. Assume, however, that the cost of producing a bottle is seven cents, while the cost of producing a can is eight cents. As long as bottles are sold at the competitive price, the beer bottlers will prefer bottles and the competition from cans will be, at best, "potential." But should the bottle industry ever be cartelized or come under the control of a monopolist, the bottle seller's power to sell at a supra competitive price will be limited by the existence of the can market. If the bottle sellers attempt to charge more than eight cents, beer bottlers will switch to cans.

2. The *Continental Can* decision makes one thing clear: our definition of a particular merger as a "conglomerate" or "potential competition" merger is entirely a function of our definition of the relevant markets. To say that two firms operate in the same product and geographic markets is to say that they compete; to say that one or both of the markets are different, however, is to conclude that their competition is only "potential." Sometimes, the question whether two firms operate in the same market is controversial, as it was in *Continental Can.* In that case, the

conclusion that they are in the same market, plus the application of the fixed market share rules of *Brown Shoe, Von's Grocery,* or *Philadelphia Bank* can yield a certain amount of over-reaching, can they not? This is so because, although the level of competition that exists between any two firms is a continuum, antitrust analysis has tended to group all pairs of firms into two categories: they are either competitors or they are not. As Justice Harlan's dissent suggests, although Continental Can and Hazel-Atlas "compete," they probably do not compete as much as did the parties in *Brown Shoe, Von's Grocery,* or *Philadelphia Bank.* In that case, does it make sense to use the same kind of market share analysis? *See* Werden, *Section 7 of the Clayton Act and the Analysis of Semihorizontal Mergers,* 27 ANTITRUST BULL. 135 (1982); Areeda & Turner, *Conglomerate Mergers: Extended Interdependence and Effects of Interindustry Competition as Grounds for Condemnation,* 127 U. PA. L. REV. 1082 (1979).

3. The Court observed that before the merger, the glass container companies were competing vigorously, both to develop new uses for glass bottles and to convince customers that they would be better off with glass. The metal container companies carried on similar research and development. The Court assumed that once Continental Can and Hazel-Atlas come under common control, they would lose the incentive to do this, for gains in the can market would come only at the expense of losses in the glass bottle market, and vice versa. Is the Court correct? Hazel-Atlas manufactured approximately 10% of the market's glass containers. Suppose that the "Can" division of the post-merger firm developed a superior can that stole 1,000,000 units per year away from glass manufacturers. Because Hazel-Atlas/Continental is the developer of this new can, it will get all the 1,000,000 sales of the new can, at least initially, until it is copied by competitors. However, the glass division, which has 10% of the productive capacity for glass containers, will suffer only 10% of the loss in sales. Thus the post-merger firm would realize a net gain of 900,000 units. On the other hand, if a competing firm developed the new can, Hazel-Atlas/Continental would lose all 1,000,000 sales. Wouldn't the post-merger firm have just as much incentive to innovate after the merger as it did before?

4. The question of what is vertical and what is horizontal, and of what products potentially compete with each other, is often a dynamic one that shifts with technology and consumer preferences. The FTC has recently (2013) had occasion to again examine the relationship between glass and other kinds of containers in examining the merger of Ardagh Group and Saint-Gobain Containers, Inc. As of this writing the FTC's complaint is pending. That complaint, which can be found at http://www.ftc.gov/os/adjpro/d9356/130701ardaghcmpt.pdf, alleges a "glass only" market for certain kinds of products and in certain geographic markets.

5. *Mergers of firms producing complementary goods.* The *Continental Can* merger involved goods (cans and bottles), which are imperfect *substitutes* for each other. By contrast, the merger in *Sidney W. Winslow,* reprinted *supra,* was among producers of *complements,* which are goods that are used together, such as toasters and bread, automobiles and spark plugs, or hardware and software. Such mergers do not typically eliminate competition between the merging firms, but they have been thought to facilitate other kinds of practices, such as tying or reciprocity. The theory has not been used much in recent decades. *See* 5 P. AREEDA & H. HOVENKAMP, ANTITRUST LAW ¶¶ 1143–1144 (3d ed. 2009).

FTC v. PROCTER & GAMBLE CO.
386 U.S. 568 (1967)

JUSTICE DOUGLAS delivered the opinion of the Court.

This is a proceeding initiated by the Federal Trade Commission charging that respondent, Procter & Gamble Co., had acquired the assets of Clorox Chemical Co. in violation of § 7 of the Clayton Act. . . . The charge was that Procter's acquisition of Clorox might substantially lessen competition or tend to create a monopoly in the production and sale of household liquid bleaches.

. . . .

At the time of the merger, in 1957, Clorox was the leading manufacturer in the heavily concentrated household liquid bleach industry. It is agreed that household liquid bleach is the relevant line of commerce. The product is used in the home as a germicide and disinfectant, and, more importantly, as a whitening agent in washing clothes and fabrics. It is a distinctive product with no close substitutes. Liquid bleach is a low-price, high-turnover consumer product sold mainly through grocery stores and supermarkets. The relevant geographical market is the Nation and a series of regional markets. Because of high shipping costs and low sales price, it is not feasible to ship the product more than 300 miles from its point of manufacture. Most manufacturers are limited to competition within a single region since they have but one plant. Clorox is the only firm selling nationally; it has 13 plants distributed throughout the Nation. Purex, Clorox's closest competitor in size, does not distribute its bleach in the northeast or mid-Atlantic States; in 1957, Purex's bleach was available in less than 50% of the national market.

At the time of the acquisition, Clorox was the leading manufacturer of household liquid bleach, with 48.8% of the national sales — annual sales of slightly less than $40,000,000. Its market share had been steadily increasing for the five years prior to the merger. Its nearest rival was Purex, which manufactures a number of products other than household liquid bleaches, including abrasive cleaners, toilet soap, and detergents. Purex accounted for 15.7% of the household liquid bleach market. The industry is highly concentrated; in 1957, Clorox and Purex accounted for almost 65% of the Nation's household liquid bleach sales, and, together with four other firms, for almost 80%. The remaining 20% was divided among over 200 small producers. Clorox had total assets of $12,000,000; only eight producers had assets in excess of $1,000,000 and very few had assets of more than $75,000.

In light of the territorial limitations on distribution, national figures do not give an accurate picture of Clorox's dominance in the various regions. Thus, Clorox's seven principal competitors did no business in New England, the mid-Atlantic States, or metropolitan New York. Clorox's share of the sales in those areas was 56%, 72%, and 64% respectively. Even in regions where its principal competitors were active, Clorox maintained a dominant position. Except in metropolitan Chicago and the west-central States Clorox accounted for at least 39%, and often a much higher percentage, of liquid bleach sales.

Since all liquid bleach is chemically identical, advertising and sales promotion are vital. In 1957 Clorox spent almost $3,700,000 on advertising, imprinting the value of its bleach in the mind of the consumer. In addition, it spent $1,700,000 for other promotional activities. The Commission found that these heavy expenditures went far to explain why Clorox maintained so high a market share despite the fact that its brand, though chemically indistinguishable from rival brands, retailed for a price equal to or, in many instances, higher than its competitors.

Procter is a large, diversified manufacturer of low-price, high-turnover household products sold through grocery, drug, and department stores. Prior to its acquisition of Clorox, it did not produce household liquid bleach. Its 1957 sales were in excess of $1,100,000,000 from which it realized profits of more than $67,000,000; its assets were over $500,000,000. Procter has been marked by rapid growth and diversification. It has successfully developed and introduced a number of new products. Its primary activity is in the general area of soaps, detergents, and cleansers; in 1957, of total domestic sales, more than one-half (over $500,000,000) were in this field. Procter was the dominant factor in this area. It accounted for 54.4% of all packaged detergent sales. The industry is heavily concentrated — Procter and its nearest competitors, Colgate-Palmolive and Lever Brothers, account for 80% of the market.

In the marketing of soaps, detergents, and cleansers, as in the marketing of household liquid bleach, advertising and sales promotion are vital. In 1957, Procter was the Nation's largest advertiser, spending more than $80,000,000 on advertising and an additional $47,000,000 on sales promotion. Due to its tremendous volume, Procter receives substantial discounts from the media. As a multiproduct producer Procter enjoys substantial advantages in advertising and sales promotion. Thus, it can and does feature several products in its promotions, reducing the printing, mailing, and other costs for each product. It also purchases network programs on behalf of several products, enabling it to give each product network exposure at a fraction of the cost per product that a firm with only one product to advertise would incur.

Prior to the acquisition, Procter was in the course of diversifying into product lines related to its basic detergent-soap-cleanser business. Liquid bleach was a distinct possibility since packaged detergents — Procter's primary product line — and liquid bleach are used complementarily in washing clothes and fabrics, and in general household cleaning. As noted by the Commission:

> "Packaged detergents — Procter's most important product category — and household liquid bleach are used complementarily, not only in the washing of clothes and fabrics, but also in general household cleaning, since liquid bleach is a germicide and disinfectant as well as a whitener. From the consumer's viewpoint, then, packaged detergents and liquid bleach are closely related products. . . . Since products of both parties to the merger are sold to the same customers, at the same stores, and by the same merchandising methods, the possibility arises of significant integration at both the marketing and distribution levels."

. . . The Commission found that the substitution of Procter with its huge assets and advertising advantages for the already dominant Clorox would dissuade new entrants and discourage active competition from the firms already in the industry due to fear of retaliation by Procter. The Commission thought it relevant that retailers might be induced to give Clorox preferred shelf space since it would be manufactured by Procter, which also produced a number of other products marketed by the retailers. There was also the danger that Procter might underprice Clorox in order to drive out competition, and subsidize the underpricing with revenue from other products. The Commission carefully reviewed the effect of the acquisition on the structure of the industry, noting that "[t]he practical tendency of the . . . merger . . . is to transform the liquid bleach industry into an arena of big business competition only, with the few small firms that have not disappeared through merger eventually falling by the wayside, unable to compete with their giant rivals." Further, the merger would seriously diminish potential competition by eliminating Procter as a potential entrant into the industry. Prior to the merger, the Commission found, Procter was the most likely prospective entrant, and absent the merger would have remained on the periphery, restraining Clorox from exercising its market power. If Procter had actually entered, Clorox's dominant position would have been eroded and the concentration of the industry reduced. . . .

. . . .

The anticompetitive effects with which this product-extension merger is fraught can easily be seen: (1) the substitution of the powerful acquiring firm for the smaller, but already dominant, firm may substantially reduce the competitive structure of the industry by raising entry barriers and by dissuading the smaller firms from aggressively competing; (2) the acquisition eliminates the potential competition of the acquiring firm.

The liquid bleach industry was already oligopolistic before the acquisition, and price competition was certainly not as vigorous as it would have been if the industry were competitive. Clorox enjoyed a dominant position nationally, and its position approached monopoly proportions in certain areas. The existence of some 200 fringe firms certainly does not belie that fact. Nor does the fact, relied upon by the court below, that, after the merger, producers other than Clorox "were selling more bleach for more money than ever before." In the same period, Clorox increased its share from 48.8% to 52%. The interjection of Procter into the market considerably changed the situation. There is every reason to assume that the smaller firms would become more cautious in competing due to their fear of retaliation by Procter. It is probable that Procter would become the price leader and that oligopoly would become more rigid.

The acquisition may also have the tendency of raising the barriers to new entry. The major competitive weapon in the successful marketing of bleach is advertising. Clorox was limited in this area by its relatively small budget and its inability to obtain substantial discounts. By contrast, Procter's budget was much larger; and, although it would not devote its entire budget to advertising Clorox, it could divert a large portion to meet the short-term threat of a new entrant. Procter would be able to use its volume discounts to advantage in advertising Clorox. Thus, a new entrant would be much more reluctant to face the giant Procter than it would have been to face the smaller Clorox.[8]

---

[8] [FN 3] The barriers to entry have been raised both for entry by new firms and for entry into new geographical markets by established firms. The latter aspect is demonstrated by Purex's lesson in Erie,

Possible economies cannot be used as a defense to illegality. Congress was aware that some mergers which lessen competition may also result in economies but it struck the balance in favor of protecting competition.

The Commission also found that the acquisition of Clorox by Procter eliminated Procter as a potential competitor. The Court of Appeals declared that this finding was not supported by evidence because there was no evidence that Procter's management had ever intended to enter the industry independently and that Procter had never attempted to enter. The evidence, however, clearly shows that Procter was the most likely entrant. Procter had recently launched a new abrasive cleaner in an industry similar to the liquid bleach industry, and had wrested leadership from a brand that had enjoyed even a larger market share than had Clorox. Procter was engaged in a vigorous program of diversifying into product lines closely related to its basic products. Liquid bleach was a natural avenue of diversification since it is complementary to Procter's products, is sold to the same customers through the same channels, and is advertised and merchandised in the same manner. Procter had substantial advantages in advertising and sales promotion, which, as we have seen, are vital to the success of liquid bleach. No manufacturer had a patent on the product or its manufacture, necessary information relating to manufacturing methods and processes was readily available, there was no shortage of raw material, and the machinery and equipment required for a plant of efficient capacity were available at reasonable cost. Procter's management was experienced in producing and marketing goods similar to liquid bleach. Procter had considered the possibility of independently entering but decided against it because the acquisition of Clorox would enable Procter to capture a more commanding share of the market.

It is clear that the existence of Procter at the edge of the industry exerted considerable influence on the market. First, the market behavior of the liquid bleach industry was influenced by each firm's predictions of the market behavior of its competitors, actual and potential. Second, the barriers to entry by a firm of Procter's size and with its advantages were not significant. There is no indication that the barriers were so high that the price Procter would have to charge would be above the price that would maximize the profits of the existing firms. Third, the number of potential entrants was not so large that the elimination of one would be insignificant. Few firms would have the temerity to challenge a firm as solidly entrenched as Clorox. Fourth, Procter was found by the Commission to be the most likely entrant. These findings of the Commission were amply supported by the evidence.

Pennsylvania. In October 1957, Purex selected Erie, Pennsylvania — where it had not sold previously as an area in which to test the salability, under competitive conditions, of a new bleach. The leading brands in Erie were Clorox, with 52%, and the "101" brand, sold by Gardner Manufacturing Company, with 29% of the market. Purex launched an advertising and promotional campaign to obtain a broad distribution in a short time, and in five months captured 33% of the Erie market. Clorox's share dropped to 35% and 101's to 17%. Clorox responded by offering its bleach at reduced prices, and then added an offer of a $1-value ironing board cover for 50 cents with each purchase of Clorox at the reduced price. It also increased its advertising with television spots. The result was to restore Clorox's lost market share and, indeed, to increase it slightly. Purex's share fell to 7%.

NOTES AND QUESTIONS

1.   What did Justice Douglas mean in *Procter & Gamble* when he wrote that "[p]ossible economies cannot be used as a defense to illegality." Did he mean, as *Brown Shoe* suggested, that the merger was bad *because* it produced certain economies and therefore injured competitors of the post-merger firm? Or did Justice Douglas mean merely that once a merger was shown to have sufficient anticompetitive effects to justify condemnation, the Court would not recognize the creation of economies as an affirmative defense? The difference between the two views can be quite significant. See the note on efficiency defenses in merger cases, *supra*, Section II[B] of this chapter.

2.   Justice Douglas said that Procter's acquisition of Clorox was bad because it raised "barriers to entry" in the bleach industry. He then cited economies in advertising as such an entry barrier: the fact that a large firm like P&G can obtain advertising cheaply makes it more difficult and expensive for a smaller firm to enter the market. Under this usage, isn't the phrase "barrier to entry" simply a synonym for efficiency? Every cost-reducing practice of a firm already in the market makes entry by others more difficult. See the note on entry barriers in monopolization and merger cases, Chapter 6, *supra*.

One problem with the term, as Justice Douglas used it, is that it fails to distinguish barriers to persons outside the market who want to get in and barriers to persons who are already inside the market. P&G's advertising economies injured existing rivals just as much as prospective entrants. A true barrier to entry should *protect* incumbents while it excludes outsiders.

3.   Justice Douglas believed that Procter's presence as a potential entrant into the bleach industry made the bleach industry more competitive, even though Procter was not manufacturing bleach. This "potential entrant" argument has taken two forms. One version is that an acquisition is bad if one firm would have entered the other firm's market anyway had the merger not occurred. If the alternative way is less anticompetitive than the merger, the merger ought to be condemned. This is known as the "actual potential entrant" doctrine. It is in effect an argument, not that a market is less competitive as a result of a merger, but that the market could have been more competitive if the acquiring firm had entered in a different way.

The second version of the argument appeared in both *Procter* and *El Paso Natural Gas.* It is that the acquiring firm was *perceived* as an entrant by the firms already selling in the market. Because they feared entry, they behaved more competitively. However, if the "perceived potential entrant" should actually acquire one of the firms in the market, then its status as a perceived potential entrant would disappear and the market would become less competitive. Unlike the actual potential entrant doctrine, the perceived potential entrant doctrine does argue that a particular merger lessens competition, not merely that it diminishes the chances for increased competition in the future. For that reason, courts have been somewhat more willing to accept the perceived potential entrant doctrine than they have the actual potential entrant doctrine.

For example, *United States v. Falstaff Brewing Corp.*, 410 U.S. 526 (1973), involved the acquisition by Falstaff Brewing of Narragansett Brewing Co. Falstaff was a very large brewer, but it did not sell beer in the Northeastern United States. Narragansett was a regional brewer which had the largest share of the New England market — about 20%. The government argued the case under the actual potential entrant doctrine. The government said that Falstaff should have entered the New England market *de novo* or else by means of a "toehold" acquisition — that is, by acquiring a small company in New England rather than the largest seller there. Entry by either of these means, argued the government, would have increased competition in the New England market. Entry by the mechanism that Falstaff chose, however, did not.

The Supreme Court held that the merger might violate Section 7, but the Court relied on the perceived potential entrant doctrine rather than the actual potential entrant doctrine. It held that Falstaff might have been perceived by New England beer sellers as a potential entrant into their market. This perception caused them to price beer more competitively because they knew that Falstaff would be attracted into the market by high profits. Once Falstaff acquired Narragansett, however, it was already in the market and no longer exercised a downward pressure on prices. Thus it was possible that Falstaff's presence on the edge of the market made the market more competitive, and the market became less competitive as a result of Falstaff's entry. The Court remanded for determination whether Falstaff was actually perceived as a potential entrant by firms already inside the market. The district court decided that it was not and dismissed the complaint. *United States v. Falstaff Brewing Corp.*, 383 F. Supp. 1020 (D. R.I. 1974). The government did not appeal.

4. During the 1980s, the lower courts considered several merger challenges under both the perceived and actual potential entrant doctrines. In *Yamaha Motor Co. v. FTC*, 657 F.2d 971 (8th Cir. 1981), *cert. denied*, 456 U.S. 915 (1982), the court enforced a divestiture order, based on the actual potential entrant doctrine. Yamaha and Brunswick had formed a joint venture for making small outboard motors. Both firms manufactured motors, but they had always sold them in different countries, although Yamaha had once tried unsuccessfully to market a small motor in the United States. The FTC concluded that Yamaha was a potential entrant into the American market, and if it had entered without a joint venture with Brunswick, Yamaha and Brunswick would have been competitors in the American market. Because the joint venture included an agreement allocating sales territories, however, such competition would never occur under the joint venture agreement.

In general, however, the circuit courts have looked at the potential competition doctrines with a great deal of skepticism. For example, *Tenneco, Inc. v. FTC*, 689 F.2d 346 (2d Cir. 1982), rejected a challenge to a merger between a major automobile parts manufacturer (excluding shock absorbers) and a major automobile shock absorber manufacturer. The shock absorber market was highly concentrated, with a CR4 exceeding 90, and entry barriers were found to be very high. Nevertheless, the Second Circuit disagreed with the FTC's decision condemning the merger:

> To establish a violation of section 7 in this case based upon the elimination of actual potential competition, . . . the Commission must show: (1) that the relevant market is oligopolistic; (2) that absent its

acquisition of Monroe, Tenneco would likely have entered the market in the near future either *de novo* or through toehold acquisition; and (3) that such entry by Tenneco carried a substantial likelihood of ultimately producing deconcentration of the market or other significant procompetitive effects. . . .

The record establishes that the structure, history and probable future of the market for replacement shock absorbers are all consistent with the Commission's finding. The extraordinarily high concentration ratios have remained stable over many years with the same firms occupying the top four positions since at least the late 1960s. Substantial barriers to entry severely limit the number of firms likely to provide additional competition. The industry has been highly profitable, and despite recent indications that profit margins may be decreasing, industry experts, including Tenneco executives, foresee a bright future. . . .

Nevertheless, we reject the Commission's finding that Tenneco was an actual potential entrant likely to increase competition in the market for replacement shock absorbers. The record lacks substantial evidence supporting the Commission's finding that Tenneco was likely to have entered the market for replacement shock absorbers in the near future either *de novo* or through toehold acquisition. . . .

We also conclude that the record contains inadequate evidence to support the Commission's conclusion that Tenneco's acquisition of Monroe violated section 7 by eliminating Tenneco as a perceived potential competitor in the market for replacement shock absorbers. . . .

There is abundant evidence that the oligopolists in the market for replacement shock absorbers perceived Tenneco as a potential entrant. Industry executives testified that they considered Tenneco one of very few manufacturers with both the incentive and the capability to enter the market. This perception was based on Tenneco's financial strength and on the compatibility of shock absorbers with exhaust system parts produced by Tenneco's Walker Division. This testimony was enhanced by evidence that the negotiations between Tenneco and DeCarbon were initiated by an independent broker and that the negotiations that eventually led to the Tenneco-Monroe merger were initiated by Monroe, indicating that those in the industry were aware of Tenneco's interest. This, especially when combined with the fact that industry participants were apparently not privy to the lack of success in Tenneco's toehold acquisition negotiations, is more than sufficient to satisfy the substantial evidence requirement with respect to industry perceptions of Tenneco as a potential entrant.

However, the analysis does not end here. The Commission's conclusion that the perception of Tenneco as a potential entrant actually tempered the conduct of oligopolists in the market must also be supported by substantial evidence. It is not.

. . . [The Commission] must produce at least circumstantial evidence that Tenneco's presence probably directly affected competitive activity in the market. . . . [But the] testimony constitutes direct evidence that Tenneco had no direct effect on Maremont's business decisions or competitive activity. In the face of this contrary and unchallenged direct evidence, the substantiality of circumstantial evidence arguably suggesting an 'edge effect' vanishes. . . .

The court then dismissed the complaint. For further discussion of the potential competition doctrine, see 5 P. AREEDA & H. HOVENKAMP, ANTITRUST LAW ¶¶ 1121–1134 (3d ed. 2009); H. HOVENKAMP, FEDERAL ANTITRUST POLICY §§ 13.4–13.5 (4th ed. 2011); E.T. SULLIVAN & J. HARRISON, UNDERSTANDING ANTITRUST AND ITS ECONOMIC IMPLICATIONS, ch. 7 (5th ed. 2008).

5. In *United States v. Penn-Olin Chem. Co.*, 378 U.S. 158 (1964), the Supreme Court held that the potential competition doctrine applied to a joint venture, in this case, by the formation of a new corporation owned jointly by Pennsalt and Olin to make sodium chlorate in the southeastern United States. One parent corporation, Pennsalt, made sodium chlorate in the Northwest. The other, Olin, was both a purchaser and a distributor of sodium chlorate and had patented certain uses of the product. The court acknowledged that a joint venture can in fact create a new actual competitor in a market, as it did in this case, while a merger generally eliminates an actual or potential competitor. Nevertheless, it held that the same considerations applied to Section 7 analysis of a joint venture as to a potential competition merger:

> Just as a merger eliminates actual competition, this joint venture may well foreclose any prospect of competition between Olin and Pennsalt in the relevant sodium chlorate market. . . . The existence of an aggressive, well equipped and well financed corporation engaged in the same or related lines of commerce waiting anxiously to enter an oligopolistic market would be a substantial incentive to competition which cannot be underestimated. . . . This same situation might well have come about had either Olin or Pennsalt entered the relevant market alone and the other remained aloof watching developments.

> Here the evidence shows beyond question that the industry was rapidly expanding; the relevant southeast market was requiring about one-half of the national production of sodium chlorate; few corporations had the inclination, resources and know-how to enter this market; both parent corporations of Penn-Olin had great resources; each had long been identified with the industry, one owning valuable patent rights while the other had engaged in sodium chlorate production for years; each had other chemicals, the production of which required the use of sodium chlorate; right up to the creation of Penn-Olin, each had evidenced a long-sustained and strong interest in entering the relevant market area; each enjoyed a good reputation and business connection with the major consumers of sodium chlorate in the relevant markets . . . ; and, finally, each had the know-how and capacity to enter that market and could have done so individually at a reasonable profit. Moreover, each company had compelling reasons for entering the southeast market. Pennsalt needed to expand its sales to the southeast, which it could not do economically without a plant in that area. Olin was motivated by 'the fact that [it was] already buying and

using a fair quantity [of sodium chlorate] for the production of sodium chlorite. . . . ' Unless we are going to require subjective evidence, this array of probability certainly reaches the prima facie stage. As we have indicated, to require more would be to read the statutory requirement of reasonable probability into a requirement of certainty. This we will not do.

The court then remanded for determination whether either Pennsalt or Olin would have entered the southeast market independently. If they would have, the merger violated the potential competition doctrine. For thoughtful analysis of the problem of joint ventures and merger policy, see Brodley, *Joint Ventures and Antitrust Policy*, 95 Harv. L. Rev. 1521, 1523–1538 (1982).

POTENTIAL COMPETITION
MERGERS UNDER THE 1984 JUSTICE DEPARTMENT MERGER GUIDELINES

Although horizontal mergers are governed by the 2010 Horizontal Merger Guidelines, reprinted in Appendix A, potential competition mergers continue to be governed by the substantive standards articulated in the 1984 Justice Department Merger Guidelines. In all likelihood, however, questions pertaining to market definition and entry barriers will be resolved under the 2010 Guidelines. Respecting potential competition mergers, the 1984 Guidelines note the following:

§ 4.111. Harm to 'Perceived Potential Competition'

By eliminating a significant present competitive threat that constrains the behavior of the firms already in the market, the merger could result in an immediate deterioration in market performance. The economic theory of limit pricing suggests that monopolists and groups of colluding firms may find it profitable to restrain their pricing in order to deter new entry that is likely to push prices even lower by adding capacity to the market. If the acquiring firm had unique advantages in entering the market, the firms in the market might be able to set a new and higher price after the threat of entry by the acquiring firm was eliminated by the merger.

§ 4.112. Harm to 'Actual Potential Competition'

By eliminating the possibility of entry by the acquiring firm in a more procompetitive manner, the merger could result in a lost opportunity for improvement in market performance resulting from the addition of a significant competitor. The more procompetitive alternatives include both new entry and entry through a "toehold" acquisition of a present small competitor.

If it were always profit-maximizing for incumbent firms to set price in such a way that all entry was deterred and if information and coordination were sufficient to implement this strategy, harm to perceived potential competition would be the only competitive problem to address. In practice, however, actual potential competition has independent importance. Firms already in the market may not find it optimal to set price low enough to deter all entry; moreover, those firms may misjudge the entry advantages of a particular firm and, therefore, the price necessary to deter its entry.

§ 4.12. Relation Between Perceived and Actual Competition

§ 4.13. Enforcement Standards

. . . .

The factors that the Department will consider are as follows:

§ 4.131. Market Concentration

Barriers to entry are unlikely to affect market performance if the structure of the market is otherwise not conducive to monopolization or collusion. Adverse competitive effects are likely only if overall concentration, or the largest firm's market share, is high. The Department is unlikely to challenge a potential competition merger unless overall concentration of the acquired firm's market is above 1800 HHI (a somewhat lower concentration will suffice if one or more of the factors discussed in Section 3.4 indicate that effective collusion in the market is particularly likely). Other things being equal, the Department is increasingly likely to challenge a merger as this threshold is exceeded.

§ 4.132. Conditions of Entry Generally

If entry to the market is generally easy, the fact that entry is marginally easier for one or more firms is unlikely to affect the behavior of the firms in the market. The Department is unlikely to challenge a potential competition merger when [entry is easy].

If more than a few firms have the same or a comparable advantage in entering the acquired firm's market, the elimination of one firm is unlikely to have any adverse competitive effect. The other similarly situated firm(s) would continue to exert a present restraining influence, or, if entry would be profitable, would recognize the opportunity and enter. The Department is unlikely to challenge a potential competition merger if the entry advantage ascribed to the acquiring firm (or another advantage of comparable importance) is also possessed by three or more other firms. Other things being equal, the Department is increasingly likely to challenge a merger as the number of other similarly situated firms decreases below three and as the extent of the entry advantage over non-advantaged firms increases.

§ 4.133. The Acquiring Firm's Entry Advantage

If the evidence of likely actual entry by the acquiring firm is particularly strong, however, the Department may challenge a potential competition merger, notwithstanding the presence of three or more firms that are objectively similarly situated. In such cases, the Department will determine the likely scale of entry, using either the firm's own documents or the minimum efficient scale in the industry. The Department will then evaluate the merger much as it would a horizontal merger between a firm the size of the likely scale of entry and the acquired firm.

Entry through the acquisition of a relatively small firm in the market may have a competitive effect comparable to new entry. Small firms frequently play peripheral roles in collusive interactions, and the particular advantages of the acquiring firm may convert a fringe firm into a significant factor in the market.

§ 4.134. The Market Share of the Acquired Firm

The Department is unlikely to challenge a potential competition merger when the acquired firm has a market share of five percent or less. Other things being equal, the Department is increasingly likely to challenge a merger as the market share of the acquired firm increases above that threshold. The Department is likely to challenge any merger satisfying the other conditions in which the acquired firm has a market share of 20 percent or more.

PROBLEM 7.4

Alpha Corp. is an American firm that manufactures and sells Responders in the United States. A Responder is a piece of high-tech hardware used in American defense applications. There are no known substitutes. Alpha proposes to acquire all the stock of Beta Corp., a Japanese firm that manufactures Responders for foreign defense applications. Currently, however, Beta Corp. does not sell Responders to the United States government, or in the United States at all. Alpha is the largest supplier of Responders in the United States, accounting for about 25% of United States' sales. Beta is much larger than Alpha and provides 40% of world demand for Responders outside the United States. If Beta wished to make sales in the United States, it would take at least 18 months for it to establish sufficient distribution facilities. Thus, assume that the relevant geographic market is the United States.

NOTE: THE COMMON CARRIER IMMUNITY FROM § 7

Section 7 of the Clayton Act contains this limitation on its prohibition of mergers:

Nor shall anything herein contained be construed to prohibit any common carrier subject to the laws to regulate commerce . . . from extending any of its lines through the medium of the acquisition of stock or otherwise of any other common carrier where there is no substantial competition between the company extending its lines and the company whose stock, property, or an interest therein is so acquired.

15 U.S.C. § 18. In *South Austin Coalition Community Council v. SBC Communications*, 274 F.3d 1168 (7th Cir. 2001), *cert. denied*, 537 U.S. 814 (2002), the court held that this language immunized a merger between two very large "Baby Bell" telephone systems, SBC and Ameritech. Clearly, regulated telephone systems are common carriers and the merger, which linked two systems that operated in contiguous but non-overlapping territories, was a line extension.

The court noted that the original House version of the proviso used the word "railroad," while the Senate substituted "common carrier" and the House acquiesced. The Senate Report then explained that the purpose of the amendment was to make the exemption "apply to any common carrier, thus including telephone and pipe lines." Telephone companies, in particular, were placed under ICC jurisdiction in 1910, and from that time treated as common carriers for federal purposes. Both the plain language of the statute and its legislative history suggest a broad reading, including any firm that is by common law or statutory definition a common carrier.

In any event, any challenge to such a merger would have to come under one of the potential competition doctrines, which are rarely applied today. Would the provision exempt a merger between two *non*-contiguous Bell carriers? And query: because mergers are condemned under the Sherman and Clayton Acts under pretty much the same standards, but the Sherman Act contains no common carrier immunity, could a plaintiff avoid the problem simply by challenging the merger under the Sherman Act?

IV   THE FAILING COMPANY DEFENSE

CITIZEN PUBLISHING CO. v. UNITED STATES
394 U.S. 131 (1969)

JUSTICE DOUGLAS delivered the opinion of the Court.

Tucson, Arizona, has only two daily newspapers of general circulation, the Star and the Citizen. . . . Prior to 1940 the two papers vigorously competed with each other. While their circulation was about equal, the Star sold 50% more advertising space than the Citizen and operated at a profit, while the Citizen sustained losses. Indeed the Star's annual profits averaged about $25,825, while the Citizen's annual losses averaged about $23,550.

In 1936 the stock of the Citizen was purchased by one Small and one Johnson for $100,000 and they invested an additional $25,000 of working capital. They sought to interest others to invest in the Citizen but were not successful. Small increased his investment in the Citizen, moved from Chicago to Tucson, and was prepared to finance the Citizen's losses for at least awhile from his own resources. It does not appear that Small and Johnson sought to sell the Citizen; nor was the Citizen about to go out of business. The owners did, however, negotiate a joint operating agreement between the two papers which was to run for 25 years from March 1940, a term that was extended in 1953 until 1990. By its terms the agreement may be canceled only by mutual consent of the parties.

The agreement provided that each paper should retain its own news and editorial department, as well as its corporate identity. It provided for the formation of Tucson Newspapers, Inc. (TNI), which was to be owned in equal shares by the Star and Citizen and which was to manage all departments of their business except the news and editorial units. The production and distribution equipment of each paper was transferred to TNI. The latter had five directors — two named by the Star, two by the Citizen, and the fifth chosen by the Citizen out of three named by the Star.

The purpose of the agreement was to end any business or commercial competition between the two papers and to that end three types of controls were imposed. First was *price fixing*. The newspapers were sold and distributed by the circulation department of TNI; commercial advertising placed in the papers was sold only by the advertising department of TNI; the subscription and advertising rates were set jointly. Second was *profit pooling*. All profits realized were pooled and distributed to the Star and the Citizen by TNI pursuant to an agreed ratio. Third was a *market control*. It was agreed that neither the Star nor the Citizen nor any of their stockholders, officers, and executives would engage in any other business in Pima County — the metropolitan area of Tucson — in conflict with the agreement. Thus competing publishing operations were foreclosed.

All commercial rivalry between the papers ceased. Combined profits before taxes rose from $27,531 in 1940 to $1,727,217 in 1964.

. . . .

The case went to trial on . . . a charge brought under § 7 of the Clayton Act. The . . . charge arose out of the acquisition of the stock of the Star by the shareholders of the Citizen pursuant to an option in the joint operating agreement. Arden Publishing Company was formed as the vehicle of acquisition and it now publishes the Star.

. . . .

The only real defense of appellants was the "failing company" defense — a judicially created doctrine. . . . That defense was before the Court in *International Shoe Co. v. FTC*, 280 U.S. 291, where § 7 of the Clayton Act was in issue. The evidence showed that the resources of one company were so depleted and the prospect of rehabilitation so remote that "it faced the grave probability of a business failure." There was, moreover, "no other prospective purchaser." It was in that setting that the Court held that the acquisition of that company by another did not substantially lessen competition within the meaning of § 7.

In the present case the District Court found:

> "At the time Star Publishing and Citizen Publishing entered into the operating agreement, and at the time the agreement became effective, Citizen Publishing was not then on the verge of going out of business, nor was there a serious probability at that time that Citizen Publishing would terminate its business and liquidate its assets unless Star Publishing and Citizen Publishing entered into the operating agreement."

The evidence sustains that finding. There is no indication that the owners of the Citizen were contemplating a liquidation. They never sought to sell the Citizen and there is no evidence that the joint operating agreement was the last straw at which the Citizen grasped. Indeed the Citizen continued to be a significant threat to the Star. How otherwise is one to explain the Star's willingness to enter into an agreement to share its profits with the Citizen? Would that be true if as now claimed the Citizen was on the brink of collapse?

The failing company doctrine plainly cannot be applied in a merger or in any other case unless it is established that the company that acquires the failing company or brings it under dominion is the only available purchaser. For if another person or group could be interested, a unit in the competitive system would be preserved and not lost to monopoly power. So even if we assume, arguendo, that in 1940 the then owners of the Citizen could not long keep the enterprise afloat, no effort was made to sell the Citizen; its properties and franchise were not put in the hands of a broker; and the record is silent on what the market, if any, for the Citizen might have been.

Moreover, we know from the broad experience of the business community since 1930, the year when the *International Shoe* case was decided, that companies reorganized through receivership, or through Chapter X or Chapter XI of the Bankruptcy Act often emerged as strong competitive companies. The prospects of reorganization of the Citizen in 1940 would have had to be dim or nonexistent to make the failing company doctrine applicable to this case.

The burden of proving that the conditions of the failing company doctrine have been satisfied is on those who seek refuge under it. That burden has not been satisfied in this case.

NOTES AND QUESTIONS

1. Both the House and Senate Reports on the 1950 amendments to Section 7 of the Clayton Act contemplated some kind of "failing company" defense. On the surface at least, such a defense is attractive: if a firm is on the verge of bankruptcy and is not a viable competitor to begin with, then how much competition can a merger eliminate? Furthermore, the defense has an appeal to those who believe that antitrust should occasionally protect small business, inefficiency notwithstanding. It provides small businesses with a "parachute" in case things go bad.

Clearly the failing company defense gives a certain amount of protection to small businesses when they are the partners to the prospective merger. However, it may injure small businesses when they are competitors with the failing company that is being acquired, for one result of the acquisition may be that the failing company will be a better competitor than it was before. See *Brunswick Corp. v. Pueblo Bowl-O-Mat, Inc.*, 429 U.S. 477 (1977), for one instance when a small business was injured by a merger that might have been legal because of the failing company defense.

Can the failing company defense be justified on the alternative grounds that it is efficient? Suppose that a market contains five firms of equal market shares and that Firm C is certainly failing. If it goes out of business altogether, total output in the market is likely to decline because capacity has declined. Suppose Firm A acquires Firm C. A is not likely to acquire C merely to close C's plant; C's imminent failure would do that. Rather, A intends to operate C's plant, thus suggesting that total market output will be greater with the acquisition than without it. As a general rule, a firm with large capacity maximizes its profit at a higher rate of output than a firm with a small capacity, even if it is a monopolist, provided that price is higher than average variable cost. In that case, the acquisition will yield an output increase by A, and output increases are generally good. So a tradeoff would have to be computed between (1) any increase in market power or likelihood of collusion that may result from the merger; and (2) resulting efficiencies, including the effects of maintaining a larger amount of productive capacity on the market. For rival views about how these competing concerns should be evaluated, see Campbell, *The Efficiency of the Failing Company Defense*, 63 TEX. L. REV. 251 (1984); McChesney, *Defending the Failing-Firm Defense*, 65 NEB. L. REV. 1 (1985); Friedman, *Untangling the Failing Company Doctrine*, 64 TEX. L. REV. 1375 (1986).

The failing company defense can operate so as to legalize some very anticompetitive mergers. For example, if a market contains four competitors of roughly equal size and one is on the verge of bankruptcy, the failing company defense might result in the acquisition of one of the remaining competitors of 50% of the market, while the other two have 25% each. Absent the defense, we would expect the three remaining firms to divide the failing firm's customers among themselves, and each would end up with about one-third of the market.

Courts today generally agree that before the failing company defense will apply, the target company must be shown to be unable to recover through bankruptcy — that is, but for the merger the target company's assets will be scrapped or sold to the highest bidder.

The failing company defense is an affirmative defense: it becomes necessary only after we have decided that a merger poses a sufficient threat to competition that it would otherwise be enjoined under Section 7.

For general discussions of the defense, see 4A P. AREEDA, H. HOVENKAMP, & J. SOLOW, ANTITRUST LAW ¶¶ 951–954 (3d ed. 2009); H. Hovenkamp, Federal Antitrust Policy § 12.8 (4th ed. 2011).

2. In 1970, Congress passed the Newspaper Preservation Act, 15 U.S.C. § 1801 (1988), which permits "joint newspaper operating arrangements" similar to the one disapproved in the *Citizen Publishing* case. The act permits two or more newspapers to enter into an agreement or joint venture for the purpose of sharing production facilities, distribution mechanisms, solicitation of advertising, and circulation, and even for setting joint advertising and circulation rates. It expressly prohibits the member newspapers from having joint editorial or reportorial staffs, or from creating joint editorial policies. In order to qualify under the Act, the joint operating arrangement must have the prior written consent of the United States Attorney General, and it must show that all or all but one of the member newspapers were "failing newspapers" — that is, that each was unlikely "to remain or become a financially sound publication." Finally, the Act provides that parties to a joint newspaper operating arrangement will be subject to antitrust liability for activities not expressly exempted by the Newspaper Preservation Act. Today several large cities have pairs of daily newspapers that operate pursuant to such joint newspaper operating arrangements.

In *Michigan Citizens for an Independent Press v. Thornburgh*, 493 U.S. 38 (1989), an equally divided Supreme Court affirmed a decision by the District of Columbia Circuit which interpreted the Newspaper Preservation Act phrase "probable danger of financial failure" to mean that one of two newspapers seeking permission to enter a joint operating agreement must be suffering losses that more than likely cannot be reversed by unilateral action. While the Attorney General must approve the initial joint venture, she apparently does not need to approve subsequent amendments. *See Mahaffey v. Detroit Newspaper Agency*, 969 F. Supp. 446 (E.D. Mich. 1997) (because the Newspaper Preservation Act contained no procedure for amending a JOA or any statement of the consequences of such an amendment, an amendment to an existing JOA did not lose its antitrust immunity simply because the Justice Department had not approved the amendment). On the Newspaper Preservation Act, see Areeda, Hovenkamp & Solow, *id.* at ¶ 955.

In *Reilly v. The Hearst Corp.*, 107 F. Supp. 2d 1192 (N.D. Cal. 2000), the court held that one newspaper's acquisition of its registered partner under the Newspaper Preservation Act was lawful because the acquired paper qualified for the failing company defense. Projections indicated that the acquired paper (the San Francisco *Examiner*) would lose money, and it had been a financial drain on the joint operating agreement. Further, the paper had made a reasonable effort to seek out alternative inquirers. The case is idiosyncratic, however, because the *Examiner* was not a free-standing firm to begin with, but a newspaper without significant production resources of its own, and operating only under the joint operating agreement. As a result, the fact of failure had to be analyzed on the basis of predictions about how the *Examiner* would fare as an independent enterprise rather than any track record of independent entrepreneurship. The court concluded that:

> . . . the evidence establishes that the *Examiner*, operating as a general circulation metropolitan daily and Sunday newspaper outside the JOA and independent of the *[San Francisco] Chronicle*, would have to overcome a 4:1 circulation disadvantage to achieve not only future profitability, but profitability sufficient to recoup any losses that Hearst would incur during the period of losses. A circulation disadvantage of this magnitude is considerably greater than that which Hearst or any commercially motivated publisher could surmount to achieve profitability.

V PRIVATE ENFORCEMENT OF SECTION 7

Congress unquestionably intended that private persons should sometimes be permitted to enforce the antimerger laws. Section 4 of the Clayton Act, 15 U.S.C. § 15, creates a private action for treble damages plus attorneys' fees for injuries caused by "anything forbidden in the antitrust laws," and Section 1 of the Clayton Act, 15 U.S.C. § 12, includes the Clayton Act in "antitrust laws." Congress is even more explicit in Section 16 of the Clayton Act, 15 U.S.C. § 26, which creates a private right of injunctive relief from antitrust violations and expressly includes Section 7 in its coverage.

Nevertheless, private actions under Section 7 pose some problems not generally shared by private actions under the other antitrust statutes. First of all, Section 7 is an "incipiency" statute. Courts condemn mergers because of their tendency to create market power in the post-merger firm, or to facilitate collusion in the market affected by the merger. However, even the relatively tolerant Horizontal Merger Guidelines condemn mergers long before they give the post-merger firm substantial market power. As a result, there are few private cases alleging, for example, that a horizontal merger enabled the post-merger firm to price monopolistically and that the plaintiff was injured by being required to pay a monopoly overcharge. The private injuries caused by mergers are much more subtle.

Unquestionably, mergers that are marginally illegal under the incipiency test or the new Merger Guidelines do cause substantial private injuries. Often, however, these injuries are caused by the increased efficiency of the post-merger firm, not by its increased market power. The efficiencies that result from mergers are present in all mergers, whether legal or illegal. Present, measurable market power, however, comes only from mergers that are far beyond the threshold for legality. Furthermore, mergers are "public" offenses: as a general matter, merging firms cannot conceal their merger either from the general public or from enforcement agencies. As a result, the vast majority of mergers occur only after at least one of the parties to the merger has made some kind of calculation that the merger will not be found illegal in court. Mergers that give the post-merger firm measurably increased market power do not often occur unless someone has made a rather serious miscalculation.

Because all mergers can create efficiencies, but only some of them increase measurably the post-merger firm's market power, the danger of overdeterrence in private merger litigation is high. The threat of treble damage lawsuits plus attorney's fees might encourage many firms to forego a merger that would in fact provide large efficiency gains and have relatively insignificant effects on market power. This danger of overdeterrence makes it very important for courts to distinguish the private costs created by mergers from the social costs.

Anyone who is injured by a merger suffers a private cost. This may include persons who are charged a monopoly price because the merger has created monopoly power. However, it may also include the management of a company which is the target of a tender offer from another firm. Likewise it may include a business which has a difficult time competing with a firm that has become more efficient as the result of a merger, or it may include an independent distributor whose contract is terminated because a firm has vertically integrated by merger.

The social costs of mergers accrue not from the post-merger firm's greater efficiency, but from its increased market power. If the post-merger firm is able to reduce market output and charge a higher price than the participating firms did before the merger, and if these losses are not outweighed by efficiency gains, then the merger is socially costly. By contrast, if the result of the merger is that the post-merger firm can sell a better product at a lower price — as was the case, for example, in *Brown Shoe* — then the merger is socially useful, even though it may injure certain people, such as the competitors of the post-merger firm, or people whose business services to the firm become unnecessary as a result of the merger.

Although there is no general "efficiency defense" in merger cases, the danger of overdeterrence requires that private plaintiffs alleging injuries from mergers be able to show that they are injured by the post-merger firm's increased market power, not by its increased efficiency. This, in large part, is the lesson of the Supreme Court in *Brunswick Corp. v. Pueblo Bowl-O-Mat, Inc.*, 429 U.S. 477 (1977), reprinted in Chapter 3, *supra*. The plaintiff was a competitor of a merging firm who alleged that it was injured because its competitor was more efficient after the merger than it had been before. In fact, the plaintiff argued that the competitor would have gone out of business but for the merger, and that as a result of the merger, the plaintiff was forced to continue to be a competitor where it otherwise would have been a monopolist.

When the facts are stated as boldly as they are above, something immediately strikes us as wrong. The merger laws were designed to encourage competition and decrease monopoly, not vice versa. In fact, however, many damages actions alleging illegal mergers are much more ambiguous, and it takes a fair amount of analysis to discern whether the plaintiff was injured by the post-merger firm's market power or its increased efficiency. For example, how would you deal with a competitor's charge that as a result of a merger, a firm engaged in predatory pricing? Perhaps the plaintiff's theory is that predatory pricing requires a predator with a deep pocket, and the relatively large parent company that acquired the competitor had the necessary funds to finance a long period of below marginal cost selling.

Such a theory might be plausible. (*See* the discussion of predatory pricing in Chapter 6.) One thing seems clear, however. Whether or not such price predation was facilitated by an illegal merger, the plaintiff is complaining about predatory pricing, not about an illegal merger. The merger may be absolutely illegal under current law; but a plaintiff claiming that it was injured by predatory pricing financed by a merger must nevertheless prove that the pricing was truly predatory. How does it do this? Probably by employing the same test that courts apply generally in predatory pricing cases. Many times, a price reduction following a merger will appear "predatory" from a competitor's view. Such a price reduction may be a function of nothing more than the increased efficiency of the firm that went through the merger.

One way to solve this problem is to restrict private damages actions in merger cases to "overcharge" injuries or injuries that are directly attributable to a post-merger firm's reduction of output. An alternative is to eliminate the damages action arising immediately under Section 7, on the theory that private injuries that result from mergers are the result of some kind of post-merger exclusionary practice, and we already have a barrage of antitrust laws to protect private plaintiffs from such activities. For example, the competitor complaining that a merger facilitated predatory pricing must prove predatory pricing — and as a general rule, it will not be able to collect additional damages because it can show that the defendant was guilty of both predatory pricing and an illegal merger. Likewise, a distributor who has been terminated because of a post-merger output reduction may have a cause of action for monopolization under Section 2 of the Sherman Act. If it cannot prove monopolization (perhaps because it cannot prove that the post-merger defendant has market power), that is good evidence that the termination was the result of the post-merger firm's increased efficiency, not of monopolistic practices. *See* Hovenkamp, *Merger Actions for Damages*, 35 HASTINGS L.J. 937 (1984).

CARGILL, INC. v. MONFORT OF COLORADO, INC.

479 U.S. 104 (1986) (This decision is reprinted in Chapter 3.)

NOTES AND QUESTIONS

1. In *Chrysler Corp. v. General Motors Corp.*, 589 F. Supp. 1182 (D.D.C. 1984), the court decided that Chrysler Motor Co., a competitor, had standing to challenge a joint venture created by General Motors Corp. and Toyota Motor Corp. for the manufacture of automobiles. (A month earlier, the Federal Trade Commission had approved the joint venture.) The court did not suggest how Chrysler might be injured by the venture. The case was later settled out of court. The settlement shortened the period of "active cooperation" between General Motors and Toyota from 12 to 8 years.

How is a firm injured by a merger or joint venture of two or more of its competitors? If the joint venture between General Motors and Toyota reduces competition in the automobile industry and enables the post-merger firm to charge a higher price, Chrysler will be better off, will it not? It will be able to charge a higher price too, protected by the "umbrella" created by the larger firm. By contrast, if the merger creates efficiencies that permit General Motors and Toyota to charge *lower* prices, Chrysler will be injured. What would you think of a rule that a competitor may *never* have standing to challenge a horizontal merger? *See* Easterbrook, *The Limits of Antitrust*, 63 TEX. L. REV. 1 (1984); Markovits, *The Limits to Simplifying Antitrust: A Reply to Professor Easterbrook*, 63 TEX. L. REV. 41 (1984).

2. Just as problematic as the private action for damages resulting from an illegal merger is the private injunctive action seeking divestiture. Once a merger has taken place, the entire market reorients itself to the structure of the new firm. As a result, divestiture can cause repercussions throughout the economy and create an entire new set of private injuries. Furthermore, it is often impossible for divestiture to restore the market to anything resembling the pre-merger situation. In *California v. American Stores Co.*, 495 U.S. 271 (1990), the Supreme Court held that the remedy of divestiture was available to a private party (in this case, the state of California acting as parens patriae). The Court found no evidence in the legislative history that Congress intended to exclude divestiture from the scope of Section 16 of the Clayton Act, granting "injunctive relief" to private antitrust plaintiffs. The issue is discussed further in Chapter 3.

3. Suppose that Firm *A* attempts to acquire Firm *B* through a tender offer for Firm *B*'s shares. Firm *B*'s managers are opposed to the takeover however, fearing that they will lose their jobs. They file a suit seeking a preliminary injunction, alleging that the merger would be illegal under Section 7 of the Clayton Act. Should tender offer targets have standing to bring such actions? The courts are divided. Among those granting standing are *Marathon Oil Co. v. Mobil Corp.*, 669 F.2d 378, 383–384 (6th Cir. 1981), *cert. denied*, 455 U.S. 982 (1982); *Grumman Corp. v. LTV Corp.*, 665 F.2d 10, 11 (2d Cir. 1981). Those denying standing include *Central Nat'l Bank v. Rainbolt*, 720 F.2d 1183 (10th Cir. 1983), holding that injury alleged by the takeover target that "is not the result of diminution in competition but rather the

effect of change in . . . control" does not come within the "ambit of the antitrust laws." In *Carter Hawley Hale Stores v. The Limited, Inc.*, 587 F. Supp. 246 (C.D. Cal. 1984), the plaintiff Carter Hawley Hale (CHH) objected that a planned tender offer would (1) result in lessened competition in the apparel market; (2) produce "disruption and uncertainty" in CHH's business affairs; and (3) permit the defendant to learn CHH's trade secrets. As to the second and third allegations the court replied:

> [E]ach of these alleged injuries does not result from the possibility of substantially lessened competition, but rather derives from the fact that after a successful, albeit unfriendly, merger, two corporate entities become one. Put another way, each of these 'injuries' to CHH would occur in the event of a merger, whether or not the merger would substantially lessen competition. Thus, CHH has not alleged an 'antitrust injury'. . . .

Id. at 250. But even with respect to the allegation that the merger would lessen competition between the two firms, the court found that CHH lacked standing to raise the issue. "If the proposed merger is completed, CHH will be a part of the very entity it claims will have a super competitive advantage, i.e., it suffers no antitrust harm." As a result, "it is inconsistent for CHH to complain of this outcome on *antitrust* grounds." *Id.*

PROBLEM 7.5

Ten firms sell pre-wrapped dessert snacks (such as Twinkies and Hostess Buns) in the Philadelphia area. Of these, Alpha, the largest, sells 18%, and Beta, the second largest, sells 10%. Delta, the fourth largest firm, sells 5%. Total revenue of all firms selling dessert snacks is far smaller than the total revenue of firms selling bread, and about equal to the total revenue of yet another group of firms that sell pre-wrapped bakery fresh cookies. Most stores in Philadelphia have shelf space to display only three brands of dessert snacks, and competition among the 10 firms is keen to acquire this shelf space.

In 1988, Alpha Co. acquires Beta Co. The acquisition is approved by the Justice Department. However, Delta Company challenges the acquisition, alleging that (1) the merger will facilitate collusion in the Philadelphia dessert snack market; (2) the post-merger Alpha-Beta Co. will engage in predatory pricing against its rivals, and has already cut price by 25% to selected Philadelphia stores; (3) Alpha-Beta Co. now insists that in order to get either Alpha brand dessert snacks or Beta brand dessert snacks, stores must stock and display both; as a result, competitors face a much more limited opportunity to obtain shelf access.

VI INTERLOCKING DIRECTORATES UNDER SECTION 8 OF THE CLAYTON ACT

Section 8 of the Clayton Act forbids a person from serving as a director or other corporate officer in two different corporations, where the prerequisites of the Act are satisfied. First, the statute applies only "if such corporations are or shall have been theretofore, by virtue of their business and location of operation, competitors, so that the elimination of competition by agreement between them would constitute a violation of any of the provisions of any of the anti-trust laws." 15 U.S.C. § 19. Second, the statute applies to companies with more than 10 million dollars each in capital, surplus, and undivided profits. 1990 amendments to the statute provide "safe harbors" even if the 10 million dollar threshold is met: (1) if the competitive sales of either corporation are less than one million dollars, (2) if the competitive sales of either corporation are less than 2% of that corporation's total sales, or (3) if the competitive sales of each corporation are less than 4% of that corporation's sales.

Banks and related associations and common carriers are generally exempted from Section 8. In 1983, the Supreme Court decided that this exemption applies if *either* of two interlocked directorates is a bank. As a result, Section 8 did not apply to an interlock between a bank and an insurance company. *BankAmerica Corp. v. United States*, 462 U.S. 122 (1983).

The statute explicitly requires that the two corporations be "competitors." Thus, it does not apply to so-called "vertical interlocks" — in which a common director or officer sits on the board of, say, a manufacturer and one of the manufacturer's independent distributors or retailers. On the other hand, if the two corporations are in fact competitors, then a common director or officer violates the statute, even if each corporation is sufficiently small that a merger between them would be legal, provided that the relationship does not qualify for one of the safe harbor exemptions outlined above. *See United States v. Sears, Roebuck & Co.*, 111 F. Supp. 614 (S.D.N.Y. 1953).

VII   SHOULD WE REGULATE BIGNESS?

From the time the Sherman Act was passed up to the present day, people have been concerned with business bigness, or, as they have sometimes put it, "the rising tide of concentration" in industry. The expressed concerns with raw business size have been both economic and noneconomic — although if one looks at the attitudes of Congress and antitrust policy makers throughout the twentieth century, noneconomic concerns appear to dominate. People have argued that bigness in business is bad for a host of reasons, some of which contradict each other: big business is able to take advantage of certain cost savings and drive smaller businesses into bankruptcy; big business is too large to be efficient; big business places too much political power in relatively few hands; and big business makes too much money.

At various times, both Congress and the Executive Branch have considered legislation to control business bigness. These proposals have taken widely different forms. Some have been directed against mergers, but some would force large corporations to divest certain assets even if all their growth had been internal. For a survey of such proposals, see H. Blake, *Legislative Proposals for Industrial Deconcentration, in* H. GOLDSCHMID, H.M. MANN & J.F. WESTON, INDUSTRIAL CONCENTRATION: THE NEW LEARNING, 340–359 (1974).

The proponents of some kind of legislation regulating industrial concentration have relied on two rather controversial empirical conclusions. The first is that large corporations make more money than smaller ones, and that there is a positive correlation between industrial concentration and profitability. The second conclusion, which is more controversial than the first, is that many firms today are far larger than the minimum size necessary to take advantage of all available economies of scale.

In 1951, Professor Joe S. Bain published a pioneering study of the relationship between profitability and market concentration in 42 industries. Bain, *Relation of Profit Rate to Industry Concentration: American Manufacturing, 1936–1940*, 65 Q.J. ECON. 293, 293–324 (1951); for a critique, see Phillips, *A Critique of Empirical Studies of Relations Between Market Structure and Profitability*, 24 J. INDUS. ECON. 241, 241–249 (1976). Professor Bain found that in general, the more highly concentrated the industry, the higher its profit rates. In the last 30 years, Bain's findings have been subjected to a number of criticisms and a number of people have rallied to Bain's support. Most economists have concluded that there *is* a positive correlation between concentration and high profits — although they disagree about the numbers. After 30 years of debate, we do not have a very precise view of the relationship that exists between profitability and concentration, but economists rather persistently find that firms in highly concentrated industries generally make higher profits than firms in unconcentrated industries. A survey of the literature on the relationship between concentration and profitability is contained in Goldschmid, Mann & Weston, *supra*, at 162–245; and F.M. SCHERER & D. ROSS, INDUSTRIAL MARKET STRUCTURE AND ECONOMIC PERFORMANCE, 440–444 (3d ed. 1990).

How do we explain persistent high profits in concentrated industries? The way that comes immediately to mind when we think about industries that have relatively few competitors is either express or tacit collusion, or oligopolistic interdependence. If the collusion is express and we can catch the conspirators in the act, our problem would be simple. Unfortunately, that is not often the case. The problem of judicial remedy in cases of oligopoly pricing has been often analyzed and considered insoluble (see the discussion of oligopoly, *supra*). Courts cannot force firms in concentrated industries simply to ignore the pricing behavior of their competitors. Put more simply, reduction of output and pricing at above marginal cost may be inherent in oligopoly situations, especially where there are fewer than four or so firms in the market, and any other kind of pricing behavior would be irrational. To some antitrust theorists, such as those who proposed the statutes described above, this has justified structural relief: forced divestiture until the market is sufficiently diffuse that oligopolistic interdependence is no longer likely to occur. *See, e.g.*, C. KAYSEN & D. TURNER, ANTITRUST POLICY, 27 (1959).

This kind of structural relief comes with one immense problem of its own, however: what if certain markets are concentrated because the most efficient size for firms in that market is very large? If that is the case, forced divestiture could impose costs in the form of diseconomies of size that far outweigh any inefficiency caused by the oligopolistic pricing itself. For one concise argument to this effect, see Peltzman, *The Gains and Losses from Industrial Concentration*, 20 J.L. & ECON. 229 (1977); and see the responses in 22 J.L. & ECON. 183–211 (1979). *See also* Meehan & Larner, *The Structural School, Its Critics, and Its Progeny: An Assessment, in* ECONOMICS AND ANTITRUST POLICY 179 (R. Larner & J. Meehan eds., 1989).

For this reason, proponents of forced deconcentration generally rely on a second empirical premise. This premise — that most big firms in concentrated industries are far larger than economies require — is much more controversial. The biggest problem is that the word "economies" applies to a wide range of phenomena that differ substantially from one industry to the next. One must determine the most efficient size of the single plant, whether a firm can realize certain multi-plant economies, and whether there are transactional economies that can be achieved by integration of operations. For example, it is probable that a plant capable of producing 5% to 10% of the American market for automobiles is large enough to realize all available economies of plant size. However, certain multi-plant economies, such as advertising, can be achieved at much larger outputs. The cost of developing an advertisement or slogan is the same, whether one's production of automobiles is 1,000 units per year or 10,000,000. However, such economies become less significant as one reaches very high outputs because the cost as distributed per unit of output becomes quite small. For some of the problems involved in measuring the economies that industries can achieve by size and integration, see Scherer & Ross, *supra*, at 97–151; for a somewhat different approach, see G. Stigler, *The Economies of Scale*, 1 J.L. & ECON. 54, 54–71 (1958).

F.M. Scherer and others have made several studies of representative American industries and have concluded that a few firms are as much as 10 times as large as the "Minimum Efficient Size" (MES) required for their particular industry, and that many firms are about four times as large as the MES. The MES represents a firm large enough to take advantage of all available economies. Thus, if MES is properly computed, a firm larger than MES would not be more efficient than an MES firm, but it could be less efficient if a larger plant size generated diseconomies. That is, if a certain plant or firm becomes too large, it will operate inefficiently and its cost of production will begin to rise. The findings and the literature are surveyed in Scherer & Ross, *supra*, at 97–151; and in Goldschmid, Mann & Weston, *supra*, at 15–113, which includes an insightful dialogue between Professor Scherer and Professor John S. McGee.

Critics have faulted Scherer and his followers for failing to make exhaustive lists of the efficiencies that large size can generate. As John S. McGee puts it, "a so-called minimum optimum size that does not exhaust all of the economies is simply not a minimum-cost size." McGee may have pointed to a serious flaw in the MES approach: no list of available economies can really be exhaustive, for technology is constantly changing the list, and the list is already very long and complex. To understand fully the kinds of economies that can be achieved in, say, automobile production, one must consider engineering, transportation costs, market location, availability of natural resources and other materials, labor, federal, state, and local tax laws and regulations, and management, to name only a few things.

Furthermore, the establishment of a minimum plant size for optimal efficiency does not necessarily mean that larger firms cannot be equally efficient. If the MES in a particular market is a plant capable of producing 2% of market demand, but firms do not begin to suffer from diseconomies of excessive size until they occupy a 30% share or greater, we would not expect to find an industry full of identical firms occupying 2% of the market. We would expect to find firms operating in the entire range from 2% to 30%. In the real world, not all firms behave in the same way, not all have equally effective management, and not all have the same run of good or bad luck. If all firms in the 2% to 30% range are capable of being equally efficient, we would expect some of them to grow far beyond the 2% minimum size, some to stay there, and some to go broke even though they are within the efficiency range (that is to say, not all firms of an efficient size are necessarily efficient firms). Additionally, if our computation of MES overlooked just one nontrivial economy, it might be profitable for two firms in that market whose combined share was less than 30% to merge. In short, in the natural course of things, we expect firms to be larger than MES, right up to the maximum size they can be without suffering from diseconomies of large size.

Some of the proponents of forced industrial deconcentration have gone even further than the argument that many American firms are larger than MES. They have argued that some American firms, particularly conglomerates, are too large to be efficient, and that they could actually operate at reduced cost if they were smaller. Conglomerates have been accused of continuing to produce certain products after demand for them disappeared, but subsidizing the losses from profits earned in other sectors. They have been accused of exhibiting managerial "sluggishness," because top management is deluged with too much information from too many different sources. They have been accused of purchasing and selling among their own subsidiaries not because the transactions were most efficient, but because necessary information was so readily available. Finally, large conglomerates have often been accused of being poor innovators. These arguments and others are summarized in Scherer & Ross, *supra*, at 668–672. For generally conflicting views, see the essays collected in ANTITRUST, INNOVATION, AND COMPETITIVENESS (T. Jorde & D. Teece eds., 1992). As discussed *supra*, in recent years there has been a revival of Schumpeterian arguments that large firms (or joint ventures) innovate more than small ones, and that the gains from giving innovation free rein far exceed any losses from the industrial concentration that results. *See, e.g.*, J. SCHUMPETER, CAPITALISM, SOCIALISM, AND DEMOCRACY, chs. 7–8 (1942).

In short, we sometimes expect to find plants that are smaller than optimal for the manufacture of a particular product. However, we do not expect to find plants that are too large for efficient production unless there has been a miscalculation. For example, someone might think that a market for 500,000 widgets will maintain itself indefinitely, and build a plant of size B. A few years later, however, demand drops to 250,000 and the firm is stuck with an excessively large plant.

The argument above is only an extension of an argument we have seen in a different context. Faced with a choice between buying something in the marketplace or doing something for itself (vertical integration), a profit-maximizing firm will choose the cheapest course. If integration will produce substantial diseconomies of size, the firm will be more likely to purchase the service in the market. Thus, there might be some basis for concluding that firms are larger than the minimum size necessary to achieve optimal efficiency. However, there is little basis in either logic or evidence to conclude that firms are larger than the maximum size that will permit them to operate efficiently.

As a result, forced divestiture is not likely to produce efficiency gains (except perhaps a reduction of monopoly pricing) but may very well produce substantial losses in efficiency. The American economy could pay a large price if firms were divided in the absence of specific evidence of inefficient practices. If large businesses have no economic advantage over smaller rivals, then they will be able to maintain high rates of profit only by means of inefficient exclusionary practices. If we have no evidence of such practices, then we have at least a basis for an inference that the large size is a result of efficiency. In that case, forced divestiture could cost American consumers heavily. Worse yet, it could mean that American business could lose its competitive position in world markets, at least if other countries are inclined to permit businesses to seek out their most efficient size in unrestrained markets.

American antitrust policy has always been guided by a concern for bigness. However, the law itself has always tempered that concern by establishing various bad conduct requirements. The reasons for this are clear. It is extraordinarily difficult — perhaps impossible — to look at an established business of a given size and pronounce that business as too big to be efficient. Economists have debated such questions for decades and have failed to reach agreement. To believe that we can perform such a task in litigation is questionable.

By contrast, we have more confidence about specific practices that we have labeled exclusionary or monopolistic. To be sure, some of these practices are more obviously inefficient than others. For example, we have a great deal of confidence about industrial sabotage, price-fixing, patent fraud, and perhaps predatory pricing at below marginal cost. We have less confidence about tying arrangements, reciprocity, and intentional building of excess capacity. This suggests strongly that antitrust policy should focus heavily on issues of conduct, not merely on issues of structure.

By establishing bad conduct requirements for antitrust liability, however, we at least increase the chances that we are really attacking inefficient rather than efficient practices, and that American consumers will come out gainers as a result.

To be sure, this may leave us with the uncomfortable situation that firms in concentrated industries make more money than we would like them to make. Consumers would be better off if they would price their output more competitively — that is, if they behaved more like competitors. But, as we have noted before, there are good reasons to believe that the deadweight loss that results from supra competitive pricing in oligopolistic markets is far less than the loss that would result if we forced firms to operate at less than their most efficient size.

Chapter 8

SECONDARY-LINE DIFFERENTIAL PRICING AND THE ROBINSON-PATMAN ACT

Because it is taught infrequently, the full text of Chapter 8 on the Robinson-Patman Act is now posted online and free for anyone to use. This chapter covers all issues related to secondary-line enforcement, the "cost justification," "meeting competition," and other defenses, as well as buyers' liability. Primary-line enforcement is still covered with the materials on predatory pricing in Chapter 6. The full text of Chapter 8 is available under this title at abstract number SSRN 2319067. Users, kindly acknowledge the source and the authors, as E. Thomas Sullivan, Herbert Hovenkamp, Howard A. Shelanski & Christopher R. Leslie, Antitrust Law, Policy and Procedure: Cases, Materials, Problems (7th ed. 2014).

Chapter 9

ANTITRUST, OTHER FORMS OF REGULATION, AND EXEMPTIONS

INTRODUCTION

"Regulation" is government intervention in the marketplace. Government price controls, output controls, quality controls, and restrictions on entry are all common forms of regulation. The federal antitrust laws themselves are a form of regulation, as are common law rules and the litigation process itself.[1]

This chapter briefly examines the relationship between the federal antitrust laws and these other forms of regulation.

The relationship between antitrust and regulation is complicated by the fact that, not only does regulation come in many varieties, but it is also imposed by a variety of sovereigns. Federal, state, and local governments all regulate. The potential for conflict between antitrust and other forms of regulation arises at all three levels.

This chapter is divided into three sections. Section I considers the relationship between the antitrust laws and the classical "regulated industries" generally. Section II considers questions about private liability for "petitions" to the government (the *Noerr-Pennington* doctrine). These petitions can take the form of requests for regulation, but they can also take the form of litigation before a court or regulatory agency. Section III considers the special problems of federalism that arise in the case of conflict between federal antitrust policy and regulation imposed by state or local government.

I ANTITRUST AND AGENCY REGULATION

[A] Overview

Broadly defined, a "regulated industry" is one whose behavior is controlled in part by legislative or governmental agency decision rather than by free market forces. Virtually all American industries are regulated to some degree. Today the term "regulated industry" refers more specifically to a collection of industries in which pricing, entry and exit, or method of operation are determined substantially by a regulatory agency rather than by the market. The agencies include (among others) the Federal Communications Commission, the Federal Energy Regulatory

---

[1] On the "regulatory" role of the Antitrust Division of the Justice Department, see Sullivan, *The Antitrust Division as a Regulatory Agency: An Enforcement Policy in Transition*, 64 Wash. U. L.Q. 996 (1986).

Commission, the Surface Transportation Board (formerly the Interstate Commerce Commission), the Securities and Exchange Commission, the Commodity Futures Trading Commission, the Federal Reserve System, and the Federal Maritime Commission. In addition, there are a host of state and local regulatory agencies that control everything from land use, to the price of taxicab rides, to the cost of trash collection. *See generally* S. BREYER, REGULATION AND ITS REFORM (1982); C. SUNSTEIN, AFTER THE RIGHTS REVOLUTION: RECONCEIVING THE REGULATORY STATE (1990); HERBERT HOVENKAMP, THE OPENING OF AMERICAN LAW: NEOCLASSICAL LEGAL THOUGHT, 1870–1970 (2013).

Just as there are almost no American industries completely free of statutory regulation, there are also few regulated markets in which competitive forces are unimportant. Businesses are extraordinarily creative in their ability to compete with one another. If a regulatory agency determines the retail price in a certain market, the sellers in that market will concentrate on nonprice competition. For example, when air fares were price-regulated several years ago, the airlines competed vigorously in different ways: by offering cabin services; movies; stereo music; more frequent flights; "free" ground transportation; or other amenities. Other industries are no exception. It would be impossible for a legislature or regulatory agency to develop a regulatory scheme so comprehensive and detailed that it eliminated all forms of competition among providers in the same market in the regulated industry.

As a result, antitrust enforcement has found a place in most of the regulated industries. The common law nature of federal antitrust permits a certain amount of "after the fact" judgment of a particular firm's activity that even the most comprehensive of regulatory schemes could not foresee. Today there is substantial antitrust litigation in the communications, interstate transportation, and public utility industries, all of which remain subject to agency regulation. Yet as the materials that follow demonstrate, there are often hard questions about the applicability and scope of antitrust enforcement in regulated industries.

[B] Theories of Regulation and the Movement Toward Deregulation

Industries have generally become economically regulated for one of five reasons: (1) they are (or are thought to be) natural monopolies; (2) some other form of "market failure" prevents the competitive processes from allocating resources properly within a certain market; (3) some scarce natural resource is thought to require allocation in a way the unregulated market is unlikely to yield; (4) the market itself is thought to be unable to provide consumers with adequate information about the product; or (5) some interest group has successfully persuaded a legislative body that its particular industry should be protected from competitive forces by means of a regulatory scheme. *See* S. BREYER, REGULATION AND ITS REFORM 13–35 (1982).

Several developments have prompted skepticism about regulation and have motivated recent moves toward deregulation in many markets. One such development is a growing belief that many industries have been regulated for political rather than economic reasons, and that often regulation results in the protection of inefficiency, higher product prices, and extraordinarily high public costs in running the regulatory process itself. Other developments have involved the economic theories of competition and natural monopoly. Finally, technological change has altered the scope and undermined the rationale for regulation in several industries.

[1] The Rise and Rationale of Regulation

The era of federal regulation dates back to the late nineteenth century. The Interstate Commerce Commission was the first federal agency created to supplant competition with various forms of regulation in a large American industry: the railroads. At that time and throughout the first half of the nineteenth century, the prevailing theory of regulation was that it was passed in the "public interest" to protect American consumers from price gouging or other unfair practices that would prevail in certain industries if they were not restrained by regulatory agencies.

Eventually many economists, historians, and political scientists began to argue, however, that the biggest beneficiaries of the regulatory process were the regulated industries themselves. In the period before the Interstate Commerce Commission was created in 1887, and during the early years of its operation, railroads had been subject to serious overdevelopment. Excess capacity had led to giant rate wars that had driven many of them into bankruptcy. One effect of state and federal regulation of railroads was to limit new entry into the industry, and eventually guarantee the incumbent rail carriers "fair" profit. *See* G. KOLKO, RAILROADS AND REGULATION, 1877–1916 64–83 (1965); REGULATION IN PERSPECTIVE: HISTORICAL ESSAYS (T. McCraw ed., 1981); T. McCRAW, PROPHETS OF REGULATION (1984); H. Hovenkamp, *Regulatory Conflict in the Gilded Age: Federalism and the Railroad Problem*, 97 YALE L.J. 1017 (1988).

More recently, there has been a growing skepticism about both the reasoning behind government regulation and the effects of that regulation. On one hand, price regulation may put a ceiling on a firm's power to price monopolistically. On the other hand, regulation might protect inefficiency in business by guaranteeing a fair rate of return which is calculated from cost data most often submitted by the regulated firms themselves. This effect is sometimes revealed by the political process. For example, when the movement for price deregulation in the interstate trucking industry began, the loudest objections were raised by members of the trucking industry themselves — good evidence, it seems, that the chief danger of deregulation was not monopoly pricing, which would benefit the deregulated firms, but more intense competition.

In addition, we have become aware that the regulatory process itself imposes enormous costs, often larger than the costs of the competitive marketplace. If every rate change, every decision to enter or withdraw from a particular market, or every significant change in the service to be delivered must be approved by an agency after a fact-finding procedure, the costs of regulation can be enormous, perhaps larger than the costs that would result from unregulated monopoly pricing. *See* S. Breyer, *supra*, at 184–284; Posner, *Natural Monopoly and Its Regulation*, 21 STAN. L. REV. 548, 619 (1969); Robert W. Hahn & Robert E. Litan, *Counting Regulatory*

Benefits and Costs: Lessons for the United States and Europe, 8 J. INTL. ECON. L. 473 (2005).

Finally, regulation becomes more difficult as a practical and theoretical matter as economic and technological events change the structures of regulated industries. With these changes, the potential costs and benefits of regulation just discussed have come under even greater scrutiny.

[2] Natural Monopoly, Contestability, and Deregulation

The second reason for the growing trend toward deregulation involves important changes in the economic theory of competition and natural monopoly. These changes have been brought about by one rather general development in the economic theory of property rights, and one quite specific development.

The general development is the Coase theorem, which states that two parties bargaining over a legal entitlement will reach the efficient, or joint-maximizing result, assuming transaction costs are low. *See* Coase, *The Problem of Social Cost*, 3 J.L. & ECON. 1 (1960). Importantly, the Coase theorem does not depend on the existence of competitive or even moderately competitive markets. Indeed, most of the illustrations in Coase's famous article (such as the rancher and farmer bargaining over damage done by grazing cattle) were bilateral monopolies — situations where a monopoly seller faces a monopoly buyer. In law and economics, the Coase theorem serves greatly to weaken the premise that only "perfect competition" yields efficient results. One result has been a great deal of interest in institutional settings designed to make competition work better by lowering transaction costs.

The more specific development is the theory of franchise bidding and its more technical offspring, the doctrine of contestable markets. These theories call into question the robustness of the traditional economic theory of natural monopoly. A "natural" monopoly is a market that can be served most efficiently by a single incumbent firm. In more technical terminology, a natural monopoly is a market where costs decline as output increases through the entire range of market demand. Figure 1 illustrates such a market. The market demand curve (D) crosses the average total cost curve (AC) to the left of the lowest point on the AC curve. Over the long run, a single firm operating in this market would have to recover its total costs, which it could do by setting its price at the intersection of D and AC. This would yield a price of Pc and output of Qc. Technically speaking, this is not the "competitive" price and output, for price is well above marginal cost. However, it is the price that most regulatory agencies strive to achieve and is one way of identifying the lowest price consistent with profitability over the full volume of market demand.

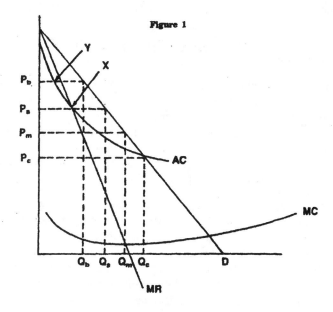

Figure 1

Because the average cost curve in Figure 1 slopes downward through the entire relevant range, any firm that produced less than Qc would be less efficient and would face higher costs. Suppose, for example, that two equally efficient and equal-sized sellers shared the market in Figure 1. Each would fill half the demand, so their joint output would lie on a point along the average cost curve midway between the vertical axis and the demand curve: point X. At that point, each firm could sell one half the output in the market at a price equal to its average total costs. However, the combined output of the firms would be lower than the output of a single firm in the market would be, and the price would be higher. Two equal-sized firms would have a combined output of Qa and they would charge a price of Pa. If three identical firms shared this market, the loss of efficiency would be even more severe, output would be even lower, and prices would be higher. In that case, each firm would have costs equal to the point on the AC curve one-third of the distance between the vertical axis and the demand curve — point Y. The three firms would have a total output of Qb and each would charge a price of Pb. The more firms that occupied the market, the lower total output would be and the higher the market price would be. Such a market behaves most favorably to consumers when it is occupied by a single seller which sets its price equal to its average costs. *See generally* R. Schmalensee, The Control of Natural Monopolies (1979).

The last part of the preceding sentence is critical to the theory of regulation. A natural monopolist is a monopolist. Although the natural monopoly behaves optimally when it is occupied by a single seller pricing at average cost, there is little reason to believe that a monopolist in such a market will price at average cost. Unless restricted, the monopolist will set its price at the intersection of its marginal cost and marginal revenue curves, just like any other monopolist. In Figure 1, the unregulated monopolist would sell at Pm and produce at a rate of Qm. Whether Pm is above or below Pa or Pb varies from situation to situation. By contrast, if the industry were regulated a single incumbent (such as an electric utility) would be given the entire market but a regulatory agency would try to ensure that the price approached Pc rather than Pm.

The theory of natural monopoly has justified price regulation by federal, state, or local governments in many markets — electricity, natural gas, water, telephone and telegraph, cable television, the railroad industry, and — quite inappropriately — even commercial air traffic and trucking. In recent years, however, the natural monopoly model has been challenged by the theory of contestable markets. This attack formed an important justification for the deregulation movement of the 1970s and 1980s, particularly in commercial air traffic.

The theories of franchise bidding and contestable markets view the traditional economic model for natural monopoly as flawed in one very important way: although it describes competition (or the lack of it) *within* the market very well, it completely ignores the question of competition *for* the market. Assuming that the market in Figure 1 is operated most efficiently by a monopolist, how do we determine who that monopolist will be? One way is by taking competitive bids, with the bid being awarded to the firm that agrees to sell in the market for, say, two years at the lowest bid price. If there were no collusion among the bidders, we would expect the bids to come in at around price Pc.

Once a firm is in the market and operating, however, what incentive does it have to continue to price competitively? No firm can be expected to charge the same price forever. Any requirement that it can pass increased costs on to its customers will amount to little more than the creation of a regulatory agency that will supervise the firm's request for price increases and make sure that they are reasonable in comparison with its increased costs.

One solution would be to renew the bidding periodically. For example, if Firm *A* wins the initial bid it will operate as a monopolist in the market and charge the bid price for two years. Then there will be a new round of bids in which *A* can attempt to remain in the market by submitting the most favorable bid, and potential competitors can attempt to steal the market away from *A* by bringing in a lower bid.

The initial bid might well yield a competitive price for the first two-year period. *A* may have a substantial advantage over potential competitors, however, in the second and all subsequent bids. Suppose that *A* is a gas pipeline company that was successful in an original bid to supply natural gas from Nevada to Los Angeles. After winning the bid, company *A* builds a pipeline from Nevada to Los Angeles and for two years provides natural gas at the bid price. At the end of the two-year period, the market is opened for new bidding. Now, however, *A* already owns the pipeline. All potential competitors must calculate the costs of building a pipeline into their bids. These additional costs, which must be borne by *A*'s competitors but not by *A* itself, give *A* considerable latitude for monopolistic pricing. For example, if *A* knows that any competitor must face $1,000,000 in entry costs that have already been "sunk" by *A* itself, then *A* will be able to add any amount short of $1,000,000 in monopoly profits to a competitive price and still win the bid. *A*'s sunk costs (that is, money that *A* has already invested and that it is unlikely to recover if it leaves the market) become the means by which it can engage in monopolistic pricing.

The higher A's relative sunk costs, the more power A will have to price monopolistically in a particular natural monopoly market. A natural monopoly such as a gas pipeline, where sunk costs are very high, contains a great deal of room for monopoly pricing. In other markets, sunk costs are far lower. For example, a city might award a single trash hauling contract each year to bidders who already own a fleet of trucks. In that case, the incumbent may not have a significant advantage over newcomers, and can retain its position only by bidding a competitive price.

A perfectly contestable natural monopoly market will behave just as competitively as a perfectly competitive market with 100 identical incumbents. As soon as the incumbent in the perfectly contestable market raises its price above cost it becomes a target for entry by another firm which can undercut the monopolist by a slight amount, reap the profits, and impose large losses on the incumbent. In theory, *all* natural monopoly markets can be made into contestable markets. Even the natural gas pipeline, for example, could become contestable if the pipeline itself were owned by the State, which periodically took bids for its operation. In that case, the incumbent would not have the advantage of having large sunk costs in the pipeline. It would have to bid competitively or lose the market to a lower bid. The theory of contestable markets and its implications for industry regulation have produced a gigantic literature. Perhaps the most seminal historical contribution is Demsetz, *Why Regulate Utilities?*, 11 J.L. & Econ. 55 (1968). The general formulation of the theory is contained in W. Baumol, J. Panzar & R. Willig, Contestable Markets and the Theory of Industry Structure (1982), which is highly technical. For a discussion of some of the implications for antitrust policy in particular markets, see Brodley, *Antitrust Policy Under Deregulation: Airline Mergers and the Theory of Contestable Markets*, 61 B.U. L. Rev. 823 (1981). For a less optimistic view of contestability, see Williamson, *Franchise Bidding for Natural Monopolies — In General and with Respect to CATV*, 7 Bell J. Econ. & Mgmt. Sci. 73 (1976).

The theory of contestable markets has come under a good deal of criticism, largely because there appear to be no markets that approach perfect contestability. That is to say, although there is a robust "pure" theory of contestability, the "applied" theory of contestability leaves much to be desired. For example, protagonists of contestability presented the passenger airline industry as the paradigm example of a contestable market. But a host of airline mergers in the mid- and late 1980s revealed that when the number of actual, incumbent competitors on an airline route declines, prices go up. Why should this be true in a "contestable" market? Probably because, although airplanes themselves are highly mobile across markets, other parts of the airlines' "plant" are not. For example, gate space is in short supply at most airports; as a result, new carriers either cannot get in, have a long wait, or may have to pay someone else a premium. Further, one cannot easily enter such markets offering a single flight, but must offer convenient connecting flights as well — customers may be willing to pay a premium for the convenience of not having to change carriers en route. Finally, although airplanes are very mobile pieces of equipment, ground service and labor are not. One thinks twice before uprooting and transferring personnel, or training new personnel for a new market. Several studies have concluded that airlines are either imperfectly contestable or not particularly contestable at all. See Borenstein, *The Evolution of U.S. Airline*

Competition, 6 J. Econ. Perspectives 45 (1992), a readable article concluding that contestability is "no substitute for actual competition," and that airport concentration is the culprit. Equally critical is Dempsey, Flying Blind: the Failure of Airline Deregulation (1990).

In general, the process of deregulation has been concentrated in those industries where sunk costs are low, and where contestability appears to work quite well without the need for major restructuring of the industries themselves. Such deregulation has been substantial in the commercial airline industry and the trucking industry, for example. *See* Airline Deregulation Act of 1978, 49 U.S.C. § 1301, Pub. L. No. 95-504, 92 Stat. 1705 (codified at scattered sections of 49 U.S.C.; Motor Carrier Deregulation Act of 1980), 49 U.S.C. § 11101 Pub. L. No. 96-296, 94 Stat. 793 (codified at scattered sections of tit. 18 and 49 U.S.C.). Significant price regulation remains, however, in natural monopolies where sunk costs are high, such as pipelines, electric utilities at the retail level, and most forms of communication that depend on wire or cable connections between the communicating parties. But the world is changing quickly.

The general thrust of contestability theory and the deregulation movement is to take markets that were once considered to be regulated natural monopolies and treat them instead as competitive. To the extent that they are less regulated and more competitive, traditional regulatory concerns give way to antitrust concerns. The result is growing room for antitrust enforcement in these industries. *See* H. Hovenkamp, Federal Antitrust Policy, ch. 19 (4th ed. 2011).

[3]   Network Deregulation, Interconnection, and Antitrust

As noted above, deregulation is easier in industries where sunk costs are low and the competitive process with which antitrust law concerns itself — a process that improves with firms' ease of market entry and exit — can operate more smoothly. One notable case in which deregulation has progressed in an industry with high sunk costs is telecommunications. Telecommunications has high fixed costs (many of which are "sunk" in the sense that the assets cannot be easily recovered or redeployed if the firm wants to exit the business) and low marginal (or average variable) costs. Nonetheless, long-distance telephony was increasingly deregulated over the 1990s as a result of competition that took off after the break-up of AT&T in the early 1980s. Retail prices for long-distance calling are essentially deregulated today. Local telephony is still under significant retail price regulation, but in other important respects was deregulated by the federal Telecommunications Act of 1996 (to be discussed, infra). Several factors contributed to this deregulatory shift. One factor was increased skepticism about the existence and scope of natural monopoly in the delivery of telecommunications. By the 1970s the FCC and the Justice Department were no longer of the view that the purported natural monopoly properties of local telephone networks extended to the long distance networks that connected local networks to each other. The result was an antitrust suit, and eventual settlement, that broke up AT&T into seven separate, regional local phone companies and one, completely independent long-distance company that would have to compete with two new market entrants, MCI and Sprint. *United States v. Western Electric Co.*, 552 F. Supp. 131 (D.D.C. 1982), *aff'd mem. sub nom. Maryland v. United States*, 460 U.S. 1001 (1983). As competition in the long-distance market developed, retail price regulation was slowly removed to the point that long-distance telephony today is an unregulated business in which any anti-competitive conduct would likely be addressed by the antitrust agencies rather than (or along with) the FCC.

Another factor leading to telecommunications deregulation was the recognition that the network structure of telecommunications did not imply monopoly and regulation. One of the early reasons that competition failed in U.S. telecommunications was that the leading firm, AT&T, did not interconnect with its competitors to exchange customers' calls. The result was that customers of rival telephone companies could not call customers of AT&T, and vice versa. Without statutory authority for regulators to mandate such interconnection or a developed antitrust law basis for requiring a firm to deal with its rivals, AT&T capitalized on its "network externality" to become a monopoly. A network externality arises when the value of a service rises for each individual consumer as more consumers use the service. The more people attached to a telecommunications network, the more people each subscriber can call and the more valuable that particular network becomes. Now, consider a potential new customer deciding which network to subscribe to: the bigger network or the smaller (i.e. fewer customers) network. The customer will see that at a given price the bigger network offers more potential correspondents per dollar, and will sign up with that network. The process becomes self reinforcing as the lead network only becomes more attractive to each prospective customer as more people subscribe. Such network externalities are rare, but telecommunications is one industry in which there is broad consensus that they arise. The result was that AT&T became a monopoly that, for a variety of reasons, became regulated by state regulatory commissions and, after 1934, the Federal Communications Commission.

Did AT&T have to become a monopoly, regulated by a host of retail price and other rules? The answer is probably no. If telephone companies had instead been required to interconnect, then there might have been viable competition among them and no need for retail price regulation. To be sure, to the extent interconnection has costs it might need to be priced. In that case, interconnection might substitute wholesale price regulation for retail regulation. But if such regulation is easier, perhaps because the regulator has several firms from which to gather information and judge costs rather than just one monopoly, then it might lead to a more efficient and competitive system for consumers.

In recent years, regulatory policy has begun to move in the direction of trying to promote competition through means like preemption of legal entry barriers and interconnection, while moving away from trying to restrain and govern a monopoly. As competition begins to enter these liberalized markets — of which electricity generation and telephone service are the most prominent examples — the roles of conventional monopoly regulation and antitrust may evolve, with the latter increasing in importance. With the shift from regulated monopoly to competition comes a shift in the kind of conduct with which regulators, whether antitrust enforcement agencies or industry-specific regulatory agencies, are concerned. In particular, regulators have less reason to worry about retail pricing as competition begins to erode market power, but they have increased reason to focus on vertical discrimination and other exclusionary strategies incumbents may use to block new firms from successfully entering the market. How this shift in focus might affect the interaction between regulation and antitrust in traditionally regulated sectors is complicated.

With respect to the behavior of incumbent firms toward consumers, there is good reason for antitrust to take the place of rate regulation. When there is a monopolist in the marketplace, the regulator has a large margin of error in setting a regulated retail price. So long as that regulated price covers costs and is below what the monopolist would have charged unrestrained, the regulator likely improves consumer welfare. The regulator thus has a large target to hit in setting rates. As an industry moves toward competition, however, that target may narrow considerably. For example, mandated retail rates that are set too low may deter new entrants, especially if those entrants are coming into the market with the need to finance high fixed costs to compete against incumbents whose costs are already amortized. Or, those rates may induce new entrants to come into the market only in profitable, low-cost markets. In the face of competition, regulators must therefore consider not only the welfare effects of rates for consumers and the incumbent firm, but on the very new entrants that regulators want to encourage and that could provide the competition that renders any regulation unnecessary. As the risks of incorrect regulation grow, the case for dispensing with such *ex ante* controls on incumbents in favor of *ex post* antitrust enforcement against specific anticompetitive behavior grows. The hard question for regulators will be to decide when competition is sufficiently on track for regulation to be withdrawn. Consumers could be harmed if regulation is withdrawn when competition is purely speculative. Competition itself could be harmed if regulators hang on too long the rules go from protecting consumers to harming them by interfering with the development of competition and the even greater consumer benefits it can create. *See* Howard A. Shelanski, *The Case for Rebalancing Antitrust and Regulation*, 100 MICH. L. REV. 683 (2001).

With respect to vertical discrimination by the incumbent against new entrants, the balance of antitrust and regulation raises harder questions. Some kinds of vertical discrimination or refusals to deal are harmless and may even be precompetitive. On the other hand, others instance of discrimination can stand in the way of emerging competition. It might be hard to craft an *ex ante* rule that separates the latter from the former. For that reason, *ex post* antitrust enforcement that would look case-by-case to see if a particular instance of discrimination is anticompetitive or not is attractive. But there may be substantive limits on the ability of antitrust to govern such behavior. One of the most common complaints of new entrants is that the incumbents will not provide them access to some facility the entrant claims to be essential to competition. As we saw earlier in Chapter 6, however, the Supreme Court's 2004 *Trinko* decision places very stringent limits on the Sherman Act's imposition of a unilateral duty to deal. As a result, the substitution of antitrust for regulation may be less feasible for such vertical conduct so long as vertical discrimination poses a genuine anticompetitive threat in the industry as it transitions from regulation to competition.

The end result is that traditionally regulated network industries are likely to see a mix of deregulation and re-regulation, where antitrust will play an increasing role but will not fully supplant industry-specific rules. In telecommunications, then, interconnection rules that provide access for new entrants will become more important while regulation that governs firms' behavior toward consumers might cede its place to antitrust enforcement.

[4] Technological Change and Deregulation

Technological change can alter the competitive structure of markets. New technology can, for example, make entry and competition economical in industries once thought to be natural monopolies. The telecommunications industry provides a good example of the strong relationship that exists between technology and the economics of regulation. When telecommunications required overhead or underground lines linking all buildings provided with telephone service, the entire telephone system (except for the instruments) was arguably a natural monopoly. The cost of two or more competing systems, when one was sufficient to carry the entire load, would be very high, particularly if a substantial cost of providing telephone services is the installation of the physical system itself, while marginal costs (the cost of one additional phone call) are very low. Once microwave and other forms of wireless communication became a part of the system, however, the system's status as a natural monopoly began to erode. For example it might be economic for two or more firms in competition to provide wireless communication between distant cities. These changes in technology were the principle economic reason behind the break-up of the American Telephone & Telegraph Co.'s telephone monopoly in the United States, in which the local operating companies were separated AT & T's long-distance operations. *United States v. AT & T*, 552 F. Supp. 131 (D.D.C. 1982), *aff'd sub nom. Maryland v. United States*, 460 U.S. 1001 (1983). *See* S. Breyer, Regulation and Its Reform, 285–314 (1982).

If the costs of pervasive agency regulation are higher than the costs of competition (and many economists believe they are significantly higher), then the most efficient regulatory scheme will permit price-regulated monopolies to exist only to the extent that they are bona fide natural monopolies: that is, only in those areas where competition of incumbents would not produce lower prices and higher output. The telephone companies once took the position that not only the lines, but even the manufacture and sale or lease of telephone instruments should be a monopoly. For many years it was either impossible or else very expensive for a customer to lease a phone line from the telephone company without obtaining telephone instruments from the company as well. The telephone companies generally argued that a monopoly in the instruments was necessary because improperly designed instruments could damage the telephone lines themselves. Both the FCC and the courts eventually rejected that argument. *See Litton Sys. v. AT & T*, 700 F.2d 785 (2d Cir. 1983), *cert. denied*, 464 U.S. 1073 (1984); *Phonetele, Inc. v. AT&T*, 664 F.2d 716 (9th Cir. 1981), *cert. denied*, 459 U.S. 1145 (1983); *Hush-A-Phone Corp. v. United States*, 238 F.2d 266 (D.C. Cir. 1956). *See also* Brennan, *Why Regulated Firms Should Be Kept Out of Unregulated Markets: Understanding the Divestiture in* United States v. AT & T, 32 Antitrust Bull. 741 (1988). As technological innovation began to erode the economic arguments that had long justified AT&T's integrated monopoly, Congress, the courts, and the Federal Communication Commission all began to rethink AT&T's monopolies over services as well.

Shortly after the AT&T divestiture in 1984, the long-distance market grew in competition and the FCC slowly rolled back regulation of the long-distance market in favor of competition. About a decade after the AT&T divestiture, Congress began to have doubts about whether the local telephone networks — the networks that connect each household and business to a central switch that in turn routes calls to others on the local network or onto the long-distance lines — were natural monopolies. The rise of wireless telephone service and the technological possibility of using the cable network to provide voice services in competition with conventional telephone networks led Congress to pass the Federal Telecommunications Act of 1996. The 1996 Act significantly deregulates, and in important respects re-regulates, telecommunications. Notably, the Act preempts state-law barriers to entry into the local telephone market, provides mandates and incentives for incumbent local telephone monopolies to provide new entrants with access to parts of the incumbent network, and requires the incumbents to interconnect with new entrants for the purpose of exchanging customer traffic (as discussed in the previous note). *See* 47 U.S.C. §§ 251, 252, and 261. The purpose of the 1996 was to transition the industry away from regulated monopoly and toward competition, as process through which antitrust enforcement would appear naturally to assume a greater role in telecommunications markets. Congress included in the 1996 Act and express antitrust "savings clause" which provides that ". . . nothing in this Act or the Amendments made by this Act shall be construed to modify, impair or supersede the applicability of any antitrust laws." 47 U.S.C. § 601(b)(1).

Despite the savings clause, or perhaps because of it, for several years after the 1996 Act went into effect the Circuit Courts were in disarray on questions concerning the role of the antitrust laws in enforcing interconnection when ILECs, or incumbent local exchange carriers, seem to be recalcitrant in fulfilling their interconnection agreements. In *Goldwasser v. Ameritech Corp.*, 222 F.3d 390 (7th Cir. 2000), the Seventh Circuit suggested there was considerable potential for conflict if state and federal regulatory agencies could assess the legality of the same conduct, perhaps under different standards than the courts apply under antitrust law. But the Eleventh Circuit disagreed in *Covad Communications Co. v. Bellsouth Corp.*, 299 F.3d 1272 (11th Cir. 2002), at least to the point of holding that it would not decide the issue of agency conflict on a motion to dismiss. And in *Law Offices of Curtis V. Trinko v. Bell Atlantic*, 305 F.3d 89 (2d Cir. 2002), *cert. petition filed*, the Second Circuit also refused to dismiss an antitrust complaint, noting that this was a consumer class action, not a competitor suit. The all important difference between a competitor suit and a consumer suit is that competitors are parties to interconnection agreements and have the right to petition regulatory agencies when they have a problem with the local ILEC. Consumers, by contrast, typically have no automatic right of access to the regulatory agencies, leading Mr. Trinko to sue under the antitrust laws. The Supreme Court rejected Trinko's suit on the merits in *Verizon Communications, Inc. v. Law Offices of Curtis V. Trinko*, 540 U.S. 398 (2004), discussed *supra* in Chapter 6. As we will discuss, *infra*, the Supreme Court's decision in *Trinko* has important implications not just for the substantive law of Section 2 of the Sherman Act, but also for the application of antitrust law in regulated industries.

To what extent should these decisions be governed by the antitrust "savings clause" contained in the 1996 Telecommunications Act? Does such an antitrust savings clause "save" only substantive liability provisions? Or does it also "save" the background principles that the antitrust courts have always used to determine when deference to a regulatory agency is appropriate? As the cases below demonstrate, even if Congress does not expressly preempt antitrust law in a regulatory statutes, indeed even if Congress expressly "saves" the operation of antitrust in the regulated sector, the Supreme Court has come to take an expansive view of the deference due to regulatory agencies and an increasingly narrow view of the substantive scope of antitrust in regulated industries.

[C] Jurisdictional and Prudential Problems of Antitrust Enforcement in Regulated Industries

CREDIT SUISSE SECURITIES LLC v. BILLING
551 U.S. 264 (2007)

JUSTICE BREYER delivered the opinion of the Court.

A group of buyers of newly issued securities have filed an antitrust lawsuit against underwriting firms that market and distribute those issues. The buyers claim that the underwriters unlawfully agreed with one another that they would not sell shares of a popular new issue to a buyer unless that buyer committed (1) to buy additional shares of that security later at escalating prices (a practice called "laddering"), (2) to pay unusually high commissions on subsequent security purchases from the underwriters, or (3) to purchase from the underwriters other less desirable securities (a practice called "tying"). The question before us is whether there is a "'plain repugnancy'" between these antitrust claims and the federal securities law. *See Gordon v. New York Stock Exchange, Inc.*, 422 U.S. 659, 682 (1975) (quoting *United States v. Philadelphia Nat. Bank*, 374 U.S. 321, 350–351 (1963)). . . .

The underwriting practices at issue take place during the course of an initial public offering (IPO) of shares in a company. An IPO presents an opportunity to raise capital for a new enterprise by selling shares to the investing public. A group of underwriters will typically form a syndicate to help market the shares. The syndicate will investigate and estimate likely market demand for the shares at various prices. It will then recommend to the firm a price and the number of shares it believes the firm should offer. Ultimately, the syndicate will promise to buy from the firm all the newly issued shares on a specified date at a fixed, agreed-upon price, which price the syndicate will then charge investors when it resells the shares. When the syndicate buys the shares from the issuing firm, however, the firm gives the syndicate a price discount, which amounts to the syndicate's commission. *See generally* L. LOSS & J. SELIGMAN, FUNDAMENTALS OF SECURITIES REGULATION 66–72 (4th ed. 2001).

At the heart of the syndicate's IPO marketing activity lie its efforts to determine suitable initial share prices and quantities. At first, the syndicate makes a preliminary estimate that it submits in a registration statement to the Securities and Exchange Commission (SEC). It then conducts a "road show" during which syndicate underwriters and representatives of the offering firm meet potential investors and engage in a process that the industry calls "book building." During this time, the underwriters and firm representatives present information to investors about the company and the stock. And they attempt to gauge the strength of the investors' interest in purchasing the stock. For this purpose, underwriters might well ask the investors how their interest would vary depending upon price and the number of shares that are offered. They will learn, among other things, which investors might buy shares, in what quantities, at what prices, and for how long each is likely to hold purchased shares before selling them to others.

On the basis of this kind of information, the members of the underwriting syndicate work out final arrangements with the issuing firm, fixing the price per share and specifying the number of shares for which the underwriters will be jointly responsible. As we have said, after buying the shares at a discounted price, the syndicate resells the shares to investors at the fixed price, in effect earning its commission in the process.

In January 2002, respondents, a group of 60 investors, filed two antitrust class-action lawsuits against the petitioners, 10 leading investment banks. . . . . The investors stated that between March 1997 and December 2000 the banks had acted as underwriters, forming syndicates that helped execute the IPOs of several hundred technology-related companies. Respondents' antitrust complaints allege that the underwriters "abused the . . . practice of combining into underwriting syndicates" by agreeing among themselves to impose harmful conditions upon potential investors — conditions that the investors apparently were willing to accept in order to obtain an allocation of new shares that were in high demand.

These conditions, according to respondents, consist of a requirement that the investors pay "additional anticompetitive charges" over and above the agreed-upon IPO share price plus underwriting commission. In particular, these additional charges took the form of (1) investor promises "to place bids . . . in the aftermarket at prices above the IPO price" (i.e., "laddering" agreements); (2) investor "commitments to purchase other, less attractive securities" (i.e., "tying" arrangements); and (3) investor payment of "non-competitively determined" (i.e., excessive) "commissions," including the "purchas[e] of an issuer's shares in follow-up or 'secondary' public offerings (for which the underwriters would earn underwriting discounts)." The complaint added that the underwriters' agreement to engage in some or all of these practices artificially inflated the share prices of the securities in question.

The underwriters moved to dismiss the investors' complaints on the ground that federal securities law impliedly precludes application of antitrust laws to the conduct in question. . . . The District Court agreed with petitioners and dismissed the complaints against them. . . . The Court of Appeals for the Second Circuit reversed . . . . And we now reverse the Court of Appeals.

Sometimes regulatory statutes explicitly state whether they preclude application of the antitrust laws. Compare, e.g., Webb-Pomerene Act, 15 U. S. C. § 62 (expressly providing antitrust immunity), with § 601(b)(1) of the Telecommunications Act of 1996, 47 U.S.C. § 152 (stating that antitrust laws remain applicable). *See also*

Verizon Communications Inc. v. Law Offices of Curtis V. Trinko, LLP, 540 U.S. 398, 406–407 (2004) (analyzing the antitrust saving clause of the Telecommunications Act). Where regulatory statutes are silent in respect to antitrust, however, courts must determine whether, and in what respects, they implicitly preclude application of the antitrust laws. Those determinations may vary from statute to statute, depending upon the relation between the antitrust laws and the regulatory program set forth in the particular statute, and the relation of the specific conduct at issue to both sets of laws. . . .

Three decisions from this Court specifically address the relation of securities law to antitrust law. In *Silver* [*v. New York Stock Exchange*, 373 U.S. 341 (1963),] the Court considered a dealer's claim that, by expelling him from the New York Stock Exchange, the Exchange had violated the antitrust prohibition against group "boycott[s]." The Court wrote that, where possible, courts should "reconcil[e] the operation of both [i.e., antitrust and securities] statutory schemes . . . rather than holding one completely ousted." It also set forth a standard, namely that "[r]epeal of the antitrust laws is to be regarded as implied only if necessary to make the Securities Exchange Act work, and even then only to the minimum extent necessary." And it held that the securities law did not preclude application of the antitrust laws to the claimed boycott insofar as the Exchange denied the expelled dealer a right to fair procedures.

In reaching this conclusion, the Court noted that the SEC lacked jurisdiction under the securities law "to review particular instances of enforcement of exchange rules"; that "nothing [was] built into the regulatory scheme which performs the antitrust function of insuring" that rules that injure competition are nonetheless "justified as furthering" legitimate regulatory "ends"; that the expulsion "would clearly" violate "the Sherman Act unless justified by reference to the purposes of the Securities Exchange Act"; and that it could find *no such justifying purpose* where the Exchange took "anticompetitive collective action . . . *without according fair procedures.*"

In *Gordon*, supra, the Court considered an antitrust complaint that essentially alleged "price fixing" among stockbrokers. It charged that members of the New York Stock Exchange had agreed to fix their commissions on sales under $500,000. And it sought damages and an injunction forbidding future agreements. The lawsuit was filed at a time when regulatory attitudes toward fixed stockbroker commissions were changing. The fixed commissions challenged in the complaint were applied during a period when the SEC approved of the practice of fixing broker-commission rates. But Congress and the SEC had both subsequently disapproved for the future the fixing of some of those rates.

In deciding whether antitrust liability could lie, the Court repeated *Silver's* general standard in somewhat different terms: It said that an "implied repeal" of the antitrust laws would be found only "where there is a 'plain repugnancy between the antitrust and regulatory provisions." It then held that the securities laws impliedly precluded application of the antitrust laws in the case at hand. The Court rested this conclusion on three sets of considerations. For one thing, the securities law "gave the SEC direct regulatory power over exchange rules and practices with respect to the fixing of reasonable rates of commission" (internal quotation marks omitted). For another, the SEC had "taken an active role in review of proposed rate changes during the last 15 years," and had engaged in "continuing activity" in respect to the regulation of commission rates. Finally, without antitrust immunity, "the exchanges and their members" would be subject to "conflicting standards."

This last consideration — the conflict — was complicated due to Congress's, and the agency's, changing views about the validity of fixed commissions. As far as the past fixing of rates was concerned, the conflict was clear: The antitrust law had forbidden the very thing that the securities law had then permitted, namely an anticompetitive rate-setting process. In respect to the future, however, the conflict was less apparent. That was because the SEC's new (congressionally authorized) prohibition of (certain) fixed rates would take effect in the near-term future. And after that time the SEC and the antitrust law would *both* likely prohibit some of the ratefixing to which the plaintiff's injunction would likely apply.

Despite the likely compatibility of the laws in the future, the Court nonetheless expressly found conflict. The conflict arose from the fact that the law permitted the SEC to supervise the competitive setting of rates and to "reintroduc[e] . . . fixed rates" (emphasis added) under certain conditions. The Court consequently wrote that "failure to imply repeal would render nugatory the legislative provision for regulatory agency supervision of exchange commission rates." The upshot is that, in light of potential future conflict, the Court found that the securities law precluded antitrust liability even in respect to a practice that both antitrust law and securities law might forbid.

In [*United States v. National Assn. of Securities Dealers, Inc.*, 422 U.S. 694 (1975) NASD], the Court considered a Department of Justice antitrust complaint claiming that mutual fund companies had agreed with securities broker-dealers (1) to fix "resale" prices, i.e., the prices at which a broker-dealer would sell a mutual fund's shares to an investor or buy mutual fund shares from a fund investor (who wished to redeem the shares); (2) to fix other terms of sale including those related to when, how, to whom, and from whom the broker-dealers might sell and buy mutual fund shares; and (3) to forbid broker-dealers from freely selling to, and buying shares from, one another.

The Court again found "clear repugnancy," and it held that the securities law, by implication, precluded all parts of the antitrust claim. In reaching this conclusion, the Court found that antitrust law (e.g., forbidding resale price maintenance) and securities law (e.g., permitting resale price maintenance) were in conflict. In deciding that the latter trumped the former, the Court relied upon the same kinds of considerations it found determinative in *Gordon*. In respect to the last set of allegations (restricting a free market in mutual fund shares among brokers), the Court said that (1) the relevant securities law "enables [the SEC] to monitor the activities questioned"; (2) "the history of Commission regulations suggests no laxity in the exercise of this authority"; and hence (3) allowing an antitrust suit to proceed that is "so directly related to the SEC's responsibilities" would present "a substantial danger that [broker-dealers and other defendants] would be subjected to duplicative and inconsistent standards."

As to the other practices alleged in the complaint (concerning, e.g., resale price maintenance), the Court emphasized that (1) the securities law "vested in the SEC final authority to determine whether and to what extent" the relevant practices "should be tolerated"; (2) although the SEC has not actively supervised the relevant practices, that is only because the statute "reflects a clear congressional determination that, subject to Commission oversight, mutual funds should be allowed to retain the initiative in dealing with the potentially adverse effects of disruptive trading practices"; and (3) the SEC has supervised the funds insofar as its "acceptance of fund-initiated restrictions for more than three decades . . . manifests an informed administrative judgment that the contractual restrictions . . . were appropriate means for combating the problems of the industry." The Court added that, in these respects, the SEC had engaged in "precisely the kind of administrative oversight of private practices that Congress contemplated." . . .

This Court's prior decisions also make clear that, when a court decides whether securities law precludes antitrust law, it is deciding whether, given context and likely consequences, there is a "clear repugnancy" between the securities law and the antitrust complaint — or as we shall subsequently describe the matter, whether the two are "clearly incompatible." Moreover, *Gordon* and *NASD*, in finding sufficient incompatibility to warrant an implication of preclusion, have treated the following factors as critical: (1) the existence of regulatory authority under the securities law to supervise the activities in question; (2) evidence that the responsible regulatory entities exercise that authority; and (3) a resulting risk that the securities and antitrust laws, if both applicable, would produce conflicting guidance, requirements, duties, privileges, or standards of conduct. We also note (4) that in *Gordon* and *NASD* the possible conflict affected practices that lie squarely within an area of financial market activity that the securities law seeks to regulate.

These principles, applied to the complaints before us, considerably narrow our legal task. For the parties cannot reasonably dispute the existence here of several of the conditions that this Court previously regarded as crucial to finding that the securities law impliedly precludes the application of the antitrust laws.

First, the activities in question here — the underwriters' efforts jointly to promote and to sell newly issued securities — is central to the proper functioning of well-regulated capital markets. The IPO process supports new firms that seek to raise capital; it helps to spread ownership of those firms broadly among investors; it directs capital flows in ways that better correspond to the public's demand for goods and services. Moreover, financial experts, including the securities regulators, consider the general kind of joint underwriting activity at issue in this case, including road shows and book-building efforts, essential to the successful marketing of an IPO. Thus, the antitrust complaints before us concern practices that lie at the very heart of the securities marketing enterprise.

Second, the law grants the SEC authority to supervise all of the activities here in question. Indeed, the SEC possesses considerable power to forbid, permit, encourage, discourage, tolerate, limit, and otherwise regulate virtually every aspect of the practices in which underwriters engage . . . private individuals who suffer harm as a result of a violation of pertinent statutes and regulations may also recover damages.

Third, the SEC has continuously exercised its legal authority to regulate conduct of the general kind now at issue. It has defined in detail, for example, what underwriters may and may not do and say during their road shows. It has brought actions against underwriters who have violated these SEC regulations. And private litigants, too, have brought securities actions complaining of conduct virtually identical to the conduct at issue here; and they have obtained damages. *See, e.g., In re Initial Pub. Offering Securities Litigation*, 241 F. Supp. 2d 281 (S.D.N.Y. 2003).

The preceding considerations show that the first condition (legal regulatory authority), the second condition (exercise of that authority), and the fourth condition (heartland securities activity) that were present in *Gordon* and *NASD* are satisfied in this case as well. Unlike Silver, there is here no question of the existence of appropriate regulatory authority, nor is there doubt as to whether the regulators have exercised that authority. Rather, the question before us concerns the third condition: Is there a conflict that rises to the level of incompatibility? Is an antitrust suit such as this likely to prove practically incompatible with the SEC's administration of the Nation's securities laws?

Given the SEC's comprehensive authority to regulate IPO underwriting syndicates, its active and ongoing exercise of that authority, and the undisputed need for joint IPO underwriter activity, we do not read the complaints as attacking the bare existence of IPO underwriting syndicates or any of the joint activity that the SEC considers a necessary component of IPO-related syndicate activity. [The Court cited evidence that syndicated underwriting was the norm and had been lawful for decades.]

We nonetheless can read the complaints as attacking the manner in which the underwriters jointly seek to collect "excessive" commissions. The complaints attack underwriter efforts to collect commissions through certain practices (i.e., laddering, tying, collecting excessive commissions in the form of later sales of the issued shares), which according to respondents the SEC itself has already disapproved and, in all likelihood, will not approve in the foreseeable future. In respect to this set of claims, they contend that there is no possible "conflict" since both securities law and antitrust law aim to prohibit the same undesirable activity. Without a conflict, they add, there is no "repugnance" or "incompatibility," and this Court may not imply that securities law precludes an antitrust suit.

We accept the premises of respondents' argument — that the SEC has full regulatory authority over these practices, that it has actively exercised that authority, but that the SEC has *disapproved* (and, for argument's sake, we assume that it will continue to disapprove) the conduct that the antitrust complaints attack. Nonetheless, we cannot accept respondents' conclusion. Rather, several considerations taken together lead us to find that, even on these prorespondent assumptions, securities law and antitrust law are clearly incompatible.

First, to permit antitrust actions such as the present one still threatens serious securities-related harm. For one thing, an unusually serious legal line-drawing problem remains unabated. In the present context only a fine, complex, detailed line separates activity that the SEC permits or encourages (for which respondents must concede antitrust immunity) from activity that the SEC must (and inevitably will) forbid (and which, on respondents' theory, should be open to antitrust attack).

For example, in respect to "laddering" the SEC forbids an underwriter to "solicit customers prior to the completion of the distribution regarding whether and at what price and in what quantity they intend to place immediate aftermarket orders for IPO stock." But at the same time the SEC permits, indeed encourages, underwriters (as part of the "book building" process) to "inquir[e] as to a customer's desired future position in the longer term (for example, three to six months), and the price or prices at which the customer might accumulate that position without reference to immediate aftermarket activity."

It will often be difficult for someone who is not familiar with accepted syndicate practices to determine with confidence whether an underwriter has insisted that an investor buy more shares in the immediate aftermarket (forbidden), or has simply allocated more shares to an investor willing to purchase additional shares of that issue in the long run (permitted). And who but a securities expert could say whether the present SEC rules set forth a virtually permanent line, unlikely to change in ways that would permit the sorts of "laddering-like" conduct that it now seems to forbid?

Similarly, in respect to "tying" and other efforts to obtain an increased commission from future sales, the SEC has sought to prohibit an underwriter "from demanding . . . an offer from their customers of any payment or other consideration [such as the purchase of a different security] in addition to the security's stated consideration." But the SEC would permit a firm to "allocat[e] IPO shares to a customer because the customer has separately retained the firm for other services, when the customer has not paid excessive compensation in relation to those services." . . .

[E]vidence tending to show unlawful antitrust activity and evidence tending to show lawful securities marketing activity may overlap, or prove identical. Consider, for instance, a conversation between an underwriter and an investor about how long an investor intends to hold the new shares (and at what price), say a conversation that elicits comments concerning both the investor's short and longer term plans. That exchange might, as a plaintiff sees it, provide evidence of an underwriter's insistence upon "laddering" or, as a defendant sees it, provide evidence of a lawful effort to allocate shares to those who will hold them for a longer time.

Similarly, the same somewhat ambiguous conversation might help to establish an effort to collect an unlawfully high commission through atypically high commissions on later sales or through the sales of less popular stocks. Or it might prove only that the underwriter allocates more popular shares to investors who will help stabilize the aftermarket share price.

Further, antitrust plaintiffs may bring lawsuits throughout the Nation in dozens of different courts with different nonexpert judges and different nonexpert juries. In light of the nuanced nature of the evidentiary evaluations necessary to separate the permissible from the impermissible, it will prove difficult for those many different courts to reach consistent results. And, given the fact-related nature of many such evaluations, it will also prove difficult to assure that the different courts evaluate similar fact patterns consistently. The result is an unusually high risk that different courts will evaluate similar factual circumstances differently. See Hovenkamp, *Antitrust Violations in Securities Markets*, 28 J. Corp. L. 607, 629 (2003) ("Once regulation of an industry is entrusted to jury trials, the outcomes of antitrust proceedings will be inconsistent with one another . . . ").

Now consider these factors together — the fine securities-related lines separating the permissible from the impermissible; the need for securities-related expertise (particularly to determine whether an SEC rule is likely permanent); the overlapping evidence from which reasonable but contradictory inferences may be drawn; and the risk of inconsistent court results. Together these factors mean there is no practical way to confine antitrust suits so that they challenge only activity of the kind the investors seek to target, activity that is presently unlawful and will likely remain unlawful under the securities law. Rather, these factors suggest that antitrust courts are likely to make unusually serious mistakes in this respect. And the threat of antitrust mistakes, i.e., results that stray outside the narrow bounds that plaintiffs seek to set, means that underwriters must act in ways that will avoid not simply conduct that the securities law forbids (and will likely continue to forbid), but also a wide range of joint conduct that the securities law permits or encourages (but which they fear could lead to an antitrust lawsuit and the risk of treble damages). And therein lies the problem.

This kind of problem exists to some degree in respect to other antitrust lawsuits. But here the factors we have mentioned make mistakes unusually likely (a matter relevant to Congress' determination of which institution should regulate a particular set of market activities). And the role that joint conduct plays in respect to the marketing of IPOs, along with the important role IPOs themselves play in relation to the effective functioning of capital markets, means that the securities-related costs of mistakes is unusually high. It is no wonder, then, that the SEC told the District Court (consistent with what the Government tells us here) that a "failure to hold that the alleged conduct was immunized would threaten to disrupt the full range of the Commission's ability to exercise its regulatory authority," adding that it would have a "chilling effect" on "lawful joint activities . . . of tremendous importance to the economy of the country."

We believe it fair to conclude that, where conduct at the core of the marketing of new securities is at issue; where securities regulators proceed with great care to distinguish the encouraged and permissible from the forbidden; where the threat of antitrust lawsuits, through error and disincentive, could seriously alter underwriter conduct in undesirable ways, to allow an antitrust lawsuit would threaten serious harm to the efficient functioning of the securities markets.

Second, any enforcement-related need for an antitrust lawsuit is unusually small. For one thing, the SEC actively enforces the rules and regulations that forbid the conduct in question. For another, as we have said, investors harmed by underwriters' unlawful practices may bring lawsuits and obtain damages under the securities law. Finally, the SEC is itself required to take account of competitive considerations when it creates securities-related policy and embodies it in rules and regulations. And that fact makes it somewhat less necessary to rely upon antitrust actions to address anticompetitive behavior. See 15 U.S.C. §77b(b) (instructing the SEC to consider, "in addition to the protection of investors, whether the action will promote efficiency, competition, and capital formation"); § 78w(a)(2) (the SEC "shall consider among other matters the impact any such rule or regulation would have on competition") . . . .

We also note that Congress, in an effort to weed out unmeritorious securities lawsuits, has recently tightened the procedural requirements that plaintiffs must satisfy when they file those suits. To permit an antitrust lawsuit risks circumventing these requirements by permitting plaintiffs to dress what is essentially a securities complaint in antitrust clothing. See generally Private Securities Litigation Reform Act of 1995, 109 Stat. 737; Securities Litigation Uniform Standards Act of 1998, 112 Stat. 3227.

In sum, an antitrust action in this context is accompanied by a substantial risk of injury to the securities markets and by a diminished need for antitrust enforcement to address anticompetitive conduct. Together these considerations indicate a serious conflict between, on the one hand, application of the antitrust laws and, on the other, proper enforcement of the securities law. . . .

The upshot is that all four elements present in Gordon are present here: (1) an area of conduct squarely within the heartland of securities regulations; (2) clear and adequate SEC authority to regulate; (3) active and ongoing agency regulation; and (4) a serious conflict between the antitrust and regulatory regimes. We therefore conclude that the securities laws are "clearly incompatible" with the application of the antitrust laws in this context.

The Second Circuit's contrary judgment is

Reversed.

JUSTICE KENNEDY took no part in the consideration or decision of this case. [A concurring opinion by JUSTICE STEVENS and a dissent by JUSTICE THOMAS are omitted.]

NOTES AND QUESTIONS

1.   Many federal statutes creating regulatory regimes say little or nothing about the impact of agency regulation on possible antitrust scrutiny of the regulated firms. As a result the courts have had to develop rules for determining when antitrust actions can proceed or must give way. Under the doctrine of "primary jurisdiction" the antitrust laws, which are general, must give way to the more specific provisions of a federal regulatory statute when it is clear that enforcement of the antitrust laws would frustrate the specific regulatory scheme. This generally means that allegedly anticompetitive conduct in these industries is evaluated initially by some federal agency other than the Department of Justice, the Federal Trade Commission, or the courts. If the particular activity alleged to be an antitrust violation is mandated by the regulatory agency, or if it has been approved by the agency after a full consideration of the consequences for competition, then the antitrust laws have been preempted. *See Hughes Tool Co. v. Trans World Airlines*, 409 U.S. 363 (1973). If the agency's approval of activity initiated by the firm is merely pro forma, however, or if the agency did not fully evaluate the activity in order to determine the effects on competition, then there would appear to be considerable room for antitrust enforcement. *See* 1A P. AREEDA & H. HOVENKAMP, ANTITRUST LAW ¶¶ 240–246 (4th ed. 2013).

2. In *Square D Co. v. Niagara Frontier Tariff Bur.*, 476 U.S. 409 (1986), the Supreme Court reaffirmed the so-called Keogh doctrine, established in *Keogh v. Chicago & Nw. R.R.*, 260 U.S. 156 (1922), that a rate which has been filed and approved by the Interstate Commerce Commission cannot form the basis of a treble damage action based on the theory that those proposing the rate were engaged in price fixing.

Keogh's rationale, as Justice Brandeis explained in the Court's opinion, was to honor "the paramount purpose of Congress — prevention of unjust discrimination . . . ." In fact, a principal purpose of regulated rates in the late nineteenth and early twentieth centuries was to defeat the attempts of large companies to drive smaller firms out of business by obtaining discriminatorily low rates from railroad companies. For example, Standard Oil Co. was alleged to have acquired its monopoly in this way.

The regulatory world has changed a great deal since Keogh, however. First, the principal stated purpose of rate regulation today is not to prohibit price discrimination but rather to force efficient pricing in monopoly markets (although many regulated markets are not monopolies). In fact, a certain amount of price discrimination is actually encouraged. Second, procedural devices such as class action suits and offensive collateral estoppel tend to make antitrust damages awards against regulated firms nondiscriminatory — i.e., all firms who paid a cartel rate would be in an equally good position to collect damages. Finally, and perhaps most significantly, one of the most important consequences of the deregulation movement has been to inject more antitrust into the regulated industries, although as we will see there may be legal limits to how far antitrust enforcement can go into industries still governed, even if less so, by a regulatory statute. The law against cartelization, whose anticompetitive effects are most easily recognized, would seem to be a good place to start.

Nevertheless, the Supreme Court ruled in *Square D* that *Keogh* "represents a longstanding statutory construction that Congress has consistently refused to disturb, even when revisiting this specific area of law." For example, when Congress passed the Motor Carrier Act of 1980, which greatly deregulated the trucking industry, it made no attempt to change the doctrine. "If there is to be an overruling of the Keogh rule, it must come from Congress, rather than from this Court." The Court noted, however, that *Keogh* did not confer antitrust immunity on the defendants; it merely held that they could not be liable for treble damages. They could still be found liable in a civil or criminal government action.

Suppose that a private plaintiff alleges not that a filed rate is the result of price fixing but that the rate is predatory, designed to exclude a rival from the market? The circuit courts do not agree about whether a competitor can challenge a filed rate. *See In re Lower Lake Erie Iron Ore Antitrust Litig.*, 998 F.2d 1144 (3d Cir. 1993) (permitting a competitor challenge); *Barnes v. Arden Mayfair*, 759 F.2d 676 (9th Cir. 1985) (same); *City of Kirkwood v. Union Elec. Co.*, 671 F.2d 1173, 1178 (8th Cir. 1982), *cert. denied*, 459 U.S. 1170 (1983) (same). *But see Pinney Dock & Transp. Co. v. Penn Cent. Corp.*, 838 F.2d 1445 (6th Cir. 1988), interpreting *Keogh* to require that the regulatory commission be "the sole source of the rights not only of shippers, but of the entire public, including competitors." On the filed rate doctrine, see 1A P. AREEDA & H. HOVENKAMP, ANTITRUST LAW, at ¶ 247.

Consider the impact of the filed rate doctrine when the relevant agency is state rather than federal. The "state action" doctrine, discussed *infra*, permits a state to immunize a restraint only when the state "clearly articulates" its wish to do so and "actively supervises" any private conduct that results. By contrast, the filed rate doctrine requires no more than that a rate be "filed." This can effectively create an antitrust immunity, something the Supreme Court purports to disfavor, for conduct that never could have qualified for the "state action" exemption. For example, a state provision may authorize an exclusionary tariff, giving no thought to competitive consequences. The state agency in turn may approve such requests with little or no evaluation. While the provision in question is unlikely to survive scrutiny under the state action doctrine, the tariff filing itself may have effective immunity under the filed rate doctrine. The Third Circuit's *McCray* decision applied the filed rate doctrine to price fixing among title insurers, expressly rejecting the argument that application required the defendant's to show "meaningful review" by the state regulator. *McCray v. Fid. Nat'l Title Ins. Co.*, 682 F.3d 229 (3d Cir. 2012), *cert. denied*, 133 S. Ct. 1242 (2013). The court found "no apparent requirement" that the "state action" and filed rate doctrine be "reconciled." The court did suggest that the requirements for state action immunity would probably have been met in any event. *See also New Jersey Title Ins. Litig.*, 683 F.3d 451 (3d Cir. 2012).

3. In *Town of Concord v. Boston Edison Co.*, 915 F.2d 17, 25 (1st Cir. 1990), the court considered charges of a price "squeeze" by a regulated electric utility. The utility was accused of selling wholesale power at a high price to smaller municipal power companies, but of charging a low retail price for its own electricity. This allegedly made it difficult for the smaller utilities to compete with the defendant for new customers along the common boundaries of their service areas. Without finding a regulatory exemption, the court dismissed the complaint, holding that the presence of comprehensive regulation greatly undermined the plausibility of the plaintiffs' claims. In this case, regulation of both utility prices and of new entry by others diminishes the likelihood of "entry barrier" harm, namely the risk that (1) prices will rise because (2) new firms will hesitate to enter a market and compete after (3) a squeeze has driven pre-existing independent competitors from the marketplace. All three propositions are made doubtful by regulation.

Further, the court noted, any rule forbidding such price squeezes would add a new dimension to the problem of determining the utility's optimal rates. Regulatory agencies are generally incapable of making any more than rough judgments about the optimal rate for a regulated company to charge. Any kind of innovative pricing technique could injure competing firms not undertaking the innovation:

> [C]ourt involvement in the rate-setting process could easily discourage utilities from proposing, and commissions from considering, such innovative, economically based, energy-conserving pricing systems as off-peak pricing (charging higher prices for electricity used during peak periods), incremental-cost pricing (charging prices for certain services reflecting the higher costs of hypothetical new construction), or even traditional Ramsey pricing (tailoring rates to reflect the comparative likelihood that higher rates will force customers to discontinue service).

[1]   Prudential Considerations After *Trinko*

Even in cases where Congress has expressly saved the operation of antitrust law in a regulated sphere, hard questions arise about the extent of antitrust enforcement and how it interacts with regulation. In *Verizon Communications, Inc. v. Law Offices of Curtis V. Trinko*, 540 U.S. 398 (2004), the Supreme Court took a very modest view of the scope of antitrust law in regulated industries, even those undergoing deregulation and the transition to competition. Chapter 6, *supra*, discusses *Trinko* in detail. Here we revisit the case specifically for the Court's discussion of the boundary between antitrust and regulation.

VERIZON COMMUNICATIONS, INC. v. LAW OFFICES OF CURTIS V. TRINKO, LLP
540 U.S. 398 (2004)

Justice Scalia delivered the opinion of the Court.

. . . Antitrust analysis must always be attuned to the particular structure and circumstances of the industry at issue. Part of that attention to economic context is an awareness of the significance of regulation. As we have noted, "careful account must be taken of the pervasive federal and state regulation characteristic of the industry." United States v. Citizens & Southern Nat. Bank, 422 U.S. 86, 91 (1975); see also IA P. Areeda & H. Hovenkamp, Antitrust Law, p. 12, ¶ 240c3 (2d ed.2000). "[A]ntitrust analysis must sensitively recognize and reflect the distinctive economic and legal setting of the regulated industry to which it applies." Concord v. Boston Edison Co., 915 F.2d 17, 22 (C.A.1 1990) (Breyer, C.J.) (internal quotation marks omitted).

One factor of particular importance is the existence of a regulatory structure designed to deter and remedy anticompetitive harm. Where such a structure exists, the additional benefit to competition provided by antitrust enforcement will tend to be small, and it will be less plausible that the antitrust laws contemplate such additional scrutiny. Where, by contrast, "[t]here is nothing built into the regulatory scheme which performs the antitrust function," Silver v. New York Stock Exchange, 373 U.S. 341 (1963), the benefits of antitrust are worth its sometimes considerable disadvantages. Just as regulatory context may in other cases serve as a basis for implied immunity, see, e.g., United States v. National Assn. of Securities Dealers, Inc., 422 U.S., at 730 735, it may also be a consideration in deciding whether to recognize an expansion of the contours of § 2.

The regulatory response to the OSS failure complained of in respondent's suit provides a vivid example of how the regulatory regime operates. When several competitive LECs complained about deficiencies in Verizon's servicing of orders, the FCC and PSC responded. The FCC soon concluded that Verizon was in breach of its sharing duties under § 251(c), imposed a substantial fine, and set up sophisticated measurements to gauge remediation, with weekly reporting requirements and specific penalties for failure. The PSC found Verizon in violation of the PAP even earlier, and imposed additional financial penalties and measurements with daily reporting requirements. In short, the regime was an effective steward of the antitrust function.

Against the slight benefits of antitrust intervention here, we must weigh a realistic assessment of its costs. Under the best of circumstances, applying the requirements of '2 "can be difficult" because "the means of illicit exclusion, like the means of legitimate competition, are myriad." United States v. Microsoft Corp., 253 F.3d 34, 58 (C.A.D.C.2001) (en banc) (per curiam). Mistaken inferences and the resulting false condemnations "are especially costly, because they chill the very conduct the antitrust laws are designed to protect." Matsushita Elec. Industrial Co. v. Zenith Radio Corp., 475 U.S. 574, 594 (1986). The cost of false positives counsels against an undue expansion of '2 liability. One false positive risk is that an incumbent LEC's failure to provide a service with sufficient alacrity might have nothing to do with exclusion. Allegations of violations of § 251(c)(3) duties are difficult for antitrust courts to evaluate, not only because they are highly technical, but also because they are likely to be extremely numerous, given the incessant, complex, and constantly changing interaction of competitive and incumbent LECs implementing the sharing and interconnection obligations.

NOTES AND QUESTIONS

1. How should lower courts interpret the Supreme Court's *Trinko* decision when faced with antitrust claims in a regulated market? Is the Supreme Court simply saying that regulatory statutes cannot enlarge the scope of settled antitrust law? The court certainly is saying that, which makes sense, but the Court is also saying more. The excerpt above suggests that, at very least, the Court does not think regulated industries whose governing statutes address competition are a context in which antitrust should test its outer boundaries. Indeed, the Court might be read to be saying that antitrust should not even apply to its full extent in such regulated industries and should instead be particularly deferential to the regulatory scheme. Which reading is correct? Which should be correct as a matter of policy?

2. *Trinko* is notable for the skepticism the Supreme Court expresses about antitrust in general. Note the Court's discussion of false positives and its focus on the costs of antitrust enforcement. What is the Court's basis for assuming regulation will work better? In the presence of the express antitrust savings clause at issue in *Trinko*, the Court's decision to emphasize regulation is hard to attribute to judicial deference to Congress. Is the Court making its own judgment about the comparative institutional competencies of antitrust enforcement and regulation? If so, is the Court right?

3. The Court is clear that antitrust should defer only in the presence of a statute that is concerned with competition. But does the competition regulation have to be actively enforced or is its presence on the books enough to trigger the *Trinko* doctrine? This is a key question in the wake of the case, because if a presumption against antitrust can apply absent active enforcement of a regulatory statute that ostensibly "performs the antitrust function," then the technicality of regulation without the substance could displace meaningful competition enforcement in regulated industries.

4. In the end, the *Trinko* decision demonstrates that the role of antitrust in regulated industries, even those undergoing deregulation, will be subject to some restraint by the courts so long as the right kind of regulatory statute is in place.

Tying this back to the example of telecommunications, while there would appear to be a growing role for antitrust in the industry in the aftermath of the economic and technological changes the industry has undergone, antitrust enforcement is likely to play a complementary and secondary role to regulation so long as the current statutory regime remains in place.

5. For a different view of the role between antitrust and regulation, see *F.T.C. v. Actavis, Inc.*, 133 S. Ct. 2223 (2013), which implicated the patent system and regulation of pharmaceutical drugs under the Hatch-Waxman Act. The issue was "pay for delay" settlements of patent infringement suits, in which the patentee plaintiff pays the defendant, a maker of generic drugs, a large sum of money to stay out of the plaintiff's market. Reverse payments are apparently unique, or nearly unique, to these Hatch-Waxman Act settings. They result from the fact that the statute gives the first generic to declare its entry and risk patent litigation an exclusivity period that lasts 180 days from the time the generic began to produce. During that period no one else can either challenge the patent or enter into production of that drug. Although the drafters clearly did not foresee it, one consequence was to give the patentee and the first generic a strong incentive to preserve the patent monopoly but divide the profits. You may recall that the profit-maximizing price and output of a cartel is the same as for a monopolist, and ordinarily much more profitable than when two firms enter into competition with one another. "It may well be that Hatch-Waxman's unique regulatory framework, including the special advantage that the 180-day exclusivity period gives to first filers, does much to explain why in this context, but not others, the patentee's ordinary incentives to resist paying off challengers (*i.e.*, the fear of provoking myriad other challengers) appear to be more frequently overcome." 133 S. Ct. at 2235.

One important question was whether patent policy or antitrust policy should control the outcome. Justice Breyer held that if the payment was significantly higher than litigation costs plus any services that the generic supplied to the patentee, then antitrust should control under a truncated rule of reason inquiry. As a result, a tribunal could condemn the settlement without making an inquiry into the validity of the patent. This made sense principally for two reasons. First, the very high payment was itself a sign that the patent was very likely invalid, otherwise the patentee would not have been willing to pay so much. Second, while the Patent Act expressly authorizes patentees to give others licenses to *produce*, it nowhere even hints at authorization for payments made to keep nonpatentees out of the market. The Chief Justice (joined by Justices Scalia and Thomas) dissented. The decision is reprinted, *supra*, Chapter 4.

[D]   Antitrust Exemptions

[1]   Labor Organizations

At common law, courts considered labor unions to be nothing more than cartels. Combinations of sellers of labor were dealt with in the same way as combinations of sellers of products. This judicial hostility toward labor unions increased after the Sherman Act was passed, largely because the statute contained no exception for labor organizations. *See* H. HOVENKAMP, ENTERPRISE AND AMERICAN LAW, 1836–1937, chs. 18–19 (1991). But in 1914, Congress created the first labor exemption in the Clayton Act.

Section 6 of the Clayton Act provides that the antitrust laws shall not be construed to "forbid the existence and operation" of labor organizations, or to "forbid or restrain individual members of such organizations from lawfully carrying out" their "legitimate objects." In addition, labor organizations are not to be construed as illegal combinations or conspiracies in restraint of trade under the antitrust laws. 15 U.S.C. § 17. Section 20 of the Clayton Act provides that strikes and other specified labor activities are not to be considered "violations of any law of the United States."

Originally, the Supreme Court read this labor exemption narrowly. Section 6 immunizes only activities "lawfully carrying out" a union's "legitimate objects." The Court reasoned that because a secondary boycott by a labor union was neither "lawful" nor a "legitimate object," it was not protected by the Clayton Act. *Duplex Printing Press Co. v. Deering*, 254 U.S. 443, 468–469 (1921).

In 1932, Congress passed the Norris-LaGuardia Act, which deprived federal courts of the power to issue injunctions in most labor disputes, including secondary boycotts. This Act, which ostensibly had nothing to do with antitrust law, nonetheless triggered reconsideration of the labor exemption by the Supreme Court. In *United States v. Hutcheson*, 312 U.S. 219 (1941), the Court gave a new, and much broader, reading to the exemption. The Court read what it termed the "interlacing" statutes — the Sherman Act, the Clayton Act, and the Norris-LaGuardia Act — as the equivalent of a single, unified provision, and concluded that conduct protected by the Clayton and Norris-LaGuardia Acts would not violate the Sherman Act. Under this new formulation,

> [i]f the facts . . . come within the conduct enumerated in § 20 of the Clayton Act they do not constitute a crime within the general terms of the Sherman Law. . . . So long as a union acts in its self-interest and does not combine with non-labor groups, the licit and the illicit under § 20 are not to be distinguished by any judgment regarding the wisdom or unwisdom, the rightness or wrongness, the selfishness or unselfishness of the end of which the particular union activities are the means.

Id. at 232.

The statutory exemption for labor organizations does not apply when a union enters into an agreement with a nonlabor group. Agreements or arrangements between unions and employers are neither expressly barred nor expressly permitted by the Clayton or Norris-LaGuardia Acts. *See United Mine Workers v. Pennington*, 381 U.S. 657, 662 (1965). The statutory exemption thus applies to unilateral acts by unions, but not to agreements with employers.

The difficulty with this formulation is obvious: the labor policy of the United States favors collective bargaining and the formation of contracts between employers and employees. These contracts necessarily are agreements "in combination with" employers, who are a nonlabor group. Many of these contracts contain provisions that can restrain trade. To resolve this conflict between labor and antitrust policy, the courts have created a "limited nonstatutory exemption from antitrust sanctions" for employer-union agreements. *See Connell Constr. Co. v. Plumbers Local 100*, 421 U.S. 616, 622 (1975).

If the court finds a combination with a nonlabor group, the next question becomes whether the union is acting in its self-interest. The line drawing is problematic. Agreements affecting wages, for example, are plainly matters of direct interest to labor unions. It is permissible for a union to bargain with a multi-employer unit — a group of employers who bargain together as a single unit — and sign contracts that fix wages for many competitors. A union is free to fix a wage scale and attempt to force each employer it bargains with to adhere to that scale. But when a union agrees with one group of employers to impose a certain wage scale on other employers without bargaining with the latter group, it forfeits its exemption — at least where there is evidence of intent to drive other employers out of business. *United Mine Workers v. Pennington*, 381 U.S. 657, 665–666 (1965) (three justice plurality).

The nonstatutory exemption also requires that the challenged agreement must affect principally only the bargaining parties. In *Continental Maritime v. Pacific Coast Metal*, 817 F.2d 1391 (9th Cir. 1987), the Ninth Circuit approved an agreement between a union and two Portland, Oregon shipbuilders to work temporarily for lower wages. The agreement was challenged by a competing shipbuilder from San Francisco, with whom the unions refused to negotiate a similar agreement, who alleged a combination among the parties to injure its business. As the court suggested, however, the requirement that the agreement affect principally the bargaining parties applies to effects made explicit in the agreement itself, not generally to effects that an agreement may have on the market.

The means chosen by the union to implement its self interest must not restrict the market more than is necessary to achieve legitimate union goals. *H.A. Artists & Assocs. v. Actors' Equity Ass'n*, 451 U.S. 704, 722 (1981). Agreements between unions and employers to deny other competitors entry into the market are not exempt from antitrust sanctions, for they restrict the market more than is necessary. For example, a union-employer agreement that contractors will buy only from local union manufacturers, and that manufacturers will sell only to local union contractors, violates the antitrust laws. *Allen Bradley Co. v. Local Union No. 3*, 325 U.S. 797, 809 (1945) (union's involvement was only part of a general conspiracy among local businesses to restrain trade). The Court reached a similar result in *Connell Constr. Co. v. Plumbers Local 100*, 421 U.S. 616 (1975) (union and employer with whom union had no relationship could not agree to subcontract work only to contractors who had contracts with local union). But unions legitimately may be concerned about preserving work traditionally done by union members, and agreements restricting the employer's ability to deal may be the key to such job preservation. *National Woodwork Mfrs. Ass'n v. NLRB*, 386 U.S. 612 (1967).

Other conditions of employment are also proper subjects for agreement. For example, a union may agree with grocery stores to set fixed hours for sales of meat for all stores in a metropolitan area because the union had a significant interest in the hours worked by its butchers. *Amalgamated Meat Cutters Local 189 v. Jewel*

Tea Co., 381 U.S. 676 (1965) (plurality opinion). The issue is whether the restriction is "intimately related to wages, hours and working conditions" and is not undertaken "at the behest of or in combination with nonlabor groups." *Id.* at 689–690.

In *Brown v. Pro Football, Inc.*, 518 U.S. 231 (1996), the Supreme Court interpreted the nonstatutory labor exemption to immunize a horizontal agreement among a group of employers — in this case, professional football teams seeking to cap the salaries of certain classes of players. Importantly, the action was taken in response to ongoing collective bargaining that had reached an impasse. The Court wrote:

> As a matter of logic, it would be difficult, if not impossible, to require groups of employers and employees to bargain together, but at the same time to forbid them to make among themselves or with each other any of the competition-restricting agreements potentially necessary to make the process work or its results mutually acceptable. Thus, the implicit exemption recognizes that, to give effect to federal labor laws and policies and to allow meaningful collective bargaining to take place, some restraints on competition imposed through the bargaining process must be shielded from antitrust sanctions. . . .

> Consequently, the question before us is one of determining the exemption's scope: Does it apply to an agreement among several employers bargaining together to implement after impasse the terms of their last best good-faith wage offer? We assume that such conduct, as practiced in this case, is unobjectionable as a matter of labor law and policy. On that assumption, we conclude that the exemption applies. . . .

> Although the caselaw we have cited focuses upon bargaining by a single employer, no one here has argued that labor law does, or should, treat multiemployer bargaining differently in this respect. Indeed, Board and court decisions suggest that the joint implementation of proposed terms after impasse is a familiar practice in the context of multiemployer bargaining. . . .

> Multiemployer bargaining itself is a well-established, important, pervasive method of collective bargaining, offering advantages to both management and labor. See Appendix (multi-employer bargaining accounts for more than 40% of major collective-bargaining agreements, and is used in such industries as construction, transportation, retail trade, clothing manufacture, and real estate, as well as professional sports). . . . The upshot is that the practice at issue here plays a significant role in a collective-bargaining process that itself comprises an important part of the Nation's industrial relations system.

> In these circumstances, to subject the practice to antitrust law is to require antitrust courts to answer a host of important practical questions about how collective bargaining over wages, hours and working conditions is to proceed — the very result that the implicit labor exemption seeks to avoid. And it is to place in jeopardy some of the potentially beneficial labor-related effects that multi-employer bargaining can achieve. That is

because unlike labor law, which sometimes welcomes anticompetitive agreements conducive to industrial harmony, antitrust law forbids all agreements among competitors (such as competing employers) that unreasonably lessen competition among or between them in virtually any respect whatsoever. . . .

For these reasons, we hold that the implicit ("nonstatutory") antitrust exemption applies to the employer conduct at issue here. That conduct took place during and immediately after a collective-bargaining negotiation. It grew out of, and was directly related to, the lawful operation of the bargaining process. It involved a matter that the parties were required to negotiate collectively. And it concerned only the parties to the collective-bargaining relationship.

Our holding is not intended to insulate from antitrust review every joint imposition of terms by employers, for an agreement among employers could be sufficiently distant in time and in circumstances from the collective-bargaining process that a rule permitting antitrust intervention would not significantly interfere with that process. . . . We need not decide in this case whether, or where, within these extreme outer boundaries to draw that line. Nor would it be appropriate for us to do so without the detailed views of the Board, to whose "specialized judgment" Congress "intended to leave" many of the "inevitable questions concerning multi-employer bargaining bound to arise in the future."

By contrast *California ex rel. Brown v. Safeway, Inc.*, 615 F.3d 1171 (9th Cir. 2010), *aff'd*, 651 F.3d 1118 (9th Cir. 2011), held that the nonstatutory labor immunity did not preclude applying the Sherman Act to an agreement among multiple grocery chains to contribute to a fund in the event that one of them was the subject of a labor strike. As the court observed,

. . . defendants' profit sharing conduct has not traditionally been regulated under labor law principles, nor does it raise issues either on its face or in its practical implementation that are suitable for resolution as a matter of labor law, by the NLRB, or by the courts that review or implement Board rulings. There is no well-defined set of NLRB rules or principles that would govern the circumstances in which such conduct would be permissible, and the conduct does not involve any mandatory subject of collective bargaining. Perhaps most important, profit sharing is not "needed to make the collective bargaining process work." To the contrary, collective bargaining has worked and does work quite well from the standpoint of employers without the need to engage in such basic violations of the antitrust system.[2]

And looking from the other side:

Profit sharing implicates the core concerns of the antitrust laws, and such concerns are best resolved by courts steeped in antitrust law and its principles. Such is the historic means by which profit sharing, market

---

[2] *Id.* at 1196–1197.

allocation and price fixing agreements have been adjudicated. The only relationship of profit sharing agreements to labor matters is the possibility that they would unbalance the existing, carefully drawn process, and strengthen the hand of employers in labor disputes by means that would otherwise violate well-established antitrust policies — means that have not been historically authorized for use as part of the collective bargaining process.

For comprehensive treatment of the labor exemption, see 2A P. AREEDA & H. HOVENKAMP, ANTITRUST LAW ¶¶ 255–257 (4th ed. 2013).

In *Clarett v. NFL*, 369 F.3d 124 (2d Cir. 2004), the court approved a National Football League rule requiring entry level draft players to be at least three full college seasons beyond high school. The court concluded that the rule addressed a mandatory subject of collective bargaining and thus qualified for the nonstatutory exemption. In this case, the eligibility rule did not appear in the collective bargaining agreement itself but was in the NFL Constitution and Bylaws when the agreement was negotiated. However, language in the collective bargaining agreement appeared to refer to these bylaws as if they were a part of the agreement.

The district court had ruled against the NFL, concluding that (1) the rules excluded strangers to the collective bargaining agreement; (2) the rules in question do not concern wages, hours or working conditions of current NFL players; and (3) given that the rules were not in the collective bargaining agreement itself, they were not the product of bona fide arm's-length negotiations that led to the collective bargaining agreement. The court of appeals rejected all three contentions.

First, "the eligibility rules constitute a mandatory bargaining subject because they have tangible effects on the wages and working conditions of current NFL players." For example, "the complex scheme by which individual salaries in the NFL are set, which involves, inter alia, the NFL draft, league-wide salary pools for rookies, team salary caps, and free agency, was built around the longstanding restraint on the market for entering players imposed by the eligibility rules and the related expectations about the average career length of NFL players. The eligibility rules in other words cannot be viewed in isolation, because their elimination might well alter certain assumptions underlying the collective bargaining agreement between the NFL and its players union."

The court also noted that "by reducing competition in the market for entering players, the eligibility rules also affect the job security of veteran players." As the court explained, "Because the size of NFL teams is capped, the eligibility rules diminish a veteran player's risk of being replaced by either a drafted rookie or a player who enters the draft and, though not drafted, is then hired as a rookie free agent."

On the plaintiff's argument that the eligibility rules were improper because they affect players outside the union, the court replied: ". . . [S]imply because the eligibility rules work a hardship on prospective rather than current employees does not render them impermissible. The eligibility rules in this respect are not dissimilar to union demands for hiring hall arrangements that have long been recognized as mandatory subjects of bargaining. *See* Associated Gen. Contractors of

America, Houston Chapter, 143 N.L.R.B. 409, 412, *enforced*, 349 F.2d 449 (5th Cir. 1965) (" '[E]mployment' connotes the initial act of employing as well as the consequent state of being employed."). In such hiring hall arrangements, the criteria for employment are set by the rules of the hiring hall rather than the employer alone. Nevertheless, such an arrangement constitutes a permissible, mandatory subject of bargaining despite the fact that it concerns prospective rather than current employees."

Further,

> Clarett would have us hold that by reaching this arrangement rather than fixing the eligibility rules in the text of the collective bargaining agreement or in failing to wrangle over the eligibility rules at the bargaining table, the NFL left itself open to antitrust liability. Such a holding, however, would completely contradict prior decisions recognizing that the labor law policies that warrant withholding antitrust scrutiny are not limited to protecting only terms contained in collective bargaining agreements. The reach of those policies, rather, extends as far as is necessary to ensure the successful operation of the collective bargaining *process* and to safeguard the "unique bundle of compromises" reached by the NFL and the players union as a means of settling their differences.

Finally, speaking of the threat of monopoly, the court noted:

> The disruptions to federal labor policy that would be occasioned by Clarett's antitrust suit, moreover, would not vindicate any of the antitrust policies that the Supreme Court has said may warrant the withholding of the non-statutory exemption. This is simply not a case in which the NFL is alleged to have conspired with its players union to drive its competitors out of the market for professional football. Nor does Clarett contend that the NFL uses the eligibility rules as an unlawful means of maintaining its dominant position in that market. This lawsuit reflects simply a prospective employee's disagreement with the criteria, established by the employer and the labor union, that he must meet in order to be considered for employment. Any remedies for such a claim are the province of labor law.

PROBLEM 9.1

The Detroit Auto Dealers Association entered into an agreement that new car dealers in Detroit would limit showroom hours by closing on Saturday and on three weekday evenings. When the Federal Trade Commission sought an injunction, the defendants, 90 auto dealers and their trade association, argued that the conduct was exempted from the Sherman Act by the labor exemption. Defendants asserted that the closing restrictions were an attempt to defend themselves against the possibility of unionization of sales people and against the threats (and acts) of violence which often accompanied unionization attempts in the Detroit area. Does the labor exemption apply to defendants' agreement? Would your answer change if the unions were also parties to the agreement that restricted hours? *See Detroit Auto Dealers Ass'n v. FTC*, 955 F.2d 457 (6th Cir. 1991), *cert. denied*, 506 U.S. 973 (1992).

[2] Export Associations

Fostering competition is a major goal of American antitrust policy. But American companies operating on a worldwide scale often are faced with competition from foreign cartels, which may not be restricted by such laws. Congress has on two occasions provided an exemption from the Sherman Act for American businesses engaged in the export trade. The Webb-Pomerene Act was passed in 1918 to "aid and encourage" American manufacturers to extend the nation's foreign trade. "Congress felt that American firms needed the power to form joint export associations in order to compete with foreign cartels. But . . . the exemption created was carefully hedged to avoid substantial injury to domestic interests." *United States v. Concentrated Phosphate Export Ass'n*, 393 U.S. 199, 206 (1968). Section 2 of the Webb-Pomerene Act, 15 U.S.C. § 62, exempts any "association" whose "sole purpose" is engaging in export trade, so long as (1) its actions do not restrain trade within the United States or restrain the export trade of its domestic competitors; and (2) it does nothing that "artificially or intentionally enhances or depresses the prices" or substantially lessens competition or restrains trade *within* the United States. The "unfair methods of competition" provisions of the FTC Act *are* applicable to export associations, however. *Id.* § 64.

To qualify for the exemption, export associations must file a number of documents with the Federal Trade Commission, and must make annual reports to the FTC. *Id.* § 65. The FTC has the power to investigate the association. If it finds a prohibited restraint, it may issue "recommendations" to the association for "readjustment" of its business. If the association fails to comply, the FTC may refer the case to the Attorney General for prosecution. In this event, because the association has forfeited its exemption, it also leaves itself open to ordinary antitrust remedies. *See United States Alkali Export Ass'n v. United States*, 325 U.S. 196 (1945).

Because of the antitrust liability uncertainties surrounding the interpretation of the law governing export trade, Congress in 1982 passed the Export Trading Company Act. 15 U.S.C. §§ 4001–4021. Its purpose was to encourage exports by facilitating the formation and operation of export trading companies, export trade associations, and the expansion of export trade service. *Id.* § 4001(b). Under the 1982 Act, the Department of Commerce has the authority, with the concurrence of the Department of Justice, to certify export trading companies.

Four antitrust standards must be met before certification can be granted. Section 4013(a) requires the applicant to show that the proposed conduct will

> (1) result in neither a substantial lessening of competition or restraint of trade within the United States nor a substantial restraint of the export trade of any competitor of the applicant;

> (2) not unreasonably enhance, stabilize, or depress prices within the United States . . . ;

> (3) not constitute unfair methods of competition against competitors engaged in the export of goods, wares, merchandise, or services of the class exported by the applicant; and

(4) not . . . reasonably be expected to result in the sale for consumption or resale within the United States of the goods, wares, merchandise, or services exported of the class by the applicant.

Once the export trading company obtains a certificate, it is immunized from antitrust suits brought by federal or state enforcement officials "whenever the conduct that forms the basis of the action is specified in, and complies with, the terms of the certificate. Conduct which falls outside the scope of, or violates the terms of, the certificate is 'ultra vires' and would not be protected." H.R. Rep. No. 924, 97th Cong., 2d Sess. 7 (1982).

Section 4016 provides for private antitrust actions for injunctive relief or actual damages against the export certificate-holder if specific antitrust standards set out in Section 4013 have been violated. The statute of limitations for a private action is two years from notice of the violation. The certificate itself creates a presumption of legality for conduct specified in the certificate. A successful defendant is entitled to recover reasonable costs and attorney's fees.

Finally, Title IV of the Act (the Foreign Trade Antitrust Improvements of 1982, 96 Stat. 1246), which supplements the antitrust certification provisions of Title III, amended the Sherman Act and the FTC Act to require that before they can serve as a jurisdictional threshold for enforcement actions against exporting entities, such conduct must have a "direct, *substantial*, and reasonably foreseeable effect" on commerce in the United States, or on the export commerce of a United States resident. 15 U.S.C. § 6a; *Id.* § 45(a)(3). *See also National Bank of Canada v. Interbank Card Ass'n*, 666 F.2d 6, 8 (2d Cir. 1981). The statute also permits the Secretary of Commerce to issue a certificate regarding specific export trading practices, the effect of which insulates, under certain circumstances, the holder of the certificate from treble damage suits.

[3] Insurance

The McCarran-Ferguson Act, 15 U.S.C. §§ 1011–1012, specifically provides that the Sherman Act, the Clayton Act, and the FTC Act are only "applicable to the business of insurance to the extent that such business is not regulated by State law." A particular practice that under normal circumstances would violate the antitrust laws (e.g., price fixing), is immune from attack if it is done in the course of activities authorized and regulated by state law. There are two requirements for application of the exemption: (1) the questioned activity must be part of the "business of insurance," and (2) it must be authorized and regulated by the state.

The first requirement demands a definition of "business of insurance." An "indispensable characteristic of insurance" is the "spreading and underwriting of a policyholder's risk," which "strongly suggest[s] that Congress understood the business of insurance to be the underwriting and spreading of risk." *Group Life & Health Ins. Co. v. Royal Drug Co.*, 440 U.S. 205, 211–212, 220–221 (1979). *Royal Drug* held that agreements entered into by an insurance company, under which it set the maximum price it would pay for drugs, and which enabled it to "minimize costs and maximize profits," were outside the "business of insurance" and were therefore not immunized by the McCarran-Ferguson Act. *Id.* at 214. The relationship of insurer to insured ("the 'business of insurance'"), not that of insurer to non-insureds ("the business of insurance companies"), was the subject that Congress intended to immunize. *Id.* at 215–217. The primary concern of Congress, said the Court, was that "cooperative ratemaking efforts be exempt." *Id.* at 221.

In *Union Labor Life Ins. Co. v. Pireno*, 458 U.S. 119 (1982), the Supreme Court distilled the *Royal Drug* holding into a three-prong test for determining whether a particular practice was part of the "business of insurance":

> *[F]irst*, whether the practice has the effect of transferring or spreading a policyholder's risk; *second*, whether the practice is an integral part of the policy relationship between the insurer and the insured; and *third*, whether the practice is limited to entities within the insurance industry. None of these criteria is necessarily determinative in itself. . . .

Id. at 129. At issue in *Pireno* was an insurance company's use of a physician peer review panel to determine whether a particular physician's treatments and rates were "reasonable." Because the peer review panel served only to keep the insurer's costs (and, therefore, the insureds' premiums) down, but played no part in the spreading and underwriting of a policyholder's risk, it was not exempt from antitrust attack. *Id.* at 130–131. *See also United States v. Title Ins. Rating Bur. of Ariz.*, 700 F.2d 1247 (9th Cir. 1983), holding that an agreement among title insurers to fix escrow fees was not exempt because many other businesses, such as banks and escrow companies, offered the same services, and the services themselves were unrelated to the spreading of any risk.

The second requirement of the statute is normally easier to satisfy. The actual setting of rates and regulation of insurer-insured relations is normally done by state insurance commissions. The activities of insurance rate bureaus (which set rates for policies) are exempt from antitrust attack if they are licensed and supervised by the state. *See McCray v. Fld. Nat'l Title Ins. Co.*, 2010 U.S. Dist. LEXIS 76616 (D. Del. July 29, 2010), *aff'd*, 682 F.3d 229 (3d Cir. 2012).

The McCarran-Ferguson exemption does not apply to acts of "boycott, coercion, or intimidation." In *St. Paul Fire & Marine Ins. Co. v. Barry*, 438 U.S. 531 (1978), the Supreme Court found that an agreement among insurers to insure medical malpractice only if it occurred during the period covered by the policy constituted a "boycott." The ruling seems odd in one respect: joint drafting of insurance policies is protected by the Act, and any such drafting is effectively a refusal to deal or "boycott" of buyers unwilling to accept the terms of a policy. Suppose a group of insurers agree with each other not to insure people with two or more drunk driving convictions? Other kinds of "boycotts" are less problematic. For example, *Malley-Duff & Assocs. v. Crown Life Ins. Co.*, 734 F.2d 133 (3d Cir. 1984), held that an agreement between an insurance company and one agent to terminate a second agent was a nonexempt boycott. Likewise, *In re Workers Compensation Ins.*, 867 F.2d 1552 (8th Cir.), *cert. denied*, 492 U.S. 920 (1989), found a boycott in an insurers' agreement to exclude from a trade association other insurers who charged lower prices than the defendants.

In its most recent decision on the McCarran exemption, the Supreme Court found that qualifying "boycotts" had been alleged but narrowed the meaning of that term. In *Hartford Fire Ins. Co. v. California*, 509 U.S. 764 (1993), several state attorneys general alleged that primary insurers unlawfully agreed to reduce their policy coverages so as to eliminate losses that occurred outside the policy period, or upon which claims were made outside the policy period, and losses caused by certain forms of "sudden and accidental" pollution. Although a simple agreement to develop a new insurance form with reduced coverage was exempt "business of insurance," the plaintiffs alleged that the defendants entered collateral agreements with two other entities. The first was an agreement with Insurance Services Office (ISO) that the latter would not supply risk data for risks that the conspirators no longer wished to cover. Several nonconspiring insurers would have continued to write the larger risks, but they could not do so without adequate risk data. Secondly, the defendant insurers allegedly agreed with foreign sellers of reinsurance that the reinsurers would not provide their services to the nonconspiring insurers either. Reinsurers sell insurance to primary insurers, enabling the latter to reduce their own risk from catastrophic losses. In finding a boycott, the Court noted:

> It is . . . important . . . to distinguish between a conditional boycott and a concerted agreement to seek particular terms in particular transactions. A concerted agreement to terms (a "cartelization") is "a way of obtaining and exercising market power by concertedly exacting terms like those which a monopolist might exact." The parties to such an agreement (the members of a cartel) are not engaging in a boycott, because: "They are not coercing anyone, at least in the usual sense of that word; they are merely (though concertedly) saying "we will deal with you only on the following trade terms."

The critical issue was whether the agreement covered only the terms of the contract under negotiation, or whether it reached further. For example, if a group of tenants agreed with each other that they would not renew their leases unless they received lower rents from the landlord, they would be negotiating the contract at hand. They would not be "boycotting" anyone. However, if the tenants also refused to engage in unrelated transactions — for example, if they refused to sell their landlord food or other supplies until he lowered the rents — this latter agreement would be a boycott. "[T]his expansion of the refusal to deal beyond the targeted transaction . . . gives great coercive force to a commercial boycott: unrelated transactions are used as leverage to achieve the terms desired." Applying this definition, the Court found that the plaintiffs' allegations contained several qualifying "boycotts." For example, the reinsurers allegedly refused to write reinsurance on any policy given by a firm that also wrote a policy containing the coverages that the defendants wanted removed from the market.

Recently, Congress has entertained proposals to repeal the McCarran-Ferguson antitrust exemption for insurance, or reduce its scope. Would such an action greatly increase insurers' antitrust exposure? Insurance is heavily regulated by state law, and some of the activities now exempted by McCarran-Ferguson would probably also be exempted under the "state action" doctrine. (*See* Section III, *below.*) The principal difference between the "state action" doctrine and the insurance exemption is that the former contains an "active state supervision" requirement while the latter does not. As a result, many insurer activities that are not effectively supervised by the state are, nonetheless, exempt from the antitrust laws. Would repeal of the special exemption for insurance be a good idea?

For further discussion of the insurance exemption, see 1 P. AREEDA & H. HOVENKAMP, ANTITRUST LAW ¶¶ 219, 220 (4th ed. 2013).

[4] Agricultural Organizations

Section 6 of the Clayton Act exempts from the antitrust laws "agricultural [and] horticultural organizations, instituted for the purpose of mutual help, and not having capital stock or conducted for profit." The Capper-Volstead Act of 1922, 7 U.S.C. § 291, extended the exemption to capital stock agricultural cooperatives, which had not been covered under the Clayton Act. The exemption authorizes persons engaged in the production of agricultural products, such as farmers, ranchers, planters, dairymen, or nut or fruit growers, to act together in cooperatives, collectively processing, preparing for market, handling, and marketing agricultural products.

The purpose of the exemption is to allow farmers to act together in cooperatives, like a corporation, within the framework of the antitrust laws. *Maryland & Va. Milk Producers Ass'n v. United States*, 362 U.S. 458 (1960). Thus, while the creation and internal operations of a farmer cooperative are immune from attack, the external activities of the cooperative are judged by the same standards as any other business. These cooperatives may, however, voluntarily combine to fix prices at which they will sell their products, provided that no nonfarmer or other organization is a party to the combination. *United States v. Maryland Coop. Milk Producers, Inc.*, 145 F. Supp. 151 (D.D.C. 1956).

The cooperative is subject to other traditional antitrust prohibitions. For example, a cooperative may not use its legal monopoly power to suppress competition among independent producers and processors. *Maryland & Va. Milk Producers Ass'n v. United States*, 362 U.S. 458 (1960) (purchase of independent dairy with intent to suppress competition). Nor may it coerce individual producers to join it, or coerce other organizations into complying with its demands. *North Texas Producers Ass'n v. Metzger Dairies*, 348 F.2d 189 (5th Cir. 1965).

The Secretary of Agriculture is given authority to issue cease and desist orders whenever he finds that an organization is monopolizing or restraining trade "to such an extent that the price of any agricultural product is unduly enhanced." 7 U.S.C. § 292.

[5] Professional Sports

Professional sports are big business in America. The very nature of the business requires mutual dependence among the teams that make up the sport. It would be difficult for a professional team to survive without operating in a league, and the members of a league *must* cooperate on a wide variety of issues that in other industries might well be serious restraints of trade. Moreover, professional sports teams, while they compete with each other on the field, arguably are not competing with each other in a business sense; they compete with other forms of entertainment in their own communities. The hybrid nature of professional sports leagues — half business, half sport — has forced courts to deal with the issue of how to promote competition within the business without damaging the sport.

Professional baseball is in a unique position relative to other sports. As the result of an early case, *Federal Baseball Club of Baltimore, Inc. v. National League of Prof. Baseball Clubs*, 259 U.S. 200 (1922), the national pastime is exempt from the antitrust laws. Although the Supreme Court has recognized that *Federal Baseball* was decided on highly questionable grounds (the Court actually found no interstate commerce involved in the game of baseball), it has refused to repeal the judicial exemption. *See Flood v. Kuhn*, 407 U.S. 258 (1972). Congress arguably gave implied approval to the exception in 1961, by providing that nothing contained in an act relating to telecasting of sporting events "shall be deemed to change, determine, or otherwise affect the applicability or nonapplicability of the antitrust laws to . . . football, baseball, basketball, or hockey." 15 U.S.C. § 1294.

The Supreme Court has refused to extend the judicial exemption to any other sport. *See Haywood v. National Basketball Ass'n*, 401 U.S. 1204 (1971); *Radovich v. National Football League*, 352 U.S. 445 (1957). Thus, professional sports other than baseball are generally covered by the antitrust laws. A federal court, for example, has enjoined enforcement of National Football League rules barring N.F.L. owners from acquiring teams in other sports. *See North Am. Soccer League v. National Football League*, 465 F. Supp. 665 (S.D.N.Y. 1979). The draft rules of various sports leagues have also been attacked, and have frequently been found unreasonable. *See Smith v. Pro Football, Inc.*, 593 F.2d 1173 (D.C. Cir. 1978); *Mackey v. National Football League*, 543 F.2d 606 (8th Cir. 1976), *cert. denied*, 434 U.S. 801 (1977).

In *Major League Baseball v. Crist*, 331 F.3d 1177 (11th Cir. 2003), the court rejected a state antitrust challenge to Major League Baseball's decision to drop two teams. The court noted that the contraction was clearly part of the "business of baseball," and that the federal baseball immunity thus prevented the challenge under federal law. In addition, however, the need for national uniformity on the subject entailed that federal antitrust law in this particular case preempted inconsistent state antitrust law. The court quoted this language from the Supreme Court's decision in *Flood v. Kuhn*, 407 U.S. 258, 284 – 285 (1972): The petitioner's argument as to the application of state antitrust laws deserves a word. [The district court] rejected the state law claims because state antitrust regulation would conflict with federal policy and because national "uniformity (is required) in any regulation of baseball and its reserve system." The Court of Appeals, in affirming, stated, "[A]s the burden on interstate commerce outweighs the states' interests in regulating baseball's reserve system, the Commerce Clause precludes the application here of state antitrust law." As applied to organized baseball, and in the light of this Court's observations . . . and despite baseball's allegedly inconsistent position taken in the past with respect to the application of state law, these statements adequately dispose of the state law claims.

Interestingly, beginning with Justice Holmes's decision in *Federal Baseball Club of Baltimore v. Nat'l League of Prof'l Base Ball Clubs*, 259 U.S. 200 (1922), the basis of the Supreme Court's refusal to apply the Sherman Act was that baseball was not "commerce." Justice Holmes wrote:

> The business is giving exhibitions of base ball, which are purely state affairs. It is true that in order to attain for these exhibitions the great

popularity that they have achieved, competitions must be arranged between clubs from different cities and States. *But the fact that in order to give the exhibitions the Leagues must induce free persons to cross state lines and must arrange and pay for their doing so is not enough to change the character of the business.* According to the distinction insisted upon in *Hooper v. California*, 155 U.S. 648, 655, 15 S. Ct. 207, 39 L. Ed. 297, *the transport is a mere incident, not the essential thing.* That to which it is incident, the exhibition, although made for money would not be called trade of commerce in the commonly accepted use of those words. As it is put by defendant, personal effort, not related to production, is not a subject of commerce. That which in its consummation is not commerce does not become commerce among the States because the transportation that we have mentioned takes place. 259 U.S. at 208–209 (emphasis added).

Since the "commerce" language in the Sherman Act tracks that in the Commerce Clause, that holding was tantamount to one that the Commerce Clause did not permit Congress to regulate organized baseball. But the function of the Commerce Clause is to allocate regulatory power as between the federal government and the states. As a result, *Federal Baseball Club* is best read not as an antitrust policy decision that baseball should not be regulated at all, but as a conclusion that in the assignment of regulatory powers, the power to regulate baseball fell to the states rather than the federal government.

[6] National Sovereign Immunity

In *United States Postal Service v. Flamingo Industries (USA), Ltd.*, 540 U.S. 736 (2004), the Supreme Court held that the Post Office (USPS) was not a "person" subject to federal antitrust liability. The plaintiff, Flamingo, sued under the antitrust laws as well as other statutes when its contract to supply the USPS with mail sacks was terminated. The rather vague antitrust allegations were that USPS was seeking to monopolize the market for mail sacks by procuring them from cheaper foreign sources than Flamingo.

The Supreme Court observed that a federal statute, the Postal Reorganization Act (PRA), contemplated that the Post Office would be less political than other federal agencies, and also that it behave to some extent as a competitor in the market for mail and parcel delivery. For example, it was required to price its services in a way that reflected the costs of providing them. Nevertheless, the Post Office remained an "independent establishment of the executive branch of the Government of the United States," and that status indicated immunity unless there has been a specific waiver. While federal legislation waived the Post Office's immunity from other types of lawsuits, there was no waiver with respect to antitrust liability. The Court noted its decision in *United States v. Cooper Corp.*, 312 U.S. 600 (1941), which held that the United States was not a "person" who could be a plaintiff in an antitrust case. The Court reasoned that one difficulty with permitting the United States to be a plaintiff was that the word "person" in the Sherman Act did not distinguish between plaintiffs and defendants. As a result, permitting the United States to be a plaintiff would also subject the United States to antitrust liability as a defendant. Thereafter Congress amended the antitrust laws to permit the federal government to be an antitrust plaintiff in a damages action. Significantly, it did so not by redefining the word "person" to include the United States, which would have changed the federal government's status as both defendant and plaintiff. Rather, it added a new section to the Clayton Act entitling the United States to sue:

Although Congress was well aware of the view the Court indicated in *Cooper Corp.*, that Congress had not described the United States as a 'person' for Sherman Act purposes, Congress addressed only the direct holding in that case — the ruling that the United States was not authorized to proceed as a Sherman Act treble damage action plaintiff. The Court elaborated:

> The PRA gives the Postal Service a high degree of independence from other offices of the Government, but it remains part of the Government. The Sherman Act defines "person" to include corporations, and had the Congress chosen to create the Postal Service as a federal corporation, we would have to ask whether the Sherman Act's definition extends to the federal entity under this part of the definitional text. Congress, however, declined to create the Postal Service as a Government corporation, opting instead for an independent establishment. The choice of words likely was more informed than unconsidered, because Congress debated proposals to make the Postal Service a Government corporation before it enacted the PRA . . . .

> Our conclusion is consistent with the nationwide, public responsibilities of the Postal Service. The Postal Service has different goals, obligations, and powers from private corporations. Its goals are not those of private enterprise. The most important difference is that it does not seek profits, but only to break even, which is consistent with its public character. It also has broader obligations, including the provision of universal mail delivery, the provision of free mail delivery to the certain classes of persons, and, most recently, increased public responsibilities related to national security. Finally, the Postal Service has many powers more characteristic of Government than of private enterprise, including its state-conferred monopoly on mail delivery, the power of eminent domain, and the power to conclude international postal agreements.

> On the other hand, but in ways still relevant to the non-applicability of the antitrust laws to the Postal Service, its powers are more limited than those of private businesses. It lacks the prototypical means of engaging in anti-competitive behavior: the power to set prices. This is true both as a matter of mechanics, because pricing decisions are made with the participation of the separate Postal Rate Commission, and as a matter of substance, because price decisions are governed by principles other than profitability. Similarly, before it can close a post office, it must provide written reasons, and its decision is subject to reversal by the Commission for arbitrariness, abuse of discretion, failure to follow procedures, or lack of evidence. The Postal Service's public characteristics and responsibilities indicate it should be treated under the antitrust laws as part of the Government of the United States, not a market participant separate from it.

What about native American tribes? Federal law has a complex array of provisions that recognizes federal sovereign immunity, although with some limitations. In particular, a federal statute applies to Indian tribes only if Congress expressly states its wish to do so. *See Miller v. Wright*, 705 F.3d 919 (9th Cir. 2013) (tribal immunity precluded application of Sherman Act where Congress had never unequivocally expressed its wish to apply federal antitrust laws to tribes). A native American tribe can immunize conduct occurring on its land without qualifying for the state action exemption. The plaintiff had alleged that a tribe's imposition of a sales tax on non-native American cigarette purchasers on tribal land was an unlawful antitrust conspiracy with the state of Washington. What about a "sham" petition to a tribal court? In that case the conduct is purely private and one can assume that tribal councils and courts do not authorize sham petitions.

II   PETITIONS TO THE GOVERNMENT

[A]   Political Process, "Rent- Seeking," and the Antitrust Laws

Perhaps the world's greatest creator of monopoly is government itself. For example, the surest way for a firm to maintain its exclusive position in some market is to convince the sovereign to pass a statute forbidding others from entering. At common law, a "monopoly" was not a firm that had simply come to dominate a market; rather, it was someone with an exclusive grant, or franchise, from the state.

The political process in a democratic country becomes a means by which firms attempt to earn monopoly profits. They engage in "rent-seeking" by urging governments to guarantee profit margins, give them exclusive privileges to operate in a market, authorize their own innovations for sale, or refuse to authorize the innovations of their competitors (see the *Allied Tube* case reprinted below). Many of the things that private firms request from government are downright anticompetitive. Worse yet, government often obliges them. *See* D. FARBER & P. FRICKEY, LAW AND PUBLIC CHOICE: A CRITICAL INTRODUCTION (1991); Hovenkamp, *Legislation, Well-Being and Public Choice*, 57 U. CHI. L. REV. 63 (1990).

But the purpose of the antitrust laws is not to prevent people from asking the government for what they want. The purpose of antitrust is not even to prohibit the government from granting anticompetitive requests. Ever since its decision in *Eastern R.R. Presidents Conf. v. Noerr Motor Freight, Inc.*, 365 U.S. 127 (1961), the Supreme Court has recognized that individuals have a right, grounded in the First Amendment, to petition the government. This right is protected no matter how anticompetitive the petitioners' intent, and whether they conduct the petitioning singly or in concert. *Noerr* held that the antitrust laws proscribe only trade restraints that result from private action, not those that result from valid government action.

The conduct challenged in *Noerr* was a concerted campaign by railroads to lobby for legislation restricting competition from the trucking industry. *Id.* at 136. The Court's conclusion, which rested not on the First Amendment but on the

Sherman Act itself, was that the antitrust laws do not prohibit two or more persons from associating together in an attempt to persuade the government to take a certain regulatory action, no matter how anticompetitive. "[N]o violation of the [Sherman] Act can be predicated upon mere attempts to influence the passage or enforcement of laws." Further,

> [w]e think it equally clear that the Sherman Act does not prohibit two or more persons from associating together in an attempt to persuade the legislature or the executive to take particular action with respect to a law that would produce a restraint or a monopoly. Although such associations could perhaps, through a process of expansive construction, be brought within the general proscription of "combination[s] . . . in restraint of trade," they bear very little if any resemblance to the combinations normally held violative of the Sherman Act. . . .
>
> In a representative democracy such as this, these branches of government act on behalf of the people and, to a very large extent, the whole concept of representation depends upon the ability of the people to make their wishes known to their representatives. To hold that the government retains the power to act in this representative capacity and yet hold, at the same time, that the people cannot freely inform the government of their wishes would impute to the Sherman Act a purpose to regulate, not business activity, but political activity, a purpose which would have no basis whatever in the legislative history of that Act. Secondly, and of at least equal significance, such a construction of the Sherman Act would raise important constitutional questions. The right of petition is one of the freedoms protected by the Bill of Rights, and we cannot, of course, lightly impute to Congress an intent to invade these freedoms. . . .

Further,

> [t]he right of the people to inform their representatives in government of their desires with respect to the passage or enforcement of laws cannot properly be made to depend upon their intent in doing so. It is neither unusual nor illegal for people to seek action on laws in the hope that they may bring about an advantage to themselves and a disadvantage to their competitors. . . . A construction of the Sherman Act that would disqualify people from taking a public position on matters in which they are financially interested would thus deprive the government of a valuable source of information and, at the same time, deprive the people of their right to petition in the very instances in which that right may be of the most importance to them. . . .

The court reiterated this conclusion in *UMW v. Pennington*, 381 U.S. 657 (1965). In *California Motor Transp. Co. v. Trucking Unlimited*, 404 U.S. 508 (1972), it held that the First Amendment required such a limitation on the Sherman Act. The *California Motor* case is discussed further below.

ALLIED TUBE & CONDUIT CORP. v. INDIAN HEAD, INC.
486 U.S. 492 (1988)

JUSTICE BRENNAN delivered the opinion of the Court.

. . . .

I

The National Fire Protection Association (Association) is a private, voluntary organization with more than 31,500 individual and group members representing industry, labor, academia, insurers, organized medicine, firefighters, and government. The Association, among other things, publishes product standards and codes related to fire protection through a process known as "consensus standard making." One of the codes it publishes is the National Electrical Code, which establishes product and performance requirements for the design and installation of electrical wiring systems. Revised every three years, the National Electric Code (Code) is the most influential electrical code in the nation. A substantial number of state and local governments routinely adopt the Code into law with little or no change; private certification laboratories, such as Underwriters Laboratories, normally will not list and label an electrical product that does not meet Code standards; many underwriters will refuse to insure structures that are not built in conformity with the Code; and many electrical inspectors, contractors, and distributors will not use a product that falls outside the Code.

Among the electrical products covered by the Code is electrical conduit, the hollow tubing used as a raceway to carry electrical wires through the walls and floors of buildings. Throughout the relevant period, the Code permitted using electrical conduit made of steel, and almost all conduit sold was in fact steel conduit. Starting in 1980, respondent began to offer plastic conduit made of polyvinyl chloride. Respondent claims its plastic conduit offers significant competitive advantages over steel conduit, including pliability, lower installed cost, and lower susceptibility to short circuiting. In 1980, however, there was also a scientific basis for concern that, during fires in high-rise buildings, polyvinyl chloride conduit might burn and emit toxic fumes.

Respondent initiated a proposal to include polyvinyl chloride conduit as an approved type of electrical conduit in the 1981 edition of the Code. Following approval by one of the Association's professional panels, this proposal was scheduled for consideration at the 1980 annual meeting, where it could be adopted or rejected by a simple majority of the members present. Alarmed that, if approved, respondent's product might pose a competitive threat to steel conduit, petitioner, the nation's largest producer of steel conduit, met to plan strategy with, among others, members of the steel industry, other steel conduit manufacturers, and its independent sales agents. They collectively agreed to exclude respondent's product from the 1981 Code by packing the upcoming annual meeting with new Association members whose only function would be to vote against the polyvinyl chloride proposal.

Combined, the steel interests recruited 230 persons to join the Association and to attend the annual meeting to vote against the proposal. Petitioner alone recruited 155 persons — including employees, executives, sales agents, the agents' employees, employees from two divisions that did not sell electrical products, and the wife of a national sales director. Petitioner and the other steel interests also paid over $100,000 for the membership, registration, and attendance expenses of these voters. At the annual meeting, the steel group voters were instructed where to sit and how and when to vote by group leaders who used walkie-talkies and hand signals to facilitate communication. Few of the steel group voters had any of the technical documentation necessary to follow the meeting. None of them spoke at the meeting to give their reasons for opposing the proposal to approve polyvinyl chloride conduit. Nonetheless, with their solid vote in opposition, the proposal was rejected and returned to committee by a vote of 394 to 390. Respondent appealed the membership's vote to the Association's Board of Directors, but the Board denied the appeal on the ground that, although the Association's rules had been circumvented, they had not been violated.[3]

In October 1981, respondent brought this suit in Federal District Court, alleging that petitioner and others had unreasonably restrained trade in the electrical conduit market in violation of § 1 of the Sherman Act. 26 Stat. 209, 15 U.S.C. § 1. . . .

. . . .

II

Concerted efforts to restrain or monopolize trade by petitioning government officials are protected from antitrust liability under the doctrine established by *Noerr*. The scope of this protection depends, however, on the source, context, and nature of the anticompetitive restraint at issue. "[W]here a restraint upon trade or monopolization is the result of valid governmental action, as opposed to private action," those urging the governmental action enjoy absolute immunity from antitrust liability for the anticompetitive restraint. In addition, where, independent of any governmental action, the anticompetitive restraint results directly from private action, the restraint cannot form the basis for antitrust liability if it is "incidental" to a valid effort to influence governmental action. The validity of such efforts, and thus the applicability of *Noerr* immunity, varies with the context and nature of the activity. A publicity campaign directed at the general public, seeking legislation or executive action, enjoys antitrust immunity even when the campaign employs unethical and deceptive methods. But in less political arenas, unethical and deceptive practices can constitute abuses of administrative or judicial processes that may result in antitrust violations.

In this case, the restraint of trade on which liability was predicated was the Association's exclusion of respondent's product from the Code, and no damages were imposed for the incorporation of that Code by any government. The relevant context is thus the standard-setting process of a private association. Typically,

---

[3] [FN 1] . . . The Association subsequently approved use of polyvinyl chloride conduit for buildings of less than four stories in the 1984 Code, and for all buildings in the 1987 Code.

private standard-setting associations, like the Association in this case, include members having horizontal and vertical business relations. See generally 7 P. Areeda, Antitrust Law ¶1477, p. 343 (1986) (trade and standard-setting associations routinely treated as continuing conspiracies of their members). There is no doubt that the members of such associations often have economic incentives to restrain competition and that the product standards set by such associations have a serious potential for anticompetitive harm. Agreement on a product standard is, after all, implicitly an agreement not to manufacture, distribute, or purchase certain types of products. Accordingly, private standard-setting associations have traditionally been objects of antitrust scrutiny. When, however, private associations promulgate safety standards based on the merits of objective expert judgments and through procedures that prevent the standard-setting process from being biased by members with economic interests in stifling product competition, those private standards can have significant procompetitive advantages. It is this potential for procompetitive benefits that has led most lower courts to apply rule of reason analysis to product standard-setting by private associations.

Given this context, petitioner does not enjoy the immunity accorded those who merely urge the government to restrain trade. We agree with the Court of Appeals that the Association cannot be treated as a "quasi-legislative" body simply because legislatures routinely adopt the Code the Association publishes. Whatever *de facto* authority the Association enjoys, no official authority has been conferred on it by any government, and the decisionmaking body of the Association is composed, at least in part, of persons with economic incentives to restrain trade. "We may presume, absent a showing to the contrary, that [a government] acts in the public interest. A private party, on the other hand, may be presumed to be acting primarily on his or its own behalf." The dividing line between restraints resulting from governmental action and those resulting from private action may not always be obvious. But where, as here, the restraint is imposed by persons unaccountable to the public and without official authority, many of whom have personal financial interests in restraining competition, we have no difficulty concluding that the restraint has resulted from private action.

Noerr immunity might still apply, however, if, as petitioner argues, the exclusion of polyvinyl chloride conduit from the Code, and the effect that exclusion had of its own force in the marketplace, were incidental to a valid effort to influence governmental action. Petitioner notes that the lion's share of the anticompetitive effect in this case came from the predictable adoption of the Code into law by a large number of state and local governments. Indeed, petitioner argues that, because state and local governments rely so heavily on the Code and lack the resources or technical expertise to second-guess it, efforts to influence the Association's standard-setting process are the most effective means of influencing legislation regulating electrical conduit. This claim to *Noerr* immunity has some force. The effort to influence governmental action in this case certainly cannot be characterized as a sham given the actual adoption of the 1981 Code into a number of statutes and local ordinances. Nor can we quarrel with petitioner's contention that, given the widespread adoption of the Code into law, any effect the 1981 Code had in the marketplace of its own force was, in the main, incidental to petitioner's genuine effort to influence governmental action. And, as petitioner persuasively argues, the claim of *Noerr* immunity cannot be dismissed on the ground that the conduct at issue involved no "direct" petitioning of government officials, for *Noerr* itself immunized a form of "indirect" petitioning. See *Noerr*, 365 U.S. 127 (1961) (immunizing a publicity campaign directed at the general public on the ground that it was part of an effort to influence legislative and executive action).

Nonetheless, the validity of petitioner's actions remains an issue. We cannot agree with petitioner's absolutist position that the *Noerr* doctrine immunizes every concerted effort that is genuinely intended to influence governmental action. . . . We . . . conclude that the *Noerr* immunity of anticompetitive activity intended to influence the government depends not only on its impact, but also on the context and nature of the activity.

Here petitioner's actions took place within the context of the standard-setting process of a private association. Having concluded that the Association is not a "quasi-legislative" body, we reject petitioner's argument that any efforts to influence the Association must be treated as efforts to influence a "quasi-legislature" and given the same wide berth accorded legislative lobbying. That rounding up supporters is an acceptable and constitutionally protected method of influencing elections does not mean that rounding up economically interested persons to set private standards must also be protected. . . .

. . . Unlike the publicity campaign in *Noerr*, the activity at issue here did not take place in the open political arena, where partisanship is the hallmark of decisionmaking, but within the confines of a private standard-setting process. The validity of conduct within that process has long been defined and circumscribed by the antitrust laws without regard to whether the private standards are likely to be adopted into law. Indeed, because private standard-setting by associations comprising firms with horizontal and vertical business relations is permitted at all under the antitrust laws only on the understanding that it will be conducted in a nonpartisan manner offering procompetitive benefits, the standards of conduct in this context are, at least in some respects, more rigorous than the standards of conduct prevailing in the partisan political arena or in the adversarial process of adjudication. The activity at issue here thus cannot, as in *Noerr*, be characterized as an activity that has traditionally been regulated with extreme caution, or as an activity that "bear[s] little if any resemblance to the combinations normally held violative of the Sherman Act." And petitioner did not confine itself to efforts to persuade an independent decisionmaker; rather, it organized and orchestrated the actual exercise of the Association's decisionmaking authority in setting a standard. Nor can the setting of the Association's Code be characterized as merely an exercise of the power of persuasion, for it in part involves the exercise of market power. The Association's members, after all, include consumers, distributors, and manufacturers of electrical conduit, and any agreement to exclude polyvinyl chloride conduit from the Code is in part an implicit agreement not to trade in that type of electrical conduit. Although one could reason backwards from the legislative impact of the Code to the conclusion that the conduct at issue here is "political," we think that, given the context and nature of the conduct, it can more aptly be characterized as commercial activity with a political impact. Just as the antitrust laws should not regulate political activities "simply because those activities have a commercial impact," so the antitrust laws should not necessarily immunize what are in essence commercial activities simply because they have a political impact.

. . . .

. . . Although we do not here set forth the rules of antitrust liability governing the private standard-setting process, we hold that at least where, as here, an economically interested party exercises decision-making authority in formulating a product standard for a private association that comprises market participants, that party enjoys no *Noerr* immunity from any antitrust liability flowing from the effect the standard has of its own force in the marketplace.

This conclusion does not deprive state and local governments of input and information from interested individuals or organizations or leave petitioner without ample means to petition those governments. Petitioner, and others concerned about the safety or competitive threat of polyvinyl chloride conduit, can, with full antitrust immunity, engage in concerted efforts to influence those governments through direct lobbying, publicity campaigns, and other traditional avenues of political expression. To the extent state and local governments are more difficult to persuade through these other avenues, that no doubt reflects their preference for and confidence in the nonpartisan consensus process that petitioner has undermined. Petitioner remains free to take advantage of the forum provided by the standard-setting process by presenting and vigorously arguing accurate scientific evidence before a nonpartisan private standard-setting body. And petitioner can avoid the strictures of the private standard-setting process by attempting to influence legislatures through other forums. What petitioner may not do (without exposing itself to possible antitrust liability for direct injuries) is bias the process by, as in this case, stacking the private standard-setting body with decisionmakers sharing their economic interest in restraining competition.

The judgment of the Court of Appeals is *Affirmed*.

NOTES AND QUESTIONS

1. *The Causation Problem in Noerr-Pennington Cases.* Observe that Indian Head was not seeking damages for injuries caused when state and local governments enacted codes prohibiting the use of plastic conduit. Rather, it complained about the chilling effect that the restrictions in the model National Electric Code had on contractor decisions to stick with steel conduit. The first form of injury was very likely protected by *Noerr-Pennington. See Sessions Tank Liners v. Joor Mfg.*, 827 F.2d 458 (9th Cir. 1987), where the court found *Noerr* protection for a petition to a private body when the injury was caused by subsequent legislative enactment of the private body's proposal. In this case, the injury "resulted from the act of public officials, . . . not the . . . action of defendants," whose proposal "had no legal force and little injurious effect until it was adopted by local legislatures or enforced by local fire officials." *Id.* at 464.

This analysis suggests that the First Amendment may not be an integral part of the *Noerr-Pennington* exemption. Every plaintiff must show that the defendant's antitrust violation caused its injury. (*See* Chapter 3, *supra*.) Suppose that Firms *A*, *B*, and *C* petition a state agency for a regulation that burdens a competitor, Firm *D*. The agency passes the regulation and *D* sues *A*, *B*, and *C* under the antitrust laws.

Can *D* prove causation? Although *A*, *B*, and *C* asked the government to do something, the government officials presumably had discretion to do it or not do it. They may have passed the regulation without the intervention of *A*, *B*, and *C*. What must *D* show in order to establish that *A*, *B*, and *C* "caused" its injury?

2. *In United Airlines, Inc. v. U.S. Bank N.A.*, 2005-1 Trade Cas. (CCH) 74,775, 406 F.3d 918 (7th Cir. 2005), the Seventh Circuit held that the *Noerr-Pennington* doctrine immunized lenders; joint efforts to get a court to increase the amount United Airlines would owe on leased planes on which it was in default. The court suggested that, quite apart from *Noerr*, joint collection activities do not restrain trade, and are thus not antitrust violations: "Competition comes at the time loans are made; cooperation in an effort to collect as much as possible of the amounts due under competitively determined contracts is not the sort of activity with which the antitrust laws are concerned."

GF Gaming Corp. v. City of Black Hawk, Colorado, 405 F.3d 876, 2005-1 Trade Cas. (CCH) ¶ 74,752 (10th Cir. 2005), affirmed a district court's Rule 12(b)(6) dismissal of the plaintiff's complaint that the city, gaming entrepreneurs, and land owners conspired to build a bypass road that shifted traffic away from the plaintiff's facility. The court noted that the private defendants were not alleged to have engaged in any anticompetitive act other than "conspiring" with the city to build the by-pass road, excluding a few land purchases: "Standing alone, plaintiffs' allegations that the non-governmental defendants conspired with Black Hawk officials to block the southern access road is essentially an allegation that defendants met with city officials and urged them to take anticompetitive action. For purposes of *Noerr-Pennington*, there is no distinction between petitioning government officials and conspiring with them." (Citing *City of Columbia v. Omni Outdoor Adver., Inc.*, 499 U.S. 365, 383 (1991).) The court concluded that "Even if defendants' sole motive for petitioning the Black Hawk officials was to injure competition, the conduct would still be protected by" *Noerr*. Further, the "sham" exception to *Noerr* did not apply because "it was the outcome of defendants' lobbying (i.e., Black Hawk's decision to block the annexation petition) rather than the process of that lobbying that gives rise to the alleged antitrust injuries."

FTC v. SUPERIOR COURT TRIAL LAWYERS ASS'N
493 U.S. 411 (1990)

JUSTICE STEVENS delivered the opinion of the Court.

Pursuant to a well-publicized plan, a group of lawyers agreed not to represent indigent criminal defendants in the District of Columbia Superior Court until the District of Columbia government increased the lawyers' compensation. The questions presented are whether the lawyers' concerted conduct violated § 5 of the Federal Trade Commission Act and if so, whether it was nevertheless protected by the First Amendment to the Constitution.

I

The burden of providing competent counsel to indigent defendants in the District of Columbia is substantial. During 1982, court-appointed counsel represented the defendant in approximately 25,000 cases. In the most serious felony cases, representation was generally provided by full-time employees of the District's Public Defender System (PDS). Less serious felony and misdemeanor cases constituted about 85 percent of the total caseload. In these cases, lawyers in private practice were appointed and compensated pursuant to the District of Columbia Criminal Justice Act (CJA).

Although over 1,200 lawyers have registered for CJA appointments, relatively few actually apply for such work on a regular basis. In 1982, most appointments went to approximately 100 lawyers who are described as "CJA regulars." These lawyers derive almost all of their income from representing indigents. In 1982, the total fees paid to CJA lawyers amounted to $4,579,572. . . .

Bar organizations began as early as 1975 to express concern about the low fees paid to CJA lawyers. Beginning in 1982, respondents, the Superior Court Trial Lawyers Association (SCTLA) and its officers, and other bar groups sought to persuade the District to increase CJA rates to at least $35 per hour. Despite what appeared to be uniform support for the bill, it did not pass. It is also true, however, that nothing in the record indicates that the low fees caused any actual shortage of CJA lawyers or denied effective representation to defendants.

At an SCTLA meeting, the CJA lawyers voted to form a "strike committee." The eight members of that committee promptly met and informally agreed "that the only viable way of getting an increase in fees was to stop signing up to take new CJA appointments, and that the boycott should aim for a $45 out-of-court and $55 in-court rate schedule."

On August 11, 1983, about 100 CJA lawyers met and resolved not to accept any new cases after September 6 if legislation providing for an increase in their fees had not passed by that date. Immediately following the meeting, they prepared (and most of them signed) a petition stating:

> "We, the undersigned private criminal lawyers practicing in the Superior Court of the District of Columbia, agree that unless we are granted a substantial increase in our hourly rate we will cease accepting new appointments under the Criminal Justice Act."

On September 6, 1983, about 90 percent of the CJA regulars refused to accept any new assignments. Thereafter, SCTLA arranged a series of events to attract the attention of the news media and to obtain additional support. These events were well publicized and did engender favorable editorial comment, but the trial examiner found that "there is no credible evidence that the District's eventual capitulation to the demands of the CJA lawyers was made in response to public pressure, or, for that matter, that this publicity campaign actually engendered any significant measure of public pressure." . . .

Within 10 days, the key figures in the District's criminal justice system "became convinced that the system was on the brink of collapse because of the refusal of CJA lawyers to take on new cases." On September 15, they hand-delivered a letter to the mayor describing why the situation was expected to "reach a crisis point" by early next week and urging the immediate enactment of a bill increasing all CJA rates to $35 per hour. The mayor promptly met with members of the strike committee and offered to support an immediate temporary increase to the $35 level as well as a subsequent permanent increase to $45 an hour for out-of-court time and $55 for in-court time.

At noon on September 19, 1983, over 100 CJA lawyers attended a SCTLA meeting and voted to accept the $35 offer and end the boycott. . . .

II

The Federal Trade Commission (FTC) filed a complaint against SCTLA and four of its officers (respondents) alleging that they had "entered into an agreement among themselves and with other lawyers to restrain trade by refusing to compete for or accept new appointments under the CJA program beginning on September 6, 1983, unless and until the District of Columbia increased the fees offered under the CJA program." The complaint alleged that virtually all of the attorneys who regularly compete for or accept new appointments under the CJA program had joined the agreement. The FTC characterized respondents' conduct as "a conspiracy to fix prices and to conduct a boycott" and concluded that they were engaged in "unfair methods of competition in violation of § 5 of the FTC Act."

. . . [T]he FTC rejected each of respondents' defenses. It held that their "coercive, concerted refusal to deal" had the "purpose and effect of raising prices" and was illegal per se. . . . [T]he FTC refused to conclude that the boycott was harmless, noting that the "boycott forced the city government to increase the CJA fees from a level that had been sufficient to obtain an adequate supply of CJA lawyers to a level satisfactory to the respondents. The city must, as a result of the boycott, spend an additional $4 million to $5 million a year to obtain legal services for indigents. We find that these are substantial anticompetitive effects resulting from the respondents' conduct." . . .

The Court of Appeals vacated the FTC order and remanded for a determination whether respondents possessed "significant market power." It concluded . . . that "the SCTLA boycott did contain an element of expression warranting First Amendment protection." It noted that boycotts have historically been used as a dramatic means of expression and that respondents intended to convey a political message to the public at large. It therefore concluded that under *United States v. O'Brien*, 391 U.S. 367 (1968), a restriction on this form of expression could not be justified unless it is no greater than is essential to an important governmental interest. This test, the Court reasoned, could not be satisfied by the application of an otherwise appropriate per se rule, but instead required the enforcement agency to "prove rather than presume that the evil against which the Sherman Act is directed looms in the conduct it condemns." . . .

III

. . . We may assume that the preboycott rates were unreasonably low, and that the increase has produced better legal representation for indigent defendants. Moreover, given that neither indigent criminal defendants nor the lawyers who represent them command any special appeal with the electorate, we may also assume that without the boycott there would have been no increase in District CJA fees at least until the Congress amended the federal statute. These assumptions do not control the case, for it is not our task to pass upon the social utility or political wisdom of price-fixing agreements.

As the ALJ, the FTC, and the Court of Appeals all agreed, respondents' boycott "constituted a classic restraint of trade within the meaning of Section 1 of the Sherman Act." As such, it also violated the prohibition against unfair methods of competition in § 5 of the FTC Act. . . . Prior to the boycott CJA lawyers were in competition with one another, each deciding independently whether and how often to offer to provide services to the District at CJA rates. The agreement among the CJA lawyers was designed to obtain higher prices for their services and was implemented by a concerted refusal to serve an important customer in the market for legal services and, indeed, the only customer in the market for the particular services that CJA regulars offered. "This constriction of supply is the essence of "price-fixing," whether it be accomplished by agreeing upon a price, which will decrease the quantity demanded, or by agreeing upon an output, which will increase the price offered." The horizontal arrangement among these competitors was unquestionably a "naked restraint" on price and output. . . .

It is of course true that the city purchases respondents' services because it has a constitutional duty to provide representation to indigent defendants. It is likewise true that the quality of representation may improve when rates are increased. Yet neither of these facts is an acceptable justification for an otherwise unlawful restraint of trade. As we have remarked before, the "Sherman Act reflects a legislative judgment that ultimately competition will produce not only lower prices, but also better goods and services." *National Society of Professional Engineers v. United States.* This judgment "recognizes that all elements of a bargain — quality, service, safety, and durability — and not just the immediate cost, are favorably affected by the free opportunity to select among alternative offers." That is equally so when the quality of legal advocacy, rather than engineering design, is at issue. . . .

Our decision in *Noerr* in no way detracts from this conclusion. In *Noerr* we "considered whether the Sherman Act prohibited a publicity campaign waged by railroads" and "designed to foster the adoption of laws destructive of the trucking business, to create an atmosphere of distaste for truckers among the general public, and to impair the relationships existing between truckers and their customers." Interpreting the Sherman Act in the light of the First Amendment's Petition Clause, the Court noted that "at least insofar as the railroads' campaign was directed toward obtaining governmental action, its legality was not at all affected by any anticompetitive purpose it may have had."

It of course remains true that "no violation of the Act can be predicated upon mere attempts to influence the passage or enforcement of laws," even if the defendants' sole purpose is to impose a restraint upon the trade of their competitors. But in the *Noerr* case the alleged restraint of trade was the intended consequence of legislation; in this case the boycott was the *means* by which respondents sought to obtain favorable legislation. The restraint of trade that was implemented while the boycott lasted would have had precisely the same anticompetitive consequences during that period even if no legislation had been enacted. In *Noerr*, the desired legislation would have created the restraint on the truckers' competition; in this case the emergency legislative response to the boycott put an end to the restraint.

. . . .

The lawyers' association argues that if its conduct would otherwise be prohibited by the Sherman Act and the Federal Trade Act, it is nonetheless protected by the First Amendment rights recognized in *Claiborne Hardware*. That case arose after black citizens boycotted white merchants in Claiborne County, Miss. The white merchants sued under state law to recover losses from the boycott. We found that the "right of the States to regulate economic activity could not justify a complete prohibition against a nonviolent, politically motivated boycott designed to force governmental and economic change and to effectuate rights guaranteed by the Constitution itself." We accordingly held that "the nonviolent elements of petitioners' activities are entitled to the protection of the First Amendment."

The lawyers' association contends that because it, like the boycotters in *Claiborne Hardware*, sought to vindicate constitutional rights, it should enjoy a similar First Amendment protection. It is, of course, clear that the association's efforts to publicize the boycott, to explain the merit of its cause, and to lobby District officials to enact favorable legislation — like similar activities in *Claiborne Hardware* — were activities that were fully protected by the First Amendment. But nothing in the FTC's order would curtail such activities, and nothing in the FTC's reasoning condemned any of those activities.

The activity that the FTC order prohibits is a concerted refusal by CJA lawyers to accept any further assignments until they receive an increase in their compensation; the undenied objective of their boycott was an economic advantage for those who agreed to participate. It is true that the *Claiborne Hardware* case also involved a boycott. That boycott, however, differs in a decisive respect. Those who joined the *Claiborne Hardware* boycott sought no special advantage for themselves. They were black citizens in Port Gibson, Mississippi, who had been the victims of political, social, and economic discrimination for many years. They sought only the equal respect and equal treatment to which they were constitutionally entitled. They struggled "to change a social order that had consistently treated them as second class citizens." As we observed, the campaign was not intended "to destroy legitimate competition." Equality and freedom are preconditions of the free market, and not commodities to be haggled over within it.

The same cannot be said of attorney's fees. As we recently pointed out, our reasoning in *Claiborne Hardware* is not applicable to a boycott conducted by business competitors who "stand to profit financially from a lessening of competition in the boycotted market." *Allied Tube Corp. v. Indian Head*. No matter how altruistic the motives of respondents may have been, it is undisputed that their immediate objective was to increase the price that they would be paid for their services. Such an economic boycott is well within the category that was expressly distinguished in the *Claiborne Hardware* opinion itself. . . .

V

Respondents' concerted action in refusing to accept further CJA assignments until their fees were increased was thus a plain violation of the antitrust laws. The exceptions derived from *Noerr* and *Claiborne Hardware* have no application to respondents' boycott. . . .

The Court of Appeals, however, crafted a new exception to the per se rules, and it is this exception which provoked the FTC's petition to this Court. The Court of Appeals derived its exception from *United States v. O'Brien*, 391 U.S. 367 (1968). In that case O'Brien had burned his Selective Service registration certificate on the steps of the South Boston Courthouse. He did so before a sizable crowd and with the purpose of advocating his antiwar beliefs. We affirmed his conviction. We held that the governmental interest in regulating the "nonspeech element" of his conduct adequately justified the incidental restriction on First Amendment freedoms. Specifically, we concluded that the statute's incidental restriction on O'Brien's freedom of expression was no greater than necessary to further the Government's interest in requiring registrants to have valid certificates continually available.

However, the Court of Appeals held that, in light of *O'Brien*, the expressive component of respondents' boycott compelled courts to apply the antitrust laws "prudently and with sensitivity," with a "special solicitude for the First Amendment rights" of respondents. The Court of Appeals concluded that the governmental interest in prohibiting boycotts is not sufficient to justify a restriction on the communicative element of the boycott unless the FTC can prove, and not merely presume, that the boycotters have market power. Because the Court of Appeals imposed this special requirement upon the Government, it ruled that per se antitrust analysis was inapplicable to boycotts having an expressive component.

There are at least two critical flaws in the Court of Appeals' antitrust analysis: it exaggerates the significance of the expressive component in respondents' boycott and it denigrates the importance of the rule of law that respondents violated. Implicit in the conclusion of the Court of Appeals are unstated assumptions that most economic boycotts do not have an expressive component, and that the categorical prohibitions against price fixing and boycotts are merely rules of "administrative convenience" that do not serve any substantial governmental interest unless the price-fixing competitors actually possess market power. . . .

In any event, however, we cannot accept the Court of Appeals' characterization of this boycott or the antitrust laws. Every concerted refusal to do business with a potential customer or supplier has an expressive component. At one level, the competitors must exchange their views about their objectives and the means of obtaining them. The most blatant, naked price-fixing agreement is a product of communication, but that is surely not a reason for viewing it with special solicitude. At another level, after the terms of the boycotters' demands have been agreed upon, they must be communicated to its target: "we will not do business until you do what we ask." That expressive component of the boycott conducted by these respondents is surely not unique. On the contrary, it is the hallmark of every effective boycott. . . .

In sum, there is thus nothing unique about the "expressive component" of respondents' boycott. A rule that requires courts to apply the antitrust laws "prudently and with sensitivity" whenever an economic boycott has an "expressive component" would create a gaping hole in the fabric of those laws. Respondents' boycott thus has no special characteristics meriting an exemption from the per se rules of antitrust law. . . .

The judgment of the Court of Appeals is accordingly reversed insofar as that court held the per se rules inapplicable to the lawyers' boycott. The case is remanded for further proceedings consistent with this opinion.

NOTES AND QUESTIONS

1. 1. Of what significance is the fact that the lawyers' boycott was "well publicized"? Should the per se rule be reserved for secret practices, such as price fixing? Wouldn't that encourage people to bring dubious practices into the open?

2. Normally, the Federal Trade Commission has only the power to obtain a "cease and desist" order barring further antitrust violations. But the District of Columbia in this case may have an antitrust damages action under Section 1 of the Sherman Act. How would the damages be measured?

3. After the *Trial Lawyers* decision, what is the status of *Missouri v. National Organization for Women*, reprinted in Chapter 4? Was that boycott more like the one in *Trial Lawyers*, or like the one in *Claiborne Hardware*?

4. Does *Trial Lawyers* suggest a "commercial" exception to *Noerr* when the government acts as a purchaser of services rather than as a policy maker in the more abstract sense? Some courts have found such an exception, suggesting that in such cases "the government . . . is not acting as a political body but as a participant in the marketplace." *General Aircraft Corp. v. Air Am.*, 482 F. Supp. 3, 7 (D.D.C. 1979). Most lower courts have refused to recognize a commercial exception. For example, in *Airport Car Rental Antitrust Litig.*, 693 F.2d 84 (9th Cir. 1982), the Ninth Circuit found no exception for a transaction in which the antitrust defendants, car rental companies, attempted to convince state airport officials to restrict the leasing of airport space to themselves and not make it available to their competitors. However, weakly stated dicta in the Supreme Court's decision in *City of Columbia & Columbia Outdoor Advertising, Inc. v. Omni Outdoor Advertising, Inc.*, 499 U.S. 365, 375 (1991), reprinted *infra*, suggested that "immunity does not necessarily obtain where the State acts not in a regulatory capacity but as a commercial participant in a given market."

What if the antitrust plaintiff alleges that the antitrust defendant bribed a government official to take some action that worked to the plaintiff's disadvantage? On the one hand, the injury was caused by governmental, not by private, action. On the other hand, the legal political process does not include bribery, and the First Amendment does not protect it. Many plaintiffs have alleged that public officials were somehow "co-conspirators" with the antitrust defendant in creating the statutory scheme that injured the plaintiffs. *See, e.g., Affiliated Capital Corp. v. City of Houston*, 735 F.2d 1555 (5th Cir. 1984), *cert. denied* 474 U.S. 1053 (1986). *See* Calkins, *Developments in Antitrust and the First Amendment: The Disaggregation of Noerr*, 57 ANTITRUST L.J. 2 (1988). The Supreme Court's *Columbia* decision, reprinted *infra*, suggests that even bribery is protected.

5. In *Mass. School of Law at Andover v. ABA*, 107 F.3d 1026 (3d Cir.), *cert. denied*, 522 U.S. 907 (1997), the plaintiff, a law school which was denied accreditation by the ABA, alleged that many states prevented graduates from unaccredited law schools from taking the state's bar examination. The court responded that *Noerr* protected the ABA's presentation of accrediting recommendations to state governments, with the result that the government itself rather than the ABA decided which law school graduates were eligible for bar admissions.

However, the plaintiff also alleged that "independent of any bar examination requirements, it was injured by the stigmatic effect in the market place of the denial of accreditation." *Id.* at 1037. The court concluded that such injury was merely incidental to the ABA's legitimate petitioning efforts and thus protected under *Noerr* as well: "Discussing the quality and competence of its decisions is a legitimate, although somewhat indirect, way of petitioning the states to continue to follow its guidance. Yet, such activity is no more indirect than the public relations campaign held to be petitioning in *Noerr*."

[B] The "Sham" Exception

In *Eastern R.R. Presidents Conf. v. Noerr Motor Freight, Inc.*, 365 U.S. 127 (1961), the Supreme Court suggested an exception to its rule insulating petitions to the government from antitrust liability: "There may be situations in which a publicity campaign, ostensibly directed toward influencing governmental action, is a mere sham to cover what is actually nothing more than an attempt to interfere directly with the business relationships of a competitor and the application of the Sherman Act would be justified."

A decade later in *California Motor Transp. Co. v. Trucking Unlimited*, 404 U.S. 508 (1972), the Court found that such a "sham" might have existed. The antitrust defendants and antitrust plaintiffs were competing trucking companies. The plaintiffs challenged that the defendants filed a variety of administrative and judicial actions before state and federal tribunals in order to deny the plaintiffs the right to operate in parts of the California trucking market. In distinguishing the *Noerr* and *Pennington* decisions, the Court said:

> In the present case . . . the allegations are not that the conspirators sought "to influence public officials," but that they sought to bar their competitors from meaningful access to adjudicatory tribunals and so to usurp that decision-making process. It is alleged that petitioners "instituted the proceedings and actions . . . with or without probable cause, and regardless of the merits of the cases." The nature of the views pressed does not, of course, determine whether First Amendment rights may be invoked; but they may bear upon a purpose to deprive the competitors of

meaningful access to the agencies and courts. . . .

. . . [U]nethical conduct in the setting of the adjudicatory process often results in sanctions. Perjury of witnesses is one example. Use of a patent obtained by fraud to exclude a competitor from the market may involve a violation of the antitrust laws, as we held in *Walker Process Equipment v. Food Machinery & Chemical Corp.*, 382 U.S. 172, 175–177 (1965). Conspiracy with a licensing authority to eliminate a competitor may also result in an antitrust transgression. *Continental Ore Co. v. Union Carbide & Carbon Corp.*, 370 U.S. 690, 707 (1962). . . . Similarly, bribery of a public purchasing agent may constitute a violation of § 2(c) of the Clayton Act, as amended by the Robinson-Patman Act. . . .

> There are many other forms of illegal and reprehensible practice which may corrupt the administrative or judicial processes and which may result in antitrust violations. Misrepresentations, condoned in the political arena, are not immunized when used in the adjudicatory process. Opponents before agencies or courts often think poorly of the other's tactics, motions, or defenses and may readily call them baseless. One claim, which a court or agency may think baseless, may go unnoticed; but a pattern of baseless, repetitive claims may emerge which leads the factfinder to conclude that the administrative and judicial processes have been abused. . . . Insofar as the administrative or judicial processes are involved, action of that kind cannot acquire immunity by seeking refuge under the umbrella of "political expression."

The "sham" exception is most often invoked by antitrust plaintiffs challenging improperly motivated litigation, as in the following case, or complaints before administrative agencies as antitrust violations.

PROFESSIONAL REAL ESTATE INVESTORS, INC. v. COLUMBIA PICTURES INDUSTRIES, INC.
508 U.S. 49 (1993)

JUSTICE THOMAS delivered the opinion of the Court.

This case requires us to define the "sham" exception to the doctrine of antitrust immunity first identified in *Eastern R. Presidents Conference v. Noerr Motor Freight, Inc.*, 365 U.S. 127 (1961), as that doctrine applies in the litigation context. Under the sham exception, activity "ostensibly directed toward influencing governmental action" does not qualify for *Noerr* immunity if it "is a mere sham to cover . . . an attempt to interfere directly with the business relationships of a competitor." We hold that litigation cannot be deprived of immunity as a sham unless the litigation is objectively baseless. . . .

I

Petitioners Professional Real Estate Investors, Inc., and Kenneth F. Irwin (collectively, PRE) operated La Mancha Private Club and Villas, a resort hotel in Palm Springs, California. Having installed videodisc players in the resort's hotel rooms and assembled a library of more than 200 motion picture titles, PRE rented videodiscs to guests for in-room viewing. . . . Respondents, Columbia Pictures Industries, Inc., and seven other major motion picture studios (collectively, Columbia), held copyrights to the motion pictures recorded on the videodiscs that PRE purchased. Columbia also licensed the transmission of copyrighted motion pictures to hotel rooms through a wired cable system called Spectradyne. PRE therefore competed with Columbia not only for the viewing market at La Mancha but also for the broader market for in-room entertainment services in hotels. In 1983, Columbia sued PRE for alleged copyright infringement through the rental of videodiscs for viewing in hotel rooms. PRE counterclaimed, charging Columbia with violations of §§ 1 and 2 of the Sherman Act. . . . In particular, PRE alleged that Columbia's copyright action was a mere sham that cloaked underlying acts of monopolization and conspiracy to restrain trade. . . .

Columbia did not dispute that PRE could freely sell or lease lawfully purchased videodiscs under the Copyright Act's "first sale" doctrine, see 17 U.S.C. § 109(a). . . . [S]ummary judgment depended solely on whether rental of video-discs for in-room viewing infringed Columbia's exclusive right to "perform the copyrighted work[s] publicly." § 106(4). Ruling that such rental did not constitute public performance, the District Court entered summary judgment for PRE. The Court of Appeals affirmed on the grounds that a hotel room was not a "public place" and that PRE did not "transmit or otherwise communicate" Columbia's motion pictures. 866 F.2d 278 (9th Cir. 1989).

On remand, Columbia sought summary judgment on PRE's antitrust claims, arguing that the original copyright infringement action was no sham and was therefore entitled to immunity under [*Noerr*]. . . . [T]he District Court granted the motion: "It was clear from the manner in which the case was presented that [Columbia was] seeking and expecting a favorable judgment. . . . " The Court of Appeals affirmed . . . , [reasoning] that the existence of probable cause "pre-clude[d] the application of the sham exception as a matter of law" because "a suit brought with probable cause does not fall within the sham exception to the *Noerr-Pennington* doctrine." Finally, the court observed that PRE's failure to show that "the copyright infringement action was baseless" rendered irrelevant any "evidence of [Columbia's] subjective intent." It accordingly rejected PRE's request for further discovery on Columbia's intent. . . .

II

PRE contends that "the Ninth Circuit erred in holding that an antitrust plaintiff must, as a threshold prerequisite . . . , establish that a sham lawsuit is baseless as a matter of law." It invites us to adopt an approach under which either "indifference to . . . outcome," *ibid.*, or failure to prove that a petition for redress of grievances "would . . . have been brought but for [a] predatory motive," would expose a defendant to antitrust liability under the sham exception. We decline PRE's invitation. Those who petition government for redress are generally immune from antitrust liability. We first recognized in *Noerr* that "the Sherman Act does not prohibit . . . persons from associating together in an attempt to persuade the legislature or the executive to take particular action with respect to a law that would produce a restraint or a monopoly." . . . In light of the government's "power to act in [its] representative capacity" and "to take actions . . . that operate to restrain trade," we reasoned that the Sherman Act does not punish "political activity" through which "the people . . . freely inform the government of their wishes." *Noerr*, 365 U.S., at 137. Nor did we "impute to Congress an intent to invade" the First Amendment right to petition. *Id.*, at 138. *Noerr*, however, withheld immunity from "sham" activities because "application of the Sherman Act would be justified" when petitioning activity, "ostensibly directed toward influencing governmental action, is a mere sham to cover . . . an attempt to interfere directly with the business relationships of a competitor." *Id.*, at 144. In *Noerr* itself, we found that a publicity campaign by railroads seeking legislation harmful to truckers was no sham in that the "effort to influence legislation" was "not only genuine but also highly successful." *Ibid.* In *California Motor Transport Co. v. Trucking Unlimited*, 404 U.S. 508 (1972), we elaborated on *Noerr* in two relevant respects. First, we extended *Noerr* to "the approach of citizens . . . to administrative agencies . . . and to courts." Second, we held that the complaint showed a sham not entitled to immunity when it contained allegations that one group of highway carriers "sought to bar . . . competitors from meaningful access to adjudicatory tribunals and so to usurp that decisionmaking process" by "institut[ing] . . . proceedings and actions . . . with or without probable cause, and regardless of the merits of the cases." We left unresolved the question presented by this case — whether litigation may be sham merely because a subjective expectation of success does not motivate the litigant. We now answer this question in the negative and hold that an objectively reasonable effort to litigate cannot be sham regardless of subjective intent.

Our original formulation of antitrust petitioning immunity required that unprotected activity lack objective reasonableness. *Noerr* rejected the contention that an attempt "to influence the passage and enforcement of laws" might lose immunity merely because the lobbyists' "sole purpose . . . was to destroy [their] competitors." . . . "*Noerr* shields from the Sherman Act a concerted effort to influence public officials regardless of intent or purpose." *Pennington*, 381 U.S., at 670.

Nothing in *California Motor Transport* retreated from these principles. Indeed, we recognized that recourse to agencies and courts should not be condemned as sham until a reviewing court has "discern[ed] and draw[n]" the "difficult line" separating objectively reasonable claims from "a pattern of baseless, repetitive claims . . . which leads the factfinder to conclude that the administrative and judicial processes have been abused." Our recognition of a sham in that case signifies that the institution of legal proceedings "without probable cause" will give rise to a sham if such activity effectively "bar[s] . . . competitors from meaningful access to adjudicatory tribunals and so . . . usurp[s] th[e] decisionmaking process." Since *California Motor Transport*, we have consistently assumed that the sham exception contains an indispensable objective component. We have described a sham as "evidenced by repetitive lawsuits carrying the hallmark of *insubstantial* claims." *Otter Tail Power Co. v. United States*, 410 U.S. 366, 380 (1973) (emphasis added). We regard as sham "private action that is not genuinely aimed at procuring favorable government action," as opposed to "a valid effort to influence government action." *Allied Tube & Conduit Corp. v. Indian Head, Inc.*, 486 U.S. 492, 500, n. 4

(1988). And we have explicitly observed that a successful "effort to influence governmental action . . . certainly cannot be characterized as a sham." . . .

. . . In *Columbia v. Omni Outdoor Advertising, Inc.*, 499 U.S. 365 (1991), we similarly held that challenges to allegedly sham petitioning activity must be resolved according to objective criteria. We dispelled the notion that an antitrust plaintiff could prove a sham merely by showing that its competitor's "purposes were to delay [the plaintiff's] entry into the market and even to deny it a meaningful access to the appropriate . . . administrative and legislative fora." . . .

III

We now outline a two-part definition of "sham" litigation. First, the lawsuit must be objectively baseless in the sense that no reasonable litigant could realistically expect success on the merits. If an objective litigant could conclude that the suit is reasonably calculated to elicit a favorable outcome, the suit is immunized under *Noerr*, and an antitrust claim premised on the sham exception must fail. Only if challenged litigation is objectively meritless may a court examine the litigant's subjective motivation. Under this second part of our definition of sham, the court should focus on whether the baseless lawsuit conceals "an attempt to interfere directly with the business relationships of a competitor," *Noerr, supra*, at 144. . . .

Of course, even a plaintiff who defeats the defendant's claim to *Noerr* immunity by demonstrating both the objective and the subjective components of a sham must still prove a substantive antitrust violation. Proof of a sham merely deprives the defendant of immunity; it does not relieve the plaintiff of the obligation to establish all other elements of his claim. . . .

IV

We conclude that the Court of Appeals properly affirmed summary judgment for Columbia on PRE's antitrust counterclaim. Under the objective prong of the sham exception, the Court of Appeals correctly held that sham litigation must constitute the pursuit of claims so baseless that no reasonable litigant could realistically expect to secure favorable relief. The existence of probable cause to institute legal proceedings precludes a finding that an antitrust defendant has engaged in sham litigation. The notion of probable cause, as understood and applied in the common law tort of wrongful civil proceedings, requires the plaintiff to prove that the defendant lacked probable cause to institute an unsuccessful civil lawsuit and that the defendant pressed the action for an improper, malicious purpose. . . . Probable cause to institute civil proceedings requires no more than a "reasonabl[e] belie[f] that there is a chance that [a] claim may be held valid upon adjudication" (internal quotation marks omitted). *Hubbard v. Beatty & Hyde, Inc.*, 343 Mass. 258, 262, 178 N.E.2d 485, 488 (1961); Restatement (Second) of Torts § 675, Comment e, pp. 454–455 (1977). Because the absence of probable cause is an essential element of the tort, the existence of probable cause is an absolute defense. . . . Just as evidence of anticompetitive intent cannot affect the objective prong of *Noerr*'s sham exception, a showing of malice alone will neither entitle the wrongful civil proceedings plaintiff to prevail nor permit the factfinder to infer the absence of probable cause. When a court has found that an antitrust defendant claiming *Noerr* immunity had probable cause to sue, that finding compels the conclusion that a reasonable litigant in the defendant's position could realistically expect success on the merits of the challenged lawsuit. Under our decision today, therefore, a proper probable cause determination irrefutably demonstrates that an antitrust plaintiff has not proved the objective prong of the sham exception and that the defendant is accordingly entitled to *Noerr* immunity. . . . Columbia enjoyed the "exclusive righ[t] . . . to perform [its] copyrighted" motion pictures "publicly." 17 U.S.C. § 106(4). Regardless of whether it intended any monopolistic or predatory use, Columbia acquired this statutory right. . . . Indeed, to condition a copyright upon a demonstrated lack of anticompetitive intent would upset the notion of copyright as a "limited grant" of "monopoly privilege s" intended simultaneously "to motivate the creative activity of authors" and "to give the public appropriate access to their work product." *Sony Corp. of America v. Universal City Studios, Inc.*, 464 U.S. 417, 429 (1984).

When the District Court entered summary judgment for PRE on Columbia's copyright claim in 1986, it was by no means clear whether PRE's videodisc rental activities intruded on Columbia's copyrights. At that time, the Third Circuit and a District Court within the Third Circuit had held that the rental of video cassettes for viewing in on-site, private screening rooms infringed on the copyright owner's right of public performance. *Columbia Pictures Industries, Inc. v. Redd Horne, Inc.*, 749 F.2d 154 (1984); *Columbia Pictures Industries, Inc. v. Aveco, Inc.*, 612 F. Supp. 315 (MD Pa. 1985), *aff'd*, 800 F.2d 59 (3d Cir. 1986). Although the District Court and the Ninth Circuit distinguished these decisions by reasoning that hotel rooms offered a degree of privacy more akin to the home than to a video rental store, . . . copyright scholars criticized both the reasoning and the outcome of the Ninth Circuit's decision, see 1 P. Goldstein, Copyright: Principles, Law and Practice § 5.7.2.2, pp. 616–619 (1989); 2 M. Nimmer & D. Nimmer, Nimmer on Copyright § 8.14[C][3], pp. 8-168 to 8-173 (1992). The Seventh Circuit expressly "decline[d] to follow" the Ninth Circuit and adopted instead the Third Circuit's definition of a "public place." *Video Views, Inc. v. Studio 21, Ltd.*, 925 F.2d 1010, 1020, *cert. denied*, 502 U.S. (1991). In light of the unsettled condition of the law, Columbia plainly had probable cause to sue. Any reasonable copyright owner in Columbia's position could have believed that it had some chance of winning an infringement suit against PRE. Even though it did not survive PRE's motion for summary judgment, Columbia's copyright action was arguably "warranted by existing law" or at the very least was based on an objectively "good faith argument for the extension, modification, or reversal of existing law." Fed. Rule Civ. Proc. 11. . . . A court could reasonably conclude that Columbia's infringement action was an objectively plausible effort to enforce rights. Accordingly, we conclude that PRE failed to establish the objective prong of *Noerr*'s sham exception.

Finally, the Court of Appeals properly refused PRE's request for further discovery on the economic circumstances of the underlying copyright litigation. As we have held, PRE could not pierce Columbia's *Noerr* immunity without proof that Columbia's infringement action was objectively baseless or frivolous. Thus, the District Court had no occasion to inquire whether Columbia was indifferent to the outcome on the merits of the copyright suit, whether any damages for infringement would be too low to justify Columbia's investment in the suit, or whether Columbia had decided to sue primarily for the benefit of collateral injuries inflicted through the use of legal process. Such matters concern Columbia's economic motivations in bringing suit, which were rendered irrelevant by the objective legal reasonableness of the litigation. The existence of probable cause eliminated any "genuine issue as to any material fact," Fed. Rule Civ. Proc. 56(c), and summary judgment properly issued. We affirm the judgment of the Court of Appeals.

So ordered.

JUSTICE STEVENS, with whom JUSTICE O'CONNOR joins, concurring in the judgment.

. . . I disagree with the Court's equation of "objectively baseless" with the answer to the question whether any "reasonable litigant could realistically expect success on the merits." There might well be lawsuits that fit the latter definition but can be shown to be objectively unreasonable, and thus shams. . . .

. . . The label "sham" [might] apply to a plaintiff who had some reason to expect success on the merits but because of its tremendous cost would not bother to achieve that result without the benefit of collateral injuries imposed on its competitor by the legal process alone. Litigation filed or pursued for such collateral purposes is fundamentally different from a case in which the relief sought in the litigation itself would give the plaintiff a competitive advantage or, perhaps, exclude a potential competitor from entering a market with a product that either infringes the plaintiff's patent or copyright or violates an exclusive franchise granted by a governmental body. The case before us today is in the latter, obviously legitimate, category. There was no unethical or other improper use of the judicial system; instead, respondents invoked the federal court's jurisdiction to determine whether they could lawfully restrain competition with petitioners. The relief they sought in their original action, if granted, would have had the anticompetitive consequences authorized by federal copyright law.

NOTES AND QUESTIONS

1. In a footnote, the Court added the following: "We need not decide here whether and, if so, to what extent *Noerr* permits the imposition of antitrust liability for a litigant's fraud or other misrepresentations (citing *Walker Process Equipment, Inc. v. Food Machinery & Chemical Corp.*, 382 U.S. 172, 176–177 (1965))."

Professional Real Estate thus seems to apply only to decisions where the underlying claim was based on a dubious *legal* theory. This considerably narrows the impact of the decision. For example, one of the most commonly litigated areas involving the "sham" exception is wrongfully-based patent or copyright infringement suits, such as *Walker Process, ibid.* But most claims of "sham" in that context refer to the patentee's factual misrepresentations in the patent application, its knowledge that the patent was in fact unenforceable, or that the defendant in the infringement action (now the antitrust plaintiff) was not really infringing. In such cases, the element of bad faith is that the antitrust defendant knew of *facts* that undermined its own legal claim. *Professional Real Estate* appears not to apply to such cases. *See Nobelpharma v. Implant Innovations*, 141 F.3d 1059 (Fed. Cir.), *cert. denied*, 525 U.S. 876 (1998), which upheld a jury instruction that if a patentee had committed "a knowing, willful and intentional act, misrepresentation or omission" before the Patent and Trademark Office in applying for its patent, and thus knew that the patent was unenforceable, then its subsequent infringement suit could constitute the basis for an antitrust violation. The court then found that the patentee brought its infringement suit "knowing that the '891 patent was either invalid or unenforceable and with the intent of interfering directly with 3I's ability to compete in the relevant market." The appellate court agreed, concluding that "if the evidence shows that the asserted patent was acquired by means of either a fraudulent misrepresentation or a fraudulent omission and that the party asserting the patent was aware of the fraud when bringing suit, such conduct can expose a patentee to liability under the antitrust laws."

Thus, as the court noted, infringement suits can be attacked as antitrust violations in two different ways. If a patent is valid but an infringement suit is *objectively* baseless — perhaps because the infringement defendant is clearly not infringing — then PRE would permit an attack on the baseless legal claim. By contrast, if the patent is invalid or unenforceable and the patentee knows this, then the infringement suit can be attacked as an antitrust violation even if the legal theory of the lawsuit is objectively sound.

2. In stating possible criteria for determining whether an *improperly* motivated infringement suit is a "sham," the Court suggests the factor "whether any damages for infringement would be too low to justify Columbia's investment in the suit." Suppose that the damages for infringement were $100,000, but Columbia predicted only a 25% chance of collecting $200,000, thus making the case worth about $50,000. Would that suggest "sham"? Suppose that 100 hotel and resort operators around the country were doing exactly what PRE was doing, and that the suit would "send a message" to these operators as well. In that case, what is the expected value of the suit?

3. 3. Suppose a dominant firm that owns several patents threatens to sue a rival for patent infringement unless the rival abandons a certain production process that competes with the dominant firm's patented process. The suit, if filed, would be a baseless "sham." (For the relationship between patent law and antitrust, see Chapter 6, *supra*.) Should a mere threat to sue, as opposed to a lawsuit itself, receive *Noerr-Pennington* protection?

A threat to sue is not a "petition" to the sovereign the way that an actual lawsuit is. But consider the consequences of holding that a threat to sue is not protected. Firms might then be forced to sue immediately rather than writing demand letters or making other threats to sue. The threat to sue, whether in the form of a demand letter or something else, is an important device for getting people to stop doing unlawful things without the need for a lawsuit. Most courts that have addressed the issue have held that a legitimate threat to sue is protected just as the lawsuit itself. As the Fifth Circuit put it, "[t]he litigator should not be protected only when he strikes without warning. If litigation is in good faith, a token of that sincerity is a warning that it will be commenced and a possible effort to compromise the dispute." *Virginia Panel Corp. v. Mac Panel Co.*, 133 F.3d 860 (Fed. Cir. 1997), *cert. denied*, 525 U.S. 815 (1998) (threats to file infringement suit protected). *Accord In re*

Innovatio IP Ventures, LLC Patent Litigation, 921 F. Supp. 2d 903 (N.D. Ill. 2013). However, just as legitimate threats are protected by *Noerr*, unjustified threats can fall within the "sham" exception. *See CVD v. Raytheon Co.*, 769 F.2d 842, 851 (1st Cir. 1985), *cert. denied*, 475 U.S. 1016 (1986).

Suppose a dominant firm not only threatens a competitor with a lawsuit but also writes a letter to the competitor's customers, telling them their supplier is behaving illegally and warning them of the consequences of subsequent legal action. Is the letter protected under *Noerr? See Alexander v. National Farmers Org.*, 687 F.2d 1183, 1200–1203 (8th Cir. 1982), *cert. denied*, 461 U.S. 937 (1983).

4. What happens if the petitioning activities are found to be a "sham?" From that point, the antitrust plaintiff must still prove the remaining elements of its claim. That is, the "sham" petition is not itself the entire violation. For example, sham petitioning by a single firm could be monopolization or an attempt to monopolize only if the requisite market power and dangerous probability of success elements were established as well. The *Professional Real Estate* opinion makes this clear: "Proof of a sham merely deprives the defendant of immunity; it does not relieve the plaintiff of the obligation to establish all other elements of his claim. . . . " Previously, not all courts had gotten it right. *See Rickards v. Canine Eye Registration Fund*, 783 F.2d 1329 (9th Cir.), *cert. denied*, 479 U.S. 851 (1986), which found that a group of antitrust defendants lacked market power but, nevertheless, that their "sham" petition constituted an antitrust violation.

5. The term "sham" applies not only to improperly motivated litigation or administrative actions, but also to certain improperly motivated requests for legislative action. The standards are different, however. Courts have strict rules governing pleadings and setting high standards for truthfulness. By contrast, the legislative process is much more rough and tumble. *See, e.g., Mercatus Group, LLC v. Lake Forest Hosp.*, 641 F.3d 834 (7th Cir. 2011), which concluded that *Noerr* immunized a hospital's "underhanded" lobbying to a village land use board in order to exclude a proposed diagnostic imaging facility. As the court observed:

> . . . the process by which the Board considered whether to grant Mercatus approval to develop the Shepard Land was decidedly legislative or political in nature. Both Mercatus and the Hospital engaged in *ex parte* lobbying of individual Board members prior to the hearings. Mercatus executives contacted or met personally with individual Board members, and at least one Board member even took a tour of Mercatus' facilities. A number of Lake Bluff residents also contacted the Board members to voice their views on the Mercatus project. This lobbying activity by advocates on both sides was perfectly legitimate, as would not be the case in an adjudicative proceeding.

In *City of Columbia & Columbia Outdoor Advertising, Inc. v. Omni Outdoor Advertising, Inc.*, 499 U.S. 365 (1991), reprinted *infra*, the Supreme Court accepted both a "state action" and a *Noerr* defense to a claim that an influential private firm's request for an ordinance injuring the plaintiff's business violated the antitrust laws. Here, the plaintiff's purpose in petitioning the government was to obtain passage of the anticompetitive ordinance, and the ordinance was actually passed. The portion of the opinion finding a "state action" exemption is reprinted later in this chapter.

The Court also refused to find that the request for the ordinance fell within *Noerr*'s "sham" exception, stating:

> The "sham" exception to *Noerr* encompasses situations in which persons use the governmental process as opposed to the outcome of that process as an anticompetitive weapon. A classic example is the filing of frivolous objections to the license application of a competitor, with no expectation of achieving denial of the license but simply in order to impose expense and delay. . . .
>
> Neither of the Court of Appeals' theories for application of the "sham" exception to the facts of the present case is sound. The court reasoned, first, that the jury could have concluded that COA's interaction with city officials "was actually nothing more than an attempt to interfere directly with the business relations of a competitor." This analysis relies upon language from *Noerr*, but ignores the import of the critical word "directly." Although COA indisputably set out to disrupt Omni's business relationships, it sought to do so not through the very process of lobbying, or of causing the city council to consider zoning measures, but rather through the ultimate product of that lobbying and consideration, viz., the zoning ordinances. The Court of Appeals' second theory was that the jury could have found "that COA's purposes were to delay Omni's entry into the market and even to deny it a meaningful access to the appropriate city administrative and legislative fora." But the purpose of delaying a competitor's entry into the market does not render lobbying activity a "sham," unless (as no evidence suggested was true here) the delay is sought to be achieved only by the lobbying process itself, and not by the governmental action that the lobbying seeks. "If *Noerr* teaches anything it is that an intent to restrain trade as a result of government action sought . . . does not foreclose protection." Sullivan, *Developments in the Noerr Doctrine*, 56 Antitrust L.J. 361, 362 (1987). As for "deny[ing] . . . meaningful access to the appropriate city administrative and legislative fora," that may render the manner of lobbying improper or even unlawful, but does not necessarily render it a "sham." We did hold in *California Motor Transport, supra*, that a conspiracy among private parties to monopolize trade by excluding a competitor from participation in the regulatory process did not enjoy *Noerr* protection. But *California Motor Transport* involved a context in which the conspirators' participation in the governmental process was itself claimed to be a "sham," employed as a means of imposing cost and delay. ("It is alleged that petitioners 'instituted the proceedings and actions . . . with or without probable cause, and regardless of the merits of the cases.'" 404 U.S., at 512.) The holding of the case is limited to that situation. To extend it to a context in which the regulatory process is being invoked genuinely, and not in a "sham" fashion, would produce precisely that conversion of antitrust law into regulation of the political process that we have sought to avoid. Any lobbyist or applicant, in addition to getting himself heard, seeks by procedural and other means to get his opponent ignored. Policing the legitimate boundaries of such defensive strategies, when they are conducted in the context of a genuine attempt to influence governmental

action, is not the role of the Sherman Act. In the present case, of course, any denial to Omni of "meaningful access to the appropriate city administrative and legislative fora" was achieved by COA in the course of an attempt to influence governmental action that, far from being a "sham," was if anything more in earnest than it should have been. If the denial was wrongful there may be other remedies, but as for the Sherman Act, the *Noerr* exemption applies.

6. In *Baltimore Scrap Corp. v. David J. Joseph Co.*, 237 F.3d 394 (4th Cir. 2001), the Fourth Circuit found *Noerr-Pennington* immunity for a claimed "public interest" lawsuit challenging plaintiffs' zoning permit even though the suit was secretly financed by a competitor, and even though attorneys may have misrepresented that fact before the court. On the first fraud issue — failure to tell the citizen groups about who was financing "their" lawsuit, the court observed:

> This alleged fraud was solely between the parties. The defendants' failure to tell the citizen groups that they were behind the litigation did not deceive the courts because the courts were not the target of this alleged deception. As the district court noted, Baltimore Scrap's "central problem, which it is unable to overcome, is that the arguments presented by the citizens groups were legitimate, both objectively and subjectively."

On the second claim, of fraud to the court:

> The problem with Baltimore Scrap's argument remains, however, that [the lawyer's] alleged misstatements were simply not material. CHIEF JUDGE HAMMERMAN, before he ruled, stated that he saw the hand of the defendants in the lawsuit. Indeed, he presumed the defendants were involved before he issued his opinion against the citizen groups and the defendants. The result would have been the same even if [the lawyer] had admitted the defendants' role because no judicial ruling was based on the erroneous assumption that the citizens alone were pursuing the appeal and fully funding the litigation.

> If [the lawyer] did indeed misrepresent facts to the court, the proper remedy here is through Maryland law, whether it be through the sanctioning process of the state bar. . . .

The court then reiterated "that the Supreme Court has not approved a fraud exception to *Noerr-Pennington* immunity at all."

PROBLEM 9.2

Hospitals in many states cannot be built or enlarged unless the operators can acquire a "Certificate of Need." The Certificate of Need is granted only after a government agency determines that patient load in a community is sufficient to support the new hospital space. The purpose of the Certificate of Need requirement is to keep hospital costs low.

Regis and Alegis are large proprietary hospitals in a medium-sized town. Together they account for 75% of hospital capacity in the area. When their only competitor, St. Francis, a Catholic hospital, sought to add a large wing, Regis and Alegis jointly objected to the regulatory agency that there was already plenty of hospital capacity. When the agency requested Regis and Alegis to supply proof, they submitted false information about patient demand over the preceding five years. The agency denied St. Francis' request for the new wing, and St. Francis sued Regis and Alegis, charging a conspiracy to monopolize the hospital market. Regis and Alegis raise *Noerr-Pennington* as a defense. Outcome? *See St. Joseph's Hosp. v. Hospital Corp. of Am.*, 795 F.2d 948 (11th Cir. 1986).

Alternatively, suppose that when St. Francis applied for its Certificate of Need, the agency requested it to supply information justifying more hospital space. In response, St. Francis submitted false information, which exaggerated patient demand for the previous five years. The existing hospitals then sue St. Francis under the antitrust laws. Outcome?

III PROBLEMS OF FEDERALISM: PREEMPTION AND THE "STATE ACTION" DOCTRINE

All state and local government regulation is subject to the limitation imposed by the Supremacy Clause of the Constitution that it will be trumped, or preempted, by inconsistent federal legislation. The preemption doctrine in the antitrust context simply considers whether such regulation is so inconsistent with federal antitrust policy that one must give way to the other. Ordinarily, the state or local regulation gives way. But the "State Action" doctrine, developed in Part B of this Section, notes an important exception where federal antitrust policy actually defers to state and local regulation.

[A] Preemption

FISHER v. CITY OF BERKELEY
475 U.S. 260 (1986)

JUSTICE MARSHALL delivered the opinion of the Court.

The question presented here is whether a rent control ordinance enacted by a municipality pursuant to popular initiative is unconstitutional because pre-empted by the Sherman Act.

I

In June 1980, the electorate of the City of Berkeley, California, enacted an initiative entitled "Ordinance 5261-N. S., Rent Stabilization and Eviction for Good Cause Ordinance," (hereafter Ordinance). . . . [T]he Ordinance establishes a base rent ceiling reflecting the rents in effect at the end of May 1980. A landlord may raise his rents from these levels only pursuant to an annual general adjustment of rent ceilings by a Rent Stabilization Board of appointed commissioners or after he is successful in petitioning the Board for an individual adjustment. A landlord who fails to register with the Board units covered by the Ordinance or who fails to adhere to the maximum allowable rent set under the Ordinance may be fined by the Board, sued by his tenants, or have rent legally withheld from him. If his violations are willful, he may face criminal penalties.

. . . .

Recognizing that the function of government may often be to tamper with free markets, correcting their failures and aiding their victims, this Court noted in *Rice v. Norman Williams Co.*, that a "state statute is not pre-empted by the federal antitrust laws simply because the state scheme may have an anticompetitive effect." See *Exxon Corp. v. Governor of Maryland*, 437 U.S. 117, 133 (1978). We have therefore held that a state statute should be struck down on pre-emption grounds "only if it mandates or authorizes conduct that necessarily constitutes a violation of the antitrust laws in all cases, or if it places irresistible pressure on a private party to violate the antitrust laws in order to comply with the statute." 458 U.S., at 661.

Appellants argue that Berkeley's Rent Stabilization Ordinance is pre-empted under *Rice* because it imposes rent ceilings across the entire rental market for residential units. Such a regime, they contend, clearly falls within the *per se* rule against price fixing, a rule that has been one of the settled points of antitrust enforcement since the earliest days of the Sherman Act. That the prices set here are ceilings rather than floors and that the public interest has been invoked to justify this stabilization should not, appellants argue, save Berkeley's regulatory scheme from condemnation under the *per se* rule.

Certainly there is this much truth to appellants' argument: Had the owners of residential rental property in Berkeley voluntarily banded together to stabilize rents in the city, their activities would not be saved from antitrust attack by claims that they had set reasonable prices out of solicitude for the welfare of their tenants. Moreover, it cannot be denied that Berkeley's Ordinance will affect the residential housing rental market in much the same way as would the philanthropic activities of this hypothetical trade association. What distinguishes the operation of Berkeley's Ordinance from the activities of a benevolent landlords' cartel is not that the Ordinance will necessarily have a different economic effect, but that the rent ceilings imposed by the Ordinance and maintained by the Stabilization Board have been unilaterally imposed by government upon landlords to the exclusion of private control.

The distinction between unilateral and concerted action is critical here. Adhering to the language of § 1, this Court has always limited the reach of that provision to "unreasonable restraints of trade effected by a 'contract, combination . . . , or conspiracy' between *separate* entities." *Copperweld Corp. v. Independence Tube Corp.*, 467 U.S. 752, 768 (1984) (emphasis in original). We have therefore deemed it "of considerable importance" that independent activity by a single entity be distinguished from a concerted effort by more than one entity to fix prices or otherwise restrain trade, *Monsanto Co. v. Spray-Rite Service Corp.*, 465 U.S. 752, 763 (1984). Even where a single firm's restraints directly affect prices and have the same economic effect as concerted action might have, there can be no liability under § 1 in the absence of agreement. *Id.*, at 760–761; *United States v. Parke, Davis & Co.*, 362 U.S. 29, 44 (1960). Thus, if the Berkeley Ordinance stabilizes rents without this element of concerted action, the program it establishes cannot run afoul of § 1.

Recognizing this concerted action requirement, appellants argue that the

Ordinance "forms a combination between [the City of Berkeley and its officials], on the one hand, and the property owners on the other. It also creates a horizontal combination among the landlords." In so arguing, appellants misconstrue the concerted action requirement of § 1. A restraint imposed unilaterally by government does not become concerted action within the meaning of the statute simply because it has a coercive effect upon parties who must obey the law. The ordinary relationship between the government and those who must obey its regulatory commands whether they wish to or not is not enough to establish a conspiracy. Similarly, the mere fact that all competing property owners must comply with the same provisions of the Ordinance is not enough to establish a conspiracy among landlords. Under Berkeley's Ordinance, control over the maximum rent levels of every affected residential unit has been unilaterally removed from the owners of those properties and given to the Rent Stabilization Board. While the Board may choose to respond to an individual landlord's petition for a special adjustment of a particular rent ceiling, it may decide not to. There is no meeting of the minds here. The owners of residential property in Berkeley have no more freedom to resist the city's rent controls than they do to violate any other local ordinance enforced by substantial sanctions.

There may be cases in which what appears to be a state- or municipality-administered price stabilization scheme is really a private price-fixing conspiracy, concealed under a "gauzy cloak of state involvement," *Midcal, supra*, at 106. This might occur even where prices are ostensibly under the absolute control of government officials. However, we have been given no indication that such corruption has tainted the rent controls imposed by Berkeley's Ordinance. Adopted by popular initiative, the Ordinance can hardly be viewed as a cloak for any conspiracy among landlords or between the landlords and the municipality. Berkeley's landlords have simply been deprived of the power freely to raise their rents. That is why they are here. And that is why their role in the stabilization program does not alter the restraint's unilateral nature.

Because under settled principles of antitrust law, the rent controls established by Berkeley's Ordinance lack the element of concerted action needed before they can be characterized as a *per se* violation of § 1 of the Sherman Act, we cannot say that the Ordinance is facially inconsistent with the federal antitrust laws. We therefore need not address whether, even if the controls were to mandate § 1 violations, they would be exempt under the state-action doctrine from antitrust scrutiny.

The judgment of the California Supreme Court is

Affirmed.

[JUSTICE BRENNAN's dissenting opinion is omitted.]

NOTES AND QUESTIONS

1. How broad is the antitrust immunity created by *Fisher*? Does *Fisher* hold that local governments are immune from federal antitrust challenge under Section 1 of the Sherman Act when there is no allegation or proof of concerted conduct between government officials and private parties? Is this the meaning of the Court's use of the term "unilateral"? Would such a rationale create immunity under Section 2 of the Sherman Act? Or, under Section 2 or 3 of the Clayton Act? *See* D. MANDELKER, J. GERARD & E.T. SULLIVAN, FEDERAL LAND USE LAW § 11.08 (1999). *See generally Westborough Mall v. City of Cape Girardeau*, 693 F.2d 733 (8th Cir. 1982).

    2. In *Exxon Corp. v. Governor of Md.*, 437 U.S. 117 (1978), the Supreme Court held that the mere fact that a statute was anticompetitive and inconsistent with the general policies of the Sherman Act did not mandate preemption unless the law actually forced private parties to violate the Sherman Act. It approved a state statute compelling the vertical disintegration of oil companies within the state.

    3. Liquor price-posting statutes have often been found to be preempted by the Sherman Act. For example, see the *Midcal* and *Schwegmann* cases, both discussed in the *Fisher* opinion. The statutes are preempted for compelling resale price maintenance, which is illegal per se.

    But this creates a conceptual problem. Where is the "agreement" between two persons? If a statute orders wholesalers to post a price and retailers to sell at the posted price, it is not compelling the wholesalers and retailers to "agree" with each other. To be sure, they may discuss the price and agree about it before it is posted, but that is quite a different matter. As *Fisher* makes clear, the mere compliance with the statute is likewise not an agreement between the private citizen and the state.

    In order to solve this conceptual difficulty, courts in price-posting cases have developed the concept of the "hybrid" restraint. For example, in *324 Liquor Corp. v. Duffy*, 479 U.S. 335 (1987), the Supreme Court struck down a statute requiring liquor wholesalers to post wholesale prices and retailers to set their prices at 112% or more of the posted wholesale price, but permitted wholesalers to sell cases of liquor at less than the posted price. This was a "hybrid" restraint, the court explained, because the statute granted the wholesalers the power to force the retailers to set a price independently of the price that the wholesalers actually charged. For example, a wholesaler could post a price of $100 a case, thus requiring the retailer to charge a per-bottle price totaling at least $112 per case. But under the statute, the wholesaler was then free to sell the case at any price it pleased. This, as the court observed, was merely compelling a form of resale price maintenance. *See* 1 P. AREEDA & H. HOVENKAMP, ANTITRUST LAW ¶ 217 (4th ed. 2013).

[B]   The "State Action" Doctrine

    The principal purpose of the antitrust laws is to regulate private conduct, not to second-guess regulatory decisions made by state and local government. If a particular restraint is authorized or compelled by a governmental regulation, it may be exempt from federal antitrust liability under the "state action" doctrine.

    The state action exemption from the antitrust laws must be distinguished from the very broad concept of "state action" used in litigation under the Fourteenth Amendment and the federal civil rights statutes. The Fourteenth Amendment concept of state action is expansive and applies to public officials at every governmental level other than federal, and sometimes even to private persons acting under color of state law. *See* L. TRIBE, AMERICAN CONSTITUTIONAL LAW §§ 18-1 to 18-7 (2d ed. 1988). By contrast, the antitrust "state action" exemption is strictly construed and applies only to legislation and regulations of the state itself, or of governmental subdivisions whose authority to regulate comes explicitly from a state.

In 1943, the Supreme Court announced the state action doctrine in *Parker v. Brown*, 317 U.S. 341 (1943), a case which challenged California's agricultural marketing regulation which restricted competition among raisin growers and permitted the fixing of prices at which growers could sell the raisins. The defendants named in *Parker* were state officials who had administrative responsibility for approving the "production zones" and "proration programs" for raisin producers. In rejecting the Sherman Act challenge, the Supreme Court's unanimous opinion stated that "nothing in the language of the Sherman Act or in its history . . . suggests that its purpose was to restrain a state or its officers or agents from activities directed by its legislature." *Id.* at 350–351. The result suggested that state conduct authorized by the state legislature was immune from antitrust challenge regardless of the degree of anticompetitiveness. The state, in other words, was free to substitute its judgment for that of the federal statutory scheme as to how competition was to be regulated. But the conduct had to be clearly that of the state. Private conduct, which was merely encouraged or perhaps authorized by the state, was not immunized under *Parker. Id.* at 352. Lower courts interpreted the *Parker v. Brown* exemption to cover Clayton Act violations as well. *See, e.g., Feldman v. Gardner*, 661 F.2d 1295, 1304 n.76 (D.C. Cir. 1981).

Thirty-two years after *Parker*, the Supreme Court was confronted with the issue whether the setting of minimum prices by lawyers, implicitly sanctioned but not mandated by a state Supreme Court rule, was protected from antitrust challenge. The Court reasoned in *Goldfarb v. Virginia State Bar*, 421 U.S. 773 (1975), that the state action defense could be invoked only if the state, through a sovereign act, *required* the challenged practice. *Id.* at 791. Applying this test to the facts in *Goldfarb*, the Court found that the minimum-fee schedule was not required by the state Supreme Court. Thus, the price fixing arrangement was not exempt from the antitrust laws. For a time, therefore, it appeared that the exemption applied only to private activities that were "compelled" by state law.

In *Bates v. State Bar*, 433 U.S. 350 (1977), the Supreme Court clarified these requirements. It held that a rule prohibiting advertising by attorneys, which was approved and supervised by the Arizona Supreme Court under its constitutional authority to enforce disciplinary rules, was exempt from antitrust scrutiny. The restraint was compelled, the Court reasoned, at the direction of the state acting as sovereign.

The Court has frequently considered the scope of the state action doctrine when a political subdivision such as a city, acting in its authorized capacity, is charged with an antitrust violation. In rejecting the defense generally as applied to cities, the Court in *City of Lafayette v. Louisiana Power & Light Co.*, 435 U.S. 389 (1978), held that "the *Parker* doctrine exempts only anticompetitive conduct engaged in as an act of government by the state as sovereign, or, by its subdivisions, pursuant to state policy to displace competition with regulation or monopoly public service." *Id.* at 413. *Lafayette* addressed the issue whether a city, which operated an electric power company and which was charged with "various antitrust offenses in the conduct" of the utility, could seek a dismissal of the antitrust charges under the *Parker* doctrine. The plurality opinion interjected federalism as the basis for holding that cities should not automatically be treated the same as states.

> Cities are not themselves sovereign; they do not receive all the federal deference of the States that create them. . . . *Parker*'s limitation of the exemption to "official action directed by a state," . . . is consistent with the fact that the States' subdivisions generally have not been treated as equivalents of the States themselves. In light of the serious economic dislocation which could result if cities were free to place their own parochial interests above the Nation's economic goals reflected in the antitrust laws, . . . we are especially unwilling to presume that Congress intended to exclude anticompetitive municipal action from their reach.

Id. at 412–413.

The Court, then, opined that cities could come within the state action immunity if evidence demonstrated that the state intended to displace a competition policy by authorizing the anticompetitive practices. 435 U.S. at 414.

CALIFORNIA RETAIL LIQUOR DEALERS ASS'N v. MIDCAL ALUMINUM, INC.
445 U.S. 97 (1980)

JUSTICE POWELL delivered the opinion of the Court.

In a state-court action, respondent Midcal Aluminum, Inc., a wine distributor, presented a successful antitrust challenge to California's resale price maintenance and price posting statutes for the wholesale wine trade. The issue in this case is whether those state laws are shielded from the Sherman Act by . . . the "state action" doctrine of *Parker v. Brown*. . . .

Under § 24866 (b) of the California Business and Professions Code, all wine producers, wholesalers, and rectifiers must file fair trade contracts or price schedules with the State. If a wine producer has not set prices through a fair trade contract, wholesalers must post a resale price schedule for that producer's brands. No state-licensed wine merchant may sell wine to a retailer at other than the price set "either in an effective price schedule or in an effective fair trade contract. . . . "

. . . A licensee selling below the established prices faces fines, license suspension, or outright license revocation. The State has no direct control over wine prices, and it does not review the reasonableness of the prices set by wine dealers.

Midcal Aluminum, Inc., is a wholesale distributor of wine in southern California. In July 1978, the Department of Alcoholic Beverage Control charged Midcal with selling 27 cases of wine for less than the prices set by the effective price schedule of the E. & J. Gallo Winery. . . . Midcal stipulated that the allegations were true. . . . Midcal then filed a writ of mandate in the California Court of Appeal for the Third Appellate District asking for an injunction against the State's wine pricing system.

The Court of Appeal ruled that the wine pricing scheme restrains trade in violation of the Sherman Act.

. . . .

California's system for wine pricing plainly constitutes resale price maintenance in violation of the Sherman Act. The wine producer holds the power to prevent price competition by dictating the prices charged by wholesalers. As Mr. JUSTICE HUGHES pointed out in *Dr. Miles*, [*see* Casebook, p. 421] such vertical control destroys horizontal competition as effectively as if wholesalers "formed a combination and endeavored to establish the same restrictions . . . by agreement with each other." . . .

[Our earlier] decisions establish two standards for antitrust immunity under *Parker v. Brown*. First, the challenged restraint must be "one clearly articulated and affirmatively expressed as state policy"; second, the policy must be "actively supervised" by the State itself. *City of Lafayette v. Louisiana Power & Light Co.*, 435 U.S. 389, 410 (1978) (opinion of BRENNAN, J.). The California system for wine pricing satisfies the first standard. The legislative policy is forthrightly stated and clear in its purpose to permit resale price maintenance. The program, however, does not meet the second requirement for *Parker* immunity. The State simply authorizes price setting and enforces the prices established by private parties. The State neither establishes prices nor reviews the reasonableness of the price schedules; nor does it regulate the terms of fair trade contracts. The State does not monitor market conditions or engage in any "pointed reexamination" of the program. The national policy in favor of competition cannot be thwarted by casting such a gauzy cloak of state involvement over what is essentially a private price-fixing arrangement. . . .

NOTES AND QUESTIONS

1. The "state action" doctrine is judicially created. Is it justified by the legislative history of the Sherman Act? It is difficult to conceive how the framers of the Sherman Act in 1890 could have imagined such a doctrine. Under the prevailing interpretations of the Commerce Clause there was an absolute line between interstate activities, which only the federal government could regulate (*see, e.g., Wabash, St. L. & Pac. Ry. v. Illinois*, 118 U.S. 557 (1886)), and intrastate activities, which only the states could control (*for example, United States v. E.C. Knight Co.*, 156 U.S. 1 (1895)). Furthermore, state judicial jurisdiction was absolutely limited to persons and activities within the state. *See, e.g., Pennoyer v. Neff*, 95 U.S. 714 (1878). As a result, in 1890, a state statute could constitutionally be applied only to activities entirely within that state's borders. At the same time, the Sherman Act, which was passed under the Commerce Clause, could not reach wholly intrastate activities. In such a regime, the "state action" doctrine simply had no place. *Parker v. Brown* was decided in 1943, one year after the Supreme Court had greatly expanded federal jurisdiction under the commerce clause to reach intrastate activities if they merely "affected" interstate commerce. *Wickard v. Filburn*, 317 U.S. 111 (1942). Only then did the modern "state action" doctrine become possible and, perhaps, necessary.

2.   In *Hoover v. Ronwin*, 466 U.S. 558 (1984), the plaintiff, who had taken the Arizona bar examination and failed, alleged that the Committee on Examination and Admissions, responsible for administering and grading the bar examination, "had set the grading scale . . . with reference to the number of new attorneys they thought desirable [to be admitted to the bar], rather than with reference to some 'suitable' level of competence." Ronwin claimed unlawful monopolization, but the Supreme Court found that the "state action" doctrine precluded liability. The Committee on Examination and Admissions was completely controlled by the state Supreme Court, which was a part of the state itself. Once the principal actor was identified as the state itself, no authorization from any other part of the state was needed, nor was "active supervision" required, because no private conduct was being challenged.

In *Southern Motor Carriers Rate Conf. v. United States*, 471 U.S. 48 (1985), the Court found the "state action" exemption to apply, but it appeared to hold that state rate-making agencies are not part of the state itself but, rather, separate entities requiring clearly articulated authorization from the state legislature, just as a municipality would. (See the discussions of the *Boulder, Hallie*, and *Columbia* decisions, *infra*.) However, in *Charley's Taxi Radio Dispatch v. SIDA of Haw.*, 810 F.2d 869 (9th Cir. 1987), the court held that the director of the state's Department of Transportation was part of the state itself, and needed no independent authorization from the legislature. In *Cine 42nd St. Theater Corp. v. Nederlander Org.*, 790 F.2d 1032 (2d Cir. 1986), the court held that the New York Urban Development Corporation, an incorporated public agency, was not the "state" for purposes of the "state action" doctrine, because it had been designed to facilitate urban development without the bureaucratic delays that had frustrated other projects. As a result, the court concluded, the Corporation should be considered distinct from ordinary state agencies.

NOTE: FEDERALISM AND THE "STATE ACTION" DOCTRINE

Midcal's outcome notwithstanding, the "state action" doctrine is highly deferential toward state and local regulation, is it not? Under *Fisher*, the *Parker* doctrine applies only to state or local regulation found to be preempted by the antitrust laws. In most areas of federal-state conflict, that is the end of the matter. Once a state or local regulation is found to be preempted by a valid federal statute, the regulation cannot be enforced. E.T. SULLIVAN & J. HARRISON, UNDERSTANDING ANTITRUST AND ITS ECONOMIC IMPLICATIONS 65–69 (6th ed. 2013).

Midcal not only permits continued enforcement of regulations that are preempted by the federal antitrust laws, but also gives state governments virtual *carte blanche* to exempt any type of regulation they choose, no matter how anticompetitive. The record of antitrust litigation involving local governments suggests that counties and municipalities often pass inefficient, "special interest" legislation designed to benefit a relatively small constituency at the expense of the community as a whole. Commentators have made the same point. *See, e.g.*, Kitch, Isaacson & Kasper, *The Regulation of Taxicabs in Chicago*, 14 J.L. & ECON. 285 (1971). Query: Why doesn't the electoral process keep inefficient, special interest legislation from being passed? *See* Farber & Frickey, *The Jurisprudence of Public Choice*, 65 TEX. L. REV. 873 (1987); Sunstein, *Interest Groups in American Public Law*, 38 STAN. L. REV. 29 (1985). Assuming that local governments or states are prone to pass inefficient legislation, is there any reason for thinking that Congress or a federal court interpreting the antitrust laws would do any better?

Some commentators have argued that a little less deference to state or local regulation would be a good idea. *See, e.g.*, Wiley, *A Capture Theory of Antitrust Federalism*, 99 HARV. L. REV. 713 (1986), arguing that less federal deference is in order if the state or local regulation is an obvious example of special interest "capture" of the regulatory process, and the activity is not protected by a specific federally created exemption. *See also* Cirace, *An Economic Analysis of the "State-Municipal Action" Antitrust Cases*, 61 TEX. L. REV. 481 (1982), arguing that federal law should preempt any local legislation that is not justified by a perceived market failure. *And see* Hovenkamp & MacKerron, *Municipal Regulation and Federal Antitrust Policy*, 32 UCLA L. REV. 719 (1985), arguing that federal deference is in order only if the state or local government is a better regulator of the conduct at issue than the federal government is. The federal government is likely to be the superior regulator when the regulation has substantial effects, or "spillovers," outside the geographic territory controlled by the sovereign. These and other proposals are discussed more fully in H. HOVENKAMP, FEDERAL ANTITRUST POLICY §§ 20.2 to 20.3 (4th ed. 2011).

[1] The Authorization Requirement and the Antitrust Liability of Municipalities and other Governmental Subdivisions

Midcal articulated a concise two-part test for the "state action" exemption. First, the restraint had to be "clearly articulated and affirmatively expressed," or *authorized*, in state regulatory policy. Second, any private conduct performed under the state scheme had to be "actively supervised" by the state. Interpreting these requirements required several additional decisions.

One of the most important authorization issues pertains to the regulatory power of municipalities. Throughout this discussion, the term "municipal" refers to some unit of local government. It could be a municipality, county, township, or even a school or water district. The *Lafayette* decision, discussed *supra*, first considered whether a municipality may itself "authorize" anticompetitive activity. The answer was no; authorization must come from the state. Next, in *Community Commun. Co. v. City of Boulder*, 455 U.S. 40 (1982), the Court considered what it would take for a state to authorize a municipality to regulate in such a way as to meet the "clear articulation" requirement.

Boulder was an antitrust challenge to a municipal ordinance that delayed the further development of the plaintiff's cable television system for three months, pending the city's study of its needs. The City of Boulder was a "home rule" municipality, which under the Colorado constitution was "entitled to exercise 'the full right of self-government in both local and municipal matters,' and with respect to such matters the City Charter and ordinances supersede the laws of the State." The city claimed that its "home rule" status provided adequate state authorization for its ordinance. The Supreme Court disagreed, saying:

> [In *City of Lafayette* we recognized] that a State may frequently choose to effect its policies through the instrumentality of its cities and towns. It was stressed, however, that the "state policy" relied upon would have to be "clearly articulated and affirmatively expressed." . . .
>
> Respondent [argues] that through the Home Rule Amendment the people of the State of Colorado have vested in the city of Boulder " '*every power* theretofore possessed by the legislature . . . in local and municipal affairs.' " The power thus possessed by Boulder's City Council assertedly embraces the regulation of cable television, which is claimed to pose essentially local problems. Thus, it is suggested, the city's cable television moratorium ordinance is an "act of government" performed by the city *acting as the State* in local matters, which meets the "state action" criterion of *Parker*.
>
> *We reject this argument: it both misstates the letter of the law and misunderstands its spirit.* The *Parker* state-action exemption reflects Congress' intention to embody in the Sherman Act the federalism principle that the States possess a significant measure of sovereignty under our Constitution. But this principle contains its own limitation: Ours is a "*dual* system of government," which has no place for sovereign cities. As this Court stated long ago, all sovereign authority "within the geographical limits of the United States" resides either with the Government of the United States, or [with] the States of the Union. *There exist within the broad domain of sovereignty but these two.* There may be cities, counties, and other organized bodies with limited legislative functions, but they are all derived from, or exist in, subordination to one or the other of these. . . .
>
> [P]lainly the requirement of "clear articulation and affirmative expression" is not satisfied when the State's position is one of mere *neutrality* respecting the municipal actions challenged as anticompetitive. A State that allows its municipalities to do as they please can hardly be said to have "contemplated" the specific anticompetitive actions for which municipal liability is sought. Nor can those actions be truly described as "comprehended within the powers *granted*," since the term, "granted," necessarily implies an affirmative addressing of the subject by the State. The State did not do so here: The relationship of the State of Colorado to Boulder's moratorium ordinance is one of precise neutrality.

The *Boulder* decision created numerous problems for the relationship between state and local government. In several states, for example, large cities have authority to regulate under a general home-rule provision that effectively permits the city to displace state law within its boundaries. Smaller cities in the same states, however, were perceived to require less overall regulatory authority. They regulate under specific statutory grants of power, such as zoning enabling acts, rent control enabling acts, acts permitting the cities to provide their own electric power, and so on. One of *Boulder*'s ironies is that in such states the smaller cities, whose grants of regulatory authority are "market specific," may have substantially more power to regulate than larger cities that regulate under a home-rule provision. Most troubling of all was the specter of treble damages actions against municipalities (although no municipality was ever actually required to pay damages).

Responding to these concerns, Congress passed the Local Government Antitrust Act, codified at 15 U.S.C. §§ 35, 36. The statute provides that no "damages, interest on damages, costs or attorney's fees may be recovered" in private damages actions under the federal antitrust laws "from any local government, or official or employee thereof acting in an official capacity." The statute permits a prevailing plaintiff to obtain an injunction and attorney's fees in injunction actions. While the Act says nothing about when local government conduct violates the antitrust laws, its damage exclusion has reduced substantially the number of antitrust complaints filed against municipalities.

Shortly after Congress passed the Local Government Antitrust Act, Supreme Court thinking about municipal antitrust liability changed. After reading the *Hallie* and *Columbia* decisions, *infra*, consider how much of *Lafayette* and *Boulder* remains. Has the Local Government Antitrust Act become superfluous?

HALLIE v. CITY OF EAU CLAIRE
471 U.S. 34 (1985)

JUSTICE POWELL delivered the opinion of the Court.

This case presents the question whether a municipality's anticompetitive activities are protected by the state action exemption to the federal antitrust laws . . . when the activities are authorized, but not compelled, by the State, and the State does not actively supervise the anticompetitive conduct.

I

Petitioners — Town of Hallie, Town of Seymour, Town of Union, and Town of Washington (the Towns) — are four Wisconsin unincorporated townships located adjacent to respondent, the City of Eau Claire (the City). Town of Hallie is located in Chippewa County, and the other three towns are located in Eau Claire County. The Towns filed suit against the City in United States District Court for the Western District of Wisconsin seeking injunctive relief and alleging that the City violated the Sherman Act, 15 U.S.C. § 1 *et seq.*, by acquiring a monopoly over the provision of sewage treatment services in Eau Claire and Chippewa Counties, and by tying the provision of such services to the provision of sewage collection and transportation services. [T]he City had obtained federal funds to help build a sewage treatment facility within the Eau Claire Service Area, that included the Towns; the facility is the only one in the market available to the Towns. The City has refused to supply sewage treatment services to the Towns. It does supply the services to individual landowners in areas of the Towns if a majority of the individuals in the area vote by referendum election to have their homes annexed by the City, and to use the City's sewage collection and transportation services.

Alleging that they are potential competitors of the City in the collection and transportation of sewage, the Towns contended in the District Court that the City used its monopoly over sewage treatment to gain an unlawful monopoly over the provision of sewage collection and transportation services, in violation of the Sherman Act. They also contended that the City's actions constituted an illegal tying arrangement and an unlawful refusal to deal with the Towns.

II

. . . .

Municipalities . . . are not beyond the reach of the antitrust laws by virtue of their status because they are not themselves sovereign. *City of Lafayette v. Louisiana Power & Light Co.*, 435 U.S. 389, 412 (1978) (opinion of BRENNAN, J.). Rather, to obtain exemption, municipalities must demonstrate that their anticompetitive activities were authorized by the State "pursuant to state policy to displace competition with regulation or monopoly public service." . . .

It is therefore clear from our cases that before a municipality will be entitled to the protection of the state action exemption from the antitrust laws, it must demonstrate that it is engaging in the challenged activity pursuant to a clearly expressed state policy. We have never fully considered, however, how clearly a state policy must be articulated for a municipality to be able to establish that its anticompetitive activity constitutes state action. Moreover, we have expressly left open the question whether action by a municipality — like action by a private party — must satisfy [*Midcal's*] "active state supervision" requirement.

III

. . . .

A

Wisconsin Stat. § 62.18(1) (1982) grants authority to cities to construct, add to, alter, and repair sewerage systems. The authority includes the power to "describe with reasonable particularity the district to be [served]." *Ibid.* This grant of authority is supplemented by Wis. Stat. Ann. § 66.069(2)(c) (Supp. 1984), providing that a city operating a public utility

> "may by ordinance fix the limits of such service in unincorporated areas. Such ordinance shall delineate the area within which service will be provided and the municipal utility shall have no obligation to serve beyond the area so delineated."

B

The Towns contend that these statutory provisions do not evidence a state policy to displace competition in the provision of sewage services because they make no express mention of anticompetitive conduct. As discussed above, the statutes clearly contemplate that a city may engage in anticompetitive conduct. Such conduct is a foreseeable result of empowering the City to refuse to serve unannexed areas. It is not necessary, as the Towns contend, for the state legislature to have stated explicitly that it expected the City to engage in conduct that would have anti-competitive effects. Applying the analysis of *City of Lafayette*, 435 U.S. 389 (1978), it is sufficient that the statutes authorize the City to provide sewage services and also to determine the areas to be served. We think it is clear that anticompetitive effects logically would result from this broad authority to regulate. . . .

Nor do we agree with the Towns' contention that the statutes at issue here are neutral on state policy. The Towns attempt to liken the Wisconsin statutes to the Home Rule Amendment involved in *City of Boulder*, arguing that the Wisconsin statutes are neutral because they leave the City free to pursue either anticompeti-tive conduct or free-market competition in the field of sewage services. The analogy to the Home Rule Amendment involved in *City of Boulder* is inapposite. That Amendment to the Colorado Constitution allocated only the most general authority to municipalities to govern local affairs. We held that it was neutral and did not satisfy the "clear articulation" component of the state action test. The Amendment simply did not address the regulation of cable television. Under Home Rule the municipality was to be free to decide every aspect of policy relating to cable television, as well as policy relating to any other field of regulation of local concern . Here, in contrast, the State has specifically authorized Wisconsin cities to provide sewage services and has delegated to the cities the express authority to take action that foreseeably will result in anticompetitive effects. No reasonable argument can be made that these statutes are neutral in the same way that Colorado's Home Rule Amendment was.

The Towns' argument amounts to a contention that to pass the "clear articula-tion" test, a legislature must expressly state in a statute or its legislative history that it intends for the delegated action to have anticompetitive effects. This contention embodies an unrealistic view of how legislatures work and of how statutes are written. No legislature can be expected to catalog all of the anticipated effects of a statute of this kind. . . .

In sum, we conclude that the Wisconsin statutes evidence a "clearly articulated and affirmatively expressed" state policy to displace competition with regulation in the area of municipal provision of sewerage services. These statutory provisions plainly show that " 'the legislature contemplated the kind of action complained of.' " *City of Lafayette*, *supra*. This is sufficient to satisfy the clear articulation require-ment of the state action test.

. . . .

IV

Finally, the Towns argue that as there was no active state supervision, the City may not depend on the state action exemption. The Towns rely primarily on language in *City of Lafayette*. It is fair to say that our cases have not been entirely clear. The plurality opinion in *City of Lafayette* did suggest, without elaboration and without deciding the issue, that a city claiming the exemption must show that its anticompetitive conduct was actively supervised by the State. 435 U.S., at 410. In *California Retail Liquor Dealers Assn. v. Midcal Aluminum, Inc.*, a unanimous

Court held that supervision is required where the anticompetitive conduct is by private parties. In *City of Boulder*, however, the most recent relevant case, we expressly left this issue open as to municipalities. 455 U.S., at 51–52, n. 14. We now conclude that the active state supervision requirement should not be imposed in cases in which the actor is a municipality.[4]

V

We conclude that the actions of the City of Eau Claire in this case are exempt from the Sherman Act. They were taken pursuant to a clearly articulated state policy to replace competition in the provision of sewerage services with regulation. We further hold that active state supervision is not a prerequisite to exemption from the antitrust laws where the actor is a municipality rather than a private party. We accordingly affirm the judgment of the Court of Appeals for the Seventh Circuit.

NOTES AND QUESTIONS

1. In *Hallie*, the Supreme Court held that in order to qualify for the "state action" exemption a municipality's activities do not need to be either "compelled" by the state or "actively supervised" by the state. The Court justifies both of these conclusions with the observation that a municipality will presumably act in the "public interest" rather than its own interest, and therefore would not consider anything as self-serving as participation in a private price-fixing agreement. If that is the case, then why should municipalities *ever* be held liable under the antitrust laws? But more to the point, do you believe what the Court says about municipalities? Doesn't a municipality have some of the same profit incentives that a private firm has? If so, might it not be tempted to participate in a private price fixing agreement? *See Affiliated Capital Corp. v. City of Houston*, 735 F.2d 1555 (5th Cir. 1984) (en banc), which may have involved a municipality's participation in a private territorial division scheme.

2. The *Hallie* opinion left unanswered the question whether a private defendant, rather than a municipality, must be "compelled" to act by the State, rather than merely "permitted" to act. However, in *Southern Motor Carriers Rate Conf. v. United States*, 471 U.S. 48 (1985), which was decided the same day, it answered that question in the negative. The Court held that the activities of a legislatively authorized "rate bureau" (a legalized cartel in which price-regulated common carriers jointly draft and propose rates to a regulatory agency) qualified for the "state action" exemption, even though the state legislation merely authorized, and did not compel, the activities. The Court made clear, however, that its holding did not amount to a blanket rule that state compulsion is unnecessary in state action cases involving private defendants. Rather, it looked closely at the joint rate-making activities in question and found a good reason for individual firms to be given the option whether to set rates jointly or separately:

---

[4] [FN 10] In cases in which the actor is a state agency, it is likely that active state supervision would also not be required, although we do not here decide that issue. Where state or municipal regulation of a private party is involved, however, active state supervision must be shown, even where a clearly articulated state policy exists.

Most common carriers probably will engage in collective ratemaking, as that will allow them to share the cost of preparing rate proposals. If the joint rates are viewed as too high, however, carriers individually may submit lower proposed rates to the commission in order to obtain a larger share of the market. Thus, through the self-interested actions of private common carriers, the States may achieve the desired balance between the efficiency of collective ratemaking and the competition fostered by individual submissions. Construing the Sherman Act to prohibit collective rate proposals eliminates the free choice necessary to ensure that these policies function in the manner intended by the States.

In effect, the Court is arguing that a "compulsion" requirement in this case would make the states prevent the carriers from cheating on their own cartel. Are you convinced by the Court's "efficiency" argument? Would it not have been useful to discern how often a disruptive carrier requested to deviate downward from the rate set by the legal cartel?

FTC v. PHOEBE PUTNEY HEALTH SYSTEM, INC.
133 S. Ct. 1003 (2013)

SOTOMAYOR, J., delivered the opinion for a unanimous Court.

Under this Court's state-action immunity doctrine, when a local governmental entity acts pursuant to a clearly articulated and affirmatively expressed state policy to displace competition, it is exempt from scrutiny under the federal antitrust laws. In this case, we must decide whether a Georgia law that creates special-purpose public entities called hospital authorities and gives those entities general corporate powers, including the power to acquire hospitals, clearly articulates and affirmatively expresses a state policy to permit acquisitions that substantially lessen competition. Because Georgia's grant of general corporate powers to hospital authorities does not include permission to use those powers anticompetitively, we hold that the clear-articulation test is not satisfied and state-action immunity does not apply.

I

A

In 1941, the State of Georgia amended its Constitution to allow political subdivisions to provide health care services. 1941 Ga. Laws p. 50. . . . [T]he Law authorizes each county and municipality, and certain combinations of counties or municipalities, to create "a public body corporate and politic" called a "hospital authority." Hospital authorities are governed by 5- to 9-member boards that are appointed by the governing body of the county or municipality in their area of operation.

Under the Law, a hospital authority "exercise[s] public and essential governmental functions" and is delegated "all the powers necessary or convenient to carry out and effectuate" the Law's purposes. Giving more content to that general delegation, the Law enumerates 27 powers conferred upon hospital authorities, including the power "[t]o acquire by purchase, lease, or otherwise and to operate projects," which are defined to include hospitals and other public health facilities, "[t]o construct, reconstruct, improve, alter, and repair projects," "[t]o lease . . . for operation by others any project" provided certain conditions are satisfied, and "[t]o establish rates and charges for the services and use of the facilities of the authority . . . ."

B

. . . Memorial is one of two hospitals in Dougherty County. The second, Palmyra Medical Center (Palmyra), was established in Albany in 1971 and is located just two miles from Memorial. At the time suit was brought in this case, Palmyra was operated by a national for-profit hospital network, HCA, Inc. (HCA). Together, Memorial and Palmyra account for 86 percent of the market for acute-care hospital services provided to commercial health care plans and their customers in the six counties surrounding Albany. Memorial accounts for 75 percent of that market on its own.

In 2010, PPHS began discussions with HCA about acquiring Palmyra. Following negotiations, PPHS presented the Authority with a plan under which the Authority would purchase Palmyra with PPHS controlled funds and then lease Palmyra to a PPHS subsidiary for $1 per year under the Memorial lease agreement. The Authority unanimously approved the transaction.

The Federal Trade Commission (FTC) shortly thereafter issued an administrative complaint alleging that the proposed purchase-and-lease transaction would create a virtual monopoly and would substantially reduce competition in the market for acute-care hospital services, in violation of § 5 of the Federal Trade Commission Act and § 7 of the Clayton Act . . . .

The District Court held that respondents are immune from antitrust liability under the state-action doctrine. The United States Court of Appeals for the Eleventh Circuit affirmed. 663 F.3d 1369 (2011) As an initial matter, the court "agree[d] with the [FTC] that, on the facts alleged, the joint operation of Memorial and Palmyra would substantially lessen competition or tend to create, if not create, a monopoly." But the court concluded that the transaction was immune from antitrust liability. The Court of Appeals explained that as a local governmental entity, the Authority was entitled to state-action immunity if the challenged anticompetitive conduct was a " 'foreseeable result' " of Georgia's legislation. According to the court, anticompetitive conduct is foreseeable if it could have been " 'reasonably anticipated' " by the state legislature; it is not necessary, the court reasoned, for an anticompetitive effect to "be 'one that ordinarily occurs, routinely occurs, or is inherently likely to occur as a result of the empowering legislation.' . . . The court noted the "impressive breadth" of the powers given to hospital authorities, which include traditional powers of private corporations and a few additional capabilities, such as the power to exercise eminent domain. More specifically, the court reasoned that the Georgia Legislature must have anticipated that the grant of power to hospital authorities to acquire and lease projects would produce anticompetitive effects because "[f]oreseeably, acquisitions could consolidate ownership of competing hospitals, eliminating competition between them." In tension with the Court of Appeals' decision, other Circuits have held in analogous circumstances that substate governmental entities exercising general corporate powers were not entitled to state-action immunity.[5] . . .

We granted certiorari on two questions: whether the Georgia Legislature, through the powers it vested in hospital authorities, clearly articulated and affirmatively expressed a state policy to displace competition in the market for hospital services; and if so, whether state-action immunity is nonetheless inapplicable as a result of the Authority's minimal participation in negotiating the terms of the sale of Palmyra and the Authority's limited supervision of the two hospitals' operations. Concluding that the answer to the first question is "no," we reverse without reaching the second question.

II

In *Parker v. Brown*, 317 U.S. 341 (1943), this Court held that because "nothing in the language of the Sherman Act [15 U.S.C. § 1 et seq.] or in its history" suggested that Congress intended to restrict the sovereign capacity of the States to regulate their economies, the Act should not be read to bar States from imposing market restraints "as an act of government." Following *Parker*, we have held that under certain circumstances, immunity from the federal antitrust laws may extend to nonstate actors carrying out the State's regulatory program. See *Patrick v. Burget*, 486 U.S. 94, 99–100 (1988); *Southern Motor Carriers Rate Conference, Inc. v. United States*, 471 U.S. 48, 56–57 (1985).

But given the fundamental national values of free enterprise and economic competition that are embodied in the federal antitrust laws, "state-action immunity is disfavored, much as are repeals by implication." *FTC v. Ticor Title Ins. Co.*, 504 U.S. 621, 636 (1992). Consistent with this preference, we recognize state-action immunity only when it is clear that the challenged anticompetitive conduct is undertaken pursuant to a regulatory scheme that "is the State's own." Accordingly, "[c]loser analysis is required when the activity at issue is not directly that of" the State itself, but rather "is carried out by others pursuant to state authorization." *Hoover v. Ronwin*, 466 U.S. 558, 568 (1984). When determining whether the anticompetitive acts of private parties are entitled to immunity, we employ a two-part test, requiring first that "the challenged restraint . . . be one clearly articulated and affirmatively expressed as state policy," and second that "the policy . . . be actively supervised by the State." *California Retail Liquor Dealers Assn. v. Midcal Aluminum, Inc.*, 445 U.S. 97, 105 (1980).

. . . Because municipalities and other political subdivisions are not themselves sovereign, state-action immunity under Parker does not apply to them directly. See *Columbia v. Omni Outdoor Advertising, Inc.*, 499 U.S. 365, 370 (1991); *Lafayette v.*

---

[5] [FN 2] See *Kay Elec. Cooperative v. Newkirk*, 647 F.3d 1039, 1043, 1045–1047 (10th Cir. 2011); *First Am. Title Co. v. Devaugh*, 480 F.3d 438, 456–457 (6th Cir. 2007); *Surgical Care Center of Hammond, L.C. v. Hospital Serv. Dist. No. 1*, 171 F.3d 231, 235–236 (5th Cir. 1999) (en banc); *Lancaster Community Hospital v. Antelope Valley Hospital Dist.*, 940 F.2d 397, 402–403 (9th Cir. 1991).

Louisiana Power & Light Co., 435 U.S. 389, 411–413 (1978) (plurality opinion). At the same time, however, substate governmental entities do receive immunity from antitrust scrutiny when they act "pursuant to state policy to displace competition with regulation or monopoly public service." *Id.*, at 413 This rule "preserves to the States their freedom . . . to use their municipalities to administer state regulatory policies free of the inhibitions of the federal antitrust laws without at the same time permitting purely parochial interests to disrupt the Nation's free-market goals."

As with private parties, immunity will only attach to the activities of local governmental entities if they are undertaken pursuant to a "clearly articulated and affirmatively expressed" state policy to displace competition. *Community Communications Co. v. Boulder*, 455 U.S. 40, 52 (1982). But unlike private parties, such entities are not subject to the "active state supervision requirement" because they have less of an incentive to pursue their own self-interest under the guise of implementing state policies. *Hallie v. Eau Claire*, 471 U.S. 34, 46–47 (1985).

"[T]o pass the 'clear articulation' test," a state legislature need not "expressly state in a statute or its legislative history that the legislature intends for the delegated action to have anticompetitive effects." *Id.*, at 43 Rather, we explained in *Hallie* that state-action immunity applies if the anticompetitive effect was the "foreseeable result" of what the State authorized. *Id.*, at 42.

III

Applying the clear-articulation test to the Law before us, we conclude that respondents' claim for state-action immunity fails because there is no evidence the State affirmatively contemplated that hospital authorities would displace competition by consolidating hospital ownership. The acquisition and leasing powers exercised by the Authority in the challenged transaction, which were the principal powers relied upon by the Court of Appeals in finding state-action immunity, mirror general powers routinely conferred by state law upon private corporations. Other powers possessed by hospital authorities that the Court of Appeals characterized as having "impressive breadth," also fit this pattern, including the ability to make and execute contracts, to set rates for services, to sue and be sued, to borrow money, and the residual authority to exercise any or all powers possessed by private corporations.

Our case law makes clear that state-law authority to act is insufficient to establish state-action immunity; the substate governmental entity must also show that it has been delegated authority to act or regulate anticompetitively. In *Boulder*, we held that Colorado's Home Rule Amendment allowing municipalities to govern local affairs did not satisfy the clear-articulation test. There was no doubt in that case that the city had authority as a matter of state law to pass an ordinance imposing a moratorium on a cable provider's expansion of service. But we rejected the proposition that "the general grant of power to enact ordinances necessarily implies state authorization to enact specific anticompetitive ordinances" because such an approach "would wholly eviscerate the concepts of 'clear articulation and affirmative expression' that our precedents require." We explained that when a State's position "is one of mere neutrality respecting the municipal actions challenged as anticompetitive," the State cannot be said to have " 'contemplated' " those anticompetitive actions.

The principle articulated in *Boulder* controls this case. Grants of general corporate power that allow substate governmental entities to participate in a competitive marketplace should be, can be, and typically are used in ways that raise no federal antitrust concerns. As a result, a State that has delegated such general powers "can hardly be said to have 'contemplated' " that they will be used anticompetitively. *Ibid.* See also 1A P. Areeda & H. Hovenkamp, Antitrust Law ¶ 225a, p. 131 (3d ed. 2006) (hereinafter Areeda & Hovenkamp) ("When a state grants power to an inferior entity, it presumably grants the power to do the thing contemplated, but not to do so anticompetitively"). Thus, while the Law does allow the Authority to acquire hospitals, it does not clearly articulate and affirmatively express a state policy empowering the Authority to make acquisitions of existing hospitals that will substantially lessen competition.

In concluding otherwise, and specifically in reasoning that the Georgia Legislature "must have anticipated" that acquisitions by hospital authorities "would produce anticompetitive effects," the Court of Appeals applied the concept of "foreseeability" from our clear-articulation test too loosely.

In *Hallie*, we recognized that it would "embod[y] an unrealistic view of how legislatures work and of how statutes are written" to require state legislatures to explicitly authorize specific anticompetitive effects before state-action immunity could apply. "No legislature," we explained, "can be expected to catalog all of the anticipated effects" of a statute delegating authority to a substate governmental entity. *Ibid.* Instead, we have approached the clear-articulation inquiry more practically, but without diluting the ultimate requirement that the State must have affirmatively contemplated the displacement of competition such that the challenged anticompetitive effects can be attributed to the "state itself." Thus, we have concluded that a state policy to displace federal antitrust law was sufficiently expressed where the displacement of competition was the inherent, logical, or ordinary result of the exercise of authority delegated by the state legislature. In that scenario, the State must have foreseen and implicitly endorsed the anticompetitive effects as consistent with its policy goals.

For example, in *Hallie*, Wisconsin statutory law regulating the municipal provision of sewage services expressly permitted cities to limit their service to surrounding unincorporated areas. While unincorporated towns alleged that the city's exercise of that power constituted an unlawful tying arrangement, an unlawful refusal to deal, and an abuse of monopoly power, we had no trouble concluding that these alleged anticompetitive effects were affirmatively contemplated by the State because it was "clear" that they "logically would result" from the grant of authority. . . .

By contrast, "simple permission to play in a market" does not "foreseeably entail permission to roughhouse in that market unlawfully." *Kay Elec. Cooperative v. Newkirk*, 647 F.3d 1039, 1043 (10th Cir. 2011). When a State grants some entity general power to act, whether it is a private corporation or a public entity like the Authority, it does so against the backdrop of federal antitrust law. . . .

Believing that this case falls within the scope of the foreseeability standard applied in *Hallie* and *Omni*, the Court of Appeals stated that "[i]t defies imagination to suppose the [state] legislature could have believed that every geographic market in Georgia was so replete with hospitals that authorizing acquisitions by the authorities could have no serious anticompetitive consequences." . . .

Even accepting, arguendo, the premise that facts about a market could make the anticompetitive use of general corporate powers "foreseeable," we reject the Court of Appeals' and respondents' conclusion because only a relatively small subset of the conduct permitted as a matter of state law by Ga. Code Ann. § 31-7-75(4) has the potential to negatively affect competition. Contrary to the Court of Appeals' and respondents' characterization, § 31-7-75(4) is not principally concerned with hospital authorities' ability to acquire multiple hospitals and consolidate their operations. Section 31-7-75(4) allows authorities to acquire "projects," which includes not only "hospitals," but also "health care facilities, dormitories, office buildings, clinics, housing accommodations, nursing homes, rehabilitation centers, extended care facilities, and other public health facilities." § 31-7-71(5). Narrowing our focus to the market for hospital services, the power to acquire hospitals still does not ordinarily produce anticompetitive effects. Section 31-7-75(4) was, after all, the source of power for newly formed hospital authorities to acquire a hospital in the first instance — a transaction that was unlikely to raise any antitrust concerns even in small markets because the transfer of ownership from private to public hands does not increase market concentration. See 1A Areeda & Hovenkamp ¶ 224e(c), at 126 ("[S]ubstitution of one monopolist for another is not an antitrust violation"). While subsequent acquisitions by authorities have the potential to reduce competition, they will raise federal antitrust concerns only in markets that are large enough to support more than one hospital but sufficiently small that the merger of competitors would lead to a significant increase in market concentration. This is too slender a reed to support the Court of Appeals' and respondents' inference. . . .

We have no doubt that Georgia's hospital authorities differ materially from private corporations that offer hospital services. But nothing in the Law or any other provision of Georgia law clearly articulates a state policy to allow authorities to exercise their general corporate powers, including their acquisition power, without regard to negative effects on competition. The state legislature's objective of improving access to affordable health care does not logically suggest that the State intended that hospital authorities pursue that end through mergers that create monopolies. Nor do the restrictions imposed on hospital authorities, including the requirement that they operate on a nonprofit basis, reveal such a policy. Particularly in light of our national policy favoring competition, these restrictions should be read to reflect more modest aims. . . .

We recognize that Georgia, particularly through its certificate of need requirement, does limit competition in the market for hospital services in some respects. But regulation of an industry, and even the authorization of discrete forms of anticompetitive conduct pursuant to a regulatory structure, does not establish that the State has affirmatively contemplated other forms of anticompetitive conduct that are only tangentially related. . . .

Finally, respondents contend that to the extent there is any doubt about whether the clear-articulation test is satisfied in this context, federal courts should err on the side of recognizing immunity to avoid improper interference with state policy choices. But we do not find the Law ambiguous on the question whether it clearly articulates a policy authorizing anticompetitive acquisitions; it does not.

More fundamentally, respondents' suggestion is inconsistent with the principle that "state-action immunity is disfavored." *Ticor Title*, 504 U.S., at 636. Parker and its progeny are premised on an understanding that respect for the States' coordinate role in government counsels against reading the federal antitrust laws to restrict the States' sovereign capacity to regulate their economies and provide services to their citizens. But federalism and state sovereignty are poorly served by a rule of construction that would allow "essential national policies" embodied in the antitrust laws to be displaced by state delegations of authority "intended to achieve more limited ends." . . .

We hold that Georgia has not clearly articulated and affirmatively expressed a policy to allow hospital authorities to make acquisitions that substantially lessen competition. The judgment of the Court of Appeals is reversed, and the case is remanded for further proceedings consistent with this opinion.

It is so ordered.

NOTES AND QUESTIONS

1. The lower court had found "impressive breadth" in the hospital entity's power "make and execute contracts, to set rates for services, to sue and be sued, to borrow money, and the residual authority to exercise any or all powers possessed by private corporations." State chartered business corporations routinely have these powers and execute them all the time. They also have the power to acquire the stock or assets of other corporations. The lower court's reasoning would suggest that ordinary business mergers are immune "state action" simply because the merger was lawful under state corporate law. Already at the beginning of the twentieth century the Supreme Court held that mere illegality of a merger under state corporate law was not sufficient to immunize it from federal antitrust scrutiny. *See Northern Securities Co. v. United States*, 193 U.S. 197, 338 (1904). New Jersey had passed a statute permitting its corporations to own shares in other corporations. Northern Securities was a holding company that acquired most of the shares in two competing railroad lines. Nearly all of the track was outside of New Jersey. In condemning the acquisition under § 1 of the Sherman Act, the Court wrote:

> [E]ven if the state allowed consolidation, it would not follow that the stockholders of two or more state railroad corporations, having *competing lines and engaged in interstate commerce*, could lawfully combine and form a distinct corporation to hold the stock of the constituent corporations, and, by destroying competition between them, in violation of the act of Congress, restrain commerce among the states and with foreign nations. . . .
>
> It is proper to say in passing that nothing in the record tends to show that the state of New Jersey had any reason to suspect that those who took advantage of its liberal incorporation laws had in view, when organizing the Securities Company, to destroy competition between two great railway

carriers engaged in interstate commerce in distant states of the Union. The purpose of the combination was concealed under very general words that gave no clue whatever to the real purposes of those who brought about the organization of the Securities Company. If the certificate of incorporation of that company had expressly stated that the object of the company was to destroy competition between competing, parallel lines of interstate carriers, all would have seen, at the outset, that the scheme was in hostility to the national authority, and that there was a purpose to violate or evade the act of Congress.

2. The opening paragraphs of Justice Sotomayor's opinion provides a nice and compact discussion of the antitrust "state action" doctrine as it has developed over the past century, although dramatically understating the degree of division and changes of direction that the courts have taken.

3. One value that is strong in the Court's approach to state action is transparency. If the state wants to authorize anticompetitive conduct — which typically injures its own citizens — it may do so only if it is clear about its purpose. Authorizing mergers is not the same thing as authorizing anticompetitive mergers, just as authorizing companies to enter into contracts does not authorize price-fixing agreements. What about cases where anticompetitive effects are not so common or are more ambiguous? For example, the *Hallie* decision held that an action is immune if it is a foreseeable result of what the legislature authorized. The power to enter a cartel may not be a foreseeable result of the power to make a contract. But *Hallie* was a challenge to a tying arrangement. Suppose the legislature expressly authorized hospitals to offer primary, secondary, and tertiary care in the same facility. Should a plaintiff be permitted to complain that in the case of a market dominating hospital that combination is an unlawful tie? Exclusivity provisions are problematic because they can sometimes be anticompetitive but are often necessary for efficient operation. Suppose the statute authorizes a hospital to contract for its own anesthesiologists or ambulance service. Does that authorize it to enter into an exclusive contract with a particular anesthesiologist or ambulance company? Or suppose the authorization permits but does not require exclusive contracts. Should that authorize exclusive contracts by dominant hospitals that threaten to exclude rivals? Keep in mind that finding loss of immunity does not end the inquiry. The conduct must still be shown to violate the antitrust laws.

4. Justice Sotomayor stated and repeated the admonition that regulatory immunities are "disfavored." Does that signal a new direction in Supreme Court jurisprudence on the question?

PROBLEM 9.3

Euclid, like most municipalities, has a comprehensive land-use planning (zoning) scheme which regulates both residential and commercial land uses. Euclid's authority for this regulation is a standard Zoning Enabling Act, which authorizes municipalities within the state to "establish and regulate land uses and building construction within their limits." Jack has a parcel of land that is zoned residential, but he wishes to construct a retail vegetable market on it. He petitions the Euclid city council for a reclassification of the land from residential to retail. Ron currently owns a grocery store across the street from Jack's parcel, and the only grocery store within a two-mile radius. Ron (1) makes $1,500 contributions to each of the city council members for their next campaign; (2) objects vociferously at the city council meeting to Jack's request for a reclassification of his property; and (3) secretly bribes two of the council members. The city council votes 5-2 to deny Jack's request.

Jack files an antitrust complaint naming both the city council and Ron as defendants, seeking $250,000 in damages. What arguments should each defendant make? Outcome? *See Pendleton Constr. Corp. v. Rockbridge Cty., Va.*, 652 F. Supp. 312 (W.D. Va. 1987); *Whitworth v. Perkins*, 559 F.2d 378 (5th Cir. 1977). Now, consider the impact of the following decision.

CITY OF COLUMBIA & COLUMBIA OUTDOOR ADVERTISING, INC. v. OMNI OUTDOOR ADVERTISING, INC.
499 U.S. 365 (1991)

JUSTICE SCALIA delivered the opinion of the Court.

This case requires us to clarify the application of the Sherman Act to municipal governments and to the citizens who seek action from them.

I

Petitioner Columbia Outdoor Advertising, Inc. (COA), a South Carolina corporation, entered the billboard business in the city of Columbia, South Carolina (also a petitioner here), in the 1940's. By 1981 it controlled more than 95% of what has been conceded to be the relevant market. COA was a local business owned by a family with deep roots in the community, and enjoyed close relations with the city's political leaders. The mayor and other members of the city council were personal friends of COA's majority owner, and the company and its officers occasionally contributed funds and free billboard space to their campaigns. According to respondent, these beneficences were part of a "longstanding" "secret anticompetitive agreement" whereby "the City and COA would each use their [sic] respective power and resources to protect . . . COA's monopoly position," in return for which "City Council members received advantages made possible by COA's monopoly."

In 1981, respondent Omni Outdoor Advertising, Inc., a Georgia corporation, began erecting billboards in and around the city. COA responded to this competition in several ways. First, it redoubled its own billboard construction efforts and modernized its existing stock. Second, according to Omni, it took a number of anticompetitive private actions, such as offering artificially low rates, spreading untrue and malicious rumors about Omni, and attempting to induce Omni's customers to break their contracts. Finally (and this is what gives rise to the issue we address today), COA executives met with city officials to seek the enactment of zoning ordinances that would restrict billboard construction. COA was not alone in urging this course; a number of citizens concerned about the city's recent explosion of billboards advocated restrictions, including writers of articles and editorials in local newspapers.

In the spring of 1982, the city council passed an ordinance requiring the council's approval for every billboard constructed in downtown Columbia. This was later amended to impose a 180 day moratorium on the construction of billboards throughout the city, except as specifically authorized by the council. A state court invalidated this ordinance on the ground that its conferral of unconstrained discretion upon the city council violated both the South Carolina and Federal Constitutions. The city then requested the State's regional planning authority to conduct a comprehensive analysis of the local billboard situation as a basis for developing a final, constitutionally valid, ordinance. In September 1982, after a series of public hearings and numerous meetings involving city officials, Omni, and COA (in all of which, according to Omni, positions contrary to COA's were not genuinely considered), the city council passed a new ordinance restricting the size, location, and spacing of billboards. These restrictions, particularly those on spacing, obviously benefitted COA, which already had its billboards in place; they severely hindered Omni's ability to compete.

In November 1982, Omni filed suit against COA and the city in Federal District Court, charging that they had violated §§ 1 and 2 of the Sherman Act. . . . Omni contended, in particular, that the city's billboard ordinances were the result of an anticompetitive conspiracy between city officials and COA that stripped both parties of any immunity they might otherwise enjoy from the federal antitrust laws. In January 1986, after more than two weeks of trial, a jury returned general verdicts against the city and COA on both the federal and state claims. It awarded damages, before trebling, of $600,000 on the § 1 Sherman Act claim, and $400,000 on the § 2 claim.[6]

The jury also answered two special interrogatories, finding specifically that the city and COA had conspired both to restrain trade and to monopolize the market. Petitioners moved for judgment notwithstanding the verdict, contending among other things that their activities were outside the scope of the federal antitrust laws. In November 1988, the District Court granted the motion.

A divided panel of the United States Court of Appeals for the Fourth Circuit reversed the judgment of the District Court and reinstated the jury verdict on all counts.

II

. . . In recent years, we have held that *Parker* immunity does not apply directly to local governments. . . . We have recognized, however, that a municipality's restriction of competition may sometimes be an authorized implementation of state policy, and have accorded *Parker* immunity where that is the case.

---

[6] [FN 2] The monetary damages in this case were assessed entirely against COA, the District Court having ruled that the city was immunized by the Local Government Antitrust Act of 1984, 98 Stat. 2750, as amended, 15 U.S.C. §§ 34–36, which exempts local governments from paying damages for violations of the federal antitrust laws.

The South Carolina statutes under which the city acted in the present case authorize municipalities to regulate the use of land and the construction of buildings and other structures within their boundaries. It is undisputed that, as a matter of state law, these statutes authorize the city to regulate the size, location, and spacing of billboards. It could be argued, however, that a municipality acts beyond its delegated authority, for *Parker* purposes, whenever the nature of its regulation is substantively or even procedurally defective. On such an analysis it could be contended, for example, that the city's regulation in the present case was not "authorized" by S.C. Code § 5-23-10 (1976), if it was not, as that statute requires, adopted "for the purpose of promoting health, safety, morals or the general welfare of the community." As scholarly commentary has noted, such an expansive interpretation of the *Parker* defense authorization requirement would have unacceptable consequences.

> "To be sure, state law 'authorizes" only agency decisions that are substantively and procedurally correct. Errors of fact, law, or judgment by the agency are not 'authorized." Erroneous acts or decisions are subject to reversal by superior tribunals because unauthorized. If the antitrust court demands unqualified 'authority" in this sense, it inevitably becomes the standard reviewer not only of federal agency activity but also of state and local activity whenever it is alleged that the governmental body, though possessing the power to engage in the challenged conduct, has actually exercised its power in a manner not authorized by state law. We should not lightly assume that *Lafayette*'s authorization requirement dictates transformation of state administrative review into a federal antitrust job. Yet that would be the consequence of making antitrust liability depend on an undiscriminating and mechanical demand for 'authority" in the full administrative law sense." P. Areeda & H. Hovenkamp, Antitrust Law ¶ 212.3b, p. 145 (Supp. 1989).

We agree with that assessment, and believe that in order to prevent *Parker* from undermining the very interests of federalism it is designed to protect, it is necessary to adopt a concept of authority broader than what is applied to determine the legality of the municipality's action under state law. . . . It suffices for the present to conclude that here no more is needed to establish, for *Parker* purposes, the city's authority to regulate than its unquestioned zoning power over the size, location, and spacing of billboards.

Besides authority to regulate, however, the *Parker* defense also requires authority to suppress competition more specifically, "clear articulation of a state policy to authorize anticompetitive conduct" by the municipality in connection with its regulation. *Hallie*, 471 U.S., at 40. We have rejected the contention that this requirement can be met only if the delegating statute explicitly permits the displacement of competition. It is enough, we have held, if suppression of competition is the "foreseeable result" of what the statute authorizes, *id.*, at 42. That condition is amply met here. The very purpose of zoning regulation is to displace unfettered business freedom in a manner that regularly has the effect of preventing normal acts of competition, particularly on the part of new entrants. A municipal ordinance restricting the size, location, and spacing of billboards (surely a common form of zoning) necessarily protects existing billboards against some competition from newcomers.

The Court of Appeals was therefore correct in its conclusion that the city's restriction of billboard construction was *prima facie* entitled to *Parker* immunity. The Court of Appeals upheld the jury verdict, however, by invoking a "conspiracy" exception to *Parker* that has been recognized by several Courts of Appeals. . . . That exception is thought to be supported by two of our statements in *Parker*: "[W]e have no question of the state or its municipality becoming a *participant in a private agreement or combination by others* for restraint of trade, *cf. Union Pacific R. Co. v. United States*, 313 U.S. 450." *Parker*, 317 U.S., at 351–352 (emphasis added). "The state in adopting and enforcing the prorate program made no contract or agreement and entered into no conspiracy in restraint of trade or to establish monopoly but, as sovereign, imposed the restraint as an act of government which the Sherman Act did not undertake to prohibit." *Parker* does not apply, according to the Fourth Circuit, "where politicians or political entities are involved as conspirators" with private actors in the restraint of trade.

There is no such conspiracy exception. The rationale of *Parker* was that, in light of our national commitment to federalism, the general language of the Sherman Act should not be interpreted to prohibit anticompetitive actions by the States in their governmental capacities as sovereign regulators. The sentences from the opinion quoted above simply clarify that this immunity does not necessarily obtain where the State acts not in a regulatory capacity but as a commercial participant in a given market. That is evident from the citation of *Union Pacific R. Co. v. United States*, 313 U.S. 450 (1941), which held unlawful under the Elkins Act certain rebates and concessions made by Kansas City, Kansas, in its capacity as the owner and operator of a wholesale produce market that was integrated with railroad facilities. These sentences should not be read to suggest the general proposition that even governmental regulatory action may be deemed private and therefore subject to antitrust liability when it is taken pursuant to a conspiracy with private parties. The impracticality of such a principle is evident if, for purposes of the exception, "conspiracy" means nothing more than an agreement to impose the regulation in question. Since it is both inevitable and desirable that public officials often agree to do what one or another group of private citizens urges upon them, such an exception would virtually swallow up the *Parker* rule: All anticompetitive regulation would be vulnerable to a "conspiracy" charge. See Areeda & Hovenkamp, *supra*, ¶ 203.3b; Elhauge, *The Scope of Antitrust Process*, 104 Harv. L. Rev. 667, 704–705 (1991).

Omni suggests, however, that "conspiracy" might be limited to instances of governmental "corruption," defined variously as "abandonment of public responsibilities to private interests," "corrupt or bad faith decisions," and "selfish or corrupt motives." Ultimately, Omni asks us not to define "corruption" at all, but simply to leave that task to the jury: "At bottom, however, it was within the jury's province to determine what constituted corruption of the governmental process in their community." Omni's amicus eschews this emphasis on "corruption," instead urging us to define the conspiracy exception as encompassing any governmental act "not in the public interest."

A conspiracy exception narrowed along such vague lines is similarly impractical.

Few governmental actions are immune from the charge that they are "not in the public interest" or in some sense "corrupt." The California marketing scheme at issue in *Parker* itself, for example, can readily be viewed as the result of a "conspiracy" to put the "private" interest of the State's raisin growers above the "public" interest of the State's consumers. The fact is that virtually all regulation benefits some segments of the society and harms others; and that it is not universally considered contrary to the public good if the net economic loss to the losers exceeds the net economic gain to the winners. *Parker* was not written in ignorance of the reality that determination of "the public interest" in the manifold areas of government regulation entails not merely economic and mathematical analysis but value judgment, and it was not meant to shift that judgment from elected officials to judges and juries. If the city of Columbia's decision to regulate what one local newspaper called "billboard jungles" . . . is made subject to *ex post facto* judicial assessment of "the public interest," with personal liability of city officials a possible consequence, we will have gone far to "compromise the States' ability to regulate their domestic commerce," *Southern Motor Carriers Rate Conference, Inc. v. United States*, 471 U.S. 48, 56 (1985). The situation would not be better, but arguably even worse, if the courts were to apply a subjective test: not whether the action was in the public interest, but whether the officials involved thought it to be so. This would require the sort of deconstruction of the governmental process and probing of the official "intent" that we have consistently sought to avoid. . . .

The foregoing approach to establishing a "conspiracy" exception at least seeks (however impractically) to draw the line of impermissible action in a manner relevant to the purposes of the Sherman Act and of *Parker*: prohibiting the restriction of competition for private gain but permitting the restriction of competition in the public interest. Another approach is possible, which has the virtue of practicality but the vice of being unrelated to those purposes. That is the approach which would consider *Parker* inapplicable only if, in connection with the governmental action in question, bribery or some other violation of state or federal law has been established. Such unlawful activity has no necessary relationship to whether the governmental action is in the public interest. A mayor is guilty of accepting a bribe even if he would and should have taken, in the public interest, the same action for which the bribe was paid. (That is frequently the defense asserted to a criminal bribery charge and though it is never valid in law, it is often plausible in fact.) When, moreover, the regulatory body is not a single individual but a state legislature or city council, there is even less reason to believe that violation of the law (by bribing a minority of the decisionmakers) establishes that the regulation has no valid public purpose. To use unlawful political influence as the test of legality of state regulation undoubtedly vindicates (in a rather blunt way) principles of good government. But the statute we are construing is not directed to that end. Congress has passed other laws aimed at combatting corruption in state and local governments. See, e.g., 18 U.S.C. § 1951 (Hobbs Act). "Insofar as [the Sherman Act] sets up a code of ethics at all, it is a code that condemns trade restraints, not political activity." *Eastern Railroad Presidents Conference v. Noerr Motor Freight, Inc.*, 365 U.S. 127, 140 (1961).

For these reasons, we reaffirm our rejection of any interpretation of the

Sherman Act that would allow plaintiffs to look behind the actions of state sovereigns to base their claims on "perceived conspiracies to restrain trade." We reiterate that, with the possible market participant exception, any action that qualifies as state action is "ipso facto . . . exempt from the operation of the antitrust laws." This does not mean, of course, that the States may exempt private action from the scope of the Sherman Act; we in no way qualify the well established principle that "a state does not give immunity to those who violate the Sherman Act by authorizing them to violate it, or by declaring that their action is lawful."

[That portion of the opinion dealing with the "sham" exception to the Noerr-Pennington doctrine is reprinted *supra*.]

The judgment of the Court of Appeals is reversed, and the case is remanded for further proceedings consistent with this opinion.

It is so ordered.

NOTES AND QUESTIONS

1. Suppose a state passes a very general "welfare" statute that gives municipalities virtual *carte blanche*. *Wall v. City of Athens*, 663 F. Supp. 747 (M.D. Ga. 1987), involved the following state statute: "It is declared by the General Assembly of Georgia that in the exercise of powers specifically granted to [home-rule municipalities] by law, local governing authorities of cities and counties are acting pursuant to state policy. . . ." Further, "[t]his chapter is intended to articulate clearly and express affirmatively the policy of the State of Georgia that in the exercise of such powers, such local governing authorities shall be immune from antitrust liability to the same degree and extent as enjoyed by the State of Georgia. O.C.G.A. § 36-19-1 (April 4, 1984)."

The court found the attempt ineffectual. A later decision found that the same language did qualify a municipality for the exemption. *McCallum v. City of Athens*, 976 F.2d 649 (11th Cir. 1992). Which decision is more consistent with *Boulder*? With *Hallie*? With *Columbia*? With *Phoebe-Putney*? Can a state simply declare "[a]ll of our regulatory legislation follows a clearly articulated and affirmatively expressed policy to displace the federal antitrust laws."

2. The *Columbia* decision also refused to recognize a "co-conspiracy" exception to *both* the *Parker* and *Noerr* doctrines, reasoning:

> Omni urges that we should use this case to recognize a "conspiracy" exception [to *Noerr*], which would apply when government officials conspire with a private party to employ government action as a means of stifling competition. We have left open the possibility of such an exception, see, e.g., *Allied Tube, supra,* at 502, n. 7. . . .

> Giving full consideration to this matter for the first time, we conclude that a "conspiracy" exception to *Noerr* must be rejected. We need not describe our reasons at length, since they are largely the same as those set forth in Part II above for rejecting a "conspiracy" exception to *Parker*. As we have described, *Parker* and *Noerr* are complementary expressions of the principle that the antitrust laws regulate business, not politics; the

former decision protects the States' acts of governing, and the latter the citizens' participation in government. Insofar as the identification of an immunity destroying "conspiracy" is concerned, *Parker* and *Noerr* generally present two faces of the same coin. The *Noerr* invalidating conspiracy alleged here is just the *Parker* invalidating conspiracy viewed from the standpoint of the private sector participants rather than the governmental participants. The same factors which, as we have described above, make it impracticable or beyond the purpose of the antitrust laws to identify and invalidate lawmaking that has been infected by selfishly motivated agreement with private interests likewise make it impracticable or beyond that scope to identify and invalidate lobbying that has produced selfishly motivated agreement with public officials. "It would be unlikely that any effort to influence legislative action could succeed unless one or more members of the legislative body became . . . 'coconspirators'" in some sense with the private party urging such action. And if the invalidating "conspiracy" is limited to one that involves some element of unlawfulness (beyond mere anticompetitive motivation), the invalidation would have nothing to do with the policies of the antitrust laws. In *Noerr* itself, where the private party "deliberately deceived the public and public officials" in its successful lobbying campaign, we said that "deception, reprehensible as it is, can be of no consequence so far as the Sherman Act is concerned." . . .

PROBLEM 9.4

Consider the following under the Supreme Court's *Columbia* decision:

1. Three members of a five-person city council are the owners of an ambulance company. They pass an ordinance on a 3-2 vote that gives the company a monopoly of all police ambulance calls in the region. A competing ambulance company sues under the antitrust laws. A state statute authorizes the municipality to regulate local ambulance service. Are the three city council members liable as private defendants? Is the municipality liable?

2. A municipality owns a hot dog and soft drink vending service, from which it makes a great deal of money. It gives its own service the exclusive right to sell prepared food on municipal beaches, in municipal parks, and in municipal stadiums. A state statute authorizes the municipality to regulate health, safety, and vending of goods in these facilities. The municipality is sued by a competing vendor. Has it violated the antitrust laws?

[2] The "Active Supervision" Requirement

The Supreme Court's *Midcal* decision, as you recall, assessed two requirements for the "state action" exemption. First, the challenged activity must be adequately authorized in state policy. Second, any private conduct carried out pursuant to this regulatory regime must be "actively supervised" by the state or one of its agencies.

In *Patrick v. Burget*, 486 U.S. 94 (1988), the Supreme Court found that private conduct pursuant to a state regulatory policy did not qualify for the state action exemption because it was inadequately supervised. Patrick was a surgeon with staff privileges at Columbia Memorial Hospital. Most of the supervisory staff at the hospital were partners in nearby Astoria Clinic. Patrick refused to join the clinic but established an independent practice in competition with the clinic. The clinic then treated him with hostility, giving him no referrals. When Patrick was later charged with negligence, the defendant hospital and its supervisory staff hastily voted to terminate his staff privileges. Patrick challenged the dismissal under the antitrust laws, contending that "the Clinic partners had initiated and participated in the hospital peer-review proceedings to reduce competition from petitioner rather than to improve patient care. . . . " In refusing to find that the dismissal was exempt under *Parker*, the Supreme Court said the following:

> In this case, we need not consider the "clear articulation" prong of the *Midcal* test, because the "active supervision" requirement is not satisfied. The active supervision requirement stems from the recognition that "[w]here a private party is engaging in the anticompetitive activity, there is a real danger that he is acting to further his own interests, rather than the governmental interests of the State." The requirement is designed to ensure that the state action doctrine will shelter only the particular anticompetitive acts of private parties that, in the judgment of the State, actually further state regulatory policies. To accomplish this purpose, the active supervision requirement mandates that the State exercise ultimate control over the challenged anticompetitive conduct. The mere presence of some state involvement or monitoring does not suffice. The active supervision prong of the *Midcal* test requires that state officials have and exercise power to review particular anti-competitive acts of private parties and disapprove those that fail to accord with state policy. Absent such a program of supervision, there is no realistic assurance that a private party's anticompetitive conduct promotes state policy, rather than merely the party's individual interests.

The defendants had alleged that three government agencies supervised private peer review actions: the Oregon Health Division, the Oregon Board of Medical Examiners (BOME), and the Oregon court system. The Court concluded that each failed to meet the standard. The Health Division had some supervisory powers over hospital peer review, but it was largely limited to ensuring that hospitals had an active peer review process in place. "The Health Division has no power to review private peer review decisions and overturn a decision that fails to accord with state policy. Thus, the activities of the Health Division under Oregon law cannot satisfy the active supervision requirement of the state action doctrine."

Likewise, the main function of the BOME was to license physicians, but it also lacked the "power to disapprove private privilege decisions." Rather, its only role in a termination was to determine whether additional action was appropriate, such as revocation or suspension of a physician's license.

That left the state judiciary. Said the Court:

> This Court has not previously considered whether state courts, acting in their judicial capacity, can adequately supervise private conduct for purposes of the state action doctrine. All of our prior cases concerning state supervision over private parties have involved administrative agencies or state supreme courts with agency-like responsibilities over the organized

bar, see *Bates v. State Bar of Arizona*, 433 U.S. 350 (1977). This case, however, does not require us to decide the broad question whether judicial review of private conduct ever can constitute active supervision, because judicial review of privilege-termination decisions in Oregon, if such review exists at all, falls far short of satisfying the active supervision requirement.

As an initial matter, it is not clear that Oregon law affords any direct judicial review of private peer-review decisions. Oregon has no statute expressly providing for judicial review of privilege terminations. Moreover, we are aware of no case in which an Oregon court has held that judicial review of peer-review decisions is available. . . .

Moreover, the Oregon courts have indicated that even if they were to provide judicial review of hospital peer-review proceedings, the review would be of a very limited nature. The Oregon Supreme Court, in its most recent decision addressing this matter, stated that a court "should [not] decide the merits of plaintiff's dismissal" and that "[i]t would be unwise for a court to do more than to make sure that some sort of reasonable procedure was afforded and that there was evidence from which it could be found that plaintiff's conduct posed a threat to patient care." *Straube* [*supra*]. This kind of review would fail to satisfy the state action doctrine's requirement of active supervision.

FTC v. TICOR TITLE INSURANCE CO.
504 U.S. 621 (1992)

JUSTICE KENNEDY delivered the opinion of the Court.

The Federal Trade Commission filed an administrative complaint against six of the nation's largest title insurance companies, alleging horizontal price fixing in their fees for title searches and title examinations. . . . The Commission charged the title companies with violating § 5(a)(1) of the Federal Trade Commission Act, 38 Stat. 719, 15 U.S.C. § 45(a)(1), which prohibits "[u]nfair methods of competition in or affecting commerce." One of the principal defenses the companies assert is state-action immunity from antitrust prosecution, as contemplated in the line of cases beginning with *Parker v. Brown*. . . .

I

Title insurance is the business of insuring the record title of real property for persons with some interest in the estate, including owners, occupiers, and lenders. A title insurance policy insures against certain losses or damages sustained by reason of a defect in title not shown on the policy or title report to which it refers. Before issuing a title insurance policy, the insurance company or one of its agents performs a title search and examination. The search produces a chronological list of the public documents in the chain of title to the real property. The examination is a critical analysis or interpretation of the condition of title revealed by the documents disclosed through this search. The title search and examination are major components of the insurance company's services. . . .

. . . Four of respondents are the nation's largest title insurance companies: Ticor Title Insurance Co., with 16.5 percent of the market; Chicago Title Insurance Co., with 12.8 percent; Lawyers Title Insurance Co., with 12 percent; and Safeco Title Insurance Co. (now operating under the name Security Union Title Insurance Co.), with 10.3 percent. Stewart Title Guarantee Co., with 5.4 percent of the market, is the country's eighth largest title insurer, with a strong position in the West and Southwest.

. . . The Commission did not challenge the insurers' practice of setting uniform rates for insurance against the risk of loss from defective titles, but only the practice of setting uniform rates for the title search, examination, and settlement, aspects of the business which, the Commission alleges, do not involve insurance. Before the Administrative Law Judge (ALJ), the respondents defended against liability on [the ground that] their activities are entitled to state-action immunity, which permits anticompetitive conduct if authorized and supervised by state officials. . . . [After numerous dismissals] four States remain in which violations were alleged: Connecticut, Wisconsin, Arizona, and Montana. The ALJ held that the rates for search and examination services had been fixed in these four States. . . .

Rating bureaus are private entities organized by title insurance companies to establish uniform rates for their members. The ALJ found no evidence that the collective setting of title insurance rates through rating bureaus is a way of pooling risk information. Indeed, he found no evidence that any title insurer sets rates according to actuarial loss experience. Instead, the ALJ found that the usual practice is for rating bureaus to set rates according to profitability studies that focus on the costs of conducting searches and examinations. Uniform rates are set notwithstanding differences in efficiencies and costs among individual members.

The ALJ described the regulatory regimes for title insurance rates in the four States still at issue. In each one, the title insurance rating bureau was licensed by the State and authorized to establish joint rates for its members. Each of the four States used what has come to be called a "negative option" system to approve rate filings by the bureaus. Under a negative option system, the rating bureau filed rates for title searches and title examinations with the state insurance office. The rates became effective unless the State rejected them within a specified period, such as 30 days. Although the negative option system provided a theoretical mechanism for substantive review, the ALJ determined, after making detailed findings regarding the operation of each regulatory regime, that the rate filings were subject to minimal scrutiny by state regulators. In Connecticut the State Insurance Department has the authority to audit the rating bureau and hold hearings regarding rates, but it has not done so. The Connecticut rating bureau filed only two major rate increases, in 1966 and in 1981. The circumstances behind the 1966 rate increase are somewhat obscure. The ALJ found that the Insurance Department asked the rating bureau to submit additional information justifying the increase, and later approved the rate increase although there is no evidence the additional information was provided. In 1981 the Connecticut rating bureau filed for a 20 percent rate increase. The factual background for this rate increase is better developed though the testimony was somewhat inconsistent. A state insurance official testified that he reviewed the rate increase with care and discussed various components of the increase with the rating bureau. The same official testified, however, that he lacked the authority to question certain expense data he considered quite high. In Wisconsin the State Insurance Commissioner is required to examine the rating bureau at regular intervals and authorized to reject rates through a process of hearings. Neither has been done. The Wisconsin rating bureau made major rate filings in 1971, 1981, and 1982. . . . The 1982 rate increase received but a cursory reading at the office of the Insurance Commissioner. The supporting materials were not checked for accuracy, though in the absence of an objection by the agency, the rate increase went into effect. In Arizona the Insurance Director was required to examine the rating bureau at least once every five years. It was not done. . . . In Montana the rating bureau made its only major rate filing in 1983. In connection with it, a representative of the rating bureau met with officials of the State Insurance Department. He was told that the filed rates could go into immediate effect though further profit data would have to be provided. The ALJ found no evidence that the additional data were furnished.

. . . [T]he Commission held that none of the four states had conducted sufficient supervision, so that the title companies were not entitled to immunity in any of those jurisdictions. The Court of Appeals for the Third Circuit disagreed with the Commission. . . .

II

. . . Our decisions make clear that the purpose of the active supervision inquiry is not to determine whether the State has met some normative standard, such as efficiency, in its regulatory practices. Its purpose is to determine whether the State has exercised sufficient independent judgment and control so that the details of the rates or prices have been established as a product of deliberate state intervention, not simply by agreement among private parties. Much as in causation inquiries, the analysis asks whether the State has played a substantial role in determining the specifics of the economic policy. The question is not how well state regulation works but whether the anticompetitive scheme is the State's own. . . .

The respondents contend that principles of federalism justify a broad interpretation of state-action immunity, but there is a powerful refutation of their viewpoint in the briefs that were filed in this case. The State of Wisconsin, joined by Montana and 34 other States, has filed a brief as *amici curiae* on the precise point. These States deny that respondents' broad immunity rule would serve the States' best interests. We are in agreement with the amici submission.

If the States must act in the shadow of state-action immunity whenever they enter the realm of economic regulation, then our doctrine will impede their freedom of action, not advance it. The fact of the matter is that the States regulate their economies in many ways not inconsistent with the antitrust laws. For example, Oregon may provide for peer review by its physicians without approving anticompetitive conduct by them. See *Patrick, supra,* at 105. Or Michigan may regulate its public utilities without authorizing monopolization in the market for electric light bulbs. See *Cantor v. Detroit Edison Co.,* 428 U.S. 579, 596 (1976). So we have held that state-action immunity is disfavored, much as are repeals by implication. *Lafayette v. Louisiana Power & Light Co.,* 435 U.S. 389, 398–399 (1978). By adhering in most cases to fundamental and accepted assumptions about the benefits of competition within the framework of the antitrust laws, we increase the States' regulatory flexibility.

States must accept political responsibility for actions they intend to undertake. It is quite a different matter, however, for federal law to compel a result that the States do not intend but for which they are held to account. Federalism serves to assign political responsibility, not to obscure it. Neither federalism nor political responsibility is well served by a rule that essential national policies are displaced by state regulations intended to achieve more limited ends. For States which do choose to displace the free market with regulation, our insistence on real compliance with both parts of the *Midcal* test will serve to make clear that the State is responsible for the price fixing it has sanctioned and undertaken to control.

The respondents contend that these concerns are better addressed by the requirement that the States articulate a clear policy to displace the antitrust laws with their own forms of economic regulation. This contention misapprehends the close relation between *Midcal*'s two elements. Both are directed at ensuring that particular anticompetitive mechanisms operate because of a deliberate and intended state policy. In the usual case, *Midcal*'s requirement that the State articulate a clear policy shows little more than that the State has not acted through inadvertence; it cannot alone ensure, as required by our precedents, that particular anticompetitive conduct has been approved by the State.

It seems plain, moreover, in light of the amici curiae brief to which we have referred, that sole reliance on the requirement of clear articulation will not allow the regulatory flexibility that these States deem necessary. For States whose object it is to benefit their citizens through regulation, a broad doctrine of state-action immunity may serve as nothing more than an attractive nuisance in the economic sphere. To oppose these pressures, sole reliance on the requirement of clear articulation could become a rather meaningless formal constraint.

III

In the case before us, the Court of Appeals relied upon a formulation of the active supervision requirement articulated by the First Circuit: " 'Where . . . the state's program is in place, is staffed and funded, grants to the state officials ample power and the duty to regulate pursuant to declared standards of state policy, is enforceable in the state's courts, and demonstrates some basic level of activity directed towards seeing that the private actors carry out the state's policy and not simply their own policy, more need not be established,' " quoting *New England Motor Rate Bureau, Inc. v. FTC*, 908 F.2d 1064, 1071 (1st Cir. 1990). Based on this standard, the Third Circuit ruled that the active supervision requirement was met in all four states, and held that the respondents' conduct was entitled to state-action immunity from antitrust liability.

While in theory the standard articulated by the First Circuit might be applied in a manner consistent with our precedents, it seems to us insufficient to establish the requisite level of active supervision. . . . [W]e must conclude that there was no active supervision in either Wisconsin or Montana.

The respondents point out that in Wisconsin and Montana the rating bureaus filed rates with state agencies and that in both States the so-called negative option rule prevailed. The rates became effective unless they were rejected within a set time. It is said that as a matter of law in those States inaction signified substantive approval. This proposition cannot be reconciled, however, with the detailed findings, entered by the ALJ and adopted by the Commission, which demonstrate that the potential for state supervision was not realized in fact. The ALJ found, and the Commission agreed, that at most the rate filings were checked for mathematical accuracy. Some were unchecked altogether. In Montana, a rate filing became effective despite the failure of the rating bureau to provide additional requested information. In Wisconsin, additional information was provided after a lapse of seven years, during which time the rate filing remained in effect. These findings are fatal to respondents' attempts to portray the state regulatory regimes as providing the necessary component of active supervision. The findings demonstrate that, whatever the potential for state regulatory review in Wisconsin and Montana, active state supervision did not occur. In the absence of active supervision in fact, there can be no state-action immunity for what were otherwise private price fixing arrangements. . . .

This case involves horizontal price fixing under a vague imprimatur in form and agency inaction in fact. No antitrust offense is more pernicious than price fixing. *FTC v. Superior Court Trial Lawyers Assn.*, 493 U.S. 411, 434, n.16 (1990). In this context, we decline to formulate a rule that would lead to a finding of active state supervision where in fact there was none. Our decision should be read in light of the gravity of the antitrust offense, the involvement of private actors throughout, and the clear absence of state supervision. We do not imply that some particular form of state or local regulation is required to achieve ends other than the establishment of uniform prices. . . . [W]e do not here call into question a regulatory regime in which sampling techniques or a specified rate of return allow state regulators to provide comprehensive supervision without complete control, or in which there was an infrequent lapse of state supervision. Cf. *324 Liquor Corp. v. Duffy*, 479 U.S. 335, 344, n.6 (1987) (a statute specifying the margin between wholesale and retail prices may satisfy the active supervision requirement). In the circumstances of this case, however, we conclude that the acts of the respondents in the States of Montana and Wisconsin are not immune from antitrust liability.[7]

NOTES AND QUESTIONS

1. As noted in *Hallie, supra*, the "active supervision" requirement applies to the conduct of private parties. It does not apply to municipalities. But suppose that the municipality gives economic decisionmaking power to a private party. Must the private conduct be supervised? If so, who must supervise it? In footnote 10 of the *Hallie* opinion, the Supreme Court suggested that "[w]here state or municipal regulation of a private party is involved, however, active *state* supervision must be shown, even where a clearly articulated state policy exists." Was this merely a slip of the pen, or did the Court really mean to suggest that the *state* must supervise private decisionmaking in regulatory schemes created by municipalities? Courts

---

[7] [As to Connecticut and Arizona, the Court remanded for consideration whether the Third Circuit had given adequate regard to the FTC's fact findings. —eds.]

addressing the issue have held that if municipalities create regulatory schemes requiring supervision, the municipalities themselves must do the supervising. *See Englert v. City of McKeesport*, 637 F. Supp. 930 (W.D. Pa. 1986) (requiring active municipal supervision over municipally authorized private electrical inspections). *See* 1 P. Areeda & H. Hovenkamp, Antitrust Law ¶ 226 (4th ed. 2013).

In North Caroline Board of Dental Examiners, 151 F.T.C. 607 (2011), *review denied*, 717 F.3d 359 (4th Cir. 2013), the FTC concluded and the Fourth Circuit agreed that a professional dental association whose decision making was controlled by practicing dentists required both authorization and supervision, "especially when the state agency is not accountable to the public but rather to the very industry it purports to regulate . . . ." The court also agreed that because the relevant decision makers where the dentist participants the concerted action requirement was permit, permitting the group to be challenged as a cartel. The challenged rule prohibited anyone in the state except dentists from providing professional teeth whitening services. On supervision the court concluded:

> North Carolina has done far less "supervision" in this case than the Court found wanting in *Midcal*. Here, the cease-and-desist letters were sent without state oversight and without the required judicial authorization. The Board has pointed to certain reporting provisions and "good government" provisions in North Carolina law, but those fall far short of the type of supervision in *Midcal* that was nonetheless considered deficient. As the FTC explained, "[t]his sort of generic oversight . . . does not substitute for the required review and approval of the 'particular anticompetitive acts' " challenged by the FTC.

By contrast *Hass v. Oregon State Bar*, 883 F.2d 1453 (9th Cir. 1989), held that a statutorily created state bar association, like a municipality, was a governmental agency that did not need to be supervised in order for its activities to qualify for the "state action" exemption. But the bar association was made up of lawyers, and the principal interests that the bar association protected were those of the lawyers themselves. A dissenting Judge objected that

> the Bar's regulatory authority is simply not constrained by the same degree of public scrutiny typically governing other state agencies. While state agencies may not operate as democratically as municipal governments, they usually provide some opportunity for public participation in regulatory decisions. . . . The Bar, however, is not required to submit *any* of its Fund decisions for public scrutiny. Requiring active supervision of the Bar would serve the salutary purpose of ensuring that the public, either directly or through publicly accountable state officials, would have an opportunity to participate in a delegated regulatory decisionmaking process of significant public importance.

2. The Health Care Quality Improvement Act, 42 U.S.C. §§ 11101–11152, exempts medical peer review from the antitrust laws if the review was undertaken in the "reasonable belief" that it would further quality health care. The statute "does not change other immunities under the law" — so presumably the states are free to create even larger "state action" exemptions, provided the conduct is actively supervised. Under the statute, physicians' conduct in the peer review process is subjected to an *objective* standard of good faith. As a result, if physicians conduct peer review proceedings in an orderly fashion, give due notice and opportunity to be heard to the subject, and act deliberately, a disciplined or excluded physician will not be permitted to inquire into their actual state of mind. *See, e.g., Austin v. McNamara*, 979 F.2d 728 (9th Cir. 1992) (if there was an objective basis for the dismissal, statute's standard was met, even though some review board members may subjectively have been hostile toward the plaintiff); *Fobbs v. Holy Cross Health Sys. Corp.*, 29 F.3d 1439 (9th Cir. 1994), *cert. denied*, 513 U.S. 1127 (1995) (same); *Bryan v. James E. Holmes Regional Medical Center*, 33 F.3d 1318 (11th Cir. 1994) (HCQIA exempted physician disciplinary action prompted by reasonable belief that plaintiff had acted unprofessionally; numerous complaints of abusive behavior directed at subordinates; staff had made numerous attempts to control the problem by other means). *See also Imperial v. Suburban Hospital Assn.*, 37 F.3d 1026 (4th Cir. 1994) (hospital and staff immune from antitrust liability when all procedural requirements of HCQIA met); *Smith v. Ricks*, 31 F.3d 1478 (9th Cir. 1994) (HCQIA immunized hospital providing adequate notice and opportunity to be heard in physician discipline process and conducting thorough review).

3.   In *Hardy v. City Optical*, 39 F.3d 765 (7th Cir. 1994), the Seventh Circuit held that optometrists' requirement that patients obtaining their eye examinations also obtain their contact lenses in the same place could have been an unlawful tying arrangement. The requirement did not enjoy a *Parker* exemption by virtue of a statute requiring that only certain eye care professionals such as optometrists could recommend and fit contact lenses. The statute seemed to contemplate that the person conducting the eye examination could *either* supply the contact lenses herself or else write a prescription so that the patient could procure them elsewhere. Suppose that the statute *forbad* the consumer from purchasing contact lenses from anyone other than the person who performed the eye examination? Would there be any private conduct left to supervise?

In *Massachusetts School of Law at Andover v. ABA*, 107 F.3d 1026 (3d Cir.), *cert. denied*, 522 U.S. 907 (1997), the Third Circuit examined states' policies of adopting the accreditation recommendations of the American Bar Association and excluding graduates from unaccredited law schools from the states' bar exam. The plaintiff was a law school that the ABA refused to accredit after it was found not to be in compliance with several of the ABA's accreditation standards. The court noted that it was not the ABA itself that forbad the plaintiff's graduates from taking the bar exam. Rather, "[e]ach state retains" that authority. Further,

> to the extent that [the plaintiff's] alleged injury arises from the inability of its graduates to take the bar examination in most states, the injury is the result of state action and thus is immune from antitrust action. . . . The ABA does not decide who can take the bar examinations. Rather, it makes an accreditation decision which it conveys to the states, but the states make the decisions as to bar admissions. Without state action, the ABA's accreditation decisions would not affect state bar admissions requirements. Because the states are sovereign in imposing the bar admission require-ments, the clear articulation and active supervision requirements urged by MSL are inapplicable.

PROBLEM 9.5

Kansas has a liquor price-posting statute which requires liquor distributors to post their wholesale liquor prices monthly. But the statute differs from most other price-posting statutes in one respect: wholesale transactions must be made at the posted price. The state's Alcoholic Beverage Control Board establishes a minimum markup percentage for retail sales, which is published quarterly. Retailers may charge more than the posted wholesale price plus the minimum markup, but they may not charge less. The minimum markup percentages have been changed only once in the preceding 10 years. Is the statute preempted under *Fisher*? If so, is it saved by the "state action" exemption? *See Kansas ex rel. Stephan v. Lamb*, 1987-1 Trade Cas. ¶ 67521 (D. Kan. 1987), which will give you the wrong answer. Why?

PROBLEM 9.6

A state statute (1) defines the exclusive service areas for privately owned electric utilities in the state, and (2) instructs the utilities that when large new customers that straddle a utility boundary apply for service, the utility entitled to the customer is the one in whose area the customer has the largest number of square feet of space. So, for example, if a new subdivision is located 60% in utility A's territory and 40% in utility B's territory, utility A would provide the service. No agency of the state supervises the operation of this customer assignment process. Have the "state action" requirements respecting private firm conduct been met? Does it matter that the "supervisory" activity consists merely in calculating the number of square feet in each utility's territory? Would the state have to have a mechanism for resolving disputes? *See Municipal Utils. Bd. of Albertville v. Alabama Power*, 934 F.2d 1493 (11th Cir. 1991).

APPENDIX A

HORIZONTAL MERGER GUIDELINES

U.S. Dept. of Justice and Federal Trade Commission

Issued: August 19, 2010

Table of Contents

1. Overview

These Guidelines outline the principal analytical techniques, practices, and the enforcement policy of the Department of Justice and the Federal Trade Commission (the "Agencies") with respect to mergers and acquisitions involving actual or potential competitors ("horizontal mergers") under the federal antitrust laws.[1] The relevant statutory provisions include Section 7 of the Clayton Act, 15 U.S.C. § 18, Sections 1 and 2 of the Sherman Act, 15 U.S.C. § 1, 2, and Section 5 of the Federal Trade Commission Act, 15 U.S.C. § 45. Most particularly, Section 7 of the Clayton Act prohibits mergers if "in any line of commerce or in any activity affecting commerce in any section of the country, the effect of such acquisition may be substantially to lessen competition, or to tend to create a monopoly."

The Agencies seek to identify and challenge competitively harmful mergers while avoiding unnecessary interference with mergers that are either competitively beneficial or neutral. Most merger analysis is necessarily predictive, requiring an assessment of what will likely happen if a merger proceeds as compared to what will likely happen if it does not. Given this inherent need for prediction, these Guidelines reflect the congressional intent that merger enforcement should interdict competitive problems in their incipiency and that certainty about anticompetitive effect is seldom possible and not required for a merger to be illegal.

These Guidelines describe the principal analytical techniques and the main types of evidence on which the Agencies usually rely to predict whether a horizontal merger may substantially lessen competition. They are not intended to describe how the Agencies analyze cases other than horizontal mergers. These Guidelines

---

[1] These Guidelines replace the Horizontal Merger Guidelines issued in 1992, revised in 1997. They reflect the ongoing accumulation of experience at the Agencies. The Commentary on the Horizontal Merger Guidelines issued by the Agencies in 2006 remains a valuable supplement to these Guidelines. These Guidelines may be revised from time to time as necessary to reflect significant changes in enforcement policy, to clarify existing policy, or to reflect new learning. These Guidelines do not cover vertical or other types of non-horizontal acquisitions.

are intended to assist the business community and antitrust practitioners by increasing the transparency of the analytical process underlying the Agencies' enforcement decisions. They may also assist the courts in developing an appropriate framework for interpreting and applying the antitrust laws in the horizontal merger context.

These Guidelines should be read with the awareness that merger analysis does not consist of uniform application of a single methodology. Rather, it is a fact-specific process through which the Agencies, guided by their extensive experience, apply a range of analytical tools to the reasonably available and reliable evidence to evaluate competitive concerns in a limited period of time. Where these Guidelines provide examples, they are illustrative and do not exhaust the applications of the relevant principle.[2]

The unifying theme of these Guidelines is that mergers should not be permitted to create, enhance, or entrench market power or to facilitate its exercise. For simplicity of exposition, these Guidelines generally refer to all of these effects as enhancing market power. A merger enhances market power if it is likely to encourage one or more firms to raise price, reduce output, diminish innovation, or otherwise harm customers as a result of diminished competitive constraints or incentives. In evaluating how a merger will likely change a firm's behavior, the Agencies focus primarily on how the merger affects conduct that would be most profitable for the firm.

A merger can enhance market power simply by eliminating competition between the merging parties. This effect can arise even if the merger causes no changes in the way other firms behave. Adverse competitive effects arising in this manner are referred to as "unilateral effects." A merger also can enhance market power by increasing the risk of coordinated, accommodating, or interdependent behavior among rivals. Adverse competitive effects arising in this manner are referred to as "coordinated effects." In any given case, either or both types of effects may be present, and the distinction between them may be blurred.

These Guidelines principally describe how the Agencies analyze mergers between rival suppliers that may enhance their market power as sellers. Enhancement of market power by sellers often elevates the prices charged to customers. For simplicity of exposition, these Guidelines generally discuss the analysis in terms of such price effects. Enhanced market power can also be manifested in non-price terms and conditions that adversely affect customers, including reduced product quality, reduced product variety, reduced service, or diminished innovation. Such non-price effects may coexist with price effects, or can arise in their absence. When the Agencies investigate whether a merger may lead to a substantial lessening of non-price competition, they employ an approach analogous to that used to evaluate price competition. Enhanced market power may also make it more likely that the merged entity can profitably and effectively engage in exclusionary conduct. Regardless of how enhanced market power likely would be manifested, the Agencies normally evaluate mergers based on their impact on customers. The Agencies

---

[2] These Guidelines are not intended to describe how the Agencies will conduct the litigation of cases they decide to bring. Although relevant in that context, these Guidelines neither dictate nor exhaust the range of evidence the Agencies may introduce in litigation.

examine effects on either or both of the direct customers and the final consumers. The Agencies presume, absent convincing evidence to the contrary, that adverse effects on direct customers also cause adverse effects on final consumers.

Enhancement of market power by buyers, sometimes called "monopsony power," has adverse effects comparable to enhancement of market power by sellers. The Agencies employ an analogous framework to analyze mergers between rival purchasers that may enhance their market power as buyers. See Section 12.

2. Evidence of Adverse Competitive Effects

The Agencies consider any reasonably available and reliable evidence to address the central question of whether a merger may substantially lessen competition. This section discusses several categories and sources of evidence that the Agencies, in their experience, have found most informative in predicting the likely competitive effects of mergers. The list provided here is not exhaustive. In any given case, reliable evidence may be available in only some categories or from some sources. For each category of evidence, the Agencies consider evidence indicating that the merger may enhance competition as well as evidence indicating that it may lessen competition.

2.1   Types of Evidence

2.1.1   Actual Effects Observed in Consummated Mergers

When evaluating a consummated merger, the ultimate issue is not only whether adverse competitive effects have already resulted from the merger, but also whether such effects are likely to arise in the future. Evidence of observed post-merger price increases or other changes adverse to customers is given substantial weight. The Agencies evaluate whether such changes are anticompetitive effects resulting from the merger, in which case they can be dispositive. However, a consummated merger may be anticompetitive even if such effects have not yet been observed, perhaps because the merged firm may be aware of the possibility of post-merger antitrust review and moderating its conduct. Consequently, the Agencies also consider the same types of evidence they consider when evaluating unconsummated mergers.

2.1.2   Direct Comparisons Based on Experience

The Agencies look for historical events, or "natural experiments," that are informative regarding the competitive effects of the merger. For example, the Agencies may examine the impact of recent mergers, entry, expansion, or exit in the relevant market. Effects of analogous events in similar markets may also be informative.

The Agencies also look for reliable evidence based on variations among similar markets. For example, if the merging firms compete in some locales but not others, comparisons of prices charged in regions where they do and do not compete may be informative regarding post-merger prices. In some cases, however, prices are set on such a broad geographic basis that such comparisons are not informative. The Agencies also may examine how prices in similar markets vary with the number of significant competitors in those markets.

2.1.3   Market Shares and Concentration in a Relevant Market

The Agencies give weight to the merging parties' market shares in a relevant market, the level of concentration, and the change in concentration caused by the merger. See Sections 4 and 5. Mergers that cause a significant increase in concentration and result in highly concentrated markets are presumed to be likely to enhance market power, but this presumption can be rebutted by persuasive evidence showing that the merger is unlikely to enhance market power.

2.1.4 Substantial Head-to-Head Competition

The Agencies consider whether the merging firms have been, or likely will become absent the merger, substantial head-to-head competitors. Such evidence can be especially relevant for evaluating adverse unilateral effects, which result directly from the loss of that competition. See Section 6. This evidence can also inform market definition. See Section 4.

2.1.5 Disruptive Role of a Merging Party

The Agencies consider whether a merger may lessen competition by eliminating a "maverick" firm, i.e., a firm that plays a disruptive role in the market to the benefit of customers. For example, if one of the merging firms has a strong incumbency position and the other merging firm threatens to disrupt market conditions with a new technology or business model, their merger can involve the loss of actual or potential competition. Likewise, one of the merging firms may have the incentive to take the lead in price cutting or other competitive conduct or to resist increases in industry prices. A firm that may discipline prices based on its ability and incentive to expand production rapidly using available capacity also can be a maverick, as can a firm that has often resisted otherwise prevailing industry norms to cooperate on price setting or other terms of competition.

2.2 Sources of Evidence

The Agencies consider many sources of evidence in their merger analysis. The most common sources of reasonably available and reliable evidence are the merging parties, customers, other industry participants, and industry observers.

2.2.1 Merging Parties

The Agencies typically obtain substantial information from the merging parties. This information can take the form of documents, testimony, or data, and can consist of descriptions of competitively relevant conditions or reflect actual business conduct and decisions. Documents created in the normal course are more probative than documents created as advocacy materials in merger review. Documents describing industry conditions can be informative regarding the operation of the market and how a firm identifies and assesses its rivals, particularly when business decisions are made in reliance on the accuracy of those descriptions. The business decisions taken by the merging firms also can be informative about industry conditions. For example, if a firm sets price well above incremental cost, that normally indicates either that the firm believes its customers are not highly sensitive to price (not in itself of antitrust concern, see Section 4.1.3[3]) or that the firm and its rivals are engaged in coordinated interaction (see Section 7). Incremental cost depends on the relevant increment in output as well as on the time period involved, and in the case of large increments and sustained changes in output it may include some costs that would be fixed for smaller increments of output or shorter time periods.

Explicit or implicit evidence that the merging parties intend to raise prices, reduce output or capacity, reduce product quality or variety, withdraw products or delay their introduction, or curtail research and development efforts after the merger, or explicit or implicit evidence that the ability to engage in such conduct motivated the merger, can be highly informative in evaluating the likely effects of a merger. Likewise, the Agencies look for reliable evidence that the merger is likely to result in efficiencies. The Agencies give careful consideration to the views of individuals whose responsibilities, expertise, and experience relating to the issues in question provide particular indicia of reliability. The financial terms of the transaction may also be informative regarding competitive effects. For example, a purchase price in excess of the acquired firm's stand-alone market value may indicate that the acquiring firm is paying a premium because it expects to be able to reduce competition or to achieve efficiencies.

2.2.2   Customers

Customers can provide a variety of information to the Agencies, ranging from information about their own purchasing behavior and choices to their views about the effects of the merger itself.

Information from customers about how they would likely respond to a price increase, and the relative attractiveness of different products or suppliers, may be highly relevant, especially when corroborated by other evidence such as historical purchasing patterns and practices. Customers also can provide valuable information about the impact of historical events such as entry by a new supplier.

The conclusions of well-informed and sophisticated customers on the likely impact of the merger itself can also help the Agencies investigate competitive effects, because customers typically feel the consequences of both competitively beneficial and competitively harmful mergers. In evaluating such evidence, the Agencies are mindful that customers may oppose, or favor, a merger for reasons unrelated to the antitrust issues raised by that merger.

When some customers express concerns about the competitive effects of a merger while others view the merger as beneficial or neutral, the Agencies take account of this divergence in using the information provided by customers and consider the likely reasons for such divergence of views. For example, if for regulatory reasons some customers cannot buy imported products, while

---

[3] High margins commonly arise for products that are significantly differentiated. Products involving substantial fixed costs typically will be developed only if suppliers expect there to be enough differentiation to support margins sufficient to cover those fixed costs. High margins can be consistent with incumbent firms earning competitive returns.

others can, a merger between domestic suppliers may harm the former customers even if it leaves the more flexible customers unharmed. See Section 3.

When direct customers of the merging firms compete against one another in a downstream market, their interests may not be aligned with the interests of final consumers, especially if the direct customers expect to pass on any anticompetitive price increase. A customer that is protected from adverse competitive effects by a long-term contract, or otherwise relatively immune from the merger's harmful effects, may even welcome an anticompetitive merger that provides that customer with a competitive advantage over its downstream rivals.

Example 1: As a result of the merger, Customer C will experience a price increase for an input used in producing its final product, raising its costs. Customer C's rivals use this input more intensively than Customer C, and the same price increase applied to them will raise their costs more than it raises Customer C's costs. On balance, Customer C may benefit from the merger even though the merger involves a substantial lessening of competition.

2.2.3   Other Industry Participants and Observers

Suppliers, indirect customers, distributors, other industry participants, and industry analysts can also provide information helpful to a merger inquiry. The interests of firms selling products complementary to those offered by the merging firms often are well aligned with those of customers, making their informed views valuable.

Information from firms that are rivals to the merging parties can help illuminate how the market operates. The interests of rival firms often diverge from the interests of customers, since customers normally lose, but rival firms gain, if the merged entity raises its prices. For that reason, the Agencies do not routinely rely on the overall views of rival firms regarding the competitive effects of the merger. However, rival firms may provide relevant facts, and even their overall views may be instructive, especially in cases where the Agencies are concerned that the merged entity may engage in exclusionary conduct.

Example 2: Merging Firms A and B operate in a market in which network effects are significant, implying that any firm's product is significantly more valuable if it commands a large market share or if it is interconnected with others that in aggregate command such a share. Prior to the merger, they and their rivals voluntarily interconnect with one another. The merger would create an entity with a large enough share that a strategy of ending voluntary interconnection would have a dangerous probability of creating monopoly power in this market. The interests of rivals and of consumers would be broadly aligned in preventing such a merger.

3. Targeted Customers and Price Discrimination

When examining possible adverse competitive effects from a merger, the Agencies consider whether those effects vary significantly for different customers purchasing the same or similar products. Such differential impacts are possible when sellers can discriminate, e.g., by profitably raising price to certain targeted customers but not to others. The possibility of price discrimination influences market definition (see Section 4), the measurement of market shares (see Section 5), and the evaluation of competitive effects (see Sections 6 and 7).

When price discrimination is feasible, adverse competitive effects on targeted customers can arise, even if such effects will not arise for other customers. A price increase for targeted customers may be profitable even if a price increase for all customers would not be profitable because too many other customers would substitute away. When discrimination is reasonably likely, the Agencies may evaluate competitive effects separately by type of customer. The Agencies may have access to information unavailable to customers that is relevant to evaluating whether discrimination is reasonably likely.

For price discrimination to be feasible, two conditions typically must be met: differential pricing and limited arbitrage.

First, the suppliers engaging in price discrimination must be able to price differently to targeted customers than to other customers. This may involve identification of individual customers to which different prices are offered or offering different prices to different types of customers based on observable characteristics.

Example 3: Suppliers can distinguish large buyers from small buyers. Large buyers are more likely than small buyers to self-supply in response to a significant price increase. The merger may lead to price discrimination against small buyers, harming them, even if large buyers are not harmed. Such discrimination can occur even if there is no discrete gap in size between the classes of large and small buyers.

In other cases, suppliers may be unable to distinguish among different types of customers but can offer multiple products that sort customers based on their purchase decisions.

Second, the targeted customers must not be able to defeat the price increase of concern by arbitrage, e.g., by purchasing indirectly from or through other customers. Arbitrage may be difficult if it would void warranties or make service more difficult or costly for customers. Arbitrage is inherently impossible for many services. Arbitrage between customers at different geographic locations may be impractical due to transportation costs. Arbitrage on a modest scale may be possible but sufficiently costly or limited that it would not deter or defeat a discriminatory pricing strategy.

4. Market Definition

When the Agencies identify a potential competitive concern with a horizontal merger, market definition plays two roles. First, market definition helps specify the line of commerce and section of the country in which the competitive concern arises. In any merger enforcement action, the Agencies will normally identify one or more relevant markets in which the merger may substantially lessen competition. Second, market definition allows the Agencies to identify market participants and measure market shares and market concentration. See Section 5. The measurement of market shares and market concentration is not an end in itself, but is useful to the extent it illuminates the merger's likely competitive effects.

The Agencies' analysis need not start with market definition. Some of the analytical tools used by the Agencies to assess competitive effects do not rely on market definition, although evaluation of competitive alternatives available to customers is always necessary at some point in the analysis.

Evidence of competitive effects can inform market definition, just as market definition can be informative regarding competitive effects. For example, evidence that a reduction in the number of significant rivals offering a group of products causes prices for those products to rise significantly can itself establish that those products form a relevant market. Such evidence also may more directly predict the competitive effects of a merger, reducing the role of inferences from market definition and market shares. Where analysis suggests alternative and reasonably plausible candidate markets, and where the resulting market shares lead to very different inferences regarding competitive effects, it is particularly valuable to examine more direct forms of evidence concerning those effects.

Market definition focuses solely on demand substitution factors, i.e., on customers' ability and willingness to substitute away from one product to another in response to a price increase or a corresponding non-price change such as a reduction in product quality or service. The responsive actions of suppliers are also important in competitive analysis. They are considered in these Guidelines in the sections addressing the identification of market participants, the measurement of market shares, the analysis of competitive effects, and entry.

Customers often confront a range of possible substitutes for the products of the merging firms. Some substitutes may be closer, and others more distant, either geographically or in terms of product attributes and perceptions. Additionally, customers may assess the proximity of different products differently. When products or suppliers in different geographic areas are substitutes for one another to varying degrees, defining a market to include some substitutes and exclude others is inevitably a simplification that cannot capture the full variation in the extent to which different products compete against each other. The principles of market definition outlined below seek to make this inevitable simplification as useful and informative as is practically possible. Relevant markets need not have precise metes and bounds.

Defining a market broadly to include relatively distant product or geographic substitutes can lead to misleading market shares. This is because the competitive significance of distant substitutes is unlikely to be commensurate with their shares in a broad market. Although excluding more distant substitutes from the market inevitably understates their competitive significance to some degree, doing so often provides a more accurate indicator of the competitive effects of the merger than would the alternative of including them and overstating their competitive significance as proportional to their shares in an expanded market.

Example 4: Firms A and B, sellers of two leading brands of motorcycles, propose to merge. If Brand A motorcycle prices were to rise, some buyers would substitute to Brand B, and some others would substitute to cars. However, motorcycle buyers see Brand B motorcycles as much more similar to Brand A motorcycles than are cars. Far more cars are sold than motorcycles. Evaluating shares in a market that includes cars would greatly underestimate the competitive significance of Brand B motorcycles in constraining Brand A's prices and greatly overestimate the significance of cars.

Market shares of different products in narrowly defined markets are more likely to capture the relative competitive significance of these products, and often more accurately reflect competition between close substitutes. As a result, properly defined antitrust markets often exclude some substitutes to which some customers might turn in the face of a price increase even if such substitutes provide alternatives for those customers. However, a group of products is too narrow to constitute a relevant market if competition from products outside that group is so ample that even the complete elimination of competition within the group would not significantly harm either direct customers or downstream consumers. The hypothetical monopolist test (see Section 4.1.1) is designed to ensure that candidate markets are not overly narrow in this respect.

The Agencies implement these principles of market definition flexibly when evaluating different possible candidate markets. Relevant antitrust markets defined according to the hypothetical monopolist test are not always intuitive and may not align with how industry members use the term "market."

Section 4.1 describes the principles that apply to product market definition, and gives guidance on how the Agencies most often apply those principles. Section 4.2 describes how the same principles apply to geographic market definition. Although discussed separately for simplicity of exposition, the principles described in Sections 4.1 and 4.2 are combined to define a relevant market, which has both a product and a geographic dimension. In particular, the hypothetical monopolist test is applied to a group of products together with a geographic region to determine a relevant market.

4.1 Product Market Definition

When a product sold by one merging firm (Product A) competes against one or more products sold by the other merging firm, the Agencies define a relevant product market around Product A to evaluate the importance of that competition. Such a relevant product market consists of a group of substitute products including Product A. Multiple relevant product markets may thus be identified.

4.1.1 The Hypothetical Monopolist Test

The Agencies employ the hypothetical monopolist test to evaluate whether groups of products in candidate markets are sufficiently broad to constitute relevant antitrust markets. The Agencies use the hypothetical monopolist test to identify a set of products that are reasonably interchangeable with a product sold by one of the merging firms.

The hypothetical monopolist test requires that a product market contain enough substitute products so that it could be subject to post-merger exercise of market power significantly exceeding that existing absent the merger. Specifically, the test requires that a hypothetical profit-maximizing firm, not subject to price regulation, that was the only present and future seller of those products ("hypothetical monopolist") likely would impose at least a small but significant and non-transitory increase in price ("SSNIP") on at least one product in the market, including at least one product sold by one of the merging firms.[4] For the purpose of analyzing this issue, the terms of sale of products outside the candidate market are held constant. The SSNIP is employed solely as a methodological tool for performing the hypothetical monopolist test; it is not a tolerance level for price increases resulting from a merger.

Groups of products may satisfy the hypothetical monopolist test without including the full range of substitutes from which customers choose. The hypothetical monopolist test may identify a group of products as a relevant market even if customers would substitute significantly to products outside that group in response to a price increase.

Example 5: Products A and B are being tested as a candidate market. Each sells for $100, has an incremental cost of $60, and sells 1200 units. For every dollar increase in the price of Product A, for any given price of Product B, Product A loses twenty units of sales to products outside the candidate market and ten units of sales to Product B, and likewise for Product B. Under these conditions, economic analysis shows that a hypothetical profit-maximizing monopolist controlling Products A and B would raise both of their prices by ten percent, to $110. Therefore, Products A and B satisfy the hypothetical monopolist test using a five percent SSNIP, and indeed for any SSNIP size up to ten percent. This is true even though two-thirds of the sales lost by one product when it raises its price are diverted to products outside the relevant market.

When applying the hypothetical monopolist test to define a market around a product offered by one of the merging firms, if the market includes a second product, the Agencies will normally also include a third product if that third product is a closer substitute for the first product than is the second product. The third product is a closer substitute if, in response to a SSNIP on the first product, greater revenues are diverted to the third product than to the second product.

Example 6: In Example 5, suppose that half of the unit sales lost by Product A when it raises its price are diverted to Product C, which also has a price of $100, while one-third are diverted to Product B. Product C is a closer substitute for Product A than is Product B. Thus Product C will normally be included in the relevant market, even though Products A and B together satisfy the hypothetical monopolist test.

The hypothetical monopolist test ensures that markets are not defined too narrowly, but it does not lead to a single relevant market. The Agencies may evaluate a merger in any relevant market satisfying the test, guided by the

---

[4] If the pricing incentives of the firms supplying the products in the candidate market differ substantially from those of the hypothetical monopolist, for reasons other than the latter's control over a larger group of substitutes, the Agencies may instead employ the concept of a hypothetical profit-maximizing cartel comprised of the firms (with all their products) that sell the products in the candidate market. This approach is most likely to be appropriate if the merging firms sell products outside the candidate market that significantly affect their pricing incentives for products in the candidate market. This could occur, for example, if the candidate market is one for durable equipment and the firms selling that equipment derive substantial net revenues from selling spare parts and service for that equipment.

overarching principle that the purpose of defining the market and measuring market shares is to illuminate the evaluation of competitive effects. Because the relative competitive significance of more distant substitutes is apt to be overstated by their share of sales, when the Agencies rely on market shares and concentration, they usually do so in the smallest relevant market satisfying the hypothetical monopolist test.

Example 7: In Example 4, including cars in the market will lead to misleadingly small market shares for motorcycle producers. Unless motorcycles fail the hypothetical monopolist test, the Agencies would not include cars in the market in analyzing this motorcycle merger.

4.1.2   Benchmark Prices and SSNIP Size

The Agencies apply the SSNIP starting from prices that would likely prevail absent the merger. If prices are not likely to change absent the merger, these benchmark prices can reasonably be taken to be the prices prevailing prior to the merger.[5] If prices are likely to change absent the merger, e.g., because of innovation or entry, the Agencies may use anticipated future prices as the benchmark for the test. If prices might fall absent the merger due to the breakdown of pre-merger coordination, the Agencies may use those lower prices as the benchmark for the test. In some cases, the techniques employed by the Agencies to implement the hypothetical monopolist test focus on the difference in incentives between pre-merger firms and the hypothetical monopolist and do not require specifying the benchmark prices.

The SSNIP is intended to represent a "small but significant" increase in the prices charged by firms in the candidate market for the value they contribute to the products or services used by customers. This properly directs attention to the effects of price changes commensurate with those that might result from a significant lessening of competition caused by the merger. This methodology is used because normally it is possible to quantify "small but significant" adverse price effects on customers and analyze their likely reactions, not because price effects are more important than non-price effects.

The Agencies most often use a SSNIP of five percent of the price paid by customers for the products or services to which the merging firms contribute value. However, what constitutes a "small but significant" increase in price, commensurate with a significant loss of competition caused by the merger, depends upon the nature of the industry and the merging firms' positions in it, and the Agencies may accordingly use a price increase that is larger or smaller than five percent. Where explicit or implicit prices for the firms' specific contribution to value can be identified with reasonable clarity, the Agencies may base the SSNIP on those prices.

Example 8: In a merger between two oil pipelines, the SSNIP would be based on the price charged for transporting the oil, not on the price of the oil itself. If pipelines buy the oil at one end and sell it at the other, the price

---

[5] Market definition for the evaluation of non-merger antitrust concerns such as monopolization or facilitating practices will differ in this respect if the effects resulting from the conduct of concern are already occurring at the time of evaluation.

charged for transporting the oil is implicit, equal to the difference between the price paid for oil at the input end and the price charged for oil at the output end. The relevant product sold by the pipelines is better described as "pipeline transportation of oil from point A to point B" than as "oil at point B."

Example 9: In a merger between two firms that install computers purchased from third parties, the SSNIP would be based on their fees, not on the price of installed computers. If these firms purchase the computers and charge their customers one package price, the implicit installation fee is equal to the package charge to customers less the price of the computers.

Example 10: In Example 9, suppose that the prices paid by the merging firms to purchase computers are opaque, but account for at least ninety-five percent of the prices they charge for installed computers, with profits or implicit fees making up five percent of those prices at most. A five percent SSNIP on the total price paid by customers would at least double those fees or profits. Even if that would be unprofitable for a hypothetical monopolist, a significant increase in fees might well be profitable. If the SSNIP is based on the total price paid by customers, a lower percentage will be used.

4.1.3   Implementing the Hypothetical Monopolist Test

The hypothetical monopolist's incentive to raise prices depends both on the extent to which customers would likely substitute away from the products in the candidate market in response to such a price increase and on the profit margins earned on those products. The profit margin on incremental units is the difference between price and incremental cost on those units. The Agencies often estimate incremental costs, for example using merging parties' documents or data the merging parties use to make business decisions. Incremental cost is measured over the change in output that would be caused by the price increase under consideration.

In considering customers' likely responses to higher prices, the Agencies take into account any reasonably available and reliable evidence, including, but not limited to:

- how customers have shifted purchases in the past in response to relative changes in price or other terms and conditions;

- information from buyers, including surveys, concerning how they would respond to price changes;

- the conduct of industry participants, notably:

  - ☐ sellers' business decisions or business documents indicating sellers' informed beliefs concerning how customers would substitute among products in response to relative changes in price;

  - ☐ industry participants' behavior in tracking and responding to price changes by some or all rivals;

- objective information about product characteristics and the costs and delays of switching products, especially switching from products in the candidate market to products outside the candidate market;

- the percentage of sales lost by one product in the candidate market, when its price alone rises, that is recaptured by other products in the candidate market, with a higher recapture percentage making a price increase more profitable for the hypothetical monopolist;

- evidence from other industry participants, such as sellers of complementary products;

- legal or regulatory requirements; and

- the influence of downstream competition faced by customers in their output markets.

When the necessary data are available, the Agencies also may consider a "critical loss analysis" to assess the extent to which it corroborates inferences drawn from the evidence noted above. Critical loss analysis asks whether imposing at least a SSNIP on one or more products in a candidate market would raise or lower the hypothetical monopolist's profits. While this "breakeven" analysis differs from the profit-maximizing analysis called for by the hypothetical monopolist test in Section 4.1.1, merging parties sometimes present this type of analysis to the Agencies. A price increase raises profits on sales made at the higher price, but this will be offset to the extent customers substitute away from products in the candidate market. Critical loss analysis compares the magnitude of these two offsetting effects resulting from the price increase. The "critical loss" is defined as the number of lost unit sales that would leave profits unchanged. The "predicted loss" is defined as the number of unit sales that the hypothetical monopolist is predicted to lose due to the price increase. The price increase raises the hypothetical monopolist's profits if the predicted loss is less than the critical loss.

The Agencies consider all of the evidence of customer substitution noted above in assessing the predicted loss. The Agencies require that estimates of the predicted loss be consistent with that evidence, including the pre-merger margins of products in the candidate market used to calculate the critical loss. Unless the firms are engaging in coordinated interaction (see Section 7), high pre-merger margins normally indicate that each firm's product individually faces demand that is not highly sensitive to price.[6] Higher pre-merger margins thus indicate a smaller predicted loss as well as a smaller critical loss. The higher the pre-merger margin, the smaller the recapture percentage necessary for the candidate market to satisfy the hypothetical monopolist test.

Even when the evidence necessary to perform the hypothetical monopolist test quantitatively is not available, the conceptual framework of the test provides a useful methodological tool for gathering and analyzing evidence pertinent to customer substitution and to market definition. The Agencies follow the hypothetical monopolist test to the extent possible given the available evidence, bearing in mind that the ultimate goal of market definition is to help determine whether the merger may substantially lessen competition.

4.1.4   Product Market Definition with Targeted Customers

---

[6] While margins are important for implementing the hypothetical monopolist test, high margins are not in themselves of antitrust concern.

If a hypothetical monopolist could profitably target a subset of customers for price increases, the Agencies may identify relevant markets defined around those targeted customers, to whom a hypothetical monopolist would profitably and separately impose at least a SSNIP. Markets to serve targeted customers are also known as price discrimination markets. In practice, the Agencies identify price discrimination markets only where they believe there is a realistic prospect of an adverse competitive effect on a group of targeted customers.

Example 11: Glass containers have many uses. In response to a price increase for glass containers, some users would substitute substantially to plastic or metal containers, but baby food manufacturers would not. If a hypothetical monopolist could price separately and limit arbitrage, baby food manufacturers would be vulnerable to a targeted increase in the price of glass containers. The Agencies could define a distinct market for glass containers used to package baby food.

The Agencies also often consider markets for targeted customers when prices are individually negotiated and suppliers have information about customers that would allow a hypothetical monopolist to identify customers that are likely to pay a higher price for the relevant product. If prices are negotiated individually with customers, the hypothetical monopolist test may suggest relevant markets that are as narrow as individual customers (see also Section 6.2 on bargaining and auctions). Nonetheless, the Agencies often define markets for groups of targeted customers, i.e., by type of customer, rather than by individual customer. By so doing, the Agencies are able to rely on aggregated market shares that can be more helpful in predicting the competitive effects of the merger.

4.2   Geographic Market Definition

The arena of competition affected by the merger may be geographically bounded if geography limits some customers' willingness or ability to substitute to some products, or some suppliers' willingness or ability to serve some customers. Both supplier and customer locations can affect this. The Agencies apply the principles of market definition described here and in Section 4.1 to define a relevant market with a geographic dimension as well as a product dimension.

The scope of geographic markets often depends on transportation costs. Other factors such as language, regulation, tariff and non-tariff trade barriers, custom and familiarity, reputation, and service availability may impede long-distance or international transactions. The competitive significance of foreign firms may be assessed at various exchange rates, especially if exchange rates have fluctuated in the recent past.

In the absence of price discrimination based on customer location, the Agencies normally define geographic markets based on the locations of suppliers, as explained in subsection 4.2.1. In other cases, notably if price discrimination based on customer location is feasible as is often the case when delivered pricing is commonly used in the industry, the Agencies may define geographic markets based on the locations of customers, as explained in subsection 4.2.2.

4.2.1 Geographic Markets Based on the Locations of Suppliers

Geographic markets based on the locations of suppliers encompass the region from which sales are made. Geographic markets of this type often apply when customers receive goods or services at suppliers' locations. Competitors in the market are firms with relevant production, sales, or service facilities in that region. Some customers who buy from these firms may be located outside the boundaries of the geographic market.

The hypothetical monopolist test requires that a hypothetical profit-maximizing firm that was the only present or future producer of the relevant product(s) located in the region would impose at least a SSNIP from at least one location, including at least one location of one of the merging firms. In this exercise the terms of sale for all products produced elsewhere are held constant. A single firm may operate in a number of different geographic markets, even for a single product.

Example 12: The merging parties both have manufacturing plants in City X. The relevant product is expensive to transport and suppliers price their products for pickup at their locations. Rival plants are some distance away in City Y. A hypothetical monopolist controlling all plants in City X could profitably impose a SSNIP at these plants. Competition from more distant plants would not defeat the price increase because supplies coming from more distant plants require expensive transportation. The relevant geographic market is defined around the plants in City X.

When the geographic market is defined based on supplier locations, sales made by suppliers located in the geographic market are counted, regardless of the location of the customer making the purchase.

In considering likely reactions of customers to price increases for the relevant product(s) imposed in a candidate geographic market, the Agencies consider any reasonably available and reliable evidence, including:

how customers have shifted purchases in the past between different geographic locations in response to relative changes in price or other terms and conditions;

the cost and difficulty of transporting the product (or the cost and difficulty of a customer traveling to a seller's location), in relation to its price;

whether suppliers need a presence near customers to provide service or support;

evidence on whether sellers base business decisions on the prospect of customers switching between geographic locations in response to relative changes in price or other competitive variables;

the costs and delays of switching from suppliers in the candidate geographic market to suppliers outside the candidate geographic market; and

the influence of downstream competition faced by customers in their output markets.

4.2.2 Geographic Markets Based on the Locations of Customers

When the hypothetical monopolist could discriminate based on customer location, the Agencies may define geographic markets based on the locations of targeted customers.[7] Geographic markets of this type often apply when suppliers deliver their products or services to customers' locations. Geographic markets of this type encompass the region into which sales are made. Competitors in the market are firms that sell to customers in the specified region. Some suppliers that sell into the relevant market may be located outside the boundaries of the geographic market.

The hypothetical monopolist test requires that a hypothetical profit-maximizing firm that was the only present or future seller of the relevant product(s) to customers in the region would impose at least a SSNIP on some customers in that region. A region forms a relevant geographic market if this price increase would not be defeated by substitution away from the relevant product or by arbitrage, e.g., customers in the region travelling outside it to purchase the relevant product. In this exercise, the terms of sale for products sold to all customers outside the region are held constant.

Example 13: Customers require local sales and support. Suppliers have sales and service operations in many geographic areas and can discriminate based on customer location. The geographic market can be defined around the locations of customers.

Example 14: Each merging firm has a single manufacturing plant and delivers the relevant product to customers in City X and in City Y. The relevant product is expensive to transport. The merging firms' plants are by far the closest to City X, but no closer to City Y than are numerous rival plants. This fact pattern suggests that customers in City X may be harmed by the merger even if customers in City Y are not. For that reason, the Agencies consider a relevant geographic market defined around customers in City X. Such a market could be defined even if the region around the merging firms' plants would not be a relevant geographic market defined based on the location of sellers because a hypothetical monopolist controlling all plants in that region would find a SSNIP imposed on all of its customers unprofitable due to the loss of sales to customers in City Y.

When the geographic market is defined based on customer locations, sales made to those customers are counted, regardless of the location of the supplier making those sales.

Example 15: Customers in the United States must use products approved by U.S. regulators. Foreign customers use products not approved by U.S. regulators. The relevant product market consists of products approved by U.S. regulators. The geographic market is defined around U.S. customers. Any sales made to U.S. customers by foreign suppliers are included in the market, and those foreign suppliers are participants in the U.S. market even though located outside it.

5. Market Participants, Market Shares, and Market Concentration

---

[7] For customers operating in multiple locations, only those customer locations within the targeted zone are included in the market.

The Agencies normally consider measures of market shares and market concentration as part of their evaluation of competitive effects. The Agencies evaluate market shares and concentration in conjunction with other reasonably available and reliable evidence for the ultimate purpose of determining whether a merger may substantially lessen competition.

Market shares can directly influence firms' competitive incentives. For example, if a price reduction to gain new customers would also apply to a firm's existing customers, a firm with a large market share may be more reluctant to implement a price reduction than one with a small share. Likewise, a firm with a large market share may not feel pressure to reduce price even if a smaller rival does. Market shares also can reflect firms' capabilities. For example, a firm with a large market share may be able to expand output rapidly by a larger absolute amount than can a small firm. Similarly, a large market share tends to indicate low costs, an attractive product, or both.

5.1 Market Participants

All firms that currently earn revenues in the relevant market are considered market participants. Vertically integrated firms are also included to the extent that their inclusion accurately reflects their competitive significance. Firms not currently earning revenues in the relevant market, but that have committed to entering the market in the near future, are also considered market participants.

Firms that are not current producers in a relevant market, but that would very likely provide rapid supply responses with direct competitive impact in the event of a SSNIP, without incurring significant sunk costs, are also considered market participants. These firms are termed "rapid entrants." Sunk costs are entry or exit costs that cannot be recovered outside the relevant market. Entry that would take place more slowly in response to adverse competitive effects, or that requires firms to incur significant sunk costs, is considered in Section 9.

Firms that produce the relevant product but do not sell it in the relevant geographic market may be rapid entrants. Other things equal, such firms are most likely to be rapid entrants if they are close to the geographic market.

Example 16: Farm A grows tomatoes halfway between Cities X and Y. Currently, it ships its tomatoes to City X because prices there are two percent higher. Previously it has varied the destination of its shipments in response to small price variations. Farm A would likely be a rapid entrant participant in a market for tomatoes in City Y.

Example 17: Firm B has bid multiple times to supply milk to School District S, and actually supplies milk to schools in some adjacent areas. It has never won a bid in School District S, but is well qualified to serve that district and has often nearly won. Firm B would be counted as a rapid entrant in a market for school milk in School District S.

More generally, if the relevant market is defined around targeted customers, firms that produce relevant products but do not sell them to those customers may be rapid entrants if they can easily and rapidly begin selling to the targeted customers.

Firms that clearly possess the necessary assets to supply into the relevant market rapidly may also be rapid entrants. In markets for relatively homogeneous goods where a supplier's ability to compete depends predominantly on its costs and its capacity, and not on other factors such as experience or reputation in the relevant market, a supplier with efficient idle capacity, or readily available "swing" capacity currently used in adjacent markets that can easily and profitably be shifted to serve the relevant market, may be a rapid entrant.[8] However, idle capacity may be inefficient, and capacity used in adjacent markets may not be available, so a firm's possession of idle or swing capacity alone does not make that firm a rapid entrant.

5.2   Market Shares

The Agencies normally calculate market shares for all firms that currently produce products in the relevant market, subject to the availability of data. The Agencies also calculate market shares for other market participants if this can be done to reliably reflect their competitive significance.

Market concentration and market share data are normally based on historical evidence. However, recent or ongoing changes in market conditions may indicate that the current market share of a particular firm either understates or overstates the firm's future competitive significance. The Agencies consider reasonably predictable effects of recent or ongoing changes in market conditions when calculating and interpreting market share data. For example, if a new technology that is important to long-term competitive viability is available to other firms in the market, but is not available to a particular firm, the Agencies may conclude that that firm's historical market share overstates its future competitive significance. The Agencies may project historical market shares into the foreseeable future when this can be done reliably.

The Agencies measure market shares based on the best available indicator of firms' future competitive significance in the relevant market. This may depend upon the type of competitive effect being considered, and on the availability of data. Typically, annual data are used, but where individual transactions are large and infrequent so annual data may be unrepresentative, the Agencies may measure market shares over a longer period of time.

In most contexts, the Agencies measure each firm's market share based on its actual or projected revenues in the relevant market. Revenues in the relevant market tend to be the best measure of attractiveness to customers, since they reflect the real-world ability of firms to surmount all of the obstacles necessary to offer products on terms and conditions that are attractive to customers. In cases where one unit of a low-priced product can substitute for one unit of a higher-priced product, unit sales may measure competitive significance better than revenues. For example, a new, much less expensive product may have great competitive significance if it substantially erodes the revenues earned by older, higher-priced products, even if it earns relatively few revenues. In cases where customers sign long-term contracts, face switching costs, or tend to re-evaluate their suppliers only occasionally, revenues earned from recently acquired cus-

---

[8] If this type of supply side substitution is nearly universal among the firms selling one or more of a group of products, the Agencies may use an aggregate description of markets for those products as a matter of convenience.

tomers may better reflect the competitive significance of suppliers than do total revenues.

In markets for homogeneous products, a firm's competitive significance may derive principally from its ability and incentive to rapidly expand production in the relevant market in response to a price increase or output reduction by others in that market. As a result, a firm's competitive significance may depend upon its level of readily available capacity to serve the relevant market if that capacity is efficient enough to make such expansion profitable. In such markets, capacities or reserves may better reflect the future competitive significance of suppliers than revenues, and the Agencies may calculate market shares using those measures. Market participants that are not current producers may then be assigned positive market shares, but only if a measure of their competitive significance properly comparable to that of current producers is available. When market shares are measured based on firms' readily available capacities, the Agencies do not include capacity that is committed or so profitably employed outside the relevant market, or so high-cost, that it would not likely be used to respond to a SSNIP in the relevant market.

Example 18: The geographic market is defined around customers in the United States. Firm X produces the relevant product outside the United States, and most of its sales are made to customers outside the United States. In most contexts, Firm X's market share will be based on its sales to U.S. customers, not its total sales or total capacity. However, if the relevant product is homogeneous, and if Firm X would significantly expand sales to U.S. customers rapidly and without incurring significant sunk costs in response to a SSNIP, the Agencies may base Firm X's market share on its readily available capacity to serve U.S. customers.

When the Agencies define markets serving targeted customers, these same principles are used to measure market shares, as they apply to those customers. In most contexts, each firm's market share is based on its actual or projected revenues from the targeted customers. However, the Agencies may instead measure market shares based on revenues from a broader group of customers if doing so would more accurately reflect the competitive significance of different suppliers in the relevant market. Revenues earned from a broader group of customers may also be used when better data are thereby available.

5.3   Market Concentration

Market concentration is often one useful indicator of likely competitive effects of a merger. In evaluating market concentration, the Agencies consider both the post-merger level of market concentration and the change in concentration resulting from a merger. Market shares may not fully reflect the competitive significance of firms in the market or the impact of a merger. They are used in conjunction with other evidence of competitive effects. See Sections 6 and 7.

In analyzing mergers between an incumbent and a recent or potential entrant, to the extent the Agencies use the change in concentration to evaluate competitive effects, they will do so using projected market shares. A merger between an incumbent and a potential entrant can raise significant competitive concerns. The lessening of competition resulting from such a merger is more likely to be substantial, the larger is the market share of the incumbent, the greater is the competitive significance of the potential entrant, and the greater is the competitive threat posed by this potential entrant relative to others.

The Agencies give more weight to market concentration when market shares have been stable over time, especially in the face of historical changes in relative prices or costs. If a firm has retained its market share even after its price has increased relative to those of its rivals, that firm already faces limited competitive constraints, making it less likely that its remaining rivals will replace the competition lost if one of that firm's important rivals is eliminated due to a merger. By contrast, even a highly concentrated market can be very competitive if market shares fluctuate substantially over short periods of time in response to changes in competitive offerings. However, if competition by one of the merging firms has significantly contributed to these fluctuations, perhaps because it has acted as a maverick, the Agencies will consider whether the merger will enhance market power by combining that firm with one of its significant rivals.

The Agencies may measure market concentration using the number of significant competitors in the market. This measure is most useful when there is a gap in market share between significant competitors and smaller rivals or when it is difficult to measure revenues in the relevant market. The Agencies also may consider the combined market share of the merging firms as an indicator of the extent to which others in the market may not be able readily to replace competition between the merging firms that is lost through the merger.

The Agencies often calculate the Herfindahl-Hirschman Index ("HHI") of market concentration. The HHI is calculated by summing the squares of the individual firms' market shares,[9] and thus gives proportionately greater weight to the larger market shares. When using the HHI, the Agencies consider both the post-merger level of the HHI and the increase in the HHI resulting from the merger. The increase in the HHI is equal to twice the product of the market shares of the merging firms.[10]

Based on their experience, the Agencies generally classify markets into three types:

- Unconcentrated Markets: HHI below 1500

- Moderately Concentrated Markets: HHI between 1500 and 2500

- Highly Concentrated Markets: HHI above 2500

    The Agencies employ the following general standards for the relevant markets they have defined:

- Small Change in Concentration: Mergers involving an increase in the HHI of less than 100 points are unlikely to have adverse competitive effects and

---

[9] For example, a market consisting of four firms with market shares of thirty percent, thirty percent, twenty percent, and twenty percent has an HHI of 2600 ($30^2 + 30^2 + 20^2 + 20^2 = 2600$). The HHI ranges from 10,000 (in the case of a pure monopoly) to a number approaching zero (in the case of an atomistic market). Although it is desirable to include all firms in the calculation, lack of information about firms with small shares is not critical because such firms do not affect the HHI significantly.

[10] For example, the merger of firms with shares of five percent and ten percent of the market would increase the HHI by 100 ($5 \times 10 \times 2 = 100$).

ordinarily require no further analysis.

- Unconcentrated Markets: Mergers resulting in unconcentrated markets are unlikely to have adverse competitive effects and ordinarily require no further analysis.

- Moderately Concentrated Markets: Mergers resulting in moderately concentrated markets that involve an increase in the HHI of more than 100 points potentially raise significant competitive concerns and often warrant scrutiny.

- Highly Concentrated Markets: Mergers resulting in highly concentrated markets that involve an increase in the HHI of between 100 points and 200 points potentially raise significant competitive concerns and often warrant scrutiny. Mergers resulting in highly concentrated markets that involve an increase in the HHI of more than 200 points will be presumed to be likely to enhance market power. The presumption may be rebutted by persuasive evidence showing that the merger is unlikely to enhance market power.

The purpose of these thresholds is not to provide a rigid screen to separate competitively benign mergers from anticompetitive ones, although high levels of concentration do raise concerns. Rather, they provide one way to identify some mergers unlikely to raise competitive concerns and some others for which it is particularly important to examine whether other competitive factors confirm, reinforce, or counteract the potentially harmful effects of increased concentration. The higher the post-merger HHI and the increase in the HHI, the greater are the Agencies' potential competitive concerns and the greater is the likelihood that the Agencies will request additional information to conduct their analysis.

6. Unilateral Effects

The elimination of competition between two firms that results from their merger may alone constitute a substantial lessening of competition. Such unilateral effects are most apparent in a merger to monopoly in a relevant market, but are by no means limited to that case. Whether cognizable efficiencies resulting from the merger are likely to reduce or reverse adverse unilateral effects is addressed in Section 10.

Several common types of unilateral effects are discussed in this section. Section 6.1 discusses unilateral price effects in markets with differentiated products. Section 6.2 discusses unilateral effects in markets where sellers negotiate with buyers or prices are determined through auctions. Section 6.3 discusses unilateral effects relating to reductions in output or capacity in markets for relatively homogeneous products. Section 6.4 discusses unilateral effects arising from diminished innovation or reduced product variety. These effects do not exhaust the types of possible unilateral effects; for example, exclusionary unilateral effects also can arise.

A merger may result in different unilateral effects along different dimensions of competition. For example, a merger may increase prices in the short term but not raise longer-term concerns about innovation, either because rivals will provide sufficient innovation competition or because the merger will generate cognizable research and development efficiencies. See Section 10.

6.1   Pricing of Differentiated Products

In differentiated product industries, some products can be very close substitutes and compete strongly with each other, while other products are more distant substitutes and compete less strongly. For example, one high-end product may compete much more directly with another high-end product than with any low-end product.

A merger between firms selling differentiated products may diminish competition by enabling the merged firm to profit by unilaterally raising the price of one or both products above the pre-merger level. Some of the sales lost due to the price rise will merely be diverted to the product of the merger partner and, depending on relative margins, capturing such sales loss through merger may make the price increase profitable even though it would not have been profitable prior to the merger.

The extent of direct competition between the products sold by the merging parties is central to the evaluation of unilateral price effects. Unilateral price effects are greater, the more the buyers of products sold by one merging firm consider products sold by the other merging firm to be their next choice. The Agencies consider any reasonably available and reliable information to evaluate the extent of direct competition between the products sold by the merging firms. This includes documentary and testimonial evidence, win/loss reports and evidence from discount approval processes, customer switching patterns, and customer surveys. The types of evidence relied on often overlap substantially with the types of evidence of customer substitution relevant to the hypothetical monopolist test. See Section 4.1.1.

Substantial unilateral price elevation post-merger for a product formerly sold by one of the merging firms normally requires that a significant fraction of the customers purchasing that product view products formerly sold by the other merging firm as their next-best choice. However, unless pre-merger margins between price and incremental cost are low, that significant fraction need not approach a majority. For this purpose, incremental cost is measured over the change in output that would be caused by the price change considered. A merger may produce significant unilateral effects for a given product even though many more sales are diverted to products sold by non-merging firms than to products previously sold by the merger partner.

Example 19: In Example 5, the merged entity controlling Products A and B would raise prices ten percent, given the product offerings and prices of other firms. In that example, one-third of the sales lost by Product A when its price alone is raised are diverted to Product B. Further analysis is required to account for repositioning, entry, and efficiencies.

In some cases, the Agencies may seek to quantify the extent of direct competition between a product sold by one merging firm and a second product sold by the other merging firm by estimating the diversion ratio from the first product to the second product. The diversion ratio is the fraction of unit sales lost by the first product due to an increase in its price that would be diverted to the second product. Diversion ratios between products sold by one merging firm and products sold by the other merging firm can be very informative for assessing unilateral price effects, with higher diversion ratios indicating a greater likelihood of such effects. Diversion ratios between products sold by merging firms and those sold by non-merging firms have at most secondary predictive value.

Adverse unilateral price effects can arise when the merger gives the merged entity an incentive to raise the price of a product previously sold by one merging firm and thereby divert sales to products previously sold by the other merging firm, boosting the profits on the latter products. Taking as given other prices and product offerings, that boost to profits is equal to the value to the merged firm of the sales diverted to those products. The value of sales diverted to a product is equal to the number of units diverted to that product multiplied by the margin between price and incremental cost on that product. In some cases, where sufficient information is available, the Agencies assess the value of diverted sales, which can serve as an indicator of the upward pricing pressure on the first product resulting from the merger. Diagnosing unilateral price effects based on the value of diverted sales need not rely on market definition or the calculation of market shares and concentration. The Agencies rely much more on the value of diverted sales than on the level of the HHI for diagnosing unilateral price effects in markets with differentiated products. If the value of diverted sales is proportionately small, significant unilateral price effects are unlikely.[11]

Where sufficient data are available, the Agencies may construct economic models designed to quantify the unilateral price effects resulting from the merger. These models often include independent price responses by non-merging firms. They also can incorporate merger-specific efficiencies. These merger simulation methods need not rely on market definition. The Agencies do not treat merger simulation evidence as conclusive in itself, and they place more weight on whether their merger simulations consistently predict substantial price increases than on the precise prediction of any single simulation.

A merger is unlikely to generate substantial unilateral price increases if non-merging parties offer very close substitutes for the products offered by the merging firms. In some cases, non-merging firms may be able to reposition their products to offer close substitutes for the products offered by the merging firms. Repositioning is a supply-side response that is evaluated much like entry, with consideration given to timeliness, likelihood, and sufficiency. See Section 9. The Agencies consider whether repositioning would be sufficient to deter or counteract what otherwise would be significant anticompetitive unilateral effects from a differentiated products merger.

6.2   Bargaining and Auctions

In many industries, especially those involving intermediate goods and services, buyers and sellers negotiate to determine prices and other terms of trade. In that process, buyers commonly negotiate with more than one seller, and may play sellers off against one another. Some highly structured forms of such competition are known as auctions. Negotiations often combine aspects of an auction with

---

[11] For this purpose, the value of diverted sales is measured in proportion to the lost revenues attributable to the reduction in unit sales resulting from the price increase. Those lost revenues equal the reduction in the number of units sold of that product multiplied by that product's price.

aspects of one-on-one negotiation, although pure auctions are sometimes used in government procurement and elsewhere.

A merger between two competing sellers prevents buyers from playing those sellers off against each other in negotiations. This alone can significantly enhance the ability and incentive of the merged entity to obtain a result more favorable to it, and less favorable to the buyer, than the merging firms would have offered separately absent the merger. The Agencies analyze unilateral effects of this type using similar approaches to those described in Section 6.1.

Anticompetitive unilateral effects in these settings are likely in proportion to the frequency or probability with which, prior to the merger, one of the merging sellers had been the runner-up when the other won the business. These effects also are likely to be greater, the greater advantage the runner-up merging firm has over other suppliers in meeting customers' needs. These effects also tend to be greater, the more profitable were the pre-merger winning bids. All of these factors are likely to be small if there are many equally placed bidders.

The mechanisms of these anticompetitive unilateral effects, and the indicia of their likelihood, differ somewhat according to the bargaining practices used, the auction format, and the sellers' information about one another's costs and about buyers' preferences. For example, when the merging sellers are likely to know which buyers they are best and second best placed to serve, any anticompetitive unilateral effects are apt to be targeted at those buyers; when sellers are less well informed, such effects are more apt to be spread over a broader class of buyers.

6.3   Capacity and Output for Homogeneous Products

In markets involving relatively undifferentiated products, the Agencies may evaluate whether the merged firm will find it profitable unilaterally to suppress output and elevate the market price. A firm may leave capacity idle, refrain from building or obtaining capacity that would have been obtained absent the merger, or eliminate pre-existing production capabilities. A firm may also divert the use of capacity away from one relevant market and into another so as to raise the price in the former market. The competitive analyses of these alternative modes of output suppression may differ.

A unilateral output suppression strategy is more likely to be profitable when (1) the merged firm's market share is relatively high; (2) the share of the merged firm's output already committed for sale at prices unaffected by the output suppression is relatively low; (3) the margin on the suppressed output is relatively low; (4) the supply responses of rivals are relatively small; and (5) the market elasticity of demand is relatively low.

A merger may provide the merged firm a larger base of sales on which to benefit from the resulting price rise, or it may eliminate a competitor that otherwise could have expanded its output in response to the price rise.

Example 20: Firms A and B both produce an industrial commodity and propose to merge. The demand for this commodity is insensitive to price. Firm A is the market leader. Firm B produces substantial output, but its operating margins are low because it operates high-cost plants. The other suppliers are operating very near capacity. The merged firm has an incentive to reduce output at the high-cost plants, perhaps shutting down some of that capacity, thus driving up the price it receives on the remainder of its output. The merger harms customers, notwithstanding that the merged firm shifts some output from high-cost plants to low-cost plants.

In some cases, a merger between a firm with a substantial share of the sales in the market and a firm with significant excess capacity to serve that market can make an output suppression strategy profitable.[12] This can occur even if the firm with the excess capacity has a relatively small share of sales, if that firm's ability to expand, and thus keep price from rising, has been making an output suppression strategy unprofitable for the firm with the larger market share.

6.4   Innovation and Product Variety

Competition often spurs firms to innovate. The Agencies may consider whether a merger is likely to diminish innovation competition by encouraging the merged firm to curtail its innovative efforts below the level that would prevail in the absence of the merger. That curtailment of innovation could take the form of reduced incentive to continue with an existing product-development effort or reduced incentive to initiate development of new products.

The first of these effects is most likely to occur if at least one of the merging firms is engaging in efforts to introduce new products that would capture substantial revenues from the other merging firm. The second, longer-run effect is most likely to occur if at least one of the merging firms has capabilities that are likely to lead it to develop new products in the future that would capture substantial revenues from the other merging firm. The Agencies therefore also consider whether a merger will diminish innovation competition by combining two of a very small number of firms with the strongest capabilities to successfully innovate in a specific direction.

The Agencies evaluate the extent to which successful innovation by one merging firm is likely to take sales from the other, and the extent to which post-merger incentives for future innovation will be lower than those that would prevail in the absence of the merger. The Agencies also consider whether the merger is likely to enable innovation that would not otherwise take place, by bringing together complementary capabilities that cannot be otherwise combined or for some other merger-specific reason. See Section 10.

The Agencies also consider whether a merger is likely to give the merged firm an incentive to cease offering one of the relevant products sold by the merging parties. Reductions in variety following a merger may or may not be anticompetitive. Mergers can lead to the efficient consolidation of products when variety offers little in value to customers. In other cases, a merger may increase variety by encouraging the merged firm to reposition its products to be more differentiated from one another.

If the merged firm would withdraw a product that a significant number of customers strongly prefer to those products that would remain available, this can constitute a harm to customers over and above any effects on the price or quality of any given product. If there is evidence of such an effect, the Agencies may

---

[12] Such a merger also can cause adverse coordinated effects, especially if the acquired firm with excess capacity was disrupting effective coordination.

inquire whether the reduction in variety is largely due to a loss of competitive incentives attributable to the merger. An anticompetitive incentive to eliminate a product as a result of the merger is greater and more likely, the larger is the share of profits from that product coming at the expense of profits from products sold by the merger partner. Where a merger substantially reduces competition by bringing two close substitute products under common ownership, and one of those products is eliminated, the merger will often also lead to a price increase on the remaining product, but that is not a necessary condition for anticompetitive effect.

Example 21: Firm A sells a high-end product at a premium price. Firm B sells a mid-range product at a lower price, serving customers who are more price sensitive. Several other firms have low-end products. Firms A and B together have a large share of the relevant market. Firm A proposes to acquire Firm B and discontinue Firm B's product. Firm A expects to retain most of Firm B's customers. Firm A may not find it profitable to raise the price of its high-end product after the merger, because doing so would reduce its ability to retain Firm B's more price-sensitive customers. The Agencies may conclude that the withdrawal of Firm B's product results from a loss of competition and materially harms customers.

7. Coordinated Effects

A merger may diminish competition by enabling or encouraging post-merger coordinated interaction among firms in the relevant market that harms customers. Coordinated interaction involves conduct by multiple firms that is profitable for each of them only as a result of the accommodating reactions of the others. These reactions can blunt a firm's incentive to offer customers better deals by undercutting the extent to which such a move would win business away from rivals. They also can enhance a firm's incentive to raise prices, by assuaging the fear that such a move would lose customers to rivals.

Coordinated interaction includes a range of conduct. Coordinated interaction can involve the explicit negotiation of a common understanding of how firms will compete or refrain from competing. Such conduct typically would itself violate the antitrust laws. Coordinated interaction also can involve a similar common understanding that is not explicitly negotiated but would be enforced by the detection and punishment of deviations that would undermine the coordinated interaction. Coordinated interaction alternatively can involve parallel accommodating conduct not pursuant to a prior understanding. Parallel accommodating conduct includes situations in which each rival's response to competitive moves made by others is individually rational, and not motivated by retaliation or deterrence nor intended to sustain an agreed-upon market outcome, but nevertheless emboldens price increases and weakens competitive incentives to reduce prices or offer customers better terms. Coordinated interaction includes conduct not otherwise condemned by the antitrust laws.

The ability of rival firms to engage in coordinated conduct depends on the strength and predictability of rivals' responses to a price change or other competitive initiative. Under some circumstances, a merger can result in market concentration sufficient to strengthen such responses or enable multiple firms in the market to predict them more confidently, thereby affecting the competitive incentives of multiple firms in the market, not just the merged firm.

7.1   Impact of Merger on Coordinated Interaction

The Agencies examine whether a merger is likely to change the manner in which market participants interact, inducing substantially more coordinated interaction. The Agencies seek to identify how a merger might significantly weaken competitive incentives through an increase in the strength, extent, or likelihood of coordinated conduct. There are, however, numerous forms of coordination, and the risk that a merger will induce adverse coordinated effects may not be susceptible to quantification or detailed proof. Therefore, the Agencies evaluate the risk of coordinated effects using measures of market concentration (see Section 5) in conjunction with an assessment of whether a market is vulnerable to coordinated conduct. See Section 7.2. The analysis in Section 7.2 applies to moderately and highly concentrated markets, as unconcentrated markets are unlikely to be vulnerable to coordinated conduct.

Pursuant to the Clayton Act's incipiency standard, the Agencies may challenge mergers that in their judgment pose a real danger of harm through coordinated effects, even without specific evidence showing precisely how the coordination likely would take place. The Agencies are likely to challenge a merger if the following three conditions are all met: (1) the merger would significantly increase concentration and lead to a moderately or highly concentrated market; (2) that market shows signs of vulnerability to coordinated conduct (see Section 7.2); and (3) the Agencies have a credible basis on which to conclude that the merger may enhance that vulnerability. An acquisition eliminating a maverick firm (see Section 2.1.5) in a market vulnerable to coordinated conduct is likely to cause adverse coordinated effects.

7.2   Evidence a Market is Vulnerable to Coordinated Conduct

The Agencies presume that market conditions are conducive to coordinated interaction if firms representing a substantial share in the relevant market appear to have previously engaged in express collusion affecting the relevant market, unless competitive conditions in the market have since changed significantly. Previous express collusion in another geographic market will have the same weight if the salient characteristics of that other market at the time of the collusion are comparable to those in the relevant market. Failed previous attempts at collusion in the relevant market suggest that successful collusion was difficult pre-merger but not so difficult as to deter attempts, and a merger may tend to make success more likely. Previous collusion or attempted collusion in another product market may also be given substantial weight if the salient characteristics of that other market at the time of the collusion are closely comparable to those in the relevant market.

A market typically is more vulnerable to coordinated conduct if each competitively important firm's significant competitive initiatives can be promptly and confidently observed by that firm's rivals. This is more likely to be the case if the terms offered to customers are relatively transparent. Price transparency can be greater for relatively homogeneous products. Even if terms of dealing are not transparent, transparency regarding the identities of the firms serving particular customers can give rise to coordination, e.g., through customer or territorial allocation. Regular monitoring by suppliers of one another's prices or customers can indicate that the terms offered to customers are relatively transparent.

A market typically is more vulnerable to coordinated conduct if a firm's prospective competitive reward from attracting customers away from its rivals will be significantly diminished by likely responses of those rivals. This is more likely to be the case, the stronger and faster are the responses the firm anticipates from its rivals. The firm is more likely to anticipate strong responses if there are few significant competitors, if products in the relevant market are relatively homogeneous, if customers find it relatively easy to switch between suppliers, or if suppliers use meeting-competition clauses.

A firm is more likely to be deterred from making competitive initiatives by whatever responses occur if sales are small and frequent rather than via occasional large and long-term contracts or if relatively few customers will switch to it before rivals are able to respond. A firm is less likely to be deterred by whatever responses occur if the firm has little stake in the status quo. For example, a firm with a small market share that can quickly and dramatically expand, constrained neither by limits on production nor by customer reluctance to switch providers or to entrust business to a historically small provider, is unlikely to be deterred. Firms are also less likely to be deterred by whatever responses occur if competition in the relevant market is marked by leapfrogging technological innovation, so that responses by competitors leave the gains from successful innovation largely intact.

A market is more apt to be vulnerable to coordinated conduct if the firm initiating a price increase will lose relatively few customers after rivals respond to the increase. Similarly, a market is more apt to be vulnerable to coordinated conduct if a firm that first offers a lower price or improved product to customers will retain relatively few customers thus attracted away from its rivals after those rivals respond.

The Agencies regard coordinated interaction as more likely, the more the participants stand to gain from successful coordination. Coordination generally is more profitable, the lower is the market elasticity of demand.

Coordinated conduct can harm customers even if not all firms in the relevant market engage in the coordination, but significant harm normally is likely only if a substantial part of the market is subject to such conduct. The prospect of harm depends on the collective market power, in the relevant market, of firms whose incentives to compete are substantially weakened by coordinated conduct. This collective market power is greater, the lower is the market elasticity of demand. This collective market power is diminished by the presence of other market participants with small market shares and little stake in the outcome resulting from the coordinated conduct, if these firms can rapidly expand their sales in the relevant market.

Buyer characteristics and the nature of the procurement process can affect coordination. For example, sellers may have the incentive to bid aggressively for a large contract even if they expect strong responses by rivals. This is especially the case for sellers with small market shares, if they can realistically win such large contracts. In some cases, a large buyer may be able to strategically undermine coordinated conduct, at least as it pertains to that buyer's needs, by choosing to put up for bid a few large contracts rather than many smaller ones, and by making its procurement decisions opaque to suppliers.

8.   Powerful Buyers

Powerful buyers are often able to negotiate favorable terms with their suppliers. Such terms may reflect the lower costs of serving these buyers, but they also can reflect price discrimination in their favor.

The Agencies consider the possibility that powerful buyers may constrain the ability of the merging parties to raise prices. This can occur, for example, if powerful buyers have the ability and incentive to vertically integrate upstream or sponsor entry, or if the conduct or presence of large buyers undermines coordinated effects. However, the Agencies do not presume that the presence of powerful buyers alone forestalls adverse competitive effects flowing from the merger. Even buyers that can negotiate favorable terms may be harmed by an increase in market power. The Agencies examine the choices available to powerful buyers and how those choices likely would change due to the merger. Normally, a merger that eliminates a supplier whose presence contributed significantly to a buyer's negotiating leverage will harm that buyer.

Example 22: Customer C has been able to negotiate lower pre-merger prices than other customers by threatening to shift its large volume of purchases from one merging firm to the other. No other suppliers are as well placed to meet Customer C's needs for volume and reliability. The merger is likely to harm Customer C. In this situation, the Agencies could identify a price discrimination market consisting of Customer C and similarly placed customers. The merger threatens to end previous price discrimination in their favor.

Furthermore, even if some powerful buyers could protect themselves, the Agencies also consider whether market power can be exercised against other buyers.

Example 23: In Example 22, if Customer C instead obtained the lower pre-merger prices based on a credible threat to supply its own needs, or to sponsor new entry, Customer C might not be harmed. However, even in this case, other customers may still be harmed.

9.   Entry

The analysis of competitive effects in Sections 6 and 7 focuses on current participants in the relevant market. That analysis may also include some forms of entry. Firms that would rapidly and easily enter the market in response to a SSNIP are market participants and may be assigned market shares. See Sections 5.1 and 5.2. Firms that have, prior to the merger, committed to entering the market also will normally be treated as market participants. See Section 5.1. This section concerns entry or adjustments to pre-existing entry plans that are induced by the merger.

As part of their full assessment of competitive effects, the Agencies consider entry into the relevant market. The prospect of entry into the relevant market will alleviate concerns about adverse competitive effects only if such entry will deter or counteract any competitive effects of concern so the merger will not substantially harm customers.

The Agencies consider the actual history of entry into the relevant market and give substantial weight to this evidence. Lack of successful and effective entry in the face of non-transitory increases in the margins earned on products in the relevant market tends to suggest that successful entry is slow or difficult. Market values of incumbent firms greatly exceeding the replacement costs of their tangible assets may indicate that these firms have valuable intangible assets, which may be difficult or time consuming for an entrant to replicate.

A merger is not likely to enhance market power if entry into the market is so easy that the merged firm and its remaining rivals in the market, either unilaterally or collectively, could not profitably raise price or otherwise reduce competition compared to the level that would prevail in the absence of the merger. Entry is that easy if entry would be timely, likely, and sufficient in its magnitude, character, and scope to deter or counteract the competitive effects of concern.

The Agencies examine the timeliness, likelihood, and sufficiency of the entry efforts an entrant might practically employ. An entry effort is defined by the actions the firm must undertake to produce and sell in the market. Various elements of the entry effort will be considered. These elements can include: planning, design, and management; permitting, licensing, or other approvals; construction, debugging, and operation of production facilities; and promotion (including necessary introductory discounts), marketing, distribution, and satisfaction of customer testing and qualification requirements. Recent examples of entry, whether successful or unsuccessful, generally provide the starting point for identifying the elements of practical entry efforts. They also can be informative regarding the scale necessary for an entrant to be successful, the presence or absence of entry barriers, the factors that influence the timing of entry, the costs and risk associated with entry, and the sales opportunities realistically available to entrants.

If the assets necessary for an effective and profitable entry effort are widely available, the Agencies will not necessarily attempt to identify which firms might enter. Where an identifiable set of firms appears to have necessary assets that others lack, or to have particularly strong incentives to enter, the Agencies focus their entry analysis on those firms. Firms operating in adjacent or complementary markets, or large customers themselves, may be best placed to enter. However, the Agencies will not presume that a powerful firm in an adjacent market or a large customer will enter the relevant market unless there is reliable evidence supporting that conclusion.

In assessing whether entry will be timely, likely, and sufficient, the Agencies recognize that precise and detailed information may be difficult or impossible to obtain. The Agencies consider reasonably available and reliable evidence bearing on whether entry will satisfy the conditions of timeliness, likelihood, and sufficiency.

9.1   Timeliness

In order to deter the competitive effects of concern, entry must be rapid enough to make unprofitable overall the actions causing those effects and thus leading to entry, even though those actions would be profitable until entry takes effect.

Even if the prospect of entry does not deter the competitive effects of concern, post-merger entry may counteract them. This requires that the impact of entrants in the relevant market be rapid enough that customers are not significantly harmed by the merger, despite any anticompetitive harm that occurs prior to the entry.

The Agencies will not presume that an entrant can have a significant impact on prices before that entrant is ready to provide the relevant product to customers unless there is reliable evidence that anticipated future entry would have such an effect on prices.

9.2   Likelihood

Entry is likely if it would be profitable, accounting for the assets, capabilities, and capital needed and the risks involved, including the need for the entrant to incur costs that would not be recovered if the entrant later exits. Profitability depends upon (a) the output level the entrant is likely to obtain, accounting for the obstacles facing new entrants; (b) the price the entrant would likely obtain in the post-merger market, accounting for the impact of that entry itself on prices; and (c) the cost per unit the entrant would likely incur, which may depend upon the scale at which the entrant would operate.

9.3   Sufficiency

Even where timely and likely, entry may not be sufficient to deter or counteract the competitive effects of concern. For example, in a differentiated product industry, entry may be insufficient because the products offered by entrants are not close enough substitutes to the products offered by the merged firm to render a price increase by the merged firm unprofitable. Entry may also be insufficient due to constraints that limit entrants' competitive effectiveness, such as limitations on the capabilities of the firms best placed to enter or reputational barriers to rapid expansion by new entrants. Entry by a single firm that will replicate at least the scale and strength of one of the merging firms is sufficient. Entry by one or more firms operating at a smaller scale may be sufficient if such firms are not at a significant competitive disadvantage.

10.   Efficiencies

Competition usually spurs firms to achieve efficiencies internally. Nevertheless, a primary benefit of mergers to the economy is their potential to generate significant efficiencies and thus enhance the merged firm's ability and incentive to compete, which may result in lower prices, improved quality, enhanced service, or new products. For example, merger-generated efficiencies may enhance competition by permitting two ineffective competitors to form a more effective competitor, e.g., by combining complementary assets. In a unilateral effects context, incremental cost reductions may reduce or reverse any increases in the merged firm's incentive to elevate price. Efficiencies also may lead to new or improved products, even if they do not immediately and directly affect price. In a coordinated effects context, incremental cost reductions may make coordination less likely or effective by enhancing the incentive of a maverick to lower price or by creating a new maverick firm. Even when efficiencies generated through a merger enhance a firm's ability to compete, however, a merger may have other effects that may lessen competition and make the merger anticompetitive.

The Agencies credit only those efficiencies likely to be accomplished with the proposed merger and unlikely to be accomplished in the absence of either the proposed merger or another means having comparable anticompetitive effects. These are termed merger-specific efficiencies.[13] Only alternatives that are practical in the business situation faced by the merging firms are considered in making this determination. The Agencies do not insist upon a less restrictive alternative that is merely theoretical.

Efficiencies are difficult to verify and quantify, in part because much of the information relating to efficiencies is uniquely in the possession of the merging firms. Moreover, efficiencies projected reasonably and in good faith by the merging firms may not be realized. Therefore, it is incumbent upon the merging firms to substantiate efficiency claims so that the Agencies can verify by reasonable means the likelihood and magnitude of each asserted efficiency, how and when each would be achieved (and any costs of doing so), how each would enhance the merged firm's ability and incentive to compete, and why each would be merger-specific.

Efficiency claims will not be considered if they are vague, speculative, or otherwise cannot be verified by reasonable means. Projections of efficiencies may be viewed with skepticism, particularly when generated outside of the usual business planning process. By contrast, efficiency claims substantiated by analogous past experience are those most likely to be credited.

Cognizable efficiencies are merger-specific efficiencies that have been verified and do not arise from anticompetitive reductions in output or service. Cognizable efficiencies are assessed net of costs produced by the merger or incurred in achieving those efficiencies.

The Agencies will not challenge a merger if cognizable efficiencies are of a character and magnitude such that the merger is not likely to be anticompetitive in any relevant market.[14] To make the requisite determination, the Agencies consider whether cognizable efficiencies likely would be sufficient to reverse the merger's potential to harm customers in the relevant market, e.g., by preventing price increases in that market.[15] In conducting this analysis, the Agencies will not simply

---

[13] The Agencies will not deem efficiencies to be merger-specific if they could be attained by practical alternatives that mitigate competitive concerns, such as divestiture or licensing. If a merger affects not whether but only when an efficiency would be achieved, only the timing advantage is a merger-specific efficiency

[14] The Agencies normally assess competition in each relevant market affected by a merger independently and normally will challenge the merger if it is likely to be anticompetitive in any relevant market. In some cases, however, the Agencies in their prosecutorial discretion will consider efficiencies not strictly in the relevant market, but so inextricably linked with it that a partial divestiture or other remedy could not feasibly eliminate the anticompetitive effect in the relevant market without sacrificing the efficiencies in the other market(s). Inextricably linked efficiencies are most likely to make a difference when they are great and the likely anticompetitive effect in the relevant market(s) is small so the merger is likely to benefit customers overall.

[15] The Agencies normally give the most weight to the results of this analysis over the short term. The Agencies also may consider the effects of cognizable efficiencies with no short-term, direct effect on prices in the relevant market. Delayed benefits from efficiencies (due to delay in the achievement of, or

compare the magnitude of the cognizable efficiencies with the magnitude of the likely harm to competition absent the efficiencies. The greater the potential adverse competitive effect of a merger, the greater must be the cognizable efficiencies, and the more they must be passed through to customers, for the Agencies to conclude that the merger will not have an anticompetitive effect in the relevant market. When the potential adverse competitive effect of a merger is likely to be particularly substantial, extraordinarily great cognizable efficiencies would be necessary to prevent the merger from being anticompetitive. In adhering to this approach, the Agencies are mindful that the antitrust laws give competition, not internal operational efficiency, primacy in protecting customers.

In the Agencies' experience, efficiencies are most likely to make a difference in merger analysis when the likely adverse competitive effects, absent the efficiencies, are not great. Efficiencies almost never justify a merger to monopoly or near-monopoly. Just as adverse competitive effects can arise along multiple dimensions of conduct, such as pricing and new product development, so too can efficiencies operate along multiple dimensions. Similarly, purported efficiency claims based on lower prices can be undermined if they rest on reductions in product quality or variety that customers value.

The Agencies have found that certain types of efficiencies are more likely to be cognizable and substantial than others. For example, efficiencies resulting from shifting production among facilities formerly owned separately, which enable the merging firms to reduce the incremental cost of production, are more likely to be susceptible to verification and are less likely to result from anticompetitive reductions in output. Other efficiencies, such as those relating to research and development, are potentially substantial but are generally less susceptible to verification and may be the result of anticompetitive output reductions. Yet others, such as those relating to procurement, management, or capital cost, are less likely to be merger-specific or substantial, or may not be cognizable for other reasons.

When evaluating the effects of a merger on innovation, the Agencies consider the ability of the merged firm to conduct research or development more effectively. Such efficiencies may spur innovation but not affect short-term pricing. The Agencies also consider the ability of the merged firm to appropriate a greater fraction of the benefits resulting from its innovations. Licensing and intellectual property conditions may be important to this enquiry, as they affect the ability of a firm to appropriate the benefits of its innovation. Research and development cost savings may be substantial and yet not be cognizable efficiencies because they are difficult to verify or result from anticompetitive reductions in innovative activities.

11. Failure and Exiting Assets

Notwithstanding the analysis above, a merger is not likely to enhance market power if imminent failure, as defined below, of one of the merging firms would cause the assets of that firm to exit the relevant market. This is an extreme instance of the more general circumstance in which the competitive significance of one of the

---

the realization of customer benefits from, the efficiencies) will be given less weight because they are less proximate and more difficult to predict. Efficiencies relating to costs that are fixed in the short term are unlikely to benefit customers in the short term, but can benefit customers in the longer run, e.g., if they make new product introduction less expensive.

merging firms is declining: the projected market share and significance of the exiting firm is zero. If the relevant assets would otherwise exit the market, customers are not worse off after the merger than they would have been had the merger been enjoined.

The Agencies do not normally credit claims that the assets of the failing firm would exit the relevant market unless all of the following circumstances are met: (1) the allegedly failing firm would be unable to meet its financial obligations in the near future; (2) it would not be able to reorganize successfully under Chapter 11 of the Bankruptcy Act; and (3) it has made unsuccessful good-faith efforts to elicit reasonable alternative offers that would keep its tangible and intangible assets in the relevant market and pose a less severe danger to competition than does the proposed merger.[16]

Similarly, a merger is unlikely to cause competitive harm if the risks to competition arise from the acquisition of a failing division. The Agencies do not normally credit claims that the assets of a division would exit the relevant market in the near future unless both of the following conditions are met: (1) applying cost allocation rules that reflect true economic costs, the division has a persistently negative cash flow on an operating basis, and such negative cash flow is not economically justified for the firm by benefits such as added sales in complementary markets or enhanced customer goodwill;[17] and (2) the owner of the failing division has made unsuccessful good-faith efforts to elicit reasonable alternative offers that would keep its tangible and intangible assets in the relevant market and pose a less severe danger to competition than does the proposed acquisition.

12.   Mergers of Competing Buyers

Mergers of competing buyers can enhance market power on the buying side of the market, just as mergers of competing sellers can enhance market power on the selling side of the market. Buyer market power is sometimes called "monopsony power."

To evaluate whether a merger is likely to enhance market power on the buying side of the market, the Agencies employ essentially the framework described above for evaluating whether a merger is likely to enhance market power on the selling side of the market. In defining relevant markets, the Agencies focus on the alternatives available to sellers in the face of a decrease in the price paid by a hypothetical monopsonist.

Market power on the buying side of the market is not a significant concern if suppliers have numerous attractive outlets for their goods or services. However, when that is not the case, the Agencies may conclude that the merger of competing buyers is likely to lessen competition in a manner harmful to sellers.

---

[16] Any offer to purchase the assets of the failing firm for a price above the liquidation value of those assets will be regarded as a reasonable alternative offer. Liquidation value is the highest value the assets could command for use outside the relevant market.

[17] Because the parent firm can allocate costs, revenues, and intra-company transactions among itself and its subsidiaries and divisions, the Agencies require evidence on these two points that is not solely based on management plans that could have been prepared for the purpose of demonstrating negative cash flow or the prospect of exit from the relevant market.

The Agencies distinguish between effects on sellers arising from a lessening of competition and effects arising in other ways. A merger that does not enhance market power on the buying side of the market can nevertheless lead to a reduction in prices paid by the merged firm, for example, by reducing transactions costs or allowing the merged firm to take advantage of volume-based discounts. Reduction in prices paid by the merging firms not arising from the enhancement of market power can be significant in the evaluation of efficiencies from a merger, as discussed in Section 10.

The Agencies do not view a short-run reduction in the quantity purchased as the only, or best, indicator of whether a merger enhances buyer market power. Nor do the Agencies evaluate the competitive effects of mergers between competing buyers strictly, or even primarily, on the basis of effects in the downstream markets in which the merging firms sell.

Example 24: Merging Firms A and B are the only two buyers in the relevant geographic market for an agricultural product. Their merger will enhance buyer power and depress the price paid to farmers for this product, causing a transfer of wealth from farmers to the merged firm and inefficiently reducing supply. These effects can arise even if the merger will not lead to any increase in the price charged by the merged firm for its output.

13.   Partial Acquisitions

In most horizontal mergers, two competitors come under common ownership and control, completely and permanently eliminating competition between them. This elimination of competition is a basic element of merger analysis. However, the statutory provisions referenced in Section 1 also apply to one firm's partial acquisition of a competitor. The Agencies therefore also review acquisitions of minority positions involving competing firms, even if such minority positions do not necessarily or completely eliminate competition between the parties to the transaction.

When the Agencies determine that a partial acquisition results in effective control of the target firm, or involves substantially all of the relevant assets of the target firm, they analyze the transaction much as they do a merger. Partial acquisitions that do not result in effective control may nevertheless present significant competitive concerns and may require a somewhat distinct analysis from that applied to full mergers or to acquisitions involving effective control. The details of the post-acquisition relationship between the parties, and how those details are likely to affect competition, can be important. While the Agencies will consider any way in which a partial acquisition may affect competition, they generally focus on three principal effects.

First, a partial acquisition can lessen competition by giving the acquiring firm the ability to influence the competitive conduct of the target firm. A voting interest in the target firm or specific governance rights, such as the right to appoint members to the board of directors, can permit such influence. Such influence can lessen competition because the acquiring firm can use its influence to induce the target firm to compete less aggressively or to coordinate its conduct with that of the acquiring firm.

Second, a partial acquisition can lessen competition by reducing the incentive of the acquiring firm to compete. Acquiring a minority position in a rival might significantly blunt the incentive of the acquiring firm to compete aggressively because it shares in the losses thereby inflicted on that rival. This reduction in the incentive of the acquiring firm to compete arises even if cannot influence the conduct of the target firm. As compared with the unilateral competitive effect of a full merger, this effect is likely attenuated by the fact that the ownership is only partial.

Third, a partial acquisition can lessen competition by giving the acquiring firm access to non-public, competitively sensitive information from the target firm. Even absent any ability to influence the conduct of the target firm, access to competitively sensitive information can lead to adverse unilateral or coordinated effects. For example, it can enhance the ability of the two firms to coordinate their behavior, and make other accommodating responses faster and more targeted. The risk of coordinated effects is greater if the transaction also facilitates the flow of competitively sensitive information from the acquiring firm to the target firm.

Partial acquisitions, like mergers, vary greatly in their potential for anticompetitive effects. Accordingly, the specific facts of each case must be examined to assess the likelihood of harm to competition. While partial acquisitions usually do not enable many of the types of efficiencies associated with mergers, the Agencies consider whether a partial acquisition is likely to create cognizable efficiencies.

APPENDIX B

SELECTED ANTITRUST STATUTES

SHERMAN ACT

Section 1   [15 U.S.C. § 1]

Every contract, combination in the form of trust or otherwise, or conspiracy, in restraint of trade or commerce among the several States, or with foreign nations, is declared to be illegal. Every person who shall make any contract or engage in any combination or conspiracy hereby declared to be illegal shall be deemed guilty of a felony, and, on conviction thereof, shall be punished by fine not exceeding $100,000,000 if a corporation, or, if any other person, $1,000,000, or by imprisonment not exceeding 10 years, or by both said punishments, in the discretion of the court.

Section 2   [15 U.S.C. § 2]

Every person who shall monopolize, or attempt to monopolize, or combine or conspire with any other person or persons, to monopolize any part of the trade or commerce among the several States, or with foreign nations, shall be deemed guilty of a felony, and, on conviction thereof, shall be punished by fine not exceeding $100,000,000 if a corporation, or, if any other person, $1,000,000, or by imprisonment not exceeding ten years, or by both said punishments, in the discretion of the court.

Section 4   [15 U.S.C. § 4]

The several district courts of the United States are invested with jurisdiction to prevent and restrain violations of sections 1 to 7 of this title; and it shall be the duty of the several United States attorneys, in their respective districts, under the direction of the Attorney General, to institute proceedings in equity to prevent and restrain such violations. Such proceedings may be by way of petition setting forth the case and praying that such violation shall be enjoined or otherwise prohibited. When the parties complained of shall have been duly notified of such petition the court shall proceed, as soon as may be, to the hearing and determination of the case; and pending such petition and before final decree, the court may at any time make such temporary restraining order or prohibition as shall be deemed just in the premises.

Section 8   [15 U.S.C. § 7]

The word "person", or "persons", wherever used in sections 1 to 7 of this title shall be deemed to include corporations and associations existing under or authorized by the laws of either the United States, the laws of any of the Territories, the laws of any State, or the laws of any foreign country.

CLAYTON ACT

Section 1   [15 U.S.C. § 12]

"Commerce," as used herein, means trade or commerce among the several States and with foreign nations, or between the District of Columbia or any Territory of the United States and any State, Territory, or foreign nation, or between any insular possessions or other places under the jurisdiction of the United States, or between any such possession or place and any State or Territory of the United States or the District of Columbia or any foreign nation, or within the District of Columbia or any Territory or any insular possession or other place under the jurisdiction of the United States: Provided, That nothing in this Act contained shall apply to the Philippine Islands.

The word "person" or "persons" wherever used in this Act shall be deemed to include corporations and associations existing under or authorized by the laws of either the United States, the laws of any of the Territories, the laws of any State, or the laws of any foreign country.

(b) This Act may be cited as the "Clayton Act".

Section 2   [15 U.S.C. § 13, as Amended by Robinson-Patman Act]

(a)   Price; selection of customers

It shall be unlawful for any person engaged in commerce, in the course of such commerce, either directly or indirectly, to discriminate in price between different purchasers of commodities of like grade and quality, where either or any of the purchases involved in such discrimination are in commerce, where such commodities are sold for use, consumption, or resale within the United States or any Territory thereof or the District of Columbia or any insular possession or other place under the jurisdiction of the United States, and where the effect of such discrimination may be substantially to lessen competition or tend to create a monopoly in any line of commerce, or to injure, destroy, or prevent competition with any person who either grants or knowingly receives the benefit of such discrimination, or with customers of either of them: Provided, That nothing herein contained shall prevent differentials which make only due allowance for differences in the cost of manufacture, sale, or delivery resulting from the differing methods or quantities in which such commodities are to such purchasers sold or delivered: Provided, however, That the Federal Trade Commission may, after due investigation and hearing to all interested parties, fix and establish quantity limits, and revise the same as it finds necessary, as to particular commodities or classes of commodities, where it finds that available purchasers in greater quantities are so few as to render differentials on account thereof unjustly discriminatory or promotive of monopoly in any line of commerce; and the foregoing shall then not be construed to permit differentials based on differences in quantities greater than those so fixed and established: And provided further, That nothing herein contained shall prevent persons engaged in selling goods, wares, or merchandise in commerce from selecting their own customers in bona fide transactions and not in restraint of trade: And provided further, That nothing herein contained shall prevent price changes from time to time where in response to changing conditions affecting the market for or the marketability of the goods concerned, such as but not limited to actual or imminent deterioration of perishable goods, obsolescence of seasonal goods, distress sales under court process, or sales in good faith in discontinuance of business in the goods concerned.

(b) Burden of rebutting prima-facie case of discrimination

Upon proof being made, at any hearing on a complaint under this section, that there has been discrimination in price or services or facilities furnished, the burden of rebutting the prima-facie case thus made by showing justification shall be upon the person charged with a violation of this section, and unless justification shall be affirmatively shown, the Commission is authorized to issue an order terminating the discrimination: Provided, however, That nothing herein contained shall prevent a seller rebutting the prima-facie case thus made by showing that his lower price or the furnishing of services or facilities to any purchaser or purchasers was made in good faith to meet an equally low price of a competitor, or the services or facilities furnished by a competitor.

(c) Payment or acceptance of commission, brokerage, or other compensation

It shall be unlawful for any person engaged in commerce, in the course of such commerce, to pay or grant, or to receive or accept, anything of value as a commission, brokerage, or other compensation, or any allowance or discount in lieu thereof, except for services rendered in connection with the sale or purchase of goods, wares, or merchandise, either to the other party to such transaction or to an agent, representative, or other intermediary therein where such intermediary is acting in fact for or in behalf, or is subject to the direct or indirect control, of any party to such transaction other than the person by whom such compensation is so granted or paid.

(d) Payment for services or facilities for processing or sale

It shall be unlawful for any person engaged in commerce to pay or contract for the payment of anything of value to or for the benefit of a customer of such person in the course of such commerce as compensation or in consideration for any services or facilities furnished by or through such customer in connection with the processing, handling, sale, or offering for sale of any products or commodities manufactured, sold, or offered for sale by such person, unless such payment or consideration is available on proportionally equal terms to all other customers competing in the distribution of such products or commodities.

(e) Furnishing services or facilities for processing, handling, etc.

It shall be unlawful for any person to discriminate in favor of one purchaser against another purchaser or purchasers of a commodity bought for resale, with or without processing, by contracting to furnish or furnishing, or by contributing to the furnishing of, any services or facilities connected with the processing, handling, sale, or offering for sale of such commodity so purchased upon terms not accorded to all purchasers on proportionally equal terms.

(f) Knowingly inducing or receiving discriminatory price

It shall be unlawful for any person engaged in commerce, in the course of such commerce, knowingly to induce or receive a discrimination in price which is prohibited by this section.

Section 3 [15 U.S.C. § 14]

It shall be unlawful for any person engaged in commerce, in the course of such commerce, to lease or make a sale or contract for sale of goods, wares, merchandise, machinery, supplies, or other commodities, whether patented or unpatented, for use, consumption, or resale within the United States or any Territory thereof or the District of Columbia or any insular possession or other place under the jurisdiction of the United States, or fix a price charged therefor, or discount from, or rebate upon, such price, on the condition, agreement, or understanding that the lessee or purchaser thereof shall not use or deal in the goods, wares, merchandise, machinery, supplies, or other commodities of a competitor or competitors of the lessor or seller, where the effect of such lease, sale, or contract for sale or such condition, agreement, or understanding may be to substantially lessen competition or tend to create a monopoly in any line of commerce.

Section 4 [15 U.S.C. § 15]

. . . [A]ny person who shall be injured in his business or property by reason of anything forbidden in the antitrust laws may sue therefor in any district court of the United States in the district in which the defendant resides or is found or has an agent, without respect to the amount in controversy, and shall recover threefold the damages by him sustained, and the cost of suit, including a reasonable attorney's fee.

Section 4 [15 U.S.C. § 15c]

(a) Parens patriae; monetary relief; damages; prejudgment interest

(1) Any attorney general of a State may bring a civil action in the name of such State, as parens patriae on behalf of natural persons residing in such State, in any district court of the United States having jurisdiction of the defendant, to secure monetary relief as provided in this section for injury sustained by such natural persons to their property by reason of any violation of sections 1 to 7 of this title. The court shall exclude from the amount of monetary relief awarded in such action any amount of monetary relief (A) which duplicates amounts which have been awarded for the same injury, or (B) which is properly allocable to (i) natural persons who have excluded their claims pursuant to subsection (b)(2) of this section, and (ii) any business entity.

(2) The court shall award the State as monetary relief threefold the total damage sustained as described in paragraph (1) of this subsection, and the cost of suit, including a reasonable attorney's fee. . . .

Section 5 [15 U.S.C. § 16]

A final judgment or decree heretofore or hereafter rendered in any civil or criminal proceeding brought by or on behalf of the United States under the antitrust laws to the effect that a defendant has violated said laws shall be prima facie evidence against such defendant in any action or proceeding brought by any other party against such defendant under said laws as to all matters respecting which said judgment or decree would be an estoppel as between the parties thereto: Provided, That this section shall not apply to consent judgments or decrees entered before any testimony has been taken. Nothing contained in this section shall be construed to impose any limitation on the application of collateral estoppel, except that, in any action or proceeding brought under the antitrust laws, collateral estoppel effect shall not be given to any finding made by the Federal Trade Commission under the antitrust laws or under section 45 of this title which could give rise to a claim for relief under the antitrust laws.

Section 6   [15 U.S.C. § 17]

The labor of a human being is not a commodity or article of commerce. Nothing contained in the antitrust laws shall be construed to forbid the existence and operation of labor, agricultural, or horticultural organizations, instituted for the purposes of mutual help, and not having capital stock or conducted for profit, or to forbid or restrain individual members of such organizations from lawfully carrying out the legitimate objects thereof; nor shall such organizations, or the members thereof, be held or construed to be illegal combinations or conspiracies in restraint of trade, under the antitrust laws.

Section 7   [15 U.S.C. § 18]

No person engaged in commerce or in any activity affecting commerce shall acquire, directly or indirectly, the whole or any part of the stock or other share capital and no person subject to the jurisdiction of the Federal Trade Commission shall acquire the whole or any part of the assets of another person engaged also in commerce or in any activity affecting commerce, where in any line of commerce or in any activity affecting commerce in any section of the country, the effect of such acquisition may be substantially to lessen competition, or to tend to create a monopoly.

No person shall acquire, directly or indirectly, the whole or any part of the stock or other share capital and no person subject to the jurisdiction of the Federal Trade Commission shall acquire the whole or any part of the assets of one or more persons engaged in commerce or in any activity affecting commerce, where in any line of commerce or in any activity affecting commerce in any section of the country, the effect of such acquisition, of such stocks or assets, or of the use of such stock by the voting or granting of proxies or otherwise, may be substantially to lessen competition, or to tend to create a monopoly.

This section shall not apply to persons purchasing such stock solely for investment and not using the same by voting or otherwise to bring about, or in attempting to bring about, the substantial lessening of competition. Nor shall anything contained in this section prevent a corporation engaged in commerce or in any activity affecting commerce from causing the formation of subsidiary corporations for the actual carrying on of their immediate lawful business, or the natural and legitimate branches or extensions thereof, or from owning and holding all or a part of the stock of such subsidiary corporations, when the effect of such formation is not to substantially lessen competition. . . .

Nothing contained in this section shall apply to transactions duly consummated pursuant to authority given by the Secretary of Transportation, Federal Power Commission, Surface Transportation Board, the Securities and Exchange Commission in the exercise of its jurisdiction under section 79j of this title, the United States Maritime Commission, or the Secretary of Agriculture under any statutory provision vesting such power in such Commission, Board, or Secretary.

Section 8   [15 U.S.C. § 19]

(a) (1) No person shall, at the same time, serve as a director or officer in any two corporations (other than banks, banking associations, and trust companies) that are —

    (A) engaged in whole or in part in commerce; and

    (B) by virtue of their business and location of operation, competitors, so that the elimination of competition by agreement between them would constitute a violation of any of the antitrust laws;

if each of the corporations has capital, surplus, and undivided profits aggregating more than $10,000,000 as adjusted pursuant to paragraph (5) of this subsection.

(2) Notwithstanding the provisions of paragraph (1), simultaneous service as a director or officer in any two corporations shall not be prohibited by this section if —

    (A) the competitive sales of either corporation are less than $1,000,000, as adjusted pursuant to paragraph (5) of this subsection;

    (B) the competitive sales of either corporation are less than 2 per centum of that corporation's total sales; or

    (C) the competitive sales of each corporation are less than 4 per centum of that corporation's total sales.

    For purposes of this paragraph, "competitive sales" means the gross revenues for all products and services sold by one corporation in competition with the other, determined on the basis of annual gross revenues for such products and services in that corporation's last completed fiscal year. For the purposes of this paragraph, "total sales" means the gross revenues for all products and services sold by one corporation over that corporation's last completed fiscal year.

(3) The eligibility of a director or officer under the provisions of paragraph (1) shall be determined by the capital, surplus and undivided profits, exclusive of dividends declared but not paid to stockholders, of each corporation at the end of that corporation's last completed fiscal year.

(4) For purposes of this section, the term "officer" means an officer elected or chosen by the Board of Directors.

(5) For each fiscal year commencing after September 30, 1990, the $10,000,000 and $1,000,000 thresholds in this subsection shall be increased (or decreased) as of October 1 each year by an amount equal to the percentage increase (or decrease) in the gross national product, as determined by the Department of Commerce or its successor, for the year then ended over the level so established for the year ending September 30, 1989. As soon as practicable, but not later than January 31 of each year, the Federal Trade Commission shall publish the adjusted amounts required by this paragraph.

(b) When any person elected or chosen as a director or officer of any corporation subject to the provisions hereof is eligible at the time of his election or selection to act for such corporation in such capacity, his eligibility to act in such capacity shall not be affected by any of the provisions hereof by reason of any change in the capital, surplus and undivided profits, or affairs of such corporation from whatever cause, until the expiration of one year from the date on which the event causing ineligibility occurred.

Section 15 [15 U.S.C. § 25]

The several district courts of the United States are invested with jurisdiction to prevent and restrain violations of this Act, and it shall be the duty of the several United States attorneys, in their respective districts, under the direction of the Attorney General, to institute proceedings in equity to prevent and restrain such violations. . . .

Section 16 [15 U.S.C. § 26]

Any person, firm, corporation, or association shall be entitled to sue for and have injunctive relief, in any court of the United States having jurisdiction over the parties, against threatened loss or damage by a violation of the antitrust laws, including sections 13, 14, 18, and 19 of this title, when and under the same conditions and principles as injunctive relief against threatened conduct that will cause loss or damage is granted by courts of equity, under the rules governing such proceedings. . . .

FEDERAL TRADE COMMISSION ACT

Section 1 [15 U.S.C. § 41]

A commission is created and established, to be known as the Federal Trade Commission (hereinafter referred to as the Commission), which shall be composed of five Commissioners, who shall be appointed by the President, by and with the advice and consent of the Senate. Not more than three of the Commissioners shall be members of the same political party. . . . No Commissioner shall engage in any other business, vocation, or employment. Any Commissioner may be removed by the President for inefficiency, neglect of duty, or malfeasance in office. A vacancy in the Commission shall not impair the right of the remaining Commissioners to exercise all the powers of the Commission.

Section 5 [15 U.S.C. § 45]

(1) Unfair methods of competition in or affecting commerce, and unfair or deceptive acts or practices in or affecting commerce, are hereby declared unlawful.

(2) The Commission is hereby empowered and directed to prevent persons, partnerships, or corporations, except banks, savings and loan institutions described in section 57a(f)(3) of this title, Federal credit unions described in section 57a(f)(4) of this title, common carriers subject to the Acts to regulate commerce, air carriers and foreign air carriers subject to part A of subtitle VII of Title 49, and persons, partnerships, or corporations insofar as they are subject to the Packers and Stockyards Act, 1921, as amended [7 U.S.C.A. § 181 et seq.], except as provided in

section 406(b) of said Act [7 U.S.C.A. § 227(b)], from using unfair methods of competition in or affecting commerce and unfair or deceptive acts or practices in or affecting commerce.

(b) Whenever the Commission shall have reason to believe that any such person, partnership, or corporation has been or is using any unfair method of competition or unfair or deceptive act or practice in or affecting commerce, and if it shall appear to the Commission that a proceeding by it in respect thereof would be to the interest of the public, it shall issue and serve upon such person, partnership, or corporation a complaint stating its charges in that respect and containing a notice of a hearing upon a day and at a place therein fixed at least thirty days after the service of said complaint. The person, partnership, or corporation so complained of shall have the right to appear at the place and time so fixed and show cause why an order should not be entered by the Commission requiring such person, partnership, or corporation to cease and desist from the violation of the law so charged in said complaint. Any person, partnership, or corporation may make application, and upon good cause shown may be allowed by the Commission to intervene and appear in said proceeding by counsel or in person. The testimony in any such proceeding shall be reduced to writing and filed in the office of the Commission. If upon such hearing the Commission shall be of the opinion that the method of competition or the act or practice in question is prohibited by this subchapter, it shall make a report in writing in which it shall state its findings as to the facts and shall issue and cause to be served on such person, partnership, or corporation an order requiring such person, partnership, or corporation to cease and desist from using such method of competition or such act or practice.

PATENT ACT (35 U.S.C. § 1-293)

35 U.S.C § 271

. . .

(d) No patent owner otherwise entitled to relief for infringement or contributory infringement of a patent shall be denied relief or deemed guilty of misuse or illegal extension of the patent right by reason of his having done one or more of the following: (1) derived revenue from acts which if performed by another without his consent would constitute contributory infringement of the patent; (2) licensed or authorized another to perform acts which if performed without his consent would constitute contributory infringement of the patent; (3) sought to enforce his patent rights against infringement or contributory infringement; (4) refused to license or use any rights to the patent; or (5) conditioned the license of any rights to the patent or the sale of the patented product on the acquisition of a license to rights in another patent or purchase of a separate product, unless, in view of the circumstances, the patent owner has market power in the relevant market for the patent or patented product on which the license or sale is conditioned. . . .

TABLE OF CASES

[References are to pages]

[References are to pages]

[References are to pages]

D

E

[References are to pages]

[References are to pages]

[References are to pages]

[References are to pages]

[References are to pages]

INDEX

[References are to page numbers.]

[References are to page numbers.]

F

G

I

J

L

[References are to page numbers.]

V